Textbook on Immigration
and Asylum Law

Textbook on
Immigration and Asylum Law

....

Seventh edition

Gina Clayton
BA (Hons), LLM

Chapter 3 revised & updated by
Caroline Sawyer
BA (Hons), MA, PhD
Barrister and Solicitor, Wellington

Chapter 4 revised & updated by
Rowena Moffatt
BA (Hons), LLM
Barrister, Doughty Street Chambers

Chapters 8, 14, 15, and 16 revised & updated by
Georgina Firth
LLB (Hons), LLM, Barrister
Lecturer, University of Lancaster

Chapters 9 & 10 revised & updated by
Helena Wray
BA (Hons), PhD
Associate Professor of Law, Middlesex University

OXFORD
UNIVERSITY PRESS

OXFORD

UNIVERSITY PRESS

Great Clarendon Street, Oxford, OX2 6DP,
United Kingdom

Oxford University Press is a department of the University of Oxford.
It furthers the University's objective of excellence in research, scholarship,
and education by publishing worldwide. Oxford is a registered trade mark of
Oxford University Press in the UK and in certain other countries

Fourth edition 2010
Fifth edition 2012
Sixth edition 2014

Impression: 2

Public sector information reproduced under Open Government Licence v3.0
(http://www.nationalarchives.gov.uk/doc/open-government-licence/open-government-licence.htm)

Published in the United States of America by Oxford University Press
198 Madison Avenue, New York, NY 10016, United States of America

British Library Cataloguing in Publication Data
Data available

Library of Congress Control Number: 2016940609

ISBN 978–0–19–874755–0

Printed in Great Britain by
Ashford Colour Press Ltd.

OUTLINE CONTENTS

DETAILED CONTENTS

SECTION 1   Laying the foundations

SECTION 2   Enabling principles:
EU free movement and human rights

SECTION 3   The system of immigration control

SECTION 4   Entry to the UK

10 Visitors: entry for temporary purposes 370

SECTION 5   The asylum claim

11 The asylum process 389

12 Claims for international protection 437

13 Exclusion from asylum 498

SECTION 6   Enforcement

14 Detention 521

PREFACE

The topics of immigration and asylum have attracted increasing public interest during the time since the previous edition of this textbook. The photo on the beach of a small boy who had drowned, with most of his family, trying to reach safety in Europe, prompted a surge of public interest in the hundreds of thousands of people making this journey. There has been huge public support for welcoming refugees and an interest in where they have come from and why they are coming. There has also been a backlash and fear as to how European countries can cope with the numbers arriving. The Schengen agreement and aspects of the Common European Asylum System look fragile. At the same time, the UK government has developed an increasingly hostile rhetoric, which constructs immigration as a problem. Migrants have become targets of restrictive policies, and the government's repeatedly expressed aims of curbing entry to the UK and access to its benefits have become substantial political forces driving a movement to leave the EU. Immigration has been identified as the cause of numerous social ills, and opinion polls suggest that views about immigration and asylum are significant political drivers for many people.

It is to be hoped that this surge of interest is reflected in interest in immigration and asylum law, since those who are caught in its complex and restrictive web are in need of imaginative and well-informed lawyers who can cut through the complexity and uphold whatever rights are remaining. Current developments in Calais have shown that committed lawyers on the ground can make a difference. The Tribunal decision in the case of *ZAT*, discussed in chapters 6 and 11, resulted in children from the Calais camp being reunited with their siblings in the UK. The charity Detention Action pursued repeated and determined litigation challenging the Detained Fast Track system in which asylum applicants were held in detention throughout their claim, under conditions which made proper preparation of the case almost impossible. The system had attracted criticism since it began. Finally, in July 2015 it was suspended as a result of Detention Action's work.

The Immigration Act 2014 has removed the right of appeal from most immigration decisions. It has been replaced in those cases by an internal Home Office administrative review which has a much lower success rate for the applicant than did appeals. The new appeals system is fraught with uncertainty as to when it applies. Surprisingly, it may provide an appeal in some situations where there was previously no appeal.

The Immigration Act 2014 implemented the government policy to make it easier to deport foreign criminals. This has been a repeated policy of governments of different political hues from at least 2006 onwards. The 2014 Act's contribution was to introduce the power to 'deport first, appeal later', also inserted into the EEA regulations. According to a government factsheet, in the first year nearly 1,500 people were deported using these powers.

The Immigration Bill 2015/16 is now near to completing its passage through Parliament. Although the public policy justification seems nowhere near as compelling, the Bill proposes to extend this power to remove people before their appeal to include human rights appeals against removal where the removal is based on lack of immigration status, not criminal offences.

Another policy implemented by the 2014 Act was that of the 'hostile environment'. The Immigration Bill 2015/16 takes this further. The hostile environment is purportedly targeted on those who have no immigration permission to be in the UK. However, its effects go much wider. The 'right to rent' or 'landlord checking' provisions of the 2014 Act introduced a prohibition on renting for those with no immigration permission to be in the UK. There are various exemptions, but the broad scheme was effected by requiring landlords to check the immigration status of their tenants, on pain of a civil penalty if they did not. This scheme was not yet in force when the 2015/16 Bill was published, making letting to an unauthorized person a criminal offence. Other provisions in a similar vein in the Bill make it an offence to drive in the UK without having immigration permission to be in the country, and an offence to hold a driving licence. Holding a bank account is prohibited and bank accounts can be closed or frozen without notice. Tenants can be evicted on the order of the Secretary of State. The scope for mistakes and discrimination are obvious. All those drawn into implementing the hostile environment are affected.

It is some years since the then government announced an intention to simplify immigration law. Any such idea is now very far from realization. Not only is the content of legislation more restrictive of migrants' rights, but its architecture is astoundingly complex and obscure. For instance, the 2014 Act commencement provisions take the form of exceptions to exceptions and later orders amending earlier ones.

The policy behind these legislative changes is reflected in case law in the Tribunal considering what it means to say that a person's status is 'precarious'. For instance, this passage from the judgment of the Upper Tribunal in *AM (S 117B) Malawi* [2015] UKUT 260 (IAC) in which the Tribunal holds (against the tenor of ECtHR decisions on the issue) that all those with limited leave hold an immigration status that is precarious.

Even if the individual genuinely holds a legitimate expectation that their leave will ultimately be extended . . . they have no absolute right to insist that this will occur, whether or not they meet the requirements of the Immigration Rules at the date of their application . . . the individual will need to meet at some future date the requirements of the Immigration Rules that are then in force . . . The ability of the individual to do so is not capable of prediction in advance.

The previous understanding and application of the concept of precariousness, as established by the House of Lords in *EB (Kosovo)*, was that, if a person knows that they have no right to stay, they form relationships in the knowledge that these may be precarious. As time goes on, if the person is not removed from the UK, that sense of uncertainty naturally fades. In *AM Malawi* and other tribunal cases the concept is turned on its head. Rather than expressing a human experience, it is appropriated as a tool of state control of the migrant.

This is now the repeated message of government to anyone who wants to enter the UK, including refugees. Home Secretary Theresa May made this clear in her message to those in Calais. In effect, 'we will not let you in if you make your own efforts.' Please wait in your home country or a border camp. Entry to the UK is by grace and favour.

The first edition of this textbook quoted Stephen Legomsky, that efforts to be neutral in presenting immigration law only succeed in replicating the value system embedded in that law. This is now more true than ever. Despite this, the textbook endeavours to present the law as it stands at 1 February 2016.

Following reviewers' comments, the human rights chapter has been reinstated, and incorporates the material previously included in the final chapter. However, human rights material remains distributed throughout the book, since it belongs also particularly in the chapters on family life, asylum, and removal.

The chapter on the EU's external controls has also gone. Otherwise, the structure remains the same as in the last edition.

This time the team has said 'goodbye' to Helen Toner, with thanks for her years of contribution to the EU section, and warmly welcomes Rowena Moffatt, who brings a wealth of experience to the EU free movement chapter. Georgina Firth has increased her input, taking on the whole of the enforcement section, bringing her clarity of combined practical and academic experience. Caroline Sawyer and Helena Wray have very kindly continued to contribute their enormous expertise to the nationality, PBS, and visitor chapters, and I am very grateful for their constant input and professionalism, edition after edition. My heartfelt thanks to all the contributors.

Thanks also to OUP for continuing to support this book. Although advisers now have handbooks to refer to, this is still the only student textbook, and the subject is now of critical importance.

Finally, thanks as ever to my husband Mike Fitter, who continues to support and encourage my efforts with this book, with great kindness and grace.

Gina Clayton
March 2016

GUIDE TO USING THE BOOK

Incorporated in this textbook are a number of features that are designed to help you in your studies.

SUMMARY

This chapter examines the definition of a 'refugee' fou[n]
Relating to the Status of Refugees 1951 and the Refug[e]
Although at the time of drafting the Convention this p[a]
preoccupation of contracting states, every phrase of it [
courts and tribunals worldwide.

Chapter summaries provide an overview of what will be addressed in each chapter, so you are aware of the key learning outcomes for each topic.

Key Case

EM (Lebanon) v SSHD [2008] UKHL 64

The appellant's asylum claim failed and she faced re[turn]
Lebanon. The accepted evidence was that if returned [
tody of the child to her husband who had previously[
Saudi Arabia and had subjected her to extreme violen[ce]
automatically give custody to the father if he did not ap[

Key case boxes highlight important cases in each subject area and provide a valuable summary of the significant points to note.

QUESTIONS

1 Was the ECJ right to refuse entitlement to b[
  with the Commission's view that Article 18 [
  the Union should not be impeded by being [
  After all, Mr Collins would only have qualif[
  was genuinely seeking work.

2 Do you agree with the Court in *Akrich* that [
  rights arising from *Surinder Singh*?

3 *Akrich* and *Metock* take very different views [
  States and Community law in relation to co[
  of EU citizens. Which do you find more con[

4 In *Forster*, the Advocate General takes a diff[erent]
  differences, which you prefer, and why.

 For guidance on answering questions, visit w[

At the end of each chapter is a selection of **questions**. These allow you to check your understanding of the topics covered, and help you engage fully with the material in preparation for further study, writing essays, and answering exam questions.

Guidance on answering these questions is available on the Online Resource Centre: **www.oxfordtextbooks.co.uk/orc/clayton7e/**

FURTHER READING

Buck, Trevor (2006) 'Precedent in Tribunals and the Dev[
  Quarterly no. 25, October, pp. 458–484.
Buxton, Richard 'Application of Section 13(6) of the Trib[
  to Immigration Appeals from the Proposed Upper Trib[
  pp. 225–227.
Carnwath, Robert 'Tribunal Justice – A New Start' [2009]
Chowdhury, Zahir 'The Concept of "Error of Law" in Pu[blic]
  Immigration Cases' *Immigration Law Digest* vol. 15, no.[

Each chapter concludes with a list of recommended **further reading**.

These suggestions include books and journal articles, and will help to supplement your knowledge and develop your understanding of the subjects covered.

ONLINE RESOURCE CENTRE

www.oxfordtextbooks.co.uk/orc/clayton7e/

This book is accompanied by an Online Resource Centre—a website providing free and easy-to-use resources designed to support the book.

> Clayton is able to keep the reader up to date with the textbook's on-line companion website, which is easily accessible and very useful in this particular area.
> *Legal Information Management*

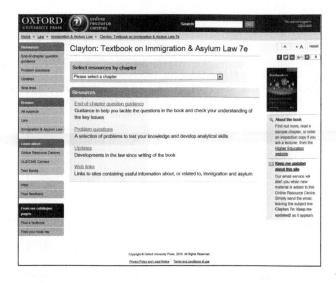

- Yearly updates provide easy access to changes and developments in the law, helping you to stay up-to-date in this fast-moving area.

- Problem questions develop your analytical skills and put your knowledge to the test.

- Guidance on answering end-of-chapter questions allows you to check your understanding of the key issues.

- A selection of web links allow you to research topics of particular interest.

TABLE OF CASES

*Cases and page references in **bold** indicate a 'Key Case'*

TABLE OF STATUTES

TABLE OF STATUTORY INSTRUMENTS

TABLE OF EU LEGISLATION

TABLE OF TREATIES AND CONVENTIONS

TABLE OF IMMIGRATION RULES

LIST OF ABBREVIATIONS

AIT	Asylum and Immigration Tribunal
AITOCA	Asylum and Immigration (Treatment of Claimants, etc.) Act 2004
APG	Asylum Process Guidance
API	Advance Passenger Information
API	Asylum Policy Instruction
ARC	Application registration card
BAPIO	British Association of Physicians of Indian Origin
BCIA	Borders, Citizenship and Immigration Act 2009
BDTC	British dependent territories citizenship
BIOT	British Indian Ocean Territory
BN(O)	British national (overseas)
BNA	British Nationality Act
BOC	British overseas citizen
BOTA	British Overseas Territories Act
BOTC	British overseas territories citizen
BPP	British protected person
BRP	Biometric residence permit
CAS	Confirmation of Acceptance for Studies
CAT	Convention Against Torture
CEAS	Common European Asylum System
CEDAW	Convention on the Elimination of All Forms of Discrimination Against Women
CEFR	Common European Framework of Reference for Languages
CERD	Convention on Ending Racial Discrimination
CG	Country Guidance (or Guideline) (case)
CIG	Country Information and Guidance
CJEU	Court of Justice of the European Union
CO	Crown Office
COI	Country of Origin Information
CRC	Convention on the Rights of the Child
CRD	Case Resolution Directorate
CRE	Commission for Racial Equality
CTA	Common Travel Area
CUKC	Citizen of the UK and Colonies
DFT	Detained fast track
DL	Discretionary leave
DoH	Department of Health
ECG	Entry Clearance Guidance
ECHR	European Convention on Human Rights
ECO	Entry clearance officer
ECtHR	European Court of Human Rights
EEA	European Economic Area
EIG	Enforcement Instructions and Guidance
ELR	Exceptional leave to remain
ESOL	English for speakers of other languages
EURODAC	European Dactyloscopy

EWCA	England and Wales Court of Appeal
FCC	Five Countries Conference
FCO	Foreign and Commonwealth Office
FGM	Female genital mutilation
GCC	Gulf Cooperation Council
GCI	Government-controlled Iraq
HASC	Home Affairs Select Committee
HMIP	Her Majesty's Inspector of Prisons
HP	Humanitarian protection
HRLR	Human Rights Law Reports
HSMP	Highly skilled migrants programme
IAA	Immigration and Asylum Act 1999
IAGCI	Independent Advisory Group on Country Information
IANA	Immigration, Asylum and Nationality Act 2006
IANL	Journal of Immigration, Asylum and Nationality Law
IAT	Immigration Appeal Tribunal
ICAR	Information Centre about Asylum and Refugees
ICCPR	International Covenant on Civil and Political Rights
IDI	Immigration Directorate Instructions
ILM	immigration liaison manager
ILPA	Immigration Law Practitioners' Association
ILR	Indefinite leave to remain
IND	Immigration and Nationality Directorate
INLP	Immigration and Nationality Law and Practice
INLR	Immigration and Nationality Law Reports
JCHR	(Parliamentary) Joint Committee on Human Rights
JCWI	Joint Council for the Welfare of Immigrants
KAZ	Kurdish Autonomous Zone
LAA	Legal Aid Agency
LASPO	Legal Aid, Punishment and Sentencing of Offenders Act 2012
MAC	Migration Advisory Committee
MOU	Memorandum of Understanding
NAM	New Asylum Model
NGO	Non-governmental organization
NI	Nationality Instructions
NIAA	Nationality Immigration and Asylum Act 2002
NSA	Non-suspensive appeal
OGNs	Operational Guidance Notes
OISC	Office of the Immigration Services Commissioner
PBS	Points-based system
QD	Qualification Directive
QMV	Qualified majority voting
RALON	The Risk and Liaison Overseas Network
SAWS	Seasonal Agricultural Workers Scheme
SBS	Sectors Based Scheme
SEF	Statement of Evidence Form
SIAC	Special Immigration Appeals Commission
SIS	Schengen Information Systems
SOCA	Serious Organised Crime Agency
SSHD	Secretary of State for the Home Department

TCEA	Tribunals Courts and Enforcement Act 2007
TCNs	Third country nationals
TFEU	Treaty on the Functioning of the European Union
TPIM	Terrorism Prevention and Investigation Measure
UDHR	Universal Declaration of Human Rights
UKBA	United Kingdom Border Agency
UKVI	United Kingdom Visas and Immigration
UNHCR	United Nations High Commissioner for Refugees
UNHRC	United Nations Human Rights Committee
UTIAC	Upper Tribunal Immigration and Asylum Chamber
VAC	visa application centre

SECTION 1

Laying the foundations

1

....

History and sources of immigration law

SUMMARY

This chapter divides into two parts. The first gives a brief history of immigration law in the United Kingdom (UK), focusing on key legislative developments and noting the themes which arise in that history. The second part introduces the reader to the sources of immigration law, including the immigration rules and policies.

1.1 Introduction

One of the reasons for having at least a passing acquaintance with the history of immigration law in the UK is that themes repeat themselves over time, and it is possible to gain a greater perspective and understanding when we know that the current trend is not new. Particular kinds of legal provisions are created, abolished, and then recreated. For instance, sanctions on airlines for carrying passengers who do not carry full documents were introduced in the latter part of the twentieth century by the Immigration (Carriers Liability) Act 1987, but in 1905 the Aliens Act had provided for fines to be levied on carriers of unauthorized passengers.

Bevan identified nine themes in UK immigration policy: lack of planning, the Commonwealth, the importance of the European Community, international law, bipartisan policy, concern for civil liberties, race relations, the question of assimilation or diversity, and the use of language (1986:22–8). These themes are still important in the twenty-first century, though the balance has changed since 1986. We would now need to add the preoccupation with deterring false asylum claims and terrorism. Each of these will emerge to varying degrees in the course of this book. In enabling us to see that the issues of today are not new, a historical perspective creates the possibility of learning from history.

1.1.1 Attitudes to immigration

Government stance in relation to what is called 'public opinion' is a critical factor in the direction of immigration law and policy. Every history of immigration shows that in Britain each new group of arrivals has been regarded with suspicion and hostility. Allegations against Jews at the turn of the twentieth century, West Indians in the 1950s, people from the Asian subcontinent in the 1960s, and in the 1990s, and at the turn of the twenty-first century, against asylum seekers, are all remarkably similar: 'every mass immigrant group was liable to be pronounced unconventional, unclean, unprincipled and generally unwelcome' (Jones in Juss 1993:71). They may also be accused of being inveterate liars and scrounging from, or alternatively taking the jobs of, native British people, sometimes even the last two at the same time. The history is less often written of tolerance, welcome, solidarity, inter-marriage, cultural exchange, and economic contribution.

In the lives of the population, prejudice and hostility, actual social benefits and actual social problems, friendliness and hospitality, are of course all part of reality. Commentators including Alibhai-Brown and Layton Henry observe that as inward migration grew in the 1950s, public responses were 'complex but not fixed'. However, the opportunity was missed by government to promote a climate of welcome, and this opportunity has been repeatedly missed since.

The absence of this voice from political leadership has left governments with a very limited base from which to make policy and law. Integration policies exist in limited spheres, but have little backing, and the law is mainly about restriction. The question of whether government follows or leads public opinion may be useful to have in mind in reading the history which follows.

In Bevan's themes, race relations and the question of assimilation or diversity are related to these issues of attitudes. The assertion that the issue is not one of race but of numbers has been correlated with a political objective of assimilation rather than diversity. If an immigrant group gains sufficient strength in numbers, it is thought that it will have more capacity to retain an identity distinct from that of the host population. Immigrant groups are thought to be assimilable in small numbers (see, for instance, the report of Political and Economic Planning discussed in Dummett and Nicol 1990:174). In larger numbers they are said to generate resentment in the host population. Established immigrant groups have sometimes also supported this line of argument, though others have opposed any form of immigration controls. Examples of the latter are the action of Jewish trade unions in the nineteenth century and the Indian, West Indian, and Pakistani Workers Associations in the twentieth century (see Cohen, Humphries, and Mynott 2002).

The former Home Affairs Select Committee on Race Relations and Immigration's report of 1990 asserted that 'the effectiveness and fairness of immigration controls affect both the maintenance of good race relations at home and Britain's standing in the world'. The European Court of Human Rights did not accept this argument for immigration rules that discriminated against women (*Abdulaziz, Cabales and Balkandali v UK* (1985) 7 EHRR 471). The Commission did not accept that the restriction on the entry of husbands was justifiable on grounds which included the protection of employment opportunities for the indigenous population and the maintenance of 'public tranquillity'. No link had been demonstrated between excluding such men and 'good race relations'. The effect could equally be the reverse, in that although the rules addressed the fears of some members of the population, they could create resentment in others, particularly the immigrant population that would regard the rules as unfair (para 77). The Court endorsed the Commission's view (para 81).

Lester and Bindman identify 'the ambivalence of public policies. One face confronts the stranger at the gate; the other is turned towards the stranger within' (1972:13–14). Roy Hattersley, who at one time considered that strict immigration control was necessary to maintain good race relations, ultimately came to the conclusion that:

Good community relations are not encouraged by the promotion of the idea that the entry of one more black immigrant into this country will be so damaging to the national interest that husbands must be separated from their wives, children denied the chance to look after their aged parents and sisters prevented from attending their brothers' weddings. It is measures like the Asylum and Immigration Bill—and the attendant speeches—which create the impression that we cannot 'afford to let them in'. And if we cannot afford to let them in, then those of them who are already here must be . . . doing harm. (*The Guardian* 26 February 1996)

1.2 History of immigration law

In studying immigration, we are focusing on movement *into* a country, in this case the UK. However, this is only one small part of a worldwide movement of peoples which has gone on since time immemorial. Until at least around 1994 (Home Affairs Committee, Fifth Report 2005–06, para 8), the UK was a country of net emigration; in other words, more people left the UK than entered it. Many of the people who have come to the UK have done so from areas with a long history of migration, and in paying attention to their arrival in the UK we are only selecting a tiny portion of history.

A complex body of statute, rules, and case law governing entry into the UK is a twentieth-century phenomenon. Before this there was not a developed body of law, but there were numerous provisions controlling the movement of 'aliens'. Aliens were people who did not owe allegiance to the Crown, defined as those who were not British subjects (British Nationality and Status of Aliens Act 1914 s 27; see chapter 3). Sometimes sweeping measures have been employed; for example, in 1290, Edward I, following an increasing campaign of hatred against Jews, expelled all Jews from England. Some of those expelled would have been aliens, and some British subjects. The latter, according to Magna Carta, had a right to remain in the kingdom and travel freely in and out; the royal decree was illegal as well as immoral, but there was no remedy.

Measures controlling the movement of aliens were often connected with hostilities with other countries. In the sixteenth century, when England was at war with Spain, Ireland gave assistance to the Spaniards, and Ireland and England were in continual conflict. There were by this time a significant number of Irish people resident in England. As Dummett and Nicol comment, regardless of the individual views or affiliations of these people, Queen Elizabeth I issued a proclamation that 'no manner of person born in the realm of Ireland . . . shall remain in the realm' (1990:45). The Irish were either expelled from England or imprisoned. Again, in 1793, a statute was passed to control the entry of aliens, this time directed towards travellers from France; following the French Revolution, it was feared they might stir up similar fervour in England. While some echoes of these earlier practices may be detected in modern law, by and large the immigration law of the last 100 years is a very different creature from the Royal Proclamations of Edward and Elizabeth.

The beginning of modern-day immigration control can be traced to the persecution of Jews in Eastern Europe at the end of the nineteenth century. From being an envied and romanticized minority as they had been in the nineteenth century, Jews once again became a target of violence and hostility. Many took refuge in Western Europe, including England. However, such movements of hatred are not generally confined within national boundaries, and the new arrivals also found themselves the subject of a campaign in Britain. They were concentrated in areas of poor housing and working conditions, and Parliament debated as it does now whether the immigrants exacerbated these conditions, or whether their industry and creativity were an asset. A Jewish family living in overcrowded rooms, and taking in lodgers to cover the rent, was said to be 'lowering the social standard very greatly' (HL Debs 5 July 1898 vol 60 col 1098). The counter-argument was made that overcrowding should be dealt with by domestic law, not immigration control (HL Debs 20 June 1898 vol 59 col 729). 'Foreigners' were few in number: 'but they settle down in one or two limited areas, and this handful of foreigners becomes a very large quantity in these limited areas' (col 738).

Debates in the House of Lords noted, then as now, the contrary nature of maintaining both that immigrants were taking jobs and keeping down wages *and* refusing to work and taking up welfare provision (HL Debs 20 June 1898 vol 59 col 729).

A campaign against alien workers followed, and the government responded by setting up a Royal Commission to investigate the effect of immigrant workers upon housing and employment conditions and upon public health and morals, the allegations being that they were unclean and spread disease and crime. The conclusion of the Royal Commission was that there was no threat to the jobs and working conditions of British workers, and immigrants did not create poverty, disease, and crime. There was a slightly higher rate of crime among some alien groups, though Dummett and Nicol suggest that 'the figures were crude and took no account of social class' (1990:101), and immigrants were living in overcrowded housing. The balance of the report was not obviously in favour of immigration control; nevertheless, the Royal Commission recommended control. The result was the Aliens Act 1905, the first major piece of modern immigration legislation.

This Act marked the inception of the immigration service and the appeals system. It set up an inspectorate which operated at ports of entry to the UK. It was called the Aliens Inspectorate and its officers (the first immigration officers) had the power to refuse entry to aliens who were considered 'undesirable'. Undesirability was defined as lacking in the means to support oneself and dependants, and lacking in the capacity to acquire such means; mentally ill; likely through ill health to become dependent on the public welfare system or to endanger the health of others; or having been previously expelled or convicted abroad of an extraditable non-political crime. As a result of successful argument in Parliament, those opposed to controls on aliens had managed to limit the inspectorate's powers to those who travelled on the cheapest tickets (steerage class) on immigrant ships, which were defined as those carrying more than 20 aliens. These categories bear a striking similarity to the requirements for entry in modern-day immigration rules. Under present rules, all categories of entrant are required to show that they will not be reliant on public funds, long-term entrants are required to undergo a medical examination (HC 395 para 36) and the commission of criminal offences may give grounds for deportation (Immigration Act 1971 s 3(5)(a)). Note also that the standards in the Act do not clearly correspond to the findings of the Royal Commission; instead, they compromise between averting real problems that had been identified and pandering to fears which had been shown to be unfounded. The overall effect is somewhat mitigated by the arguments in Parliament of those concerned with civil liberties. Here we see Bevan's themes of lack of planning and bipartisan policy enacted, the latter meaning that political parties would tend to take opposing positions on immigration (though it would also be true to say that it is an issue which does not always split on party lines).

The Act also marked the beginning of an appeals system, by providing for Immigration Appeals Boards. They were set up in every major port of entry and immigrants refused leave to enter had a right of appeal to them.

As we have seen in relation to earlier conflicts with France and Spain, war has been used to impose severe restrictions upon foreigners. During the First World War, the Aliens Restriction Act 1914 s 1 gave the Secretary of State a great deal of power to regulate the entry, stay, and deportation of aliens, and even to pass regulations 'on any other matters which appear necessary or expedient with a view to the safety of the realm'. The

Aliens Restrictions (Amendment) Act 1919 extended these wartime powers to apply at any time, subject to a yearly review. This was the pattern also with Prevention of Terrorism Acts, introduced in 1974 as an emergency measure subject to annual review, but culminating in a permanent Terrorism Act in 2000. The effects of the 1919 Act were far-reaching. Not only did the wide powers given to the Secretary of State for wartime now also apply in peacetime, but the Act also set the pattern, as Bevan describes, for the legal structure of immigration control. The legislation, like many modern statutes, was skeletal in form, having few substantive provisions but giving wide powers to the Secretary of State to make rules.

Visas were instituted during the First World War for all those who were not nationals of Commonwealth countries. After the war, visas remained available as an ad hoc mechanism and were used for temporary controls for particular groups, including, even then, to deter refugees. For instance, in 1938, anticipating Jewish refugees, the UK reinstated a visa requirement for Austria and Germany (see Dummett and Nicol:157).

The 1919 Act was followed by the Aliens Order of 1920, which laid out the more detailed control of aliens and initiated today's system of work permits. Both passports and work permits grew out of wartime controls, as before 1914 it was possible to travel between a number of countries without a passport.

The Second World War had a very significant effect upon patterns of immigration to the UK. War was declared at a time when the Commonwealth was a strong bond that held together a number of nations in allegiance to the monarch of the UK. The UK was regarded by many as the 'mother country'. The fact that British and Commonwealth soldiers were fighting alongside one another contributed to the development of the idea of family, a sense of partnership, and belonging. Additionally, some Commonwealth service people had contributed to the war effort by doing essential work in the UK and so developed real familiarity with Britain. The media talked in terms of loyalty and gratitude to other Commonwealth citizens. This sense of belonging was not a thought-out policy based on a concept of rights enforceable by individuals, but more of a pleasing sentiment which was not expected to have any legal effect.

The reality of post-war entry to the UK was somewhat different. Spencer (1997) describes the deliberations of an interdepartmental working party set up in 1948, and also the later work of a committee of the Ministry of Labour, to consider where there were labour shortages and whether citizens from Commonwealth countries could or should be recruited to make up any shortfall. Writers differ as to the extent of any labour shortage and of recruitment policies aimed at remedying such shortage. The main focus was on the West Indies, and the question of whether workers should be recruited from there. Spencer reports negative conclusions as far as the recruitment of West Indians was concerned; they were not considered suitable workers or acceptable to the unions in the UK. Spencer also reports a refusal by the unions to cooperate with a recruitment scheme, and a preference by the government committees for workers from the continent of Europe. The reasons for this preference were that European workers would integrate more easily and it would be easier for the government to return them when no longer needed. The latter is in part because European workers would not have any claim as British subjects whereas Caribbean workers would. That Europeans would be regarded as easier to integrate could be surprising in view of the fact that English would be a native language for Caribbean workers though not for any European. However, Spencer's analysis of the Cabinet papers of the time, released under the 30-year rule, strongly suggests that colour was at the root of the government's objection to West Indian workers. An analysis of Cabinet papers of the following few years relating to attempts to restrain immigration in the early 1950s reveals the same concerns (Carter, Harris, and Joshi 1987).

All the authors previously mentioned, whose work is based on Cabinet papers, recount obstructive practices that were instituted in the Caribbean, West Africa, India, and Pakistan, making it more difficult for citizens of those countries to travel to Britain despite their being Commonwealth citizens. Examples of tactics employed were the delay in issuing passports and the omission of the reference to British subject status on travel documents, even though the holder was entitled to such a reference.

The passage of the British Nationality Act in 1948 did not affect right of entry into the UK; it dealt with nationality rather than immigration. However, it did so in a rather theoretical sense, being more a matter of labelling than of delivering enforceable rights. Indeed, it was not within the contemplation of those who produced this legislation that the millions of Commonwealth citizens and citizens of the UK and Colonies would attempt to use their right to enter the UK. It expressed the rather theoretical and symbolic idea that legislators had of the meaning of British subject status, and began the division between citizens of independent Commonwealth countries and other British subjects, which laid the foundation for the later development of immigration control (see chapter 3).

Despite the disincentives mentioned earlier, immigration into Britain continued. There were opportunities for work, and these were attractive. By far the largest number of entrants was from Ireland and the countries known as the Old Commonwealth, that is, Australia, Canada, and New Zealand. Immigration from the Caribbean was also rising, though not keeping pace with Ireland and the old Commonwealth. Until the release of the Cabinet papers relating to the 1950s, it was widely believed that there was a disproportionate rise in that period of immigration from the Caribbean and of social problems associated with this immigration. The popular account also entailed that the government was dedicated to retaining the rights of British subjects from the Caribbean to enter the UK, but then as social problems escalated, they were reluctantly forced to legislate in the form of the Commonwealth Immigrants Act 1962 to restrict the right of some Commonwealth citizens. Political speeches of the time focused on the familiar theme of numbers. Only a certain number of immigrants, it was asserted, could be assimilated—in other words absorbed—into the majority culture in Britain without noticeable impact or making demands. The studies mentioned earlier suggest a contrary view, namely that in working parties established specifically to consider the role of 'coloured' workers, the link of immigrants with social problems was not proven, and immigrants from the West Indies were far outnumbered by those from Ireland and the Old Commonwealth. The initiative to control black immigration seemed to come, not from the identification of a social problem, but from an independent agenda within the Home Office and Cabinet Office. The government moved to impose a quota system on immigrants from the West Indies. However, official descriptions of them became more favourable after arrivals increased from India and Pakistan. Those who were formerly lazy were now industrious and English-speaking, and it was the South Asians who were 'unassimilable'. The British government succeeded in obtaining cooperation from West Indian, Indian, and Pakistani governments to restrain migration, and Paul comments:

The range of administrative methods used by territories of origin and the United Kingdom to prevent colonial migration was so extensive that one might suggest that those migrants who did succeed in obtaining a passport, completing an English language interview, bearing up to scrutiny and accepting the propaganda at its true value were indeed hardy souls. (1997:153)

After years of political debate and manoeuvring, the Commonwealth Immigrants Act was finally passed in 1962. The significance of the Act was immense. For the first time, there was a restriction on the rights of certain Commonwealth citizens to come to the UK.

The Act distinguished between Commonwealth citizens based on parentage. Those who were born in the UK or Ireland or who held a passport issued by the government of those countries would not be subject to immigration control; others would. The immigration control consisted of conditions that a Commonwealth citizen would have to satisfy to gain entry. Whether these conditions were satisfied was to be determined by an immigration officer who was given a wide measure of discretion.

One of the peculiar features of British immigration law, to which we shall return time and again, is the heavy reliance on formerly unpublished instructions, guidelines, and concessions. These less formal sources in practice often determine the outcome of applications. In the course of the implementation of the Commonwealth Immigrants Act 1962, it was made clear by internal guidance that the discretion given to immigration officers to refuse entry on the basis that requirements were not met, would not be applied in practice to immigrants from Canada, Australia, or New Zealand. The system of control that was established therefore discriminated at two levels against black would-be entrants. Initially, the terms of the Act itself, while neutral on their face as regards race or colour, were based on a requirement of birth in the UK or possession of a passport issued by the UK government, both of which would be satisfied more often in practice by white people. At the second level of internal instructions, the discrimination was closer to being explicit. As with the Jews in the thirteenth century, though less publicly, the distinction was made on the basis of ethnicity, not nationality.

For the Commonwealth citizens subject to immigration control, a three-tier system of work vouchers was instituted. Dummett and Nicol comment that this founded a bureaucratic system for processing immigration rather than a method of controlling it. The actual effect of the Commonwealth Immigrants Act was very different from the government's intention. There was a substantial rise in immigration from the Indian subcontinent in particular around the time of the 1962 Act. The Act has often been presented as the response to this increased immigration, but as Spencer (1997) and Bevan (1986) recount, it is more likely to have caused it. Spencer suggests four ways in which the Commonwealth Immigrants Act actually encouraged immigration, as follows.

First, the build-up to the legislation had taken years. The proposal to restrict immigration was therefore known long in advance and during the years 1960–2 this created a rush to 'beat the ban'.

Second, prior to the 1962 Act, those who had come from the Indian subcontinent to Britain were mainly men who had come for a temporary period to work and to send money back to their families. Often this was in a tradition in their original locality, and they came to Britain because at that time there was a good chance of employment, particularly in the textile industry in the north of England. These men's travels were therefore not immigration as it is sometimes understood 40 years later, that is, they had not come to settle. The 1962 Act made it less likely that the men retiring from this role could be replaced by younger relatives as the work voucher system would not have favoured their entry. The Act therefore tended to encourage those men to apply for leave to remain in the UK.

Following on from the last point, the Act permitted unification of families, and so for the men who had come as sojourners, the provisions of the Act combined to make remaining in the UK and being joined by their families the more viable option. It might be said (though Spencer does not make this point) that the Act encouraged and established the growth of an immigrant population modelled on British assumptions of working and family life, rather than an understanding of what migration meant to those who were doing it.

Spencer's final point is also made by Dummett and Nicol (1990): that the Act established a regime that regulated and therefore to a degree allowed people to enter the UK, namely the system of entry control and work vouchers.

The 1962 Act was formative in that it laid the foundation of the distinction between entry as a right and entry subject to the fulfilment of conditions, and did so by using the criterion of connection with the UK. The particular history of this Act reminds us not to take at face value assertions of cause and effect in relation to legislation; it also introduces the role of internal guidance in the operation of immigration law.

The history of the Commonwealth Immigrants Act 1968 is discussed by many writers including Shah, P. (2000), Bevan (1986), and Dummett and Nicol (1990). It provides a stark illustration of the difference between immigration policy based on loyalty to those whom the Empire and then the Commonwealth gave the status of British subject, and immigration policy based on fear of admission of numbers of non-white people. The key events were the independence of, first, Kenya and, later, Uganda and Tanzania. Each of these countries at independence had an established minority population which had come from the Indian subcontinent, some of whom had been introduced into East Africa by Britain which, as colonial power, had employed them on construction projects. Many had left India before its independence and before the creation of Pakistan, and their only citizenship was that of the UK and Colonies. The East African countries, on attaining independence, pursued a policy of Africanization that required residents to demonstrate their allegiance to the new state. Many Asians either did not fulfil the conditions for acquiring the new citizenship or did not register within the time limit, preferring to wait and see how their fortunes were likely to go in the new regime before committing themselves. Some may have been reluctant to lose their British connection. For many of those who did not acquire the new citizenship, serious consequences ensued. They lost their employment or their livelihood, and sought to use whatever protection being a citizen of the UK and Colonies (CUKC) could offer them. Their passports had been issued by the British High Commission and, therefore, under the 1962 Act they were not subject to immigration control. They had, as British subjects, right of entry into the UK. Inflated figures of likely entrants were quoted in the media, and the Commonwealth Immigrants Act 1968 was rushed through Parliament. The new Act provided that British subjects would be free from immigration control only if they, or at least one of their parents or grandparents, had been born, adopted, registered, or naturalized in the UK. The issue of a passport by a British High Commission thus ceased to be a qualification for entry free of control. For those subject to control, another voucher system was introduced. This one was based on tight quotas, reflecting the government's contention that numbers were the problem.

The story of the East African Asians illustrates how a British government was prepared to mix together issues of nationality and immigration. This is one of the themes identified by Bevan. While the East African Asians retained their CUKC status, it was in effect worthless as it no longer conferred a right of entry to their country of nationality.

The next step was to introduce a mandatory requirement to evidence entitlement to enter. A written parliamentary answer in 1969 announced a system of entry certificates for Commonwealth men seeking entry to join wives and fiancées. This was rapidly followed by inserting a requirement in the Immigration Appeals Act 1969 for all dependent relatives to obtain an entry certificate. Those who were required to apply for an entry certificate had in theory a right to enter. However, the application system created notorious delays, which operated as an illegitimate form of immigration control (*R v SSHD ex p Phansopkar* [1975] 3 WLR 322 CA).

The 1969 Act was also accompanied by a visa list. This was the beginning of the present system, which requires that nationals of a visa national country must obtain entry clearance (a visa) to come to the UK. For both entry certificates and visas, the process was daunting. Information was gathered largely from interviews. Entry clearance posts were not well distributed, so an applicant might have a long and arduous journey. On arrival, an applicant could be exhausted and not really fit for an important interview. Despite this, researchers reported that applicants would never answer in the negative the standard question asked by the entry clearance officer (ECO) as to whether they were fatigued, nervous, or unwell. The reason was the fear that if they were unfit for interview on arrival, the interview would be postponed for a long period (CRE:36).

ECOs used the discrepancy system—interviewing separately members of the same family, then turning down claims to be related from people who differed in minor detail in their accounts of events which might have been years in the past. The issue of colour (which was the terminology then used, and which was quite accurate) continued to dominate public debate about immigration. When the Immigration Act 1971 was passed, the racial definition of those with rights of entry and those without was complete. While later statutes have made substantial changes to the immigration process and the rights of immigrants, the 1971 Act remains the source of Home Office and immigration officers' powers to make decisions on entry, stay, and deportation. Its significance in terms of the history we are now tracing is its division of the world into patrials and nonpatrials. Previously, UK law had divided the world into British subjects and aliens. This was the fundamental category which determined whether a person had right of entry into the UK. Legislation then, as we have seen, restricted the rights of some British subjects to the extent that these rights became practically worthless. The Immigration Act 1971 gave right of abode in the UK to those it defined as 'patrials'. These were:

(i)   citizens of the UK and Colonies who had that citizenship by birth, adoption, naturalization, or registration in the UK;

(ii) citizens of the UK and Colonies whose parent or grandparent had that citizenship by those same means at the time of the birth of the person in question;

(iii) citizens of the UK and Colonies with five years' ordinary residence in the UK;

(iv) Commonwealth citizens whose parent was born or adopted in the UK before their birth;

(v)   Commonwealth citizens married to a patrial man.

Commonwealth citizens who had been settled in the UK for five years when the Act came into force (1 January 1973) also had the right to register and thus possibly the right of abode. Others would be subject to immigration controls. Apart from the five-year residence qualification, the right to live in the UK and to enter free from immigration control was determined by birth or parentage, not by nationality. The British Nationality Act 1981 carried this classification into British nationality law, and it is still the case that there are some, though a dwindling number, of British nationals who do not have a right of entry to the UK. More detail is given of all these provisions in chapter 3.

On the same day that the Immigration Act 1971 came into force, the UK entered the European Community (EC). One of the cornerstones upon which the EC is built is freedom of movement, not only of goods but also of workers and their families. Despite this timing, the Immigration Act made no reference to European membership or the principle of freedom of movement. It continues to be the case up to the present that UK immigration law has developed quite separately from European law on freedom of movement (*R v IAT and Surinder Singh ex p SSHD* [1992] Imm AR 565) and that, at the same time that immigration restrictions were confirmed for Commonwealth citizens with a traditional allegiance to Britain, a new category of privilege was created for European nationals. The free movement rights of EU nationals are implemented in UK law by separate regulations: the Immigration (European Economic Area) Regulations 2006, SI 2006/1003 as amended. Although the UK government seeks now to exercise more control over European Economic Area (EEA) nationals, this cannot be done by directly applying UK immigration law (see *Sanade* chapter 5).

Primary immigration, that is, of people coming to establish a life on their own rather than to join family members, virtually ceased with the Acts of 1968 and 1971; nevertheless, in the 1980s, the general trend in immigration provisions remained towards increasing restriction. Attention switched from primary immigration to family settlement, and more demanding rules for the entry of spouses were introduced. These raised such a political storm that, most unusually, there was a debate in Parliament concerning new immigration rules (see the discussion in chapter 8).

Major studies in the 1980s, later work by Juss (1997), research conducted into family visitor appeals, and the working holiday-maker scheme, continued to reveal concerns with the quality of entry clearance decisions. These included delays in processing the application; cursory or poor quality consideration of the application; oppressive conduct and conditions of interview; and use of the discrepancy system.

Towards the end of the twentieth century, immigration policy (as distinct from asylum) played a less prominent part in the political life of the UK. The Labour government's abolition of the infamous primary purpose rule in 1997 was a reversal of one of the most punitive provisions on family settlement (again see chapter 8) and the reduced tension around immigration and increased awareness of rights made this possible. The increasingly restrictive nature of immigration law did not arise from concerns about immigration as such, but from concerns about increased asylum claims. The rapid growth of a visa regime, now affecting travellers from potentially any country in the world, is an example of this (see chapter 6). The Immigration and Asylum Act 1999 made significant inroads into the rights of appeal of those alleged to be in breach of immigration law, but this was to address the backlog of cases at the Home Office and to expedite the removal of unsuccessful asylum seekers. The backlog, rather than issues of entry and entitlement, became the immigration scandal of the late 1990s in its own right.

The other major development in immigration law particularly in the last 20 years has been the introduction of internal controls. This entails the requirement for housing officers, benefits officers, employers, registrars of births, marriages, and deaths, and airline officials to interpret immigration status, upon which entitlement to civil benefits such as housing or employment increasingly depends. Juss dates the introduction of these provisions from the first report of the Select Committee on Race Relations and Immigration in 1978. The effect has been to exclude from social benefits those people who have, or who may have, or who may be thought to have, a questionable immigration status. The introduction of biometric identity documents for foreign nationals in 2007 heralded the entrenchment of immigration status into everyday life.

Both the development of internal controls and the reduction of appeal rights ride on the back of the issue which has attracted public attention since the 1990s—that of asylum. The bulk of the case law reported in the Immigration Appeal Reports for some years concerned asylum rather than immigration issues. There was an escalation of

legislation principally aimed at controlling asylum seekers: the Asylum and Immigration Appeals Act 1993, Asylum and Immigration Act 1996, Immigration and Asylum
Act 1999, Nationality, Immigration and Asylum Act 2002, the bizarrely named Asylum
and Immigration (Treatment of Claimants, etc.) Act 2004, and the Immigration, Asylum and Nationality Act 2006. However, although the target group is different, the
themes are recognizable.

The 1993 Act introduced an appeal right for asylum seekers, but also the concept of a
claim 'without foundation' (Sch 2 para 5). Again, this is based on the idea of a potential
entrant as dishonest. Claims so certified would attract only limited appeal rights, the
government's avowed intention being to speed through the system claims which could
be identified at an early stage as unmeritorious. This provision is based not only on the
idea of the deceptive applicant but also on addressing the backlog. Juss gives a sting-
ing account of the origins of the 1993 Act in which he suggests that the problem of the
backlog was self-inflicted, resulting from a recruitment freeze in the Immigration and
Nationality Department (IND). Opportunities for applicants to manipulate the system
arose as a result of increasing delays, and these manipulations in turn extended the
delays. His account may be borne out by the fact that the backlogs were tackled in the
year 2000 by recruiting extra personnel in the IND.

Delay and cheating the system, and the relationship between the two, became the
political issues of the 1990s. The alleged cheating was both at the point of entry (the
concept of the 'bogus' asylum seeker) and after entry (the concept of the 'scrounger').
These ideas underlie further provisions in the Asylum and Immigration Act 1996 such
as, for instance, the creation of a new offence of obtaining leave to remain by deception
(s 4). The kinds of claims that would be subjected to restricted appeal rights (known
then as the short procedure) were extended to include those from a designated country
of origin. Designation, according to the promoting minister in Parliament, would be
on the basis that there had been a high number of applications and a high number of
refusals from that particular country and that there was, in general, no serious risk of
persecution in that country (HC Debs 11 December 1995 col 703). This provision has a
similar basis to the 'without foundation' provision, that of expediting applications on
the basis that they may be identified without full examination as being unmeritorious.
Similar provisions followed in the 1999 Act ('manifestly unfounded') and in the 2002
Act ('clearly unfounded'). The list of designated countries became known as the 'White
List'. It was abandoned after a successful challenge, in *R v SSHD ex p Javed and Ali* [2001]
Imm AR 529, to the inclusion of Pakistan because of known widespread discrimination
against women and against Ahmadis, which had been accepted in the higher courts
in the UK (*Shah and Islam v IAT and SSHD* [1999] Imm AR 283 and *Ahmed (Iftikhar) v
Secretary of State for the Home Department* [2000] INLR 1). Where sectors of society could
be said to be at risk, it could not be reasonable to say there was, in general, no serious
risk of persecution. A new list of safe countries of origin was produced in the 2002 Act.
It has been extended by ministerial orders and is now in regular use (see chapter 11).

Section 2 of the 1996 Act also introduced a power for the Secretary of State to certify
that asylum seekers could be returned, before their claim was considered, to a 'safe
third country'. This was the beginning of the UK's effort to stop asylum seekers being
'bounced around' Europe, that is, shuttled from one country to another, each one declining to hear their asylum application but finding a reason to return them to another
Member State. The UK was a signatory to the Dublin Convention, the treaty by which
EC countries sought to find a way of determining which state should hear an asylum
application. As the Common European Asylum System came into effect, the treaty has
been superseded by a binding regulation, discussed in chapter 11.

Other provisions of the 1996 Act continued the dual themes of deception and internal controls. More criminal offences were devised, targeting the racketeering of those who arrange entry to the UK for gain (s 5), and more internal controls were set up, including recruiting employers into the system of detection of residents with potentially irregular immigration status (ss 8 and 9).

The history of immigration law is full of examples of legislation swiftly introduced to reverse higher court decisions. Section 11 of the 1996 Act was one such example. The Social Security (Persons from Abroad) Miscellaneous Amendment Regulations 1996, SI 1996/30, had removed benefits from almost everyone who was subject to immigration control. The regulations were declared *ultra vires* by Simon Brown LJ because they were beyond the tolerance level of a 'civilised nation'. 'Something so uncompromisingly draconian can only be achieved by primary legislation' (*R v Secretary of State for Social Security ex p JCWI* [1997] 1 WLR 275). As Macdonald puts it: 'The government duly obliged, enacting the condemned regulation as section 11 of the 1996 Act' (2001:9).

The Immigration and Asylum Act 1999 continued the trend by, according to Statewatch, 'hugely increasing surveillance, monitoring and compulsion'. Registrars of births, marriages, and deaths were brought into the internal control system (s 24). Penalties for carrying passengers without full documentation increased once again, being extended to include trains, buses, and coaches to cover entry via the Channel Tunnel (Part II of the Act). There were also provisions for penalizing private car and lorry drivers who carried clandestine entrants. Asylum seekers were excluded from the mainstream benefits system, and a dispersal system was instituted which would distribute them around the country (Part VI). Appeal rights were further curtailed, both for asylum seekers and other deportees (Part IV). Limited appeal rights for family visitors were reinstated. The 1990s had seen a massive increase of asylum seekers detained in detention centres and prisons. One of the anomalous features of immigration detention generally, including that of asylum seekers, is that it is not subject to any compulsory supervision by the courts, and there is no presumption of a right to bail, as there is when someone is charged with a criminal offence. In the 1999 Act, the government took the opportunity to address this issue by introducing a routine bail hearing (Part III). However, these provisions were never implemented, and were repealed by the Nationality, Immigration and Asylum Act 2002. The 1999 Act contained the first statutory presumptions of the safety of a third country to which an asylum seeker could be returned. This appeared to be a government reaction to having the Secretary of State's certificates of safety issued under the 1996 Act regularly struck down by the courts. In the Immigration and Asylum Act 1999 s 11, the certificates in relation to European countries were made immune to judicial review by a statutory presumption that such countries were deemed safe. This proved unassailable (*R (Thangasara) v SSHD* [2002] UKHL 36).

The 1999 Act was proclaimed as a radical overhaul of the immigration and asylum system. It expressed the political agenda of its day—suspicion that there is a large volume of unmeritorious asylum claims; the cost of welfare benefits obtained by people who made such claims; the progressive extension of internal controls; the problem of backlog and delay in the system both before dealing with claims and before removal from the country of those who did not succeed; and the shifting of blame to the morally more acceptable targets of 'racketeers' rather than the obviously vulnerable asylum seekers. There was another influence at the time of debates on the 1999 Act, namely, the Human Rights Act 1998 (HRA), which had received Royal Assent but was not yet in force. The 1999 Act removed some rights to have an appeal heard in the UK. The counterbalance was to provide an in-country appeal on human rights grounds. The 1999 Act provided the first statutory right of appeal against immigration decisions on human rights grounds (s 65, now in the Nationality, Immigration and Asylum Act 2002 s 84).

1.2.1 Twenty-first century

Six immigration statutes have been passed already in this century, with a seventh imminent at the time of writing. There have also been five anti-terrorism statutes, three of which derived from and interact with policies to restrict the activities of foreign nationals. Amendments to terrorism legislation have been contained in numerous other statutes. Provisions restricting immigration status, removing rights of appeal, and restricting admissible evidence have been inserted into statutes mainly dealing with criminal justice and security issues (Criminal Justice and Immigration Act 2008, Crime and Courts Act 2013, Justice and Security Act 2013, Counter-Terrorism and Security Act 2015).

In parallel throughout this same period the higher courts have been working out the application of the Human Rights Act to immigration and immigration-related decisions. At first the tension was severe between the government which had drafted, promoted, and secured the passage of the Human Rights Act through Parliament and the judiciary who were applying it to immigration and asylum cases. Amidst a 'gathering storm in relations' between the executive and judiciary (Rawlings 2005:380), the government attempted to stop all immigration and asylum issues from being heard by the courts, whether on appeal or review, by means of an ouster clause in the Asylum and Immigration (Treatment of Claimants, etc.) Bill 2003.

In 2012 the government introduced immigration rules aimed at curtailing the powers of judges to apply and interpret human rights (discussed in chapters 5, 7, and 8). Since the government desired more control over the application and interpretation of human rights than the rules achieved, the Immigration Act 2014 introduced measures to restrict the application of Article 8.

This is in the context of the wider debate, not only concerning migrants and refugees, in which the UK government has made it clear in numerous ways that it would like to curtail the impact of the Strasbourg Court in the UK.

During the same period there has been an intensified focus on security. This predated 11 September 2001, but was accelerated by government responses to the attack on the World Trade Center that day. Also during this period, the completion of the first phase of the Common European Asylum System followed by the acquisition by the Court of Justice of the EU of competence in immigration and asylum matters meant that first EU legislation on asylum, and then EU case law, have a direct effect in the UK.

At the time of the passing of the 1999 Act, it was widely predicted there would be another immigration statute within three years, and so it turned out (see, for this point and generally, McKee 2002). The Nationality, Immigration and Asylum Act 2002 was preceded by a White Paper: *Secure Borders, Safe Haven; Integration with Diversity in Modern Britain* (Cm 5387), announced by Home Secretary David Blunkett in the following terms:

The White Paper takes forward our agenda by offering an holistic and comprehensive approach to nationality, managed immigration, and asylum that recognises the interrelationship of each element in the system. No longer will we treat asylum seekers in isolation or fail to recognise that there must be alternative routes to entry into this country. (HC Debs 7 February 2002 col 1028)

The Act deals with changes to nationality law, the provision of accommodation centres for asylum seekers, restrictions on the asylum support system, the provision of removal centres and expansion of powers of detention and removal, extension and amendment of the carriers' liability scheme, and the introduction of further criminal offences. At least as much as the 1999 Act, this Act was dominated by objectives concerning the asylum system.

McKee refers to 'divergent and contradictory goals', specifically:

- to keep asylum seekers out, but to provide a welcome for genuine refugees;
- to integrate refugees and ethnic minorities into mainstream British culture, but to celebrate cultural diversity;
- to include a raft of authoritarian and repressive measures under the same anodyne umbrella of 'modernisation' as liberal measures to allow economic migration and facilitate easier travel. (2002:181)

Within the broad purposes identified by McKee, the Act and the White Paper have a number of underlying policy themes which may be characterized as:

1. developing an all-pervasive control system for asylum seekers;
2. a controlled development of the possibility of entry for work;
3. the creation of a class of people without rights or status;
4. development of extra-territorial immigration control;
5. combating terrorism; and
6. the strengthening of executive power.

Taking each of these in turn: the all-pervasive control system was an attempt to repair the damaged credibility of the asylum system, which had been criticized for unfairness, inefficiency, and delay. Accommodation and removal centres were elements in this development. Restrictions on welfare support which made it conditional on reporting or residence also tightened the level of continuous control that the government is able to exercise over asylum seekers. Increased powers of detention and removal served the same purpose.

The second policy underlying the 2002 White Paper was a cautious encouragement of economic migration. This was the first evidence for decades that immigration policy might be directed towards encouragement of entry, and received a general welcome. Shah, R. (2002:315), for instance, saw this as evidence of 'a new dynamism' in the Home Office. However, this apparent shift in policy was not reflected in the 2002 Act. Extensions of various schemes permitting entry of workers were implemented by concessions and developments in administrative practice which, in some cases, resulted in changes to the immigration rules. The retention of government control over entry into the UK is presaged in the White Paper, para 12: 'We have taken steps to ensure that people with the skills and talents *we need* are able to come to the UK on a sensible and managed basis' (emphasis added). The retention of control outside statute and the words emphasized lend support to the argument of Cohen that such proposals represent nothing new; rather, they replicate a historical tendency to manipulate overseas labour, 'labour which can be turned on and off like a tap' (2002). Bevan made the same comment in relation to earlier provisions (1986:278). Scepticism, it seems, was warranted. A further White Paper in 2005 announced a tiered system of managed migration that aimed to bring entry for work and study into a more routinized, bureaucratized system, dominated by immigration control. But this is to anticipate.

The growth of a class of people without rights or status is evident in a number of disparate developments, and three provisions of the 2002 Act are examples. Section 4 for the first time allowed the Secretary of State to deprive a person of their British nationality if they were born British (see chapter 3). Although this could not be done if they would be left stateless, as the Joint Parliamentary Committee on Human Rights pointed out:

deprivation of British citizenship would entail loss of British diplomatic protection; loss of status; loss of the ability to participate in the democratic process in the United Kingdom; and serious damage to reputation and dignity. The Home Office argument assumes that the real threat to human rights would derive from any subsequent decisions taken as part of the immigration control process. In that process, there would usually be adequate opportunity to ensure that effect is given to Convention rights, and that other rights are given appropriate weight. However, we are concerned about the wider implications of loss of British citizenship. (Parliamentary Joint Committee on Human Rights Session 2001–02 Seventeenth Report para 26)

While recognizing that there is no right to British nationality, the Committee was concerned that if the other country refused a passport, the alternative nationality would be 'an empty shell' (para 26). The Committee's report reveals that the civic limbo in which persons would find themselves was not recognized by the Home Office. The difficulties of being left in a condition of no status or rights revealed in *Ahmed v Austria* 24 EHRR 62 had resulted in Mr Ahmed taking his own life.

Section 76 of the 2002 Act enables the Secretary of State to revoke a person's indefinite leave to remain if the person 'is liable to deportation but cannot be deported for legal reasons'. The legal reasons which would prevent deportation are likely to be that the person would face a serious violation of their human rights in their country of origin and no other country is willing to accept them. Without indefinite leave to remain, a person may neither work nor claim benefits. They are without status and without means.

The 2002 Bill was amended in the House of Lords so that citizenship by birth (though not by application) could only be removed in reliance on acts committed after s 4 came into force (1 April 2003). However, indefinite leave to remain may be revoked in reliance on anything done before s 76 came into force (10 February 2003) and leave granted before that date may be revoked, giving the section retrospective effect.

The third provision is s 67(2) in combination with its interpretation in *R v SSHD ex p Khadir (Appellant)* [2005] UKHL 39, which means that a person who is granted temporary admission—a status without rights—may remain in that position for years, even though there is no possibility of being removed (see chapter 14). The government has maintained that people on temporary admission are not 'lawfully present' for the purpose of social security rules and housing rules. Arguments on this and other issues have even led to the legal fiction that people temporarily admitted are not present at all, let alone lawfully. This was scotched in *Szoma v Secretary of State for the Department of Work and Pensions* [2005] UKHL 64, in which their Lordships held that the appellant was lawfully present.

The concern with undocumented migrants both throughout Europe and further afield is marked by this paradox; ever-increasing control measures are developed alongside measures to exclude some people from the system altogether. The Criminal Justice and Immigration Act 2008 contained a further power of this kind, though never implemented.

The development of extra-territorial immigration control is strongly signalled in the 2002 White Paper but barely appears in the Act. It was indeed a very significant development, but was introduced by a single enabling section. Ann Dummett submitted to the Parliamentary Joint Committee on Human Rights (JCHR) that the chief threat which the 2002 Bill represented to human rights arose from

the character it shares with all the immigration legislation of the twentieth century: it is an enabling Bill . . . Many of its provisions are vague and general, allowing for subsequent, more precise provisions contained in statutory instruments and rules. The nature of these precise provisions is to be to a very large extent discretionary. (Memorandum 5 to JCHR 17th Report Session 2001–02)

The detail of the export of immigration control is contained in secondary legislation and administrative arrangements. The notable exceptions are in Sch 8, which extends and amends the liability of carriers (lorry drivers, rail companies, and so on) for clandestine entrants hidden in their vehicles. Section 141 permits a law of the UK to have effect abroad. This enabling section laid the foundation for UK immigration control to operate at French ports. In fact, the legislative foundation for exporting the border in other ways had already been laid in the 1999 Act. Nevertheless, posting immigration officers alongside their counterparts at European ports, with the aim of deterring asylum claims constituted a significant change. These measures are discussed fully in chapter 6.

Combating terrorism is a thread which runs throughout legislation and government policy much more strongly since 11 September 2001. The Anti-terrorism, Crime and Security Act 2001 contains significant provisions affecting refugee claims, discussed in chapter 13, but the agenda of preventing terrorism is not explicit in the Immigration Acts. There are not, for instance, sections headed 'terrorism'. Nevertheless, in the 2002 Act, the strengthened and extended border controls, the new offences created, and the intensive monitoring of asylum seekers all have security as a background theme and objective (see McKee 2002 and Shah, R. 2002).

The asylum support provisions of the 2002 Act were among its most contentious. Despite research suggesting that welfare policies are not an effective deterrent (Home Office Research Study 243, 2003), the government was dedicated to a path of reducing welfare provision. As welfare support is not covered as a subject in its own right in this book, the main issues will be outlined here. The crucial provision in the 2002 Act was s 55, which provided that the Secretary of State has no obligation to provide welfare support (money or accommodation) where a claim for asylum has not been made 'as soon as reasonably practicable' unless this is necessary to avoid a breach of the claimant's human rights. Challenges to denial of benefit multiplied in the High Court. In the first year of the Act, judges made over 800 emergency orders for the payment of interim benefit (Sedley LJ annual Legal Action Group lecture November 2003). After people were refused support even when they claimed asylum on the day of their arrival in the UK, the case of *R (on the application of Q) v SSHD* [2003] EWCA Civ 364 considered the meaning of s 55. The Court of Appeal accepted that the asylum seeker's circumstances should be taken into account in determining what was 'as soon as reasonably practicable' and this could include advice given by someone arranging their passage. In January 2004, the government was obliged to introduce fairer procedures and a three-day period to allow people to find their way to relevant government offices (Macdonald and Webber 2005:868).

The government still pursued to the House of Lords the question of whether actual or imminent destitution would amount to a breach of Article 3—the right to be free of inhuman or degrading treatment. The House of Lords found that it did (*R v SSHD ex p Adam, Limbuela and Tesema* [2005] UKHL 66).

Welfare support continued to be a major preoccupation in the 2004 Act. The proposal in the consultation letter preceding the Act which provoked the most opposition was that welfare support and accommodation should be withdrawn from failed asylum seekers with families. The 1999 Act had already withdrawn support from childless asylum seekers whose claim had failed, but it was not thought appropriate then to inflict destitution on children. In 2003, the government had a different solution—take the children into care. Section 9 enabled support to be withdrawn once a claim has failed and appeals are exhausted in a case where the Secretary of State certified that the claimant 'has failed without reasonable excuse to take reasonable steps to leave the UK voluntarily' (s 9 of the 2004 Act, inserting para 7A into Sch 3 of the 2002 Act). Section 10 drew almost as much criticism as it enables the Secretary of State to make regulations making continuation of accommodation for a failed asylum seeker dependent upon performing community service.

The Parliamentary Joint Committee on Human Rights noted that an asylum seeker 'who has exhausted their rights of appeal, cannot return to their country for reasons beyond their control and who has no other means of support is in an analogous position to a UK citizen or any other person in the UK who is entitled to emergency state assistance to prevent destitution' (Fourteenth Report 2003–04 HL 130/HC 828 para 18). An obligation to perform community service as a condition of receiving emergency social assistance was not, as claimed by the government 'a normal civic obligation'. On the contrary, it was 'without precedent or even analogy' (para 15). There was a significant risk of breach of Article 4(2) ECHR through forced or compulsory labour (para 16). Singling out asylum seekers would breach Article 14 as it was unjustifiably discriminatory (para 21), and a withdrawal of support if someone did not perform the labour could breach Article 3 by subjecting them to inhuman and degrading treatment (para 24). In the event, s 10 proved impossible to implement as no community organizations could be found who were willing to provide the community service in question.

The operation of s 9 was piloted in late 2005 in East London, Manchester, and West Yorkshire. Organizations representing social workers lobbied against it as their members baulked at taking asylum seekers' children into care when this would not be in the children's best interests. The Joint Committee on Human Rights considered that it would be difficult to implement s 9 without breaches of Articles 3 and 8 (Session 2003–04 Fifth Report HL Paper 35 HC 304 para 45). Reports of children's charities and refugee organizations concluded that the pilot of s 9 had caused enormous distress and destitution. Families were considered to be at low risk of absconding, but some did disappear when faced with the prospect of parents being separated from children (Refugee Action and Refugee Council 2006). The Immigration Asylum and Nationality Act 2006 contains a provision (s 44) allowing s 9 to be repealed by ministerial order, but this has not been implemented. Instead, in the 2015/16 Bill, the government seeks to reintroduce the idea. This time the proposal is extremely complex, and at the time of writing is subject to further amendments. Broadly, the Bill proposes to prevent families whose asylum claim has been refused from continuing on asylum support, *and* from being supported under the Children Act 1989. However, the Bill necessarily makes provision for those who demonstrate they are unable to return to their home country. The result is uncertain, presenting a risk of destitution for families, but with provisions so complex that interpreting and applying them will also contribute to the problem.

The 2002 Act demonstrated the strength of executive power not only in its content but also in its passage through Parliament. One of the most hotly debated provisions in the Bill was the proposal that the Secretary of State should be able to certify asylum claims 'clearly unfounded' and that this certificate should prevent any appeal from taking place in the UK. This late amendment prevented proper parliamentary scrutiny of the removal of appeal rights for people who, if they have been wrongly refused, may face the most serious human rights violations. This was announced after the end of the Commons Standing Committee, leaving any effective debate only to the House of Lords. A further amendment to this clause was one of many announced even after Committee stage in the House of Lords. This led to the unusual step of the Bill being sent back to the Lords Committee for further consideration.

This practice of introducing late amendments on significant matters was a characteristic of the passage of both the 2002 and 2004 Act and has recurred in the Immigration

Act 2014. The Parliamentary Joint Committee on Human Rights commented adversely on the Home Office practice in relation to the 2002 Act of not replying to the Committee's questions until crucial parliamentary stages had been passed (JCHR Session 2001–02 Seventeenth Report para 4). In relation to the 2004 Act 'we find ourselves once again in the very same position so soon after having made clear that such a practice undermines parliamentary scrutiny of legislation for compatibility with human rights' (JCHR Session 2003–04 Fourteenth Report HL 130 HC 828 para 3). Lord Lester commented that an unfortunate effect of this lack of scrutiny is that 'the matter will end up in court' (HL Debs 6 July 2004 col 722) as, in fact, happened on the very matter upon which that comment was made (regulations on marriage, discussed in chapter 8).

Haste and lack of consultation characterized the 2003 AITOC Bill. It was introduced in November 2003, with minimal consultation and during the currency of a Home Affairs Committee inquiry into Asylum Applications. The Committee had to break off its work to provide a response to the Bill, and said:

we have not had the benefit of a draft Bill, nor—in common with other interested parties—were we given more than a few weeks' notice of the proposals even in outline. In view of the fact that since March 2003 we have been conducting a major inquiry into asylum applications, we find this regrettable. (Home Affairs Committee Session 2003–04 Second Report HC 218 para 3)

The Bill contained a clause which would have prevented all higher courts from hearing any immigration or asylum case whether by way of appeal or review. The government's stated reason was to streamline the appeals process and end unmeritorious appeals, but the measure contained no means of separating the meritorious from the unmeritorious, and that decision is precisely the one the courts can make. In addition to the plain injustice to foreign nationals, the development of international refugee law would be denied the contribution of the British House of Lords.

There was unanimous opposition from the legal establishment. The Law Society, Bar Council, Joint Parliamentary Committee on Human Rights, and senior judiciary, including two former Lord Chancellors, agreed the ouster clause violated the rule of law. Matrix Chambers published an opinion quoting Lord Denning: 'If tribunals were at liberty to exceed their jurisdiction without any check by courts the rule of law would be at an end' (*ex p Gilmore* [1957] 1 QB 574 at 586). The Constitutional Affairs Committee said:

The new proposals do little to address the failings at the initial decision making level and the low level of Home Office representation at initial appeals, which must add to the delays in the system. We think it unlikely that the abolition of a tier of appeal can by itself increase 'end to end' speed and achieve improvements in the quality of judicial decisions. We doubt whether many of the proposals contained in the new Bill are necessary to deal with the current issues in relation to asylum and immigration appeals. (Constitutional Affairs Committee Session 2003–04 Second Report HC 211 summary)

The government was forced to concede, and on introducing the Bill for its second reading in the House of Lords the Lord Chancellor Lord Falconer accepted that the ouster clause could not stand (HL Debs 15 March 2004 col 51).

The Bill contained other reforms of the appeals system which, after reformulation, gained acceptance in Parliament. The principal one was collapsing the former two-tier system of immigration appeals into one.

The 2004 Act added a number of enforcement powers. It is a fairly short miscellany of mainly punitive or enforcement measures, the Bill being referred to by Lord Lester as 'mean spirited and reactionary' (2004:263). It received Royal Assent on 22 July 2004.

In February 2005, the White Paper entitled *Controlling our Borders: Making Migration Work for Britain* (Cm 6472) was announced as a 'five-year strategy for asylum and immigration'. The Immigration, Asylum and Nationality Act 2006 was said to provide the legislative base for implementing the proposals, but includes fresh initiatives not raised in the White Paper; it is apparent that the White Paper is not a five-year plan in any comprehensive sense. Much of its content referred to changes that had already been agreed or made. New proposals included:

- the introduction of a points system for all migration for work or study, privileging the most skilled and ending settlement rights for the low skilled;
- detaining more failed asylum seekers;
- giving recognized refugees only temporary leave (five years);
- abolishing appeals against work and study immigration decisions;
- increasing use of new technology and intelligence coordination at borders, and reintroducing exit monitoring.

Most of these did not require legislation, and the majority of the 2006 Act provisions concern tightening enforcement powers, whether through immigration officers' powers or sanctions on employers.

The most radical and far-reaching proposals of *Controlling our Borders* were those to end appeal rights and to institute a comprehensive points system for work and study. The points-based system (PBS) was modelled on that of other countries, for instance Australia, in which a certain number of points are required to gain entry, and these are gained for qualifications and other characteristics such as age, available money, and so on. Once published, the PBS consisted of five tiers to encompass all routes to entry for work and study. The vision promoted by the government was of a routinized system, with applications beginning with an online self-assessment form for the applicant to check whether they would qualify for entry, and applications for entry made at overseas posts instead of through the specialized system at Work Permits (UK). The first stage of implementation, for highly skilled people, started in March 2008, and by March 2009 all five tiers were in force. The PBS is discussed in chapter 9.

As each tier of the PBS came into effect, appeal rights for that tier were removed using s 4. It removed the right of appeal against refusal of entry clearance on grounds other than human rights and race discrimination in all but specified family visitor and dependant cases. The new system encompasses students and almost all those who apply to work in the UK. The change was radical. A swell of opposition to the removal of appeal rights from students and the enlistment of universities in immigration control, including from University Vice-Chancellors and Principals (letter from Universities UK to *Financial Times*, Tuesday, 5 July 2005), was to no avail.

The government said that appeal rights would be less important in the PBS because of the claimed objectivity. However, the points system had not been published in any detail at the time of parliamentary debate on the Bill. This made it difficult for Parliamentarians to debate the Bill effectively and test the government's assertion that the new system would guarantee fair and objective decisions, warranting removal of the right of appeal. Eventually, at report stage in the House of Lords, the government agreed that the tiered migration system would be published before their Lordships went on to the third reading, so that they could assess the safeguards for themselves. This was done by publishing an outline in the document, 'A Points Based System: Making Migration Work for Britain', and the Bill was passed.

Lest we be tempted to think that haste and lack of consultation are purely modern practices, the requirement for entry certificates, which laid the foundation for the whole system of entry clearance, was a last-minute amendment to the Immigration

(Appeals) Act 1969. The draconian Commonwealth Immigrants Act 1968 was rushed through Parliament in only five days. One difference now is that statutes are prefaced with a declaration that they are compatible with the Human Rights Act (under HRA s 19), but often there has not been enough consideration of whether this is the case.

The PBS extends the policy of end-to-end monitoring to all who enter for work and study. A key feature of the system is 'compliance checking': this involves sponsors reporting that migrants are here and are doing what their terms of entry permitted them to do, and whether people have left the UK at the end of their permitted period of stay. Educational institutions are sponsors of overseas students, and employers of their employees.

In the meantime, entry for work became less welcome after all. Romanian and Bulgarian workers were given more limited rights to work than A8 nationals, and the terms of entry for medical graduates and highly skilled workers were dramatically restricted during 2006 (see chapter 9). Families once again came under the government spotlight, as a certificate of approval scheme was introduced for marriages of foreign nationals (see chapter 8), and proposals issued to raise the age for marriage once again (implemented in 2008) and introduce language testing for spouses. The first two of these initiatives have since been found to be unlawful by the Supreme Court (see chapter 8). The third has been implemented, though found to be capable of inflicting serious hardship in individual cases (*R (on the applications of Ali and Bibi) v SSHD* [2015] UKSC 68, see chapter 8)

The 2006 Act, in addition to removing rights of appeal as mentioned previously, develops the provisions for information exchange between carriers and immigration control personnel, including a power for the Secretary of State or an immigration officer to compel disclosure to them of passenger lists. This is an element in 'exporting the border', as introduced in the 2002 White Paper. The Act's other miscellaneous provisions are enforcement oriented, including a provision which makes it far easier to exclude people charged with terrorist-related offences from the protection of the Refugee Convention (s 54; see chapter 13). As discussed earlier, the 2002 Act made it possible for the first time for people to lose British nationality acquired by birth or parentage. The 2006 Act made this substantially easier, equating the grounds with the grounds for deportation—simply that the deprivation of nationality was 'conducive to the public good' (s 56).

Continuing the control theme, *Controlling our Borders* introduced a 'new asylum model' (NAM), an administrative system designed to streamline applications and make greater use of detention. The accommodation centres proposed in the 2002 Act did not prove viable, and induction centres were introduced as another attempt to process as many asylum claims as possible while keeping the claimant in some form of controlled accommodation. In tandem with the NAM, in July 2006, the Home Office announced that there was a 'legacy' of 450,000 cases that were outstanding and would not come within the NAM, and they undertook to clear this backlog within five years. The 'Case Resolution' directorate was set up within the Home Office to be proactive in achieving this. By the deadline of July 2011, some 18,000 cases remained officially to be completed, and were transferred to a new unit: Case Assurance and Audit. Another 98,000 asylum cases were placed in a 'controlled archive'. As these were reviewed, it began to appear that the majority might be duplicate files for cases that had already been concluded but many were files of people who were in fact regularly reporting to the Home Office and not untraceable, as had been recorded. Fifty-six per cent of the outcomes in July 2011 were 'other'—that is, duplicates, errors (for instance, the person was an EU national), or placed in the controlled archive. In parallel with the passage of the 2006 Act through Parliament, the Home Affairs Committee was conducting an inquiry into immigration control. Perhaps their main message was that the immigration system was stuck in the era of seeing itself, and being seen, as concerned with preventing entry. They recommended that the focus should move also towards facilitation of legitimate travel and control of immigration after arrival in the country. When people's leave to remain expired, the government should be aware of that and able to act on it.

Also in 2006, the Home Office instituted a root and branch review of the immigration system, following the disclosure that foreign prisoners had been released without being considered for deportation. The review went beyond this issue, resulting in a programme of far-reaching organizational reforms (see chapter 2).

With each step, as appeal rights were removed, the government appointed an independent monitor to oversee the quality of the decisions in question. By 2007 this had resulted in a number of monitors, each with a different remit. Following consultation, the government abolished the monitors, and appointed instead an Independent Chief Inspector whose remit covers all the work connected with borders and immigration.

Developing the policy of internal controls, the UK Borders Act 2007 introduced a scheme of biometric identity documents for foreign nationals. Sections 5 to 15 provide that any non-EEA national in the UK, whether lawfully resident or not, may be required to apply for a 'biometric immigration document' (see chapter 2). This means any kind of document recording external physical characteristics including, in particular, fingerprints, features of the iris, and digital photographs which may be scanned by facial recognition technology. Section 19 removed the right to introduce new documentary evidence at appeals against a refusal to vary leave under the points-based system, thus underscoring the policy of the PBS that the first decision should be the final decision (see chapter 9).

The 2007 Act introduced automatic deportation for those who have committed certain criminal offences (ss 32–39). Although the Home Affairs Committee endorsed this idea for 'serious criminals', it may be doubted whether all those caught by this provision could really be described as such (see chapter 15 for discussion). A further provision in the Criminal Justice and Immigration Act 2008 removed all status from people who cannot be deported for legal reasons. This was to prevent the government from being obliged to give a protective status to people who have been convicted of a criminal offence, but cannot be returned to their home country because of feared human rights abuses. The Act also provides for powers to restrict residence and work, and for electronic tagging. This is another example of the government legislating to overturn a decision of the courts, this time the decision in the Afghan hijackers' case, discussed in chapter 2. The 2008 regime has not been implemented, but instead a policy of restricted leave is in place.

The 2006 Act gave increased powers of arrest to immigration officers. The 2007 Act gave them increased powers of detention. The 2006 Act created a duty for immigration, revenue, and customs officers to share information. These steps contributed to the creation of the unified border force, announced by the Prime Minister in July 2007. This heralded a major new development in immigration control. The defining document, *Security in a Global Hub*, proclaimed the new agency as an integration of the Immigration Department of the Home Office, UKVisas (the entry clearance operation overseas), and the border operations of HM Revenue and Customs. The UK Border Agency came into being in April 2008. UKBA, located in the Home Office, survived until 2013. The intelligence- and technology-led system established under the auspices of UKBA is described in chapters 2 and 6.

Alongside these institutional changes, the government attempted to achieve a goal often referred to by earlier administrations, that of consolidating all immigration statutes into one. The aim of consolidation was itself consolidated with another aim, to 'simplify' immigration law. In July 2008, a 'Draft Partial Simplification Bill' was published. The Bill was not a great success, the House of Commons Home Affairs research paper describing it as 'not what one might call "simple": it is still full of complex clauses, sub-clauses, exceptions, qualifications, and cross-references, and in some cases reproduces sections of previous Acts wholesale'. On 11 November 2008, the Home Affairs Committee suspended its scrutiny of the Bill, taking the view that it was unable to continue until the whole Bill had been published, and the Bill was withdrawn.

Elements of the Bill which dealt with a new idea of an earned progression towards citizenship were skeletally enacted in the Borders, Citizenship and Immigration Act 2009, in particular by providing for the status of 'probationary citizenship'. This was intended to place a hurdle between temporary and indefinite leave, and to allow government to change the criteria and qualification periods from time to time depending upon policy. The then government envisaged a PBS for settlement, which could incorporate various tests of integration, again depending on 'current interests' ('Earning the Right to Stay: A New Points Test for Citizenship'). These plans were abandoned in November 2010.

The main body of the 2009 Act is concerned with provisions for officials of UKBA to carry out the functions of HMRC and other related powers which progressed the creation of the single border agency. The Act contains a short miscellany of other items, including a new duty on the Secretary of State to make arrangements to ensure that immigration, asylum, and nationality functions are discharged 'having regard to the need to safeguard and promote the welfare of children' who are in the UK (s 55). This recognized the UK's withdrawal of its reservation to the UN Convention on the Rights of the Child. The Parliamentary Joint Committee on Human Rights said that this represented 'a most welcome change in policy' (Legislative Scrutiny: Borders, Citizenship and Immigration Bill, Ninth Report of Session 2008–09 HL 62, HC 375), which would provide an opportunity to begin to address the serious human rights concerns the Committee had previously expressed, including the inappropriate detention of children, the effect on them of 'heavy handed enforcement methods such as dawn raids and forced removals', and inappropriate methods for testing their age (para 1.14). Joint guidance on the performance of the new duty has been issued by the Home Office and the Department for Children, Schools and Families, and its importance was emphasized by the Supreme Court in *ZH (Tanzania)* [2011] UKSC 4 (see chapter 8).

The Coalition government that came to power in May 2010 made a commitment to reduce net immigration. Detailed consultations in 2011 on family migration and on settlement were promulgated in this context. Proposals in *Family Migration: A Consultation* include introducing specified detailed questions to ascertain whether the marriage is 'genuine', setting a minimum income threshold to sponsor a partner or relative, extending the probationary period for partners from two years to five years, abolishing immediate settlement for partners with a four-year relationship, giving immigration control functions to marriage registrars, and introducing a probationary period for elderly relatives. All of these provisions were included in a lengthy and very complex set of immigration rules implemented in July 2012 (see chapter 8). The Coalition government has also made numerous and frequent changes to entry for work, discussed in chapter 9, including abolishing the domestic worker category, together with the protections for domestic workers that accompanied that route. The government has abolished the right of most students to be accompanied by their families. It has also made significant steps towards ending the immigration detention of children (see chapter 14).

The development of immigration law in 2012/13 took place in a government atmosphere of increasingly aggressive control of migrants and migration and of refugees. This is briefly elaborated upon in chapter 2. This was the context of the Immigration Bill

2013 which heralded major changes in immigration law. Its initial progress through Parliament was at breakneck speed. It was introduced in Parliament on 10 October 2013, and completed its passage through the House of Commons as far as the Committee stage within six weeks. The government's intention was to complete the Commons stage before Christmas, so that in January 2014 the Bill would go straight to the Lords. The final stage of EU law restrictions on Bulgarian and Romanian workers was due to be lifted on 31 December 2013, and a backbench Conservative MP put down an amendment to the Bill at Committee stage which would retain the restrictions for a further five years. The amendment attracted significant backbench support, although it would have been illegal under EU law. In order to avoid confrontation and possible defeat, the Prime Minister deferred the report stage and third reading of the Bill to 2014, allowing time for negotiations and for the 31 December deadline to pass. This was part of the genesis of proposals to limit the access of EEA nationals to welfare benefits in the UK, proposals which formed part of the Prime Minister's renegotiation of EU membership.

The delay also allowed for a further development. When the Bill came back to the House of Commons the Home Secretary introduced an amendment allowing her to strip naturalized British citizens of their nationality even if this left them stateless, if she is satisfied that they have conducted themselves 'in a manner which is seriously prejudicial to the vital interests of the UK'. The clause was enacted with the qualification that the power could only be exercised if the Secretary of State had 'reasonable grounds for believing' that the person was able to acquire another nationality.

The key provisions of the Immigration Act 2014 include removing the right to appeal an immigration decision except a human rights or protection claim. The only grounds for appeal are human rights or asylum grounds. It will be recalled from the history so far that governments have tried before to prevent migrants from having access to appeals. The 2003 proposal met with uproar from the legal establishment and was defeated. However, since then a number of appeal rights have been removed step by step. This clause, which was one of the most controversial in the House of Commons, removed rights of appeal for all migrants (students, workers, family members). The government offered instead the remedy of administrative review. Figures at the time the provision was debated showed that approximately 18 per cent of administrative reviews result in the original decision being remade whereas 50 per cent of immigration appeals succeeded.

Decisions in the courts mitigated the government's attempts to make Article 8 ECHR subject to the immigration rules (see chapters 5, 7, 8, and 15). The Immigration Act 2014 goes further and contains obligatory factors to which the court must have regard in deciding Article 8 appeals. Section 19 introduces a definition of the 'public interest' which must form part of the court's consideration in deciding on a possible infringement of Article 8. It provides that 'little weight should be given to a private life established by a person at a time when the person's immigration status is precarious' (clause 117B (5); see chapter 5). The Act has a curious feature in that it contains its own internal policy justification:

It is in the public interest, and in particular in the interests of the economic well-being of the United Kingdom, that persons who seek to enter or remain in the United Kingdom are able to speak English, because persons who can speak English—
(a) are less of a burden on taxpayers, and
(b) are better able to integrate into society. (clause 117B (2)).

Provisions of the Immigration Act 2014 are discussed in relevant chapters of this book: 'deport first, appeal later' and restricted appeals in chapters 5, 7, and 15; the factors defining Article 8 in chapters 5 and 15; the marriage restrictions in chapter 8; removal powers in chapter 16; the spread of immigration powers into civil society in chapter 2; deprivation of nationality in chapter 3.

The Act is a draconian piece of legislation which seeks to create a 'hostile environment' for those migrants who are deemed not welcome (see chapter 2). In the context of preceding developments, it is clear that the 2014 Act is a new way to achieve some of the goals that previous governments have aimed at. These include removing rights of appeal from migrants, restricting settlement, and preventing human rights appeals so far as possible from being heard in the UK. One step in the opposite direction is in section 5, which provides that unaccompanied children should not be detained except in short-term holding facilities or the Cedars (see chapter 14).

The Legal Aid Sentencing and Punishment of Offenders Act 2012 is discussed in chapter 7. It removed legal aid from immigration and some human rights cases, and created a massively complex set of rules for public funding in judicial review. No sooner was it in force than further cuts in legal aid for migrants were proposed: a residence test for eligibility. This was declared ultra vires by the Supreme Court in *R (on the application of the Public Law Project) v Lord Chancellor* on 18 April 2016.

At the same time, new fast tracks to settlement were opened up for the super-rich, who need not speak English (see chapter 9), and fast-track electronic visa waivers were introduced for visitors from Qatar, Oman, and the United Arab Emirates.

Before all the provisions of the 2014 Act were in force, the government introduced the Immigration Bill 2015/16. This criminalizes many of the matters which were introduced in the 2014 Act as civil matters. For instance, the scheme whereby landlords are obliged to check the immigration status of their tenants (see chapter 2) now subjects the landlord to criminal penalties if they let to a person who has no right to rent. Working without permission will become an offence for the worker as well as the employer. This proposal has given rise to fears that it will harden exploitative employment practices as workers become more fearful of speaking out.

The Bill also proposes, as discussed already, to remove asylum support from families whose claims have failed, to reduce conditions of availability of support for single people whose claims have failed, and to remove the right of appeal against refusal of asylum support for both groups except where they have made prompt new submissions.

Despite the concern of the JCHR and House of Lords about destitution, successive governments have pursued a policy of maximizing destitution, testing the limits that the law will allow. The proposals in the 2015/16 Bill continue the policy on the basis that people will leave the UK if they are forced to by being made destitute. (see chapter 2).

One further legal development should be mentioned here. Following a series of legal challenges, the Detained Fast Track system of processing asylum claims was suspended by the government in July 2015. The system had been shown in numerous ways to be placing vulnerable people at risk. An interim instruction permits detention of asylum seekers only on normal detention grounds (see chapter 14). A replacement scheme is promised.

1.3 Sources of immigration law

There is no doubt that immigration control is an exercise of executive power; that is, it is exercised by the executive arm of government, in this case principally by the Home Secretary, Home Office civil servants, immigration officers, and ECOs. Less clear are the source and limits of that power. Immigration law is, in a sense, all about the exercise of executive power and the limits upon it. A characteristic that will be encountered over and over again in the study of immigration law is the retention of discretion, which is of course less amenable to control than the application of specific rules. The discretionary nature of immigration law is at the root of much of the criticism that has been directed at it. While challenges to decisions and initiatives towards accountability and openness seek to put limits on the power of the executive, in other ways the scope to use discretion is continually reasserted. In order to ascertain the extent to which decisions can be challenged, it is necessary to consider the source of the power that is exercised. A purely statutory power is subject to public law constraints and perhaps the exercise of appeal rights; something with a more nebulous origin may be harder to control. So we will begin with that question—where does it come from?

1.3.1 **Prerogative origins?**

The right of nation states to control the entry and expulsion of foreign nationals is often said to be an essential aspect of sovereignty, and arguably exercised under the prerogative. The prerogative was originally the power of the Crown. The Bill of Rights 1689 decreed that the prerogative could not be extended any further and that statute could supersede the prerogative. From this time on, the prerogative had a residual character (see, for instance, Loveland, *Constitutional Law; Administrative Law and Human Rights: A Critical Introduction* 2003). In the present day, relevant prerogatives, if any, are at the disposal of the government, which now holds the authority of the Crown for most purposes. There are personal prerogatives of the monarch such as dispensing certain honours, but we are not concerned with these.

The extent of the prerogative has been a matter of argument even in quite recent times. In *R v Secretary of State ex p Northumbria Police Authority* [1989] QB 26, the Court of Appeal found that there was a prerogative to keep the peace even though it had not been written down anywhere. However, Vincenzi argues that there are specific recognized areas of prerogative power, not an amorphous pool which could be used for purposes convenient to the government (1992:300). Following *CCSU v Minister for the Civil Service* [1985] AC 374 (the GCHQ case), in which the House of Lords decided that the exercise of the prerogative was reviewable, a number of prerogative powers have been considered, and the reviewability of each decided as a separate question (see, e.g., *R v Secretary of State for Foreign and Commonwealth Affairs ex p Everett* [1989] QB 811 CA, *R v SSHD ex p Bentley* [1993] 4 All ER 442). This seems to support Vincenzi's argument. Indeed, this approach seems to flow from Lord Diplock's list in the GCHQ case of potentially non-reviewable prerogative powers, and the question was not resolved in *ex p Northumbria Police Authority*.

Those prerogative powers which have been identified include matters such as the conduct of foreign affairs, the power to conduct the internal affairs of the civil service, and the issue of passports (Vincenzi 1998). It would be a brave person now who suggested that there was a major prerogative power left undiscovered, and in the area of immigration control it is reasonable to assume that whatever prerogative power exists is known about. Chapter 4 of Vincenzi's book explores the relationship between the prerogative and immigration control, and reference should be made to that for a full account. All the authorities agree that there is a prerogative power to deal with aliens, but there is disagreement over its extent.

Immigration control in the UK is now largely governed by statute and immigration rules made pursuant to the statutory power to do so (Immigration Act 1971 s 3(2)). The Immigration Act 1971, however, expressly reserves a prerogative power in mysterious terms: 'This Act shall not be taken to supersede or impair any power exercisable by Her Majesty in relation to aliens by virtue of her prerogative' (s 33(5)). In its reference only to aliens, the subsection conforms with the established view that the prerogative does not apply to those who owe allegiance to the Crown, that is, British and Commonwealth citizens (cp. *DPP v Bhagwan* [1972] AC 60 and *R v IAT ex p Secretary of State for the Home Department* [1990] 3 All ER 652). However, what power over 'aliens' does the section reserve, and over which 'aliens'? Vincenzi suggests that the only non-contentious prerogative in relation to aliens is to imprison enemy aliens, that is, nationals of those countries with whom the UK is at war. This is consistent with the first appearance of a reservation of a prerogative power in the Aliens Restriction Act 1914, passed at the outbreak of the First World War, apparently ensuring that the Crown did not, by the Act, diminish its power to deal with the enemy. The Supreme Court in *Alvi* and in *Munir*, discussed later, confirmed this understanding, quoting Lord Windlesham who spoke for the government in the debate on the Immigration Bill:

The prerogative powers in question . . . include the power in the Crown at times of war to intern, expel or otherwise control enemy aliens at its discretion, . . . The Government do not think it necessary to surrender these powers, which go back many years. We are talking about residuary prerogative powers for the kind of exceptional circumstances which have arisen in this century only on the occasions of the two World wars. (*Munir* para 25)

The concept of immigration control is a modern one, originating in the Aliens Act 1905. The innovation that the Act represented is clear from parliamentary debates. For instance, Sir Charles Dilkes, the MP for Gloucestershire, Forest of Dean, said that the measure 'for the first time' would prevent 'free men' [sic] from coming to a 'free country' (HC Debs 29 March 1904 vol 132 col 991). The basis of the Bill was that statutory power was needed to interfere with the entry of aliens.

The reason this issue is discussed here is that if immigration control is seen as a 'prerogative power clothed in statute' (Vincenzi p. 101), its amenability to regulation is that much less. If it is seen as a purely statutory power, it must be exercised in accordance with the power granted by that statute and in accordance with principles of statutory interpretation, and not otherwise.

Although it was unlikely that the prerogative was the source of immigration control, the government continued to assert that there was a prerogative power, and that when doing something outside the rules they were exercising it. The idea even continued to appear in dicta of the senior judiciary (see *Odelola* [2009] UKHL 25).

The alleged prerogative source of immigration law has now been laid to rest by the Supreme Court.

 **Key Case**

R (on the application of Munir) v SSHD [2012] UKSC 32

The case concerned the withdrawal of a policy. DP 5/96, upon which the appellants sought to rely, allowed for leave to remain to be granted to families where children had been resident in the UK for seven years or more. The Secretary of State argued that policies such as these were issued under the prerogative. Although Mr Munir lost his case because the Supreme Court held that the Secretary of State was entitled to change her policy, they held that this was not on the basis of the prerogative. The Court noted that the long title of the 1971 Immigration Act was that it was to amend '*and replace*' the immigration laws then in

force. The Court reviewed the history and purpose of the Immigration Act and concluded
that:

> the power to make immigration rules under the 1971 Act derives from the Act itself and
> is not an exercise of the prerogative. As its long title indicates, the purpose of the 1971
> Act was to replace earlier laws with a single code of legislation on immigration control.
> (para 26)

There is undoubtedly a power to make immigration decisions outside the immigration
rules, but this derives from the wide powers in the statute to give or refuse leave to enter
or remain (Immigration Act 1971 ss 3A, 3B, and 4), and there is no need to employ the
prerogative as an explanation. Judgment was given on the same day in another case
which also dealt with the prerogative as a source of power to control immigration:

 Key Case

R (on the application of Alvi) v SSHD [2012] UKSC 33

Mr Alvi held a work permit as a physiotherapy assistant under the previous system of leave to
enter and remain in the UK for work. He applied for further leave to remain after the points-
based system had come into effect, and was refused on the basis that the job of assistant
physiotherapist was below NVQ/SVQ level 3 and thus did not fulfil the requirements of the
code of practice for leave to remain for skilled work. Initially he was refused on the basis that
he had failed to fulfil the requirements of the immigration rules since the code of practice
was referred to in the rules. In judicial review proceedings before the Supreme Court the
Secretary of State argued that it was open to her to control immigration in ways not set out
in the rules, because she could rely on the prerogative.

The Supreme Court held that the 1971 Act 'should be seen as a constitutional landmark
which, for all practical purposes, gave statutory force to all the powers previously exercisable
in the field of immigration control under the prerogative' (para 31).

The Secretary of State's argument that she could 'control immigration in a way not covered by the immigration rules in the exercise of powers under the prerogative' was rejected
(para 33). Dicta in *Odelola* were wrong.

Following *Alvi* and *Munir*, it is beyond doubt that immigration control is exercised pursuant to the statute. It is not empowered by a mysterious source which somehow lurks
behind the rules.

1.3.1.1 A modern equivalent?

The danger of relying on the prerogative is that it allows reliance upon a supposed
reserve of undefined power to supplement explicit provisions. However, even without
reliance on the prerogative, two other principles, sovereignty and the judgment of the
executive, may be observed in more recent case law to be playing a similar role. The first
is explanatory and the second is justificatory.

Sovereignty in dealing with foreign nationals is curtailed by treaties to which the
state is a party, such as, in the UK's case, the European Convention on Human Rights,
and the 1951 UN Convention Relating to Refugees. In the age of internationalism, the

development of international human rights norms, and an international criminal court, the nation state can no longer be properly regarded as the ultimate legal authority. It was well recognized that national legal authority must now be tempered by regard for international law, and that international regulation is a fact of life.

Ironically, it is through the Human Rights Act 1998, bringing the rights of the European Convention into UK law, that the idea of sovereignty seemed to make something of a comeback. In immigration cases, the European Court of Human Rights routinely begins its reasoning with the statement that states have the right, as a recognized principle of international law, and subject to their treaty obligations, to control the entry of non-nationals (see *Abdulaziz Cabales and Balkandali* (1985) 7 EHRR 471 para 67). This statement has an understandable place in the judgment of an international court, but has been transposed into the UK courts' and tribunals' reasoning in human rights cases. It is not inaccurate, but is unnecessary in the national context, where the task of the decision-maker is to apply and interpret law which is already made by the sovereign law-maker (Parliament) or is of a lesser status (immigration rules) or is case law which arises or can be argued to have a place in the jurisdiction. Sovereignty, if it arises at all, is being exercised, not challenged, and the reiteration of it in national courts has an effect similar to that noted by Evans in relation to the prerogative. This was demonstrated in *R v SSHD ex p Saadi, Maged, Osman and Mohammed* [2002] 1 WLR 3131, HL, in which the principle of sovereignty was itself used to interpret, and thus restrict, human rights (see chapter 14). The outcome was endorsed by the European Court of Human Rights (ECtHR). As Dauvergne comments, 'Migration law is transformed into the new last bastion of sovereignty' (2004:588), and correspondingly, sovereignty is invoked to buttress the state's right to control migration. A number of writers now argue that the territorial notion of sovereignty is also breaking down (e.g., Thomas and Kostakopoulou, Dauvergne), and that sovereignty is now exercised over people and information more than over territory. The shift in the UK's border control strategy could be argued to demonstrate just that.

In the early days of the Human Rights Act, the idea that immigration control is a matter for the executive influenced the courts and tribunals as they began to explore the application of qualified rights, which require them to judge the proportionality of the harm done to the individual against the public interest. The doctrine of deference to the executive was developed from judicial review, but in *Huang and Kashmiri v SSHD* [2007] UKHL 11, the House of Lords held that deference is not really a proper constitutional principle at all. The judiciary are competent to decide whether in a particular case they should give special weight to the Secretary of State's judgment or not. To argue for deference is not the same thing as to argue for a prerogative power, but the effect may be similar in that, in both instances, it is posited that there is an area of exercise of judgment which is somehow the special preserve of the government. For instance, in the case of indefinite detentions of foreign nationals, the Court of Appeal deferred to the judgment of the executive that discrimination on grounds of nationality was necessary for security reasons (*A v SSHD* [2002] EWCA Civ 1502). In the House of Lords, Lord Bingham in particular set out the UK's obligations under international treaties as an important part of the reasons why this deference was not warranted (*A v SSHD* [2004] UKHL 56).

1.3.2 Statutory origins

As is now accepted, the present-day legal source of the power of immigration control is statutory. The main statutes are the Immigration Act 1971, the Immigration and Asylum Act 1999, the Nationality, Immigration and Asylum Act 2002, the Asylum and Immigration (Treatment of Claimants, etc.) Act 2004, the Immigration, Asylum and Nationality Act 2006, the UK Borders Act 2007, the Borders Citizenship and Immigration Act 2009, and the Immigration Act 2014. All of these have been discussed earlier.

The fundamental legal authority for the power to control immigration is found in the Immigration Act 1971 s 4(1), which says:

The power under this Act to give or refuse leave to enter the United Kingdom shall be exercised by immigration officers, and the power to give leave to remain in the United Kingdom, or to vary any leave under section 3(3)(a) (whether as regards duration or conditions), shall be exercised by the Secretary of State.

Perhaps surprisingly, the statutes contain none of the specific provisions which govern whether a person may gain entry to the UK or leave to remain, although they do contain the basic grounds upon which they may be expelled. The requirements to be met to gain entry or leave to remain are mainly contained in the immigration rules.

1.3.3 **Immigration rules**

Immigration Act 1971 s 1(4) contains the only requirement as to the content of the rules. They must:

include provision for admitting (in such cases and subject to such restrictions as may be provided by the rules . . .) persons coming for the purpose of taking employment, or for the purposes of study, or as visitors, or as dependants of persons lawfully in or entering the UK.

Section 3(2) provides that this:

shall not be taken to require uniform provision to be made by the rules as regards admission of persons for a purpose or in a capacity specified in section 1(4) (and in particular, for this as well as other purposes of this Act, account may be taken of citizenship or nationality).

The rules are now voluminous and run into thousands. Numbering stops at 417 but this is not indicative as many numbered paragraphs are expanded by additional lettered paragraphs: A to Z and so on and major new bodies of rules are included in Appendices, of which there are now 26. All changes since 1994 are amendments to the rules issued in that year: HC 395, so HC 395 is still the name of the rules. They are frequently amended in major or minor respects. The rules govern almost all immigration cases and also have an impact on asylum cases. They contain the practical substance of immigration law.

On reading the rules, it is apparent that they are the language of the administrator rather than the lawyer. They are practical and descriptive, stating what action should be taken in given sets of circumstances. This being the case, they should not be treated as a legal text in the English tradition, namely as language which has been created with great precision and therefore must be interpreted strictly. The accepted approach (*Alexander v IAT* [1982] 2 All ER 766) to interpretation is:

These Rules are not to be construed with all the strictness applicable to the construction of a statute or a statutory instrument. They must be construed sensibly according to the natural meaning of the language which is employed. (para 11)

This was confirmed again by the House of Lords in *Odelola* and in *Mahad and others v ECO* [2009] UKSC 16. The rules have become more specific over the years. They have also become more and more comprehensive, as matters formerly dealt with by concessions and policies are absorbed into the rules.

The immigration rules may be divided roughly into points-based rules and the rest. Although the non-points-based rules have also become more specific in their requirements, they still contain some scope for judgment as to whether specified criteria are met, for instance whether a couple intend to live together as husband and wife. This is not a discretion in a pure sense, but it is a matter on which an entry clearance officer and an applicant could disagree. By comparison in the points-based rules, the idea of adequacy of maintenance was replaced by specified sums, and subjective states such as 'intention to leave' do not appear. Interestingly, some of the most recent changes in the PBS have reintroduced elements of judgment (students may now be required to attend an interview, and entrepreneurs must show the viability of their plans). For details of the PBS see chapter 9.

The status of the immigration rules has been a subject of much legal argument. The Immigration Act 1971 s 3(2) says that the Secretary of State 'shall from time to time lay before Parliament statements of the rules . . . to be followed in the administration of this Act'. They are thus in form not delegated legislation. The House of Lords, in *Odelola*, thought that this section did not impose a statutory duty to make the rules, but rather that the duty was procedural—to lay them before Parliament, subject to the negative resolution procedure. The Supreme Court in *Munir* held that although there is no explicit duty to make immigration rules, it is implicit, because this is how a level of democracy and accountability is achieved. *Pearson v IAT* [1978] Imm AR 212 has been followed, and confirmed in *Odelola*, that the Rules are not delegated legislation or rules of law, but rules of practice for the guidance of those who administer the Act. Despite this, the rules have a status well beyond that of normal administrative guidelines. Sedley LJ in *SSHD v Pankina and others* [2010] EWCA Civ 719 said:

In my judgement the time has come to recognize that, by a combination of legislative recognition and executive practice, the rules made by Home Secretaries for regulating immigration have ceased to be policy and have acquired a status akin to that of law. (para 17)

Sedley LJ confirmed that the rules are not subordinate legislation. The arrangements for their creation are 'not merely unusual but unique' (para 13), and he draws his conclusion that they have a status akin to law in part from the requirement that they be laid before Parliament.

The rules are subject only to very limited parliamentary scrutiny, and if Parliament wants to reject them it must reject the rules as a whole: there is no provision for amendment (though in February 2008, a debate in Parliament secured promises from the government to deal with some objections to new grounds for refusing leave to enter the UK). Rules have been rejected on very few occasions, the most notable perhaps being in December 1982 (HC Debs 15 December 1982 col 355) when the Labour Party opposition succeeded in defeating the Conservative government's proposed new marriage rules. New immigration rules are produced on average at least once a month, and it is rare even to secure parliamentary time to debate them. A further exception was the controversial HC 194 in July 2012, whose provisions included a fixed maintenance figure for partners, abolition of the 14-year residence rule, and an attempt to fix the meaning of Article 8 (see chapters 5, 6, 7, 8, and 15). In *Huang and Kashmiri v SSHD* [2007] UKHL 11, the House of Lords rejected an argument that the negative resolution procedure meant that the immigration rules were the product of democratic debate. The immigration rules are 'not the product of active debate in Parliament, where non-nationals seeking leave to enter or remain are not in any event represented' (para 17).

Key Case

SSHD v Pankina and others [2010] EWCA Civ 718

Applicants for leave to remain under the points-based system met the requirement of the rules to have £800 in their bank accounts, but did not meet the requirements in the guidance for this sum to be in their accounts for a continuous period of three months prior to their application. The Secretary of State purported to incorporate this guidance into the rules, although it had not been laid before Parliament. The Court of Appeal held that although there was no obstacle in principle to incorporating a policy into a legally enforceable measure, a policy was simply guidance as to the usual case, and was to be interpreted. So if an applicant's bank balance fell below £800 for one day, there would be consideration of whether the spirit and intention of the policy was nevertheless met. In this case the Secretary of State did not rely on the guidance as policy, but as an extension of the rule and thus mandatory. This was impermissible as it had not been laid before Parliament, affected individuals' status and entitlement, and could be changed at any time by the Secretary of State. If the provision was to have the force of law (as an immigration rule did) it must be certain (para 33).

Pankina is now confirmed by *Alvi*. The Supreme Court held that, where a requirement must be satisfied as a condition of being given leave to enter or remain then it is a rule (Lord Dyson para 94). Also, a provision laying down the period and conditions of leave is a rule (para 94). In that case, the provisions in the code of practice which said that a physiotherapy assistant would not meet the required level were in effect immigration rules because they must be met in order to obtain leave. They had not been laid before Parliament and thus could not be enforced as a basis to refuse leave to Mr Alvi.

In theory the rules are subject to challenge by way of judicial review on the usual grounds of illegality, irrationality, and procedural impropriety (following Lord Diplock's classification in *CCSU v Minister for the Civil Service* [1985] AC 374). Unsuccessful attempts have been made to challenge the rules on the basis that they fetter discretion, this being an aspect of illegality (*R v Secretary of State for the Home Department ex p Rajinder Kaur* [1987] Imm AR 278). For the purpose of a challenge for irrationality, the rules are treated like by-laws, and so may only be struck down if they are 'impartial or unequal in their operation as between classes; manifestly unjust; made in bad faith; or involving such oppressive or gratuitous interference with the rights of those subject to them as could find no justification in the minds of reasonable persons' (*Kruse v Johnson* [1898] 2 QB 91). This has succeeded on one occasion, when the rule on admission of family dependants was challenged for its requirement that the elderly dependent relative, in order to gain entry, must be living at a standard substantially below that in their country. This discriminated against applicants in poor countries, for whom even a small amount of financial help would lift their standard of living above a low level for their country (*R v IAT ex p Manshoora Begum* [1986] Imm AR 385).

The rules are subject to directly applicable EC law, and in *R (on the application of Ezgi Payir) v SSHD* [2005] EWHC 1426 (Admin), the High Court made a declaration that former rr 92–4 were unlawful insofar as they purported to exclude the right to an extension of stay for a Turkish au pair, contrary to Article 6 of Decision 1/80 of the Council of the Association between the EU and Turkey. This outcome was upheld on a preliminary reference to the ECJ (Case C–294/06).

The decision in *Odelola*, that the rules were not subordinate legislation, meant that the Interpretation Act 1978 did not apply to them, and so the appellant did not obtain that Act's protection against retrospective effect. In similar wording, the Human Rights Act defines subordinate legislation in s 21(1) as including 'rules . . . made under primary legislation'. *Pankina* proceeded on the basis, though not fully argued, that the immigration rules are not included in s 21 HRA. The effect of this is that the interpretive duty in HRA s 3 does not apply to the rules. This was the view of the Court of Appeal in *AM (Ethiopia), and others v Entry Clearance Officer* [2008] EWCA Civ 1082, though in a passing comment.

Even without s 3, those who implement the rules are public authorities under s 6 and their actions must be in accordance with the Convention. In effect, immigration rules must be applied in a way that upholds Convention rights, as Sedley LJ said in *Pankina*:

In exercising her powers, whether within or outside the rules of practice for the time being in force, the Home Secretary must have regard and give effect to applicants' Convention rights. (para 45)

The Court of Appeal in *R (on the application of Syed) v SSHD* [2011] EWCA Civ 1059 confirmed this interpretation.

The judgment in *Huang* referred to earlier held that the immigration rules do not already embody human rights standards. The consideration of a human rights claim begins once an applicant has failed under the rules. Human rights standards are additional to the rules, which, as previously discussed, are simply guidance in the administration of the powers to grant and refuse leave to enter or remain.

There has been some change since *Huang* in that the government has made rules which embody the Secretary of State's interpretation of Article 8 (see *Izuazu* and *MF (Nigeria)*, and discussion in chapters 5 and 8). In the case of the rules relating to deportation these were said to amount to a 'complete code'. Nevertheless, the courts have accepted that the rules may not secure those rights. The rules themselves contemplate this by their anticipation of 'exceptional circumstances' and in such cases the normal Article 8 proportionality exercise must be carried out. Where the rules were not made with the intention of incorporating human rights, the Court will allow less latitude to the Secretary of State in asserting that there is no violation of rights (*SS (Congo) v SSHD* [2015] EWCA Civ 387), since she has not already put her mind, in the construction of the rule, to the protection of the right, and so the rule cannot be said to represent the Secretary of State's view as to where the public interest lies.

If the rules as they stand are incapable of delivering decisions which respect human rights, then they may be unlawful for this reason. They were found to be so by the Supreme Court in *R (on the application of Quila and another) v SSHD* [2011], where the lower age limit of 21 for a spouse visa was not capable of being interpreted as applicable only to forced marriages. It was disproportionate to the legitimate aim of preventing them.

By comparison in *Bibi*, the Supreme Court said that holding a nationality of an 'English-speaking country' was a 'reasonable proxy' for fluency in English language, and the condition of English-speaking as a condition of entry was not generally disproportionate as long as exceptions could be made where hardship was caused.

Aikens LJ in *MM* [2014] EWCA Civ 985 summed up the situation in this way: ('IRs' are immigration rules):

134. First, Laws LJ [in *AM Ethiopia*] was dealing with the principles of construction of IRs. IRs are not to be construed upon the presumption that they will guarantee compliance with the relevant Convention right. Secondly, therefore, a particular

IR does not, in each case, have to result in a person's Convention rights being 'guaranteed'. In a particular case, an IR may result in a person's Convention rights being interfered with in a manner which is not proportionate or justifiable on the facts of that case. That will not make the IR unlawful. But if the particular IR is one which, being an interference with the relevant Convention right, is also incapable of being applied in a manner which is proportionate or justifiable or is disproportionate in all (or nearly all cases), then it is unlawful.

135. Where the relevant group of IRs, upon their proper construction, provide a 'complete code' for dealing with a person's Convention rights in the context of a particular IR or statutory provision, such as in the case of 'foreign criminals',[152] then the balancing exercise and the way the various factors are to be taken into account in an individual case must be done in accordance with that code, although references to 'exceptional circumstances' in the code will nonetheless entail a proportionality exercise. But if the relevant group of IRs is not such a 'complete code' then the proportionality test will be more at large, albeit guided by the *Huang* tests and UK and Strasbourg case law.

Another critical issue concerning the effect of the rules is the question of which set of rules applies if the rules are changed between the date of the application and the date of the decision, as happened in *Odelola* (see 1.3.3). The House of Lords' answer was that the applicable rules are those in force at the date of the decision. Different considerations applied in the special case of an integrated scheme for highly skilled migrants which proclaimed itself as a route to settlement (*R (on the application of HSMP Forum Ltd) v SSHD* [2008] EWHC 664 (Admin)).

1.3.4 Policies and concessions

Internal government instructions are highly influential in the implementation of immigration law as they guide immigration officers and Home Office officials in their response to individual cases. These may be of a formal or informal kind. Mention has already been made of the exclusion of black passport-holders from the UK by means of internal government instructions which accompanied the Commonwealth Immigrants Act 1962. These, of course, were not the kind of instructions to which the public would have access. The secrecy, which was a hallmark of immigration law, has changed in recent years, and a body of internal instructions is now disclosed on the Home Office website. Internal instructions as they now exist may be roughly classified as follows.

First, there are policy documents that give guidance on the exercise of a discretion. The criteria for immigration detention are found entirely in guidance documents of this kind, disclosed on the government website in the Enforcement Instructions and Guidance.

Second, there is guidance on the application of the immigration rules. Lord Justice Sedley in *ZH (Bangladesh) v SSHD* [2009] EWCA Civ 8 described this guidance as being directions about the implementation of the rules (para 26). The Court said that Home Office officials should not depart from the IDIs (Immigration Directorate Instructions) without good reason. This reflected the legal obligation of the government not to act inconsistently with its own policy unless there was a good reason for doing so (*British Oxygen v Board of Trade* [1971] AC 610, *ZH* para 33). On the other hand, the IDIs did not have the force of law. They were not an aid to construction of the immigration rules, but sat 'within the four corners of the rule' to which they related (para 32). An example is guidance on what kind of behaviour might warrant a refusal of leave to enter at the port on 'non-conducive' grounds (HC 395 para 320 (19); see chapter 6).

These kinds of guidance are mainly disclosed on the government website, but the location of particular subjects is often unpredictable and the usability is marred by poor indexing and lack of dating (so that it is difficult to tell whether the particular guidance was in force at the date of a decision, as in *R (on the application of I and O) v SSHD* [2005] EWHC 1025 (Admin)). Some subjects are covered in a set called 'Modernised Guidance'.

One of the features of immigration law is the extent of provision which has been contained in discretionary practices outside the rules. Sometimes these have been standard practices, established for many years. An example of this was the grant of indefinite leave to remain to a person who attained refugee status. This had the appearance of an established rule, as it was invariable practice for some years, but when practice was changed in August 2005, it was done simply by an announcement. Such announcements have been given, for instance, by notice on the Home Office website, in Parliament, or by letter to interested organizations (and see *Munir*).

The judgments in *Alvi* and *Munir* were followed by a host of provisions which had been in guidance being incorporated into the immigration rules. Perhaps that period represented the low water mark of established policy and practice being maintained outside the rules. The new and wide powers of removal in the Immigration Act 2014 and the unknown parameters of its appeal provisions require, in the interests of good administration, guidance as to the exercise of powers. Enforcement Instructions and Guidance and Immigration Directorate Instructions therefore contain new guidance as to how these new provisions should be implemented. Some of this could be described as policy establishing normal practice (e.g., the issue of various forms and notices in relation to removal). These may not explicitly be substantive provisions like the former practice of giving refugees indefinite leave to remain since many have a more procedural character. Nevertheless, in time these provisions may come to establish new norms which are found to have substantive implications. There is an inherent tension for government. To take wide powers means to issue guidance to govern its exercise. To limit powers in statute or rules gives scope for direct legal challenge.

Another category of guidance is the volumes of Asylum Policy Instructions (APIs), governing the asylum process. Some of these may have implications for substantive fairness later on (e.g., the applicant's right to request an interpreter of their own gender). APIs also govern the substance of asylum decision-making. While the law (see chapter 12) is the foundation of asylum decision-making, a great deal of guidance is given to decision makers applying that law (e.g., *Gender Issues in the Asylum Claim*).

There are also temporary concessions, often in periods of upheaval or emergency. An example was a policy not to return people to active war zones, a policy which has now been revoked.

What all these forms of guidance have in common is that if an individual comes within their terms they can expect to be treated in accordance with the policy. These may not usually be enforced by appeal, though failures to follow guidance may be relevant in an appeal. A breach of policy may give rise to judicial review (see chapter 7). *R v SSHD ex p Amankwah* [1994] Imm AR 240 was the first case which held that even if the policy was undisclosed, if its existence was known, a decision which did not take the policy properly into account was unreasonable and unfair. The existence of a policy on marriage and deportation had become known by accident, having been referred to in a Home Office letter in a previous case.

The Home Office should apply the policy in a relevant case even if the individual is unaware of it (*R (on the application of Rashid) v SSHD* [2005] EWCA Civ 744; see chapter 7).

Individual exceptions may be made, and it is possible to argue that the particular circumstances of the case warrant more lenient treatment than the rules seem to provide. The source of the power for Home Office and immigration officers to do this has been discussed earlier, and is the Immigration Act 1971, not the prerogative.

Guidance in the PBS is a different phenomenon. It is referred to in the immigration rules as binding and is phrased in mandatory terms. It is addressed not only to Home Office officials, as are the policies discussed earlier, but to applicants on what is required of them, and is mainly procedural (what kind of documents are accepted, when to submit them, and so on). This guidance was described by the Tribunal in *NA & Others (Tier 1 Post-Study Work-funds)* [2009] UKAIT 00025 as a 'hybrid of a new kind' (para 46). As held by the Court of Appeal in *Pankina*, guidance cannot be given the same force as a rule, and the Supreme Court in *Alvi* has now laid down a clear demarcation between such guidance or policy, and a rule. As a consequence, many of the provisions which were formerly in guidance are now in rules so that they can be treated as compulsory.

1.3.5 Tribunal decisions

Another specialist source of law in the immigration and asylum field is the body of case law emanating from the Tribunal. The structure of the Tribunal and grounds of appeal to it are discussed more fully in chapter 7. Here we simply consider Tribunal decisions as a source of law.

Studies by Buck (2006) and Thomas examine the unique phenomenon of the Tribunal and its case law. The early idea of tribunals, as fact-finding bodies which were somehow closer to the people and the facts than the courts could be, is a misleading picture of the Tribunal which hears immigration and asylum appeals. Its characteristics are described by Thomas as: high volume; fact-based; compulsory (in that claimants have little alternative); no compromise is possible; serving public interest; not bound by usual rules of evidence; and an exceptionally high rate of challenge.

Buck notes that the intention of Tribunal case law was that it would not be binding in the way that the decisions of higher courts are. Wade and Forsyth (*Administrative Law* Oxford: OUP) say that the Tribunal's duty is to reach the 'right decision in the circumstances of the moment'.

The authority of the new Upper Tribunal is enhanced by its constitution in 2007 as court of record, explicitly equal in the court hierarchy with the High Court. The transfer to the unified Tribunal structure has highlighted the nature and authority of Tribunal case law. In *AH (Sudan)*, Baroness Hale said that rarely should the decision of a specialist Tribunal be interfered with, unless it was plainly wrong in law. However, the specialist quality of the Tribunal has been doubted, on the grounds that its jurisdiction is too diverse to permit of real specialization, and that many decisions are taken by an immigration judge sitting alone, unlike other Tribunal jurisdictions in which lay people with relevant expertise act as wing members (Chowdhury 2009). In the transfer of judicial review jurisdiction to the Upper Tribunal, there is potentially a trade-off between Tribunal specialism and the capacity of High Court judges to maintain coherence with the wider body of law, in particular public law principles (see Thomas 2009). Tribunal decisions are not all reported, and a practice direction prevents unreported cases from being cited in tribunals except in defined circumstances, although the new tribunal website gives easier access to unreported decisions. The decision as to which decisions are reported is made by a Reporting Committee, following guidance published by the President of the Upper Tribunal Immigration and Asylum Chamber (Guidance note 2011 no. 2). The procedure of the Reporting Committee has been questioned as contravening the principles of fairness and due administration of justice (Toal 2012). There is a system of factual precedents called country guidance cases, discussed in chapter 11.

Tribunal decisions may be accessed by searching on www.bailii.org or https://tribunalsdecisions.service.gov.uk/utiac/decisions.

1.4 **Conclusion**

Whether the focus of attention is the Jews in the nineteenth century, West Indians in the 1960s, East African Asians in the 1970s, or more recently asylum seekers, immigration legislation is passed with a target group in mind. The political agenda of the day moulds the law in a very direct way. The current targets include the illegally resident population, and terrorists. The result is a concentration on security and the dissemination of points of immigration control through many aspects of life. Another current target, to restrict entry for work, has become enmeshed in similar processes.

QUESTIONS

1 How have the themes identified by Bevan in 1986 developed in the present day?

2 The minister introducing a Draft Immigration Bill in 2009 said that it would 'ensure that Parliament and not case law determines immigration policy'. To what extent is this a realistic or desirable objective, given the nature and sources of immigration law?

3 Given the use and origin of the immigration rules, it appears that the Secretary of State both makes and implements much of immigration law. Is this a problem?

 online resource centre For guidance on answering questions, visit the Online Resource Centre www.oxfordtextbooks.co.uk/orc/clayton7e/.

FURTHER READING

Bevan, Vaughan (1986) *The Development of British Immigration Law* (Beckenham: Croom Helm).

Bingham, Lord (2007) 'The Rule of Law' *Cambridge Law Journal* 66, pp. 67–85.

Carter, Bob, Harris, Clive, and Joshi, Shirley [1987] *The 1951–55 Conservative Government and the Racialisation of Black Immigration* Policy Papers in Ethnic Relations no. 11 CREC.

Chowdhury, Zahir (2009) 'The Doctrine of Deference to Tribunal Expertise and the Parameters of Judicial Restraint' *Immigration Law Digest* vol. 15, no. 3, Autumn, pp. 15–21.

Cohen, Steve, Humphries, Beth, and Mynott, Ed (eds) (2000) 'Never Mind the Racism . . . Feel the Quality' *Immigration and Nationality Law and Practice* vol. 14, no. 4, pp. 223–6.

Cohen, Steve, Humphries, Beth, and Mynott, Ed (eds) (2002) *From Immigration Controls to Welfare Controls* (London: Routledge).

Dauvergne, Catherine (2004) 'Sovereignty, Migration and the Rule of Law in Global Times' *Modern Law Review* vol. 67, no. 4, pp. 588–615.

Dummett, Ann and Nicol, Andrew (1990) *Subjects, Citizens, Aliens and Others* (London: Weidenfeld and Nicolson).

Fryer, Paul (1984) *Staying Power: The History of Black People in Britain* (London: Pluto).

Gillespie, Jim (1996) 'Asylum and Immigration Act 1996: An Outline of the New Law' *Immigration and Nationality Law and Practice* vol. 10, no. 3, pp. 86–90.

Gilroy, Paul (2002) *There Ain't no Black in the Union Jack* (London: Routledge).

Harvey, Colin (2005) 'Judging Asylum' in Shah, P. (ed.) *The Challenge of Asylum to Legal Systems* (London: Cavendish).

Joint Council for the Welfare of Immigrants (JCWI) (2005) *Recognise Rights, Realize Benefits, JCWI analysis of the five-year plan* (London: JCWI).

Juss, Satvinder (1993) *Immigration, Nationality and Citizenship* (London: Mansell).

Layton-Henry, Zigg (1992) *The Politics of Immigration* (Oxford: Blackwell).

Macdonald, Ian and Toal, Ronan (2014) *Macdonald's Immigration Law and Practice*, 9th edn (London: Butterworths), chapter 1.

McKee, Richard (2002) 'Fitting the Bill? A survey of the main proposals in the Nationality, Immigration and Asylum Bill and some related developments' *Immigration Asylum and Nationality Law* vol. 16, no. 3, pp. 181–8.

McKee, Richard (2006) 'The Immigration, Asylum and Nationality Act 2006 and other developments' *Journal of Immigration, Asylum & Nationality Law* vol. 20, no. 2, pp. 86–93.

Moore, Robert and Wallace, Tina (1975) *Slamming the Door* (London: Martin Robertson and Co.).

Paul, Kathleen (1997) *Whitewashing Britain: Race and Citizenship in the Postwar Era* (New York: Cornell).

Rawlings, Richard (2005) 'Review, Revenge and Retreat' *Modern Law Review* vol. 68, no. 3, pp. 378–410.

Shah, Prakash (2000) *Refugees, Race and the Legal Concept of Asylum in Britain* (London: Cavendish).

Singh, Rabinder (2004) 'Equality: The Neglected Virtue' *European Human Rights Law Review* 2, pp. 141–57.

Spencer, Ian (1997) *British Immigration Policy since 1945: The Making of Multi-Racial Britain* (London: Routledge).

Stevens, Dallal (1998) 'The Asylum and Immigration Act 1996: The Erosion of the Right to Seek Asylum' *Modern Law Review* vol. 61, no. 2, pp. 201–22.

Stevens, Dallal (2001) 'The Immigration and Asylum Act 1999: A Missed Opportunity?' *Modern Law Review* vol. 64, no. 3, pp. 413–38.

Stevens, Dallal (2004) 'The Nationality, Immigration and Asylum Act 2002: Secure Borders, Safe Haven?' *Modern Law Review* vol. 67, no. 4, pp. 616–31.

Stevens, Dallal (2004) *UK Asylum Law and Policy* (London: Sweet & Maxwell), chapters 1 and 2.

Thomas, Robert (2003) 'Asylum Appeals Overhauled Again' *Public Law* Summer, pp. 260–71.

Thomas, Robert (2009) 'Tribunalising Immigration and Asylum Judicial Reviews' *Immigration Law Digest* vol. 15, no. 4, Winter, pp. 2–4. (2003)

Toal, Ronan (2012) 'The Reporting Committee of the Upper Tribunal, Immigration and Asylum Chamber: Country Guidance Decisions' *Journal of Immigration Asylum and Nationality Law* vol. 26 no.1 pp. 64–7.

Vincenzi, Christopher (1992) 'Extra-statutory Ministerial Discretion in Immigration Law' *Public Law* Summer, pp. 310–21.

Vincenzi, Christopher (1998) *Crown Powers, Subjects and Citizens* (London: Cassell).

Virdee, Satnam (1999) 'England: Racism, Anti-racism and the Changing Position of Racialised Groups in Economic Relations' in Dale, G., and Cole, M. (eds) *The European Union and Migrant Labour* (Oxford: Berg).

Webber, Frances (2012) *Borderline Justice* (London: Pluto).

2

....

Policy, politics, and the media

SUMMARY

This chapter is an introduction to some of the policy issues which shape immigration law. These issues are raised so that as they appear, embedded within the law throughout this book, they may be more easily recognized. The role of the media is discussed, because it is a powerful actor in moulding immigration and asylum policy, though in discussing the law, usually an invisible one. Some of the provisions which govern the treatment in the UK of asylum seekers are also covered here. These, too, have no other place in this book, not being an aspect of the law of entry, but they affect and are affected by the climate of policy on entry, and give rise to human rights issues. The institutions of immigration control are introduced as both a tool and an expression of policy.

2.1 Introduction—migration policy in a global context

In 2006, shortly after taking up his post as Home Secretary, John Reid pronounced that the immigration system was 'not fit for purpose'. His comment, dramatic, publicly given, and headline-catching, obscures the assumption behind it—that there is a recognized or agreed purpose for the immigration system. The Home Affairs Committee, in a measured introduction to the report of their inquiry into immigration control, posed the question, 'what is the purpose of the immigration system in the twenty-first century?' (Fifth Report of Session 2005–06 HC 775 para 5).

Before considering how this question is answered in policy and practice in the UK, we will take a step back to look through a wider lens. The study of migration is a vast field, engaging many disciplines including economics, politics, history, philosophy, international relations, as well as law. The main subject of this book is a tiny corner of that field: the national law which regulates entry to the UK. Though the policies implemented are national, the context for them is international. Evidence to the Home Affairs Committee was that:

the great contradiction in migration today is that it is a global issue that people try to manage at a national level

and

the root causes of migration are so powerful—it is about underdevelopment, disparities in demographic processes, in development, and in democracy—that to an extent . . . immigration control is treating the symptom rather than the cause. (para 7)

One of the key questions in the study of migration is 'what causes people to migrate?' Views that are held about this may in turn influence policy if policy makers seek to influence behaviour. Yash Ghai (1997) suggests that the market was historically, and remains, the key determinant of international movement. From the establishment of plantations and their demand for labour, the aspirations of employers fuelling illicit migration, and the balancing demand of the market for stability, labour mobility, and competition, these economic forces, he argues, predominate. Demetrios Papademetriou (2003) suggests that two drivers are particularly important in the present era: political, social, and cultural intolerance, which at the extreme turns into gross, group-based violations of human rights; and the systematic failure of governments to address multiple disadvantages faced by their populations. Papademetriou acknowledges that these phenomena are always present, and suggests additional factors influence the actual pattern of migration:

- a long-term political, social, and economic relationship between the country of origin and destination country;
- economic benefits of migration sufficient to motivate the destination country to organize structures to receive migrants;
- a mature and influential 'anchor' ethnic community in the destination state, who may welcome and facilitate new arrivals; and
- interest groups in the destination state who oppose the circumstances from which migrants are escaping, thus carving out a social space into which they can be welcomed, and political support for permissive migration policies.

It may be noted that of the two drivers Papademetriou identifies as being particularly relevant at the present time, flight from human rights violations is one which would generate a need for international protection, perhaps a claim for refugee status. The failure of governments to address disadvantage might have that result, but might also generate what is often called economic migration. The trigger factors do not sit neatly in either category. While the law, particularly in Western countries, distinguishes sharply between economic migration and asylum-seeking, the actual causes of international movement are not necessarily so sharply distinguished. Savitri Taylor (2005:6) regards the attempt to make this distinction as problematic. She says that 'the explanation for most international migration is to be found in a combination of economic and non-economic factors'. She considers that Western governments' attempts to *control* 'irregular' migration by controlling borders are an attempt to do the impossible. She proposes cooperation with countries of origin to *manage* migration for the benefit of all concerned at the same time as the long-term work of tackling root causes—poverty, armed conflict, and human rights abuse.

This kind of approach, seeing the management of migration as requiring international cooperation, is reflected in the work of the Global Commission on Migration, convened to move 'beyond the political deadlock which had effectively paralysed international discussion on migration for more than a decade' (Grant 2006:13). The Commission proposed that migration should become 'an integral part of national, regional and global strategies for economic growth' (2005:2). Moving beyond the deadlock involved recognizing migration as a potential benefit for the host country, the country of origin, and the migrants themselves, and developing policies that enable all those benefits to flow freely. Their recommendations included measures to prevent the benefit to states of origin from being lost. For instance, a 'brain drain' should be replaced by a 'brain circulation', and taxation or appropriation of remittances—the money that migrants send home—should be prevented. The money sent in remittances is 'second only to foreign direct investment in countries. In some countries remittances can be higher than official development assistance' (DFID 2007:13).

The Global Commission set an ambitious objective:

Women, men and children should be able to realise their potential, meet their needs, exercise their human rights and fulfil their aspirations in their country of origin, and hence migrate out of choice rather than necessity. Those women and men who migrate and enter the global labour market should be able to do so in a safe and authorised manner, and because they and their skills are valued and needed by the states and societies that receive them. (2005:11)

These ideas echo a view put forward by the economist John Maynard Keynes, that migration is 'the oldest action against poverty', and recognized in the UK by the Department for International Development (DFID):

migration and development are linked . . . The objectives of both fields are more likely to be achieved if migration and development policies begin to acknowledge the benefits and risks of migration for poor people and developing countries. (DFID 2007:33)

Interestingly, the UK government's 2008 consultation paper, *Earning the Right to Stay: A New Points Test for Citizenship*, contained a section headed 'Migration and International Development'. This section set out some ideas for encouraging circular migration in order to reduce the impact of a brain drain on developing countries. It suggested, for instance, developing codes of practice for different sectors, such as the one in force with the National Health Service (NHS) whereby the UK reduces active recruitment from countries with vulnerable healthcare systems, or giving credits in the earned citizenship scheme for development work in a migrant's home country.

This consultation was abandoned. Indeed, it is difficult now to perceive any meaningful level of transnational perspective in the UK's immigration policy. Like other states, the UK attempts to influence the behaviour of migrants through law.

By way of example, there may be a trade-off between rights and the availability of opportunities for migrants to work. Martin Ruhs (2009) cites as extremes the Gulf States and Sweden. In 2005, migrants accounted for a relatively high percentage of the population in the Gulf States, ranging between 24.4 per cent in Oman and 78.3 per cent in Qatar. He describes labour migration in the Gulf States as an 'employer-led, large-scale guest worker programme', entailing minimal rights without opportunities for settlement. In Sweden, by contrast, labour migration is minimal; perhaps 400 people per year, but rights are comprehensive. He argues that this trade-off should be acknowledged, recognizing that the opportunity for migration has value and is conducive to human development, but also that a core minimum of rights should be identified.

The simple figures presented show how governments attempt to influence behaviour through law, and that these attempts can have an impact, though from this brief information we cannot deduce the whole effect. The operation of laws is influential on migration in ways that are not fully understood. Economics, human rights, and regulatory laws are part of a complex web which interacts with the subjective reasons that people have for moving.

Papademetriou warns that: 'The attempt to manage . . . complex transnational processes through unilateral and single purpose policies will be of ever diminishing value.' He cites three escalating drivers of migration in the twenty-first century: exclusion of ethnic or religious groups, the deterioration of ecosystems, and flight from natural and human-made disasters. These are events for which border-oriented long-term policy responses are unlikely to be adequate. Papademetriou finds present policy constructs for dealing with migration dated and 'disturbingly binary'. Categories of 'sending and receiving' countries, 'permanent and temporary migrants' and 'economic migration and seeking refuge' are not, he suggests, an adequate foundation for policy.

Yash Ghai observes that the law is contradictory, as its underlying principles are confused. Although 'governments welcome economic flows—especially of finance and trade'—they are more ambivalent on flows of people (Castles 2007:12).

From the broader perspective, there is unlikely to be a simple answer to the question which the Home Affairs Committee posed: the purpose of the immigration system. How the answer is currently seen in the UK is indicated by where responsibility is located in government.

2.2 Institutional basis of immigration control—an overview

A number of parts of government have a significant role to play in migration policy: the Department for Business, Innovation and Skills in relation to overseas students and opportunities for workers; local authority social service departments in relation to children at risk; the police in relation to immigration offences; and so on. As a result of the Home Affairs Committee's recommendation, a Cabinet sub-committee was created to remedy 'the absence of any place within government with overall responsibility . . . for determining . . . migration strategy'. In so recommending, the Home Affairs Committee was drawing attention, not to an absence of immigration control, which is a more limited activity, but to an absence of an overall migration strategy. Migration policy in the UK has tended to be strongly identified with immigration control—a more familiar phrase, and the title of this section. Publicly available documentation does not suggest that this sub-committee survived the 2010 General Election, and policy across government in relation to migration is now largely presented in terms of prevention. Bodies such as the Migration Advisory Committee make a contribution to migration strategy, but any public commitment to migration management has been largely abandoned in favour of immigration control.

The authority to control immigration is given by Immigration Act 1971 s 4(1) to 'the Secretary of State'. Though the Act does not specify which Secretary of State, in long-standing policy and practice this has been the Home Secretary. In *Pearson v IAT* [1978] Imm AR 212, the Court of Appeal held that the Secretary of State, referred to throughout the immigration statute, must 'by reason of the subject matter' be the Home Secretary. We might note in passing that the Department of Health guidance which prohibited doctors who had qualified in another country from getting work in English hospitals—although it was the subject of a successful challenge in the courts—was so in part precisely because another government department than the Home Office had unlawfully attempted to lay down an immigration measure (*R (on the application of BAPIO Action Ltd) v SSHD and Department of Health* [2008] UKHL 27; see chapter 9).

The immigration service, although answerable to the Home Secretary, was originally a distinct service. Immigration officers' powers concerned entry, and the Secretary of State's powers, exercised through Home Office civil servants (*Carltona Ltd v Commissioner of Works* [1943] 2 All ER 560) were to deal with those already in the country by making decisions on further leave to remain or deportation (Immigration Act 1971 s 4). The distinction between the Secretary of State's powers and immigration officers' powers has diminished (Immigration and Asylum Act 1999 s 1) and is now of limited significance.

The 1971 Act did not deal with work permits, which remained the responsibility of the Secretary of State for Employment. Entry clearance officers remained answerable to the Foreign and Commonwealth Office. At the turn of this century, there were substantial changes. Chapter 1 has related how the Immigration and Asylum Act 1999 began to enlist more of society in immigration control, a process which has intensified in the Immigration Act 2014, and laid the foundations to export the UK's border, the detail of which is discussed in chapter 6. This policy of pervasive control was mirrored in institutional changes. In 2000, the Home Office and Foreign Office set up a joint unit to manage entry clearance. Following this, the Entry Clearance operation was rebranded 'UKVisas', and is now the overseas part of UK Visas and Immigration, a section in the Home Office. In June 2001, responsibility for work permit applications transferred from the Department of Education and Employment to the Home Office. It retained a separate identity as 'Work Permits UK' until 2008, with the creation of the UK Border Agency (UKBA) and the introduction of the points-based system (PBS). Now it is subsumed within UK Visas and Immigration in the Home Office. As immigration control was both extended beyond the UK's border and introduced into civil affairs, so the Home Office became the department with overall control.

2.2.1 Reviews and inquiries

From December 2005 to June 2006, the Home Affairs Select Committee (HASC) of the House of Commons conducted a major inquiry into immigration control. During the period of that inquiry, there was a public outcry over the release of foreign national prisoners who had not been considered for deportation. An observer would be forgiven for thinking that this was due to 'weak laws' or possibly even the Human Rights Act. Neither of these was the case, and the problem was poor communication within the Home Office. The affair as treated in the media is discussed later in the chapter. It was in response to this that the incoming Home Secretary John Reid instituted a review, looking at strategic objectives, core processes, culture, and organization of the Immigration and Nationality Directorate (as it then was) (as stated to the Committee, HC 775 para 537).

The first published fruit of the review, issued shortly before the Home Affairs Committee reported, included an intention to 'make IND a more powerful agency, more clearly accountable to Parliament and the public'. The objectives were to:

- strengthen borders; use tougher checks abroad so that only those with permission can travel to the UK; monitor who leaves 'so that we can take action against those who break the rules';
- fast-track asylum decisions, removing those who fail, and integrating those who need protection;
- enforce compliance with immigration laws, 'removing the most harmful people first and denying the privileges of Britain to those here illegally'; and
- boost Britain's economy by bringing the right skills here from around the world, and ensuring that this country is easy to visit legally' (*Fair, Effective, Transparent and Trusted*, July 2006).

These largely repeated the objectives of the five-year strategy launched in 2005. The agency was divided into regions. The message was that the immigration system was to be run in a way that ordinary people understood. Strategic direction was divided into management areas: asylum; borders; enforcement; human resources and organizational development; managed migration; and resource management; and the Director of UKVisas was given a seat on the board.

The Case Resolution Directorate was established to deal with the backlog of cases. The New Asylum Model was introduced for all asylum claims made after April 2007 (see chapter 11). Speed of decision-making became a highly prized quality in response to problems and injustice caused by delay. Already by this time, the prevailing governmental approach to a need to show achievement was to work to targets, mainly described in terms of numbers and time (e.g., 30,000 removals per year). The Home Affairs Committee identified the following problems with targets:

- Major political targets meant that other work may have been side-lined or even deliberately manipulated (para 572).
- For instance, prioritizing asylum claims and asylum removals had created backlog in other areas, and contributed to the foreign prisoner issue not being acted on more quickly.
- Targets were set for one part of a system without considering the effects elsewhere.
- This includes a problem with numerical targets per se in that, if a target of dealing with 90 per cent of claims in a certain time is met, 'what happens to the remaining 10 per cent is irrelevant from the point of view of meeting targets' (para 583); so a target culture can also contribute to a black hole into which more difficult cases disappear because nobody can afford to spend the time on them.
- Targets on speed had a negative impact on quality.
- Targets might be met, but still have no impact on the underlying objective because they were the wrong targets. They might be set because they could be met rather than because they were designed to address a problem.

Despite these criticisms the culture of speed and targets intensified after the 2006 reviews, most strikingly exemplified by the publication of 'milestones'. Some effects of speedier initial decision-making in asylum cases are discussed in the section on the treatment of asylum seekers.

2.2.2 UKBA

In early 2007, the Home Secretary announced that the Home Office would be split into two. What was then the Department for Constitutional Affairs took control of probation, prisons, and prevention of re-offending and was renamed the Ministry of Justice. The focus of the new Home Office was to be terrorism, policing, security, and immigration. This allocation gave a clear signal about the way that immigration was perceived, and the direction that further institutional change would take. One of the effects was that the international protection nature of the work of dealing with asylum claims was even more invisible. Within the new enforcement-oriented Home Office, on 25 July 2007 the government announced the creation of a unified border force, the UKBA. This was an idea that as late as November 2006 had been described by the Minister for Immigration, Nationality and Citizenship as 'damaging, distracting and disruptive' and 'rooted in a concept of a frontier that is long past' (HC Debs 2 November 2006 col 182WH). UKBA came into being as a shadow agency in April 2008, incorporating immigration and visa work, the border work of HM Revenue and Customs, and closer cooperation with the police Special Branch and with transport organizations, and regulators. Interestingly, the public launch did not come from the Home Secretary but from the Prime Minister in the Cabinet Office report *Security in a Global Hub* (2007). Migration in this vision was more a matter of border security than of foreign relations. The border as envisaged was not a 'purely geographical entity' (para 6). Much of the improved security that the document promised is delivered by 'exporting the border'. This is described in chapter 6, where we follow the various processes of border crossing. It relies on biometric data and cross-database checking at entry clearance posts, advance passenger information and juxtaposed controls in France and Belgium. *Security in a Global Hub* is an extensive document, describing a strategy of deterrence, intelligence sharing, and an integrated operation of policing and immigration control. Passengers are checked electronically against databases and watch lists, in advance through a visa application and again at the border.

On 1 March 2008, the first regulations took effect which created a duty to share information between immigration authorities, police, and revenue and customs in relation to a range of matters including 'passenger information' and 'notification of non-EEA arrivals on a ship or aircraft'. These were made under powers that already existed (Immigration, Asylum and Nationality Act 2006 (Duty to Share Information and Disclosure of Information for Security Purposes) Order 2008, SI 2008/539). The legislative foundation for closer cooperation between the three bodies was developed in the UK Borders Act 2007.

By April 2009, UKBA was fully established. The public face of UKBA was markedly security and enforcement oriented, inevitably if not only because immigration functions were institutionally combined with the work of crime prevention and raising revenue. Strategic objectives in UKBA's Business Plan April 2009–March 2012 were stated as articles of intent:

We will protect our border and our national interests.

We will tackle border and tax fraud, smuggling and immigration crime.

We will implement fair and fast decisions.

It would be easy to lose sight of the purposes of immigration control as anything other than these. However, in its response to a report from the House of Lords Committee on Economic Affairs: 'The Economic Impact of Immigration' (session 2007–08 HL 82) the government said that the objectives of Britain's immigration system were threefold:

- to offer humanitarian protection to people requiring sanctuary and fleeing persecution;
- to welcome the loved ones of UK citizens and those with permission to be in the UK who want to be re-united with their families;
- to attract those with the skills who can make a positive contribution to the UK, through work and study.

These objectives attracted little attention in UKBA's business plan. UKBA marked a consciously different approach from its predecessor, the Borders and Immigration Agency, who stated their purpose as being to 'manage immigration in the interests of Britain's security, economic growth and social stability', in keeping with the tenor of the 2002 White Paper, *Secure Borders, Safe Haven: Integration with Diversity in Modern Britain* Cm 5387. Management instead of control implies dealing with a resource, something that is inherently beneficial, and while setting rules and processes for how to handle the resource, getting the best out of it. The reversion to the language of control marks a more hard-nosed attitude to economic migration, and a more absolute approach to enforcement and border control.

The HASC remained intensely interested in the workings of UKBA, and instituted a practice of requiring four-monthly reports on its performance. The resulting picture was not a happy one. In the words of the HASC, UKBA:

continued to perform poorly in several areas, such as tackling the asylum and immigration backlog, and dealing with foreign national offenders when they are released from prison, and processing in-country visa renewals. (HASC, The Work of the UK Border Agency October to December 2012 Fourth Report of Session 2013–14 HC 486 para 3)

The HASC added that the Independent Chief Inspector of Borders and Immigration 'frequently reported' problems with the Agency, 'as has the Parliamentary Ombudsman, who noted that almost two-thirds of complaints that had to be sent back to organisations in 2011–12 were about the Agency' (para 3).

In November 2011, following differences of understanding between ministers and senior UKBA officials about the scope of a pilot of risk-led border controls, the Home Secretary announced the creation of a Border Force, taking the border control function out of the UKBA. In 2012, in the words of the HASC, 'matters came to a head' when the ICIBI found that the HASC had 'consistently been supplied with misleading information about the immigration and asylum backlogs'. The Committee Report goes on:

Mr Vine's oral evidence to us was remarkably consistent with Dr Reid's evidence to our predecessors six years previously—there was a lack of transparency and 'shockingly poor' customer service, and the Agency was divided into isolated 'silos'. (para 5)

The day after this report was published the Home Secretary announced that UKBA was to be abolished. The Agency status had created a 'closed, secretive and defensive culture'. The work of UKBA was divided into four new units in the Home Office:

(a) Border Force: a law enforcement command which carries out immigration and customs controls for people and goods entering the UK;

(b) UK Visas and Immigration: migration casework, visas, asylum casework, appeals, and business, growth and premium services;

(c) Immigration Enforcement: removals and detention, operational intelligence, foreign national offenders and immigration crime; and

(d) Operational Systems Transformation: responsible for modernizing technology; identity and data integrity; performance, assurance and compliance; business strategy; strategic risks and analysis; external engagement on growth; and joint working across the immigration system.

The HASC was surprised to note the immediate reassurance given by the Permanent Secretary: 'Most of us will still be doing the same job in the same place with the same colleagues for the same boss' (para 14). In its final report on UKBA, the HASC was sceptical about whether reorganization had or would have any impact on the effectiveness of its work (HASC, The Work of the UKBA January to March Eighth Report of Session 2013–14 HC 616).

The HASC still receives regular reports on the work of the Immigration Directorates. The HASC and the Independent Chief Inspector of Borders and Immigration each provide a level of public scrutiny of the work of the immigration directorates. The work of the Chief Inspector, established by the UK Borders Act 2007, has provided an important source of independent and detailed scrutiny. The Chief Inspector has power to conduct unannounced inspections of the work of the Immigration Directorates, and may for instance observe officers at work in airports, in local immigration teams where decisions are made, and in visa offices abroad. Reports are published regularly, and recent topics in addition to visas and border controls include Removals, Illegal Working, Settlement Casework, and the Monitoring of Tier 4 Licences.

The HASC recorded in their thanks to the retiring inspector John Vine 'his ability to discover information from within the Home Office that seems to have bypassed the entire management structure including the board of the Visas and Immigration Department.'

The fact that one individual working in a small team has managed to find so many errors begs the question of why there is not proper internal oversight. (HC 712 para 30)

In this context both the inspector and the committee were concerned by a practice adopted by the government in 2014 of delaying publication of the inspector's reports (HASC *The Work of the Immigration Directorates (January to June 2014)* Ninth report of session 2014–15 HC 712 para 71). For five years reports had been presented to the Home Secretary then published within 30 days. Despite the HASC requiring the Secretary of State to resume the former good practice, delay in publishing the reports continues.

2.3 A technological border

In 2003 work commenced on a programme aimed at delivering a new system of immigration control called e-borders. As described by the Chief Inspector of Borders and Immigration, this involved collecting Advance Passenger Information (API)

for all scheduled inbound and outbound passengers, in advance of travel. The intention was to 'export the border,' preventing passengers from travelling where they were considered a threat to the UK, while at the same time delivering a more efficient model of immigration control, targeting resources to risk and improving passenger clearance times through the immigration control. (ICIBI 2013 para 1)

E-borders relied on electronic recording, transfer, and checking of personal details becoming the paramount form of immigration control. UKBA aimed to create a comprehensive record of passenger movements, which it considered will strengthen security by:

- identifying in advance passengers who are a potential risk;
- telling us who plans to cross our border;
- checking travellers against lists of people known to pose a threat; and
- enabling us to link a person's journeys in order to form a detailed travel history, so that we can provide background checks to other agencies and compile a profile of suspect passengers and their travel patterns and networks.

E-borders linked immigration control closely with security issues as expressed in the Prime Minister's 'Statement on Security' in Parliament on 25 July 2007:

Our first line of defence against terrorism is overseas at other countries' ports and airports where people embark on journeys to our country, and from where embassies issue visas.

The e-borders scheme was also intended to deliver exit checks. It was eventually abandoned as it was not delivering the promised benefits, although many elements of the intended technological border are fundamental to current immigration control and are still being developed.

The requirement to provide biometric information for a visa application was the first step in the creation of e-borders and remains a key element in the present system. The Prime Minister goes on:

The way forward is electronic screening of all passengers . . . at ports and airports . . . The Home Secretary will enhance the existing E-borders programme to incorporate all passenger information.

The second line of defence is at our borders where biometrics . . . are already in use.

Since 30 November 2009, those people who arrive with biometric entry clearance have their fingerprints scanned on arrival to ensure that they match the prints of the person to whom entry clearance was issued.

British citizens also need to be able to travel in and out of the UK through electronic borders. The UK is moving towards embedding biometric details in the passports of British citizens, at the same time trying to ensure technological compatibility with new minimum security standards for European passports, including biometric fingerprint and facial data (reg 2252/2004), although the Regulation is part of the Schengen *acquis* which does not apply to the UK.

Since 2007 personal interviews have been used for first-time British passport applications, at which identity is confirmed through biographical details, facial features are scanned, and fingerprints taken. The information is recorded in a microchip which is read by an electronic reader at immigration control. The Identity Documents Act 2010 s 10 allows orders to be made compelling disclosure of information from other government departments for the purposes of issuing a passport.

For non-EEA nationals, the Immigration (Biometric Registration) Regulations 2008, SI 2008/3048 (as amended) require all applicants for leave to remain in the UK, and their dependants, to apply for a BRP. SI 2009/819 extends the requirement to those who are updating their passport or travel document and SI 2012/594 extends it to those to whom the Secretary of State decides to grant leave. Thus, at the point of grant or application, foreign nationals are brought into the electronic system. Details of leave granted are held on a chip in the BRP, and are therefore machine-readable and capable of being compared electronically with databases. From 2015, an application for a BRP has become a compulsory part of the entry clearance application process in some cases. Where this system is used, the applicant receives a temporary biometric entry clearance. Their leave to enter expires if they do not collect the BRP within the required time after arrival in the UK (see chapter 6).

Electronic collection and transmission of data has enabled the UK to enter into an agreement with the Five Countries Conference (FCC) nations: the USA, Canada, Australia, and New Zealand. Under a Protocol, the five countries are each able to check an agreed number (initially 3,000) per year of fingerprint sets in immigration cases against databases of the other FCC countries. The UK uses the Protocol primarily to check asylum cases where, for example, the person cannot be identified or there is reason to believe the person may be known to another FCC country, and to check foreign nationals who have been convicted of criminal offences but are difficult to remove due to questions about identity and documentation. The UK, Australia, and New Zealand have opened a shared Visa Application Centre in Singapore.

Electronic document recognition at borders has also enabled a number of fast-track simple entry procedure for 'trusted travellers'. The most recent of these is the 'Registered Traveller' Scheme for regular travellers from the United States of America, Canada, Japan, Australia, New Zealand, Hong Kong (Special Administrative Region passports), Singapore, South Korea, and Taiwan (passports with personal ID number).

E-borders was subsumed within a wider Border Systems Programme, which has responsibility for all technological and information systems including the Warnings Index—a security log of people with significant criminal records, suspected terrorists, or others excluded from the UK (see chapter 6 for the effect of checks on entry).

2.4 Policy drivers

In the introduction to this chapter and in chapter 1 we noted that a number of political agendas typically have a major influence on migration policy. We now briefly identify some of the current drivers of UK policy.

2.4.1 **Security**

Security has been high on the government and public agenda since the attacks on the World Trade Center on 11 September 2001. The presence of terrorist networks in the UK, many of whose members were born abroad, brought allegations that the government did not know who was in the UK. Increasingly, immigration control became wrapped up with the anti-terrorism programme. Refugee law has been changed by the drive against terrorism, and the climate created by connecting the two has contributed towards the ease with which detention and criminalization have been visited upon asylum seekers. Chapters 12 and 13 of this book include a more detailed exploration of these matters.

Criticism of the immigration system was compounded on 26 July 2005 when, immediately after failed attempts at bombings in London, one of the suspects departed on Eurostar. This brought to public attention that there was no longer any monitoring of people leaving the country, as controls on departure had been abolished in the 1990s. The Prime Minister's statement on security on 5 August 2005 set out a number of anti-terror measures that would be taken, all of which have had a significant effect:

- extending grounds for deportation to include 'unacceptable behaviour' such as 'glorifying terrorism'. Following this, a policy was adopted of relying on such behaviour as evidence that deportation or exclusion met the statutory requirement that it was 'conducive to the public good' (see, for instance, *Naik v SSHD*, chapter 5). At the same time, the new offence of encouraging terrorism was introduced in the Terrorism Act 2006. The UK Borders Act 2007 was an attempt to make deportation automatic for criminal offences (see chapter 15);
- action on nationality law. This included reviewing the oath of allegiance and language testing, and expanding the grounds for depriving British citizens of their nationality (Immigration, Asylum and Nationality Act 2006 s 56). These matters are discussed in chapter 3;
- implementation of the e-borders scheme;
- measures to make it easier to prevent anyone with terrorist connections from obtaining refugee status (e.g., ss 54 and 55 of the Immigration, Asylum and Nationality Act 2006, discussed in chapter 13). Likelihood of causing harm was also a reason for prioritizing an asylum decision within the backlog dealt with by the Case Resolution Directorate.

Since these measures there have been regular interventions in legal procedure geared to restricting status or rights of appeal for people who are suspected of terrorist activities. For instance, appeal rights against deportations based on national security were further restricted in the Crime and Courts Act 2013, and the Immigration Act 2014 deprives people of British nationality on the grounds that they have acted in a way that is seriously prejudicial to the UK's vital interests (see chapter 3).

In all of the developments of the electronic borders security is one of the key drivers. Facilitating international exchange of information as among the FCC countries and in the EU is in large part a security measure.

The law barely deals with the question of what really is security. It is not confined to combating terrorism, however, as the deportation of serious criminals is also said to be in aid of public security. Security is usually concerned with a threat to the public or a section of the public. In *SSHD v Rehman* [2001] 3 WLR 877, the House of Lords said that the Secretary of State was the only proper judge of what was *in the interests of* national security (see chapter 15), but it was within their jurisdiction to decide that an action which threatened the security of another country was a matter of national security in the UK.

There is a great volume of writing on the effect of increased security measures on immigration and on asylum-seeking in the UK, in Europe, and worldwide. Much of it charts increased monitoring and controls, and examines the risks of asylum claims being wrongly prevented or denied. While the rhetoric of governments often counterposes civil liberties and security, writers make the point that these can be on the same side. Related to this, some writers question the notion of 'security' as used in these debates. For instance, Nana Poku, Neil Renwick, and John Glenn argue that the idea of security which underlies the panoply of legal provisions is an outdated one tied to a national society, seen as military security and political and territorial integrity. They argue for replacing this with an idea of 'human security' (as opposed to 'state security') which values basic welfare of the population. This would entail taking into account that the pressures causing migration often have their source outside the borders of a state, and that these may be events which fundamentally affect the security of a population, such as environmental degradation, economic deprivation, and conflict. They give examples of where such causes of insecurity have come from outside a state's borders: the 'speculative activities that resulted in the economic meltdown in South East Asia which led to the mass expulsion of "guest" workers from those states', and 'the sale of armaments to oppressive regimes'. They conclude that acknowledging this causal interdependence 'lies at the heart of sustainable common security'. This is an interesting counterpart to the House of Lords' identification of the security of one nation with the security of another—or of all.

2.4.2 Economic growth and economic migration

While there has been pressure on the UK government to close the border to entry for work, encapsulated in the slogan 'British jobs for British workers', the actual economic impact of migration is complex, and very different in different sectors of the economy. The Migration Advisory Committee is an expert group which takes evidence from an extensive range of sources and has the job of advising the government on the need for, and to an extent the impact of, migrant workers, in particular on where there are shortages of skilled workers that could appropriately be filled by migration. Government decisions on controlling the opportunities to enter for work are based on advice from this body (for discussion of its work see chapter 9). Problems for government in relation to entry for work include attracting the people with the skills for which there is an unmet demand and tackling illegal working.

The Global Commission commends the practice of granting settlement to those who enter for work. Granting the right to stay often contributes to economic growth in the destination country and plays a role in meeting the needs of migrants. However, they also point out two disadvantages. One is that the public mood is not always welcoming, and may be less willing to accept long-term migrants. The other is that countries of origin stand to gain more if migrants return. Although it is difficult to devise programmes of temporary entry for work that protect migrant workers' rights, the Commission advises that this should be attempted as well as settlement routes. In such cases, workers' rights, including access to proper working conditions, information and to transfer employers, should be respected (2005:17–18).

These standards support the capacity of migration to alleviate poverty. If routes to work within the law are too restricted so that enterprising migrants are pushed into using illegal means, there is an overall loss (though note the arguments of Ruhs earlier, which suggest that there may be an optimum balance). The individual migrant may suffer poor or dangerous living and working conditions, never be able to earn enough to pay off debts owed to smugglers or traffickers, let alone send home, and yet not be able to bring any of their troubles to the attention of the authorities because of their own illegal status. In the meantime, their country of origin may receive little or no benefit from their migration. The host country loses taxation, working conditions for other workers may be driven down, the immigration system is brought into disrepute, and migrants suffer from being associated with illegality. Where the rights of migrant workers are respected, their autonomy increases and they are able to leave abusive employers, send money home, return home when they are ready, or if they want to settle in the new country are free to do so lawfully rather than 'disappearing' into the illegal economy (see Ryan MRN 2006).

In the UK, entry for work has been subject to intense scrutiny following the government's commitment to cut net immigration to tens of thousands. Students account for the largest group of immigrants (50 per cent of non-EEA visas in 2014), although the HASC argues that they should not be included in immigration figures unless and until they apply to stay after their studies, which the vast majority do not. Those coming for work accounted for 43 per cent in the same year. Human rights and domestic race relations are critically involved in family settlement, so this is difficult to control. Similarly, EEA nationals account for significant numbers of immigrants, but have a right to enter. In 2011 the government introduced a yearly 'cap' of 20,700 non-EEA workers who can enter for skilled work, and in December 2010 closed the general category for entry for highly skilled workers to all except 'those who have won international recognition in scientific and cultural fields, or who show exceptional promise', limited to 1,000 grants of entry clearance. There are now new Tier 1 routes for entrepreneurs; all these categories are discussed in detail in chapter 9.

The frequency with which categories of entry for work open and close demonstrates the attempts of the government to juggle responding to employers' demands for flexibility in their work force, and appearing to meet political commitments to reduce immigration. The HASC observed that 'the proposed cap—unless it is set close to 100 per cent—will have little significant impact on overall immigration levels' (para 31). The Migration Advisory Committee was unequivocal that the target could only be achieved by 'cutting net migration on study and family routes'. HASC advised the government 'not to treat the routes it can control too stringently in order to compensate for the routes it cannot control' (*Immigration Cap* First Report of Session 2010–11 HC 361 para 28). Employers' organizations opposed capping the numbers of intra-company transfers, which accounted for about 60 per cent of entries for skilled work. The HASC also advised against including intra-company transfers, while pointing out that without doing so there would be minimal impact on numbers, and intra-company transfers remain outside the cap, and are the most popular route for entry for work. Recent reports suggest that the cap is restricting non EU entry for work, but this is balanced out by an increase in EU nationals coming for work (HASC *Immigration: Skills Shortages* Fifth Report of Session 2015–16 HC 429 para 25). The HASC commented in relation to the cap:

The Tier 2 cap of 20,700 appears to play a very limited role in Government attempts to restrict net migration. There are no immediate consequences if the Government fails to reach its overall target to reduce migration to the tens of thousands. There are real consequences if the cap on Tier 2 visas is reached, as was discovered in June 2015. Reaching the monthly quota of Certificates of Sponsorship means employers, who had done all that was asked of them, and who had fulfilled the same criteria as those applying in the previous month, were unable to bring in skilled workers who had a definite offer of a job. . . . We welcome the decision of the Migration Advisory Committee to look again at how the system for Tier 2 skilled worker visas operates which we see as an acknowledgement that the imposition of restrictions has the potential to damage the UK economy (para 32).

Following a MAC review, which heard evidence from health professions, nursing was listed as a shortage occupation to prevent nurses from being caught by salary limits and prevented from staying in the UK (para 44).

2.4.3 Undocumented migrants and removal

A previous director of immigration enforcement and removals, when asked by the Home Affairs Committee how many illegal migrants there were in the UK, famously replied: 'I have not the faintest idea' (HC 775 para 74). The media seized upon this since effecting the timely and humane departure of those who have no right to be here has been an espoused political objective, and is often treated as a litmus test of the credibility of government's immigration policy. Thus, attempts to show that something is being done about this are another potent driver of immigration policy. However, there is much confusion and misinformation about who such people are, how many there are, and what harm their continued presence does, if any. The undocumented or 'irregular' population (sometimes estimated at around half a million) consists mainly of people who have overstayed their original leave, people who have entered clandestinely or on false documents without being detected, and people whose removal has been directed, but who have not left, such as asylum seekers whose claim has failed (see, e.g., JCWI 2006). There are also many migrants who are legitimately in the UK but who are in breach of their conditions of stay, for instance by working. Irregular migrants include those who have been trafficked. So when figures, known or guessed at, are used in debating these matters, it is generally unknown who is included. Describing such people as 'illegal' carries connotations of criminality that are often quite inappropriate. 'Illegal immigrant'—the term beloved of the media—has no precise meaning. To describe someone as an illegal immigrant who has worked in breach of their conditions of stay is equivalent to describing someone who has committed a speeding offence as an 'illegal driver'.

The circumstances of people with irregular status are more various than imagination can encompass. For instance, the history that led to the Court of Appeal case of *Bibi and others v SSHD* [2007] EWCA Civ 740 was that a man had entered the UK in the 1960s using documents that were not his, and obtained a British passport in that identity. He had worked in the UK ever since, and made regular trips home to Bangladesh. It was only after his death when the rights of his family were affected that his deception came to light. He had probably lived and worked and paid taxes with nothing apparently to distinguish his situation from that of another naturalized British citizen. This man's situation was very different from that of the cockle-pickers who died in Morecambe Bay, and others who live in hiding because their illegal status and, in effect, debt bondage to their traffickers means that they have no option but to hide from the authorities.

Evidence given to the Home Affairs Committee in 2006 suggested that by far the largest number among undocumented migrants are people who have at some point been lawfully resident, and may still be so. A number of NGOs take the same view:

Anecdotal evidence suggests that pressures exist with the experiences of migration which buffet against plans and intentions to remain lawfully and which convert a minority of migrants into rule breakers and overstayers. Many of these pressures are financial, involving the discovery that recovery of the cost of the original investment in migration (visa fees, student fees, travel costs, legal advice and other facilitation, etc) is not as easily recoverable from the meagre wages available to migrants as had been thought. In other instances migrants will come under pressure from family abroad to remain to take full advantage of earnings opportunities which can be remitted abroad. In these cases migrants may be tempted to work more hours than permitted or overstay their leave in order to claim to the benefits of migration. (MRN 2007)

The weight of evidence and opinion is that action needs to be taken on many different fronts to tackle this problem, but that some regularization of existing irregular migrants and the protection of migrant workers' rights are important elements. Enforcement by removal is not the only strategy. Ruhs and Anderson (2007) point out some non-compliance is tolerated by all concerned. For instance, how does the law evaluate a request by a student's employer that she works a couple of extra hours so that she exceeds the permitted hours that week? These compromises, they suggest, need to be understood.

Even when a removal decision has been made and directions issued to carry it out, carrying this into effect is not a simple matter. The obstacles to removal are real, and not always understood by critics. As JCWI relates:

Removal of failed asylum seekers may be impeded for a variety of practical reasons, such as a lack of travel documents, a lack of co-operation from the authorities of the country of origin in issuing such documents, or because there are no safe routes of return, or simply because that country is unsafe to return to. (2006:17)

These obstacles to removal are discussed in chapter 16. In addition to these reasons, Phuong discusses a host of other practical factors. Airlines may be reluctant to take on scheduled flights people who are being removed against their will:

Each person to be removed from the UK is subject to a risk assessment in order to determine his suitability for escorted or unescorted removal via commercial air services . . . In any case, the International Air Transport Association . . . has decided that the number of persons to be removed should be limited to one escorted and three unescorted on each flight. (2005:124)

Additionally, many passengers do not like to see people forced onto a plane and 'may take their business to another airline' (2005:125). In Germany, under pressure from the public, Lufthansa decided it would not carry passengers who were resisting deportation (2005:125). Because of the limited flights to removal destinations and the growing reluctance of commercial airlines, governments including the UK now charter planes to countries to which there are high numbers of returnees, and there are regular charter flights returning people to Afghanistan, Pakistan, Jamaica, and Nigeria. Charter flights have also been used for returns to Iraq and Sri Lanka. Clearly this is an expensive method, as planes with a capacity of hundreds of passengers may only carry a few dozen returnees at any one time (2005:125), although flights to, for example, Afghanistan have been known to carry as many as 90 passengers. Related to this, the Home Office identify 'reserves' for each flight. This means that extra people are given removal directions, and may be taken to the airport, but will only board if others do not fly because of last minute injunctions or other reasons. Those not flying are returned to detention. This practice has been criticized by HMIP.

The Home Affairs Committee noted that, despite the tone of much public debate, public opinion is another factor which explains the low number of removals relative to government targets and the numbers of those who are liable in law to removal (para 418; see also 2.6 on media). Phuong notes that, although public opinion may be in favour of removals in the abstract, when it comes to people being removed by force, and sometimes even injured or killed in the attempt, especially if they know them personally or they 'seem likeable (especially if they are well educated and have small children) they can become quite opposed to a particular forced removal' (2005:126).

In almost any government statement of immigration policy objectives in recent years, 'increase removals' has appeared as a key item. The practical reality is that it is a hard and unpleasant business for all involved and often unfeasible. Phuong concludes that one should also ask 'why are there so many people to be removed in the first place?' She, too, speculates that limited routes to legal migration may be part of the reason, and that opening up economic migration could assist. The Global Commission on International Migration recommends: 'States should address the conditions that promote irregular migration by providing additional opportunities for regular migration and by taking action against employers who engage migrants with irregular status.' The Commission also recommends 'dialogue and cooperation among states' (2005:36). Other commentators, too, consider that action on illegal working would alleviate the problems of undocumented migrants. Ryan (2006) explains that giving migrants the same basic workers' rights as other employees could solve some of the problems of exploitation not only directly but also indirectly, and help resolve immigration irregularity at the same time.

The conduct of removals is also a cause for concern. This is discussed in chapter 16 along with legal controls over the removal process.

2.4.4 **The UK in Europe**

A growing policy driver is a desire to distance the UK from the rest of Europe. Although successive governments repeat a wish to stay in the EU they increasingly argue for doing this on 'British terms'. The present Prime Minister's proposals to limit welfare benefits for EEA migrants are part of this. This tendency also affects the attitude to the Human Rights Act. The Coalition government which took power in 2010 set up a Commission to consider a proposal for a 'British bill of rights'. Consultation responses were largely to the effect that the Human Rights Act already fulfilled the need, and no change was proposed. The Conservative Party manifesto published in 2015 promised to 'scrap the Human Rights Act and curtail the role of the European Court of Human Rights, so that foreign criminals can be more easily deported from Britain'. However, as chapter 5 shows, the legal situation is not this simple.

The UK government is attempting to distance the UK from responsibility in what is called the 'refugee crisis'. A million people crossed into the EU in 2015 through Greece, Bulgaria, Italy, Spain, Malta, and Cyprus. At the time of writing in early 2016 the flow of people continues, and shows no sign of slowing. By far the greatest number of people are from Syria, about half of whose population is said to have been displaced over the five years of its civil war. Over 4 million Syrians have left the country, and the majority of these are still in Turkey, Lebanon, and Jordan. Some of those who moved in 2015 had already spent years in refugee camps. The vast majority of the passengers come by sea and land in Greece, often on the islands where facilities are minimal, and their survival is assisted by volunteers.

The EU was unable to respond effectively to the numbers arriving. An agreement was reached for some EU countries to take quotas totalling 120,000, but the UK refused to participate.

When some EU countries closed their borders against the queues of people arriving it became apparent that the refugee crisis was threatening the very existence of the Common European Asylum System and freedom of movement within the Schengen area. The pressure to reimpose border controls increased after the attacks by the Islamic

State in Paris in November 2015. In December 2015 the European Commission proposed that the security checks which apply to non-EEA nationals at the external borders of the EU would henceforth apply to EEA nationals.

After record numbers of migrants travelled to southern Germany through Austria, Germany reimposed controls on its border with Austria. Austria restricted road and rail traffic on its border with Hungary. Hungary built a fence on its border with Serbia (which is not in the EU), and later on its borders with Slovenia and Croatia. Denmark and Sweden imposed identity checks at their borders.

Most of the refugees coming to Europe are from Syria. The most common countries of origin after Syria are Eritrea, Afghanistan, Kosovo, and Iraq. The UK stated it would take 20,000 Syrian refugees over a five-year period, and then in January 2016 agreed that it would take an unspecified number of unaccompanied children. However, the UK government's policy is to take these refugees from refugee camps, not from the borders of the UK—which means not those waiting in Calais.

2.5 Control within the borders

The concern with controlling and being seen to control the presence and numbers of irregular migrants has become a major preoccupation in government policy. This reached a new extreme in 2013 with the creation of the 'Hostile Environment Working Group'. The aim was to make the UK a hostile environment for the undefined population of unwanted immigrants. Following Liberal Democrat objections, the group was renamed the Inter-ministerial Group on Migrants' Access to Benefits and Public Services. Despite the change of name, the intention to create a 'hostile environment' was publicly espoused by the Home Secretary Theresa May as the aim of the Immigration Act 2014 (*Immigration bill: Theresa May defends plans to create 'hostile environment'* The Guardian 10 October 2013). It is now an explicit government policy, escalated by the 2015/16 Bill which introduces criminal penalties for breach of many of the restrictions introduced in the 2014 Act.

2.5.1 The hostile environment

The hostile environment is developed in the 2014 Act by measures which include requiring landlords to check prospective tenants' immigration status, letting only to those with verifiable permission to reside in the UK and making access to bank accounts and driving licences dependent on immigration status. The 2015/16 Bill includes clauses which criminalize letting premises to those without leave to remain, possessing a driving licence without authority, and illegal working.

The landlord provisions of the 2014 Act came into force nationally on 1 February 2016. They require landlords to check the immigration status of those to whom they propose to rent property, with a civil penalty of up to £3,000 if they let to someone who does not have a right to rent, that is, those who do not have leave to remain in the UK (2014 Act ss 21 and 22). The scheme was piloted in the West Midlands for six months from 1 December 2014. An evaluation conducted by the Joint Council for the Welfare of Immigrants revealed that 42 per cent of landlords were less likely to let to people who did not have a British passport; 27 per cent were reluctant to engage with those with a foreign passport or name. Sixty-five per cent of landlords were much less likely to rent to those who could not produce documents immediately. An evaluation conducted by the Home Office focused on measuring compliance with the scheme and information about it. It found 'potential' for discrimination.

The Home Office evaluation found that 'Right to Rent Referrals', including enquiries made with the Landlords Checking Service, brought to their notice 109 individuals who did not have a right to remain in the UK, including 63 previously unknown to the Home Office. The situation for these individuals as at 14 September 2015 was:

- six could not be progressed due to lack of detailed information;
- nine had been removed from the UK;
- five were pending removal, in a detention centre, or in the assisted voluntary returns process.
- 25 had barriers to removal, broken down as: 19 without valid travel documents, four with an outstanding judicial review, one not removable due to their nationality, and one with further representations—their cases were being progressed;
- two were involved in criminal cases including one in prison;
- 15 were being progressed as family cases;
- 28 had outstanding cases such as asylum applications;
- nine were granted leave to stay in the UK;
- nine had been ordered to report to Immigration Enforcement but had failed to do so; and
- one was deceased.

Clearly the landlord provisions are envisaged as a doorway to enforcement. However, this is the tip of the iceberg of a complex picture. Many of those identified had ongoing legal matters at the time of compiling this information. The issues named suggest that many would qualify for statutory support, whereas previously they had been unknown to the Home Office and living outside any statutory system. The findings reveal that describing the population which is the target of the hostile environment as 'illegal' is too broad. It also suggests that people living under the radar are not exercising rights they may have. It raises questions about access to legal advice, and the cost–benefit analysis of these provisions.

2.5.2 Hostile control after entry

While the political statements are that the hostile environment is created for those with no permission to be in the UK, the hostility spills out onto lawful residents who are subject to immigration control. JCWI's research into the landlord scheme revealed incidents such as that of a Syrian tenant with leave to remain who was evicted because the landlord found his documents complicated and did not want the trouble or the risk. The hostility also arguably affects those who are required to administer the increasing number of internal immigration controls. Landlord organizations opposed this scheme. The population generally, working in banks, hospitals, the DVLA, letting agencies, marriage registrars, and so on, are recruited into vetting their customers, clients, and patients.

Chapter 8 (at 8.7) describes the more onerous marriage provisions introduced by the 2014 Act, some of which apply to all marriages and some to all marriages involving a non-EEA national. These include an active investigation power for the Secretary of State, which she may decide to exercise. The measures provide a disincentive to marry for anyone without leave to remain, since they will come to the notice of the Home Office and be investigated. They also provide extra hurdles for all non-EEA nationals, whatever their immigration status.

From 6 April 2015, as part of the application process for entry to the UK, or for leave to remain, migrants must pay an Immigration Health Surcharge (IHS, Immigration Act 2014 s 38). The charge is £150 per year for students and £200 per year for others, and must be paid up front at the time of application for all the years for which leave is being applied for. The charge also applies to each dependent member of the family. So a family of four coming on a visa for five years pays an IHS of £4,000.

This charge was introduced at very short notice and applied immediately, with no transitional provision. Application fees to renew discretionary leave (DL) were introduced at the same time and were also charged per person. The impact on some lawful residents was devastating. Families with children who were due to renew their DL to remain were suddenly faced with bills of thousands of pounds. Non-payment of the charges at the time of application could mean that the application was rejected as invalid, the applicant lost their leave to remain, and any future application would be treated as out of time and thus invalid. In one fell swoop they could lose their permission to be in the UK, their job, and their home.

The government also aims in 2016 to deny access to health services to destitute refused asylum seekers. Critics have argued that there is a point beyond which health services cannot be curtailed without impact on the service as well as the life and health of the individual. For instance, vulnerable pregnant women refused antenatal care may have a health crisis resulting in an emergency hospital admission which could have been prevented. While the present regime prevents access to non-urgent secondary care for refused asylum seekers who are not on asylum support, urgent and primary care are available. At the time of writing the government is renewing the proposal to remove all health care from people in this position (*Making a fair contribution: A consultation on the extension of charging overseas visitors and migrants using the NHS in England*, Department of Health, December 2015). There is no legal obligation to carry the BRP, but it becomes more necessary with the progressive introduction of the use of immigration status to qualify for access to public services, education, or employment. This generates potential for discrimination if cards are demanded where access to the benefit in question does not in fact depend on immigration status, or where the BRP is not well understood. Beynon reported a speech of the former Home Secretary to the effect that BRPs were to be used to 'refine and upscale a project already in hand—the enforced destitution of irregular migrants such as failed asylum applicants and visa overstayers so as to encourage them to return to their sending countries' (2007:328). The policy of enforced destitution is considered further in the next section.

The use of BRPs to access health care is in keeping with the government's programme of attempting to end access to the NHS for groups of foreign nationals.

This book does not cover access to welfare benefits and public services, but as context to the hostile environment policy, and its effect on lawful residents as well as those without leave to remain, it is important to be aware that most people subject to immigration control already have very limited access to public resources. The majority of people subject to immigration control do not have access to public housing. Most migrants granted leave to enter the UK are granted that leave on condition of having no recourse to public funds. The benefits rules, which prohibit access to most welfare benefits for most non-EEA migrants, therefore to a great extent mirror the immigration conditions. There are many complex exceptions, but the point here is that the broad prohibition on access to welfare benefits or public housing already applies not only to irregular migrants but also to lawful ones. Access to the NHS depends on immigration status. All school age children are entitled to attend school, but access to higher education is in practice limited by whether the student is treated as eligible to pay home or overseas fees. This is judged by whether students are 'ordinarily resident' in the UK. The Supreme Court held that this could not imply a requirement to have indefinite leave to remain (*R (on the application of Tigere) v Secretary of State for Business, Innovation and Skills* UKSC [2015] 57).

The integration policy behind recent legal changes and proposals is marked by a tendency to harmonize to an idea of British life that is based on a particular conception of the majority culture. Tests of English language ability are now required for most categories of entry except visitors and the very rich. The 'life in the UK' test, initially a condition of obtaining British citizenship, is now required for all applicants for indefinite leave to remain.

The growth of internal immigration controls has entailed the increasing recruitment of public officials and private citizens into the business of immigration control. To mention a few: marriage registrars, local authority housing officers, lorry drivers, employers, landlords, DVLA, banks and building societies, and universities. The residence test for eligibility for legal aid would involve solicitors checking their clients' immigration status. There is another dimension of this development of pervasive immigration control which needs to be mentioned to give a picture of migration control in today's Britain and that is the privatization of government activities. The contracting out of Home Office housing for asylum seekers will be mentioned later. In addition to that, in 2012 the 'business process management and outsourcing solutions' company Capita obtained a contract to reduce the 'Migration Refusal Pool', which is the number of people who have been refused leave but who have not left the UK. Towards the end of the period of that contract the HASC said:

Backlogs at the UKVI have always been a concern to this Committee under successive governments. The current backlog of cases remains at 318,159. There has therefore been an increase between Q1 and Q2. As we have said previously, the biggest contributor to the backlog is the Migration Refusal Pool. In its response to this Report, we expect the Home Office to set out a timetable for further reduction of this backlog. We are now coming to the end of the £4 million contract awarded to Capita with the view to the Migration Refusal Pool backlog being reduced. We would like a full assessment of this contract before there is any possibility of renewal. (HC 512 para 62).

Capita sent texts to thousands of people, but there were unanswered questions as to how they obtained the mobile numbers or on what basis recipients were selected. Those who received texts telling them to leave the UK included British citizens who had lived lawfully in the UK for over 30 years and who had never given the Home Office their mobile phone number. An immigration adviser received letters for 31 of his clients demanding that they go back to India. They were IT specialists who had been on short-term contracts providing services to a UK company. The letters (like the texts) stated: 'You no longer have the right to remain in the United Kingdom' and 'you must make immediate arrangements to leave the United Kingdom and provide proof you have done so'. They had all left Britain in 2008, and the Home Office had been advised of this (BBC news, *Capita tells departed migrants to leave the UK*, 4 January 2013).

Clearly these actions, like the 'Go Home' campaign discussed later, are part of creating the 'hostile environment' and contribute to a growing haze over the distinction between the activities of various 'outsourcing' companies and the actions of the Home Office.

2.5.3 **Treatment of asylum seekers**

This section concerns the conditions of support for asylum seekers during their time in the UK.

The Tenth Report of the Parliamentary Joint Committee on Human Rights in Session 2006–07, *The Treatment of Asylum Seekers*, was an important public document, saying:

12. The treatment of asylum seekers is important for the men, women and children seeking asylum in the UK. But it is also important for those of us who are not asylum seekers. This is because the UK's approach to migration—and its treatment of asylum seekers in particular—says something about the society we live in and the kind of country we want to be. The human rights principles and values of democratic societies must guide the country's behaviour towards asylum seekers and its relationships with other countries from which asylum seekers originate.

Asylum seekers who have no other means of material support are entitled to a basic level of assistance and accommodation while their claim is being considered (Immigration and Asylum Act 1999 s 95). The financial support is £36.95 per person per week. This can be refused if they do not claim asylum as soon as reasonably practicable after their arrival (Nationality, Immigration and Asylum Act 2002 s 55). As discussed in chapter 1, the application and interpretation of this section initially left hundreds (at least) of asylum seekers destitute. Following the *Limbuela* judgment, discussed in chapter 1, people with an outstanding asylum claim or appeal should not be denied support where they are destitute. Following the *Limbuela* judgment witnesses to the JCHR enquiry, including from the Home Office confirmed that s 55 of the 2002 Act was still being used to deny support to people who had somewhere to sleep but no food. In deciding whether someone had delayed in claiming, the difficulties of finding one's way to an unknown location in an unknown country, perhaps not speaking the language, and without the information that this journey was necessary and how to do it, were minimized or overlooked (para 78). The Committee concluded that the continued application of s 55 did not comply with the *Limbuela* judgment, that there were clear breaches of Article 3 ECHR, and that s 55 ought to be repealed. It was not, although its use declined, and it is now applied infrequently.

Where an asylum claim has failed and appeals are exhausted, entitlement to support under s 95 ends. A refused asylum seeker may be able to claim support under s 4 of the 1999 Act if they are taking all reasonable steps to go home, or the Secretary of State accepts that they are physically not able to leave, either because of illness or there is no viable route of return, or failure to support would entail a breach of their human rights. These conditions do not apply to the majority of refused asylum seekers. Section 4 support consists of accommodation and a card (Azure card) credited with £35.39 per week, and usable only at certain shops. The 2015/16 Bill proposes scrapping s 4, though it allows for support to be available where the person has outstanding further submissions with the Home Office which have not been responded to within a period to be specified (expected to be five days), or (s 95A) faces genuine obstacles to leaving the UK, or has an outstanding judicial review. These conditions are not very different from those for s 4. The key differences are:

- the Bill proposes to abolish the right of appeal against refusal of s 95A support;
- it avoids a grant of support to a refused asylum seeker where further submissions are responded to promptly (this is current policy, not always implemented);
- it attempts to change the priority between Home Office and local authority support for children;

- it abolishes automatic continued support for families with children on the refusal of their claim, and provides a different scheme of possible short-term support from the Home Office or Local Authority.

Asylum seekers are not permitted to work, though see *ZO Somalia* discussed later in this chapter.

The JCHR criticized frequent moves of asylum seekers who were on asylum support, interrupting children's schooling and causing other hardship, the use of vouchers to buy food and toiletries—once abandoned by the government as too degrading and inefficient but revived in the form of the Azure card—and the poor housing provided as the only option, sometimes overcrowded with collapsing ceilings. With the prohibition on doing paid work, there was no escape from the degrading conditions. The Committee concluded:

The treatment of asylum seekers in a number of cases reaches the Article 3 threshold of inhuman and degrading treatment. This applies at all stages of the asylum process.

The HASC 2013 Inquiry into Asylum also reported on housing conditions for asylum seekers following contracting out the provision of accommodation to multinational companies. There were problems with poor standards in housing, lack of housing, and slowness in responding to complaints. Although some problems were remedied by individuals at a local level, at the systemic level it appeared that some at least of the contractors were unable to deliver what they had promised.

Funding for English classes for asylum seekers has also been intermittently stopped and started. The Refugee Council commented:

The removal of automatic ESOL and FE funding for asylum seekers is a major blow toward their ability to function and communicate effectively during the time when their claim is being considered . . . English language brings greater self-sufficiency which, amongst other benefits, means less reliance on support services. It also allows people to make connections with the local community that they would not have otherwise. We are particularly concerned that these changes further disempower people who have already undergone significant loss. (ESOL and Further Education Funding Changes 2007/08 announced by the Learning and Skills Council. Briefing November 2007)

The HASC in 2013 recommended that English provision be restored to its former level, as for those obtaining leave to remain as refugees lack of English language provision is a bar to integration. This has not happened, and there have been further cuts in funding with the result that even asylum seekers on asylum support now cannot get access to English classes in many parts of the country.

2.5.3.1 Destitution

While life on s 4 support is virtual destitution, most refused asylum seekers do not qualify for s 4, and are entirely destitute. In 2006 an independent group of people began to investigate the asylum system in depth. This became the Independent Asylum Commission, which reported in 2008 on whether the asylum system was 'fit for purpose yet'. The foreword to their final report said:

We lose control over the movements of the asylum seeker at exactly the point—after refusal —that the incentive for the asylum seeker to maintain contact disappears. And we lose moral authority by using destitution to 'encourage' refused asylum seekers to return home 'voluntarily'.

Their recommendations included that 'robust independent research should be undertaken into the reasons why different categories of refused asylum seeker do not return home voluntarily, and the results should inform a pilot project to increase take-up of voluntary return'. Certainly many would say that their first asylum decision was badly made and the appeal system was unable to put that right (see chapter 11 for some reasons as to why that might be and for coverage of the asylum application process). Destitution at this stage is not an accident. The JCHR said:

We have been persuaded by the evidence that the government has indeed been practising a deliberate policy of destitution of this highly vulnerable group. We believe that the deliberate use of inhumane treatment is unacceptable.

Since then there have been numerous reports on destitution, all of which confirm that the largest groups of destitute asylum seekers come from countries where there is severe conflict and human rights abuses. For instance, research by the Joseph Rowntree Trust revealed that the largest groups of destitute refused asylum seekers were from Eritrea (25 per cent), Sudan (14 per cent), and Iran (12 per cent). This may in part be an indicator of the very real obstacles to return even when an individual asylum claim has failed. A refused asylum seeker may still be in fear of what would happen to them on return. This overriding fear may make the thought of return intolerable. In addition, there are obstacles to return, which have been considered earlier and are also examined in chapter 16.

For such a person, fast progress through the asylum system may mean that they are plunged more rapidly into destitution or, one of the few options for survival, illegal working. Other options are charities, begging, sleeping rough, or staying with friends. The most recent study, by the Red Cross, found that 66 per cent of participants in the study reported hunger, without being able to satisfy it, on a weekly basis. Twenty-three per cent experienced hunger every day of a given week. Eighteen per cent did not have at least one person they could go to for help with a serious problem. For a fuller account of survival strategies see Crawley, Hemmings, and Price (2011).

2.5.3.2 The right to work

EC Reception Directive 2003/9 Article 11(2) requires that if an asylum decision has not been taken within one year through no fault of the applicant, the Member State must 'decide the conditions for granting access to the labour market for the applicant'.

 **Key Case**

ZO (Somalia) and MM (Burma) v SSHD [2010] UKSC 36

The Supreme Court held that Article 11(2) of the Directive also applied to fresh claims for asylum, so that if a person whose first claim had failed later found further evidence and was able to make a fresh claim, that would trigger the start of a further 12-month period after which permission to work could be sought. Many asylum seekers do make further representations which they say amount to a fresh claim. The government's common practice was to decide that further representations did not amount to a fresh claim but the representations might be waiting for years for a decision as to whether they met the requirements (see chapter 11) to be treated as a fresh claim. During that period the Home Office would not treat time as running for the purposes of permission to work. The Court said that to interpret the rules in that way deprived the right to apply for permission to work of all utility. Time now runs from when further submissions are made.

The judgment of the Court of Appeal was to the same effect as that of the Supreme Court, but was never implemented. Once the Supreme Court judgment was given, UKBA introduced a policy that the only work for which asylum seekers could be considered was that in the list of shortage occupations. The HASC, in its 2013 Inquiry into Asylum, compared the UK with other European countries that allow the right to work after shorter periods and with less onerous conditions. See for detail Asylum Information Database Annual Report 2014/15.

2.6 **Media**

The final subject in this chapter is the media. They have been present, though without mention, in much of what has gone before. Policy is presented and framed in the way it is because the government expects that the media will publicize what they have said. Without the news media, many of the policy statements we have been discussing might not be made at all. Lord Woolf described the relationship between the media and the judiciary as one of a common interest, and a need to be independent of one another while also recognizing that each has some power to uphold the other's independence. The media and judiciary each act as a check on the power of government, particularly when that government has a large majority and can become 'impatient of interference and criticism' (2003). When there is tension in the relationship between the judiciary and executive, the media is an interested party.

Constitutional Reform Act 2005 s 3 affirms convention by requiring ministers to uphold the independence of the judiciary. The House of Lords Constitution Committee explained that this does not mean that ministers may not comment on individual cases. They may, but they should say that they disagree with the decision and that they will appeal if that is the case, and not imply that there is something wrong with the judge for making that decision (2006–07 Sixth Report para 40).

This convention has been infringed in immigration and asylum cases in recent years. In a number of cases, the judge has come under personal attack. Even more than this, ministers have implied that there is something unconstitutional and anti-democratic in the judges upholding the rights of asylum seekers and migrants. Remarkably, in relation to *R (on the application of Q and M) v SSHD* [2003] 2 All ER 905, the then Home Secretary David Blunkett said that he would not put up with judges interfering with the democratic process in this way. The case was one of statutory interpretation, using the Human Rights Act to interpret the Nationality, Immigration and Asylum Act 2002. Commenting on Mr Blunkett's response, Geoffrey Bindman in *The Independent* newspaper in February 2003 pointed out that it is the constitutional task of the judiciary to interpret legislation, and in a democracy, judicial review is the essential constitutional check by the judiciary of the executive.

In the case of *R (on the application of S and others) v SSHD* [2006] EWCA Civ 1157, the government apparently used the media to publish a distorted account of a court case, with damaging results for the courts, the Human Rights Act and the appellants. This case was serious enough that, in combination with two other incidents, it prompted an enquiry by the JCHR.

Briefly, this was the case of nine people who had hijacked a plane as a desperate measure to leave Afghanistan. They were members of a group opposed to the government, and were in fear for various reasons, including that one member of their group had been tortured, killed, and then delivered to their door. After an eight-day hearing by a specially convened Tribunal, their claims for asylum were turned down because of the crime they had committed by hijacking the plane, but it was held that they should have temporary protection because of their fears of human rights abuses. This would entail a grant of DL. They were convicted of the hijacking and served prison sentences, though later cleared by the Court of Appeal because the jury had been misdirected on the question of duress.

The government accepted before the Tribunal that the appellants did not present any security risk to the UK, but refused to accept the ruling of the Tribunal. They did not challenge it, but just failed to implement it. They kept the appellants on temporary admission, even though there was no basis in law for this. DL, although temporary, would entitle them to work or claim benefits, neither of which they could do on temporary admission.

As the hijack itself was such a high-profile event, the media would be interested in the fate of the appellants, so anticipation of press coverage must have been in the government's mind in the conduct of this case. The question was whether the government was willing to take the lead in explaining to the public that the hijackers had paid the penalty in law for their criminal actions, what they had suffered, why they needed protection, and to take credit for Britain upholding its proud tradition of giving sanctuary, albeit temporary. Unfortunately, they did nothing, leaving the appellants in limbo for 18 months.

When the case eventually came to the High Court, and Sullivan J ordered that the Secretary of State act lawfully and grant DL, the government appealed to the Court of Appeal. The High Court judgment was castigated in the press and by the Prime Minister as 'an abuse of common sense'. The response of the Prime Minister and Home Secretary implied that the High Court had only just decided that the claimants could not return for human rights reasons and that they were amazed and outraged by this, rather than acknowledging that the human rights decision had been made 18 months earlier and was no surprise. Their response also implied that these people had hijacked a plane and got off scot-free. Crucially, the Home Secretary commented in the press:

When decisions are taken which appear inexplicable or bizarre to the general public, it only reinforces the perception that the system is not working to protect or in favour of the vast majority of ordinary decent hard-working citizens in this country.

The media did not apparently notice that the 'ordinary decent hard-working citizens of this country' were not in any way adversely affected by the decision, but were being invoked in support of the indignation of the Home Secretary and Prime Minister. Over the next few days, they picked up the case as a call to repeal the Human Rights Act. *The Telegraph* contrasted the 'hijack at gunpoint' with the right to stay. There was no mention of the basis for the appellants' fear, nor the abuse of power by the Home Secretary. The press coverage painted the claimants as the villains of the piece, and the Home Secretary as amazed and outraged. Eventually the Court of Appeal applauded Sullivan J's judgment as 'impeccable'.

At the special inquiry by the Parliamentary Joint Human Rights Committee, the Lord Chancellor was asked whether he regarded Sullivan J's judgment as 'impeccable' or 'inexplicable and bizarre'. His response sets out a fairly standard piece of legal reasoning, which implicitly endorses that it was 'impeccable'.

Comment has not all been in one direction. As discussed in chapter 1, in recent years, there has sometimes been a high level of tension between the executive and judicial branches of government. One indication of this was that senior judiciary broke their time-honoured tradition of not commenting on government policy. The battle over the proposed ouster clause in the AITOC Bill brought out the senior and retired judiciary in powerful opposition, not only in Parliament but also outside it. Lord Woolf's trenchant criticism in his Squire Centenary lecture marked a new point in executive–judicial relations. Lord Steyn was prepared to count himself out of hearing the challenge to the British government's role in detention in Guantanamo Bay, which he described as a 'legal black hole' (2004:256), in order to be free to warn publicly against an 'unprincipled and exorbitant executive response' (*The Independent* 26 November 2003).

The use of the media in relation to *S* was a low watermark. However, the release of foreign prisoners reported in 2006 was, if anything, a lower point. In this case, neither the judiciary nor the Human Rights Act had any part to play. Journalism revealed a failing in government, and the government then blamed the judiciary and the Human Rights Act. The story is best told in the words of the JCHR report:

22. When it came to light that a substantial number of foreign prisoners had been released at the end of their sentences without being considered for deportation, some of whom had re-offended, the then Home Secretary, Rt Hon Charles Clarke MP announced plans, in a statement to the House of Commons on 3 May 2006, to change the system governing deportation of foreign prisoners.
23. The new Home Secretary, Dr Reid, said in a newspaper article on 7 May: 'the vast majority of decent, law-abiding people . . . believe that it is wrong if court judgments put the human rights of foreign prisoners ahead of the safety of UK citizens. They believe that the Government and their wishes are often thwarted by the courts. They want the deportation for foreign nationals [sic] to be considered early in their sentence, and are aware that this was overruled by the courts' (*News of the World*).

The cause of the prisoners not being considered for deportation was actually a failure of communication between different parts of the Home Office, and nothing at all to do with the Human Rights Act. This was admitted by the government in evidence given to the JCHR enquiry. This admission of course gained almost no press coverage by comparison with the outcry over the release of the prisoners, which was full of misinformation of all kinds. After the assertion by the Home Secretary that the Human Rights Act was to blame, the Prime Minister followed up in Parliament with a speech referring to the government's plans to change the law on deportation, and said that the vast majority of people 'would be deported, irrespective of any claim that they have that the country they are returning to may not be safe' (HC Debs 17 May 2006 col 990). The implication was not only that the Human Rights Act was to blame but also that the government had the power to legislate to override fundamental rights. The press coverage also implied that the prisoners *would* have been deported if they had been considered, but deportation is a discretion to be exercised on the merits of the individual case. There were said to be 1,000 prisoners freed without consideration of their cases, but the fact that this total was accumulated over seven years was lost from public view.

A serious result of the media outcry was that the government was under pressure to find and deport as many of the freed prisoners as they could. This meant that recently released foreign nationals, even if they would not normally be deported on the facts of their case, were at higher risk. One such case was that of Sakchai Makao, a popular young Thai man who had lived in Shetland most of his life. After one crime that was out of character, he served an eight-month prison sentence, but was welcomed back to Shetland. He was re-arrested for deportation in the aftermath of the foreign prisoners issue, but the islanders said he had been picked up as a 'soft target', and they campaigned for him to stay. The Tribunal agreed he should.

Not only foreign nationals were at risk in this operation. Some of the alleged foreign national prisoners turned out to be British. It seemed that prisoners' nationalities were not routinely checked (see Shah, R. 2007).

None of this was to do with the Human Rights Act or, in fact, the state of the law at all, but it was nevertheless a platform upon which the government could launch its idea of 'automatic' deportation for serious offences. In chapter 15 we discuss how automatic this actually is. Although the UK Borders Act 2007 has created a strong presumption in a wide range of criminal cases, even the strongest presumption cannot displace human rights, as the JCHR noted. Government representatives before the Committee were forced to agree. Nevertheless, human rights of migrants have continued to be a target, and as discussed in chapters 5, 7, 8, 16, and elsewhere, the government has continued to legislate to try to exclude human rights particularly of those with criminal convictions. The real issues have at times been obscured by remarks probably designed for the media but not necessarily true, for instance, the Home Secretary's famous complaint that a particular appellant had been protected from deportation because he owned a cat (BBC news, *Theresa May under fire over deportation cat claim* 4 October 2011). This was of course not so, and the judiciary, who were implicitly trivialized by this false account, entered the media arena with the Royal Courts of Justice issuing a statement that the cat 'had nothing to do with' the deportation being overturned.

The foreign national prisoners issue also provoked a published letter from the Prime Minister to the Home Secretary, in which he alleged that British courts overruled the government in a way that was inconsistent with other EU countries' interpretation of the ECHR. A parliamentary question and inquiries by the JCHR were unable to unearth any such case, but if they had, the implication that this would be somehow illegal, unethical, or unconstitutional is simply wrong. The suggestion was withdrawn before the JCHR, but again without media attention.

Sometimes, of course, the press itself misrepresents the law, and has also done this in a way that inaccurately disparages the Human Rights Act. An instance of this was press coverage of the case of Learco Chindamo, the young man who killed Philip Lawrence. A teenager killing a respected head teacher generated particularly strong feeling, and once again the Human Rights Act was wrongly credited with the fact that the Asylum and Immigration Tribunal held that he could not be deported. Chindamo, as an EU national, could only be deported 'on imperative grounds of public policy', which would not apply in this case where he was agreed not to present a future risk. Undeterred by facts, the *Daily Mail* and other newspapers reported that the Human Rights Act was the reason for the ruling, which was described as 'profoundly stupid and amoral' (21 August 2007). The Shadow Home Secretary was apparently also taken in, saying that the case demonstrated 'a stark demonstration of the clumsy incompetence of this Government's human rights legislation'. In fact, it was an EC Directive which bound the Tribunal.

The concern in cases of this kind, and one reason that *S* and the foreign prisoners issue warranted investigation by the JCHR, was that such inaccurate reporting, and particularly when led by government, undermines attempts to build a human rights culture. It feeds racism, though this was not discussed by the JCHR, as the implication of the Home Secretary's remark, not voiced openly by him but quickly picked up on by newspapers such as the *Daily Mail*, is that human rights are delivered to failed asylum seekers in preference to long-term residents. There was no foundation for this in the cases in question.

Press outrage over decisions which uphold the rights of foreign nationals has now become routine. The events discussed here provided a political backdrop for the continual readjustments of the law in relation to deportation and human rights, which continues to the present with the 'deport first, appeal later' strategy launched in the Immigration Act 2014.

The role and power of the press in creating a climate around asylum and immigration has been researched in a number of studies. Greenslade for the Institute of Public Policy Research shows that press reports have encouraged ill-feeling against migrants since the early part of the twentieth century, including anti-Jewish material in the newspapers of the late 1940s and press coverage of street fighting in Notting Hill in the 1950s, inaccurately reported as 'race riots'. The study shows how 'newspapers, either by exaggerating race disputes or covering them in such a way as to suggest that migrants were the cause of trouble, helped to set the political agenda which led to immigration legislation' (2005:17). A similar story may be told about disturbances in Brixton in 1981, also inaccurately dubbed 'race riots'. Greenslade gives examples of misinformation in newspapers which directly resulted in violence. For instance, the misleading claim that 'luxury pads' were being prepared for asylum seekers resulted in homes being broken into and damaged before refugees had moved in.

In October 2003, the Press Complaints Commission issued a brief guidance note to editors about terminology. It explained, for instance, that an asylum seeker is 'someone currently seeking refugee status or humanitarian protection'. Consequently 'there can be no such thing in law as an "illegal asylum seeker"'. This guidance on terminology, while welcome, only scratched the surface. The JCHR recommended the PCC go further and provide practical guidance on professional practice of journalists in reporting matters of legitimate public interest, while not encroaching on free speech (para 366).

A study for the Information Centre about Asylum and Refugees (ICAR) in the UK assessed the impact of media and political images of refugees and asylum seekers on community relations in London (ICAR Media Image, Community Impact 2004). This report uses a range of methods and is a theoretically grounded study. It was inconclusive about the link between unbalanced press reporting and violence against asylum seekers. It did find under-reporting of violence against asylum seekers and refugees, and the frequent use of emotive language and inaccurate information. The writers noted that 'local papers were more likely than national ones to interpret their role as providing a balanced picture on issues that affect local people' (2004:98). This finding was repeated in a later study by ICAR of the effect of the Press Complaints Commission Guidelines (ICAR 2007).

The 2007 ICAR research found that the most inaccurate reporting was in the daily newspapers with the top six circulation figures. The study found most political reporting to be 'tired, repetitive and unquestioning'.

This is endorsed by Philo, Briant, and Donald (2013), whose extensive study of media treatment of refugees finds:

- persistent and overwhelmingly hostile coverage of refugees and asylum in the national media;
- confusion in news accounts between refugees, asylum seekers, and other migrants;
- relative absence of the voices of refugees or those who represent them;
- adverse consequences for the stability of existing communities;
- consequences for refugees, particularly in compounding their isolation and stigma.

The book documents many kinds of abuses including those found by earlier researchers: false adverse portrayal of migrants and refugees, and false presentation of the impact of the law, in particular the Human Rights Act. It demonstrates how the construction of questions by journalists contributes to an adverse climate by defining problems and asking how politicians have solved them. The book also covers a new and significant form of use of the media—advertising by the immigration authorities. There is discussion of television programmes such as *UK Border Force*, a series funded by the government to portray what an interviewee for the authors' research described as 'a simple good and bad vision of the world'. While the funding for the programme was handed back because of controversy, there was a larger budget which UKBA spent on sponsoring TV coverage.

Finally, the government resorted to an extraordinary use of media in the 'Go Home' campaign. A van travelling around London bore the slogan:

In the UK illegally? Go home or face arrest. Text HOME to 78070 for free advice, and help with travel documents. We can help you return home voluntarily without fear of arrest or detention.

The exercise was considered ill-judged. The HASC thought that there would be a 'more effective and less menacing' way to deliver this message. Likewise, it advised the Home Office to reconsider its use of Twitter feeds—also used as advertising for government policy but potentially misleading.

There is enormous power attributed in the immigration and asylum field to an invisible factor called 'public opinion'. There is now a range of initiatives by non-governmental organizations (NGOs) and by individuals and community groups to tackle 'public opinion' directly by the provision of direct information about and contact with refugees and asylum seekers and their human experience. As government solutions to an ill-defined problem proliferate, so do the solutions of civil society, migrants themselves, activists, and people at various levels of organization. See, for instance, the London-based Strangers into Citizens campaign and the growth of the City of Sanctuary movement, an initiative to build a climate of welcome and hospitality. A coalition of over 60 organizations formed a campaign called 'Still Human Still Here', which aims to end the destitution of refused asylum seekers.

An important role played by the media in immigration and asylum issues is in investigative journalism. Journalists have revealed many human stories and uncovered malpractice in government, for instance when a chief immigration officer was alleged to have pressurized an 18-year-old asylum seeker for sex in return for asylum status (*The Observer* 21 May 2006). Sometimes press reports from their country of origin may also be an important source of evidence for asylum seekers. It is difficult to establish their claim outside their country, but they may be able to obtain newspaper articles through contacts or online, or occasionally witness statements from investigative journalists (for instance, in *BK (DRC)* [2007] UKAIT 00098).

Some of the major human rights violations occurring in connection with migration have been uncovered by investigative journalists, for instance, the Joseph Rowntree Foundation note in their report on contemporary slavery a 'formidable body of work by investigative journalists' (2007:24) which has uncovered stories of trafficking adults and children for sex and other forms of forced labour, and abuse. John Pilger's film, *Stealing a Nation*, brought the little-known story of the Chagos Islanders (see chapter 3) to the attention of the general public when it was shown on ITV. Possibly the most extraordinary public response in decades came as a result of an action by the media. The photograph of three-year-old Alan Kurdi, dead on a Turkish beach, made a huge impact on people in Europe. He drowned on 2 September 2015, along with his mother and brother. The family were Syrian, Kurdish, and basically non-political. They were fleeing after repeated bombing and then questioning from the security forces. This finally brought public attention to the so-called 'refugee crisis', described above.

2.7 **Conclusion**

This chapter just touches on some of the issues surrounding the making of legal policy. This is the edge of a very large field. Some other policy issues are addressed throughout this book as they arise.

QUESTIONS

1 Under what conditions is it possible to make immigration policy in a way that is truly democratically accountable? Is this desirable?

2 What elements would you like to see in a code of practice for the media on reporting on immigration and asylum issues?

 online resource centre For guidance on answering questions, visit the Online Resource Centre www.oxfordtextbooks.co.uk/orc/clayton7e/.

FURTHER READING

Anderson, Bridget (2013) *Us and Them? The Dangerous Politics of Immigration Control* (Oxford: Oxford University Press).

Arcarazo, Diego Acosta and Wiesbrock, Anja (eds) (2015) *Global Migration Old Assumptions, New Dynamics* (Santa Barbara: Praeger)

Beynon, Rhian (2007) 'The Compulsory Biometric Registration of Foreign Nationals in the UK: Policy Justifications and Potential Breaches of Human Rights' *Journal of Immigration, Asylum and Nationality Law* vol. 21, no. 4, pp. 324–33.

Billings, Peter and McDonald, Ian (2007) 'The Treatment of Asylum Seekers in the UK' *Journal of Social Welfare and Family Law* vol. 29, no.1, March 2007, pp. 49–65.

Birnberg Peirce & Partners, Medical Justice and NCADC (2008) *Outsourcing Abuse* (London: Medical Justice).

Crawley, Heaven, Hemmings, Joanne, and Price, Neil, (2011) 'Coping with Destitution: Survival and Livelihood Strategies of Refused Asylum Seekers Living in the UK' Centre for Migration Policy Research (CMPR), Swansea University (Swansea: Oxfam and Swansea University).

Department of International Development (DFID) (2007) 'Moving out of Poverty—Making Migration Work better for Poor People' (London: DFID).

Fancott, Nancy and York, Sheona, (2008) 'Enforced Destitution: Impediments to Return and Access to Section 4 "Hard Cases" Support' *Journal of Immigration, Asylum and Nationality Law* vol. 22, no. 1, pp. 5–26.

Flynn, Don and Williams, Zoe (eds) (2007) 'Towards a Progressive Immigration Policy' (London: Migrant Rights Network).

Ghai, Yash, (1997) 'Migrant Workers, Markets and the Law' in Wang Gungwu (ed.), *Global History and Migration* (Boulder, CO: Westview Press), pp. 145–82.

Global Commission on International Migration (GCIM) (2005) 'Migration in an Interconnected World: New Directions for Action' (GCIM).

Grant, Stephanie (2006) 'GCIM Report: Defining an "Ethical Compass" for International Migration Policy' *International Migration* vol. 44, no. 1, pp. 13–19.

Greenslade, Roy (2005) 'Seeking Scapegoats' IPPR Asylum and Migration Working Paper (London: Institute for Public Policy Research).

Home Office, *Fair, Effective, Transparent and Trusted: Rebuilding Confidence in our Immigration System* (Policy document, July 2006) (London: Home Office).

House of Commons Home Affairs Committee (2013) *The Work of the UK Border Agency* January–March 2013 HC 616, and earlier reports in the series.

House of Commons Home Affairs Committee (2012) *Rules Governing Enforced Removals from the UK* 18th report of session 2012–12 HC 563.

Independent Asylum Commission (IAC) (2008) *Deserving Dignity* (London: IAC).

Independent Chief Inspector of Prisons (2011) *Detainees under Escort: Inspection of escort and removals to Jamaica* 24–25 March 2011 (London: ICIP).

Independent Chief Inspector of Prisons (2011) *Detainees under Escort: Inspection of escort and removals to Nigeria* 20–21 April 2011 (London: ICIP).

Information Centre about Asylum and Refugees (ICAR) (2004) *Media Image, Community Impact* (London: ICAR).

Information Centre about Asylum and Refugees (ICAR) (2006) *Reporting Asylum: the UK Press and the Effectiveness of PCC Guidelines* (London: ICAR).

Joint Council for the Welfare of Immigrants (JCWI) (2006) 'Recognising Rights, Recognising Political Realities: The Case for Regularising Irregular Migrants' (London: JCWI).

Joint Parliamentary Committee on Human Rights *The Treatment of Asylum Seekers*, Tenth Report of 2006–07 HL Paper 81 HC 60.

Migrants Rights Network (2007) 'Enforcement Policy: The Heart of Managed Migration?' (London: Migrants Rights Network).

Moses, Jonathon (2006) *International Migration: Globalization's Last Frontier* (London: Zed Books).

Philo, Greg, Briant, Emma and Donald, Pauline (2013) *Bad News for Refugees* (London: Pluto Press).

Papademetriou, Demetrios (2003) *World Migration* (Geneva: International Organisation for Migration).

Phuong, Catherine (2005) 'The Removal of Failed Asylum Seekers', *Legal Studies* vol. 25, no. 1, 117–41.

Poku, Nana, Renwick, Neil, and Glenn, John (2000) 'Human Security in a Globalising World' in David T. Graham and Nana K. Poku (eds) *Migration, Globalisation and Human Security* (London: Routledge), pp. 9–12.

Ruhs, Martin (2009) 'Migrant Rights, Immigration Policy and Human Development' Human Development Research Paper 2009/23, United Nations Development Programme (UNDP).

Ruhs, Martin and Anderson, Bridget (2006) 'Semi-Compliance in the Migrant Labour Market' Compas Working Paper 30 (Oxford: Compas).

Ryan, Bernard (2008) 'Integration Requirements: A New Model in Migration Law' *Journal of Immigration, Asylum and Nationality Law* vol. 22, no. 4, pp. 303–16.

Shah, Ramnik (2007) 'The FNP Saga' *Journal of Immigration, Asylum and Nationality Law* vol. 21, no. 1, pp. 27–31.

Somerville, Will (2007) *Immigration under New Labour* (Bristol: Policy Press).

Taylor, Savitri (2005) 'From Border Control to Migration Management: The Case for a Paradigm Change in the Western Response to Transborder Population Movement' *Social Policy and Administration* vol. 39, no. 6, December pp. 563–86 (24).

Woolf, Lord (2003) 'Should the Media and the Judiciary be on Speaking Terms?' www.judiciary.gov.uk/media/speeches/2003/should-media-judiciary-be-on-speaking-terms.

3

Nationality, citizenship, and right of abode

SUMMARY

Nationality law lies behind issues of immigration and asylum. The question of who belongs to a nation may be answered in various ways, and the way a country defines its own nationals may change over time. This chapter considers the bases of nationality and citizenship and traces the development of British nationality law, focusing on changes from 1948 to the present day. Those changes are characterized to a significant extent by progressive exclusion of particular groups previously recognized as British from the right to live in or come to the UK. The bases for obtaining British nationality by registration and naturalization are discussed, as are the developing powers of deprivation of citizenship.

3.1 Introduction

Nationality law has consequences for immigration law. The greatest incident of nationality or citizenship is the right to enter and live in one's own country. As Juss says (1993:48), 'those individuals who are nationals of a state are deemed . . . to be its citizens . . . and the state uses its immigration law to prevent the entry and residence of non-nationals'. Not all British nationals have the right to enter the UK; some non-nationals, however, such as European citizens, do.

Some countries have nationality systems within which all their people are regarded as 'citizens' of the political entity, reserving the word 'nationality' for an identity within that overarching category. Thus, for example, in the old Soviet Union, a person would be a citizen of the Soviet Union but have a subsidiary and essentially ethnic identity, which would also appear on their passport. The UK has used the terms 'nationality' and 'citizenship' in its laws since 1948, but the former has tended to refer to a more historical, inclusive, and imperial version of Britishness and the latter to a more modern political adherence to the state. Some non-citizens may have the right of abode (the right to live) in the UK because of their status in countries that used to be part of the British Empire. This structure had no official acknowledgement of ethnic diversity but broadened the right of residence to those with citizenship outside the UK's boundaries. The fundamental trajectory of change to UK nationality law is the shedding of the remnants of post-imperial rules, long after the Empire itself has been officially disposed of.

British nationality law was historically riddled with inequalities of sex and birth status where British people sought to pass citizenship to their children born abroad or outside marriage. Although the discriminatory aspects of citizenship by descent have largely been dealt with at the legal level, those changes mean that events in the distant past must be proved, which can produce difficulties. The UK's attitude to race discrimination in nationality law remains hard to pinpoint. The UK refused to accept an opinion of the European Commission of Human Rights in 1973 that elements of its laws were racist (*East African Asians v UK* (1973) [1981] 3 EHRR 76), and the Race Relations (Amendment) Act 2000 made a partial exclusion for nationality functions as it did for immigration functions. This was, however, removed by s 6 of the Nationality, Immigration and Asylum Act 2002, so nationality functions are now included within the general duty on public authorities to avoid race discrimination. An ethnic group, as defined in law for the purposes of the Race Relations Act 1976, involves a shared history and some of the practices regarded as culture, such as language or sometimes religious practice (*Mandla v Dowell Lee* [1983] 2 AC 548 HL). Thus, Sikhs are an ethnic group, as are the English, and Roma (also called Gypsies). Nationality functions are not, however, the same as nationality laws, so that the latter may still indirectly discriminate by tending in effect to exclude some ethnic groups more than others. The construction of citizenship rules is outside the remit of the European Convention on Human Rights (ECHR), and European Union (EU) law defines European citizenship as a consequence of citizenship of a Member State, the definition of which is left to the Member States (see chapter 4). Citizenship, in European as in international law, is politically fundamental to state sovereignty.

3.1.1 Nature of nationality and its structure

Nationality and citizenship law is inherently controversial, because the question of how a state defines who belongs is itself disputed. A country may be defined by its geographical boundaries. It may be defined by its members, when it is often described as a 'nation'. If a country is identified by its existence as a political entity, it will often be referred to as a 'state'. The definitions may conflict: a group of people within a state may define itself as a nation that is politically subjugated by another nation. Some groups who feel they constitute nations, or states, may not be recognized as such by more established countries. Andrew Grossman (2001) has described how nationality may function for people who feel that they ought to have a country but have not achieved self-determination, pointing out how some of the trappings of individual citizenship may work, such as being able to use travel documents. It is also commonplace that even long-established states and populations may have continuing political disputes. The tendency in earlier centuries for political leaders to desire power over a wide population, perhaps including those in overseas territories, was largely reversed by the rise of welfare systems. The desire to shed responsibility especially for impoverished populations and individuals has influenced both immigration and citizenship laws.

Law is often unclear too, and the nationality laws of other countries are increasingly relevant across jurisdictions: if a person is to be expelled from Britain, another country must take them in, and this may give rise to legal and practical difficulties (see, e.g., the discussion in *MS (Palestinian Territories)* [2010] UKSC 25). An entitlement to citizenship elsewhere may deprive a person of the benefit of British refugee law (*ST (Ethnic Eritrean—nationality—return) Ethiopia CG* [2011] UKUT 00252 (IAC)), or may mean they can be deprived of British nationality as the deprivation would not leave them stateless (*Al-Jedda v SSHD* SIAC Appeal no SC/66/2008 18 July 2014, and see 3.5.2 on Deprivation).

Different countries have different rules of national belonging, but there are four basic ideas that may lie behind it: geography, allegiance, descent, or choice. The Universal Declaration of Human Rights (UDHR) Article 15 and the International Covenant on

Civil and Political Rights Article 24(3) assert the individual's right to a nationality, but there is no means of obliging any country to accept any individual as a national. The coexistence of a variety of citizenship attribution systems means that some people are eligible for more than one citizenship—though some countries do not allow their citizens to be citizens of other countries at the same time—and some people are stateless and have no citizenship at all.

The simplest way of recognizing someone as a national is perhaps by geography, ascribing membership to anyone born in the territory. This is the *jus soli* (law of the soil) principle. Allegiance is perhaps a still more ancient system of defining membership. It belongs to a world in which power was obtained by claiming territories through conquering their peoples. The system of allegiance is also inclusive, and children born within the monarch's territory in this type of system are generally born nationals, owing allegiance, whoever their parents are.

Membership by descent is the idea sometimes referred to as 'bloodlines' or the *jus sanguinis* (law of blood), so that the children of nationals are themselves born nationals, regardless of where they are born, and this may carry through many generations of a family living abroad. The pure form of this system means that the children of non-nationals are by definition also non-nationals even if they are born in the territory to lawful residents, and one cannot become a national if born outside it. A system of this type was operated in Germany until 2000, leading to large populations of German-born and -educated people who were regarded as foreigners because their parents were from, say, Turkey. Although there were limited provisions for naturalization (becoming a national), this was, in effect, racially discriminatory, and was eventually changed.

Most countries do have some system for granting citizenship to the children of nationals who are born abroad, usually with a limit of one or two generations. This is also known as a 'law of return'. In the UK, nationality has long been transmissible at least one generation, and there are advantageous provisions for the second generation born abroad to register as citizens, as well as obtaining favourable 'Ancestry' work visas.

In addition, a country may admit a person who requests membership, perhaps after the satisfaction of requirements such as a period of residence in the territory or commitment to certain national values. The basis on which naturalization is allowed varies amongst countries; in the UK, the most striking element is probably its fundamentally discretionary nature.

3.1.2 International and regional law on nationality and statelessness

Although Article 15 of the UDHR of 1948 says that 'everyone has the right to a nationality', not only is international law rarely enforceable in any way, but also no system of working out which nationality any individual ought to have is prescribed. The provision may be a sign of the national conflicts that gave rise to the UDHR itself. In Europe in the 1930s and 1940s, many people found themselves stateless as they did not fall within the nationality definition of any existing country, often following widespread deprivations of citizenship. There are also UN Conventions that relate to statelessness, but these have attracted relatively few signatories. Nevertheless, many countries, including the UK, have provisions in their domestic laws which grant citizenship to people born in the territory if they did not get a nationality at birth and so were born stateless. The UK has ratified the Convention on the Reduction of Statelessness 1961, but has not signed the Convention on the Status of Stateless Persons 1954.

There also exists a European Convention on Nationality, made by the Council of Europe in 1997. The UK has not even signed it so it is not a useful legal tool in Britain, but its contents are interesting as an example of some contemporary consensus. Until the later twentieth century, Europe showed a wide range of systems of nationality law, but by the earliest years of the twenty-first century, they had converged, on a broadly similar basis to the 1997 Convention. That asks states to recognize those born in the territory to parents who are lawfully resident, and to make provision for granting citizenship to lawful foreign residents of ten years' standing, or certain residents who are stateless. It does not invite states to operate the *jus soli*, by which a country recognizes as nationals all those born in the territory. It does require an element of the *jus sanguinis*, in that it asked states to recognize the children of citizens, even if those children are born abroad. Its provisions in relation to deprivation of citizenship require that it should not be arbitrary, and that, with some exceptions, it should not be used so as to leave a person stateless. Avoidance of statelessness is one of the objectives of the Convention, according to its preamble, and its Article 4 provides that the rules of each state party should be based on the principles that everyone has a right to a nationality and that statelessness should be avoided. British law now broadly accords with its provisions in relation to the attribution of citizenship, though perhaps not in relation to deprivation of nationality, where its provisions are close to arbitrariness. However, the Convention on the Reduction of Statelessness allows a relatively wide latitude in relation to supervening statelessness, but only if there is sufficiently good factual cause in the individual case which, in the broad British process, may not easily be established (see 3.2.4 on statelessness).

It should be noted that the ECHR contains no right to citizenship, nor a positive right to live in one's own country. The right not to be expelled from one's own country might seem a basic incident of citizenship, and perhaps one particularly apposite to the circumstances of civil collapse that gave rise to the ECHR itself. However, that right is contained only in Optional Protocol No. 4, which the UK has so far not signed, although it has been acknowledged that it contains important rights. In the White Paper, *Bringing Rights Home*, which presaged the Human Rights Act of 1998, the incoming Labour government of Tony Blair said that the Protocol should be ratified 'if potential conflicts with our domestic law can be resolved' (para 4.11), these 'conflicts' being the position of British nationals from outside the UK who were not permitted to enter the UK. The ECHR, unlike most other international instruments, is enforceable at the instance of the individual victim. The omission of nationality rights from the core of the ECHR, and the failure of the UK to sign up to Protocol No. 4, is therefore of very practical significance. Part 1 of the Counter-Terrorism and Security Act 2015 allows the making of a 'temporary exclusion order' preventing a British citizen who has gone overseas and is suspected of involvement in terrorism from re-entering the UK if, and for so long as, the Secretary of State thinks it necessary for the protection of the public. Orders can last for up to two years but can also be renewed any number of times. The making of an order must be referred to a court, but '[T]he function of the court on the application is to determine whether the relevant decisions of the Secretary of State are obviously flawed.' (s 3 (2)). This power of exile applies very broadly, including to British citizens by birth who have no other nationality, though a person may still be deported back to Britain.

A further practical point in relation to the structure of British nationality law in the European context is that citizenship of the European Union, a very valuable status giving rise to rights all over the continent, is defined by the membership rules of each individual Member State. UK-British citizens are European citizens, but this does not include overseas British nationals. In December 1992, on the point of joining the European Community (EC), Britain issued a Declaration stating that overseas British nationals—those who were subject to immigration control in the UK—would not be

British for the purpose of EC law. This was later confirmed in the European Court of Justice at Luxembourg in Case C-192/99 *R v Secretary of State for the Home Department ex p Manjit Kaur* [2001] ECR I-1237. More recently, deprivation of European citizenship has been raised as a defence by those being deprived of British citizenship, but this has been unsuccessful: European 'citizenship' is a right to free movement across Europe rather than a substantive 'citizenship' as such (*McCarthy and Others* [2014] EUECJ C-202/13).

3.1.3 Belonging in the UK: settlement, citizenship, and residence

The first clear legal affirmation of the principle that anyone born in the monarch's realm was therefore a subject of the monarch was *Calvin's Case [1608] 7 Co. Rep 1a; 11 Digest 496, 2*, confirming that a person born in Scotland after the union of England and Scotland was a subject of the monarch. This established the *jus soli* in the UK, which was formally codified in the British Nationality and Status of Aliens Act 1914. Section 1 of the 1914 Act said that a person 'born within His Majesty's dominions and allegiance' was a British subject. By then, the British Empire covered about 20 per cent of the world and everyone in it was equally British by birth—or this was at least the theoretical position: Shah has discussed the way in which in reality non-white British people were subjected to institutionalized racial prejudice (Shah 2000:70). Nevertheless, the *jus soli* meant that by the end of the Second World War there were about 600 million British people eligible to enter and live in the UK and exercise full civic rights while they lived here.

After the Second World War, British nationality law gradually became more restrictive. The British Nationality Act (BNA) 1948 provided for citizens of the newly-independent former colonies and dominions to remain British nationals (see 3.1.4), but Britain began to close the doors of the UK to overseas British nationals from the 1960s onwards. In 1983, the principle of the *jus soli* was removed from British law, marking a great break of principle by removing automatic entitlement to British nationality from those born in the UK. The effect on day-to-day rights was not immediate. At the level of everyday life then, access to social benefits such as health care or education depended on need or place of residence, not nationality or immigration status. As Hale LJ said in *O v London Borough of Wandsworth; Bhika v Leicester City Council* [2000] EWCA Civ 201, the National Assistance Act was 'about needs, not morality', and she also pointed out that status was difficult to determine. However, from the 1990s onwards, those without status were gradually excluded from such benefits, in a process which is still continuing, though the political focus has changed to the welfare benefits obtainable by lawful EU migrants.

The loss of the pure *jus soli* in 1983 marked a fundamental change from the traditional system of belonging in the UK, which reflected the mediaeval system of settlement within a parish. 'Settlement' remains a term used within the UK system, and the concept is often still more important than that of citizenship (see chapter 6). One might say that indefinite leave to remain (ILR) reflects the formal mediaeval concept of 'denizenship', bringing most of the benefits of Britishness without naturalization. The lack of focus on citizenship and formerly on immigration status as the fount of social entitlement has meant that these areas are not a major part of a general legal education, and this remains the case. The political climate has moved on, though, so that the government's appointee, Peter Goldsmith, who wrote a report on *Citizenship: Our Common Bond* in 2007, could be bemused at the lack of a bright line between citizens and others, speaking of 'a muddle that probably exists for honourable reasons' (Goldsmith 2007:77). It is, however, simply the traditional structure.

Many foreign nationals have lived in the UK for very protracted periods on ILR. Some will have travel documents in another nationality. People with refugee status will have UK-issued travel documents. Living in the UK on ILR is often useful for those whose countries of origin do not allow dual nationality, but who are unwilling to renounce their original nationality for some reason. For Mr Al-Rawi, whose family left Iraq and settled in New Malden, the reason was that he was the family member 'chosen' to maintain Iraqi nationality and so retain claims on land in Iraq. However, when Mr Al-Rawi was then detained in Guantanamo Bay, and the British government obtained the release of British citizens, this meant that because he was not a British citizen he was not released. In *Al-Rawi v SSHD* [2006] EWCA Civ 1279, the Court held that despite his not being a citizen as such, the UK had the right to intervene with the US about how he was treated. However, following *R (on the application of Abbassi) v Secretary of State for Foreign and Commonwealth Affairs* [2003] UKHRR 76, the Court did not have the power to compel the government to do that in any particular way.

The fact that these cases on the difference between citizens and non-citizen residents are tested so late in the development of nationality laws is a symptom of the long-standing fuzziness of the dividing lines between the two. It is also interesting to see that it is opposite in thrust to the previous notable case law where a defendant accused of treason tried to establish that he was not British enough to be convicted. William Joyce, who was also known as 'Lord Haw-Haw' because of his haughty manner of speaking, had made broadcasts from Nazi Germany during the Second World War. He was a citizen of the United States of America, but had travelled to Germany on a British passport obtained because his father had been Irish when Ireland was under British rule. On that basis, it was held that he had obtained the protection of Britain and so owed allegiance. Joyce was hanged for treason in 1946 (*Joyce v DPP* [1946] AC 347).

Many long-term British residents have neither British citizenship nor ILR. There is a variety of other statuses, and both the meaning of the statuses and the entitlements of those who hold them are often unclear. Many people live and work in the UK who are not strictly entitled to do so. Others may be entitled to live in the UK but only have conditional access, for example, to the NHS or welfare benefits. The position may be further confused by legal concepts such as 'habitual residence' or 'ordinary residence', which also apply to British people, and whose use as a test for welfare entitlements is still developing.

3.1.4 **British nationality in transition: restructuring the Empire**

British nationality was originally based on birth in the land controlled by the monarch, wherever it was. It was after the Second World War that the distinction between UK-based and non-UK-based British people began to be drawn. Former colonies became independent, their populations largely transferring their allegiance into the new countries. These newly independent countries often did not allow dual nationality and required people, in order to belong as a citizen of the new country, to cease to be British. Canada passed its own citizenship laws in 1946; India followed shortly afterwards. Britain responded with the BNA 1948, acknowledging the control of the newly independent states over their own affairs and at the same time retaining some idea of universal Empire. This was embodied in the concept of the Commonwealth, which has moral but not political power. Most current members are former British territories, though Mozambique is a longstanding member and Rwanda joined in 2009. Applications to join have also been made by, for example, the Palestinian National Authority. Not all former British territories are members: Ireland left on independence and other countries such as South Africa, Zimbabwe, and Fiji have variously been suspended as a measure of disapproval. Australia alone regards other Commonwealth states as 'foreign powers' (see *Sue v Hill* [1999] HCA 30).

The BNA 1948 retained the overall status of 'subject' for all British people in the Empire, but superimposed on it the new (to British law) idea of 'citizenship'. The idea was that people would be either citizens of the UK and Colonies (CUKCs) in the UK or where their countries of residence remained colonies, or, where their countries gained independence, they would be citizens of those countries and British subjects as well. CUKCs were people born, adopted, registered, or naturalized in the UK or the Colonies, or whose father was such a person. The 1948 Act itself had no immediate impact on the status of members of either group. There was also movement between the two groups. Citizens of independent Commonwealth countries, or of Ireland, had the right to register as CUKCs if they had been resident in the UK or a colony for 12 months, though later the Commonwealth Immigrants Acts would affect these registration rights: whether such registrations were made can affect unforeseen British citizenship issues for future generations. CUKCs would, if they met any necessary criteria, become citizens of independent Commonwealth countries when their home country gained independence.

Some people, however, fell outside both categories of citizenship (ss 13 and 16 BNA 1948), if their country of residence became independent but for some reason they did not gain citizenship of it. These people became British subjects without citizenship. Others were not British subjects because they were born, not in a British colony, but in a British protectorate such as Iraq. The difference between colonies and protectorates was established during the Empire, when colonies were countries governed by Britain where the common law applied, whereas at least in theory in protectorates government was by local rulers, and the common law did not apply. Those who were connected with protectorates were not CUKCs but British Protected Persons (BPPs), and because this status could not be transmitted to children, there are now few of them left.

3.1.5 **The end of Empire: the Commonwealth Immigrants Acts and the East African Asians**

After the war, the structure and infrastructure of Britain needed rebuilding, inviting substantial labour immigration, especially from the British Caribbean, in the 1950s. There was also substantial non-white, visible immigration to the UK from Africa, for reasons connected with Empire and decolonization. The reaction of the newly independent former colonies in East Africa to past white domination was policies of Africanization. Kenya, Tanganyika (Tanzania), and Uganda had substantial populations of Asian descent, often families who had for generations served in the British civil service. Many decided against renouncing their status as CUKCs, or even BPPs, in favour of the new African citizenship, so that if life became too difficult they could go to the UK.

Following the initial post-war rebuilding, the UK began to close its borders to British nationals from outside the UK. This began with restrictions on non-white immigration from East Africa, in a domestic climate of growing racial tension. In 1962, the Commonwealth Immigrants Act made British subjects subject to immigration control unless they had a UK passport issued by the UK government rather than the government of a colony, or by a High Commission even in a colony; Irish citizens also retained the right of abode. The 1968 Commonwealth Immigrants Act then divided CUKCs into those who could enter the UK without restriction, and those who could not. The atmosphere of racial tension in which this legislation was passed was not universally discouraged by government figures: the speech made by Enoch Powell, MP for Wolverhampton South West, in April 1968 is still famous as the 'Rivers of Blood speech'. In it, he talked of rioting by white people against the non-white population unless immigration was stopped. In this climate, the Commonwealth Immigrants Act 1968 passed through Parliament with great rapidity. Though Powell was sacked from the Shadow Cabinet for his speech, the effects of the Acts remained in place and were consolidated in the Immigration Act 1971, which is still in force.

The effect of these Acts was to divide British people into those who had the 'right of abode' in the UK and those who were subject to immigration control, with the former being described in the original terms of s 2 of the 1971 Act as 'patrials'. CUKCs who were born, adopted, naturalized, or registered in the UK (s 2(1)(a)), or whose parents or grandparents were (s 2(1)(b)), were 'patrials'. So were CUKCs who had been ordinarily resident in the UK for five years (s 2(1)(c)). The right of abode was more restricted for Commonwealth citizens, who had it if they had a parent born or adopted in the UK (s 2(1)(d)) or were married to patrial men (s 2(2)). The ancestral connection for Commonwealth citizens thus needed to be closer than for CUKCs in order to obtain the right of abode. The value of a British passport for those without the requisite parental connections suddenly diminished. The Act took away the right of abode for the majority of East African Asians, who were thus left with no country in which they had any right to live. Their chance of entry to the UK depended on a voucher scheme, which operated on a quota system.

Section 1 of the 1968 Act was the subject of the challenge before the European Commission of Human Rights in *East African Asians v UK (1973)* [1981] 3 EHRR 76. The successful basis of the claim was that the Act was racially discriminatory and that such treatment was degrading and thus in breach of Article 3 of the Convention. This decision was of historic importance in finding as fact that the statute was passed with a racial motive. This was strenuously denied by the government on the basis that requiring a familial connection had nothing to do with colour but only with defining who 'belongs' to the UK. However, the evidence for this emerges clearly from the Cabinet papers and other official records of the time, which refer to 'coloured' immigration (see Lester 2002) and the Commission was satisfied about the effects of the legislation:

persons who belong to the category of 'patrials' have the 'right of abode' in the United Kingdom . . . such persons would normally be white Commonwealth citizens. . . . The Asian citizens of the United Kingdom and Colonies in East Africa, on the other hand, would not normally be 'patrials' and thus have no 'right of abode' in the United Kingdom, the State of which they are citizens. (*East African Asians v UK* para 202)

The second significant aspect of the Commission's decision was the finding that racial discrimination can amount to a breach of Article 3 in itself. If it is sufficiently severe it amounts to degrading treatment, doing away with the need to identify another Convention right in respect of which discrimination may be alleged under Article 14. If the UK had ratified Protocol 4 of the Convention the applicants would have had a very strong case under Protocol 4, being nationals denied entry, and also under Article 14 read with Protocol 4. However, the decision could be said to have greater significance because of the use of Article 3, though the Strasbourg Court has tended to be less radical since then in its defence of rights of nationality and citizenship.

The right of abode has occasionally resurfaced as a separate issue, as for example in *Vogel v SSHD* [2015] UKUTUR IA26033/2013. The applicant sought a certificate of entitlement to the right of abode on the basis that her British father had registered her birth in South Africa with the British authorities there. However, he had not registered her as a CUKC. Therefore, her father being a citizen by descent, she had no right of abode. Article 8 ECHR was engaged because of the applicant's life in the UK, but it was found to be proportionate to require her to return to South Africa and apply from there for readmission to the UK.

3.2 **British citizenship under the British Nationality Act 1981**

There are six categories in British nationality law: British citizens (the most privileged category, and the only one that always carries a right of abode in the UK); British Overseas Territories citizens (BOTCs); British Overseas citizens (BOCs); British subjects; British nationals (Overseas); and BPPs. The trajectory of the development of British nationality law since the Act has been to focus on British citizens and to lose the other categories.

3.2.1 **Acquisition of British citizenship by birth**

Section 1 of the BNA 1981 deals with the acquisition of British citizenship by people born after the commencement of the 1981 Act on 1 January 1983. It provides that a person born in the UK after commencement is a British citizen if, at the time of their birth, their mother or father is a British citizen or settled in the UK. This ended the longstanding tradition of the *jus soli*, establishing instead a form of the *jus sanguinis*, tempered by broad provisions for registration and naturalization of those born outside the UK. For the first time, the UK-born children of, say, migrant workers or refugees could be born stateless in the UK if they did not gain a nationality through their parents.

The British Overseas Territories Act 2002 (BOTA) Sch 1 amended BNA 1981 s 1 so that since 21 May 2002, birth in an overseas territory also results in British citizenship if the child's parents are British or settled in the territory. Their parents are likely now to be British following s 3 of BOTA, which is discussed more fully at 3.3.1. British Overseas Territories are currently: Anguilla, Bermuda, the British Antarctic Territory (so-called, although this is also claimed by Chile and Argentina and has no inhabitants), British Indian Ocean Territory, Cayman Islands, Falkland Islands, Gibraltar, Montserrat, Pitcairn, Henderson, Ducie and Oeno Islands, St Helena and Dependencies, Turks and Caicos Islands, and the Virgin Islands. The sovereign base areas on Cyprus are British Overseas Territories, but birth there does not give rise to British citizenship. Under BNA 1981 s 1, British citizenship is acquired by birth in the UK if the child's parents are either British or settled. To be settled means to be ordinarily resident in the UK without any immigration restrictions (Immigration Act 1971 s 33). Settlement is discussed more fully in chapter 6. European nationals exercising free movement rights in the UK used to be regarded as settled for nationality purposes, that is, their child born in the UK could have British nationality. However, this was later limited to those who have acquired permanent residence under those regulations. Children born to European Economic Area (EEA) nationals who are exercising EC rights in the UK will be British if born before 2 October 2000, but not if born after that date unless their parents have permanent residence in the UK. Section 42 of the Borders, Citizenship and Immigration Act 2009 provides that British citizenship is transmissible to children by serving members of the British armed forces even if they are not themselves British or settled.

3.2.2 **Acquisition under the Act by those born before commencement**

Section 11 of the BNA 1981 gave British citizenship to anyone born before commencement of the Act (1 January 1983) who was a CUKC with right of abode before the Act. In other words, it gave British citizenship to patrial CUKCs as defined in the old s 2 of the 1971 Act, discussed earlier. These were the people with a parental or grandparental connection with the UK who were citizens of the UK itself, or a colony, but not Commonwealth countries.

On 21 May 2002, British citizenship was also acquired by existing BOTCs listed earlier (British Overseas Territories Act 2002 s 3), whatever their date of birth.

3.2.3 British citizenship by descent

Citizenship by birth in the UK was historically a matter of the common law; citizenship by descent, which is of the essence of the *jus sanguinis*, has always been statutory, beginning with the statute De Natis Ultra Mare 1351. At the time of implementation of the 1971 Immigration Act, nationality passed through men to the children of their marriage, and through women only to non-marital children. A person born to married parents could therefore only acquire CUKC status by birth if their father was British, and if they were born outside the UK and Colonies the CUKC citizenship so acquired was citizenship by descent, which in UK law cannot be passed to a child also born outside the UK. Transmission of nationality outside the UK and Colonies could only occur for one generation, and this is still the position under s 2 of the 1981 Act, although rights of registration under s 3 help the next generation (see 3.4.1).

Where a person is born to a British parent (or, under s 42 BCI Act 2009, a serving member of the British armed forces) outside the UK, they are a British citizen by descent (BNA s 2). Therefore, if a British couple, A and B, go abroad, say to work, and have a child C while they are abroad, but later return, C's children, if born in the UK, will be British, and the line of British citizenship continues unbroken. If, however, C stays abroad, or goes to work abroad herself and has children there, they will not be British unless their other parent is British otherwise than by descent. C's children have an entitlement to register as British if they meet certain conditions (set out at 3.4.1), but this ends with them, and is not available to their children. The provision maintains a distinction between those who are British and those who are settled. The children of a settled couple, neither of whom is British, are British if born in the UK, but otherwise are not. The exception, since 21 May 2002, is that birth in an overseas territory to British parents will now give rise to British citizenship otherwise than by descent (i.e., full British citizenship), regardless of whether the parents are settled in the UK or in the overseas territory where the birth takes place. British citizenship by descent in the overseas territories continues only for those who had that status before 2002.

Prior to the 1981 Act, citizenship could pass only through a married father. The 1981 Act provided for citizenship, including of the British Dependent Territories, to pass through the mother also. Section 13 of the Nationality, Immigration and Asylum Act 2002 inserted s 4C into the BNA 1981 and allowed those born between 7 February 1961 and 1 January 1983 to register as British if they would have been British by descent if, at the time of their birth, nationality could pass through a woman (see *SSHD v Hicks* [2006] EWCA Civ 400). Section 45 of the Borders, Citizenship and Immigration Act 2009 extended that right to include those born earlier. Section 45 of the Immigration Act 2014 amended s 4 BNA 1981 by inserting paragraphs 4E–4J, extending entitlement to register to children who would otherwise be unable to do so only because their natural father was not married to their mother. In an interim case, *R on the application of Montana v SSHD* [2001] 1 WLR 552 CA, a British citizen man had a son born in Norway to a Norwegian mother to whom the father was not married. Registration of the child as a British citizen was declined on the basis that the child had insufficient connection with the UK. That argument prevailed on judicial review, against that of Article 8, the right to respect for private and family and Article 14, freedom from discrimination in relation to Convention rights: the Court of Appeal considered registration to be unlike citizenship by descent, and held that common nationality was not a requirement of family life, so Article 8 was not engaged.

Retrospectivity may, however, throw up its own issues. In *Romein, Re Judicial Review* [2014] ScotCS CSOH_174, the applicant for registration was born in the USA in 1978, her father having been born in the USA and her mother in South Africa. Her mother was British by descent as her father was Welsh, and said she would have registered the applicant as British in South Africa under s 7 of the BNA 1948 but she had been told there was no point because citizenship could not be transmitted through the female line. The application was refused because the mother had not registered the birth with the British authorities, registration as a CUKC being a different matter from simple registration of the birth.

3.2.4 Statelessness and British nationality

Statelessness is a problem for the individual who has no state to call upon for protection and a practical problem as well as one of principle for the countries they live in. Despite the attempts of the influential Paul Weis, the international provisions relating to statelessness, such as the Convention on the Status of Stateless Persons 1954 (based on the Refugee Convention) and the Convention on the Reduction of Statelessness 1961 refer only to those who are *de jure*, or legally, stateless. They do not include those who are merely *de facto* stateless—who have no useful or effective nationality, but may have the citizenship of a country they do not know and may never have lived in. The general idea of the Conventions is that, to keep the problem to a minimum, states should accept certain stateless people as theirs, particularly those born on their territory, and should look after the others. The Statelessness Conventions have never attracted the widespread ratification of the Refugee Convention, though Britain takes its obligations under the 1961 Convention seriously.

There are several provisions related to statelessness in the BNA 1981, especially in Schedule 2. Children born in the UK who would otherwise be stateless are BOTCs, BOCs, or British subjects if either parent has such a status (Sch 2, para 1); similar rules apply for those born stateless in British Overseas Territories (Sch 2, para 2)—this now means only those born in the British bases on Cyprus. The children and grandchildren of Hong Kong BDTCs who became BOCs in 1997 because they would otherwise have been stateless benefit from a like right. Children born on British ships or aircraft who would otherwise be stateless will be British citizens under s 50 (7, 7A, 7B). For those born stateless outside the UK to parents who are British nationals, it is also possible to register with those statuses, or to naturalize, under the usual rules. Parental residence requirements for naturalization may be waived for a child born stateless.

Claims to a right to live in Britain on the basis of statelessness are sometimes made by those who make a concurrent or alternative claim for asylum. Being stateless does not bring a right to remain in Britain of itself, nor does it make a person a refugee (*Revenko v SSHD* [2000] EWCA Civ 500). The growth in issues of statelessness was reflected in the new Part 14 of the immigration rules made in May 2013, which deals with applications for leave to remain on the basis of statelessness. It confirms that it applies only to those who are *de jure* stateless, who are in the UK, and who are not excluded for reasons tantamount to those that exclude a person from recognition as a refugee (receiving UN protection; holding in effect permanent residence rights elsewhere; being a war criminal, having committed a serious non-political crime before coming to the UK; being guilty of acts contrary to the purposes and principles of the UN). A person not so excluded may apply for limited leave to remain as a stateless person, which will be refused if they are considered a danger to security or public order, or fall to be refused under Rule 322 (including false representations made or false documents or information submitted or matters concealed; being subject to deportation; or convictions, character, or associations or being a threat to national security). If leave is given, it will be for up to 30 months, which may be curtailed if the person commits offences or is a danger to security or public order, or may be renewed or followed by a grant of indefinite leave if they have been lawfully in the UK continuously for five years. Spouses, civil partners, or *de facto* partners of two years' standing, or dependent children aged under 18 may also apply for leave as the family member of a stateless person who has leave on that basis; they may have leave granted, curtailed, or refused on the same bases as the principal applicant. For indefinite leave as a family member, the relationship must still be subsisting and, for a dependent child, they must not have become independent.

Applicants nevertheless have to show that they are stateless. In *Riaz v SSHD* [2014] UKUTUR AA00241/2014, a woman from the disadvantaged and often stateless south Asian Rohingya population was found not to have shown that she was stateless, particularly because on the evidence she held a Pakistani passport. People from countries where there have been changes of political ordering may have been left technically stateless when their countries were reorganized. It was in this context that the practice arose of regarding people as not stateless if they could obtain a nationality by application, and it was codified as s 40 (4A) (c) of the BNA 1981 by s 66 IA 2014: deprivation is available where 'the Secretary of State has reasonable grounds for believing that the person is able, under the law of a country or territory outside the United Kingdom, to become a national of such a country or territory'. Echoing the issues in *Pham* (see 3.5.2), in *Semeda, R (on the application of) v Secretary of State for the Home Department* [2015] UKUT 658 (IAC), the Secretary of State had found that a person claiming to be an undocumented Kuwaiti Bidoon had 'a claim to' Libyan nationality and was therefore not technically stateless. The Upper Tribunal, quashing that decision, held that the question was whether the relevant government recognized the claimant as one of its nationals at the time the decision was taken, and moreover that it was the relevant government's position rather than the letter of the law that was determinative. The Tribunal also commented on a claimant's duty to cooperate with the Secretary of State in establishing their nationality position.

In *JM, R (on the application of) v Secretary of State for the Home Department (Statelessness: Part 14 of HC 395) (IJR)* [2015] UKUT 676 (IAC), the Upper Tribunal UKUT 676 (IAC) considered s 40(4A)(c) BNA 1981 and HC 395 403 (c), which refers to a person not being admissible to their country of former habitual residence or any other country, and held that a person is not stateless if they can register as a national with another country.

3.2.5 British nationality in European law

For the purposes of EC law Britain has defined 'British nationals' as British citizens, British Overseas Territories citizens deriving their citizenship from Gibraltar (though since the British Overseas Territories Act 2002 s 3 came into force these people have been British citizens), and British subjects with the right of abode. This excludes BOCs (see *Manjit Kaur*), British protected persons, and Commonwealth citizens with the right of abode.

3.3 Other categories of British nationality

The less privileged classes of British nationality were created to answer immigration concerns at particular moments in history, and can best be understood in the context of the UK's relationship with the groups who were the targets of the legislation. This relationship is complex and different in each case; the subsidiary British national statuses were designed to deal with problems that were otherwise very difficult to resolve.

3.3.1 British Overseas Territories Citizens

In older documentation and in the BNA 1981, this nationality status is referred to as British Dependent Territories Citizenship. The category was created for those who had been born in a former colony to a parent who was born or settled in a colony. Under s 23 BNA 1981, such a person who had been a CUKC by birth, naturalization, or registration or had a parent or grandparent who was, became a BDTC (later a BOTC). This status could be acquired or passed on. It did not however give the right to enter other dependent territories, or to enter Britain. However, these people had generally already lost the right of abode in Britain following the Commonwealth Immigrants Acts of the 1960s. The citizenship was renamed to recognize that these territories had thriving rather than 'dependent' communities (see White Paper, *Partnership for Progress and Prosperity* (Cm 4264)). Most people involved became British citizens under the British Overseas Territories Act 2002 or through some other provision.

The territory of Gibraltar, in southern Spain, has long been the subject of a sovereignty dispute between Britain and Spain. In order not to weaken the British claim, Gibraltarians were included in the UK's declaration of British nationality for EU purposes, and Gibraltarian BDTCs were given the right to register as British citizens by s 5 BNA 1981. In a similar move, following the attempted military seizure of the Falklands Islands, a British territory off the coast of South America, by Argentina in 1983, the islanders were granted British citizenship under the British Nationality (Falkland Islands) Act 1983. Had these provisions not been made, Gibraltarians and Falkland Islanders would have benefited from the British Overseas Territories Act 2002 by becoming British citizens in any event. This brings all the advantages of EU citizenship, as with the overseas lands or 'régions d'outre-mer' of France, such as Guadeloupe and Martinique.

Hong Kong had been leased to Britain by China for 99 years in 1898, and was to be returned to Chinese hands in 1997. During the parliamentary debate on the 1981 Act, when opposition members argued for citizenship concessions for Gibraltar and the Falklands, no one was prepared to argue for concessions for Hong Kong. The concern was that the 2.6 million Hong Kong Chinese population would leave and come to the UK when Hong Kong returned to China. There was however an alternative worry, namely that plans agreed with the Chinese government for Hong Kong's continuance as a financial trading centre would be jeopardized if the most powerful businesspeople involved left, as they would be well placed to do. Accordingly 50,000 'key' people were given British citizenship, as insurance that, if they stayed, their personal position would not be compromised; they could leave later for the UK if it became necessary. A further interim provision under Article 4 of the Hong Kong (British Nationality) Order 1986 created the British National (Overseas) category of citizenship. Under this, applicants (mostly ethnically Chinese and therefore also Chinese citizens) could obtain rights similar to those which Hong Kong BDTCs had in any event under s 4(1) BNA 1981 in relation to obtaining British citizenship after residence in the UK. Following s 14 NIAA 2002, no one could register as a BOTC by virtue of a connection with Hong Kong. It was only after much pressure that those persons ordinarily resident in Hong Kong but left legally adrift—who were not entitled to Chinese nationality by reason of ethnicity, who held a form of British nationality that did not carry the right of abode, or were British Protected Persons—were entitled to register as British citizens. A discretionary right to register was also given to Hong Kong war widows.

However, the status of BOTC remains important because naturalization after residence in an overseas territory leads to BOTC status rather than British citizenship (British Nationality (British Overseas Territories) Regulations 2007, SI 2007/3139), and because the overseas territories include the Sovereign base areas in Cyprus (Akrotiri and Dhekelia). The government was keen to ensure that those territories, 'at an important crossroads between the middle east and Europe', did not attract people to go to Cyprus trying to seek asylum (Ben Bradshaw, Foreign Office Minister, to Standing Committee D, 6 December 2001).

Here we see the development of trends as described in chapter 1. Whereas in the mid-twentieth century, a desire to curb non-white immigration drove immigration law and policy and that of nationality, by the end of the twentieth century, a desire to curb asylum claims was the driver, including here, in relation to an obscure provision of nationality law.

3.3.1.1 The Chagos Islands

The nationality story of the Chagos Islanders (also, and perhaps more properly, known as the Ilois) is overshadowed by the political tale. The Chagos Islands form part of the British Indian Ocean Territory, which until 1965 was part of the British colony of Mauritius but then became a separate dependent territory. Mauritius itself was to become independent in 1968, but well before then the US had identified the largest island, Diego Garcia, as somewhere it would like to build a military base. The UK agreed to lease it to them and went on to expel the islanders, by a mixture of trickery and legislation, largely to Mauritius and the Seychelles. Eventually, the Chagos Islanders began to fight their expulsion through the courts. In 2000, the Divisional Court found in *R v Secretary of State for the Foreign and Commonwealth Office ex p Bancoult* [2001] 2 WLR 1219 that the British government had abused its "power to make laws for the 'peace, order and good government' of a territory" saying this 'required its people to be governed, not removed', and Mr Bancoult won the right for the Chagossians to return. Though a Foreign Office minister claimed in 2001 that 'such treatment would be impossible today' (HC Standing Committee D 6 December 2001), it was only after lobbying, the case of *Bancoult*, and an amendment to the Bill that those Chagossians who had lost the opportunity of BDTC status were included in the provisions of the 2002 Act, which gave those born between 1969 and 1981 British citizenship by descent. Had there been no exile, they would however have been British citizens under the 2002 Act like other BOTCs. The government's justification was that they were now free to return to the Chagos Islands, and if they did so their children would be British citizens, as with any other British citizen abroad.

However, no practical arrangements for return were made. The British government then claimed the islands were not habitable, and a claim for compensation by the Islanders was dismissed in the QBD by Ouseley LJ in 2003 (*Chagos Islanders v AG HMs BIOT Commissioner* [2003] EWHC 2222). On 10 June 2004, hidden behind the publicity given to European and local election day, two Orders in Council were signed by the Queen. The British Indian Ocean Territory (Constitution) Order appointed a Commissioner to the territory, stated that no person has any right of abode in it and restricted access to it save by a restrictive system of permits under the British Indian Ocean Territory (Immigration) Order. These orders were made under the Royal Prerogative and, in the words of Baroness Symons 'restore the legal position to what it had been understood to be before the High Court decision' in *ex p Bancoult* (HL Debs 15 June 2004 col WS27): the executive had overturned the judicial decision. This undermined the justification offered by the government for limiting the Ilois' nationality entitlement and meant they could not pass British citizenship to their children.

It also prompted Mauritius to threaten to withdraw from the Commonwealth so it could sue the UK in the International Court of Justice. The UK government responded by excluding from its acceptance of the jurisdiction of the International Court of Justice not only current Commonwealth countries (an existing exception retained by a number of Commonwealth members) but also former Commonwealth countries (Hansard 7 July 2004 col 294WH). In other words, Mauritius would not be able to sue in any event. The Orders in Council were challenged by judicial review and once again found unlawful (*R (on the application of Bancoult) v SSFCA* [2006] EWHC 1038 (Admin); *SSFCA v R (on the application of Bancoult)* [2007] EWCA Civ 498). The government's argument was that Orders in Council were not subject to judicial review, but the Court of Appeal held that it was a fiction to regard these Orders as acts of the monarch and they were in reality acts of the executive and as such subject to judicial review. It held that, for the population of the Chagos Islands, the case concerned 'not its governance, but its elimination as a population' (para 66) and that the prerogative Orders that later removed the Chagossians' right to return were a defeat of a substantive legitimate expectation and were 'so profoundly unfair . . . as to amount to an abuse of power' (para 73). However, on appeal the House of Lords found for the government. In (*R (on the application of Bancoult) v SSFCA* [2008] UKHL 61), they held that although the right of abode was 'fundamental and, in the informal sense in which that is necessarily used in a United Kingdom context, constitutional' (per Lord Mance, para 151), nevertheless by a 3:2 majority they found for the government, holding that the right of abode was in the gift of Parliament, and that what Parliament had given, Parliament could also take away. A commentator suggested that 'their Lordships' deference fails to reflect a judicial commitment to substantive legality' (Cohn 2009).

Some Islanders came to the UK as British citizens and found establishing a life here difficult because of the rules excluding people without a period of residence from welfare provisions, which in this context may appear ironic ([2007] UKSSCSC CJSA_1223_2206). The Chagos Islanders complained to Strasbourg in 2004, under Articles 3, 8, 6, and 14 of the ECHR, (Application no. 35622/04), but on 11 December 2012 the Grand Chamber held that the applicants' claims had been satisfied by the acceptance in 1982 of money and land by way of compensation. However, the use of Diego Garcia, the biggest island, by the US remains politically controversial, especially following confirmation that it was used as a refuelling stop for US 'extraordinary rendition' flights, carrying terrorism suspects to places where they could be tortured. In 2010, the UK announced that a marine reserve was to be established in the Islands, and a US cable made public on Wikileaks suggested that one motivation was to engage environmental arguments to defeat any subsequent return by the islanders. Mauritius contested the plans, and in March 2015, with the US lease on Diego Garcia due to expire in 2016, the Permanent Court of Arbitration found largely for Mauritius. The British government has again been consulting on whether the islanders may return in future. The US lease on Diego Garcia expires in 2016, but may be renewed for a further twenty years. Another British territory with exceptional nationality arrangements is Ascension Island, which is administratively part of the territory of St Helena, and like Diego Garcia is devoted largely to military use. Here, no one has a right of abode. A Foreign Office promise to grant this was revoked in early 2006, government policy being that 'All those working and living on Ascension Island are required by Ascension law to leave once their contracts expire' (Geoff Hoon, SSFCA, Hansard Written Answers 23 May 2007 col 1311W).

3.3.2 **British Overseas Citizens**

This kind of nationality was created by s 26 BNA 1981 to cover those CUKCs who did not at commencement obtain British citizenship or British Dependent Territories citizenship. It carries no right of abode in the UK (see *AL and others (Malaysia BOCs) Malaysia* [2009] UKAIT 00026), and the number of people holding this status is diminishing as it cannot be transmitted to children. It mostly affected people of Asian origin living in East African countries. The situation of people and families from India and Pakistan who had moved to Kenya and Uganda has been briefly described in chapter 1. The legislative history is one of the longest-running human rights issues in UK nationality and immigration law.

East African Asians did not have the necessary connection with the UK to obtain British Citizenship on 1 January 1983 (see 3.1.5), nor with an overseas territory to become a BDTC. Accordingly, under the BNA 1981 they obtained the residual status of BOC with no right of abode and no transmission to children, in sharp contrast to those citizens of overseas territories who attained full British citizenship. The government's reason for not including BOCs in the 2002 Act—that many had access to or had acquired dual nationality, or had access to the UK through the voucher scheme—was generally correct for most people with BOC status, namely those of Malaysian nationality living in Singapore, but it was not true of East African Asians. They could only use the discretionary voucher system, which was ended without warning on 4 March 2002, on the basis that it was not much used (Angela Eagle, Minister of State for Home Office HC Debs 5 March 2002 col 162W), though evidence given in *ECO Mumbai v NH (India)* [2007] EWCA Civ 1330 para 6 was that there were then 500 applications per year. A late amendment to the Nationality, Immigration and Asylum Bill 2002 provided at s 4B BNA 1981 that BOCs could register as British citizens if they had no other nationality or had not deprived themselves of such nationality after 4 July 2002. BOCs who can obtain leave to enter the UK can therefore register as British citizens after five years' residence, including as dual nationals. BOCs without nationality may therefore register as British citizens, provided they do not relinquish another nationality to do so, but will not have the option of dual nationality; their dependents may seek entry under the usual rules, rather than the less stringent rules under the voucher system (which applied, however, only to 'heads of household').

Although the new rights were intended to right a historic wrong, the lack of transitional provisions meant that they caused numerous problems. In *ECO Mumbai v NH* [2007] EWCA Civ 1330, the Court of Appeal found for a woman who wished to sponsor the entry of her adult son from India. Although the immigration rules did not allow for his entry, to refuse it to 'families like this . . . prevented for over thirty years from settling in the country of which some or all of their members once were, and are now again, citizens' (para 21) was a disproportionate interference with the right to family life under Article 8 ECHR. The legislation that had prevented the family from settling was racially discriminatory, and the refusal to accept the sponsor as a head of household because she was a married woman discriminated against her on the grounds of sex. What was necessary in a democratic society was 'consideration of all the circumstances including the previous history of any previous wrongful act' (para 18, quoting the Tribunal). However, in later cases such as *JB and others (children of former BOC—limits of NH) India* [2008] UKAIT 00059, it was held by a tribunal considering applications by over-age children of former BOCs that the 'historic wrong' did not create an Article 8 right of itself. In *PV & ors* [2009] UKAIT 00033, the Tribunal found that the BOC sponsor's limited financial position justified a refusal of entry to his family, because Article 8 did not override the maintenance requirements of the Rules.

The UK's declaration on nationality for purposes of EU membership still excludes BOCs. Therefore, BOCs do not, by virtue of that status, obtain citizenship of the European Union (*Manjit Kaur*), though following the introduction in 2003 of s 4B BNA 1981, the discrimination inherent in this situation is much reduced.

3.3.3 British subjects under the Act

This name is given by the 1981 Act to the people known under earlier nationality statutes as British subjects without citizenship. If such people acquire any other citizenship, they lose their British subject status. In addition to those mentioned in the historical section, this group includes some Irish citizens who exercised a right to retain their British subject status. They have effective right of abode in the UK by virtue of the Common Travel Area (see chapter 6) though most others do not. The right to register for citizenship under BNA 1981 s 4B applies also to this group.

3.3.4 British Protected Persons

Before the majority of countries that had been under British rule during the Empire obtained independence, millions of people were BBPs. There are now very few, so—in accordance with the general trend that overseas groups are gradually excluded from the right of abode until they become numerically insignificant—they may now register under BNA 1981 s 4B.

3.4 Becoming British: registration and naturalization

If a person is not a national or citizen of a country, they might want to become one. British law historically had two very separate ways of doing this, but the processes of registration and naturalization are now much closer to each other than they used to be. Traditionally, registration is for those not born British but, nevertheless, entitled to be recognized as such because of specified connections with the UK, such as UK-born British ancestors or certain types of established residence in the UK, and naturalization was for anyone else. The two processes are converging particularly as requirements of good character have crept into the registration process, making it more akin to an exercise of discretion.

3.4.1 Registration

Registration broadly provides a method for those who fall just outside the provisions for British citizenship to apply for it nevertheless. The process has been available for a very long time, as the case of *Bibi and others v SSHD* [2007] EWCA Civ 740 shows. Mr Jabbar entered the UK using someone else's identity and after five years of residence registered as a CUKC in 1967. After he died, his widow and children claimed that they had right of abode through his citizenship. The Court of Appeal held that his registration as a CUKC was void. The person identified on the documents had not been in the UK for five years, so no registration had taken place. Thus, the family had no basis upon which to claim right of abode.

The Secretary of State may register any minor child as a British citizen, at her discretion, if an application is made while the child is still a minor (s 3 (1)). Children registered under s 3(1) are British citizens by descent if one of their parents was British at the time of their birth (s 14(1)(c)). This discretion may be used to fill gaps in the entitlements listed previously, for instance where a child has been adopted abroad by British parents, though it paradoxically means that the children of British parents are disadvantaged by comparison to the children of foreign nationals, since citizenship by descent is a less privileged status (see *Azad Ullah*, later in the chapter). Nationality Instructions chapter 9 gives guidance on the exercise of the discretion. Section 9.17.2 says 'the most important criterion is that the child's future should clearly be seen to lie in the UK'. If the child and family seem to have an established way of life in the UK, then the Home Office 'should accept at face value that the child intends to live here'. The parents' immigration status is relevant to this. Where the mother had ILR and had applied for British citizenship, the Home Office was wrong to place emphasis on the fact that the father's leave was still limited (*R (on the application of Ali) v SSHD* [2007] EWHC 1983 (Admin)). He had also applied for ILR. The reason it had not yet been granted was delay in the Home Office, and his application showed where the children's future lay.

Some people are entitled to register as British citizens, namely:

(a) Children of a British citizen by descent, if the application is made while the child is a minor and either one parent is the child of a grandparent who was a British citizen otherwise than by descent and that parent had lived in the UK for three years before the child's birth (s 3(2) and (3)) or the child and both parents have lived in the UK for three years prior to the date of the application and both parents consent (BNA 1981 s 3(5): subsection (6) provides that one parent suffices in situations of legal separation, divorce or death). The first entitlement deals with the situation where a British citizen by descent lives in the UK with their child, demonstrating an intention to make the UK their home; it recognizes the child's ancestral UK connection. Where the child is not resident, a stronger blood tie with the UK is required (s 3(3). See 3.2.3).

(b) British Overseas Territories Citizens, British Nationals (Overseas), British Overseas Citizens, British subjects under the 1981 Act, and British Protected Persons, so long as they have been resident in the UK for five years, are entitled to register as British citizens under BNA 1981 s 4. This means that someone who has naturalized as a BOTC has a right to register as a British citizen if they meet the residence conditions. As mentioned earlier, since the British Overseas Territories Act 2002, there are now very few other BOTCs remaining who are not already also British citizens, and BOCs, BPPs, and British subjects under the Act who have no other nationality can now register under s 4B without the five-year residence condition. British Nationals (Overseas) were included in this provision under s 44 BCI Act 2009.

(c) Children born in the UK whose parent becomes British or settled, providing the application is made while they are still minors (BNA s 1(3)).

(d) Children born in the UK who live here until they are 10 years old (BNA s 1(4)).

(e) Persons born stateless in the UK, providing they have lived in the UK for five years at the date of the application and apply before they reach the age of 22 (BNA Sch 2 para 3, as amended by the Nationality, Immigration and Asylum Act 2002).

(f) The children of non-British serving members of the armed forces who are born abroad (s 4D BNA 1981).

Section 47 of the BCI Act 2009 controversially inserted a 'good character' requirement for most types of registration where the applicant is an adult or a child aged over ten years. In *SA, R (on the application of) v Secretary of State for the Home Department* [2015] EWHC 1611 (Admin), the High Court quashed a refusal of registration on the basis of a conviction for possession of cannabis. It found that the applicant's Article 8 ECHR rights were engaged, and that the rules and practices as to want of good character did not comply with the UK's obligations under the United Nations Convention on the Rights of the Child.

3.4.2 **Naturalization**

Naturalization is the way that a person without the British connections to register as British (see 3.4.1) can obtain British nationality by application, and in Britain is at most a couple of centuries old; the process has been made more restrictive in recent years. Naturalization in Britain has always been in theory an aspect of the Royal Prerogative, so there is no right to it, but as the exercise of the Secretary of State's discretion has accrued statutory requirements and published criteria, it has become open to judicial review on the usual administrative law grounds (see 3.6). Some restrictions are structurally built in—BOCs who become British have a more restricted status than outright foreigners who naturalize, and British citizens by descent cannot naturalize in order to 'switch' to being British citizens otherwise than by descent, which they might wish to do in order to rid themselves of the disadvantage of the secondary British citizenship status. In *SSHD v Azad Ullah* [2001] EWCA Civ 659, Mr Ullah was a British citizen by descent who had lived in the UK for some time with his Indian wife. Their children born in the UK were British citizens otherwise than by descent because Mr Ullah was British, but the Ullahs planned to spend a protracted period in India and wanted any children who might be born to them there to be British. Mr Ullah therefore applied to naturalize as a British citizen otherwise than by descent. The Court of Appeal held that this was not permissible.

The most visible aspects of the process of naturalization were reformed during the early twenty-first century. The oath of allegiance had previously been made privately before a solicitor, with the process of naturalization being completed by post. Under the Nationality, Immigration and Asylum Act 2002, along with a 'Knowledge of Life in the UK' test, citizenship ceremonies were introduced, making the oath and pledge of allegiance much more public and ceremonial. The content of the process, however, did not change a great deal. The considerable media attention devoted at the time to the introduction of the new pledge and oath of allegiance, and to the obligation on those naturalizing to be able to speak English (or, in fact, Welsh or Scots Gaelic), was misplaced, as these were both longstanding provisions. The method of testing for language skills is more formalized than it used to be, though for fluent English-speakers a pass is inferred from passing the 'Life in the UK' test (see 3.4.2.6).

Naturalization became an actively contested issue in the early twenty-first century. There was a period of close government concern with promoting 'citizenship' in its meaning of 'being a good citizen', especially with reference to voluntary work, amidst some of the periodic public questioning as to what it is to be British. The former Attorney-General, Peter Goldsmith, reported in 2007 on *Citizenship: Our Common Bond*, and a Green Paper, *The Path to Citizenship* and then a 'Simplification Bill', which aimed to replace the accumulation of immigration and nationality laws with one clear and workable piece of legislation, followed in 2008. The Bill was felt to be neither clear nor workable and was withdrawn, but followed by the Borders, Citizenship and Immigration Act 2009, which extended the periods for which many people have to live in the UK before being eligible for naturalization.

The requirements which must be fulfilled in order to qualify to apply for naturalization are found in BNA 1981 s 6 and Sch 1. Applications may only be made by persons of 'full age and capacity', and applicants must fulfil residence and character requirements. The Home Secretary's discretion must be exercised without regard to the race, colour, or religion of the applicant (s 44(1) BNA 1981). The British Nationality (General) (Amendment No. 3) Regulations 2015 introduced a requirement that persons with an EU law-based right of permanent residence obtain a residence document as evidence of that right in order to naturalize. However, the right of permanent residence itself brings a person within s 50 of the BNA 1981 without the need for any documentation, so the regulation effectively conflicts with primary legislation and may be ineffective.

3.4.2.1 Capacity

Full capacity is defined in BNA 1981 s 50(11) as 'not of unsound mind'. The Nationality Instructions chapter 18 annex A says that the question is whether the applicant is sufficiently mentally competent to know that they want to become British citizens. Where applicants have lodged their own applications, it should be assumed that they meet the requirement 'unless there is information on the Home Office papers to cast doubt on this'. By Immigration, Asylum and Nationality Act 2006 s 49, the Secretary of State may waive the capacity requirement 'if he thinks it in the applicant's best interests'. This is a very minimal standard compared with the demanding approach of the tests of knowledge of English language and life in the UK, but this, too, may be waived in suitable cases (see later).

3.4.2.2 Period of residence

Naturalization requires a period of residence in the UK. The present qualifying period is three years for a person married to or in a civil partnership with a British citizen (s 6(2)), otherwise, it is five years (s 6(1)). Schedule 1 allows certain periods of absence from the UK without jeopardizing the application (270 days for spouses or 450 days for others, provided that not more than 90 of these days are in the last 12months), and there is a discretion to disregard the residence requirement, at least to an extent (see NI chapter 18 annex B paras 4 and 5). The exceptions to the rule that there is no discretion to waive the requirement for presence at the beginning of the qualifying period are very limited.

The discussion about voluntary work and 'earned citizenship' that was politically live during the passing of the Borders, Citizenship and Immigration Act 2009 led to that Act changing the provisions for naturalization, including requiring longer residence from applicants for citizenship who had not 'earned' citizenship by carrying out unpaid work (ss 39–41). These provisions lie on the statute book, but appear likely to be amongst those legal changes passed in a climate of high political fever which are, however, never brought into force.

3.4.2.3 Type of residence

Residence during the majority of the qualifying period is only required to be physical presence, not a particular immigration status. However, at the date of application a spouse or civil partner, and for the last year of residence a s 6(1) applicant, must be free of immigration restrictions on their stay (Sch 1 para 1(2)(b)). Residence must also not have been in breach of immigration laws (1(2)(d)), though once again there is a discretion to regard periods so spent as lawful (para 2(d)). Nationality Instructions chapter

18 annex B para 8.10 gives examples of when the Home Office would normally exercise discretion to disregard a breach, which it would not normally do 'when the breach was substantial and deliberate' or could affect the good character requirement (see 3.4.2.4). Because of the historical complexity and laxity of the immigration system, many people, especially asylum seekers, could be in breach of immigration laws, and it is not always easy to say how far someone's status may be lawful.

BNA 1981 Sch 1 gives a discretion to regard periods of 'technical absence' as residence for naturalization purposes: this is generally used for members of the forces and diplomatic staff. People in detention without leave are physically present in the UK but in immigration law they are not legally present. Those on temporary admission used not to be considered legally present, but since the House of Lords' decision in *Szoma v DWP* [2005] UKHL 64 have been so, albeit this is implemented in a grudging and limited manner.

3.4.2.4 Good character requirement

Schedule 1 para 1(1)(b) requires 'that he is of good character'. Home Office guidance on how this is to be interpreted is to be found in chapter 18 annex D of the Nationality Instructions. Criminal activity is clearly an indication that the person may be regarded as not of good character: however, not all criminal activity will debar an applicant (though an extant Deportation Order will). A criminal record will mean a delay before naturalization, or, if it attracted a sentence of four years' imprisonment or more, will normally mean that naturalization will be refused. The Home Office guidance is mostly detailed and clear, but some elements are restricted and not for disclosure. These include some details of the discovery and treatment of pending prosecutions, extradition requests, involvement with gangs or association with known criminals, and 'war crimes, terrorism and other non-conducive activity'. The approach of the relatively new Deprivation Screening Team, a part of the Home Office in Liverpool, includes considering whether a bankruptcy involved recklessness, fraud or concealment of assets; benefit fraud or deliberate failure to pay council tax will result in a refusal. 'Notoriety' will also lead to a refusal of naturalization, but it is expressly stated that marital or domestic problems; promiscuity or sexual preference within the law; drinking or gambling; eccentricity, including beliefs, appearance, and lifestyle; and unemployment, working habits, or other legitimate means of support are not normally relevant. Only if the scale and level of behaviour has made a person notorious in their local or the wider community and reflects so poorly on the person's character will notoriety mean application should be refused. The risk that the decision will attract public attention or press reaction invites decision-makers to discuss the case with the Deputy Chief Caseworker. Deception and dishonesty, particularly in relation to immigration-related matters such as marriages of convenience, are likely to lead to refusal, and repeat applications within ten years of a refusal for reason of false statements in applying for citizenship will also be refused. Involvement in war crimes is a good reason for refusal (*Amirifard, R (on the application of) v Secretary of State for the Home Department* [2013] EWHC 279 (Admin)), but refusal for reason of a speeding conviction was found to require revisiting (*Hiri v Secretary of State for the Home Department* [2014] EWHC 254 (Admin))

In *Rushiti & Anor, R (on the application of) v Secretary of State for the Home Department* [2014] EWHC 3931 (Admin) and *R (Kurmerkaj) v Secretary of State for the Home Department* [2014] EWHC 1701 (Admin), applicants for naturalization had previously claimed to be Kosovar refugees and had obtained ILR under the legacy programme (see chapter 11). When they applied for naturalization, their false claim to be Kosovar was found to indicate a lack of good character and their application was refused. It was irrelevant whether they had gained any benefit from the deception, as a deception practised on the immigration authorities was held to be serious of itself. In *SSHD v Okere* [2014] UKUTUR DC00003/2014, the respondent had previously made immigration applications under a different name and obtained naturalization separately in each name. There was no suggestion of his hiding or gaining anything, but the Home Office regarded it as 'major immigration fraud' using 'multiple identities', and (notwithstanding that British law allows for a name change merely by usage) the Upper Tribunal allowed the Secretary of State's appeal as to his deprivation.

3.4.2.5 Language requirement

Applicants for British citizenship have long been required to have 'sufficient knowledge of the English, Welsh or Scottish Gaelic language' (Sch 1 para 1(1)(c) BNA 1981). Sufficient language ability used to be assumed unless there was evidence to the contrary, but positive requirements began to be introduced under the Nationality, Immigration and Asylum Act 2002. Now applicants from non-majority-English-speaking countries must have a speaking and listening qualification in English at B1 of the Common European Framework of Reference for Languages or higher, or equivalent; or an academic qualification recognized as equivalent to a UK degree, from a majority-English-speaking country (not Canada). If, however, it would be unreasonable to expect a person to fulfil these requirements 'because of the applicant's age or physical or mental condition' (Sch 1 para 2(e) BNA 1981) then the requirement may be waived.

3.4.2.6 Knowledge of British society

The highly contentious requirement that an applicant show 'that he has sufficient knowledge about life in the United Kingdom' was also introduced by the 2002 Act. The proposal was a controversial manifestation of the government's then policy to make citizenship meaningful and to link it with nationality by ensuring that successful applicants for naturalization would understand the UK's cultural habits and practices and usual ways of behaving, as well as the basics of the country's history. Against the background of a debate that continued the questions of Jim Marshall MP as to whether the measure was concerned 'to improve civic participation and awareness' or to 'promote cultural uniformity' (HC Debs 24 April 2002 col 366), the test has unfortunately attracted much criticism and even some ridicule. The recommended, even compulsory, handbook for the test is the 3rd edition of the *Life in the United Kingdom Handbook: A Guide for New Residents*, and there are also practice tests available. The fee for the test is £50.

Since April 2007, Knowledge of Life in the UK and the language tests have also been part of the requirements for ILR (see chapter 6).

3.4.2.7 Pledge

Along with the requirement for knowledge of British society was the institution of a pledge to be taken as well as the oath of allegiance, which is the formal moment at which new citizenship is acquired. Contrary to much of the media discussion at the time of the 2002 Bill, the oath of allegiance to the monarchy had always been part of obtaining citizenship. However, it was previously administered by a Commissioner for Oaths (usually a solicitor) or magistrate, in private and without ceremony.

The additional pledge, in Sch 1 to the 2002 Act, is as follows:

I will give my loyalty to the United Kingdom and respect its rights and freedoms. I will uphold its democratic values. I will observe its laws faithfully and fulfil my duties and obligations as a British Citizen.

This is administered in formal ceremonies for nationality applications made after 1 January 2004.

Part of the legacy of the focus on immigration considerations as a basis for nationality law is that the 'duties and obligations' of a British citizen have never been identified and most people who are British by birth or descent would have no idea what these are. It is therefore debatable whether those who acquire their nationality by a formal process should be asked to promise to fulfil them.

3.4.2.8 Intention to live in UK

The final requirement for naturalization is that the applicant intends to make their future home in the UK (Sch 1 para 1(1)(d)). Where the applicant has an established home in the UK, or there is no reason to doubt this intention, then the requirement will be regarded as met (NI chapter 18 annex F para 2). An intention to travel should not debar the applicant unless it appears that they do not intend to return.

3.4.2.9 Becoming British by adoption

A child can become British by adoption if at least one of the adoptive parents is a British citizen on the date of adoption, and the adoption order is made by a court in a British territory, or after May 2003 under the 1993 Hague Convention on Intercountry Adoption and the adopters are habitually resident in the UK at the relevant date. (If, e.g., the parents are resident overseas and this does not apply, it may be possible to register the child as British; an application for registration should be made before the child is eighteen, and would be likely to succeed if the child would have been British had s/he been the adopters' biological child: see 3.4.1.) The child's British status will survive any annulment of an adoption order. More interestingly, if a British person is adopted abroad, they do not cease to be British for that reason.

3.5 Renunciation and deprivation of nationality

3.5.1 Renunciation

It is possible to renounce British citizenship: s 12 BNA 1981. Renunciation takes effect only when accepted by the Secretary of State, who will not accept any renunciation of British citizenship that would leave the individual in question stateless. A common reason for renouncing British citizenship is that the person concerned wishes to take up the nationality of a country that does not allow dual citizenship. In such cases, British citizenship may subsequently be resumed as of right (subject to any good character requirement), but only once (s 13). All other resumptions of British citizenship after renunciation are discretionary, like ordinary naturalization.

3.5.2 Deprivation of nationality, citizenship, and the right of abode

Section 40 of the BNA 1981 deals with deprivation of citizenship. The provision that citizenship obtained by fraud, false representation, or concealment of a material fact may be removed is of long standing. Where a person registers as a British citizen on a factual basis that later turns out to be untrue, the fact that this was simply due to mistake will not cure the withdrawal of the passport or the invalidity of the claim to British citizenship, even if this results in statelessness: see *Burnett's Application* [2010]

NICA 2. The Secretary of State also had the power to deprive a person of their citizenship if he was satisfied that the person had been guilty of 'disloyalty or disaffection to Her Majesty', helping an enemy in time of war, or a criminal offence within five years of obtaining citizenship. These provisions have been considerably extended during the twenty-first century.

The Nationality, Immigration and Asylum Act 2002, passed amidst a media scandal about the difficulty of deporting Abu Hamza al-Masri, an Egyptian Muslim cleric who had naturalized following marriage to a British woman, allowed deprivation of citizenship if the person had done something seriously prejudicial to the vital interests of the UK or a British Overseas Territory. That this also applied to those born British in the UK was new and caused considerable public disquiet at the time. It also did not work in respect of Mr al-Masri, because he would have been left stateless, which was prohibited.

A later influential case was that of *SSHS v Hicks* [2006] EWCA Civ 400, dealing with the application of a detainee at Guantanamo Bay, to register as a British citizen under s 4C BNA 1981, because his mother had been British by descent. David Hicks was an Australian citizen who was detained in Guantanamo Bay as a suspected terrorist. He wanted to assert the benefit of the arrangements made for the release of British citizen detainees. However, the Secretary of State declined to register him and alternatively proposed, should he have the right to register, to deprive him of that citizenship simultaneously with granting it, on the grounds of 'disloyalty and disaffection'. The Court of Appeal held that Mr Hicks was entitled to register and, on the wording of the section, alleged 'disloyalty and disaffection' before his registration could not count against him.

The response of the government to this, and to the devastating terrorist bombings in London on 7 July 2005 (see chapter 15), was to give the Secretary of State the power to deprive a person of their citizenship if s/he 'is satisfied that it is conducive to the public good' (s 56 IANA 2006), though with the limit that a person could not thereby be left stateless. This provision applies even to those born British in the UK, though it is, as Majid (2008) pointed out, the criterion previously applied in relation to deportation of foreign nationals. The government indicated at the time that the kind of behaviour which could found deprivation of citizenship under this subsection would include that in the 'list of unacceptable behaviours' made public by the Home Secretary on 24 August 2005 (Standing Committee E 27 October 2005 col 254) as part of the government's counter-terrorism strategy. Mr Hicks was deprived almost immediately. A corresponding provision relates to deprivation of the right of abode (s 57 IANA 2006). Section 58 of the IANA 2006 also introduced a requirement of good character that would have made it possible for the Home Office to refuse to register Mr Hicks' citizenship in the first place (see 3.4.1.)

Wide and draconian powers brought in on the back of attempts to exclude and expel Islamicists with British citizenship, have made nationality more fragile, and more conditional upon conduct. In the case of people who had obtained nationality by registration or naturalization, the possibility that they could be left stateless if they have obtained it by fraud always conveyed a powerful message. The broadening of deprivation powers has made the process more routine. A Deprivation Screening Team (DST) has been established. The DST also screens applications for naturalization. Deprivation is made by notifying the person to be deprived, which can be done by post. Since appeals are non-suspensive, the person may be deported even if they lodge an appeal, or they may be deprived while they are out of the country, so that they cannot come back. It has been held that depriving someone in this way may be a justifiable tactic: *L1 v SSHD* [2014] UKSIAC SC_100_2010.

As mentioned in chapter 1, the Parliamentary Joint Committee on Human Rights raised early concerns with the Home Office about the use of deprivation of nationality, particularly 'loss of British diplomatic protection; loss of status; loss of the ability to participate in the democratic process in the United Kingdom; and serious damage to reputation and dignity' (Joint Committee on Human Rights Session 2001–02 Seventeenth Report para 26). The Home Office, somewhat disingenuously, replied that the person would have another nationality and so the harm to them would be limited, but did not mention that this may not be the case where nationality is removed because of fraud; with the further rise of concerns about terrorism, the political agenda has since hardened. Between 1915 and 1948, when the British Empire was spread across the world, and there were two global wars, there were 287 deprivations. Between 1949 and 1973, there were ten. After 1973, there were no deprivations until after the Nationality, Immigration and Asylum Act 2002. After 2006, numbers of deprivations on 'conducive' grounds increased, and attempts to obtain information have become, themselves, the subject of legal contest (*Home Office v Information Commissioner and Cobain (Final Decision) (Information rights: Freedom of information—absolute exemptions)* [2015] UKUT 27 (AAC) (20 January 2015)).

The long-running case of Hilal al-Jedda led to fierce Parliamentary and media debate on deprivation of citizenship and ensuing statelessness. Mr al-Jedda was an alleged terrorist who had naturalized as British having previously been an Iraqi citizen. The Secretary of State deprived him of citizenship and in *Al-Jedda v SSHD* [2013] UKSC 62, the Supreme Court held that that had been unlawful as he did not hold any other nationality at the date of deprivation. In fact, Article 8 of the Convention on the Reduction of Statelessness 1961 allows a person to be left stateless on deprivation both if they have obtained the citizenship by fraud and if they have committed acts seriously prejudicial to their country of citizenship, and the UK had entered a reservation to the 1961 Convention by which it retained 'the right to deprive a naturalised person of his nationality . . . [if he had] . . . in disregard of an express prohibition of Her Britannic Majesty, rendered or continued to render services to, or received or continued to receive emoluments from, another State, or [h]as conducted himself in a manner seriously prejudicial to the vital interests of Her Britannic Majesty'. Following the Supreme Court case, Mr al-Jedda was deprived of his citizenship for a second time, and the court also affirmed that no issues of EU law or European citizenship were engaged by Mr al-Jedda's deprivation, including any obligations there might have been to make a minimum disclosure to him of the reasons for his deprivation.

Section 66 of the Immigration Act 2014 amended s 40 BNA 1981 by providing that a person might be deprived of citizenship if they obtained it by naturalization; the Secretary of State was satisfied that the deprivation was conducive to the public good because the person, whilst a British citizen, had behaved in a manner seriously prejudicial to the country's vital interests; and the Secretary of State had reasonable grounds for believing that the person was able to become a national of another country under its laws. These issues were considered by the Supreme Court in *Pham v Secretary of State for the Home Department* [2015] UKSC 19. As a child, Mr Pham had come to Britain from Vietnam as a refugee with his family. After naturalizing as British and converting to Islam, he went to Yemen where he attended an al-Qaida training camp, according to the Secretary of State, who deprived him of his citizenship. Mr Pham both denied the allegations of terrorism and said that deprivation left him stateless. The family had never had Vietnamese passports, but had also not renounced Vietnamese nationality. After his deprivation, Vietnam had refused to confirm that it considered him one of its nationals. The Special Immigration Appeals Commission (SIAC) allowed his appeal because it held the deprivation had left him stateless (*B2 v SSHD* Appeal No: SC/114/2012 29th June 2012), but the Court of Appeal allowed the government's appeal saying that he was a Vietnamese national under Vietnamese law despite the attitude of the Vietnamese government (*B2 v Secretary of State for the Home Department* [2013] EWCA Civ 616). The Supreme Court agreed with the Court of Appeal on that point, but remitted the case to the SIAC on the issue of proportionality, without clearly accepting or rejecting the relevance of EU law.

Deprivation is, however, not used only against those suspected or convicted of terrorism. In *Deliallisi (British citizen: deprivation appeal: Scope) Albania* [2013] UKUT 439, Deliallisi, an Albanian, had been granted asylum as a Kosovar, and later naturalized. He later married an Albanian woman and they had two children. However, when his parents visited, their visa application revealed that Deliallisi was actually Albanian. His wife was at first refused naturalization, though later she succeeded. His own appeal against deprivation, however, failed.

3.5.3 Nullity

The Nationality Instructions chapter 55 give an account of the difference between fraud which means that nationality will be taken away, and fraud which means that the original grant of nationality was a nullity—that is, had no effect. In *Bibi and others v SSHD* [2007] EWCA Civ 740 discussed previously at 3.4.1, the grant was a nullity because Mr Jabbar took on the identity of another person, so a grant of nationality to him did not happen. If he had falsified certain details, such as the time he had spent in the UK, the grant of nationality would have taken effect. He could have been deprived of it once the fraud came to light, but he would have actually been a British Citizen in the interim. In some cases, (though problematic on the facts of that case as he had died) this difference could affect the rights of relatives.

The Home Office has recently increased the use of nullity apparently as a method of avoiding the right of appeal that comes with deprivation of citizenship. Though there is no appeal, there may, however, be a judicial review. In *Kaziu & Ors v Secretary of State for the Home Department* [2014] EWHC 832 (Admin), again Albanians had obtained a grant of naturalization having previously told the Home Office that they were Kosovars. Although she had previously said that deprivation proceedings were unlikely as a consequence of that, the Secretary of State subsequently told the applicants that their naturalizations were a nullity for reason of 'impersonation', and the court declined their application for judicial review of that decision. In *Rasheed, R (On the Application of) v Secretary of State for the Home Department (Rev 1)* [2015] EWHC 2052 (Admin), the court held that *Kaziu* had established the principles for nullity, whilst affirming that the burden of proof of fraud and materiality was on the Secretary of State. The Secretary of State succeeded similarly in *Hysa & Ors, R (On the Application of) v Secretary of State for the Home Department* [2015] EWCA Civ 1195, but Sales LJ expressed some concern at para 64: 'the interpretation of the 1981 Act given by those authorities is one which is problematic in various respects. I think this is an area in which it would be desirable for Parliament to clarify the law by express statutory provision.'

3.6 Challenging nationality decisions

Under the old s 40, a proposal to make an order depriving a person of their citizenship could be referred to a committee of inquiry. The 2002 Act introduced a full right of appeal to the Tribunal, but not if the Secretary of State certifies that the decision was taken wholly or partly in reliance on information which in his opinion should not be made public in the interests of national security or the relationship between the UK and another country, or 'otherwise in the public interest'. This is a very wide provision, and given the grounds for deprivation in s 40(2) there is potential for it to apply in almost any case. An appeal then lies, however, to the SIAC. As discussed in chapter 7, the proceedings of this Commission may be closed to the public and information and evidence may be withheld from the appellant, and attempts to challenge this on the basis of European law requirements have not succeeded. Under the Asylum and Immigration (Treatment of Claimants, etc.) Act 2004, appeals against deprivation orders were made non-suspensive, so that a person deprived of citizenship could not stay in the country while they appealed against deprivation.

The grounds on which refusal of citizenship can be challenged are limited. Since nationality issues are a matter of the Royal Prerogative, it used to be asserted that they were entirely discretionary and no reasons for refusal need be given. However, after Mohammed al Fayed's well-known challenge to the Home Secretary's refusal of his naturalization application, the Court of Appeal held that in some cases the Secretary of State was under a duty to give reasons (*Fayed v SSHD* [1997] 1 All ER 228). The Secretary of State announced after *Fayed* that reasons would generally be given, and the 2002 Act subsequently repealed s 44(2) and (3) BNA 1981, which had previously provided that no reasons should be given. There is, however, no appeal, so a decision has to be obviously wrong enough to be susceptible to judicial review. Moreover, it may be asserted that applicants for citizenship cannot be told the grounds for their refusal for security reasons.

Judicial review presents high hurdles of argument and expense. In practice, if an application fails through not meeting the factual criteria, the remedy would be to re-apply when the criteria were met, or point out the Home Office error if there has been one. In *R (MH and others) v SSHD* [2008] EWHC 2525 (Admin), Blake J considered applications from ten people who wished to be able to challenge refusals of naturalization by judicial review. Nine had been rejected for reasons to do with association with hostile parties; in the tenth case, reasons were withheld for reason of the public interest. Blake J expressed the way such challenges are treated: 'In general terms with the abolition of citizenship by registration for adults, no claimant has a right to British citizenship but only a right to have an application fairly considered under the statutory scheme.'

In *SSHD v AHK, GA, AS, MH, FT and NT and FM v SSHD* [2009] EWCA Civ 287, the Court of Appeal dealt with both the general principles for dealing with refusals of citizenship applications—that reasons should be given and the declined applicant shown all the material on which the refusal was based—as well as the exceptions, where the applicant is considered to be not of good character on the basis of material that should not be revealed on public interest grounds, including national security (para 37). In these cases, the judge may consider that material or justice may require that a special advocate be appointed (see chapter 7). The Court was specifically concerned that '[t]hese principles should not be diluted on the grounds of administrative convenience' (para 37(e)). In *R (on the application of Chockalingam Thamby) v SSHD* [2011] EWHC 1763 (Admin), a refugee from Sri Lanka had been refused naturalization because he had been a member of the 'Tamil Tigers', a violent political liberation movement, and had failed to declare details of that. He sought judicial review of the refusal, and Sales J referred to the 'Guide AN' for applicants for naturalization and annex D to the Nationality Instructions, including the War Crimes Guidance.

Human rights challenges have also been attempted in relation to nationality claims. In *Harrison v SSHD* [2003] INLR 284, the appellant had wanted to be recognized as

British through a disputed ancestral claim, but was refused. He cited his right under Article 6 ECHR to a fair trial in relation to matters of his civil rights, but the Court of Appeal held that being recognized as a citizen was not a civil right within the meaning of Article 6 ECHR. It did, however, say that Mr Harrison could apply to the Court for a declaration of his citizenship and that this hearing would follow normal requirements of fairness. As with Mr Fayed, this amounts to much the same thing. As will be seen elsewhere in this book, the courts are reluctant to imply any private rights for affected parties to challenge the state's power to control its membership or borders. The application of Article 6 is considered more fully in chapter 5.

In very recent years, particular difficulties with challenging deprivation decisions have become apparent. One is that the very broad ground of deprivation—that the Secretary of State is satisfied it is conducive to the public good—was apparently meant to allow no contradiction—if the Secretary of State certifies herself satisfied, there could be no gainsaying it. However, in *Hilal Abdul-Razzaq Ali al Jedda v SSHD* SC/66/2008 SIAC 7 April 2009, the SIAC rejected this idea as 'profoundly unattractive' (para 4), even though the SIAC Act 1997 did not contain an equivalent to the former s 86 NIAA 2002, requiring an appeal to be allowed against a decision insofar as it was not in accordance with law or where a discretion should have been exercised differently. This wider approach has now become the normal interpretation of the scope of the statutory right of appeal, which also includes human rights considerations. In *Delial-lisi (British citizen: deprivation appeal: Scope)* [2013] UKUT 439(IAC), the Upper Tribunal found that Article 8 might be engaged, including under the principles in *Beoku-Betts* [2008] UKHL 39 that meant taking into account the effects on those close to the person to be deprived. Invoking *Zambrano (European Citizenship)* [2011] EUECJ C-34/09, the Upper Tribunal also said that 'the CJEU requires importance to be attached to the rights and benefits derived from EU citizenship', and found that use of EU citizenship rights, especially the right to work in other EU states, might mean that deprivation would weigh more heavily, so that deprivation 'may well require a greater degree of justification on the part of the national authorities'. This discussion did, however, treat deprivation of citizenship as now being a relatively run-of-the-mill operation. Human rights arguments have not, however, been as effective in challenges to deprivation of citizenship as they have been in challenging immigration and deportation decisions. Although the possibility of deprivation of citizenship breaching a person's Article 8 rights was recognized by the ECtHR in the case of *Karassev v Finland* (1999) 28 *EHRR* CD132 5, that referred to 'arbitrary' deprivation, and no British deprivation has yet been characterized as 'arbitrary'.

The only limitation on the power to deprive for the newest reason—that the Secretary of State is satisfied that it is conducive to the public good—is that the person may not be left stateless. This has meant a number of cases in which the matter being considered is the nationality system of the country the appellant is claimed to belong to. The SIAC in *Y1 v SSHD* [2012] SIAC 112/2011 found 'there is something unrealistic about the exercise', but investigated Afghan citizenship law nevertheless, and found Y1 to be Afghan. There have been many cases in which the English courts have debated foreign nationality laws in order to decide this issue, but the amendment made by the 2014 Act (see 3.5.2) probably means that there will be fewer such cases in future, as statelessness will often not be available as a defence.

As also previously mentioned, a person may be deprived of citizenship by notice when they are outside Britain, so they cannot come back. Anyone deprived in this way is likely to have to take any appeal to the SIAC, as it probably involves security evidence the Secretary of State would not want to reveal. The practical difficulties of giving any instructions for the conduct of a SIAC case from overseas, especially in a hostile environment, were discussed in *K2 v SSHD* Appeal No: SC/96/2010, 18 December 2014, but the court did not find they meant it could not proceed. The contentions of the appellant in *G1 v SSHD* [2012] EWCA Civ 867 included an assertion of a common law right to be present at one's own appeal, but the Court held there was no such right. G1 also asserted that he was being deprived of an in-country right of appeal, contrary to European law requirements of an effective remedy and non-discrimination; again, the Court did not accept that argument, emphasizing that laws of the attribution and deprivation of nationality were strongly within individual states' competence. Whilst the availability and scope of European rights are still not entirely clear, even after *Pham* in the Supreme Court, it appears likely that European citizenship (which is in substance more akin to an open visa) will continue to be regarded as entirely dependent on citizenship of a Member State and liable therefore to fall with it, without any separate recourse, and that European rights to disclosure will make few inroads into the Special Advocate process used in the SIAC.

3.7 Conclusion

This chapter has sought to show that in the second half of the twentieth century, the UK's nationality law was shaped largely by the desire to restrict immigration from former colonies. From the early part of the twentieth century when hundreds of millions of people could claim the status of British subject and therefore come to and live in Britain, now those rights are restricted to British citizens or those few people who separately hold the right of abode. From being broad and inclusive, covering the Empire, the category of belonging to Britain has become restricted almost entirely to those with a family connection with Britain itself. Though a few people whose connection is with a strategic British territory such as Gibraltar or the Falkland Islands are now included, some people born in Britain are excluded from British status.

As noted at the beginning of this chapter, the exclusive power of the state to determine who are its nationals has passed through its earlier preoccupation with the question of who 'belongs' to the UK, largely seen in terms of birth and parentage. Discrimination as to gender or parental marriage status has been largely eradicated. Naturalization and registration have become contingent on conduct, and, beginning with the changes under Nationality, Immigration and Asylum Act 2002, even those born in Britain can be deprived of citizenship on the grounds that the Secretary of State is satisfied that deprivation is conducive to the public good. That power is being used more widely, along with a new power to exclude even British-born citizens with no other citizenship from the UK. British citizenship is now less a matter of intrinsic personal identity and more a matter of a contingent privilege, which may be removed on the posting of a letter.

QUESTIONS

1 Are the UK's nationality laws closer to a principle of *jus soli* or *jus sanguinis*? Whichever you think, what elements can you find in UK nationality law of the other principle?

2 How do registration and naturalization fit in with the way the UK embodies the *jus soli* or *jus sanguinis* principles?

3 Is it possible to give content to the idea of 'belonging' to a country? How does British nationality law do it? How would you do it?

4 How would you structure a law of deprivation of nationality or citizenship? What safeguards would you put in place?

5 What legal responses to *de jure* and *de facto* statelessness exist in the UK? Are they appropriate?

 online resource centre For guidance on answering questions, visit the Online Resource Centre www.oxfordtextbooks.co.uk/orc/clayton7e/.

FURTHER READING

Anderson, Benedict (2006) *Imagined Communities* (new edn) (London: Verso).

Blake, Charles (1982) 'Citizenship, Law and the State: The British Nationality Act 1981' *Modern Law Review* vol. 45, pp. 179–97.

Clayton, Gina (2008) 'Right of Abode and National Insecurity', *Immigration Law Digest* vol. 14, no. 4, Winter, pp. 2–9.

Cohn, Margit (2009) 'Judicial Review of Non-Statutory Executive Powers after *Bancoult*: A Unified Anxious Model' *Public Law* pp. 260–86.

Dummett, Ann and Nicol, Andrew (1990) *Subjects, Citizens, Aliens and Others* (London: Weidenfeld and Nicolson), chapter 7.

Fransman, Laurie (2011) *British Nationality Law* (3rd edn) (London: Bloomsbury), this, with updates, is the major authoritative work, for reference on all issues.

Goldsmith, Peter (2008) *Citizenship: Our Common Bond* (London: The Stationery Office).

Grossman, Andrew (2001) 'Nationality and the Unrecognised State' *International and Comparative Law Quarterly* vol. 50, pp. 849–76.

Hogenstijn, Maarten and van Middelkoop, Daniel (2005) 'Saint Helena: Citizenship and Spatial Identities on a Remote Island' *Tijdschrift voor Economische en Sociale Geografie* vol. 96, no. 1, pp. 96–104.

Immigration Law Practitioners' Association (2000) 'The Overseas Territories White Paper and Protocol 4 of the ECHR—the ILPA response' *Journal of Immigration, Asylum and Nationality* vol. 14, no. 3, pp. 142–50.

Kiwan, Dinah (2007) 'Becoming a British Citizen: A Learning Journey', Goldsmith Citizenship Review, Ministry of Justice.

Lester, Anthony (2002) 'Thirty Years On: The *East African Asians Case* Revisited' *Public Law* Spring, pp. 52–72.

Lester, Anthony (2008) 'Citizenship and the Constitution' *Political Quarterly* vol. 79, no. 3, pp. 388–403.

Majid, Hina (2008) 'Protecting the Right to Have Rights: The Case of Sect. 56 of the Immigration, Asylum and Nationality Act 2006' *Immigration, Asylum and Nationality Law* vol. 22, no. 1, pp. 27–44.

Mole, Nuala (1995) 'Constructive Deportation and the European Convention' *European Human Rights Law Review* launch issue, pp. 63–71.

Paul, Kathleen (1997) *Whitewashing Britain: Race and Citizenship in the Postwar Era* (New York: Cornell University Press), chapter 1.

Sawyer, Caroline (2005) 'Civis Europeanus Sum: The citizenship rights of the children of foreign parents' *Public Law* pp. 475–82.

Sawyer, Caroline (2006) 'Not Every Child Matters: The UK's Expulsion of British Children' *International Journal of Children's Rights* vol. 14, no. 2, pp. 157–85.

Sawyer, Caroline (2013) '"Civis Britannicus Sum" No Longer: Deprivation of British nationality' *Journal of Immigration, Asylum and Nationality Law* pp. 23–40.

Shah, Prakash (2000) *Refugees, Race and the Legal Concept of Asylum* (London: Cavendish), chapter 5.

Shah, Ramnik (2003) 'Special Voucher Scheme Abolished' *Journal of Immigration, Asylum and Nationality Law* vol. 16, pp. 108–10.

Shah, Ramnik (2003) 'A Wrong Righted: Full Status for Britain's "Other Citizens"' *Journal of Immigration, Asylum and Nationality Law* vol. 17, pp. 19–24.

Smith, Anthony D. (1996) *Nations and Nationalism in a Global Era* (Cambridge: Polity Press).

Tomkins, Adam (2001) 'Magna Carta, Crown and Colonies' *Public Law* pp. 571–85.

Winder, Robert (2013) *Bloody Foreigners* (London: Little Brown).

SECTION 2

Enabling principles: EU free movement and human rights

4

Freedom of movement for EU nationals

SUMMARY

This chapter introduces freedom of movement within the European Union (EU). The focus is on rights of entry and residence, particularly for employed workers and their families.

4.1 Introduction

EU free movement law differs in a fundamental way from domestic immigration law as it is based on EU rights of entry and residence as opposed to the permission of an immigration officer. This has a number of effects in practice: first, EU free movement rights are contained not in the Immigration Rules but in separate secondary legislation (the Immigration (European Economic Area) Regulations 2006, SI 2006/1003 (EEA Regulations)); secondly, EU nationals are not required to obtain entry clearance, visas, or leave to enter—the only formal requirement at a Member State border is a passport or identity document; and thirdly, residence documentation issued by a host Member State under EU law is evidence of a right to reside but not constitutive of it since the source of the right is EU law not an administrative decision of the host Member State. The focus of this chapter is on EU free movement law as implemented by the UK. It is not a general account of EU law, for which regard should be had to general EU law textbooks.

Economic freedom of movement (workers, establishment, and services) was present in the EU Treaties (and their predecessors) since the inception of the EU. However, since the Treaty of Maastricht in 1992 the possibilities (and limitations) of freedom of movement based on EU citizenship alone have developed. There have been a number of Treaty amendments since the founding treaties, the most recent being the Treaty of Lisbon in 2009 which renamed the former EC Treaty the 'Treaty on the Functioning of the European Union' (TFEU). The new numbering of Treaty articles after amendment by the Treaty of Lisbon is used in this chapter, with the old number in brackets (for example, 'Article 45 TFEU (ex 39 EC)') so that the connection can be made with older cases and materials.

Whilst the UK has an opt-out which it has exercised in part in respect of the EU provisions on immigration and asylum for non-EU nationals, known in European law as third country nationals (TCNs), this is not currently the position in relation to the free movement of EU citizens (and their TCN family members). However, the renegotiation of the UK's EU membership sought by Prime Minister David Cameron on the terms currently sought would substantially alter the UK's obligations in relation to the free movement of EU citizens. It is also clear that in the event of Brexit, the basis on which EU citizens may enter and reside in the UK would be fundamentally changed.

As already noted, this chapter concerns the law which governs the free movement of people within the EU. As such, it is principally about the movement of EU nationals, but the movement of TCNs may come within the ambit of EU law as a result of their connection with EU nationals, for instance, as a spouse or employee. The chapter concentrates on the rights of EU nationals as workers (and also simply as citizens) to move within the EU. The rights of establishment and to provision of services are not covered in detail, and for these, as for a fuller account of free movement generally, reference should be made to textbooks on EU law.

4.2 **Sources of law**

Free movement law is primarily contained in the TFEU and secondary legislation (primarily Directive 2004/38/EC on the right of citizens of the Union and their families to move and reside freely within the territory of Member States), and is given effect in UK law by statute and regulations. In the event of a European provision not being given effect by these mechanisms, the main relevant provisions are directly effective, and take precedence over any inconsistent national provision (Case 6/64 *Costa v ENEL* [1964] ECR 585). Thus, EU law takes effect where UK law fails to deliver an enforceable EU right, but does not prevent UK law from giving greater rights than are contained in EU law.

Appeals against administrative decisions made under the European provisions are made to the same appellate bodies as other UK immigration appeals (EEA Regulations, part 6). This means that there are decisions of the Upper Tribunal, High Court, and appellate courts on European free movement issues that are binding on both administrative decision-makers and the First-tier Tribunal. In general terms, the repeal of rights of appeal undertaken by the Immigration Act 2014 does not affect European Economic Area (EEA) cases, since EEA rights of appeal are governed by the EEA Regulations (reg 26) rather than the Nationality Immigration and Asylum Act 2002. Some EEA decisions, however—for example decisions under the EC-Turkey Association Agreement—no longer have a right to an appeal but only to an administrative review (see further chapter 5). Domestic courts may rule on matters of EU law, but where it is necessary, under Article 267 TFEU (ex 234 EC) any court or tribunal may refer a question to the Court of Justice of the EU (CJEU, previously ECJ) for a preliminary ruling, which will then return to the domestic court for application. Only courts against whose decision there is no legal remedy are obliged to refer, and even this obligation is subject to the exception that a reference need not be made if the point is abundantly clear (Case 283/81 *CILFIT* [1982] ECR 03415).

On 30 April 2006, Directive 2004/38/EC became binding on Member States. This Directive replaced many of the earlier directives and regulations concerning entry and residence. Commonly known as the Citizens' Directive, it is now a major source of law which consolidates and enhances free movement rights. The detailed implementation in UK law is by the EEA Regulations 2006, (as subsequently amended), intended to give effect to the Citizens' Directive, though whether they do so fully is a matter we shall consider. The EEA Regulations are supplemented on an operational level by guidance published by the Home Office (formerly European Casework Instructions and currently labelled 'modernised guidance' on EEA and Swiss nationals and EC association agreements).

Section 7 of the Immigration Act 1988 implements in UK law the basic principle of free movement by providing that those who have an 'enforceable Community [EU] right' shall not require leave to enter under the Immigration Act 1971. This means that although they are technically subject to immigration control, within that system of control they have a right to enter to exercise their freedom of movement. This may be seen at any port of entry to the UK where there is a channel for EU citizens who are normally waved through on presentation of proof of right to travel. Those with an enforceable EU right are nationals of the EEA, that is, EU countries, Iceland, Norway, and Liechtenstein, and the UK Regulations include Swiss nationals also (EEA Regulations, reg 2(1)). From January 2014, nationals of Croatia are currently the only EEA nationals subject to transitional provisions limiting their rights to work and permitting Member States to retain national measures restricting access to the labour market.

4.2.1 Determination of EU citizenship

Nationality of a Member State—and thus EU citizenship—is determined by each Member State (Article 20(1) TFEU (ex Article 18 EC)). This leaves matters primarily in the hands of Member States but the CJEU has held that Member States must have due regard for EU law in determining the conditions for acquisition and loss of nationality, and therefore it is not out of the question that certain determinations or revocations of nationality may be questionable under EU law. In Case 21/74 *Airola v Commission* [1975] ECR 221, this entailed that staff regulations should be applied so as to disregard a nationality imposed on a female employee by operation of a discriminatory domestic law over which she had no control. Normally, however, the Court, as in Case C-369/90 *Micheletti* [1992] ECR I-4329 (a case of dual Italian/Argentinian nationality) and Case C-200/02 *Chen* (an unusual case of Irish nationality acquired by birth in Northern Ireland, even though this was UK territory), will expect one EU Member State to recognize the nationality conferred on an individual by another. However, mere possession of another Member State nationality by a dual national who had never been economically active in their state of residence nor exercised any Treaty rights abroad in another Member State was held to involve a purely internal situation in Case C-434/09 *McCarthy* [2011] ECR I-3375. Deprivation of nationality (and thus of EU citizenship and its benefits) where the individual does not also have a second EU Member State nationality is also to some extent a matter of EU law (see Case C-135/08 *Rottmann* [2010] ECR I-1449). In *Rottmann*, the Court held that Germany's withdrawal of German nationality from a former Austrian national (who had lost Austrian nationality by operation of law upon acquiring a second nationality) must respect the EU principle of proportionality. Before domestic courts, however, the view that EU law applies to the deprivation of British nationality has been rejected (see *GI (Sudan) v SSHD* [2012] EWCA Civ 867).

4.2.2 UK nationals for EU purposes

A number of Member States, including the UK, have made declarations, appended to the Maastricht Treaty, as to whom they regard as their nationals for EU purposes. The UK's Declaration ([1983] OJ C23/1) defines as nationals for EU purposes British citizens, British subjects with the right of abode in the UK, and British 'Dependent' (now Overseas) Territories citizens who acquire that citizenship from connection with Gibraltar. This appears to exclude Commonwealth citizens with right of abode in the UK, unless the Immigration Act 1971 definition of 'British citizens' can be implied into the declaration. Such people are treated by the Immigration Act 1971 as British citizens, indeed their right of abode in the UK is the same as that of a British citizen. However, it appears they do not obtain freedom of movement rights in the EU, even though they may well have lived in the UK all their lives, have the right to vote, and are in every other respect the equivalent in law of a British citizen. The exclusion of British Overseas Territories citizens (BOTCs) who are not from Gibraltar no longer has any significance: they became British citizens by virtue of the British Overseas Territories Act 2002 (it may be noted that the Act did not give other European nationals the right to enter the British Overseas Territories). Other categories of British national remain excluded, namely British Overseas citizens, British nationals (overseas), and British subjects under the Act or British protected persons.

A challenge to the exclusion of British overseas citizens arose before the CJEU in Case C-192/99 *Manjit Kaur* [1992] ECR I-35, an attempt to reverse the underprivileged immigration status of British overseas citizens, as discussed in chapter 3. The CJEU, however, reaffirmed the pre-Maastricht principle that it was for Member States, with due regard to EU law, to determine who would be their nationals and thus nationals of the Union. The Court would therefore not interfere with Ms Kaur's status as determined by Britain. The High Court in *ex parte Zaunab Upadhey* 31 January 2000 (unreported) ILU vol. 3 no. 13 confirmed that a British protected person was also not a British national for EU purposes.

4.3 Free movement of Union citizens

The free movement of persons is one of the foundational principles of EU law. This freedom has primarily developed in connection with economic activities but the Treaty on European Union created EU citizenship, and in what is now Article 20 TFEU (ex 18 EC), a general right for EU citizens to move and reside freely within the territory of the Member States.

The CJEU suggested, in cases such as Case C-184/99 *Grzelczyk* [2002] 1 CMLR 19 (a student lawfully residing in another Member State could claim a benefit available to Belgian students), that EU citizenship and Article 20 meant that free movement is increasingly to be detached from the exercise of economic activity. As we shall see, this has been increasingly recognized, but economic status remains highly relevant in some situations.

4.3.1 Union citizens' rights of entry and residence

Article 5.1 of the Citizens' Directive provides that Member States must allow Union citizens entry simply on production of an identity card or passport, and no entry visa requirement or similar may be imposed. Where a Union citizen or family member does not have the necessary travel documents, they must be given every opportunity to obtain them or have them brought before they are turned back at a border between Member States (Article 5.4). On production of an identity document or passport and confirmation of employment an EU state national must be issued with a registration certificate (Article 8.3). This is proof of the existing entitlement to free movement rights, and so possession of such a document cannot be required as a condition of exercising the rights (Case C-85/96 *Martinez Sala* [1998] ECR I-2691). These provisions are implemented in the UK by Regulations 11 (right of admission to the UK) and 16 (issue of Registration Certificate) of the EEA Regulations. There are also special provisions for temporary permits for seasonal workers, those on short-term temporary contracts, and frontier workers. Third country national family members who qualify under the Directive are to be issued with residence cards, not registration certificates (Article 9 of the Citizens' Directive; reg 17 EEA Regulations).

Member States must, 'acting in accordance with their laws', issue identity documents or passports to their own nationals (Article 4.3). A failure to issue a passport in the UK could be challenged as a breach of the Citizens' Directive, which may only be permitted on the restricted grounds allowed by Article 27 (public policy, public security, public health—see 4.8). Several cases have recently arisen from Bulgaria (Case C-430/10 *Gyadov* [2011] ECR I-11637, Case C-434/10 *Aladzhov* [2011] ECR I-11659, Case C-249/11 *Byankov* [2013] 1 CMLR 15) in which the CJEU condemns the generality of the Bulgarian provisions under which exit bans have been made more or less automatically in cases of serious criminality (drug dealing) and debts (both tax obligation and private debt). At the same time the Court did not rule out that in particular individual cases drug trafficking convictions or the enforcement of tax obligations could be a sufficiently serious reason to prevent exit and, in the case of tax collection, could be presented as not being for purely economic reasons. Individual scrutiny is clearly required by national courts to establish a sufficiently serious case, but it is unclear quite how exceptional a case would have to be for it to be a proportionate response.

Having entered, any Union citizen and their family members have an initial right to reside for three months without any qualifying conditions (Article 6; reg 13). After the first three months there is a further indefinite right of residence so long as qualifying conditions exist (Article 7; reg 14). The conditions are that the person is a worker, self-employed, economically self-sufficient, a student with adequate means and sickness insurance, or the family member of any of these. How these conditions are met is discussed more fully later. In principle, it appears that removal of persons not exercising Treaty rights because they satisfy none of these conditions is not excluded by the Directive, although recourse to public funds must not 'automatically' result in revocation of a right of residence and subsequent removal (Case C-140/12 *Pensionsversicherungsanstalt v Brey* [2014] 1 CMLR 37). Questions and concerns have been raised about attempts to remove homeless EEA nationals from the UK (see further at 4.8.2.5). From 1 January 2014 the Home Office has adopted a more stringent policy towards EEA nationals whom they believe are not exercising Treaty rights. For the first three months an EEA national may be resident without exercising any other Treaty rights, and so without restriction. The new policy promotes removal where a person is considered to have left and re-entered the UK in order to have another initial three-month period. In addition, the EEA Regulations now permit a re-entry ban for 12 months following administrative removal of EU citizens insofar as they cannot provide evidence that they are now qualified persons.

4.3.1.1 Permanent residence

Article 17(1)(b) of the Directive gives a right to remain to those who have ceased work through permanent incapacity, either through pensionable industrial disease or injury, having lived in the Member State continuously for two years or more. This is implemented in the same terms in the EEA Regulations, Regulation 5(3). Article 17(1)(a) gives the right to remain to workers who retire in a Member State, having lived there for three years and worked there for one year, prior to retirement. Regulation 5(2) of the EEA Regulations implements this in the UK. There is also a right of permanent residence for those who, after three years' continuous employment and residence in the host

Member State, obtain employment in another Member State, but who return at least weekly to the first Member State (reg 5(4) EEA Regulations).

In addition to these particular situations, Article 16 (reg 15 EEA Regulations) gives a right of permanent residence to all Union citizens and their families after five years of continuous lawful residence. Provisions are made about breaks in continuity. According to the EFTA Court, this right includes the right to have accompanying family members enter and join the migrant, without complying with the 'sufficient resources' condition (Case E-4/11 *Clauder* EFTA Court Rep 216). Another important question concerning the interpretation of this right has recently been clarified. There was a view, based on recital 17 in the preamble to the Directive, that Article 16 refers to five years' residence in accordance with the Directive, in other words, exercising a right given by the Treaty or Directive for those five years. Case C-162/09 *Lassal* [2010] ECR I-9217 confirms that this is not the case in so far as five years of residence before the Directive came into force does confer the right to permanent residence, but Case C-325/09 *Dias* [2011] ECR I-6387 also makes clear that a formal residence card which had not been revoked is not in itself proof of ongoing compliance with conditions of stay under EU law if the individual had not in fact complied with conditions that would have made the residence lawful throughout the five years. It also indicated that, once this five-year period is completed, periods of absence or periods of residence that do not fully comply with the Directive's conditions before the 2006 date do not necessarily interrupt the continuity of residence to result in loss (or rather, non-acquisition) of the permanent residence status. Case 424/10 *Ziolkowski* [2011] I-14035 raises the question of lawful residence under national law of an A8 (that is, nationals of Czech Republic, Poland, Hungary, Slovakia, Slovenia, Estonia, Latvia, and Lithuania—the so called 'A8' countries which joined the EU in 2004) national prior to accession and acquisition of the status of EU citizen. The case indicates that such prior residence may be counted, but the applicant must have complied in substance with the conditions set out in the Directive.

As for the impact of imprisonment on the acquisition of permanent residence, in Case C-378/12 *Onuekwere* [2014] ECR nyr the CJEU held that imprisonment interrupts the continuity of residence for the purposes of the acquisition of permanent residence (see also Case C-400/12 *MG* [2014] ECR C-400/12 and *Essa* [2013] UKUT 11316).

4.4 Freedom of movement for workers

Free movement of persons is one of the four fundamental freedoms of the EU. Case law and secondary legislation flesh out the content of the free movement right, but it begins with Article 45 TFEU (ex 39 EC), which reads as follows:

1. Freedom of movement of workers shall be secured within the Union.

2. Such freedom of movement shall entail the abolition of any discrimination based on nationality between workers of the Member States as regards employment, remuneration, and other conditions of work and employment.

3. It shall entail the right, subject to limitations justified on grounds of public policy, public security, or public health:

   (a) to accept offers of employment actually made;

   (b) to move freely within the territory of Member States for this purpose;

   (c) to stay in a Member State for the purpose of employment in accordance with the provisions governing the employment of nationals of that State laid down by law, regulation, or administrative action;

(d) to remain in the territory of a Member State after having been employed in that State, subject to the conditions which shall be embodied in implementing regulations to be drawn up by the Commission.

4. The provisions of this Article shall not apply to employment in the public service.

Paragraph 1, setting out the objective of the Article, may be regarded as an agenda for the Court in its decisions and for the other EU bodies in making secondary legislation. In terms of achieving the purpose set out in para 1, the listed rights a, b, c, and d within para 3 may be regarded as the minimum content of the freedom. Paragraph 2 expresses one of the key policies of the EU, the abolition of discrimination based on nationality. Paragraph 4, on the other hand, represents a concession to the sovereignty of states, permitting them, for national security or related purposes, to retain some posts specifically for their nationals. In a series of cases, Article 45 has been held to be sufficiently clear, precise, and unconditional to be directly effective: for example, Case 167/73 *Commission v French Republic* [1974] ECR 359. It may therefore be relied upon directly by a worker to protect their freedom of movement, which means it may be used as a basis for argument in national courts.

4.4.1 Personal scope—to whom Article 45 applies

The definition of who is a worker has been consistently held by the Court to be a matter of EU law, not domestic law, so Member States cannot narrow the effect of Article 45 TFEU by using their own definition. As such, in the EEA Regulations, Regulation 4(1), 'worker' is defined by reference to a worker within the meaning of Article 45. However, there is no single definition of 'worker' in EU law, 'it varies according to the area in which the definition is to be applied' (Case C-85/96 *Martinez Sala* [1998] ECR I 2691). Accordingly, as will be seen later, Article 45 includes within it job-seekers, vocational or occupational trainees, the involuntarily unemployed and sick, injured and retired workers, and pregnant women who give up work or job-seeking due to the physical constraints of the late stages of pregnancy and the aftermath of childbirth, provided they return to work or find another job within a reasonable period after the birth of the child (*Yusuf (EEA—ceasing to be a jobseeker; effect)* [2015] UKUT 00433 (IAC)).

4.4.1.1 People in work

The term 'worker' refers to someone who is or has been employed. The rights of self-employed people are dealt with separately by the provisions on the rights of establishment and provision of services. Case C-66/85 *Lawrie-Blum* [1986] ECR 2121 held that a worker in EU law was someone who, for a period of time, performs services under the direction of another in return for remuneration. Case C-53/81 *Levin* [1982] ECR 1035 confirmed that part-time work that paid less than the minimum subsistence level of income, i.e. the minimum on which someone could live, fell nonetheless within Article 45. In so finding, the CJEU distinguished between work that was 'genuine and effective' and activities 'on such a small scale as to be marginal and ancillary' that are excluded from the ambit of Article 45. Case 139/85 *Kempf* [1986] ECR 1741 established that low-paid work may be supplemented not only by the earnings of other family members, but also from other sources including public funds. In *Kempf* the applicant was a music teacher who taught 12 lessons per week and supplemented his income by a claim on public funds.

Further, whilst remuneration is crucial to worker status, it need not be in the form of a wage. The economic nature of the work is the key, and provision for basic needs such as accommodation, food, pocket money, and so on, in return for participation in the activities and work of a religious community can satisfy this—Case 196/87 *Steymann* [1988] ECR 6159. However, in Case 344/87 *Bettray* [1989] ECR 1621, the applicant did not convince the CJEU that he was a worker as the work that he did was rehabilitative in purpose and not economic. This was so even though he was paid a wage for his work because the work was selected because of its suitability for him rather than he for the work. In Case C-456/02 *Trojani* [2004] ECR I-07573, the CJEU held that a resident in a homeless hostel working for about 30 hours a week under its direction, as part of a personal re-integration programme in return for benefits in kind and 'pocket money' cash, could claim residence as a worker if the paid activity was real and genuine (*Steymann*) rather than rehabilitative (*Bettray*). It would be for the national court to examine the facts to discover if this was the case.

In Case 413/01 *Ninni-Orasche* [2003] ECR I-13187 the CJEU held that the fact that the employment contract was for a fixed short term and that she knew that in advance did not affect Ms Ninni-Orasche's claim to receive the benefits of a worker. The question is an objective one as to whether the employment is effective and genuine. Likewise, in the situation of a 'zero hours' contract, of which there has been significant discussion recently, the status of worker is not ruled out: the national court will determine, on the basis of all the circumstances, whether there is genuine and effective employment (Case C-379/89 *Raulin* [1992] ECR I-01027).

4.4.1.2 Work-seekers

Article 45 itself does not mention job-seeking, but the CJEU has interpreted the provision to include those who have not yet secured a job offer in another European country but wish to work there in order to give full effect to the freedom of movement for workers. In Case 316/85 *Lebon* [1987] ECR 2811, the CJEU held that those who were seeking work should be entitled to equality of treatment in access to employment under Article 45. Case C-292/89 *Antonissen* [1991] ECR I 745 considered more fully the position of unemployed job-seekers. Mr Antonissen, a Belgian national, had entered the UK, but did not find work. The UK government proposed to deport him following his conviction for drugs offences. Part of his challenge was to the immigration rule then in force, which limited to six months the stay of an EU national seeking work. The Court held that a job-seeker should be allowed a reasonable period within which to become acquainted with the job opportunities available in the country to which s/he had moved, and that, in the context of that case, six months was a reasonable period. However, at the end of that time the person could still not be deported if it could be shown that s/he was continuing to seek employment and there was a genuine prospect of being employed. The definition of job seeker refers both to those entering a state for the first time to seek employment ('first-time job seekers') and those who have had a job and are again seeking work ('second-time job seekers') (*Shabani (EEA—jobseekers, nursery education)* [2013] UKUT 315 (IAC); *Yusuf (EEA—ceasing to be a jobseeker; effect)* [2015] UKUT 00433 (IAC)). The EEA Regulations expressly include a job-seeker as a 'qualified person', that is, a beneficiary of EU rights (reg 6). However, there has been substantial recent amendment of the rights of job-seekers under the Regulations. In particular, the effect of the latest amendments (in force from November 2014, Immigration (European Economic Area) (Amendment) (No.3) Regulations 2014 (SI 2014/2761)) is to impose upper time limits on the period of time that a person may qualify as a job-seeker for the purposes of EU law. The upper limit is ninety-one days in the case of persons who wish to assert a right of residence as a job-seeker and six months for those who wish to assert that they retain their right of residence as a worker whilst unemployed (see later): Regulation 6(4)–(11).

Beyond this, 'compelling evidence' of a continuing search for employment and a genuine prospect of being engaged is required in order for a person to be a qualified person: Regulation 6(7). Guidance issued by the Secretary of State for Work and Pensions identifies 'compelling evidence' as a definite job offer of genuine and effective work or evidence of a change of circumstances that makes it likely that a person will receive a job offer imminently (DWP Decision Makers Guide). Arguably both the Regulations and the guidance are inconsistent with EU law. *Antonissen* does not provide an upper limit on the period during which a person may qualify as a job-seeker and the extra requirement to provide 'compelling evidence' in the EEA Regulations goes beyond what is said in that judgment.

In *Lebon and Antonissen*, a job-seeker was not treated as a worker for all purposes. The right to remain to seek work was simply a necessary corollary of Article 45, required to give effect to the freedom of movement for workers, but not in itself giving entitlement to all the rights which attach to a worker. Thus, the Upper Tribunal in *Yusuf (EEA—ceasing to be a jobseeker; effect)* [2015] UKUT 00433 (IAC) held that a person who had acquired the status of worker for the purposes of Article 45 TFEU only through being a job-seeker, who is a qualified person under Regulation 6(1)(a), does not retain the status of worker on ceasing to be a jobseeker.

4.4.1.3 Unemployment after having been in work

In the case of unemployment, as appears from the cases discussed earlier, there is a distinction between retaining the status of worker in the context of social rights, and the status of worker giving a right to reside in a Member State. The Citizens' Directive provides that the status of worker will be retained where: s/he is temporarily unable to work because of illness or accident; s/he has been in employment for more than one year and is now involuntarily unemployed, registered and seeking work; s/he has been in employment for less than a year and is now involuntarily unemployed, though in this case the status may only be retained for a further six months; or s/he embarks on vocational training. If the unemployment was voluntary, then the vocational training must be related to the previous employment (Directive 2004/38 Article 7(3)). This enacts the decision in Case C-39/86 *Lair* [1988] ECR 3161, and Regulation 6(2) of the EEA Regulations implements these provisions. The Citizens' Directive provides that where the worker becomes involuntarily unemployed during the first 12 months the status of worker is retained for a minimum of six months after that (Article 7(3)(c)). The UK Regulations purport to implement this by requiring, in respect of workers who have been employed for at least one year, that during the six months the worker retains the status if s/he can provide evidence of seeking employment in the UK and of a 'genuine chance of being engaged' and after six months if s/he can provide 'compelling evidence' of the same (reg 6(2)(b)). In respect of workers who have been employed for less than one year, there is a cap of six months on retained worker status (reg 6(2)(ba) & (2A)) (see earlier discussion for questions over the compatibility of these provision with EU law).

In *RP (EEA Regs—worker—cessation)* [2006] UKAIT 00025, the appellant entered the UK in 1999, worked for four months, and was then unemployed for five years, except for one week in 2001. The Tribunal held that he was a worker in 1999, and for some time thereafter. They were not convinced that he had been genuinely seeking work since then, and the week of employment in 2001 was 'marginal and ancillary'. Thus, at some time before his application for an EEA residence document in 2004, he had lost the status of worker. He was thus no longer a qualified person under the EEA regulations.

4.4.1.4 Pregnant women

The question of whether a pregnant worker who ceases work (or job-seeking) for reasons related to pregnancy retains the status of worker during that time and for a reasonable time after the birth was answered in the affirmative by the Court of Justice in Case C-507/12 *Saint-Prix* [2015] ECR nyr. The CJEU held that retention of worker status in these circumstances was required by EU law provided that the women return to work or find another job within a reasonable period after the birth of the child. Domestic courts have subsequently considered and applied the CJEU's ruling. In its judgment in *Secretary of State for Work and Pensions v SSF and others* [2015] UKUT 0502 (AAC) the Upper Tribunal (Administrative Appeals Chamber) held that pregnant EU citizens may, ordinarily, expect to retain 'worker' status for a year when off work. Importantly, for the purposes of claiming social welfare benefits, a right to remain on a *Saint-Prix* basis may be established prospectively such that there is no need for a woman to prove at the outset that she will return to work or find another job (although on the expiry of the reasonable period, the right is likely to be terminated). The Immigration and Asylum Chamber of the Upper Tribunal have also considered the effect of *Saint-Prix*. In *Weldemichael and another (St Prix [2014] EUECJ C-507/12; effect)* [2015] UKUT 00540 (IAC), the Tribunal found that ordinarily the retention of worker status due to pregnancy starts 11 weeks prior to birth, but this may be displaced if 'cogent evidence . . . that the woman was physically constrained from working or seeking work' is provided.

4.4.2 Material scope—the content of free movement rights for workers

The underlying premise of European free movement law is that equality in conditions after arriving in another Member State, such as rights to social benefits or access to employment, all support the freedom to move. Though this book's focus on migration and constraints of space means that the main emphasis is on rights of entry and residence, we briefly touch here on some of the social rights.

4.4.2.1 Entry and residence

Article 45(3) provides the right to enter the territory of another Member State and to reside there in order to take up an offer of employment. Directive 2004/38 ensures that there are not administrative obstacles to the exercise of this right, and the right of entry for workers is as described at 4.3.1 for all Union citizens.

4.4.2.2 Working conditions

One of the fundamental principles of the Treaty is the abolition of discrimination between nationals of Member States. Article 45(2) requires the abolition of discrimination between workers of Member States as regards 'employment, remuneration and other conditions of work and employment'. The provision has been held to apply to obvious working conditions such as the length and security of employment contracts, for example, in Case C-272/92 *Maria Chiara Spotti* [1993] ECR I-5185. It also applies to matters not within the direct province of the employer such as the refund of tax deductions (Case C-175/88 *Biehl* [1990] ECR I-2779).

Regulation 1612/68 has now been updated in Regulation 492/2011—Article 7 (in both versions of the Regulation) which governs equality in relation to social and tax advantages may be interpreted to give effect to the right of non-discrimination in relation to working conditions (see, for instance, Case C-195/98 *Österreichischer Gewerschaftbund, Gewerkschaft Öffentlicher Dienst v Austria* [2000] ECR I-10497).

4.4.2.3 Access to employment

The most fundamental right relating to work is of course the opportunity to obtain a job in the first place. Domestic legal systems must not put in place provisions which discriminate against other Member State nationals in being able to obtain such an offer of employment (Article 45(2) and Regulation 492/2011 (codifying the rights formerly in Regulation 1612/68)). Indirectly discriminatory provisions, that is, those which apply both to foreign and home state nationals but which would deter other Member State nationals, are prohibited in addition to directly discriminatory provisions, that is, those which discriminate between home and foreign workers. One of the best-known cases dealing with this principle is the *Bosman* case from the world of football.

 Key Case

**Case 415/93 *Union Royale Belge des Sociétés de Football Association v Bosman*
[1995] ECR I-4921**

Bosman was a goalkeeper with the Belgian team, RC Liege, who challenged the nationality rules which limited the number of foreign players a club could field in official matches (he also challenged the post-contract transfer fee rules, but this raised different issues involving restrictive rules that did not discriminate on the grounds of nationality). The CJEU ruled in his favour. The Court said that a limit on the matches in which foreign players could appear obviously discouraged a club from employing them.

One of the arguments used by the Belgian Football Association was that the rules promoted cultural identity and thus were supported by Article 162 TFEU (ex 151(1) EC), which was one of the measures introduced by the TEU 'to contribute to the flowering of the cultures of the member states'. The TEU marked a move away from the strictly economic base of EU law and began the process of increasing the EU's competence in educational and cultural areas. The Court rejected this argument as applied to *Bosman*. It said that sport and culture should not be confused, and that the case concerned the freedom of professional sportspeople to move between Member States. *Bosman* was controversial, partly because it put players more in charge and partly because it meant that there was nothing to stop a football club from fielding a team which included no 'home' players from the home nation. UEFA has subsequently entered into an agreement to try to protect the number of locally trained players, but this agreement has also proved controversial. Intergovernmental discussions have not yet exempted sport from freedom of movement provisions, though the sporting bodies have promoted that view. The Court has restated that sportspeople are protected by Article 45 in Case C-176/96 *Lehtonen* [2001] 1 All ER (EC) 97, though accepting rules to ensure the regularity of sporting competitions, subject to a test of necessity. Most recently, in Case C-325/08 *Olympique Lyonnais*, the Court appears to have refined its position confirming that trainee players may be subject to a proportionate regime to ensure some compensation to their training club if they chose not to continue playing there if offered a contract, but to move elsewhere. A further and more general discussion of sport is found in the Commission's Communication COM(2011)12.

Some job requirements may have a genuine cultural purpose, which would be protected by the Treaty, even though they are discriminatory in their effect. One of the most obvious is language, and explicit provision is made for this in Article 3 of Regulation

492/2011. This was considered in Case 379/87 *Groener*. Groener was a Dutch national who had been working in Ireland as a part-time art teacher. After two years she applied for a full-time post and was recommended for the job. However, she was not appointed as she failed a mandatory Irish language test, even though the lessons would be given in English. Groener argued that as Irish would not be required for the lessons it could not be required by reason of the nature of the post to be filled. However, the Court supported the lawfulness of the Irish government's policy, which was that the use of Irish was being promoted in schools as a means of expressing national culture and identity. The requirement was not disproportionate to this objective, and could be upheld.

Even where a condition of employment explicitly or implicitly constitutes an obstacle to the free movement of workers, by, for instance, requiring prior experience in the host state, it may be lawful if it pursues a legitimate aim compatible with the Treaty, is justified by pressing reasons of public interest, and if application of the measure ensures achievement of that aim and does not go beyond what is necessary for that purpose. This has been illustrated in numerous cases in the CJEU, of which the following are but recent examples.

Case C-40/05 *Kaj Lyyski* concerned a Swedish government scheme to recruit and train teachers to remedy a shortage. Candidates had to be employed in a Swedish school. This would indirectly discriminate against non-Swedish candidates. The CJEU accepted that the scheme's aim was legitimate, and that it was more difficult to monitor practical training if it was taking place outside Sweden. However, as some colleges were exempting trainees from the practical part of the training, and as candidates could be allowed to carry out their training at a different school from the one where they were employed, it could not be said that current employment in a Swedish school was necessary to achieve the Swedish government's aim. In Case C-371/04 *Commission v Italy*, the Member State directly refused to take into account experience gained in other Member States when recruiting for the civil service, on the grounds that the recruitment process in other Member States would be different from that in Italy. The CJEU held that this justification was insufficient. The aim of getting qualified people for the job was appropriate, but if someone was doing equivalent work in a different Member State their experience was what counted and Italy could not discount that experience on the basis of how the person was employed.

4.4.2.4 Social and tax advantages

Article 7 of Regulation 492/2011 is central in creating a legal basis for equality of social condition and opportunity. The social advantages covered by the Article are not confined to those arising from employment, as a result of Case 207/78 *Ministère Public v Even* [1979] ECR 2019. Mr Even was a French national working in Belgium. He took early retirement, and his pension was reduced accordingly. This was the usual practice, but it did not apply to Belgian nationals who received a war service pension. Mr Even received a French war service pension and so argued that his pension should not be subject to the early retirement reduction. Like nationality, war service is regarded as a quasi-personal relationship between the individual and the state, and the Belgian provision was to give the country's own nationals 'an advantage by reason of the hardships suffered for that country'. Therefore, Mr Even lost his claim. However, the statement of principle made by the Court in the case has wider impact:

The advantages which this regulation extends to workers who are nationals of other Member States are all those which, whether or not linked to a contract of employment, are generally granted to national workers primarily because of their objective status as workers or by virtue of the mere fact of their residence on the national territory.

This principle has been built upon in succeeding cases. For example, Case 65/81 *Reina* [1982] ECR 33 demonstrates that this objective approach may prevent a national social policy from creating disadvantage for other Member State nationals. In *Reina*, an Italian couple living in Germany applied for a discretionary childbirth loan. The loan could only be granted where one member of the couple was German. It was means tested and based on a policy of promoting population growth in Germany. The Landeskreditbank refused the Reinas' application, and defended their claim in the CJEU on the basis that the political objective meant that the loan was not an Article 7(2) social advantage. The CJEU looked at the question from the point of view of the impact upon workers. The actual effect of denying the loan to non-German families was that families from other Member States would be living with less material support than German families. This flew in the face of the purpose and the wording of the Regulation. Article 7(2) could include benefits granted on a discretionary basis, and the CJEU was not debarred from making decisions on social advantages which might have a political effect.

Case 137/84 *Mutsch* [1985] ECR 2681 invoked *Even* to endorse the right of a Luxembourg national to use the German language in certain court proceedings, as Belgians were allowed to do. This social advantage had no connection with employment, and was unlikely to influence nationals of other Member States in their desire or otherwise to travel to Belgium for work. However, the Court recognized that the ability to conduct court proceedings in their own language 'plays an important role in the integration of a migrant worker and his family into the host country, and thus in achieving the objective of free movement for workers'. The objective of the law is not only to ensure equality in working conditions, but also to remove obstacles to the social integration of workers in pursuit of a vision of a European Union in which people are genuinely free to live wherever their occupation takes them.

The judgment in Case 249/83 *Hoeckx* [1985] ECR 973 showed that Article 7(2) of Regulation 492/2011 may be used to fill a gap left by another provision, in this case Regulation 1408/71 on social security benefits. The minimum income allowance, the 'minimex', was granted to people who could show five years' residence in Belgium, which the applicant could not as her residence in Belgium had been interspersed with periods in France. The Court found that the benefit was not one of those covered by Regulation 1408/71, but that it did constitute a social advantage in accordance with Article 7(2). Moreover, the residence condition discriminated against nationals of other Member States in access to this social advantage. It did not apply to Belgian nationals, but even if did it would still be indirectly discriminatory as non-nationals would be less likely to be able to fulfil it.

4.4.2.5 Social assistance

However, Regulation 492/2011 does not give entirely open access for Union citizens to the welfare benefits systems of Member States. Not all benefits of a host state are open to Union citizens who migrate there for work, and conversely migrants may, in moving, lose benefits that would have been payable in their home state. For full coverage of this subject, including discussion of the coordination of social security systems and payments under what was Regulation 1408/71, now Regulation 883/04, reference should be made to EU law sources such as those listed at the end of this chapter. It is a fast-moving and complex area but the following cases illustrate some of the main principles.

In *Lebon*, the Court held that a work-seeker did not qualify for equal social and tax advantages under Article 7 of Regulation 492/2011. The outcome was similar in Case C-138/02 *Collins* [2005] QB 145, although here the CJEU, significantly, affirmed the possibility of a work-seeker claiming social benefits intended to facilitate access to the labour market. In Case C-22/08 *Vatsouras*, benefit claims by work-seekers were argued to be excluded by Article 24(2) of the Citizens' Directive. Article 24(2) allows derogation from the provision of social assistance during the first three months of residence and longer for job-seekers. Although the Court considered—and implicitly upheld the validity of—Article 24(2), it distinguished between different kinds of benefits, stating that 'benefits of a financial nature which, independently of their status under national law, are intended to facilitate access to the labour market cannot be regarded as constituting social assistance within the meaning of Article 24(2) of Directive 2004/38'. This means that such benefits will apparently not be covered by the legislative exclusion from equal treatment laid down in Article 24(2). See further on the distinction Case C-140/12 *Peter Brey*. The fact that the Austrian equivalent of pension credit was not classed as 'social assistance' in the Social Security Regulation did not prevent it from being so in Directive 2004/38.

In respect of claims to social assistance by economically inactive EU citizens, the CJEU in *Brey* held that there should be individualized 'assessment of the specific burden which granting that benefit would place on the social assistance system as a whole by reference to the personal circumstances characterising the individual situation of the person concerned' (para 77). Automatic exclusion of economically inactive EU citizens from welfare benefits is therefore not compatible with individualized assessment. However, in Case C-333/13 *Dano* [2015] ECR nyr, the Court made clear Member States may refuse claims of social assistance to EU citizens who have no intention to work. The trajectory of the case law was confirmed in Case C-67/14 *Alimanovic* [2015] ECR nyr, in which the CJEU held that the German restriction of social assistance to an upper limit of six months following the cessation of employment was compatible with EU law.

4.4.2.6 The 'right to reside' test and *Patmalniece*

In 2004, in an attempt to enforce the limits of entitlement to benefits by migrant EU citizens, particularly those newly arrived, a new test was introduced by the UK government for access to a range of income-related benefits. This involved both factual habitual residence and a legal right to reside in the UK (we leave aside the special position of the Common Travel Area and Irish citizens). Naturally this 'right to reside' was satisfied by UK nationals but only by some EU citizens—and in particular it excluded those not entitled to reside under EU law. In *Patmalniece* [2011] UKSC 11, this was held by the House of Lords to be indirectly discriminatory, drawing on the CJEU's reasoning in *Bressol* (see 4.4.2.7), in which Belgium had incorporated a fairly similar (but 'permanent') right to reside test in its student admissions policy in certain university sectors. However, the Court considered the test justified in the particular case, pension credit, which was covered by the specific Social Security Regulation (at the time Regulation 1408/71). The Commission has started infringement proceedings against the UK in respect of the right to reside test being applied to a range of benefits covered by the social security co-ordination Regulation, 883/04. The government is defending its position on this, and formal court proceedings before the CJEU were initiated in 2013. The CJEU has considered a similar matter from a different Member State in the *Brey* case, discussed already. The Austrian pension credit benefit was considered to be a social assistance benefit for the purposes of Directive 2004/38, and could be made contingent on demonstrating a legal right to reside in the host state. The fact that the individual was entitled to a means-tested benefit of this nature could be an indication that they lacked sufficient resources not to be an unreasonable burden on the host state. However, this conclusion could not be drawn without an individualized assessment.

4.4.2.7 Education

Education is the subject of specific provisions in secondary legislation. Article 7(3) of Regulation 492/2011 gives workers access to vocational schools and retraining on the same basis as national workers. As we have already seen, in the Citizens' Directive the status of worker is retained where training following work was either linked to the former occupation (an example of which might be the situation in *Saint-Prix* where a teaching assistant worker subsequently enrols in a teacher training PGCE course) or was necessary re-training after the worker had become involuntarily unemployed.

Articles 165 and 166 TFEU (ex 126 and 127 EC) provide for the development of education and vocational training within the EU. Students have a specific right of residence for education by virtue of Directive 2004/38 (Article 7(1)(c)) provided they can satisfy the relevant national authority: *(a)* that they have sufficient resources to avoid becoming a burden on the social assistance system of the host Member State; *(b)* they are enrolled in a recognized educational establishment for the principal purpose of following a course of study; and *(c)* they are covered by sickness insurance in respect of all risks in the host state. In common with many other 'self-sufficient' residents, students here for more than six months are entitled to NHS treatment, but the status of this entitlement as fulfilling or defeating the condition of having comprehensive medical insurance remains somewhat problematic. Case C-209/03 *Bidar* [2005] ECR I-02119 established that student maintenance support was no longer entirely outside the scope of the Treaty. Although requiring evidence of integration into the host society by a period of residence before granting such assistance is permissible, it also suggested that Member States must not act disproportionately in setting the conditions of eligibility, including any period of residence required. In the case, UK Regulations had effectively precluded Bidar from attaining 'settled' status even though his length of prior residence was sufficient, and this was seen as disproportionate. However, the subsequently finalized Directive 2004/38 restricts any obligation of payment of maintenance grants by the host state until permanent residence is obtained, usually five years (Article 24) and this raises an interesting tension between the proportionality approach suggested by *Bidar* and the clear rule inserted into the Directive. Case C-158/07 *Forster* [2008] I-08507 suggests that Member States will not be prevented from relying on the Directive to maintain a clear 'bright-line' rule of five-year residence before allowing access to student maintenance support. Case C-184/99 *Grzelczyk* [2001] ECR I 6193, however, established that general social assistance payments may be available for migrant students where they are to host state-national students and that recourse to such benefits should not be an automatic reason for ending a student's lawful residence status, particularly where the individual has been resident for some time. Case C-73/08 *Bressol* [2010] ECR I-02735 affirmed the theoretical possibility of placing numerical restrictions on non-resident students entering specific higher education courses. The Court accepted that this was indirectly discriminatory (the Belgian residency test included satisfying not just a test of residence but other criteria including having a permanent right to reside in Belgium), but insisted that such must be justified. Whilst suitable and proportionate measures to guard against real risks of future shortages of health professionals could be a possible public health justification for imposing indirectly discriminatory conditions on access to university training courses, vague assertions of securing future workers to provide health services in the host state in question were scrutinized somewhat sceptically as a measure justifying the kind of residency tests and quotas applied, although the final decision will rest with the national court. The exportation of student benefits for those studying abroad has also arisen. Germany's regulations both requiring a year of study in Germany prior to exporting support (Case C-11/06 *Morgan* [2007] ECR I-09161), and later of three years' continuous residence before qualifying for the exportation of student support for the entire duration of the course (the applicant's support was limited to one year) has been ruled to be disproportionate (Case C-523/11 *Prinz v Region Hanover*).

By Article 12 of Regulation 492/2011, children dependent on a worker have the same right of access to the education system of the host country as do nationals of that state.

4.5 **Family members**

Through secondary legislation and case law, EU law confers a number of rights on family members of EU citizens. The primary right to be accompanied by family members is contained in the Citizens' Directive and family members of 'qualified persons', as defined by Regulation 7 of the EEA Regulations, are accorded the same rights of entry and residence as their EU citizen sponsors. Rights are granted to members of Union citizens' families without reference to the nationality of those family members, and this is one of the ways in which a third country national may come directly within the ambit of EU law. As rights derive from the relationship with the Union citizen, the family member may be left vulnerable if that relationship is disrupted by, for instance, death, divorce, or migration. The Citizens' Directive goes some way to enhance the rights of family members, though TCNs still have fewer rights than EEA nationals and, as we shall see, the EEA Regulations do not fully implement the Directive.

4.5.1 **Who is a family member?**

'Family member' is a term of art under the Citizens' Directive. It applies to the Union citizen's spouse, their registered partner if the *host* Member State treats such partnerships as equivalent to marriage, children, or grandchildren under 21, dependent children or grandchildren if over 21, parents or grandparents if they are dependent, in each case, on either partner. Being recognized as a family member, as defined, entitles a person to full rights under the Directive. According to Article 3, Member States must also facilitate the admission of other dependants of the Union citizen, including where health grounds strictly require personal care by them, and a partner with whom the Union citizen has 'a durable relationship, duly attested'. This wider group of family members is called in the Directive 'beneficiaries'. In the EEA Regulations, they are called 'extended family members' (reg 8). The precise meaning of 'facilitation' was considered by the Court of Justice in Case C-83/11 *Rahman*. It is clear that, whilst falling short of a directly effective right of entry, provisions enabling extensive examination of the individual circumstances and a reasoned refusal open to review are necessary.

In relation to all except partners and children under 21, rights only accrue where the family member is 'dependent' on the Union citizen. The CJEU has confirmed in Case C-423/12 *Reyes v Sweden* that dependency is a question of fact in EU law. The dependency must be genuine (not contrived) but if it is found that a family member's essential needs are met by the material support of an EEA national, there is no need to enquire as to the reasons for the dependency and there is no need to show emotional dependency. In *Reyes* the applicant was a national of the Philippines, aged 26. Her mother was married to an EU citizen who had exercised his right to free movement. The applicant had trained as a nurse but was unemployed and had not claimed benefits in the Philippines.

Instead, she was financially supported by her EU citizen step-father. Her claim for a residence permit as a dependent family member was rejected by the Swedish authorities. In the course of proceedings challenging that decision, the Swedish courts referred questions to the CJEU. In particular, the Swedish courts were unsure whether in order to establish dependence, it was necessary to show that the applicant could not work or claim benefits in the country of origin. The Court held that it was necessary to demonstrate a situation of real dependence between the family member and the EU citizen but that this would be met in circumstances such as those in Ms Reyes' case where an EU citizen 'regularly, for a significant period, pays a sum of money to that descendant, necessary in order for him to support himself in the State of origin' (para 24). It was not necessary, therefore, for the applicant to show that she could not obtain work or benefits in the Philippines. *Reyes* confirmed and clarified the Court of Justice's earlier judgments in cases pre-dating the Citizens' Directive, in particular, Case C1/05 *Jia v Migrationsverket* [2007] ECR I-1 and Case 316/85 *Centre Public d'Aide Sociale, Courcelles v Lebon* [1987] ECR 2811. It is also clear that the existence of dependency is not necessarily negated by the fact that the family member applies for or receives social assistance (*Lebon*) or by the fact that a family member chooses not to support him or herself through savings (*Lim (EEA—dependency)* [2013] UKUT 00437 (IAC)).

As to the timing of dependency, Regulation 8(2) of the EEA Regulations sets out when dependency must be shown in order for a person to qualify as an extended family member. Dependency prior to entry in the host Member State does not necessarily have to be shown if it can be demonstrated that the applicant was, prior to departure, a member of the EEA national's household. Equally, present dependency need not be shown if the applicant is presently a member of the EEA national's household. However, some combination of prior dependency or membership of the EEA national's household and present dependency or membership of the EEA national's household must be demonstrated: *Dauhoo (EEA Regulations—reg 8(2))* [2012] UKUT 79 (IAC); *Oboh v Secretary of State for the Home Department* [2013] EWCA Civ 1525, [2014] 1 WLR 1680. But as the CJEU clarified in Case C-83/11 *Rahman,* the dependency situation should have been in the country from which the family member comes, rejecting suggestions that it need be in the country from which the Union citizen has come. In other words, it is not necessary to have resided in the same state as the EEA national or to have been dependent on the EEA national before or at the time that s/he entered the host Member State. Further, although Regulation 8(2) permits the dependent relatives of an EEA national's spouse/ civil partner to qualify as extended family members provided the relevant conditions are met, the Court of Appeal in *Soares v Secretary of State for the Home Department* [2013] EWCA Civ 575 [2013] 3 CMLR 847 confirmed that the dependency must be on the EEA national and not his or her spouse/civil partner.

Children may include not only biological children of the EU citizen but, for instance, in *Baumbast* the worker's stepchild benefited from what was then Regulation 1612/68. This is in keeping with the purpose of European secondary legislation and family life as defined by Article 8 of the ECHR, which takes account not only of biological relationships but also of the actuality of relationships.

4.5.2 Family rights of entry and residence

Under Directive 2004/38, family members acquire rights in parallel with their Union citizen family member: to entry; to three months' residence without conditions (Article 6); to a longer period of residence while the Union citizen is a 'qualified person', that is, a worker, self-employed, self-sufficient, or a student (Article 7), or a permanent resident pursuant to Article 16; and to an independent right of permanent residence after five years' residence. This is implemented in the EEA Regulations at Regulations 13–15. Additionally, the family member acquires rights to residence in the particular circumstances detailed at 4.5.4 where their relationship with the Union citizen is severed. Exceptionally, family members may acquire rights to residence outside the provisions of the Directive to make the right of the Union citizen effective (see discussion on *Chen, Surinder Singh,* and *Zambrano* at 4.5.5–7).

Family members should be admitted on proof of their entitlement, that is, of their identity and relationship. For third country nationals, this includes a passport, though for EU nationals identity may be proved by a national identity card. The right of entry of a non-EU family member may be subject to a visa requirement, but it is disproportionate and therefore prohibited to send them back at the border for lack of a visa provided they are able to prove their identity and relationship and there is no evidence to suggest they present a risk to public policy, and so on (Case C-459/99 *Mouvement Contre le Racisme, l'Antisemitisme et la Xenophobie Asbl (MRAX) v Belgium* [2002] 3 CMLR 25). The right only applies to the family member in the host state where the sponsor is residing, not if the family member remains in the sponsor's state of origin whilst the sponsor moves (Case C-40/11 *Iida*).

As originally enacted, the UK Regulations on the issue of a family permit departed from the requirements of the Directive. Regulation 12 required that the family member be either lawfully resident in another Member State, or meet the requirements of the UK immigration rules. This applied to all family members, whether a spouse, child, parent, or other relative. This Regulation relied on *Akrich,* in which the CJEU ruled that a family member must have been lawfully resident in one Member State in order to benefit from free movement rights in another state. The interpretation adopted by the UK, although supported by some other governments, was controversial and departed from the traditional understanding of the scope of EU law rights. Further clarification was required and a challenge was inevitable. Ireland had introduced rules similar to those in the UK immigration rules and these were challenged in Case C-127/08 *Metock* [2008] ECR I-06241, which made it clear that, on this point, *Akrich* was no longer to be relied upon. It also clarified that a TCN national spouse of an EU citizen benefits from the provisions of the Citizens' Directive 'irrespective of when and where their marriage took place and of how the national of a non-member country entered the host Member State' (para 99). In 2011, Regulation 12 of the EEA Regulations was amended to take into account the CJEU's judgment in *Metock.*

4.5.3 Extended family members

As mentioned earlier, the Directive provides that Member States must facilitate the entry of extended family members in accordance with national law. These are defined to include:

- a partner in a duly attested durable relationship;
- another family member who is either dependent on the Union citizen, or lived as a member of their household, or 'on serious health grounds, strictly requires the personal care of the EEA national or their registered partner' (see also EEA Regulations, reg 8).

The EEA Regulations implement the Directive by providing that extended family members *may* be issued with a family permit to join or accompany an EEA national if 'in all the circumstances, it appears to the ECO appropriate to issue' it. By comparison, the ECO must issue a family permit for immediate family members. The effect is that a married or registered civil partner may enter as of right, but an unregistered partner only does so technically as a matter of discretion.

The Tribunal in *AK (Sri Lanka)* [2007] UKAIT 00074 relied on the requirement in Article 3.2 of the Citizens' Directive that the admission of extended family members be facilitated in accordance with national law. They held (upholding *AP and FP (Citizens' Directive Article 3(2); discretion; dependence) India* [2007] UKAIT 00048) that this referred to the substantive national law, and the facilitation was procedural, meaning that difficult hurdles should not be put in the way of such relatives. However, they rejected the argument for the appellant that, as a relative who did not come within the terms of the Regulations (a cousin who had not been dependent on the Union citizen nor a member of her household), he gained a right of residence directly from the Directive. Article 3.2 did not, they thought, create rights of residence; it only defined who would benefit from the requirement to have their entry facilitated. Thus, the Secretary of State was permitted to apply the immigration rules, and a cousin's entry would be a matter of discretion. Although *Metock* concerned close family members, the Court of Appeal in *Bigia v ECO* [2009] EWCA Civ 79 has clarified that a general requirement of prior residence in another EU Member State is not applicable to 'extended'/ 'other' family members either for the same reasons.

4.5.4 Residence without the Union citizen

Family members may acquire or retain rights of residence in certain circumstances even if their relationship with the Union citizen comes to an end. In these cases, there is an explicit difference in the Directive between family members who are not nationals of a Member State and those who are. For family members who are nationals of a Member State, their right of residence is not affected by the death or departure from the country of the Union citizen, nor by divorce, annulment of marriage, or termination of registered partnership. This means that such right as they already have is not affected. In order to obtain permanent residence they must themselves become a worker, self-employed, student, or self-sufficient, or once again become a family member joining or accompanying a Union citizen who satisfies these conditions (Articles 12.1 and 13.1).

Third country national family members are subject to additional requirements. In the case of death of the Union citizen the family member's rights are not affected if they lived as family for one year prior to the death. There is no provision for protecting a TCN where the Union citizen leaves the country. In the case of divorce, annulment, and partnership termination, there are four circumstances in which the right of residence is retained: the marriage or registered partnership lasted three years, at least one of which was in the host state; the TCN has custody of the Union citizen's children; residence is warranted because of particularly difficult circumstances such as domestic violence; or the third country national partner has access rights to a minor child and the Court has ruled that access must happen in the host state. Third country national family members may only acquire permanent residence in these circumstances if they become workers, self-employed, self-sufficient, or if they are members of a family 'already constituted in the host state' of a person who fulfils these conditions. This presumably means that a child of a marriage between a third country national and a Union citizen, who has not acquired an EU nationality, would acquire permanent residence after their parents' divorce if their TCN parent acquired it, say, by being a worker. However, if their TCN parent could not establish their own right to permanent residence but remarried another EU national, then the rights of both child and parent would depend on those of the new EU partner (Articles 12.2 and 13.2).

In the EEA Regulations, children at school of a qualified person (EU worker, self-employed, self-sufficient, or student) who has died or left the UK retain rights of residence (reg 10(3)) as do parents with custody of such a child (reg 10(4)). Third country nationals retain residence under any of the conditions listed in the Directive for the ending of the relationship but only if they themselves are workers, self-employed or self-sufficient, or they are still a family member of an EEA national in one of these categories (reg 10(5)). This creates a substantial disadvantage for TCN family members in the Regulations as compared with the Directive. Further, UK courts have interpreted Article 13 of the Citizens' Directive to mean that a TCN does not acquire a right of residence upon divorce unless the EEA national was in the United Kingdom and exercising Treaty rights at the date of the lawful termination of the marriage: *Amos* [2011] EWCA Civ 552 and *Ahmed (Amos; Zambrano; reg 15A(3)(c) 2006 EEA Regs)* [2013] UKUT 00089 (IAC). Additionally, if a TCN's EU partner dies s/he obtains a permanent right of residence if s/he lived with the qualified person immediately before their death and for the two years preceding, or the death was due to industrial accident or injury (reg 15(e)). So, if a TCN spouse lived with his/her EU citizen spouse for two years and then that person dies, permanent residence is acquired. If a TCN spouse retains his/her right of residence due to having custody of a child and being self-employed, at the end of five years' residence (subject to points which follow) s/he acquires permanent residence.

A family member who retains the right to reside obtains permanent residence after five years' residence, as they would if their relationship had continued without disruption (reg 15(1)(f)). The condition above concerning death of a partner under Regulation 15(e) of the EEA Regulations applies also to EU citizens. Strangely, no provision is made in the EEA Regulations for EU national partners on the end of a relationship, except as the parents of children at school. They would of course have a right to work, and to acquire rights of residence as workers, and permanent residence after five years as a custodial parent or worker and so on.

The failure in the UK Regulations to provide for the departure of the Union citizen is in line with court and tribunal decisions based on the earlier Regulations. In *DA (EEA— revocation of residence document)* [2006] UKAIT 00027, the Tribunal held that where the EU spouse had left the UK the Secretary of State was entitled to revoke a residence document on the basis that the appellant was no longer the spouse of a qualifying person. This was because the qualifying person had ceased to qualify, having left the country; see also *Kungwegwe v SSHD* [2005] EWHC 1427 (Admin). The 2006 Regulations make it clear that a residence document can be revoked where the holder has 'ceased to have a right to reside' under the Regulations.

Case C-267/83 *Diatta v Land Berlin* [1985] ECR 567 held that, while a couple are still married, the non-EU spouse retains rights of residence whether or not they continue to live under the same roof. In the light of the EEA Regulations it seems that this right is retained for an EU spouse, but only for a non-EU spouse if the Union citizen can be proved to be still exercising Treaty rights in the UK or if the relationship is legally ended and one of the conditions set out in Regulation 10(5) applies.

4.5.5 Derived rights from economic freedoms: *Surinder Singh & Carpenter* type cases

As noted earlier, in certain circumstances family members may derive a right to reside outside of the terms of the provisions of the Citizens' Directive. The case of *Surinder Singh*, Case C-370/90, [1992] ECR I-4265 is an early example of this principle. In that case, a British national entered the UK with her Indian husband after they had both been living and working in Germany. If she had never left the UK, she would have had to use domestic UK immigration law to bring her husband in. However, as she had exercised her rights of free movement by going to work in another EU country, it was held that her husband had the right of entry with her under EU law when she returned to her home state, the UK. The reasoning for the judgment is that failing to confer on EU citizens equivalent rights of family reunion to those enjoyed whilst exercising EU rights in another Member State would act as an obstacle and a deterrent to free movement. In Case C-109/01 *Akrich*, the appellants sought to use this principle to rely on EU rights for the husband on returning to the UK after the couple had spent what might be termed a 'working holiday' of six months or so in Dublin. The Court held that the reasons for the couple's attempting to exercise Treaty rights in this way were irrelevant, providing the marriage was genuine. This aspect of the Court's reasoning in *Akrich* still seems sound even though other aspects have been overruled (see 4.5.2, *Metock*).

In 2014 the EEA Regulations were amended so as to include the *Surinder Singh* principle (reg 9). Regulation 9 includes a requirement that the British national had transferred the 'centre of his/her life' to another EU Member State, before seeking to re-enter with his/her TCN spouse. Shortly after the amendment, the CJEU revisited the *Surinder Singh* case in Case C-456/12 *O & B*. The Court confirmed the earlier jurisprudence and held that although EU citizens returning home fall outside the scope of the Citizens' Directive, it should be applied by analogy. As such, the rules on family reunion—under the Directive—which applied to the EU citizen whilst exercising free movement rights in another Member State should be applied by analogy when the citizen returns home. As to the length of time that the returning citizen must spend in another Member State, the CJEU again turned to the Directive to highlight three months as the dividing line between a right to move and a right to reside. It found, thus, that a three-month period would be sufficient to engage the *Surinder Singh* principle. This would appear to cast considerable doubt over the apparently more stringent requirements of the EEA Regulations. A recent Upper Tribunal decision has, however, held the *ratio decidendi* of *Surinder Singh* to be fact-sensitive, finding it to be authority for the 'principle of efficacious enjoyment of Community law rights and the principle of non-discrimination' but no more specific rights: *Osoro (Surinder Singh)* [2015] UKUT 00593 (IAC). Importantly, in both the *Surinder Singh* and *O & B* case, the EU citizens were exercising economic EU free movement rights.

Another circumstance in which there may be a right to family reunion in EU terms for a EU citizen in his/her home Member State is articulated by the CJEU in Case 60/00 *Carpenter* [2002] ECR I-6279, and, more recently, in C-457/12 *S & G*. Both cases involved situations where denial of family reunion for an EU citizen in his home Member State constituted an obstacle to economic free movement rights. Mr Carpenter was a UK national living in the UK, from where he ran a business which had clients in, and involved some travel to, other Member States. Mrs Carpenter was a Philippine national who had overstayed her visitor's visa and married Mr Carpenter. She was refused leave to remain in the UK because of her irregular immigration status at the time of her marriage. She challenged the decision that she should return to the Philippines to apply for entry clearance and a residence permit on the basis that she had EU law rights. The fundamental question in the case was whether these EU rights were engaged at all. The CJEU concluded that they were: Mr Carpenter was exercising his rights under Article 56 TFEU (ex 49 EC) to provide services in another Member State. His capacity to do this was hindered by the disruption to his family life (amongst other things, his wife had to return to the Philippines and so could not look after the children during his absences) but it is not clear how heavily these practical issues weighed with the Court compared with the basic issue of the separation of a married couple (as to this, see consideration of Article 8 ECHR later).

In *S & G*, however, the CJEU was clear that the issue was one of restrictions on free movement (rather than human rights). In that case, both applicants were resident in their home Member State (the Netherlands) but worked either exclusively (in the case of Mr G) or partially (in the case of Mr S) in another Member State. They both had children who were looked after by third country national family members (in Mr G's case, his wife, and in Mr S's case, his mother-in-law). The CJEU held that insofar as re-fusal to grant a right of residence to TCN family members 'discourages the worker from effectively exercising his rights under Article 45 TFEU', that article must be interpreted as conferring a derived right of residence on the TCN family members. It held that the question of whether a worker was so discouraged was a question of fact for the refer-ring court to determine. The CJEU did find, however, in relation to S's case that '[t]he mere fact that it might appear desirable that the child be cared for by the third-country national who is the direct relative in the ascending line of the Union citizen's spouse is not . . . sufficient in itself to constitute such a dissuasive effect' (para 43). It seems, therefore, that more than mere personal preference is required, potentially financial constraints or the fact that both parents work and are not available to take care of the child may suffice, but this will be a subject of future litigation.

4.5.6 *Chen*—the self-sufficient child

Case law has also developed a right to reside for TCN parents where their presence is necessary to give effect to the right of an EU citizen national child, but this right is hedged about with many qualifications and conditions. In Case C-413/99 *Baumbast v SSHD* [2002] 3 CMLR 23, the Court considered the situation of a German man who had been running a business in the UK, but when that failed, left his Colombian wife and children in the UK, which he considered his family home, while he worked outside the EU. The CJEU held that the child of an EU national former worker had a right to remain in education in the host state, and the fact that the EU national parent was now mainly working elsewhere would not affect that right. To hold otherwise would interfere with the mobility of workers within the EU. To make the child's right effective, Mrs Baumbast, too, must have a right to reside with the child. Children and their accompanying TCN parent (still married but separated), need not be self-sufficient if the children remain for education in a *Baumbast*-type situation after one parent has exercised rights as a worker (see Cases C-310/08 *Ibrahim* and C-480/08 *Teixeira*).

Then, Case C-200/01 *Zhu and Chen v SSHD* [2004] Imm AR 333 broke new ground in establishing the right to be accompanied by a parent.

 **Key Case**

Case C-200/02 *Zhu and Chen v SSHD* [2004] Imm AR 333

The claimants were a mother and her child. The mother and her husband were Chinese nationals who worked for a large chemical production company which exported to various parts of the world. In the course of the husband's work he frequently travelled to the EU in-cluding the UK. The couple wished to have a second child, against China's one child policy, and decided to have the child in Northern Ireland. The effect of Irish law at the time was that a child born on the island of Ireland acquired Irish nationality. The baby was an EU citizen and so had free movement rights within the EU. As she had adequate sickness insurance and sufficient resources, she had a right of residence for an indeterminate period of time under then Directive 90/36, now the Citizens' Directive (para 78).

The mother and daughter sought to remain in the UK to exercise this right. The mother was not the daughter's dependant, but she had a right to reside with the child in order to give effect to the child's right. The child was too young to live alone and her right of residence was otherwise meaningless. The conscious use by the couple of EU law was not an abuse because it did not distort the purpose and objectives of EU law, but rather 'took advantage of them by legitimate means to attain the objective which the EU provision sought to uphold; the child's right of residence' (para 122).

Following *Chen*, a range of cases came to the Tribunal and the Court of Appeal in which parents sought to establish a right to reside. In particular, the question of whether the child's economic support may come from the parent's employment in the host Member State arose. The Chens had sufficient income, so the question did not arise for them. The UK immigration rules prevented the family income from coming from employment in the UK. This has also been the approach in the Tribunal, confirmed in the Court of Appeal in *W (China) and X (China) v SSHD* [2006] EWCA Civ 1494, *ER and others (Ireland)* [2006] UKAIT 00096, *GM & AM* [2006] UKAIT 00059, and in *Ali v SSHD* [2006] EWCA Civ 484. However, Case C-34/09 *Zambrano* [2011] ECR I-1177 suggests that Member States may be required to permit a parent to work (see further discussion of the *Zambrano* case later). Regulation 15A integrates, restrictively, the *Chen, Zambrano, Ibrahim, and Teixeira* cases into the EEA Regulations.

4.5.7 *Zambrano* carers

The *Zambrano* case was an innovation as it appeared to apply the logic of *Chen* but in an 'internal situation' (see further 4.6), that is, where the EU citizen children in question were born in their home Member State and had never exercised free movement rights.

 **Key Case**

C-34/09 *Ruiz Zambrano v Office national de l'emploi* [2011] ECR I-1177

In Case C-34/09 *Zambrano*, the question of the internal effect of Articles 18 and 20 TFEU (ex 12, 17, and 18 EC) was raised to question whether EU citizens in their state of birth and sole EU Member State of nationality could assert a right of residence under EU law and rely on the *Chen* principle to acquire residence for a TCN parent/carer. As alluded to earlier, the Court established the capacity of EU law and the status of EU citizenship to protect the residence right of the whole family in this situation, on the basis that the family otherwise faced exile from the whole of the EU and this would be a denial of the genuine enjoyment of the substance of citizenship rights of the infant EU citizen. The Court comments that 'Article 20 TFEU precludes national measures which have the effect of depriving citizens of the Union of the **genuine enjoyment of the substance of the rights conferred by virtue of their status as citizens of the Union** (see, to that effect, *Rottmann*, paragraph 42) . . . A refusal to grant a right of residence to a third country national with dependent minor children in the Member State where those children are nationals and reside, and also a refusal to grant such a person a work permit, has such an effect . . . It must be assumed that such a refusal would lead to a situation where those children, citizens of the Union, would have to leave the territory of the Union in order to accompany their parents. Similarly, if a work permit were not granted to such a person, he would risk not having sufficient resources to provide for himself and his family, which would also result in the children, citizens of the Union, having to leave the territory of the Union. In those circumstances, those citizens of the Union would, in fact, be unable to exercise the substance of the rights conferred on them by virtue of their status as citizens of the Union' (paragraphs 42–4, emphasis added).

Since *Zambrano,* there has been substantial litigation of what, precisely, the CJEU meant by 'genuine enjoyment of the substance' of EU rights. The Court in *Dereci* appeared, however, to give a strong indication.

 **Key Case**

C-256/11 *Murat Dereci v Bundesministerium für Inneres* [2011] ECR I-11315

In Case C-256/11 *Dereci*, the Court still maintained that the Zambrano family faced the choice of staying in Belgium or exile from the entire EU. It emphasized, however, that in the normal situation of a married couple or adult children, who wish to reunite the family in the EU citizen's home Member State, the frustration of that wish by the home Member State's immigration regulations will not necessarily lead to the loss of the core of the EU citizenship right by being obliged to leave the entire EU territory. The Court commented that 'the criterion relating to the denial of the genuine enjoyment of the substance of the rights conferred by virtue of European Union citizen status refers to situations in which the Union citizen has, in fact, to leave not only the territory of the Member State of which he is a national but also the territory of the Union as a whole . . . the mere fact that it might appear desirable to a national of a Member State, for economic reasons or in order to keep his family together in the territory of the Union, for the members of his family who do not have the nationality of a Member State to be able to reside with him in the territory of the Union, is not sufficient in itself to support the view that the Union citizen will be forced to leave Union territory if such a right is not granted' (paragraphs 66 and 68).

The EEA Regulations were amended to reflect the *Zambrano* principle as interpreted restrictively by *Dereci*. Regulation 15(4A) (iii) provides that the British citizen must be 'unable to reside in the United Kingdom if the appellant were to leave.' Yet, the application of the *Zambrano* principle in practice has been the subject of much domestic litigation. In *Damion Harrison (Jamaica) & AB (Morocco) v SSHD* [2012] EWCA Civ 1736 the appellants (TCNs) were facing deportation. Each had British citizen children and in each case it had been found at first instance that if the appellant were removed from the United

Kingdom, the British children would not be compelled to leave. The appellants argued, however, that their deportation would adversely affect their British children's quality of life, and as such the *Zambrano* principle was engaged. The Court of Appeal rejected this submission. Elias LJ (giving the judgment of the court) held that there was no basis for the claim that *Zambrano* extends to cover 'anything short of a situation where the EU citizen is forced to leave the territory of the EU' [63]. He held, therefore, that if the relevant EU citizen would not in practice be compelled to leave the UK if the non-EU family member were to be refused the right of residence, EU law is not engaged. Rights under Article 8 ECHR may be relevant, however (see 4.5.7). The Upper Tribunal in *Sanade (British children—Zambrano—Dereci)* [2012] UKUT 00048(IAC), also in the deportation context, came to a similar conclusion. It found that the *Zambrano* principle would only apply where the British citizen child was dependent on the third country national facing deportation for the exercise of his/her EU right of residence. Where, therefore, another parent had a right to remain in the UK, the principle was found not to apply. The Upper Tribunal in *Sanade* also found that as a result of the *Zambrano* case law, it is not open to the Secretary of State or tribunal to find that it would be reasonable to require a British citizen to relocate outside the EU.

The meaning of 'genuine enjoyment of the substance' of EU rights has also been examined in the context of welfare benefits. In *R (Sanneh) v the Secretary of State for Work and Pensions* [2013] EWHC 793 (Admin) the TCN appellants were the primary carers of British children present in the UK. Each was unable to work and had sought some form of social assistance on the same basis as EU citizens resident in the UK. This had been refused in each case on the basis of regulations that had entered into force on 8 November 2012 (SI 2012/2587, SI 2012/2588, and SI 2012/2612). These regulations expressly excluded TCN primary carers of British children, such as the appellants, from receiving mainstream income-related benefits (including income support, jobseeker's allowance, employment allowance, housing benefit, council tax benefit, and child tax credit). The Administrative Court upheld the refusals (and the lawfulness of the regulations under which the decisions were made). In essence, the effect of the Court's judgment was to find that whilst British citizens must not be forced to leave by economic necessity, their TCN primary carers do not have a right to a particular level of subsistence or quality of life and so they are not entitled to the same levels of assistance as EU citizens.

The question was also revisited by the Upper Tribunal in *Ayinde and Thinjom (Carers—Reg 15A—Zambrano)* [2015] UKUT 00560 (IAC). In that case, the British citizens in question were elderly adults, cared for by TCNs. The Tribunal contrasted this factual matrix with the situation in *Zambrano* to find that whilst '[i]t is beyond the range of proportionate responses that a minor should be required to go into some form of alternative care (be it adoption, foster-care or residential care) in order to enjoy his EU rights were both his parents required to leave. The same consideration does not normally apply in relation to the infirm or elderly.' As such, the Tribunal held that it could not be assumed that an elderly British citizen would be forced to leave the UK and this is a question of fact to be determined. In particular, the tribunals should 'examine critically a claim that a British citizen will leave the Union if the benefits he currently receives by remaining in the United Kingdom are unlikely to be matched in the country in which he claims he will be forced to settle.'

4.5.8 Article 20

Although the CJEU has accepted in *Baumbast* that the right of residence now in Article 20(2)(a) TFEU (ex 18 EC) is directly effective, arguments that this right is entirely unconstrained by the requirements of self-sufficiency in secondary legislation have been unsuccessful. The text of Article 20 TFEU is qualified: 'in accordance with the conditions and limits defined by the Treaties and by the measures adopted thereunder'. Although this qualification is expressed slightly differently from the previous text, there is nothing to indicate that the effect will be any different. In *Chen* itself, the CJEU held that a child had a right to reside under Article 20, which she could exercise because she was economically self-sufficient, as required by secondary legislation. If she had not been able to fulfil these requirements, Article 20 would not have provided an independent right. *Baumbast* and *Grzelczyk* do suggest that, in suitable cases, proportionality may be invoked to place some restraint on the application of the strict letter of the law in the implementation of secondary legislation, but *Trojani* clearly indicates that there are limits to this. Equally the *Zambrano* right has, as seen earlier, been strictly contained.

4.5.9 Article 8 ECHR

The *Carpenter* case discussed earlier was used as an example of a case where an obstacle (Ms Carpenter's removal from the UK) to the exercise of economic free movement (Mr Carpenter's Article 56 rights) was relevant to deriving a right of residence. However, as noted already, it is not clear how heavily the interference with the economic rights weighed in the decision vis-à-vis the interference with the couple's family life under Article 8 ECHR caused by the envisaged enforced separation. Thus, in *Carpenter*, the interference in Mr Carpenter's service provision to other Member States brought the case within the scope of EU law (as to this, see 4.6), which in turn permitted reliance on fundamental rights. The CJEU placed emphasis on the infringement of Article 8 ECHR, which was entailed by separating Mr and Mrs Carpenter. Removal was disproportionate as, although Mrs Carpenter had infringed immigration law, there was no other complaint against her. It is significant that in the other—more recent—case discussed above (*S & G*), the CJEU avoids entirely the question of fundamental rights.

Both here and in the context of expulsion (see 4.8), ECHR rights are in principle highly relevant but in practice the well-established secondary free movement law (Directive 2004/38) often gives as much, or better, protection. Indeed, this was why Mrs Carpenter and Mr Akrich sought to rely on EU law.

4.5.10 Social and tax advantages

Article 24 of the Citizens' Directive provides that family members who obtain a right to remain are entitled to equality of treatment. In Case 32/75 *Fiorini* [1975] ECR 1085, an Italian woman and her children were resident in France. She was the widow of an Italian man who had worked in France and died in an industrial accident. During his life, he had been entitled to a fare reduction card for large families, but when she claimed this after his death it was refused on the grounds that she was not French. She claimed nationality discrimination in breach of Article 18 TFEU (ex 12 EC) and of Article 7(2) Regulation 492/2011 (then 1612/68). This case predated *Even*, but the CJEU still took the view that the social advantages referred to in Article 7(2) did not have to arise from a contract of employment. The Article was intended to refer to all social and tax advantages. As the family had a right to remain in France after Mr Fiorini's death, pursuant to Regulation 1251/70, they also had a right to equal treatment in relation to these social advantages. Combining the effects of Article 7 of Regulation 1251/70 and Article 7(2) of (what is now) Regulation

492/2011 they were entitled to the fare reduction card, as would be any French family in a comparable situation.

An important right for families established in Article 11 of Regulation 1612/68 and continued in Article 23 of Directive 2004/38 is to 'take up any activity as an employed person throughout the territory of that same state'. Case C-10/05 *Mattern and Cikotic* [2006] ECR I-03145 emphasized that the spouse's right to work is to work in the host state, not another Member State.

As mentioned earlier, the worker's children's right to education is the same as that of host state nationals, and continues after their parent has ceased work. Entitlement to educational grants is now dealt with in the Citizens' Directive Article 24(2), and benefits families of workers, the self-employed, and those with permanent residence.

4.5.11 Marriages of convenience

A spouse is held not to qualify as a spouse for the purpose of the Treaty or secondary legislation if the marriage is one of convenience (see *Akrich* at 4.5.1). The EEA Regulations incorporate this in the definition section (reg 2(1)). Civil partnerships are included in the EEA Regulations as being the UK's form of registered partnerships, which are recognized as being equivalent to marriage (as provided for in Article 2(b) of the Citizens' Directive). As such, civil partnerships of convenience are also excluded from the protections of the Directive. By a non-binding resolution of 4 December 1997, the European Council defines marriage of convenience as a marriage entered into 'with the sole aim of circumventing the rules on entry and residence'. This is a more stringent test than the old primary purpose rule in UK law. Evasion must be the *sole* aim of the marriage, rather than one motive among many. The resolution sets out a list of factors which may provide grounds for believing that the marriage is one of convenience. They include, for instance, that the parties do not live together after the marriage, that they do not speak a language understood by both, and they are inconsistent about details such as each other's nationality and job. A European Commission Communication of 2 June 2009 (COM (2009) 313 Final), which provides guidance to Member States on the implementation of the Citizens' Directive, confirms the earlier EU guidance. The Communication lists a set of 'indicative criteria' that suggest where a marriage is unlikely to be one of convenience, and a separate set where it is likely to be one. The Communication was referred to in the leading UK case on marriages of convenience, *Papajorgji (EEA spouse—marriage of convenience) Greece* [2012] UKUT 00038 (IAC). Whilst recognizing that it was not binding, the Upper Tribunal in *Papajorgji* held that it should assist judges and the Home Office in decision-making. *Papajorgji* confirmed that there is no burden of proof on TCN spouses (or civil partners) to establish that they are not party to a marriage of convenience unless the circumstances known to the decision-maker give reasonable grounds for suspicion of such. In the event that reasonable grounds for suspicion exist, the spouse/civil partner should be invited to respond to the basis for these grounds with evidence. In 2014, the EU Commission published a Handbook ('Handbook on addressing the issue of alleged marriages of convenience between EU citizens and non-EU nationals in the context of EU law on free movement of EU citizens'), which further confirms and develops the EU's approach to marriages and civil partnerships of convenience.

The Citizens' Directive permits measures to combat fraud or abuse of rights, including marriages of convenience (Article 35), but these must be proportionate and subject to the procedural safeguards in Articles 30 and 31 of the Directive. On 1 January 2014, amendments to the EEA Regulations came into effect conferring on the Secretary of State the power to make an 'EEA decision' where there are reasonable grounds to suspect fraud or abuse and it is proportionate to do so given all the circumstances of the case (reg 21B). The types of behaviours listed in Regulation 21B specifically include entering, attempting to enter, or assisting another person in entering or attempting to enter a marriage of convenience (21B(1)(c)). Regulation 19(3) states that a person may be removed from the UK if the Secretary of State has found that that person's removal is justified on grounds of abuse of rights under reg 21B(2). Guidance issued by UK Visas and Immigration provides a list of factors to be undertaken in deciding whether it is proportionate to make a decision against a person on grounds of abuse of rights. These include the level of the abuse, the personal circumstances of the individual, and the nature of the decision (e.g., revocation of documentation, refusal of documentation, or removal from the UK).

4.6 Scope of EU law and internal situations

In a number of cases, applicants have sought to use rights granted by European law in situations that have not involved the crossing of national borders. Traditionally, the CJEU has held that these situations must be regarded as internal to Member States and thus not involving freedom of movement and not engaging EU law. In Case C-175/78 *R v Saunders* [1979] ECR 1129, a British national from Northern Ireland who was convicted of an offence in England was required to return to Northern Ireland and keep out of England and Wales for three years. The Court declined to interfere with this. They took the position that the state was entitled to impose restrictions within the Member State upon its own nationals where this was done in the course of criminal law.

Cases 35 and 36/81 *Morson & Jhanjhan* [1982] ECR 3723 took a similar approach in relation to family rights and Cases C-64 and 65/96 *Uecker & Jaquet* [1997] ECR I-3171 confirmed that EU citizenship does not in the Court's view alter this fundamentally. A number of commentators have suggested that if borders within the EU are to be removed, the requirement of movement across borders in order to trigger family reunion rights is artificial. The artificiality was recognized by the Commission in early drafts of the Family Reunion Directive in proposing to abolish this discrimination in respect of family reunion, but this did not survive to the final version of the directive. In *Carpenter, Surinder Singh*, and *Chen* (all discussed earlier—as well as subsequent cases building on these principles), the CJEU rejected the argument that the situation was purely internal and found sufficient link to the exercise of EU law rights—the time spent working in Germany, the services provided regularly in other Member States, and the residence as an Irish national in the UK. The *Zambrano* case, discussed in detail earlier, also is an example of an apparently 'internal' situation (the Zambrano children were Belgian nationals who had never left Belgium) which nevertheless had been found by the CJEU to come within the scope of EU law. Initially, it appeared that in the *Zambrano* judgment the Court was distancing itself from the 'internal situation' limitation on EU rights. However, the case law that has followed emphasizes that the reach of EU law into apparently 'internal situations' is by no means fully settled yet.

 **Key Case**

C-434/09 *Shirley McCarthy v SSHD*

In addition to the subsequent case law directly on the *Zambrano* principle discussed earlier, Case C-434/09 *McCarthy* is perhaps another indication that *Zambrano* does not herald the end of the 'internal situation' for good. The CJEU perhaps rather surprisingly refused to recognize the effect of the dual (Irish/British) nationality of a British resident wife who wished to assert her Irish nationality as defeating the 'internal situation' argument so that her Jamaican husband could rely on EU rights rather than the domestic UK immigration regulations. She had apparently never worked in the UK or Ireland and was dependent on benefits. The Court comments that 'no element of the situation of Mrs McCarthy, as described by the national court, indicates that the national measure at issue in the main proceedings has the effect of depriving her of the genuine enjoyment of the substance of the rights associated with her status as a Union citizen, or of impeding the exercise of her right to move and reside freely within the territory of the Member States, in accordance with Article 21 TFEU. Indeed, the failure by the authorities of the United Kingdom to take into account the Irish nationality of Mrs McCarthy for the purposes of granting her a right of residence in the United Kingdom in no way affects her in her right to move and reside freely within the territory of the Member States, or any other right conferred on her by virtue of her status as a Union citizen . . . by contrast with the case of *Ruiz Zambrano*, the national measure at issue in the main proceedings in the present case does not have the effect of obliging Mrs McCarthy to leave the territory of the European Union. Indeed, as is clear from paragraph 29 of the present judgment, Mrs McCarthy enjoys, under a principle of international law, an unconditional right of residence in the United Kingdom since she is a national of the United Kingdom' (paragraph 50).

Zambrano and *McCarthy* sit uneasily together and it is clear that the reach of EU law in situations where the 'internal situation' argument is raised still remains in a state of uncertainty. Indeed, the question of the scope of EU law within the citizen's own state has continued to raise issues. *Iida* confirms that the migrant sponsor's family member staying in the sponsor's state of origin is not protected by EU law, nor is the new third country national step-parent who has married the TCN parent of an EU citizen after the breakdown of the initial marriage to the initial EU citizen sponsor (Case C-356 and 357/11 *O and S*), unless the effect of this is to deny the genuine enjoyment of the substance of the citizenship rights of the child. The latter point is a question for the national court. Case C-87/12 *Ymeraga* re-iterates the 'denial of the genuine enjoyment of the substance of the rights' test, indicating that in a case where a Kosovan migrant had acquired Luxembourg nationality, his parents and brothers could not rely on EU law to seek residence with him in Luxembourg. It appears that the CJEU is directing national courts to consider whether in such circumstances (indicated to be 'exceptional') there is 'an intrinsic connection with the freedom of movement of the EU Citizen which prevents the right of entry and residence being refused to those nationals in the Member State of residence of that Citizen, in order not to interfere with that freedom'. *Ymeraga* re-iterates that the (entirely understandable and normal) desire to bring about reunification of the family in the sponsor's state of residence and nationality is not in itself sufficient to demonstrate this.

4.7 **Public service exceptions**

The TFEU recognizes that some kinds of work may require a particular affiliation to the state, and where this is the case it may be legitimate for the state to restrict work to its own nationals. Accordingly, Article 45 TFEU (ex 39 EC) includes an exception for employment in the public service, giving the state the right to discriminate on the basis of nationality in opportunities to be admitted to such jobs.

What this exception covers is one of those issues, like the definition of a worker, which the CJEU regards as a matter of EU law. The definitions of Member States will not be conclusive, as this would give them power to define the terms of their own exemption, which would not be appropriate. Two approaches to the question have been identified: the 'institutional approach' and the 'functional approach'. The institutional approach says that because a person is employed by a particular body, say, a national railway, this employment is defined as employment in the public service. The functional approach looks at what is entailed in the work and determines whether this should qualify as public service. The CJEU prefers the latter approach, while Member States have tended to argue (unsuccessfully) in favour of the former.

In Case 149/79 *Commission v Belgium*, the Court set out some characteristics which could bring employment within the definition of public service. First, the post presumes on the part of the employee and employer a 'special relationship of allegiance to the State'. Second, there is a reciprocity of rights and duties which form the foundation of the bond of nationality. Third, the post must involve the exercise of powers conferred by public law and duties designed to safeguard the general interests of the state.

If and when a non-national is actually employed in public service, Article 45(4) cannot be used to treat them less favourably than national workers. In Case 195/98 *Österreicher Gewerkschaftbund, Gewerkschaft Öffentlicher Dienst v Austria* [2000] ECR I-10497, a union challenged the practice of discounting periods of service spent in other Member States when reckoning periods of service for the purposes of pay and promotion. The government argued that teachers were employed in the public service and therefore exempt under Article 45(4). This argument was doomed as it was already settled law that teachers were not covered by the public service exception, but the Court also held that non-recognition of earlier periods of service was not a matter connected with access to employment but to conditions of employment once in post, and thus not covered by Article 45(4).

For the self-employed, the exception in Article 51 (and 62) TFEU (ex 55 and 66 EC) takes effect in relation to 'activities which in that state are connected, even occasionally, with the exercise of official authority'. In Case 2/74 *Reyners v Belgium* [1974] ECR 631, a Dutch lawyer had obtained his legal education in Belgium, but was refused admission to the Belgian bar on the grounds that he was not of Belgian nationality. The Court said that the extension of the exception to the whole profession was not permissible where activities connected with the exercise of official authority were separable from professional activity as a whole. The exercise of official authority in the legal profession was the exercise of judicial authority by judges, and not contact with the courts by advocates.

4.8 **Decisions taken on public policy, public security, and public health grounds**

The public policy, security, and health exception is the only basis for deportation of an EEA national, and should be compared with grounds for other foreign nationals, discussed in chapter 15. Substantial differences will be seen, as the deportation of an EU citizen is in almost every case an interference with their Treaty right to freedom of movement. Any ECHR rights are additional to this. The EEA Regulations transpose Articles 27–29 of the Citizen's Directive on public policy, security, and health at Regulation 21.

4.8.1 Public health

This may be dealt with briefly. Article 29 of the Directive says:

1. The only diseases justifying measures restricting freedom of movement shall be [those] with epidemic potential as defined by . . . the World Health Organization and other infectious or contagious parasitic diseases if they are the subject of protective provisions applying to nationals of the host Member State.
2. Diseases occurring after three months from the date of arrival shall not constitute grounds for expulsion from the territory.

Medical examinations may only be required 'where there are serious indications that it is necessary' within the first three months after arrival. This is transposed by Regulation 21(7) of the EEA Regulations.

4.8.2 Public policy

This is the more contentious and frequently used ground, which also encompasses public security. There is no definition of public policy in the Directive or by the CJEU, but the Court interprets the Directive restrictively in order not to interfere with the purposes of the Treaty.

Article 27(2) of the Directive provides:

Measures taken on grounds of public policy or public security shall comply with the principle of proportionality and shall be based exclusively on the personal conduct of the individual concerned. Previous criminal convictions shall not in themselves constitute grounds for the taking of such measures.

The personal conduct of the individual concerned must represent a genuine, present and sufficiently serious threat affecting one of the fundamental interests of society. Justifications that are isolated from the particulars of the case or that rely on considerations of general prevention shall not be accepted.

This is transposed by Regulation 21(1)–(6) of the EEA Regulations. To appreciate the radical nature of this paragraph comparison needs to be made with grounds for UK deportations discussed in chapter 15, where it will be seen that a general policy of deterrence has often been accepted by the courts as justifying an individual deportation. This new element in Article 27(2) reinforces the social objectives of free movement law, showing that the power of the state in relation to the individual is curbed by EU law.

Accordingly, one of the earliest and foundational decisions on the application of the public policy exception would almost certainly not be decided the same way today. Case 41/74 *Van Duyn* [1974] ECR 1337, concerned whether association with an organization could amount to personal conduct. Ms Van Duyn was a member of the Church of Scientology and was refused leave to enter the UK to work for the Church because the UK government considered its activities to be socially harmful. The CJEU concluded that this was within the permissible range of discretion for a Member State, and this was the case even if (as was the case here) the organization had not been made unlawful, and its nationals could participate in it without legal sanction. It would be an undesirable distortion of social policy to require a government to outlaw an activity so that it could prevent people from entering the country to take part in it. The Court would, however, expect to see some administrative measure taken against the activity. In the *Van Duyn* case a statement in Parliament sufficed for that.

Case 115/81 *Adoui and Cornouaille* [1982] ECR 1665 takes a different approach, and one more likely to be used if *Van Duyn* were heard again today. The CJEU would be concerned to see that effective measures were taken against nationals who engaged in the activity in question before regarding it as a suitable basis for excluding a non-national. Prostitution was not illegal in Belgium and there was not a strong enough policy reason to exclude non-nationals for engaging in an activity that was not prohibited, or at least subject to effective repressive and deterrent measures, for nationals.

EU nationals should not be deported as a sanction for administrative lapses or irregularities. In Case C-215/03 *Oulane* [2005] ECR I-1215, it was disproportionate to detain and deport a French national who did not produce proof of identity on two occasions when requested.

4.8.2.1 Criminal convictions

The most common basis for expulsion on grounds of public policy is criminal conduct. The CJEU has reinforced on a number of occasions that previous convictions do not in themselves constitute grounds for exclusion or expulsion, although such convictions may be taken into account in determining whether someone should be deported on the grounds of public policy. A leading case is Case 30/77 *R v Bouchereau* [1977] ECR 1999. The defendant, a French national working in the UK, was convicted for a second time of unlawful possession of drugs. The sentencing court wished to recommend that he be deported and referred two questions to the CJEU. The Court ruled, first, that a recommendation for deportation was a 'measure' within Article 3; and, second, that 'the existence of previous criminal convictions can only be taken into account in so far as the circumstances which gave rise to that conviction are evidence of personal conduct constituting a present threat to the requirements of public policy'. Elaborating, the Court went on, 'recourse . . . to the concept of public policy presupposes . . . a genuine and sufficiently serious threat to the requirements of public policy affecting one of the fundamental interests of society'. However, the Court also issued a caveat that, in sufficiently serious cases, conduct alone might warrant deportation. Directive 2004/38 adopts these words from *Bouchereau*.

By contrast, the personal conduct of the applicant in Case 67/74 *Bonsignore* [1975] ECR 297 could not be said to pose any threat to public policy affecting one of the fundamental interests of society. He was an Italian worker resident in Germany who, while handling a gun (which he had purchased illegally) accidentally but negligently killed his younger brother. The incident was a tragic accident, and there was no reason to deprive Mr Bonsignore of his German residence on the grounds of public policy.

There is thus no scope for *automatic* expulsion connected to the commission of criminal offences (Case C-50/06 *Commission v Netherlands* [2007] ECR I4383, also Case C-348/96 *Donatella Calfa* [1999] ECR I-0011). This is recognized in the EEA Regulations, at Regulation 21(5)(e), which states in terms that 'a person's previous criminal convictions do not in themselves justify the decision [to deport]'. Equally, the UK Borders Act 2007 ss 32–39, which introduce compulsory deportation for certain criminal convictions (see chapter 15), contains an exception for those protected by EU law so that deportation will not be automatic, although now the threshold for *consideration* for removal of even EU/EEA nationals in cases of drugs, violent, or sexual offences has recently been reduced from sentences of two years to 12 months.

4.8.2.2 Weighing up the conduct

We can usefully compare the EU public policy proviso with the UK law concept of a deportation being 'conducive to the public good'. Theoretically, the emphasis in both is not on what the individual has done in the past but on the effect on society of their continued presence but the European law standard makes more demands on the state than the UK law standard, as the state's argument must be sufficient to outweigh the right of freedom of movement, within a system in which this freedom is the primary purpose, and the Court has repeatedly stated that this power of derogation must be interpreted restrictively.

In UK courts and tribunals, the caveat in *Bouchereau*, permitting deportation when past conduct is sufficiently serious, has been applied in offences involving Class A drugs—for instance, the case of *Marchon* [1993] Imm AR 384 in which a Portuguese doctor had been convicted of importing 4.5 kilos of heroin. This view has been re-garded as 'unsound as a matter of Community law' by the Tribunal in *MG and VC (EEA Regulations 2006; 'conducive' deportation; Ireland)* [2006] UKAIT 00053. In *Essa* [2012] EWCA Civ 1718, the Court of Appeal considered the relevance of rehabilitation in deportation decisions. It found that, applying the CJEU authorities discussed earlier, that in applying Regulation 21, the decision-maker must consider whether a decision to deport may prejudice the prospects of rehabilitation in the host Member State and this must be weighed in the balance in considering proportionality under Regulation 21(5)(a).

In cases where the proposed deportee has a family or private life in the UK, the dis-ruption to this must be proportionate to the public interest pursued in accordance with Article 8 ECHR, and various factors relevant to such a balancing assessment are enumerated in Article 28 of Directive 2004/38 (and transposed in reg 21(6)). These are equivalent to the widest possible interpretation of Article 8 ECHR, including 'social and cultural integration into the host member state'. The very restrictive interpreta-tions on the application of Article 8 ECHR that have been inserted into the Rules (and that now appear in primary legislation)—see further chapters 5 and 15—do not apply to EU citizens. However, it appears that it is the practice of the Secretary of State, in the expressed interests of 'consistency and fairness in the application of Article 8' to apply these provisions by analogy. This approach is arguably contrary to EU law.

4.8.2.3 Protection for long-term residents

In addition to the general principles applying to all EU citizens, Directive 2004/38 also contains further protections against expulsion where the individual has long residence in the host state. This means that there are now three tiers of protection against expul-sion decisions, as follows:

1. A decision against any Union citizen or their family member, only on grounds of public policy, public health, or public security. Considerations as just discussed, Article 27(1) and Regulation 21(2), (5), and (6).

2. An expulsion decision against a Union citizen or their family member who has the right of permanent residence may only be taken on 'serious grounds of public policy or public security', Article 28(2) and Regulation 21(3).

3a. An expulsion decision against a Union citizen who has resided for 10 years may only be taken on 'imperative grounds of public security', Article 28(3)a and Regulation 21(4)(a).

3b. An expulsion decision against a minor, unless expulsion is necessary for the best interests of the child, also may only be taken on 'imperative grounds of public security', Article 28(3)b and Regulation 21(4)(b).

It is clear that expelling an EU national is intended to be a rarity.

'Imperative grounds of public security' were interpreted in *MG and VC* [2006] UKAIT 00053 to mean something more than 'the ordinary risk to society arising from the commission of further offences by a convicted criminal' (para 34). The Home Office representative suggested that what was intended was the commission or suspicion of terrorist offences, but the Court of Appeal in *LG (Italy) v SSHD* [2008] EWCA Civ 190 said that 'imperative grounds of public security' did not necessarily connote a terrorist threat.

 **Key Case**

Case C-145/07 *Land Baden-Württemberg v Panagiotis Tsakouridis*

Tsakouridis was a Greek national who was born and had lived in Germany all his life and had an unlimited residence permit there since 2001. He then went back briefly to Greece a couple of times in 2004/5 but was returned under an arrest warrant and eventually convicted of various narcotics offences. In 2007 he was sentenced to six and a half years in prison. This was not his first conviction, however, as he had a criminal record going back to 1998. He was informed that his permanent residence was revoked and he was liable to expulsion to Greece, relying (apparently decisively and exclusively) on the five-year sentence threshold in relevant German regulations. This expulsion was overturned on appeal to the Stuttgart Administrative Court on the grounds that there were no 'imperative' grounds of public security and that crossing the five-year sentence threshold making expulsion *possible* did not *automatically* lead to this conclusion. On reference to the Court of Justice during the course of a further appeal against the quashing of the expulsion, the CJEU made it clear that narcotics offences were not necessarily excluded from being viewed either as 'serious grounds of public policy or security' or as 'imperative reasons of security' if they were serious enough. However, it also made clear that any national regulation purporting to use the length of sentence alone as an indication of such 'serious' or 'imperative' reasons being established without taking into account all the factors involved could not be sustained. On this point the initial decision seems to have been unsustainable and its quashing by the Stuttgart Administrative Court justified, although the case would not automatically be precluded for *consideration* as one of 'imperative reasons of public security' purely because it involved a drugs offence, if it were serious enough.

Since this case, it has been made clear that serious sexual offences are also capable of being such 'imperative reasons' if the circumstances of the offence are sufficiently serious (Case C-348/09 *P.I.*). The case in question concerned prolonged child sexual abuse within a step-family setting. The Advocate General suggested that an effect on the public at large (which perhaps could be argued as not necessarily the case with crime committed in a domestic setting) should be required. However, he also suggested that the circumstances of the abuse had contributed to its remaining hidden for so long and thus to the appellant deriving the enhanced protection, as he would have been deported much sooner had the offences come to light at an earlier stage. The Advocate General thought that this should not be permitted if the enhanced protection had been gained through the criminality. The Court satisfied itself with saying that the circumstances must disclose 'particularly serious characteristics' and repeated the general guidance that the need to show a present and serious threat to the fundamental interests of society implies propensity to offend in the future, and that all the circumstances of the individual concerned must be taken into account before any removal decision is made.

As noted earlier, the CJEU has now determined that imprisonment interrupts the continuity of residence for the purposes of accruing five or ten years' residence (see Case C-378/12 *Onuekwere* [2014] ECR nyr).

4.8.2.4 Procedural rights

Directive 2004/38 provides for a right to judicial procedures for all expulsion decisions. Furthermore, it provides that where an application is made for an interim order to suspend enforcement, with limited exceptions for repeat cases and where expulsion is based on 'imperative grounds of national security', no enforcement action may be taken until that application has been heard. Regulation 26 of the EEA Regulations provide rights of appeal to the First-tier Tribunal (with onward appeal to the Upper Tribunal and ordinary appellate courts) for the majority of decisions made under the Regulations. In general, therefore, EEA decisions survive the cull of rights of appeal enacted by the Immigration Act 2014 (see chapters 1 and 7).

An important decision in terms of European law's impact in the UK was C-357/98 *R v SSHD ex p Yiadom* [2000] ECR I-9265. A decision refusing leave to enter after the applicant had been in the UK for seven months on temporary admission was in reality a decision to remove her, not a decision on entry. This would therefore attract a right under what was then Article 9 Directive 64/221 to have an appeal before removal, which was not available to a non-European. As mentioned in chapter 1, one of the sub-themes of immigration and asylum law in the UK at present is the creation of a kind of non-status; a condition of being present in body but not in law. Here, the CJEU took a very realistic approach. It is not appropriate to give someone a temporary status in the country, then make a decision which means they must leave, but to label it a decision on entry rather than removal and so deprive them of appeal rights (compare *Khadir*, discussed in chapter 14).

In the case of *ZZ* (Case C-300/11) the UK's Special Immigration Appeals Commission and Special Advocate processes were considered. There were allegations of terrorist links and activities and some closed material was relied on to deny re-entry to the UK in 2005 to a dual French-Algerian national who had been granted permanent residence in the UK 2004 after nearly 15 years of residence. The CJEU indicated that any refusal to disclose the full evidence on which an expulsion or exclusion is based must be 'limited to that which is strictly necessary' and that the applicant 'must be informed, in any event, of the essence of those grounds in a manner which takes due account of the necessary confidentiality of the evidence'.

However, despite the generally strong procedural protections in the Citizens' Directive, it permits Member States to exclude 'the individual concerned from their territory pending the redress procedure.' However, Member States 'may not prevent the individual from submitting his/her defence in person, except when his/her appearance may cause serious troubles to public policy or public security or when the appeal or judicial review concerns a denial of entry to the territory' (Article 31(4)). Recent amendments to the EEA Regulations have made use of this provision of the Directive. Regulation 27 now permits EU citizens to be removed from the UK pending their appeal in a number of circumstances, primarily, deportation decisions. There is no right of appeal against such decisions.

The Upper Tribunal in *R (Bilal Ahmed) v Secretary of State for the Home Department (EEA/s 10 appeal rights: effect) IJR* [2015] UKUT 00436 (IAC) considered the case of expulsion decisions that are not taken on grounds of public policy, security, and health. It found that there was no general principle of automatic suspensive effect applying to expulsion decisions taken against EEA nationals and/or their family members. The Tribunal held therefore that Third Country National family members with a right of appeal under Regulation 26 of the EEA Regulations against a decision to refuse them a residence card may be removed under s 10 of the Immigration and Asylum Act 1999 pending the hearing of their appeal (see further chapter 16). Whilst interim relief against removal in these circumstances may be secured through judicial review proceedings, the Upper Tribunal indicated that insofar as the Secretary of State reasonably suspects that a person is party to a marriage of convenience, a judicial review application against removal based on that marriage will not succeed.

4.8.2.5 Expulsion of those not exercising Treaty rights: the case of homeless EEA nationals

The UK authorities have indicated their intention to enforce more strictly the limits of EU residence rights against those not in fact entitled to be here because they are not, or are no longer, 'qualified persons' exercising Treaty rights (see Weiss, IANL 2010). This is recognized in the EEA Regulations, which now expressly contain removal powers against EEA nationals and/or their family members who do not have or cease to have a right to reside: Regulation 19(3)(a). As noted at 4.3.1, this appears to be permitted by EU law, after individual consideration (and provided it is not automatic) on the basis of being or becoming an 'unreasonable burden' on the social assistance system. Some, however, have questioned the use of removal powers against those who are, by and large because of the 'right to reside' test (see 4.4.2.6), not entitled to claim income-related welfare benefits. If such individuals are not entitled under national legislation to such assistance, how, Weiss argues, can they be an 'unreasonable burden' on the system from which they are excluded by law?—although after the Court of Appeal judgment in *Lekpo-Bouza* [2010] EWCA Civ 909, his suggestion that reliance on access to NHS care would normally fulfil rather than negate the 'health insurance' condition may be more questionable. The legality of removals on the basis of lack of exercise of Treaty rights on both points (means and health insurance) remains to be fully clarified. The recent case of *R (Kondrak) v Secretary of State for the Home Department* [2015] EWHC 639 (Admin) shows, however, that where EU rights are discounted by the Home Office, this may result in claims for substantial damages. In that case, the Claimant was a Polish national who had been either working or work-seeking during his stay in the UK. At times, he was forced to sleep rough and whilst doing so was encountered by the Home Office and detained, pending removal. He was detained for over five months and when he was released he was prohibited from working. The Home Office sought to remove him as someone who was not exercising EU Treaty rights but the difficulty with this position was that it was the Home Office who had engineered that situation since both the detention and prohibition on working prevented him from exercising his EU rights to work and seek work. The Administrative Court found that Mr Kondrak had been unlawfully detained and the Home Office conceded that the restriction on work was unlawful.

4.9 European enlargement and freedom of movement

The fundamental status of Union citizen applies to nationals of states recently acceded to the EU. There is no status such as 'new union citizen'. Nevertheless, the right reserved to old Member States to phase in their recognition of the rights of nationals of the states that acceded in 2004 and 2007 delayed the full implementation of rights for nationals of the states that acceded in 2004 and 2007 and still remain relevant for Croatian nationals. It seems highly likely that any future accessions may well also be subject to similar arrangements.

4.10 Conclusion

The Citizens' Directive represents a significant advance in developing rights of free movement. However, in the UK, the interpretation of the Directive by the courts and in Regulations maintains a consistently restrictive approach. While, in theory, Article 20 TFEU provides a right of residence, in practice the extent of rights are still largely dictated by and subject to the limitations and conditions laid down in secondary legislation. Probing the limits of these rights under EU law remains a fertile source of litigation, as will undoubtedly be the case in respect of any renegotiation of the rights of EU citizens that may be secured by the current Conservative government.

QUESTIONS

1　Do you have any sympathy with the view that Article 20 TFEU (ex 18 EC) requires that the mobility of citizens of the Union should not be impeded by being unable to claim benefits while they look for work?

2　Do you agree with the Court in *Akrich* that motivation is irrelevant to claiming EU law rights, such as those rights arising from the *Surinder Singh* or *Chen* cases?

3　What are the boundaries of 'internal effect' following *Zambrano* and *McCarthy* (and subsequent cases)? What is the test (or tests) for the engagement of EU law rights?

4　Why do you think the CJEU relied on Article 8 ECHR in *Carpenter* but not *S & G*? Was the CJEU right not to refer to human rights in the latter case?

5　Do you agree with the CJEU's assessment of the meaning of 'genuine enjoyment of the substance of EU rights' in *Dereci* and the subsequent judgments of the English courts discussed earlier?

 online resource centre For guidance on answering questions, visit the Online Resource Centre www.oxfordtextbooks.co.uk/orc/clayton7e/.

FURTHER READING

Barnard, Catherine (2013) *The Substantive Law of the EU: The Four Freedoms* (4th edn) (Oxford: Oxford University Press).

Berry, Adrian (2014) 'Deprivation of nationality and citizenship: the role of EU law' *Journal of Immigration, Asylum and Nationality Law* vol. 28, no. 4, pp 355–66.

Carlier, Jean-Yves (2005) 'Case Note on *Chen*' *Common Market Law Review* vol. 42, pp. 1121–31.

Costello, Cathryn (2009) 'Free Movement and "Normal Family Life" in the Union' *Common Market Law Review* vol. 46, p. 587.

Cox, Simon (2014) 'Case Comment: *Saint Prix v Secretary of State for Work and Pensions*' *Journal of Immigration Asylum and Nationality Law* vol. 28, no. 3, pp 288–90.

Craig, Paul and de Búrca, Gráinne (2015) *EU Law: Text, Cases and Materials* (6th edn) (Oxford: Oxford University Press).

Currie, Samantha (2006) '"Free" Movers? The Post-accession Experience of Migrant Workers in the UK' *European Law Review*, April, pp. 207–99.

Currie, Samantha (2009) 'Accelerated Justice or a Step too Far? Residence Rights of Non-EU Family Members and the Court's ruling in *Metock*' *European Law Review* vol. 34, no. 2, p. 310.

Dautricourt, Camille and Thomas, Sebastian (2009) 'Reverse Discrimination and Free Movement of Persons under Community Law: All for Ulysses, nothing for Penelope?' *European Law Review* vol. 34, no. 3, p. 433.

Guild, Elspeth (ed.) (1999) *The Legal Framework and Social Consequences of Free Movement of Persons in the European Union* (London: Kluwer Law International).

Guild, Elspeth (2014) 'Case Comment: *S v Minister voor Immigratie, Integratie en Asiel* (C-457/12)/*O v Minister voor Immigratie, Integratie en Asiel* (C-456/12)' *Journal of Immigration, Asylum and Nationality Law* vol. 28, no. 3, pp. 284–8.

Handoll, John (1988) 'Article 48(4) EEC and Non-National Access to Public Employment' *European Law Review* vol. 13, no. 4, pp. 223–41.

Jacqueson, Catherine (2002) 'Union Citizenship and the Court of Justice: Something New under the Sun? Towards Social Citizenship' *European Law Review* vol. 27, no. 3, pp. 260–81.

Journal of Immigration, Asylum and Nationality Law vol. 21, no. 3 is a special issue devoted to EU law, focusing on the implementation of the Citizens' Directive in the UK. All seven articles are relevant.

Kochenov, D. (2013a) 'The Right to Have what Rights? EU Citizenship in Need of Clarification' *European Law Journal* vol. 19, no. 4, pp. 502–16.

Kochenov, D. (2013b) 'The Essence of EU Citizenship Emerging from the Last Ten Years of Academic Debate: Beyond the Cherry Blossoms and the Moon' *International & Comparative Law Quarterly* vol. 62, pp. 97–136.

Kochenov, D. and Plender, R. (2012) 'EU Citizenship: From an Incipient Form to an Incipient Substance? The Discovery of the Treaty Text' *European Law Review* vol. 37 no. 4, pp. 369–96.

Kubal, Agnieszka (2009) 'Why Semi-legal? Polish Post-2004 EU Enlargement Migrants in the United Kingdom' *Journal of Immigration, Asylum and Nationality Law* vol. 23, no. 2, p. 148.

McKee, Richard (2007) 'Regulating the Directive? The AIT's Interpretation of the Family Members Provisions in the EEA Regulations' *Journal of Immigration, Asylum and Nationality Law* vol. 21, no. 4, pp. 334–40.

Moffatt, Rowena (2015) 'Case Comment: *Sanneh and others v Secretary of State for Work and Pensions and others*',*Journal of Immigration Asylum and Nationality Law* vol. 29, no. 2, pp. 232–3.

Oosterom-Staples, Helen (2005) 'Case Note on *Collins*', *Common Market Law Review* vol. 42, pp. 205–233.

Reynolds, S. (2013) 'Exploring the Intrinsic Connection between Free Movement and the Genuine Enjoyment Test: Reflections on EU Citizenship After Iida' *European Law Review* vol. 38, no. 3, pp. 376–92.

Richards, Tom (2012) '*Zambrano, McCarthy* and *Dereci:* reading the leaves of EU citizenship jurisprudence' *Judicial Review* vol. 17, no. 3, pp. 272–85.

Spaventa, Eleanor (2005) 'Case Note on *Akrich*', *Common Market Law Review* vol. 42, pp. 225–239.

Spaventa, Eleanor (2008) 'Seeing the woods for the trees? On the scope of Union Citizenship and its effects' *Common Market Law Review* vol. 45, p. 13.

Toner, Helen (2004) '*Chen*—Judgment of the ECJ' *Journal of Immigration, Asylum and Nationality Law* vol. 18, no. 4, pp. 265–6.

Toner, Helen (2006) 'New Regulations Implementing Directive 2004/38' *Journal of Immigration, Asylum and Nationality Law* vol. 20, no. 3, pp. 158–78.

Van Eijken, H. and de Vries, S. (2011) 'A New Route Into the Promised Land? Being a European Citizen After Ruiz Zambrano' *European Law Review* vol. 36, p. 704.

Van Eulsweg, P. and Kochenov, D. (2011) 'On the Limits of Judicial Intervention' EU Citizenship and Family Reunification Rights' *European Journal of Migration and Law* vol. 13, no. 1, p. 443.

Wiesbrock, A. (2011) 'Disentangling the "Union Citizenship Puzzle" the *McCarthy* case' *European Law Review* vol. 37, p. 861.

5

Immigration law and human rights

SUMMARY

This chapter discusses the relationship between human rights law and immigration law in the UK. There is a detailed discussion of the application of Article 3 and Article 8 to immigration situations, briefer treatment of the remaining Articles, and a discussion of the impact of immigration rules and statutory provisions designed to govern the interpretation of Article 8.

5.1 The relationship between immigration law and human rights

There is an obvious connection between migration and human rights. In moving between countries fundamental rights are often being exercised; for instance, to be reunited with one's family or to be free from torture or discrimination. Some accounts of human rights would include the right to freedom of movement itself, or the right to work. Immigration law enforcement may involve *prima facie* violations of rights; for instance, people who are not even suspected of crime can be detained under immigration powers. However, there is no human right to move to a particular country. States have the right to a system of law which, within the constraints of international law, regulates who may enter. Whatever the origins of that power, which we briefly considered in chapter 1, immigration law is primarily concerned with defining and giving enforceable substance to it. It has been concerned with regulating the numbers, origin, and material and other circumstances of those to whom entry will be granted, not primarily with the protection of their rights.

In the context of migration and human rights, seeking asylum is a special case because an application for asylum is an application for a specialized form of international human rights protection. This chapter is not concerned with making an asylum claim, which is dealt with in Section 5 of this book, but is concerned with the application of human rights law in the UK in immigration decision-making, including to a person whose asylum claim has failed. This chapter will focus on the use of the European Convention on Human Rights in the UK, both directly and through the Human Rights Act 1998. But many other international conventions may be relevant to immigration cases, for instance, the International Covenant on Civil and Political Rights (ICCPR), the Convention on Ending Racial Discrimination (CERD), the Convention on the Elimination of All Forms of Discrimination Against Women (CEDAW), the Convention Against Torture (CAT), the Convention on the Rights of the Child (CRC) and the EU Charter of Fundamental Rights. Human rights principles may also be drawn from the deliberations of bodies whose work is to develop human rights, for instance the United Nations

Commission on Human Rights. Case law from other jurisdictions where there are constitutionally enshrined rights is relevant, including in particular from Commonwealth jurisdictions and judgments of the Privy Council.

The rights of foreign nationals have been controversial throughout the life of the European Convention on Human Rights and, in the UK, of the Human Rights Act. Adverse political reactions to the prospect and the actuality of rights granted to foreign nationals have had a significant impact on the development of human rights law. When the UK first ratified the European Convention on Human Rights (ECHR), it did not immediately grant the individual right of petition. This meant that, although the UK was a party to the Convention in international law, no one in the UK's jurisdiction who suffered an infringement of their rights could actually go to the Court of Human Rights and complain. The delay may be attributed to the government's fear of applications from overseas territories, of which Britain had 42 in 1953 when the Convention was ratified. Macdonald cites a minister in Parliament: 'among emerging communities political agitators thrive and one may well imagine the use which political agitators would make of the right of individual petition' (Blake and Fransman 1999:vii). By the end of 1966, when the UK granted the individual right of petition, the number of overseas territories had dropped to 24.

Since the right of individual petition was granted, successive UK governments have attempted to exclude the rights of foreign nationals from the reach of the Convention, or limit their access to it. In *Abdulaziz, Cabales and Balkandali v UK* (1985) 7 EHRR 471, the UK government argued that Protocol 4, Article 4, which simply says: 'Collective expulsion of aliens is prohibited', was the only reference in the Convention to immigration control, and that accordingly no other immigration decision came within the reach of the Convention. The European Court of Human Rights (ECtHR) rejected this argument. The Court's judgment established the principle that Convention rights, and in this case the right to respect for family life (Article 8), do apply to a state's immigration decisions. They made the following important statement:

the right of a foreigner to enter or remain in a country was not as such guaranteed by the Convention, but immigration controls had to be exercised consistently with Convention obligations, and the exclusion of a person from a State where members of his family were living might raise an issue under Article 8. (para 59)

This principle remains a crucial foundation of the relationship between immigration decisions and human rights. Immigration decisions are acts of the state with the potential to affect the rights of individuals. Where rights are affected, interference with them may be challenged in the ECtHR, or in the UK's national courts in reliance on the Convention rights secured by the Human Rights Act 1998.

Since *Abdulaziz* the application of Convention rights to immigration decisions has been litigated in a wide range of situations. As the scope of human rights law has expanded, its principles have become more sophisticated and its limits tested. The body of this chapter will explore in more detail the expansion of the application of Convention rights, and the contrary developments by which their application has been restricted.

Pursuant to the Lisbon Treaty (the Treaty on the Functioning of the European Union OJ C 83/49), the CJEU acquired jurisdiction in immigration and asylum matters, and the fundamental rights contained in the EU Charter of Fundamental Rights became justiciable in EU law. This has introduced the first binding supranational authority in relation to human rights applied to immigration and asylum issues. The first judgment on these points was in C-411/10 *NS v SSHD* and C-493/10 *ME and others v Refugee Applications Commissioner and Minister for Justice, Equality and Law Reform*.

 **Key Case**

C-411/10 *NS v SSHD* and C-493/10 *ME and others v Refugee Applications Commissioner and Minister for Justice, Equality and Law Reform*

The applicants were asylum seekers who had travelled through Greece and claimed asylum in the UK and Ireland respectively. The legal challenges were to the UK and Ireland's practice and legislation, which allowed no opportunity for the asylum seekers to argue that their return to Greece, pursuant to the EC regulation known as Dublin II, would breach their human rights. In the UK, return to Greece was deemed safe by the Asylum and Immigration (Treatment of Claimants, etc.) Act 2004, and as such could not be challenged.

The judgment of the CJEU Grand Chamber was delivered after that of the ECtHR in *MSS v Belgium and Greece*. In *MSS* the ECtHR had accepted evidence from 'regular and unanimous reports of international non-governmental organizations' to reach a conclusion that the fundamental rights of asylum seekers under Article 3 ECHR were infringed in Greece. The CJEU concluded that 'there existed in Greece at the time of the transfer of the applicant MSS, a systemic deficiency in the asylum procedure and the reception conditions of asylum seekers' (para 89).

The CJEU held that, contrary to the submissions of governments, the discretion that Member States have to decide an asylum application themselves, instead of sending the applicant to another Member State under the Dublin Regulation, is a discretion which implements EU law. Accordingly, it must be exercised consistently with the principles of EU law including respect for fundamental rights. The Court held that where the Member State could 'not be unaware' that systemic deficiencies existed in the asylum procedure in the receiving country such that there were substantial grounds for believing that there was a real risk of violations of Article 4 of the Charter (equivalent to Article 3 ECHR) then the Charter prohibited an asylum seeker from being transferred to that country. EU law prohibited a conclusive presumption that the destination state complied in its asylum procedures with the Charter of Fundamental Rights.

The workings of the Dublin regulation and the case of *MSS* are discussed more fully in chapter 11. The point here is the radical effect of the CJEU's human rights judgments in the EU. While the Court said that minor infringements would not nullify Dublin transfers, in the face of evidence of real risk of inhuman or degrading treatment or punishment, or torture, regulations made for the operation of the Common European Asylum System would give way to human rights.

5.2 Human rights in immigration law since the Human Rights Act

The arrival of the human rights jurisdiction in the UK changed the legal landscape and context for immigration decisions. The Human Rights Act required acts of public authorities to be compatible with the Convention rights derived from the ECHR. It established a binding legal basis for those seeking leave to enter or remain in the UK, or opposing their removal, to assert their fundamental human rights, as a counterpoint to the state's assertion of immigration control. Although claiming a human right does not mean that it will prevail in the particular case, this changed the dynamics of claims and litigation. It also brought the judiciary into a politically charged arena.

From October 2000 (and even before that—see earlier editions of this textbook) two very different strands were evident in the UK courts' and tribunals' interpretation of what human rights meant for immigration appeals. One strand, demonstrated in Court of Appeal cases such as *Edore v SSHD* [2003] 3 All ER 1265, held that the human rights jurisdiction of the courts and tribunals was limited to considering whether the Secretary of State had acted reasonably. It was equivalent to a standard judicial review jurisdiction. Although case law developed around the *intensity* of review in a human rights case, creating such concepts as 'anxious scrutiny', the basic approach was that immigration decisions were within the remit of the Secretary of State, and deference should be accorded to that by the judiciary whose role was more remote. A body of jurisprudence grew up around this concept, challenging the notion of 'deference' in various ways, but the concept itself endured.

The other strand, evident in early cases such as *Nhundu and Chiwera* 01/TH/00613, held that the judiciary on appeal were required and competent to assess any alleged infringement of rights directly and fully, as a matter of law within their jurisdiction, not as a mere check on the actions of the executive.

The matter was settled by the House of Lords in *Huang and Kashmiri v SSHD* [2007] UKHL 11 when they held that, in an Article 8 appeal concerning the right to respect for family life, 'it is the Court's task to . . . weigh up the competing considerations on each side and according appropriate weight to the judgment of a person with responsibility for a given subject matter and access to special sources of knowledge and advice' (para 16). The following year a series of judgments in the House of Lords developed the judicial approach to human rights in immigration. *Chikwamba v SSHD* [2008] UKHL 40, *Beoku-Betts v SSHD* [2008] UKHL 39), and *EB (Kosovo) v SSHD* [2008] UKHL 41 established a humane approach to the application of the principle of proportionality, taking account of the impact of immigration control in individual human situations, and exercising jurisdiction to decide on the proportionality of a potential violation as a matter of law (see 5.11.4).

The two different strands, however, remained apparent in judicial decision-making. For instance, in Article 8 cases considering whether the life of the family could continue abroad, different tests were selected from ECtHR case law which raised higher or lower thresholds for the family to surmount.

The government also was not content to accept the courts exercising full jurisdiction as a matter of law over the adjudication of human rights. The July 2012 immigration rule changes, which are discussed in detail at 5.11.9 and chapter 8, were intended to embed within the rules the Secretary of State's interpretation of Article 8 ECHR. The interpretation of the relationship between the rules and Article 8 remains live and is awaiting a judgment from the Supreme Court at the time of writing (*SS (Congo) v ECO Nairobi*).

The next step was for the government to embed an interpretation of Article 8 into statute, since this would be binding on the judiciary. They did this in the Immigration Act 2014, and the specific provisions are discussed at 5.11.10 and chapter 15.

The governmental effort to restrict the rights of foreign nationals has become a party political issue. After a consultation carried out under the Coalition government indicated that there was little to be gained by repealing the Human Rights Act, the issue was quietly dropped. It has been picked up again by the Conservative government with the explicit aim of preventing people abroad suing for the actions of British troops, and preventing foreign nationals from using 'spurious' human rights arguments to prevent their deportation, and freeing UK courts from being bound by the Strasbourg Court. It is surprising that this argument persists, since the Human Rights Act s 2 provides that UK courts are not bound by decisions of the ECtHR but only need to take them into account (Human Rights Act s 2). As regards direct interventions by Strasbourg, in 2014 the Court delivered 27 judgments on UK cases. Violations were found in five (*A British Bill of Rights?* briefing paper 7193 House of Commons Library 2015).

These more recent government attempts to curb the rights of foreign nationals come after the UK courts have delivered some progressive judgments in asylum and immigration cases. They have acted perhaps in the spirit encouraged by Sir Nicolas Bratza, a former UK judge and President in the ECtHR, endorsing Baroness Hale, that the national courts should 'sometimes consciously leap ahead of Strasbourg'. In addition to the 2008 House of Lords cases, examples include *Limbuela*, in which the House of Lords held that actively subjecting asylum seekers to destitution constituted a breach of Article 3, and *EM (Lebanon) v SSHD* [2008] UKHL 64, in which the House of Lords upheld the rights of a child not to be parted from his mother, and established an approach to engaging the state's responsibility for a breach of Article 8 abroad (these decisions are discussed at 5.6.1 and 5.4.2).

In *Quila*, the Supreme Court broke new ground by expressly declining to follow *Abdulaziz v UK* (1985) 7 EHRR 471. This was not a radical departure in Article 8 case law, because the Supreme Court cited a number of cases since *Abdulaziz* which showed that the direction of ECtHR case law had changed (see chapter 8). However, it demonstrated the independent growth of UK human rights jurisprudence. Lord Wilson said:

Having duly taken account of the decision in *Abdulaziz* pursuant to section 2 of the Human Rights Act 1998, we should in my view decline to follow it. It is an old decision. There was dissent from it even at the time. More recent decisions of the ECtHR, in particular *Boultif* and *Tuquabo-Tekle* [2006] 1 FLR 798, are inconsistent with it. There is no 'clear and consistent jurisprudence' of the ECtHR which our courts ought to follow: see *R (Alconbury Developments Ltd) v Secretary of State for the Environment, Transport and the Regions* [2001] UKHL 23, [2003] 2 AC 295 at para 26, per Lord Slynn. (para 43)

The most keenly fought issues in UK human rights law applied to immigration are not between UK judges and Strasbourg but between those seeking to exercise human rights and the government which seeks to restrain them. Two declarations of incompatibility have been made by the courts about powers taken by the government against foreign nationals. The declarations were in relation to the Church of England exemption from the certificate of approval scheme, which required the Secretary of State's consent to the marriage of foreign nationals (*SSHD v Baiai and Trzcinska, Bigoku and Agolli and Tilki* [2007] EWCA Civ 478, discussed in chapter 8) and the regime of indefinite detention imposed on foreign suspected terrorists by the Anti-terrorism, Crime and Security Act 2001, which was declared incompatible with Article 14 (*A v SSHD* [2004] UKHL 56).

The ECtHR is not a precedent-setting court. Nevertheless, the court does attempt to create a consistent jurisprudence, so ECtHR case law will give an indication of how the ECtHR might approach an issue. If a decision is old, and the subject matter is one in which there have been significant developments, then the decision may provide less reliable guidance as to how the court may approach a similar matter now.

Commonly, legal reasoning uses both ECtHR and UK cases when interpreting the Convention, and this is the practice followed in this book. In the course of discussing one topic, we may move from ECtHR case law to UK case law and back again.

5.3 Who may make a human rights claim?

Anyone present in the jurisdiction may make a human rights claim. There is no requirement of lawful presence. Article 1 ECHR provides that the rights and freedoms of the Convention must be secured to everyone within the state's jurisdiction. This

Article was not included in the HRA, but the statute contains no exclusions of people on grounds of their status, and anyone may apply who claims that their Convention rights have been violated, 'if he would be a victim for the purposes of Article 34 of the Convention if proceedings were brought in the ECtHR' (Human Rights Act s 7). This requires that the applicant be directly affected by the act or omission in question.

The meaning of a 'human rights claim' is discussed in chapter 7, where it is explained that only certain decisions are appealable on human rights grounds. Where those appeals are available they are made on the basis that the decision 'would be unlawful under s 6 of the Human Rights Act 1998' (Nationality, Immigration and Asylum Act 2002 s 84(1)).

Section 82(1) does not permit an appeal to be brought by someone else whose human rights are interfered with by an immigration decision. However, in Article 8 cases, the Article 8 rights of others cannot in practice be separated from those of the appellant (*Beoku-Betts v SSHD* [2008] UKHL 39).

 **Key Case**

Beoku-Betts v SSHD [2008] UKHL 39

The appellant was a citizen of Sierra Leone who came to the UK as a student in 1997 after a coup, during which, as members of a politically active family, he and his elder brother had been subject to mock executions. His asylum claim failed and his case continued to the House of Lords on the basis of his Article 8 claim. He had a close relationship with his family, most of whom were in the UK, and their needs and interests as well as the close-knit quality of the family had been treated as important by the adjudicator who had allowed the appeal. The Secretary of State objected to this approach.

The House of Lords said:

To insist that an appeal to the Asylum and Immigration Tribunal consider only the effect upon other family members as it affects the appellant, and that a judicial review brought by other family members considers only the effect upon the appellant as it affects them, is not only artificial and impracticable. It also risks missing the central point about family life, which is that the whole is greater than the sum of its individual parts. The right to respect for the family life of one necessarily encompasses the right to respect for the family life of others, normally a spouse or minor children, with whom that family life is enjoyed. (para 4 *per* Baroness Hale)

The House held that the life of the family could be considered on an appeal based on Article 8, and the parties agreed that this principle applied to decisions of the Secretary of State, so that initial Home Office decisions must also be made with regard to the rights of other family members. The application of *Beoku-Betts* is discussed in chapter 8.

Where a human rights challenge touches on a question of policy, or affects a wider group of people than just the claimant, a public interest organization may be involved in the case. Where an organization is directly affected by the action it may be joined as an interested party. Alternatively, the organization may provide expert evidence on the impact of the issue on their client group, or apply to appear as intervenors in order to argue wider points that may not be made by the parties. In appeals and judicial review, you will sometimes notice that a human rights or refugee organization appears in the title to the case. For instance, in *R (on the application of Q) v SSHD* [2003] EWCA Civ 364, a challenge to withholding benefits from asylum seekers, both Liberty and the Joint Council for the Welfare of Immigrants were represented. In *Quila* the AIRE Centre, the Asian Community Action Group, Southall Black Sisters, and the Henna Foundation all intervened. The United Nations High Commissioner for Refugees sometimes intervenes in asylum cases of particular significance.

In *R (Sehwerert) v SSHD* [2015] EWCA Civ 1141 a group of MPs whose Article 10 rights were engaged were claimants in a judicial review challenging the refusal of entry clearance to Mr Sehwerert.

5.4 **Geographical scope—expulsions**

Many human rights cases in the immigration and asylum context are concerned with the effect of removing a person from the country, and this includes both the damage to their life here and what may happen to them abroad. As the consequence may be experienced outside the UK, expulsions engage the question of geographical scope.

5.4.1 **Article 3**

The case of *Soering v UK* (1989) 11 EHRR 439 was the first to establish that, where a state expelled a person to face treatment in breach of a Convention article, the expelling state could be held to be in breach. This is not vicarious liability for the actions of the other state, but because the expulsion itself amounts to a breach. In *Soering* a German national challenged extradition to the US state of Virginia to face the death penalty on a charge of murdering his girlfriend's parents. The threat to his life could not be challenged because Article 2, the right to life, permits the death penalty and at that time the UK had not ratified Protocol 6 which outlaws it. However, the ECtHR decided that expulsion to face the phenomenon of being on death row was a breach of Article 3 because of the inordinate delays and suspense, during which the condemned person might wait for years to know whether they would be killed or not. *Cruz Varas v Sweden* [1991] 14 EHRR 1 confirmed that expulsion itself may amount to a violation in the case of deportation as well as extradition. The principle is expressed in *Soering* as follows:

A decision by a contracting State to expel a fugitive may give rise to an issue under Article 3, and hence engage the responsibility of that State under the Convention, where substantial grounds have been shown for believing that the person concerned, if extradited, faces a real risk of being subjected to torture or inhuman or degrading treatment or punishment in the requesting country. The establishment of such responsibility inevitably involves an assessment of conditions in the requesting country against the standards of Article 3 of the Convention. Nonetheless, there is no question of adjudicating on or establishing the responsibility of the receiving country, whether under general international law, under the Convention, or otherwise. Insofar as any liability under the Convention is or maybe incurred, it is liability incurred by the extraditing Contracting State by reason of its having taken action which has as a direct consequence the exposure of an individual to proscribed treatment. (para 91)

This phenomenon is referred to loosely as 'extra-territorial' application of the Convention right. This is a convenient shorthand as the expulsion is a breach because of what is likely to happen elsewhere. In *R v SSHD ex p Bagdanavicius (FC) & another* [2005] UKHL 38 the House of Lords explained that the assessment of risk on return does not mean that the court is making a decision in law about that receiving country, which after all is not represented in the court. It only means there has to be an assessment of risk to the appellant (para 22).

Although most cases involve Article 3, it is established that the same principle of 'extra-territoriality' applies to Article 2.

5.4.2 **Breach of qualified rights abroad**

Soering and *Cruz Varas* put the application of Article 3 to expulsions beyond doubt. Engagement of the responsibility of the sending state has been more contentious where the feared breach abroad is of a qualified right.

In *Bensaid v UK* (2001) 33 EHRR 205, the applicant failed in his challenge to removal, but the ECtHR found no obstacle to his arguing a feared breach of Article 8. In the early days of the Human Rights Act, a number of cases, without deciding the point, assumed the possibility of extra-territorial application of qualified rights, that is, those which allow the state to interfere with the right when necessary for the protection of listed public interests. See, for instance, *Nhundu and Chiwera* 01TH00613 and *SSHD v Z, A v SSHD, M v SSHD* [2002] Imm AR 560, *Kacaj* [2002] Imm AR 213.

The question of responsibility where breaches of qualified rights are feared abroad was settled by the House of Lords in *R v Special Adjudicator ex p Ullah and Do v SSHD* [2004] UKHL 26.

 Key Case

R v Special Adjudicator ex p Ullah and Do v SSHD [2004] UKHL 26

Both Mr Ullah and Ms Do feared infringement of their rights to freedom of religion (Article 9), and Mr Ullah additionally freedom of expression (Article 10) and freedom of association (Article 11) on return to their countries of origin. They had each claimed asylum as they feared persecution for their religious beliefs, but their asylum claims had failed. Mr Ullah was a citizen of Pakistan and a member of the Ahmadhiya, a minority faith. Ms Do was a Roman Catholic teacher from Vietnam.

The House of Lords held that:

- theoretically, a real risk of breach of *any* Convention right on return may make the expulsion a breach of the UK's obligations (overturning the CA that only Article 3 could be engaged in an extra-territorial case);

- such a feared breach would need to be flagrant, or in the case of a qualified right, amount to a fundamental denial of that right in order to engage the responsibility of the UK (departing from CA in which a breach of any other right would only be so regarded if it amounted to a breach of Article 3);

- it is not the case that the Convention rights were not intended to interfere with the state's sovereign rights in relation to foreign nationals (refuting the CA's *obiter* comments in this respect);

- the expelling state cannot relieve itself of responsibility by saying the breach happens elsewhere. The action of expulsion takes place within the jurisdiction;

- *Soering* and *Cruz-Varas* clearly stated the law and may be followed. They are not exceptions.

On the facts, the appellants failed in their claims, but the points of principle are important. The third point refutes the argument made for the UK government in *Abdulaziz* and which did not find favour with the ECtHR in that case. Indeed, 20 years of ECtHR case law since *Abdulaziz* had proceeded on the basis that immigration decisions are subject to human rights considerations.

Although the House of Lords held in *Ullah and Do* that expulsions may engage qualified rights as a result of anticipated treatment in the destination state, this is not a straightforward matter to assess. The appeals in *SSHD ex p Razgar* [2004] UKHL 27 concerned claims based on Articles 3 and 8, that the claimants would suffer deterioration in their mental health if returned to France or Germany. The House of Lords held that the right to respect for private life can be engaged by the foreseeable consequences for health or welfare of removal from the UK when removal does not violate Article 3, if the facts relied on by the appellant are sufficiently strong. The threshold is said to be a high one. Such a claim could not be successfully made simply by showing relative disadvantage in care between the sending and receiving state (para 9 and see 5.11.11). Where the consequences of removal for family or private life are felt in the UK, the House of Lords called this a 'domestic' case. It is settled law that removal can engage Article 8 because of the consequences for family or private life in the UK, and this is dealt with extensively later. Where the consequences are feared abroad, they called it a 'foreign' case. The difference between these two is expressed by Baroness Hale:

42. . . . In a domestic case the state must always act in a way which is compatible with the Convention rights. There is no threshold test related to the seriousness of the violation or the importance of the right involved. Foreign cases, on the other hand, represent an exception to the general rule that a state is only responsible for what goes on within its own territory or control . . . the Strasbourg court has not yet explored the test for imposing this obligation in any detail. But there clearly is some additional threshold test indicating the enormity of the violation to which the person is likely to be exposed if returned.

43. . . . Lord Bingham also refers to a third, or hybrid category. Here 'the removal of a person from country A to country B may both violate his right to respect for private and family life in country A and also violate the same right by depriving him of family life or impeding his enjoyment of private life in country B' . . . On analysis, however, such cases remain domestic cases. There is no threshold test of enormity or humanitarian affront. But the right . . . protected by Article 8 is a qualified right, which may be interfered with if this is necessary to pursue a legitimate aim. What may happen in a foreign country is therefore relevant to the proportionality of the proposed expulsion.

The authority now on the breach of qualified rights abroad is that of *EM (Lebanon) v SSHD* [2008] UKHL 64.

 Key Case

EM (Lebanon) v SSHD [2008] UKHL 64

The appellant's asylum claim failed and she faced removal with her ten-year-old child to Lebanon. The accepted evidence was that if returned to that country she would lose custody of the child to her husband who had previously attempted to remove the child to Saudi Arabia and had subjected her to extreme violence. This was because the law would automatically give custody to the father if he did not approve the mother as custodian. She claimed that removal would breach her right to respect for family life under Article 8.

The House of Lords held that where the appellant claimed a breach of qualified rights abroad, the question was whether the treatment she feared would constitute a flagrant breach so as to amount to a nullification or destruction of the very essence of the right. This was a single question, and there was no distinction between a flagrant breach and a complete denial of the right (as the Court of Appeal had suggested).

Their Lordships said that, in the absence of exceptional circumstances, an appellant could not claim entitlement to remain in the UK to escape the discriminatory effects of family law in their country of origin. However, exceptional circumstances were present here. The appellant's son had never had a personal relationship with his father. All he knew of him was as someone who had inflicted serious violence on his mother before he was born. There would be no opportunity in Lebanon for the appellant to oppose the transfer of custody. There was a close relationship between mother and son and a real risk that the mother would not be permitted any contact with her son at all. Consequently, the removal of mother and son to Lebanon would breach their Article 8 rights. The breach was flagrant because the mother would not have any opportunity to oppose the award of custody to the father.

5.4.3 Breach of other rights abroad

Soering itself seems to suggest there may be scope for extraterritorial application of Article 6, and this was applied in *Othman (Abu Qatada) v UK* application no. 8139/09 in which the ECtHR held for the first time that unfairness of a trial abroad would mean that expulsion breached Article 6. The House of Lords in the same case, *B (Algeria) v SSHD; OO (Jordan) v SSHD* [2009] UKHL 10, confirmed that the flagrant breach standard applies to the risk of violation of Articles 5 and 6 abroad. They held that Mr Othman (Abu Qatada) was unlikely to be detained without trial for the legal maximum of 50 days in Jordan, but even if he was, this was not a flagrant or fundamental breach of Article 5. The ECtHR agreed with this. However, the House of Lords held that the risk that evidence used against him in trial had been obtained by torture did not amount to a flagrant or fundamental breach of Article 6. Here the ECtHR disagreed. The Court considered that the use at trial of evidence obtained by torture would amount to a flagrant denial of justice (*Othman v UK* para 263). The Court did not consider it necessary to determine whether a flagrant denial of justice only arose when the unfair trial would have serious consequences for the applicant (para 262). The central issue was the use of evidence obtained by torture.

Regarding the test of a flagrant breach applied to Article 6, in *Al-Nashiri v Poland* [2014] ECHR 833 the ECtHR said:

A flagrant denial of justice goes beyond mere irregularities or lack of safeguards in the trial procedures such as might result in a breach of Article 6 if occurring within the Contracting State itself. What is required is a breach of the principles of fair trial guaranteed by Article 6 which is so fundamental as to amount to a nullification, or destruction of the very essence, of the right guaranteed by that Article. (para 563)

In relation to the use of torture evidence:

The Court has taken a clear, constant and unequivocal position in respect of the admission of torture evidence. No legal system based upon the rule of law can countenance the admission of evidence—however reliable—which has been obtained by such a barbaric practice as torture. The trial process is a cornerstone of the rule of law. Torture evidence irreparably damages that process; it substitutes force for the rule of law and taints the reputation of any court that admits it. Torture evidence is excluded in order to protect the integrity of the trial process and, ultimately, the rule of law itself. The prohibition of the use of torture is fundamental. (para 564)

Both Mr Al-Nashiri and the applicant in *Husayn (Abu Zubaydah) v Poland* [2014] ECHR 834 had been detained in secret locations in Poland and then handed to the CIA, and subject to extraordinary rendition, resulting in imprisonment in Guantanamo Bay. Findings of violations were made against Poland in relation both to the detention on Polish territory and to the transfer of the applicants out of Polish territory as there was a real risk of flagrant breaches of Articles 3, 5, and 6. The risk of a flagrant breach of Article 5 was said by the ECtHR to be 'inherent where an applicant has been subjected to "extraordinary rendition", which entails detention . . . "outside the normal legal system" and which, "by its deliberate circumvention of due process, is anathema to the rule of law and the values protected by the Convention"' (para 452).

In summary, there is no doubt that a real risk of a breach of Article 2 or 3 abroad engages the responsibility of the sending state in the act of removal. Removal cases in the UK based on these Articles normally concern disputes about the existence or level of the risk or harm, and not the UK's responsibility as such. Risks of other violations abroad must be of a flagrant violation in order to engage the Convention and the Human Rights Act.

5.5. Geographical scope—entry decisions

The description of immigration control in chapter 6 shows that whether someone is outside the UK or not when they apply for leave to enter is in part a matter of factual accident. Decisions on leave to enter may now be made anywhere in the world. The Court of Appeal in *Naik v SSHD* [2011] EWCA Civ 1546 remarked that:

It is difficult to see any logic in treating an applicant less favourably because he takes the sensible course of applying for entry clearance from abroad, rather than simply arriving at border control at Heathrow. (para 31)

In the early days of the Human Rights Act, some argued that human rights did not apply to entry clearance on the basis that these decisions are taken outside the jurisdiction. This argument is no longer made and could not be sustained. See discussion in earlier editions of this textbook on the consular exception to territorial jurisdiction in *Bankovic v Belgium* (2001) 11 BHRC 435, *R (on the application of B) v Secretary of State for Foreign and Commonwealth Affairs* [2004] EWCA Civ 1344 and on jurisdiction by exercising control in *Al-Skeini v UK* [2011] ECHR 1093. The exercise of jurisdiction through physical control has been reinforced by recent decisions such as *Al-Saadoon & Ors v Secretary of State for Defence* [2015] EWHC 715 (Admin).

Both case law and the immigration rules treat Article 8 as applying in entry cases. For instance, the House of Lords in *Chikwamba v SSHD* [2008] UKHL 40 (discussed later in the chapter) based their decision on the expectation that if the appellant were required to leave the UK and apply for entry clearance to join her spouse, she would have a right of appeal under Article 8 against a refusal. Immigration rules accompanying the restrictive appeals provisions of the Immigration Act 2014 acknowledge the availability of human rights appeals in family-based entry cases (Appendix AR). Case law discussed later in this chapter shows the application also of Article 10 to entry.

In *Tuquabo-Tekle v Netherlands* the Netherlands government attempted to raise a late objection to the admissibility of the application on the basis that the applicant for a residence permit was outside the territory. The Court did not allow the point to be argued, as the case had already been accepted as admissible.

The direction of the case law both in Strasbourg and the UK is to minimize any difference between the application of Article 8 to entry and removal decisions. Interestingly, in the Calais cases discussed in chapters 6 and 11, it was common ground between the applicants and Secretary of State that the applicants were entitled to rely on Article 8, and the Tribunal's decision ultimately rested on their application of Article 8, in a situation in which the refusals were

not imbued with any *special sources of knowledge and advice*. . . we take into account, as did the Court of Appeal recently in *R (Sehwerert) v Secretary of State for the Home Department* [2015] EWCA Civ 1141, at [46], that lesser weight is to be accorded to the Secretary of State's assessment of the balance to be struck between the public interest and the rights of the individual in circumstances where the Secretary of State's insistence upon full adherence to the Dublin Regulation embodies a generalised assessment, a broad brush, to be contrasted with a specific, considered response and decision on a case by case basis . . . . the platform upon which the Secretary of State has contested these proceedings is quite unrelated to the individual circumstances, needs and merits of any of the seven Applicants. (*R (on the application of ZAT and Others) v SSHD (Article 8 ECHR—Dublin Regulation—interface—proportionality)*, para 57)

Having established that Convention rights apply to both entry and removal decisions, we will look at the substance of those rights, before considering how the balance is struck in more detail in the UK context.

5.6 Convention rights—Article 3

This section will concentrate on those rights commonly encountered in the immigration and asylum contexts and to the extent they are not covered elsewhere in the textbook.

5.6.1 Treatment contrary to Article 3

Article 3 provides that:

No one shall be subjected to torture or inhuman or degrading treatment or punishment.

In relation to persecution, Goodwin-Gill and Macadam say that it is 'a concept only too readily filled by the latest examples of one person's inhumanity to another, and little purpose is served by attempting to list all its known measures' (2007:93–4). The same could be said of treatment that contravenes Article 3. Cross-reference may be made here to discussion of 'severe harm' in the refugee definition discussed in chapter 12, and no catalogue of violations is attempted in either chapter. Treatment that falls short of torture may be inhuman or degrading treatment but it must pass a certain threshold of severity in order to come within Article 3. The Convention moves with the times, and in *Selmouni v France* (1999) 29 EHRR 403 the ECtHR held that the interrogation techniques (hooding, exposure to noise, deprivation of food and drink, deprivation of sleep, and enforced standing against a wall) found to be degrading and inhuman in *Ireland v UK* (1978) 2 EHRR 25 would now be found to be torture. The absolute nature of the Article means that torture or inhuman treatment cannot be justified by any belief in its effect. The police force cannot, for instance, say that such treatment is necessary to extract a confession.

Adverse treatment on grounds of race may amount to degrading treatment if it is institutionalized, as in the *East African Asians cases* (1981) 3 EHRR 76. Here, the ECHR found that the refusal of entry to the UK to the British passport holders resident in Uganda, Tanzania, and Kenya (discussed in chapter 3) amounted to institutionalized racism and was degrading, passing the threshold of severity to amount to a violation of Article 3.

A breach of Article 3 normally requires actual or threatened physical or psychological ill-treatment which is deliberately applied. This can include a government's regime of action directed against asylum seekers, including enforced destitution (*R v SSHD ex p Adam, Limbuela and Tesema* [2005] UKHL 66). If the asylum seeker has, by some other means, for instance, friends or a charity, obtained shelter, sanitary facilities, and some money for food, the denial of benefit does not reach the threshold to be regarded as degrading (*R (on the application of S, D, T) v SSHD* [2003] EWHC 1951 (Admin)). This is confirmed by the ECtHR's judgment in *MSS v Belgium and Greece* [2011] ECHR 108. The Court held that in the light of the particular vulnerability of destitute asylum seekers, and their absolute dependency on the host state for their material needs, the conditions in which MSS lived were in breach of Article 3. He had no accommodation, and no regular source of food or shelter. He slept in a park.

Article 3 played a part in developments in 'the jungle' in Calais. The Upper Tribunal in *R (on the application of ZAT and Others) v SSHD (Article 8 ECHR—Dublin Regulation—interface—proportionality)* IJR [2016] UKUT 61 (IAC) quoted an order dated 2 November 2015 made by the Tribunal Adminstratif de Lille:

As a result of manifestly inadequate access to water and toilets and the lack of refuse collection operations, the population at the camp are living in conditions which do not meet their basic needs in terms of hygiene and access to drinking water and which expose them to health risks; **As a result, there is a serious and manifestly unlawful breach of their right not to be subjected to inhuman and degrading treatment**. [Emphasis added.] (*ZAT* para 15)

The Court had ordered the Prefet of Pas-de-Calais to take specified measures, to be commenced within eight days:

the provision of water access points; the installation of 50 toilets; the introduction of a refuse collection operation; the cleaning of the site; and the creation of internal access routes to facilitate the emergency services. (*ZAT* para 15)

Article 3 can entail a positive duty to investigate alleged breaches which may occasionally be relevant in immigration and asylum matters. It was held to extend to alleged breaches of Article 3 in the administration of a detention centre in the UK (*R (on the application of AM) v SSHD and Kalyx, BID intervening* [2009] EWCA Civ 219).

A present issue, when many asylum applicants come from conditions of war, is whether removal can be opposed on the basis of conditions of general violence or deprivation, not harm which is targeted on the applicant. In this respect the judgment of the ECtHR in *Sufi and Elmi v UK* represented a development.

 **Key Case**

Sufi and Elmi v UK 8319/07 [2011] ECHR 1045

The Court found, in applications made by refused asylum seekers against their removal to Somalia, that 'the violence in Mogadishu is of such a level of intensity that anyone in the city, except possibly those who are exceptionally well-connected to 'powerful actors', would be at real risk of treatment prohibited by Article 3' (para 250). In relation to risks in other parts of the country the Court made detailed findings, including for instance that an applicant might not be at risk in parts of central and southern Somalia if they had close family who could protect them. In regions controlled by Al-Shabaab, or in the camps for internally displaced people, a returnee would be at risk of treatment contrary to Article 3.

Issues of this kind may now be raised under Article 15(C) of the Refugee Qualification Directive (see chapter 11), since this provides specifically for situations of violence. In relation to return to Mogadishu, the UK now has Country Guidance which departs from *Sufi and Elmi* (*MOJ & Ors (Return to Mogadishu) Somalia CG* [2014] UKUT 00442 (IAC)).

Applications that removal will breach Article 3 are made in numerous cases of proposed removal under the Dublin Regulation to poor or discriminatory reception conditions in another EU country (see chapter 11). Few have succeeded in the UK, but the ECtHR in *Tarakhel v Switzerland* (Application no. 29217/12) found that there were deficiencies in the reception system for families in Italy, such that the Swiss authorities were in breach of Article 3 unless they obtained specific assurances from the Italian authorities, before returning the family, of reception facilities that would be adequate for them.

5.6.2 Medical treatment and Article 3

Applications opposing removal on the basis of a breach of Article 3 have been made by claimants who are receiving medical treatment in the UK and who will die if that treatment is withdrawn. The case of *D v UK* (1997) 24 EHRR 423 broke new ground in this respect, although it has generally been distinguished in subsequent cases where applicants have sought to rely on it. The Secretary of State sought to deport D after he had served a long prison sentence for supplying prohibited drugs. He was by this time in an advanced stage of AIDS and receiving terminal care in a hospice. The treatment he had been undergoing had slowed down the progress of the disease and relieved his symptoms, and he was receiving support as he faced death. His life expectancy was short in any event, but if he was deported to St. Kitts the treatment upon which he depended would not be available at all, and he had no family or social network to support him. The end of his life would be marked by much greater suffering. The ECtHR held that to return him in these circumstances would breach Article 3.

The leading case in relation to Article 3 and medical care is that of *N v SSHD* [2005] UKHL 31.

 Key Case

N v SSHD [2005] UKHL 31

N was an AIDS sufferer facing deportation to Uganda. In the UK, where she had been living for five years, her condition had stabilized on medication. This medication would not be available to her in Uganda. Her brothers and sisters had died of AIDS and her life expectancy would be reduced to a year or two. The House of Lords unanimously and carefully distinguished *D v UK*. It held that in *D*, the removal was a breach of Article 3 because it would mean that his death, which was imminent, would take place in far more distressing circumstances.

Here, death was not imminent, although their Lordships acknowledged there could be no real difference in humanitarian terms between removing someone to face imminent death and removing someone to face death within a year or two. The difference came in that the Convention could not be taken to have imposed upon the parties an obligation to provide medical treatment. Lord Brown identified *D* as concerning a negative obligation—not to deport D to 'an imminent, lonely and distressing end' (*N v SSHD* [2005] UKHL 31 para 93). *N*, he thought, concerned a positive obligation—to provide N with medical treatment. Not to allow N to remain but not give her medical care would not answer her needs.

All their Lordships expressed strong sympathy with N, and distaste for having to make this decision. In the end, social policy considerations had to be overt in order to make sense of this case. Lord Nicholls and others acknowledged 'If the appellant were a special case I have no doubt that, in one way or another, the pressing humanitarian considerations of her case would prevail'. However, given the prevalence of AIDS in Africa in particular and the shortage of treatment, her case was 'far from unique' (para 9). Their Lordships saw the issue as being outside their capacity to resolve. The problem arose from 'Uganda's lack of medical resources compared with those available in the UK' (para 8) and the better answer than migration and human rights claims was, in the words of Lord Hope, 'for states to continue to concentrate their efforts on the steps which are currently being taken, with the assistance of the drugs companies, to make the necessary medical care universally and freely available' (para 53).

The ECtHR by a majority of 14 to 3 confirmed the House of Lords decision (*N v UK* (2008) 47 EHRR 885). They considered that Article 3 usually only applied to intentional acts or omissions of a state or non-state body. In medical cases, Article 3 applied only in very exceptional circumstances. The Convention was essentially directed to the protection of civil and political rights, and a fair balance between the interests of the community and the rights of the individual was inherent in the Convention. Article 3 could not be relied upon to address the disparity in medical care between contracting states and an applicant's state of origin.

The court in *N v UK* applied Article 3 in a very different way from that used when the risk on return is a risk of torture, arguably treating Article 3 more like a qualified right. In reported cases at least, it remains, following *N*, extremely difficult for anyone to resist removal on health grounds using Article 3. This is now confirmed in *GS India and others* [2015] EWCA Civ 40. The appellant GS had only one kidney, and was dependent on dialysis every two or three days for his survival. The Secretary of State decided to remove him. In India the nearest hospital to his home that could provide dialysis was 300 kilometres away, and GS had no means to pay for that treatment or support himself near the hospital. Without dialysis he would die within a week or two. Four of the other appellants were also in end-stage kidney failure, receiving dialysis, and the sixth was at an advanced stage of HIV infection.

The Court of Appeal dismissed all their appeals on Article 3 grounds, following *N*. The exception was that for one appellant, GM, a kidney donor had been identified, and the Court suggested that GM should put this before the Home Office as a fresh claim under Article 3. KK was facing deportation for criminal offences. He had always had leave to remain during his time in the UK, so there could be no suggestion that he had attempted to stay just for medical treatment. The Court of Appeal said that this made no difference and did not prevent the Secretary of State from removing him (para 74).

A risk of suicide may mean that removal is a breach of Article 3.

Key Case

Y and Z (Sri Lanka) v SSHD [2009] EWCA Civ 362

The appellants, who were brother and sister, were Sri Lankan Tamils. They had been tortured by the Sri Lankan security forces as suspected LTTE members or sympathizers, both had been raped in captivity, and suffered from post-traumatic stress disorder and depression. The second appellant's husband and daughter were killed by the security forces. Two cousins had been executed by the security forces, and their mother (the appellants' aunt) had starved herself to death in a public protest.

Their asylum claim in the UK failed because it was found that, although they had suffered such serious violations, there was no real risk of repetition. After their arrival in the UK, 50 members of their extended family were killed in the 2004 tsunami. The appellants claimed to be at risk of suicide if they were returned.

Sedley LJ in the Court of Appeal said that, in applying *J*, in relation to suicide, what mattered was whether there was a real and overwhelming fear, not whether it was well-founded. Where there was considered to be no objective risk to the asylum seeker on return, but the individual was said to be at risk of suicide if returned, it was right to scrutinize the claim with care. But there came a point at which an undisturbed finding that an appellant had been tortured and raped in captivity had to be conscientiously related to credible and uncontradicted expert evidence that the likely effect of the psychological trauma, if return was enforced, would be suicide. In such a case, return was a breach of Article 3.

The cause of the suicide risk is relevant only to the extent that it has a bearing on whether the risk will materialize. Assessing this may include considering the availability of care to prevent suicide in the UK and the receiving country. It also includes assessing the risk at three stages: prior to anticipated removal; during removal; on arrival.

5.6.3 Absolute right under challenge

Article 3 confers an absolute right, the breach of which cannot be justified by any interest of the state. The ECtHR confirmed in *Chahal v UK* (1996) 23 EHRR 413 that this means that even a person who may be a danger to national security cannot be expelled to face torture. This simple assertion, confirmed in *N v Finland* (2005) 43 EHRR 12, has become the focal point of an international debate, in which states bent on defeating terrorism seek ways to circumvent the absolute nature of this prohibition.

In the UK, a previous government talked of withdrawing from the whole European Convention, and then re-ratifying without Article 3. Legal opinion obtained in response to the proposal, unsurprisingly, was that 'it is strongly arguable that the ECHR does not permit a contracting state to use the power of denunciation . . . as a device to secure a reservation which could not otherwise validly be made, and therefore the proposal floated by the Prime Minister would be invalid and unlawful' (29 January 2003, Blackstone Chambers, D. Pannick and S. Fatima, for Liberty). The absolute nature of the prohibition on returning someone to a risk of torture was energetically reasserted by the ECtHR in *Saadi v Italy*, and subsequent decisions in the ECtHR have followed that judgment.

 **Key Case**

Saadi v Italy **[2008] ECHR 179**

Italy wanted to deport the applicant to Tunisia, where he would face a risk of torture. The Italian government gave evidence that he was a risk to national security. The UK intervened to support the Italian government's argument that an expelling state should be able to balance the risk to its society against the risk to the deportee. The ECtHR disagreed. The Court held unanimously that the protection of Article 3 against torture was absolute and fundamental in a democratic society. The fact that the feared ill-treatment would take place abroad did not prevent the responsibility of the contracting state from being engaged nor did it affect the standard of proof. In attempting to deal with the threat of terrorism, states were not permitted to weigh any threat to the security of the host state against the risk of torture in the destination state. These two risks were of different kinds.

5.6.3.1 Memoranda of understanding (MOU)

Another way for the government to effect returns is to obtain assurances from receiving governments that returnees will not be subject to torture. Memoranda of understanding (MOU) that returnees will not be tortured have been signed with countries including Ethiopia, Jordan, Libya, and Lebanon. The reliability of assurances has been seriously doubted (see Human Rights Watch 2005, Amnesty International 2007 and 2010 and Metcalf). The courts have maintained the position that it is for them to determine 'the factual question of whether an individual faces a substantial risk of torture on his return, and in reaching that decision the courts will properly take into account the assurances given as part of all the relevant evidence, including evidence about the likelihood of those assurances being delivered in practice' (Counter-Terrorism Policy and Human Rights Joint Committee on Human Rights Third Report of sessions 2005–06 HL 75–I, HC 561–I para 145).

Thus, the means and standard of evaluation of the reliability of assurances is said not to be a question of law, but rather one of assessing evidence to draw a conclusion of fact (see, e.g., *BB v SSHD* [2006] UKSIAC 39/2005 para 4, confirmed in *RB, U and OO v SSHD* [2009] UKHL). The Special Immigration Appeals Commission (SIAC) said that the following conditions should be fulfilled for assurances to be adequate:

(i) the terms of the assurances must be such that, if they are fulfilled, the person returned will not be subjected to treatment contrary to Article 3;

(ii) the assurances must be given in good faith;

(iii) there must be a sound objective basis for believing that the assurances will be fulfilled;

(iv) fulfilment of the assurances must be capable of being verified.

In the House of Lords, one of the issues was that the appellants wanted to challenge SIAC's assessment of the reliability of the memoranda of understanding, or assurances. However, the House of Lords held that this could only be challenged before them if SIAC had made its decision unreasonably, that is, if its decision would be susceptible to challenge in judicial review. Their Lordships held that there was nothing in SIAC's assessment of the reliability of the memoranda of understanding which suggested an error of that kind. Lord Phillips said that the ECtHR cases did not establish that assurances must eliminate all risk of inhuman treatment before they could be relied upon.

Metcalfe is highly critical of SIAC's assessment, considering that SIAC showed little awareness of the difficulties involved in detecting torture and ill-treatment, and minimized the need for scrutiny and redress.

In *AS & DD (Libya) v SSHD, Liberty intervening* [2008] EWCA Civ 289, SIAC had found that Libya signed the MOU in good faith, but assurances would be honoured when Colonel Qadhafi or his regime considered it was in their interests to do so. Colonel Qadhafi's assessment of his interests was unpredictable, and, based on past conduct, he might at times act in ways that the outside world thought damaged his long-term interests, but which he would assess according to a different priority. The Court of Appeal approved this approach by SIAC, and the assurances were held not to give sufficient protection. Accordingly, deportation to Libya risked breaching Article 3.

The ECtHR has taken a similar approach in that it has decided each case of MOU on its merits. *Saadi v Italy* was itself a case of assurances, in which the ECtHR said that even if the Tunisian government had provided more detailed assurances

that would not have absolved the Court from the obligation to examine whether such assurances provided, in their practical application, a sufficient guarantee that the applicant would be protected against the risk of treatment prohibited by the Convention. The weight to be given to assurances from the receiving State depends, in each case, on the circumstances obtaining at the material time. (para 148)

This fairly robust approach to assurances was maintained in another case against Italy and three against Russia in the following two years; in each case the ECtHR found diplomatic assurances insufficient. The foundational case in affirming the absolute nature of Article 3, *Chahal v UK*, was also a case of assurances which the Court found unconvincing. Against the trend, in *Mamatkulov v Turkey* [2005] 41 EHHR 25, the Court decided that assurances by Uzbekistan were sufficient to prevent Turkey from being in breach by returning the applicant, and the assurances of Jordan, which were given at a very high level and specifically in relation to Mr Othman (Abu Qatada), were held to be sufficient protection for him against torture (*Othman (Abu Qatada) v UK*).

The UK's practice of sending people back to countries with proven records of torture on the basis of diplomatic assurances was strongly criticized by Thomas Hammarberg, the Commissioner for Human Rights of the Council of Europe, in a report following his visit to the UK in 2008 (CommDH(2008)23 Strasbourg, 18 September 2008). In the Amnesty International report, *Dangerous Deals*, the UK was described as 'the most influential and aggressive promoter in Europe of the use of diplomatic assurances to forcibly return people it considers threats to national security to countries where they would face a real risk of serious human rights violations' (2010:27). The report says that the UK has relied on post-return monitoring arrangements to strengthen the assurances. However, the reality of post-return monitoring is described by the report as inadequate (and in an Ethiopian case was found to be so—see *XX v SSHD* [2010] UKSIAC 61/2007). Detainees are not visited in conditions where they may remain anonymous. The fear of reprisals is therefore a major constraint. The monitoring bodies have no powers of enforcement.

The House of Lords in *RB* held that effective verification was essential for assurances to be protective. Verification could be achieved by means, formal and informal, of which monitoring was only one. Other means could include contact by the British Embassy and investigation by Amnesty International and other non-governmental agencies. The question of assurances arises most often in the context of extradition, and as such is not pursued further in this textbook.

5.6.3.2 Evidence obtained by torture

This issue has already been addressed in the context of unfair trials. The absolute nature of Article 3 is undermined if evidence is accepted that has been obtained by torture. In no case would evidence obtained by torture within the UK be admissible (*A v SSHD* [2005] UKHL 71), but the question of admitting evidence which may have been obtained by torture abroad has arisen in deportation or exclusion cases in which the evidence obtained suggests that a person poses a risk to national security. It may also arise in exclusion from refugee status on account of acts said to have been committed abroad (*Al-Sirri v SSHD* [2009] EWCA Civ 222).

In *A and others v SSHD* [2005] UKHL 71, a committee of seven Law Lords unanimously rejected the Secretary of State's argument that evidence which might have been obtained by torture could, as a matter of law, be admitted before SIAC. The judgment is a complex one, and the distinctions between the majority and minority views are not easy to follow—as Lord Brown expresses (para 173). The majority (Lords Brown, Rodger, and Hope) considered that SIAC should refuse to admit the evidence if it concluded, on a balance of probabilities, that the evidence *was* obtained by torture. Lords Bingham and Hoffmann thought that evidence should be excluded if there was a *real risk* that it had been obtained by torture, probably meaning that it should be excluded if SIAC was not satisfied that evidence had *not* been obtained by torture. In *RB, U & OO*, the House of Lords held that no higher standard than that which applied in SIAC could be applied to the risk of Mr Othman being convicted abroad in a trial in which evidence might have been obtained by torture. This was the issue on which the ECtHR disagreed with the national Court. The Strasbourg Court found that:

- admitting evidence obtained by torture would only serve to legitimate indirectly the sort of morally reprehensible conduct which the authors of Article 3 of the Convention sought to proscribe;

- torture evidence is excluded because it is 'unreliable, unfair, offensive to ordinary standards of humanity and decency and incompatible with the principles which should animate a tribunal seeking to administer justice' (quoting Lord Bingham in *A and others*);

- fundamentally, no legal system based upon the rule of law can countenance the admission of evidence—however reliable—which has been obtained by such a barbaric practice as torture. The trial process is a cornerstone of the rule of law. Torture evidence damages irreparably that process; it substitutes force for the rule of law and taints the reputation of any court that admits it. Torture evidence is excluded to protect the integrity of the trial process and, ultimately, the rule of law itself (para 264).

In *Al-Sirri v SSHD* [2009] EWCA Civ 222, the Court of Appeal held that it was wrong to admit evidence which had *probably* been obtained by torture. This was in the context of a decision to exclude the appellant from refugee status on the grounds of convictions obtained abroad.

In an interim report to the UN General Assembly on 1 September 2004, the UN Special Rapporteur on Torture criticized attempts by governments to circumvent the absolute nature of the prohibition on torture and other inhuman treatment on the ground of combating terrorism. The UN General Assembly in November 2011 repeated its stand against torture, passing a resolution which included condemnation of

any action or attempt by States or public officials to legalize, authorize or acquiesce in torture and other cruel, inhuman or degrading treatment or punishment under any circumstances, including on grounds of national security or through judicial decisions.

The resolution urged states not to expel a person to another state 'where there are substantial grounds for believing that the person would be in danger of being subjected to torture', and recognized that 'diplomatic assurances, where used, do not release States from their obligations under international human rights, humanitarian and refugee law, in particular the principle of non-refoulement' (doc. A/C.3/66/L.28/Rev.1). The ECtHR's judgment in *Othman (Abu Qatada)* reinforces that resolution.

5.6.3.3 Extraordinary rendition

The practice of 'extraordinary rendition' is that of transporting people to extra-territorial locations for interrogation 'in circumstances that make it more likely than not that the individual will be subjected to torture or cruel, inhuman or degrading treatment' (All Party Parliamentary Group on Extraordinary Rendition, December 2005). These locations include US bases and countries known for their record of torture (Amnesty International 2005:4). It is relevant here since it is a means of exporting torture, with the aim of avoiding the territorial jurisdiction of any country the All Party Parliamentary Group on Extraordinary Rendition has successfully challenged the secrecy surrounding these practices and the denial by the UK government that it has had any role in the US' extraordinary rendition programme. The Council of Europe's Committee for the Prevention of Torture in its seventeenth report in September 2007 concluded that, 'in the light of information now in the public domain, there can be little doubt that the interrogation techniques applied in the CIA-run facilities concerned have led to violations of the prohibition of torture and inhuman or degrading treatment'.

There was a breakthrough in December 2011 when the Court of Appeal granted an application for a writ of habeas corpus in relation to a Pakistani national who had been captured by UK forces in Iraq, handed over to US forces, and detained for seven years in Bagram in Afghanistan (*Rahmatullah v Secretary of State for the Foreign and Commonwealth Affairs and the Ministry of Defence* [2011] EWCA Civ 1540). The Court accepted that, under the MOU and the Geneva Conventions, the UK had sufficient control of Mr Rahmatullah that the UK government was able to make a request of the US government to release Mr Rahmatullah. Initially the UK government had denied that Mr Rahmatullah was detained. A US tribunal had found in 2010 that he was not an enduring security threat, but he remained in detention.

This decision, the Court of Appeal said, was not inconsistent with *Abbassi* [2002] EWCA Civ 1598 and *Al-Rawi* [2008] QB 289, in which the Court had refused, in judicial review, to make an order that the Foreign and Commonwealth Office use its diplomatic powers in relation to detainees in Guantanamo Bay. The basis of the successful habeas corpus application was that Mr Rahmatullah was within the control of the UK. To require the government to demand his release was not trespassing on the forbidden area of foreign relations. The Supreme Court agreed ([2012] UKSC 48).

Successful claims have been made in the ECtHR on the basis of extraordinary rendition, as described at 5.4.3.

5.6.4 Relationship with asylum claims

There is a substantial overlap between the treatment which might form the substance of an asylum claim and treatment which would breach Article 3. The majority of Article 3 claims are thus from people whose asylum claim has failed or are made concurrently with an asylum claim. The case of *Kacaj* established that the standard of proof is the same for a refugee claim and for a human rights claim. The standard to be applied is to enquire whether there is a real risk of the feared treatment occurring. This was further explained by Sedley LJ in *Batayav v SSHD* [2003] EWCA Civ 1489: 'If a type of car has a defect which causes one vehicle in ten to crash, most people would say that it presents a real risk to anyone who drives it, albeit crashes are not generally or consistently happening' (para 38).

Kacaj also established that the approach in the asylum case of *Horvath v SSHD* [2000] 3 WLR 370 to the question of state protection applies in Article 3 cases. In that case, the Roma applicant had been subjected to attacks by skinheads, and the case in the House of Lords turned on whether the system of criminal law in Slovakia gave him adequate protection. It was held that where there is a system of criminal law which makes violent attacks punishable, and a reasonable willingness by the enforcement agencies to enforce that law, then the state is held to protect its citizens sufficiently. Therefore, when treatment contrary to Article 3 is feared from people who are not part of the state machinery themselves, if there is such a system in place there will be no sustainable claim under Article 3.

The ECtHR has now said in a line of cases that:

the existence of the obligation not to expel is not dependent on whether the source of the risk of the treatment stems from factors which involve the responsibility, direct or indirect, of the authorities of the receiving country. Having regard to the absolute character of the right guaranteed, Article 3 may extend to situations where the danger emanates from persons or groups of persons who are not public officials. What is relevant in this context is whether the applicant is able to obtain protection against and seek redress for the acts perpetrated against him or her. (*Auad v Bulgaria* [2011] ECHR 1602)

An Article 3 claim may succeed where an asylum seeker is unable to prove that the ill-treatment they fear is for a reason laid down by the Refugee Convention (see chapters 11 and 12). See, for instance, *AS (Appeals raising Articles 3 and 8) Iran* [2006] UKAIT 00037 where the immigration judge found that there was a real risk of punishment by lashes but not for a reason recognized by the Refugee Convention. This treatment would contravene Article 3.

5.7 Convention rights—Article 2

Article 2(1) provides that:

Everyone's right to life shall be protected by law. No one shall be deprived of his life intentionally save in the execution of a sentence of a court following conviction of a crime for which this penalty is provided by law.

Article 2 does not outlaw the death sentence. This is done by Protocol 13, which the UK ratified on 10 October 2003. Protocol 13, unlike Protocol 6, outlaws the death penalty in all circumstances. The inclusion of Protocol 13 in the rights in Sch 1 to the Human Rights Act means that there are substantial constitutional problems in the way of any future government that might wish to re-introduce the death penalty, including in time of war.

Article 2(1) entails both that the state must take some positive steps to prevent life being taken and that the state must not itself take life.

5.7.1 Positive obligation

The positive duty to protect life is of a limited kind. In *Osman v UK* (2000) 29 EHRR 245, the police were aware that a schoolteacher who had developed an obsession with his pupil was harassing him. The ECHR held that there was no breach of Article 2 in their failure to apprehend him and to prevent the killing he committed, because there was no decisive stage at which the police knew or ought to have known that the lives of the applicant family were at real and immediate risk. The corollary of this is that if, in another case, there were such a decisive stage at which the risk was real and immediate then there could be a breach of Article 2. Case law on this protective aspect of Article 2 more often concerns the death of someone who was already in the care of the state, for instance in custody. More generally, in *Osman*, the Court interpreted the duty of protection in Article 2 to mean that the state has a general duty to establish and maintain an effective system of criminal law to deter, detect, and punish offenders.

5.7.2 Negative obligation

The negative obligation not to take life is qualified by Article 2(2), which sets out possible defences the state may be able to maintain where death results accidentally from the use of force which is no more than absolutely necessary:

(a) in defence of any person from unlawful violence;

(b) in order to effect a lawful arrest or to prevent the escape of a person lawfully detained; and

(c) in action lawfully taken for the purpose of quelling a riot or insurrection.

The terms of this paragraph are strictly construed by the Court, and in determining whether the use of force was no more than absolutely necessary attention may be paid to whether adequate guidelines for the situation were in place and followed. This was demonstrated in the case of *McCann v UK* (1996) 21 EHRR 97 (the 'deaths on the Rock' case) where the lack of training in shooting to wound rather than to kill was one of the reasons that the UK government was found in breach of Article 2 for the killing of IRA suspects in Gibraltar.

The negative aspect of the duty is less likely to be relevant as a defence to removal but is relevant to the conduct of immigration functions in the UK. There have been two deaths at the hands of officials during deportations in the UK. In 1993, a woman called Joy Gardner suffocated to death when she was bound and gagged by the police Alien Deportation Group. Prosecution and complaints failed. In October 2010 an Angolan man, Jimmy Mubenga, died while being restrained by escorts employed by a private security firm as he was being put onto a plane for deportation. What Article 2 may add to legal routes is a further element of state responsibility. If the individuals were exonerated because sufficient justification was found for their actions at the time, given their training, responses, and state of knowledge, this does not exonerate the state from providing a level of training that would prevent such incidents from occurring. In the case of *McCann*, the SAS officers were not trained to shoot to wound rather than kill. They were not held individually to blame but the state was in breach of Article 2. In the case of Joy Gardner, it seems that the officers were insufficiently aware of the effect of binding someone's head with 13 feet of surgical tape. The positive obligation also requires diligent and prompt investigation of a death at the hands of the state (*Kaya v Turkey* (1999) 28 EHRR 1). The Supreme Court in *In the matter of an application by Brigid McCaughey and another for Judicial Review (Northern Ireland)* [2011] UKSC 20 held that an inquiry into a death must comply with the procedural requirements of Article 2, even if the death occurred before the commencement of the Human Rights Act. This meant that the inquests could, as the Coroner proposed, consider the purpose and planning of the operation in which the deceased met their deaths. The inquest would thus be capable of considering whether they were, as their surviving relatives alleged, the victims of a 'shoot to kill' policy. The Supreme Court was following a development in the ECtHR in *Silih v Slovenia* (2009) 49 EHRR 37 where the Court held that the duty to investigate deaths had evolved into a separate and autonomous duty.

5.7.3 Article 2 and expulsions

Article 2 is relevant in the case of threatened expulsion of someone from the UK to a risk of death. This would usually refer to deliberate killing against which there is insufficient protection in the destination country, and not to the circumstances in *N*. Earlier case law suggested that the risk of death must be 'near certain' in order to engage the responsibility of the expelling state, following a Commission decision, *Dehwari v Netherlands* (2001) 29 EHRR CD 74. However, in *A v SSHD* [2003], the Court of Appeal applied the same standard to a risk of violation of Article 2 as to Article 3, namely that there was a 'real risk'. This is now the correct standard, and is consistent with Article 3. Note that also the EC Refugee Qualification Directive provides for subsidiary protection to be granted where someone faces a real risk of 'death penalty or execution', which is a form of 'serious harm' under Article 15C (a).

It is immaterial whether the danger comes from the state or, as in *A*, criminal gangs, if there is a real risk that the applicant will not be protected. This confirms the approach in *Kacaj*, referred to previously, in relation to state responsibility.

5.7.4 Death penalty

If the danger to life comes from the state, this may be by way of extra-judicial killing or by the death penalty. The imposition of the death penalty is now outlawed by the inclusion of Protocol 13 in the ECHR. A minister in a parliamentary written answer (WA 40 28 November 2001) confirmed that there would not be expulsions from the UK to face the death penalty. Extradition requests to the UK now contain an assurance that the death penalty will not be imposed.

The way in which the death penalty is carried out may involve an expelling state in a breach of Article 3. This is a small extension of the outcome of *Soering*, and is demonstrated in cases such as *Jabari v Turkey* [2001] INLR 136. Here, the applicant was granted refugee status by the UNHCR in Turkey, but, because she had not made her application within five days, under Turkish law she was still vulnerable to expulsion from Turkey. There was a real risk that if returned to Iran she would face death by stoning for adultery. Returning her to face this was held to be a breach of Article 3.

5.8 Convention rights—Article 4

Article 4 is potentially relevant to protect victims of trafficking, and where domestic workers are kept in forced conditions. An important development in the ECtHR is *Rantsev v Cyprus and Russia* Application no. 25965/04, [2010] ECHR 22. Here the police had handed a young woman back to her employer who had taken her to the police, asking for her to deported, without investigating whether she might have been trafficked. The ECtHR found Cyprus to have violated Article 4. The case is discussed in chapter 12.

Article 4 can be relied on in a removal case where there is a real risk of re-trafficking. It is also relevant to the UK's obligations to people making asylum and human rights claims in the UK. If the facts disclosed suggest that the individual may have been trafficked, or subject to forced labour in the UK, there is an obligation on a Home Office official to refer to the National Referral Mechanism (see chapter 11).

5.9 **Convention rights—Article 6**

Article 6, the right to a fair hearing, is one of the most litigated Articles in the Convention. It sets out minimum requirements of a fair hearing which apply to the determination of 'civil rights and obligations' and criminal trials and provides further minimum rights for a person charged with a criminal offence, for instance to have information of the charge, facilities and time for preparing a defence, and so on.

In addition to the express rights set out, Article 6 also imports a general requirement of fairness into trials, which is open to interpretation by the Court. It has been held to require access to a court (*Golder v UK* (1979–80) 1 EHRR 524), the right to put one's case on equal terms with one's opponent, which may, depending on the circumstances entail the right to legal representation, and the right to participate effectively in proceedings (e.g., *Goddi v Italy* (1984) 6 EHRR 457).

5.9.1 **Article 6 and immigration**

Where an immigration offence such as illegal entry is charged, then Article 6 applies as to any other criminal matter. However, the majority of immigration issues only come within the ambit of Article 6(1) if they are regarded as civil rights. In the case law of the ECtHR civil rights are personal to the individual, and are distinguished from public or administrative matters (*Salesi v Italy* (1993) 26 EHRR 187, *Adams & Benn v UK* (1996) 23 EHRR 160 CD). In *Uppal v UK* (1979) 3 EHRR 391, the Commission found that decisions to deport were of an administrative nature and so not covered by Article 6(1). Challenging extradition (*Farmakopoulous v Greece* (1990) 64 DR 52), nationality (*S v Switzerland* (1988) 59 DR 256), and entry for employment (*X v UK* (1977) 9 DR 224) were all found by the Commission not to qualify as civil rights for Article 6.

The issue of immigration decisions came before the Grand Chamber of the ECtHR in the case of *Maaouia v France* (2001) 33 EHRR 42.

 Key Case

Maaouia v France (2001) 33 **EHRR 42**

Mr Maaouia was unaware of a deportation order made against him as it was not served on him. The following year, he went to the Nice Centre for Administrative Formalities to regularize his immigration status and was served with the deportation order. He refused to leave the country in compliance with the order, and was sentenced to one year in prison and ten years' exclusion from French territory. He appealed through the French system against his exclusion, but his appeals were finally dismissed in 1994 on the ground that he had not challenged the deportation order in the lower courts, though it was eventually quashed because it had not been served. Mr Maaouia then applied for rescission of the exclusion order, which clearly could not stand as the deportation order on which it was based no longer existed. Rescission is a remedy available on mainly humanitarian grounds. He continued to take steps to regularize his immigration status. Eventually, in 1998, the exclusion order was rescinded and he obtained a residence permit.

Mr Maaouia claimed in the ECtHR that the four-year delay in rescinding the exclusion order was unreasonable and thus a breach of Article 6 as he had not had a fair hearing within a reasonable time in determination of his civil rights (6:1).

The Court, by a majority of 15 to 2, decided that Article 6:1 did not apply. Rescission of the exclusion order was not a criminal matter because the original merits of the criminal charges were not examined. The majority also thought that the exclusion order was not a penalty but an administrative measure particular to immigration control. It was also not 'civil' within the meaning of Article 6, for two principal reasons. The first was the view which the majority took of the existence and rationale of Protocol 7 Article 1, which provides procedural safeguards relating to the expulsion of aliens. They considered that the purpose of this Protocol was to give protection to aliens, which had not previously existed. If there had been no previous protection, then it must be the case that Article 6 did not apply to aliens faced with expulsion.

The Court's second main reason was that the Commission had previously expressed a consistent view, in cases such as those referred to earlier, that the rights of aliens faced with expulsion were not within Article 6. Given that the matter was referred to a full court because of its importance and the lack of previous decisions of the Court, for the Court to follow the less authoritative earlier decisions rather than look at the matter afresh is disappointing.

Personal and economic effects of rescission were not considered sufficient to bring the matter within Article 6. The Court said 'the fact that the exclusion order incidentally had major repercussions on the applicant's private and family life and on his prospects of employment cannot suffice to bring those proceedings within the scope of civil rights'.

Powerful dissenting judgments from Judges Loucaides and Traja argued that Article 31 of the Vienna Convention on the Law of Treaties required that if a term is capable of more than one interpretation, the meaning which enhances individual rights should be preferred. Their view of the history of Article 6 was that the phrase 'civil rights and obligations' was meant to catch all non-criminal matters, rather than to develop a new and specialized meaning. The result of limiting its application to private law matters is that the individual has less protection against the power of the state than against other individuals, which they said was 'absurd' and flouted the purpose of the Convention. Their view of Protocol 7 was that it was designed to furnish 'additional special protection' for people liable to be expelled. It refers to administrative rather than judicial safeguards, and it was the latter that were the realm of Article 6.

As the sole judgment on this matter of a full court, *Maaouia* has been consistently followed as an authority and the non-applicability of Article 6 to immigration matters is treated as settled law. The boundaries of this principle have been tested in numerous contexts without success. See *Harrison v SSHD, MH and others v SSHD* and *K2 v SSHD* SC/96/2010, all discussed in chapter 3, and holding that disputes about refusal of nationality did not relate to the determination of civil rights or obligations.

The Court of Appeal in *W (Algeria) v SSHD* [2010] EWCA Civ 898 confirmed that, in a case where the appellant was the subject of both a control order under the Terrorism Act and a deportation order, Article 6 applied to the control order, so that he must be 'provided with the essence of the allegations against him' (following *A v UK* [2009] ECHR 301) but not to the deportation order, following *Maaouia* (see also *SSHD v MB and AF* [2007] UKHL 46). The SIAC rejected the application of Article 6 to a bail application by a person detained pending deportation (*R on the application of BB v SIAC and SSHD* [2011] EWHC 2129 (Admin)).

Following this consistent exclusion of Article 6, Article 47 of the EU Charter of Fundamental Rights seems to offer new possibilities since the Article provides:

Everyone whose rights and freedoms guaranteed by the law of the Union are violated has the right to an effective remedy before a tribunal in compliance with the conditions laid down in this Article.

In principle it appears that Article 47 is capable of applying to immigration issues, although in *R (on the application of MK(Iran)) v SSHD* [2010] EWCA Civ 115 it was not found to give the appellant the right to a prompt determination of his asylum claim. In *AZ* [2015] EWHC (Admin) 3695 the Court accepted that since the applicant's right to a Convention Travel Document, although qualified, was given by EU law, he could rely on Article 47, but this did not give a right to full disclosure of the reasons for refusal. The Qualification Directive allowed for refusal of a travel document if there were 'compelling reasons' of national security. In *ZZ v SSHD* [2014] EWCA Civ 7 the Court of Appeal applied the CJEU's judgment (Case C-300/11, *ZZ v SSHD*) to reach a conclusion that proceedings in SIAC had not given ZZ the minimum level of disclosure that Article 47 required. He was entitled to 'the essence of the grounds' on which the decision to exclude him was based.

The majority of procedural issues which would affect a fair hearing in the immigration appeal tribunals are covered in the Tribunal's procedure rules. However, the rules contain no right to be represented, and the abolition of legal aid for immigration cases, combined with very narrow guidance on when exceptional case funding was to be allowed, produced a new challenge to fairness in immigration cases.

In *Gudanaviciene and others v The Director of Legal Aid Casework and Lord Chancellor* [2014] EWCA Civ 1422 the applicants challenged the fairness of the legal aid guidance on exceptional case funding. The Court of Appeal's findings included that, although Article 6 does not apply in immigration cases, Article 8 carries procedural rights. Following ECtHR jurisprudence, the Court held:

- the procedural protections inherent in article 8 are necessary in order to ensure that article 8 rights are practical and effective (para 69);
- the test for article 8 . . . (whether those affected have been involved in the decision-making process, viewed as a whole, to a degree sufficient to provide them with the requisite protection of their interests) differs from the test for article 6(1) (whether there has been effective access to court) (para 70);
- nevertheless they doubted whether there was any real difference between the two formulations in the present context (para 70).

The Court of Appeal's rulings on exceptional case funding (ECF) in immigration cases were:

- eCF does not involve an exceptionality test and is to be assessed by reference to the requirements of the ECHR and the EU Charter. Legal aid would have to be granted if the Legal Aid Agency concluded there would be a breach, or if not, if it was appropriate to grant legal aid having regard to any risk of a breach;
- the Guidance was incompatible with Article 6 ECHR and Article 47 of the Charter because it sent a signal to caseworkers that the refusal of legal aid would breach Art 6 only in rare and extreme cases (para 45);
- the Guidance was incompatible with Article 8 ECHR in immigration cases. In the context of legal aid, the standards were the same as those under Article 6 ECHR.
- the key requirements were effectiveness and fairness (para 72);
- the decision-maker should not apply a 'very high threshold' (para 76);
- deportation cases are of particular concern, not least because of the importance of the interests at stake (para 77).

5.10 **Convention rights—Article 8**

Article 8 is discussed at length here because of its central relevance to immigration and asylum cases. Applications to enter to join family members and challenges to a removal or deportation that would break up a family are the substance of many cases in the courts and tribunals. The House of Lords in *Huang and Kashmiri* stated the 'core value' which Article 8 exists to protect:

Human beings are social animals. They depend on others. Their family, or extended family, is the group on which many people most heavily depend, socially, emotionally and often financially. There comes a point at which, for some, prolonged and unavoidable separation from this group seriously inhibits their ability to live full and fulfilling lives. (para 18)

This expresses the importance of the Article 8 right, which in immigration control may come into direct conflict with the exercise of state power. Thus, legal doctrine surrounding it has become highly developed, and its application raises all the difficult questions about proportionality and jurisdiction.

The text of the Article is:

(8.1) Everyone shall have the right to respect for his private and family life, his home and correspondence.

(8.2) There shall be no interference with the exercise of this right except such as is in accordance with the law and is necessary in a democratic society in the interests of national security, public safety or the economic well-being of the country, for the prevention of disorder or crime, for the protection of health or morals, or for the protection of the rights and freedoms of others.

A structured approach is used to applying the Article, and Lord Bingham's 'five steps' in *Razgar* (para 19) are the accepted exposition of this:

(1) Will the proposed removal be an interference by a public authority with the exercise of the applicant's right to respect for his private or (as the case may be) family life?

(2) If so, will such interference have consequences of such gravity as potentially to engage the operation of article 8?

(3) If so, is such interference in accordance with the law?

(4) If so, is such interference necessary in a democratic society in the interests of national security, public safety or the economic well-being of the country, for the prevention of disorder or crime, for the protection of health or morals, or for the protection of the rights and freedoms of others?

(5) If so, is such interference proportionate to the legitimate public end sought to be achieved?

Razgar was a case about the application of Article 8 to the health consequences of removal, abroad as well as in the UK. As discussed previously in relation to extraterritorial scope, where the feared breach of qualified rights is abroad, the threshold is much higher (*EM (Lebanon)*). Court of Appeal cases have confirmed that it is a mistake to elevate Lord Bingham's point 2 to create a high threshold for the engagement of Article 8 where, as is usually the case, the claim is for protection of family or private life in the UK. See *AG (Eritrea)* [2007] EWCA Civ 801 para 28, *VW (Uganda) v SSHD and AB (Somalia) v SSHD* [2009] EWCA Civ 5, and Baroness Hale's refutation in *Razgar* of a threshold in domestic cases, set out at 5.4.2. With this caveat, the five steps are a widely accepted formulation, and we now examine each in turn.

5.10.1 **Does private or family life exist?**

Private and family life are ECHR concepts which are given their meaning by the ECtHR. In accordance with HRA s 2, the UK courts are obliged to take account of these meanings. The current approach to identifying private and family life is described in chapter 8 at 8.4.1, and see the discussion of *Kaur (visit appeals; Article 8* [2015] UKUT 487 (IAC)) in chapter 10 for the Catch 22 that may result when the strength of ties establishes family life but casts doubt on whether the applicant would leave at the end of a visit.

The ECtHR in *Niemietz v Germany* (1992) 16 EHRR 97 has said that it is not possible or desirable to define all the situations to which the concept of private life can apply. In *Marckx v Belgium* (1979) 2 EHRR 330, the Court identified the central purpose of Article 8 as to protect the individual from arbitrary interference by public authorities, and this principle may be used to help determine new situations that may come within the protection of Article 8.

The anti-discrimination provisions of Article 14 mean that the marital status of the parents should not make any difference to the degree of respect accorded to the family under Article 8. The case of *Marckx v Belgium* expounded on this point:

Article 8 makes no distinction between the legitimate and illegitimate family. Such distinction would not be consonant with the word 'everyone' in Article 1 and this is confirmed by Article 14 with its prohibition . . . of discrimination grounded on birth.

In the UK, following the Civil Partnership Act 2004 and the inclusion of registered partners in the immigration rules, there is no justification for distinguishing between couples on the basis of whether they are of the same or different sexes. Between adults other than couples, often the Court looks for 'more than normal emotional ties' (see chapter 8). The ECtHR is moving away from placing reliance on the distinction between private and family life. See *Omojudi v UK* [2009] ECHR 1942 and this passage in *AA v UK* [2011] ECHR 1345:

An examination of the Court's case-law would tend to suggest that the applicant, a young adult of 24 years old, who resides with his mother and has not yet founded a family of his own, can be regarded as having 'family life'. However, it is not necessary to decide the question given that, as Article 8 also protects the right to establish and develop relationships with other human beings and the outside world and can sometimes embrace aspects of an individual's social identity, it must be accepted that the totality of social ties between settled migrants and the community in which they are living constitutes part of the concept of 'private life' within the meaning of Article 8. Thus, regardless of the existence or otherwise of a 'family life', the expulsion of a settled migrant constitutes an interference with his right to respect for private life. While the Court has previously referred to the need to decide in the circumstances of the particular case before it whether it is appropriate to focus on 'family life' rather than 'private life', it observes that in practice the factors to be examined in order to assess the proportionality of the deportation measure are the same regardless of whether family or private life is engaged. (para 49)

This approach was followed in *RG (Automatic deportation Section 33(2)(a) exception) Nepal* [2010] UKUT 273(IAC) in which the Tribunal found, in the case of a young man of 20, that the essence of the case was one of a family that 'have strong mutual links and that have always lived together and who expected to continue to live together in the UK'. They concluded that 'substantial respect was due to those links by way of family life or private life different in kind from the mere number of years of residence here' (para 28).

The evaluation of the contact between family members raises particular difficulties where adult children and parents are living in different countries. There must be 'an irreducible minimum' of actual and effective relationship (*Kugathas v SSHD* [2003] INLR 170 CA).

5.10.2 What does 'respect for private or family life' entail?

What a positive obligation of respect requires depends upon the situation. The implications of this are considered more fully in chapter 8, in the context of family settlement.

As discussed there, the trend in the courts is increasingly to make no real distinction of principle between what respect requires when a removal threatens to break up a family and what respect requires when a person applies to join their family in the UK. In *Tuquabo-Tekle v The Netherlands* [2006] 1 FLR 798 the Court asserted that boundaries between the state's positive and negative obligations under Article 8 did 'not lend themselves to precise definition', and that the applicable principles were similar. Also, the practical reality may be that decisions on entry merge with those on removal. For instance, the leading case of *Huang and Kashmiri v SSHD* [2007] UKHL 11 concerned applications for leave to remain in the UK, though as both applicants were in the UK, in practice they also concerned the prospect of removal.

5.10.3 Has there been an interference with the right?

There is normally little doubt about the act of interference in the immigration context. The most obvious and damaging interference with family life by a removal is the break-up of the family. The upheaval and disruption of support networks, wider family relationships, and so on is an interference with family and private life, and the upheaval to the whole family must be considered as the potential breach (*Beoku-Betts*). The Tribunal in *Nhundu* said that where a family is established, removal will constitute an interference with family life. In some later cases, this has been doubted, but this has generally been based on an erroneous interpretation of Lord Bingham's second step to create a high threshold for engagement of Article 8. In *DM (Zambia) v SSHD* [2009] EWCA Civ 474, the Court said:

Once the existence of private or family life in the UK is established, its character and intensity affect the proportionality of the proposed interference with it, not its existence or the engagement of Article 8. (para 17)

In other words, the real issue in Article 8 cases is whether the upheaval caused by removal or refusal of entry is proportionate to the public interest served. This is now affirmed by the Supreme Court in *Quila*, which held that 'forcing a married couple to choose either to live separately for some years or to suspend their plans to live in one place and go to live where neither of them wishes to live' was 'a colossal interference' with their right to respect for family life (paras 32 and 72). 'The only sensible enquiry can be into whether the refusals were justified.' (para 43).

The ECtHR does not hesitate to find an interference in removal cases, but has also gone beyond this to find that prolonged uncertainty and insecurity of status generated by immigration decisions can also amount to an interference. For instance, in *Shevanova v Latvia* (Application no 58822/00) a deportation order amounted to an interference with private life even though it was never enforced, because of the uncertainty and insecurity it created, and in *Sisojeva v Latvia* (Application no. 60654/00) prolonged refusal to recognize a stateless Russian family's right to permanent residence in Latvia constituted an interference with their right to respect for their family life.

5.11 **Can the interference with the right be justified?**

This is the main question in the majority of Article 8 cases. It is governed by Article 8.2, which, like the other qualified rights, has the following substantive requirements. The interference with the right, to be permitted, must be:

- in accordance with the law;
- in pursuit of a legitimate aim;
- necessary in a democratic society in the interests of that aim; and
- proportionate to the aim pursued.

Finally, the reasons given by the state must be relevant and sufficient (see *Handyside v UK*). These are established principles of Convention case law, referred to in almost every ECtHR case decided using the qualified rights. According to the ECtHR in *Smith and Grady v UK* (1999) 29 EHRR 493, these principles 'lie at the heart of the Court's analysis of complaints under Article 8 of the Convention' (para 138). We shall consider each in turn.

5.11.1 **In accordance with the law**

This has the same meaning as 'prescribed by law', which is the wording used in the other qualified Articles. It requires that the provision that interferes with the right not only complies with domestic law, but also that the law itself is accessible (*Silver v UK* (1983) 5 EHRR 347) and precise enough to enable an individual to regulate their conduct accordingly (*Sunday Times v UK* (1979) 2 EHRR 245). In immigration and asylum cases, this requirement is very rarely an issue. The interference normally arises from the application of statute or rules, which easily meet these criteria. A rare case of an immigration provision not being 'in accordance with the law' was *KK (Jamaica)* [2004] UKIAT 00268, which concerned a concession that children under 12 only needed to show adequate accommodation with their parent in order to obtain settlement. The terms of the concession were held to be insufficiently precise as it was not clear whether it only applied to entry clearance cases, nor whether the applicant had to be informed that the concession applied to them.

In *Estrikh v Latvia* [2007] ECHR 57 the ECtHR, held that a deportation was not in accordance with the law because it had taken place on the day that the applicant lodged an appeal against the deportation, in contravention of the Criminal Procedure Code, which, as in the UK, deemed that the order was not final until appeals had been exhausted.

In the UK, the inaccessibility of policies governing immigration-related decisions has been an important basis of challenge. These challenges are more usually brought on public law principles rather than Convention rights, and more often concern detention, and so potentially Article 5 ECHR, rather than Article 8. See *Lumba and Mighty* in chapter 14.

5.11.2 **In pursuit of a legitimate aim**

This requirement is rarely the subject of case law, but in immigration cases the importance of identifying the aim correctly has been recognized. See, for instance, *AA v UK* where the Court takes pains to identify which legitimate aim the government contends is served, before going on to consider whether deportation is proportionate. The legitimate aims are listed in para 2 of the qualified Articles (see Article 8 earlier in the chapter). They differ slightly as between the different qualified rights.

Importantly, this list of aims is exhaustive. The Court in *Golder v UK* said that the words 'There shall be no interference . . . except such as . . .' left 'no room for the concept of implied limitations' (para 44). Article 18 provides that restrictions on Convention rights cannot be used for any purposes other than those prescribed. Indeed, for this to be otherwise would subvert the purpose of the Convention, which is to control the situations in which governments can legitimately interfere with the rights of individuals. The aims listed are quite wide in their coverage, and it is not usually problematic for a government to bring their action within them. In the case of deportations, 'prevention of disorder or crime' or 'protection of health or morals' are usually cited as public interests served by the deportation. Other removals are usually directed towards immigration enforcement, but this is not listed in para 2 as a legitimate aim. Blake and Husain (*Immigration, Asylum and Human Rights* 2003:190) summarize the position as follows:

Immigration control has consistently been held by the European Court to relate to the preservation of the economic well-being of the country, the prevention of disorder or crime, the protection of health and morals, and the protection of the rights and freedoms of others. Exclusions and expulsions of illegal entrants are therefore likely to fall easily within a permissible competing interest under Article 8(2). It is important to note that immigration control is not of itself a valid end capable of justifying an interfering measure; it is rather the medium through which other legitimate aims are promoted.

See now s 117B discussed at 5.11.6 and 5.11.10. The identification of the legitimate aim is a fundamental requirement for considering proportionality. Without identifying the legitimate aim, there is nothing to which the interference must be proportionate. Richards LJ in *JO (Uganda) and JT (Ivory Coast) v SSHD* [2010] EWCA Civ 10 stressed that in deportation cases (based on criminal behaviour) and in removal cases (based on immigration enforcement):

The difference in aim is potentially important because the factors in favour of expulsion are in my view capable of carrying greater weight in a deportation case than in a case of ordinary removal.

There must be a rational connection between the aim and the means by which it is pursued (*de Freitas v Permanent Secretary of Ministry of Agriculture, Fisheries, Lands and Housing* [1999] 1 AC 69). This means not just that the aim generally is a legitimate one, but that it can be served by interfering with individual rights in this particular case.

Following *Huang and Kashmiri*, it is the Court's task to investigate the connection between the aim and the measures employed, and whether the interference is proportionate *to the aim pursued*. In a similar vein to Richards LJ quoted earlier, the Supreme Court in *ZH (Tanzania) v SSHD* [2011] UKSC 4 remarked, in the context of considering whether the removal of a parent of British children was in the interests of the economic well-being of the country, that:

Each of the legitimate aims . . . may involve individual as well as community interests . . . In reality, however, an argument that the continued presence of a particular individual in the country poses a specific risk to others may more easily outweigh the best interests of that or any other child than an argument that his or her continued presence poses a more general threat to the economic well-being of the country. (para 28)

5.11.3 Necessity in a democratic society

The question of whether the interference is necessary in a democratic society was said by the ECtHR in *Smith and Grady* to be the core of rights protection. Necessity has been equated with serving a 'pressing social need' (*Sunday Times v UK*). The characteristics of a democratic society according to the ECtHR in freedom of expression cases are tolerance, pluralism, broad-mindedness, and willingness to tolerate ideas that shock or offend (*Handyside v UK*). A democratic society is evidently not one in which all people think or behave in the same way. Necessity should be distinguished from reasonableness.

Necessity in a democratic society is rarely explicitly mentioned in UK immigration cases, and often proportionality and necessity flow into each other. In *Miao v SSHD* [2006] EWCA Civ 75, Sedley LJ said that to treat the two issues separately is to overcomplicate the issue.

As a rare exception, the concept was applied in the case of *ECO Mumbai v NH (India)* [2007] EWCA Civ 1330. Here, the Court of Appeal endorsed the Tribunal's examination of the history of discriminatory legislation preventing British East African Asians from obtaining residence in the UK in deciding whether it was proportionate to refuse entry to an 18-year-old son of the sponsor. The Tribunal said:

We regard this history and context as of the utmost relevance. We agree with the Appellants' representatives that the assessment of what is necessary in a democratic society in Article 8 terms should involve a consideration of all the circumstances including the previous history of any previous wrongful act and an understanding of how the convention rights have to be enforced. We accept the submission that '*in Strasbourg cases the Courts have looked at the history of development of legislation in assessing what is the right thing to do in the modern context when acknowledgements of past wrongful treatment are made*'. (quoted in CA para 18)

5.11.4 Proportionality

Proportionality is a relatively new concept in UK law, though it is established in the ECHR and in European law. It is relevant in all qualified rights. A classic formulation may be found in *de Freitas*, which was a Privy Council case from Antigua and Barbuda. Here, Lord Clyde observed, at p. 80, that in determining whether a limitation on a right was arbitrary or excessive the Court should ask itself:

whether: (i) the legislative objective is sufficiently important to justify limiting a fundamental right; (ii) the measures designed to meet the legislative objective are rationally connected to it; and (iii) the means used to impair the right or freedom are no more than is necessary to accomplish the objective.

In the context of Convention rights, point (i) here overlaps with identifying the legitimate aim and the question of necessity in a democratic society. The second and third points are a useful guide in considering the question of whether an infringement of a right is proportionate to the aim pursued. Proportionality requires a rational connection between the interference and the aim pursued, and that the interference is no more than is necessary.

The *de Freitas* formulation was added to by the House of Lords in *Huang and Kashmiri*, saying that 'the need to balance the interests of society with those of individuals and groups' was something 'which should never be overlooked or discounted' (para 19). This statement of the need for balance between society and the individual was said by the House of Lords in *Razgar* to be 'inherent in the whole of the Convention' (para 20).

Proportionality is very fact-specific. It is only possible to form a judgment about the infringement of an individual's rights in the light of all the circumstances of a particular case. Often, in judgments, one sees the phrase 'in all the circumstances'. In the context of proportionality, these are not empty words but may actually be the nub of the issue. It may be justifiable policy in general to remove people who have entered the UK illegally, and still disproportionate in a particular case, given that person's situation. Where human rights are concerned, even within the context of a policy, the state must justify an infringement on the merits of the individual case. The question of proportionality involves a close examination of facts but it is not a factual question, it is a judgment based upon an investigation into facts. In *A v SSHD* [2004] UKHL 56, Lord Bingham said: 'The European Court does not approach questions of proportionality as questions of pure fact . . . Nor should domestic courts do so' (para 44).

The nature of the proportionality exercise has been a vital and contentious question since the inception of the Human Rights Act. Many of the questions that have been debated were settled by the House of Lords in *Huang* in the following way:

> The question for the appellate immigration authority is whether the refusal of leave to enter or remain, in circumstances where the life of the family cannot reasonably be expected to be enjoyed elsewhere, taking full account of all considerations weighing in favour of the refusal, prejudices the family life of the applicant in a manner sufficiently serious to amount to a breach of the fundamental right protected by article 8. If the answer to this question is affirmative, the refusal is unlawful and the authority must so decide. (*Huang* para 20)

The House of Lords rejected many of the doctrines which have complicated the issue. Determining proportionality, they say, 'is not, in principle, a hard task to define, however difficult the task is, in practice, to perform' (para 14).

It has proved in many immigration cases to be the nub of the responsibility given to the judges by Parliament in the Human Rights Act. It is also, of course, a requirement of primary decision-makers in the Home Office. The proportionality exercise is not a special one for the judges.

Chikwamba v SSHD [2008] UKHL 40, unlike *Huang*, did not deal with the structure or principles of proportionality but with its application. The House of Lords held unanimously and in vigorous terms that it was disproportionate to expect the wife of a Zimbabwean refugee, herself a Zimbabwean, to return to Zimbabwe with her small child to make an application for entry clearance. All that prevented her Article 8 application to remain to live with her husband from being decided in the UK was a rule that as she did not have entry clearance for this purpose she should leave to obtain it. To require this was to elevate a policy beyond reason. This case is discussed in chapter 8.

In *EB (Kosovo) v SSHD* [2008] UKHL 41 the House of Lords said that the proportionality exercise required consideration of whether the individual could 'reasonably be expected to follow the removed spouse to the country of removal'. All the factors related to the possibility of family life elsewhere should be taken into account. These include, for instance, whether the spouse who is settled in the UK can speak the language of the other country or has any connections there; the impact on the couple's employment opportunities; their family ties in the UK; health needs; children's education; and so on. In the particular case, Lord Bingham said that the decision of the adjudicator had not 'accurately or adequately addressed the human problems' raised by the appeal, in that he had not considered the proportionality of separating the appellant from his girlfriend, informally adopted child, and expected child, or alternatively, of requiring his girlfriend 'to move to a country which was entirely unfamiliar and whose language she could not speak' (para 18).

The next sections examine some particular kinds of factual situations, and the way that these have been approached by the courts in the UK and Strasbourg. As the House of Lords said in *Huang*, the Strasbourg cases 'are of value in showing where, in many different factual situations, the Strasbourg Court, as the ultimate guardian of rights, has drawn the line' (para 18).

Nothing, however, displaces the fact that proportionality is an individual assessment. In the words of Lord Bingham in *EB (Kosovo) v SSHD* [2008] UKHL 41 at para 12:

there is in general no alternative to making a careful and informed evaluation of the facts of the particular case. The search for a hard-edged or bright-line rule to be applied to the generality of cases is incompatible with the difficult evaluative exercise which article 8 requires.

5.11.5 Settled people

There is a substantial body of case law in the ECtHR applying the principle of proportionality to the expulsion of individuals from a country where they are settled.

The most extreme case is that of someone who has lived lawfully in that country for all or most of their life, and now faces expulsion because of criminal offences. People in this position are sometimes referred to as 'integrated aliens', or 'quasi-nationals'. The fact that they are not a national of their country of residence may be because of that country's restrictive nationality law, or of decisions made by their parents. They may have lived in the country for longer than some of its nationals have, or have greater ties with it.

The ECtHR has considered this issue on many occasions, and the Grand Chamber laid down relevant principles in *Üner v The Netherlands* [2006] ECHR 873. The Court referred to Recommendation 1504 (2001), in which the Parliamentary Assembly of the Council of Europe recommended that the Committee of Ministers invited Member States to guarantee that long-term migrants who were born or raised in the host country could not be expelled under any circumstances. A number of contracting states have enacted legislation or adopted policy or rules to that effect, but the UK has moved in the opposite direction by introducing the power to revoke indefinite leave to remain (s 76 2002 Act), by weakening the presumption of a grant of indefinite leave after long residence (see chapter 6), and by introducing broader powers to deprive a person of their British citizenship (see chapter 3).

The Court in *Üner* held that an absolute right not to be expelled could not be derived from Article 8 (para 55). Even if a non-national held a very strong residence status and had attained a high degree of integration, his or her position could not be equated with that of a national when it came to the power of expulsion (para 56). However, the Court continued that its case law 'amply demonstrates' that expulsion could violate Article 8, and the Court would 'have regard to the special situation of aliens who have spent most, if not all, their childhood in the host country, were brought up there and received their education there' (para 58). The Court held that 'the totality of social ties between settled migrants and the community in which they are living constitute part of the concept of "private life" within the meaning of Article 8'. Thus, in human rights law, any long residence gives some protection against expulsion under Article 8, even if the person does not have family in their country of residence, though whether it will outweigh the reasons for expulsion is a matter which must be considered in the light of all the circumstances.

The ECtHR in *Maslov v Austria* [2007] ECHR 224 emphasized the importance of age and of youth spent in the host country:

For a settled migrant who has lawfully spent all or the major part of his or her childhood and youth in the host country, very serious reasons are required to justify expulsion; and this is all the more so where the person concerned committed the relevant offences as a juvenile (para 75)

Maslov was applied in the UK in *MJ (Angola) v SSHD* [2010] EWCA Civ 557 in which the Court held that:

the fact that (i) the appellant had lived in the UK since he was 12 years of age, (ii) most of his offending had been committed when he was under the age of 21 and (iii) he had no links with Angola meant that very serious reasons were required to justify the decision to deport him. (para 42)

In *SSHD v HK (Turkey)* [2010] EWCA Civ 583 Sedley LJ said: 'The number of years a potential deportee has been here is always likely to be relevant; but what is likely to be more relevant is the age at which those years began to run. Fifteen years spent here as an adult are not the same as fifteen years spent here as a child' (para 35).

In *DM (Zimbabwe)* [2015] EWCA Civ 1288 the Court of Appeal, drawing on *Jeunesse v The Netherlands* (Application no. 12738/10), considered the principle in *Maslov* that where the applicant had 'spent all or the major part of his or her childhood and youth in the host country very serious reasons are required to justify expulsion' and held that it did not apply to someone who did not have a lawful immigration status in the UK. Being 'settled' in the sense used by the ECtHR entailed 'having been granted formally a right of residence' (*Jeunesse* para 104). 'Very serious reasons' does not have to mean 'very serious offences' (*Akpinar* [2014] EWCA Civ 937).

Appeals against removal from the UK on the basis of the right to respect for a private life accumulated in the country are now affected by the July 2012 immigration rules and the Immigration Act 2014 discussed later. For EU citizens, the rules in Directive 2004/38 on expulsion are also relevant if they have acquired rights of permanent residence (see chapter 4).

In a reflection of the debate on Article 8 rights, in *Secretary of State for the Home Department v MG* [2014] CJEU C-400/12, the Luxembourg Court considered the effect of Directive 2004/38, which requires that expulsion of EU citizen migrants who have integrated in a host EU state should be limited in accordance with the principle of proportionality, taking account of the length of their residence, the degree of their integration, their age, state of health, family and economic situation, and their links with their country of origin. Expulsion of long-term residents, especially the native-born, should occur 'only in exceptional circumstances, where there are imperative grounds of public security'.

5.11.6 Status is precarious

This concept has been growing in relevance. In *EB (Kosovo)* Lord Bingham said:

An immigrant without leave to enter or remain is in a very precarious situation, liable to be removed at any time. Any relationship into which such an applicant enters is likely to be, initially, tentative, being entered into under the shadow of severance by administrative order. . . . But if months pass without a decision to remove being made, and months become years, and year succeeds year, it is to be expected that this sense of impermanence will fade and the expectation will grow that if the authorities had intended to remove the applicant they would have taken steps to do so. This result depends on no legal doctrine but on an understanding of how, in some cases, minds may work and it may affect the proportionality of removal. (para 15)

In *Jeunesse* the ECtHR applied the oft-quoted words from *Rodrigues da Silva and Hoogkamer v Netherlands* (2006) 44 EHRR 34:

Another important consideration is whether family life was created at a time when the persons involved were aware that the immigration status of one of them was such that the persistence of that family life within the host State would from the outset be precarious. (para 108)

In *Jeunesse* the applicant was aware of the precariousness of her residency status as she had made a number of applications for permission to remain in the Netherlands, all of which had been unsuccessful. The majority gave some weight to this factor, but set against it that at birth she had been a Netherlands national; she had lost that nationality through action of law when Suriname became independent, not by her own choice. They also took into account that although the Netherlands authorities had refused her residence, they had never attempted to remove her.

In *Jeunesse* the applicant had no leave to remain in the Netherlands. This is the situation in which the concept of precarious status is normally used in the ECtHR, though it is used to refer to a range of situations, and some applicants have had leave at some point in the past. Since the concept now appears in case law, statute, and policy its meaning has become important.

In the UK, the higher courts (e.g., the Court of Appeal in *SS (Congo)* [2015] EWCA Civ 387) have adopted the approach in *R (on the application of Nagre) v SSHD* [2015] EWHC 720 (Admin) to so-called 'precarious' cases. In *Nagre* the appellant had had leave as a visitor but had overstayed for some years. He sought leave on the basis of his relationship with his partner. The Court of Appeal cited such a case, of a person with no children whose status was precarious, as an example of when leave on the basis of Article 8 would only exceptionally be allowed outside the immigration rules (para 29). This fitted with the Home Office guidance. Sales J's 'careful review of Strasbourg case law' in *Nagre* was approved by the Court of Appeal in *Singh and Khalid v SSHD* [2015] EWCA Civ 74, again describing the immigration status of someone with no leave to remain as 'precarious'.

Section 117B(5) of the 2002 Act, inserted by the Immigration Act 2014, requires a tribunal to give little weight to a private life established at a time when immigration status was 'precarious'. The Upper Tribunal in *AM (S 117B) Malawi* [2015] UKUT 260 (IAC) has taken the interpretation in a much narrower direction, saying:

- A person's immigration status is 'precarious' if their continued presence in the UK will be dependent upon their obtaining a further grant of leave.

- In some circumstances it may also be that even a person with indefinite leave to remain, or a person who has obtained citizenship, enjoys a status that is 'precarious' either because that status is revocable by the Secretary of State as a result of their deception, or because of their criminal conduct. In such circumstances the person will be well aware that he has imperilled his status and cannot viably claim thereafter that his status is other than precarious.

The Tribunal explained this interpretation on the basis that s 117B distinguishes those whose status is 'precarious' from those whose status is 'unlawful'. Therefore, those whose status is 'precarious' *must* have had a lawful grant of leave. In an apparent rejection of preceding jurisprudence on proportionality the Tribunal said: 'Nor does the statute oblige the FtT to descend to adopting the approach of affording subtle gradations of 'little weight' to the elements of private life established during different periods of time.' (para 24). *Deelah and others (section 117B—ambit)* [2015] UKUT 515 (IAC) confirmed *AM (Malawi)* trenchantly in this respect, and in particular finding that student leave was 'precarious'. Both decisions cite ECtHR cases of those with *no* leave in support of the argument that *limited* leave is precarious.

Section 117B(5) does not apply to family life. Twelve days after *AM (Malawi)* the Administrative Court found that the immigration status of family members was not precarious 'throughout the period of ten years that their decisions were being unlawfully delayed by the SSHD' (*R (on the application of Said) v SSHD* [2015] EWHC 879 (Admin) para 420). The applicants had made valid, in-time applications for indefinite leave to remain, but these had simply not been decided. It is difficult to see how the judgment of 'precariousness' can be anything other than fact-sensitive. No doubt this will not be the end of the issue.

5.11.7 Criminal offences

Article 8 cases commonly concern the expulsion of people because of criminal offences they have committed. In UK law, such expulsions are likely to be deportations (see chapter 15). The weighing of the qualified rights of individuals under Article 8 and the rights of the state to deport criminals has been the focus of particular political, media, and public concern. The issue had a substantial ECHR case-law background by the time the domestic immigration rules were amended in July 2012. In *Boultif v Switzerland* [2001] ECHR 497, the ECtHR gave guidance on factors to be considered when the expulsion of a criminal interferes with family life. These were:

- the nature and seriousness of the offence committed by the applicant;
- the length of the applicant's stay in the country from which he or she is to be expelled;
- the time elapsed since the offence was committed and the applicant's conduct during that period;
- the nationalities of the various persons concerned;
- the applicant's family situation, such as the length of the marriage, and other factors expressing the effectiveness of a couple's family life;
- whether the spouse knew about the offence at the time when he or she entered into a family relationship;
- whether there are children of the marriage, and if so, their age; and
- the seriousness of the difficulties which the spouse is likely to encounter in the country to which the applicant is to be expelled.

Üner v The Netherlands [2006] ECHR 873 added two more considerations:

- the best interests and well-being of the children, in particular the seriousness of the difficulties which any children of the applicant are likely to encounter in the country to which the applicant is to be expelled; and
- the solidity of social, cultural, and family ties with the host country and with the country of destination.

Before *Boultif* and *Üner*, in *Beldjoudi v France* (1992) 14 EHRR 801, a life of crime was held not sufficient to outweigh the fact that the applicant had spent almost all his life in France, and had a French wife with whom his marriage would probably be destroyed if he were deported. On the other hand, in *Boughanemi v France*, the retention of links with Tunisia meant that the deportation was proportionate, though in other respects the facts were quite similar. In *Bouchelkia v France* (1998) 25 EHRR 686, the applicant had lived in France since the age of two, and was living with his family of origin, but the ECtHR held that his deportation following conviction for rape was proportionate. In *Nasri v France* (1996) 21 EHRR 458, the applicant had been involved in a gang rape, and some petty offences. He was deaf and mute, and the ECtHR held that to deport him would interfere with his right to respect for family and private life under Article 8(1).

Rogers (2003) identifies *Boultif* as promoting a trend towards a more realistic assessment of the difficulties facing family members required to relocate and the actual harm which would be inflicted by continuing residence. She says: 'The judgement is significant for its recognition that in cases where there are real barriers such as lack of ties for some of the family members or language difficulties, the Court is likely to conclude that the family cannot be expected to follow the deportee' (p. 62). The development towards assessment of the actual harm risked by allowing the non-national to remain is confirmed in *Maslov v Austria*, where the Grand Chamber said that the criteria in *Boultif* and *Üner* were 'designed to help evaluate the extent to which the applicant can be expected to cause disorder or to engage in criminal activities' (para 70).

In the case of *Kaya v Germany* [2007] ECHR 538, the applicant's cruelty to his partner and another woman and his attempt to shift responsibility to a co-defendant suggested to the Court that, even though all his offending happened in a short period of time, it was not 'mere juvenile delinquency' and he was not taking responsibility for his actions. Although he was born and brought up in Germany, his removal to Turkey was not a violation of his right to respect for private life. By contrast, Mr Maslov's offences, though they were many, were committed within a short period of time and were typical of juvenile delinquency and to deport him was a breach of Article 8 (*Maslov v Austria* [2007] ECHR 224). Both *Kaya* and *Maslov* concerned second-generation immigrants, in relation to whom one can say that, but for the particular provisions of nationality law into which they were born, they would be nationals of their home state, and so not deportable.

There are numerous cases from the UK. By way of example, in *Grant v UK* [2009] ECHR 26, the applicant had come to the UK at the age of 14. He had four British children ranging in age from 12 to 25. He had last lived in Jamaica 34 years ago. Nevertheless, the Court took account of the 'sheer number' of offences and the time span during which they occurred. With the exception of 1991 to 1995, there was no prolonged period during which the applicant was out of prison and did not reoffend. There was no evidence that he had addressed the underlying problem of drug addiction, and deportation was proportionate. By comparison, in *Omojudi v UK* [2009] ECHR 1942, the claimant had committed a sexual assault which was also a breach of trust. However, the short sentence revealed that it was not at the most serious end of the scale. The applicant and his wife had lived in the UK for 23 years, and had three children and a grandchild, who all lived with them. Mr Omojudi was deported, but the ECtHR held that deportation was disproportionate to the legitimate aim pursued.

The Court in *Üner* takes into account the effect of the deportation on the applicant themselves, given what they will face in their destination and their stage of life. In *Jakupovic v Austria* [2004] 38 EHRR 27, which concerned the proposed expulsion of a teenager with a fairly minor criminal record to Bosnia, the Court said, 'very weighty reasons have to be put forward to justify the expulsion of a young person (16 years old), alone, to a country which has recently experienced a period of armed conflict with all its adverse effects on living conditions and with no evidence of close relatives living there' (para 29). In *Grant v UK* [2009] ECHR 26, the Court took into account that deportation was not permanent. In a maximum of ten years, the applicant would be able to return. Note that since the 2008 rule changes in the UK, someone with Mr Grant's record is precluded from return under the rules (see chapter 6), but the courts clearly contemplate applications from abroad to revoke deportation orders, after a period of years, on the basis of Article 8 (see, e.g., *Sanade and others (British children—Zambrano—Dereci)* [2012] UKUT 00048 (IAC), discussed at 5.11.8).

Chapter 15, at 15.7.1, discusses the interaction between deportations rendered 'automatic' by the operation of s 32 of the UK Borders Act and the grounds which the immigration rules allow to be raised as defences to deportation. These provisions in the rules were intended by the government to define and determine the way that Article 8 is applied in deportation cases. As described in chapter 15 at 15.7.1, the restrictive rules were followed by the Immigration Act 2014 s 19 introducing an attempted statutory definition of 'the public interest question' to be considered in Article 8 cases (2002 Act s 117A–D). At the same time the immigration rules were further amended to reflect the statute, including removing the exception to deportation for someone with a 'genuine and subsisting relationship' with a partner in the UK who is a refugee or has humanitarian protection.

Reference should be made to chapter 15 for the public interest factors relevant to deportation, the exceptions introduced by s 117C, and early case law on the meaning of 'unduly harsh' in this context.

5.11.8 **Can the family reasonably be expected to live abroad?**

This question is posed in almost all cases of removal involving a family. As identified by the Tribunal in *VW and MO (Article 8—insurmountable obstacles) Uganda* [2008] UKAIT 00021, ECtHR cases use a range of terms when considering the family's prospects of life elsewhere:

- 'whether there are insurmountable obstacles in the way of the family living in the country of origin of one or more of them' (e.g., *Da Silva and Hoogkamer; Headley v UK* Application no. 39642/03 1 March 2005; *Konstatinov*);
- 'whether the applicant's family could reasonably be expected to follow the applicant to' (e.g., *Keles; Üner*); and
- 'the seriousness of the difficulties which the spouse is likely to encounter in the country to which the applicant is to be expelled' (e.g., *Boultif; Üner; Keles*).

These terms are not used in the ECtHR as a 'test', but are context-specific. The House of Lords in *Huang* established that the proper question is whether 'the life of the family cannot reasonably be expected to be enjoyed elsewhere' (para 20, and see chapter 8). This was repeated by the House of Lords in *EB (Kosovo)*, and the Court of Appeal has affirmed that, following *EB (Kosovo)*, assessing the proportionality of an interference with the right to respect for family life requires a judgment of what could reasonably be expected in the light of all the material facts, including whether a settled spouse could reasonably be expected to relocate abroad (see *VW (Uganda) and AB (Somalia) v SSHD* [2009] EWCA Civ 5, *TF (Angola) v SSHD* [2009] EWCA Civ 905 and *YD (Togo) v SSHD* [2010] EWCA Civ 214). The Court of Appeal in *SS (India) v SSHD* [2010] EWCA Civ 388 held that:

the tribunal has to consider and assess as a whole how serious the difficulties would be if the family were to follow the deportee. As Richards LJ pointed out at paragraph 26 of *JO (Uganda)*, the precise wording used by a tribunal when making its decision is less important than whether it is clear that the matter has been examined as a whole and that no limiting test (such as 'insurmountable problem') has been applied. (para 52)

In *MT (Zimbabwe) v SSHD* [2007] EWCA Civ 455, the Court accepted that 'because of shared experiences in Zimbabwe and the recovery from those experiences by mutual life together continuing in the UK, Ms T was more than normally emotionally dependent on Mr G and his family' (para 26).

Boultif gives the nationality of family members as a relevant factor. If a spouse is British, the Court in *AB (Jamaica)* [2007] EWCA Civ 1302 said that it was necessary to give:

detailed and anxious consideration to the situation of a British citizen who has lived here all his life before it is held reasonable and proportionate to expect him to emigrate to a foreign country in order to keep his marriage intact. (para 20)

The position of British children has been changed by the case of *ZH (Tanzania) v SSHD* [2011] UKSC 4 (see chapter 8). The rights of a child to preserve their national identity, with all that goes with this, now weigh in the balance in considering an objection to removal under Article 8. *ZH (Tanzania)* makes a significant addition to the protection that Article 8 gives to the residence of children. The Supreme Court drew on the ECtHR case of *Rodrigues da Silva, Hoogkamer v Netherland* (2007) 44 EHRR 34 in which the Court held that a mother who had had 'a cavalier attitude to the Dutch immigration rules' should nevertheless not be removed from the Netherlands. She and her daughter Rachael's father had separated, and the Dutch courts found that it was in Rachael's best interests to remain with her father and his family in the Netherlands, even if this meant that she would have to be separated from her mother. In practice, her care was shared between her mother and paternal grandparents. The ECtHR concluded:

In view of the far reaching consequences which an expulsion would have on the responsibilities which the first applicant has as a mother, as well as on her family life with her young daughter, and taking into account that it is clearly in Rachael's best interests for the first applicant to stay in the Netherlands, the Court considers that in the particular circumstances of the case the economic well-being of the country does not outweigh the applicants' rights under article 8, despite the fact that the first applicant was residing illegally in the Netherlands at the time of Rachael's birth. (para 44)

As discussed in chapter 8, the Supreme Court in *ZH (Tanzania)* concluded that treating the best interests of a child as a primary consideration was required by s 55 BCIA 2009 and entailed asking whether it was reasonable to expect the child to live in another country:

Relevant to this will be the level of the child's integration in this country and the length of absence from the other country; where and with whom the child is to live and the arrangements for looking after the child in the other country; and the strength of the child's relationships with parents or other family members which will be severed if the child has to move away. (para 29)

The effect on children's rights and interests of their parents' expulsion, and thus the reverse influence, were considered in *Zambrano v Office National de L'Emploi* (2011) CJEU (Case C-34/09) and *Dereci & Others* [2012] EUECJ (Case C-256/11), as the Luxembourg Court followed the Strasbourg Court in developing strong family rights (see chapter 4). The interaction between the legal provisions was considered in *Sanade and others (British children—Zambrano—Dereci)* [2012] UKUT 00048 (IAC). These were appeals against deportation by parents who had committed offences including indecent assault, drug-dealing, and theft. All were married to British citizen women and had British citizen children. There were three legal issues:

- Application of the EU cases of *Zambrano* and *Dereci*: since all the children had British mothers on whom they could rely, the deportation of their fathers did not engage *Zambrano*. The children were not dependent on the parent being removed for the exercise of their Union right of residence.
- The s 55 duty as interpreted in *ZH (Tanzania)*. This had to be considered in any case, most obviously the impact on the children of losing their father's regular presence.
- Article 8 in an automatic deportation: the Tribunal rejected the view that, in an automatic deportation case, an Article 8 claim had to be exceptional in order to defeat the deportation. Article 8 itself provided an exception to deportation. The Tribunal considered the particular families in the light of ECHR case law (*Boultif, Uner,* and *Maslov*) and held two deportations to be proportionate and one not.

In *Jeunesse v Netherlands* the ECtHR included an evaluation of the best interests of the children, on the basis of '[t]he broad consensus, including in international law, in support of the idea that in all decisions concerning children, their best interests are of paramount importance'. They said:

national decision-making bodies should, in principle, advert to and assess evidence in respect of the practicality, feasibility and proportionality of any such removal in order to give effective protection and sufficient weight to the best interests of the children directly affected by it. (para 120)

In this case:

Given the common background of the applicant and her husband and the relatively young age of their children, that there were no insurmountable obstacles for them to settle in Suriname. However, they would experience a degree of hardship if they were forced to do so.

119. Noting that the applicant takes care of the children on a daily basis, it is obvious that their interests are best served by not disrupting their present circumstances by a forced relocation of their mother from the Netherlands to Suriname or by a rupturing of their relationship with her . . . [T]he applicant's husband provides for the family by working full-time in a job that includes shift work. He is, consequently, absent from the home on some evenings. The applicant—being the mother and homemaker—is the primary and constant carer of the children who are deeply rooted in the Netherlands of which country—like their father—they are nationals. The materials in the case file do not disclose a direct link between the applicant's children and Suriname, a country where they have never been.

It was disproportionate to refuse her a permit to live in the Netherlands.

The best interests of the children in an Article 8 case is an aspect of a case awaiting judgment in the Supreme Court: *Makhlouf v SSHD (NI)*.

5.11.9 Article 8 and the immigration rules

There are three sets of rules which purport to embody Article 8: para 276ADE–276DH, providing for applications for leave to remain on grounds of private life; Appendix FM, providing for applications based on family life, and paras 398–399D relating to deportation.

In *Izuazu (Article 8—new rules)* [2013] UKUT 45 (IAC) the Upper Tribunal endorsed the decision in *MF (Article 8—new rules) Nigeria* [2012] UKUT 00393 (IAC) and, whilst acknowledging the rules as relevant to the striking of the Article 8 balance, held that 'the rules cannot over-ride either the legal duty imposed by statute or the existing learning on that duty supplied by the higher courts' (para 30). The Upper Tribunal found that the First Tier decision against MF failed to take proper account of the position of his British citizen wife and stepchild, especially the latter, and despite the validity of the Secretary of State's case for deporting him, found for MF. On the Secretary of State's appeal to the Court of Appeal in *MF (Nigeria) v SSHD* [2013] EWCA Civ 1192, the Court cited Lord Bingham's discussion in *Huang* [2007] UKHL 11, but said that at the time of that judgment the rules 'were not required to guarantee compliance with Article 8 and did not strike the balance' (para 7). The position was now different, as the Secretary of State had attempted to strike the balance required by Article 8 within the rules.

The language of 'exceptional circumstances' in the deportation rules was problematic since it appeared that the Secretary of State might have intended to reintroduce an exceptionality test, 'thereby flouting the Strasbourg jurisprudence' (para 41). However, this was clarified. The Court of Appeal concluded that the new rules appeared to amount to a complete code, with the exceptional circumstances mentioned being itself the requisite proportionality test; nevertheless, if the rules were not a complete code, the proportionality test would have to be applied in any event (paras 44, 45). The Upper Tribunal had made no errors in coming to the decision in favour of MF, though it was a finely balanced case, and the Secretary of State's appeal was dismissed.

It has been clear since *MF (Nigeria)* that there is scope for considering Article 8 in a case which fails under the rules. The question is how much scope. For instance, a judge allowed an appeal against entry clearance for the Indian wife of a British pensioner who could not meet the new financial requirements on the basis that the judge who had previously allowed the wife's appeal had 'embarked on a free-wheeling Article 8 analysis, unencumbered by the rules' (*Gulshan (Article 8—new Rules—correct approach)* [2013] UKT 640 (IAT), para 27).

In *SS (Congo) and others v SSHD* the Court of Appeal considered the gap between the immigration rules and Article 8. They said that, where the Secretary of State in making the rules had made a 'conscientious' attempt to strike 'the appropriate balance under Article 8' this would mean that any gap between the Rules and what Article 8 required would be comparatively narrow, and the Court would 'more readily give weight' to the Secretary of State's assessment when making its own decision (para 17). They also said, following *Huang*, that 'it cannot be maintained as a general proposition that LTR or LTE outside the Immigration Rules should only be granted in exceptional cases.' (para 29). They continued:

However, in certain specific contexts, a proper application of Article 8 may itself make it clear that the legal test for grant of LTR or LTE outside the Rules should indeed be a test of exceptionality. This has now been identified to be the case, on the basis of the constant jurisprudence of the ECtHR itself, in relation to applications for LTR outside the Rules on the basis of family life (where no children are involved) established in the United Kingdom at a time when the presence of one or other of the partners was known to be precarious : see *Nagre*, paras. [38]–[43], approved by this court in *MF (Nigeria)* at [41]–[42]. (para 29)

There have been challenges to the legality of sections of the new immigration rules. So far none has succeeded on a systemic challenge, but *SS(Congo)* is currently on appeal to the Supreme Court together with *MM (Lebanon), SJ (Pakistan) and Master AF*, challenging the minimum income requirement in the July 2012 immigration rules, and its relationship with Article 8. A challenge to the compatibility of the deportation rules with Article 8 is awaiting judgment in the Supreme Court (*Hesham Ali v SSHD* appealing [2014] EWCA Civ 1304).

5.11.10 Public interest and proportionality in Part 5A 2002 Act

Part 5A is a short insertion into the 2002 Act, headed 'Article 8 of the ECHR: public interest considerations'. It applies when a court or tribunal is required to decide whether an immigration decision breaches Article 8 (s 117A). Section 117A defines the 'question of whether an interference with a person's right to respect for private and family life is justified under Article 8.2' as the 'public interest question'. It requires that, when considering that question, the court or tribunal must 'have regard' to the considerations listed in s 117B. As the Tribunal found in *Dube (ss 117A–117D)* [2015] UKUT 90 (IAC), the listed factors are thus an elaboration of the fifth question in *Razgar*'s five stage approach (see 5.10). The first four questions must be addressed first. The Tribunal in *Dube* also held that the listed factors 'are not an a la carte menu of considerations that it is at the discretion of the judge to apply or not apply. Judges are duty-bound to "have regard" to the specified considerations' (para 21) but the list is not exhaustive. The obligation to have regard to them does not exclude other relevant considerations. Nor does it override the need to take a structured approach or 'modify existing learning as to when it is or is not an error of law for a judge to have express regard to specific elements of a structured approach' (para 26).

The factors in section 117B are, firstly, that 'the maintenance of effective immigration controls is in the public interest'. Secondly, the section says that it is in the public interest, and in particular in the interests of the economic well-being of the UK, that those who seek to enter or remain in the UK are able to speak English and are financially independent, because they (a) are less of a burden on taxpayers, and (b) are better able to integrate into society. This is a very unusual provision, stating social policy within the statute itself. The only case so far to interpret this paragraph, *AM (S 117B) Malawi*, rejected the argument of the appellants that their fluency in English and financial independence should weigh in their favour in the consideration of Article 8.

Next, subsection 4 provides that 'little weight' should be given to a private life or a relationship formed with a qualifying partner (i.e., British or settled) which is established when the person whose rights are in issue was in the UK unlawfully. The Tribunal in *Deelah and others (section 117B—ambit)* [2015] UKUT 515 (IAC) rejected the submission that this referred only to when a relationship began, and held that it referred to its duration.

Subsection 5 contains the provision already discussed: 'Little weight should be given to a private life established by a person at a time when the person's immigration status is precarious.' Note that this factor refers to private and not family life.

Finally, '[i]n the case of a person who is not liable to deportation, the public interest does not require the person's removal where (a) the person has a genuine and subsisting parental relationship with a qualifying child, and (b) it would not be reasonable to expect the child to leave the United Kingdom.' A qualifying child is a British citizen, or one who has lived in the UK for seven years (s 117D).

Section 117C contains extra factors to be taken into account in deportation cases, and these are discussed in chapter 15.

The impact of these statutory provisions on the courts' consideration of Article 8 cases is beginning to be felt though case law is still in its early stages. One of the key questions was given an initial answer by the Tribunal in *Deelah and others (section 117B—ambit)*. The headnote says: 'Section 117B(4) and (5) of the 2002 Act, which instruct Judges to attribute "little weight" to the considerations specified therein, do not give rise to a constitutionally impermissible encroachment on the independent adjudicative function of the judiciary.' However, although the contrary argument was made, the Tribunal accepted that the question did not arise in the case, since the decision under appeal did not rely on subsections 4 and 5. Obviously much remains to be seen as to how judges will interpret the duty to give 'little weight' and to 'have regard'.

5.11.11. **Article 8 and health care**

In *Razgar* the House of Lords held that the right to respect for private life can be engaged by the foreseeable consequences for health or welfare of removal from the UK, and endorses a holistic concept of private life which extends 'to those features which are integral to a person's identity or ability to function socially as a person' (para 9). While this principle remains intact, giving effect to it in Article 8 claims is difficult. *GS India*, which follows *N v UK*, reinforces that Article 3 will only very rarely provide a remedy even to a person who is terminally ill and faces death within weeks of return to their home country. Article 8, which is qualified by the state's interests, cannot by itself provide a basis for leave to remain for health treatment where Article 3 does not. However, health is one of many aspects of the whole of a person's private life. In *GS (India)* the Court of Appeal did not change that. The Court said:

If the Article 3 claim fails (as I would hold it does here), Article 8 cannot prosper without some separate or additional factual element which brings the case within the Article 8 paradigm—the capacity to form and enjoy relationships—or a state of affairs having some affinity with the paradigm. (para 86)

However, when those factors are present, an application based on Article 8 can be made. This was demonstrated in *Akhalu (health claim: ECHR Article 8)* [2013] UKUT 400 (IAC) where Ms Akhalu had substantial other elements in her UK private life as well as her need for health care. The Tribunal said that difficulty accessing health care in her home country was 'a material consideration of central importance to the individual concerned'. At the same time 'the countervailing public interest in removal will outweigh the consequences for the health of the claimant because of a disparity of health care facilities in all but a very few rare cases.' (para 43) Ms Akhalu's case was one of those rare cases, applying *MM (Zimbabwe) v Secretary of State for the Home Department* [2012] EWCA Civ 279.

Other factual situations may also give rise to a claim under Article 8. For instance, in *JA (Ivory Coast) and ES (Tanzania) v SSHD* [2009] EWCA Civ 1353, the Court found that the appellants had been given leave to remain in the UK specifically for medical treatment for AIDS, then had the continuation of that leave refused. The UK had made a de facto commitment to ES. The Court said it was insufficient to follow *N v UK*, which did not deal with the application of Article 8. The Court held that ES could return to Tanzania and obtain treatment, but JA's position was more finely balanced and needed to be assessed by the Tribunal. In the Court of Appeal, in *DM (Zambia)* [2009] EWCA Civ 474, Sedley LJ said that to remove an AIDS sufferer 'from free care and treatment in one of the best health services in the world, which had rescued her from what would otherwise have been a terminal condition', was a 'clear interference with her physical and psychological integrity and thus an invasion of her private life requiring justification', although justification was found in that case because DM, like ES, was found to have access to resources in her home country.

Also in *GS*, one of the appellants (EO) had a kidney transplant during the course of the appeal proceedings. The Home Office invited further submissions based on Article 8 in the light of this development.

5.12 Other qualified rights

Article 10, which protects freedom of expression, is regarded as one of the most central Articles of the Convention. It protects freedom of expression in written or spoken words, action, and through any medium such as theatre, film, photography, or painting. The Courts have accepted that it is engaged in immigration decisions where an exclusion order or a refusal of leave to enter is based specifically on preventing the exercise of the right (*Farrakhan* [2002] 3 WLR 481, relying on the ECtHR cases of *Piermont v France* [1995] 20 EHRR 301, *Swami Omkarananda and Divine Light Zentrum v Switzerland* (1997) 25 DR 105, and *Adams and Benn v UK* (1997) 88A DR 137). Where the interference with freedom of expression is incidental to the immigration decision then the right is less likely to be engaged.

Instances of the engagement of Article 10 have included the exclusion of Nation of Islam leader Louis Farrakhan on the basis of feared disorder as a reaction to his speaking tour (*Farrakhan*, see chapter 6); and of Dr Zakir Naik, who planned to visit the UK on a public lecture tour. The Secretary of State regarded some of his public statements as contrary to the Home Office's published policy on so-called 'unacceptable behaviours' (see chapters 2 and 15), and as supporting the 9/11 attacks and anti-Jewish (*Naik v SSHD and ECO Mumbai* [2011] EWCA Civ 1546). The Court of Appeal held that the exclusion of Dr Naik and Mr Farrakhan were legitimate restrictions on the right within Article 10.2.

An Article 10 challenge to an exclusion reached the Supreme Court in *R (Lord Carlile of Berriew and Others) v SSHD* [2014] UKSC 60.

The case began with a request by Lord Carlile of Berriew QC, on behalf of himself and two other members of the House of Lords, for a meeting with the Home Secretary to discuss lifting the exclusion order that had been in force since 1997 against Maryan Rajavi, a leading figure in an opposition movement in Iran, the People's Mojahedin Organisation of Iran (PMOI), also called Majahedin e-Khalq (MeK). The PMOI had been proscribed but was deproscribed in the UK and the EU as it was accepted that it had not been involved in terrorist activities since 2001. The purpose of lifting the exclusion was 'to enable her to address meetings in the Palace of Westminster on democracy, human rights and other policy issues relating to Iran' (para 4).

The Home Secretary declined to meet, maintained the exclusion of Ms Rajavi, and said it was not based on the proscription of the PMOI. The Supreme Court summarized the Secretary of State's case as

that Mrs Rajavi's admission to the United Kingdom for the purpose of discussions with Parliamentarians would pose an appreciable risk of (i) reprisals, either instigated by the Iranian government or resulting from an 'uncontrolled public reaction', against persons for whose safety Britain is responsible such as locally engaged staff of the British Embassy in Tehran and British nationals inside and outside Iran; (ii) damage to British property still in Iran, and (iii) a significant impairment of the United Kingdom's ability to engage diplomatically with Iran on important issues, including nuclear non-proliferation, the Middle East and human rights.

The Supreme Court rejected an argument by the appellants, now including a cross-party group of MPs and peers, that the Secretary of State was not entitled to have regard to the potential reaction of a foreign state which did not subscribe to the values of the ECHR. Their argument went as far as to say that the case was different from that of Naik and Farrakhan because in this case the Secretary of State had no objection to the views of the proposed visitor. The Supreme Court rejected that suggestion as 'contrary to principle'. Rather, '[t]he question whether the visitor's presence or activities in the United Kingdom is conducive to the public good must depend on its effects, and not on whether his or her opinions command general or ministerial assent.' (para 17).

In a majority judgment the Court held that it had no basis on which to contest the assessment of consequences which the Home Secretary had made. There was no error of law in the Home Secretary's reasoning. Furthermore:

a decision based on the possibility of an adverse reaction of a foreign government, and consequential risk of damage to the United Kingdom's diplomatic and economic interests, and to the well-being of United Kingdom citizens and employees abroad, is very much at that end of the spectrum where a court should be extremely diffident about differing from a ministerial decision, at least where the only challenge is based on proportionality. (para 70).

Despite dismissing the appeal, all members of the Court made important comments on the role of the judiciary in a human rights appeal. In the words of Lord Neuberger:

whatever the issue, once a Convention right is affected by a decision of the executive, the court has a duty to decide for itself whether the decision strikes a fair balance between the rights of an individual or individuals and the interests of the community as a whole. (para 57)

Applying this, in *Sehwerert v ECO* [2015] EWCA Civ 1141 the Court of Appeal for the first time allowed an appeal against a refusal to admit a foreign national on Article 10 grounds. This was a refusal of entry clearance on the mandatory grounds of having a conviction and sentence over four years (HC 395 para 320(2) see chapter 6). However, the conviction and sentence were the very reason that Mr Seherwet sought entry clearance.

 **Key Case**

Sehwerert v ECO [2015] EWCA Civ 1141

The appellant was one of five Cuban nationals, known as the 'Cuban Five', who were convicted in the USA in June 2001 on charges relating to their activities as intelligence agents for the Cuban government. The appellant was sentenced to 15 years' imprisonment. Serious concerns had been expressed over many years by international human rights organizations about the convictions, sentences, and the fairness of the trial. In 2014 a group of UK parliamentarians invited the appellant to meet with them in the Palace of Westminster to discuss the case. The appellant's application for entry clearance to visit the UK for that meeting was refused pursuant to paragraph 320(2) of the Immigration Rules by reason of his conviction and sentence. The appellant applied for judicial review of the refusal but was refused. On appeal the MPs intervened and argued that refusing entry clearance was a disproportionate interference with their Article 10 rights.

The Court drew on the judgments of the Law Lords in *Lord Carlile of Berriew*, especially in relation to the importance of political speech, which is at the top of the hierarchy of expression protected by Article 10. But that case concerned 'weighty public interest considerations, which are very different from anything to be found in the present case' (para 30).

The Court noted that rule 320(2) had not been formulated as a considered response by the Secretary of State to circumstances like those in this case. This meant that 'in the relevant proportionality analysis rather lesser weight attaches to the generalised assessment of the Secretary of State regarding the balance to be struck between the public interest and individuals' rights, as reflected in the general rule in paragraph 320(2), than would otherwise be the case: see *SS (Congo) v SSHD* [2015] EWCA Civ 387' (para 46).

The Court concluded that refusal of entry clearance for a visit of a few days was disproportionate in these circumstances.

5.13 **Other derogable rights**

Article 12 provides that:

Men and women of marriageable age have the right to marry and to found a family according to the national laws governing the exercise of this right.

What the law requires by way of respect for this right in the context of immigration policy has been considerably strengthened by case law. In the UK the decision of the Supreme Court in *Quila* (see chapter 8) has given more substance to the right to marry, although no breach of Article 12 was found in that case. Whereas Article 8 protects respect for existing marriages, Article 12 protects the right to enter into the marriage. Normally this right is not interfered with by immigration control since, as the Supreme

Court said in *Quila*, Article 12 'does not include the right to marry in any particular place, at least if it is possible to marry elsewhere' (para 78). However, in *R (on the application of Baiai and others) v SSHD* [2008] UKHL 53, discussed in chapter 8, the House of Lords held that the right to marry was fundamental, and not subject to the same qualifications as the right to respect for family life. Article 12 allowed for the right to be subject to national laws governing its exercise, but these should govern regulatory matters. Any rules of substance must only be for a generally recognized public interest and must never impair the substance of the right. The fixed fee of £295 impaired the essence of the right to marry. The condition that a person must have a certain number of months' leave remaining was not related to the genuineness of the marriage and was an unreasonable restriction on the right, and there was a breach of Article 12. The ECtHR also came to the conclusion that the scheme of certificates of approval for marriage was a breach of Article 12 (*O'Donoghue and Others v the UK* (Application no. 34848/07)). The Court's objections were that the scheme did not differentiate between genuine and sham marriages (the supposed purpose of the scheme) but imposed a blanket requirement on marriages based purely on immigration status. The fee was prohibitive for some couples.

Article 14 is potentially of wide application. The full text of Article 14 is:

The enjoyment of the rights and freedoms set forth in this Convention shall be secured without discrimination on any ground such as sex, race, colour, language, religion, political or other opinion, nationality or social origin, association with a national minority, birth or other status.

Article 14 was successfully used by the applicants in *Abdulaziz, Cabales and Balkandali v UK*. In that case, the applicants succeeded in pleading sex discrimination in the application of Article 8 rights, even though no breach of Article 8 was found.

 Key Case

Abdulaziz, Cabales and Balkandali v UK (1985) 7 EHRR 471

Three women who were settled in the UK challenged the immigration rules then in force (HC 394) on the basis that they discriminated against women. The rules allowed virtually automatic admission of wives of British men, but there were more hurdles to be overcome for the husbands of British women.

The ECtHR found that the rules were discriminatory. The British government's response to this was to alter the rules to make the more restrictive process applicable to wives as well as husbands. The inequality between the sexes was thus rectified, but British citizens of different ethnic origins were more sharply differentiated as more people who have family connections abroad are likely to want to marry someone from abroad. The Court considered this question in relation to Mrs Balkandali, who was a British citizen born outside the UK, but concluded that the government was not obliged to provide equal rights between citizens of different ethnic origins. They said: 'there are in general persuasive social reasons for giving special treatment to those whose link with a country stems from birth within it' (para 88).

Article 14 guarantees non-discrimination in the delivery of the other Convention rights, but is not a free-standing right. In order to lodge a claim under Article 14, it is necessary that discrimination is alleged in some area that is within the ambit of one of the other Convention rights. For instance, in *Abdulaziz*, the applicants alleged that

the immigration rules interfered with their Article 8 rights to family life and discriminated against them as women, because it would have been easier for men to bring their
spouses into the country. The Court found in their favour on the discrimination issue
but not on the family life issue, as it was not impossible for them to set up family life
in another country. It was necessary to claim under Article 14 that the Article 8 issue of
the interference with family life was involved, but there was no need for a violation of
Article 8 in order for the applicants to succeed under Article 14.

Discrimination for Article 14 entails a difference in treatment which is not based
upon 'an objective and reasonable justification' and is not proportionate to the social objective of that difference in treatment. These principles were established in the
Belgian Linguistics case (No. 2) (1968) 1 EHRR 252. Although the wording of Article 14
makes no reference to any defences or justification, this potential defence is held to be
inherent in the concept of discrimination, that is, it is differential treatment which
cannot be justified. The principles of discrimination and its justification are not fully
developed in the law of the ECHR, but by analogy with cases in the Court of Justice of
the EU the defence must be strictly construed, and the justification must exist independently of any discriminatory reasoning (Case 170/84 *Bilka Kaufhaus GmbH v Weber von
Hartz* [1986] ECR 1607).

In *R (on the application of Ali and Bibi)* (see chapter 8) the Supreme Court rejected an argument that the pre-entry language requirement for spouses was a breach of Article 14
taken with Article 8. While it did discriminate on grounds of nationality, this discrimination could be justified as 'being a national of an Anglo-phone country is a reasonable
proxy for a sufficient familiarity with the English language' (para 58).

One of the most significant decisions on Article 14 in recent times concerned not
immigration, but why it was discriminatory to categorize an issue as one of immigration. The challenge by those detained under the powers of indefinite detention in the
Anti-terrorism, Crime and Security Act 2001 was mounted partly on the basis that the
statutory power was discriminatory as it allowed the detention of only foreign nationals (*A v SSHD* [2004] UKHL 56). The government's case was that the power was not
discriminatory as these detainees could not be deported because they faced a real risk of
treatment contrary to Article 3, and the relevant comparison was with non-UK nationals who *could* be deported. The House of Lords accepted the appellants' argument that
the appropriate comparator for the purpose of assessing discrimination was a British
suspected international terrorist. The difference in treatment between British and non-
British suspects (i.e., the detention) had no bearing on the objective of defeating terrorism but was purely immigration or nationality related, an impermissible basis under
Article 14. The Home Office's proposed comparator group were not the appropriate ones
because they did not share the most relevant characteristics of the appellants, namely
non-removability. British nationals did share that characteristic, and to say that they
were not comparable because they had a right of abode whereas the appellants could
not be removed, as did the Court of Appeal, was to accept the Secretary of State's treatment of the matter as an immigration issue, which it patently was not. The decision is
discussed again in chapter 14.

The marriage provisions challenged in *R (on the application of Baiai and others) v SSHD*
were also found to be in breach of Article 14 as they made an unwarranted exception
for Church of England marriages.

Article 5 protects the right to liberty and security of person and is discussed in chapter 14. Immigration detention raises many human rights issues. At the same time, immigration detention in the UK has been frequently criticized because of its lack of fixed
time limit and the regular and unjustified detention of vulnerable people. The most

recent report is *Review into the Welfare in Detention of Vulnerable Persons*: a report to the Home Office by Stephen Shaw, January 2016.

Article 5 is the Article from which the UK has derogated on a number of occasions. The first derogations were all in relation to overseas territories during their struggles for independence. Later, there was a derogation from Article 5 in relation to detention in Northern Ireland, which was withdrawn as part of the peace process. In 2001, there was the derogation discussed earlier in relation to 'international terrorists', also discussed further in chapter 14.

The UK government has no plans to sign Protocol 12 ECHR, which provides for a free-standing right not to be discriminated against in any action by a public authority and in delivery of 'rights set forth by law' (see their response to the Parliamentary Joint Committee on Human Rights report on the International Covenant on Economic Social and Cultural Rights, Session 2005–06 Eighth Report HC 850 HL paper 104).

5.14 Conclusion

In simple terms, human rights are a counterbalance to the exercise of executive power. While the human rights era initially shifted the balance, it also threw existing tensions into sharper relief. House of Lords' decisions, particularly in *Huang and Kashmiri, Chikwamba, EB (Kosovo), Beoku-Betts* and *ZH (Tanzania)*, laid out humane principles as a foundation for a distinctive UK jurisprudence in Article 8 cases. This has been tested by the introduction of immigration rules and statutes laying down interpretations of Article 8. It is interesting that in *Sehwerert*, a case challenging the use of a mandatory exclusion power, and based on a different qualified right, the fundamental principles were reiterated, that the judiciary decide whether there has been a violation of rights. The scope of Article 3 protection is limited by political and economic considerations in medical cases, though remains absolute where there are real risks of torture or inhuman or degrading treatment.

Both internationally and within the UK there are now serious challenges to maintaining effective human rights protection.

QUESTIONS

1 How would you have decided the case of *N*?

2 Does it or should it make any difference to rights under Article 8 whether family life has been formed while waiting for an asylum claim to be processed or while spending time in the UK as, say, a student?

3 Is proportionality really a question of law?

online resource centre For guidance on answering questions, visit the Online Resource Centre www.oxfordtextbooks.co.uk/orc/clayton7e/.

FURTHER READING

All Party Parliamentary Group on Extraordinary Rendition (December 2005) *Briefing: Torture by Proxy: International Law Applicable to 'Extraordinary Renditions'*.

Amnesty International (2007) *United Kingdom: Deportations to Algeria at all Costs*, AI Index: EUR 45/001/2007.

Bratza, Nicholas (2011) 'The Relationship between the UK Courts and Strasbourg' *European Human Rights Law Review* vol. 5, pp. 505–12.

Clayton, Gina (2008) 'Article 3 Jurisprudence—*N v UK*: Not a Truly Exceptional Case?' *Immigration Law Digest* vol. 14, no. 3, Autumn, pp. 6–14.

Clayton, Richard (2004) 'Judicial Deference and Democratic Dialogue: The Legitimacy of Judicial Intervention under the Human Rights Act' *Public Law* 33–47.

Dunlop, Rory (2009) 'Case Analysis: *Y & Z (Sri Lanka) v SSHD*' *European Human Rights Law Review* vol. 6, pp. 805–10.

Gough, Roger, McCracken, Stuart, and Tyrie, Andrew (2011) *Account Rendered: Extraordinary Rendition and Britain's Role* (London: Biteback Publishing).

Hickman, Tom (2008) 'The Court and Politics after the Human Rights Act: A Comment' *Public Law* Spring, pp. 84–100.

Klug, Francesca and Wildbore, Helen (2010) 'Follow or Lead? The Human Rights Act and the European Court of Human Rights' *European Human Rights Law Review* vol. 6, pp. 621–30.

MacDonald, Ian (2008) 'ECHR Article 8: Bringing UK Courts back in Step with Strasbourg' *Journal of Immigration, Asylum and Nationality Law* vol. 22, no. 4, pp. 293–302.

McKee, Richard (2008) 'Deference Deferred: Article 8 Appeals: Recent House of Lords Decisions' *Immigration Law Digest* vol. 14, no. 4, Summer, pp. 8–15.

Metcalfe, Eric (2009) 'The False Promise of Assurances against Torture' *JUSTICE Journal* vol. 6, no. 1, pp. 63–92.

Mole, Nuala (2007) 'Asylum and the European Convention on Human Rights' AIRE Centre, Council of Europe.

Schaefer, Max (2011) 'Al-Skeini and the Elusive Parameters of Extraterritorial Jurisdiction' *European Human Rights Law Review* vol. 5, pp. 566–81.

Shah, Prakash (2000) 'The Human Rights Act 1998 and Immigration Law' INLP vol. 14, no. 3, pp. 151–58.

Shah, Sangeeta and Poole, Thomas (2009) 'The Impact of the Human Rights Act on the House of Lords' *Public Law* April, pp. 347–71.

Steyn, Lord (2005) 'Deference—A Tangled Story' *Public Law* pp. 346–59.

Weiss, Wolfgang (2011) 'Human Rights in the EU: Rethinking the role of the ECHR after Lisbon' *European Constitutional Law Review* vol. 7, no. 1, pp. 64–95.

Section 3

The system of immigration control

6

··

Crossing the border and leave to remain

SUMMARY

This chapter is concerned with the legal processes of crossing the border to enter the UK and the stages at which that crossing is encountered before and on arrival. The extra-territorial powers of immigration officers and the role of new technologies are discussed as characteristics of an increasingly diffuse, intelligence-based, and security-oriented system. The chapter describes the role and powers of ECOs and immigration officers, and considers the general grounds for refusal of leave or entry clearance. There is a short account of some offences which may be committed in the course of entry. The Common Travel Area (CTA) is introduced. Finally, there is discussion of the grant of leave, and of how the most secure immigration status of settlement may be achieved.

6.1 Introduction

The legal processes described in this chapter apply to all those who are subject to immigration control (Immigration Act 1971 s 3(1)). The law relating to the various categories of entry such as spouse, dependent child, or worker, is dealt with in the fourth part of this book and asylum claims in the fifth part. The provisions discussed in this chapter apply to those whose applications are discussed in Section 4 of this book, and, where relevant, to asylum seekers.

The development of immigration control from the Aliens Act 1905 up to the end of the twentieth century was increasingly complex in detail but quite simple in concept. At the borders, whether sea or air, immigration officers determined whether a passenger needed leave to enter, and if so whether and on what terms to grant it. The exceptions to this were the CTA (see 6.9), since the land border between Britain and Ireland required a more flexible approach, and, from 1969, entry clearance, which formalized a pre-entry stage of immigration control in British embassies and High Commissions abroad.

At the end of the twentieth century, this traditional model was dissolving, in part as a result of membership of the EU. Although the UK has opted into few of the immigration provisions made under the Treaty of Amsterdam, it is a full partner in the Common European Asylum System, and participates in security measures such as the Schengen information system and the Eurodac fingerprinting system. The UK's movement towards harmonization with the rest of Europe brings a dual preoccupation with freedom of movement on the one hand, and security on the other. Increasingly sophisticated international intelligence networks and communication media make this possible. As described in chapter 2, immigration control is becoming a matter of interception, policing, and international information exchange, not granting leave by a stamp in a passport at a port of entry.

Chapter 2 describes the spread of immigration control into civil society. This chapter focuses on the control of entry to the UK.

6.2 Who is subject to immigration control?

British citizens and Commonwealth citizens with right of abode, as defined and discussed in chapter 3, are not subject to immigration control (Immigration Act 1971 s 3(1)). The following groups are, strictly speaking, subject to immigration control but do not need leave to enter: nationals of the European Economic Area (EEA) (Immigration Act 1988 s 7); air and sea crews making a lawful stop, service people, diplomats, and their households (1971 Act s 8); people arriving from another part of the CTA (1971 Act s 1(3)); and prisoners brought to the UK to give evidence in drug-trafficking cases (Criminal Justice (International Co-operation) Act 1990 s 6). Certain representatives of governments and those benefiting from immunities conferred by Orders in Council referring to international tribunals and other international bodies are exempt from immigration control under the Immigration (Exemption from Control) Order 1972, SI 1972/1613, as amended. All other passengers need leave to enter.

Although people seeking asylum need leave to enter, this cannot be granted until their asylum claim has been processed. This may take a long time (see chapter 11), and asylum seekers are normally given a status called temporary admission pending determination of their claim (Immigration Act 1971 Sch 2 para 21); alternatively, they may be detained. See chapter 11 for the asylum process; detention and temporary admission are discussed in chapter 14.

6.2.1. Entry clearance

Entry clearance is defined in the Immigration Act 1971 as 'a visa, entry certificate or other document which, in accordance with the immigration rules, is to be taken as evidence [or the requisite evidence] of a person's eligibility, though not [a British citizen] for entry into the UK' (s 33). Despite the critical role of entry clearance in immigration control, the Act itself makes no provision for its use, and it was only ever statutory for a brief period during the currency of the Immigration Appeals Act 1969. Where entry clearance is mandatory, this is achieved by the immigration rules. According to para 24, visa nationals, and all non-EEA nationals who intend to stay for more than six months, need entry clearance, which must be obtained at an entry clearance post overseas. The list of visa national countries is appended to the immigration rules.

The number of visa national countries is around 112. To put that number in perspective, the United Nations currently recognizes 191 countries. Countries have often been added to the visa list when circumstances suggested that asylum claims from there would increase. For instance, during the three months of July to September 2002, a total of 2,105 Zimbabweans sought asylum in the UK, almost as many as in the whole of 2001. In November 2002, the Secretary of State announced that Zimbabwe would become a visa national country.

Recognized refugees also need entry clearance to come to the UK because from 11 February 2003 the UK suspended its participation in the 1959 Council of Europe

Agreement on the Abolition of Visas for Refugees. The grounds cited were that refugees were 'travelling to the United Kingdom and either remaining illegally or making asylum applications in false identities in order to access the benefits system' (Declaration of suspension contained in a letter from the Permanent Representative of the United Kingdom, dated 7 February 2003).

Those people for whom entry clearance is not mandatory may apply for entry clearance as a precaution (HC 395 para 24) to establish their eligibility for entry and so avoid the risk of being turned away at the port. From January 2014 there is an exception to the requirement for entry clearance for visitors from the Gulf Cooperation Council (GCC) states—Qatar, Oman, and the United Arab Emirates—who can register biographic and travel information online and obtain an electronic visa waiver without the need to give biometric information or attend a VAC (see 6.3). Visitors from the GCC spend an average of $3,417 per person per visit—significantly more than other visitors. There are other exemptions also. For the full list see the appendix to the immigration rules dealing with visitors' visas.

6.3 Applying for entry clearance

Entry clearance applications are granted or refused by entry clearance officers (ECOs) based in British posts abroad, that is, in embassies, high commissions, and consulates. ECOs are not mentioned in any of the legislation, and until June 2000 they were answerable to the Foreign and Commonwealth Office (FCO) rather than to the Home Office. The defining reference to ECOs in the immigration rules is in para 26, which says that where appropriate the term 'entry clearance officer' should be substituted for 'immigration officer'. The gov.uk website gives access to the Entry Clearance Guidance (ECG) used by ECOs, although this is not always up to date.

In the early days of entry clearance applications, the main basis for an entry clearance decision was information gathered in an interview. The interview might follow a long and arduous journey, for instance, as described in a research report by the UK Immigration Advisory Service:

The train journey from Sylhet to Dacca alone takes 13 hours, added to that, of course, the cumbersome boat, bus journey, including miles of walking to reach Sylhet town from the village. [Most wives were also] carrying an infant and other children of very young age through the long journey. (p. 11, as quoted by Juss:73)

Now the majority of the information on which an entry clearance decision is based is gathered electronically, although interviews were reintroduced mainly for student entry clearance in response to evidence of non-compliance with the terms of student visas (see Independent Chief Inspector of Borders and Immigration (ICIBI) 2014).

Applications for entry clearance are made online. The initial application is submitted on a form on the UK Visas and Immigration (UKVI) website. Following this the applicant will normally attend a commercially run Visa Application Centre (VAC) where they provide biometric data, and submit a paper copy of their application form. The fee may be collected electronically at the time of submitting the application or in some cases paid at the VAC. The VAC sends the documents to the British Embassy or High Commission where ECOs make the decision. The post making the decision may not be in the country where the application was made, since smaller diplomatic posts may report to a larger one in a different country (see chapter 2).

ECOs may work closely with RALON (the Risk and Liaison Overseas Network of the Home Office) as an intelligence-gathering arm of UKVI and may employ field officers, both of which are geared to assessing risk of immigration infringements prior to the grant of leave or prior to travel. For an example of this working relationship see the December 2013 report on the operation of the Dhaka visa section by the Independent Chief Inspector of Borders and Immigration.

The authorization to discriminate issued under the Equality Act and discussed at 6.6.4 applies to entry clearance decisions, so that leave to enter granted outside the UK (i.e., including by means of entry clearance) may be refused on the basis of legalized discrimination (see discussion at 6.6.4).

6.3.1 Biometrics

Digital photographs and fingerprinting are a compulsory requirement in any visa application (Immigration (Provision of Physical Data) Regulations 2006, SI 2006/1743). This method makes it easier to transfer to other parts of the border control operation unique information about applicants. The scanned fingerprints are checked against police and immigration records to identify if a prospective traveller has already been fingerprinted in the UK by the immigration authorities, has been arrested, charged, cautioned or convicted, is on a security watch-list, or has made an asylum application in the UK. Failure to provide biometric data is a discretionary reason for refusing entry clearance (HC 395 para 320(20)).

Entry clearance may be refused when a match with police, immigration, or security records indicates that the applicant has a criminal record, is a security risk, or has a previous immigration history that founds a reason for refusal. This can happen through the fingerprint match revealing that the applicant is now using, or has in the past used, a false document (such as a forged passport) to gain entry, or through information coming to light which the applicant had not disclosed, if this is material to the present application or dishonestly withheld (HC 395 para 320(7A) see discussion at 6.8.7).

In theory, fingerprints and photographs are no more than evidence of identity supporting an application, but a match is difficult to challenge, and few applicants for entry have a right of appeal against refusal (see chapter 7). A few cases concerning disputed fingerprint matches come from asylum appeals, and these show that human mistakes are made, for instance asserting that there is a fingerprint match when there is not (e.g., *Kamara v SSHD* [2013] EWHC 959 (Admin)). In the context of the Eurodac system (the European database that records fingerprints of asylum claimants), the Tribunal held that it was right to require further evidence in addition to a bare assertion that the prints matched in order to be satisfied that the fingerprint records proved that the claimant had made a previous claim for asylum in Italy (*YI (Previous claims—fingerprint match—EURODAC) Eritrea* [2007] UKAIT 00054). An example of such further evidence would be a photograph of the person who supplied the prints said to be matched by the claimant's. This was in the context of an allegation of fraud, and the High Court in *R (on the application of YZ, MT and YM) v SSHD* [2011] EWHC 205 (Admin) held that this did not give a right to challenge the Eurodac system. In *RZ (Eurodac—fingerprint match—admissible) Eritrea* [2008] UKAIT 00007, the Tribunal held that the standard of proof was the balance of probabilities, though the burden of proof was on the Secretary of State to show the accuracy of the match. A successful challenge would be difficult to mount as the evidence was that the system was highly reliable.

Most applicants for leave to enter or remain in the UK are now required to apply for Biometric Residence Permits (see chapter 2). In 2015 the Home Office began to roll out a new process entailing that an application for a BRP is part of the entry clearance application. When the application succeeds, a 'short term' (30-day) biometric entry clearance visa is granted. During its currency the applicant must travel to the UK and collect their BRP from a designated post office (Modernised Guidance *Biometric Information: Introduction*). This entry clearance is treated as leave to enter on a single occasion (The Immigration (Leave to Enter and Remain) (Amendment) Order 2015, SI 2015/434).

6.3.2 Monitoring entry clearance applications

The remit of the Independent Chief Inspector of Borders and Immigration includes the entry clearance operation, also including grants of entry clearance as well as refusals. The inspector is unable to make recommendations in individual cases, and systemic recommendations are not enforceable. Entry clearance was one of the first areas of work to which the Inspectorate's attention turned, and there are reports of the entry clearance operation in Abuja, Rome, Guangzhou, Chennai, Kuala Lumpur, Amman, Istanbul, New York, Nairobi, Pretoria, Abu Dhabi, Islamabad, Madrid, and Accra.

Against this background, we consider the legal effect of entry clearance once granted. The grounds upon which entry clearance may be refused are almost identical to reasons for refusal of leave to enter, and are discussed later in that context.

6.3.3 Effect of entry clearance

Before the changes introduced by the Immigration and Asylum Act 1999, entry clearance and leave to enter were two distinct stages of the entry control process. Although possession of entry clearance made it highly likely that leave to enter would be granted on arrival, it was not in itself a grant of leave. From 28 April 2000, the Immigration (Leave to Enter and Remain) Order 2000, SI 2000/1161 enabled entry clearance to have effect as leave to enter, provided it specifies the purpose for which the holder wishes to enter the UK, and is endorsed with any conditions to which it is subject or a statement that it is to have effect as indefinite leave (Article 3). In most cases now, therefore, entry clearance functions as leave to enter. The exception is for refugee travel documents. Entry clearance endorsed on these after 27 February 2004 does not have effect as leave to enter (Immigration (Leave to Enter and Remain) (Amendment) Order 2004, SI 2004/475).

As a consequence of this extended effect of entry clearance, the role of immigration officers at the port of entry has changed to more of a policing function, checking the traveller's identity and the validity of existing documents. Immigration Act 1971 Schedule 2 para 2A says that, in the case of a passenger who arrives with leave, the powers of the immigration officer are to examine that person to ascertain whether any grounds exist to cancel that leave, and, as discussed at 6.8, in limited circumstances the immigration officer has the authority to refuse entry to someone holding an entry clearance (para 321 of the rules). In *Khaliq v Immigration Officer, Gatwick* [2011] UKUT 00350(IAC) the appellant had entry clearance as a student. On arrival in the UK, it was apparent that he did not meet the college's minimum requirement for English language, and he accepted that he had bought the certificate purporting to verify his level of English. However, the points-based system did not require examination of qualifications by an entry clearance or immigration officer; the offer letter issued by the college is conclusive. There was no evidence before the Tribunal as to whether the language certificate had been sent to the college. There was therefore no evidence that the appellant had made any false representation in relation to his application for leave, and the entry clearance was conclusive of his entitlement to enter.

The grant of entry clearance, which has effect as leave to enter, bears two dates, one when the entry clearance becomes effective, 'valid from . . . ' and one which marks its expiry, 'valid until . . . '. The passenger may travel once the entry clearance/leave to enter is effective. ECOs are permitted to make the entry clearance/leave to enter valid from a date up to three months after the date when they granted it (ECO Guidance ECB9.5).

If a person arrives before the 'valid from . . . ' date, the immigration officer on arrival has a discretion to cancel the entry clearance (HC 395 para 30C) and grant a new period of leave (para 31A). This discretion must, of course, be exercised reasonably.

6.4 Development of the exported border

A flow of measures to export border control has been built upon the power in the Immigration (Leave to Enter and Remain) Order 2000, SI 2000/1161, to grant leave to enter outside the UK. The power to grant or refuse leave to enter from abroad was not only granted for convenience of some travellers, but also for deterrence of others, namely asylum seekers. Simon Brown LJ in *European Roma Rights Centre and Others v Immigration Officer, Prague Airport and SSHD* [2003] 4 All ER 247 explains:

There are difficulties, however, of a political nature in imposing a visa regime on certain friendly states and so Parliament in 1999 authorized the Home Secretary to introduce in addition a scheme enabling the immigration rules to be operated extra-territorially rather than simply at UK ports of entry. Intending asylum seekers would in this way be refused leave to enter the UK by immigration officers operating abroad and so be unable to travel to the UK to claim asylum here. (para 2)

First, we consider the Order itself, then the uses that have been made of it so far.

6.4.1 Immigration (Leave to Enter and Remain) Order 2000, SI 2000/1161

The Immigration (Leave to Enter and Remain) Order 2000 was made pursuant to a widely phrased power in Immigration and Asylum Act 1999 s 1 (which inserted a new section 3A into the Immigration Act 1971):

1. The Secretary of State may by order make further provision with respect to the giving, refusing or varying of leave to enter the United Kingdom.
2. An order under subsection (1) may, in particular, provide for leave to be given or refused before the person concerned arrives in the United Kingdom;
   (a) the form or manner in which leave may be given, refused or varied;
   (b) the imposition of conditions;
   (c) a person's leave not to lapse on his leaving the common travel area.

This was the first time since the 1971 Act that there had been a substantive change in the power to grant or refuse leave to enter. It should be noted that the power in s 3A is simply to 'make further provision with respect to the giving, refusing, or varying of leave to enter'. The specific powers that follow in subsection 2 are not necessarily an exhaustive account of how this power will be exercised.

The power was first exercised by making the Immigration (Leave to Enter and Remain) Order 2000, SI 2000/1161. By Article 7 of that order, 'an immigration officer *whether or not in the United Kingdom*, may give or refuse a person leave to enter the United

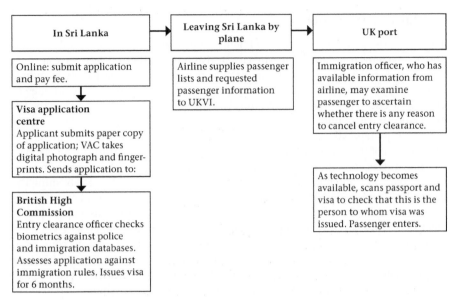

Figure 6.1 Stages of immigration control—visitor from Sri Lanka

Kingdom *at any time before his departure for, or in the course of his journey to*, the United Kingdom' (emphases added). This means that neither the immigration officer nor the grant of leave are fixed to the port of entry. Leave may be given before or during travel, and the immigration officer need not be based at the port. Article 8 provides that notice giving or refusing leave to enter, instead of being given in writing as required by s 4(1) of the 1971 Act, may be given to visitors orally, including by telephone, and in all cases where it is given in writing it may be given by fax or e-mail (Article 8ZA inserted by Immigration (Leave to Enter and Remain) (Amendment) Order 2013, SI 2013/1749), including to an authorized representative (Article 9). The key substantive change introduced by the 2013 Order was that, where attempts were unsuccessful to serve a notice by the specified means, it could be served by recording the reasons and putting the notice on file. The 2013 Order applied this rule to non-appealable decisions for the first time. The notice provisions apply to decisions refusing leave to remain as well as leave to enter, and the provision for notice to be given on file is more likely to be relevant in those cases. Article 8A, inserted by Immigration (Leave to Enter and Remain) (Amendment) Order, SI 2010/957, implements e-borders by providing for leave to be given as a visitor by entry through an automated gate under specified conditions.

This flexibility in the means of communicating a grant of leave to enter may have drawbacks if, for instance, a question of proof arises at a later date; the burden of proof is on the person claiming that they have leave to enter to prove that is the case (Article 11). It was said to be for the convenience of those regarded as 'low risk' passengers on school trips or other organized tours. In these cases, a passenger list may be presented and endorsed with leave to enter, even before setting out on the trip, and this is intended to minimize delay at the port of entry.

In addition to grant by entry clearance, and advance clearance for groups of 'low risk' passengers, the power to grant or refuse leave to enter before travel is designed for schemes established abroad to deter unauthorized passengers.

6.4.2 **Juxtaposed control**

The first of these initiatives considered here is known as 'juxtaposed control'. This involves a reciprocal arrangement whereby British immigration officers work at ports abroad, and border guards of those countries work in the ports in the UK, each country carrying out its immigration controls *before* the passenger embarks on the journey to cross the border. Presently, these reciprocal arrangements are in place between the UK and France and Belgium.

The first juxtaposed controls were a development of the Channel Tunnel project, as the opening of the Channel Tunnel was seen to create new opportunities for clandestine migrants to enter the UK by hiding in containers and lorries. The Sangatte Protocol to the Treaty of Canterbury was agreed between France and the UK, establishing the principles of and authorizations for juxtaposed controls. This is given effect within the UK's legal system, by the Channel Tunnel (International Arrangements) Order 1993, SI 1993/1813 (the 1993 Order), made using powers in the Channel Tunnel Act 1987.

The Sangatte Protocol and the 1993 Order provide for officials of each country to carry out their functions in a 'control zone' in the other. Control zones are: 'the part of the territory of the host State determined by mutual agreement between the two Governments within which the officers of the adjoining state are empowered to effect controls'. The actions of these officials were to be governed by 'frontier control enactments' of each state which were permitted by the Sangatte Protocol to have effect in the control zone in the other.

These first controls operated on the shuttle trains that carried road vehicles, and also enabled immigration officers of each state to operate on board Eurostar passenger trains. However, an increase in undocumented arrivals and asylum claims at Waterloo led to an Additional Protocol being agreed between France and the UK authorizing juxtaposed controls in railway stations. Following amendments because of changes to the Eurostar route, and an agreement with Belgium, juxtaposed controls for Eurostar passengers are now operating in London St Pancras, Ebbsfleet International, and Ashford on British territory, Paris Gare du Nord, Calais Fréthun, and Lille-Europe on French territory, and the Gare du Midi in Brussels. Juxtaposed controls hit the headlines in 2013 with the disclosure of the 'Lille loophole' whereby passengers were buying tickets in Brussels for Lille, but staying on the train to London.

While the first Channel Tunnel juxtaposed controls were wide-ranging, dealing with animal health, consumer goods, and traffic issues as well as immigration, the Eurostar controls were purely aimed at immigration, and in particular at the deterrence of asylum claims. The Additional Protocol Article 3 provided that controls exercised by the state of departure were to check whether the person was free in law to leave its territory, and controls by the state of arrival were to check whether the passenger was in possession of the necessary travel documents and fulfilled any other conditions for entry to its territory. Additionally, to meet the UK government's interest in preventing asylum seekers from reaching the UK through the Tunnel, the Additional Protocol with France provided that claims for refugee status must be made and processed in the state of departure if made at any time before the train doors closed at the last scheduled stop in that state (Article 4). The responsibility for receiving asylum claims was thus imposed, by agreement, on France. The same applies to a claim for protection made on the basis of human rights rather than as a refugee.

A main source of impetus for the extension of juxtaposed controls to sea ports was the furore surrounding the Red Cross refugee camp at Sangatte in northern France. There were daily entries to the UK by asylum seekers waiting in the camp; and this, with the associated breaches of security, danger, and injury to individuals, and delays to freight and other traffic, created a three-year dispute over causes and responsibilities between the two governments. Accordingly, in 2002, British immigration officers began working alongside French border police in Calais, in an informal arrangement to cooperate, and for this a new legal foundation was needed.

In 2003, France and the UK entered into a Frontier Control Treaty at le Touquet 'concerning the implementation of frontier controls at the sea ports of both countries on the Channel and North Sea' (Cm 5832, in force on 1 February 2004). The Treaty is given effect in UK law by the Nationality, Immigration and Asylum Act 2002 (Juxtaposed Controls) Order 2003, SI 2003/2818, made under the power in the Nationality, Immigration and Asylum Act 2002 s 141. This power broke new ground in allowing an order to provide for 'a law' of England and Wales to have effect in a specified area outside the UK.

The Treaty says that the powers which may be exercised in sea port control zones are 'all the laws and regulations of the Contracting Parties concerning immigration controls and the investigation of offences relating to immigration' (Article 2). However, the 2003 Order specifically lists those statutes which apply.

As new enforcement powers are effected in the UK, many have been added to the sea port juxtaposed control regime. For instance, the Nationality, Immigration and Asylum Act 2002 (Juxtaposed Controls) (Amendment) Order 2006, SI 2006/2908, extends to a control zone the power to take fingerprints of someone who fails to provide a valid passport or equivalent on arrival. The offences of absconding from detention and obstructing a search (Immigration, Asylum and Nationality Act 2006 ss 40 and 41) are also extended to the control zone. By means of these incremental changes the control zones are increasingly treated as part of UK jurisdiction, and the network of border control is established outside the actual territory, including by the use of new detection technology to find people hiding in vehicles. However, in relation to appeal rights, control zones are not treated as part of the territory. Any appeal rights which exist in theory are treated as 'out-of-country' appeals (see chapter 7) and there is no case law concerning the exercise of such rights. Any such appeal rights are not supported by practical arrangements for their exercise. Where a person's leave to enter is cancelled in a control zone for reasons which would otherwise attract a right of administrative review, they may not exercise that right of administrative review until they have 'left or been removed from' the control zone (HC 395 Appendix AR AR4.3). The Home Office's Control of Immigration Statistics show that between 23 per cent and 30 per cent of 'non-asylum' refusals of entry at ports of entry are at juxtaposed controls. As an asylum claim cannot be made to the destination country in a control zone, these figures do not reveal how many of those refused might have had asylum as their ultimate aim, or what happened to them.

In the 'refugee crisis' of 2015, the number of people staying in makeshift camps in Calais rose to around 6,000 people ('Calais "Jungle": anger over fate of child refugees denied UK asylum hearing' *The Guardian* 9 January 2016). The camps became a health and security concern, with reports that many unaccompanied children were staying there, as well as the risks associated with the attempts to board lorries bound for the UK. Efforts to encourage people to claim asylum in France met with some success (House of Commons Home Affairs Committee *The work of the Immigration Directorates: Calais* Eighteenth Report of Session 2014–15 HC 902 para 16) but many were deterred by the actions of the French police, who attacked the camps with riot gear including pepper sprays, water cannons, and truncheons.

Reports of poor conditions in the asylum process and a hostile response also deterred people from claiming asylum in France, and created a legal limbo, since the control zone regime prevented them from making their claim to the UK authorities. However, under the Dublin Regulation (see chapter 11) some would have a basis for their asylum claim to be heard in the UK. The rigid approach of the UK authorities to applying juxtaposed controls prevented these applications being heard, including from unaccompanied minors. This refusal was challenged by judicial review. In *R (on the application of ZAT and Others) v SSHD (Article 8 ECHR—Dublin Regulation—interface—proportionality)* IJR [2016] UKUT 61 (IAC) the Upper Tribunal held that refusal to allow the applicants swift admission to the UK was an infringement of their Article 8 rights if they could be regarded as asylum applicants. On the condition that they registered a claim with the French authorities, the Tribunal ordered that they should be admitted to the UK. The Tribunal accepted that a written claim to the French authorities would suffice. Within two days after the ruling they had submitted their claim and arrived in the UK (*Syria refugees from Calais arrive in UK after legal ruling* BBC news 22nd January 2016). See chapter 11 for more detail of this case.

Following an order of the Lille Administrative Court, the French authorities erected shipping containers to house the people camping at Calais and prepared to bulldoze some of the tented areas.

6.4.3 Immigration liaison managers—RALON

Another role taken abroad by immigration officers is as immigration liaison managers (ILMs), to advise airlines on the validity of documents presented to them for travel to the UK. ILMs do not grant or refuse leave to enter, but advise airlines, which may then refuse to allow the passenger to board. They work as part of RALON. In answer to a question in Parliament, the immigration minister said that in the five years up to January 2009, the immigration liaison network had assisted in preventing nearly 210,000 people from boarding planes, 'equivalent to about two jumbo jets a week' (HC Debs 27 January 2009 288W). The liability of the officers for wrong advice is a matter of concern, given that there is no appeal against what is in formal terms advice to the airline rather than an immigration decision (see discussion of *Farah v British Airways & Home Office* TLR 26 January 2000 at 6.5.3.5). Asylum seekers may travel on false documents as this may be the only way to leave their country. For obvious reasons, the effect on asylum seekers turned away from flights after such advice is unknown, although RALON staff are bound by the International Air Transport Association/Control Authorities Working Group Code of Practice, and where a passenger who is refused boarding expresses a fear of persecution they should be referred to UNHCR.

RALON provides an intelligence link between posts overseas and the UK, enabling individuals to be targeted more easily if they are identified as a threat. When a requirement for visas is implemented in relation to nationals of a country, RALON provides country-specific risk assessments. RALON also connects with SOCA (the Serious Organised Crime Agency) to track stolen British passports and detect or prevent their re-use.

6.4.4 Passenger information

As part of developing the Schengen area, the UK opted into EC Directive 2004/82, binding from 5 September 2006. This entails that Member States have systems requiring carriers to transmit passenger data to immigration authorities. The Immigration and Asylum Act 1999 first required carriers to provide immigration officers 'such information relating to the passengers carried, or expected to be carried . . . as may be specified' (Immigration Act 1971 Sch 2 para 27(2) as amended). An additional power was inserted by the Asylum and Immigration (Treatment of Claimants, etc.) Act 2004 to require provision of 'a copy of all or part of a document that relates to the passenger'. The 2006 Act has added powers for the police to require passenger and freight information (ss 32 and 33) and a duty for the immigration authorities, police, and HMRC to share information among themselves (s 36). Passenger information may be provided electronically and so may be checked against 'multi-agency watchlists' prior to boarding.

The Immigration and Police (Passenger, Crew and Service Information) Order, SI 2008/5 and Immigration Act 1971 Schedule 2 paras 27 and 27B provide that an immigration officer or the police may require a responsible person in respect of a ship or aircraft to provide a passenger list showing the names and nationality of passengers on board, whether arriving in or leaving the UK. They may also be required to provide, if they have it, dozens of items of data specified in the Order, including, for instance, in relation to passengers the number of pieces and description of any baggage carried, their ticket number, its date and place of ticket issue, the identity of any person who made the reservation, and more. Information must be provided electronically.

Successive governments have promised systems of electronic checks at the border, but have met with obstacles. The House of Commons Home Affairs Committee has requested regular reports on these developments since it appeared that targets for implementation would not be met.

Advance passenger information requirements were ill-suited to ferry and rail travel, and would breach EU law if they imposed a requirement other than the simple production of ID or a passport as a condition of entry on those exercising EU free movement rights. The EU Commission set out guarantees that would be required to make the API programme compatible with EU law.

In the end the Home Office implemented a limited 'authority to carry scheme'. Since 2012 provision of advance passenger information has been mandatory on non-EU flights. For EU flights, carriers could be required to seek authority to carry those subject to deportation orders or travel bans (The Nationality, Immigration and Asylum Act 2002 (Authority to Carry) Regulations 2012/1894). The Independent Chief Inspector reported in 2013 that:

[f]or EU flights, API could only be provided to the extent that the carrier processed the information under its terms and conditions of carriage, where the passenger gave consent and where the country in which the data was collected did not object on data protection grounds. The provision of API was not mandatory for maritime or rail passengers. As of March 2013, 138 carriers were providing API covering 4,412 routes and 142 million passengers, representing 65% of all passenger movements annually.

6.4.5 Pre-clearance

Successive Home Secretaries have asserted that it would be desirable to pre-sift asylum claims abroad, and the third initiative discussed here is an example of an attempt to do this. The pre-clearance scheme at Prague in the Czech Republic was an experiment in overseas activity of the British immigration service aimed at deterring unauthorized passengers from travelling, and targeting Roma asylum seekers. In this case, leave to enter was granted or refused before embarkation on a flight for the UK. In *European Roma Rights Centre (ERRC) v Immigration Officer at Prague Airport and SSHD* [2002] EWHC 1989 (Admin), the evidence of the Secretary of State confirmed that 'the Prague operation is not a pre-screening which is a prelude to a subsequent consideration of eligibility at a United Kingdom airport. Rather it takes the place of that consideration of that eligibility' (para 25). The judgments in the Court of Appeal [2003] 4 All ER 247 and House of Lords [2004] UKHL 55 confirmed what critics and the UK government had agreed upon, namely that the effect of such a scheme was to prevent asylum claims being made. The difference between the parties was whether this was lawful or not. This case was a dramatic illustration of the potential of the Immigration (Leave to Enter and Remain) Order 2000. Where an asylum claim is made at a UK port of entry there is an obligation implied by the 1951 UN Convention Relating to the Status of Refugees to consider it. However, the Courts in the *ERRC* case found there was no obligation to allow the claimant to reach the UK in order to make that claim. The House of Lords found this scheme to be discriminatory on racial grounds and therefore unlawful.

The Prague scheme ran from 18 July 2001 to 26 February 2003. Following the Czech Republic's accession to the EU in 2004, the scheme would have no basis. However, the idea of selecting refugees before arrival at the border continues to appear in political statements, for example, that of the Home Secretary Theresa May in 2015 in response to the 'refugee crisis' (speech to Conservative Party conference, 6 October 2015).

6.5 Trans-border controls—carriers' liability

The trend of government policy is to extend the responsibility for immigration control to people in many walks of life. Liability placed on those who transport people and goods is not a new phenomenon, but until the 1980s it was relatively unimportant. Its use has expanded enormously in the UK since 1987 and it now represents a major plank in the government's policy to control asylum claims.

6.5.1 International context

Not only EU countries, but also the USA, Canada, and Australia have introduced measures imposing liability on carriers for the transport of passengers who either hide themselves and gain entry without being detected ('clandestine entrants') or who do not have the appropriate documents for travel, for instance, their passport is forged or stolen or does not show the requisite entry clearance ('inadequately documented' passengers). Articles 26 and 27 of the Schengen Convention, which became part of EC law following the Treaty of Amsterdam, require the imposition of carrier sanctions by means of legislation, and the UK has been active in these measures.

6.5.2 Summary of legislative history

Under the Aliens Act 1905, a shipping company committed an offence punishable by a fine if a person subject to immigration control disembarked without leave to enter. If an immigrant who needed leave was admitted to the UK but expelled within six months, the Home Office could recover the cost of the return journey from the shipping company that had brought that passenger. Similar provisions persist to the present day. Immigration Act 1971 Schedule 2 paras 26 and 27 set out duties of shipping companies and airlines, which show how closely these commercial bodies are required to cooperate with the immigration service. For instance, if they carry passengers who require leave to enter, ships or aircraft may only call at designated ports of entry, and must ensure that passengers disembarking pass through designated control areas. Liability could be imposed without any fault on the part of the carriers. For this reason, the Independent Chief Inspector suggests that carriers would welcome government officers using their statutory power to grant or refuse leave to enter abroad, rather than just the advisory power that ILMs currently have.

Although the risk of penalties gave an incentive to carriers to check the documentation of passengers and refuse passage where they had doubts as to someone's status, there was no statutory obligation to do so until the Immigration (Carriers' Liability) Act 1987. The Act imposed fines on airlines and shipowners or their agents of £1,000 for each person carried by them who entered without a valid passport, and, where required, visa. The fine was increased to £2,000 in 1991. This amount was per passenger, not per journey. Therefore, if 50 inadequately documented passengers were found on one ship, the fine imposed on the owner or agent would be £50,000, or, after 1991, £100,000. In 1993, the Asylum and Immigration Appeals Act 1993 s 12 added liability for carrying people who did not have the required transit visas. In 1998, legislation was introduced to include trains following the opening of the Channel Tunnel (Channel Tunnel (Carriers' Liability) Order 1998, SI 1998/1015).

In 1999, the Immigration and Asylum Act introduced liability for clandestine entrants as opposed to just passengers with improper documentation, and increased the scope of legislation to cover road transport. Later amending regulations have included rail freight (Carriers Liability (Clandestine Entrants) (Application to Rail Freight) Regulations 2001, SI 2001/280). These provisions represented an enormous extension of liability. Whereas a professional passenger carrier such as an airline would have in place procedure for checking documentation, the extension to clandestine entrants and road transport meant that other commercial organizations and individuals, who had no professional expertise in transporting passengers, could be held liable to a penalty for people who had hidden in their car or lorry. The Immigration (Carriers' Liability) Act 1987 was repealed. Current law is governed by the 1999 Act, as amended by Nationality, Immigration and Asylum Act 2002 Schedule 8 and the Carriers' Liability Regulations 2002, SI 2002/2817, amending regulations and codes of practice.

6.5.3 The statutory scheme of carriers' liability

6.5.3.1 Liability for clandestine entrants

Section 32(5) of the 1999 Act imposed liability for clandestine entrants arriving in the UK on the owner or captain of the ship or aircraft, the owner, hirer, or driver of another vehicle, including, if the vehicle is a detached trailer, its operator. Since amendment by the 2002 Act, a penalty is imposed for each clandestine entrant, the maximum being £2,000 (Carriers' Liability Regulations 2002, SI 2002/2817, reg 3). In respect of each clandestine entrant, a penalty may be collected from more than one responsible person. In this case, there is a maximum aggregate penalty of £4,000 per entrant (reg 3). If the driver is an employee of the vehicle's owner or hirer, the employer is jointly and severally liable for the penalty. The maximum applies to the passenger, not the carrier. So, up to £4,000 may be paid by a number of different carriers for the one clandestine entrant, but if a carrier carries several clandestine entrants, the maximum penalty is £2,000 per passenger.

The definition of 'clandestine entrant' in s 32(1) as amended is striking. There are two aspects to it, first of all the concealment. A person is a clandestine entrant if they arrive concealed in a vehicle, ship, rail freight wagon, or aircraft or pass or attempt to pass through immigration control concealed in a vehicle. Arrival includes in a control zone as prescribed for the purposes of juxtaposed control (Carriers' Liability (Amendment) Regulations 2004, SI 2004/244). The definition catches both a person who stowed away on a ship, but disembarks on foot, and someone who continues or attempts to continue through immigration control hidden in a vehicle. The second part of the definition is that the person evades, or attempts to evade, immigration control, or, which is more surprising, they claim, or indicate that they intend to claim, asylum in the UK. There can be no doubt that this provision catches a genuine asylum claimant. The penalty is on those who transport them rather than the clandestine entrants themselves, but of course the effect of this is to make carriers more wary of carrying clandestine entrants. There is a non-statutory scheme of refunding penalties paid for carrying inadequately documented travellers where the passenger ultimately succeeds in an asylum claim (see *Charging Procedures—a Guide for Carriers* para 8.3). A successful asylum claim might of course be years down the line and so of small comfort to the carrier.

There is a defence in s 34 to liability for the penalty if the carrier can show that they were acting under duress, or that they had an effective system for preventing the carriage of clandestine entrants, which was operated properly, and they did not know, and had no reasonable grounds for suspecting, that someone might be concealed. The Guidance also sets out circumstances when charges might be waived, which include where the clandestine entrant was in imminent danger, and when the carrier could not have known or acted otherwise. In the case of imminent danger where the carrier cannot verify the person's identity they are advised to contact UNHCR or a UK port or UK representative for advice.

In determining whether a carrier's system is effective, account will be taken of the code of practice for vehicles issued by the Secretary of State under s 32A. The code contains detailed provision for road haulage and other commercial vehicles concerning the sealing of containers and repeated inspections. It also contains provisions for buses and coaches concerning the locking of doors and inspections and even for private vehicles such as cars and caravans, making equivalent provision.

Following the extension of liability to rail freight operators by the Carriers' Liability (Clandestine Entrants) (Application to Rail Freight) Regulations 2001, SI 2001/280, a Code of Practice for securing rail freight has also been adopted, and a further code for rail freight shuttle wagons.

The carrier may serve a notice of objection to the penalty (Carriers' Liability Regulations 2002, SI 2002/2817) which the Secretary of State must consider. If the notice is upheld, the Secretary of State may sue to recover the amount of the penalty. Importantly, following the *Roth* case discussed shortly, the 2002 Act introduced a right of appeal to a court against the imposition of the penalty (1999 Act s 35A; *International Transport Roth GmbH and Other v SSHD* [2002] 3 WLR 344).

The penalty is backed up by the power in s 36(1) for a senior officer to detain vehicles pending payment of the charge, if 'there is a significant risk that the penalty will not be paid' and no satisfactory alternative security. This power was extended by the 2002 Act to detaining a vehicle while the matter is being considered (1999 Act s 36(2A) and (2B)). The Court may order the release of a transporter if it considers that there is satisfactory security, or there is no significant risk that the penalty will not be paid or it considers that the penalty was not payable (s 37(3A) and (3B)). If the Court does not order the release of the transporter and the penalty is not paid within 84 days, the transporter may be sold (s 37(4)).

6.5.3.2 Improperly documented passengers

Since the 2002 Act, liability for improperly documented passengers does not apply to bus, coach, and train operators but only to owners of ships or aircraft. The penalty is payable on demand to the Secretary of State like an 'on the spot' fine. Section 40(4) provides a defence if the carrier can show that the passenger embarked with the proper documentation. The *Charging Procedures—Guide for Carriers* sets out situations in which the penalty will be waived, including that the carrier acted on the advice of an airline liaison manager.

6.5.3.3 Effect of scheme

The new carrier provisions in the 1999 Act came into effect between 6 December 1999 and 18 September 2000. Simon Brown LJ, in the case of *International Transport Roth GmbH & Others* at para 10, described the effect as follows:

By June 2001, 988 penalty notices had been served in respect of 5,433 clandestine entrants. 249 vehicles had been detained, of which 190 were subsequently released on payment of the penalty or a substantial security. In some 25 per cent of cases where clandestine entrants were discovered, either no penalty notice was served or, following the carrier's notice of objection, the Secretary of State decided, under section 35(8), that the penalty was not payable. The average penalty payable is some £12,000 (in respect, therefore, of six clandestine entrants). The bulk of the penalties are paid by companies, but some 10 per cent are paid by individuals including occasional car drivers. By October 2001 the value of the penalties paid or agreed to be paid was £2,432 million. In some cases instalment payments have been agreed, in the most extreme case at the rate of £40 per month for 12.5 years (£6,000).

In the *Roth* case, three of the appellants only discovered clandestine entrants when they were travelling up the motorway to London. They 'would never have been penalized had they not themselves alerted the police'.

The effect on small businesses of these penalties may be imagined, and the scheme generated an outcry. It was subject to a number of challenges.

6.5.3.4 Redress for carriers

When the system under the 1999 Act came into effect, there was no appeal against the imposition of a penalty. In *R (on the application of Balbo B &C Auto Transport Internazionale) v SSHD* [2001] 1 WLR 1556, the Secretary of State had decided to uphold the penalty and in the absence of a right of appeal the claimants applied for judicial review of that decision. The Administrative Court held that judicial review was not appropriate, but when the Secretary of State began enforcement proceedings then liability could be challenged.

The claimants in *Roth* challenged the harshness of the scheme, demonstrated by the fixed penalty, by the carriers bearing the burden of establishing that they were not blameworthy, and the lack of compensation for loss of business while a vehicle was detained, even if the carrier was determined not to be liable in the end. They suggested this was a disproportionate response to the problem of clandestine entrants. They challenged the lack of discretion and flexibility and the lack of provision for a fair hearing or a right of appeal, alleging under the Human Rights Act 1998 a breach of Article 6 and of Protocol 1, Article 1.

The specific procedural requirements of a fair trial in Article 6 apply only to a criminal matter, though the general principle of fairness applies also to the determination of civil rights and obligations. The requirements of fairness would therefore be greater if the proceedings were regarded as criminal. In the Act the charge levied is referred to as a 'civil penalty', there is no criminal charge and the penalty is recoverable as a civil debt. However, what a proceeding is called by the domestic authorities is not conclusive of whether it will be regarded as criminal or civil for the purposes of Article 6 ECHR. The Court of Appeal agreed (by a majority) with the carriers that the penalty scheme should be regarded as criminal, mainly because the carriers were in fact being punished, and the punishment meted out was severe.

It was a small step from this conclusion to decide that the scheme violated Article 6, though not necessarily for the reasons advanced by the carriers. Simon Brown LJ held: 'The hallowed principle that the punishment must fit the crime is irreconcilable with the notion of a substantial fixed penalty' (para 47). He accepted the claimants' characterization of the scheme as 'harsh', and this was his main reason for finding a breach of Article 6. In a similar vein, he concluded that the heavy burden on the carriers violated the principle of proportionality inherent in Protocol 1, Article 1, and that even if there was no violation of Article 6, then there was of this Article.

Jonathan Parker LJ found the scheme incompatible with Article 6 for a different reason, namely that the Secretary of State had an exclusive role in determining liability, and the role of the courts was subsidiary. 'Accordingly, for the simple yet fundamental reason that the scheme makes the Secretary of State judge in his own cause, the scheme in my judgment is plainly incompatible with Article 6' (para 157).

Following the Court of Appeal's decision, a right of appeal and a flexible penalty were introduced.

In March 2013 the government launched a consultation which proposed to increase penalties to between £7,000 and £10,000. The Independent Chief Inspector had commented that the scheme was not frequently used, and respondents to the consultation pointed out that preventing unauthorized travel through more sophisticated document checking and the advice of ILMs was more effective than penalties.

6.5.3.5 Redress for travellers

The carriers' liability scheme, particularly in relation to clandestine entrants, also carries particular hazards for potential passengers. The greatest hazard of the scheme is to an asylum seeker, who may lack proper documents, and who is turned away from a flight, or discovered and removed from a lorry, perhaps directly into the hands of the authorities whose persecution they seek to escape. There is also a potential problem for any traveller whose documents are not correctly understood.

This problem arose in *Farah v British Airways & Home Office* (*The Times* 26 January 2000). In this case, the Somali appellants had been prevented from embarking on a flight from Cairo to London. One had a passport. The other four appellants, all members of the same family, had declarations of identity documents issued by the British Embassy in Addis Ababa. The immigration liaison officer advised the airline that the passengers were incorrectly documented and should not be allowed to travel. As a consequence, they were detained in Cairo airport for five days, then deported to Ethiopia. *The Times* report is of the Court of Appeal's judgment that the judge should not have struck out the part of the particulars of claim which claimed negligence. This was held to be an arguable matter which would turn on the particular facts and should be heard.

The liability of airlines and of ILMs in this situation is as yet undetermined, though the *European Roma Rights Centre* case found that the Race Relations (Amendment) Act 2000 applied to decisions of immigration officers abroad (see 6.4.5).

The Council of Europe's Parliamentary Assembly considered the issue of sanctions against airlines in 1991 and commented:

Airline sanctions . . . undermine the basic principles of refugee protection and the rights of refugees to claim asylum, while placing a considerable legal, administrative and financial burden upon carriers and moving the responsibility away from the immigration officers.

Research on people illegally resident in the UK shows that different routes of entry are more likely to be taken by people of different nationalities. It would suggest that airline controls impact more on travellers from West and Sub-Saharan Africa, and carrier sanctions would bite more on travellers from Albania, Ukraine, and Sri Lanka (Home Office 20/05 chapter 4).

The use of carrier sanctions has remained steady in absolute numbers, while travel has increased enormously.

6.6 Immigration officers' powers on arrival

On arrival at a UK port, a passenger with or without entry clearance will encounter an immigration officer. Since March 2012 they are employed by the UK Border Force, which is a law enforcement command in the Home Office with dual responsibility for immigration and customs. Immigration officers have extensive powers including to conduct an examination of the passenger, and to search or detain them (Sch 2, 1971 Act). The Immigration and Asylum Act 1999 gave powers to immigration officers very similar to those possessed by the police in the investigation of crime and the apprehension of suspects. These enhanced powers apply both to dealing with people suspected of immigration offences (Immigration Act 1971 Part III) and to carrying out immigration functions under Schedule 2. In addition, immigration officers may be designated as, and exercise the powers of, customs officials (Borders Citizenship and Immigration Act 2009 s 3).

Where a person arrives in the UK at a port, they are deemed not to have entered until they have passed through the designated area for immigration control (Immigration Act 1971 s 11). The repercussions of this are as shown in Table 6.1.

6.6.1 Grant or refuse leave to enter

By s 4(1) of the 1971 Act, immigration officers have statutory power to give or refuse leave to enter. Since all passengers entering for more than six months require entry clearance, in practice leave granted on arrival will now normally be only for non-visa national visitors. Until April 2000, leave to enter was granted at the port of entry by means of a date stamp in the passport. For travellers receiving leave to enter at the port it may still be granted by this method, unless and until technological developments make that redundant. Leave to enter may be refused on any of the grounds discussed at 6.8.

An immigration officer must act in accordance with the immigration rules and instructions given by the Secretary of State (Immigration Act 1971 Sch 2 para 1(3)). However, since the 2014 Act substitution of s 82 of the 2002 Act on 20 October 2014, there has been no right of appeal against refusal on arrival for a passenger unless their application is treated as a human rights or asylum claim (see chapter 7).

Where a passenger has entry clearance which functions as leave to enter, the immigration officer may cancel that leave on grounds set out at 6.9 or suspend it during examination (Sch 2 para 2A(7)).

6.6.2 **Examination**

The most widely applicable of the immigration officer's powers is to examine any person arriving (Sch 2 para 2). This includes where entry clearance has been granted (para 2A) and even where leave to enter is not required, as Immigration Act 1971 s 1(1) provides that freedom to come and go, enjoyed for instance by British citizens, may be hindered 'to enable their right to be established'. Any person arriving may be examined to ascertain whether they need leave to enter, and may be required to produce 'either a valid passport with photograph or some other document satisfactorily establishing his identity and nationality or citizenship' (Immigration Act 1971 Sch 2(1) and (4)). Therefore, a British passport-holder must show their passport to gain entry, even though they do not need leave to enter, and without such proof they may be refused entry (see also Immigration Act 1971 s 3(9) and HC 395 para 12). A 'valid' passport means a current one. The case of *Akewushola v Immigration Officer Heathrow* [2000] 2 All ER 148 CA established that an expired passport plus other proof of identity was not sufficient. Case C 378/97 *Wijsenbeek* [1999] I-6207 established that an EEA national passenger could be required to prove their entitlement despite their right to free movement, although a valid identity card is all that is necessary to establish the right to travel. In the case of other nationals, passports or refugee travel documents will be required (Table 6.1).

The legal process called 'examination' is at minimum a cursory inspection of a passport, and may go on from there (*R (on the application of Ogilvy) v SSHD* [2007] EWHC 2301 (Admin)) to involve an interview or a series of interviews. These may be on different dates so that the whole examination may be spread over a considerable period of time. The examination also includes other investigations carried out by the immigration officer, which may not involve the passenger directly (*Thirukumar* [1989] Imm AR 270). In between interviews, the applicant may be in detention or released in the UK on a status known as temporary admission (Sch 2 para 21). Paragraph 4 imposes a duty on people who are undergoing examination to provide all information required for the examination including documentation. There is no 'duty of utmost good faith' to disclose everything which might conceivably be relevant, however, silence as to a material fact is capable of amounting to deception or fraud depending on the circumstances (*Khawaja* [1984] AC 74, HL). It is a criminal offence to refuse to submit to examination, not to produce documents

Table 6.1 Entry and arrival

Method of arrival and entry decision	Consequence for entry
At a port. No leave granted but allowed physically to remain pending further inquiries (probably on temporary admission—see chapter 14)	Has arrived but not entered
At a port. Leave granted or already held and not cancelled	Arrives on disembarking from ship or boat and enters lawfully when passes through immigration control
Not at a port. Crosses land border (Republic of Ireland to N. Ireland). Leave granted or already held and not cancelled	Arrives and enters lawfully on crossing border (see *R v Javaherifard and Miller* [2005] EWCA Crim 323)
Not at a port. Arrives by sea or air (e.g., on a remote beach). No leave	Arrives on disembarking. Enters at time of arrival, but not lawfully
Not at a port. Arrives by sea or air (e.g., private landing strip). Has leave	Arrives on disembarking. Enters at time of arrival, lawfully

that are requested, or to knowingly make a false statement (s 26 Immigration Act 1971), but recalling *Khaliq*, referred to earlier, where the passenger is not making an application at the port of entry, a certificate produced at that time is not a representation for the purposes of obtaining leave. The collection and advance electronic transmission of passenger data now means that when a traveller arrives at a UK port, advance information about them may already be available to the immigration officer.

6.6.3 Retention of documents and search

Documents, including a passport, may be retained by the immigration officer until the examination is over (1971 Act Sch 2 para 4(2A) and (4)) and even until the person 'is about to depart or be removed' (Immigration, Asylum and Nationality Act 2006 s 27). In other words, a passport can be retained throughout a person's stay in the UK. The immigration officer also has power to search the passenger and their luggage (Sch 2 para 4). The UK Borders Act 2007 provides that trained immigration officers may be 'designated', and these designated officers may detain a person suspected of a listed immigration offence (ss 1 and 2). The Immigration Act 2014 Schedule 8 allows other 'designated' persons to conduct examinations and require production of passports. This is likely to be used to delegate and assign immigration functions to private contractors.

6.6.4 Authorization to discriminate

The Equality Act 2010 s 29 prohibits discrimination, victimization, or harassment by public bodies, but this is made subject to wide exceptions in relation to immigration by Schedule 3 part 4. The protection of section 29 on grounds of disability is excluded for decisions on leave to enter or remain. It is excluded for discrimination based on religion or belief for decisions on entry, or leave to remain, or exclusion from the UK where these are taken on the basis that they are conducive to the public good. It is excluded for the exercise of functions in relation to the Immigration Acts and Special Immigration Appeals Commission Act for discrimination based on age (para 15A), nationality, or 'ethnic or national origins' (para 17(1)). The functions in relation to which discrimination is permitted are those exercised by a Minister of the Crown personally, or by a person acting in accordance with an authorization given, with respect to a particular case or class of case, by a Minister of the Crown; or with respect to a particular class of case, by relevant legislation or an instrument made under it (para 17(4)). Ten authorizations are in place at the time of writing. See https://www.gov.uk/government/uploads/system/uploads/attachment_data/file/262793/annex-ee.pdf.

An authorization to discriminate under the Equality Act, issued in February 2011, permits an immigration officer, on the basis of a passenger's nationality, to subject them to more rigorous examination, to exercise any of their powers related to examination (asking for documents, retaining documents, etc.), to detain them, to prioritize them for removal, to decline to give notice of the grant or refusal of leave to enter in the prescribed form, and to set conditions of temporary admission (Equality (Transit Visa, Entry Clearance, Leave to Enter, Examination of Passengers and Removal Directions) Authorisation 2011). The condition for exercising these powers to discriminate is that the passenger is or claims to be of a nationality listed by the minister. The grounds for the minister to list a nationality are that:

(a) there is statistical evidence showing that in at least one of the preceding three months, the total number of adverse decisions or breaches of the immigration laws and/or the immigration rules by persons of that nationality exceeds 50 in total and 5 for every 1,000 admitted persons of that nationality; or

(b) there is specific intelligence or information which has been received and processed in accordance with the IND Code of Practice for the recording and dissemination of intelligence material and which suggests that a significant number of persons of that nationality have breached or will attempt to breach the immigration laws and/or the immigration rules; or

(c) there is statistical evidence showing an emerging trend of adverse decisions or breaches of the immigration laws and/or the immigration rules by persons of that nationality that exceeds the criteria expressed in paragraph 8(ii)(a) within a time-frame shorter than a single month.

In relation to decisions affecting transit visas, the figures in (a) are 150 in total and 50 for every 1,000 admitted persons of that nationality.

This authorization under the Equality Act is on the same stated basis as authorizations which preceded it under the Race Relations Act 1976, as amended in 2000. However, there is a major difference in terms of transparency and accountability in that under the Equality Act there is no obligation to disclose the authorizations. No public information is given about which nationalities are targeted. Since the statute permits this, it follows that authorizations may be made on grounds of ethnicity as well as nationality without this being disclosed. Reinforcing this secrecy, ECOs are prohibited by internal instructions from referring to the list when making decisions (FOI request 17943). The purpose of evidence-based statutorily authorized discrimination as introduced in 2000 was in part to make the basis of decisions more accountable and transparent. The Equality Act version has the reverse effect. The only way for an affected individual to find out whether an authorization has affected them is to compel disclosure in legal proceedings.

A principle laid down in the first challenge to the authorizations in the 1976 Act was that, as the actions permitted are acts of discrimination which would otherwise be unlawful, on principle they should be construed narrowly (*R (on the application of Tamil Information Centre) v SSHD* [2002] EWHC 2155 (Admin)). There is no reason to think that this principle no longer applies, but the difficulty under the Equality Act is not that the principle does not apply, but rather getting disclosure that an authorization has been relied on.

The Equality Act s 149 also contains a duty to have regard to the need to combat discrimination. There are exceptions in relation to immigration and nationality functions, but these do not extend to powers of arrest and search.

6.6.5 Extended powers in relation to terrorism

Immigration officers have powers under Schedule 7 to the Terrorism Act 2000 as amended to stop, detain, search, and question any person at an air or sea port for the purpose of determining whether that person appears to be concerned or to have been concerned in the 'commission, preparation or instigation of acts of terrorism' (s 40(1) (b)). A person at a port may have arrived in the UK from anywhere. There is a wider power in relation to journeys into Northern Ireland from the Republic of Ireland when a person may be stopped not only at the port, but also within the border area. This is defined as any place up to a mile from the border with the Republic, or, if the journey is by train, the first train stop in Northern Ireland (Sch 7 para 4). This places a limit on the freedom of movement given by the CTA, and note that these constraints on movement are not immigration restrictions but are security restrictions entailing policing activity. The Nationality, Immigration and Asylum Act 2002 (Juxtaposed Controls) Order 2003, SI 2003/2818 applies these powers to sea port control zones.

Powers under the schedule do not require a basis of reasonable suspicion. They may be exercised 'for the purpose of determining whether' the person may have terrorist involvement, in other words, simply in order to find out. This has been repeatedly criticized by David Anderson QC, the Independent Reviewer of Terrorism Legislation. These powers are also given a wide scope by the broad definition of terrorism used in s 1 (discussed more fully in chapter 13). An officer exercising powers under this schedule may require the passenger to surrender any documents of a kind that the officer specifies (para 5), and may retain for seven days any property obtained during a search of the passenger (para 11). They may download the content of a mobile phone. The exercise of these powers is subject to the usual administrative law restraints and to the positive duty not to discriminate in s 29 of the Equality Act 2010. However, both these forms of redress place the burden on the complainant to show that the powers were unlawfully exercised, rather than on the immigration officer to show that there was a reasonable basis for their actions. The authorization to discriminate, discussed earlier, does not apply to Schedule 7, which is not a power under the Immigration Acts. It is a criminal offence not to comply with the requirements of an immigration officer exercising these powers.

An immigration officer may search a ship, aircraft, or anything on or which s/he reasonably believes to have been or be about to be on a ship or aircraft (e.g., a container) 'for the purpose of satisfying himself whether there are any persons he may wish to question under paragraph 2' (para 7).

The maximum period of detention for these powers to be exercised is six hours (reduced from nine by the Anti-Social Behaviour, Crime and Policing Act 2014 (ASBCPA)), although the person may be detained for longer by the police if there are grounds for suspicion. The ASBCPA also introduced a right to have someone informed and to consult a solicitor.

The use of Schedule 7 powers has decreased in recent years but become more targeted. A total of 34,500 individuals were detained for examination in 2014/15. The majority of those examinations were short with only 1,887 lasting over an hour.

The powers came to public notice when they were exercised in August 2013 on David Miranda, the partner of a *The Guardian* journalist, on the basis that he was carrying encrypted files containing journalistic material derived from the US National Security Agency whistleblower Edward Snowden. The High Court found his detention lawful and the Court of Appeal agreed (*R (David Miranda) v SSHD and Commissioner of Police of the Metropolis, Intervenors: Liberty; Article 19, English Pen and the Media Legal Defence Initiative* [2016] EWCA Civ 6). However, the Court of Appeal held that the stop power was incompatible with ECHR Article 10 in relation to journalistic material in that it was not subject to adequate safeguards against its arbitrary exercise (para 119).

In 2011 the powers were used to stop, search, and question Sylvie Beghal, the wife of a man detained in France in relation to terrorism charges. She was returning to the UK after visiting him. Ms Beghal challenged not only the application to her of the Schedule 7 powers, but also their lawfulness. Both challenges were rejected by the Supreme Court, which found that ECHR Articles 5 and 8 were engaged but not violated, and that Article 6 was not engaged (*Beghal v DPP* [2015] UKSC 49). The Court made some obiter remarks about the Schedule 7 powers, including endorsing the Independent Reviewer's recommendation that the statute should make explicit that answers given in questioning at the port under Schedule 7 should not be admissible in criminal proceedings. Lord Kerr dissented and the case may go to the ECtHR.

6.7 **Criminal law and entry to the UK**

Immigration offences are not covered in detail in this book on the basis that they are part of criminal law, not immigration law. A brief outline is given here of the main offences which may be charged on entry. Immigration officers have power to arrest, detain, and question in relation to these offences, and when they do so they must have regard to relevant Codes of Practice issued in relation to the Police and Criminal Evidence Act 1984, as modified by order (s 45 Immigration and Asylum Act 1999).

Illegal entry is an offence committed by entering the UK without leave or in breach of a deportation order (Immigration Act 1971 s 24). Most people who enter without leave are not prosecuted, but are treated as illegal entrants and subject to removal—that is, immigration enforcement rather than criminal enforcement. The status of illegal entrant and the process of removal are discussed in detail in chapter 16.

The use of deception to seek or obtain leave to enter or remain in the UK is an offence contrary to Immigration Act 1971 s 24A (as inserted and amended by the 1996 and 1999 Acts), carrying a maximum penalty of two years in prison. The use of false or altered documents is an offence contrary to s 26(1)(d), and may also be charged as the offence of using a false instrument contrary to s 3 of the Forgery and Counterfeiting Act 1981 or possessing one contrary to s 5. In *R v Kolawole* [2004] EWCA Crim 3047, the Court gave guidance that, because of increased public concern on these matters, the appropriate sentence for having a false passport with intent to use it, 'even on a guilty plea by a person of good character, should usually be within the range of 12 to 18 months' imprisonment'. The maximum sentence is two years, and ten years for an offence under s 3.

Offences in connection with the use of false identity documents are found in the Identity Documents Act 2010. Section 4 creates an offence of having in one's possession an identity document that is false which the holder knows or believes to be false, or that was improperly obtained (i.e., by the use of false information: s 9(3)) and which the holder knows or believes to have been improperly obtained, or that relates to someone else. This offence requires the *mens rea* of intention to use the document to establish personal information about the holder or purported holder, including name, address, nationality, and immigration status. This includes a false claim to be the person in the document (see *R v Goodings* [2012] EWCA Crim 2586). There is a further offence in s 6 of simply possessing such a false document without reasonable excuse. The s 4 offence carries a maximum sentence of ten years' imprisonment; the s 6 offence carries a maximum sentence of two years. An identity document is defined in s 7 to include a passport, a driving licence, and an immigration document of any kind; this includes the biometric identity documents which are now required for foreign nationals (see chapter 2).

Commission of one of these offences on entry may also be treated as relevant to the person being an illegal entrant and thus liable for removal (see chapter 16). Prosecution for these offences is inappropriate in the case of refugees, who may have no lawful route to enter, and this issue is discussed in chapter 11 on the asylum process. Offences which control and criminalize asylum seekers are also discussed in chapter 11, where facilitation of entry for seeking asylum is also discussed. It is relevant to note here that criminal offences may be committed by people who arrange unlawful entry or stay for any immigration purpose. See, for instance, *Dhall v R* [2013] EWCA Crim 1610 in which the appellant was an immigration adviser regulated by the Office of Immigration Services Commissioner. He was convicted of assisting breaches of immigration law (s 25 Immigration Act 1971) by the preparation and submission of fraudulent Tier 1 (General) Highly Skilled Worker extension applications. Where a number of people join together in a scheme to enable breaches of immigration law, a conspiracy may be charged, as in *Bhatti, Akhtar and Mohammed v R* [2015] EWCA Crim 1305 where the college set up by the appellants 'issued dishonest documents to non-EU foreign nationals who wanted to obtain leave to enter, or to remain in, the United Kingdom as students ... without any intention of studying.' (para 10).

6.8 Refusal of entry clearance, or of leave to enter on arrival

The immigration rules contain general grounds for refusal, which apply to leave to enter or entry clearance. The grounds for refusal in para 320 are divided into those upon which leave to enter or entry clearance 'is to be refused' and those upon which leave to enter 'should normally be refused'. Before considering some of the grounds individually we shall consider their standing in administrative law.

The wording of the rules indicates that when a reason in the first group applies, refusal of leave is mandatory and when a reason in the second set applies, refusal is discretionary. Guidance on the government website gives an indication of how the Secretary of State expects discretion to be exercised. However, the administrative law principle against fettering discretion does not permit prescription of circumstances in which there must always be a refusal. The power to grant or refuse leave is given by statute (s 4(1) Immigration Act 1971), and the immigration rules may not lawfully restrict the statutory power, though they guide its exercise. An authority acts lawfully in having a policy as long as it is prepared to listen to someone who has something new to say which might justify dealing with them in a different way (*R v Port of London Authority ex p Kynoch Ltd* [1919] 1 KB 176 and *British Oxygen Co Ltd v Minister of Technology* [1971] AC 610). This principle was applied to the immigration rules by the Court of Appeal in *Pearson v Immigration Appeal Tribunal*. Paragraph 5 of the immigration rules then in force, HC 80, provided that if the Department of Employment did not approve an extension of leave for work, then the application 'should be refused'. The Court of Appeal said, at 225, that in making such a rule:

The Home Secretary did, in our opinion, make a rule as to how he would in future, as a matter of general policy, exercise his discretion, but not how he would exercise it in every case without considering the circumstances of a particular case and whether to make an exception to that policy.

Following *Pearson*, the existence of so-called mandatory reasons for refusal is not an unlawful fetter on discretion according to administrative law, because there exists a power to act outside the rules. This was confirmed more recently in *R (on the application of Thebo) v SSHD* [2013] EWHC 146 (Admin).

Where the reasons for refusal entail the immigration officer being satisfied that something is the case, the officer must form their judgment on a reasonable basis (*Secretary of State for Education v Tameside MBC* [1977] AC 1014). *JC (China) v ECO Guangzhou* [2007] UKAIT 00027 confirmed that the burden of proof is on the Secretary of State on the balance of probabilities to prove any fact upon which a refusal under para 320 relies.

Note that of the reasons for refusal in para 320, only those in sub-paras 3, 10, and 11 apply in relation to applications made under the immigration rules relating to family members (para A320). However, the 'public good' and conviction-related grounds and non-compliance grounds are reproduced in Appendix FM to the rules, and applied category by category to family and private life applications. Chapter 8 discusses family applications in detail.

6.8.1 **Reasons for refusal: purpose not within the rules**

The first reason given in para 320 is that 'entry is sought for a purpose not covered by the rules'. The obligation is on the applicant to show that the reason for entry is within the categories provided for by the rules (*Abid Hussain v ECO Islamabad* [1989] Imm AR 46). However, 'Modernised Guidance' on applications on entry says that refusal should only take place if there is no concession that could be applied, putting an obligation on the immigration officer to consider this (*General Grounds for Refusal— section 3 of 5 considering entry at a UK port*, September 2015). Since the immigration rules are increasingly tightly drawn, there is an increasing chance of an applicant falling foul of para 320(1). Modernized guidance to decision-makers on the application of the equivalent rule in relation to leave to remain says that this rule should not be used where the applicant has failed to meet the requirements of a rule, but only when they are applying outside the rules (*General Grounds for Refusal—section 4 of 5 considering leave to remain*, September 2015).

6.8.2 **Reasons for refusal: evidential, documentary, or status requirements**

A number of the general reasons for refusal relating to evidential or documentary re-quirements or other matters concerning the status of the applicant are in the following sub-paras of rule 320:

(2A) failure, if required . . . to provide a criminal record certificate from the relevant authority in any country in which they have been resident for 12 months or more, in the past 10 years. Not normally required where the applicant is 17 years old or under.

(3) failure to produce a valid national passport or other document satisfactorily establish-ing identity and nationality (this ground can be applied to family applications);

(4) failure to satisfy the Immigration Officer, in the case of a person who intends to enter another part of the common travel area, that he is acceptable to the immigration authorities there;

(5) failure, in the case of a visa national, to produce a valid and current entry clearance issued for the purpose for which entry is sought; . . .

(7D) failure, without providing a reasonable explanation, to comply with a request made on behalf of the Entry Clearance Officer to attend for interview;

(8) failure to furnish the Immigration Officer with information required for deciding whether leave to enter is required and on what terms leave should be given;

(8A) where the person seeking leave is outside the UK, failure to supply any information, documents, copy documents or medical report requested by an Immigration Officer; . . .

(10) production of a passport or travel document from a government or state not recognized by the UK (this ground applies to family applications); . . .

(13) failure, except by a person eligible for admission for settlement, to satisfy the Immigration Officer that he will be admitted to another country after a stay in the United Kingdom; . . .

(20) failure to provide physical data as required by regulations made under section 126 of the Nationality, Immigration and Asylum Act 2002; . . .

(22) where a relevant NHS body has notified the Secretary of State that the person seeking entry has failed to pay charges with a total value of at least £1000 in accordance with NHS regulations on charges to overseas visitors.

These grounds are largely self-explanatory. Sub-rule 2A was added with effect from 6 April 2015 and applies to Tier 1 Investors and Entrepreneurs. There is a discretion to waive the requirement if it is not reasonably practicable for the applicant to obtain such evidence. Guidance suggests that convictions revealed by any certificate will be judged in accordance with the usual rules on criminality (see next section). Sub-rule 8A applies only to specific requests made to an individual, not to media information generally.

6.8.3 Grounds for refusal relating to convictions or 'public good'

These grounds were extended substantially in December 2012, and there are now four sets of provisions of this kind.

The first is paragraph 320(2) which makes refusal of entry mandatory on the basis of a prison sentence for criminal convictions, or if the person is currently the subject of a deportation order. A sentence of four years or more excludes them permanently, a sentence of between 12 months and four years excludes them for ten years, and a sentence of less than 12 months excludes them for five years. The periods of exclusion are counted from the end of the sentence imposed, not the time the applicant spent in prison (Modernised Guidance *General Grounds for Refusal, Section 1 of 5*, September 2015). There is provision for exceptional circumstances or a grant of entry if refusal would breach the Human Rights or Refugee Convention. A breach of Article 10 was found in *Sehwerert v ECO* (chapter 5) where the Court of Appeal made clear that exceptional circumstances warranting a grant of entry clearance despite the mandatory reason for refusal are a separate issue from interference with ECHR rights.

The same guidance advises decision-makers that exceptions may also be made if 'there are exceptional circumstances that mean entry must be granted despite the conviction, or an applicant's conviction is for an offence not recognised in the UK'. An act that is not an offence in the UK would be, for instance, homosexuality or proselytizing.

A non-exhaustive list of factors is given to consider in deciding whether circumstances are exceptional:

Since conviction, the passage of time or the personal circumstances of the person have significantly changed such that maintaining a refusal would be so perverse as to undermine confidence in the immigration system;

There is reliable evidence to suggest the conviction was politically motivated;

The person intends to make a significant investment in the UK, for example, buying or heavily investing in a major company, so refusing entry would not be in the national interest.

Section 56A UK Borders Act 2007 exempts immigration decisions from the provisions of the Rehabilitation of Offenders Act 1974, so applicants for entry clearance or leave to enter must disclose convictions, even those which would otherwise be spent under UK law.

Paragraph 320(6) provides that leave must be refused where the Secretary of State has personally directed that the exclusion of a person from the UK is conducive to the public good. The discretionary ground in para 320(19) is similarly worded, except that it is not based on a personal direction of the Secretary of State but on the discretion of the immigration officer.

Personal directions under para 320(6) have been used when there is a perceived risk to national security when the individual has some degree of notoriety or political prominence, or there is intelligence information suggesting risk. For instance, in *Murungaru v SSHD, ECO Nairobi, British High Commissioner Nairobi* [2008] EWCA Civ 1015, the Secretary of State received information that the Kenyan MP and minister was engaging in activities concerned with corruption in Kenya during his medical visits to the UK. It was partly to show support for the Kenyan government that the Secretary of State acted quickly under para 320(6) to prevent his next visit. In *Farrakhan*, the Secretary of State had information that, because Mr Farrakhan had expressed anti-Semitic views, and because two members of the Nation of Islam had been arrested for public order offences outside the Stephen Lawrence Inquiry, his presence in the UK might give rise to disorder. The direction made by the Secretary of State that the person's exclusion is for the public good is not itself made under the immigration rules. The source of the power was discussed in case law for the first time in *Cakani v SSHD* [2013] EWHC 16 (Admin) where the Court held the power was derived from the Immigration Act 1971 and thus it was not unlawful even though guidance as to its exercise was not laid before Parliament in immigration rules (applying *Alvi* [2012] UKSC 33). See also *Naik v SSHD and ECO Mumbai* [2011] EWCA Civ 1546 and *R (on the application of Geller and Spencer) v SSHD* [2015] EWCA Civ 45. In both these cases the Secretary of State made a personal direction based on the 'list of unacceptable behaviours' (see chapters 2 and 15). Challenges to the use of the list (*Naik*) and the lawfulness of relying on it (*Geller and Spencer*) both failed. It was public, announced in Parliament, and did not consist of conditions that applicants had to fulfil (cp. *Alvi*). It simply gave information as to matters that the Secretary of State might take into account in deciding to exclude someone.

Refusal of leave to enter or entry clearance relying on para 320(6) is not restricted to high-profile or security-related cases. For instance, in *Campbell (exclusion; Zambrano)* [2013] UKUT 147 (IAC) refusal was based on common offences. The exclusion decision was made after the appellant had voluntarily left the UK. Guidance disclosed in the case of *Cakani* revealed an intention that 'a "major area(s) of future use" of the exclusion power is the case of foreign national prisoners who have taken up the offer of assistance and who have left the country as part of the Facilitated Returns Scheme' (*Cakani* para 52). The Court endorsed the use of exclusion in such a situation (see the parallel with deprivation of nationality in chapter 3).

An earlier sub-para 18 permitted refusal of entry on grounds that the applicant had been convicted of an offence carrying at least 12 months' imprisonment, as long as the immigration officer did not consider that there were compassionate circumstances which required entry to be granted. In its place the reference to compassionate circumstances has gone and there are discretionary grounds for refusal that:

(18A) within the 12 months prior to the date on which the application is decided, the person has been convicted of or admitted an offence for which they received a non-custodial sentence or other out of court disposal that is recorded on their criminal record;
(18B) in the view of the Secretary of State:
    (a) the person's offending has caused serious harm; or
    (b) the person is a persistent offender who shows a particular disregard for the law.

The breadth of discretion is substantially increased, although where a person has received an absolute or conditional discharge this is not treated as a conviction (Powers of Criminal Courts (Sentencing) Act 2000 s 14(1), confirmed in *Omenma (Conditional discharge—not a conviction of an offence)* [2014] UKUT 314 (IAC)).

Exclusion under sub-para 19 is on the basis that the immigration officer 'deems the exclusion of the person from the United Kingdom to be conducive to the public good, for example, because the person's conduct (including convictions which do not fall within paragraph 320(2)), character, associations, or other reasons, make it undesirable to grant them leave to enter.' This discretion must be reasonably exercised; however, it provides a broad basis for exclusion. The Court in *R (on the application of) Ivlev v SSHD* [2013] EWHC 1162 (Admin) said that this wording in a former version of sub-para 19:

confers a wide discretion and power of evaluation and assessment on the decision-maker to reach a judgment on what is conducive to the public good . . . For this ground of refusal, the issue is simply whether the decision-maker has formed the relevant opinion and made the relevant judgment without breaching any general rules of public law and that the opinion and judgment are ones he could rationally reach. (para 87)

In *Ivlev* the exclusion was based on the fact that there were outstanding charges against the applicant in Russia. Charges in related situations had been found to be politically motivated in other European countries, were the subject of challenge to the ECtHR, and had never successfully founded an extradition. The applicant argued that since the UK government must know that the charges were politically motivated, this was an improper use of para 320(19). The Court disagreed, holding that even if the charges were politically motivated, this did not mean that they were entirely without foundation; the UK government had a very wide discretion under para 320(19) and it was legitimate to take into account the possibility of protracted court proceedings, the impact on the public purse, and the effect on relations with Russia if entry clearance was granted.

The information founding the decision might be prior information, perhaps revealed through a fingerprint match, which would then found a refusal of entry clearance. Alternatively, it might be information gathered at the port of entry, for instance, if the passenger is found to be in possession of illegal drugs or quantities of pornography sufficient to suggest that they are intending to sell it rather than use it personally. Arguments about the rights of long-term residents to remain despite criminal convictions are considered more fully in the section on enforcement.

6.8.4 Travel bans

There are international interests in restricting certain people from travelling between countries. These centre around the prevention of crime, particularly terrorist and drugs offences, and restriction of the movements of war criminals and national leaders upon whom groups of nations wish to exert pressure. These restrictions are effected in UK law by orders made under s 8B Immigration Act 1971 (inserted by s 8 of the Immigration and Asylum Act 1999). The section provides for a category of 'excluded persons'. These are people named or referred to in a designated resolution of the United Nations Security Council or Council of the European Union. Immigration (Designation of Travel Bans) Orders have designated resolutions concerning, for instance, former President Milosevic of Yugoslavia, President Mugabe of Zimbabwe, and individuals implicated in abuses in Syria, Moldova, Belarus, Guinea-Bissau, Iran, Eritrea, Libya, Liberia, Sudan, DRC, Cote d'Ivoire, Somalia, and Yemen. The effect of these designations is that the excluded person must be refused leave to enter or leave to remain in the UK. These resolutions and orders demonstrate the increase in concerted international action on issues which are seen as relating to violations of human rights on a large scale, or to the spread of criminal activity. EU orders banning travel to the EU do not apply in the Vatican. This became publicly apparent when Robert Mugabe travelled to the Vatican for Pope John Paul II's funeral in 2005 and beatification in 2011 and again for the installation of Pope Francis in 2013.

6.8.5 Medical reasons

6.8.5.1 Medical examinations

The immigration rules require that a person who intends to remain in the UK for more than six months is referred to the medical inspector for a medical examination (HC 395 para 36). This applies to anyone who is coming to the UK to settle with family members. Referral to the medical inspector may also be made if the person seeking entry 'mentions health or medical treatment as a reason for his visit or appears not to be in good health' (para 36). An immigration officer may also refer a person for further medical examination after entry 'in the interests of public health' (Immigration Act 1971 Sch 2 para 7). Applicants for more than six months' stay, or people applying to enter as fiancé(e)s, must have a medical test for tuberculosis *before* making their entry clearance application if they come from any of the 101 countries listed in Appendix T to the immigration rules. Medical procedures related to applications for entry clearance are described in the entry clearance guidance on the government website.

Refusal to undergo a medical examination is a discretionary reason for refusal of leave to enter or entry clearance (para 320(17)) and so is failure to supply a medical report when an application is proceeding outside the UK (para 320(8A) and Immigration (Leave to Enter and Remain) Order 2000, SI 2000/1161, Article 7(4)). The effect of this is that, when an immigration officer or ECO (HC 395 para 39) refers a person for a medical examination, that person is compelled to attend the medical examination if they want leave to enter.

6.8.5.2 Refusal on medical grounds

Paragraph 320(7) provides for a mandatory refusal on the following basis:

save in relation to a person settled in the United Kingdom or where the Immigration Officer is satisfied that there are strong compassionate reasons justifying admission, confirmation from the Medical Inspector that, for medical reasons, it is undesirable to admit a person seeking leave to enter the United Kingdom.

Historically there have been ambiguities in the rules about whether the operative decision refusing entry lay with the medical inspector, who has no statutory power to exercise immigration control, or the immigration officer. The Modernised Guidance says:

Medical inspectors will only issue certificates when satisfied the person's condition is a significant risk to public health. If they do issue a medical certificate or following a medical examination they recommend the person must not enter because of medical reasons you must refuse entry or leave to remain in the UK. (*General Grounds for Refusal* p. 110)

This suggests that the substantive decision is in effect delegated to the medical inspector, whose opinion is conclusive. However, the immigration officer has a discretion to override the medical recommendation where they are satisfied that there are strong compassionate reasons justifying admission. The guidance lists reasons that an immigration officer should refer a passenger for a medical examination where their appearance or conduct suggests a health problem.

The guidance explains that

[t]he objective of the medical examination and recommendation is to prevent the entry of, or bring to notice, persons who if admitted to the UK might:

1. endanger the health of other persons in the UK; or
2. be unable for medical reasons to support themselves and/or dependants in the UK; or
3. require major medical treatment (for which an entry clearance application has not been made).

The medical inspector is a doctor employed by the Home Office to make reports on potential immigrants and asylum seekers (Immigration Act 1971 s 4(2) and Sch 2 para 1(2)). The Guidance stresses that medical inspectors should not be asked to examine passengers to discover whether they have borne children or had sexual relations nor to X-ray them to determine their age. The prohibition is worded strictly, and this is because precisely these practices were carried out in the 1970s. The former refers to the virginity tests carried out on the claimed basis that a good Muslim or Hindu woman would not engage in sexual relations before marriage, nor would a respectable man of those faiths marry someone who had. Therefore, genuine fiancées could be detected by their virginity. The ensuing scandal prompted the Commission for Racial Equality's investigation into immigration control, but the scale of the practice was only revealed in May 2011 after confidential Home Office files were disclosed ('Virginity tests for immigrants reflected "dark age prejudices" of 1970s Britain' *The Guardian* 8 May 2011).

The medical inspector's opinion may not be challenged on its own merits (*Al-Tuwaidji v Chief Immigration Officer Heathrow* [1974] Imm AR 34 followed in *Mohazeb v Immigration Officer Harwich* [1990] Imm AR 555). This ground for refusal does not apply to people with settled status who, having travelled abroad, may not be refused re-entry on medical grounds.

6.8.6 Immigration breaches

Previous breaches of immigration law used to be a discretionary reason for refusing entry clearance or leave to enter, but became mandatory on 1 April 2008 (HC 321).

In addition to making previous breaches a ground for refusal, para 320 7(B) effects a re-entry ban. It sets a mandatory ground for refusal of entry clearance or leave to enter where the applicant has breached immigration laws by: *(a)* overstaying; *(b)* breaching a condition attached to their leave; *(c)* being an illegal entrant; and *(d)* using deception in an application for entry clearance, leave to enter or remain (whether successful or not). In these cases, entry clearance or leave to enter may only be granted if certain periods of time have elapsed, as follows:

- 90 days for an overstayer who left voluntarily without expense to the Secretary of State;
- 12 months for anyone else who left the UK voluntarily not at the expense of the Secretary of State;
- 2 years for anyone who left voluntarily at the expense of the Secretary of State if they left within six months of a removal decision or exhaustion of appeal or review rights;
- 5 years for anyone else who left the UK voluntarily at the expense of the Secretary of State;
- 5 years for anyone who left or was removed from the UK as a condition of a caution issued in accordance with section 22 of the Criminal Justice Act 2003;
- 10 years for anyone who used deception in an application for entry clearance or was removed or deported.

Prior to 2008, it was only a deportation order which resulted in a period of exclusion from the UK. Through rule 320(7B), the impact of immigration enforcement extends into the future, and that future impact must be taken into account when making enforcement decisions. The Court of Appeal in *AS (Pakistan) v SSHD* [2008] EWCA Civ 1118 held that the duration of exclusion was a relevant factor to be taken into account when assessing the proportionality of deportation. The Tribunal in *NA & others (Cambridge College of Learning)* [2009] UKAIT 00031 took account of the effect of a finding against the appellants that they had used false representations to obtain leave to remain in confirming that the standard of proof for such a finding was a high one. In

MA (Nigeria) v SSHD [2009] EWCA Civ 1229, the Court of Appeal held that a failure to take account of the effect of the re-entry ban amounted to an error of law, and in *AA v SSHD* [2010] EWCA Civ 773 (see 6.8.7) the Court of Appeal was influenced by the re-entry ban in reaching its conclusion. In the same spirit, the Upper Tribunal in *Ozhogina and Tarasova v SSHD* [2011] UKUT 00197 (IAC) held that where the Secretary of State refused an application for entry clearance on the basis that the appellant had breached the UK's immigration laws by using deception in an application for entry clearance (para 320(7B)), the Secretary of State must show that a false statement was deliberately made for the purpose of securing an immigration advantage. Paragraph 320(7B) does not apply to the applications of adult partners and family members (para A320). Also, the re-entry bans only apply in relation to previous immigration breaches committed when over the age of 18 (para 320(7B)).

A further ground for discretionary refusal, added on 30 June 2008, is that the applicant 'has previously contrived in a significant way to frustrate the intentions of these Rules' (para 320(11)). The application of this paragraph is fraught with difficulty, but cases in the Upper Tribunal have begun to clarify how it should be applied. In *SD v ECO Chennai* [2010] UKUT 276 (IAC) the Tribunal held that:

- The substance of paragraph 320(11) refers to an applicant's previous history.
- If an application for entry clearance is refused on the ground of forged documents in a previous application, the Entry Clearance Officer has the burden of proof that the documents were forged.
- If there was no judicial determination of that issue, and the appellant did not admit it, there would need to be evidence to establish a forgery.

In *PS v ECO New Delhi* [2010] UKUT 440 (IAC) the appellant's asylum application had failed. He had married lawfully in the UK, and could comply with the immigration rules. He left the UK voluntarily and went to India, where he applied for entry clearance. The Tribunal overturned the refusal of the ECO and the First Tier Tribunal, observing that the automatic prohibition of entry clearance was disapplied because of his family reasons for entry (then para 320(7C), now para A320). Paragraph 320(7B) did not apply because he had left the UK voluntarily more than 12 months before he applied for entry clearance. The Tribunal thought that a proper purpose of the rules was that the provisions of para 320(7B) and (7C) encouraged a person in the position of Mr S voluntarily to leave the UK, to remain outside the UK for a significant period, and then to seek to regularize his immigration status by applying properly for leave to enter to join his wife. Refusing his entry by application of para 320(11) would defeat that proper purpose of the rules. In *Mumu (paragraph 320; Article 8; scope)* [2012] UKUT 00143(IAC) the Tribunal noted that conduct must be the personal conduct of the applicant in order to fall within para 320(11).

6.8.7 **False representations and non-disclosure of material facts**

Another rule change in 2008 was para 320 7(A), adding grounds for refusal of leave to enter or entry clearance that false representations or information have been submitted or there has been a material non-disclosure in relation to the application. The meaning of these terms was considered in the case of *AA v SSHD* [2010] EWCA Civ 773 in the context of an application for leave to remain. Previous authority (*Akhtar* [1991] Imm AR 326 CA) was that in order to be considered false, representations did not have to be fraudulent, simply inaccurate.

 **Key Case**

AA v SSHD **[2010] EWCA Civ 773**

Mr A was a student who had, at the date of his application for further leave to remain, been in the UK for nine years. He had studied and worked continuously throughout that time, had not breached the immigration rules, had obtained a first class undergraduate degree, and a masters degree, and now applied for leave to remain as a Tier 1 (post-study work) migrant.

In his application he failed to disclose that he had three convictions for driving without a licence or insurance. The application form clearly asked for disclosure of criminal offences including driving offences, but Mr A did not think that these convictions were criminal. He was refused leave on the basis that 'material facts were not disclosed' and that he had used deception. In view of the finding that he had used deception, the re-entry ban in para 320(7B) applied, dating from his leaving the UK.

Mr A's appeal to the Tribunal was refused on the basis that his statement was false, that this was a mandatory ground for refusal, and thus there was no discretion and his intention was irrelevant.

The Court of Appeal noted that deception is defined in para 6 of the immigration rules as:

> making false representations or submitting false documents (whether or not material to the application), or failing to disclose material facts.

The Court of Appeal drew on the immigration rules, guidance in the IDIs, Lord Bassam's assurance in the House of Lords that mistakes of fact would not be treated as deception, and a letter from Mr Liam Byrne MP, Minister of State at the Home Office. On the basis of these, the Court came to the conclusion that 'false' was not to be used in its meaning of 'untrue' or 'incorrect', but in its meaning of 'lying' or 'deceitful'. Consequently, 'dishonesty or deception is needed, albeit not necessarily that of the applicant himself, to render a "false representation" a ground for mandatory refusal' (para 76).

The Court noted that in *Akhtar* the representation was a dishonest one (by the husband that he had no other wife) although transmitted through someone who was not aware of that (his second wife, the applicant). Also, at the time of *Akhtar*, the finding that there had been a false statement did not result in liability to a re-entry ban of several years. For these reasons, *Akhtar* was not authority for the proposition that in the present context falsity did not require deception.

In *AA* the Court did not deal with the interpretation of the ground of material non-disclosure. However, a failure to disclose traffic-related offences has been the reason for several of the reported appeals in the Upper Tribunal based on this rule. *Ahmed v SSHD* [2011] UKUT 00351 (IAC) was a case in which the appellant, the holder of an Oyster card, had assumed that it was valid for travel to Gravesend. It was not, and he was fined £80, to which were added compensation of £4.50, a victim surcharge of £15, and costs of £35. Like Mr A, he did not think this was a criminal conviction, and so did not disclose it in his application for further leave to remain as a student. The Upper Tribunal held that the basis on which Rix LJ concluded in *AA* that dishonesty was required for 'false representations' applied equally to the interpretation of non-disclosure within the context of paragraph 322(1A). UT Judge Mckee said: 'In many, if not most, cases false representations and material non-disclosure will be opposite sides of the same coin.' A did not have a dishonest state of mind and so should not be refused on the basis of non-disclosure. In *R (on the application of Giri) v SSHD* [2015] EWCA Civ 784 the applicant had used deception in a previous application for leave to enter. The application was refused. Later he made a successful application. He stated on a further application that he had not used deception previously. The Court of Appeal accepted that this was a failure to disclose a material fact.

In *Mumu (paragraph 320; Article 8; scope)* [2012] UKUT 00143(IAC) the Upper Tribunal noted that dishonesty by someone other than the applicant could still found refusal of entry or leave to remain. They concluded that, applying Article 8, it was not disproportionate to refuse entry under para 320(7A) where a false education certificate had been relied on. The Home Office carries the burden of proving on balance of probabilities the matters alleged to amount to false representations or non-disclosure (*Singh (paragraph 320 (7A)—IS151A forms—proof)* [2012] UKUT 00162(IAC)). The standard was said in *NA & others (Cambridge College of Learning)* [2009] UKAIT 00031 to be high, though not the criminal standard. The Tribunal made the distinction between refusal of leave to remain and a criminal charge in that the former did not carry penal consequences. Refusal under the immigration rules did not inherently deprive an applicant of any right or privilege in the same way as a criminal conviction did. Nevertheless, the Tribunal agreed that the consequences of refusal could be serious, particularly as the appellants might be faced with a re-entry ban of five to ten years under para 320(7B). In *SS (Nepal) v ECO* [2013] EWCA Civ 1206 the Court of Appeal confirmed that even where the applicant would not meet the substantive requirements of the rules and so would not gain entry, he was justified in appealing because of the future impact of paras 320(7B) and 320(11) if a finding of dishonesty under para 320(7A) was left unchallenged. An appeal of this kind may be no longer possible since appeals on most grounds were abolished by the Immigration Act 2014. In *Begum (false documents and false statements)* [2015] UKUT 41 (IAC) the Upper Tribunal held that a report on the adequacy of accommodation for a visitor contained a false statement warranting refusal under para 320(7A) because it said the writer had inspected the premises when he had not and the sponsor knew he had not. The content of the report about the premises was accurate, but this did not save the situation.

6.8.8 General and specific grounds

The points-based rules (see chapter 9) have made a linkage between general and specific requirements as the rules for applications in the PBS include the requirement that: 'the applicant must not fall for refusal under the general grounds for refusal' (see, e.g., rule 245C for Tier 1 and rule 245ZD for Tier 2).

In *NA & others (Cambridge College of Learning)* [2009] UKAIT 00031, the Tribunal endorsed the general grounds for refusal of leave (to remain rather than to enter, thus under para 322(1A) of the immigration rules) as the applicants for Post-Study Work made false representations by relying on diplomas for courses that had never run. The Tribunal went on to say that even if the high standard of proof which was required to show false representations had not been met, reasonable doubts about what was proved by documents were relevant to assessing whether the appellant met the substantive requirements of the rules.

Some substantive rules permit the applicant's previous immigration history to be taken into account, that is, the rules on entrepreneurs as used in *R (on the application of Lei Zhang) v SSHD* [2015] UKUT 138 (IAC).

6.9 Cancellation, refusal, or revocation of leave to enter for holders of entry clearance

Entry clearance does not guarantee entry. Where entry clearance has effect as leave to enter, that leave may be cancelled on arrival; or, in the less common situation where entry clearance does not have effect as leave to enter, leave may be refused on arrival (HC 395 paras 321 and 321A). On the same grounds, entry clearance may be revoked before travel (para 30A), though this is rare. Cancellation does not have retrospective effect (*NM (Zimbabwe)* [2007] UKAIT 00002) so that, when the appellant in that case applied for a variation of leave before the cancellation decision, he had current leave which meant his leave was extended until his appeal was heard.

By Immigration Act 1971 Schedule 2A(2)(c) and (3) and HC 395 para 321A, leave to enter may be cancelled or refused for entry clearance holders on the four 'public good' grounds which have already been discussed in relation to refusal of entry clearance or entry on arrival (i.e., paras 320(2), (6), (18), and (19)); medical grounds and that *(a)* the leave or entry clearance was obtained by false representations; *(b)* the leave or entry clearance was obtained as a result of material facts not being disclosed; or *(c)* there has been a material change of circumstances since the leave or entry clearance was obtained (see *Khaliq* at 6.3.3). Where the person is outside the UK, failure to provide requested documents may also generate a cancellation of leave to enter (para 321A(6)). In *Murungaru v SSHD* [2008] EWCA Civ 1015, the claimant had a multiple entry visa for the UK, which was revoked without notice about three months after it had been granted. He wanted to travel to the UK to continue his private medical treatment and challenged the revocation of the visa by judicial review. One of his arguments was that the revocation interfered with his rights under Article 1 of Protocol 1 of the ECHR, the right to peaceful enjoyment of his possessions, that is, to his contract with his doctors. The Court of Appeal held that Dr Murungaru's contractual rights had none of the qualities of possessions. They were intangible, not assignable, not transmissible, not realizable, and had no present economic value. They could not be described as an asset. They did not count as a possession for the purposes of A1P1.

The power to cancel is contained in Immigration Act 1971 Schedule 2 para 2A as well as in the immigration rules. Thus, while the conditions for *refusal* of leave to enter are still governed only by the immigration rules, those for *cancelling* existing leave which was granted outside the UK are governed by statute. Paragraph 2A(2) refers to leave obtained 'as a result of' false information or failure to disclose material facts. The implication of this is that false representations or non-disclosure must be at least material and possibly decisive in order to warrant cancellation of leave. An applicant cannot oppose the cancellation or refusal of leave to enter on the basis that if the true facts had been known they would have gained entry anyway (*Bugdaycay* [1987] AC 514 HL).

A change of circumstances, in order to warrant cancellation of leave to enter or revocation of entry clearance, must be so fundamental that it undermines the basis upon which the original application was made. In the case of a visitor who changes their itinerary or their sponsor, the change would not normally be regarded as fundamental. It is in each case a question of fact and degree (*Immigration Officer Heathrow v Salmak* [1991] Imm AR 191). An example of a change of circumstances which could warrant cancellation occurred in the case of *Shaw v SSHD* [2013] EWHC 42 (Admin) in which the immigration officer decided that Ms Shaw was returning to the UK not to study, as her leave to remain permitted, but to work. Changes in visitors' plans are discussed further in chapter 10.

Again, cancellation of leave granted by entry clearance is governed by statute (Immigration Act 1971 Sch 2 para 2A (2A)) which permits cancellation where 'the person's purpose in arriving in the UK is different from the purpose specified in the entry clearance'. The Secretary of State carries the burden of proving the changes of circumstances (*Fiaz (cancellation of leave to remain—fairness) Pakistan* [2012] UKUT 57) and see visitor rules, which also allow for refusal based on change of circumstances in chapter 10. Cancellation on the basis of change of circumstances, false information, or failure to disclose material facts attracts a right of administrative review (HC 395 Appendix AR AR 4.2).

6.10 Common Travel Area

6.10.1 Common Travel Area—introduction

Entry from another part of the CTA is an exception to the requirement for leave to enter. Agreements on absence of immigration controls between the UK and Ireland have existed in various forms since the founding of the Irish Free State in 1922. Although there were restrictions on travel during and for a short while after the Second World War, these were relaxed after an exchange of letters between the two governments in 1952 proposed a similar and mutually enforced immigration policy. This laid the foundation for the present-day CTA (see Ryan 2001). The UK implemented this by repealing the requirement for aliens to obtain leave to land from the Ireland (Aliens (No. 2)) Order 1952, SI 1952/636. The arrangement for an absence of immigration control between the two countries and mutual assistance with enforcement included passing information between governments about the movement of aliens. In particular, there was, and still is, sharing of intelligence about those who appeared on the other country's list of undesirable aliens.

The present-day CTA consists of the United Kingdom of Great Britain and Northern Ireland, the Channel Islands, the Isle of Man, and the Republic of Ireland. It was established by Immigration Act 1971 s 1(3) which provides that journeys which are purely between any of these places (i.e., they do not start or end outside the CTA) are free of immigration control. This does not mean, however, that the whole of the immigration law of the CTA is entirely harmonized or that it is subject to the same laws (see Immigration Act 1971 s 9). The UK, Islands, and Ireland remain different jurisdictions. Neither does it mean that no individual travelling is subject to any restriction, as there are exceptions to this freedom of movement. The effect of the CTA is to create an area somewhat similar to the Schengen system, in which there is mutual enforcement of each other's immigration laws but which does not facilitate entry to the area from outside. Critically, however, leave to enter the UK does not also constitute leave to enter the Republic of Ireland, and vice versa. See discussion of the case of *Emmanson* in the next section.

6.10.2 Common Travel Area—operation

While their inhabitants have British nationality, the Isle of Man and Channel Islands have their own immigration laws. In practice, the Island authorities adopt British provisions selectively; for instance, they do not permit the collection of biometric information for entry clearance, thus putting the Islands outside a major part of the UK government's borders programme. Islanders are not subject to British immigration control, and vice versa. Immigration Act 1971 Schedule 4 gives effect in the UK to the immigration laws of the Islands. The result is that limited leave granted in the UK or Islands has effect with the same limitations throughout the UK and Islands. Similarly, deportation orders made in the UK or Islands are given effect in each other's jurisdiction and illegal entry into one is illegal entry into the others.

Citizens of the Republic of Ireland on the other hand, are subject to British immigration control (and vice versa). The CTA means that British and Irish citizens may enter Ireland and Britain respectively without leave and without having to present a passport to establish their status, but like other EEA nationals they may be deported. There is an additional provision for the exclusion of Irish citizens if the Secretary of State personally directs that their exclusion is conducive to the public good (Immigration (Control of Entry through Republic of Ireland) Order 1972, SI 1972/1610 Article 3(1)(b)(iv) and (2)).

The CTA effects mutual enforcement of immigration controls. An illegal entrant to Ireland for instance is not permitted by the CTA to enter Britain, and requires leave to do so. The UK and Ireland enforce each other's deportation orders, though not without question. An Irish deportation order is a relevant consideration for entry to the UK, but an application for entry should still be considered on its merits. Visa nationals who do not, on entering another part of the CTA, have a valid visa for the UK, do not have this omission wiped out on entering the UK. They still need a visa. The Immigration (Control of Entry through Republic of Ireland) Order 1972, SI 1972/1610 Article 3(1)(b) as amended makes this plain in relation to entry through Ireland. The applicant in *R (on application of Alinta)* [2006] NIQB 61 lived in Northern Ireland but had overstayed his UK visa. On attempting to cross the border to the Republic of Ireland on a shopping trip, he was detained and in due course served with notice of removal signed by a UK immigration officer. He was escorted by security personnel back to Northern Ireland. He contended that he was not an overstayer as he was not in the UK at the time of the service of the notice, and he was not liable to removal as he had been brought back to the UK under the control of the law so his presence could not be unlawful. These ingenious arguments failed. According to Article 3 of the Order, as a person who had overstayed in the UK he needed fresh leave to re-enter. Without this, he was an illegal entrant. The mutuality provisions have the same effect in relation to the Islands.

SI 1972/1610 Article 4 allows a limited stay in the UK for certain people entering through the Republic of Ireland. If someone's leave to remain in the UK has expired while they were in Ireland, the Order itself grants seven days' leave on return to the UK, unless they were a visitor on a short visa in which case it grants one month. If they have entered Ireland from outside the CTA, they may only remain in the UK for three months and may not take paid work. The Court of Appeal in *Kaya v SSHD* [1991] Imm AR 572 confirmed that someone who exceeds this period is correctly treated as an overstayer. This provision is ambiguous and problematic (see Macdonald (2014) ch.5).

A new British-Irish visa scheme was introduced in 2014. This allows visitors from China and India, who have biometric visas for travel to Ireland, to travel on to the UK without further permission (The Immigration (Control of Entry through Republic of Ireland) (Amendment) Order 2014 SI 2475).

The CTA has been criticized as a weak point in the UK's border controls, and the Labour government in 2009 included a clause in the Borders, Citizenship and Immigration Bill which would in effect have reintroduced immigration controls within the CTA. The clause was defeated in the House of Lords. The Coalition government dropped proposals for legislative reform of the CTA but instead strengthened internal controls by changes of practice. Operation Gull was a programme introduced in November 2010, in which UKBA ended the secondment of police officers at Scottish sea ports, and increased its enforcement staff at Northern Irish sea ports. A report on the operation cited a 65 per cent increase in immigration offenders detected at Scottish and Northern Irish sea ports (*Common Travel Area: Review of Arrangements at Northern Ireland Sea Ports*). As the report explains, ferry routes between Northern Ireland and Scotland are domestic UK services 'and are, legally and in immigration control terms, no different to [sic] ferry services between ... Hampshire and the Isle of Wight'. The Northern Irish Court of Appeal in *Emmanson (Fyneface), Re Judicial Review* [2010] NICA 35 was asked to rule that checking the status of passengers on these routes was unlawful. The Secretary of State relied on Immigration Act 1971 Schedule 2 para 2A, giving a power to 'examine a person who has arrived' in order to establish whether their leave should be cancelled (see 6.6.5), and the case of *Baljinder Singh v Hammond* [1987] 1 All ER 829 where the High Court held that an immigration officer might examine a person outside the port of entry and at a date subsequent to entry, provided they had information to found an enquiry as to the person's immigration status. The Court of Appeal declined to rule on the lawfulness of Operation Gull, on the basis that Mr Emmanson had consented to the examination and so no authority had been exercised.

The case raises questions about the operation of the CTA. Mr Emmanson had obtained entry clearance to the UK as a visitor. Before he left Nigeria he had obtained both sterling and euros, and bought presents for a woman living in Dublin. He was detained on arrival in Belfast from Stranraer. Mr Emmanson said that he was not aware that as a visitor to the UK he was not allowed to visit Ireland. Indeed, the CTA operates on the usual presumption that a visitor's visa to one part of the CTA is valid for all. However, as Mr Emmanson had not declared his intention to visit Dublin, the immigration officer considered that his entry clearance had been obtained by deception and that he was an illegal entrant. The NICA endorsed this view. The effect of this decision is that an applicant for entry clearance to any part of the CTA must declare their intention to travel to other parts, otherwise they may be treated as an illegal entrant. The Chief Inspector of UKBA pointed out the vulnerability of the operation of the CTA to challenge on the basis of misuse of the power to examine. His report emphasizes that the law following *Singh v Hammond* is that examination on in-country journeys is only authorized where the immigration officer *has information* which would found an inquiry into whether the person examined had breached immigration law.

The CTA does not fit easily with the UK government's programme of creating technologically governed border, and the Isle of Man's government, the Tynwald, has made it clear that the Isle of Man will not introduce collection of data for electronic border purposes.

6.11 The leave obtained

6.11.1 Non-lapsing or continuing leave

A further change made by the Immigration (Leave to Enter and Remain) Order 2000, SI 2000/1161 was the introduction of so-called 'non-lapsing' or 'continuing' leave. Before 30 July 2000, the position was governed entirely by Immigration Act 1971 s 3(4), which provides that: 'A person's leave to enter or remain in the United Kingdom shall lapse on his going to a country or territory outside the Common Travel Area'. There were a few exceptions to this rule, but in general what it meant was that people on limited leave, such as students, could go away from the UK for a weekend break, and be refused entry on their return.

From 30 July 2000, s 3(4) remains in force, but its effects are considerably modified. Article 13(2) of the 2000 Order provides that leave will not lapse on the holder's leaving the Common Travel Area if 'it was conferred by means of an entry clearance ... or for a period exceeding six months'. The effect of this is that most people with limited leave are able to come and go during the currency of that leave without fear of being refused entry on return. Article 13(5) of the Immigration (Leave to Enter and Remain) Order 2000 applies the cancellation powers in Immigration Act 1971 Sch 2 para 2A to non-lapsing leave. The immigration officer is therefore entitled to examine people returning to discover whether any such reason applies (Immigration Act 1971 Sch 2 para 2A). In *R (on the application of Ogilvy) v SSHD* [2007] EWHC 2301 (Admin), the High Court held that this applied to someone who had indefinite leave to remain. There was suspicion that the claimant was involved in criminal offences, and the Court held that the Home Office acted lawfully in using this immigration power to hold his passport, suspend his leave, and grant temporary admission while further criminal inquiries were conducted. The power was not limited to investigation of his current immigration status. Criminal offences might be a reason to cancel leave. This meant that a long-term resident of the UK could be deprived of leave to remain, and, thus, unlike a British citizen, be unable to work or claim benefits pending trial. This is the case whether or not they are ultimately convicted and even if they would not be liable to deportation. Where leave is varied so that a person has no leave, or it is revoked, s 3D of the Immigration Act 1971 provides that leave is continued pending appeal, but this does not expressly cover the *suspension* of leave applied in *Ogilvy*. This is a temporary measure pending investigation (Sch 2 para 2A(7)) and seems to deprive the applicant of all status.

The non-lapsing provisions do not apply to leave to enter as a visitor, but Article 4 of the 2000 Order has a similar effect, providing that a visit visa 'during its period of valid-ity, shall have effect as leave to enter the United Kingdom on an unlimited number of occasions'. Visit visas, though usually valid for six months, may be granted for periods of up to five years, on the basis that any stay as a visitor is limited to six months, but permitting multiple entries during the five-year period. These visas are particularly used by business people. The leave to enter lapses on the visitor leaving the Common Travel Area (2000 Order Article 13(2)) but on their return within the period of validity of the visa it operates as leave to enter again (Article 13(2)). The Immigration (Leave to Enter and Remain) (Amendment) Order 2005, SI 2005/1159, makes an exception to this provision for visitors under an Approved Destination Status Agreement with China. These visas are normally for one entry unless endorsed for two.

The visitor who does not benefit from the 2000 Order is the non-visa national visitor who obtains leave to enter at the port which lapses on their departure (Article 13(2)), but who does not possess a visa which can operate as leave to enter on their return. Therefore, they must re-apply for leave to enter on arrival at the port on each occasion.

6.11.2 **The 24-hour rule**

The 24-hour rule has effectively been nullified by the Immigration (Leave to Enter and Remain) Order 2000, SI 2000/1161 Article 12, but it remains on the statute book and is briefly discussed here so that Article 12 may be understood. It applied to lawful en-trants applying at the port for leave to enter for a limited period. This is now restricted to non-visa nationals wishing to enter as a visitor. Immigration Act 1971 Schedule 2 para 6(1) provides that if the immigration officer fails to give notice of their decision to the passenger within 24 hours of the conclusion of the examination, the passenger is automatically granted six months deemed leave with a prohibition on working. This is equivalent to the leave that a visitor would be routinely granted. Article 12 provides that notice given *on any date* after the end of the examination is to be regarded as having been given within the period of 24 hours specified in paragraph 6(1) of Schedule 2 (emphasis added). The 24-hour rule is thus deemed to be satisfied in any case in which a decision is made, thereby largely neutralizing it.

6.11.3 Limited leave to enter or remain

Leave to enter may be for an indefinite or a limited period of time. Limited leave may be subject to conditions:

- restricting or prohibiting employment;
- requiring the holder to maintain themselves and any dependants without recourse to public funds;
- requiring the holder to register with the police;
- of reporting to an immigration officer or the Secretary of State; and
- about residence (Immigration Act 1971 s 3(1)(c)).

The last two conditions were added by UK Borders Act 2007 s 16 as part of the government's intention to keep track of people, particularly asylum seekers and unaccompanied children seeking asylum. There were objections (e.g., from Liberty, see Public Bill Committee 1 March 2007 col 121) about the width of the condition about residence. There is no limit on the face of the condition as to *what* can be specified about residence, so it could in theory be used like house arrest. A proposal to insert a test of necessity and explicit human rights protection in the clause was defeated. No other conditions are possible. If and when the time limit is lifted on the holder's stay in the UK, any conditions will also be lifted, as indefinite leave may not be subject to conditions (s 3(3)).

If the holder of limited leave does not intend to leave the country on the expiry of the leave, an application to extend or vary the terms of leave must be made before it expires, otherwise the person becomes an overstayer and is liable to removal as a person who needs leave but does not have it (Immigration and Asylum Act 1999 s 10 as substituted by Immigration Act 2014 s.1). Such an application to vary or extend leave is an application for leave to remain. Leave to remain for a person already in the UK is granted by the Secretary of State under the power in Immigration Act 1971 s 4(1). The power includes giving further limited leave to remain, either by way of extending the existing leave or by varying it to a different immigration category, or giving indefinite leave to remain. Where limited leave is extended or varied, the Secretary of State may also vary or continue any conditions attaching to the earlier leave (Immigration Act 1971 s 3(3) and HC 395 para 31). The Immigration (Leave to Enter and Remain) Order 2000, SI 2000/1161 Article 13(6) extends the scope of the power to vary leave by providing that it may be exercised while the holder of leave is outside the UK (immigration rules para 33A).

Section 3C of the Immigration Act 1971 provides a statutory extension of leave where an application for variation is made within the currency of existing leave. This prevents the injustice of a person being treated as an overstayer simply because their application had not been decided before their existing leave expired. Section 3C extends the existing leave, on the existing conditions if any, until the decision has been taken and any appeal finally determined. The Immigration Bill 2015/2016 adds a power to cancel s 3C leave on the basis of a breach of condition of the leave, or that the person has used deception in seeking leave to remain (whether successfully or not).

6.11.3.1 Leave to enter granted in the UK

As mentioned at 6.6, entry to the UK is a legal event which may or may not coincide with physical arrival. So a person may be living in the UK for a period of months or even years on temporary admission, but still not be treated as having entered.

In 1971 the statute contemplated a division of function between immigration officers and other Home Office civil servants. Immigration officers were to have power to give or refuse leave to enter (s 4(1)), and the Secretary of State, in practice the Immigration Department, had power to give leave to remain or to vary leave. These are 'in-country' decisions, contrasted with border control decisions allocated by s 4 to the immigration service. Before 2001, decisions granting or refusing leave to enter to an asylum seeker used to be sent back to be made by the immigration service after Home Office civil servants or the courts had determined the asylum claim. This added administrative complexity and was nonsensical in the case of someone who had been living in the UK on temporary admission for years. Accordingly, the Immigration (Leave to Enter) Order 2001, SI 2001/2590, made under Immigration Act 1971 s 3A, provides that the Secretary of State may give or refuse leave to enter to an asylum or human rights applicant, and exercise all the powers of an immigration officer (examination, requiring medical examinations, etc.) for that purpose.

6.11.4 No-switching rules

The 'no-switching' rules restrict the categories between which changes may be made. These restrictions are apparent from the immigration rules. Permissible switching is now very limited. Until 2003, all categories could change to spouse, though not fiancé(e), but rule changes following the 2002 White Paper *Secure Borders, Safe Haven*, Cm 5387 prevented visitors from staying in the UK for marriage (see HC 395 para 284(i)). Some provisions for students and visitors are covered in chapters 9 and 10. For full details of current permitted and prohibited switches, reference should be made to the immigration rules for the category into which a switch is sought. Where the change of category is permitted, there must be an application for a variation of leave.

6.11.5 Indefinite leave

When leave is indefinite no further contact with the Home Office is required and there is no further stage to pass through in terms of immigration status. For most entrants, indefinite leave to remain may only be granted after a period of limited leave. Indefinite leave on entry is granted to some dependent relatives, but the criteria for this have become difficult to fulfil (see chapter 8).

Many immigration categories cannot lead to indefinite leave, and the individual must leave at the end of their permitted time, unless they can make a successful application to vary their leave under the immigration rules, or removal would breach their human rights. For instance, leave to enter or remain as a student or Tier 5 worker cannot be converted directly to indefinite leave. By contrast, people who have leave to enter or remain as a spouse or a Tier 1 worker may apply for indefinite leave once they have fulfilled the qualifying number of years' residence without breach of conditions. With effect from 6 April 2011, applicants for indefinite leave to remain must show that they have no unspent convictions (as defined by the Rehabilitation of Offenders Act 1974). This requirement has been added to each rule which provides for indefinite leave to remain.

A person with indefinite leave to remain has full access to the National Health Service (NHS) and may freely change employment as no conditions may be attached to indefinite leave (Immigration Act 1971 s 3(3)(a)). They may have recourse to public funds, unless their sponsor has signed an undertaking to support them for a fixed period after entry during which no claim for welfare benefits may be made by them or on their behalf.

Since 2 April 2007, applicants for indefinite leave to remain must pass a test on Life in the UK and now must also meet the requirements showing they have sufficient knowledge of the English language (Appendix KoLL to the immigration rules). Sufficient knowledge of English language is demonstrated by being a national of a listed English-speaking country, holding a degree-level academic qualification taught in English, or passing an ESOL language test at no less than ESOL Entry level 3, or an English language test in speaking and listening at minimum level B1 of the Common European Framework of Reference for Languages. EEA nationals are exempt from this requirement, but must comply with it if they apply for British nationality. There are also exemptions for certain medical conditions and those under 18 or over 66, and the requirement may be deemed met in certain cases of long residence. The Life in the UK test must be taken by any non-exempt person who is applying for indefinite leave, on any basis. If the applicant has not passed the test by the time their existing leave expires, they can be granted an extension for this purpose.

Residence without immigration restriction is one of the qualifications to apply for naturalization as a British citizen (British Nationality Act 1981 Sch 1 paras 1 and 3). Once a person gains indefinite leave they may begin to count time towards qualifying to naturalize as British if they so wish.

UK practice was to grant indefinite leave to people on acquisition of refugee status, but since 31 August 2005, a grant of five years has been normal practice. In the last month of the five-year period the refugee may apply under what is called the Protection Route, for indefinite leave.

There are other concessions entailing a grant of indefinite leave. One which attracted public attention was that Commonwealth citizens who have served in the armed forces may obtain indefinite leave to remain in the UK if they were discharged from service in the UK. This concession was incorporated into the immigration rules in 2004. It did not apply to Gurkhas, Nepalese soldiers of the Gurkha Brigade, as, due to the agreement made between India, the UK, and Nepal at the time of the formation of the Brigade, Gurkhas were to return to Nepal at the end of their service and so were not discharged in the UK. There was a discretion to grant ILR to Gurkhas who fell outside that rule.

In *R (on the application of D.P. Limbu, C.P. Limbu, Shrestha, Rai, Gurung and Mukhiya) v SSHD, ECO Kathmandu and ECO Hong Kong* [2008] EWHC 2261 (Admin), a number of ex-members of the Gurkha Brigade challenged the refusal to them of indefinite leave under the discretionary policy. Part of the reason for the discretionary policy was to honour the exceptional service record of Gurkhas. These claimants had given long and distinguished military service and served in the UK's military campaigns, including the Falklands. The judge concluded that it was irrational to refuse them leave, and quashed the refusal.

On 24 April 2009, the government published guidance for applications for settlement from Gurkhas who were discharged before 1 July 1997, but requiring 20 or more years of service. The standard length of army service by Gurkhas was 15 years. After a public campaign (famously spearheaded by the actress Joanna Lumley) a Liberal Democrat motion in the House of Commons voted to overturn the government policy and give Gurkhas equal rights of residence, and on 21 May 2009 the Home Secretary announced that any former Gurkha with more than four years' service who had been discharged from the Brigade of Gurkhas before 1 July 1997 would be eligible for settlement in the UK (HC Debs 16 July 2009 col 251W). This is now in the immigration rules at paras 276E–K.

6.11.6 Long residence

It is appropriate that people who have been living for a long time in a country should have some security of residence, when they have not otherwise obtained a secure immigration status. This principle used to be given effect in the UK by a concession for people with ten years' or more continuous lawful residence or 14 years' or more continuous residence of any legality. The concession gave effect to Article 3(3) European Convention on Establishment, which the UK ratified on 14 October 1969, and which provides that nationals of any contracting party who have been lawfully residing for more than ten years in the territory of another party may only be expelled for reasons of national security or for particularly serious reasons relating to public order, public health, or morality. The concession went beyond the requirements of the Convention in three respects:

- it included all foreign nationals, not just those of contracting states;
- granting indefinite leave rather than simply refraining from removing such a person; and
- allowing those who had been in the UK illegally to benefit.

However, the concession did not give immunity from expulsion, nor limit the grounds for it in the way that the Convention suggests.

The concession was abandoned in April 2003, and protection given by the immigration rules which replaced it has been steadily eroded.

There is still a rule based on ten years' lawful residence. This no longer contains a presumption of a grant of leave, but says that indefinite leave may be granted if 'having regard to the public interest there are no reasons why it would be undesirable'. The rule requires that reasons not to grant leave should be ascertained in the light of the individual circumstances such as age, domestic circumstances, personal history, including character, conduct, associations, and employment record, and this also weakens the presumption (para 276B(ii)). The rules allow for a 28-day break in legality due to overstaying (para 276B(v)).

Short absences from the UK of up to six months will not break continuity if the person has leave when they left and when they return (para 276A(a)). There are exceptions, and the person's intention is also relevant. Sometimes, longer ones will also be accepted as part of the period of residence, depending on the intention shown. In *LL (China) v SSHD* [2009] EWCA Civ 617, the appellant failed in her application for leave based on ten years' residence. She had undergone all her schooling in the UK from the age of 13, and then completed an undergraduate degree, and began a full-time course in accountancy. Her residence had been lawful at all times, but she had gone home to China in all her school and university holidays. As a consequence, her cumulative absences totalled more than 18 months—a limit set in the rules para 276A (a)(v). She was not accepted to have the requisite period of continuous residence.

The 14-year rule was abolished in 2012. It had enabled overstayers, people in breach of condition, and illegal entrants to declare themselves to the Home Office and obtain a status that enables lawful working, an application to be joined by relatives, entitlement to welfare benefits, and so on. The rule that replaced it allows an application on the basis of respect for private life, based on 20 years' residence (para 276ADE). The requirements of the rule are stringent as the applicant must not fall for refusal under the general grounds of refusal, and if their application succeeds, they will only be granted 30 months' leave to remain. After four such periods, amounting to 120 months' leave, they may apply for indefinite leave. In other words, it will take such a person 30 years of residence to qualify for indefinite leave to remain in the UK.

The tribunal in *Ogundimu (Article 8—new rules) Nigeria* [2013] UKUT 60 (IAC), in the context of a deportation appeal, held that Article 8 ECHR is not displaced by the 2012 immigration rules. The ECtHR in *Maslov v Austria* [2008] ECHR 546 held that:

74. Although Article 8 provides no absolute protection against expulsion for any category of aliens (see *Üner*, §55), including those who were born in the host country or moved there in their early childhood, the Court has already found that regard is to be had to the special situation of aliens who have spent most, if not all, their childhood in the host country, were brought up there and received their education there (see *Üner*, §58 *in fine*).
75. In short, the Court considers that for a settled migrant who has lawfully spent all or the major part of his or her childhood and youth in the host country very serious reasons are required to justify expulsion. This is all the more so where the person concerned committed the offences underlying the expulsion measure as a juvenile.

This was settled law and not displaced by the immigration rules. The Tribunal faced with an appeal by someone who has been refused under the rules but spent the majority of their life in the UK must still consider that person's right to respect for their private life, and whether this is outweighed by the public interest in immigration control. As the Tribunal held in *MF (Article 8—new rules) Nigeria* [2012] UKUT 393 (IAC), the rules must be applied, but if the applicant fails under the rules, Article 8 must still be considered, and is engaged in a case where the migrant has spent most of their life in the UK.

Paragraph 276ADE allows for claims on the basis of respect for private life based on shorter periods of residence as follows:

(iv) under the age of 18 years and has lived continuously in the UK for at least 7 years (discounting any period of imprisonment) and it would not be reasonable to expect the applicant to leave the UK; or

(v) aged 18 years or above and under 25 years and has spent at least half of his life living continuously in the UK (discounting any period of imprisonment); or

(vi) subject to sub-paragraph (2), is aged 18 years or above, has lived continuously in the UK for less than 20 years (discounting any period of imprisonment) but there would be very significant obstacles to the applicant's integration into the country to which he would have to go if required to leave the UK.

6.11.7 Returning residents

A person with indefinite leave has no immigration restrictions on their stay in the UK, but they are still subject to immigration control in that if they leave the country they may be examined by an immigration officer on their return and refused entry on limited grounds. Prior to the Immigration (Leave to Enter and Remain) Order 2000, SI 2000/1161, the position of such people was governed by the so-called returning resident rules, found in HC 395 paras 18–20. These rules were based on the fact that indefinite leave lapsed when the holder left the UK, but enabled the holder to be re-admitted provided they had not been absent for more than two years, that when they last entered they had indefinite leave, that they now returned for settlement and that they did not leave the UK with the assistance of public funds (i.e., using a government repatriation scheme). These rules are still in existence, but must now be read together with SI 2000/1161. The effect of the 2000 Order is that leave does not lapse during an absence of less than two years. So, a person with indefinite leave who returns within two years no longer has to re-apply for leave. The effect of the change removes the basis for confusion and distressing refusals of leave to enter provided the person returns within two years. They may only be examined at the port to see if the leave should be cancelled, for the reasons discussed in the earlier section on this subject.

After two years, even so-called non-lapsing leave actually lapses (Immigration (Leave to Enter and Remain) Order 2000, SI 2000/1161 Article 13(4)). Outside the two-year period, re-entry is a matter of discretion, but if the only factor preventing return is that the person has been away too long, they should be admitted if, for example, they have lived in the UK for most of their life (HC 395 para 19). This is a wide discretion, and the example of when it should be exercised is no more than an indication of a basis for exercising it. Reference may be made to the IDIs for more examples. Visa nationals returning after more than two years will need a new entry clearance.

Returning residents may be refused readmission on grounds under para 320, in the limited situations where these are relevant, but not on medical grounds. Refusal is possible on grounds of exclusion being conducive to the public good, and para 320(9) gives the basis for refusal of leave where the requirements of para 18 are not met.

6.11.8 Revoking indefinite leave

The security of indefinite leave to remain is somewhat undermined by the power in Nationality, Immigration and Asylum Act 2002 s 76. Under this section the Secretary of State may revoke a person's indefinite leave to enter or remain if the person is liable to deportation but 'cannot be deported for legal reasons'. In a similar vein, under s 76(2) indefinite leave can be revoked if it was obtained by deception but the person cannot be removed for legal or practical reasons. A person whose leave is revoked will not be able to work or claim benefits and therefore will have no basis for economic support unless they are detained or work illegally. Their children will not be British, and depending on the laws of their country of nationality may be born stateless. They will have no right to be joined by other members of their family. This raises the prospect of a new group of people forced into destitution. There is no exemption in the section for children. Section 76 does not require that national security is in issue and the application of this section may raise issues under Human Rights Act Articles 3, 8, and 14. Those with indefinite leave but not with British nationality do not have a right to the protection of the state nor a formal obligation of allegiance (see *Al-Rawi* and chapter 3).

In *R (on the application of) George v SSHD* [2014] UKSC 28 the Supreme Court held that where a deportation order had been revoked the appellant's indefinite leave was not automatically revived. The Secretary of State could grant periods of limited leave, according to her assessment of the applicant's situation.

6.12 Settlement

The terms 'settlement' and 'settled' are used widely in immigration law, and it is important to grasp their meaning. Settled status must be distinguished from right of abode, indefinite leave to remain, and ordinary residence.

The Immigration Act 1971 s 33(2)A defines a person who is 'settled' as subject to no immigration restrictions on length of stay and ordinarily resident in the UK. These two components of the definition are both important. Someone who has no immigration restrictions on their length of stay may be in that position either because they have indefinite leave to remain or because they have right of abode. Right of abode, it may be recalled from chapter 3 on nationality, is the right to come and go 'without let or hindrance' (Immigration Act 1971 s 1) and is held only by British citizens and relatively few Commonwealth citizens. Settlement includes indefinite leave to remain but carries the additional requirement of ordinary residence.

The meaning of the term 'ordinary residence' was considered by the House of Lords in *Shah v Barnet London Borough Council* [1983] 2 AC 309; not an immigration but an education case, concerning a student's entitlement to a grant, which also, under statute, depended upon 'ordinary residence'. The House of Lords held that it was possible to have more than one ordinary residence. The country of ordinary residence was the person's home, chosen as part of a settled way of life for the time being. It could be of long or short duration and did not imply permanence. The reason for being present was irrelevant providing it was voluntary, and immigration status had no bearing on the matter, providing the person was not in breach of immigration law. This meant that someone with limited leave could be ordinarily resident. In the context of defining 'settled status' it means that there is no need to prove that the person intends to be in the UK for the rest of their life. The case of *Chugtai* [1995] IAR 559 developed *Shah* in holding that a person could be ordinarily resident in two countries at the same time. In *AB Bangladesh* [2004] UKIAT 00314 the Tribunal held that this could include where the appellant intended to spend six months of each year in each country. He could therefore be said to be coming to the UK 'for settlement'.

Colloquially, it is often said that when a person obtains indefinite leave to remain they 'get settlement'—as, for instance, when a worker has lived for five years in the UK and obtains indefinite leave to remain, or a spouse whose restrictions are lifted after their probationary period. The terms 'settlement' and 'indefinite leave to remain' are often used interchangeably and for practical purposes this is quite valid. However, the two are not exactly the same. Settled status is not awarded by the Secretary of State explicitly. It is a description of a state of affairs rather than an immigration status awarded. It is necessary to be able to identify when a person is settled as important rights accrue to someone with settled status. Children born in the UK to a settled person will be British (British Nationality Act 1981 s 1), and in the immigration rules a settled person is qualified to sponsor a partner or relative to come to the UK (HC 395 Appendix FM).

In practical terms, settlement and indefinite leave to remain are virtually coterminous. As we have seen, a person with indefinite leave to remain who stays away from the UK for more than two years may lose that leave. Therefore, an ordinary residence requirement is implied in retaining indefinite leave to remain. Although it is technically accurate to refer to a British citizen ordinarily resident in the UK as 'settled', these entitlements are of greater real significance to people who are not British. In general, therefore, the word 'settled' is used to refer to people who have indefinite leave to remain and are ordinarily resident in the UK.

Settled status in this usual sense does not carry full rights of citizenship. A settled person can be deported on the ground that deportation is conducive to the public good (Immigration Act s 3(5)(a)) and does not have the right to vote or stand for Parliament. In these respects, as well as the possible loss of status after two years' absence, settled status is less secure than right of abode.

6.13 **Conclusion**

This chapter has considered some of the legal provisions relating to crossing the UK's borders and obtaining an immigration status here. The border itself is described as an increasingly distributed, intelligence-led, and security-focused system, rather than a geographical boundary. The processes of control begin well before arrival and are encountered before and at the border. The other trend observed in this chapter has been the development of restrictions on return to the UK—the re-entry bans; increased grounds for refusal of entry; and increased use of exclusion for those who have left voluntarily. The most radical measures affecting migrants' ability to challenge decisions on entry are the removal of immigration law from the scope of legal aid and the abolition of appeal rights. These issues are not expressly addressed in this chapter, but they form a backdrop to it, and the chapter should be read with this background in mind.

QUESTIONS

1 How do you think the Immigration (Leave to Enter and Remain) Order 2000 changes the substance and nature of immigration control?

2 What would you consider to be appropriate medical grounds for refusal of leave to enter and who do you think should make that decision? How does your idea compare with the present law?

3 In December 2012 the boxer Mike Tyson was refused entry to the UK under para 320(2) of the immigration rules. See www.thebookseller.com/news/mike-tyson-event-cancelled-after-uk-entry-refusal.html. Compare this with the case of *R v SSHD ex Bindel* [2001] Imm AR 1. Use this is a basis for commentary on the development of rules excluding individuals on the basis of criminal convictions.

 online resource centre For guidance on answering questions, visit the Online Resource Centre www.oxfordtextbooks.co.uk/orc/clayton7e/.

FURTHER READING

Aliverti, Ana (2013) *Briefing: Immigration Offences: Trends in Legislation and Criminal and Civil Enforcement* (Migration Observatory, University of Oxford).

Anderson, David (2015) *The Terrorism Acts in 2014: Report of the Independent Reviewer on the Operation of the Terrorism Act 2000 and Part 1 of the Terrorism Act 2006*, September

Cabinet Office (2007) *Security in a Global Hub* (London: Cabinet Office).

Commission for Racial Equality (1985) *Immigration Control Procedures: Report of a Formal Investigation* (London: Commission for Racial Equality), chapter 3.

Coussey, Mary (2004, 2005, and 2006) *Annual Reports of the Independent Race Monitor* London UKBA).

Free Movement blog: *Secret Race Discrimination:* www.freemovement.org.uk/2011/05/31/secret-race-discrimination/.

Guild, Elspeth (2000) 'Entry into the UK: The Changing Nature of National Borders' INLP vol. 14, no. 4, pp. 227–38.

House of Commons Home Affairs Committee (2011) *UK Border Controls* 17th report of session 2010–12 HC 1647.

House of Commons Home Affairs Committee (2015) *The Work of the Immigration Directorates: Calais* 18th report of session 2014–15 HC 902.

Independent Chief Inspector of Borders and Immigration (2013) *An Inspection of e-Borders October 2012 to March 2013.*

Independent Chief Inspector of Borders and Immigration (2013) *An Inspection of Juxtaposed Controls November 2012–March 2013.*

Independent Chief Inspector of Borders and Immigration (2013) *An Inspection of the UK Visas and Immigration Visa Section Dhaka April to July 2013.*

Independent Chief Inspector of Borders and Immigration (2014) *An Inspection of Visa Interviewing March–August 2014.*

Juss, Satvinder (1997) *Discretion and Deviation in the Administration of Immigration Control* (London: Sweet & Maxwell).

Ryan, Bernard (2001) 'The Common Travel Area between Britain and Ireland' *Modern Law Review* vol. 64, November 2001, pp. 855–74.

Shah, Ramnik (2007) 'Language Test for Permanent Residents' *Journal of Immigration, Asylum and Nationality Law* vol. 21, no. 1, pp. 26–7.

Statewatch Bulletin 'UK: E-Borders Plan to Tackle "Threats"' vol. 15, no. 3/4.

Toal, Ronan (2008) 'The New "General Grounds for Refusal"' *Journal of Immigration, Asylum and Nationality Law* vol. 22, no. 2, pp. 135–46.

United Kingdom Borders Agency (UKBA) (2011) 'Common Travel Area: Review of new arrangements at Northern Ireland Sea Ports' (London: UKBA).

Wray, Helena (2006) 'Guiding the Gatekeepers: Entry Clearance for Settlement on the Indian Sub-Continent' *Journal of Immigration, Asylum and Nationality Law* vol. 20, no. 2, pp. 112–29.

7

Challenging decisions: appeals, administrative and judicial review

SUMMARY

This chapter describes the structure of the Tribunal and the Special Immigration Appeals Commission, and examines rights of appeal and administrative review. It also describes the importance of judicial review and outlines the changes made by the Immigration Act 2014 to appeal rights. The chapter ends with a section on immigrants and asylum seekers' access to legal representation.

7.1 Introduction

Since 6 April 2015, when the final changes to appeals brought by the Immigration Act 2014 came into effect, appeals to the Tribunal have only been available on asylum or human rights grounds. Substantive asylum law is covered in chapter 12, and human rights law in chapter 5. This chapter explains in outline the structure and process of the appeals system. The more technical aspects of law relating to appeals are outside the scope of this book, and for this reference should be made to practitioner works such as Macdonald's *Immigration Law and Practice*.

7.2 The Appeal Tribunal

A two-tier system of immigration appeals was instituted in 1969 for Commonwealth citizens and in 1973 for all immigrants. There was an initial appeal to an adjudicator, with a second appeal to an Immigration Appeal Tribunal (IAT). The Asylum and Immigration (Treatment of Claimants, etc.) Act 2004 abolished that two-tier system, replacing it with a single tier, Asylum and Immigration Tribunal (AIT), with effect from 4 April 2005. The system of challenging a decision of the AIT was complex. In brief, challenge was by way of an application for 'reconsideration' to a panel of the Tribunal, the underlying idea being that the Tribunal on reconsideration was constitutionally the same judicial body, looking again at their decision, even though different personnel of different seniority would be involved (see *DK (Serbia)* [2006] EWCA Civ 1747). This resulted in complex and sometimes inconsistent rules, found partly in the procedure rules but developed in case law, to deal with issues such as whether findings of fact of the first Tribunal were binding at the reconsideration hearing, and whether issues of law on the reconsideration hearing should be restricted to those which had been identified by the judge who decided to order reconsideration (see *HS (Afghanistan) v SSHD* [2009] EWCA Civ 771).

The AIT was in turn abolished. The Tribunals, Courts and Enforcement Act (TCEA) 2007 created a unified Tribunal structure, to encompass all areas of law. On 15 February 2010, the functions of the AIT were incorporated into that structure (Transfer of Functions of the Asylum and Immigration Tribunal Order 2010, S1 2010/21). The Tribunal once again has two tiers: the First Tier and the Upper Tribunal, each of which has an Immigration and Asylum Chamber. Article 3 of the Transfer of Functions Order provided for immigration judges of the AIT to be transferred in as First-tier Tribunal judges. The 2004 Act created a new tier of 'designated immigration judges' to create a supervisory structure within the Tribunal. They were transferred in as First-tier Tribunal judges and deputy judges of the Upper Tribunal. Senior immigration judges and non-legal members became judges and members of the Upper Tribunal. The Upper Tribunal was newly created as a court of record.

Appeals may be made from the First Tier to the Upper Tribunal on the grounds of error of law. As discussed later in relation to appeals to the Court of Appeal, an error of law must be more than a disagreement on the outcome. By way of not uncommon example, in *AP (Trinidad and Tobago) v SSHD* [2011] EWCA Civ 551 the Court of Appeal held that the First-tier Tribunal had *not* made an error of law in deciding that the public interest in deporting the appellant because of his offending did not outweigh his right to respect for family life. If all the relevant facts have been carefully considered, with reasons given, there is unlikely to have been an error of law.

Permission for an appeal is sought from the First-tier Tribunal in the first instance, and if refused, then directly from the Upper Tribunal. On hearing an appeal, the Upper Tribunal can decide the matter for itself, or remit the case back to the First Tier if it considers that the matter needs to be reheard (TCEA s 12). If the Upper Tribunal refuses permission to appeal, this decision is not appealable (TCEA s 13(8) (c)). TCEA s 13(6) empowered the Lord Chancellor to make permission to appeal to the Court of Appeal conditional on that court considering that the proposed appeal raises an important point of principle or practice, or that there is some other compelling reason to hear the appeal. The Joint Committee on Human Rights argued that this extra test should not apply to immigration and asylum appeals (see Buxton 2009), but their proposal was resisted. The Lord Chancellor made the order, and its application to immigration and asylum cases is discussed later (*PR (Sri Lanka) v SSHD* [2011] EWCA Civ 988).

In addition to concern about the threshold for permission to appeal from the Upper Tribunal to the Court of Appeal, the statutory conditions for the new Tribunal presented questions for asylum and immigration judicial review cases:

- Would final decisions of the Upper Tribunal be open to judicial review, and if so, what would be the threshold for granting an application for permission?
- Some judicial review functions of the High Court were to be transferred to the Upper Tribunal. Would this include immigration and asylum matters?

In immigration and asylum law an important non-appealable decision of the Upper Tribunal is its refusal of permission to appeal from a decision of the First-tier Tribunal. This was the substance of MR's challenge in the case of *Cart* before the Supreme Court.

In *R (on the application of Cart, U and XC) v Upper Tribunal and SIAC* [2009] EWHC 3052 (Admin), government parties—the Secretary of State for Justice, the Secretary of State for the Home Department, and the Child Maintenance and Enforcement Commission—initially argued that the designation of the new Upper Tribunal as a superior court of record prevented its decisions from being susceptible to judicial review. This argument was rejected by the High Court, which held that as a court of limited jurisdiction the Upper Tribunal could not in principle be unreviewable. The case reached the Supreme Court on the issue of what test the Court should apply in considering whether to grant permission for judicial review of a decision of the Upper Tribunal.

 **Key Case**

*R (on the application of Cart) v Upper Tribunal and R (on the application of MR (Pakistan))
v Upper Tribunal and SSHD* [2011] UKSC 28

The Supreme Court held that it would be inconsistent with the new structure introduced by the 2007 Act to distinguish between the scope of judicial review in the various jurisdictions which had been gathered together in the new structure (para 37). There was no question of ousting the judicial supervision that judicial review provided; the question was, the threshold at which this should be permitted. The Court was faced with three alternative propositions:

1. Judicial review of the tribunal was limited to 'pre- *Anisminic* excess of jurisdiction and the denial of fundamental justice'.
2. Nothing had changed—judicial review of the new tribunal could be granted on the same basis as before.
3. Judicial review of Upper Tribunal decisions should be limited to the grounds upon which permission to make a Second-tier appeal to the Court of Appeal would be granted.

The Court chose the third option as a 'rational and proportionate' solution. The Lord Chancellor had made an order under s 13(6) TCEA, that the grounds upon which permission to make a Second-tier appeal to the Court of Appeal may be granted are that '(a) the proposed appeal would raise some important point of principle or practice; or (b) there is some other compelling reason for the relevant appellate court to hear the appeal' (Appeals from the Upper Tribunal to the Court of Appeal Order 2008, SI 2008/2834, art 2). Second-tier appeals are those where the decision of the Upper Tribunal is itself a decision on appeal. Lord Dyson said:

Care should be exercised in giving examples of what might be 'some other compelling reason', because it will depend on the particular circumstances of the case. But they might include (i) a case where it is strongly arguable that the individual has suffered what Laws LJ referred to at para 99 as 'a wholly exceptional collapse of fair procedure' or (ii) a case where it is strongly arguable that there has been an error of law which has caused truly drastic consequences. (para 131)

Litigation in the High Court on the application of the *Cart* standard has determined that it applies to the permission stage of judicial review, but not the substantive hearing. This is now in the Civil Procedure rules, rule 54.7A, which also says that permission will only be granted if:

there is an arguable case, which has a reasonable prospect of success, that both the decision of the Upper Tribunal refusing permission to appeal and the decision of the First Tier Tribunal against which permission to appeal was sought are wrong in law.

At the substantive hearing, normal principles of judicial review are applied (*R (on the application of HS) v Upper Tribunal (Immigration and Asylum Chamber)* [2012] EWHC 3126 (Admin)).

The threshold for judicial review having been settled, in *PR (Sri Lanka) v SSHD* [2011] EWCA Civ 988, the Court of Appeal considered whether the threshold in the Lord Chancellor's order should be applied to immigration and asylum appeals, and how it should be interpreted. In particular, what could be encompassed in the phrase 'some other compelling reason'? The Court held that the test should be applied the same way in immigration and asylum cases as in other matters. The Supreme Court's judgment in *Cart* rejected any special test. Lady Hale quoted Sullivan LJ in the Court of Appeal:

The immigration and asylum jurisdiction was not the only one in which claimants might be unrepresented, or particularly vulnerable, or where fundamental human rights were involved, or where the law was complex. (para 36)

Part of the rationale of the new unified tribunal system was that access to appeals did not depend on the subject matter under appeal (para 28). The Court said: ' "compelling" means *legally* compelling, rather than compelling, perhaps, from a political or emotional point of view, although such considerations may exceptionally add weight to the legal arguments' (para 36).

The Court said in *PR (Sri Lanka)* that applying a more stringent test to permit an appeal to the Court of Appeal is justified because the case has 'failed twice in the tribunal system'. This is not necessarily the case, as demonstrated in *JD (Congo) and others v SSHD* [2012] EWCA Civ 327. JD and two other appellants had succeeded in their appeal to the First-tier Tribunal, but this decision had been set aside on the basis of error of law by the Upper Tribunal, which had made a new decision dismissing the appeal. The Court of Appeal held that this was relevant but not decisive in applying the test of 'some other compelling reason'. It would be relevant, but again not decisive, to consider whether the applicant had *in substance* received only one level of judicial consideration (para 31).

The TCEA s 19 mandated the transfer of judicial reviews to the Upper Tribunal when specified conditions were met. Asylum and immigration judicial reviews were originally excluded from such transfers. The Joint Human Rights Committee thought that cases which raised complex issues of fact and law, or in which human rights such as life, liberty or freedom from torture were at stake should continue to be heard by High Court judges. However, the transfer went ahead, and from 1 November 2013 most immigration and asylum judicial reviews are heard in the Upper Tribunal (Crime and Courts Act 2013 s 22). The exceptions are challenges to validity of legislation or rules, the lawfulness of detention, decisions of the Upper Tribunal or SIAC, those regarding the register of sponsors, nationality law and citizenship, asylum support or accommodation, declarations of incompatibility under the Human Rights Act, and decisions taken on by the Secretary of State based on national security (Practice Direction 21 August 2013, amended on 17 October 2014). Arguably judicial reviews of EEA free movement decisions are also excluded as they are not 'decisions under the Immigration Acts' nor 'relating to leave to enter or remain' (Practice Direction para 1).

On 19 December 2011 the payment of fees was introduced for immigration and asylum appeals. Appeals against most enforcement processes are exempt from fees, and appellants on asylum support are exempt. There is also a procedure for applying for individual exemption (HM Courts and Tribunals Service: Immigration and Appeals Tribunal fees guidance). See chapter 1 for comment on the work of the Tribunal.

7.2.1 The procedure of the Tribunal

The Tribunal Procedure (First-Tier Tribunal) (Immigration and Asylum Chamber) Rules 2014, SI 2604 form the foundation for the practice of the First Tier Tribunal. The overriding objective of procedure rules provides a principle by which they can be interpreted and which may guide discretionary decisions. In the current rules the overriding objective is 'to deal with a case fairly and justly'. This includes:

(a) dealing with the case in ways which are proportionate to the importance of the case, the complexity of the issues, the anticipated costs and the resources of the parties and of the Tribunal;

(b) avoiding unnecessary formality and seeking flexibility in the proceedings;

(c) ensuring, so far as practicable, that the parties are able to participate fully in the proceedings;

(d) using any special expertise of the Tribunal effectively; and

(e) avoiding delay, so far as compatible with proper consideration of the issues. (rule 2)

Firstly, in order to exercise their right of appeal, the individual must receive the notice of the decision against which they are appealing. The Immigration (Notices) Regulations 2003 SI 658 provide that the decision-maker must give written notice of any appealable immigration decision or EEA decision (reg 4), and written notice of (a) the person's right of appeal and the statutory provision on which this is based; (b) whether or not such an appeal may be brought while in the UK; (c) the grounds on which an appeal may be brought; and (d) the facilities available for advice and assistance in connection with such an appeal (reg 5).

Previous Tribunal procedure rules calculated the time period for giving notice of appeal from the date when the immigration decision was received or deemed to have been received. Even the calculation of these time periods may be complex and critical. For instance, the method of sending a notice, and the time of day at which it was received may be relevant (see *R (on the application of Semere) v AIT* [2009] EWHC 335 (Admin) decided in relation to former rules).

The 2014 rules calculate the time for appealing as 14 days not from when the decision was received but from when it was 'sent'. This has created a new problem in that the rules do not define whether 'sent' means leaving the Home Office—that is, posted or faxed—or leaving the desk of the writer. The decision notice itself may contain a date which the Home Office calculates is the time for appealing, and this may run 14 days from the date of the decision, but several days may elapse before posting, thus shortening the appellant's time to appeal.

Where the only right of appeal is from outside the UK, time runs 28 days from the person leaving the country.

The rules allow for appellants to apply for permission to appeal out of time, and the Tribunal must decide that as a preliminary issue (rule 20). The rules also give the Tribunal discretion to decide whether to proceed with a hearing in a party's absence if it (a) is satisfied that the party has been notified of the hearing or that reasonable steps have been taken to notify the party of the hearing; and (b) considers that it is in the interests of justice to proceed. (rule 28)

Initial appeals to the First-tier Tribunal are a hearing of the whole case, and the Tribunal may 'consider evidence about any matter which it thinks relevant to the substance of the decision' (Nationality, Immigration and Asylum Act 2002 s 85(4)). The Tribunal has wide powers to govern the conduct of hearings—to call for witnesses and evidence, and decide on the admissibility of evidence (rule 14). Hearings are normally public, but the Tribunal can direct that the case is heard in private (rule 27). In particular, the Tribunal may do that if the judge considers that the protection of vulnerable witnesses or appellants requires it (Practice Direction 2008 and Joint Presidential Guidance Note 2010: *Child, Vulnerable Adult and Sensitive Appellant Guidance*).

In the interests of fairness and full disclosure there is some obligation on the Tribunal to operate in the direction of a more inquisitorial process, rather than being simply an arbiter between two arguments. This should not be taken to the point of excessive intervention in cross-examination, taking hostile points against the appellant which the Home Office had not thought fit to raise (*XS Serbia and Montenegro* [2005] UKIAT 00093). In *AM (Pakistan) v SSHD* [2011] EWCA Civ 872 the Court of Appeal did not accept an argument that the immigration judge had been in error for failing to view a video which was central to the appellant's claim. Neither the appellant's representative nor the Home Office had asked for it to be viewed. When it finally was viewed by the Upper Tribunal it became clear that it would have made a substantial difference to the case. Still the Court of Appeal declined to place any responsibility on the Tribunal for the examination of evidence.

As the House of Lords said in the case of *Bugdaycay v SSHD* [1987] AC 514, an asylum claim involves matters of such great importance that judicial bodies should subject each case to 'the most anxious scrutiny'. Evidence should be admitted of 'any matter which the Tribunal thinks relevant to the substance of the decision, including evidence which relates to a matter after the date of the decision' (2002 Act s 85(4)). The same applies to a human rights appeal which concerns future risk.

An amendment introduced by the Immigration Act 2014 (Nationality Immigration and Asylum Act 2002 s 85(5) and (6)) provides that the Tribunal may not hear a 'new matter' unless the Secretary of State has consented. A 'new matter' is a ground of appeal (i.e., protection or human rights, see 7.3) which the Secretary of State has not previously considered, whether in the original decision or a response to a later notice to the appellant to state all their reasons for staying in the UK (by a so-called s 120 notice). In other words, this section says that the appellant cannot, on the day of the hearing, introduce asylum grounds when they had previously only appealed on human rights grounds. However, the appellant can raise evidence of events that have occurred after the date of the decision (2002 Act s 85(4)). This is inherent in the nature of appeals on protection grounds since these are future focused—the appellant argues that removal *would* create a real risk of harm.

The Tribunal may hold a case management review hearing, at which the appellant and Home Office must give details of witnesses they intend to call, interpreters, the timescale for evidence to be ready, and any other necessary steps to ensure that all will be ready for the hearing date. The Tribunal may do this in any case, but does so routinely in an asylum appeal.

The Tribunal's written decision must be sent to the parties as soon as reasonably practicable after it is made (Procedure rule 5). There is no time within which the Tribunal must make a decision. Normally the decision is reasoned, and must be in a protection or human rights appeal.

The burden of proof is on the appellant. In deciding whether an appeal can be brought there are broadly three questions to consider:

- Is this the kind of decision against which an appeal may be brought?
- Are there grounds for the appeal?
- Is the appeal available in the UK or only from abroad?

Section 82 of the Nationality Immigration and Asylum Act 2002 sets out the decisions against which appeals may be brought. Before the Immigration Act 2014 these were all the major decisions made in relation to a person's stay in the UK, including refusal of leave to enter, refusal of entry clearance, refusal to vary leave, a decision to remove, and a decision to deport. Now the only appealable decisions are the refusal of a protection claim, the refusal of a human rights claim or the revocation of protection status (2002 Act s 82(1) as substituted).

7.2.2 **Appealable decisions**

A protection claim is defined as a claim that to remove the claimant from the UK would breach the UK's obligations under the Refugee Convention or in relation to a person eligible for a grant of humanitarian protection. Protection status is defined as including refugee status and 'a person eligible for a grant of humanitarian protection' (s 82(2)(c)). The statute rather oddly defines humanitarian protection 'in accordance with the immigration rules' (s 82(2)(d)). Humanitarian protection (see chapter 11) is the UK's name for an international protection status established in the Qualification Directive. The absence of reference to any international source in the UK's definition of humanitarian protection in the immigration rules reflects the UK government's stance on separating itself from European accountability for its human rights performance. This may be the subject of litigation if it is used to narrow the rights of those who fear serious harm abroad.

The meaning of 'human rights claim' attracted little attention before the Immigration Act 2014 appeals regime, but now takes on a new importance. 'What is a human rights claim?' is a new question under the 2014 Act. Does the human rights element of an application need to be explicit in order for it to be a human rights claim, or is the exercise of human rights implicit, for example, in an application to enter the UK for family reasons? And if the latter, what is the place of established case law in the definition of the existence and exercise of human rights?

The 2002 Act s 113 as amended contains the following definition of 'human rights claim' for the purposes of the appeals provisions:

a claim made by a person to the Secretary of State at a place designated by the Secretary of State that to remove the person from or require him to leave the United Kingdom or to refuse him entry into the United Kingdom would be unlawful under section 6 of the Human Rights Act 1998

There are now some applications that attract a right of appeal on human rights grounds that did not do so before 6 April 2015, although at the time of writing, which these are is not yet fully resolved. The Home Office published guidance to caseworkers: *Requests for reconsiderations of human rights or protection based claims refused without right of appeal before 6 April 2015*, which give criteria for when such requests for reconsideration can be granted (mainly situations involving children). The implication is that refusal will generate a right of appeal, although this is not stated and not an inevitable inference.

Guidance as to which applications the Home Office considers attract a right of appeal since 6 April 2015 is to be found in the immigration rules relating to administrative review (Appendix AR). Administrative review is described further at 7.4.3, and is an alternative remedy where no right of appeal is available. Appendix AR A3.2 says that decisions on applications based on the following immigration rules will attract a right of appeal under s 82:

1. Paragraph 276B (long residence, see chapter 6).

2. Paragraphs 276ADE(1) or 276DE (private life, see chapters 5, 6, and 8).

3. Paragraphs 276U and 276AA (partner or child of a member of HM Forces).

4. Paragraphs 276AD and 276AG (partner or child of a member of HM Forces) where the sponsor is a foreign or Commonwealth member of HM Forces and has at least four years' reckonable service in HM Forces at the date of application.

5. Part 8 of the Rules (family members) where the sponsor is present and settled in the UK (unless the application is made under paragraphs 319AA to 319J, or under para 284, 287, 295D, or 295G where the sponsor was granted settlement as a Points Based System Migrant) or has refugee or humanitarian protection status in the UK (see chapter 8).

6. Part 11 of the Rules (asylum, see chapter 12).

7. Part 4 or Part 7 of Appendix Armed Forces (partner or child of a member of HM Forces) where the sponsor is a British citizen or has at least four years' reckonable service in HM Forces at the date of application.

8. Appendix FM (family members), but not where an application is made under section BPILR (bereavement) or section DVILR (domestic violence), see chapter 8.

This provides a useful starting point for identifying applications which may be treated as human rights claims.

The existence of an appealable decision was a litigated point before the 2014 Act. This was problematic where people were refused leave to remain, but then not served with a removal decision. In *TE (Eritrea) v SSHD* [2009] EWCA Civ 174 and *Sapkota v SSHD* [2011] EWCA Civ 132 the Court of Appeal held that this could be unfair. The problem for the individual is that if they lose an appeal against the refusal of leave to remain, they no longer have leave to be in the UK, cannot work or claim benefits, but also they do not have a forum in which they can argue why they should not be removed from the UK. They are thus without means to continue their usual life but also without a forum to argue their case in full.

The Supreme Court in *Patel and others v SSHD* [2013] UKSC 72 held that the decision to remove was a discretion which the Secretary of State could not be compelled to exercise. The statutory power which enabled the Secretary of State to issue a notice requiring the appellant to state all their grounds together or lose the opportunity of arguing them (s 120 Nationality Immigration and Asylum Act 2002) did not mean that there was an overarching and binding statutory policy of considering all grounds together which constrained the discretion of the Secretary of State. Since the start of the Immigration Act 2014 appeals regime, similar problems may still arise where no appealable decision is made.

Challenges from individuals who were refused EU documents (this being a decision under the EEA regulations) and who sought to argue human rights grounds on appeal under the pre-Immigration Act s 84 were caught by the same problem and the absence of a s 120 notice. In *TY (Sri Lanka) v SSHD* [2015] EWCA Civ 1233 the Court of Appeal rejected an argument that the appellants could rely on Article 8 in an appeal against refusal to issue EU documents. The outcome was similar in the earlier case of *Amirteymour v SSHD* [2015] UKUT 466 in the Upper Tribunal.

7.2.3 **EEA Appeals**

Prior to amendments made by the 2014 Act, breach of EU rights was a ground of appeal to the Tribunal against an immigration decision (s 84 (1)(d) 2002 Act before amendment). Since 6 April 2015, EU rights no longer appear as grounds for appeal in the 2002 Act.

As described in chapter 4, EEA decisions are governed by the EEA regulations (Immigration (European Economic Area) Regulations 2006/1003 as amended). These EEA regulations have always provided that provisions of the 2002 Act have effect in relation to appeals against decisions under the EEA regulations *as if they were* decisions under the 2002 Act. Amendments in SI 2015/694, effective from 6 April 2015, restrict the applicable sections of the 2002 Act and provide that they apply

As though the sole permitted ground of appeal were that the decision breaches the appellant's rights under the EU Treaties in respect of entry to or residence in the United Kingdom. (SI 2015/694 schedule 1 para 15 amending schedule 1 2006 regs).

This, in terms of the effect, was the direction of travel approved by the Court of Appeal in *TY (Sri Lanka)* before the 2015 amendments, but this issue is likely to go further. Rights under the EU Treaties entail respect for fundamental rights, and there is likely to be argument that the EU ground for appeal against decisions under the EEA regulations has implications in terms of human rights.

It remains the case that EEA appeals are brought under the EEA regulations, not under the 2002 Act. The Tribunal in *Amirteymour* emphasized that the Schedule to the EEA regulations says 'as if it were' a decision under the 2002 Act.

The relationship between the immigration rules and human rights is complex, and is considered in more detail in chapter 5.

7.3 Grounds of appeal to the Tribunal

Grounds of appeal to the Tribunal in the substituted s 84 2002 Act are set out in full here.

(1) An appeal against the refusal of a protection claim must be brought on one or more of the following grounds:
 - Removal of the appellant from the UK would breach the UK's obligations under the Refugee Convention;
 - Removal of the appellant from the UK would breach the UK's obligations in relation to persons eligible for a grant of humanitarian protection;
 - Removal of the appellant from the UK would be unlawful under s.6 Human Rights Act 1998.

(2) An appeal against refusal of a human rights claim must be brought on the ground that the decision is unlawful under s.6 Human Rights Act 1998.

(3) An appeal against revocation of protection status must be brought on one or more of grounds that:
 - The decision breaches the UK's obligations under the Refugee Convention;
 - The decision breaches the UK's obligations in relation to persons eligible for a grant of humanitarian protection.

Breach of obligations under the Refugee Convention includes the obligation of *non-refoulement* and other obligations to those with refugee status. For these and the requirements to be fulfilled to obtain refugee status see chapters 11 and 12. Obligations to a person eligible for a grant of humanitarian protection are similar, and are set out in the Qualification Directive. Unlawfulness under the Human Rights Act is dealt with in chapter 5. Following the Immigration Act 2014 changes there are no other grounds of appeal.

7.3.1 **Appeals from abroad**

As described in chapter 11, asylum and human rights claims may be certified as clearly unfounded with the result that appeal against refusal can only be made from abroad. The Immigration Act 2014 adds that a human rights claim made while the person is abroad can only be appealed from abroad (s 92(4) as substituted). This largely repeats the situation before the 2014 Act and means that entry clearance refusals can only be appealed from abroad. Section 92(5) provides that revocation decisions made while the person was abroad can only be appealed from abroad. This may be cross-referenced with the powers to deprive a person of their nationality while they are abroad (see chapter 3). A person who has refugee status or humanitarian protection granted in the UK is highly unlikely to have any right to reside elsewhere. A person whose protective status is revoked while they are abroad is likely to be left in a limbo of insecurity and potentially illegality if, for instance, they are visiting a third country on a short-stay visa.

The Immigration Act 2014 introduced a further power to certify human rights claims of people who are liable to deportation. Section 94B allows the Secretary of State to certify the human rights claim of a potential deportee, even while an appeal is under way or has not begun. The certificate is that 'the Secretary of State considers that . . . removal . . . pending the outcome of an appeal . . . would not be unlawful under s.6 Human Rights Act' (s 94B(2)). The grounds upon which the Secretary of State may issue a certificate include, in particular, that the person would not, 'before the appeals process is exhausted, face a real risk of serious irreversible harm if removed.' (s 94B (3)).

If this certificate is issued, any appeal must be brought or continued from abroad. This new 'deport first, appeal later' provision is an attempt to fulfil the political objective stated by numerous governments since 2006 that appeals of foreign national offenders should not prevent their deportation.

In *R (on the application of Kiarie and Byndloss)* [2015] EWCA Civ 1020 (see chapter 15) the Court of Appeal identified a flaw in the Secretary of State's approach to certification under s 94B. Richards LJ noted that the statutory condition for certifying is that the Secretary of State considers that removal would not be unlawful under s 6 HRA. That requires the Secretary of State to

form her own view on whether removal pending an appeal would breach Convention rights . . . For that purpose, in an article 8 case such as the present, she has to make relevant findings of fact and conduct a proportionality balancing exercise in relation to the facts so found. (para 33)

The Secretary of State's guidance, and approach in the individual cases before the Court, focused on the criterion of serious irreversible harm. The Court said:

That ground does not, however, displace the statutory condition in subsection (2), nor does it constitute a surrogate for that condition. Even if the Secretary of State is satisfied that removal pending determination of an appeal would not give rise to a real risk of serious irreversible harm, that is not a sufficient basis for certification. She cannot certify in any case unless she considers, in accordance with subsection (2), that removal pending determination of any appeal would not be unlawful under section 6 of the Human Rights Act. (para 35)

The risk of serious irreversible harm 'is not the overarching test'.

The Court considered whether compelling the appellants to appeal from abroad would breach their procedural rights under Article 8, and concluded that it would not. There was an established practice of out-of-country appeals for entry clearance cases, and although the conditions for appeal might not be as favourable as if the appellants were in the UK, they were sufficient.

In deciding that requiring the appellants to appeal from abroad did not breach their substantive rights under Article 8, the Court took into account that the time pending appeal would be short. Therefore, they did not think it necessary to take into account factors such as difficulty integrating in that country.

7.3.2 Appeal to the higher courts

A determination of the Upper Tribunal may be appealed to the Court of Appeal, with permission, on a point of law. What an individual must show to obtain permission was discussed earlier in relation to *PR (Sri Lanka)* and *Cart*. It is not always easy to distinguish between an error of fact and an error of law. In *E v SSHD and R v SSHD* [2004] EWCA Civ 49, there was a delay of some months between the hearing and the Tribunal decisions being promulgated. During that period, human rights reports were produced on the country to which the appellants would be sent. These reports significantly affected the factual basis on which the decisions had been made. The Court of Appeal held that the Tribunal could have reviewed its decision. They made the further important statement that:

It was time to accept that a mistake of fact giving rise to unfairness was a separate head of challenge in an appeal on a point of law, at least in those statutory contexts where the parties shared an interest in cooperating to achieve the correct result. Asylum law was such an area. For a finding of unfairness there must have been a mistake as to an existing fact, including a mistake as to the availability of evidence on a particular matter. The fact or evidence must have been 'established' in the sense that it was uncontentious and objectively verifiable. The appellant must not have been responsible for the mistake and the mistake must have played a material part in the tribunal's reasoning.

In immigration and asylum cases, a wide and flexible approach is taken to the concept of error of law. The Court in *R (Iran) v SSHD* [2005] EWCA Civ 982 gave guidance on the kinds of errors of law that might arise in immigration proceedings, including, for example, failing to give any or adequate reasons for findings on material matters or to take into account or resolve conflicts of fact. A recent Tribunal decision on the duty to give reasons may be cross-referenced with the discussion of credibility in chapter 12. The Tribunal in *MK (duty to give reasons) Pakistan* [2013] UKUT 00441 (IAC) said that:

[i]f a tribunal finds oral evidence to be implausible, incredible or unreliable or a document to be worth no weight whatsoever, it is necessary to say so in the determination and for such findings to be supported by reasons.

The Supreme Court has urged the Court of Appeal not to be quick to 'characterise as an error of law what is no more than a disagreement with the AIT's assessment of the facts' (*MA (Somalia) v SSHD* [2010] UKSC 49).

7.4 Special Immigration Appeals Commission

There is a separate system for appeals involving national security. This used to be a secret procedure before a panel of advisers, known as the 'Three Wise Men', but the conduct of these proceedings was very restricted. The panel was required to make the case against the person known to them as far as they considered national security would allow, but there was no obligation to disclose evidence or identify witnesses. The individual had no right to legal representation, and perhaps most strangely of all, no right to see the decision in their case.

Article 5(4) ECHR requires that someone who is detained should have the right to challenge their detention in a court. The applicant in the case of *Chahal v UK* (1997) 23 EHRR 413 was detained for a total of six years following a decision to deport him on national security grounds. The ECtHR held that there was a violation of Article 5(4) of the Convention in that there was no provision for him to challenge his detention before a court as the 'Three Wise Men' procedure could not be called a court. The ECtHR recognized that there may be a necessity for matters to be heard in a private forum where disclosure of some issues to the public could cause harm to national security. Nevertheless, some countries, Canada for example, had devised procedures which gave more protection to the rights of the individual while still taking account of the state's need for security. The procedure was also found to breach Article 13 of the Convention, as the panel of special advisers did not provide an effective safeguard for Mr Chahal against removal from the UK to a place where he could suffer torture or inhuman or degrading treatment or punishment in breach of Article 3.

In response to the judgment of the ECtHR, the UK replaced the 'Three Wise Men' with the Special Immigration Appeals Commission (SIAC), set up by the Special Immigration Appeals Commission Act 1997 (SIACA). The Commission must consist of one member who has held (or holds) high judicial office, one member who either is or has been an immigration judge and a third member who is normally someone with experience of national security matters (SIACA 1997 Sch 1 and see *Zatuliveter v SSHD (Deportation—The hearing of an application by the appellant—Refused)* [2011] UKSIAC 103/2010). The Commission has power to exclude anybody from a hearing, including the appellant and their representative if the Commission accepts a submission from the Secretary of State that it is necessary to rely on 'closed' material—that is, material which it would be against the public interest to disclose, even to the appellant. If the Commission decides to hold a closed hearing, the interests of the appellant are represented by a Special Advocate, appointed by the Attorney-General (in Scotland, by the Lord Advocate) for that purpose. The Special Advocate is not at liberty to discuss those proceedings with the appellant. This procedure is intended to comply with Article 5 ECHR, while still providing some protection for government concerns about national security.

7.4.1 **Jurisdiction**

The jurisdiction of the SIAC is complex and consists of both appeals and reviews. SIAC can hear appeals against refusal of human rights or protection claims, or revocation of status (the same scope as s 82 Nationality Immigration and Asylum Act 2002), and against deprivation of nationality, where the Secretary of State certifies that s/he took the decision personally, wholly or partly in the interests of national security or the relationship between the UK and another country (Nationality, Immigration and Asylum Act 2002 s 97, Special Immigration Appeals Commission Act 1997 s 2 and British Nationality Act 1981 s 40A(2)). Section 99 2002 Act allows the Secretary of State to issue a certificate under s 97 while an appeal is pending before the Tribunal, thereby compelling its transfer to SIAC.

The Justice and Security Act 2013 s 15 added to the jurisdiction of SIAC the power to hear applications on judicial review grounds challenging decisions which do not carry a right of appeal: exclusion and refusal of citizenship. The Home Secretary may certify that the exclusion or refusal is conducive to the public good, and is made wholly or partly in reliance on information which should not be made public in the interests of (i) national security, (ii) the relationship between the UK and another country, or (iii) otherwise in the public interest (ss 2C and 2D SIACA). Challenges to such a decision were previously heard in the general courts by way of judicial review. In that forum the government would be required to argue for keeping evidence out of the public domain. This amendment brings the challenges within the jurisdiction of SIAC and places the burden on the applicant of proving that secrecy is not warranted.

The most recent addition to the jurisdiction of SIAC is the power to review, on judicial review grounds, a deportation decision based on national security grounds which, following the Immigration Act 2014, carries no right of appeal to SIAC (s 2E)

The Commission can hear appeals on the same grounds as those which may be raised in the Tribunal (1997 Act s 2(2)(e), as substituted by 2002 Act Sch 7 para 20), that is, now protection and human rights.

In *SSHD v Rehman* [2001] 3 WLR 877, the first case to come before SIAC, the House of Lords agreed with the Court of Appeal and SIAC that the Commission's role was to review the merits of the case in full, which could include reviewing the Secretary of State's findings of fact. The deportation appeals heard by SIAC are discussed fully in chapter 15.

Appeals from SIAC are to the Court of Appeal on a point of law (SIACA s 7). In *B (Algeria) v SSHD; OO (Jordan) v SSHD* [2009] UKHL 10, there was a challenge to SIAC's assessment of the reliability of assurances given by the governments of Jordan and Algeria that the appellants would not be tortured if they were returned there. The House of Lords held that the Court of Appeal had been wrong to overturn SIAC's assessment. This should only be done if their assessment was clearly not sustainable on the evidence such that their judgment on this factual issue amounted to an error of law. In this particular case the appellant (Abu Qatada) obtained a different result from the ECtHR, but the point here is that SIAC is the assessor of fact.

In *J1 v SSHD* [2013] EWCA Civ 279 the Court of Appeal held that SIAC cannot delegate any part of the decision it has to make to the Secretary of State. That case also concerned evaluating the protection of human rights by formal assurances from the government of the country to which the appellant was to be deported. SIAC held that there was work to be done before the Ethiopian Human Rights Committee would have developed capacity for monitoring, but that there would be no breach of human rights by deporting the appellant because the Secretary of State would not deport him before that work had been done. The Court of Appeal held that this was an ineffective and unlawful delegation of SIAC's obligation to assess the risk to the appellant at the date of the hearing.

7.4.2 Evidence and procedures in SIAC

The standard of proof that SIAC generally applies as regards allegations of past actions is the balance of probabilities (*ZZ v SSHD* [2008] UKSIAC 63/2007), even though in content and implications for an unsuccessful appellant the proceedings have much in common with criminal cases. The assessment of risk to national security is, however, a speculative matter, which is considered to be chiefly within the remit of the executive (see discussion in chapter 15). The House of Lords in *A and others v SSHD* [2005] UKHL 71 held that SIAC could not admit evidence if there was evidence that it could have been obtained by torture (see chapter 5 for full discussion).

Two aspects of SIAC's procedure have attracted particular attention. One is the use of closed evidence. The other is the role of the Special Advocate. Both of these have spread to other jurisdictions outside SIAC, and in 2010 there were at least 21 different contexts in which special advocates were used in the UK (JCHR 2010 para 58).

After an inquiry by the Constitutional Affairs Committee, the procedure rules were amended to improve the fairness of the process (Special Immigration Appeals Commission (Procedure) (Amendment) Rules 2007, SI 2007/1285). The House of Lords and the ECtHR have both laid down requirements for the fair use of closed material.

The ECtHR heard a challenge from people who had been subjected to indefinite detention under the 2001 Act (see chapter 14), including a challenge under Article 5(4) to the fairness of the procedure before SIAC, which determined whether the Secretary of State was reasonable in believing each applicant to be a risk to national security and in suspecting them of involvement in international terrorism (*A v UK* (2009) 49 EHRR 29). The ECtHR said that 'in view of the dramatic impact of the lengthy—and what appeared at that time to be indefinite—deprivation of liberty on the applicants' fundamental rights, Article 5 para 4 must import substantially the same fair trial guarantees as Article 6 para 1 in its criminal aspect' (para 217). The Court accepted the reasons for keeping some evidence secret, but held that where full disclosure was not possible, Article 5(4) required that the detainee must be provided with sufficient information about the allegations to enable him to give effective instructions to the special advocate and to challenge the allegations against him, even if the detail and sources of evidence remained undisclosed. An example was the allegation that several of the applicants had attended a terrorist training camp. If a stated location and dates were given, an applicant could have provided an alibi or an alternative explanation for his presence there. Where, however, the open material consisted purely of general assertions and SIAC's decision was based to a decisive degree on closed material, the procedural requirements of Article 5(4) would not be satisfied (para 220).

In the UK courts this standard of disclosure has been held not to apply in SIAC proceedings concerning deportation or exclusion (*W (Algeria) v SSHD* [2011] EWCA Civ 898). In *RB (Algeria) v SSHD; OO (Jordan) v SSHD* [2009] UKHL 10 the House of Lords said that Article 6 ECHR did not apply to SIAC proceedings since the appellants were not facing a charge against them.

The SIAC procedure rules leave considerable discretion with SIAC as to whether evidence should be disclosed or not. Withholding evidence from the appellant has been challenged on numerous occasions on grounds of fairness. At the same time, the government has been frustrated by the court's exercise of discretion, manifested in the context of civil (non-immigration) proceedings in *Al-Rawi v Security Service* [2011] UKSC 34 and *Binyam Mohamed v Secretary of State for Foreign and Commonwealth Affairs* [2010] EWCA Civ 65.

Then in *W (Algeria) (FC) and BB (Algeria) (FC) and others v Secretary of State for the Home Department* [2012] UKSC 8 the Supreme Court affirmed this discretion in SIAC proceedings, and held that SIAC may decide that the identity of a witness before SIAC, and the substance of their evidence, must remain confidential, and may do so in an absolute order made *ex parte*. SIAC would only do this if it is satisfied that the evidence would be capable of belief and could be decisive, or at least highly material, on the issue of safety of return and it has no reason to doubt that the witness genuinely and reasonably fears that he and/or others close to him would face reprisals if his identity and evidence were disclosed (para 34). This was an unusual case in that it was the appellant who wished to call a witness whose identity needed to be protected because of risk to them.

A restricted standard of disclosure for some proceedings in SIAC is now statutory in Justice and Security Act 2013 s 15, as mentioned earlier.

Under the procedure rules as amended in 2007, the Special Advocate may call evidence and cross-examine witnesses. The Secretary of State must search for and serve on the appellant any evidence which might tend to show that the allegations against the appellant are untrue ('exculpatory evidence'). The rules also give the Commission a power to order the Secretary of State to serve a summary of the closed evidence on the appellant. There are still restrictions on the Special Advocate's role, however. They may not take instructions upon the closed evidence. Even if evidence in closed material shows that the case in the open material is flawed, they may not deal with this in an open hearing or take further instructions on inconsistencies. See chapter 4 at 4.8.2.4 for the application of SIAC procedures to an EU national (*ZZ v SSHD* Case C-300/11).

7.5 Administrative review

Part of the scheme of the Immigration Act 2014, and the removal of appeal rights which predated it under other provisions, is to replace a right of appeal with an administrative review. Administrative review is now governed by the immigration rules: Appendix AR, and Modernised Guidance: *Administrative Review*. The guidance at the time of writing is version 6, December 2015.

The administrative review is internal to the Home Office and is conducted by a different team from the one which made the initial decision. Administrative review considers only whether there has been a 'case-working error'. These are defined as:

- a decision to refuse or cancel leave on grounds of deception etc. or change of circumstances (in relation to listed rules) was 'incorrect';
- the decision to refuse an application on the basis that the date of application was beyond a time limit in the Rules was incorrect;
- the decision not to request specified documents under the flexibility policy in paragraph 245AA of these Rules was incorrect;
- the original decision maker otherwise applied the Immigration Rules incorrectly;
- the original decision maker failed to apply the Secretary of State's relevant published policy and guidance in relation to the application; or
- in relation to certain Tier 4 decisions, an error in calculating the correct period or conditions of immigration leave either held or to be granted.

The flexibility policy in the immigration rules provides that the decision-maker may, but need not, request documents or pages that appear to be missing from a series or a document in a correct format (see *Mandalia* in chapter 9).

Appendix AR lists the decisions that are eligible for administrative review. These include decisions on leave to remain made while the applicant is in the UK, and decisions on entry clearance. The decisions on leave to remain are listed decisions under the Points-Based System (PBS) (AR3.2). The entry clearance decisions are broadly all that do not engage the family-based rules or are for visit visas.

A fee of £80 is charged for an application for administrative review. Applications must be made on specified forms, by specified means (HC 395 para 34 U and V), and are also subject to time limits. An application in the UK must be made within 14 days, or 7 days if the applicant is in detention. The limit is 28 days for an entry clearance decision or a decision made at juxtaposed controls (HC 395 para 34R). An applicant may not be removed from the UK while an application for administrative review is pending (Appendix AR AR 2.8).

7.6 **Asylum appeals**

The Aliens Act 1905 gave the courts jurisdiction over the question of whether a person's circumstances would exempt them from deportation where political asylum could be claimed. When the 1905 Act was repealed and replaced by the Aliens Restriction Acts 1914 and 1919 that power disappeared. Now it is the Secretary of State who grants refugee status (*SSHD v R (on the application of Bakhtear Rashid)* [2005] EWCA Civ 744 para 37 and *Bugdaycay* [1987] AC 514).

However, the Court of Appeal has said that 'in asylum cases the appellate structure . . . is to be regarded as an extension of the decision-making process' (*Ravichandran v SSHD* [1996] Imm AR 97 at p. 112). The Appeal Tribunal shares the public duty to ascertain whether there is a need for international protection. An asylum appeal is forward looking; it is an assessment of the risk if the applicant is returned to their home country. Thus the case in the Tribunal is based on all the available evidence up to the date of the hearing. In this sense the appellate structure is 'an extension of the decision-making process', and this practice of assessing the case at the date of the hearing is known as the *Ravichandran* principle. If the Tribunal allows the appeal on asylum (now 'protection' grounds), the Home Office sends out the letter granting refugee status after the Tribunal office has sent its decision and reasons for allowing the appeal.

Although matters up to the date of the hearing are relevant in an asylum claim, as in other litigation the parties are still required to comply with procedure rules and serve evidence on the other side within a specified time before the hearing. This time is set by the Tribunal giving directions at the case management review hearing. The Tribunal has power to shorten or extend the time for submitting evidence (rule 4) and may make directions requiring particular evidence or evidence in a particular form (rule 14).

The 'anxious scrutiny', which should be applied to asylum appeals, is relevant in decisions about the conduct of hearings. In *MD Pakistan* [2004] UKIAT 00197 the appellant was present and ready and willing to give oral evidence. Although his statement had been filed late, the Tribunal held that there was no prejudice to the Home Office in admitting the statement. In *SA Sri Lanka* [2005] UKIAT 00028 the Tribunal held that the anxious scrutiny required in an asylum claim meant that the adjudicator should have admitted a medical report which had a bearing on the appellant's credibility. The Home Office had not sent a representative to the hearing but the Tribunal held that by this omission they had deprived themselves of the opportunity to comment on it, and the appellant should not be penalized on that account.

The future focus of an asylum appeal and the admission of late evidence raise the question of finality in legal proceedings. When does the asylum claim cease? If it is focused on future risk, and there is a substantial change in the asylum seeker's country of origin the day after s/he has lost her appeal in the Tribunal, what then? Although the Tribunal is concerned with the risk to the appellant of persecution on return, the state of affairs which is under consideration is that at the date of the hearing. If this were not so, the matter could go on being re-opened indefinitely. A change of circumstances after the date of the hearing may be dealt with by further submissions if the appeal is lost and the change would affect the outcome.

The first appeal to an immigration judge from the decision of the Home Office is a hearing of all the issues. Any further appeal must be on a point of law, not a question of fact. This may make it difficult to argue that a challenge in the Upper Tribunal can be made on the basis of new evidence, as evidence usually contributes to a finding of fact rather than law. However, as discussed at 7.2.1, a mistake as to fact may, in the circumstances stipulated, amount to an error of law and thus be appealable, particularly in asylum cases (*E and R v SSHD* [2004] EWCA Civ 49).

In civil litigation generally, evidence can be admitted on the principles derived from the case of *Ladd v Marshall* [1954] 1 WLR 1489. These are: that the fresh evidence could not have been obtained with reasonable diligence for use at the trial (here, the Tribunal hearing); if given, it would probably have an important influence on the result; it is apparently credible though not necessarily incontrovertible (*E and R* para 23). These principles may be departed from in asylum cases in exceptional circumstances when the interests of justice so require (*E and R* para 91).

The evidence of psychologists and psychiatrists has an important role to play in explicating for decision-makers the psychological effects of trauma. One difficulty that the legal system has had with evidence of psychological symptoms is that, to a greater extent than physical, they are self-reported. However, psychiatric reports should not be dismissed on this account (*XS (Serbia and Montenegro)* [2005] UKIAT 00093). The weight to be given to psychiatric evidence must depend upon the authority of the witness and their independence.

Expert evidence about conditions in a country may be very significant to the claim. Academics and others with direct and broad experience of the country concerned may be instructed for the asylum seeker. The Tribunal in *LP (Sri Lanka CG)* [2007] UKAIT 00076 held that significant weight should be given to evidence from the British High Commission as it was 'compiled by professional diplomats who are skilled and trained in the observation and acquisition of knowledge in the countries in which they are based' (para 205).

7.6.1 Credibility

The standard of proof in an asylum appeal is the same as in the original asylum claim: is there a reasonable degree of likelihood or a 'real risk' (see *Sivakumaran and Karanakaran*, chapter 12) that the feared persecution will come about?

The issue of credibility in asylum decision-making in the Home Office is discussed in chapter 11. Credibility is an important issue on appeal, as well as at the initial decision-making stage. In the hearing before the First-tier Tribunal all issues in the claim are open for new findings of fact to be made by the immigration judge. Thus the immigration judge will normally make their own findings on whether and to what extent the appellant's account is credible. Guidance on the proper approach to assessing credibility comes from case law, the immigration rules, and statute. Immigration rules governing credibility are discussed in chapter 11.

7.6.1.1 Case law

The case of *Chiver (10758)* is an authority on the proper approach. The adjudicator in that case pointed to the discrepancies in the respondent's story in order to, in the words of the Tribunal:

list the matters which were adverse to the respondent's case and to reflect his belief that they did not affect the kernel of his story. He adopted the approach which is urged upon adjudicators i.e. to weigh up the evidence and to indicate that which is believed and that which is not.

From this it may be gleaned that some inconsistencies are not fatal to the claim. The question is whether the immigration judge believes the core of what is claimed, or, in the oft quoted words in *Chiver*, whether 'the centerpiece of the story stands'. In the same case the Tribunal pointed out that there may be perfectly valid and understandable reasons for exaggeration or not telling the truth, which do not mean the asylum claim is not valid. For instance, a claimant may embroider their story if they fear it is not strong enough or change facts which they fear will be thought implausible. Gorlick (2002) quotes Hathaway as making the same point, that dishonesty, though not to be encouraged, is explicable, for instance, 'when bad advice is received from traffickers or others viewed by an asylum seeker as an expert'.

Immigration judges are warned about judging facts to be implausible. Hathaway (1991:81) points out that it is not in the nature of repressive societies to behave reasonably. In *HK v SSHD* [2006] EWCA Civ 1037 the Court characterized the facts as 'unusual and remarkable'. Nevertheless, the evidence was consistent and there was no contradictory evidence. The Court gave important guidance:

Inherent probability, which may be helpful in many domestic cases, can be a dangerous, even a wholly inappropriate, factor to rely on in some asylum cases. Much of the evidence will be referable to societies with customs and circumstances which are very different from those of which the members of the fact-finding tribunal have any (even second-hand) experience. Indeed, it is likely that the country which an asylum-seeker has left will be suffering from the sort of problems and dislocations with which the overwhelming majority of residents of this country will be wholly unfamiliar. (para 29)

The concept of inherent improbability is inappropriate where the decision-maker has no experience of what would be inherent in a situation. The UNHCR warned that assessments of this kind may be based on 'subjective assumptions, preconceptions, conjecture, speculation and stereotyping rather than accurate, objective and current evidence' (2013 p. 177). The Court of Appeal in *Gheisari v SSHD* [2004] EWCA Civ 1854 took a slightly different tack, saying that just because something is inherently improbable does not mean it is not true.

It is still legally permissible to find the claimant's account inherently implausible, even though such a conclusion should be reached with extreme care. In *MM (DRC— Plausibility) Democratic Republic of Congo* [2005] UKIAT 00019, the appellant claimed to have escaped leaving his clothes in the hands of a soldier who was restraining him, and then to have vaulted a six-foot wall while six other soldiers were outside the house in which he and his family had been seized. His advocate at the Tribunal advanced possible explanations, but the Tribunal held that, where there were possible explanations, these should be advanced by the claimant, not speculated upon by his representative. In the absence of such alternative explanations, the adjudicator had not been wrong to find this account inherently implausible, and to do so it did not need to be outside the realm of human experience, thus declining to follow an Australian decision, W148/00 *A v Ministry for Immigration and Multicultural Affairs* [2002] FCA 679.

In *MM*, the Tribunal gave further guidance on the treatment of the claimant's evidence. A decision-maker should be wary of relying on the demeanour of a witness. Conclusions drawn from this are too likely to be subjective and rely on interpretation of behaviour. It is the *content* of evidence rather than the way it is given that should inform credibility.

It is difficult to overturn credibility findings on appeal to the Upper Tribunal, because it is difficult to establish that a First-tier immigration judge's decision on credibility amounts to an error of law. Like any other finding by the First-tier Tribunal judge, the adequacy of their reasoning is relevant (*B v SSHD* [2006] EWCA Civ 922 para 18). In *MK (duty to give reasons) Pakistan* [2013] UKUT 00641 (IAC) the Tribunal held that:

[i]f a tribunal finds oral evidence to be implausible, incredible or unreliable or a document to be worth no weight whatsoever, it is necessary to say so in the determination and for such findings to be supported by reasons. A bare statement that a witness was not believed or that a document was afforded no weight is unlikely to satisfy the requirement to give reasons.

In *Koca v SSHD* [2005] CSIH 41, the Court held that the Adjudicator should have put to the appellant the discrepancies upon which she based her adverse credibility findings. In *HH (Somalia) v SSHD* [2010] EWCA Civ 426 the Tribunal suggested that the finding that the appellant had lied disabled them from reaching a conclusion on an Article 3 risk. The Court of Appeal said this was mistaken:

They first have to ask whether there is other evidence, independently of his unreliable testimony, casting light on the appellant's particular situation. If so, they must have regard to that evidence. (para 118)

Even a mendacious appellant is entitled to protection from *refoulement* if objective evidence shows a real risk that return will place his life and limb in jeopardy. (para 125)

This was put beyond doubt in *RT (Zimbabwe) v SSHD* [2012] UKSC 38 in which the Supreme Court held that even in a case of an appellant who had been completely disbelieved, the question for the Court was how that person would be perceived and treated on return.

The treatment of expert evidence is also important in relation to credibility. In *Mibanga v SSHD* [2005] EWCA Civ 367 the Court of Appeal found that the adjudicator should have looked at all the evidence, including that from the Medical Foundation and a professor with extensive knowledge of the Democratic Republic of Congo, before forming a view of the claimant's credibility. It was not appropriate to treat the claimant as not credible and then discount other evidence on the basis of that. This continues to be the proper approach (see, e.g., *KM (Somalia) v SSHD* [2009] EWCA Civ 466, and see the guidance in *JL (medical reports-credibility) China* [2013] UKUT 145 (IAC)).

AJ Cameroon [2005] UKIAT 00060 warned against immigration judges making their own assessment of scars. In the rare case where an immigration judge 'has specific skills, qualifications, knowledge and experience, then he or she should disclose them to the parties and make clear what use, if any, it is intended to put them to in the course of the hearing and determination process' (para 34). An immigration judge should not conduct physical examinations in the hearing. Conversely, a medical expert should not draw conclusions on credibility (*HH (Ethiopia) v SSHD* [2007] EWCA Civ 306, and see *KV (scarring—medical evidence) Sri Lanka* [2014] UKUT 230 (IAC) for recent guidance).

Freedom from Torture (formerly the Medical Foundation) and other organizations that support torture victims say that insufficient attention is given to the effects of trauma on memory when assessing inconsistencies. The UN Committee Against Torture also advises that these effects should be taken into account. Jane Herlihy and Stuart Turner draw attention to 'a great deal of empirical literature concerning the tendency for repeated interviews to introduce inconsistency, particularly in the more vulnerable applicant' (2009:187, see chapter 11 further reading list). Juliet Cohen, an experienced medical examiner at Freedom from Torture, describes how new memories of actual but forgotten events and innocently constructed memories of things that never happened can be introduced by repeatedly interviewing a claimant.

7.6.1.2 Section 8 AITOC

Asylum and Immigration (Treatment of Claimants etc) Act 2004 s 8 creates an obligation for a 'deciding authority' to take into account as damaging the claimant's credibility factors which that authority 'thinks' are deliberately misleading. It further sets out a list of behaviours which *shall* be treated as designed to conceal information or mislead. These include, without reasonable explanation, failure to produce a passport, destruction of documents, and failure to answer a question. Other matters are listed without provision for a reasonable explanation: production of a document which is not a valid passport as if it were and failure to claim in a safe third country or make a claim before an immigration decision or arrest under an immigration provision.

This extraordinarily draconian provision (so says Macdonald 2008:948) contradicts the core principle that an evaluation of all the facts is necessary, and deception about one matter does not necessarily mean that the claim itself is false. In *SM Iran* [2005] UKAIT 00116, an early case on the use of s 8, the Tribunal made it clear that it was not going to be overly bound by this parliamentary attempt at inroads into the decision-making process, saying that there was

no warrant at all for the claim . . . that the matters identified by section 8 should be treated as the starting point of a decision on credibility. The matters mentioned in s 8 may or may not be part of any particular claim; and their importance will vary with the nature of the claim that is being made, and the other evidence that supports or undermines it. (paras 7 and 9)

The Court of Appeal in *JT (Cameroon) v SSHD* [2008] EWCA Civ 878 is the present authority, endorsing that approach.

Key Case

JT (Cameroon) v SSHD [2008] EWCA Civ 878

The appellant was a citizen of Cameroon who arrived in the UK using false papers. He used two identities while in the UK. He claimed asylum following his arrest for offences connected with the use of false documents. His claim was refused. On appeal, the Tribunal did not accept that the appellant had escaped from detention in the way he had described, nor that he had any political profile in Cameroon or faced serious harm on return. The Tribunal said that very serious damage had been done to the appellant's credibility by the operation of s 8.

The Court agreed that the statute required that the matters listed in s 8 must be taken into account when assessing credibility, and were capable of damaging it, but the section did not dictate that damage to credibility inevitably resulted. The section could be read as if it said 'potentially damaging the claimant's credibility'. Section 8 was no more than a reminder to fact-finding tribunals that conduct coming within the categories stated should be taken into account in assessing credibility. The weight to be given to it was entirely a matter for the fact-finder. The case was remitted to a different tribunal.

7.7 Judicial review

Because appeal rights in immigration and asylum matters have been so frequently curtailed, and their scope limited, judicial review has been and continues to be a very important recourse. Immigration decisions are subject to judicial review in accordance with usual public law principles, including on the basis that they infringe Convention rights. Indeed, a number of general principles of administrative law have been established in immigration cases. Examples include: the Court's power to examine the factual basis of a decision-maker's exercise of power where this is necessary to see that the decision-maker has jurisdiction (*Khawaja v Secretary of State for the Home Department* [1983] AC 74 concerning illegal entry); the publication of an express promise or undertaking will lead to a legitimate expectation of its being honoured (*Attorney General for Hong Kong v Ng Yuen Shiu* [1983] 2 AC 629); the right to reasons for a decision (*R v Secretary of State for the Home Department ex p Fayed* [1998] 1 All ER 228, CA, a challenge to refusal of British nationality); and the obligation to hear both sides of a case which affects fundamental rights, even where strict rules of natural justice do not apply (*R v Secretary of State for the Home Department ex p Moon* (1996) 8 Admin LR 477, concerning the issue of entry clearance).

In accordance with the normal rules of judicial review, any relevant appeal rights must first be exhausted (e.g., *Cinnamond v British Airports Authority* [1980] 2 All ER 368). This means that, where there is a right of appeal against removal, the right of appeal must be exercised in preference to judicial review, even if this can only be exercised from abroad. This was reiterated in *R (on the application of Mehmood and Ali) v SSHD [2015] EWCA Civ 744, R (RK (Nepal)) v SSHD* [2009] EWCA Civ 359; and *R (Anwar and Adjo) v SSHD* [2010] EWCA Civ 1279. In *SSHD v R (on the application of Lim and another)* [2007] EWCA Civ 773, Mr Lim, a work-permit holder, was detained with removal directions set for the following day for the minor immigration infraction of being thought to be working at a different restaurant from the one for which he had permission (see chapter 16). The Court of Appeal found that the appeal mechanism was the correct one, except in cases where the facts showed there was no jurisdiction to remove. Precedent facts involved in a decision to remove could be the subject of judicial review. Such facts would include the identity of the person being removed and whether they were a British citizen. In relation to other factual issues on which the decision to remove was based, the Court should 'calibrate the use of judicial review . . . to the nature of the issue or issues'. There is room for argument that circumstances are exceptional, where an appeal from abroad would fail to avert the harm that would occur once the person is removed. However, a factual dispute usually would not amount to an exceptional situation (*Mehmood and Ali*). Nor, said the Court in *Mehmood and Ali*, would procedural unfairness.

In immigration and asylum law, as elsewhere, the remedy judicial review provides is a limited one, since the Court cannot substitute its own decision, but only set aside the previous decision and determine the principles upon which a new decision can be made.

Most judicial reviews concern the application of law or policy. Occasionally, its actual making is subject to challenge. Examples include the case of *R (on the application of BAPIO Action Ltd) v SSHD and Department of Health* [2008] UKHL 27, the facts of which are given in chapter 9. BAPIO challenged guidance issued by the Department of Health to NHS employers that international medical graduates with limited leave should only be offered a vacant training post if the resident labour market criterion was satisfied. This was in effect an immigration restriction, but discussions between the DoH and the Home Office to achieve the restriction had broken down, as the Home Office considered that a fundamental change in the immigration rules would be required (para 60). So the DoH went ahead anyway. The guidance was found unlawful. The challenges to the Detained Fast Track system, which resulted in its suspension (see chapter 14), were brought by judicial review.

Specialist areas of application of judicial review appear throughout this book, as well as application of the usual public law principles to a wide range of immigration and asylum decisions. Key areas of application are challenges to the lawfulness of detention (chapter 14), to procedural problems in the asylum decision-making system, particularly those involving abuse of power or a collapse of standards of fairness (chapter 11), and to removal (chapter 16). However, its use is not restricted, and it is employed in many other situations including work and visit decisions where there is no right of appeal, age disputes for minors, and more.

Judicial review itself has become subject to restrictions on its availability. All applications for judicial review may of course only be made with the permission of the court, which must be sought 'promptly and in any event within three months' of the impugned decision. From October 2012 the Civil Procedure rules have provided that applications for permission for judicial review of a decision of the Upper Tribunal refusing permission to appeal to itself are subject to a 16-day time limit instead of the usual judicial review time limit of 3 months (Civil Procedure Rules rule 54.7A).

The availability of representation for judicial review proceedings is affected by the changes to eligibility for legal aid described at 7.7.

7.8 Is there a right to a (fair) hearing in immigration and asylum decisions?

Given the increasing restrictions on the availability of appeals for immigration decisions, and the limitations on judicial review as a remedy, the reader may wonder if Article 6 ECHR can be relied on to fill some of the gaps, and whether there is a common law right to a hearing or a fair hearing.

7.8.1 Article 6 ECHR

Article 6 ECHR sets out minimum requirements of a fair hearing which apply to the determination of 'civil rights and obligations' and criminal trials. As discussed in chapter 5, case law has established that Article 6 does not apply to immigration and asylum matters. However, there are procedural rights implied in Article 8, and Article 47 CJEU is now sometimes invoked. These issues are discussed in chapter 5. Article 8 procedural rights underpinned the findings in *Gudanaviciene*, where the Court of Appeal found the Legal Aid Agency guidance unlawful (see 7.7 and chapter 5).

In *Gudanaviciene* the Court of Appeal accepted the summary of case law concerning the right to representation which was advanced by counsel for the appellants:

(i) the Convention guarantees rights that are practical and effective, not theoretical and illusory in relation to the right of access to the courts (*Airey* para 24, *Steel and Morris* para 59);

(ii) the question is whether the applicant's appearance before the court or tribunal in question without the assistance of a lawyer was effective, in the sense of whether he or she was able to present the case properly and satisfactorily (*Airey* para 24, *McVicar* para 48 and *Steel and Morris* para 59);

(iii) it is relevant whether the proceedings taken as a whole were fair (*McVicar* para 50, *P,C and S* para 91);

(iv) the importance of the appearance of fairness is also relevant: simply because an applicant can struggle through 'in the teeth of all the difficulties' does not necessarily mean that the procedure was fair (*P,C and S* para 91); and

(v) equality of arms must be guaranteed to the extent that each side is afforded a reasonable opportunity to present his or her case under conditions that do not place them at a substantial disadvantage vis-à-vis their opponent (*Steel and Morris* para 62). (para 46)

7.8.2 **Natural justice and fairness**

Administrative law recognizes a distinction between a judicial function and an administrative function. To characterize extremes, a judicial function is one which decides between competing arguments on the basis of evidence, and determines an outcome that will be decisive of rights or entitlements (e.g., *Ridge v Baldwin* [1964] AC 40), for example, imposing a criminal sentence or granting compensation. An administrative function is to process an application or otherwise follow a procedure according to the rules and principles governing that action. This may include the use of discretion where the rules permit. So, for instance, issuing a driving licence is an administrative matter. To oversimplify, while administrative decisions must be made fairly and in accordance with relevant procedures, a judicial decision must be made in accordance with the principles of natural justice, giving both sides a fair hearing and acting without bias. Sometimes fairness and natural justice are equated, for instance in *Lloyd v McMahon* [1987] AC 625.

There is not in reality a clear distinction between administrative and judicial decisions, and immigration decisions have qualities of each. In *Re HK* [1967] QB 617, Lord Parker CJ held that in making inquiries to ascertain the age of a child seeking to enter the UK the immigration officer should act fairly, 'only to that limited extent do the so-called rules of natural justice apply, which in a case such as this is merely a duty to act fairly'. The role of immigration officers in deciding applications was considered in *R v SSHD ex p Mughal* [1973] 3 All ER 796 not to be a judicial but an administrative one. The same goes for entry clearance officers (ECOs) and Home Office officials. Strictly, this means they are not bound by the rules of natural justice, but they are bound to act fairly.

Many of the specific elements of fairness are now dealt with in immigration rules, procedure rules, or Home Office guidance, interpreted by case law. These may change often and the resulting picture is complex.

As an example, in chapter 11 we note the Court of Appeal's decision in *R (on the application of Dirshe) v SSHD* [2005] EWCA Civ 42 that, where an asylum applicant has no public funding either for a representative or for their own interpreter, the overall fairness of the process requires that the applicant be able to tape record their asylum interview. This has been translated into Home Office policy as a requirement that the applicant be told, in the letter inviting them to their asylum interview, that they have a right to request tape recording *in advance*. Home Office guidance to caseworkers on interviewing now includes the refinement that, if the applicant had not requested tape recording in advance, there is no need to mention it again when they arrive for their interview, and if they request it on arrival there is no need to provide it. Thus this provision on fairness for an unrepresented asylum applicant is made subject to minor practical details of communication, rather than the other way round. Different methods of recording the content of asylum interviews are being tried at the time of writing.

In these two examples it may be seen that the absence of an underlying right to a fair hearing including equality of arms (the Court of Appeal in *Dirshe* confirms this absence) means that the specific rights come and go with the ebb and flow of different legal interventions.

In asylum and human rights cases, it is said that the matters at stake are of such importance that only the highest levels of fairness are sufficient, and despite instances such as the aforementioned tape recording, where the principle laid down by the Court of Appeal is eroded by policy and practice, fundamental principles may still be found and applied. In *R v SSHD ex p Anufrijeva*, the appellant's asylum claim had been turned down but she was not informed. Shortly after that, the welfare benefits she had received as an asylum seeker (then 90 per cent of the usual income support rate) were stopped as her asylum claim was no longer current, but she was not given a reason. She argued that the asylum decision could not be treated as effective because she had not been notified. Her case was not isolated as this practice was part of Home Office policy at the time. Lord Steyn said:

> The arguments for the Home Secretary ignore fundamental principles of our law. Notice of a decision is required before it can have the character of a determination with legal effect because the individual concerned must be in a position to challenge the decision in the courts if he or she wishes to do so. This is not a technical rule. It is simply an application of the right of access to justice. That is a fundamental and constitutional principle of our legal system. (para 26)

He referred to the view that an uncommunicated administrative decision could bind an individual as 'an astonishingly unjust proposition' (para 30). Where the individual is excluded not from an administrative but a judicial process, as we saw in *FP (Iran)*, there may be a breach of natural justice.

The Court of Appeal applied principles of natural justice in reaching the conclusion in *AK (Iran) v SSHD* [2008] EWCA Civ 941 that when an appellant's representative withdrew the day before the hearing, the immigration judge should have adjourned the hearing to give him a fair chance to secure representation. He was an Iranian national, and a transsexual, and was afraid that he would be perceived as homosexual in Iran and persecuted as such. The appellant had been found credible, but two previous immigration judges had made opposite assessments of the objective evidence. The importance of legal representation was clear. Sedley LJ made the point that a review based on natural justice was not confined to questions of rationality, but must consider what was 'right', in the light of what fairness required.

In *R (on application of AM (Cameroon)) v AIT and SSHD (interested party)* [2008] EWCA Civ 100, allegations concerning the immigration judge in connection with the hearing of the asylum claimant's appeal included that he had refused to allow oral evidence to be admitted by telephonic link from a barrister whom the claimant said had represented her in getting her out of detention. The fact of her detention was doubted by the Home Office and in issue in the asylum claim. The judge also refused an adjournment to allow the claimant's medical condition to stabilize and described as 'mere supposition' a medical report stating that AM's blood pressure was critically high. After AM collapsed, the judge granted an adjournment to a date when her representative was not available, refusing a longer adjournment as requested by her doctor. On the renewed date, the hearing proceeded without the participation of either the appellant or her representative, although the claimant's credibility was a live issue in the case.

The Court of Appeal held that the appellant's allegations raised the question of whether the immigration judge should have continued to hear the case, and there needed to be a process that could wipe that hearing and decision from the slate. A challenge based on natural justice was able to do this, where an appeal was not. This was a rare situation where a challenge to an interlocutory decision was appropriately brought by way of judicial review because these issues of natural justice could only be decided in that forum.

7.9 Representation

In such a complex and powerful system, effective, knowledgeable, and affordable representation is essential. Procedural points are often essential to the outcome of an immigration case, and many issues can only be tested on judicial review, which is a virtually impossible task for an unrepresented applicant. The importance of the matter to the individual also will often mean that representation is highly desirable.

Organizations of experienced representatives also have an important role in commenting on the almost continuous flow of legislation and policy-making and in responding to consultations. In fact, they are in a better position than most to assist government to see the implications of their proposals. This has political significance also as immigration and, to a greater extent, asylum are fields in which political battles are fought with legal tools. However, immigration and asylum law practice is under-funded and highly regulated, and since April 2013 legal aid has not been available for most immigration matters.

Prior to 2000 it was possible for unqualified people to represent clients both in dealings with the Home Office and at tribunals. Unscrupulous individuals set themselves up as immigration practitioners and charged high fees for work of dubious quality and sometimes of no value at all. Poor practice was not the preserve of the unqualified. It was also the case that, due perhaps partly to the absence of immigration law from most legal professional training, bad work for high prices was done by legal professionals. Added to this was the vulnerability of immigration and asylum clients due to the profound importance to them of the matter, the scarcity of sound knowledge of the subject, and the possibility that they may not be fluent in English.

7.9.1 Regulatory system

Part V of the Immigration and Asylum Act 1999 provides statutory controls of the provision of immigration advice and representation by prohibiting such work from being done by an unqualified person (s 84(1)). A qualified person is, broadly speaking, an authorized member of a legal professional body (the Law Society, Institute of Legal Executives, or General Council of the Bar) or someone registered with the Immigration Services Commissioner. Voluntary organizations such as citizens' advice bureaux, and other publicly funded organizations providing immigration advice must comply with the requirements of the scheme. To provide immigration advice outside these provisions is an imprisonable offence under s 91.

The Immigration Services Commissioner's role is (s 83) to promote good practice in immigration advice and representation and to maintain a register of qualified advisers (s 85). Their powers and duties include preparing a code setting standards of conduct which applies to registered individuals and exempt bodies, that is, all except legal professionals and government employees (Sch 5). The Commissioner's Rules and Codes of Standards allow for registration at a number of different levels, depending on the scope and level of competence of the organization or registered individual. This does not include representation in immigration offences as these are a branch of criminal law. The 2004 and 2014 Acts amended and increased the OISC's powers, introducing powers of entry and search of premises and seizure of documents including a power to seize materials that are subject to legal privilege (2004 Act s 38) and inspection (2014 Act Schedule 7). The 1999 Act also makes provision, in s 87, for an Immigration Services Tribunal which hears complaints from those aggrieved by a decision of the Commissioner, or disciplinary matters referred by the Commissioner. Non-practising barristers must apply for regulation with the Office of the Immigration Services Commissioner.

Both the Law Society and the Bar Council set up voluntary accreditation schemes, but the greater impact on legal professionals is from compulsory accreditation for publicly funded work. This was instituted by the Law Society and Legal Services Commission in 2005, and now all lawyers carrying out publicly funded immigration and asylum work must be accredited or supervised by an accredited person.

7.9.2 **Funding**

While the regulation of legal advice has improved quality, the availability of publicly funded legal advice has become a major issue.

Following nine years of steady reductions in legal aid, in April 2013 the Legal Aid, Sentencing and Punishment of Offenders (LASPO) Act 2012 removed legal aid from immigration and human rights cases. Asylum work remains within the scope of legal aid, as does work related to immigration detention, but there are complex limitations on the kind of judicial review work that can be funded.

The LASPO Act includes a provision for exceptional case funding (ECF) where:

   (a) it is necessary because failure to provide legal aid would be a breach of

      (i) the individual's Convention rights (within the meaning of the Human Rights Act 1998), or

      (ii) any rights of the individual to the provision of legal services that are enforceable EU rights, or

   (b) it is appropriate to do so, in the particular circumstances of the case, having regard to any risk that failure to do so would be such a breach (s 10(3)).

The Lord Chancellor's Exceptional Funding Guidance ('the Guidance') to Legal Aid Agency decision makers suggested that ECF would only rarely be granted.

 Key Case

Gudanaviciene and others v The Director of Legal Aid Casework and Lord Chancellor [2014] **EWCA Civ 1422**

The appellants had all been refused exceptional case funding under the LASPO Act and challenged the refusals and the Guidance in judicial review.

The Court of Appeal held that the Guidance was not compatible with Article 6(1) of the ECHR and article 47 of the EU Charter of Fundamental Rights. 'It impermissibly sends a clear signal to caseworkers and the Director that the refusal of legal aid will amount to a breach only in rare and extreme cases.' (para 181). It was also not compatible with Article 8 of the Convention in immigration cases. Having considered the case law, 'the critical question is whether an unrepresented litigant is able to present his case effectively and without obvious unfairness. The answer to this question requires a consideration of all the circumstances of the case' (para 56). No special high threshold was needed or even permissible.

The effect of these radical cuts, removing 30–40 per cent of immigration legal aid according to the House of Commons Justice Committee (HC 2010–11 681-I), had barely begun when the government launched a further consultation: *Transforming Legal Aid*. This proposed a residence test for all civil legal aid, which in its initial form would have excluded refugees for their first year after the grant of refugee status, all refused asylum seekers, and all foreign nationals for their first year of lawful residence. The regulations introducing these proposals were declared *ultra vires* by the Supreme Court on 18 April 2016 in *Public Law Project v The Lord Chancellor*. The legal aid reforms of recent years have included the introduction of contracts, so that firms are only permitted to do legally aided work for which they have a contract. This has been controversial in relation to immigration detention, since detainees have no choice, and was commented upon by the Court of Appeal in *BA and others v SSHD* [2012] EWCA Civ 944 where the Court had to decide whether it was an abuse of process for a person in detention to challenge the legality of their detention by judicial review, and to begin a new action in the County Court or the Queen's Bench Division for damages for the unlawful detention. The claimant had no option of pursuing both together since her immigration and asylum solicitors did not have a franchise for other public law work.

In the climate of reductions in funding it has been difficult for NGOs to continue to provide immigration and asylum advice, and the two main NGO providers of advice and representation went into administration: Refugee and Migrant Justice in 2010 and Immigration Advisory Service in 2011. Despite regulation, obtaining reliable legal representation and the assurance of proper standards in relation to immigration and asylum legal work remains a huge challenge.

7.10 Conclusion

The final subject treated here, the restricted availability of legal representatives and the abolition of legal aid for immigration matters, in practice has an enormous impact on the actual accessibility of courts and tribunals to people affected by immigration and asylum decisions. Obtaining good legal advice is a significant hurdle for would-be appellants to cross, before the highly technical rules concerning the scope and availability of appeals can be navigated effectively.

QUESTIONS

1 Consider the case for and against transferring judicial review cases to the Upper Tribunal.
2 If immigration decisions are administrative, does the new administrative review system meet the requirements of fairness for immigration applications?
3 Who should decide whether legal advisers are abusing the system?

 online resource centre For guidance on answering questions, visit the Online Resource Centre www.oxfordtextbooks.co.uk/orc/clayton7e/.

FURTHER READING

Barnes, John (2004) 'Expert Evidence: The Judicial Perception in Asylum and Human Rights Appeals' *International Journal of Refugee Law* vol. 16, no. 3, pp. 349–57.

Buck, Trevor (2006) 'Precedent in Tribunals and the Development of Principles' *Civil Justice Quarterly* no. 25, October, pp. 458–84.

Buxton, Richard (2009) 'Application of Section 13(6) of the Tribunals Courts and Enforcement Act 2009 to Immigration Appeals from the Proposed Upper Tribunal' *Judicial Review* vol. 14, no. 3 pp. 225–7.

Carnwath, Robert (2009) 'Tribunal Justice—A New Start' *Public Law* January, pp. 48–69.

Chowdhury, Zahir (2009) "The Concept of 'Error of Law' in Public Law and its Application in Immigration Cases" *Immigration Law Digest* vol. 15, no. 2, Summer, pp. 8–20.

Good, Anthony (2004) 'Expert Evidence in Asylum and Human Rights Appeals: An Expert's View' *International Journal of Refugee Law* vol. 16, no. 3, pp. 358–80.

Kapadia, Amit, (2008) 'Experiencing Judicial Review' *Judicial Review* vol. 13, no. 3, pp. 191–2.

Office of the Immigration Services Commissioner—codes and standards, press releases, annual reports, accessed at: http://oisc.homeoffice.gov.uk/.

Rhys-Jones, David, and Verity-Smith, Sally (2004) 'Medical Evidence in Asylum and Human Rights Appeals' *International Journal of Refugee Law* vol. 16, no. 3, pp. 381–410.

Thomas, Robert (2005) 'Asylum Appeals: The Challenge of Asylum to the British Legal System' in P. Shah, (ed.), *The Challenge of Asylum to Legal Systems* (London: Cavendish), pp. 205–26.

Thomas, Robert (2005) 'Evaluating Tribunal Adjudication: Administrative Justice and Asylum Appeals' Legal Studies vol. 25, no. 3, pp. 462–98.

Thomas, Robert (2008) 'The Immigration Appeals Consultation Paper' *Immigration Law Digest* vol. 14, no. 3, Autumn, pp. 2–5.

UNHCR (2013) *'Beyond Proof: Credibility Assessment in EU Asylum Systems'* (Brussels: UNHCR).

SECTION 4

Entry to the UK

8

....

Family life

SUMMARY

This chapter mainly concerns non-European Economic Area (EEA) nationals who wish to live permanently with family members who are settled in or are nationals of the UK although the family members of those coming to work or study and of refugees are also briefly considered. It starts by considering some preliminary issues before examining marriage-related applications, that is, applications to join a spouse, fiancé(e), civil or long-term partner. The rules relating to adult family members and to children are then considered. At the end of the chapter, there is brief consideration of those with limited leave, and finally of refugees and asylum seekers.

8.1 Introduction

Family migration most commonly occurs through marriage or parenthood as rules for admission of other relatives are very restrictive. In 2015, 37,859 non-EEA family members were granted visas to enter the UK. Of this total 29,577 were spouses, fiancé(e)s, and civil partners, while just over 3,000 were children. Around 5,000 other family members also entered and were given indefinite leave immediately (Home Office *Immigration Statistics: October to December 2015*).

Since family migration first became an issue in the mid-1960s, the main focus has been on the admission of family members from Asia. This has always been the largest region of origin, although it has become less important as migration from other regions has increased. Home Office statistics show that, in March 2015, 24 per cent of spouses granted entry to the UK were from Pakistan and India (*Home Office Immigration Statistics: October to December 2015*). As Charsley (2012a) points out, the range of nationalities involved in family migration should not be overlooked. She has identified more than 70 nationalities involved in spousal migration, with significant numbers settling in the UK from countries such as the Philippines, South Africa, China, and the US. She has also shown (2012b) that refusal rates of spousal migrants have risen in the past few years and vary widely between countries of origin.

Family migration presents a particular challenge for the government. A decision to admit a migrant for work or business can be made purely on the basis of the UK's economic or other interests. However, the admission of family members involves a tension between the personal interests of British residents and permitting the entry of those who would not qualify under other channels and whom the government would prefer not to admit. This tension has been evident since family migration first became a controversial issue in the mid-1960s and has again come to the fore, most recently in the government's Family Migration Consultation. There are two perspectives: that of the government seeking to manage migration on behalf of the country and that of the UK resident or national who wishes to re-unite with their family member. Very often, it has been the former which is foregrounded and the issue is seen primarily as one of immigration control.

8.2 The politics of family life

Much contention surrounds family settlement applications as a result of differences and perceived differences between the practices of immigrant and host communities, raising questions about marriage and child-rearing practices, concepts of the family, individual freedom, and family duties. The law has often been dominated by an overriding concern with preventing abuse and the entry of undesirable migrants. Marriage, in particular, has 'offered an opportunity to vent a gamut of powerful and well-rehearsed emotions' (Bevan 1986:253) and has 'attracted the most controversial immigration rules' (Jackson, *Immigration Law and Practice* 1996:395). These emotions have intensified in recent years due to concerns about forced marriage and the integration of foreign spouses, resulting in new measures, some of which have been legally problematic.

Over the years, many of the measures regulating entry through marriage have particularly affected arranged marriages, as practised in UK-based communities of South Asian origin. This is not accidental. Many members of these communities have continued to marry spouses from their region of origin, leading to concerns about chain migration, the continued entry of unskilled non-English-speaking migrants, and the perpetuation of forms of family life that some consider archaic and oppressive.

Husbands have often been suspected of being disguised economic migrants and this has been reflected in the rules. The first major attempt to control marriage migration to the UK after the Commonwealth Immigrants Act 1962 involved a ban between 1969 and 1974 on the entry of Commonwealth husbands unless 'special features' were present. In the 1970s and 1980s, the 'primary purpose' rule, which was removed in 1997, was a more focused means of minimizing the entry of spouses, particularly husbands from the Indian subcontinent, while wives and children were affected by controversial administrative methods adopted by the entry clearance system. The entry of very young spouses and of more than one spouse in a polygamous marriage was ended between 1986 and 1990.

There have been two major themes in recent regulation: firstly, encouraging the integration of spouses and protecting the victims of forced marriage, and, secondly, preventing bogus or sham marriages. The 2002 White Paper, *Secure Borders, Safe Haven* (Cm 5387), the subtitle of which was *Integration with Diversity in Modern Britain*, suggested that young people from British Asian families should consider marrying someone who lived in the UK (p. 18). Incoming spouses must now pass the knowledge of language and life in the UK tests before settlement. The government also introduced a pre-entry language requirement for spouses in 2010, using arguments more commonly associated with labour migration even though partners are not required to work. This requirement was challenged in *R (on the applications of Ali and Bibi) v SSHD* [2015] UKSC 68. The appeal failed on the basis that the policy was not disproportionate due to the availability of exemptions, although the Supreme Court has invited further submissions in relation to whether Home Office guidance on when exceptions should be made to the rule may be so restrictive as to be unlawful. The minimum age for sponsorship and entry was raised to 18 in 2003 and 2004, respectively, in response to concerns about forced marriage and to 21 in 2008, although this was found by the Supreme Court to breach Article 8 ECHR (European Convention on Human Rights) and was withdrawn in late 2011. The government also adopted an inflexible approach to the maintenance of migrant family members by their extended family, a position that was undermined by the Supreme Court (see *Mahad (Ethiopia) and others v ECO* [2009] UKSC 16, discussed later in the chapter) but which has now resurfaced in the new minimum income requirements.

Despite some sympathetic decisions such as *Mahad*, cultural differences in attitudes towards marriage and family are also sometimes visible in the case law, particularly in marriage. For example, disapproval of polygamous marriage arrangements may be detected in the interpretation of the requirement to show intention to live together in *AB Bangladesh* [2004] UKIAT 00314.

Meanwhile, rules governing other forms of family life have been liberalized, reflecting changing values amongst the majority population. Unmarried and civil partners are now recognized within the rules. Although aspects of these provisions are problematic, such as the protection for victims of domestic violence, their presence suggests that 'modern' values and relationships have achieved a degree of official acknowledgement that often still eludes 'traditional' forms of family life.

Further, several cases now show an increasing level of engagement by the higher courts in questions involving respect for the family life of migrants under Article 8 ECHR or, in the case of *Baiai*, Article 12, the right to marry. Several government policies have been successfully challenged in the courts using human rights. For example, many claims for leave to remain as a spouse are made by those who have married a UK or EEA national after entering the UK. This has given rise to suspicions of sham marriages, particularly when the spouse entered on short-term leave (for example, as a visitor) or was without leave (including many asylum seekers). In 2002, the government prohibited these migrants from 'switching' into marriage, requiring them to return to their country of origin to make an entry clearance application, a policy substantially undermined by the House of Lords (*Chikwamba v SSHD* [2008] UKHL 40). The Certificates of Approval scheme, established by Asylum and Immigration (Treatment of Claimants, etc.) Act 2004, required non-EEA nationals to obtain permission of the Secretary of State to marry, which was almost always refused when migrants did not have long-term leave. Aspects of the scheme were found by the House of Lords to be incompatible with Convention Rights (*R (on the application of Baiai and others) v SSHD* [2008] UKHL 53) and the scheme was abolished in 2011, although this issue has resurfaced in the Immigration Act 2014 (see 8.7). The current Conservative government is committed to a vast reduction in 'net migration', a problematic objective discussed in chapter 2, and family migration is included in this target for reduction. In July 2011, the (then coalition) government launched a consultation on family migration which contained many radical proposals intended to reduce the numbers and change the characteristics of family migrants. The Foreword by the Home Secretary, Theresa May, set the tone:

This government is determined to bring immigration back to sustainable levels and to bring a sense of fairness back to our immigration system . . . Of course, those with a legitimate right to come here must still be able to do so. But we need to crack down on abuse of the family route and to tighten up the system.

Not all of the proposals set out in the consultation (referred to here as the Family Migration Consultation) were adopted. However, those that found their way into the rules will be discussed at relevant points in this chapter.

As Wray (2013a) has noted, many of the proposed changes to the control of family migration resembled those implemented elsewhere in Europe, for example, raising the age of entry and sponsorship of spouses, minimum income requirements, pre-entry language testing, more demanding integration criteria, and so on. This would seem to suggest that policy developments ought now to be analysed in a European context (see, e.g., the work of Van Oers, Ersbøll, and Kostakopoulou (2010) or Groenendijk (2011)). However, a report by the Migration Policy Group cited by Symonds states that, even before the changes came into place, 'the UK creates more obstacles for migrant workers and residents to reunite with their families . . . than most European countries' (Symonds 2011) and this trend looks set to continue. Furthermore, it must be borne in mind that all of the changes to the rules, discussed throughout this chapter, exist in a wider context. The removal of legal aid for some immigration cases and appeals in 2013, as a consequence of the provisions of the Legal Aid, Punishment and Sentencing of Offenders (LASPO) Act 2012, dramatically limits the ability of those subject to the new measures to obtain expert legal advice and representation (see Meyler and Woodhouse 2013).

8.3 Legal context

There is no enshrined right for a British resident to be joined in the UK by their family members. Section 1(4) Immigration Act 1971, which obliges the Secretary of State to make rules to govern certain types of entry, does not require these to cover the admission of family members, an omission that cannot be challenged under the Human Rights Act 1998 as this is an omission of the legislature which is immune from action (s 6(3)). Entry is governed by the Immigration Rules and the applicant is not the UK resident but the foreign national family member who wishes to enter and who must meet the requirements of the Rules.

As discussed in chapter 1, the legal status of the immigration Rules is ambiguous. Recent case law, such as *Odelola* and *Mahad*, has confirmed that they represent statements of policy rather than legal rights but they are nonetheless binding on the government, as *Pankina* and *Alvi* demonstrated. As we have already seen, the Immigration Rules are made by a minister after, usually, cursory scrutiny by Parliament and the requirements change frequently. While consultation exercises take place in immigration as elsewhere, there is no duty to consult nor to abide by the outcome of a consultation. The lack of statutory grounding for the entry of family migrants makes it easier to restrict rights in line with popular or government concerns.

Whether a family member gets leave to enter depends upon the judgment of an entry clearance officer as to whether they fulfil the requirements of the rules. Where an unsuccessful applicant can appeal, the appellant remains abroad and it is the sponsor in the UK who attends the appeal and whose presence is, in practice, often decisive. However, under the rules, they have no official standing, reflecting the absence of any positive right attaching to UK residents to be joined by their family members.

Immigration law and practice in the UK are affected by both European Union law and human rights norms. As explained in chapter 4, free movement rights in EU law have often permitted British nationals to avoid restrictive UK rules on family migration. These rights are an increasingly important backdrop to the law and policy discussed in this chapter. Human rights, particularly under Article 8 ECHR (right to respect for private and family life), have also been influential in the development of the recent law. The application of Article 8 in particular family situations is discussed as it arises in this chapter.

Some restrictive government policies have been successfully challenged in the courts, often using human rights, particularly Article 8 ECHR. The government is unhappy at such constraints on its power and, in the Family Migration Consultation, Theresa May referred to a government-established commission to investigate the creation of a UK Bill of Rights and expressed her 'sincere hope that the commission w[ould] bring some common sense back to this, admittedly difficult, area'. Indeed, the government clearly tried to take back some control of this area in the changes made to the Immigration Rules following the consultation (Appendix FM, EX.1). These changes were said to codify the approach case owners and judges should take when considering family life under Article 8. The purpose of the rules was set out in GEN1.1 of Appendix FM and first appearances seemed to suggest that the aim was to shift the role of the courts from reviewing the proportionality of the action in each case to directing the Court as to where the decision should be made, by limiting the circumstances in which interference with a person's family life is deemed appropriate. This approach appeared to be at odds with previous case law on Article 8 and, in particular, the need for a case-specific consideration of all of the facts in the Article 8 proportionality balancing exercise (*JO (Uganda) JT (Ivory Coast)* [2010] EWCA Civ 10 at 28). Lawyers and commentators concerned with immigration law generally greeted the new rules with disbelief. Warren commented that they appeared to be:

[a]n unlawful attempt to overturn the edifice of human rights law through the immigration rules and a fettering of the decision maker's discretion. They represented an attempt to reintroduce the rejected tests of 'insurmountable obstacles' and 'exceptionality' and placed judges in a position of conflict between the stated purpose of the rules and their obligations under the Human Rights Act. (Warren 2013)

As we will see later in this chapter, the government's attempt to regain some control over the application of Article 8 in the courts initially met with little success. As a consequence, the Government has now addressed this area in primary legislation (Part 5A NIAA 2002 as amended by s 19 of the Immigration Act 2014).

This chapter will now go on to consider the application of Article 8 in family immigration cases before moving on to look more specifically at the Immigration Rules.

8.4 Right to respect for private and family life

The right to respect for private and family life is not confined to the ECHR but is a universally recognized fundamental human right. It is included in the Universal Declaration of Human Rights 1948 and the International Covenant on Civil and Political Rights 1966, both of which forbid arbitrary and unlawful interference with family life. The International Covenant on Economic, Social and Cultural Rights 1966 says, in Article 12, that 'the widest possible protection and assistance should be accorded to the family, which is the natural and fundamental group unit of society'. The European Charter of Fundamental Rights says, at Article 7, that '[e]veryone has the right to respect for his or her private and family life, home and communications'.

In domestic law, remedies for breach of the right are available through the Human Rights Act 1998, particularly under Article 8 ECHR, the right to respect for private and family life. Section 82(1)(b) Nationality, Immigration and Asylum Act 2002 provides that a person may appeal to the Tribunal if the Secretary of State has decided to refuse a human rights claim made by the claimant. This would appear to include family visas, overstayers, and illegal entrants where human rights grounds are explicitly raised.

The Article provides:

1. Everyone has the right to respect for his private and family life, his home and his correspondence.
2. There shall be no interference by a public authority with the exercise of this right except such as is in accordance with the law and is necessary in a democratic society in the interests of national security, public safety, or the economic well-being of the country, for the prevention of disorder or crime, for the protection of health or morals, or for the protection of the rights and freedoms of others.

The application of Article 8 requires a structured approach that considers the determinative issues in an ordered way. The relevant issues are:

- Does family or private life exist?
- What does 'respect for family or private life' require?
- Has there been an interference with the exercise of this right?
- Is the interference in accordance with the law?
- Is it necessary in a democratic society to protect one of the interests set out in Article 8(2)?
- If so, is the interference proportionate to the legitimate aim pursued?

Most disputed cases centre on the Article 8(2) question of proportionality. However, it is not always clear from the courts' reasoning whether it is proportionality or the existence of, or interference with, family or private life that is being decided. Nor is it always clear which Article 8(2) interest is protected by immigration control. Immigration control is usually presumed to serve one or more of these interests and the question does not receive detailed consideration. However, identifying the interest served by interference affects the weight of the case for interference. In *JO (Uganda) v SSHD* [2010] EWCA Civ 10, Lord Justice Richards, at para 29, pointed out that deportation cases, where the migrant has been involved in wrong-doing, serve the interests of preventing disorder or crime, issues not at stake in ordinary removal cases. Thus, where an appellant's drink-driving convictions had been insufficient to merit a deportation order, they were also insufficient to refuse indefinite leave to remain as a spouse where economic aims were in issue (*LD (Article 8—best interests of a child) Zimbabwe* [2010] UKUT 278 (IAC)).

Critically, as discussed in chapter 5, *Huang* made it clear that it is for the Court or Tribunal to reach its own decision on proportionality, a point made again by the Supreme Court in *Quila*, which proceeded to carry out its own detailed examination of proportionality, discussed later in this chapter. The Immigration Rules do not necessarily represent the correct balance between the interests of the individual and the interests of the state, and it is for the state to justify the proportionality of the Article 8(2) interference. Cases must be decided on their particular facts and, in the words of Lord Bingham in *EB (Kosovo) v SSHD* [2008] UKHL 41 at para 12:

there is in general no alternative to making a careful and informed evaluation of the facts of the particular case. The search for a hard-edged or bright-line rule to be applied to the generality of cases is incompatible with the difficult evaluative exercise which article 8 requires.

As mentioned in the introduction to this section, despite a Home Office statement of 13 June 2012 (entitled 'Immigration Rules on Family and Private Life: Grounds of

Compatibility with Article 8 of the European Convention on Human Rights') recognizing the courts' role in determining proportionality, the new Immigration Rules on family life in Appendix FM appeared to be seeking to fetter judicial discretion in this area. However, the first cases challenging the new rules showed the courts robustly defending their role as decision-makers whilst at the same time, recognizing the legitimacy of the rules as an expression of the Secretary of State's position (*MF (Article 8—new rules) Nigeria* [2012] UKUT 00393 (IAC); *Izuazu (Article 8—new rules)* [2013] UKUT 00045 (IAC); *Ogundimu (Article 8—new rules) Nigeria* [2013] UKUT 00060 (IAC)). In *Nagre v SSHD* [2013] EWHC 720 (Admin), the High Court rejected a challenge to legality of the new rules but gave some guidance on their application, which has been followed in *Green (Article 8—new rules)* [2013] UKUT 00254 (IAC). Finally, the Court of Appeal reached the same conclusions (albeit on a different basis) in *MF (Nigeria) v SSHD)* [2013] EWCA Civ 1192.

As a consequence, the government resorted to primary legislation and s 19 of the Immigration Act 2014, which inserts a new part 5A into the Nationality, Asylum and Immigration Act 2002, sets out statutory public interest considerations to which courts and tribunals *must* have regard. This duty is not unlike the duty in s 8 of the Asylum and Immigration (Treatment of Claimants) Act 2004 concerning credibility findings (see chapter 11) save that it applies only to judges and not Home Office decision makers and, similarly, it requires only that judges have regard to the criteria rather than requiring them to make certain findings. Part 5A took effect immediately (*YM (Uganda) v Secretary of State for the Home Department* [2014] EWCA Civ 1292).

The substance of the new human rights considerations are set out in ss 117B and 117C and state that the following factors are presumed to be in the public interest:

- The maintenance of effective immigration control.
- The ability of the claimant to speak English in order to better integrate into society and not be a burden on the taxpayer.
- Financial independence.

They continue that little weight should be given to any private or family life established whilst a person is in the UK unlawfully or at a time when a person's immigration status is precarious. An exception is made where a person has a genuine and subsisting parental relationship with a 'qualifying child' and it would not be reasonable to expect the child to leave the UK. There are further considerations in s 117C that apply only in cases concerning foreign national criminals (see chapter 15).

It is clear that the new statutory scheme in combination with the new Immigration rules attempt to segment aspects of Article 8 so that they are considered alone rather than collectively. This contrasts with the holistic approach previously approved by the courts and it remains to be seen what impact this may have on the outcome of cases invoking Article 8. At present, the tribunal case law appears to be conflicting on the approach to be taken (see *Dube* (ss 117A–117D) [2015] UKUT 90 (IAC) and *AM (S 117B) Malawi* [2015] UKUT 260 (IAC)). It is worth recalling the words of their Lordships in *Huang and Kashmiri* (para 18), when they referred to the 'core value' of Article 8:

Human beings are social animals. They depend on others. Their family, or extended family, is the group on which many people most heavily depend, socially, emotionally and often financially. There comes a point at which, for some, prolonged and unavoidable separation from this group seriously inhibits their ability to live full and fulfilling lives.

The tension between humans' emotional needs and the complex individual evaluation demanded by Article 8, on the one hand, and the demands of a generally applicable and often restrictive immigration policy, on the other, has driven much case law as discussed in this chapter.

8.4.1 Does private or family life exist?

The application of a family member to enter the UK engages the positive obligation in Article 8 to 'respect' private and family life. While the other qualified Articles use the formula 'everyone has the right to freedom' whether of religion, expression or assembly, Article 8 does not provide a right to family life, but to 'respect for' private or family life. This has two implications. First, Article 8 does not provide a right to establish a private or family life. To the extent that this is covered in the Convention, it is dealt with in Article 12, the right to marry and found a family. The prior existence of private or family life must therefore be established under Article 8(1). These are ECHR concepts which have been given their meaning by the ECtHR and in accordance with HRA s 2, the UK courts are obliged to take account of those meanings.

8.4.1.1 Private life

The concept of private life in Article 8 is a wide one. For the purposes of this chapter, it is worth noting the judgment in *Niemietz*, where private life was held to 'comprise to a certain degree the right to establish and develop relationships with other human beings'. This includes the most intimate relationships as in *Dudgeon v UK* (1981) 4 EHRR 149 and may include professional relationships, especially where these are not easily separated from the rest of life. More recently, in the case of *Maslov v Austria* [2008] ECHR 546, the European Court of Human Rights (ECtHR) held that 'the totality of social ties between settled migrants and the community in which they are living constitutes part of the concept of "private life" within the meaning of Article 8'.

Private life can also be established when the individual knows that their stay in the country is temporary, as in *MM (Tier 1 PSW; Art 8; 'private life') Zimbabwe* [2009] UKAIT 00037. MM had been a student in the UK and then obtained limited leave for post-study work. In the UK she had developed social and professional ties and relationships, and her daughter was at school. The temporary nature of the immigration leave held by someone like MM does not displace the fact that she has a private life in the UK, but is relevant when the proportionality of not extending leave is considered.

The courts have made distinctions between family and private life, depending on the gender and legal relationship of the partners. However, this distinction is breaking down in favour of an approach which focuses on the reality of relationships. In *JN (Uganda)* [2007] EWCA Civ 802, the appellant had lived a 'decent and industrious' life in the UK for 12 years. She was doing paid work, voluntary work, was deeply involved with her church, and had a relationship with a man whom she had not married in case she was returned to Uganda. This was accepted as private life. The Court held that the reasoning of the House of Lords in *Huang* concerning respect for family life applied equally to private life (para 16).

8.4.1.2 Family life

Family life includes the society of close relatives. The ECtHR regards a 'lawful and genuine' marriage as amounting to family life, even if the couple has not yet been able to establish a home together (*Abdulaziz, Cabales and Balkandali v UK* and *Berrehab v Netherlands*).

Minor children are regarded as having a relationship of family life with biological or adoptive parents, even if they do not live together, and the ECtHR has repeatedly held that in the absence of exceptional circumstances the parent–child relationship automatically gives rise to family life. In *Berrehab*, the parents were not married and no longer lived together. Nevertheless, the father had contact with the child four times a week for several hours at a time. The Court found that family life between father and child had not been broken by the ending of the partnership between parents.

In the case of adult siblings or adults and their parents, the approach of the courts has been to treat the quality of emotional ties as relevant in determining whether there is family life. In assessing whether or not a family life exists, the ECtHR has stated that 'the existence or non-existence of "family life" for the purposes of Article 8 is essentially a question of fact depending upon the real existence in practice of close personal ties' (*Lebbink v Netherlands* (Application no. 45582/99) para 36; *Singh v Secretary of State for the Home Department* [2015] EWCA Civ 630). Furthermore, the concept of family life must be understood in the context of the UK's multicultural society.

The need for an established family life can have hard results where compassionate factors are present but pre-existing family life cannot be shown. The Tribunal in *ECO Lagos v Imoh* [2002] UKIAT 01967 held that Article 8 did not apply where a four-year-old girl wanted to move to the UK to live with her aunt whom she had only visited once. The minimal prior contact meant that this would be to establish family life, not to respect family life that was already extant. It may also mean that the type of family life that is protected under Article 8(1) may be reduced due to circumstances beyond the parties' control. The Court of Appeal in *MB (Somalia) v ECO* [2008] EWCA Civ 102 found that a ten-year involuntary separation of an elderly mother and adult son after he came to the UK as a refugee adversely affected the quality of established family life for the purposes of Article 8.

8.4.2 What requires respect and what respect requires

The courts have emphasized that family life may take many forms and it is the family life in the particular case that must be respected. In *EM (Lebanon) v SSHD* [2008] UKHL 64, Lord Bingham said (at para 37):

Families differ widely, in their composition and in the mutual relations which exist between the members, and marked changes are likely to occur over time within the same family. Thus there is no pre-determined model of family or family life to which article 8 must be applied.

Here, the family consisted of a mother and her 12-year-old son. If the family were returned to Lebanon, the son's father, who had been violent to the mother and who had not seen his son since birth, would be entitled to custody and the mother, at best, to visits. Lord Bingham found that the family life in this case involved, not only practical matters of physical care, but a bond of 'deep love and mutual dependence' (para 40) and returning them to Lebanon would 'flagrantly violate, or completely deny and nullify' their right to respect for that family life (para 42).

Family life that takes other forms must also be respected. In *MS (Ivory Coast)* [2007] EWCA Civ 133, the appellant could not live with her children due to her previous violence but she was applying for a contact order. The Court of Appeal held that she was entitled to consideration of her Article 8 rights. In *R (on the application of Fawad and Zia Ahmadi)* [2005] EWCA Civ 1721, Zia, a refugee, suffered from schizophrenia. His brother, Fawad, was refused refugee status but provided effective support to Zia. Fawad claimed that respect for his family life required the opportunity to do that. Although the Secretary of State had certified that the claim was 'clearly unfounded' (see chapter 11), the Court disagreed and held that it should be considered.

The wording of Article 8(1) implies a positive obligation on the part of the state to respect existing private and family life (*Marckx v Belgium*) not just a negative duty to avoid expulsion. However, for many years, it was assumed that any positive obligation would rarely extend to admission. This belief was established by the majority view in *Abdulaziz v United Kingdom*, at para 68: 'The duty imposed by article 8 cannot be considered as extending to a general obligation on the part of a contracting state to respect the choice by married couples of the country of their matrimonial residence and to accept the non-national.'

In cases since *Abdulaziz*, the European Court of Human Rights has questioned the clear-cut nature of the demarcation. In *Sen v Netherlands* (2003) 36 EHRR 7, refusal to admit a minor child was found to breach Article 8 ECHR. In *Tuquabo-Tekle v the Netherlands* [2006] 1 FLR 798, the daughter's admission was sought in order to allow reunification with her family. The Court observed at paras 41 and 42, that 'the boundaries between the state's positive and negative obligations under this provision do not lend themselves to precise definition' and that 'the applicable principles are, nonetheless, similar'. In *Rodrigues da Silva, Hoogkamer v Netherlands* (2006) 44 EHRR 729, the mother was entitled to remain in the Netherlands to continue contact with her daughter, a finding that the Court acknowledged entailed a positive act. See also *Jeunesse v The Netherlands* (Application no. 12738/10).

In the Supreme Court case of *R (on the application of Quila and another) v SSHD* [2011] UKSC 45 (discussed further later in the chapter), Lord Wilson declined to follow *Abdulaziz* because later cases, including those just cited, were inconsistent with it. As Lady Hale observed in the same case, what the later cases taken together show is that each case demands its own examination and where family life exists, a similar approach to interference should now be taken in all types of cases.

This seems a correct approach and not only because it recognizes the development of the European jurisprudence since *Abdulaziz*. A rigid demarcation between the negative duty to refrain from expulsion and the positive duty to admit is artificial. A married couple is regarded as having family life so an application to join one's spouse engages the right to respect for family life even if they have never lived together. There is also a strong presumption of family life between minor children and their parents. Thus, while Article 8 only protects family life that already exists, its existence does not necessarily depend upon there already being cohabitation (even if that is what its respect ultimately requires). The distinction is even more tenuous when migrants are physically present but lack status as allowing them to stay involves both the positive act of granting leave and the negative act of refraining from expulsion. It is not clear why, in terms of establishing interference, these cases are materially different from those cases where the migrant has limited leave (although compliance with immigration law may be a factor in determining proportionality).

While all forms of family life must be respected and the engagement of the state's positive and negative obligations arises in similar ways, it does not follow that respect will require cohabitation in the same country in all instances. For some relationships, contact through letters, phone calls, and visits is sufficient to maintain family life. This is particularly so as regards adult family members who are not in a relationship of dependency and who do not normally expect to live together, although each situation needs to be considered on its own facts and cohabitation may be required in some cases.

8.4.3 Whose family life?

In 2008, the House of Lords found in *Beoku-Betts v SSHD* [2008] UKHL 39 that s 84(1) of the Nationality, Immigration and Asylum Act 2002 should be construed widely and the family unit considered as a whole for Article 8 purposes. In the words of Baroness Hale (at para 4), a narrow approach is not only artificial and impracticable but 'risks missing the central point about family life, which is that the whole is greater than the sum of its individual parts'.

The difference that the judgment in *Beoku-Betts* might make was highlighted in *obiter dicta* of Baroness Hale in a subsequent House of Lords decision *AS (Somalia) v SSHD* [2009] UKHL 32. The case concerned two war orphans from Somalia whose care was undertaken by the sponsor's mother and, after she died, the sponsor and then, following forcible separation, the sponsor's mother-in-law. When the sponsor was granted refugee status in the UK, the two children and the sponsor's natural daughter applied for entry. The natural daughter was admitted but the other two children had no right of entry under the Immigration Rules and their Article 8 claims, heard before *Huang* and *Beoku-Betts*, failed. Baroness Hale commented, at para 26, that, had the totality of family life enjoyed by the sponsor and all three of the children been looked at in the round, the initial decision might have been different.

Just how family life is more than the sum of its parts is illustrated by the Court of Appeal decision in *ZB v SSHD* [2009] EWCA Civ 834. Here, the applicant's husband, eight adult children, and 19 grandchildren lived and were settled in the UK. The AIT considered that she could not show sufficient family life with any single member of the family (she had voluntarily lived apart from her husband for substantial periods of the marriage). The Court of Appeal found that this failed to consider family life as a whole rather than as a series of disconnected segments.

If there is a failure to respect family life, the question moves on to whether the interference is necessary in a democratic society for a reason permitted in Article 8(2).

8.4.4 Living together abroad

An important issue is whether the family can continue its family life by living together abroad. The issue often arises in removal cases where one party has established a family life in the UK without having the appropriate leave or any leave at all and this is discussed more fully in chapter 5. It may also arise when parties make an entry clearance application but, for whatever reason, are unable to meet the requirements of the Immigration Rules. If it is found that the family can satisfactorily be reunited abroad, there is no breach of Article 8. Thus, the ECtHR found in *Abdulaziz* that there were no obstacles to establishing family life elsewhere or 'special reasons why that could not be expected of them' (*Abdulaziz* para 68). More recent ECtHR cases on refusal of admission weigh the factors which indicate whether the family could live together elsewhere and regard this as an important question but not necessarily critical (see, for instance, *Gul v Switzerland* (1996) 22 EHRR 93, *Ahmut v Netherlands* (1996) 24 EHRR 62, *Sen v Netherlands* (2003) 36 EHRR 7, and *Jeunesse v The Netherlands* (Application no. 12738/10)). The issue has been confused by the use in certain ECtHR cases of the term 'insurmountable obstacles' to living abroad. The phrase was used by Lord Phillips in *R (on the application of Mahmood) v Home Secretary* [2001] 1 WLR 840 and was subsequently deployed to establish an unnecessarily high hurdle in Article 8 cases without a full appreciation of the term's meaning in the context in which it had been used.

After some years in which many Article 8 cases failed because there were not found to be 'insurmountable obstacles' to the family living abroad, the question received much needed clarification. The proper approach was identified in *Huang and Kashmiri v SSHD* [2007] UKHL 11 as a question of whether 'the life of the family cannot reasonably be expected to be enjoyed elsewhere' (para 20). In *EB (Kosovo) v SSHD* [2008] UKHL 41,

Lord Bingham (at para 12) found that it would rarely be proportionate to remove a spouse, where there is a close and genuine bond and the other spouse 'cannot reasonably be expected' to go abroad or the effect would be to sever the relationship between parent and child. In *Muse and others v ECO* [2012] EWCA Civ 10, the Court of Appeal pointed out that deciding if it is reasonable for the UK-based family member to move abroad is not straightforward and 'the harshness of such an expectation is a matter of degree which forms part of an overall evaluation whether or not a decision refusing entry would be disproportionate' (para 34). Despite the wording of Appendix FM, EX.1, this approach may still be followed under the new Rules (*Izuazu (Article 8—new rules)* [2013] UKUT 00045 (IAC) (paras 67 and 68)), although the effect that the 'public interest' considerations in s 117B Nationality, Asylum and Immigration Act 2002 may have on this issue are not yet clear.

8.4.5 Removal to make an entry clearance application

For a long period, government policy was to regard the removal of adult relatives as proportionate because there is the opportunity to apply for entry from abroad and the entry clearance officer must take Article 8 considerations into account. In this way, those who were not entitled to be in the UK or to switch status were said not to gain an unfair advantage over those who apply from abroad and wait their turn. The numbers affected by this approach increased after 2002, when those present without leave or on short-term leave were banned from switching into marriage.

This policy was problematic, however, as even temporary removal often risks destabilizing family life and financial self-sufficiency (which might jeopardize the outcome of the entry clearance application). In *LH (Truly exceptional—Ekinci applied) Jamaica* [2006] UKIAT 00019, for example, the applicant's child was disabled and the mother was unable to cope alone. The applicant would lose his job as a result of removal, putting the family onto benefits. Nonetheless, he had to return to Jamaica to make an entry clearance application.

These problems were exacerbated where removal was to a country that was unstable and might not even have entry clearance facilities. For instance, in *HC (Availability of Entry Clearance Facilities) Iraq* [2004] UKIAT 00154, it was considered reasonable for the applicant to return to Iraq (shortly after the Second Gulf War), obtain travel documents, negotiate Jordanian border controls, and endure the cost and danger of travelling from Iraq to Jordan to make a visa application.

After much litigation on the question, the House of Lords considered the question in *Chikwamba v SSHD* [2008] UKHL 40. The case involved a failed asylum seeker from Zimbabwe. Removals to Zimbabwe had been suspended and she was not returned. She married a Zimbabwean refugee and had a child. Once removals were reinstated, the Secretary of State sought her removal, arguing that she could apply for entry clearance from Zimbabwe. The House of Lords upheld an appeal against that decision and judgments were given in unusually frank terms. Lord Scott (at paras 3–4) expressed astonishment that the case had come this far and said that:

policies that involve people cannot be, and should not be allowed to become rigid inflexible rules. The bureaucracy of which Kafka wrote cannot be allowed to take root in this country and the courts must see that it does not.

Lord Brown (at paras 39–42) was sceptical about the government's argument that the policy was necessary to prevent applicants 'jumping' the entry clearance queue, suggesting (at para 41) that the 'real rationale' of the policy was 'the rather different one of deterring people from coming to this country in the first place without having obtained entry clearance and to do so by subjecting those who do come to the very substantial disruption of their lives involved in returning them abroad'. He found (at para 44) that:

only comparatively rarely, certainly in family cases involving children, should an article 8 appeal be dismissed on the basis that it would be proportionate for the appellant to apply for leave from abroad.

Requiring applicants to leave and reapply for entry clearance is not always disproportionate, but all the relevant circumstances of the case must be taken into account (see para 42). Not of relevance, however, is the likelihood that an entry clearance application will succeed or fail (para 36).

Chikwamba was an important case and alleviated the difficulties of many applicants with families. It is consistent with the approach taken in *Beoku-Betts* promulgated on the same day and discussed earlier. However, their Lordships distinguished the situation of the appellant in *Chikwamba* from those in previous authorities, notably *R (on the application of Ekinci) v SSHD* [2003] EWCA Civ 765. While the appellant in *Ekinci* had a child, he was also described as having 'an appalling immigration history' (para 30) and he would only be required to travel to Germany and wait a month for a visa. *Chikwamba* does not assist every migrant who wishes to have their spouse claim decided in-country, although the Court of Appeal, in *MA (Pakistan) v SSHD* [2009] EWCA Civ 953, observed that the principle in the case is not confined to cases where children are involved and the Upper Tribunal in *Hayat (nature of Chikwamba principle) Pakistan* [2011] UKUT 00444 (IAC) found that it need not involve a relationship with a UK-settled party. Whether a case falls outside the scope of *Chikwamba* is a question that must be determined on a case by case basis. Home Office policy after *Chikwamba* states that '[r]eturning an applicant to his/her home country in order to make an entry clearance application may still be proportionate in a small number of cases. All cases must therefore be considered on their own merits.'

In his lead judgment in *Chikwamba*, Lord Brown (at para 43) indicated factors to consider when deciding if return is proportionate. These included the immigration history, the length of time needed to process the application, the disruption to the family, delay by the government in dealing with the applicant's case while in the UK, and whether the ECO abroad is better placed than the UK authorities to investigate the claim. *R (on the application of Kotecha and Das) v SSHD* [2011] EWHC 2070 (Admin) illustrates where the line may be drawn. Mr Kotecha was an overstayer from Tanzania working in the UK, having originally been granted leave as a student. He married a British woman who studied and worked but there were no children. An entry clearance application would take only one month to decide and it was found that the parties could either go together to Tanzania or accept a short separation. The claim failed, the judge being uncertain whether Article 8(1) was even engaged in these circumstances.

By contrast, Mrs Das' claim succeeded. She was a Bangladeshi national who entered with her husband and infant son. Her husband died and she remained in the UK, assisted by her husband's brother, who had indefinite leave and with whom she first had a child and then married some two years after her first husband's death by which point, she had overstayed. Her new husband's job and connections were in the UK and her eldest child was at school. Making an entry clearance application would take between one and four months. Given her childcare responsibilities and her husband's employment, it was not realistic for the family to travel to Bangladesh nor for her to go alone and requiring her return would be disproportionate.

A drawback of succeeding in a *Chikwamba*-type case is that an applicant, even one who meets all the requirements for entry clearance save that of valid leave, may receive leave under the new rules for a period of 30 months, under which an entitlement to indefinite leave arises only after ten years compared to five years under a spouse visa. A claim for judicial review on this point on the previous rules failed (*R (on the application of Abdelghani) v SSHD* [2010] EWHC 1227 (Admin)).

8.5 Maintenance and accommodation

The Immigration Rules require that all family member applicants must show that they will have financial support to a standard laid down in the rules. The pre-2012 rules required that applicants would be adequately maintained and accommodated without recourse to public funds. This was a question of judgment and is still retained in some of the present rules. Many of the post-2012 rules include specific financial requirements which no longer entail judgments as to whether income is adequate. The maintenance requirement aims to protect the public purse and prevent migrants and their families falling into extreme poverty. Its application, however, has caused considerable controversy.

8.5.1 Maintenance

For cases post July 2012 involving partners (spouse, fiancé(e), unmarried, or same-sex partner) and children of parents with limited leave, controversial financial requirements have been introduced, which will be discussed later in this section. For cases prior to July 2012, the wording of the maintenance requirements in Part 8 of the Rules was slightly different for each type of family member. For spouses and allied categories, the requirement in para 281 was that 'the parties will be able to maintain themselves and any dependents adequately without recourse to public funds'. Under para 297(v), children 'can, and will, be maintained adequately by the parent, parents or relative the child is seeking to join without recourse to public funds'. For adult dependent relatives, the criterion was that the applicant 'can, and will, be maintained adequately, together with any dependents, without recourse to public funds' (para 317(iva)). The possible differences of meaning of these various formulations, together with the different contexts in which each appears, caused considerable difficulty, which was clarified by the Supreme Court in *AM (Somalia) and others v ECO* [2009] UKSC 16. For cases post July 2012, Part 8 of the Rules must be read in conjunction with Appendices FM and FM-SE (discussed later in this chapter).

The essence of both the old and new rules is that the family's financial position must be sufficiently strong to avoid the need to claim the state benefits found in para 6 of the Immigration Rules (although recent migrants are anyway ineligible for most of them). In *Konstatinov v Netherlands* (Application no. 16351/03), the ECtHR said that there was no objection in principle to rules that require a minimum level of income sufficient to meet the basic costs of subsistence of family members (para 50). The list of public funds in para 6 includes virtually all means-tested and disability benefits, apart from emergency provision, including child benefit and housing support. National Health Service (NHS) treatment and state education are not classified as public funds. However, health care for migrants is a controversial issue and the Family Migration Consultation suggested requiring future family migrants to obtain medical insurance before entry, which would, at best, impose a heavy additional financial burden and, at worst, exclude the elderly and infirm who may be uninsurable. This was not implemented but from 6 April 2015, all nationals from outside of Europe coming to live in the UK for longer than six months are required to pay a 'health surcharge' in order to gain access to the NHS.

'Recourse to public funds' means recourse to additional public funds over and above those to which the sponsor is already entitled (para 6A). The fact that a new claim might be made in future is not an issue. The test is whether maintenance would be adequate without a claim.

8.5.1.1 Financial support

Prior to July 2012, the question of adequacy focused on whether the admission of the spouse gave rise to the risk of additional public funds being required and the answer to this question turned on the particular facts of the case. Adequacy was treated as an objective standard even if some families could live more frugally *(KA (Pakistan)* [2006] UKAIT 00065 para 6). In determining adequacy, the yardstick was income support together with passport benefits (such as housing benefit, council tax benefit, and free school meals and prescriptions; *KA (Pakistan)* [2006] UKAIT 00065, approved by the Court of Appeal in *AM (Somalia) and others v ECO* [2008] EWCA Civ 1082 at para 79). It was not necessary to show there was sufficient money for an indefinite period *(Ishtiaq Ali* (11568)) and savings could be taken into account in deciding whether maintenance was adequate *(Jahangra Begum and others (maintenance—savings) Bangladesh* [2011] UKUT 00246 (IAC)).

The Family Migration Consultation of July 2011 argued that too many family migrants were reliant on the low wages of their sponsor and risked needing welfare support. As a consequence of the Consultation, sponsors, save those in receipt of certain disability benefits, must now demonstrate a minimum gross annual income of £18,600 (more where there are dependent children). This can be evidenced through employment, non-employment income, and/or cash savings. However, if savings are relied upon to meet a shortfall in income, they must amount to 2.5 times the shortfall over and above a £16,000 threshold. Neither the foreign spouse's overseas employment income nor any prospective income from a job offer in the UK can be taken into account.

The government's own figures, prior to the implementation of the new rules, predicted that 45 per cent of applicants eligible under the old rules would be excluded by the new financial provisions. This was considered a conservative estimate in research on the potential effects of the rules by both the Oxford University Migration Observatory and the Joint Council for the Welfare of Immigrants, which highlighted the devastating impact of these provisions on the young and the less wealthy. That these worrying predictions were correct can be seen in the response to a freedom of information request (Reference 26625, 24 April 2013) by Colin Yeo of the Free Movement Blog. This showed that, in the 6 months since the introduction of the new rules, there was a significant reduction in the number of visas issued (78.3 per cent generally and 83.6 per cent where the sponsor is likely to be female) compared to the previous period.

The new maintenance requirements under Appendix FM were considered in some detail by the High Court in *MM v SSHD* [2013] EWHC 1900 (Admin). The Court, whilst refusing to strike down the Rules, noted that they represented 'a radical departure from the norm in the European Union based on the Family Reunion Directive' (para 145). Mr Justice Blake stated that:

to set the figure significantly higher than even the £13,400 gross annual wage effectively denies young people and many thousands of low wage earners in full time employment the ability to be joined by their non EEA spouses from abroad unless they happen to have wealthy relatives or to have won the lottery. (para 126)

The Court further held that the earnings threshold could be considered disproportionate if combined with any of the other four requirements in the rules, for example, an inability to supplement a shortfall in income with savings unless the savings were over £16,000, and urged the Home Secretary to adjust them. Mr Justice Blake suggested a variety of less intrusive responses that could be taken by the Secretary of State when assessing adequacy, such as reducing the minimum income required of the sponsor alone to £13,400, permitting account to be taken of the earning capacity of the spouse after entry or the maintenance undertakings of third parties, and reducing to 12 months the period for which the pre-estimate of financial viability is assessed (para 147).

The Secretary of State was granted permission to appeal and decisions where the minimum income requirement had not been met were put on hold.

 **Key Case**

MM v SSHD (2014) EWCA Civ 985

On 11 July 2014, the Court of Appeal overturned the High Court's decision following an appeal by the Home Secretary. The general tenor of the decision indicates an unwillingness to interfere with government decisions and contrasts markedly with an increasing engagement of the Supreme Court in questions involving the respect for family life of migrants (see *Baiai* [2008] UKHL 53 and *Quila* [2011] UKSC 45). Essentially, the Court of Appeal held that the requirements are lawful and refused to analyse the basis of the Secretary of State's decision to introduce the requirements into the Immigration Rules as they are merely statements of administrative policy.

Lord Justice Aikens commented that the right to marry and found a family in the UK is not an absolute right (para 137). He accepted that the minimum income threshold is a very significant interference with the right to family life but considered it justified in public law terms (paras 138, 156). Unfortunately, in reaching its decision, the court seemed to pay little heed to the detailed evidence presented by claimants' lawyers and set out in the High Court judgment. Instead, the judgment followed a line of reasoning it has adopted in other recent immigration decisions (see *Bibi* [2013] EWCA Civ 322) stating that it was enough that the Secretary of State should have a rational belief that the requirements will achieve an identified aim.

The policy aim here was to safeguard the economic well-being of the country and to facilitate social integration of new arrivals. During the hearing, the Home Office pursued the questionable argument that the rich will integrate into society better than the poor. This position was not scrutinized by the Court of Appeal. Lord Justice Aikens commented that such a belief is not susceptible of empirical proof, but that a belief in the link between higher income and the likelihood of better integration is rational and so the judgment of the Secretary of State 'cannot be impugned' (para 150). The case has been appealed further and is now due to be heard by the Supreme Court in early 2016.

Colin Yeo has argued that an analogy ought to be drawn between the minimum age for sponsorship and minimum income (Free Movement, 11 July 2014). In *Quila*, the Supreme Court held that an increase in the minimum age for sponsorship from 18 to 21 was unlawful. Yeo argues that income for some people is as immutable as age and so the same principles ought to apply. Many people on the national minimum wage, however many hours they work, simply cannot achieve the required income level and will never be able to change this.

Reports from the Children's Commissioner, the All-Party Parliamentary Group on Migration (APPG) and JCWI have clearly evidenced the significant effect that the new rules have had on the number of family members who can meet the conditions of entry and that the rules have disproportionately impacted the less wealthy, young families and children within divided families. Further, as Wray has argued and the reports demonstrate, they are also likely to fail in their main aim of preventing welfare dependency, as a single person is more likely to claim benefits than a couple, where both are able to seek work and contribute to the family finances (Wray 2013b). A wider question is whether such a policy ought to have been adopted at all, given that it ignores the reality of relationships in a modern globalized world. In June 2013, a report by members of the APPG on Migration called for an independent review of the requirement and its impact. A 2015 comparison of immigration policies across 38 developed states concluded that the UK's immigration policies are the least 'family-friendly', in part due to the financial requirement (2015 Migrant Integration Policy Index).

8.5.1.2 Disabled sponsor

Some disabled sponsors receive additional benefits because of their greater needs and it has often been argued that these can be used to support a spouse (who might also perform caring duties that would otherwise be performed, for pay, by others). Tribunal cases had been inconsistent but the Court of Appeal, in *MK Somalia* [2007] EWCA Civ 1521, found by a majority that the sponsor could use the benefit in question (disability living allowance) howsoever she chose, including to maintain a spouse. Pill LJ, dissenting, feared that disabled sponsors might, as a result, be placed under pressure to use their funds in this way (at para 15), perhaps reflecting concerns that have been expressed elsewhere about the exploitation of disabled sponsors in international marriages. Although it was not an issue in *Mahad*, Lord Brown noted the finding and seemed to suggest, as would be logical, that it was not confined to spouse applications.

The decision in *MK Somalia* assists those disabled sponsors who can save out of their additional benefits. However, the Tribunal suggested in *NM (Disability Discrimination) Iraq* [2008] UKAIT 00026 that this will arise only occasionally. Disabled individuals will often find it difficult to meet the maintenance requirement due to their weak financial position, which may continue for all their lives so that they are indefinitely precluded from sponsorship. However, the Tribunal in *NM* did not consider that this disadvantage amounted to unlawful discrimination either under the Disability Discrimination Act 1995 or Article 14 ECHR. The Court of Appeal came to the same conclusion, after detailed consideration, on Article 14 (the DDA point not being argued) in *AM (Somalia) v ECO* [2009] EWCA Civ 634. Disabled sponsors are exempt from the new rules and remain subject to the previous maintenance requirements (Appendix FM E-ECP 3.3).

8.5.1.3 Third-party maintenance

One of the major questions concerning maintenance has been whether the applicant must be supported from his or her own resources and those of the sponsor or whether they may rely on support from the wider family or from friends to meet the requirements of the rule.

In 2009, the issue came before the Supreme Court.

Key Case

Mahad and others v ECO [2009] UKSC 16

This case was an appeal by some of the appellants in *AM (Ethiopia)* and the appellant in *AM (Somalia)*, discussed previously, whose disability discrimination claim had been rejected by that Court and who also wished to rely on third party support. The Supreme Court found that, in the words of Lord Kerr, the overall purpose of the maintenance provisions 'is to ensure that there is no resort to public funds by family members entering the United Kingdom . . . If it can be shown that funds are reliably available from a third party, that eventuality is avoided and the purpose of the rules is fulfilled' (para 51).

In his lead judgment, Lord Brown found that all three categories of family member should be treated according to the same principles, despite the differences in wording. The particular wording used in relation to children was stated to be purely a protection measure designed to ensure that children lived with the relatives named in the application. He observed that third-party maintenance was not materially different from nor less reliable or harder to ascertain than other types of support already accepted, such as employment or help with accommodation, and that, unlike passages elsewhere in the rules, a prohibition on such support was not apparent from the wording of the rules. As the rules, as construed by him, already permitted third-party support, it was not necessary to decide whether a construction in accordance with Article 8 was required or whether Article 8 rights should remain the subject of a separate application outside the rules. He also found that it was open to ECOs to ask a third party to become a joint sponsor and give an undertaking.

The decision recognized the plurality of family norms and the mutual support that members of migrant communities and extended families often provide for each other. The decision was strictly *obiter* so far as the maintenance of children is concerned as none of the applications were made under para 297, but the views of their Lordships were unambiguous and appeared to effectively settle the question for all applicants.

The Immigration Directorate Instructions (chapter 8, Annex F, para 5.1) were amended to recognize that third-party support for all relatives was permitted provided that satisfactory evidence is provided, and that joint sponsorship was possible. However, the Family Migration Consultation proposed a review of third-party support and the rules were amended to exclude its application in all cases (Immigration Directorate Instructions chapter 8, Annex FM 1.7, para 4.2). Whilst, as we have already seen, a general challenge to the lawfulness of the new financial provisions has failed in the Court of Appeal (*MM v SSHD* [2014] EWCA Civ 985), the previous decision in the High Court did urge the Secretary of State to reconsider her position in relation to, amongst other things, third-party support. Concerns about this issue have also been raised in reports from the APPG on Migration and the Children's Commissioner.

8.5.2 Accommodation

In addition to financial maintenance, the rules require that new entrants must be accommodated adequately. *Mushtaq* (9342) established a base-line requirement that accommodation is 'adequate' if occupation would not be an offence. This means that it is not statutorily overcrowded according to the standard laid down by the Housing Act 1985 s 326. Reports from independent Environmental Health Officers are often prepared to establish that standards are met and the Family Migration Consultation considered (but has not yet implemented) making such a report obligatory.

Compliance with the overcrowding standard does not in all cases automatically mean that the accommodation is adequate. In *S (Pakistan)* [2004] UKIAT 00006, the Tribunal held that a small terraced house, although it would not be statutorily overcrowded, was not adequate for two adult couples and four small children. There were three bedrooms and a through living-room from which the stairs went up.

HC 395 para 6A applies equally in the case of accommodation. Consequently, the provision of accommodation without recourse to public funds means without additional recourse. In *Rahman* (14257) INLP (1997) vol. 11(4), p. 135, a husband applied to join his wife who lived at her parents' house and was not working. Housing costs were met by housing benefit. The Tribunal held that the question it had to consider was whether there would be any additional claim as a consequence of his arrival. As there would not, his appeal was allowed on the accommodation issue.

The accommodation must be owned or occupied exclusively by the parties. Ownership may be of any form of legal interest in land, freehold or leasehold. Occupation must be by virtue of some legal right to occupy, but this can be as a licensee or a lodger. The requirement to own or occupy exclusively was introduced into the Immigration Rules in 1994. There was concern that it would discriminate against people living as an extended family. A letter from Nicholas Baker MP, Minister of State for the Home Office, to Giles Shaw MP in October 1994 said that:

Arrangements whereby the applicant joins his or her married partner in an established household with other residents are . . . acceptable providing . . . the applicant and their married partner have at least a small unit of accommodation e.g. a bedroom for their exclusive use.

The Immigration Directorate Instructions reflect the correct position but the presence of the word 'exclusively' may still cause difficulty, as shown in *KJ ('Own or occupy exclusively') Jamaica* [2008] UKAIT 00006. Here, the applicant lived with his girlfriend and her son in a two-bedroom flat of which she was the tenant. There was no overcrowding even if his own son, with whom he did not live, stayed overnight. However, the application was refused by the Home Office because it could not be said that the applicant had 'exclusive' occupation of any part of the property. The Tribunal disagreed and declined to give the word a technical legal meaning, finding it to mean that:

there is somewhere that the person or people in question can properly, albeit without any legal accuracy, describe as their own home.

As long as this condition is met and satisfactory evidence is provided, it is not necessary that the parties pay a market rent; third-party assistance with accommodation is permitted (*AB (Third party provision of accommodation)* [2008] UKAIT 00018), a position approved by the Supreme Court in *Mahad*.

8.6 Immigration rules for married partners

When the Civil Partnership Act 2004 was implemented in December 2005, the Immigration Rules on married partners were amended to include civil partners, and the rules are now the same for the two groups. The terms 'married partner' or 'spouse' are used here to include both groups.

Anyone who is subject to immigration control (i.e., is not an EEA national and does not have right of abode) who wants to enter the UK as the married partner of someone settled here, must obtain prior entry clearance even if they do not come from a visa national country. The requirements are set out in Appendix FM of the current Immigration Rules. Entry clearance obtained as a married partner will also operate as leave to enter providing its duration and any conditions are endorsed on it (Immigration (Leave to Enter and Remain) Order 2000, SI 2000/1161).

Most of the requirements to obtain leave as a married partner are the same, whether the applicant is applying for entry clearance from abroad or is already in the UK in another capacity. Therefore, case law on a leave to remain case may sometimes be used to illustrate the same point on leave to enter.

8.6.1 Present and settled sponsor

The first requirement is that 'the applicant is married to a person present and settled in the UK or who is on the same occasion being admitted for settlement'. This person is referred to as the 'sponsor'. Paragraph 6 of the rules provides that 'sponsor' means:

the person in relation to whom an applicant is seeking leave to enter or remain as their spouse, fiancé, civil partner, proposed civil partner, unmarried partner, same-sex partner or dependent relative.

Appendix FM GEN 1.3(b) says that the sponsor must be 'present and settled or on the same occasion being admitted for settlement'. As discussed in chapter 6, a 'settled' person includes both a person who has acquired indefinite leave to remain under immigration law and one who has a right of abode. Settled immigrants, Commonwealth citizens with right of abode, and British citizens therefore all qualify as sponsors, providing they are settled, that is, are ordinarily resident in the UK (Immigration Act 1971 s 33(2)(A)) or are entering on the same occasion for settlement. The Entry Clearance Guidance (SET 3.4) notes that, strictly speaking, someone with the right of abode is not 'being admitted for settlement' but, where there is the intention to return to the UK to reside, they should be regarded as present and settled. In *Rourke v ECO Pretoria* [2002] UKIAT 05666, the sponsor was regarded as present and settled although he had been living and working abroad since 1992. In *Zarda Begum* [1983] Imm AR 175, the Tribunal took the view that the rule permits an applicant to join a partner ordinarily resident in the UK but not to be installed there while their partner lives elsewhere. This does not prevent a settled person, including a British citizen, from having a home in the UK where their partner lives, and another outside the UK, providing they can be said to be ordinarily resident in their UK home (*AB Bangladesh* [2004] UKIAT 00314). The applicant will normally be awarded leave for 33 months initially and can apply for settlement after five years. Following the Family Migration Consultation, the probationary period of five years now also applies to those who have lived together abroad for at least four years.

8.6.2 That the applicant has passed a test in English speaking and listening from an approved English language test provider

This requirement entered the rules in November 2010. It requires applicants (subject to narrowly drawn exemptions for age, infirmity, and 'exceptional compassionate circumstances') to take and pass an English language speaking and listening test to A1 standard (the lowest level of the Common European Framework of Reference for Languages).

Nationals of countries deemed to be 'majority English speaking' (which includes Canada but not, e.g., Nigeria or Ghana) or where a single test centre is not available, and those with certain higher education qualifications in English, are also exempt.

This apparently simple and undemanding new criterion has proven to be highly problematic in practice. Access to suitable tuition can be a major hurdle for those living in rural areas and some individuals find learning a new language particularly difficult although they do not qualify for exemptions. However, the largest problem has been the small number of approved test providers and the unavailability of tests that only involve speaking and listening. Most tests require literacy in English either to pass the test (as only a combined grade for reading, writing, speaking, and listening is given) or to take it (as literacy skills are needed to take the speaking and listening test, for example, to read a passage aloud or to select multiple choice answers). In addition, the benefits for post-entry integration of requiring proven competence in English at such a low level have not been established. In other European countries where such a test has been implemented, the outcome has been a reduction in the number of spousal migrants (see Groenendijk 2011).

As already mentioned, the compatibility of the test with Articles 8, 12, and 14 ECHR was unsuccessfully challenged in *Bibi*. The Supreme Court found that the rule did not breach Article 8 of the European Convention on Human Rights, but has invited further submissions from the parties on whether the operation of the current guidance is incompatible with Article 8 where compliance with the rule is impracticable.

8.6.3 That the parties have met

The next requirement, that the parties have met, is usually straightforward for married couples. Proxy marriages are valid in some countries (see, e.g., *CB (Validity of marriage: proxy marriage) Brazil* [2008] UKAIT 00080). Muslim marriages may also sometimes take place by proxy, provided there is an offer and acceptance before witnesses (e.g., as in the case of *Akhtar 2166*) but this is relatively rare. The requirement to have met may also affect fiancé(e)s who meet online or enter very traditional arranged marriages.

The requirement to have met was introduced into the rules in 1979 by a newly elected Conservative government, alongside other proposals including the prohibition on the entry of more than one wife to a polygamous marriage, a question discussed further at 8.6.7.2. The proposed changes were so far-reaching that the rules (HC 394) were debated in the House of Commons. The opposition accused the government of equating arranged marriages with marriages of convenience. Alex Lyon MP went on: 'it is intended to hit the genuine arranged marriages of Asian girls, whether or not they were born in this country' (HC Debs 14 November 1979 col 1336). The Home Secretary in his response did not deny that this was the case, but revealed another objective for the rule:

I remember the Hon. Member for Ealing, Southall telling me that in the future it will increasingly be the practice that Asian girls in this country will wish to marry Asian boys in this country. I should have thought that was a position that we should encourage.

HC 394 was challenged in *Abdulaziz, Cabales and Balkandali*, but the ECHR found that the requirement for the parties to have met was not racially discriminatory under Article 14 of the Convention.

Where there has not been a recent meeting, the test in *Meharban v ECO Islamabad* [1989] Imm AR 57 may be applied. In that case, the sponsor and her fiancé had played together as children, but she could not recall his appearance or other characteristics.

His application for entry clearance was refused. The Tribunal found that, while there was no need for the parties to have met each other in the context of marriage or marriage arrangements, they should have an appreciation of each other's appearance or personality. In *Hashmi* (4975), the families found a way to satisfy both the Immigration Rules and their religious tradition. The fiancé and his parents stayed for a few days at the same house as the sponsor and her mother. This was arranged in order to comply with the rule, but, because of religious tradition, they did not speak to each other. The Tribunal accepted that there had been a 'meeting' within the rule.

The Entry Clearance Guidance (SET 3.10) does not refer to *Hashmi* but cites the earlier case of *Jaffer* (4284). Here, the parties had stayed in the same house when the sponsor was 14 and had seen each other from one room to another but had not spoken. They were found not to have met. There is a tension between this case and *Hashmi* and the entry clearance service prefers the more restrictive interpretation.

8.6.4 Intention to live permanently with each other

The parties must show that 'each of the parties intends to live permanently with the other as his or her spouse or civil partner' (Appendix FM E-ECP.2.10). The rule provides an opportunity to test the genuine nature of the marriage. Anxiety about marriages of convenience, or 'sham' or 'bogus' marriages as they have more recently been described, has been a recurrent theme in immigration control, although Wray (2006a) has argued that measures to combat them have often gone much wider, targeting unwanted migrants in genuine marriages. Before considering application of the test of intention to live together therefore, it is worth considering briefly both problems with the concept of a sham marriage and the historical context from which the rule has emerged.

8.6.4.1 What is a sham marriage?

There have been several attempts to define a sham marriage in legislation. Perhaps the clearest has been that used in EU law: a marriage concluded 'with the sole aim of circumventing the rules on entry and residence' (Council Resolution 97/C 382/01 of 4 December 1997). If a marriage has no purpose except to gain admission to another country and the parties do not intend to have a married life, measures to prevent that happening are unobjectionable. However, measures under UK law have often targeted marriages where intentions are more mixed. As Wray (2006a) points out, motives for choosing a spouse may include the social and economic benefits, including immigration, which will flow from the marriage even though the parties fully intend to live together and may be deeply attached.

As a result, there is a substantial grey area where immigration plays a role in decision-making but the relationship is entirely genuine. It includes not only marriages where immigration status is an added inducement but marriages that take place sooner than they otherwise might to secure immigration status and parties to arranged marriages where the families have negotiated the marriage bearing in mind the immigration consequences. Such marriages are far removed from a sham marriage, which may be entered into for money and where the parties have no relationship and no intention to live together yet may easily be caught by measures purporting to prevent only sham marriages as may marriages where there is no immigration motive at all. An example of such broad measures is the 'primary purpose rule', removed from the Immigration Rules in 1997 and discussed in the next section, and the Certificates of Approval scheme discussed later in this chapter and also now abolished.

8.6.4.2 The historical context

Entry through marriage first became a prominent issue in the mid-1960s. After Commonwealth immigration controls were imposed by the Commonwealth Immigrants Act 1962, migrants had to decide whether to return definitively to their country of origin or remain in the UK and bring over their families, as male migrants were entitled to do under the Act. The issue particularly affected South Asian workers who had often left their families behind, envisaging only a temporary sojourn. The result was a large increase in the number of wives and children arriving. Growing hostility to their arrival led to claims of abuse and long queues at airports while their credentials were checked. The problem was eventually exported through the imposition of a compulsory entry clearance system under the Immigration Appeals Act 1969, leading to long delays and a suspicious approach to decision-making on the subcontinent and elsewhere that led to lasting resentment. These applicants often lacked official documentation, such as birth or marriage certificates, to prove their status and there was heavy reliance on the so-called 'discrepancy system', under which different family members were interviewed separately and asked about their lives and homes, sometimes in great detail. If their answers differed, this would be used to cast doubt upon their relationship and applicants were rejected as being 'not related as claimed'. Some years later, DNA testing revealed that most of those who had been refused were telling the truth.

As they reached marriageable age, some young women of migrant origin in the UK entered marriages with men from their country of origin and sought to bring them to the UK. As it was more usual for a wife to move to her husband's place of residence, these marriages were regarded with great suspicion, even though such customs are liable to evolve as circumstances change and this new pattern represented a pragmatic response to a new situation in which the wife's place of residence offered more opportunities. However, the entry of non-white men of working age was seen as unacceptable and, in 1969, the entry of all Commonwealth husbands was banned unless there were 'special features'. The ban proved unpopular as its effects were felt well beyond migrant communities. Following extensive campaigning, it was removed in 1974 and, over the succeeding years, a new tool evolved: the 'primary purpose rule'. This rule required the applicant to prove that 'the marriage was not entered into primarily to gain admission to the UK' (HC 395 para 281 before amendment). Applicants were faced with the difficult task of proving a negative, that any immigration motivation was *not the* primary purpose of the marriage. For those who had entered arranged marriages, this was particularly difficult as the reasons for marriage that are familiar in the West, such as romantic attachment, were often absent at this early stage and marriages were entered into for reasons of family obligation that could easily be presented as driven by emigration. Many thousands of husbands, particularly from South Asia, were refused during the currency of the rule, although, as time went on, some concessions were made for long-lasting marriages.

The primary purpose rule was rarely applied outside South Asia and the Caribbean. Macdonald and Blake said in 1991 that they had 'still to hear of an American, Australian or New Zealander who [had] failed the primary purpose test' (1991:260–1). It is unsurprising that Macdonald later referred to the 'primary purpose' rule as one which 'generated more anger and anguish than perhaps any of the other Immigration Rules' (1995:343).

In accordance with its manifesto commitment, the incoming Labour government removed 'primary purpose' from the Immigration Rules in June 1997. The test of 'intention to live together', which had been present in the rules since 1977 but little used in the era of primary purpose, became the main way of determining whether the marriage is genuine.

8.6.4.3 Applying 'intention to live together'

While the 'primary purpose' rule was criticized for going beyond the detection of sham marriages, the test of 'intention to live together' relies on a major characteristic of most genuine marriages. Most spouses intend to live with each other, although a few couples prefer to maintain separate homes or to spend substantial periods apart. Nonetheless, 'intention to live together' is a test that is designed to fulfil its stated purpose of distinguishing between genuine and sham marriages. Most couples are able to satisfy the test by providing evidence of their relationship or that their marriage conforms to the norms of their culture. There seem to be relatively few refusals on 'intention' alone. Compared to the era of primary purpose, acceptance rates improved and the issue lost much of its heat.

Nonetheless, some problems have been associated with its application, particularly in the Indian subcontinent (see Wray 2006b). Some entry clearance officers have had difficulty understanding the difference between 'primary purpose' and 'intention'. The former is concerned with the motives for the marriage and the latter with the parties' intentions for the future, regardless of the reasons for the marriage. Even if emigration was one or even the major reason for the marriage, if the parties intend to cohabit, the 'intention' test is satisfied, a point made explicitly in the case of *Canas* (20557) INLP vol. 13(3) (1999) p. 109. In *Alaezihe v ECO Dublin* [2002] UKIAT 01168, the Tribunal overturned the adjudicator's decision because he had placed too much reliance on the appellant's adverse immigration history, from which he had gleaned an intention to come to the UK. This, however, was not the question. The appropriate question was, given that the parties were married, whether they had the intention to live together permanently.

The discrepancy approach has also sometimes been inappropriately applied to the requirement to show intention to live together. In *Anju Malik v ECO New Delhi* [2002] UKIAT 00738, the point was made that discrepancies do not have the same significance in an arranged marriage as in a love match, a point also made in the cases of *Sabar Gul v ECO Islamabad* TH/5118/99 and *Choudhury v ECO Dhaka* [2002] UKIAT 00239. In both these cases, the adjudicator had looked for evidence of personal knowledge of each other's circumstances, which should not be expected where the marriage had been arranged and the parties had little prior direct knowledge of each other.

Intention to live together does not require a willingness to cohabit anywhere. It is present even if the parties are willing to cohabit only in the UK (*R (on the application of Olofunisi) v IAT* [2002] EWHC 2106), although the Entry Clearance Guidance (SET 3.6) suggests that the entry clearance service regards this as relevant. A couple may intend to live permanently together even though present circumstances, such as work or family commitments, prevent them from cohabiting all the time, as in *Kumar* (17779) INLP vol. 13(3) p. 109 (1999), *Niksarli* (21663) (INLP vol. 14, no. 2, p. 110), and *Satnam Singh* (19068) INLP vol. 13(2) (1999) p. 78. On the other hand, where a sponsor had, at the time of the marriage, committed an offence leading to a nine-year prison sentence, the Tribunal held that no intention to live together could be formed. An intention is more than a wish (*Shabbana Bibi v ECO Islamabad* [2002] UKIAT 06623).

Past periods of separation are irrelevant if future intention is established. In *Janat Bi* (16929), the couple had lived together for 11 years followed by separation during most of the next 40 years because of the wife's family commitments. Their intention to live together was accepted. In *Barlas* TH/03975/2000, there were four years of separation before the appellant applied to come to the UK. The Tribunal did not see this as counting against intention to live together, particularly in the context of an arranged marriage. However, there are limits to the types of separation that will be countenanced. In *AB Bangladesh* [2004] UKIAT 00314, the Tribunal held that the appellant's intention to live six months of each year with his British wife and the other six months with his wife in Bangladesh could not amount to an intention to live permanently together.

Cohabitation does not require sexual relations but the precise content of 'living together' sometimes seems elusive. In *ZB and HB (Validity and recognition of marriage) Pakistan* [2009] UKAIT 00040, the applicant wished to join her severely disabled spouse. Although the central issue was that of capacity, the Tribunal was not persuaded that intention to live together was present, saying that the requirements of the rule 'are not met simply by a wish to share a house, nor by a wish to look after the sponsor, or a wish to alleviate the care responsibilities imposed upon the sponsor's mother by her relatives' (para 16). Given that the parties had a sex life and a child, it is difficult to pinpoint exactly what the Tribunal required although it seems that the lack of mutual interaction and previous visits was a decisive factor, a finding that is reminiscent of primary purpose with its emphasis on the motivation for the marriage.

Generally, a balanced approach should be taken, looking at the marriage as a whole, not one episode or aspect of it. In *Bryan* (14694) INLP vol. 11(3) (1997), immigration officers apparently caught the sponsor on a bad day. When they called, he expressed his doubts about the appellant, thought she might be having a relationship with another man, that the marriage was just being used to enable her to stay in the UK, and so on. She was not interviewed. The Tribunal allowed her appeal, saying that the question of intention to live together did not turn upon the credibility of what was said or done on a particular day, but on the position in the light of all the evidence. As *Noisaen* and a number of other cases such as *Chowdhury* (16080), *Hanif* (17561) both INLP vol. 12, (4), p. 146 (1998), and *Iqbal* (17293) in June 1999 demonstrate, enquiries into intention should be confined to whether the surrounding circumstances and context of the marriage suggest that intention exists. The fact, for example, that the parties have a house that they intend to live in together is more important than the particular conversations that they have had about the house (*Chowdhury*).

8.6.5 **The marriage is genuine and subsisting**

Appendix FM E-ECP.2.6 also requires that the marriage be genuine and subsisting. In *GA ('subsisting' marriage) Ghana* [2006] UKAIT 00046, the Tribunal treated this as a separate requirement to legal validity and to intention to live together. A subsisting marriage, they said, is one which has some real substance in terms of relationship. This couple had lived apart for 20 years and there was a legal tie, but the marriage was not subsisting. This was a starred decision and the ruling was therefore binding on subsequent tribunals, overturning the earlier view in *BK* [2005] UKAIT 00174 that 'subsisting' only meant the marriage was current in law.

Following the Family Migration Consultation, the government has published, in casework guidance, a list of factors that may be associated with a genuine and non-genuine relationship (IDI Annex FM, section FM 2.0). These include a common account of the 'core facts' of the relationship, a common language, the parties' relative ages, the nature of the wedding celebrations, and the parties' immigration histories. Whilst the guidance states these factors do not constitute a checklist, many genuine marriages may fail under one or more of those headings and there is a danger that such indicators will be used to reinforce pre-existing stereotypes about which migrants engage in bogus marriages, despite suggestions in the guidance that caseworkers should take religious and cultural differences into account (IDI Annex FM 3.0). As Clayton and Wray (2012) have noted, the new guidance will inevitably lead to 'a more intrusive interrogation' into the lives of family members and 'higher expectations of conduct'.

8.6.6 Time when requirements must be met

What happens if an application is refused, but circumstances change so that by the time of the appeal, the rules have been met, for example, through employment or an offer of accommodation? After the Court of Appeal judgment in *R v IAT ex p Kotecha* [1982] Imm AR 88, account could be taken of arrangements which were positively and reasonably foreseeable at the time of the decision. Section 85(5) Nationality, Immigration and Asylum Act 2002 provides that, in entry clearance cases, the Tribunal 'may consider only the circumstances appertaining at the time of the decision to refuse', that is, in existence at the time of the decision to refuse. Therefore, in an entry clearance application, evidence which arises after the date of the decision will not be admissible except to the extent that it sheds light on the situation at the date of the decision. What is not admissible, however, is evidence of a fact necessary for entry when that fact arises only after the decision has been made. In *SF (Afghanistan) v ECO* [2011] EWCA Civ 758, the Court of Appeal found that the applicant could not rely on a job offer made after the decision because there was no evidence put forward at the time of the decision to show that such an offer was at all probable.

The exclusion of post-decision evidence, except when light is shed on the state of affairs at the time of the decision, does not apply to a refusal of an application of leave to remain as a spouse made in-country. In *AS (Somalia) v SSHD* [2009] UKHL 32 at para 9, Lord Phillips considered that the distinction was justified because, in applications made outside the jurisdiction, the entry clearance officer is best placed to make factual judgments. The exception for entry clearance applications was not, in itself, incompatible with Article 8, although there might be particular cases where its effects, in terms of delay and expense, would be disproportionate.

8.6.7 Legal issues concerning marriage and divorce

Applicants must establish a valid marriage, required under the rules by inclusion of the simple phrase in Appendix FM E-ECP.2.7 'is married'. The validity of the marriage is adjudged at the date of the marriage and is established by showing that both parties had the legal capacity to marry and that the celebration took place in accordance with appropriate formalities. The second of these requirements is the more straightforward to apply in law, although there may be practical difficulties in obtaining evidence. If the marriage is properly conducted according to the law of the country in which it is celebrated, its formal validity is accepted in English law (the principle of *lex loci celebrationis*). This means that in a country where same-sex marriage is recognized, a properly conducted same-sex marriage will be recognized for immigration purposes.

The country in which the marriage is celebrated is usually where both parties are physically present. The only exceptions are where the marriage is conducted by telephone or by proxy. The Entry Clearance Guidance says at SET 3.17 that in countries where marriage consists of an offer by a man accepted by a woman, a telephonic marriage is celebrated in the country where the woman is. Therefore, where the wife is resident in the UK and the offer made from overseas, the marriage is considered as having been celebrated in the UK and so not valid in UK law. If the husband is in the UK and the wife in a country where telephone marriages are valid and the formalities are observed, the marriage should be valid. However, the Entry Clearance Guidance and the Immigration Directorate Instructions (IDI) state that a telephone marriage celebrated whilst one of the parties is in the UK is not valid. In *J (Pakistan)* [2003] UKIAT 00167, it was conceded that a telephonic marriage where the man was present and domiciled in the UK was not valid as the law of the UK governed his personal capacity to marry and does not recognize telephonic marriages.

This approach is arguably incorrect. The rules on domicile, which govern these matters, are concerned with capacity to enter the marriage (matters such as age, consanguinity, etc.) and not the form of the marriage. If the marriage is entered in a country where telephone marriages are valid, the location and domicile of the other party should be irrelevant. The current IDI has been amended to state that in such cases, the Home Office 'cannot deny that the marriage is valid' (IDI chapter 8, section FM 1.3, para 3.2). In *KC and NNC v City of Westminster* [2008] EWCA Civ 198, the Court of Appeal accepted a telephone marriage between a man in the UK and a woman in Bangladesh as valid in Bangladesh (although the point was not fully argued). Its non-recognition by the Court was because of the husband's mental incapacity.

Proxy marriage is lawful in some countries and such marriages, provided they are celebrated according to local rules, are valid regardless of the domicile of the parties (*CB (Validity of marriage: proxy marriage) Brazil* [2008] UKAIT 00080). The Tribunal in *CB*, relying on *Apt v Apt* [1947] P 127, found that there was no public policy reason to invalidate proxy marriages. This is acknowledged in IDI chapter 8, section FM 1.3, para 3.1.

Aside from such rare situations, a marriage certificate is normally enough to prove formal validity. In *Babul* (16466), it was held that where a marriage certificate is produced that provides *prima facie* proof of a valid marriage, the party asserting that the marriage is not valid has the burden of proof to a high standard. If a finding is made that the marriage is not valid, this only has a direct effect for immigration purposes. There would need to be a separate declaration under the Family Law Act 1986 to affect the marriage for any purpose other than immigration. The issues which have a greater effect on the recognition of marriages in the UK are the questions of the legal capacity to enter into the marriage in question and the recognition of previous divorces.

8.6.7.1 Capacity

The capacity to marry is determined for each individual separately, and is governed by the law of the country which is their domicile. *Halsbury's Laws* (vol. 8(1) para 680) explains:

A person is domiciled in that country in which he [sic] either has or is deemed by law to have his permanent home. Every individual is regarded as belonging, at every stage in his life, to some community consisting of all persons domiciled in a particular country . . . Although a person may have no permanent home, the law requires him to have a domicile.

Domicile differs from ordinary residence, in that a person may have more than one ordinary residence but not more than one domicile. Domicile may also differ from nationality and the personal civil law which applies to an individual is the law of their domicile. Domicile of origin is acquired at birth and is the domicile of the father for a child born inside marriage and of the mother for a child born outside marriage. *Cramer v Cramer* [1986] Fam Law 333 CA confirms an old rule that there is a strong presumption in favour of retaining one's domicile of origin. A domicile of choice is acquired by residence in a country where one intends to stay permanently. This intention must be proved by objective criteria. Statements of intention will not suffice. The House of Lords in *Mark v Mark* [2005] UKHL 42 held that, if a person's presence is illegal in immigration law, this does not affect their domicile. The House of Lords made the distinction between a status which would give some benefit against the state, when illegality ought not to benefit an individual, and domicile, which is a private law matter and a question of fact. Domicile simply determines which legal system will govern private law matters such as divorce proceedings. The burden of proving that the domicile of origin has been lost rests on the person making the assertion. If they do not succeed in discharging the burden of proof, the domicile remains the domicile of origin.

To say that the law of a person's domicile governs their capacity to marry means that conditions for entering into a marriage, such as age and mental capacity, are according to that country's law. The law of the UK requires that a person must be 16 years old and not married to anyone else in order to enter a valid marriage. Although the age at which someone may sponsor their married partner is now 18 (after rising to 21), this does not prevent the marriage taking place at whatever age is allowed by the law of the parties' domicile. It only means that a married partner cannot enter the UK until both parties are 18.

Domicile is also relevant where one party lacks the capacity to marry under English law but may do so under the law where the marriage is celebrated. The issue has become prominent in the recent past because of a number of marriages between mentally disabled adults resident in the UK and applicants living abroad. From a UK perspective, these marriages may be regarded, in the words of Wall LJ in *KC* as, 'exploitative and indeed abusive' (para 45). Motives may, however, on examination, prove less malign than they first appear, being concerned with procuring long-term care for the relative rather than their abuse, although these marriages are controversial, particularly where they also involve sexual relations.

8.6.7.2 Polygamy

Where a polygamous marriage has been validly entered into in another country, English law does not recognize it as valid where one party to the marriage is domiciled in the UK (Matrimonial Causes Act 1973 s 11(d)). *Hussain v Hussain* [1982] 3 All ER 369 CA found that this applied to the marriages of British women to men domiciled in countries that permitted polygamy and celebrated in that country, as they were potentially polygamous. The Private International Law (Miscellaneous Provisions) Act 1995 s 5 provided that s 11(d) only applies to *actually* polygamous marriages. The effect is that where the practical reality of the marriage is that it is monogamous it will be treated as such by UK law, wherever it is celebrated.

Where a marriage is in fact polygamous, if one of the parties is domiciled in the UK, the marriage is void under s 11(d). If neither party is domiciled in the UK, the validity of the polygamous marriage is recognized if it was recognized in the country where the parties are domiciled. However, para 278 of the Immigration Rules prevents entry clearance being granted to a wife where another wife of the same man has, since her marriage to him, visited the UK or been granted entry clearance or a certificate of entitlement.

8.6.7.3 Recognition of divorce

Because the UK does not recognize polygamy for people domiciled in the UK and does not permit entry of further married partners, entry clearance will be refused where an earlier divorce is not recognized as the person will be regarded as still married to the previous spouse. Religious divorces, such as the Islamic talaq divorce or the Jewish Get, if obtained in the UK, will not be regarded as valid as, within the jurisdiction, divorce may only be granted by a civil court (see, for instance, *ECO Islamabad v Tanzeela Imran* [2002] UKIAT 07383). A divorce obtained partially in the UK and partially abroad is not recognized in the UK even if it follows the formalities of the other country. This is the outcome of the House of Lords decision in *R v SSHD ex p Ghulam Fatima* [1986] AC 527. In that case, a talaq was pronounced in the UK and notice sent to the Union Council in Pakistan. The House of Lords found that it should not be recognized in the UK, a decision that was criticized for prolonging 'limping marriages' where the divorce is recognized in one jurisdiction and not in another.

The law in relation to recognition of divorces obtained entirely in other countries is set out in Family Law Act 1986 ss 44–54. A divorce obtained in a foreign jurisdiction will be recognized if it complies with the legal requirements of the country where it was obtained, if it was obtained by proceedings and if either party was habitually resident, domiciled in, or a national of that country (Family Law Act 1986 s 46(1)).

The majority of divorces obtained abroad, including many talaq divorces, are obtained through proceedings and are capable of recognition under s 46(1). For example, in Bangladesh and most of Pakistan, the Muslim Family Law Ordinance of 1961 requires registration of the talaq with the Union Council. The divorce then becomes effective in civil law after a period allowed for reconciliation. A talaq so registered will be recognized in UK law if the other conditions for recognition are met. This should be distinguished from the situation in *Naseem Akhtar* (15412) INLP vol. 12(1) (1998), p. 30, where there had been ancillary proceedings carried out after a bare talaq. This was not sufficient to convert a bare talaq into a talaq by proceedings.

The Tribunal in *Baig v ECO Islamabad* [2002] UKIAT 04229 laid down guidance as to the proper approach to ascertaining whether a divorce was obtained by proceedings. The Tribunal made an important distinction between tradition and proceedings. The talaq in question in this case was not a bare talaq, but a talaq al-hasan, which entailed formal declarations of divorce at monthly intervals. The appellant argued that this was by way of proceedings as it entailed more ritual and process than a bare talaq. The Tribunal said, however, that talaq al-hasan:

lacks any formality other than the ritual performance. It lacks the invocation or assistance of any organ of the state. It does not even require an organ of the state to act as a registrar or recorder of what has happened. (para 39)

Accordingly, it was regarded as a purely personal act and not a divorce obtained by proceedings. Section 46(2) of the Family Law Act 1986 provides that a divorce obtained otherwise than by means of proceedings may still be recognized if it is effective in the country in which it was obtained, both parties are domiciled in a country which recognizes the divorce, and neither party was habitually resident in the UK for a period of one year prior to the divorce. This assists parties who are relying on a divorce obtained before commencing residence in the UK. For example, in *NC (bare talaq—Indian Muslims recognition) Pakistan* [2009] UKAIT 00016, both parties had previously been divorced using the bare talaq procedure but as both had been domiciled and resident in countries that permitted bare talaq (the Kashmir region of Pakistan and India), the earlier divorces were recognized.

Recognition of marriage and divorce is made even more complex by the prevalence in some countries of customary unofficial ceremonies for which there is little or no paperwork. In the past, the absence of formal documentation was used regularly as a means to divide families who were clearly related. Registration in countries such as India has become more commonplace and the issue has become less prominent. Nonetheless, there are still frequent reports of instances when applicants have had difficulty establishing their entitlement with consequences in terms of delay, expense, and refusal (see Menski 2007; Shah 2011a, 2011b).

Where written evidence of a customary marriage or divorce is not available, evidence may be provided by a statutory declaration or affidavit from family members or others able to confirm that the ceremony took place. There is no obligation to register a ceremony if to do so is optional under local law (*NA (Customary marriage and divorce—evidence) Ghana* [2009] UKAIT 00009). The Entry Clearance Guidance provides that evidence of a marriage may also be obtained through separate interview of the parties (SET 3.15).

If a person is not free to marry another, their application to enter as a married partner cannot be treated as an application to enter as a fiancé(e) and granted on that basis (*ECO Islamabad v Mohammad Rafiq Khan 01/TH 2798 and ECO Islamabad v Shakeel* [2002] UKIAT 00605).

8.6.8 Leave to enter and the probationary period

Under the new rules, the criteria discussed in the previous section (relationship requirements) are known as eligibility criteria. Each new rule also contains 'suitability' criteria. These largely replace the general grounds for refusal (discussed in chapter 6) and must be met at the same time as the eligibility requirements. If all these conditions are met, together with those relating to maintenance and accommodation, a married partner is given leave to enter the UK for up to 33 months.

Following the Family Migration Consultation, the spouse probationary period has been extended from two years to five years with a prohibition on receiving means-tested benefits for the whole of that period. The effect of this is that couples must maintain not only their relationship but their economic independence, accommodation etc. for a much longer period than previously. Where a marriage breaks down or jobs or homes are lost before the five years have expired, the migrant spouse would become liable to removal. A likely outcome, particularly where there are children, will be an increase in claims under Article 8 ECHR.

8.6.8.1 Indefinite leave to remain

Shortly before the end of the five-year period, the married partner may apply for indefinite leave to remain if they continue to meet the requirements of the rules as to maintenance and accommodation, valid and subsisting marriage, intention to live together, have passed the knowledge of life and language in the UK test, have English speaking and listening skills at level B1 or above and do not have any unspent convictions (Appendix FM and Appendix KoLL).

Appendix FM requires the applicant to have received leave as the spouse of the party upon whom the indefinite leave application is based and to have lived in the UK for five years.

Once indefinite leave is granted, the married partner from abroad is free of immigration restrictions on their stay, may claim benefits, and may come and go freely, subject to the requirements of para 18 of the rules (see chapter 6). After three years' residence as a married partner, they may apply to become a British citizen (British Nationality Act 1981 s 6 and Sch 1, amended by Civil Partnership Act 2004 Sch 27 para 72), but until they acquire that citizenship, the married partner with indefinite leave remains liable to deportation and may lose their status if they leave the UK for a period of two years (see chapters 3 and 6 on naturalization and settlement).

8.6.8.2 Leave to remain as a married partner

As mentioned earlier, a person with limited leave under some other categories of the Immigration Rules may apply in the UK to stay as a married partner (Appendix FM, section R-LTRP). Rules as to accommodation and maintenance, the marriage, and so on, apply as for an application for entry clearance and the applicant must not have remained in breach of immigration laws. The 2002 White Paper, *Secure Borders, Safe Haven* (Cm 5387), argued that many marriages entered into by people who had been in the UK for less than six months were not genuine (para 7.11). Consequent rule changes ended the possibility of extending leave to stay as a married partner for those granted six months' leave or less. Where a person who is not eligible to switch into marriage wishes to remain on that basis, their application may be considered in accordance with Article 8 ECHR.

An applicant for an extension of stay as a married partner will be granted leave for 30 months in the first instance, placing them on a similar footing to a married partner who comes directly from abroad and they will be subject to conditions as to public funds.

8.6.9 Domestic violence and bereavement

On the basis of the rules discussed so far, a married partner has no claim to remain if the marriage breaks down or their partner dies during the first five years. This caused particular anguish to those bereaved and serious problems for those who suffer violence from their spouse during the probationary period. The latter group could not remain safely in their marriage but might feel unable to leave, particularly if return to their country of origin was financially or socially impossible.

Under Appendix FM, section BPILR, the bereaved may obtain indefinite leave if the relationship was still in existence at the time of death. Appendix FM, section DVILR of the Immigration Rules provides for indefinite leave for victims of domestic violence under certain conditions. It applies to those who have entered or been given leave as a spouse, civil partner, or as an unmarried or same-sex partner but not, the Tribunal has found, to partners granted discretionary leave outside the Immigration Rules (*Guzman Barrios (domestic violence—DLR—Article 14 ECHR) Columbia* [2011] UKUT 00352 (IAC)). The relationship must have broken down permanently as a result of domestic violence before the expiry of limited leave. Violence is not confined to physical violence but includes '[a]ny incident of controlling, coercive or threatening behavior, violence or abuse (psychological, physical, sexual, financial or emotional)' (Modernised Guidance 'Victims of Domestic Violence', p. 9) although a certain minimum threshold of seriousness must be crossed (*AN (Pakistan) v SSHD* [2010] EWCA Civ 757). While the Guidance sets out the kinds of evidence required to prove domestic violence, that cannot be taken to limit the discretion implicit in the rule to admit whatever evidence the decision-maker thinks fit (*AI (Pakistan) v SSHD* [2007] EWCA Civ 386).

The violence must cause the relationship to break down before the probationary period expires and the rule cannot not be used to remedy overstaying (*IN (domestic violence IDI policy)* [2007] UKAIT 00024). However, a domestic violence sufferer may lose track of time or may be prevented from applying for indefinite leave as part of the abuse. Cultural factors also inhibit some victims from coming forward when the violence first occurs. The Modernised Guidance does envisage that out-of-time applications may be made (p. 17) but the violence must have caused the breakdown before the end of the probationary period, and that can be difficult to establish retrospectively. In *IN*, the wife told her GP that she did not report the violence before 'because of the Asian culture'. While there was evidence of earlier abuse, her attempts at reconciliation meant that she could not show that the marriage had ended during the probationary period.

The violence does not have to be the immediate or the only cause of the breakdown (*R (on the application of B) v SSHD* [2002] EWCA Civ 1797; *AG (India) v SSHD* [2007] EWCA

Civ 1534). The Tribunal in *LA (Pakistan) v SSHD* [2009] UKAIT 00019 sensibly pointed out that, while a relationship usually ends at the moment one or both parties declare an intention to leave, the cause of the breakdown, here the 'boorish conduct' of the husband over an extended period, can only be assessed by looking at the relationship as a whole.

8.7 Restricting the right to marry

Section 24 of the Immigration and Asylum Act 1999 imposed a duty on marriage registrars to report to the Secretary of State any marriage which they have reasonable grounds for suspecting is a 'sham marriage'. A 'sham marriage' is defined in s 24(5) as amended by Part 4 of the Immigration Act 2014 as one entered into by a person who is neither a British Citizen nor a national of an EEA state, there is no genuine relationship between the parties to the marriage, and either or both of the parties enter into the marriage for one or more of these purposes: avoiding the effect of one or more provisions of the UK immigration law or rules and/or enabling a party to the marriage to obtain a right conferred by that law or those rules to reside in the UK.

The number of reports by registrars under the 1999 Act rose from 756 in 2001 to 2,712 in 2003, and 2,251 in just the first half of 2004 (Hansard 15 June 2004 col 681). This rise, which may have been due to increased incidence or increased reporting, was cited in support of the 'Certificates of Approval' scheme introduced under ss 19–25 Asylum and Immigration (Treatment of Claimants, etc.) Act 2004 (AITOCA).

AITOCA s 20 requires those subject to immigration control and who wish to marry outside the Church of England to give notice of their marriage in specified form to designated registrars. Section 25 formerly provided that the registrar could enter the marriage in the marriage notice book (necessary for the marriage to proceed) only if the party or parties subject to immigration control had entry clearance for the purpose of marriage (i.e., a fiancé(e) or marriage visitor visa), written permission of the Secretary of State to marry, or belonged to a class exempted from the Act by the Secretary of State.

Implementation of s 25 was highly controversial. All those subject to immigration control but without indefinite leave or a fiancé(e) or marriage visit visa had to apply for a certificate of approval to marry, costing £135 later raised to £295. Those on short-term leave, without leave, or whose leave would shortly expire were refused unless compassionate circumstances (narrowly defined) were present. Given the blanket ban and the discrimination in favour of Church of England marriages, legal challenge was inevitable. The government was defeated in the High Court, the Court of Appeal, and, finally, the House of Lords.

Key Case

R (on the application of Baiai and others) v SSHD **[2008] UKHL 53**

The applicants in this case all wished to marry but at least one of the parties in each relationship needed a certificate of approval to do so. These had initially been refused because of their immigration status. The genuine nature of the relationships had not been challenged. The House of Lords found that the right to marry under Article 12 was a strong right, which could be regulated by national law but could not be subject to conditions that impaired the essence of the right. While governments could impose conditions on the marriages of foreign nationals in order to ascertain whether there was a marriage of convenience, the scheme as implemented breached Article 12 ECHR (the right to marry) because of its broad and over-inclusive nature. The fee of £295 for each party needing a certificate could also be expected to 'impair the essence' of the right to marry. These were matters determined by regulations and guidance and did not affect the compatibility of the statute with Convention rights. The statutory scheme itself was discriminatory only because of the exemption for marriages in the Church of England. The government having accepted this conclusion, the declaration of incompatibility was set aside.

The effect of the judgment was that the government could still require foreign nationals to obtain permission from the government before getting married but those marrying in the Church of England must not be treated differently, the cost of the application must be reasonable, and permission must not be refused on the basis of immigration status alone.

In addition to the *Baiai* judgments, the scheme was found to breach Articles 12 and 14 ECHR by the European Court of Human Rights in *O'Donoghue and others v UK* (Application no. 34848/07 [2010] ECHR 2022). The Court was particularly critical of the blanket nature of the scheme based purely on immigration status, the fee, and of the exemption for Church of England marriages.

After the *Baiai* judgment the scheme was eventually abandoned. However, the Government returned to this area in Part 4 of the Immigration Act 2014, which came into effect on 2 March 2015. Under the Act, notice of *all* marriages in England and Wales has doubled from 15 to 28 days. Further, where one of the parties to the marriage is a non-EEA national marrying in the Church of England, the parties need to undertake civil preliminaries and will no longer be able to use Banns instead. Where one of the parties is a non EEA national, both parties to a marriage will need to attend in person to give notice at a designated Registry Office and for notice to be taken specified evidence, including specified evidence of nationality, must be provided. Where one of the parties is a non EEA national and might gain 'immigration advantage', the notice of marriage must be referred to the Home Office. In addition, if the registrar has reasonable grounds for suspecting that the marriage will be a sham marriage as defined in s 24 (5) Immigration and Asylum Act 1999 then a s 24 notice is also sent to the Home Office.

If the Home Office decides not to investigate then the Home Office should inform the registrar and the marriage can proceed after the conclusion of the normal 28-day notice period. If the Home Office does decide to investigate further, then the notice period is extended to 70 days to allow time for the investigation. The Home Office may prevent the marriage taking place where the parties fail to cooperate with the investigation. Risk factors are said by the Home Office to be where a party to a marriage:

- is of a nationality at high risk of involvement in a sham, on the basis of objective information and intelligence about sham cases;
- holds a visa in a category linked by objective information and intelligence to sham cases;
- has no immigration status or holds leave which is due to expire shortly.
- has had an application to remain in the UK refused;
- has previously sponsored another spouse or partner to enter or remain in the UK;

- his or has been the subject of a credible s 24/24A report, which explains, for example, how the couple could not communicate in a common language and did not know basic information about each other.

The effect of these rules would seem to be that it is likely that the Secretary of State may become more involved at an earlier stage in proposed marriages where one party is not exempt and that couples may face increasing scrutiny of their relationship prior to the marriage. There is no statutory definition of the meaning of 'genuine' in the new definition of sham marriage and it would seem that the Home Office will be guided by their policy on genuine and subsisting relationships (Annex FM, Section FM 2.0).

8.8 Forced marriages

Forced marriages have become a prominent issue in the recent past, with many government initiatives aimed at protecting victims. The issue of forced marriage goes far beyond immigration but the discussion here is confined to how forced marriages are treated in immigration law.

The Forced Marriage Unit was created by the Home Office and Foreign and Commonwealth Office in 2005 and operates out of the Foreign and Commonwealth Office. It also has units at some entry clearance posts and particularly assists those forced into marriage abroad. Where the victim of a forced marriage is willing to state publicly that they have been coerced, a marriage visa may be refused on the grounds that there is no intention to live together or the marriage is not subsisting. However, in many cases, victims are too frightened of reprisals to acknowledge their situation openly. Given the need to give reasons for a refusal and the existence of appeal rights, it is difficult to refuse a spousal visa application if the victim is not willing to speak out.

In response to concerns about forced marriage, the minimum age for both sponsorship and entry was raised to 18 in 2003 and 2004. In December 2007, the government published a Consultation Document (Home Office/Border and Immigration Agency, *Marriage to Partners From Overseas*). This proposed several measures to prevent forced marriages including raising the minimum age for entry and sponsorship to 21 and this happened in 2008 (HC 1113). New guidance for entry clearance staff on forced marriage was inserted into the IDI (chapter 8, section FM, Annex 1.2).

Providing assistance to victims of forced marriages is vital but there was uneasiness about the increase in the age of entry and sponsorship. In part, this is based on history. The 'reluctant sponsor' was often invoked by those hostile to the continuation of arranged marriages, and forced and arranged marriages were often conflated. For example, in 1985, following newspaper reports about Asian girls being 'sold' by their parents, the Home Secretary, David Waddington, commented that '[t]he so-called 'primary purpose' rule has been much attacked but these stories show that it can protect women against exploitation' ('Scandal of the Brides for Sale' *Daily Mail* 5 August 1985). There was also concern that raising the minimum age for sponsorship and entry is not the most effective means of preventing forced marriages which do not only involve that age group. It was argued that raising the age limit would mean only that victims were held abroad until of age to sponsor. The campaigning group, Southall Black Sisters, gave evidence to the Home Affairs Committee that this happened after the age was raised from 16 to 18 (HC 263-II Ev 334). Research commissioned by the Home Office but not published by them questioned the effectiveness of the proposal and the Home Affairs

Select Committee, while sympathetic to arguments for raising the age, recommended more research before implementation (HC263-I p. 139).

The measure affected all who wished to enter early marriages, not just those who are forced into it and, in 2011, the Supreme Court found that the policy breached Article 8 ECHR:

 Key Case

Quila and others v SSHD [2011] UKSC 45

Appeals were brought by parties to two unforced marriages involving partners under 21. The Supreme Court (Lord Brown dissenting) accepted that, as married couples, family life existed even if it was relatively undeveloped and that refusal to allow the overseas spouse admission amounted to an interference, described by Lord Wilson as 'colossal' (para 32), so as to engage Article 8 ECHR. As discussed earlier in this chapter, the Court declined to follow the majority finding in the ECtHR case of *Abdulaziz v UK* (1985) 7 EHRR 471 that Article 8 was more difficult to engage in entry cases, on the grounds that it was an old decision and inconsistent with later jurisprudence. In carrying out its own review of the proportionality of the rule, in accordance with the principle established in *Huang*, the Court found that, while the rule was rationally connected to the aim of preventing forced marriage, the government had failed to establish that it was no more than necessary to accomplish its objective nor that it struck a fair balance between the rights of parties to unforced marriages and the interests of the community in preventing forced marriage: 'On any view it is a sledge-hammer but she [the Secretary of State] has not attempted to identify the size of the nut' (Lord Wilson, para 58). While the findings were confined to the particular couples in the case, in the words of Lady Hale (at para 80), 'it is difficult to see how she [the Home Secretary] could avoid infringing article 8 whenever she applied the rule to an unforced marriage'.

In November 2011, the government amended the Immigration Rules so that the minimum age of entry and sponsorship reverted to 18. In the Family Migration Consultation, the government proposed the creation of a criminal offence of forcing someone into marriage as well as sponsorship bans for those convicted of domestic violence or forced marriage offences and the involvement of social services in international marriages involving vulnerable sponsors. The Anti-social Behaviour, Crime and Policing Act 2014, ss 120 and 121 creates offences of forced marriage and breach of a Forced Marriage Protection Order.

8.9 Unmarried couples

The right of unmarried couples to be reunited in the UK did not obtain a stable place in the Immigration Rules until 2 October 2000. In April 2003, the requirement for a legal obstacle to marriage was abolished and the minimum prior period of cohabitation reduced to two years. The current rule (Appendix FM) mirrors the requirements for leave to enter as a fiancé(e) or civil partner with the additional requirement that the applicant and their partner must show that they have been living together in a relationship akin to marriage or civil partnership for at least two years prior to the application.

Appendix FM provides that those who already have leave to enter or remain in the UK may switch into leave as an unmarried partner subject to similar conditions that govern switching as a married partner. In calculating the two-year period, IDI section FM 1.0, section 3.2.3 concedes 'short breaks apart for up to six months are acceptable for good reason, such as work commitments or looking after a relative', provided it is clear that the relationship continued throughout the period. Visiting often will not amount to cohabitation, but the cohabitation does not have to have been in one country, and there does not need to be an established joint home if they have, for instance, been living alternately at each other's separate homes using the 'visitor' category.

8.10 Fiancé(e)s

Finally, it is possible for an individual engaged to be married to a settled person to apply for entry clearance as a fiancé(e). The requirements are set out in Appendix FM and are similar to the requirements for a married partner except that some conditions will apply only after marriage and the fiancé(e) must show they are seeking leave to enter *for* marriage or civil partnership with a settled person.

If the application succeeds, leave is granted for a period of six months, during which time the ceremony must take place, there is a prohibition on working and leave is conditional on not having recourse to public funds. If the marriage does not take place during the six-month period, a further extension (Appendix FM, E-LTRP, at 1.11) may be granted to enable the marriage to take place, provided the Home Office is satisfied that there is good cause for the delay, there is satisfactory evidence that the marriage will take place within the next six months, and all the other conditions for leave to enter continue to be met.

8.11 Other adult relatives

8.11.1 Admissible relatives

The adult dependent relative visa category enables relatives of British citizens or settled persons to come to live in the UK. Successful applicants are granted permanent settlement immediately.

Under the previous rules (para 317), parents or grandparents aged 65 or over were eligible if they were wholly or mainly dependent on the UK-based member for money, did not have other close relatives in their country to support them, and could be adequately maintained and accommodated in the UK without recourse to public funds.

Other relatives (parents and grandparents under 65, adult children, siblings, uncles and aunts) could also be considered outside the rules, but only where there was a close emotional bond and very strong compassionate circumstances. Thus, only a very narrow range of relatives could enter and under the new rules, as we shall see, the range is narrower still.

Applications submitted on or after July 2013 are subject to strict eligibility requirements (Appendix FM, section EC-DR) and it could now be argued that the right to be joined by an elderly or dependent relative has been, in most cases, abolished (Wray

2013b). Firstly, uncles and aunts of UK-based sponsors and applicants with unspent convictions in the UK or overseas are no longer eligible. Further, relatives must demonstrate that they require a high level of long-term personal care, as a result of age, illness, or disability, which can only be provided by their relative in the UK and without recourse to public funds. If the relative is able to access this care in their own country with practical and financial help from the UK-based sponsor, they will not be eligible for a visa. In addition, the UK-based sponsor will have to sign an undertaking that the sponsor will be responsible for maintenance, accommodation, and care (without recourse to public funds) for the first five years.

8.11.2 Require long-term personal care as a result of age, illness, or disability

The new rules require that the adult dependent must be incapable of performing everyday tasks for themselves such as washing, dressing, and cooking. The IDI (Appendix FM, section 6.0, at 2.2.1) suggests that this condition may have been arrived at recently, for example, as a result of a serious accident resulting in long-term incapacity or it may be as a result of deterioration in the applicant's condition over several years. Medical evidence will be required to substantiate this and under paras 36–39 of the Immigration Rules, an Entry Clearance Officer has the power to refer the applicant for a medical examination and to require that this be undertaken by a doctor or other health professional on a list approved by the British Embassy or High Commission.

Previously, adult relatives who were under 65 had to show, in addition to the other conditions, that they were 'living alone in the most exceptional compassionate circumstances' and the case law on this area may provide some guidance to the types of cases that will succeed under the new rules, since the rules are clearly designed to limit the number of adult relatives who will be able to join their family in the UK to the most vulnerable. In case law on the previous rules, the courts held that being financially dependent on a relative in the UK and having no other close relatives to turn to did not, on their own, amount to exceptional compassionate circumstances (*Nessa* (16391) INLP vol. 13(2) (1999), p. 75) and families have been kept apart because there is nothing exceptional about their situation. The Court of Appeal held that it is not a breach of Article 8 for the government 'to confine the circumstances in which dependent relatives of persons living in the United Kingdom are permitted indefinite leave to enter in the way that they have done in paragraph 317' (*Husna Begum* para 12).

Living alone did not always require that there was literally no other person in the home, but that there is no one able to meet the needs of the applicant. Severe mental or physical disabilities without the necessary care being available were normally regarded as the most exceptional compassionate circumstances (e.g., *Visa Officer Islamabad v Sindhu* [1978] Imm AR 147). On the old rules, compassionate circumstances that had arisen since the applicant's arrival in the UK, if they have been here for instance on a visit, could be considered (*Alyha Begum* (17162) INLP vol. 13(3) (1999)). However, the new rules prevent adult relatives switching into this category whilst in the UK. They will be required to apply from overseas.

8.11.3 Unable to receive the required level of care in the country where they are living

The guidance on this section (Appendix FM, section 6.0, at 2.2.2) suggests that applicants will have to establish that they cannot access the required level of care in the country where they are living, even with the practical and financial help of the UK-based sponsor. This could be because (a) it is not available and there is no person in that country who could reasonably provide it, or (b) because it is not affordable. Again, it is likely that medical evidence will be required to substantiate this part of the case (IDI Appendix FM, section 6.0, at 2.3.3).

Previously, the applicant had to be without close relatives in their own country to whom they could turn for financial support. The rule did not initially include the words 'for financial support' and the leading judgment on its meaning concerned its previous formulation. Dillon LJ in the Court of Appeal case of *R v IAT ex p Swaran Singh* [1987] 1 WLR 1394 read the phrase 'as importing "to turn to in case of need"—any sort of need which may afflict elderly parents'. He gave examples of illness or accident and said that the rule was one of 'broad humanity'. Family relationships should be borne in mind, and where relatives are hostile or unwilling to help, they are clearly not relatives to turn to. In a more recent case, the Tribunal found that the issue of dependency and no close relative to turn to are 'two sides of the same coin'. Where a person was found to be dependent as of necessity on the sponsor, this would normally mean that there was no other close relative to whom they could turn (*Parekh* (14016) INLP vol. 11 (2) (1997), p. 73).

There were broadly two approaches taken to the previous rule. One, following *Swaran Singh*, construed the rule as one of 'broad humanity', which therefore should not be interpreted in a strict and literal way. The other, which became more dominant, denied that the rules embody any such policy. In particular, Dyson LJ in *MB (Somalia)* observed that the rule represented a policy decision as to where the balance should be struck between humanity and immigration control so that stating that the rule is one of broad humanity does not assist in assessing the legality of the policy. The new rules clearly rely on the latter approach and it remains to be seen how the courts will interpret the new provisions.

8.11.4 Financial dependency

Previously, all applicants in this category had to be 'financially wholly or mainly dependent on the sponsor'. Until November 2011, the rules specified that relatives under 65 had to be 'mainly dependent on relatives living in the UK' whereas now only the support of the sponsor can be considered (IDI, Appendix FM, section FM 6 at 2.2.4(c)).

The term 'dependency' has been removed from the new rules and there has clearly been a shift in emphasis. The previous case law indicated that dependency must be of necessity as 'the question of dependency has to be construed in the context of immigration control. The question of genuineness runs through all the immigration regulations . . . dependants have to show their genuine need' (*Chavda v ECO Bombay* [1978] Imm AR 40). This not only interpreted the term narrowly, but also involved a judgment as to what is necessary, a concept which may vary between cultures.

This was illustrated in the case which established the test of 'necessary dependence', *Zaman v ECO Lahore* [1973] Imm AR 71. An elderly farmer and his wife applied to join their son in the UK. They were financially dependent upon him because, in accordance with custom, Mr Zaman gave the modest income from the farms to his sons who were still resident in Pakistan. The Tribunal held that their dependence was not necessary. This case contrasts with *ECO New Delhi v Malhan* [1978] Imm AR 209. Here, the appellant's eldest son had voluntarily taken over his mother's support out of a desire to fulfil his moral obligations. The Tribunal held that she was entitled to look to him for support and not to 'more distant' relatives (her brother and father).

What steps to maximize income should an applicant take? In *Chavda*, it was accepted that a widow could not compel her three sons, who lived with her, to work and the dependency on her eldest son in the UK was necessary and not contrived. Where sons can clearly get work this might be different, as in *Hasan v ECO Bombay* [1976] Imm AR 28. In *Piara Singh* (19579) INLP vol. 13(3) (1999), p. 107, elderly parents had a spare room which they kept for visits by family members. It was held that they should not be expected to let this out to reduce their financial dependency on the sponsor.

In *Bibi v ECO Dhaka* [2000] Imm AR 385, the Court of Appeal confirmed that financial dependency may be in the form of money or money's worth. If someone has their needs for accommodation, clothing, food, and other necessities provided in kind, they are financially dependent on the provider. Here, the appellant lived with her son, daughter-in-law, and their children, and was applying to join another son in the UK who regularly sent money to the family. This was used mainly for the children's education. The Court of Appeal found that the true situation was that the family had some dependency on the sponsor, but the appellant was dependent on the family she lived with, not the sponsor in the UK. The principle, therefore, is that there must be direct financial dependency. This was confirmed in *VS (para 317(iii) no 3rd party support)* [2007] UKAIT 00069. Here the sponsor, who was severely disabled, sent a regular £100 per month to the appellant, but it was provided by a distant relative who gave evidence that he was willing and able to continue this support into the future. The Tribunal held that the sponsor was just a conduit for the relative's money, and that the appellant was not financially dependent on him.

The new rules are clearly intending to treat the remittance of funds to dependent relatives not as evidence of a claim to enter but as an alternative means of meeting their needs. The result is a Catch 22. Without showing dependency, the claim for entry will fail. If dependency is shown, it will be argued that this can continue. The desire of many families to spend time with and care for their elderly relatives is thus treated as irrelevant and, as already discussed in this chapter, Article 8 will offer little assistance as it protects only the existing life of family members, not the life they wish to have. It is clear that the new rules are not intended to be a means by which people settled in the UK may make arrangements for the care of their elderly relatives, and in this respect a settled UK family of immigrant descent does not have the choices available to families whose extended family live in the UK. The new rule depends largely on material and physical need and is more of a safety net than a positive support to family life. It is worth noting that between 9 July 2012 and 31 October 2012 only one visa was issued in this category (Barnden 2013) and in the view of the All-Party Parliamentary Group on Migration (APPG) this visa category has 'in effect been closed'.

8.11.5 Terms of stay for a successful relative

Entry clearance for dependent relatives will function as leave to enter and remain indefinitely providing the entry clearance is endorsed to that effect (Immigration (Leave to Enter and Remain) Order 2000, SI 2000/1161). There is no probationary period.

Maintenance and accommodation requirements must be met for the application to succeed. The Family Migration Consultation initially proposed introducing a minimum income requirement in line with partner applications but this change was not made. Paragraph E-ECDR 3.2 of the rules gives power to immigration authorities to require the sponsor (if a British citizen or settled in the UK) to sign an undertaking that they will be responsible for their relative's maintenance, accommodation, and care. The effect of this is to disbar the sponsored relative from any claim to key means-tested benefits for five years from the date of admission to the UK. If the relative does make a claim, the paying authorities may seek to recover from the person who gave the undertaking.

An undertaking is a formal document. In *Ahmed v Secretary of State for Work and Pensions* [2005] EWCA Civ 535, the Court of Appeal held that a statement by the sponsor that he was 'able and willing' to maintain and accommodate his uncle was designed to show to the entry clearance officer that the requirements for granting entry clearance were met and did not amount to an undertaking, which was a solemn promise for the future. The sponsor's uncle therefore was not debarred from a claim for backdated benefit on the grounds of being a person who had leave to enter the UK 'as a result of a maintenance undertaking' (Immigration and Asylum Act 1999 s 115).

There were clearly concerns in the Family Migration Consultation about the potential burden that these migrants may place on public services. These have been dealt with by way of placing very severe restrictions on those who will be eligible to enter and through sponsor undertakings in respect of benefit claims.

8.12 **Children**

8.12.1 **Introduction**

The migration of children involves domestic and private international law provisions concerning abduction, custody, and adoption as well as complex nationality rules. The UK's immigration law on children is only a small part of the picture which cannot effectively be considered in isolation. This is an area of increasing complexity now warranting specialist texts (see, for instance, Coker, Finch, and Stanley 2002). This section is therefore limited in its aim and scope. It aims to explain some of the particular Immigration Rules relating to the admission of children for settlement.

In November 2008, the UK withdrew its reservation to the UN Convention on the Rights of the Child, which had exempted the UK from the Convention in relation to immigration matters and had been widely criticized. The obligations in the Convention extend to children within the jurisdiction of the contracting state, which, in this context, means within the territory of the UK and there is no obligation to ensure that the rules governing the entry of children are compliant. Moreover, the Convention does not give rise to directly enforceable rights. However, the government will have to report on its compliance to the UN Committee on the Rights of the Child.

Article 3(1) of the Convention provides that the best interests of the child shall be a 'primary consideration'. Following withdrawal of the reservation, s 55 Borders, Citizenship and Immigration Act 2009 imposed a duty on the Secretary of State to ensure that immigration- and asylum-related duties are carried out having due regard to the need to safeguard and promote the welfare of children who are in the United Kingdom. Lady Hale, at para 23 of *ZH (Tanzania)*, regarded this as representing 'the spirit, if not the precise language' of the obligation and also found, at para 24, that the ECHR requires national states to make children's interests 'a primary consideration' so that a decision made without such consideration would not be 'in accordance with the law' for the purposes of Article 8(2). The acknowledgement of such a principle moves immigration decision-making about children who are in the UK much further towards welfare principles, an advance that may be contrasted with the situation that still obtains in entry cases, where immigration considerations still predominate.

The s 55 obligation may also affect decisions that are made about those who are caring for a child as *ZH (Tanzania)* demonstrated.

 **Key Case**

ZH (Tanzania) v SSHD [2011] UKSC 4

The case involved a Tanzanian woman national whose immigration history was described as 'appalling'. There was little doubt that, were only her own interests at stake, she would have been unable to resist removal. However, she had two children born in the UK to a British father and who were British citizens. Their father had serious health problems and it was doubtful that he could care for them if the mother was removed. Her removal would therefore almost inevitably entail their departure with her to Tanzania.

As Lady Hale noted, the duty to make a child's interests 'a primary consideration' is not the same as to make them 'the primary consideration' or 'the paramount consideration', as required by s 1(1) Children Act 1989 in respect of decisions regarding a child's upbringing. Immigration decisions generally do not affect a child's upbringing directly and the s 55 obligation is to make a child's interests the first consideration although the strength of other factors may still outweigh them. However, Lord Kerr said, at para 46:

> This [best interests] is not, it is agreed, a factor of limitless importance in the sense that it will prevail over all other considerations. It is a factor, however, that must rank higher than any other. It is not merely one consideration that weighs in the balance alongside other competing factors. Where the best interests of the child clearly favour a certain course, that course should be followed unless countervailing reasons of considerable force displace them.

As the government conceded, the principle applies not only to the care of children pending immigration decisions but to the decisions themselves. Lady Hale enumerated the matters that might be relevant in such an assessment including nationality and its connection with lifestyle, the social and linguistic disruption of children's childhood and the loss of homeland, the loss of educational opportunities, and loss of contact with wider family members.

The children's nationality, while not a 'trump card', was of particular importance in assessing their best interests. They had an unqualified right of abode and had lived in the UK for their entire lives, were being educated and had other social links there, and a good relationship with their father. They also had citizenship rights, which they would be unable to exercise if they could not remain. While there were strong countervailing factors, they did not outweigh, in this case, the interests of the children. Even if the children had been conceived in the hope of strengthening the mother's claim to remain, they themselves were innocent of her shortcomings.

The decision in *ZH* is congruent with the decision of the CJEU, reached on different legal grounds, in *Zambrano v Onde* (C-34/09) delivered a month later in March 2011 and discussed in chapter 4. Although the main application of *ZH* is in relation to removal or deportation, dealt with in chapter 5, it will also be relevant when children or parents make further claims to remain in the UK under the Immigration Rules. It was cited, for example, in *R (on the application of Mansoor) v SSHD* [2011] EWHC 832 (Admin) which concerned a citizen father and seven children who had indefinite leave. The mother was admitted for a two-year probationary period. Shortly before it expired, the husband lost his job, was obliged to claim benefits, and her claim for indefinite leave was refused. The refusal was overturned, amongst other reasons, for its failure to consider the interests of the children as a primary consideration.

While *ZH* focused on the weight to be awarded to nationality, the findings as to the importance of the child's interests apply to all children present in the UK, irrespective of their nationality. Subsequent cases have explored further the nature of the obligation. Where children have another nationality, particularly one that is shared with their parents, the arguments against return will have less force, particularly for young children whose interests are still primarily wrapped up in their immediate family life which will continue overseas. Even so, other factors concerning their interests—education, social links, and so on—will apply and the issue is to be decided as part of the overall Article 8 assessment with, however, the children's interests addressed first as a distinct enquiry. Decision-makers must be proactive in establishing what those interests are as well as the child's own wishes and views (accorded due weight according to the child's age and maturity) and must give proper and informed consideration to them (*AJ (India) and others v SSHD* [2011] EWCA Civ 1191; *R (on the application of Tinizaray) v SSHD* [2011] EWHC 1850 (Admin); *E-A (Article 8—best interests of child) Nigeria* [2011] UKUT 00315 (IAC); *MK (best interests of child) India* [2011] UKUT 00475 (IAC); *EV (Philippines) & Ors v Secretary of State for the Home Department*[2014] EWCA Civ 874).

Section 55 is stated to apply only to children in the UK so that it does not apply in entry cases where immigration concerns carry much greater weight. However, Lady Hale's observation in *ZH (Tanzania)* that the interests of children are a primary consideration under Article 8(2) should apply equally when ECHR issues arise in entry cases. The s 55 guidance, to which regard must be had under s 55(3) of the 2009 Act, states at para 2.34, that 'UK Border Agency staff working overseas must adhere to the spirit of the duty and make enquiries when they have reason to suspect that a child may be in need of protection or safeguarding, or presents welfare needs that require attention'. Thus, there does seem to be an obligation on UKVI to consider the welfare of children. The Upper Tribunal in *T (s.55 BCIA 2009—entry clearance) Jamaica* [2011] UKUT 00483 (IAC) found that s 55 indeed does not apply to children outside the UK but that the application of the Immigration Rules, Article 8, and the guidance should all be taken into account and investigations made if necessary. As Lady Hale suggested in *ZH*, it is difficult to envisage a situation in which s 55 applied and the outcome would be different from that required by Article 8. This is now reflected in the guidance to Appendix FM, EX.1.

The rules for the admission of children for settlement are found in paras 297–303 HC 395. These rules have not been substantially changed following the Family Migration Consultation, save that the new financial requirements will apply to applications by parents with limited leave to remain in the UK as a partner or parent (Appendix FM). The child must be under 18 at the time of the application. If s/he reaches 18 before a decision is made, they will not be refused for that reason (para 27). The IDI (chapter 8, Annex FM 3.2, para 2.2) says that a child who reaches 18 after issue of the visa but before entry should not be refused entry for that reason alone. However, the Family Migration Consultation suggested that children, in future, should be no more than 17 years and 6 months at the time of the application so that they enter before they are 18. Children who are close to 18 would no longer be given indefinite leave but finite leave to expire on their eighteenth birthday, when they 'will be able to apply for leave to remain in the UK in their own right', even though the options for such young adults are very limited. It was also proposed that children aged 16 or above should demonstrate a basic level of English before admission. Neither of these proposals has yet found their way into the rules. However, the government is still considering them.

According to para 6 of the rules, a parent includes a step-parent, an adoptive parent, and an unmarried father, if paternity is accepted or proved. If, after DNA testing, the child turns out, as happened in *ECO Accra v Attafuah* [2002] UKIAT 05922, not to be the father's natural child, it seems there is no provision parallel to that in nationality law to treat the child as the child of that person. However, the Entry Clearance Guidance (SET 7.11.8) emphasizes the need for discretion and says that where an illegitimate child has been brought up as a child of the family, it would normally be appropriate to admit the child under para 297(i)(f), that there are serious and compelling family or other considerations why exclusion is undesirable.

When children come to join both parents or where one parent is dead, the position is relatively straightforward. Principles of accommodation and maintenance are already familiar, and the only additional requirement is that the child is 'not leading an independent life, is unmarried and has not formed an independent family unit' (para 297(iii)).

Adequate accommodation was given an unusually extended meaning by the Court of Appeal in *M & A v ECO* [2003] EWCA Civ 263. Other children of the same parents had been taken into care, and one had died as a result of abuse. The Court had, at that time, no remit to consider welfare in an entry case but the gap in the protective capacity of the rules was filled by the Tribunal's creative decision that the accommodation was not adequate because the children would not be safe.

There are special rules which apply when the child is only joining one parent or relative. Either the sponsoring parent must have sole responsibility for the child or there must be serious and compelling family or other considerations which make exclusion of the child undesirable.

8.12.2 Sole responsibility

When the other parent of the child is still living, it must be shown that the sponsoring parent has 'sole responsibility' for them (HC 396 para 298(i)(c)). Given that the sponsor will usually have been living in the UK without the child, sole responsibility does not mean sole care or most applications would fail as relatives, not only the other parent, may also share care. If there is a residence order in favour of the UK parent, this is a strong indicator of sole responsibility for immigration purposes. Some custody orders obtained overseas are similarly regarded (IDI chapter 8, Annex FM 3.2, para 4.4). Otherwise, both the Instructions (IDI Annex FM 3.2, para 4.3) and the Entry Clearance Guidance (SET 7.8) set out some relevant factors. These include the legal relationship between all the parties, financial support, and arrangements for care. It is expected that the child will have been cared for by the sponsor's own relatives and not those of the other parent.

The sole responsibility rule does not give separated parents and children the power to choose where the child should live. An example given in the IDI makes this apparent:

Two foreign nationals living abroad have a child, then separate. One parent comes to the United Kingdom and obtains settlement. The child remains with the parent abroad for several years, then at the age of 13+ wishes to join the parent in the United Kingdom to take advantage of the educational system. There is no reason why the child should not remain with the parent who lives abroad. In this case the parent who lives in the United Kingdom would not be considered to have sole responsibility. (chapter 8, Annex FM 3.2, para 4.1)

The example cited here implies manipulation of the immigration system; however, the outcome would be the same if the child and custodial parent had started to argue and the family thought it was time for a change in the interests of the child.

The Court of Appeal in the case of *Nmaju v IAT* [2001] INLR 26 held that there were two points of principle in determining sole responsibility. One is the quality of control, the other is for what period of time that control must be exercised. The quality of control which will give rise to a finding of sole responsibility requires retention of ultimate responsibility for the child even if someone else is doing the day-to-day care provided this is 'under the direction' of the responsible parent. The parent would be expected to show a continuous interest in the child's welfare and upbringing.

Where there are two parents actually involved, the Tribunal in the case of *Zahir* 00/TH/02262 held that sole responsibility is still capable of arising, for instance, if one parent's role was clearly subsidiary, though it was not so on the facts in that case. *TD Yemen* [2006] UKAIT 00049 sets out the approach to sole responsibility cases:

(i) The question of sole responsibility is a factual one.

(ii) 'Responsibility' may be undertaken by individuals other than a child's parents and may be shared. The issue of sole responsibility is not just a matter between the parents.

(iii) If both parents are involved in the upbringing of the child, it will be exceptional that one will have sole responsibility.

(iv) If it is said that one is not involved, one of the indicators will be that they have abandoned or abdicated their responsibility.

(v) If day-to-day responsibility (or decision-making) is shared with others (such as relatives or friends) that does not prevent the parent having sole responsibility within the meaning of the Rules.

(vi) The test is whether the parent has continuing control and direction of the child's upbringing including making all the important decisions in the child's life. If not, responsibility is shared and not 'sole'.

In *TD*, the child had lived with his mother in Yemen and been brought up by her. His father phoned him every week and was entirely responsible for his financial support. He took part in major decisions, though there had been few of these. The Tribunal concluded that responsibility was shared, not sole. They referred to the underlying purpose of para 297 as being 'to effect family unity'. This, they thought, would be undermined if the provision was interpreted so as to allow a child to join a parent who was not, in fact, solely responsible for them (para 48).

The other issue in *Nmaju* is the period of time for which sole responsibility must be assumed. In that case, three children were left in the care of their father who, in September 1996, said that he was too old to look after them any longer and left them in the care of a maid. In November of that year, their application to join their mother was refused on the basis that, if she had sole responsibility, it was only for two months and that was too short a period of time. The reality of the situation at the time of the entry clearance decision was that the mother had sole responsibility and this was sufficient to meet the requirements of the rule. *TD Yemen* confirms this result.

8.12.3 Exclusion undesirable

The welfare of the child takes greater priority under the next sub-paragraph of the rule, 'that there are serious and compelling family or other considerations which make exclusion of the child undesirable'. This is not a question of whether it would on balance be better for the child to move to the UK. For instance, in *Dawson v ECO Accra* 01/

TH/1358, the Tribunal, in refusing the appeal on this ground, noted that there was no evidence of mistreatment of the appellant or of his mother or stepfather according him a lack of respect.

The rule may be used to join a relative other than a parent, although it was suggested in *OU (Nigeria) and others v SSHD* [2008] EWCA Civ 128 that this must be a blood relative. The IDI (chapter 8, Annex FM 3.2, para 1) emphasize that this basis for entry is only to be used when parents or relatives in the child's own country are *unable* to care for him or her and the circumstances surrounding the child are exceptional in relation to those of other children living in that country.

Where a child is seeking to join a parent, the circumstances of the UK parent, both of an emotional and of a physical nature, for example, illness or infirmity, may be taken into account. Where the application is to join another relative, the relative's circumstances should not form part of the consideration. This appears to be an attempt to avoid children being brought in as carers for other relatives in need.

Previous case law suggested that only if the living conditions in the child's country of origin were intolerable would entry to the UK be considered on this ground. However, it was later found that an overall view must be taken, including such factors as the willingness and availability of the overseas adult to look after the child; the living conditions available for them; the greater vulnerability of small children; and the need for family unity *(Hardward* 00/TH/01522). In *Hardward* itself, there is still an emphasis on conditions abroad as a starting point, although, in that case, the appellant was already in the UK. The appellant lost because, although there were compelling family reasons why she should remain, it was not shown that her father in Jamaica was unable to care for her.

The case of *Hardward* predated the implementation of the Human Rights Act by a few months. The application under the 'exclusion undesirable' rule was turned down, but the Tribunal considered whether, given the imminence of the Human Rights Act, it should make a recommendation using Article 8. The Tribunal suggested that para 298(i) of the rules was incompatible with the Human Rights Act:

the onus of justifying that interference under Art 8(2) shifts to the immigration authorities. That is in clear contrast with the wording of the rule set out at paragraph 298(i) which places the burden throughout on the appellant to justify why her exclusion would be undesirable. (para 19)

This argument seems to have much force.

8.12.4 **Adoption**

Inter-country adoption is a growing and complex subject, combining immigration and family law. This brief coverage just raises some issues associated with it. It is necessary to distinguish between adoption of a non-British child in the UK, and adoption overseas with the intention or consequence that the child moves to the UK.

8.12.4.1 Adoption in the UK

The adoption of a non-British child in the UK by a British citizen confers British nationality immediately upon the making of the adoption order (British Nationality Act 1981 s 1(5)). In the case of *In re B (a minor (AP))* [1999] 2 AC 136, the House of Lords established new principles for immigration considerations in the adoption of children in the UK.

In re B (a minor (AP)) [1999] 2 AC 136

B had visited the UK with her mother. She attended school in Leeds while they stayed with her grandparents, and appeared to be thriving, so her mother left her there and returned to Jamaica. B and her grandparents applied for exceptional leave for B to stay in the UK as it appeared to be in her best interests, all the more as her father in Jamaica had now died, and her mother and sister were living in reduced circumstances. Her application was refused. The parties were advised that B could only stay in the UK if she was adopted by her grandparents. Her mother consented, but the Home Secretary intervened to oppose the adoption. He also made it clear that if just a residence order were made in favour of the grandparents, he would still seek to deport B. As Lord Hoffmann says in his judgment at 140:

> Ms B had only two years of minority left. And although the benefits to her from being able to spend those two important years living with her grandparents and going to school in Leeds were plain and obvious, it would not ordinarily be necessary for her to be adopted. Were it not for her precarious immigration status, she could simply have stayed with her grandparents or, if the situation needed to be formally regulated, the Court could have made a residence order under the Children Act 1989. But the Home Office made it clear that if the Court merely made a residence order, it would nevertheless order her deportation. Thus the acquisition of British citizenship by adoption was an essential element in securing her the advantages of living with her grandparents and continuing at her school.

The Court of Appeal had accepted the Home Office's proposition that 'the court should ignore benefits which would result solely from [a] change in immigration status when determining whether the child's welfare calls for adoption' (at 141). As the acquisition of the right of abode was the main benefit, it discharged the adoption order. The House of Lords considered that this interpretation flouted the terms of the Adoption Act, which required the judge to 'have regard to "all the circumstances" and to treat the welfare of the child "throughout his childhood" as the first consideration'. It was impossible to ignore the immigration benefits of the adoption. Lord Hoffmann continues with a passage (at 141) which has great significance for adoptions:

No doubt the views of the Home Office on immigration policy were also a circumstance which the court was entitled to take into account, although it is not easy to see what weight they could be given. Parliament has not provided, as I suppose it might have done, that the adoption of a non-British child should require the consent of the Home Secretary. On the contrary, it has provided that the making of an adoption order automatically takes the child out of the reach of the Home Secretary's powers of immigration control. The decision whether to make such an order is entirely one for the judge in accordance with the provisions of section 6. In cases in which it appears to the judge that adoption would confer real benefits upon the child during its childhood, it is very unlikely that general considerations of 'maintaining an effective and consistent immigration policy' could justify the refusal of an order. The two kinds of consideration are hardly commensurable so as to be capable of being weighed in the balance against each other.

The criteria for deciding whether an adoption order should be made were amended after *Re B* was heard. In *B v S* [2009] EWHC 2491 (Fam), the High Court considered that these changes did not affect the underlying position which was that, where an adoption is merely to facilitate immigration and there is no genuine transfer of parental control, it is unlikely to be in the child's interests and would fail under the criteria. Where there is a true intention to adopt, the child's welfare is paramount and would not be outweighed by breaches of the Immigration Rules although courts should be on their guard against misuse of adoption proceedings.

8.12.4.2 Adoption outside the UK

A child adopted outside the UK in accordance with the 1993 Hague Convention on the Protection of Children and Co-operation in Respect of Inter-Country Adoptions will be a British citizen if one of the parents is a British citizen and both parents are habitually resident in the UK (s 1(5) British Nationality Act 1981). In that case, the immigration authorities do not need to be involved. However, where parents are settled in the UK but not citizens, the child will not be a British citizen and is subject to immigration control. In such cases, a child may enter the UK for settlement if the requirements of HC 395 para 310 are met. As will be demonstrated in this section, the rules are not entirely satisfactory, particularly where intra-family adoptions are involved. If the child cannot be admitted under the adoption rules, it may be possible to apply using the rule that exclusion is undesirable (*SK ('Adoption' not recognised in UK) India* [2006] UKAIT 00068). However, a further UK adoption procedure may be necessary after entry.

Two types of adoption are recognized under para 310: those made by the competent authorities in countries of origin or residence whose adoption orders are recognized by the UK under the Adoption (Recognition of Overseas Adoptions) Order 2013 (SI 2003/1801), and *'de facto'* adoptions. Alternatively, a child may be admitted, under para 316A, to join parents with a view to adoption under UK law after entry.

De facto adoptions must comply with the conditions set out in para 309A. The adoptive parent or parents, if both are involved, must have been living abroad (together if a couple) and have assumed the role of the child's parents for at least 18 months prior to the application and the child must have lived with the adoptive parent or parents for the 12 months immediately preceding the application. These provisions aim to provide for situations where a child has been treated as part of the family prior to the family's entry. The lengthy period of residence abroad means that it is rarely appropriate for UK-based parents who want to adopt from abroad. It is also often unsuitable for refugees who have cared for orphaned or abandoned children in areas of conflict. By the time that refugee status has been granted and an application for their entry made, the relationship no longer qualifies as a de facto adoption (although Article 8 may sometimes assist); *MK (Somalia) v ECO* [2008] EWCA Civ 1453; *Mohamoud (paras 352D and 309A—de facto adoption) Ethiopia* [2011] UKUT 00378 (IAC).

Recognition of the country's adoption process (or of a *de facto* adoption) is not enough to bring the child within the requirements of the Immigration Rules as there are additional criteria to be met. Paragraph 310 requires that, at the time of the adoption, both of the adoptive parents were resident together abroad or that either or both were settled in the UK. In addition, it lays down requirements for the adoption, namely that the adopted child has the same rights and obligations as any other child of the marriage; that the child was adopted due to the inability of others to care for them; that there is a genuine transfer of parental responsibility to the adoptive parents; that the child has lost or broken ties with their family of origin; and that the adoption is not one of convenience to facilitate admission to the UK. These requirements are more stringent than those for an adoption order in the UK which would not necessarily require that the child was adopted 'due to the inability of others to care for them' nor that the child has lost or broken ties with their family of origin. Indeed, it is no longer thought good practice in family law to insist upon a child severing contact with their family of origin. In *Boadi v ECO Ghana* [2002] UKIAT 01323, the Tribunal took account of this in its interpretation of the rule, holding that severing ties with a family of origin did not mean severing emotional ties, but just that the adoption was not an arrangement which could be seen as reversible. A different view of the rules had been taken in the case of *Kamande v ECO Nairobi* [2002] UKIAT 06129 a few months earlier, in which the Tribunal refused to recognize the adoption for the purposes of the rules because, although responsibility had been transferred, the appellant still retained a strong emotional relationship with his grandparents who had brought him up.

When an adoption is arranged within the family, for instance the adoption of a niece or nephew, it may not be possible to show that the parents are unable to care for the child or that all ties have been severed with the birth family. Case law on this has been mixed. *In H (A Minor) (Adoption: Non-Patrial), Re* [1997] 1 WLR 791, the Court of Appeal declined to overturn an adoption when the motivation arose from the adoptive parents' infertility. In *J (A Minor) (Adoption: Non-Patrial), Re* [1998] 1 FLR 225, the Court of Appeal, in a comparable case, again refused to overturn the adoption order. The Court distinguished between deception used to gain entry to achieve a genuine adoption and deception as to the nature of the adoption itself. The Court expressed a view that, while the adoption rules were so restrictive, it was difficult to argue that they should not be circumvented by genuine applicants (see Macdonald 2001:455).

In *Radhika Sharma v ECO New Delhi* [2005] EWCA Civ 89, the Court of Appeal adopted a strict interpretation of the requirement to show that the birth family cannot care for the child. They held that inability to care did not include unwillingness, as in the present case. This seems a harsh finding which ignores the psychological factors that may cause rejection of a child and that it may be in the child's interests to live with willing adoptive parents rather than reluctant birth parents. The decision here was perhaps connected to doubts about the veracity of the sponsor's story.

By contrast, in *Singh v ECO New Delhi* [2004] EWCA Civ 1075, the Court had to consider an application for entry clearance following an intra-family adoption which could not meet the requirements of the Immigration Rules because the child had not severed ties with his family of origin. Indeed, he was being cared for well by his birth parents while he waited to join his adoptive parents, his aunt and uncle, with whom he had a strong relationship. The case had a very protracted background, including a decision by the ECtHR that an application was admissible because the refusal to recognize adoptions carried out in India was *prima facie* discriminatory. The Court of Appeal heard and decided an application purely upon Article 8 grounds. It had no doubt that the substantial relationship between the child and adoptive parents amounted to family life. That it did not meet the UK's stringent immigration requirements should not impede genuine family life and entry clearance should be granted. However, as the earlier discussion on *MN* demonstrates, it is relatively unusual that an adoption case will demonstrate sufficient pre-existing family life for an Article 8 claim to succeed.

Singh did not decide anything about the validity of the restrictions on adoption in the Immigration Rules. The Court simply rejected a 'rigid and formulaic approach' (para 33) which would require adherence to legal form at the expense of particular facts. The Tribunal decision in *SK India* [2006] UKAIT 00067 held that the non-recognition of Indian adoptions was not a matter that the Tribunal could or should overrule, as adoptions had a wider significance than immigration and there were other effects to be reckoned with. The UK was entitled to require certain formalities of an adoption. This approach was, as indicated, endorsed in *MN India* [2007] UKAIT 00015, where the Tribunal rejected an argument that the rules were discriminatory (see Chowdhury 2007 for discussion of the issues and a critique of these decisions).

There are other regulations also governing adoption of children abroad. The Adoptions with a Foreign Element Regulations 2005, SI 2005/392, as amended, lay down an extensive system of regulation and approval for adoptive parents. However, they only apply to adoptions under the Hague Convention, adoptions of a foreign child in the UK, or adoptions abroad effected less than six months before the child enters the UK, and so not all those that are permitted in the Immigration Rules. The Children and Adoption Act 2006 also provides for special restrictions on adopting children from abroad where there is a suspicion of harm to children.

8.12.5 **Parents of children in the UK**

So far, this chapter has focused on children who wish to enter the UK to join their parents. The Immigration Rules also make provision for separated or divorced parents who need to enter for contact with children under 18. Under Appendix FM, where an applicant has either sole parental responsibility for the child or access rights to the child and is able to provide evidence that they are taking, and intend to continue to take, an active role in the child's upbringing, then entry clearance for an initial period of up to 33 months will be granted, subject to requirements of maintenance, accommodation, and required levels of English language competency.

Leave to remain may also be granted under Appendix FM (E-LTRPT) to those who have leave to remain as spouses or partners of the parent of the child in question subject to similar conditions. Indefinite leave is available to either category after 60 months.

Since July 2012, the rules have been changed in Appendix FM EX.1 to provide a longer (ten-year) route to settlement to parents who are present without leave and who cannot meet some of the criteria relating to accommodation and English language requirements. This section was brought into the rules to deal with the welfare principle in s 55 BCIA 2009, as a reaction to cases such as *ZH (Tanzania)* and *Zambrano* (discussed earlier in this chapter) but also as an attempt to reframe the understanding of how the Immigration Rules are to be interpreted when considering Article 8. The new rule also appears to re-introduce the seven-year benchmark in cases involving children that was previously found in a Home Office Policy abolished in December 2008.

EX.1 applies to applicants who have a 'genuine and subsisting' parental relationship with a child who is either settled or has lived continuously in the UK for a period of seven years prior to the application and it would not be reasonable to expect the child to leave the UK. In relation to the seven-year period, the IDI (Appendix FM) permits time spent in the UK with and without valid leave and excludes short periods outside the UK for holidays or family visits. The IDI provides that in cases where the applicant seeking leave is the sole carer, it is likely that it would be unreasonable for the child to leave the UK with that parent and so leave to remain will be granted.

8.13 **Family life for those with limited leave**

The preceding material in this chapter has dealt with applications to join people settled in the UK. People entering for a limited time—for instance, for work or study—may have the right to bring their immediate family with them. Those entering under Tiers 1, 2, and 4 (but, in most cases, only graduate students coming for at least 12 months), and Tier 5 (Temporary Worker) (collectively described in the rules as 'Relevant Points

Based Migrants') may bring family members with them subject to the conditions set out in para 319A–J of the rules. Rules similar to those for spouses and relating to valid and subsisting marriage, the length and nature of any unmarried partnership, and intention to live together apply to the spouses, civil partners, unmarried or same sex partners of relevant PBS migrants. (*R (Zhang) v SSHD* [2013] EWHC 891 (Admin)) suggests that the *Chikwamba* principle may also apply in suitable cases where switching from one type of visa to another (in this case, 'general' to 'partner') is not permitted by the rules from within the UK. Those entering for 12 months or more may work and all must not intend to stay in the UK beyond the expiry of their partner's leave. Children of the same categories of PBS migrants are permitted to enter, subject to the conditions of para 296. The specific maintenance requirements for the family members of each Tier are set out in Appendix E.

Migrants regarded as purely temporary do not have the right to be accompanied by family members. These include visitors, seasonal workers, those on the sectors-based scheme, Tier 5 (Youth Mobility), and the currently unimplemented Tier 3. The children of people with limited leave who are born in the UK will not be British, as their parents are not settled.

Following the Family Migration Consultation, spouses and partners of PBS migrants must now complete five years in the UK with temporary leave to remain (in a route that leads to settlement) before they will be eligible for permanent settlement. Adult dependents applying for indefinite leave to remain from October 2013 have to pass the Life in the UK test and achieve English language speaking and listening skills at CEFR level B1 in order to qualify for permanent settlement.

8.14 Refugees and asylum seekers

Once a person has obtained refugee status or, after 30 August 2005, a grant of humanitarian protection, they may be joined by a partner and minor children whom they left behind in their country of origin. However, the right only accrues once status has been granted and applies only to relationships that existed and to children who were part of the household prior to departure from the country of origin. Children who have been adopted informally, a common occurrence in strife-torn countries where birth parents may die or disappear, are not covered by the right and must rely on Article 8 (*MK (Somalia) and others v ECO* [2008] EWCA 1453).

The spouse of such a person must also show that the parties intend to live together and the marriage is subsisting, and the applicant would not, themselves, be excluded by Article 1F of the Refugee Convention (see chapter 13 (para 352A(iii))). Minor children may also apply to join a refugee provided they are under 18, not married or leading an independent life, were part of the family unit before the refugee sponsor left the country of origin, and would also not be excluded under Article 1F (para 352D). Similar rules apply to the family members of those granted humanitarian protection (paras 352FA and FD and 352FG).

Around 12 per cent of refugee claims are made by minors but there is no provision in the rules nor in current policy for such children to be joined by their parents, a policy that appears to be at odds with the government's obligations under s 55 Borders, Citizenship and Immigration Act 2009.

The refugee family reunion rules are more generous than those for citizens and residents as maintenance and accommodation requirements do not apply. In *ZN (Afghanistan) v ECO* [2010] UKSC 21, the Supreme Court held that the Immigration Rules, as then worded, permitted a naturalized refugee to rely on the refugee family reunion rules. The government responded by amending the rules so that, now, only those who are 'currently' refugees or have humanitarian protection can sponsor relatives under these more expansive provisions. The Court of Appeal has found that those granted indefinite leave as the spouse of a refugee cannot, themselves, rely on the refugee family reunion rules to sponsor other family members (*MS (Somalia) v SSHD* [2010] EWCA Civ 1236).

Since 30 August 2005, refugees have been given five years' leave, which is renewed in the light of conditions in the country of origin (previously, they received indefinite leave at once). Their family members are given limited leave, to run for the same period as the refugee. This policy contributes to instability and uncertainty for refugee families who must decide whether to remain separated or undergo the upheaval of relocation for a possibly finite period.

The rules left an extraordinary lacuna that operated against a refugee who formed a family after departure from the country of origin and whose partner did not themselves have settled status in the UK. As the refugee had five years' leave rather than indefinite leave they did not qualify as a sponsor under the marriage rules for settled people. As their new relationship post-dated their departure, they could not qualify as a sponsor under the refugee rules. However, it is unrealistic to expect refugees, who may well have been single when they left, not to form relationships over such a prolonged period.

In *A (Afghanistan) v SSHD* [2009] EWCA Civ 825, the Court of Appeal considered this restriction. In the previous hearing, the Tribunal had been unable to identify any relevant public interest and the Home Office could not do so in time for this hearing. The Court held that there was therefore nothing which could be weighed against the interference with Article 8, the breach of which was disproportionate. Policy arguments were put forward by the government in the subsequent Upper Tribunal case of *FH (Post-flight spouses) Iran* [2010] UKUT 275 (IAC), presided over by Lord Justice Sedley, but were found unpersuasive. The Tribunal concluded that, where an applicant met all the requirements for entry as a spouse of a settled resident (including maintenance and accommodation), exclusion was unlikely to be proportionate. They also recommended giving urgent attention to amending the rules. In 2011, the rules were amended to allow those with limited leave as refugees or through humanitarian protection to sponsor spouses, civil partners, unmarried partners, and minor children on a similar basis to settled residents and nationals (paras 319L and 319U). This means that post-flight spouse and child applications submitted after 9 July 2012 are subject to the new financial requirements (Appendix FM). Fiancé(e)s were originally not included in the amended rules nor under the rules applicable to pre-flight family members. In *Aswatte (fiancé(e)s of refugees) Sri Lanka* [2011] UKUT 0476 (IAC), the Tribunal found that where, as here, there was a long-standing relationship, the principle in *FH* applied and refusal to allow entry under the fiancé(e) rules for settled residents was disproportionate. Post-flight fiancé(e) applications are covered under the new rules in Appendix FM.

8.15 Conclusion

The rules on family settlement still carry the burden of policy on integration and diversity. The continuing proposals for change and the reasons given for these changes indicate that they continue to be instruments of social policy.

In comparison with the 1960s and 1970s, the law relating to family settlement is now relatively transparent. The IDI and entry clearance guidance are published and concessions are increasingly integrated into the rules. This greater transparency, combined with the albeit limited effect of Article 8, is no more than is necessary and appropriate, given that decisions about family members have a fundamental effect on the welfare and happiness of those settled in the UK. In substance, however, the rules continue to restrict the possibilities for family life of such residents. Family migration continues to be an area of frequent and continuing intervention. The contrast with the position of EEA nationals exercising Treaty rights in the UK, and discussed in chapter 4, has become even more pronounced following the implementation in the rules of many of the controversial proposals in the Family Migration Consultation (see Barnden 2013).

QUESTIONS

1 What is the purpose of the probationary period for partners? Why do you think that the government has not implemented a probationary period for other adult relatives?
2 What role is there for immigration control in the prevention of forced marriages?
3 Why are governments resistant to allowing third-party support to meet the maintenance requirement?
4 Draft your own immigration rule for the admission of children, taking into account the policy priorities you would consider most important. How does this compare with the existing rules?

 online resource centre For guidance on answering questions, visit the Online Resource Centre www.oxfordtextbooks.co.uk/orc/clayton7e/.

FURTHER READING

All-Party Parliamentary Group on Migration (2013) 'Report of the Inquiry into the New Family Migration Rules' (June 2013).

Barnden, Tim (2013) 'Family Reunification Requirements: Barrier or facilitator to integration' *Journal of Immigration, Asylum and Nationality Law* vol. 27, no. 2, pp. 174–81.

Charsley, Katharine (2012a) 'Marriage-related migration to the UK' *International Migration Review* vol. 46, issue 4, pp. 861–90.

Charsley, Katharine and Benson, Michaela (2012b) 'Marriages of Convenience and Inconvenient Marriages: Regulating Spousal Migration to Britain' *Journal of Immigration Asylum and Nationality Law* vol. 26, no. 1, pp. 10–26.

Children's Commissioner (2015) 'Family Friendly? The impact on children of the Family Migration Rules: A review of the financial requirements' (August).

Chowdhury, Zahir (2007) 'Recognition of Foreign Adoption: The Immigration Rules and English Conflict of Laws' *Immigration Law Digest* vol. 13, no. 2, Summer, pp. 10–16.

Clayton, Gina (2008) 'Section 3 of the Human Rights Act and the Immigration Rules' *Immigration Law Digest* vol. 14, no. 1, Spring, pp. 7–13.

Clayton, Gina and Wray, Helena (2012) 'Editorial' *Journal of Immigration, Asylum and Nationality Law* vol. 26, no. 3, pp. 218–19.

Coker, Jane, Finch, Nadine, and Stanley, Alison (2002) *Putting Children First: A Guide for Immigration Practitioners* (London: Action Group).

Drew, Sandhya and Nastic, Dragan (2009) 'The Immigration Reservation to the Convention on the Rights of the Child: An Insuperable Difficulty no More' *Journal of Immigration, Asylum and Nationality Law* vol. 23, no. 2, pp. 119–34.

Finch, Nadine (2007) 'Family and Immigration Cases: Implications for Practice' *Family Law* vol. 37, August, pp. 716–20.

Groenendijk, Kees (2011) 'Pre-departure Integration Strategies in the European Union: Integration or Immigration Policy? ' *European Journal of Migration and Law* vol. 13, pp. 1–30.

James, Charles (2006) '50 Years of Family Immigration: Changes in British Legislation for Partner and Family Immigration: 1955–2005' *Journal of Immigration, Asylum and Nationality Law* vol. 20, no. 1, pp. 21–36.

JCWI (2014) 'Harsh, Unjust, Unnecessary: Report on the Impact of the Adult Dependent Relative Rules on Families & Children' (July 2014).

Jones, Adele (2002) 'A Family Life and the Pursuit of Immigration Controls', in S. Cohen, B. Humphries, and E. Mynott (eds), *From Immigration Controls to Welfare Controls* (London: Routledge).

McKee, Richard (1999) 'Primary Purpose by the Back Door? A Critical Look at "Intention to Live Together"' *Immigration and Nationality Law and Practice* vol. 13, no. 1, pp. 3–5.

Menski, Werner (2007) 'Dodgy Asians or Dodgy Laws? The Story of H' *Journal of Immigration, Asylum and Nationality Law* vol. 21, no. 4, pp. 284–94.

Meyler, Frances and Woodhouse, Sarah (2013) 'Changing the Immigration Rules and Withdrawing the Currency of Legal Aid: The impact of LASPO 2012 on migrants and their families' *Journal of Social Welfare and Family Law*, vol. 51, no. 1, pp. 55–78.

Mole, Nuala (1987) *Immigration: Family Entry and Settlement* (Bristol: Jordan & Sons).

Pearl, David (1986) *Family Law and the Immigrant Communities* (Bristol: Jordan & Sons).

Pearl, David and Menski, Werner (1998) *Muslim Family Law* (3rd edn) (London: Sweet & Maxwell).

Pilgram, Lisa (2009) 'Tackling "Sham Marriages": The Rationale, Impact and Limitations of the Home Office's "certificate of approval" scheme' *Journal of Immigration, Asylum and Nationality Law* vol. 23, no. 1, pp. 24–40.

Rogers, Nicola (2003) 'Immigration and the ECHR: Are New Principles Emerging?' *European Human Rights Law Review* 1, pp. 53–64.

Sachdeva, Sanjiv (1993) *The Primary Purpose Rule in British Immigration Law* (Stoke on Trent: Trentham).

Shah, Prakash (2002) 'Children of Polygamous Marriage: An Inappropriate Response' *Immigration and Nationality Law and Practice* vol. 16, no. 2, pp. 110–12.

Shah, Prakash (2011a), 'When South Asians Marry Trans-jurisdictionally: Some reflections on immigration cases by an "expert"' in Holden, L. ed.*Cultural Expertise and Litigation: Patterns, Conflicts, Narratives* (London: Routledge).

Shah, Prakash (2011b) *Transnational Family Relations in Migration Contexts: British Variations on European Themes* available at: www.religareproject.eu/content/transnational-family-relations-migration-contexts-british-variations-european-themes.

Sondhi, Ranjiv (1987) *Divided Families: British Immigration Control in the Indian Subcontinent* (London: Runnymede Trust).

Stanley, Alison (2006) 'Children First, Migrants Second' *Legal Action* March, pp. 7–8.

Symonds, Steve (2011) 'Family Migration' *Journal of Immigration, Asylum and Nationality Law* vol. 25, no. 4, pp. 324–6.

Symonds, Steve (2012) 'Family Migration' *Journal of Immigration, Asylum and Nationality Law* vol. 26, no. 3, pp. 220–2.

Van Oers, Ricky, Ersbøll, Eva, and Kostakopoulou, Dora (2010) *A Re-Definition of Belonging? Language and Integration Tests in Europe* (Leiden: Martinus Nijhoff).

Wray, Helena (2006a) 'An Ideal Husband? Marriages of Convenience, Moral Gate-Keeping and Immigration to the UK' *European Journal of Migration and Law* vol. 8, pp. 303–20.

Wray, Helena (2006b) "Hidden Purpose: Ethnic Minority International Marriages and 'Intention to Live Together'" in P. Shah and W. Menski (eds) *Migration, Diasporas and Legal Systems in Europe* (London and New York: Routledge-Cavendish), pp. 163–84.

Wray, Helena (2009) 'Moulding the Migrant Family' *Legal Studies* vol. 29, no. 4, pp. 592–618.

Wray, Helena (2011) *Regulating Marriage Migration into the UK: A Stranger in the Home* (Farnham: Ashgate).

Wray, Helena (2013a) 'Greater than the Sum of their Parts: UK Supreme Court decisions on family migration' *Public Law* pp. 838–60.

Wray, Helena (2013b) 'Editorial' *Journal of Immigration, Asylum and Nationality Law* vol. 27, no. 3, pp. 196–7.

Yeo, Colin (2009) 'Raising the Spouse Visa Age' *Journal of Immigration, Asylum and Nationality Law* vol. 23, no. 4, pp. 365–70.

9

Entry for work, business, and study: the points-based system

SUMMARY

This chapter deals with the law relating to entry for work, self-employment, and study, the areas covered by the points-based system (PBS), which was implemented from 2008. It is organized around the five Tiers of the PBS but makes reference to some of the old rules as well as providing some historical perspective. It also considers those few schemes remaining outside the PBS and, briefly, illegal working.

9.1 Introduction

Until implementation of the points-based system (PBS), entry for work, business, or study was governed by many disparate schemes within the immigration rules. Most of these were incorporated into the PBS or eliminated. Leave to enter for work or study is always for a limited period. Although some routes lead to settlement, the current policy trend is to reserve this only for the wealthy or the most skilled workers.

The provisions of this chapter do not apply to those who do not need the permission of the immigration authorities to work in the UK. These are:

(a) British citizens and those with a right of abode in the UK (see chapter 3);

(b) Irish citizens, who are exempted from immigration control in the Common Travel Area (Immigration Act 1971 s 1(3) and see chapter 6);

(c) European Economic Area (EEA) nationals, who have freedom of movement under the European Community (EC) Treaties, although the ability to work is limited for Croatian nationals (see 9.9.1 and chapter 4);

(d) those with indefinite leave to remain in the UK (see chapter 6);

(e) those with entry clearance in the form of a certificate of entitlement (see chapter 6);

(f) those on their 'probationary period' as a married, civil, or unmarried partner (see chapter 8);

(g) refugees.

This section is followed by a short history of the law prior to the PBS. There is then a general introduction to the PBS before consideration of each Tier and, finally, routes outside the PBS.

9.2 **A brief history of entry to the UK to work and the development of the work permit scheme**

Work permits began in 1916 as a form of permission to undertake certain types of skilled work and were issued only to aliens, that is, non-Commonwealth citizens including Europeans, although Dummett and Nicol (1990:111) comment that the purpose of the scheme was 'not very clear'. Relatively few foreign nationals came to work in the UK at that time and the scheme was, in part, a carryover from the wartime practice of monitoring the presence of 'aliens'. Commonwealth citizens were British subjects and had, in theory, an unfettered right to enter the UK, though few actually did so.

After the Second World War, there was active recruitment to fill Britain's labour needs. Thousands of work permits were issued for specific groups and purposes, for example, to Italian men for coalmining. In 1945, the government instituted the European Voluntary Workers' Scheme (EVWS), which, for six years, recruited Europeans in refugee camps for three-year contracts in jobs assigned by the Ministry of Labour. These were single people without dependants and, initially, settlement rights. Paul's (1997:84) work reveals that, despite its short-term origins, the government soon began to think of 'the benefits that come from the assimilation of virile, active and industrious people into our stock' and permitted the long-term settlement and integration of this much-needed labour, although not of those who '"through ineptitude or general low mental capacity" or "undesirable character" proved useless' or who were disabled refugees or married women with children (Paul 1997:79). The welcome was conditional and strongly controlling, but national resources were devoted to making it work.

The EVWS met local opposition from, for example, the National Union of Mineworkers (Dummett and Nicol 1990:176). In the meantime, Commonwealth citizens, who did not need work permits, were filling vacancies. As described in chapter 1, Commonwealth nationals who had served Britain during the Second World War returned to make a living and a future in the UK. Others were recruited locally during the 1950s by major employers, for example, London Transport and the British Hotels and Restaurants Association, with inducements such as the payment of fares. Much of this work was low paid. As with the EVWS, public opinion was ambivalent. Paul argues that the government was hostile towards the 492 British subjects who arrived from the West Indies on the *Empire Windrush* in 1948: 'The colonials were met and housed to avoid "disorder" and with the determination that this was to be a once-only affair' (1997:118). British subjects from the Commonwealth could not be controlled in terms of their conditions and length of stay, unlike alien workers. The latter were also seen as more easily assimilated, being white and European. The links between labour market issues and race are covered in chapter 1, and the reader is referred to that chapter for fuller discussion.

During this period, then, there were two systems of entry for work operating in parallel. For foreign nationals, the work permit system continued. Public attention, however, focused on Commonwealth citizens, who entered by virtue of their right as British subjects. Under the Commonwealth Immigrants Act 1962, they became subject to a voucher system, allocated primarily according to skills and need for labour. Vouchers, unlike the work permits issued to aliens, carried a right to immediate settlement but, as Commonwealth citizens already had the right to settle, the scheme represented a curtailment of rights. The voucher system was an attempt to subject Commonwealth citizens to the UK's market needs and their settlement was a necessary concession (see, for instance, Bhabha, Klug, and Shutter (eds), and Holmes (1988)).

The 1965 White Paper restricted entry under the voucher system further. The Immigration Act 1971 completed the process by bringing foreign nationals and Commonwealth citizens into the same work permit scheme, and work vouchers were abolished. The remaining work-related advantages of being a Commonwealth citizen were lost, with the exception of the right of entry for Commonwealth citizens with a UK-born grandparent, discussed briefly later in this chapter. On the same day that the 1971 Act came into force, the UK became a member of the European Communities, giving European nationals the right to travel to the UK for work.

In 1979, a time of high unemployment, the work permit scheme was reviewed and work permits made more difficult to obtain, becoming available only for workers with high levels of skill, qualifications, or experience. In 1989, economic circumstances were different, and a further review had a different outcome. Devine and Barrett-Brown (2001) note that 'there was sustained economic growth with an increasing demand for highly skilled labour, an increase in internationalization in the way business was operating and substantial inward investment by foreign companies'. The Department of Employment, then responsible for the work permit scheme, modified its traditional policy of protecting the resident labour force to support the development of an enterprise economy. Applications that were clearly furthering business growth and investment would be processed more quickly with fewer demands on employers. The result was a two-tier system within the work permit scheme.

Early twenty-first-century labour market conditions were different again as were the terms of debate. A research report for the Home Office, *International Migration and the UK: Recent Patterns and Trends*, summarized the issues as being 'the contribution labour migration can make to alleviating the possible impacts of demographic change; a need to compete in a global skills market to remain economically competitive; and a need to recruit overseas workers to meet specific labour shortages' (Dobson, Koser, Mclaughlan, and Salt 2001). Projections of the numbers of migrant workers needed to sustain European economies briefly became headline news, although the Labour Migration Survey cast doubt on these projections. The Minister for Immigration, Barbara Roche, announced a change of policy, including a new route of primary immigration for the highly skilled (*The Independent* 21 July 2000). The 2002 White Paper *Secure Borders, Safe Haven* (Cm 5387) indicated, for the first time since the 1960s, that there might be a positive role for new primary 'managed migration'. Globalization meant that transnational companies needed to move their own skilled workers about the globe, and economic development increased the supply of skilled labour and demand for study. After a review, the work permit scheme was significantly opened up in 2001. The qualifications needed were reduced, applications to fill shortage occupations were expedited, and switching employers within the UK became easier. In June 2001, Work Permits (UK) was transferred from the Department of Education and Employment to the Home Office and their powers extended to the issue of work permit extensions and in-country grants of leave, without a separate application to the immigration department. The new lawful routes for economic migration proposed in the 2002 White Paper were implemented, not through primary legislation but in schemes and rules, for instance the Highly Skilled Migrants Programme (HSMP), aimed at the most skilled and which led to settlement. Anticipating the PBS, both the HSMP and a new Innovators' scheme were based on a points system, common in other Commonwealth countries but not previously used in the UK. There was expansion of the Working Holiday Makers scheme and of the Seasonal Agricultural Workers Scheme (SAWS), both considered later in this chapter, and, in May 2003, a new Sectors Based Scheme (SBS), also discussed later, was introduced extending the work permit scheme from its traditional professional base through short-term permits in food-processing and the hotel and catering industry.

On 1 May 2004, ten countries acceded to the European Union (EU). The UK, unlike most of its European partners, granted nationals of the new Member States an immediate right to work, subject to registration under the Workers' Registration Scheme. Accession Monitoring Reports showed Accession State nationals engaged in a wide range of occupations, including bus, lorry, and coach drivers, care workers, teachers, researchers, classroom assistants, and health-related posts, but the immediate impact was primarily in agriculture and fishing, where employment grew sharply (Portes and French 2005).

The positive tone towards economic migration which emerged in the 2002 White Paper was not sustained. In 2004, quotas were introduced and then reduced in SAWS and quotas were reduced also in the SBS. Criteria for the Working Holiday Makers scheme tightened again soon after having been relaxed. In April 2004, the government announced a '"top to bottom review" of managed migration routes to assess the extent to which they were subject to abuse or otherwise open to improvement' (*Selective Admission* para 4.8). The results were a number of measures tightening immigration control. In February 2005, the publication of the White Paper, *Controlling our Borders: Making Migration Work for Britain* (Cm 6472), announced plans for a tiered points system encompassing all immigration for work or study and favouring the most skilled both for entry and settlement. In July, a consultation document was published, entitled *Selective Admission*, in which the criteria were uncompromisingly economic. Details of the new managed migration scheme were published in March 2006 as Cm 6741, *A Points-Based System: Making Migration Work for Britain*. Implementation started in 2008 and now covers almost all migrants coming for work or study.

The implementation of the PBS coincided with a sharp recession, rising unemployment, and new concerns about immigration and security. The trend has been towards more restriction and this is evident in many aspects of the PBS discussed later in the chapter. While 2008 saw a record number of foreigners living in the UK (*ONS Population Trends No. 138*), government rhetoric began to suggest that the principal effect of the PBS would not be to manage migration, as originally conceived, but to reduce it. This theme continued in even more marked terms after the Coalition government came to power in 2010 and under the Conservative government elected in 2015. The continuing commitment to reducing net migration to the 'tens of thousands' means that very few (1,000 per year) highly skilled migrants without a job offer may now enter the UK while the number of skilled work migrants filling vacancies has been capped and new restrictions placed on students.

9.3 **The points-based system (PBS): Introduction**

The structure of the PBS is similar to the outline in the consultation paper. Most non-family migration routes were consolidated into one of five Tiers, although some were deleted and a decreasing number, discussed later, still operate outside the PBS. To qualify in each Tier, applicants must have sufficient points according to the criteria of the scheme. The government vigorously promoted the transparency, objectivity, and flexibility of the PBS.

The Select Committee on Home Affairs reported on the PBS in July 2009 (*Managing Migration: The Points Based System*, Thirteenth Report of Session 2008–09 HC 217–I). Some of its specific findings are discussed later in the chapter. Its overall conclusion was that, while the scheme as a whole, received a 'cautious welcome', several key structures required further consideration. Since then, however, the PBS has become less flexible, more complex and more restrictive, and there are reports of considerable delays in dealing with in-country applications (Home Affairs Committee (2013) *The Work of the UK Border Agency (January–March 2013)* Eighth Report of Session 2013–14, p. 62). In its current form, the PBS lacks any of the flexibility that is the usual characteristic of points systems while the insertion of new conditions, for example, as to genuineness, require subjective judgments by decision-makers that work against predictability and consistent decision-making.

An applicant under the PBS pays a substantial fee to have one shot at getting a complex application right with only limited scope for rectifying mistakes (discussed later). There were problems with the quality of decision-making from the outset (see Wray 2009:239). A 2010 report by the UK Council for International Student Affairs found that 10 per cent of student applicants believed that their first application had been unreasonably refused, affecting perceptions of the UK as a welcoming destination (UKCISA (2010) *Students' Experiences of Extending their Visas in the UK under Tier 4*). The Chief Inspector's inspection of Tier 2 applications in 2010 found much to commend in staff practice and attitudes but also an over-complex system and inconsistencies in practice between posts (Chief Inspector UK Border Agency (2010) *A Thematic Inspection of the Points-Based System: Tier 2 (Skilled Workers) July–August 2010*). Later reports have been more positive but still found problems with the quality of service in student applications (Independent Chief Inspector of Borders and Immigration (2012) *An Inspection of Tier 4 of the Points-Based System (Students) April–July 2012*). A 2011 survey by UKCISA found improvements but also that poor information, the pace of change, refusal due to minor errors, the cost of the application process, and the reintroduction of judgments on English language proficiency caused problems for a significant number of applicants (UKCISA (2011) *The UKCISA Tier 4 Student Survey 2011*).

9.3.1 Flexibility

The defining characteristic of a points system is that applicants who do not fully meet one criterion can compensate by scoring well elsewhere. That type of flexibility was initially present in Tiers 1 and 2 to a limited extent but has now entirely disappeared. Elsewhere within the PBS, applicants have always been required to attain full points by meeting a specific requirement. A Tier 4 student, for example, needs 30 points for attributes. These can be obtained only by obtaining a 'Confirmation of Acceptance for Studies'. Ten points are needed for maintenance. These can be awarded only by possession in the manner specified of the sum specified in Appendix C. In other words, points are simply another way of saying that the applicant must meet all the requirements of the immigration rules and, as early as 2009, the Select Committee noted the scheme's 'rigidity and inflexibility'. Since then, the PBS has been a victim of government determination to reduce immigration, and repeated and accumulated changes mean that, far from being a flexible and transparent system, it is now prescriptive, difficult to understand, and very complicated so that an applicant can easily make a mistake that is fatal to the application.

An error made when applying from abroad means refusal, loss of the fee, and possibly loss of a job or educational opportunity. Refusal also makes obtaining a later visa from the UK or elsewhere more difficult. In-country applicants may find that they become inadvertent overstayers with drastic consequences for lives built up over many years. In principle and as discussed later, Article 8 may be engaged but, so far, no case has succeeded on that basis. Paragraph 34C of the immigration rules renders an application invalid, that is, as if it had not been made, if it does not comply with all the formal requirements as to, for example, the correct fee or completion of mandatory sections. Section 3C Immigration Act 1971 (which extends expiring leave until a decision on an in-time extension application has been determined) does not apply as no valid application has been made. While applications may still be made from within the UK within 28 days of former leave expiring, by the time an application is rejected as invalid, that window may have passed. In any event, under para 14 of Appendix C of the rules, an out-of-time applicant will not have 'an established presence' in the UK and so must meet the higher financial requirements that apply to out-of-country applicants, leading to further rejection. This is precisely what happened to the claimant in *R (on the application of Behary) v SSHD* [2013] EWHC 3575 (Admin); the applicant, who was a student, and her family had been in the UK lawfully for more than six years. Her application for further leave was sent one day late due to illness and a closed post office. It was refused because she did not provide evidence of meeting the higher out-of-country financial requirements. Her claim for judicial review failed on several grounds, including the value of clear rules in the administration of immigration control. The Court of Appeal in *Iqbal and others v SSHD* [2015] EWCA Civ 838 confirmed the principle. One of the appellants, Mr Iqbal, for example, had submitted his application in time but with the incorrect fee, having failed to realize that the fee had increased. His application was rejected as invalid with the result that he no longer had valid leave to be in the UK.

The Select Committee in its 2009 report recommended that an applicant should be able to submit additional paperwork, where this is requested, without having to make a fresh application or pay another fee. In his report on Tier 2, the Chief Inspector made a similar recommendation and noted variable practice in that regard. Since 2014, para 34C has permitted (but not required) the decision maker to give the applicant an opportunity to correct any omission or error within ten working days.

With respect to missing or incorrect documents, in 2011, the government introduced a flexibility policy and then, in December 2012, paras 245AA(b) into the rules. These provide that, while decision-makers will only consider documents that have been submitted with the application, they may invite applicants to submit documents that are missing from a sequence, or a document in the correct format, that is an original of a copy or in order to have complete information. A document which is missing altogether (such as a language certificate) will not be requested and a request will not be made if the decision-maker does not anticipate that this will lead to a grant of the application because it will be refused for other reasons.

The nature of the obligations in respect of flexibility (although under the policy rather than the rule) was discussed by the Supreme Court in *Mandalia*.

 **Key Case**

Mandalia v SSHD [2015] UKSC 59

Mr Mandalia came to the UK from India in 2008 to study. In 2012, he applied to extend his stay in order to study accountancy. His application was in order except that, instead of supplying bank statements showing the required amount in his account over 28 days, his statements showed only the requisite balance over 22 days. The application was refused.

The government argued that the flexibility policy did not apply because it was expressed to apply only where documents in a sequence were missing and, here, the documents were missing at the beginning or end of the series. The Supreme Court unanimously dismissed this argument. In his lead judgment, Lord Wilson said that he considered 'the Secretary of State's submission to be misplaced even at the high level of pedantry on which it has been set' (para 33). The policy, as it was worded, required the decision-maker to request the missing bank statements.

The *Mandalia* decision affirmed that the government is bound by its own policy unless there is a good reason to depart from it, even where, as here, the applicant is unaware of its existence. This was based not on the doctrine of legitimate expectation, which is not appropriate to such a situation, but a related, freestanding doctrine of good administration. The interpretation of a policy is a matter of law which courts can decide. Both these findings offer a degree of support to applicants whose applications have been refused due to minor failings in the application, and the rules were amended in November 2015 to make failure to request a document as required by the rules a case-working error for the purposes of administrative review. However, while the government must apply its flexibility policy if it has one, the decision does not require such a policy to exist or determine its minimum content.

In some cases, the common law duty to act fairly may ensure fair process (*Marghia (procedural fairness)* [2014] UKUT 00366 (IAC)). So, where the Secretary of State had withdrawn sponsor status from a college to issue CAS letters, fairness required that the student have a reasonable opportunity to find another college (*Naved (Student—fairness—notice of points)* [2012] UKUT 14 (IAC); *Patel (revocation of sponsor licence—fairness) India* [2011] UKUT 00211 (IAC)). It was also unfair to refuse an application because of failure to supply documentation which was not requested (*Thakur (PBS Decision—Common Law Fairness) Bangladesh* [2011] UKUT 00151 (IAC)); see also the discussion later on the position of students affected by revocation of sponsorship. Where an applicant's bank statements dipped below the minimum figure required because UK Visas and Immigration had erroneously taken a fee and failed to return it in good time, the Secretary of State was required at least to consider exercising discretion particularly given her compliance for many years with immigration control (*R (on the application of Solaja) v SSHD* [2013] EWHC 3431 (Admin)). In general, however, it is not unfair to reject an application for failure to meet any of the requirements of the PBS or when the fault does not lie with the government: 'The PBS is a very detailed scheme, and, in order to secure predictability and consistency in a decision making process which has to consider a very large number of applications, it is highly prescriptive' (Sullivan LJ in *Alam and others v SSHD* [2012] EWCA Civ 960 [43]). There was no unfairness involved in refusing an application when sponsorship had been wrongly withdrawn without the applicant's knowledge. Any remedy lay against the sponsor not the government (*EK (Ivory Coast) v SSHD* [2014] EWCA Civ 1517, although see the dissenting judgment by Floyd LJ).

9.3.2 Complexity

The PBS is difficult to navigate successfully. Criteria for entry are set out in the immigration rules and must be cross-referenced with the appendices. There is additional lengthy guidance for each Tier and in relation to each application form. The Tier 2 Guidance, for instance, is 75 pages long.

Guidance outside the immigration rules has long existed in the form of the Immigration Directorate Instructions and Entry Clearance Guidance. However, the PBS guidance is of a different order of complexity and specificity, is addressed to applicants or sponsors not to officials, and is changed frequently. It is not subject to even the limited legislative scrutiny of the immigration rules. However, when the PBS was implemented, applicants would be refused because of non-compliance with the guidance. This caused immense difficulties for applicants and eventually the issue came before the Supreme Court.

 **Key Case**

Alvi v SSHD [2012] UKSC 33

This case has already been discussed in chapter 1, because of what it says about the constitutional position of the immigration rules. Mr Alvi was a Pakistani national who entered the UK as a student and remained to work as a physiotherapy assistant. When he applied for further leave, he was refused on the grounds that his job was not a skilled occupation as now required by the rules. The designation of his occupation was not in the rules themselves but in a separate Code of Practice referred to in the rules. As discussed in chapter 1, the Court found that 'any requirement which a migrant must satisfy as a condition of being given leave to enter or leave to remain, as well as any provision "as to the period for which leave is to be given and the conditions to be attached in different circumstances"' must be laid before Parliament under s 3(2) of the Immigration Act 1971, that is, must be contained in the immigration rules.

As the designation of Mr Alvi's occupation would determine his application, it must be contained in the immigration rules not in a separate Code of Practice which could be amended without going through the process of scrutiny required by the 1971 Act. There remained a role for guidance outside the rules but it should not contain 'rules', that is, prescriptions which the applicant must meet to qualify. Making the distinction between rules and guidance depends on facts and context and was recognized not to be straightforward; their Lordships themselves were divided over whether the advertising requirements in the Resident Labour Market Test (discussed later in this chapter) were a rule.

Alvi established an important point of principle and also assisted applicants and their advisers who had been unable to predict when and how detailed guidance might change, a serious problem in the period before the *Alvi* decision. The government did not use the *Alvi* decision however to adopt a less prescriptive approach but simply transferred much of the content of the guidance into the immigration rules. The result is that the rules have become highly complex and difficult to navigate or understand and are liable to even more frequent change (they were changed ten times during 2012 and a further ten times before the end of November 2013). In the words of Jackson LJ in *Pokhriyal v SSHD* [2013] EWCA Civ 1568 [4], the rules 'have now achieved a degree of complexity which even the Byzantine Emperors would have envied'. However, there is now at least notice of changes to the rules and Parliament has the opportunity to scrutinize or even reject them, although the volume of change must make effective examination difficult.

9.3.3 **Accountability**

There has never been a right of appeal against refusal of a PBS application made through entry clearance, except on human rights or (formerly) on race discrimination grounds.

This was justified by the 'objective and verifiable' criteria of the PBS (*Controlling Our Borders* 2005 p. 2), yet there is no evidence that human error has been eliminated. Independent appeal rights were replaced by a system of administrative review and scrutiny by the Independent Chief Inspector of Borders and Immigration. Administrative review mirrors a long-standing system whereby an entry clearance manager reconsiders a refusal. These were previously criticized as ineffective (see National Audit Office (2004) *Visa Entry to the United Kingdom: The Entry Clearance Operation* HC 367 at p. 27). A freedom of information request in October 2013 (FOI 29305/VCT 166359) showed that between July 2012 and June 2013, only 18 per cent of administrative reviews resulted in a changed decision although the success rate for appeals was over 50 per cent. A 2013 survey of UK Council for International Student Affairs found that educational sponsors regarded administrative review as subjective, cursory, and lacking independence (UK-CISA (2013) *Tier 4 Credibility Interviews: UKCISA Survey Report* pp. 11–12).

Appeal rights remained in place for in-country applications for some years although they were attenuated further by s 19 UK Borders Act 2007, which prohibited the introduction of new evidence at a PBS appeal (unless the appeal is on human rights or EU free movement grounds) even if this evidence related to the state of affairs at the time of the application, for example, bank statements that showed that the applicant possessed the requisite funds when the application was made. The outcome was that only evidence included in the application could be taken into account. The argument was that the government's low success rate (it won under half of appeals in this area) was because appellants introduced evidence at the appeal that should have been presented with the application. However, implementation of the measure did not improve the government's success rate and the Select Committee on Home Affairs observed that: 'The Agency's poor results in appeals must therefore be due to poor initial decision making or inadequate legal representation' (*The Work of the UK Border Agency (December 2011–March 2012)* Fifth Report of Session 2012–13, vol. I, p. 27). However, rather than improve the standard of decision-making, the government removed this layer of accountability. Section 15 Immigration Act 2014 removed all appeal rights except for claims based on human rights or protection grounds (which will rarely arise in the PBS context). From now on, all applicants must rely on administrative review (which costs £80 for in-country applicants) which can only correct errors in the decision-making process that should not have been made. Section 16 of the Immigration Act 2014 requires the Home Secretary to request the Chief Inspector of Borders and Immigration to inspect the effectiveness of administrative review. The report is due in February 2016 but the comments submitted by Immigration Law Practitioners' Association (ILPA) suggest that it is not a satisfactory way to eliminate errors. The Chief Inspector also monitors the PBS but this is also not a substitute for appeal rights. Only a small sample of decisions is examined and there is no power to overturn poor decisions. The Select Committee on Home Affairs (Fifth Report of Session 2007–8 HC 425, Conclusions and Recommendations) recommended that the Chief Inspector should have the power to investigate individual cases and provide appropriate remedies.

Judicial review remains available but, as *Rhandawa v SSHD* [2008] EWHC 3042 (Admin) demonstrates, that is not equivalent to an appeal. Here, an application under the Highly Skilled Migrant Programme had been refused because of evidence of false claims about employment which were challenged by the applicant. Mr Justice Sullivan said that, had this been an appeal on the merits, he might have been cautious about accepting the unfavourable evidence but that, in a judicial review, he was confined to deciding whether the defendants had been unreasonable to rely on it.

Where applicants have built up a life in the UK, they may argue that refusal breaches their article 8 private or family rights but this is unlikely to succeed. Sedley LJ, in *SSHD v Pankina and others* [2010] EWCA Civ 719, found that, in applying the immigration rules, the government must have regard to applicants' Convention rights. An in-country applicant may have established an Article 8 private or family life that will suffer interference if an application for further leave fails and refusal for minor errors that do not affect the applicant's substantive eligibility may be disproportionate. In *CDS (PBS: 'available': Article 8) Brazil* [2010] UKUT 00305 (IAC), the Upper Tribunal observed out that there is no hard and fast rule about which aspects of the Rules may be overlooked to render a decision compliant: 'even central requirements are not determinative if the countervailing claim is of sufficient weight'. This, however, does not mean that Article 8 is 'a means whereby the immigration rules can be ignored or re-written, because a judicial fact-finder regards a person as having only narrowly failed to comply with the relevant rules' (*MM and SA (Pankina: near miss) Pakistan* [2010] UKUT 481 (IAC)). Nor may serious breaches be ignored. In *SAB and others (students—serious breach of conditions—Article 8) Ghana* [2010] UKUT 441, the applicant had worked in excess of the hours permitted under his Tier 4 visa, a flagrant breach that could not be overlooked. The Court of Appeal in *JK (India) v SSHD* [2013] EWCA Civ 1080 agreed that refusal to extend student leave might breach Article 8 but stressed the importance of looking at the applicant's life and conduct before the date of the application. Here, the earlier submission of a forged document, even if it had been unintentional, and her failure to pursue qualifications with any vigour meant that the claim fell far short of the threshold. In *Patel v SSHD* [2013] UKSC 72, the Supreme Court made the point that, although the context of the rules (including the margin by which they have been missed) may be relevant to the consideration of proportionality, this cannot be equated with a formalized 'near-miss' or 'sliding scale' principle. Article 8 is concerned with private or family life, not the right to remain for work, education, or another purpose.

When all else fails, MPs may make representations to the UK Visas and Immigration Section on behalf of their constituents. The Home Affairs Select Committee in 2009 foresaw that these would increase as a result of the removal of appeal rights and was critical of the existing quality and speed of responses.

9.3.4 **Role of the sponsor**

All PBS applicants, except those for Tier 1, need a sponsor. This will be the employer for Tier 2, the educational establishment for Tier 4, or may be a religious body, charity, sporting, or cultural body or even a government under Tier 5. Tier 2 and Tier 5 sponsors are rated 'A' or 'B'. The 'B' rating is regarded as transitional and the sponsor must either improve their performance under a 'sponsorship action plan' or lose their licence.

Sponsors are drawn deeper into the control of migrants under the PBS. They now have many positive obligations. For instance, employer and student sponsors must report the following:

- failure to turn up for the first day of work or enrolment at college (or other educational establishment);
- unauthorized absences from work of more than ten working days or from ten 'expected contacts' at college;
- termination of the contract of employment or termination of studies;
- changes in circumstances or information that indicate that the employee or student is breaching their conditions of entry.

Because retention of a Tier 4 sponsor's licence depends on the profile and conduct of students (e.g., a Tier 4 sponsor must not have more than a 20 per cent entry clearance refusal rate), sponsors are becoming reluctant to accept students who have previously been refused or who come from particular countries or regions, however suitable they may be in other respects (UK Council for International Student Affairs (2013) *Tier 4 Credibility Interviews: UKCISA Survey Report* pp. 13–14). There is also the temptation to over-report possible violations and more than 35,000 reports were made by educational institutions in just two years ('UK Universities "over-report" on foreign students' *University World News* 2 October 2011).

The loss of a sponsorship licence is very serious for all involved. As the High Court explained in *R (on the application of The London Reading College Ltd) v SSHD* [2010] EWHC 2561 (Admin), at para 9:

> . . . establishing a college and achieving both accreditation and licensing is a substantial business undertaking for an establishment. Having achieved this status and opened for business teaching students, the college will inevitably have made substantial financial commitments. The loss of a licence would have the most serious professional and financial consequences for the college and its proprietors. It would also have a serious impact upon both its current students and its prospective students.

Despite its significance, the system of licensing is not based on statute, is administered according to guidance which changes with 'bewildering frequency' (Lord Sumption in *New London College* [15]), and may be challenged only by judicial review. However, this rarely succeeds as, in most cases, the government is found to be acting lawfully in withholding or revoking licences from institutions whose compliance does not meet prescribed standards. Unsurprisingly, the legal authority for the sponsorship system was questioned in the courts.

 **Key Case**

R (on the application of New London College Ltd) v SSHD **[2013] UKSC 51**

Two colleges, one which had its licence revoked and another which had been refused 'highly trusted sponsor status', challenged the lawfulness of the licensing guidance. It was agreed that many parts of the guidance had the character of a rule as defined in *Alvi*. It was argued that, as having a licensed sponsor was critical to a migrant obtaining leave in these categories, the system came within s 3(2) of the Immigration Act 1971 and had to be included within the immigration rules. This argument was rejected because obtaining a sponsor licence is not a condition that the migrant him/herself must fulfil but was part of a system to which sponsors voluntarily submitted themselves.

It was also argued that the sponsorship system had no other statutory foundation and, given the absence of prerogative power in immigration, represented an unlawful exercise of power. This argument was rejected by Lord Sumption for the majority: the statutory power of the Secretary of State to administer the system of immigration control includes ancillary and incidental administrative powers necessary for the administration of control. Provided these do not conflict with the Immigration Act, the immigration rules, or other legal obligations, they are lawful. Lord Carnwath came to the same conclusion but for different reasons. He considered the sponsorship licensing scheme to be an adjunct, not of the immigration control system in general, but of the specific power to provide for entry for study under s 1(4) of the 1971 Act. The exercise of those powers in respect of the licensing system was consistent with the immigration rules as currently drafted. He doubted whether the principle in *Alvi* was material to the case because that case concerned requirements that were very clearly within the scope of s 3(2) of the Act whereas here, the issue was a 'complete and self-contained regulatory code' [41].

Since the *New London College* judgment, judicial reviews of sponsorship revocations have been brought on a regular basis and a few have succeeded. More commonly however, the courts have taken the view that colleges who admit overseas students have a heavy responsibility to ensure the route is not abused and they have not discharged this. The legal principles were usefully summarized by Mr Justice Haddon-Cave in *Raj and Knoll Ltd v SSHD* [2015] EWHC 1329 Admin:

- the essence of the system is that the Secretary of State imposes 'a high degree of trust' in sponsors in implementing and policing immigration policy;
- the authority to grant sponsorship is a privilege which carries great responsibility and the sponsor is expected to carry out its responsibilities as rigorously and vigilantly as the immigration authorities and to maintain records with assiduity;
- the introduction of the Points-Based System has created a system of immigration control in which the emphasis is on certainty and detail rather than discretion and broad guidance;
- there no need to wait until there has been a breach of immigration control caused by the acts or omission of a sponsor before suspending or revoking sponsorship;
- the primary judgment about the appropriate response to breaches by sponsors is made by the government and the role of the court is supervisory;
- the courts should respect the experience and expertise of immigration officials when reaching conclusions as to a sponsor's compliance.

9.3.5 Settlement

The rights attaching to migrant status are dependent upon the Tier in which entry is granted which, in turn, is largely determined by the migrant's skills and education. In particular, only Tier 1, Tier 2, and a very few Tier 5 migrants may settle. Following a consultation in 2011 (Home Office/UK Border Agency (2011) *Employment-Related Settlement, Tier 5 and Migrant Domestic Workers: A Consultation*), the criteria that must be met for settlement have become more demanding, including more rigorous language and knowledge tests (see chapter 6) and a minimum salary threshold for skilled workers not in shortage occupations (see later in the chapter). The conditions for further leave and settlement are set out in the rules and require migrants to continue to meet the original terms of entry on each occasion. Research commissioned by the Equalities and Human Rights Commission was concerned that women and other less favoured groups may be adversely affected by requirements such as the need to maintain employment at minimum income levels for a prolonged period (Kofman et al 2009).

UK Visas and Immigration guidance to applicant advises that '[i]f you are considering applying for settlement in the future, please note that the Immigration Rules are subject to change. You must meet all the requirements of the Immigration Rules as they apply **at the time you make your application for settlement**. They may not be the same as the requirements for settlement when you first obtain leave to enter the UK' (emphasis added). This warning is a wise precaution after the government tried and failed to change the terms upon which those who had already entered the UK under the Highly Skilled Migrant programme (HSMP; now replaced by Tier 1) could obtain further leave to remain. The HSMP was amended without notice in November 2006, applying new criteria to extension of leave applications by those who had already migrated to the UK. The reason given by the government was that many were not in highly paid employment as the scheme envisaged, but were working as, *inter alia*, taxi drivers (Letter of Minister of State to JCHR 18 May 2007).

The High Court found, in *R (on the application of HSMP Forum Ltd) v SSHD* [2008] EWHC 664 (Admin), that the HSMP scheme from entry to settlement composed one whole and could not be retrospectively amended for those who had already embarked upon it. The position was different for new entrants. Similarly, the extension of the minimum period of leave before settlement from four to five years also could not be retrospectively applied (*R (on the application of HSMP Forum (UK) Ltd) v SSHD* [2009] EWHC 711 (Admin)).

The HSMP scheme had particular characteristics, which enabled these claims to succeed. It was aimed at those planning to migrate permanently and applicants had to intend to make the UK their main home for their application to succeed. The Court observed that the government could have prevented its difficulties by expressly stating that there was no guarantee that the criteria for further stay would not change.

The underlying issue in the HSMP litigation, that is, the extent to which the government can change the terms of continuing leave after entry, has also arisen in other work-related contexts. The terms on which overseas medical graduates may complete their medical training or work in the UK have changed frequently in the past 20 years. In 2006, the options for foreign medical graduates to complete their training and obtain work in the UK were dramatically reduced by the removal of provision for permit-free medical training in the UK. The government also tried to prevent doctors who could no longer qualify under the permit-free provisions from qualifying under the HSMP, not, as might be expected, by changing the HSMP rules but by sending guidance to NHS employers advising them that overseas medical graduates should only be employed if certain conditions were met.

 **Key Case**

R (on the application of BAPIO Action Limited) v SSHD [2008] UKHL 27

The situation of the second claimant to the original High Court challenge, Dr Imran Yousaf, was representative of the difficulties faced by those affected by the changes although Dr Yousaf tragically took his own life shortly before the High Court decision. He had obtained his primary medical qualification in Pakistan, working there as a junior doctor for two years. He came to the UK in 2004 to continue his training, taking and passing the necessary conversion tests. The test and visa fees and the costs of travel represented a significant commitment and he had incurred considerable debts. However, he did not obtain a post before the abolition of permit-free training, and transitional arrangements did not apply to him.

In the House of Lords, the outstanding issue was the legality of the guidance issued to NHS employers, which aimed to prevent those in Dr Yousaf's position from remaining in the UK under the HSMP. It was found that the guidance was unlawful because, in effect, it changed the terms of leave without complying with the requirements in the Immigration Act 1971 for amendment of the immigration rules. Two of their Lordships also found that those doctors who had already been admitted under the HSMP (so, not Dr Yousaf) had a legitimate expectation that they could proceed to settlement under that scheme.

These cases, although decided under pre-PBS rules, highlight a major tension within the government's thinking about skilled migration. Skilled migrants are unlikely to come to the UK if they do not have the option of long-term residence for themselves and their families. Yet, the government wishes to retain the power to adjust rights as it deems necessary. As will be seen, the PBS requires migrants to prove their worth on entry, when they apply for further leave and again on settlement. As the position is clear from the outset, migrants cannot claim that they have been misled. However, the greater degree of uncertainty that migrants now face may be a disincentive to those whose skills allow them to choose between destinations.

9.3.6 **The Migration Advisory Committee**

The Migration Advisory Committee (MAC) has played an extensive role in the development of the PBS. It is an independent, non-time limited, non-statutory committee established by the government in 2007 and is central to government claims that the PBS is determined by objectively assessed criteria. According to its website, it is:

responsible for providing transparent, independent and evidence-based advice to the government on migration issues. Our reports cover issues including:

- the impacts of immigration
- the limits on immigration under the points based system
- skills shortages within occupations.

Although the MAC has several functions, the most significant are to identify which jobs come within the description of graduate-level employment for the purposes of Tier 2 and to review the list of shortage occupations. It has also, at the request of government, carried out other tasks including, most recently, assessing whether nurses should appear on the shortage occupation list and a review of Tier 2 although the government does not always follow their recommendations.

9.4 **Tier 1 migrants**

Tier 1 provides a route to entry as a highly skilled worker, entrepreneur, or investor and is the only Tier for which a sponsor is not required. Entry clearance is always required before entry and switching in-country is possible only in limited circumstances. Tier 1 replaced a range of schemes such as the HSMP, Writers, Composers and Artists, Innovators and Investors, not all of which have their equivalents under Tier 1. The Coalition government substantially reduced the ability of migrants to enter under this Tier through the closure of Tier 1 (General) and its replacement by the much more restrictive Tier 1 (Exceptional Talent). Similarly, the closure of the Tier 1 (Post-Study Work) route prevented many former overseas students from staying on to work in the UK after graduation. There are four sub-categories in the Tier: Exceptional Talent, Entrepreneurs, Investors, and Graduate Entrepreneurs.

9.4.1 **Tier 1 (Exceptional Talent) and Tier 1 (General)**

Tier 1 (Exceptional Talent) was introduced in August 2011 to replace the Tier 1 (General) which closed to new entrants at the same time. Tier 1 (General) had been a popular scheme, with almost 14,000 main visas and more than 10,000 dependant visas issued in 2009. It was a primary target in the Coalition government's drive to reduce net migration through a cap on numbers. In June 2010, the government asked the MAC to advise on the level at which the Tier 1 and 2 caps should be set in 2011/12. The Committee concluded that, on balance, Tier 1 and 2 migrants make a small but cumulatively significant positive net fiscal contribution, that is, the benefits of their presence outweigh the costs, but that, if the objective was to reduce migration, those who entered should be the most productive. It therefore proposed a small reduction in the number of Tier 1 visas, more regular recalibration of the points awarded and a requirement of graduate level employment at the renewal stage. These cautious proposals were not in line with the government's radical plans and, in July 2010 before publication of the MAC report, the government announced an interim cap of 600 Tier 1 (General) acceptances per month.

The government argued that many Tier 1 migrants were not doing highly skilled work. In October 2011, the government published research which showed that only 25 per cent of Tier 1 visa holders were working in skilled occupations and earning over £25,000 pa. although this data was drawn only from Tier 1 migrants with dependants (Home Office/UK Border Agency *Points Based System Tier 1: An Operational Assessment*). In March 2011, Damian Green, Minister for Immigration, said that this tier 'supposedly the route for the best and the brightest—has not attracted highly-skilled workers. At least 30 per cent of Tier One migrants work in low-skilled occupations such as stacking shelves, driving taxis or working as security guards and some don't have a job at all.' The closure of the Tier 1 (General) route was announced in November 2010 and implemented from December 2010 for overseas applications and from August 2011 for in-country applicants, when Tier 1 (Exceptional Talent) also opened.

The Exceptional Talent scheme is much more restrictive than Tier 1 (General). Its purpose, according to para 245B of the rules, is to provide a route for 'exceptionally talented individuals . . . who are already internationally recognised at the highest level as world leaders in their particular field, or who have already demonstrated exceptional promise and are likely to become world leaders in their particular area.' Applicants must usually apply from outside the UK. They need a minimum of 75 points under Appendix A (para 245BB), which can be obtained only through endorsement by a Designated Competent Body, defined in para 4(b) of Appendix A as the Arts Council (allocated 250 endorsements each year for excellence in arts and culture), the Royal Society (250 endorsements for natural and medical sciences), the Royal Academy of Engineering (150 endorsements), the British Council (150 endorsements for humanities and social sciences), and Tech City UK (200 endorsements for digital technology). Thus, in each year, only 1,000 migrants can enter under this sub-category. There are no language or maintenance requirements.

Admission will be for up to five years and four months. It is subject to conditions as to public funds, registration with the police, and some limits on employment. Further leave is obtainable provided the applicant is economically active in their expert field through employment or self-employment, and the Designated Competent Body has not withdrawn its endorsement. Indefinite leave is obtainable after five years as a Tier 1 or Tier 2 migrant subject to meeting the same requirements as before regarding economic activity and the other criteria for settlement, including having passed the knowledge of life in the UK test and, unless exempted, an approved English language test at level B1 Common European Framework of Reference for Language Learning (CEFR).

Tier 1 (Exceptional Talent) is not an equivalent to Tier 1 (General) being capped, far more restrictive and lacking the flexibility of a points system. Tier 1 (General) was not only uncapped but had a more flexible system for awarding points. Those who scored less well under one heading might make them up under another. Points could be earned under the headings of Qualifications, Previous Earnings, UK Experience, and Age although it was impossible to score sufficient points without scoring highly in either Qualifications or Previous Earnings. It was one of the very few instances of a true points-based approach within the PBS and was open to anyone who qualified, unlike the new regime which is capped.

9.4.2 Tier 1 (Entrepreneur)

Paragraph 245D of the immigration rules explains that this route is for migrants who wish to establish, join, or take over one or more businesses in the UK. A business means an enterprise as a sole trader, a partnership, or a UK-registered company. The applicant must have 75 points under the relevant paragraphs of Appendix A, 10 under Appendix B (English language), and 10 under Appendix C (maintenance).

A new applicant can gain the 75 points for attributes under Appendix A by having access to at least £200,000 or to at least £50,000 from various approved sources, held in one or more regulated financial institutions and disposable in the UK. The rules explain the meaning of 'regulated financial institution' and 'disposable in the UK'. The applicant must also have a minimum of ten points for English language under Appendix B, acquired through reaching level B1 or above of the CEFR, having a degree taught in English, or nationality of an English speaking country. The applicant also needs 10 points for maintenance under Appendices C and E, which stipulate that the applicant must show that he has £3,310 for him/herself and £1,890 for each dependant available to him for a period of 90 consecutive days. The funds must not be the same as those on which the application is based and must not be held in a financial institution listed in Appendix P against which satisfactory verification checks cannot be made.

Numbers applying for this route increased by a factor of more than 15 after closure in 2012 (discussed later) of the Post-Study Work (PSW) route. In 2014, 5,488 visas were issued, of which roughly 80 per cent were issued in-country. The Chief Inspector of Borders and Immigration, in a report published in 2013, found that the decision-making was unsatisfactory. The rules now require the decision-maker to be satisfied on the balance of probabilities that the applicant has either already invested the funds within the previous twelve months or genuinely has the money available and intends to become involved in and invest their funds in a UK business within six months. The decision-maker may request additional evidence to support the application or call the applicant for interview. A business plan must also be provided. Relevant factors for deciding the application include the evidence submitted, the viability and credibility of the source of funds, the business plan and market research, the applicant's previous educational and business experience (or lack thereof), and their immigration history and previous activity in the UK.

It is clear that fear of fraud means that the type of discretionary decision-making which the PBS was designed to replace has been reintroduced but now without the accountability of appeal rights. It also appears that some nationalities are affected more than others by fears of fraud. A response to a freedom of information request (FOI Reference: 37230 12 November 2015) showed that, in 2014, 105 applications were made from the US, none were called for interview and no application was refused. In the same period, 475 applications were made in Pakistan, there were 305 interviews and 295 applications were refused. In the first six months of 2015, there were 55 applications, five referrals for interview, and 50 acceptances in the US while the corresponding figures for Pakistan were 205, 135, and 60.

It seems that the route is unsatisfactory in other ways. In a report published in September 2015, *Review of the Tier 1 Entrepreneur and Graduate Entrepreneur Routes*, the Migration Advisory Committee found that many applications did not bring substantial economic benefits to the UK and suggested major reform for those who are planning to bring £200,000 to the UK. In their view, the genuineness test should be replaced by an assessment by industry experts, there should be better monitoring of progress during the initial three-year period and further leave should be subject to a wider range of considerations. Initial leave to enter is for three years and four months. Switching from other skilled or student categories is permitted. Leave is subject to conditions as to public funds, police registration, and no employment except in the businesses upon which the application was based. Under para 245DE(c), leave may be curtailed if, within six months of entry or the grant of leave to remain, the applicant has failed to register with HM Revenue and Customs as self-employed, register a new business of which they are a director, or register as a director of an existing business. It may also be curtailed if, at any time, the funds cease to be available. When an application for further leave is made, the applicant must show, as well as meeting language and maintenance criteria, that they fulfilled and continue to fulfil the entry criteria, that they invested the funds upon which they founded the application directly into one or more businesses in the UK and that, as a consequence, two new full-time UK jobs (or equivalent) have been created.

A Tier 1 (Entrepreneur) migrant may obtain indefinite leave after five years in that category or former related categories or three years if the applicant has created at least ten new jobs or created a business worth more than £5 million.

9.4.3 Tier 1 (Investor)

According to para 245E of the rules, the purpose of this category is to provide a route 'for high net worth individuals making a substantial financial investment to [sic] the UK'. It is consistent with schemes run in a number of countries which aim to attract wealthy individuals through preferential schemes. To obtain the 75 points needed under Appendix A, a first-time applicant must have at least £2 million of his own under his control and at his disposal for investment in the UK. The Tier 1 (Investment) route was considered by the Migration Advisory Committee in a report published in February 2014 (*Tier 1 (Investor) Route: Investment thresholds and economic benefits*). The MAC was sceptical that the benefits to British residents were as substantial as claimed. They recommended raising the threshold from £1 million to £2 million (subsequently implemented) and encouraging alternative investments to gilts. It also suggested that some slots might be auctioned, proposals which have not, so far, been pursued. The MAC Chair, Professor Sir David Metcalf, in evidence to the Home Affairs Select Committee, said that the Tier 1 (Investor) visa was 'giving settlement away' and described the scheme as 'absolutely not fit for purpose.' Transparency International, in a 2015 report, *Gold Rush: Investment visas and corrupt capital flows into the UK*, identifies the Tier 1 (Investor) visa as a conduit for corrupt capital flows into the UK.

The application will be refused if there is reason to believe funds are not under the applicant's control or come from a tainted source. These conditions aim to avoid money laundering and also followed reports that wealthy individuals were giving their employees the funds to apply in this category in order to bypass the restrictive domestic worker route (see later). There are no language or maintenance requirements. Leave is granted for three years and four months in the first instance and then for a further two years. Leave may be curtailed if the applicant does not invest all the capital within three months in UK government bonds or share or loan capital in active and trading UK companies (other than property investment companies) and maintain that investment or equivalent investment throughout the period of leave.

The period of time before settlement is obtainable depends upon the wealth of the applicant. The super-rich who have £10 million under their control in the UK may settle after two years provided they have invested 75 per cent of that £10 million in UK government bonds or companies and the remainder is on deposit in a UK regulated financial institution. Those with £5 million so available and so invested can settle after three years while the merely wealthy who have £2 million under their control and invested in the UK must wait five years. The other usual conditions for settlement must also be met.

9.4.4 Tier 1 (Graduate Entrepreneur)

This scheme was introduced in 2013 to replace the Tier 1 (PSW) which closed in April 2012. The PSW visa permitted international graduates who had studied in the UK to stay for up to two years after graduation to do any sort of work as a bridge to long-term skilled work under Tiers 1 and 2. However, the government believed that, given high levels of graduate unemployment in the UK, overseas graduates should no longer have open access to the labour market, even for a limited period. Closure was also a possible disincentive to overseas students who could no longer count on working after graduation to recoup the cost of their overseas studies and the Select Committee on Home Affairs recommended reform rather than abolition (Select Committee on Home Affairs *Student Visas* Seventh Report of Session 2010–11 para 58). Its abolition has been cited as a negative factor in decisions on destination for overseas study (UKCISA (2011) *The UKCISA Tier 4 Student Survey 2011* p. 4). The government's attitude towards overseas students is further discussed at 9.7.

The PSW scheme was replaced by the Graduate Entrepreneur Scheme which can be found in para 245F–FC. It is available to MBA and other UK graduates who have been identified by approved institutions as having developed genuine and credible business ideas and entrepreneurial skills or by UK Trade and Investment as elite global graduate entrepreneurs. Applicants must be endorsed by the institution from which they have graduated with at least a Bachelor's degree. The endorsement must confirm that the applicant has a genuine and credible business idea and will spend the majority of his working time on developing business ventures, a tall order for an academic institution.

There is a language requirement which will usually be met through having graduated from an English language university and a requirement to have £1,890 available although that may be certified by the sponsor. Leave is for one year and may be renewed once; it is not a direct route to settlement. The number of visas available is capped at 2,000 per year. In 2014, only 564 visas were issued to graduate entrepreneurs, predominantly in-country.

9.4.5 Tier 1 discussion

Tier 1 has seen dramatic changes as a result of the government's policy of reducing net migration. It was perhaps inevitable that a government seeking to reduce immigration would target open-ended schemes such as Tier 1 (General) although reductions could have been obtained by tightening the criteria rather than its destruction. However, the creation of the Exceptional Talent route was a politically useful way of emphasizing the government's willingness to consider entry for a small elite. There is also a marked emphasis on attracting the wealthy and entrepreneurial with accelerated settlement available for those shown to have made a particularly large contribution in terms of investment or job creation. This contrasts with the closure of other routes in this Tier and reflects government policy. Damian Green said in March 2011 that '[e]ntrepreneurs and investors can play a major part in our economic recovery, and I want to do everything I can to ensure that Britain remains an attractive destination for them. Last year we issued far too few visas to those who wish to set up a business or invest in the UK—I intend to change that.'

9.5 Tier 2 migrants

9.5.1 The work permit scheme

Tier 2, which was implemented in November 2008, replaced the long-established work permit scheme. This had been seen as an efficient and responsive system (see, for example, Home Affairs Committee *Managing Migration: Points-Based System Oral Evidence* HC217–iv, Qs.227, 228). Entry was in two stages. The prospective employer applied for a work permit and, if that was issued, the applicant applied for entry clearance and/or leave to enter or remain. The immigration decision was usually secondary to the work permit decision (although see the discussion of the Sectors Based Scheme later in this chapter for an instance of when immigration considerations predominated).

The legal basis for the work permit scheme was uncertain (for more discussion, see earlier editions of this book). Their issue was an area of executive power largely beyond democratic or judicial scrutiny, although it was subject to judicial review. The conditions of eligibility were in guidance notes, which, over time, became publicly available on government websites. However, their discretionary and non-statutory basis meant that, as with the PBS guidance, they could be amended without debate or scrutiny. The only appeal was against the immigration decision, which was unlikely to succeed as lack of a work permit was a valid reason for refusal of leave. Parties argued unsuccessfully that the Secretary of State had therefore unlawfully confined his discretion under the immigration rules, as the immigration decision was dependent on the work permit decision (*Pearson v IAT* [1978] Imm AR 212). Although now of historical importance only, the Court of Appeal in *Miah v SSHD* [2012] EWCA Civ 1719 found that the legality of the work permit scheme had survived the decision in *Alvi*, as it had always been intended to operate outside the system of immigration control.

9.5.2 Structure of Tier 2

According to para 245H of the rules, the purpose of Tier 2 (other than the Intra-Company Transfer route which is dealt with under separate rules) is to 'enable UK employers to recruit workers from outside the EEA to fill a particular vacancy that cannot be filled by a British or EEA worker'. All applicants coming from outside the UK need entry clearance. There are four sub-categories within Tier 2: General; Minister of Religion; Sportsperson; and Intra-Company Transfer.

Those applying under the General, Minister of Religion, and Sportsperson routes are all dealt with under para 245H. All must have sufficient points for attributes, language, and maintenance under Appendices A, B, and C, be at least 18 (or have parental consent if between 16 and 18), and have a sponsor which is not a company in which they own more than 10 per cent of the shares (unless the gross salary is £153,500 or above). Initial leave is for the shorter of the period of engagement plus one month or five years and one month for Tier 2 (General) or three years and one month for other categories. Periods of further leave are granted, subject to the applicant still qualifying for sufficient points. Conditions of leave include a prohibition on working except for the sponsor and voluntary work or, for a sportsperson, employment by the national team while that team is in the UK. Supplementary working is sometimes permitted. A new application must be made if the employee changes jobs or their conditions of employment change so that they no longer work under the same job classification or within the shortage occupation list or their pay is reduced below the level indicated on the Certificate of Sponsorship. Switching is permitted from other work-related categories. Settlement is possible after five years have been spent in a work-related category with the last part as a Tier 2 migrant, provided the employer confirms that the applicant's services are still required and, for Tier 2 (General) that the salary is at the appropriate rate for the job. In its report published in 2016, *Review of Tier 2*, the MAC recommended implementation of a skills charge to be paid by employers recruiting through Tier 2, and changes to the Intra-Company Transfer route but not wider reform of Tier 2. The Immigration Bill 2015 contains a provision for the skills levy.

9.5.3 Tier 2 (General)

These migrants need 50 points for attributes from Appendix A, 10 points for language from Appendix B, and 10 points for maintenance from Appendix C. Attributes are found in paras 76–84A of Appendix A. Thirty points are awarded if there is a certificate of sponsorship for a job which passes the Resident Labour Market Test, the Resident Labour Market Test exemption applies, the job is on the shortage occupation list, or the salary is above £155,300 pa. The remaining 20 points are gained through having an 'appropriate salary' which, for a new entrant, must be at least £20,800 pa and not less than the appropriate rate for the post stated in Appendix J. The Migration Advisory Committee, in a report published in January 2016, *Review of Tier 2 Migration,* found that there was little evidence of undercutting of salaries by Tier 2 migrant workers except in a few sectors (medical professions and teaching) but saw a case for raising the threshold as this had been calculated in 2009 when the minimum skill requirement had been much lower and for some variation across occupations.

All applicants need a Certificate of Sponsorship. Under Appendix A, para 77H, the decision-maker must be satisfied that the job is a genuine vacancy. The Certificate must relate to a job that is on the list of occupations at level 6 (degree level) or above of the National Qualifications Framework listed in Appendix J, is one of a number of creative occupations skilled to level 4, or is a shortage occupation skilled to level 4 listed in Appendix K. The salary must be at or above the appropriate rate for the job. Under para 80 of Appendix A, the Secretary of State may limit the number of Certificates of Sponsorship available in any specific period and, in addition to meeting the other criteria for entry, new applicants will be awarded a visa only if that limit has not been reached or they are to be paid a salary of at least £153,300. The current limit is 20,700 per year. Croatian nationals, who are subject to different rules under the terms of Croatia's EU accession and are not restricted in number, are included in the total, reducing the overall number available to other nationalities. 2,550 Certificates of Sponsorship are available in the first month of each year (i.e., from 6th April), and 1,650 Certificates of Sponsorship in each subsequent month. If there are insufficient qualifying applications, they will be rolled over until the next month.

If there are more applications than Certificates available, then under a complex formula set out in para 83 of Appendix A, preference will be given to applications in shortage occupations or which are very highly skilled or well-paid. For example, when the cap was exceeded for the first time in June 2015, the threshold became a salary of £46,000 per annum. After the cap was introduced, numbers of applications were generally lower than the maximum allocation with the result that, by November 2013, there were 6,296 certificates of sponsorship available for allocation in December 2013. The reasons are unclear but the Home Affairs Select Committee in its 2012 report suggested that many employers prefer to use the Intra-Company Transfer route which remains uncapped although economic conditions may also have been a factor. The monthly cap was reached for the first time in June 2015 and again in July 2015, which may have been connected to graduate recruitment rounds and the Home Affairs Select Committee (*Immigration: Skill Shortages—Fifth Report of Session 2015–16*) recommended removing graduate training schemes from the cap. However, it is likely that, in an expanding economy, the limit will be reached regularly leaving employers unable to recruit sufficient skilled workers. The system for allocating points based on salary means that new entrants, less well-paid professions, such as nursing, and employers outside London will be disproportionately affected. ILPA members reported that many of those affected were professionals, including experienced workers, working in less well paid fields, small and medium sized enterprises and start-ups, and businesses outside South East England. Rejected applications included engineers, teachers, lawyers, IT and technology workers, architects, nurses and healthcare professionals and those in the creative industries. The Migration Advisory Committee recommended, in its 2016 report, *Reform of Tier 2*, that there should be more flexibility in the allocation process so that new entrants and those in lower paid occupations are not excluded.

9.5.3.1 The shortage occupation list

The shortage occupation list identifies those skilled occupations where domestic labour shortages make it sensible to recruit outside the EEA. The list is now included in the immigration rules as Appendix K. Appearing on this list means that the job is exempt from the Resident Labour Market Test and will be awarded 30 points for attributes provided that a minimum salary is payable.

It is drawn up by the government following recommendations by the MAC who review the list periodically. Occupations may be added or removed from the list in line with market conditions and the tendency in the recent past has been for the list to contract. By February 2013, around 180,000 posts were covered by the list compared to around 1 million in 2007 (although, of course, not all these posts had been filled by migrants). In fact, take-up of shortage occupation posts is quite low; 1,395 entered in the year ending in September 2014 compared to more than 45,000 entering under other Tier 2 routes.

There are some problematic areas in the list. In 2009, the MAC found that many chefs did not meet its definition of skilled work but, recognizing shortages in that area, recommended their inclusion subject to a minimum pay and experience threshold. The problem is that skills learnt within one tradition may not transfer to other cultures. The need to speak the language of the restaurant and to appreciate its overall culture (as well as the willingness to work long unsocial hours) were cited by the MAC in its 2009 report as reasons why shortages persisted even in a recession Others, however, have argued that EEA nationals of ethnic minority origin could be trained in these skills, reducing the need for imported labour ('Caterers Call for School of Curry in UK' *The Observer* 15 March 2009). However, there is still a perceived need for highly skilled chefs at top end restaurants and chefs remain on the shortage occupation list but only where there is a sufficient level of skill and the salary is above a minimum figure. The result has been reports of vacancies in less prestigious restaurants ('The Curry Crisis' *The Guardian* 8 January 2012).

When applying for further leave, the applicant must again be awarded points under Appendix A but, if an occupation has moved out of the shortage occupation list, 30 points will still be awarded for continuing to work in the same occupation for the same sponsor.

9.5.3.2 Graduate level occupations

Paragraph 77E of Appendix A requires that a new applicant for a Tier 2 (General) post not on the shortage occupation list must be entering for a job that is included in the list of occupations which are at Level 6 of the National Qualifications Framework (equivalent to a Bachelor's degree) and contained in Appendix J or one of the creative occupations listed in the paragraph and skilled to Level 4. The requirement to be working at graduate level was introduced in April 2011 and reflects the Coalition government's concern to limit immigration only to the highly skilled. As a consequence, 71 formerly eligible occupations were excluded.

Some skilled work may exist independently of formal qualifications. Care work, for example, involves interpersonal skills that are not easily measurable and many experienced care workers have few academic qualifications. Care workers were excluded from the first list of skilled occupations published by the MAC in September 2008. In its April 2009 review, the MAC recommended inclusion of senior skilled care workers if criteria were met including qualifications at NVQ level 2, minimum experience and pay, and supervisory responsibility in the post to which they are recruited. They thus returned to the list but were again removed when occupations below graduate level became ineligible. As senior care workers are not on the current shortage occupation list, this occupation cannot currently form the basis of a new application.

9.5.3.3 Resident Labour Market Test

If a graduate level post does not appear on the shortage occupation list, the employer must carry out the Resident Labour Market Test (RLMT). The test is designed to ensure that EEA labour is not available to fill the post. To pass the test, the vacancy must be advertised to settled workers as required in Table 11B of Appendix A at the necessary skill level and at the market rate. Subject to a few exceptions, the post must be advertised through Jobcentre Plus and one other method set out in Table 11C of Appendix A. The employer cannot refuse to employ an EEA national only because of the absence of skills or qualifications not specifically requested in the advertisement. If no suitable resident worker applies, a Certificate of Sponsorship may be issued within a specified period, usually six months, of the advertisement appearing.

The RLMT has been criticized as too undemanding and the Home Affairs Committee recommended in 2009 that its operation be reviewed to ensure its rigorous enforcement. There have also been repeated calls, during the recession, for the test to be withdrawn so that only occupations on the shortage list may be filled by migrants. Given that only a small fraction of jobs are filled through the shortage list, this would have almost ended skilled labour migration into the UK. This question was, at the government's request, investigated by the MAC who did not find that there was an economic case for the RLMT route to be closed although it made some recommendations for change, including a longer period of advertisement, later implemented, and more enforcement measures.

9.5.3.4 English language and maintenance

Tier 2 General Migrants applying for entry clearance must gain 10 points under Appendix B for English language competence at level B1 CEFR whether or not this is required for the post. However, the Home Affairs Committee (2009) regarded it as necessary for living in and integrating into British society.

Applicants also must have held £945 in funds for themselves to gain the 10 points needed under Appendix C for maintenance and £630 for each family member under Appendix E for a consecutive 90-day period and in an institution not listed in Appendix P. The maintenance requirements are waived if an A-rated sponsor undertakes to provide maintenance and accommodation for the family for the first month of employment.

9.5.3.5 Settlement under Tier 2 (General)

Settlement is possible for Tier 2 (General) migrants after five years, subject to the usual conditions and, in addition, a salary, which, from April 2016, must be at least £35,000 pa, increasing incrementally to £36,200 from April 2020 (para 245HF(d)). The £35,000 + minimum does not apply to those in shortage or PhD level occupations (such as scientists and university academics) or to those entering before April 2011 but it may cause difficulty for other skilled workers whose incomes tend to rise modestly, such as nurses. In November 2015, nurses were added to the shortage occupation list pending a review by the Migration Advisory Committee and this will avoid problems for nurses who enter through this route and apply for indefinite leave if their pay does not meet the threshold. The Migration Advisory Committee will advise whether nurses should be placed long term on the shortage occupation list.

9.5.4 Tier 2 (Minister of Religion)

Before the PBS, the immigration rules enabled minority faiths to recruit fully trained ministers from abroad and to undertake exchanges although these were subject to complex rules and instructions. The White Paper of 2002, *Secure Borders, Safe Haven*, argued that religious leaders needed to be able to communicate effectively with leaders of other faiths (para 3.31), and in 2004, an English language requirement was introduced. This anticipated the introduction of language requirements in the naturalization, then settlement, and finally entry requirements for other migrants.

Ministers of religion coming to the UK for an extended period now fall within Tier 2, while temporary religious workers come under Tier 5 and are discussed at 9.8.1.3. A minister of religion entering under Tier 2 must score 50 points under paras 85–92 of Appendix A, which are awarded for possession of a Certificate of Sponsorship. The Certificate of Sponsorship Checking Service entry must confirm that the applicant is being sponsored to perform mainly religious (and not non-pastoral) duties and, if the Sponsor's organization is a religious order, confirm that the applicant is a member of that order and will receive pay and conditions at least equal to those given to settled workers in the same role and which comply with national law. In addition, the sponsor must confirm that the RLMT has been performed, the applicant is qualified to do the job, intends to base himself in the UK, will comply with the conditions of his leave, and will be accommodated and maintained by the sponsor. The Resident Labour Market Test is met if the role is supernumerary, that is, additional to the sponsor's normal staffing requirements, or involves living as part of a religious order. Alternatively, the sponsor may hold national records of all available individuals for the role and confirms that the records show that no suitable settled worker is available, or the sponsor may undertake a national recruitment search in the usual way.

Under Appendix B, ministers of religion must demonstrate a higher level (B2 CEFR) of English language competence than other Tier 2 migrants. The Appendix C and E maintenance requirements apply to new applicants unless the sponsor undertakes to maintain the applicant and his family for the first month.

9.5.5 Tier 2 (Sportsperson)

Applicants in this category also need 50 points under paras 93–100 of Appendix A which are awarded for possession of a Certificate of Sponsorship. The sponsor must confirm that the applicant is qualified to do the job, has been endorsed by the sport's governing body as being internationally established at the highest level, will make a significant contribution to the sport's development, and the post could not be filled domestically. The migrant must intend to base him/herself in the UK and will comply with the conditions of his leave. Maintenance and a basic English language requirement apply.

9.5.6 **Intra-company transfer**

The intra-company transfer (ICT) route 'enables multinational employers to transfer their existing employees from outside the EEA to their UK branch for training purposes or to fill a specific vacancy that cannot be filled by a British or EEA worker' (para 245G HC 395). Numbers entering as ICTs increased from 33,645 in 2004 to 49,710 in 2008. In 2009, they accounted for 60 per cent of all Tier 2 visas and 40 per cent of Tier 1 and 2 combined (Select Committee on Home Affairs (2010) *Immigration Cap* First Report of Session 2010–11). The Chair of the MAC criticized the ITC route as prone to abuse and used to bypass the more rigorous demands of the Tier 2 (General) route, particularly in IT ('Migration Adviser Says Companies Should Train UK Staff' *The Guardian* 20 March 2009). The MAC recommended, alongside improved enforcement, that ICTs should no longer be a route to settlement and that the minimum period of prior employment should be extended to 12 months. Graduate trainees should enter on a separate scheme, involving a three-month minimum period of prior employment and a 12-month maximum stay.

However, restricting ICTs is not straightforward. The UK is subject to various international agreements and international businesses expect to transfer staff globally with relative ease. They were thus not included in the numerical cap imposed on other Tier 2 migrants. However, they were made the subject of further regulation introduced in April 2011 and the ICT route is now divided into four sub-categories:

- short-term staff coming for 12 months or less;
- long-term staff coming for more than 12 months;
- graduate trainees; and
- skills transfer.

However, they are still numerically significant. In the year ending in September 2014, 36,635 migrants entered on the intra-company route compared to 15,288 on the Tier 2 (General) route and 588 on the other Tier 2 routes.

All ITC applicants need 50 points under Appendix A. Thirty points are available for the Certificate of Sponsorship and 20 points are available for the appropriate salary. Understanding the criteria, in practice, requires close reading of the rules (paras 245 G–GF) and Appendix A, not an easy task given the complex exceptions and convoluted paragraphs. In essence, the position is that:

- the ICT applicant must be coming to do a job that is on the list of graduate level occupations in Appendix J or one of the named creative occupations and qualified to level 4 (with exceptions only in respect of further leave for those who entered under the old rules). The entry clearance officer must be satisfied that a genuine vacancy exists. In its 2016 report, *Reform of Tier 2,* the Migration Advisory Committee recommended more detailed scrutiny of the role that the transferee will undertake and the creation of a separate route, requiring a high minimum salary, where the transferee is being transferred to fulfil a contract with a third party;
- short-term and long-term staff must have been employed by the sponsor for a continuous period of 12 months immediately prior to the date of application (with allowances for parental and long-term sick leave). In its 2016 report, *Reform of Tier 2,* the Migration Advisory Committee recommended that this be extended to two years;
- graduate trainees must be taking part in a structured graduate training programme, and have been working for the sponsor outside the UK for at least three months. No more than five such trainees may be sponsored by a single employer in a single year;

- skills transfer applicants must be entering for the sole purpose of transferring skills to or from the sponsor's UK work environment and the appointment is additional to staffing requirements;
- long-term staff must be paid a salary of at least £41,500 per year and the other sub-categories at least £24,800 per year and not less than the appropriate rate published in Appendix J. Staff who qualify for the nine-year long term route must earn at least £155,300 pa;
- applicants must meet the maintenance requirements for Tier 2 migrants;
- short-Term, Graduate Trainee and Skills Transfer applicants for entry must not have been present on a Tier 2 visa in the 12 months preceding the application. They may however re-apply to enter as a Long-Term ICT, or in the same category if they are to be paid at least £152,100;
- short-Term and Graduate Trainee ICTs may enter for one year maximum, Skills Transfer ICTs for six months and Long Term ICTs for up to five years or nine years if they earn above £153,300 pa;
- entry clearance prohibits recourse to public funds and working except for the sponsor as permitted, supplementary employment, and voluntary work;
- further leave in the Long-Term sub-category is possible provided the employer remains the same, up to a maximum of five years in total or nine years if the applicant is to be paid at least £153,300. Short-Term and Graduate Trainee staff can apply for further leave in the same sub-category with the same employer up to a maximum of 12 months in total. Skills Transfer ICT staff can apply for further leave up to six months in total. In all cases, the points requirement must be met;
- previously, those who completed five years as an ICT could apply for indefinite leave. In its settlement consultation (Home Office/UK Border Agency (2011) *Employment Related Settlement, Tier 5 and Overseas Domestic Workers: A Consultation*) the government proposed removing the entitlement of ICTs to settle in the UK. The rules now provide that, to qualify for indefinite leave, an ICT must have received leave under the rules previously in place so that those who have entered since 2010 are not eligible. In addition, the sponsor must still hold their licence and certify that the employee is still needed and is paid at the appropriate rate.

9.6 Tier 3 migrants

Tier 3 was designed for low-skilled migrants. The 2006 White Paper, *A Points Based System: Making Migration Work for Britain*, anticipated that any scheme would be open only to nationals of countries with a satisfactory returns policy, while other control options such as compulsory remittances and pre-purchased return tickets were also under consideration. Low-skilled migrants would receive only temporary visas with no dependants and no route to settlement. There was never a strong commitment to the scheme and it has never opened. The five-year strategy for immigration, published in 2005, had anticipated that new sources of EEA labour would fill low-skilled vacancies. The Home Affairs Committee in 2009 heard evidence of a shortage of labour in the catering industry but regarded this as primarily due to poor wages and conditions.

Prior to the PBS, low-skilled migration was governed by the Sectors-Based Scheme (SBS) and the Seasonal Agricultural Workers Scheme (SAWS, discussed further at

9.9.1.2). SBS visas were short-term with no dependants, no switching, and no route to settlement. They were introduced in 2003 on a quota basis to meet shortages in the hotel and catering and food processing industries (mainly meat and fish), occupations that would not meet the usual skill requirements of the work permit scheme. In Bangladesh, in particular, there was a rush to apply for permits. However, 89 per cent of the prospective workers were refused entry clearance, usually because it was believed that they lacked intention to leave the UK. From January 2008, the SBS was available only to workers from Romania and Bulgaria aged between 18 and 30. Although deleted from the rules in 2009, it remained in place until the end of 2013 for these A2 nationals with a quota in 2012 and 2013 of 3,500 workers in food processing. In a report published in May 2013, the MAC did not foresee any negative consequences from the scheme's closure. Tier 3, meanwhile, remains indefinitely suspended.

9.7 Tier 4 (Students)

9.7.1 Introduction

There is a long tradition of travel to other countries, including the UK, in pursuit of education, and study is a common reason for entry. In its student visa consultation (Home Office/UK Border Agency (2010) *The Student Immigration System: A Consultation*) the government claimed that 468,000 people entered on student-related visas in 2009, compared to 272,000 entrants in 1999, but the higher figure includes nearly 40,000 student visitors, a short-term category that was introduced only in 2007 and may also have included an element of double counting. In 2011, around 260,000 student visas were issued, and. the figure has continued to drop slowly since then. In the year to September 2015, 213,560 student visas were issued. 33 per cent of students came from China, 7 per cent from US, 5 per cent each from India and Malaysia, and 4.5 per cent from Nigeria (Immigration Statistics 3rd quarter 2015).

Despite historical Commonwealth ties, the UK now competes for international students with other English-speaking destinations (e.g., US, Australia, or Canada) in a global marketplace, while students come to the UK from many countries outside the Commonwealth. Global education is an important tool in maintaining and creating international influence, as well as benefiting developing countries and providing an income stream for educational institutions. It follows that immigration should not be the only concern. However, although most students only remain for a limited period, the entry of students is regarded principally as an immigration issue by the government and a reduction in their numbers forms part of its strategy for reducing immigration.

Until the implementation of Tier 4 in March 2009, the rules governing the entry of students required decision-makers to determine matters such as the applicant's ability or intention to follow the course. When the PBS began, these questions, which formed the basis of many refusals and appeals under the old rules (see previous editions of this book for more information), were mostly determined by the sponsor. This seemed sensible as educational establishments are best placed to decide academic questions such as ability to follow the course. However, many of these issues are once again being decided by immigration officers although sponsors continue to have onerous reporting and other obligations in respect of their students. Implementation of Tier 4 was controversial.

Numbers of applications increased dramatically, and it was argued that this was due to fraudulent applications which officials lacked the power to refuse ('Immigration

Rules Result in Flood of Bogus Students' *Sunday Telegraph* 6 December 2009). A paper published by the UK Border Agency in March 2011 stated that holders of Tier 4 visas were responsible for 41 per cent of port refusals and 41 per cent of forgery detections in 2010. The National Audit Office reported that up to 50,000 people may have entered for work rather than study ('Students visas abused as 50,000 enter UK for employment not studies' *The Guardian* 27 March 2012). Some applications were temporarily suspended, for example applications to study English and NVQ level 3 courses at some Chinese posts. In November 2009, the then Prime Minister announced a review of the criteria for admission as a student ('Brown to Get Tough on Student Visas and Foreign Skilled Workers' *TheIndependent* 13 November 2009). In March and April 2010, restrictions were introduced on the amount of work that could be done by students studying below degree level and on the institutions that could sponsor such students.

The government regards students primarily as a source of immigration. In a speech to the Royal Commonwealth Society made on 7 September 2010 outlining the government's immigration policy, Damian Green, the Minister for Immigration, said that:

[t]he largest group of cases in our study granted visas in 2004 were to students, around 186,000. We think of students as people coming here for a short period, normally up to three years, to do a course. But more than a fifth of those 186,000 were still here after five years . . . To those who say that these are precisely the brightest and the best who Britain needs, I would say let's look at the facts. We estimate that around half, I repeat, around half of the students coming here from abroad only, are coming to study a degree level (or above) course.

In November 2010, the Coalition government launched a consultation on student visas. This proposed limiting courses below degree level, raising the language criterion, requiring academic progression if further leave is to be granted, reducing entitlements to work and to bring in dependants, and stricter accreditation procedures. As will be seen, several of these proposals have now been implemented. It has been reported that numbers have decreased substantially as a consequence (*Bogus Colleges: What about their Genuine Students* JCWI 22 November 2011). Nonetheless, the government has not capped their numbers as it has done with Tier 1 and Tier 2 migrants. This presumably reflects the economic contribution of overseas students, described by the Home Affairs Committee as the UK's seventh largest export industry and the second biggest contributor to the UK's net balance of payments (House of Commons Home Affairs Committee (2011) *Student Visas* Seventh Report of Session 2010–11, para 15) and as worth £7.9bn in 2009 (Home Affairs Committee (2013) *The Work of the UK Border Agency (December 2011–March 2012)* Fifth Report of Session 2012–13, p. 18).

9.7.2 **The sponsorship system**

Educational institutions wishing to recruit overseas students must obtain a sponsorship licence from UK Visas and Immigration. Once registered, sponsors issue a Confirmation of Acceptance for Studies (CAS) to students whom they wish to sponsor and this forms the basis of the student's visa application. Appendix A, para 116, sets out the conditions for a valid CAS and the information it must contain, including how the sponsor has assessed the applicant's English language ability. When the PBS was first implemented, students who qualified for a CAS could not be refused even if the immigration authorities suspected that they were not able or intending to study. From April 2011 it was announced that an educational institution's refusal rate must be less than 20 per cent and a system of Secure English Language Tests was established. However, in January 2014, a BBC *Panorama* programme revealed evidence of fraud in the testing system with, in particular, suggestions of 'proxy' test-takers. There was an investigation and a large number of applicants had their test results cancelled. At least 78 colleges had their sponsorship status revoked.

It also appears that institutions were sometimes put under unofficial pressure to withdraw CAS (Independent Chief Inspector (2012) *An Inspection of Tier 4 of the Points-Based System (Students) April–July 2012* pp. 3–4; see also *R (on the application of Hazret Kose) v SSHD* [2011] EWHC 2594 (Admin)). The immigration rules have now been amended so that, as well as the general grounds for refusal, students (with the exception of those from a handful of non-visa countries listed in Appendix H) may be refused if the Entry Clearance Officer is not satisfied that the applicant is 'a genuine student' (para 245ZV). Additionally, also under para 245ZV, an applicant must, if required to do so on examination or interview, demonstrate English language proficiency consistent with the standard specified in their CAS. Under para 320(7D) of the rules, a student who fails, without providing a reasonable explanation, to attend for interview may be refused. This interview may also be used to check the veracity of the contents of the sponsorship document resulting also in rejection of the CAS itself and therefore of the application (*R (Global Vision College Ltd) v SSHD* [2014] EWCA Civ 659).

This means that student applicants now face the disadvantages of the more subjective old system and the inflexibility and complexity of the new one. A survey of sponsors in 2013 by the UK Council for International Student Affairs found that many believed entry clearance officers to be demanding unrealistic levels of knowledge about institutions and programmes, evidence of detailed research into alternative courses at home, and fixed plans for the future at a stage in life when many people are still undecided. Officers also made subjective judgments about the value to an individual of a particular course or a UK qualification either on its own or in relation to its cost (even if the financial criteria had been met) and disregarded English test results if the applicant did not perform well at interview despite their own lack of training in conducting language assessments. The Chief Inspector was less critical in his report published in December 2014 (*An Inspection of Visa Interviewing March—August 2014*). However, in *R (on the application of Mushtaq) v ECO Islamabad, Pakistan (ECO—procedural fairness) IJR* [2015] UKUT 00224 (IAC), the President of the Upper Tribunal, Mr Justice McCloskey, found that common law principles of procedural fairness apply to entry clearance officer (ECO) decision-making processes, including interviews. The interview here, in which the ECO drew unwarranted conclusions from the applicant's answers, did not comply with these principles. He observed that entry clearance interviews require care and planning, the avoidance of ambiguous words and phrases and, in the interests of fairness, the opportunity for interviewees to clarify or expand on their answers: 'The nationals of impoverished and deprived countries who have invested large sums of money and whose admission to the United Kingdom is lawful if they satisfy the requirements of the relevant legal rules are deserving of no less'.

Registered sponsors have a range of obligations including record-keeping and the reporting obligations discussed earlier in the chapter. Reporting obligations extend to reporting on students even when they have been refused entry by UKVI (*Western Governors Graduate School) v SSHD* [2013] EWCA Civ 177.

As discussed earlier in this chapter, while applicants may rely on the immigration rules rather than guidance, the position of sponsors is determined by policy and guidance. Operation of the sponsorship system, however, may have serious consequences for applicants, particularly where a college loses its sponsorship licence.

There have long been allegations of bogus educational providers. After 1 January 2005, students had to enrol with educational providers on an approved list. In March

2009, this was replaced by the register of sponsors. As at May 2009, only around 1,500 educational institutions had registered as sponsors, compared to 15,000 on the old list and one quarter of applications had been refused. By December 2011, this had increased but only to 2,125. In a report published in July 2009 (*Bogus Colleges—Eleventh Report of 2008–9* HC595), the Home Affairs Committee found that previous quality assurance procedures had been insufficient, leading to increases in the numbers of bogus colleges. It considered the PBS accreditation regime to be more effective but recommended more robust inspections. The introduction of the Highly Trusted Sponsor status in September 2011 created an enhanced regulatory regime whereby only institutions who met a series of demanding criteria were permitted to continue to sponsor. This regime now applies to all sponsors, so that the term Highly Trusted Sponsor is no longer used, although new sponsors are treated as probationary initially. Institutions which are recognized as genuine but which fail to meet expectations may lose their licence as well as those that are bogus. In August 2012, London Metropolitan University had its sponsorship licence revoked, leaving more than 2,000 international students in limbo and causing huge financial and reputational damage to the university. The High Court ordered that students already in the UK with valid visas should be able to remain on or start their courses although further recruitment was still suspended ('London Metropolitan University wins reprieve in student visa row' *The Guardian* 21 September 2012). The university regained its sponsorship licence in April 2013. Since then, at least one university (Glendwr) has had its sponsorship licence suspended and two others (Bedfordshire and University of West London) were temporarily unable to recruit overseas students when their allocation was reduced to zero.

From the student's perspective, a registered sponsor is a prerequisite for obtaining leave to enter or remain. However, the increasingly rigorous regulatory regime means institutions may have their licences revoked after the CAS has been issued or during the period of study. According to JCWI writing in November 2011 (*Bogus Colleges: What about their Genuine Students* JCWI 22 November 2011), about 450 colleges had their status revoked during the previous year, affecting about 11,000 students. While more up-to-date figures are not available, press reports suggest that revocations are continuing. At least 60 institutions lost their sponsor status as a result of the *Panorama* exposé discussed earlier (James Brokenshire, Minister for Immigration, HC Deb, 7 July 2014, c56W).

Where a sponsor's licence is withdrawn, no new leave will be granted for a CAS issued by that institution and entry clearance will be cancelled if the student has not yet travelled. There is also power to curtail leave of those already present under para 323A of the rules. The Tier 4 Guidance says that, where the student is not believed to be involved in the reasons for the revocation, their permission to stay will be reduced to 60 days. The student can apply for another approved course during that period although that may be difficult in the middle of the academic year. The leave of any student already present and who 'was involved in the reasons why the Tier 4 sponsor's licence was withdrawn' will be cancelled immediately. *NA and Others (Cambridge College of Learning) Pakistan* [2009] UKAIT 00031 found that the burden of proof in these circumstances is on the government on the balance of probabilities and 'critical' or 'anxious' scrutiny of the decision would be appropriate.

Applicants who have applied in-country to a college whose licence is revoked after their prior leave expires but before the new decision are now given 60 days to find a new course. This was not previously the case under the rules although it was found that the common law duty of fairness required that such students, if they are not party to the reasons for revocation, should be notified and allowed an equivalent grace period of time to find a new course (*Thakur (PBS decision—common law fairness) Bangladesh* [2011] UKUT 00151; *Patel (revocation of sponsor licence—fairness) India* UKUT 00211 (IAC)). However, that is not the case if the original application for further leave has been made out of time (*R (on the application of Raza) v SSHD* [2016] EWCA Civ 36).

As the Home Affairs Committee acknowledged in its July 2009 report, many students attending bogus institutions are not aware of the true position before entering the UK and will have invested thousands of pounds in a UK education. Having genuinely hoped to acquire a qualification, they are also victims of the fraud and usually lose the fees they have paid while the consequences for them may be very serious, particularly if they cannot find or afford to switch to another course.

A new application for leave to remain is required if an applicant wants to change sponsor (*Bhimani (Student: Switching Institution: Requirements)* [2014] UKUT 00516 (IAC)). If a student wants to undertake further study after completion, the new course must represent academic progression from the previous programme either because it is at a higher level or the sponsor confirms that the course is related to the previous course, or the previous course and the new course in combination support the applicant's genuine career aspirations (para 120B Appendix A). The UKCISA report cited earlier found that students who have been issued a CAS are refused for lack of progression even when the new course is essential for qualification in a chosen career (e.g., a PGCE course after an MSc). The issue of a CAS creates a presumption of academic progress upon which the student can rely, provided the institution has explained on the CAS how this is occurring (which unfortunately, the student may be unable to verify) (*Pokhriyal v SSHD* [2013] EWCA Civ 1568; *Kaur v SSHD* [2015] EWCA Civ 13)). Under para 245ZT, students may not spend more than two years after the age of 18 studying courses below degree level and more than five years studying at degree level or above with exceptions in respect of four-year degree programmes or if subsequent study is at master's or PhD level and for those following professional courses such as in law, architecture, or medicine.

9.7.3 **Tier 4 (General)**

There are two categories of applicant under Tier 4; general students who are over 16 entering for studies in further or higher education and child students who must be between four and 18. There is thus some overlap between the two categories. General students who are under 18 must have their parents' support and consent for the arrangements.

The rules for leave as a Tier 4 (General Students) are found from para 245ZT onwards. All applicants need 30 points for attributes under Appendix A and 10 points for maintenance under Appendix C. The 30 points for attributes are awarded for the CAS, provided a number of other conditions are met. The CAS must contain the information required by the Sponsor Guidance and be issued by an approved sponsor no more than six months before the application, which itself must be made no more than three months before the course begins. The sponsor must not have withdrawn the CAS and must still hold its licence. The applicant must produce all the original documents cited in the CAS as evidence of the applicant's suitability for the course unless the applicant is a national of one of the countries listed in Appendix H, in which case documents need be produced only if requested. Since April 2011, applicants must demonstrate competence in English to at least B2 CEFR for degree level courses or B1 CEFR for courses below degree level. This may be demonstrated in a number of ways, and, as already mentioned, may now be tested as part of the application process.

The course applied for must meet minimum academic criteria. The minimum academic level is NFQ level 3 (below degree level) or its Scottish equivalent. English language courses must now be at level B2 CEFR or above. B2 is equivalent to a high A level grade so that only non-EEA nationals who already have a good knowledge of English may now enter to study English on a student visa although short courses at the lower level may be undertaken under separate rules, found in paras A57A–H, under which short-term students may come for up to six months on most courses and up to eleven months as English language students. They do not need a sponsor provided they are coming to a private accredited institution, can maintain themselves and are not believed to be attempting long term residence in the UK.

Entry for recognized foundation programmes for doctors and dentists, pre-sessional courses at the same institution as the main course and short-term study abroad programmes from an overseas institution are permitted. Where courses involve self-contained stages which may, incrementally, result in a higher award, it should not be assumed that a student is only applying for the first stage and an overall view should be taken (*R (on the application of Jawadwala) v SSHD* [2009] EWHC 802 (Admin)).

Courses must be full-time. A course at degree level or higher has no minimum requirement for contact hours. Other courses must involve a minimum of 15 hours per week organized daytime study and, except in the case of a pre-sessional course, lead to a qualification below bachelor degree level. There are restrictions on the time that may be spent on work placements. Applicants for postgraduate qualifications in the scientific, medical, and engineering disciplines listed in Appendix 6 of the rules must also obtain an Academic Technology Approval Scheme (ATAS) Clearance Certificate. This is designed to ensure that applicants will not contribute to the proliferation of weapons of mass destruction.

To show adequate maintenance under Appendix C, the applicant must have had the requisite level of funds for a consecutive 28-day period in a financial institution with which UK Visas and Immigration can make satisfactory verification checks. The documents proving this must either be provided with the application or, if the applicant is a national of a country in Appendix H, they must be confirmed by the applicant and produced if required. Funds may be held in parents' bank accounts provided evidence of the parents' consent is also demonstrated. The amount needed varies according to the place of study, the length of the course, whether the applicant is already in the UK, and the applicant's personal circumstances. For instance, someone entering for a degree course in London who has a partner and a child would have to show possession of the first year's course fees and £9,135 for him/herself. The partner and child would each need £7,605 so a total of £24,345 plus the first year's fees would have to be available. Leave is granted for the length of the course plus a short additional period at either end. If further leave is needed, a new application must be made and the same points earned as on entry. Students may not apply in-country for a course that commences more than one month after their leave expires (para 245ZX(l) HC395). Leave includes leave granted under s 3C Immigration Act 1971 pending a decision on an application made before but decided after leave expires on the original visa (*QI (Pakistan) v SSHD* [2011] EWCA Civ 614).

As leave is granted for the whole course, most students should not need further leave for the same course and immigration officers no longer engage with questions of progression within courses as they did under the old rules. However, a student may sometimes fail to complete their studies within the time permitted in the visa so that further leave is needed. This requires a new application and a new CAS. The student must also be engaged in study or revision classes; in other cases, they are expected to leave the UK and return as a student visitor for the resit examinations (*RS (Pakistan) v SSHD* [2011] EWCA Civ 434).

Switching into student status is permitted only from student or work related categories. This replicates a problem that existed under the previous rules in which those who enter in another capacity such as the family member of a worker and begin their studies cannot, if that leave expires, switch to student status but must instead leave the country and apply for entry clearance. A letter of 14 December 2000 from the Home Office to an International Student Adviser at Sheffield University stated that this was not a suitable case for a concession. In this instance, the student, who was writing up her PhD, would need to leave the country to obtain entry clearance to return and complete it, as her husband's student leave would expire before she had finished.

Students on degree level courses may work on placements that form up to one third of their course if it is below degree level and one half if it is at degree level or above (unless more is required by UK law). They may also work for up to 20 hours per week during term-time and for an unlimited period during vacations. Students studying below degree level but at higher education institutions may work for ten hours per week and full-time during vacations. The limitation on hours worked applies even if a student is writing up his/her thesis and has no scheduled classes (*OG (Student-thesis-term time employment)* [2008] UKAIT 00057). Self-employment is not permitted and the student must not fill a permanent full-time vacancy, work as a doctor in training except on a recognized Foundation programme, or provide services as a professional sportsperson or entertainer. In *Strasburger v SSHD* [1978] Imm AR 165 the appellant was an art student who wanted to stay in the UK as a self-employed artist. She needed to show that she could maintain herself as an artist and relied on sales of her work while a student as evidence of that capacity. The Tribunal held that this did not represent a breach of the condition against self-employment.

The partners and children of students who are admitted for more than 12 months onto postgraduate level courses may also be admitted. Leave as a student is not a route to settlement but there are limited opportunities for students to remain after their studies either under Tier 2 (which the government has proposed restricting still further) or under the Doctorate Extension Scheme, which permits universities to sponsor a doctoral student for 12 months after completion during which time they have unrestricted work rights.

9.7.4 Child students

Special rules apply to children between 4 and 17 coming to be educated in the UK. They need 30 points for attributes under Appendix A. This requires the applicant to have a CAS supplied by an independent, fee-paying school that holds a sponsor's licence. The Tier 4 sponsor guidance provides that sponsors must teach courses that are in accordance with the national curriculum or the National Qualification Framework or is subject to OFSTED or equivalent or the independent school inspection regime. They also need 10 points for maintenance. The precise amounts required depend upon whether the child is to attend a boarding school, is to stay with relatives or foster carers, or is 16 or 17 and living independently. This money may, unsurprisingly, be held by the parents rather than the child.

The child's parents or guardians must support the application and consent to the child's entry. If the child is to stay with relatives or in a foster care arrangement, there must be satisfactory evidence of the arrangements. Child students may not be accompanied by a partner or by their own child. Indeed, an applicant who has a child living with them or for whom they are financially responsible may not enter as a child student. A parent may accompany a child student under 12 under paras 276BT1–276BV1. A child student may not work under the age of 16. After that age, ten hours' weekly work in term-time and unlimited hours during the holidays are permitted. Switching is only permitted from other student categories.

9.8 Tier 5 (Temporary Workers)

This tier came into effect in November 2008, replacing a long list of entry routes including some very popular schemes such as the Working Holiday Maker. There was also a long list of smaller schemes that have now either disappeared or been subsumed into Tier 5 (for a full list, see the UKBA's Statement of Intent for Tier 5).

There are two sub-categories within Tier 5: Temporary Workers and Youth Mobility. These types of scheme, which aim to establish cultural, sporting, and other links, do not sit easily within a PBS that is predicated on short-term economic benefit. Schemes such as the Working Holiday Maker had long-term and often intangible benefits in terms of establishing connections and relationships with individuals and countries but the arrangements for Tier 5, particularly Youth Mobility, seem to be over-concerned with control.

9.8.1 Temporary workers

The rules for temporary workers are found in paras 245ZM onwards, which, as always, have to be read in conjunction with the Appendices. The route is 'for certain types of temporary worker whose entry helps to satisfy cultural, charitable, religious or international objectives' (para 245ZM). Entry clearance is always required with an exception for non-visa nationals entering for up to three months for creative or sporting engagements, although these will still need a Certificate of Sponsorship. This is critical. In one well-reported incident, the Canadian singer, Allison Crowe, was detained and then removed from Gatwick after she arrived without a Certificate of Sponsorship. The Manifesto Club has published numerous case studies of artists who have fallen foul of the Tier 5 (and other immigration) requirements (*Deported: Artists and Academics Barred from the UK*) although recent changes, discussed later, have mitigated some of the difficulties.

Thirty points are needed under paras 105–12 of Appendix A and 10 points for maintenance under Appendix C. Appendix A awards 30 points for possession of a Tier 5 (Temporary Worker) Certificate of Sponsorship. Initially, even a small organization or charity who wished to bring in an artist or volunteer for a short period had to go through the application process and fulfil the duties of sponsorship. There were reports that small sponsors were reluctant or ineligible to engage in the bureaucracy and cost of the sponsorship process, leading to a loss of small-scale and experimental work (Manifesto Club, *UK Arts and Culture: Cancelled, by Order of the Home Office*). Creative visas are often needed at short notice, for example, if an international opera singer falls ill and a suitable replacement is needed at short notice, but the visa will usually take much longer to process if biometric data is needed.

Delays can be particularly problematic for large groups whose members must apply individually and in person, and problems are exacerbated where, as in many parts of Africa, biometric collection points are sparse. This may require the entire group to relocate for the duration of the process. One report to the Home Affairs Select Committee in 2009 involved Malian musicians who had to travel for three days to their nearest visa application centre in Dakar and then wait for up to ten days while their applications were sent to Banjul in the Gambia for processing, all the time being separated from their passports and relevant documentation. For artists from poor countries or engaged in worldwide travel, such expense and delay may make the visit untenable.

The Home Affairs Committee in 2009 recommended that more biometric collection points be established, that visa issue times be reduced, and that a streamlined procedure be introduced for emergency applications (see also Manifesto Club, *Deported: Artists and Academics Barred from the UK*). In February 2012, the government announced the creation of a new category of visit visa, 'permitted paid engagements', which would permit specific fee paid activities for up to one month without the need for formal sponsorship which will obviate some of the difficulties and which is discussed in the next chapter.

If not eligible for this visitor category, sponsors, even non-profit-making ones, are subject to the same requirements and obligations as large employers even if there will not usually be an employment relationship between the sponsor and the migrant. In fact, according to the Sponsor Guidance, '[w]here a migrant is not your direct employee, we will look especially closely at your arrangements, and monitor you to ensure that you are fulfilling all of your sponsor duties. We will take action against you as set out in this guidance if we find that you are not fulfilling all of your sponsorship duties.' These duties include record-keeping and reporting obligations, a duty of cooperation and a guarantee of aspects of applicants' compliance although it is impossible to see how a sponsor can always control this. The sponsor must also demonstrate that the post cannot be filled by a domestic appointment although a recruitment exercise is not always needed. The maintenance requirements require £945 of personal savings held for 90 days or a maintenance guarantee by an A-rated sponsor. Sponsors must advise migrants that they are ineligible for and must not claim state benefits and a benefits claim made with the sponsor's knowledge may result in action against the sponsor. Switching is possible but only within the sub-category in which they entered and for the maximum time permitted. The only exception is for international footballers who can switch to Tier 2, subject to meeting Tier 2 requirements, including the English language requirement. The Select Committee (2009) regarded this as a case 'where money has spoken louder than merit' and urged removal of the exemption.

There are five sub-categories within the Temporary Worker scheme.

9.8.1.1 Creative and sporting

This sub-category is for applicants entering for up to 12 months. Creative sponsors must operate or intend to operate in the creative sector, for example, as a national body, event organizer, producer, venue, agent, or similar. Sponsors operating in dance, theatre, film, and television must follow a code of practice in recruitment and, in other fields, must take steps to ensure a resident worker is not available for the post. Group certificates may be issued to an entourage provided each member has proven technical or other specialist skills. Multiple engagements may be covered by the same sponsor on condition that no more than 14 days elapse between engagements. Otherwise, the applicant is expected to leave the UK and reapply for entry clearance. Rehearsal periods may be included within the period of sponsorship but the guidance warns that, if the period has been extended incorrectly—for example, to falsely extend a migrant's stay in the UK—action will be taken against the sponsor.

Sponsors in the sporting sector must be a sporting body, sports club, events organizer, or other organizer operating or intending to operate in the sporting sector. The sponsor must gain an endorsement from the governing body of the sport confirming that the applicant is established at the highest level and/or that their employment will make a significant contribution to the sport in the UK and the post could not be filled by a suitable settled worker. In issuing the Certificate of Sponsorship, sponsors guarantee that the applicant is seeking entry to the UK to work or perform in the relevant sector, is not intending to establish themselves in business, poses no threat to the resident labour force, and will comply with their visa.

Family members may also enter and may work. Those who have leave for six months or more may leave and re-enter the UK during the currency of their leave.

9.8.1.2 Charity workers

Migrants coming as charity workers should only be undertaking voluntary activity and must not be paid or receive other benefits except for reasonable expenses. The migrant should intend to carry out fieldwork directly related to the purposes of the sponsoring organization. In issuing the Certificate of Sponsorship, the sponsor guarantees that the applicant intends only to do this, will receive only reasonable expenses, will not take up a permanent position and will comply with their visa. Charity workers may enter for up to 12 months and their family members may also enter and work.

9.8.1.3 Religious workers

This is for those coming temporarily to do preaching, pastoral, or non-pastoral work, to work in the same capacity as they already worked overseas or as a member of a religious order. The religion must not 'exclude from its community on the basis of gender, nationality or ethnicity' and must not 'operate against the public interest, or in a way that has a detrimental effect on personal or family life as these are commonly understood in the UK'.

In issuing the Certificate of Sponsorship, the sponsor guarantees that the applicant is qualified to do the job in question and will work only at the specified location. The sponsor also undertakes to accept the responsibilities of sponsorship, that it will support the applicant through sufficient funds and/or accommodation, that the applicant will not be displacing a suitably qualified resident worker, and will comply with the conditions of the visa. Leave is for up to 24 months, supplementary working is permitted, and family members may also enter and work.

9.8.1.4 Government authorized exchange

This category is for applicants coming 'through approved schemes that aim to share knowledge, experience and best practice' (Sponsor Guidance p. 77). Entry is for up to 24 months and family members may enter and work. There are four types of programme that may be approved:

- Work Experience Programmes offering work experience including volunteering, job-shadowing, internships, and work exchange programmes between the UK and non-EEA countries. The aim must be to give experience of work in the UK and the maximum leave is 12 months;
- Research Programmes which allow migrants to undertake research and fellowships, on a scientific, academic, medical, or government research project at a higher education or research institution. The maximum leave is 24 months;
- Training Programmes which offer formal, practical training in science and medicine, or by the armed forces or emergency services, including for postgraduate students who need a period of formal training to complete their qualifications before leaving the UK. Maximum leave is 24 months;
- Overseas professional language training programmes for up to 24 months that are fully or partially paid for by an overseas government or an organization affiliated to an overseas government.

This scheme cannot be used to fill job vacancies or to bring unskilled labour to the UK and the government will only approve schemes for skilled work (usually at NVQ level 3 or above) that do not damage the resident labour market.

With the exception of higher education institutions sponsoring researchers and visiting academics and government departments, there are no individual sponsors. Instead, sponsorship functions are undertaken by an overarching body supported by a government department (or executive agency), which is expected to contribute to the cost of enforcement if there is significant non-compliance. As at December 2015, there were around 70 approved schemes listed in Appendix N, involving organizations such as the Law Society, the British Council, and various educational institutions. In issuing the Certificate of Sponsorship, the sponsor guarantees that the applicant is seeking entry to work or train temporarily here through an approved exchange scheme, does not intend to establish a business, and meets the requirements of the individual exchange scheme.

9.8.1.5 International agreement

This category is available for migrants coming to provide a service covered by international law, including those coming under the General Agreement on Trade in Services (GATS) and similar agreements, employees of overseas governments and bodies, and private servants in diplomatic households. The sponsor of government employees and private servants will be the diplomatic mission or international organization or body in question not the individual employer. An application for a sponsor licence amounts to a waiver of diplomatic immunity and privileges in connection with the application and sponsor licence. Also included in this category are contractual service suppliers and independent professionals coming under international agreements such as GATS (General Agreement on Trade in Services).

The sponsor must give various undertakings according to the type of agreement that is relied upon. For example, the sponsors of domestic servants in diplomatic households must confirm that the employee is over 18, will be employed full-time on domestic tasks in the diplomatic household, will take no other work, and will leave the UK at the end of their visa. Sponsors of migrants under GATS or other international agreements confirm that the migrant works for an employer or organization of a country that is a member of the World Trade Organization (and therefore is a party to GATS) or has a bilateral agreement with the EU, will be engaged in work that accords with the international agreement and will work or provide services for the employer or client.

Migrants entering under GATS and related agreements obtain leave for up to six months. Employees of overseas governments, international organizations and diplomatic households may have leave of up to 24 months. The ability to extend the period to five years and to apply for indefinite leave has been removed from the rules.

9.8.2 **Youth Mobility Scheme**

The immigration rules say that the Youth Mobility Scheme (YMS) 'is for sponsored young people from participating countries who wish to live and work temporarily in the UK' (para 245ZI). It replaced the Working Holiday Makers scheme, which was both popular and controversial. Evaluating the YMS requires an understanding of the issues that were associated with its predecessor.

9.8.2.1 Working Holiday Makers

The Working Holiday Makers scheme was a way of maintaining Commonwealth links. Applicants had to be a national of one of around 50 Commonwealth countries listed in the immigration rules or a British Overseas Citizen (BOC), a British Overseas Territories Citizen (BOTC), or a British National (Overseas), and aged between 17 and 30. They could take only employment incidental to a holiday. The scheme was, for many years, dominated by old Commonwealth countries. In 2000, 96 per cent of applicants were from New Zealand, Australia, Canada, and South Africa. In 2002, the Home Office consulted on reform of the scheme. Respondents noted its discriminatory effects while the Home Office suggested that there was abuse by people working full-time during their stay. The result was rule changes including more freedom to work.

After these changes, some posts experienced significant increases in applications, including of over 1,000 per cent in South Asia. Refusal rates fell but were still high in some regions (62.6 per cent in South Asia, for instance, compared to between 0.2 and 0.3 per cent for Australia and the South Pacific). In February 2005, the rules changed again to limit work to one year of the applicant's two-year stay, a change that would particularly affect applicants from poorer countries less able to fund a prolonged holiday. The changes also partially restored other restrictions on working during and after the working holiday (for more details, see earlier editions of this book), reflecting government fears that the scheme was used for economic migration rather than cultural exchange. In April 2005, the government suspended applications from a number of developing countries, although an attempt to prove race discrimination failed in *SK India* [2006] UKAIT 00067.

Near the end of the period discussed here, there were moves towards making the scheme subject to bilateral agreements. This prefigured the YMS, which reflects the government's concern both to prioritize control and to avoid debate about culturally laden questions such as the meaning of 'holiday'. Unfortunately, the result is a scheme so restrictive that nationals of developing countries are likely to be indefinitely excluded from it.

9.8.2.2 Requirements of the Youth Mobility Scheme

The rules governing the scheme are found in paras 245ZI onwards. This says that: '[t]his route is for sponsored young people from participating countries who wish to live and work temporarily in the UK'. Entry clearance is compulsory. The applicant must be a national of a country listed in Appendix G of the rules or a British Overseas Citizen, British Overseas Territories Citizen, or British National (Overseas). As at December 2015, only Australia, Canada, Japan, New Zealand, Monaco, Taiwan, Hong Kong, and South Korea were listed in Appendix G. All other nationalities are ineligible.

The applicant must have 40 points under Appendix A for attributes and 10 points for maintenance under Appendix C, which requires £1,890 held on a single date within 31 days of the application, no children under 18, and no previous entry under this scheme or as a Working Holiday Maker. Entry is for two years with no recourse to public funds and most types of work may be undertaken but only limited self-employment. There is no restriction on the proportion of time that may be spent working.

Under Appendix A, 30 points are awarded for having the necessary nationality and 10 points are awarded for being between 18 and 30. There is a quota for each country, which must not be exceeded at the time the application is granted. These vary from between 1,000 places for Japan, Taiwan, South Korea, and Monaco to 38,000 places for Australia. It is not clear how applicants can know if the quota has been reached before they submit their application and pay the fee. If a country has deemed sponsor status (as at December 2015, Australia, Canada, Japan, New Zealand, and Monaco), the applicant does not have to obtain separate sponsorship and can make his/her application anywhere in the world, as may BOCs, BOTCs, and British Nationals (Overseas).

Otherwise, a certificate of sponsorship from the country of origin is needed and the application must be made there. The scheme is thus quite straightforward but the critical issue is why so few countries currently participate. The Sponsor Guidance does not explain how a country may become a sponsor. More information was contained in the Statement of Intent for Tier 5, written when the scheme was in the process of being established, but no longer published.

The Statement of Intent established that countries are eligible for inclusion only where they meet criteria as to immigration risk, returns, and reciprocity. A country must not be subject to a mandatory UK visa regime (thereby excluding most developing countries) and have an acceptable risk value according to undisclosed formulae. It must have effective return arrangements and cooperate in that process. By the date it joins the scheme, the country must provide reciprocal youth mobility arrangements for UK nationals (either aged between 18 and 30 and/or who are undergraduate or graduate students) that allow a minimum stay of 12 months, a minimum period of 12 months' work (with some minor restrictions permitted), and an annual minimum quota of 1,000 UK nationals. Where, for reasons of public policy, the UK government does not wish to admit a country to the YMS, that country will be deemed to be ineligible.

Given the restrictiveness of these criteria, it is perhaps surprising that any countries have qualified. Even qualifying countries may be removed from the list if their risk increases or they do not comply in other ways. The government may also temporarily suspend issuing entry clearances under the scheme for operational reasons. The outcome is that individuals who are entirely honest and who otherwise meet the criteria for entry are disbarred under the scheme only because of their nationality. As the discrimination is contained in the immigration rules, it is lawful under the Equality Act 2010 (see chapter 6). This restrictiveness and lack of transparency suggests that the YMS is seen primarily as a tool of international relations rather than as providing an opportunity to travel. It also reinforces the point that, despite increases in transparency in some areas, immigration remains an area in which the executive may retain almost unlimited power.

The narrowness of the YMS was criticized by the Home Affairs Committee after representations from the National Farmers' Union that the Working Holiday Makers Scheme had been a source of semi-skilled agricultural labour and that the maintenance threshold was a deterrent. The Committee recommended that the YMS be made more user-friendly, although specific recommendations were confined to reducing the maintenance requirement, and the narrowness of the scheme was not addressed.

9.9 Working outside the points-based system

There are still a few schemes that continue to operate outside the PBS and which permit entry for work or study although they have recently decreased in number.

9.9.1 A8/A2 nationals and Croatia

Until May 2011, nationals of the A8 countries that acceded to the EU in 2004 had restricted access to the labour market. They did not need permission to work but had to register with the Workers' Registration Scheme for the first year of employment. Workers and employers found registration onerous and did not always comply but this could have serious consequences. In *Zalewska v Department of Social Development* [2008] UKHL

67, the House of Lords found that the requirement to re-register if employment changed during the first year was proportionate and the appellant was therefore lawfully re-fused welfare benefits. As well as the possible refusal of benefits, non-registered workers were also liable to general exploitation by employers operating outside the system. As transitional measures could not be applied for more than seven years, the scheme was abolished on 30 April 2011.

A2 nationals (from Bulgaria and Romania) also gained the same rights as other EEA nationals to work in the UK at the end of 2013, in the face of government resistance, although they could already exercise other free movement rights such as self-employment or study.

Croatia joined the EU on 1 July 2013 and will remain subject to transitional measures for up to seven years from that date. Their position is governed by the Accession of Croatia (Immigration and Worker Authorisation) Regulations 2013/1460 as amended. They are subject to a worker authorization scheme which permits working on the same terms as permitted under the PBS as it was at the date of accession although, where these are less restrictive, the provisions in place as at 9 December 2011 (the date of the Treaty of Accession) apply. There is unlimited access to the labour market after 12 months' legal working and for the highly skilled.

9.9.2 Seasonal Agricultural Workers Scheme (SAWS)

Until the end of 2013, when it ended, this scheme had been retained outside the PBS for A2 nationals. Migration for seasonal agricultural work is an old practice in the UK and, in 1990, was formalized through SAWS (Seasonal Agricultural Workers Scheme). It was a short-term programme with maximum six months' leave and no option to bring dependants or to settle.

The scheme was appreciated by the agricultural sector. Rogaly (2006) describes how pressure from supermarkets to deliver standardized, high-quality goods to tight time-scales resulted in a preference for migrant workers, perceived as more reliable, faster, and willing to work long hours. Rogaly also noted in this context their increased vulnerability to exploitation.

From January 2008, the SAWS scheme was restricted to Bulgarian and Romanian workers. The annual quota from 2010 was 21,250. After representations from the sector about the continuing need for a circular migration system, the Home Affairs Select Committee (2009) recommended the replacement of SAWS if it was to be abolished. In its report in May 2013, the MAC concluded that SAWS was generally successful and that a failure to replace it would have some adverse effects as farmers would have difficulty obtaining the required level of seasonal labour from within the EU. Nonetheless, the government announced in September 2013 that the scheme would end and not be replaced when A2 nationals gained full access to the labour market at the end of 2013.

9.9.3 Representative of an overseas business

Revised immigration rules (paras 144–51), which took effect in October 2009, created a new category, 'representative of an overseas business'. They replaced the previous categories of sole representatives of a business and overseas media representative. The principal difference is that applicants must now demonstrate some English language competence.

The category is aimed at long-term entrants who do not qualify as business visitors (discussed in chapter 10). Entry clearance is mandatory, leave is for three years initially with extensions, dependants can accompany the main migrant, and settlement is possible after five years. The overseas business must have its headquarters and principal place of business outside the UK and no existing branch, subsidiary, or other representative in the UK.

9.9.4 Domestic workers

The rules under discussion here do not permit UK residents to recruit domestic staff from abroad but apply to workers accompanying their employer from abroad. Until April 2012, when the rules changed, about 17,000 entered each year under this route. In 1980, the Department of Employment stopped issuing work permits for unskilled workers. From then until 1998, domestic workers were permitted entry as a visitor under a concession, although they were, in reality, entering for paid domestic work. In consequence, the employee could not change employer as their entry clearance formally prohibited paid work. Such resident domestic workers were vulnerable to abuse and exploitation. Their feudal situation was changed in 1998 when the concession was altered to permit employees suffering abuse or exploitation to change employer. From September 2002, the position of domestic workers was incorporated into the rules and the prohibition on changing employer and the limitation of entry to those undertaking skilled work were removed altogether. Domestic workers could also qualify for indefinite leave after five years. This changed again in April 2012 when the maximum period of entry was reduced to six months with no right of renewal and no right to change employer.

Under the current rules, found in paras 159A–H, applicants must be between 18 and 65, have worked in the sponsor's household under the same roof or in a household that the sponsor uses for himself on a regular basis for one year prior to the application, and there must be a connection between the employee and the sponsor, demonstrated through evidence such as a letter from the employer and pay slips, contract, or other documentary proof. According to the IDI, overseas domestic workers may include cleaners, chauffeurs, gardeners, cooks, those carrying out personal care, and nannies. The employee must travel with the sponsor or their family and intend to work full-time only as a member of the sponsor's household. There must be adequate maintenance and accommodation, which is assured through an undertaking from the sponsor who must also provide a signed agreement of the main terms and conditions that show that the worker will not be paid less than the minimum wage.

Use by the sponsor of the household on a regular basis means that it must be 'habitually or customarily used' (*NG Bulgaria* [2006] UKAIT 00020), although a temporary hiatus for good reason is acceptable (*BO (Nigeria)* [2007] UKAIT 00053). Use by other relatives is not use by the sponsor 'for himself' and the 'connection' between the employer and the worker must amount to more than a contract of employment. The requirement to travel with the sponsor is intended to ensure that the employee migrates as part of the sponsor's household (*JF (Domestic Servant) Philippines* [2008] UKAIT 00085; *Wusa (para 159A (ii) 'Connection') Nigeria* [2011] UKUT 00483 (IAC)).

Domestic workers in private households were not included in the PBS but the government later proposed that they should be permitted entry for six months only on amended business visitor visas, as 'domestic assistants', rather than as 'domestic workers'. While this was consistent with the government's plans to prevent the long-term entry of unskilled workers, it was recognized that the consequences would be catastrophic for this group. Migrant domestic workers often have close caring relationships with their employee's family, particularly children, and many of them cannot easily return to their country of origin. The likely consequence would have been underground working and increased exploitation. From the employer's perspective, the inability to retain long established domestic staff might influence them against choosing the UK as a destination. Following extensive campaigning, the government was persuaded to retain the current rules for a period of two years, pending research into possible new arrangements. The Home Affairs Committee in its report, *The Trade in Human Beings: Human Trafficking in the UK* (Sixth Report of Session 2008–9 HC 23–I), believed that the current arrangements would need to be retained for much longer than two years. However, in the 2011 Settlement Consultation, the government proposed capping leave at six or 12 months and removing the right to change employers. This was justified by the recent establishment of the National Referral Mechanism for trafficking. However, critics argued that this was inadequate protection and the proposal would leave such workers highly vulnerable (see, e.g., the response of Kalayaan, which advises and campaigns on behalf of overseas domestic workers, to the consultation dated 5 August 2011). In any event, relatively few domestic workers ever stayed long enough to settle. In 2010, 15,350 visas were issued and 1,060 domestic workers obtained settlement. Even this was a higher than usual figure, probably due to changes in the rules on settlement.

These arguments did not prevail and the rules changed in 2012 to a six-month visa with no renewal. Leaving aside the difficulties of accessing legal services, migrant domestic workers now have limited legal protection against exploitation. The National Referral Mechanism is designed to offer protection for victims of trafficking. Trafficking is defined in Article 4 of the Council of Europe Convention on Action against Human Trafficking as the 'recruitment, transportation, transfer, harbouring or receipt of persons' by the use or the threat of force, fraud, deception, or abuse of power or vulnerability for the purposes or exploitation amounting to slavery or servitude. It can apply to a domestic worker who enters voluntarily and is then subjected to forced labour and the government must, in such cases, consider whether the victim needs a renewable residence permit because of her personal situation (*EK v SSHD* [2013] 00313 (IAC)). The Modern Slavery Act 2015, s 53, requires provision to be made in the immigration rules for migrant domestic workers who are victims of slavery or human trafficking to be given leave to work for another employer for at least six months. The immigration rules (HC395, para 195I–J) have implemented this in a minimal way, offering only a maximum six month stay for those who have been found to have been trafficked under the National Referral Mechanism.

As well as providing only limited assistance for trafficked workers, the Modern Slavery Act does not address the less extreme but still increased imbalance of power created by the new short-term visa which, for the reasons just discussed, makes hidden long-term exploitation more likely. Employment rights cannot be enforced against those protected by diplomatic immunity, weakening the position of workers in diplomatic households still further (*Reyes and Suradi v Al-Malki* [2015] EWCA Civ 32). The Court of Appeal found in *Onu v Akwiwu* [2014] EWCA Civ 279 (under appeal to the Supreme Court) that mistreatment of migrant domestic workers did not amount to direct or indirect discrimination. However, the Supreme Court in *Hounga v Allen* [2014] UKSC 47 found that, where discrimination had been established, the illegality of the employment contract did not provide a defence.

Kalayaan found that the effect of the rule change on the working conditions of migrant domestic workers was dramatic (Kalayaan (2013) *Slavery by another name: the tied migrant domestic worker visa*). The position since then has not improved. In May 2015, Kalayaan reported that the conditions of tied domestic workers continued to be much worse than those who had entered on the previous visa. Twenty-eight per cent of tied workers reported physical abuse, compared with 11 per cent who weren't tied; 68 per cent of tied workers were not allowed to leave the house freely, compared to 38 per cent of those not tied; 70 per cent of tied workers had no time off, compared with 49 per cent of non-tied workers; and 38 per cent of tied workers reported that they were not paid at all, compared with 14 per cent of workers who were not tied (*Britain's forgotten slaves; Migrant domestic workers in the UK three years after the introduction of the tied Overseas Domestic Worker visa*). Since implementation, the tied visa has been criticized by Human Rights Watch, the United Nations special rapporteur on violence against women and two parliamentary committees (The Joint Committee on the Draft Modern Slavery Bill and the Joint Committee on Human Rights).

9.9.5 Commonwealth citizens with UK ancestry

This is a special category in the immigration rules, HC 395 paras 186–93, which provides that a Commonwealth citizen aged 17 or over, one of whose grandparents was born in the UK, may enter for five years if they intend to seek work in the UK and can maintain and accommodate themselves and any dependants without recourse to public funds. Settlement is possible after five years, even if employment has not been continuous. The Home Office suspended applications from Zimbabweans in 2004, having decided that they were abusing the scheme, although they were resumed in November 2005. The rule appears to have survived implementation of the PBS and the government announced its plans to retain it in the 2011 settlement consultation, noting both that 96 per cent of applicants come from Australia, New Zealand, Canada, and South Africa and that numbers entering and settling appear to be declining due to changed emigration patterns in the UK.

9.10 Illegal working

In the immigration context, 'illegal working' means working by those subject to immigration control who do not have leave to work or who work in ways not permitted by their leave. Illegal employment is often associated with other unlawful practices such as low pay, breach of health and safety regulations, failure to pay income tax and national insurance contributions, and so on. The Immigration Bill 2015 inserts into the Immigration Act 1971 a specific offence of working without leave although that conduct is already covered by the criminal offences in s 24 of the Act. Further criminalization is likely only to increase the fear and vulnerability of irregular migrants. This is an obstacle to seeking protection from labour exploitation, according to the Special Rapporteur on the Human Rights of Migrants (Report of the Special Rapporteur on the Human Rights of Migrants, François Crépeau, *Labour exploitation of migrants*, A/HRC/26/35, 03 April 2014).

It is an offence under s 21 Immigration, Asylum and Nationality Act 2006 knowingly to employ a person who does not have permission to work. The Immigration Bill 2015 will add those who have reasonable cause to believe that there is not permission. Section 15 of the 2006 Act also created a system of civil penalties for employing someone without permission to work, regardless of knowledge, although there is a statutory defence if the employer complies with a list of prescribed actions. There is a risk of race discrimination if employers become reluctant to hire those who, in their view, may be subject to immigration control and there is a code of practice for employers issued under s 23 of the 2006 Act. Nonetheless, employers may be torn between their duties to their employees and their fear of sanctions under immigration laws, particularly given the complexity of the latter. It is perhaps not surprising that the Migrants' Rights Network (2008) found that the regime adversely affected a much wider group than those who do not have permission to work. For example, in *Okuoimose v City Facilities Management (UK) Ltd* UKEAT/0192/11/DA, an employee of Nigerian nationality was suspended because the endorsement on her passport permitting her to work as an EEA national family member had expired. The government had failed to decide her application to renew the endorsement and advised the employer that they were liable to civil penalties if they continued to employ her. The Employment Appeal Tribunal found that her suspension had been unlawful as she had always been entitled to work.

Under s 134 Nationality, Immigration and Asylum Act 2002, the Secretary of State may require an employer to supply information about an employee whom the Secretary of State reasonably suspects of having committed particular offences under the Immigration Act 1971. Reporting obligations are now, as discussed earlier, even more extensive under the PBS. These sanctions and obligations may have an effect on well-established employers but it is more difficult to assess the effect on less well-regulated sectors. Many migrants work through operators who supply them for short-term work in particular sectors. Following the death of 24 irregular Chinese cockle-pickers in Morecambe Bay in 2004, the Gangmasters Licensing Authority (GLA) was established by the Gangmasters (Licensing) Act 2004 to protect workers from exploitation in agriculture, shellfish-gathering, and food processing and packaging. It is an offence to operate as a gangmaster without a licence or to use an unlicensed gangmaster. Licensed gangmasters are under a number of obligations which aim to prevent exploitation and dangerous working. In 2013, the government consulted on proposals to reduce the scope of the GLA and to introduce a regime of civil penalties. The Gangmasters Licensing (Exclusions) Regulations 2013/2216 set out a significant number of circumstances in which there was no longer an obligation to hold a licence. Section 55 Modern Slavery Act 2015 requires the government to consult on the role of the GLA. The consultation was launched in October 2015 and proposed to expand the powers of the GLA by establishing a statutory Director of Labour Market Enforcement, new criminal offences, increased intelligence and data sharing and a wider remit and strengthened powers. The establishment of the Director of Labour Market Enforcement with a coordinating function is provided for in the Immigration Bill. While estimating the number of irregular migrants is difficult for self-evident reasons, there are possibly more than 700,000 in the UK, many of whom will be working unlawfully and often in conditions of exploitation, leading to calls for a regularization programme (Migrants' Rights Network 2009). As suggested earlier in relation to domestic workers, there is a connection between unlawful working and trafficking.

9.11 Conclusion

The more positive, if highly instrumental, attitude towards migration heralded by the 2002 White Paper vanished in the face of recession and public disquiet. While the concept of a PBS has virtues, the system now in place is such a system only in name. The priority for some years has been to establish a complex instrument of control and this has been exacerbated by the government's drive to curtail migration which caused the end of the few remaining elements of flexibility.

There is a contradiction between the avowed intention to 'make migration work' for Britain, and the submission of applications to enter for work, study, or cultural exchange to an unresponsive and rigid decision-making process. It suggests a narrow vision of policy that is tied to short-term political calculations, a preoccupation with control, and administrative convenience. This is arguably inappropriate as regards economic migration but is surely even more so when applied to students, travellers, artists, academics, and sportspeople who wish to spend time in the UK, exchanging ideas and developing ties whose benefits may be intangible but are vital and long term.

QUESTIONS

1 Does the PBS 'work for Britain'?
2 How accountable is government for the operation of the PBS?
3 Has the government satisfactorily addressed the problem of illegal working?
4 What protections should be put in place for the protection of vulnerable migrant workers?
5 Has the government struck the right balance between promoting the UK as a destination for international students and preventing fraud?

 online resource centre For guidance on answering questions, visit the Online Resource Centre www.oxfordtextbooks.co.uk/orc/clayton7e/.

FURTHER READING

Beynon, Rhian (2007) 'Highly Skilled, No Longer Wanted' *Catalyst*, 22 January.

Bhabha, J. et al (eds) (1985), *Worlds Apart: Women under Immigration and Nationality Law* (Women, Immigration and Nationality Group (WING)).

Devine, Laura (2007) 'Is the New Highly Skilled Migrant Programme "Fit for Purpose"? If Not, the Government's Proposed Points Based Immigration System is Fundamentally Flawed' *Journal of Immigration, Asylum and Nationality Law* vol. 21, no. 2, pp. 90–108.

Devine, Laura and Barrett-Brown, Sophie (2001) 'The Work Permit Scheme—An Analysis of its Origin and Scope' *Journal of Immigration, Asylum and Nationality Law* vol. 15, no. 2, pp. 92–101.

Dobson, Janet *et al* (2001) *International Migration and the United Kingdom: Recent Patterns and Trends*, Research, Development and Statistics Occasional Paper no. 75.

Dummett, Ann and Nicol Andrew (1990) *Subjects, Citizens, Aliens and Others* (London: Weidenfeld and Nicholson).

Dzankic, Jelena (2014) 'Citizenship with a Price Tag: the Law and Ethics of Investor Citizenship Programmes' *Northern Ireland Legal Quarterly* vol. 65 (4), 387–404.

Geis, W. et al (2011) 'Why Go to France or Germany, if you Could as Well Go to the UK or the US? Selective features of immigration to the EU "big three" and the United States' *Journal of Common Market Studies* vol. 49, no. 4, pp. 767–96.

Gillespie, Jim (2000) 'Review of Work Permits' *Journal of Immigration, Asylum and Nationality Law* vol. 14, no. 2, pp. 75–6.

Harvey, Alison (2011) 'The Cap on Immigration' *Journal of Immigration, Asylum and Nationality Law* vol. 25, no. 1, pp. 7–9.

Holmes, Colin (1988) *John Bull's Island: Immigration and British Society 1871–1971* (Basingstoke: Macmillan).

Home Office (2006) *A Points-Based System: Making Migration Work for Britain* (London: Home Office).

Joint Committee on Human Rights, *Highly Skilled Migrants: Changes to the Immigration Rules* Session 2006-07 Twentieth Report HL Paper 173, HC 993.

Kalayaan/Oxfam (2008) *The New Bonded Labour: The Impact of Proposed Changes to the UK Immigration System on Migrant Domestic Workers* (London: Kalayaan/Oxfam).

Kofman, Eleonore et al (2009) *The Equality Implications of Being a Migrant in Britain* (London: Equality and Human Rights Commission).

Mantouvalou, Virginia (2015) '"Am I free now?' Overseas domestic workers in slavery" *Journal of Law and Society* vol. 42 (3), 329–57.

Mavroudi, Elizabeth and Warren, Adam (2013) 'Highly Skilled Migration and the Negotiation of Immigration Policy: Non-EEA postgraduate students and academic staff at English universities' *Geoforum* vol. 44 (January) pp. 261–70.

McLaughlan, Gail and Salt, John (2002) *Migration Policies: Towards Highly Skilled Foreign Workers* (London: Migration Research Unit, University College London).

Migrants' Rights Network (2008) Papers Please: The Impact of the Civil Penalty Regime on the Employment Rights of Migrants in the UK (MRN Migration Perspectives Paper).

Migrants' Rights Network (2009) *Irregular Migrants: The Urgent Need for a New Approach* (London: MRN Migration Perspectives Paper).

Momsen, Janet Henshall (ed.) (1999) *Gender, Migration and Domestic Service* (London: Routledge).

Murphy, Clíodhna (2013) 'The Enduring Vulnerability of Migrant Domestic Workers in Europe' *International and Comparative Law Quarterly* vol. 62, no. 3, 599–627.

Murphy, Cliodhna and Mullally, Siobhan (2014) 'Migrant Domestic Workers in the UK: enacting exemptions, exclusions, and rights' *Human Rights Quarterly* vol. 36 (2) 397–427.

Paul, Kathleen (1997) *Whitewashing Britain: Race and Citizenship in the Postwar Era* (New York: Cornell), chapters 3, 4, and 5.

Portes, Jonathan and French, Simon (2005) The Impact of Free Movement of Workers from Central and Eastern Europe on the UK Labour Market: Early Evidence DWP Working Paper no. 18.

Puttick, Keith (2006) 'Welcoming the New Arrivals? Reception, Integration and Employment of A8, Bulgarian and Romanian Migrants' *Journal of Immigration, Asylum and Nationality Law* vol. 20, no. 4, pp. 238–54.

Rogaly, Ben (2006) *Intensification of Work-Place Regimes in British Agriculture: The Role of Migrant Workers* Sussex Migration Working Paper no. 36 (Sussex Centre for Migration Research).

Stephenson, K. and Wilkins, C. (2011) 'The 2011/2012 Immigration Overhaul and the Impact on the Education Sector' *Education Law Journal* vol. 12, no. 3, pp. 197–207.

Toal, Ronan (2013) 'The Judgments of the Supreme Court in *Alvi* and *Munir' Journal of Immigration Asylum and Nationality Law* vol. 7, no. 4, 344–9.

Wray, Helena (2009) 'The Points Based System: A Blunt Instrument' *Journal of Immigration, Asylum and Nationality Law* vol. 23, no. 3, pp. 231–51.

10

Visitors: entry for temporary purposes

SUMMARY

This chapter deals with those coming to the UK as visitors for short-term or finite purposes such as tourism, business visits, sporting and entertainment engagements, or for private medical treatment.

10.1 Introduction

The majority of passengers arriving in the UK do so not for settlement but for temporary purposes, and the most common reason for temporary entry is as a visitor. In 2014, 9.15 million people were given leave to enter the UK as visitors, compared to 8.69 million the previous year and 7.69 in 2012. Only about 1.85 million visitor visas were issued so the majority seem to have come from non-visa countries such as US, Australia, Japan, Argentina, and Brazil. These visitors may obtain leave to enter at the border and do not need to obtain a visa prior to entry although they may still choose to do so.

The law relating to visitors is not much concerned with these individuals. While non-visa nationals must meet the requirements of the immigration rules, it is rare that the entry of, for example, American or Japanese tourists raises any issues when they request leave to enter. Although recent published statistics are less detailed, the immigration statistics for 2009 show that 8,445 individuals from the Americas were refused entry at the port and subsequently removed. It is probable that not all were non-visa visitors but, even if they were, they still represent only a tiny fraction (less than 0.3 per cent) of all visitors from the region. This can be compared with refusal rates for visa applications at posts such as Abuja in Nigeria where, according to the Chief Inspector's report of July 2009, there was a refusal rate of 43 per cent for applications with limited rights of appeal (around 75 per cent of which were visitor applications). Certainly, acceptance and refusal rates seem to be connected to larger global issues. Following the terrorist attacks in New York in 2001, the overall refusal rate for family visitor applications increased considerably with particularly large rises in regions such as the Middle East and South Asia (Dunstan 2004).

The law relating to visitors is therefore principally concerned with visa nationals and with the same issues as much of the rest of immigration law, and which are associated with particular regions and countries: deterring illegal and unwanted entrants, overstaying, and asylum claims. It operates on the basis of discretionary judgments challengeable by limited appeal rights, now confined to protection and human rights grounds. It affects not only those who want to spend time in the UK as a tourist or on business but also the family lives of UK residents of migrant origin seeking to maintain relationships with relatives abroad. While not overtly expressed as a requirement of the rules, the credibility of the applicant is a major factor in determining the outcome of the application and lack of credibility is frequently the underlying reason for refusal. Of course, there are more matters involved in visitor applications than these but these familiar themes are clearly present.

The visa regime itself, as we have already seen (chapter 6), is designed to prevent illegal entry and deter asylum claims. No more will be said about this here. The right of appeal against refusal of entry clearance for visitors was removed by the Asylum and Immigration Appeals Act 1993. From then, the only possibility of challenging refusal of entry clearance was by judicial review. As we have already noted, judicial review is concerned not with the merits of the decision but with the decision-making process. Usually, in the case of refusal of a visa, this is the question of whether the entry clearance officer's decision was unreasonable, and it is rarely possible to show that this was the case (see, for instance, *R v SSHD ex p Kurumoorthy* [1998] Imm AR 401 or *R v ECO Accra ex p Aidoo* [1999] Imm AR 221). One effect of a lack of appeal right is that decision-making receives little scrutiny. There are few recent Tribunal cases, and given the limitations of judicial review, there is a relatively small body of case law on the application of the rules.

The Immigration and Asylum Act 1999 ss 59 and 60 reinstated a right of appeal for family visitors. This was of particular importance to families of migrant origin who wanted relatives to come for holidays and for family events such as weddings and funerals. However, in these latter instances, not only the right but the timeliness of the appeal was critical. In practice, an appeal may not be decided until after the family event in question has taken place but it might still be brought to avoid the adverse consequences of a refusal on future applications. In its family migration consultation (Home Office/ UK Border Agency (2011) *Family Migration: A Consultation*), the government again proposed removing the enhanced appeal rights of family visitors, a proposal that was implemented in June 2013 by s 52 Crime and Courts Act 2013 and discussed further at 10.5.

The relationship between border control and visitor visas is highlighted by the inclusion of plans for reform of the visitor visa rules in the previous government's strategy document, *Securing the UK Border: Our Vision and Strategy for the Future*, published in March 2007, which set out the government's plans for expanding the border. It made a number of proposals to codify and regulate visitor status more tightly, some of which were implemented. The government also announced the intention to create, to use its own consumerist terminology, 'a new family of visa products' for short term-visits and a new category of 'Business Visitors'. A category of 'Student Visitor' had already been established. In 2008, criteria for 'Business Visitor', 'Sports Visitor', and 'Entertainer Visitor' were introduced, the latter two regularizing previous concessions. Other new categories such as 'Prospective Entrepreneur' and 'Permitted Paid Engagements' were added later. These new categories, together with the pre-existing categories of 'Child Visitor' and 'Marriage Visitor' and categories for those seeking medical treatment or visiting children at school suggested that the government wanted to exert tighter control over each group of people permitted to enter. Yet it is impossible in practice to envisage all the possible circumstances in which a person might legitimately wish to make a short visit to the UK and the rules were amended again in 2015 to create four main categories of visitor discussed below.

In March 2013, the Deputy Prime Minister Nick Clegg announced a pilot whereby visa applicants from six 'high risk' countries (India, Pakistan, Nigeria, Ghana, Sri Lanka, and Bangladesh) coming on short-term visas would deposit a £3,000 bond to be repaid on departure. The announcement caused immense concern and anger in the countries to be affected. The President of Ghana described the pilot as 'unacceptable', 'discriminatory', and 'inappropriate'. The Confederation of Indian Industry called it 'very unfortunate'. The Select Committee on Home Affairs was concerned at the damage just the proposal had done to relationships between the UK and the countries in question (*The Work of the UK Border Agency (January–March 2013)* Eighth Report of Session 2013–14). The pilot was due to take place towards the end of 2013, but was abandoned.

While there are now four categories of visitor, there are common suitability requirements found in Part V3 of Appendix V, relating to reasons for exclusion and refusal based on false information, breaches of immigration laws or other generic reasons. Failure to provide biometrics, information, or medical reports without a reasonable excuse, if these have been required, is a mandatory ground for refusal.

10.2 Standard Visitor

The rules for Standard Visitors are found in Part V4 of Appendix V. They incorporate most of the conditions that formerly applied to 'General Visitors' and include the following.

10.2.1 Has a genuine intention to visit

This means that the applicant will leave the UK at the end of their visit and will not live in the UK for extended periods through frequent or successive visits, or make the UK their main home. They must be seeking entry for a purpose that is permitted by the visitor routes (these are listed in Appendices 3, 4, and 5 of Appendix V) and will not undertake the activities prohibited in paras V4.5–V4.10.

Appendix 3 lists activities that all visitors may carry out. They include:

- tourism and leisure: visiting friends and family and/or a holiday;
- volunteering: This must be incidental to the main purpose of the visit, last no more than 30 days and be for a registered charity. More extended volunteering or where it is the central purpose of the visit comes under Tier 5 of the Points-Based System;
- business: This covers the usual activities that a person may wish to undertake during a business related visit such as attending meetings and conferences, giving presentations on a non-profit basis or negotiating and signing contracts. Until November 2008, those wishing to conduct business in the UK entered as an ordinary visitor and the range of permissible activities was not defined. The rules were then amended to create a business visitor category with a list of permitted activities. The business visitor has now been reincorporated into the general route but the list is still present and appears to be exhaustive. Business visitors were previously specifically prohibited from working or receiving payment. This is still prohibited but by the general prohibitions in paragraphs V4.5 to V4. 7;
- creative: This permits an artist, entertainer, or musician to undertake various unpaid activities or take part in one or more events on the list of permit free festivals in Appendix 5 (where payment is permitted);
- sports: This permits participation in a sports tournament or event as an individual or part of a team, personal appearances and promotional activities and other sports-related activities provided they are not paid;

- study: Visitors may carry out educational exchanges and short courses of up to 30 days in length. Previously, students on short courses of up to 11 months could enter under the visitor rules but they are now covered by separate rules in paragraphs A57A–H of the main immigration rules;

- medical treatment: This covers private (not NHS) medical treatment provided this has been arranged in advance, supporting evidence is provided and the treatment will be of a finite duration. This is one of the few instances in which a visa for more than six months is possible as an eleven month visa is possible provided there is evidence that the proposed treatment will last between six and eleven months. Unusually, a visitor visa for medical treatment may be renewed repeatedly beyond the usual six (or eleven) month period. The Tribunal in *LB (medical treatment of finite duration)* [2005] UKAIT 00175 held that treatment may last for years in a suitable case. The limit is the duration of the treatment, and, although this must be finite, it need not be short.

Other sub-categories include prospective entrepreneurs, other types of business visit, scientific, research or academic visits, film shoots and related purposes, support staff of business people, film crew or creative artists, international drivers, tour group couriers, journalists and archeologists on one-off assignments, and those coming for organ donation.

The new visitor rules appear to be an attempt to provide an exhaustive list of permitted activities. The guidance does not anticipate that leave to enter may be granted if the applicant does not fall within one of these categories. This represents a narrowing of the previous position under which a visit might be for any purpose that does not contravene the rules. This is relevant to the position of carers discussed later or to any new or unforeseen cases.

10.2.2 **Duration of visit**

A standard visit visa may be granted for up to six months but may be issued for a shorter period, particularly if there are residual doubts about the applicant's intentions. A visitor who has been given less than six months leave and continues to satisfy the requirements may apply before the expiry of their leave for a further period up to the maximum. There are reports that those who stay longer than originally planned but still leave within the currency of their visa have had later applications refused even where there are good reasons for the longer stay.

Extension beyond the maximum period is possible under the rules only for those coming for private medical visits. An academic on sabbatical leave can be granted an extension of stay up to twelve months in total (paras V8.7–V8.9).

Paragraph 8.1 says that it is not possible to switch to visitor status while in the UK where a person is in breach of immigration laws or has leave for another purpose. This means that a period as a visitor cannot be tacked onto the end of another stay. In *YT (HC 395 paragraph 44—extension of stay) Belarus* [2009] UKAIT 00003, the applicant asked to stay on after working under the sectors-based scheme, so that he could have 'the opportunity to travel in the United Kingdom'. The Tribunal found that this was permitted under the rules as they then stood. However, after that application had been made, the forerunner of para V8.1 was amended so that an individual in these circumstances would have to leave the UK and reapply for entry as a visitor.

Paragraph V4.2 requires that the decision-maker must be satisfied that the applicant will not live in the UK for extended periods through frequent or successive visits, or make the UK their main home. A similar provision was inserted in the previous rules in 2013 after two Upper Tribunal decisions. One found that the sole fact that someone wishes to spend more time in the UK, while inviting rigorous scrutiny to ensure compliance with the rules, is not, in itself, a reason for refusal (*Oppong (visitor—length of stay)* Ghana [2011] UKUT 00431 (IAC)). In *Sawmynaden v ECO* [2012] UKUT 00161 (IAC), the Upper Tribunal held that there was no restriction on the number of visits a person might make to the UK, nor any requirement that a specified time must elapse between successive visits. The reality of the arrangement had to be ascertained: was the applicant really resident in the UK and no more than a visitor to the country of origin so that the purpose of the return home is solely to gain re-admission to the UK?

The guidance advises that there is no specified maximum period which an individual can spend in the UK in any period such as '6 months in 12 months' but that, if it is clear from an individual's travel history that they are making the UK their home, the application should be refused. Relevant factors include the purpose of the visit and intended length of stay, previous visits made over the past 12 months, including the length of stay and whether this amounts to the individual spending more time in the UK than in their home country, their links with their home country and evidence that the UK is their main place of residence, for example, registration with a General Practitioner, and the history of previous applications, for example, if the visitor has previously been refused under the family rules. This latter factor creates particular problems for those who have been unable to meet the current very restrictive family rules but want to maintain contact with UK family, including partners and children (see Children's Commissioner 2015). Applicants who can show a need for repeated visits and whose circumstances and travel history are considered appropriate may be given multi-entry visas for up to ten years, permitting any number of entries within the currency of the visa. Factors set out in the guidance include a credible ongoing reason to visit such as family links or an established business connection (provided there is no intention to make the UK their home), stable personal and economic circumstances, and previous travel history. In other cases, a new application for leave will be needed for each visit.

10.2.3 Maintenance and accommodation

Under para V4.2, the applicant must satisfy the decision-maker that they have sufficient funds to cover all reasonable costs in relation to their visit without working or accessing public funds. This includes the cost of the return or onward journey, any costs relating to dependants, and the cost of planned activities such as private medical treatment. Under para V4.3, maintenance and accommodation may be provided by a third party, not necessarily a family member, where the decision-maker is satisfied that they have a genuine professional or personal relationship, are not themselves in breach of the immigration laws, and are able and willing to provide support. An undertaking in writing may be requested and failure to secure this will usually lead to refusal.

While some assurance about the applicant's financial circumstances is necessary, the purpose is only to show that the applicant has the capacity to maintain themselves and return and their finances do not need to be a model of clarity (*Osibamowo* (12116)). The assessment of this requirement involves an examination not only of the means of the visitor but also, where applicable, of those who will support them.

The guidance on credibility says that officials must consider whether the information and the reasons for the visit provided by the applicant are credible and correspond to their personal, family, social and economic background. This is a contentious area as it means that those from modest backgrounds may be treated more sceptically. The problem is illustrated by the case of *Hussain* (10037), in which the entry clearance officer (ECO) refused entry clearance on the basis that the cost of the trip was out of all proportion to the applicant's income. The IAT found that the satisfaction of seeing family was quite sufficient reason for the trip and the expenditure involved. The visit did not need to be a demonstrably wise financial move. However, the appellant still lost in this case because he could not show that he could afford the airfare home. There was a similar approach in *Kaur v ECO New Delhi* [2002] UKIAT 05692, in which the Tribunal said that the emotional value of the trip might well mean that the visitor would pay more than strict economics might dictate. However, in *Iskola* (11334) it was held to be relevant that the price of the air tickets was equivalent to one year's income from the applicant's business, and refusal of entry clearance was justified. The difficulty here is that the difference in the standard of living between the applicant's home country and the UK may make it very difficult for the applicant to show that the trip is financially viable. This is not really because of this part of the rule taken alone, but because of the way it interacts with the requirement to show intention to leave. If an individual has allocated a substantial proportion of their resources to the trip, it may be suspected that it is because they hope to remain long term.

10.2.4 Intention to leave

Under para V4.2, the applicant must satisfy the decision-maker that they will leave the UK at the end of their visit. As with all the immigration rules, the burden of proof is on the applicant to a civil standard of proof. Given that a person's intentions are, of necessity, difficult to prove, the applicant will have to adduce circumstantial evidence from which the immigration officer will make a judgment. Decision-makers will consider matters such as what incentive the applicant has to return, for example, whether they have family and work commitments in their home country. In *Aye* (10100), the Tribunal said that an apparent lack of incentive to return should not of itself be treated as a reason to refuse but could be taken into account as part of all the circumstances used to decide the applicant's intentions. Evidence from the sponsor may also help to build a picture of the applicant's intention (*DM* [2005] UKIAT 130). Entry clearance officers often expect a prospective tourist to have some idea of what they will see and reject an applicant whose plans are seen as excessively vague or inaccurate. However, it is not necessary to have a detailed itinerary for a family visit. In fact, the Tribunal has commented that too much concern with sightseeing might suggest that a family visit is not really intended (*W (Ghana)* [2004] UKIAT 00005).

In considering incentive to return, the economic circumstances in the applicant's home country by comparison with those in the UK may be taken into account. There are many cases in which this reasoning is demonstrated (see *Ashfaq Ahmad v ECO Islamabad* [2002] UKIAT 03891 discussed at 10.2.5 in the context of intention not to work). Such considerations are fraught with the potential for stereotyping and discrimination. In *R v ECO ex p Abu-Gidary* CO 965 1999, the argument was advanced for the applicant that the ECO's reasoning in this respect, if taken too far, could result in no young single women from developing or poor countries being able to obtain entry clearance as visitors. The applicant for entry clearance had made numerous previous unsuccessful applications. She was now a graduate who had a job to return to. Given local conditions, this was a considerable achievement but the ECO did not regard it as sufficient incentive to return, describing her income as 'modest'. The view of the High Court was more sympathetic. That sympathetic approach is also found in Tribunal decisions such as *Ogunkola v ECO Lagos* [2002] UKIAT 02238, in which the Tribunal endorsed the view that:

if lack of economic incentive to return to the country of origin were sufficient to found a refusal of a visit application, then no person living overseas whose standard of living was lower than that prevailing in the UK could ever come on holiday here, or visit relatives settled here. That is not the law. (para 7)

In reality, however, for those whose home lives are neither settled nor prosperous, there may be little concrete that can be put forward besides statements of good faith whose value depends on the subjective concept of credibility. The guidance points to factors such as family and economic ties in the country of residence and the UK, the political, economic and security situation in the country of residence, and previous attempts to deceive the immigration authorities not only by the applicant but by the sponsor or even other immediate family members. As the Tribunal said, in a decision on intention to return in the sectors-based scheme, it is wrong to assume that 'anyone who has the opportunity to commit an offence will do so' (*AA and others (Sectors Based Work: General Principles) Bangladesh* [2006] UKAIT 00026 para 32). Yet, decisions can easily end up being made on such a basis and, in the absence of general appeal rights, they are difficult to challenge. Because adverse findings against other family members are a factor, an unjust decision against one person may have long term ramifications not only for that individual but for those connected to him/her.

10.2.5 Prohibited activities

Paragraph V4.5 says that the applicant must not intend to work in the UK. A number of examples such as taking employment, self-employment, or direct selling are specified, in each case unless these are expressly allowed by the permitted activities and do not amount to employment or filling a role even on a temporary basis. In essence, this condition requires proof of a negative, that the visitor does not intend to work while in the UK. This is not necessarily proved by evidence that they can be maintained and accommodated. In *Ashfaq Ahmad v ECO Islamabad*, the Tribunal found that, while the sponsor could maintain and accommodate the visitor, he could not control the actions of the visitor. Whatever the sponsor's own intentions, the visitor, as a free adult, may make other choices, such as working during their stay. The sponsor could not prevent this and the application for entry clearance could be refused because of the incentive to work, given the applicant's financial circumstances.

The Tribunal in *Mistry v ECO Bombay* [2002] UKIAT 07500 put the matter rather starkly as follows: 'It comes down to the question of whether someone making a modest living in India must inevitably be regarded as too much prey to the temptations of doing much better here, at least in cash terms, to be regarded as a genuine short-term visitor' (para 7). The implied answer here was 'no', but the possibility of making such a blanket, and potentially discriminatory, judgment is clear and invokes the earlier point made about the difficulty of proving an intention in the absence of compelling evidence, which will not often be available, particularly for young, relatively poor, first-time travellers.

Ignorance of the prohibition on working can have serious consequences for those who are entering for mixed purposes. A self-employed graphic designer was lawfully refused leave to enter when it emerged that she had undertaken small amounts of work, including for UK clients, during her previous holiday even though her business was based in Israel (*Kucherov v SSHD* [2014] EWHC 3749 (Admin)). An American artist who arrived at Heathrow for a free five-day festival was detained, refused, and removed because she was carrying two small paintings which she had hopes of exhibiting or selling. The Chinese artist Huang Xu was refused a visa to attend his own exhibition because it was suspected that he would sell his work, even though the exhibition was organized by the gallery who would, as is commonplace in the art world, act as vendor (Manifesto Club (2010) *Deported: Artists and Academics Barred from the UK*).

10.2.6 Credibility

The immigration rules do not contain a heading of 'Credibility' but, as already indicated, this issue lies behind the requirements we have discussed earlier. The Guidance contains a section on genuineness and credibility. Relevant factors include:

- previous immigration and travel history, including visits to the UK and other countries;
- the duration of previous visits and whether this was significantly longer than originally stated (even if still within the period granted). As previously discussed, this has become a regular feature in refusals and seems to penalize applicants for behaviour that is lawful and authorized;
- financial circumstances and family, social, and economic background;
- personal and economic ties to their country of residence and in the UK;
- cumulative period of time spent in the UK over the last 12-month period;
- whether, in the decision-maker's judgment, the information and the reasons for the visit are not credible and do not correspond to their personal, family, social, and economic background;
- the political, economic, and security situation in the applicant's country of residence, particularly where there is instability and conflict. This can be sufficient reason for refusal on its own unless outweighed by particular circumstances, for example, a permanent right of residence in another more stable country;
- information on immigration non-compliance by individuals who applied for a visit visa from the same geographical region;
- previous deception by the applicant, their sponsor, or another immediate family member;
- discrepancies between the statements made by the applicant and the statements made by the sponsor, particularly where the sponsor could reasonably be expected to know the facts;
- that the information that has been provided or the reasons stated by the applicant are not credible.

A pattern of travel that shows the applicant has previously complied with UK immigration law or the laws in other developed countries such as the USA, Canada, Australia, New Zealand, Ireland, Schengen countries, or Switzerland is a favourable but not determinative factor and is of no assistance to a first-time traveller.

The guidance goes further than previous guidance in finding that factors unconnected with the individual are reasons for refusal. Instability in the applicant's country of residence is sufficient on its own to refuse a visa. It means that honest individuals who may have good reasons for visiting, such as very close family members, are indefinitely excluded for reasons over which they have no control.

In general, credibility is clearly relevant to subjective questions such as intention. However, it is easily elevated out of its rightful place and treated as the overriding factor. At worst, poor findings as to credibility may mean that the rest of an applicant's evidence is disregarded even where this is of good quality. Time and time again, the Tribunal stated that the issue of credibility should not be so used. However, as decisions are no longer subject to appeal rights, this cannot be challenged. In addition, the general lack of appeal rights means that other adverse findings, such as deception by others, cannot be challenged when they are made and may then be used later as the basis for refusals. It is easy to see how easily a picture may be created of a doubtful applicant based on little more than generalized assumptions and previous unchallengeable decisions.

10.2.7 Special conditions

Some applicants must meet special conditions. The position of those coming for medical treatment has already been mentioned. Paragraphs V4.11–V4.13 set out additional requirements for children. There must be adequate arrangements for their travel to, reception, and care in the UK. If the applicant is not applying or travelling with a parent or guardian in their home country who is responsible for their care, that parent or guardian must confirm their consent, in writing if required. If this does not apply, the visa must state that the child is accompanied and will be travelling with an adult identified on that visit visa or that the child is unaccompanied.

Rules for child visitors were first introduced in 2006 by HC 819 and amended under HC 120 from the beginning of 2010 to provide for educational exchange visits as well as to meet the UK's obligations under s 55 of the Borders, Citizenship and Immigration Act 2009. This requires the immigration authorities to take into account the need to safeguard and promote the welfare of children in the UK when carrying out its functions. The provisions aim to protect children who might enter the UK under private fostering arrangements, such as those used in the case of Victoria Climbié, who was ill-treated and killed by her carers, or for trafficking.

The guidance states that, if the child's parents are divorced, the consent must be given by the parent who holds legal custody or sole responsibility. This may be in the form of the application itself or a letter. Consent from both parents should be sought if the child will be travelling with a parent without legal custody, there is official notification of a risk that the child may be moved without consent, or there are other concerns that the child may be at risk.

10.3 Other visitors

As already indicated, there are some additional visitor categories.

10.3.1 Permitted paid engagements

This new category of visitor was created in the previous rules in response to complaints by those working in the cultural sector that Tier 5 was too complex for small organizations wanting to bring in an artist or others for occasional paid engagements. The criteria are set out in Part V5 of Appendix V. As well as meeting the criteria for standard visitors, an applicant to undertake permitted paid engagements must be at least 18 and intend to do one (or more) of the permitted paid engagements set out in Appendix 4, which must be arranged before the applicant travels to the UK, declared as part of the application for a visit visa or leave to enter, and evidenced by a formal invitation.

The engagements permitted under Appendix 4 are certain academic activities if carried out by an academic who is highly qualified within his or her field of expertise, assessment by an overseas designated pilot examiner of ability to meet the national aviation regulatory requirements of other countries, advocacy by a qualified lawyer and activities by a professional artist, entertainer, musician, or sports person directly relating to their profession and if invited by an appropriate UK-based organization. Leave is for a single entry for a maximum period of one month.

10.3.2 Visitors entering for marriage or civil partnership

Government scepticism about the intention of visitors to return home is illustrated by the ban implemented in 2003 to prevent switching from visitor to spouse status. The preceding *White Paper, Secure Borders, Safe Haven* (Cm 5387) said:

In 1999, 76 per cent of those granted leave to remain on the basis of marriage had been admitted to the UK for another purpose and 50 per cent of those who switched into the marriage category did so within six months of entry. As it seems unlikely that such a large percentage of this number would develop permanent relationships within such a short period of time, the indication is that many of these persons had intended to marry all along but had not obtained leave to enter on this basis and had therefore lied about their intentions to the entry clearance officer. Alternatively, they may have entered a bogus marriage to obtain leave to remain after arrival. (para 7.11)

The failure to announce an intention to marry prior to entry may be explicable in many different ways and does not, in itself, indicate dishonesty or a bogus marriage. The applicant may, for example, wish to spend more time with their partner before deciding to marry. A person who has entered as a *bona fide* visitor and formed a relationship in that time has to choose between marrying or leaving the UK with the attendant expense and delay before returning. While some bogus marriages do take place, as the House of Lords found in *Baiai*, discussed in chapter 8, it is wrong to assume that these can be detected purely on the basis of immigration status.

The ban on switching was followed by the controversial Certificates of Approval scheme, also discussed in chapter 8, which aimed to prevent those with short-term or no leave from marrying within the UK. The purpose of both that scheme and the ban on switching was to force aspiring spouses to leave the UK and make an entry clearance application from abroad. Consistent with this policy, the Marriage Visitor rules were introduced to provide for a visa that permits entrants to enter for marriage if they do not intend to remain in the UK after marriage. While the certificates of approval scheme was abolished in 2011, the marriage visitor category is relevant to the more recent sham marriage provisions, found in Part 4 of the Immigration Act 2014 and discussed in chapter 8.

Part V6 of Appendix V provides that an applicant for a marriage or civil partnership visit visa must satisfy the decision-maker that they meet the main requirements for visitors discussed above, are aged 18 or over and intend to give notice of or enter into a marriage or civil partnership (which is not a sham marriage) during their stay. The maximum permitted stay is six months and, as a visitor, the applicant must intend to leave the UK at the end of that period. If the intention is to live in the UK after the ceremony, the more demanding fiancé(e) visa is needed.

10.4 **Transit visitors**

A transit visitor is a person who travels via the UK en route to another destination country outside the common travel area. Nationals of some countries require a Direct Airside Transit Visa, provided for by the Immigration (Passenger Transit Visa) Order 2014 (as amended), just to transit airside, that is, to remain in the controlled part of the airport without entering the UK. Otherwise, under Part V7 of Appendix V, a visa national must either hold a transit visit visa or, if they meet the requirements for admission under the transit without visa scheme, they may seek leave to enter at the UK border.

To obtain a transit visa or leave to enter for transit, an applicant must satisfy the decision-maker that they are genuinely in transit, that they are taking a reasonable transit route, will not access public funds or medical treatment, work or study in the UK, and intend and are able to leave the UK within 48 hours with assured entry to the next country.

The Transit Without Visa Scheme applies when all of the above have been met, and the passenger has arrived and will be leaving by air with a confirmed booking within 24 hours. The individual must also be travelling to and from, and be resident in or have a visa for one of a small number of countries: Australia, Canada, New Zealand, or the USA, EEA, or Switzerland. However, nationals of Syria travelling to the US on temporary visas are excluded. This was introduced in the spring of 2015 because Syrians travelling on these visas were claiming asylum in the UK, described in the explanatory memorandum as 'evidenced abuse'.

10.4.1 **Carers**

There is no provision in the rules for those who want to care for a sick friend or relative in the UK. The Tribunal previously found that, provided the applicant meets the requirements of the visitor rules, the fact that she intends to spend her time in the UK caring for a relative is not a reason for refusal (*Oppong (visitor—length of stay) Ghana* [2011] UKUT 00431 (IAC)) but it is doubtful that this would still be the case now that there is an apparently exhaustive list of permitted activities.

Family members who intend to care for children may be refused on the basis that they are working as a child minder. According to the Tribunal in *Jumawan* (9385), if the intention is to take over domestic responsibilities to enable another family member to work, then refusal may be justified as this is a task which may be undertaken by a third party employed for that purpose. However, merely because a person intends to occupy some or all of their visit in the care of their grandchildren, which could be done by an employee, it does not follow that domestic employment is the applicant's object. Leave to enter as a visitor may still be granted if other conditions are met. The Guidance says that, where a family member is coming to look after a child in the UK, this is permitted provided it is for a short visit and does not amount to the relative being employed as a child-minder. This appears more accommodating (and more realistic given grandparents' and other relatives' role in child care) than the previous guidance which only permitted close relatives to do child care when neither parent had an immigration status leading to settlement and was therefore of relevance only to the relatives of temporary migrants.

10.5 **Entry clearance**

Where the requirements in Appendix V have been met, a non-visa national may be granted leave to enter at the port. Where entry clearance has been obtained beforehand, this also functions as leave to enter (Immigration (Leave to Enter and Remain) Order 2000, SI 2000/1161; see chapter 6). A visa national must obtain entry clearance for any purpose, including a visit. Visa national countries include a number of Commonwealth countries, so the belief which is sometimes held, that Commonwealth citizens may visit their UK relatives without prior entry clearance, is a false one. It depends on the Commonwealth country from which they come. For instance, Australian nationals have no such restriction; Indian nationals do.

The rate of refusal of leave to enter at the port to visitors from some non-visa national countries (notably in the Caribbean) is higher than for visitors from other countries. It can therefore be advisable for nationals of those countries to obtain entry clearance even though it is not obligatory, as it will ease the traveller's passage through immigration control and help to avoid wasted airfares and the distress of refusal at the port.

10.6 **Family visit appeals**

As mentioned previously, the Immigration and Asylum Act 1999 reinstated a right of appeal against refusal of entry clearance for visits to family members as defined in regulations. Family visit visas are controversial because of the variable refusal rates and claims of inconsistent decision-making between posts. In December 2009, it was reported that the highest rate of refusal of family visits was in Pakistan (41 per cent), followed by Bangladesh (31 per cent). The refusal rate in Pakistan has been stated to be as high as 90 per cent (Notes of Entry Clearance User Panel 22 July 2010 in ILPA members mailing August 2010). There are well-established communities from both these countries in the UK, and the inability to invite family members to important events such as weddings and funerals or merely to provide a holiday is a major cause of resentment and creates a perception of discrimination.

Successive governments have been uneasy about the continuation of family visitor appeals. In the five-year strategy published in February 2005, there was a proposal to end oral appeals, and a consultation paper in December 2007 asked if the appeal right should be 'revisited'. The Coalition government again proposed removing the general right of appeal for family members so that, in line with other visitors, appeals might be brought only on human rights or race discrimination grounds (Home Office/UK Border Agency (2011) *Family Migration: A Consultation*). The range of relatives in respect of whom an appeal could be brought was narrowed in June 2012 and family visit appeal rights were removed altogether, except in respect of race discrimination and human rights, in June 2013. The government's argument was that appeals were expensive, took too long to process, and were far more numerous than had been expected, (49,400 in 2010–11 against 20,000 that had been anticipated), representing more than a third of all appeals. It was also stated that, in many cases, new evidence was provided at the appeal which should have been submitted with the original application and that applicants should reapply rather than appeal (Letter from UK Border Agency Partnership and

Engagement Team to ILPA, 10 May 2012). That many people use appeal rights is hardly an argument for their abolition and suggests problems with the quality of information and decision-making. The success rate on appeal in family visit visa cases rose from 19 per cent in 2004 to 44.6 per cent in 2010 (calculations based on figures in *Hansard* HC, 20 January 2011: Col 974W). At that time, the Independent Chief Inspector of Borders and Immigration found that applicants are not given clear guidance about the evidence required when an application is made and that visa officers failed to take proper account of the evidence that was submitted (e.g., Chief Inspector (2010) *An Inspection of Entry Clearance in Abu Dhabi and Islamabad*, Chief Inspector (2011) *An Inspection of the UK Border Agency visa section in Amman, Jordan*, and Chief Inspector (2011) *A Short-Notice Inspection of Decision Making Quality in the Istanbul Visa Section*). Appeals on race discrimination grounds were abolished by the Immigration Act 2014, although these were rarely brought as discrimination was very difficult to prove. Even after the main right of appeal had been removed so that only claims based on human rights grounds stood any chance of success, there was a relatively high success rate. In 2014/5, 37 per cent of appeals succeeded.

Additionally, and very importantly, a refusal, particularly on the general grounds, makes future successful applications whether to the UK or elsewhere less likely and, if the allegation is that deception has been used, refusal of entry to the UK is mandatory for the next ten years under para 320(7B) of the rules. The Joint Committee on Human Rights report published in November 2012 was opposed to the removal of appeal rights (*Legislative Scrutiny: Crime and Courts Bill*, Fifth Report of Session 2012–13) and the Home Affairs Committee was concerned that appeal rights were being ended when so many appeals were successful (*The Work of the UK Border Agency (July–September 2012)* Fourteenth Report of Session 2012–13). In another report it said that '[a] poor performance in appeals should instigate a drive to improve initial casework decisions and guidance for applicants. Closing off a route of appeal . . . is not an acceptable way in which to reduce the number of appeals' (*The Work of the UK Border Agency (December 2011–March 2012)* Fifth Report of Session 2012–13). Independent appeals thus represented a necessary quality control mechanism and a way to maintain public confidence. Administrative review, in which another officer reviews the correctness of the decision, is not available for visit visas, although a reconsideration may be requested, as the government's view is that a fresh application should be made, addressing the issues that were wrong in the first application. This fails to take account of the subjectivity of decision-making, which may be replicated in a new decision, the sometimes sketchy or defective grounds of refusal, and the effect of a refusal on future attempts to obtain a visa. The Chief Inspector for Borders and Immigration, in his report on family visit visas (*An inspection of Family Visitor visa applications: August–December 2014*) published in July 2015, found no evidence that the removal of appeal rights had led to a higher refusal rate or to an overall reduction in decision quality and there had been significant improvements in decision quality at some posts. However, while the overall refusal rate did not decline, numbers of applications fell sharply after removal of appeal rights. The Chief Inspector found that, in 42 per cent of refusal notices sampled, the notice of refusal was not balanced, and failed to show that consideration had been given to both positive and negative evidence. Inconsistent decision-making criteria were also used across different posts with applicants at some posts being asked to provide additional evidence not referred to in the rules or guidance. It is likely that the wide basis for refusal, discussed earlier in this chapter, means that, even where there are errors, many applicants cannot succeed as the Chief Inspector considered that only 7 per cent of refusals were unreasonable. Where a family visit visa has been refused, the choice is between an Article 8 appeal and judicial review. The barrister Colin Yeo has published a useful guide to choosing between the two on his Free Movement blog (*Visit visa refusals: appeal or judicial review?* available at: https://www.freemovement.org.uk/visit-visa-refusals-appeal-or-judicial-review/). Judicial review is expensive and has a limited function but, as the discussion in the next section shows, an Article 8 appeal is not easy to win.

10.7 Family visits and Article 8

As just mentioned, appeals may still be brought on human rights grounds. It will be recalled from chapter 8 that what respect for family life requires, or what constitutes an interference with family life, depends to some extent on the nature of the relationship.

As we have seen, Article 8 cannot be used to *establish* family life if it does not already exist. We noted this in the case of *ECO Lagos v Imoh* [2002] UKIAT 01967, in which an Article 8 application for a girl to join her aunt failed because there was no family life in this case but rather an attempt to create one. It said: 'Article 8 requires that there is as a matter of fact family life in existence and the mere payment of money for the care of a child and one visit to see that child, is not capable of creating a family life' (para 5 of the judgment).

One might ask, though, whether Winsome Imoh would have been refused entry clearance just to visit her aunt rather than to join her as a dependant, and if so, whether she could have challenged this successfully using Article 8. The case of *Praengsamrit v ECO Bangkok* [2002] UKIAT 02791 may be considered by way of comparison. In this case, an aunt applied to visit her niece, and was turned down on the basis that there had been insufficient contact between the two of them. Article 8 was not argued, but the Vice President of the Tribunal held that:

There is no need to prove contact as an expression of devotion which one might expect between husband and wife. They are relations whose family life goes back over the period of the niece's life. That sort of relationship does not to my mind require to be demonstrated by evidence of frequent contact. It is of the essence of family life that the bond is there to be renewed as and when the occasion arises when members of a family are separated by considerable distances as in this case.

This must be a familiar idea to anyone with relatives who live at a distance from them. It suggests that the better way for the courts to approach Article 8 cases is not to consider whether family life exists, but rather what respect for family life requires in the particular instance. This will vary from one situation to another. It may not require a government to respect the choice of residence of a married couple who could live elsewhere, but it is difficult to see how it would not require at least the possibility of contact between family members. In *Ramsew v ECO Georgetown* 01/TH/2505, the Tribunal confirmed that family visit cases do normally engage family life. On the other hand, in *Hussain and Noor v ECO Islamabad* (01/TH/2746), the Tribunal held that family life was not interfered with by refusing a visit. It could be carried on by other means, for instance letters and phone calls. The approach in *Ramsew* is implicitly endorsed in *Ashrif v ECO Islamabad* 01/TH/3465, in which the Tribunal held that there did not have to be a particular reason for the visit at a particular time. 'The whole point of family visits is that the existence of the family ties of themselves will normally furnish the reason for the visit' (para 14). In *Abbasi and another (visits—bereavement—Article 8)* [2015] UKUT 463 (IAC), it was disproportionate to refuse a visa to two young Pakistani men who wished to join family in the UK for a finite period to mourn their grandfather.

However, this more expansive view of who receives Article 8 protection is not reflected in other cases. The Upper Tribunal in *Mostafa (Article 8 in entry clearance)* [2015]

UKUT 00112 (IAC) said that, where the immigration rules had been met and in the absence of a lack of candour, it was disproportionate to prevent a husband joining his wife in the UK for a visit. The Tribunal however went on to point out that this would depend upon the Article 8 right being engaged in the first place, that is, that there was a family life and there was interference. As a case involving spouses, the existence of family life was clear cut but the Tribunal said that it would only be in very unusual circumstances that a person other than a close relative would come within the scope of Article 8(1).

Thus, in *Adjei (visit visas—Article 8)* [2015] UKUT 0261 (IAC), where the relationship was between an adult daughter, her father, step-mother and step-siblings, the Tribunal did not believe that admission to the UK was necessary to allow the relationship to continue as it had existed without visits for the previous twenty years. This reflects the government's view as expressed in its guidance on human rights visitor appeals which says that only claims involving spouses, parents, and minor children engage human rights. This seems an excessively narrow view and does not reflect the Article 8 jurisprudence which does not exclude other relationships in all circumstances.

Another factor in an Article 8 claim is the extent to which there has been compliance with the rules. In *Mostafa*, the First-tier Tribunal had found that the applicants, as a matter of fact, met the requirements of the rules. In *Adjei*, the Upper Tribunal said:

a person who satisfies the Tribunal that he does meet the requirements of [the immigration rules] does not succeed on that account. He still has to demonstrate that refusal represents an unlawful infringement of rights protected by Article 8 of the ECHR. For a person who does not satisfy the requirements . . . to succeed in an appeal there would have to be cogent and compelling reasons demanding that he should succeed.

Given the breadth and discretionary character of reasons for refusal, it may not be easy for applicants to show the Tribunal that they did, as a matter of fact, meet the requirements of the immigration rules. But even if they do, that may not be sufficient if it is found that the relationship does not engage Article 8.

In *Kaur (visit appeals; Article 8)* [2015] UKUT 487 (IAC), the Upper Tribunal emphasized that compliance with the immigration rules, even though it was not the direct subject of the appeal, is material to the Article 8 determination and that judges retain their fact-finding duties in that respect. However, unless an appellant can show that there are 'compelling circumstances', the appeal is unlikely to succeed. The case also demonstrates the Catch 22 that exists in respect of family visit Article 8 claims. For the claim to succeed, particularly outside spouses and minor child/parent relationships, the ties must be particularly strong. Yet, the strength of the ties, particularly when compared to ties in the country of origin, is a reason for suspecting that the applicant will not leave the UK at the end of the visit, that is, that the applicant does not meet the requirements of the immigration rules. Here, the applicant, an elderly woman, wanted to visit her son, daughter-in-law, and grandchildren in the UK. It was not practical for all four UK-based family members to come to India for a holiday so this was the only way that they could meet. However, the strength of her ties with them combined with a lack of detail about her ties to her other children in India meant that it was considered reasonable to suspect that not only a time-limited visit was intended.

The guidance also promotes this Catch 22, saying that the strength of the human rights claim depends partly on whether family life exists for the applicant in their home country, with other family members who are residing there. This is presumably aimed at the question of dependency but also seems to mistake the nature of family ties entirely; a relationship with one adult child does not substitute for a relationship with another. It also means that an applicant's claim will fail either because there is family life in the country of origin and Article 8 is not engaged or there is no such family life, in which case the applicant will be considered as unlikely to leave the UK, meaning that the rules are not complied with and the claim is accordingly weakened.

10.8 Change of circumstances

Part V9 of Appendix V provides for cancellation of a visit visa or leave to enter or remain as a visitor on or before arrival in the UK. As well as the expected grounds, such as false information or non-disclosure of a material fact, the visa may be cancelled where there has been a change in circumstances such 'that the basis of the visitor's claim to admission or stay has been removed and the visa or leave should be cancelled'. There may also be cancellation where the visitor holds a visit visa and their purpose in arriving in the United Kingdom is different from the purpose specified in the visit visa. In the context of visit visas, circumstances might change (e.g., a family wedding might be cancelled) and the applicant would still qualify as a visitor. Nonetheless, refusals where the applicant still qualifies as a visitor have sometimes been upheld by the Tribunal. *Dapaah* (11823) upheld the principle established in *Eusebio* (4739) that the question of the effect of a change of circumstances is a question of fact and degree, particularly when the applicant is seeking entry under the same rule as the one under which they obtained entry clearance.

However, leave to enter may be refused or cancelled, even when the change of circumstances does not take the journey outside the visitor rules. In *Hiemo v Immigration Officer Heathrow* (10892), the appellant's original application had been to visit his sister. On arrival at Heathrow, he sought instead 20 days to attend a training course at the Church of Scientology in East Grinstead. His sister had gone to Germany. The Tribunal held that the change of circumstances was fundamental and the refusal was justified.

10.9 Conclusion

Non-EEA visitors are an important category of migrant numerically and in terms of their contribution to tourism and to enabling British residents to maintain family links with those living abroad. Yet, for a government preoccupied with preventing illegal working and overstaying, controlling access via the visitor visa route is critical and recent changes seek to define as tightly as possible the possible circumstances of entry, to allow refusals based on generalized characteristics rather than the individual's own position and to minimize accountability. The removal of rights of appeal for family visitors fail to acknowledge the importance of oversight, particularly given well-documented instances of poor quality decision-making at some entry clearance posts, including those that receive substantial numbers of family visit applications.

QUESTIONS

1 What is the purpose of creating different categories of visitor? Will the recently created categories fulfil these purposes?

2 What is the issue to be decided in Article 8 appeal in a visitor's application? Does this differ from Article 8 appeals in other contexts?

3 Should family visitor appeals be reinstated? Should appeal rights for all visitors be reinstated?

 For guidance on answering questions, visit the Online Resource Centre www.oxfordtextbooks.co.uk/orc/clayton7e/.

FURTHER READING

Children's Commissioner (2015) *Family Friendly? The Impact on Children of the Family Migration Rules: A Review of the Financial Requirements*

Duheric, D. (2009) 'Immigration—Business, Sport and Entertainer Visitors' *Employment Law Bulletin* vol. 89, February, pp. 5–7.

Dunstan, Richard (2003) 'Family Visitor Visa Applications: An Analysis of Entry Clearance Officer Decision-making in 2002' *Journal of Immigration and Nationality Law and Practice* vol. 17, no. 3, pp. 170–8.

Dunstan, Richard (2004) 'Family Visitor Visas: ECO Decision-making 2000–2003' *Journal of Immigration, Asylum and Nationality Law* vol. 18, no. 2, pp. 100–5.

Gelsthorpe, Verity, Thomas, Robert, Howard, Daniel, and Crawley, Heaven (2004) 'Family Visitor Appeals: An Examination of the Decision to Appeal and Differential Success Rates by Appeal Type' *Journal of Immigration, Asylum and Nationality Law* vol. 18, no. 3, pp. 167–85.

Gillespie, Jim (1994) 'The New Immigration Rules: Visitors and Students' *Immigration and Nationality Law and Practice* vol. 8, no. 4, pp. 126–8.

McKee, Richard (2007) "Tightening up? 'Managed Migration' May Manage to Make Migration more Messy" *Immigration Law Digest* vol. 13, no. 2 Summer 2007, pp. 7–9.

Thomas, R. (2004) 'Immigration Appeals for Family Visitors Refused Entry Clearance' *Public Law* Autumn, pp. 612–42.

SECTION 5

The asylum claim

11

The asylum process

SUMMARY

This chapter describes the asylum process from application through to cessation of refugee status. The chapter is divided into sections. The first deals with entering the UK to claim asylum, the second with the asylum application and decision-making, the third with the different routes through which an asylum claim can be processed, including 'safe' country of origin provisions and non-suspensive appeals, fast-track detention, and returns to third countries pursuant to the Dublin Regulation. The fourth section concerns penalties connected with seeking asylum. The final sections cover other procedures after appeal rights are exhausted, or asylum has been granted, including making a fresh claim and rights of a recognized refugee.

11.1 Entering the UK to seek asylum

There is a right in international and EU law to seek asylum (UDHR 1948 Article 14, and EU Charter Article 18) but it is difficult to exercise within the law. In *R v Naillie* [1993] AC 674 HL, the House of Lords held that arriving in the UK and requesting asylum without attempting to deceive did not make the defendants illegal entrants. However, in *R v SSHD ex p Saadi* [2002] UKHL 42, the House of Lords held that detention of asylum claimants was lawful 'to prevent unauthorized entry' (applying ECHR Article 5(1)(f)). It did not go so far as to say that unlawfulness was contemplated. Indeed, there was clear evidence that it was not. As Collins J said at first instance, the claimants were doing all they could to enter lawfully, but were detained pending determination of their claim (see chapter 14). Adding *Saadi* to *Naillie*, entry to seek asylum is not illegal but is also not authorized. *Kapoor* [2012] EWCA Crim 435 confirms that a person who claims asylum on arrival is not an illegal entrant, even though they may not possess documentation which, independently of the asylum claim, authorizes their entry.

Schiemann J in 1989 described the difficulties faced by asylum claimants in the face of visa regimes, carrier sanctions, and now we would add border control measures such as the placement of airline liaison officers and juxtaposed controls (see chapter 6) and prosecution for not producing a passport. As a consequence, he said, an asylum seeker has the option of:

1. lying to the UK authorities in his country in order to obtain a tourist visa or some other sort of visa;
2. obtaining a credible forgery of a visa;
3. obtaining an airline ticket to a third country with a stopover in the UK. (*Yassine v SSHD* [1990] Imm AR 354 at 359).

We might add a fourth option: clandestine entry.

These sanctions combine with judicial acceptance that asylum seekers may be treated in a punitive manner even without any wrongdoing *(Saadi)* to create a murky zone between legality and illegality within which an international law right exists, but can hardly be exercised without risk of penalty. In mitigation of this the Refugee Convention provides a level of protection from penalties for a refugee who uses false documents to enter. These provisions are described at 11.4.2.

An asylum seeker may well have had to commit some kind of legal infringement, simply to arrive and apply for international protection. Some of the consequences of that will appear in this chapter, which is mainly concerned with the asylum application process once the applicant has arrived in the UK.

11.2 Making an asylum application

Asylum applications may be made at the port of entry or at a later stage after legal or illegal entry. The latter are known as 'in-country' applications. Asylum claims not made at the port of entry must be made in person at the Home Office in Croydon. In the UK the responsibility for processing and deciding asylum claims lies with the Visas and Immigration Section of the Home Office, which deals with both asylum and immigration. If an asylum applicant is refused, their case then goes to the Immigration Enforcement Directorate, which also deals with immigration law infringements. This is by contrast with countries such as Canada and New Zealand, where there is a separate body responsible for refugee status determination. As the Joint Refugee Councils' 2006 submission to the Home Affairs Committee said, such immigration controls 'are a blunt instrument that do not distinguish between those fleeing persecution and irregular migrants seeking to enter a country for other purposes'. Once this merging has taken place, it appears less controversial to make extensive use of detention and other draconian control measures, such as the removal of welfare support, because dealing with asylum claims is seen as part of policing a frontier (see, for instance, Kostakopoulou and Thomas 2004 and Cornelisse 2004).

The procedures and principles by which asylum claims are decided are set out in the immigration rules paras 327–52 and in the Asylum Policy Instructions (APIs) and Asylum Process Guidance (APGs), disclosed on the government website. The procedure should be in conformity with the Procedures Directive 2005/85 EC (APD), which takes precedence over any inconsistent domestic provision, and many provisions of the Directive are in the immigration rules. The Asylum and Immigration Appeals Act 1993 defines a claim for asylum as a claim that it would be contrary to the UK's obligations under the Refugee Convention for the claimant to be removed from the UK. This refers to the *non-refoulement* obligation in Article 33 (see chapter 12).

The claim commences with a screening interview which does not deal with the substance of the claim, but determines whether the claim is to be dealt with by the Third Country Unit, or fast-tracked, or considered for certification as a non-suspensive appeal, or dealt with in the mainstream procedure. At the screening interview the applicant is required to produce their identity documents, including their passport, which will be retained for the duration of the claim. As discussed later, coming to the interview without a passport may be an offence. Applicants have fingerprints and photographs taken and are given an application registration card (ARC), which holds biometric details. A decision is taken on whether to detain the applicant or admit them on temporary admission (see chapter 14). The different outcomes of the screening interview roughly map on to a version of the asylum process introduced in 2007 and called the New Asylum Model. Although this model is no longer operating as such, Table 11.1 still gives a relevant outline of the outcomes of a screening interview.

On making their claim, asylum seekers can also apply for asylum support, which consists of accommodation and a small amount of money weekly (£36.95 per person). People only qualify for this support if they are accepted to be destitute—that is, have no accommodation or means of obtaining it or else no means of meeting their basic living needs (Immigration and Asylum Act 1999 s 95).

Although claims must be made in Croydon, the majority of asylum seekers who are not detained and who apply for asylum support are dispersed to a different region of the UK. Here they may be placed for two or three weeks in an initial accommodation centre before being allocated longer term accommodation, often in a shared house, and being assigned an appointment for their asylum interview.

Table 11.1 Outcomes of asylum screening interview

Route	Definition
1. Third country	The Home Office believes the person has, or could have, applied for asylum in a third country, usually another EU country. Some are detained whilst others are not. Referred to Third Country Unit to deal with return to third country. No asylum interview.
2. Minors	Unaccompanied minors and children in families who apply in their own right where Home Office accepts the person is under 18 or gives them the benefit of any doubt that they are. Separated children are accommodated by social services. Unless and until a social services age assessment determines that an age-disputed young person should be dealt with as an adult their case will be processed as that of a minor.
3. Potential non-suspensive appeal (NSA)	Nationals from one of the countries designated as generally 'safe' may have their case certified as clearly unfounded in which case the right of appeal has to be exercised from outside the UK. Individual asylum claims may also be certified clearly unfounded and attract only the NSA right. Some people subject to a NSA are detained whilst others are not.
4. Detained asylum casework	At the time of writing, there are interim instructions following the suspension of the detained fast track. An asylum claimant may be detained after the screening interview, but only if the general conditions for detention are met (see chapter 14).
5. General casework	Cases that do not come into any of the other categories. The individuals are usually dispersed to initial accommodation and their asylum claim will be dealt with in the region to which they are dispersed.

11.2.1 **Asylum interviews**

The asylum interview is the time when the refugee gives their story, and the body of information upon which the claim will be decided. The quality of interpretation, the fairness of the interview, the skill and understanding of the interviewer, and the resources given to the interview process, are all vital to the proper determination of the claim. The interview is a critical step in exercising the international obligation to determine an asylum claim and protect refugees, and if used properly, is not a judicial or adversarial function. Guidance on conducting the asylum interview is given in Asylum Policy Instruction (API): *Asylum Interviews*. The *UNHCR Handbook* says:

While the burden of proof in principle rests on the applicant, the duty to ascertain and evaluate all the relevant facts is shared between the applicant and the examiner. (para 196)

The Qualification Directive echoes the UNHCR's approach:

Member States may consider it the duty of the applicant to submit as soon as possible all elements needed to substantiate the application for international protection. In cooperation with the applicant it is the duty of the Member State to assess the relevant elements of the application. (Article 4)

Numerous inquiries into the asylum process have nevertheless commented on the poor and combative quality of asylum interviewing. Interviewers have been criticized for chaotic questioning, not dealing with the relevant issues, appearing adversarial and intimidating, and not dealing sympathetically or appropriately with those who have suffered trauma such as rape or torture (e.g., Asylum Aid 1999; Amnesty International 2004; and the Independent Asylum Commission 2008). Amnesty International recorded a perception by Home Office caseworkers of the interview as an opportunity to obtain material to attack the applicant's credibility by noting inconsistencies and storing them up for a later refusal letter rather than putting the inconsistency to the applicant then and there (2004:20). The Independent Asylum Commission in 2008 found that 'the style and content' of substantive interviews often fell short, citing matters including inappropriate use of leading questions and failure to implement guidelines when interviewing traumatized women. The current API sets out good practice in this respect, advising that the applicant must be asked to clarify any such discrepancies. However, more recent studies of decision-making suggest that problems continue. It appears that while the standard of the API is sometimes met, it is not maintained reliably. (Evidence to the Home Affairs Select Committee's 2013 inquiry, *Asylum*, Seventh Report of session 2103–14 HC 71 and *A Question of Credibility* Amnesty International and Still Human Still Here 2013).

Since 1 April 2004, it has not been possible in most cases for an applicant to have public funding for a representative to be present at their asylum interview. The Court of Appeal in *R (on the application of Dirshe) v SSHD* [2005] EWCA Civ 421 held that where the applicant had no public funding either for a representative or for their own interpreter, the overall fairness of the process required that the applicant be able to tape record the asylum interview, so that there is some record of it independently of that kept by the Home Office. *Dirshe* has been interpreted as an obligation to record the interview 'on request by the claimant'. The applicant is notified in the letter which invites them to interview that they can request recording in advance, but the API says that where no advance request has been made, there is no need to repeat the offer when the applicant arrives. If the interview is not recorded, admission of the interview record is not automatically unfair (*MB (admissible evidence; interview record) Iran* [2012] UKUT 00019 (IAC)). Applicants may also request an interpreter or interviewer of their gender, and such requests should be acted upon.

Paragraph 333C of the immigration rules provides that where an asylum seeker does not attend for interview, their claim may be treated as abandoned unless they show within a reasonable time that non-attendance was for reasons beyond their control.

11.2.2 **Making an asylum decision**

The immigration rules, para 339J, set out in general terms the matters which the Secretary of State must take into account in determining an asylum claim. These are:

(i) all relevant facts as they relate to the country of origin or country of return at the time of taking a decision . . . including [its] laws and regulations . . . and the manner in which they are applied;

(ii) relevant statements and documentation presented by the person including information on whether the person has been or may be subject to persecution or serious harm;

(iii) the individual position and personal circumstances of the person, including factors such as background, gender and age . . .;

(iv) whether the person's activities since leaving the country of origin or country of return were engaged in for the sole or main purpose of creating the conditions for making an asylum . . . or human rights claim, so as to assess whether these activities will expose the person to persecution or serious harm if he returned to that country; and

(v) whether the person could reasonably be expected to avail himself of the protection of another country where he could assert citizenship.

These provisions implement and repeat those in the Qualification Directive (QD) Article 4, except that the UK immigration rules include the country of return as well as the country of origin, and sometimes these may differ.

For most of these points the prime source is the substantive interview with the asylum seeker. The applicant may produce documents. At the stage of initial decision, they may well not have expert or medical reports since these are mainly obtained through instructing a solicitor, and there is rarely time between the screening and substantive interviews to obtain such documents. After the interview, the applicant or their solicitor is given five days in which to make any supplementary submissions. This is an opportunity for the asylum seeker to correct any misapprehensions that occurred in the interview.

Objective information about relevant conditions in their country may be advanced by the asylum seeker. Even if it is not, the rules and QD Article 4 make it plain that the obligation to obtain and rely on such relevant and up-to-date information lies on the decision-maker.

11.2.2.1 Country of origin information

The availability, reliability, relevance, and scope of information about an asylum seeker's country of origin are enormously important in asylum decisions and appeals (see Tsangarides). The Home Office publicizes on its website a range of documents relating to the most common countries of origin of asylum seekers. Documents are provided for about 35 countries. Some are themed reports about particular issues, for instance for Zimbabwe there are reports on women, prison conditions, sexual orientation and gender identity, and opposition to Zanu-PF. Each of these themed reports contains both country information and guidance (Country Information and Guidance (CIG)).

Guidance gives policy direction on deciding claims. Country of Origin Information (COI) is a compilation of sources giving information about the political and human rights situation in the most common countries of origin. Up until 2014, guidance, in the form of Operational Guidance Notes (OGNs), and COI in the form of Country of Origin Reports, were separate documents. Now for each country CIGs are issued which consist of both guidance and information. The Home Office Country of Origin Information Service can answer specific queries from Home Office decision makers.

An asylum seeker may also rely on the Home Office's COI and OGNs, and any other reliable information, for example, from governmental reports and non-governmental organizations, particularly those that monitor human rights.

Country of origin reports
The Home Office's country reports quote from human rights reports from the US Department of State, Amnesty International, Human Rights Watch, and other international organizations. Any of these, and other original reports may also be relied on by the asylum seeker, who, if they have the resources, can read the original reports to cross-check the Home Office interpretation.

It is rare for such a report to mention the asylum seeker personally, although this may happen, and there may be references to others with whom s/he is associated. Reports deal with a wide range of issues, including the use of torture and detention, the accountability of officials, freedom of the press, and notable events such as demonstrations, uprisings, severe repression of dissent, and so on. It is rare that an asylum seeker will have resources to compile substantial country information on their own behalf, and although independent experts may be instructed, the asylum seeker will often be reliant on information produced by organizations which do not have them or their case in mind.

The Home Office's Country of Origin Information Reports are monitored by the Independent Advisory Group on Country Information (IAGCI), which is part of the Office of the Chief Inspector of Borders and Immigration:

The IAGCI reviews the efficiency, effectiveness and consistency of approach of COI material collated by the COIS and assesses the sources, methods of research and quality control used by the Agency to help ensure that these support the production of COI material which is as accurate, balanced, impartial and up-to-date as possible. (Chief Inspector July 2011 para 4.9)

Unfortunately, IAGCI comments are often not integrated into the body of the report until the next reporting cycle, by which time they are out of date.

Reports by the Immigration Advisory Service were previously highly critical of Home Office COI reports, citing inaccuracies, misquoting and omission of relevant information, reliance on secondary sources, and a tendency to use Home Office opinion in the reports, which purport to be factual. For a robust approach by the ECtHR to assessment of background material, see *Said v Netherlands* (Application no. 2345/02). The work of IAGCI and its predecessor have brought about an improvement in the quality of country information, but the Chief Inspector's report on the use that is made of it by Home Office decision-makers indicated that to a significant extent this was selective and uncoordinated (Chief Inspector July 2011).

The crucial role of COI, and procedure for approving or challenging it, came to the fore in relation to a report in November 2014 by a Danish Immigration Service Fact Finding Mission to Eritrea (*Eritrea—Drivers and Root Causes of Emigration, National Service and the Possibility of Return*). The UK Home Office relied on the report's findings and amended their Eritrean CIG accordingly. The rate of recognition of claims from Eritreans dropped significantly. A report by the IAGCI was critical of the Danish report's methodology, and of the Home Office's reliance on it. The Home Office responded to the IAGCI, defending their approach to the Danish report. Meanwhile in Denmark, two members of the Immigration Service who were part of the Fact-Finding Mission resigned because of their disagreement with the conclusions of the report.

Country guidance cases

As may be imagined, not infrequently the same background issues fall to be proved in different cases. Laws LJ in the Court of Appeal in *S v SSHD* [2002] EWCA Civ 539 noted the waste of judicial and other resources in hearing evidence about similar factual issues repeatedly, and the need for consistency in decision-making. As a remedy for this situation, Laws LJ proposed the unusual idea of a factual precedent, which might, in asylum cases, he thought, be 'benign and practical' (para 28). From this judgment was born the practice of declaring 'country guidance' cases, which are binding as to a factual situation.

As Laws LJ pointed out in *S*, the notion of a precedent which is binding as to fact is 'foreign to the common law' (para 26). For this reason alone, the proposition should be treated with caution that findings of fact made in one case should be binding in another. *S* laid down a number of provisos, which should be strictly applied if factual precedents were to be allowed as a possibility:

- in making a decision which is intended to give guidelines on conditions in a country, the Tribunal must apply the duty to give reasons 'with particular rigour';
- such a decision must be 'effectively comprehensive. It should address all the issues capable of having a real as opposed to a fanciful bearing on the result, and explain what it makes of the substantial evidence going to each such issue';
- the facts of an individual case must still be examined;
- country guidance cases may provide a backdrop against which that individual examination takes place, recognizing that 'the impact of the political reality may vary as between one claimant and another'.

The practice of promulgating and following country guidance cases (designated CG in the case name) grew quickly after *S*. The Immigration Advisory Service carried out research and consultation on the use and nature of country guidance cases. Their work revealed concerns including the following:

- country guidance cases might be out of date for the case in hand, or worse, based on obsolete material;
- factual findings specific to a particular claimant could be elevated into country guidance;
- country guidance decisions might not be referenced properly, so that a future claimant was unable to distinguish their case from the CG because they could not identify the evidence;
- '[T]he judiciary operate under severe time constraints and a reference to a country guidance case was sometimes used as an alternative to giving reasons rather than an aid to decision-making' (p. 20);
- some country guidance cases had been designated where the dismissal of the claim was based on a *lack* of evidence; and
- even in a CG case, evidence was sometimes used and dismissed selectively without objective reasons being given, particularly by preference being given to government reports over other sources. (IAS 2005)

The IAS challenged the concept of country guidance cases as importing an artificial degree of certainty 'on an uncertain and often rapidly changing country situation'. Thomas criticizes the CG system as 'naïve'—different conclusions may be drawn from similar facts (2008). Since then, practice in country guideline cases has improved, and the Tribunal has embraced the notion. There are now hundreds of country guidance cases in relation to particular issues such as 'risk on return—Ivory Coast', 'Trafficked women—China', 'Undocumented Kurds—Syria' which are listed on the Tribunal's website. The Tribunal's practice direction goes much further than *S* in relation to their weight as precedents. It says that the most recent CG case 'shall be treated as an authoritative finding on the country guidance issue identified in the determination . . . so far as that appeal':

(a) relates to the country guidance issue in question; and

(b) depends upon the same or similar evidence' (2010, para 12.2).

Even more unequivocally: 'any failure to follow a clear, apparently applicable country guidance case or to show why it does not apply to the case in question is likely to be regarded as grounds for review or appeal on a point of law' (para 18.4 endorsed in *R & others v SSHD* [2005] EWCA Civ 982). The exception is when there is other, inconsistent authority that is binding on the Tribunal.

Country guidance cases were described by the Court of Appeal in *HM (Iraq) v SSHD* [2011] EWCA Civ 1536 as having 'a status and significance comparable to that which declarations can have in public law cases' (para 39). The Court quashed the Tribunal's country guidance in the unique situation that representation had been withdrawn for all the appellants in the proposed country guidance case just before the Tribunal hearing. The case concerned the safety of return to Iraq, relying on Article 15(c) of the Qualification Directive, and it was essential to have proper argument, not only on the law 'but also the drawing of relevant materials to the attention of the tribunal and the making of submissions as to the effect of those materials, so that the determination is based on as full and informed an analysis as possible' (para 39).

The effect of a country guidance case is to establish the factual position until it is proved to have changed. Proof of change means that the Tribunal must consider new evidence and make a new decision.

On occasions the Home Office has declared itself not bound by a country guidance case, on the basis of its view that conditions had changed, even without a new Tribunal ruling. In the case of Zimbabwe, the Home Office announced that it would not follow *RN (Returnees) Zimbabwe CG* [2008] UKAIT 00083 on the basis that it anticipated that the forthcoming decision in the case of *EM* would show that violence in Zimbabwe had reduced since the decision in *RN*. In practice the situation was managed by the Home Office refusing asylum claims on the basis it asserted, but not actually removing people to Zimbabwe on that basis while more country guidance was in the offing. The Danish reports on Eritrea discussed above contradicted country guidance cases. The potency of country guidance cases was tested again in *CM (EM country guidance; disclosure) Zimbabwe CG* [2013] UKUT 00059(IAC). An earlier CG decision had been set aside on the basis that the Home Office had not given full disclosure of relevant material. When the case was re-heard the Upper Tribunal held that there is no general duty of disclosure on the Secretary of State in country guidance cases nor in asylum appeals generally. This decision was upheld by the Court of Appeal in an unreported judgment.

11.2.2.2 Credibility

In addition to assessing objective material, the asylum decision-maker should base their decision on all the factors set out in the immigration rules para 339J, many of which entail an assessment of the asylum seeker's own testimony. This brings in the question of credibility.

Many problems with the quality of asylum decision-making result in and stem from an over-emphasis on individual credibility and/or a flawed assessment of credibility. Credibility is the term used to refer to whether or not the decision-maker believes the applicant is telling the truth. Arguably, the subject of credibility could fill a chapter on its own, or be dealt with in the next chapter, or this one, or not at all. In determining refugee claims the question of credibility is both everything and nothing. It is not an aspect of the refugee definition to be satisfied, like the matters covered in the next chapter, and yet the majority of asylum claims which are lost are lost precisely because the decision-maker does not believe the applicant.

A flawed assessment of credibility has been identified repeatedly by bodies who have criticized asylum decision-making, as discussed in the next section, but what constitutes a proper assessment of credibility?

UNHCR's report *Beyond Proof: Credibility assessments in EU Asylum Systems* points out that 'neither the Asylum Procedures Directive nor the QD explicitly or comprehensively prescribe how the credibility assessment should be carried out'. The report nevertheless draws standards of credibility assessment from those provisions which are in the Directives, particularly QD Article 4, and from UNHCR guidance and judicial decisions. The report upholds UNHCR's view that the duty to substantiate the application is shared by the applicant and the deciding authority. The QD makes an allowance for this not to be the case, and it is not so in the UK, where the burden of proof is on the applicant. Beyond this, the standards drawn from the Directives are that the assessment of the application must be carried out on an individual basis; it must be objective, impartial, evidence-based, and focus on material facts. An opportunity should be given to the applicant to comment on potentially adverse credibility findings. The credibility assessment should be based on the entire evidence, using close and rigorous scrutiny, and recognizing that it may be necessary to give the applicant the benefit of the doubt. There should be clear and unambiguous credibility findings.

The report expands on the implications of these standards. Carrying out the assessment on an individual basis entails that the applicant's statements must be considered in the context of their personal background including experiences of ill-treatment, as well as the relevant situation in their country of origin. Their statements cannot be considered in the abstract. Regarding objectivity, the report says:

It is critical to recall that the first instance procedure is not an adversarial process. On the contrary, Article 4 (1) QD explicitly states that it is the Member State's duty to assess the relevant elements of the application in cooperation with the applicant. It is, therefore, not the role of the determining authority to contest an application for international protection or strive with zeal to identify indicators of a lack of credibility. (p. 37)

And

In addition, examiners need to be aware that their perception of the applicant and his or her application should not be negatively influenced by issues that are not pertinent to the material facts of the application . . . For example, that an applicant has told a lie(s), concealed a fact(s) or submitted fraudulent documentation is not necessarily decisive in the assessment of credibility of the applicant's statements on material elements in the claim. A lie or submission of false documentary or other evidence may be re-evaluated once all the circumstances of the case are known. (p. 39)

The report refers to some of the factors which may make it difficult to be objective. These include working in a government department whose objective is to prevent irregular immigration, the repetitive nature of the task, and routine exposure to narratives of torture and other violence.

The UNHCR standards fully implemented would provide a corrective to poor practice and would influence the interpretation of the immigration rules. HC395 para 339L, implementing Article 4 of the Qualification Directive, says that where aspects of the person's statements are not supported by documentary or other evidence, those aspects will not need confirmation when all of the following conditions are met:

(i) the person has made a genuine effort to substantiate his asylum claim . . .;

(ii) all material factors at the person's disposal have been submitted, and a satisfactory explanation regarding any lack of other relevant material has been given;

(iii) the person's statements are found to be coherent and plausible and do not run counter to available specific and general information relevant to the person's case;

(iv) the person has made an asylum claim . . . at the earliest possible time, unless the person can demonstrate good reason for not having done so; and

(v) the general credibility of the person has been established.

Paragraph 339L(iv) is apt to be applied in such a way that any delay in claiming is treated as being adverse to credibility. This paragraph is based on an assumption that a person in genuine fear will claim asylum promptly. However, the reasons for not doing so may also be compelling to a person who is afraid. Hathaway and Hicks (2005, see further reading for chapter 12) describe the risks of attempts to 'objectify' the asylum seeker's state of mind with standard questions such as 'did you claim asylum at the first opportunity?' Section 8 Asylum and Immigration (Treatment of Claimants, etc.) Act 2004, discussed in chapter 7, applies to initial decisions, and permits adverse inferences on the basis of delay in claiming. The UNHCR principles, founding the assessment on the individual and their actual experience, offer an appropriate way to apply the rules.

Although the asylum seeker has to prove their case to a reasonable degree of likelihood (see *Karanakaran*, chapter 12), there is no rule of law requiring their evidence to be corroborated from another source (*SSHD v Karakas* [1998] EWCA Civ 961). This is particularly important given that an asylum seeker may have fled their country in fear and without planning, and not have been in a position to collect documentation before their departure. Furthermore, when travelling clandestinely in order to avoid the authorities, it would not be desirable to be holding information such as an arrest warrant, which would identify them as wanted by the authorities if they were stopped.

The UNHCR report advises strongly against the use of concepts such as 'inherent improbability'. This is discussed in chapter 7 in the context of asylum appeals.

11.2.2.3 Quality of initial decisions

A good quality initial decision is crucial. It may be difficult for the applicant to obtain legal representation to appeal a wrong decision, and once poorly founded decisions go unchallenged, it becomes more difficult later on to address the contested issues.

The actual quality of asylum decision-making has by no means matched its importance as an implementation of an international protection treaty. Criticism of the process has been sustained. Since 1995, numerous major reports from governmental and non-governmental organizations have been published which are critical in varying degrees of the asylum decision-making process. Some are listed in the further reading section at the end of this chapter. The reports on quality focused broadly on three areas: the interview, the reasons for refusal letter, and information about asylum seekers' country of origin. Across all the reports, concerns are found in common, including:

- medical evidence corroborating horrific abuse was dismissed or misunderstood;
- proof was required to an excessively high standard (see chapter 12 for the asylum standard of proof);
- minor ambiguities or discrepancies were used to discredit the applicants, even when these had no bearing on the basis of the asylum claim;
- insensitivity in interviewing about serious trauma, particularly torture and rape;
- ignoring evidence relating to an individual;
- but also turning down claims on the basis that country-wide human rights reports documented abuses did not refer to the applicant personally;
- unreasonable assertions about individual credibility;
- inappropriate use of standard paragraphs in reasons for refusal letters; and
- making findings at odds with the evidence.

Since the first highly critical report by Asylum Aid in 1995, the quality of decision-making has improved. The UNHCR worked in a Quality Initiative with the Border Agency from 2004 to 2009 and at the end of the programme remained involved to try to integrate good practices. Throughout this time reports were published by bodies including Asylum Aid, Freedom from Torture (formerly the Medical Foundation), the Constitutional Affairs Committee, the Home Affairs Select Committee, the House of Commons Public Accounts Committee, the Independent Race Monitor, and the Independent Asylum Commission, still critical of the quality of decision-making. In 2013 critical reports continued. Still Human Still Here and Amnesty International said:

This report highlights similar concerns to those outlined by UNHCR. In the vast majority of cases examined for this research, the refusal letter breached the credibility guidance as set out by the Home Office's UK Border Agency.

The Home Affairs Select Committee in October 2013 reported the same issues. Despite this consistent evidence there has been reluctance by governments to invest in the initial decision-making process, with a high overturn rate on appeal being treated as evidence of the need to cut appeal rights rather than invest in decision-making. For instance, the Home Affairs Select Committee thought that a 'steep rise in initial-level appeals', accompanied by a significant rise in the proportion that were successful (Second Report 2003–04 HC 218 para 122) indicated 'grounds for concern about the poor quality of much initial decision-making by immigration officers and caseworkers' (para 143). They recommended putting greater resources into achieving fair and sustainable decisions at an early stage' (HC 218 para 144), including more good-quality legal advice and interpretation, recruitment of more caseworkers with specialist knowledge of asylum seekers' countries of origin and review of the 'overall calibre and training' of those who take initial decisions (para 144). The government responded by proposing, in the Asylum and Immigration (Treatment of Claimants, etc.) Bill—which became the 2004 Act—to reduce the appeals system to one tier.

The percentage of asylum appeals successful at Tribunal stage has continued to slightly increase, reaching a steady 25 per cent in 2012/13.

11.2.2.4 Non-compliance refusals

Paragraph 339M of the immigration rules allows the Secretary of State to refuse an asylum or human rights claim where there is 'failure, without reasonable explanation, to make a prompt and full disclosure of material facts, either orally or in writing, or otherwise to assist the Secretary of State in establishing the facts of the case'. This includes failure to report for fingerprinting, or to comply with a request to attend an interview or report to an immigration officer for examination.

In *Haddad* (00HX00926), the Tribunal held that refusal must not be for noncompliance alone. The rules require, as we have seen, that applications must be determined in accordance with the Refugee Convention. Therefore, even in a case of non-compliance, whatever evidence is available about the claim, even if it is in the form of brief notes taken by the immigration officer on arrival, must be considered (API on non-compliance). See Macdonald (2009:279–80) for further discussion of the law surrounding these refusals. However, this must now be read in conjunction with para 333C referred to earlier, which allows the Secretary of State to treat the claim as abandoned if the applicant does not attend the interview.

11.3 Routes for the claim

After screening and dispersal, most asylum claims are dealt with by regional offices of the Home Office. The substantive interview is conducted in the region, and asylum support accommodation allocated there. The decision letter comes from the regional office and after the initial decision, if it is a refusal, the case continues to be handled by that office unless and until enforcement comes into play. An asylum seeker is normally required to report regularly at a Home Office reporting centre in their region as a condition of remaining on temporary admission, that is, not being detained. Some claims however, are chosen at the screening stage to follow other legal pathways.

11.3.1 'Clearly unfounded'—non-suspensive appeal

Under Nationality, Immigration and Asylum Act 2002 s 94(2), the Secretary of State has the power to certify that an asylum claim is 'clearly unfounded'. The result is that there is no appeal in the UK. These are known as 'non-suspensive appeals' (NSAs), that is, the appeal does not suspend the removal. As the claim will be refused (because the Secretary of State is saying it has no merit) the asylum seeker faces removal. An appeal from abroad, especially in a country where the person fears persecution, is worthless.

The decision to certify cannot itself be appealed, but only challenged by judicial review. In view of the serious consequences, the courts have maintained a demanding standard for the Secretary of State to show that the claim is unfounded. Case law has established that 'clearly unfounded' means 'bound to fail' (*R v SSHD ex p Thangasara and Yogathas* [2002] UKHL 36, concerning an earlier similar provision) or that the case is 'unarguable' (*R (on the application of Razgar) v Secretary of State for the Home Department* [2003] EWCA Civ 840, not overturned by the House of Lords). 'If the . . . claim cannot on any legitimate view succeed, then the claim is clearly unfounded, if not, not' (*ZL and VL v SSHD* [2003] 1 All ER 1062). The Court of Appeal put it in *NA (Iran) v SSHD* [2011] EWCA Civ 1172 that the claim is 'incapable of succeeding before an independent judicial tribunal' (para 40). In *ZT (Kosovo) v SSHD* [2009] UKHL 6, Lord Phillips said that the question of whether the claim was clearly unfounded could only have 'one rational answer. If any reasonable doubt exists as to whether the claim may succeed then it is clearly not unfounded.' Evidently, where evidence is still awaited, the claim cannot be certified. Home Office Statistics suggest that about 7 per cent of asylum claims are certified (Asylum data Tables Immigration Statistics April–June 2015 Volume 1).

11.3.1.1 'Safe' countries of origin

Some countries are treated as 'safe', so that if an applicant is from one of these countries the Secretary of State must certify their claim unless satisfied that it is not clearly unfounded (s 94(3)).

The basis upon which a country or part of a country is designated as 'safe' is that the Secretary of State is satisfied that there is 'in general' in that state or that part of the state 'no serious risk of persecution' (s 94(5)). Blanket statements of safety sit rather uneasily with the requirement to investigate whether the particular applicant is at risk. Nevertheless, the CJEU has confirmed that expediting an asylum claim on the basis of the nationality of the applicant is lawful within the APD, provided basic principles and guarantees are complied with (C-175/11 *H.I.D. v Refugee Applications Commissioner, Refugee Appeals Tribunal, Minister for Justice, Equality and Law Reform, Ireland*). Returning someone before their appeal is heard to a country where they fear persecution risks a breach of the principle of *non-refoulement*, and so the standard for designating a country as safe must be a rigorous one.

In making the decision to designate, the Secretary of State:

(a) shall have regard to all the circumstances of the State or part (including its laws and how they are applied), and

(b) shall have regard to information from any appropriate source (including other member States and international organisations). (s 94(5D))

This requirement was inserted by the Asylum (Procedures) Regulations 2007, SI 2007/3187, implementing Council Directive 2005/85/EC of 1 December 2005 on minimum standards on procedures in Member States for granting and withdrawing refugee status (the Procedures Directive). The Directive permits certification only where 'it can be shown that there is generally and consistently no persecution . . . no torture or inhuman or degrading treatment or punishment and no threat by reason of indiscriminate violence in situations of . . . armed conflict'. This subsection requires the Secretary of State to consider a broad base of evidence, whereas the section as originally enacted made no specifications as to how the Secretary of State should reach this view. Still there seems to be a gap between what the Directive requires and the amended UK statute. This may give scope for challenge in an individual case where it can be shown that the standard of the Directive is not met. There is an obligation in s 94A to make a 'European Common List of Safe Countries of Origin', if the Secretary of State thinks it necessary for the purpose of complying with the UK's obligations under Community law. However, practice within the EU is inconsistent, with some Member States using a list of 'safe' countries, and some not, and significant differences between the lists.

Under the 2002 Act the Secretary of State is obliged to certify the claim unless satisfied that there are reasons to the contrary.

Section 94(3) says:

If the Secretary of State is satisfied that a claimant is entitled to reside in a State listed in subsection (4) he shall certify the claim . . . unless satisfied that it is not clearly unfounded.

The burden of proof is therefore on the claimant to show that the claim is not clearly unfounded. The recast Procedures Directive requires that the safe country of origin concept should only be applied when the individual has not submitted serious grounds showing risk in their case (2013/32 EU). The UK has not opted into this revised

Directive. In *ZL and VL v SSHD and Lord Chancellor's Department* [2003] 1 All ER 1062, the Court of Appeal set out the decision-maker's process of reasoning to certify a claim clearly unfounded:

   (i) consider the factual substance and detail of the claim
   (ii) consider how it stands with the known background data
   (iii) consider whether in the round it is capable of belief
   (iv) if not, consider whether some part of it is capable of belief
   (v) consider whether, if eventually believed in whole or in part, it is capable of coming within the Convention. (para 57)

They concluded that there was 'no intelligible way' of certifying a claim from a listed country except by this same process (para 58). The burden of proof on the claimant, the lack of appeal against certification, the obstacles to judicial review, and the practice of fast-tracking 'NSA' claims, illustrate that in practice it is difficult to compel this individual consideration. However, in *R on the application of MD (Gambia) v SSHD* [2011] EWCA Civ 121, although the challenge to the designation (see below) of Gambia failed, the Court of Appeal held that the evidence of human rights abuses was relevant in the individual case, and the certificate relating to MD was quashed. It could not be said that his case was bound to fail.

There is a power in s 94 to add to or remove from the list by Order made by the Secretary of State. The grounds for addition are that the Secretary of State is satisfied that:

   (a) there is in general in that State or part no serious risk of persecution of persons entitled to reside in that State or part, and

   (b) removal to that State or part of persons entitled to reside there will not in general contravene UK's obligations under the Human Rights Convention (s 94(5)).

States designated under Orders are now listed in s 94 (4) and are: Albania, Jamaica, Macedonia, Moldova, Bolivia, Brazil, Ecuador, South Africa, Ukraine, India, Mongolia, Bosnia-Herzegovina, Mauritius, Montenegro, Peru, Serbia, Kosovo, and South Korea.

The 2004 Act added a further power for the Secretary of State to certify a state or part of a state safe in relation to a group of people (s 94(5A) 2002 Act). The group may be defined by gender, language, race, religion, nationality, membership of a social or other group, political opinion, or 'any other attribute or circumstance that the Secretary of State thinks appropriate.' (s. 94(5C)).

The power has been used to designate Ghana, Gambia, Kenya, Liberia, Malawi, Mali, Nigeria, and Sierra Leone as safe for men.

Criticisms could be and have been made of the inclusion of a number of these countries. For instance, it is difficult to reconcile the inclusion of Albania with the UK government's commitment to improve its policy and practice in relation to the protection of women trafficked for sex, Albania being one of the major centres of organized crime of this kind. The speed with which a claim may be refused and the person returned without an appeal hearing may give rise to real risks in individual serious cases.

11.3.1.2 Challenging designation

There are two levels of decision that may be challenged. One is the specific decision to certify the particular claim as clearly unfounded. The more fundamental challenge is to the designation of a country within s 94.

The first challenge to designation was in *R v SSHD ex p Javed and Ali* [2001] Imm AR 529, in which the designation of Pakistan under an earlier statute was found to be unlawful. The claimants relied in particular on the House of Lords' judgment concerning women in that country in *Shah and Islam* (see chapter 12) and the recorded position of Ahmadis there. These were evidence of persecution of women and religious minorities. The Court of Appeal found that the Secretary of State's decision to include Pakistan in the White List was irrational. This successful challenge made it clear that a general risk to particular social groups made Pakistan unsuitable for designation as 'safe'. The risk did not have to apply to the whole population.

This question was visited again in the successful challenge of the designation of Bangladesh in *R (on the application of Zakir Husan) v SSHD* [2005] EWHC 189 (Admin).

In *Husan* The Secretary of State said that designating a country as 'in general' one in which there is no serious risk of persecution, relied in part on the low number of successful asylum claims from a country in determining whether it can be designated. Wilson J exposed the fallacy in this reasoning. He pointed out that poor economic conditions might well drive some people to make asylum claims which would be refused, but that this did not indicate a low risk of persecution in the country. In Parliament a minister had replied that concerns about human rights in Bangladesh did not mean that 'the vast majority' of Bangladeshi nationals were at risk of having their human rights abused, confusing the question of whether there was in general a serious risk of persecution with a risk of general serious persecution. Wilson J held the inclusion of Bangladesh to be irrational and therefore unlawful in the light of a volume of evidence about widespread human rights violations in the country. Violence in politics was pervasive, the use of torture was widespread, abuse of children and violence against women and religious minorities was common and widespread and corruption endemic (*Husan* para 55). Bangladesh was removed from the list of safe countries (Asylum (Designated States) (Amendment) Order 2005, SI 2005/1016).

In the case of Sri Lanka, following pronouncements by the UN Human Rights Committee and evidence presented by human rights groups, the UK government repealed the designation of Sri Lanka in 2006.

The issue of whether a country can be designated as 'safe' when there is a real risk for particular groups was finally settled by the Supreme Court in *R (on the application of Jamar Brown (Jamaica)) v SSHD* [2015] UKSC 8. The Supreme Court addressed the meaning of 'serious' risk 'in general'. The applicant was gay, and although his claim was originally fast-tracked, after argument by his solicitor it was not certified as unfounded and on appeal he obtained refugee status, on the basis that Jamaica is a deeply homophobic society.

He then challenged the designation of Jamaica as a country in which there is in general no serious risk of persecution, since persecution of gays and lesbians is endemic. The Home Office objected that this only affects 5 to 10 per cent of the population, and thus is not in general a serious risk. The Supreme Court unanimously held, in the words of Lord Toulson:

I take section 94(5) in its natural meaning to refer to countries (or parts of countries) where its citizens are free from any serious risk of systematic persecution, either by the state itself or by non-state agents which the state is unable or unwilling to control. This is the effect of the words 'in general' and 'serious'. I do not read the words 'there is in general . . . no serious risk of persecution of persons, . . .' as meaning 'there is no serious risk of persecution of persons in general', and therefore as intended to permit the designation of a state which systematically carries out or tolerates persecution provided that it is limited so as not to affect the large majority. I read the words 'in general' as intended to differentiate a state of affairs where persecution is endemic, ie it occurs in the ordinary course of things, from one where there may be isolated incidents of persecution. (para 21)

As Lord Toulson went on to say (quoting *Husan*), persecution within the meaning of the Refugee Convention is often, by its nature, directed towards minorities, and the 'great majority of asylum and human rights claimants belong to minorities of one kind or another.' (para 22).

Lord Hughes concluded:

In the present case, however, the risk attaches to all who are homosexual, lesbian, bisexual or transsexual. That risk . . . can only properly be described as a 'general' risk in Jamaica. As Pill LJ put it in the Court of Appeal, the risk applies to 'an entire section of the community, defined by sexual orientation and substantial in numbers'. Accordingly, whilst I agree that a decision on designation is one on which reasonable people may take different views, it does not seem to me that there is more than one answer which can be given on the present facts. (para 36)

Despite the Supreme Court's judgment, Jamaica remains designated as safe under the 2002 Act. Advice to caseworkers in *Country Information and Guidance Jamaica: Sexual Orientation and Gender Identity*, July 2015, is that where a claim is refused it is 'unlikely to be certifiable under s.94'.

11.3.2 **Fast-track procedures**

In parallel with the non-suspensive appeal, from 2000 until 2015 there was a policy of detaining people whose claims appeared to be ones that can be decided quickly.

Certain detention centres, renamed 'removal centres', were designated to detain people on a 'fast track'. The system was first implemented for men at Harmondsworth, then extended to women at Yarl's Wood.

Until early 2008, selection of claims to pass through the fast track was based on a departmental list of countries of origin, compiled under the authority of a ministerial authorization to discriminate on the basis of nationality (see chapter 6). The list included some countries from which claims could be certified as NSA, but also some that could not. The list was abolished, and replaced with a policy that any asylum claim could be fast-tracked if it appeared that a quick decision could be made. A case would be suitable for the DFT where it appeared that it would not entail further enquiries, or corroborative evidence, or documents to be translated, or a need for complex legal advice (API *Detained Fast Track Processes*). Since the details of the asylum claim are not given at the screening interview, the decision to place a person in the DFT was made on the basis of very limited information. This was demonstrated in the case of *Jamar Brown (Jamaica)* discussed in relation to the designation of Jamaica, where Mr Brown's case was fast-tracked even though he said at screening that the basis was his sexuality, which would need evidencing by testimonies obtained from his home country. The Court of Appeal held that his detention was unlawful because:

no reasonable person in possession of all the information about the appellant that could and should have been available if his case had been assessed in the manner required by the DFT/DNSA policy could have been satisfied at the time of his detention that a fair and sustainable determination of his claim could be made within a period of about two weeks. (para 30)

Studies of the DFT confirmed that people with complex cases and who are in the groups listed as unsuitable for fast-track detention were placed in the DFT. These include people who are seriously mentally ill, women in the late stages of pregnancy, and families including children. The UN Committee Against Torture found that torture survivors and people with poor mental health entered the DFT:

due to a lack of clear guidance and inadequate screening processes, and the fact that torture survivors need to produce 'independent evidence of torture' at the screening interview to be recognized as unsuitable for the DFT system.

The distinguishing characteristics of the DFT were speed and the fact that the applicant was detained right through the process including not only the initial decision but also the appeal. The official timetable was that claims were to be decided in three days. Appeals were heard on the premises (i.e., in special rooms in the detention centre). Two days were allowed to give notice of appeal, two days for a respondent's notice, and the hearing must be fixed within two days after that (Schedule to the Tribunal Procedure (First-tier Tribunal) (Immigration and Asylum Chamber) Rules 2014 SI 2406. Legal representation was not automatically available. In practice the timetable was not adhered to.

Concerns about the fairness of this system were expressed by UNHCR, BID, the Independent Asylum Commission, the Joint Committee on Human Rights, Detention Action, and the Independent Chief Inspector of Borders and Immigration.

The Joint Committee on Human Rights concluded:

> 226. We are concerned that the decision to detain an asylum seeker at the beginning of the process simply in order to consider his or her application may be arbitrary because it is based on assumptions about the safety or otherwise of the country from which the asylum seeker has come. It is self-evident that some asylum seekers—most obviously torture victims and those who have been sexually abused—are unlikely to reveal the full extent of experiences to the authorities in such a short-time period, and that this problem will be exacerbated where they are not able to access legal advice and representation, and the support of organisations able to help them come to terms with their experiences.
>
> 227. We are also concerned that although fast track detention for anything more than a short, tightly controlled period of time is unlawful, some asylum seekers find themselves detained at the beginning of the asylum process for periods in excess of this. The act of claiming asylum is not a criminal offence and should not be treated as such. If asylum seekers are detained at the beginning of the asylum process, then the period of detention should be limited to a maximum of seven days. (Tenth Report 2006–07: Treatment of Asylum Seekers)

Detention Action found that people were detained for days or weeks before being told that they were in the fast track. Then the decision, refusal, and appeal process happened 'at break neck speed'.

The lawfulness of the fast track was challenged in a series of cases brought by Detention Action. Firstly, in *Detention Action v SSHD and Equality and Human Rights Commission* [2014] EWHC 2245 (Admin), a High Court judge held that there were shortcomings in the DFT process. These included restricted time for consulting a lawyer, limited effectiveness of screening in identifying appropriate cases for DFT, failures in the procedure for identifying torture victims and responding appropriately to other vulnerable applicants. None of the shortcomings in themselves was enough to make the DFT unlawful, but combined they meant that proper legal representation was essential, and this meant having enough time to instruct a legal representative in advance of the substantive interview. The judge concluded that lack of proper opportunity to consult a legal representative, in the light of the other problems, was a 'crucial failing', which was 'sufficiently significant that the DFT as operated carries with it too high a risk of unfair determinations for those who may be vulnerable applicants.'

Following this, the Home Office adjusted the operation of the DFT, including instituting a space of four clear days between instructing a lawyer and the substantive interview.

However, further challenges were brought, this time to the continued detention pending appeal in the DFT. The Court of Appeal held that detention pending a DFT appeal was unlawful unless it was justified on the grounds that would normally justify detention. These are discussed in chapter 14 and include that removal is imminent, and that the individual presents some risk such as that they are likely to abscond. The Court found that in the DFT appellants were detained purely on the basis of speed and convenience without considering whether they were at risk of absconding or whether other grounds for detention were made out. This was unlawful (*R (on the application of Detention Action) v SSHD* [2014] EWCA Civ 1634).

Detention Action then challenged the lawfulness of the rules governing fast track appeals. The procedure rules provide that appeals in the DFT must be made within two working days of receiving the decision (Tribunal Procedure (First-tier Tribunal) (Immigration and Asylum Chamber) Rules 2014 SI 2406 Schedule rule 5). The Home Office must respond within two days, the hearing is required to take place three days later (rules 7 and 8), and the decision should be given two days after the hearing (rule 10). Although in practice hearings were not arranged at the time required by the rules, the Court of Appeal held that:

the time limits are so tight as to make it impossible for there to be a fair hearing of appeals in a significant number of cases . . . The system is therefore structurally unfair and unjust. The scheme does not adequately take account of the complexity and difficulty of many asylum appeals, the gravity of the issues that are raised by them and the measure of the task that faces legal representatives in taking instructions from their clients who are in detention. (*The Lord Chancellor v Detention Action* [2015] EWCA Civ 840 para 45)

Following this judgment, the Minister of State for Immigration announced in Parliament that the DFT system was suspended (House of Commons: Written Statement (HCWS83) July 2nd 2015). New instructions were issued to Home Office staff working in the DFT system: *Detention: interim Instruction for cases in detention who have claimed asylum, and for entering cases who have claimed asylum into detention*, July 2015. People detained in the fast track were to have their detention reviewed immediately according to usual detention criteria. The instruction however still contemplates that some asylum claimants may be detained when they make their asylum claim:

Asylum claims made at the Asylum Intake Unit, at port or once apprehended as a clandestine that might be suitable for detention because there is a reasonable likelihood of certifying the claim as clearly unfounded and of removing the individual within a reasonable timeframe, or other exceptional circumstances, should be referred to the National Removals Command Gatekeeper after screening has taken place for an assessment of suitability for detention. Particular attention should be paid to any vulnerabilities that have been raised (see EIG 55.10) and the ability to conclude the claim within a reasonable timeframe. (para 17)

The instruction also contemplates that some people may receive their asylum decisions while still in detention. It suggests that decisions should normally be made within 28 days, although extensions should be considered, and the normal detention criteria kept in view.

People whose appeals were heard in the DFT should have their appeals reheard, and should only be detained if their detention is allowed within the terms of normal detention policy. The President of the Tribunal confirmed in First-tier Tribunal decisions on 4th August 2015 that people in this position cannot be removed until their appeals have been reheard.

The instruction was called 'interim' since it was issued after the suspension of the DFT which occurred after the Court of Appeal judgment in *The Lord Chancellor v Detention*

Action [2015] EWCA Civ 840. However, the Lord Chancellor has been refused permission to appeal to the Supreme Court. At the time of writing, longer term plans are awaited.

Harmondsworth, the main site of fast-track detention, is only for single men, interpreted as 'men who have no dependants on their claim' (HC Debs 16 September 2004 col 158WS). The claimant argued in *Kpandang v SSHD* [2004] EWHC 2130 Admin that his detention in Harmondsworth was unlawful because he had a partner and child. McCombe J was persuaded that 'single' meant that the detention facilities were for men on their own, not that they were unmarried. There are no facilities to detain families in the fast track, and in the cases where a person has family in the UK, detention in the fast track meant separation from their family. For detention of families generally see chapter 14. Harmondsworth has had a very troubled history. The Chief Inspector of Prisons (HMIP) has found the centre 'unsafe' (2003), and there have been a number of hunger strikes and suicides. In 2006, there was a major disturbance and the centre was closed for several months. Being run together with its neighbouring centre, Colnbrook, makes Harmondsworth the biggest immigration detention centre in Europe, with 661 beds (over 1,000 including Colnbrook). There are regular inspections and reports by HMIP and by an Independent Monitoring Board. The most recent, published in February 2015, concluded that:

Harmondsworth IRC is in large parts a depressing, dirty place and in some cases has a destructive effect on the welfare of detainees. Issues that contribute to this include: the poor maintenance of the Centre. . . detaining vulnerable detainees in unsuitable conditions. . . the continued detention of those 'unfit to be detained' . . . and the complaints process. . .

(Independent Monitoring Board Harmondsworth Immigration Removal Centre Annual Report 2014)

Yarl's Wood is for women and families. The experiences of women with the DFT persuaded the Court that there were serious problems with the way that the system responds to people who had been tortured, were suicidal, had experienced sexual violence, or were pregnant.

11.3.3 Safe third country

Safe third country provisions are a key element in the Common European Asylum System. They are not restricted to the EU; for instance, Canada has a safe third country agreement with the USA, thereby closing its land border to most asylum claims. The third country means one that is neither the refugee's home state nor the country where they have sought asylum, and the designation 'safe' means that it will not be a breach of Refugee Convention Article 33, the obligation of *non-refoulement*, to send them there.

Safe third country provisions in the European Union, the so-called Dublin provisions, were introduced for two main reasons. The first was to prevent refugees from being sent round Europe by ensuring that at least one Member State accepts an application for asylum. The second was to stop asylum seekers moving around the EU in search of the country that seems to them to offer the best prospects and to preclude multiple claims by one person in different Member States.

Maintaining this orderly system became impossible under the pressure of entry to the EU's southern and eastern borders and the Dublin system is now in question. The EU's Dublin Regulations are directly effective and directly applicable in national law without implementing measures (TFEU Article 249). Council Regulation (EC) No. 343/2003

OJ 2003 L 50/1, known as 'Dublin II', or the Dublin Regulation, which came into effect on 1 September 2003, was the governing regulation until 31 December 2013. From 1 January 2014 EU Regulation No. 604/2013, or Dublin III, came into effect. For the development of safe third country provisions prior to the implementation of Dublin II, see earlier editions of this book.

In the UK, at the initial screening interview, questions are asked to determine whether an asylum seeker has travelled through another country which could have heard their claim. As a result, an asylum application may be sent to the Third Country Unit in the Home Office, and if that unit decides that safe third country procedures should apply, the Home Office requests the third country to take back the asylum seeker. Any further consideration of their claim in the UK is halted (although, if facts which would found a safe third country decision only come to light at a later stage, this cannot stop an appeal that is already in process: *AM (Somalia) v SSHD* [2009] EWCA Civ 114). Dublin III requires that the authorities inform an asylum seeker of the consequences of moving between Member States, the criteria for applying the Dublin Regulation, the opportunities for challenging the Dublin decision, and that they give an opportunity for the asylum seeker to submit information regarding the presence of family members. The regulation requires a personal interview to determine whether the Dublin Regulation applies. No doubt the UK's procedures will come under scrutiny as regards their compliance with Dublin III.

Asylum and Immigration (Treatment of Claimants, etc.) Act 2004 Schedule 3 gives the domestic framework for making third country decisions. It establishes three kinds of lists of safe third countries. The only one which is active is the first list, which consists of 28 other countries of the European Economic Area (all except Liechtenstein and Croatia, which have not been added yet) and Switzerland. Where a claimant has travelled through a country which might be regarded as safe but which is not in this list, claims may be certified on a case-by-case basis under Part 5 of Schedule 3.

The 29 listed countries are deemed, in the following three respects, to be safe places to return an asylum claimant who is not a national of that country:

- the applicant will not face persecution contrary to the Refugee Convention in that country;
- that country will not send the applicant to another country where there is a risk of such persecution; and
- that country will not send the applicant to another country if the removal would give rise to a risk of human rights violations.

The Secretary of State is also obliged to certify that a human rights appeal against removal to that country would be unfounded, unless s/he is satisfied that it would not be. This refers to human rights implications of removal aside from the possibility of onward removal from the destination state. Examples are that family or private life in the UK will be interfered with by the removal (Article 8 ECHR), or that the applicant faces a risk of degrading treatment in the receiving state (Article 3 ECHR). The effect is that anyone who may be returned to a listed European country is returned without their asylum claim being heard unless the Secretary of State is persuaded that there would arguably be a breach of human rights in doing so. The only judicial forum in which the certificate may be challenged is judicial review. Dublin III Article 27 provides that the applicant 'shall have the right to an effective remedy, in the form of an appeal or a review, in fact and in law, against a transfer decision, before a court or tribunal'. Preliminary references before the CJEU (C-63/15*Ghezelbash* and C-155/15 *Karim*) are concerned with the scope of that review, and in due course the effectiveness of judicial review in this context may be tested.

The question of whether a person may be returned to a European country through which they have travelled is governed by a hierarchy of criteria in the Dublin Regulation (Dublin III Article 7). Firstly, the state takes responsibility for an asylum claim if the claimant has a family member who is a recognized refugee or an asylum seeker legally resident in that Member State, providing the persons concerned agree (Articles 9 and 10). Unaccompanied minors should be dealt with in the country where they make their application (Article 8). The Dublin II predecessor of this Article was interpreted by the CJEU in C-648/11 *R (on the application of MA, BT, DA) v SSHD* to mean that, because of the vulnerability of minors, it was important not to prolong more than strictly necessary the procedure for determining the Member State responsible, 'which means that, as a rule, unaccompanied minors should not be transferred to another Member State' (para 55), and Dublin III enacts this approach. Where a minor with no family members in a Member State had made an application in two Member States, and where there was no decision on the first application, the second Member State should not seek to return them, but should deal with the application (*MA and others* para 66).

A Member State which issues a residence permit or visa will be responsible normally for a claim from the holder (Article 12), unless it expired two years ago, in the case of a residence permit, or six months ago in the case of a visa. Where there is evidence of illegal entry into a Member State, the state so entered remains responsible for processing the asylum claim for 12 months. After that, or in the event of there being no evidence of illegal entry, the Member State in which the asylum seeker was living for the last five months is responsible (Article 13).

Key Case

R (on the application of ZAT and Others) v SSHD (Article 8 ECHR—Dublin Regulation—interface—proportionality)

The applicants were three 16-year olds and a 26-year old man with a psychiatric disorder. He was the brother of the third applicant, and dependent on him. The four were brothers of the three other applicants, who had refugee status in the UK. All were Syrian.

The first four applicants were living in the 'jungle' camp in Calais. Conditions described before the Upper Tribunal and before the Administrative Court in Lille were squalid and degrading. The four were desperate to join their brothers in the UK.

The Upper Tribunal heard extensive evidence of problems with the asylum system in France for unaccompanied children:

21. A report compiled by the Council of Europe Commissioner for Human Rights in September 2014 recorded that France was experiencing '*major difficulties in terms of the reception of asylum seekers*'. This gave rise to, *inter alia*, shortcomings in the provision of accommodation and other services and facilities. Deficiencies in legal and social support for asylum applicants were also highlighted. So too was the plight of unaccompanied foreign children. These concerns were echoed by other international organisations . . .

22 . . . unaccompanied foreign minors who lodged an asylum application in France and who fall within the responsibility of another Member State are not in practice transferred there . . . detailed evidence of a practising French lawyer . . . draws attention to the unavailability of public funding for legal advice at the stage of preparing and

formulating applications for asylum . . . Unaccompanied foreign minors are not legally competent to make a claim for asylum. . . . 'Take charge' requests of another Member State are unlikely to materialise until almost a year has elapsed from the beginning of the process . . . In practice, it is very rare for children to make asylum claims in France.

Ironically, since under French law a foreign unaccompanied minor was entitled to stay on the territory, child protection services took the view that there was no need to claim asylum. This meant that it was difficult for these young people to get access to a process to join their brothers.

The Tribunal confirmed, following *EM (Eritrea)*, that the Human Rights Act co-exists with the Dublin Regulation. They said that 'where the two regimes pull in different directions, full cohesion, or harmonisation, may not be achievable and some accommodation must be found.' The compromise in this case was for the four applicants in Calais to submit a written application to the French authorities, and then be allowed to travel without delay to the UK for their asylum claims to be processed.

If there are no family connections or residence documents, Article 13 allocates responsibility to the state through which the asylum seeker first entered the EU if there is evidence of illegal entry. If there is no such evidence, or if 12 months have elapsed since that entry, the country in which the claim was first made must take responsibility (Article 3.2). Article 3.2 provides the fall back after application of all these criteria above, in order. If none apply, the claim should be processed in the first Member State at which the asylum seeker lodges an application.

Article 17 is a discretionary clause. It allows a Member State to take responsibility for an asylum claim where it would not otherwise be responsible according to the criteria in the Regulation. It might do this on for instance compassionate grounds. The Article also provides that a Member State may 'request another Member State to take charge of an applicant in order to bring together any family relations, on humanitarian grounds based in particular on family or cultural considerations, even where that other Member State is not responsible under the criteria laid down in Articles 8 to 11 and 16. The persons concerned must express their consent in writing'.

Dublin II had an equivalent though weaker provision. In relation to that provision the courts consistently held that the Dublin Regulation was 'concerned with the allocation of responsibility as between states, not the creation of personal rights' (*R (MK (Iran))* [2010] 1 WLR 2059 para 42). This was supported by the Advocate General's opinion in Case C-620/10 *Kastrati* when the AG said that the applicant's withdrawal of their asylum claim did not determine how the Member State should act. This also entails that the applicant cannot insist that the UK take responsibility for their claim when there is a delay in transferring responsibility (see, e.g., *Omar v SSHD* [2005] EWCA Civ 285 and *Kheirollahi-Ahmadroghani v SSHD* [2013] EWHC 1314 (Admin)). The effect of this is that although the Member State can take responsibility for a claim, or request another state to do so if the parties agree, the individual cannot use the Dublin Regulation to compel the Member State to do either of these things. This approach must now be mitigated by the case of *ZAT* where respect for the human rights of minors suggested a compromise.

The High Court in *R (on the application of YZ, MT and YM) v SSHD* [2011] EWHC 205 (Admin) held that this absence of individual rights for the asylum seeker in the Dublin Regulation applied also to challenging fingerprint matches from Eurodac, the fingerprint database which provides the evidence that an asylum seeker entered the EU elsewhere. The Court rejected the argument that the match was a precedent fact, that is, a challengeable factual basis for the operation of the Dublin Regulation.

Dublin III, like Dublin II, provides that, if the claimant had left the EU for more than three months, then the responsibility for the claim lapses (Article 19). However, the courts have held that, once the third country has accepted responsibility, the question of whether the claimant has in fact left the EU for three months is no longer the business of the state which issued the third country certificate (*R (on the application of AR (Iran)) v SSHD* [2013] EWCA Civ 778). The repercussions of this have been that the UK was not obliged to pass on to France the asylum seeker's claim that she had returned to China (*R (on the application of Yong Qing Chen)* [2008] EWHC 437 (Admin)), and the rationality of the Secretary of State's belief that the claimant had not been back to Sri Lanka was no longer a challengeable issue in the UK Court (*R (on the application of Santhirakumar) v SSHD* [2009] EWHC 2819 (Admin)). Dublin III regularizes the procedure and sets time limits for information exchange between Member States.

The CJEU said in C-394/12 *Abdullahi v Bundesasylamt* [2013] that once a Member State has taken charge of an asylum claim through a Dublin transfer, the transfer decision can only be challenged on the limited basis that there are systemic deficiencies in the asylum and reception procedure in the receiving country, such that the asylum seeker is at real risk of being subjected to inhuman and degrading treatment.

The first indication that the legal structure of the Dublin provisions could not bear the weight of reality came with the European Court of Human Rights' judgment in *MSS v Belgium and Greece* [2011] ECHR 108.

 Key Case

MSS v Belgium and Greece (Application no. 30696/09)

MSS was an interpreter who had fled Afghanistan after, as he claimed, an attempt on his life by the Taliban. His first entry to Europe was through Greece, where he was fingerprinted but did not claim asylum. He made his asylum claim in Belgium where his fingerprints, registered on Eurodac, showed that he had passed through Greece. Pursuant to the Dublin Regulation, an order was made that he be returned to Greece. MSS lodged unsuccessful challenges with the Belgian Aliens Appeals Board. In parallel, he applied to the ECtHR to have his transfer suspended. The Court refused to make a provisional measures order (Rule 39), but informally required the Greek government to honour its obligations under the ECHR and comply with EU legislation on asylum.

MSS was removed to Greece. He was detained on arrival in a small space with 20 other detainees, had access to the toilets only at the discretion of the guards, was not allowed into the open air, was given very little to eat, and made to sleep on a dirty mattress or the bare floor. When he was released he was required to report to the Attica police station to declare his home address so that he could be informed of the progress of his asylum application. Being homeless, and believing that an address was a condition of proceeding with his claim, MSS did not report to the police station. There were other deficiencies in the procedure applied to him. For much of his time in Greece the applicant had no means of subsistence, and slept in a park.

MSS complained to the ECtHR about his treatment by both Greece and Belgium. Against Greece he alleged breaches of Article 3 ECHR by reason of his conditions of detention, his conditions of living, and a breach of Article 13 ECHR because of the deficiencies in the asylum procedure and the risk of his expulsion to Afghanistan without any serious examination of the merits of his asylum application or access to an effective remedy. His complaint against Belgium was that Belgium had breached Articles 3 and 13 by sending him to Greece and exposing him to these risks. The Court found in his favour and held that both Greece and Belgium were in violation of their obligations under Articles 3 and 13 ECHR.

This decision by the ECtHR cast doubt on the continuing operation of the Dublin Regulation as Belgium was ruled to have breached Article 3 by sending MSS to Greece, and not enquiring, given the level of evidence about conditions in Greece, whether MSS would be at risk of *refoulement* or of breaches of Article 3 in Greece itself. After the judgment in *MSS*, the Court of Justice of the European Union in C–411/10 *NS v SSHD and ME and others v Refugee Applications Commissioner* held that there is an obligation on Member States to operate the Dublin Regulation in a manner consistent with fundamental rights. In order to ensure that rights are effective, there must be a meaningful channel through which an asylum seeker can adduce evidence that there is a serious risk to them in the destination state. Member States may not transfer an asylum seeker to the 'Member State responsible' within the meaning of the Dublin Regulation

where they cannot be unaware that systemic deficiencies in the asylum procedure and in the reception conditions of asylum seekers in that Member State amount to substantial grounds for believing that the asylum seeker would face a real risk of being subjected to inhuman or degrading treatment. (*NS* para 94)

Dublin III incorporates this decision, since it provides for when a transfer is impossible due to 'systemic deficiencies' in the asylum system of the receiving state (Article 3.2).

The UK statute has not been amended following *MSS* and *NS*, but transfers to Greece were as a matter of policy suspended, and see *VT* later. To the extent that the ECtHR found that MSS was at risk of *refoulement* to Afghanistan because of the inadequacy of the Greek asylum process, the 2004 Act seems to breach the ruling, and now potentially Dublin III, since there is no forum to challenge the statutory presumption that a First List state will not *refoule* the asylum seeker. To the extent that *MSS* and *NS* rely on the failure of protection of ECtHR rights in the destination Member State (Greece), in theory the opportunity to challenge this is available in the UK by challenging the (routine) certification of the human rights claim by judicial review. *NS* did not outlaw a presumption that human rights would be respected in an EU destination country.

The relationship between the Dublin regulations and Article 3 was next considered in the Supreme Court's judgment in *EM (Eritrea)* [2014] UKSC 12.

 Key Case

EM (Eritrea) [2014] UKSC 12

Each of the four appellants in this case had suffered from gravely poor conditions in Italy. EH was severely disturbed, suffering from PTSD and depression, and there was a real risk that he would be homeless if returned to Italy. EM was destitute in Italy, but was required to pay for his asylum claim to be processed. AE had been homeless and destitute and had been raped repeatedly. She had lived in overcrowded conditions, depending on charities for food. MA had been living on the street, sleeping under bridges and relying on charities for food. Both AE and MA had refugee status.

The appellants argued that it would be a breach of Article 3 to return them to Italy. The Home Office argued that, following *NS*, only a systemic breach in the receiving country would be enough to find a breach of Article 3.

The Supreme Court held that there could be a breach of Article 3 without necessarily a breakdown in the asylum system.

The decision in *EM (Eritrea)* was very important since it allows Dublin returns to other Member States to be challenged on the basis of evidence of a breach of human rights in the receiving country.

The standard to show a breach of Article 3 is a demanding one, and so far there is no binding decision of a higher court finding a breach of Article 3 in countries other than Greece. However, numerous challenges have been mounted in the UK and in other European countries to Dublin returns. There have been many challenges to returns to Hungary. In November 2015, the Raad van State, the highest administrative court in the Netherlands, found that the Secretary of State had a duty to ascertain that the situation in another Member State would not lead to a violation of Article 3 ECHR, and had failed to do so. The Secretary of State was therefore obliged to make further investigation into whether the situation of Dublin transferees in Hungary would lead to a violation of the ECHR (Cases 201507248/1 and 201507322/1). The positive duty found in these cases is noteworthy. There have been challenges to removals to Italy on the basis that the asylum reception conditions do not secure basic human rights. The asylum system has not been found to have systemic flaws or to have broken down, but in a number of cases domestic courts have insisted on individual assessments of the conditions facing the person who would be returned (e.g., France—Administrative Court Nantes, 24 July 2015, M. S, No. 1506136 and 22 June 2015, No 1505089). In 2014 UNHCR declared that the asylum system in Bulgaria to be in a state of systemic failure (*UNHCR observations on the current asylum system in Bulgaria*, 2 January 2014), and some Dublin transfers to Bulgaria have been prevented by domestic courts on an individual basis, for example, Czech Republic—Prague Regional Court, 1 July 2015, *A. K. A., S. K. K., A. E. and K. B. v Ministry of the Interior*, 49Az 56/2015-41.

In the UK returns have been challenged not only to Hungary, Italy, and Bulgaria, but also Romania, Cyprus and Malta. At the time of writing there is no authoritative finding on systemic breaches in any of these countries, and each case is pursued individually, depending on the vulnerability of the applicant and the situation facing them.

These issues have also been pursued in the ECtHR. In *Tarakhel v Switzerland* (Application no. 29217/12), an Afghan family challenged their removal to Italy pursuant to the Dublin Regulation, on the basis of conditions in reception centres in Italy, saying that these were unsuitable for families. The Grand Chamber of the ECtHR found that there would be a violation of Article 3 if the applicants were returned to Italy without the Swiss authorities having first obtained individual guarantees from the Italian authorities that the applicants would be taken charge of in a manner suited to the age of the children, and that the family would be kept together. Reception conditions in Italy as described in the *Tarakhel* judgment were nothing like as severe as MSS had suffered in Greece, and the Court did not find that the system had broken down.

11.3.4 **Asylum seekers under 18**

Minors are dealt with through a different process. The conduct of children's asylum claims is subject to the duty in s 55 Borders Immigration and Citizenship Act 2009 to have regard to the need to safeguard and promote the welfare of children. *ZH (Tanzania) v SSHD* [2011] UKSC 4 makes it clear that children's welfare must be a primary consideration. This supplements one of the innovations brought by the Qualification Directive, which makes the best interests of a child a primary consideration in implementing social rights for refugees (Article 20.5), and recital 12 says that the best interests of the child should be a primary consideration in implementing the whole Directive. A lesser obligation has been transposed into UK law. Paragraph 350 of the immigration rules says that 'particular priority and care' is to be given to the handling of claims of unaccompanied minors.

Government policy is that those under 18 should not be detained, and although exceptions still occur, the official process is for unaccompanied children on arrival to be placed in the care of the social services department.

Minors over the age of 12 are interviewed about their asylum claim, but this should only be done in the presence of a responsible adult. If a minor's asylum claim is refused, they may only be removed from the UK if adequate care and reception arrangements are in place in their country of return (API: *Processing an asylum application from a child*). Normally, if no such arrangements are in place, they are given leave to remain until they are aged 17 and a half. This is called UASC leave (Unaccompanied Asylum-Seeking Child). When their UASC leave is due to expire they may apply for an active review, and this results in a new decision granting or refusing leave.

The care of a person under 18 is the responsibility of a local authority under the Children Act 1989. Therefore, procedures for resolving whether someone is over 18 are crucial.

11.3.4.1 Age disputes

The Home Office can request the local authority to conduct an age assessment. Where the child disputes the outcome, the only legal challenge is by judicial review. Age assessment must be conducted with care, as this process itself can compound the suffering of a traumatized young person (*R (on the application of T) v London Borough of Enfield* [2004] EWHC 2297 (Admin)). It should be borne in mind that the fact of dispute does not necessarily reflect on the asylum seeker's good faith, as the measuring, recording, and concept of age may be treated differently in their country of origin from the UK. It is the UK's measure which is determinative.

Home Office guidance on the measurement of age may be summarized as:

- a claimant *must* be treated as an adult only if their physical appearance or demeanour *very strongly* suggests that they are significantly older than 18;
- in all other cases an applicant who claims to be under 18 should be given the benefit of the doubt until an age assessment has been carried out;
- at this point the guidance applies on fulfilling the duty in s 55 Borders Citizenship and Immigration Act 2009 to ensure that arrangements are made to safeguard and promote the welfare of the child;
- Social Services age assessments which are compliant with the guidance in *R (on the application of B) v Merton LBC* [2003] 4 All ER 280 and later cases expanding on these principles should be regarded as authoritative;
- evidence submitted by the applicant *must* be considered and due weight given to it;
- unaccompanied minors must only be detained in very exceptional circumstances and then only overnight, with appropriate care, whilst alternative arrangements for their care and safety are made. (EIG 55.9.3.1 and APG on Assessing Age)

The judgment in *R (on the application of B) v Merton LBC* [2003] 4 All ER 280 held that:

- a local authority must make its own decision and not simply adopt the stance of the Home Office;
- there must be adequate information to make this assessment;
- this will include asking the child about their education, family, activities, and history;
- the assessment cannot normally be made on the basis of physical appearance alone except in an 'obvious' case.

Later case law has added to this, and the cumulative guidance is collected now in a good practice guide by the Association of Directors of Children's Services (ADCS 2015). The guidance includes:

- local authority decisions are likely to be more cogent if they are as holistic as possible and draw together multi-agency information from others who had contact with the child or young person, such as teachers, advisors and key-workers and where social workers had considered personally observing the child interact with his or her peers;
- the assessment should be undertaken by two qualified social workers who have received appropriate training and have experience of interviewing young vulnerable children;
- an appropriate adult who is independent of the local authority should attend age assessment interviews to support and assist the child and not merely as a passive observer;
- social workers should pay attention to the level of tiredness, trauma, bewilderment and/or anxiety of the child and provide appropriate breaks as necessary. If the child is ill then the interview should be rearranged;
- social workers should seek to establish a rapport with the child and should ask open-ended questions;
- social workers may hear from children who have been 'coached' or have already been asked to recount their story several times, thereby unwittingly blurring the accuracy of their answers. In these situations social workers should bear in mind that even where a child may have received coaching in relation to some aspect of his or her account, this does not necessarily mean that he or she is lying about being a child;
- if an adverse decision is made the local authority has an obligation to explain the reasons. It is best practice for these reasons to be provided in writing, with an explanation of how the child can challenge the decision;
- the reasons for a social worker's decision should be internally consistent and should not exhibit any obvious error or inadequate explanation for not accepting any apparently credible and consistent answers of the child;
- the age assessment process should be inquisitorial (not adversarial) and non-hostile, allowing for the difficulties children might face giving evidence. In particular 'due allowance should be made for the fact that a child might have a different way of recounting narratives and that proper regard should be paid to the fact that it was a child who was the subject of the age assessment process';
- the court is likely to find that a decision was unlawful if it failed to take into account the fact that a child's cultural and social background would have had a significant effect on his or her ability to provide documentary evidence of his or her age or a clear chronology of his or her previous experiences.

Reports of consultant paediatricians are relevant and should be taken into account in the age assessment (*A v London Borough of Croydon and SSHD, WK v SSHD and Kent County Council* [2009] EWHC 939 (Admin)). However, the evidence of the paediatrician Dr Stern in that case was that there was 'no reliable scientific basis for the estimation of age' and 'all the factors relied on to assess age in reality can only assess maturity and maturity and chronological age are two different things'. He added that many asylum seekers from developing countries have been subjected to deprivation and some to severe psychological stresses. Therefore, he would expect that they would have both younger psychological profiles and/or earlier measures of physical maturity than their true chronological age' (ADCS 2015).

In *R (on the application of A) v London Borough of Croydon* and *R (on the application of M) v London Borough of Lambeth* [2009] UKSC 8, the Supreme Court held that the question of whether a person was a child was a question of fact to be decided, in case of dispute, by the Court on the balance of probabilities. It was not an exercise of judgment of the kind which could be challenged only for irrationality. The limits of this decision were tested in *R (on the application of PM) v SSHD* [2010] EWHC 2056 (Admin). In this case a dental assessment had estimated PM's age as 19. By the time of his asylum Tribunal hearing this had not led to a reassessment of his age by the local authority, who had initially concluded that he was a minor. The Tribunal judge made a decision on PM's age in the course of his judgment on PM's credibility, and decided that PM was over 18 and had lied about his age for the purposes of getting leave to remain in the UK. The local authority, in the light of the Supreme Court case, thought that the judge's assessment of age was binding upon them. PM challenged this by judicial review. The Court held that the Tribunal did not have jurisdiction to decide PM's age outside the context of a finding for the purposes of the asylum claim. The local authority for its purposes was still required to form its own judgment. The case of *A and M* was about the Court's jurisdiction on appeal to decide a matter in dispute, and did not mean that judges had jurisdiction to determine age 'against all the world'. The Home Office in its guidance 'Assessing Age' says that where a Tribunal judge finds that an appellant is a child, the Agency will generally regard itself as bound by this. See also AA [2013] UKSC 49 at 14.6. The Home Office and ADCS have published Joint Working Guidance on carrying out age assessment, and guidance has been produced by the Scottish Refugee Council, including a guide for young people to help them understand the process.

11.4 Sanctions on asylum seekers

11.4.1 Attending an interview without a passport

A practice which has troubled the Home Office has been that of asylum seekers who destroy their documents while on their journey to the UK. This may be on the advice of agents who have organized their travel. The act of destroying a document does not of course give any indication of why a person concealed their identity or their means of travel, as the case might be. The desire to start a new life anonymously, or conceal a deception, or fear of persecution are clearly all possible motives.

In order to prevent this, the Asylum and Immigration (Treatment of Claimants, etc.) Act 2004 introduced an offence of attending an asylum interview without a passport or similar document (s 2), unless it is produced within a three-day grace period after the interview (s 2(3)(b)). Statutory defences include:

- to produce a false immigration document and to prove that this was used for all purposes in connection with the journey to the UK;
- to prove that he travelled to the UK without, at any stage since he set out on the journey, having possession of an immigration document;
- Reasonable excuse, which does not include destruction of the document unless that was for a reasonable cause or beyond the claimant's control.

Reasonable cause in this context does not include delaying an asylum decision, increasing one's chances of success, or complying with the instructions of a facilitator (smuggler) unless it would be unreasonable to expect non-compliance in the circumstances (s 2(7)(b)(iii)). Since asylum seekers often rely heavily on the instructions of their agent, and have no other recourse, this is problematic. The instructions to immigration officers implementing the section suggest that it would be unreasonable to expect non-compliance with advice where the asylum seeker has been threatened or intimidated so that this amounted to force.

In *R v Bei Bei Wang* [2005] EWCA Crim 293, the appellant had travelled for six months through several countries with an agent who had retained her passport at all points except for the moment of going through passport control. The Court of Appeal commented that her situation was not very different from that of someone who had not had possession of a travel document at all, or someone who travelled on forged documents. In the latter case, there would be a defence under the 2004 Act, and s 31 of the 1999 Act would provide a defence to a different criminal charge in the event of a successful asylum claim (see 11.4.2). In view also of the fact that Ms Wang was only 18 years old, a lighter sentence was appropriate.

The sentence was also reduced in *Lu Zhu Ai* [2005] EWCA Crim 936, in which the Court reiterated the very specific purpose of this offence and the distinction between s 2 and offences of fraud. The Court noted that it was difficult in these cases to take full account of individual circumstances. The components of the alleged offence could be considered, that is, the journey and to what extent the defendant had control of their travel document, but the merits of their asylum claim could not be considered at all by the criminal court. The case of *Thet v DPP* [2006] EWHC 2701 (Admin) began to set the limits of prosecutions under s 2.

 Key Case

Thet v DPP [2006] EWHC 2701 (Admin)

The defendant had entered the country on a false passport which, after passing through immigration control, he immediately handed back to the person who facilitated his entry, as instructed. As a former political prisoner, he had been unable to obtain a genuine passport in Burma. The Lord Chief Justice held that Mr Thet could rely on the defence in s 2(4)(c)—that he had a reasonable excuse for not being able to produce a document at interview of the kind referred to in s 2(1), namely one which is 'in force' and 'satisfactorily establishes his identity and nationality'. The Court held that the passport referred to in s 2 is a valid passport, not a false one.

The prosecutor wanted to rely on statements in Parliament under the rule in *Pepper v Hart* [1993] AC 593 to show that there was a parliamentary intention to prosecute people who disposed of false documents en route. The Lord Chief Justice held that the section was 'ill-drafted but not ambiguous' and so there was no *prima facie* case for using *Pepper v Hart*. If there had been, it would have been at least arguable that, where a criminal statute was ambiguous, the defendant should have the benefit of the ambiguity.

Similar facts in *R v Mohammed and R v Osman* [2007] EWCA Crim 2332 gave rise to a finding that, where the defence in s 2(4)(e) was relied on, which is that the person never had an immigration document, a defendant cannot argue that they were never in possession of an immigration document throughout the journey because the only one they had was false. This would give a defence to a possessor of a false passport who destroyed it before arrival where a possessor of a genuine passport would have no such defence, an unlikely proper effect of the statute, the Court thought. The convictions were overturned because the jury had not been properly directed on whether the defendants' reasons for giving their passports back to the agents were reasonable ones (the same defence as *Thet*), but this was too late to be of benefit to the appellants, who had already served prison sentences. Indeed, Mr Osman had been served with a deportation order, and it was only by intervention of the Criminal Cases Review Commission that his conviction had come before the Court.

Despite the speculation in *Mohammed and Osman*, in *R v Hudarey* [2008] EWCA Crim 1761, the Court of Appeal held that the appellant's guilty plea should never have been accepted, because it was clear that he had a defence under s 2(4)(c). He had not been able to obtain a genuine passport, but had, on the instructions of his agent, torn up the false one on which he travelled and flushed it down the toilet during the flight. He had a reasonable excuse for not being in possession of a genuine passport. These various outcomes can appear confusing, and, indeed, in *Thet*, Lord Phillips described the section as 'ill-drafted' and 'difficult'. It helps to be aware that the defences are alternatives, not cumulative. Therefore, for instance, failure to retain a false passport, though depriving the applicant of the defence in para (d), does not deprive them of the opportunity of arguing that they had a reasonable excuse, perhaps because of their politics as in both *Thet* and *Hudarey*, for not being in possession of a *genuine* passport.

Destruction of a passport makes it more difficult to return a person to their country of origin against their will. The s 2 offence is based on the proposition that it is not legitimate to obstruct one's return without reference to whether this is based on fear of return rather than a cynical desire to obstruct the legal system. No *mens rea* is required. The defendant is in an invidious position. If they have destroyed their passport in an attempt to ensure their own safety this fear is very relevant to the success of their asylum claim, but admitting its destruction will make them guilty of an offence and liable to imprisonment.

As Macdonald points out (2005:975), where the facts are in dispute, in the light of tightening controls by carriers, the Court may disbelieve a passenger's assertion that they never had a travel document. Section 2 may force a person fleeing persecution to prove a negative in the criminal courts. It does not target a person who attempts to remain hidden, but rather one who makes an application for international protection. The underlying mischief is the destruction of travel documents but there is no requirement on the prosecution to prove this as the *actus reus* is simply presentation at interview without the document. The burden of proof is on the defendant to show they never had one.

The Parliamentary Joint Committee on Human Rights considered whether this reverse burden meets the requirements of Article 6.2 ECHR. They did not reach a concluded view on that matter, but accepted that in principle it could be justifiable to place the burden on the defendant of showing an excuse for the destruction of a passport. This was with the caveat that immigrants should have access to information on the effect of destroying travel documents (para 23). The Committee also voiced their concern (Session 2003–04 Fifth Report HL paper 35 HC 304, para 10) that like the offences of forgery and falsification of documents, s 2 might be wrongly used, thus penalizing even more asylum seekers and breaching Article 31 (see 11.4.2). The defence of never having had a travel document was introduced to go some way towards alleviating the Committee's concerns. Nevertheless, many of the people who have been convicted under s 2 were in comparable positions to Mr Thet. His solicitor commented:

this Act . . . had an effect of criminalising genuine asylum seekers who often can only leave their own country using a false passport for which they have had to pay an agent. Due to the power the agent has over them, they usually have to return the passport to the agent or destroy the passport on arrival in the United Kingdom. (Refugee Council briefing, October 2006)

The press reported 230 asylum seekers arrested and 134 convicted in the first six months of s 2 being in force ('Asylum seekers jailed for having no passports' *The Guardian* 18 March 2005). However, cases are still coming to light in which people have been wrongly advised to plead guilty to these offences (see *Syrian asylum seekers allowed to appeal against UK convictions* bbc.co.uk/news 16 April 2015).

11.4.2 Avoiding penalties: the defences under Article 31 and section 31

Article 31 of the Refugee Convention says that refugees coming directly from the country of persecution should not be punished on account of their illegal entry or presence, provided they present themselves without delay and show good cause for this. In the case of *R v Uxbridge Magistrates Court ex p Adimi, R v Crown Prosecution Service ex p Sorani, R v SSHD ex p Kaziu* [2000] 3 WLR 434, three people who travelled on false documents were prosecuted. The purpose of Article 31 was to provide immunity for genuine refugees whose quest for asylum reasonably involved a breach of the law. The Court recognized that this could be a matter of necessity. This was related to the conduct of immigration and asylum, not to the need to punish criminal activity generally and the Court thought that the Secretary of State rather than the Crown Prosecution Service should decide when asylum seekers should be prosecuted for travelling on false documents (para 44).

A joint Memorandum of Good Practice on this subject, giving guidance for liaison between the police, the Home Office, CPS, and the Law Society, was never published (Macdonald 2009:368), and the Home Office Asylum Policy Instructions now say that the role of immigration officials is to provide information and evidence and that it is for the CPS to decide whether there is sufficient evidence and whether it is in the public interest to proceed with a prosecution. The guidance continues:

If the offender [sic] has already been granted asylum, or if it appears likely that they will be granted asylum, then the CPS would probably not consider a prosecution to be in the public interest; however, this is ultimately a decision for them. (API on Article 31 para 10)

Previous APIs said that 'it would normally be appropriate' for a decision on whether to prosecute to be deferred until the asylum decision and any appeals are concluded, but this no longer appears in present asylum instructions.

Following the judgment in *Adimi*, a statutory defence to forgery, deception, and falsification of documents was enacted in Immigration and Asylum Act 1999 s 31. It provides that there is a defence for a refugee charged with an offence to which the section applies if they:

(a) came to the UK directly from a country where their life or freedom was threatened;

(b) reported to the authorities in the United Kingdom without delay;

(c) showed good cause for their illegal entry or presence; and

(d) made a claim for asylum as soon as reasonably practicable after arrival.

Section 31 is more restricted than Article 31 and the *Adimi* judgment. For instance, the defence is available only to someone whose refugee claim succeeds, whereas *Adimi* applied Article 31 to asylum seekers.

The Court of Appeal held that 'the defendant must provide sufficient evidence in support of his claim to refugee status to raise the issue and thereafter the burden falls on the prosecution to prove to the criminal standard that he is not a refugee' (*Mateta v R* [2013] EWCA Crim 1372). If the defendant has been refused asylum, then the burden of proof is on them on the balance of probabilities to show that they are a refugee (*R v Ali Reza Sadighpour* [2012] EWCA Crim 2669).

Article 31 refers to people 'coming directly' from the country of persecution, but the Court in *Adimi* did not take this too literally. They held that there could be some element of choice by refugees as to their destination, and a short-term stopover on the journey could not be used to say that the refugee had not come to the UK directly. The Divisional Court in *R (on the application of Badur) v Birmingham Crown Court and Solihull Magistrates' Court* [2006] EWHC 539 (Admin) held that Article 31 would have permitted other considerations, for instance that the appellant was a minor at the relevant time, which might have had a bearing on whether he could have claimed asylum in a safe country. Section 31 does not allow for these factors. It limits the defence to situations where the defendant can show that in any third country at which they have stopped on the way to the UK they could not reasonably have expected to obtain refugee protection. The Court of Appeal accepted in the case of the appellant Mr Bashir in *Mateta* that his stop in Kenya was not sufficient to remove the availability of the defence, and he should have had an opportunity to make that argument before a court (paras 44–6).

UNHCR says that 'delay caused by an asylum seeker's wish to approach a lawyer or a voluntary organization first to seek advice is not unreasonable and should not preclude the protection of s 31'. They were concerned that account be taken of proper reasons for delay, such as the effects of trauma, language differences, lack of information, previous experiences which have resulted in a suspicion of authority, and a feeling of insecurity. UNHCR issued detailed advice on the API, but this has not been implemented, and the present API makes no reference to reasons for delay.

In *R (on the application of Pepushi) v Crown Prosecution Service* [2004] EWHC 798 (Admin), the Court held that there is no scope to claim the protection of Article 31 Refugee Convention, even though the protection offered by Immigration and Asylum Act 1999 s 31 is explicitly narrower. Mr Pepushi had stopped in France and Italy long enough to claim asylum. Section 31 gave no scope to extend the defence. The Court had an obligation to read the words of the statute which was intended to give effect to the Convention compatibly with the Convention; where this was not possible, parliamentary sovereignty entailed that the statute prevailed.

The Refugee Qualification Directive does not include an equivalent of Article 31, except where refugee status is refused, revoked, or terminated, when the rights set out in Article 31 apply (Article 14.6).

The defence can only apply to offences which are listed in s 31; it was extended to cover the offences under the Identity Cards Act 2006 and the Identity Documents Act 2010 (see chapter 6 at 6.7). This means that it is critical which offence is charged on a given set of facts. A practice grew up of charging with an offence not mentioned in s 31, though based on the same facts as one for which there would be a defence. The House of Lords addressed this in the case of *R v Asfaw* [2008] UKHL 31.

 **Key Case**

R v Asfaw [2008] UKHL 31

The appellant was an Ethiopian national who had very good grounds for an asylum claim. She left Ethiopia to claim asylum in the US, travelling via the UK. On arrival at Heathrow Airport, she passed through immigration control on her own passport, but was then provided with a false passport by her agent, which she presented at the check-in desk for a flight to

Washington. The official on the desk informed the police. She was arrested and charged with using a false instrument with intent contrary to s 3 of the Forgery and Counterfeiting Act 1981 and attempting to obtain services by deception, namely a Virgin Atlantic flight. She pleaded not guilty to the first count, relying on the defence in s 31 Immigration and Asylum Act 1999 and was acquitted. She was convicted on the second count which was not an offence listed in s 31.

In the House of Lords, the Secretary of State raised a new argument, that s 31 and Article 31 did not apply to offences committed in the course of leaving a country rather than entering it.

The House of Lords by a 3:2 majority held that Article 31, and accordingly s 31, which sought to implement it, covered the situation where the refugee was leaving the UK as a transit passenger if she was still in flight. This was so, even if there was no danger to the refugee in the transit country. The drafters of the Refugee Convention had not contemplated air travel nor the implications of briefly entering a country to change planes as part of flight from persecution. Their Lordships also held that, although the CPS was not wrong to bring a charge not covered by the s 31 defence, once it was clear that s 31 applied, it was an abuse of process to continue with a prosecution on a charge not covered by it.

The House of Lords judgment in *Asfaw* contains an extended examination of the history and purpose of Article 31. It also refers to how carrier sanctions were influential, the rigorous checks by Virgin Atlantic being motivated by their vulnerability to penalties if they carried a passenger using false documents. The judgment is important for its further definition of the extent of Article and s 31, and because of the House of Lords' grounding of that decision firmly in the humanitarian purpose of the Refugee Convention.

These principles, though argued, did not avail the appellants in *Sternaj v DPP and CPS* [2011] EWHC 1094 (Admin). Their convictions for offences under ss 25 and 25A were upheld for facilitating the illegal entry into the UK of the second appellant's two-year-old son. The Divisional Court held that the s 31 and Article 31 defences did not apply to offences under these sections, and it was not an abuse of process to prosecute. The Court observed in concluding that if the child had presented his own false passport, he would have had a defence, and in such a case it might be questioned whether a prosecution was in the public interest. But this was not such a case. In *R v Kamalanathan* [2010] EWCA Crim 1335 the Court of Appeal held that a month's stay in the UK meant that the appellant was not still in flight, and not therefore in a situation like that of Ms Asfaw.

The Joint Parliamentary Committee on Human Rights noted that 'a significant number of people have been wrongfully imprisoned' for offences to which s 31 should have provided a defence. Estimated figures ranged between 1,000 and 5,000 (Session 2003–04 Fifth Report HL paper 35 HC 304, para 10). People who were wrongly convicted and imprisoned have received average compensation of £40,000, but few claims have been made (Macdonald 2008:1133). Cases in the Court of Appeal have revealed that solicitors and barristers have failed to advise individuals that the s 31 defence was available to them. Where the defence was clearly available and would have been likely to have been upheld, convictions have been quashed (see *R v M, MV, M and N* [2010] EWCA Crim 2400 and *R v Jerdi* [2011] EWCA Crim 365). In *Mateta v R* [2013] EWCA Crim 1372) the Criminal Cases Review Commission had referred a series of convictions to the Court of Appeal and continues to do so. In all the decided cases the individuals concerned had received refugee status. None had received advice about the section 31 defence, and all had been convicted and served prison sentences. In every case the Court accepted that the defence would have been available and would quite probably have succeeded. Clear injustices had been done and the convictions were quashed. Most recently, in *R v Sha-bani* [2015] EWCA Crim 1924, the Court of Appeal quashed the conviction and referred the solicitor to the Solicitors Regulatory Authority because of the length of time that Mr Shabani had been wrongly imprisoned through their failure to advise.

In *SXH v CPS* [2014] EWCA Civ 90 the appellant was on remand for nearly six months awaiting trial for an offence under s 25 Identity Cards Act 2006. At the trial the prosecution accepted that she had a s 31 defence and offered no evidence. She sued for breach of Article 8 ECHR but the Court of Appeal held that the decision to prosecute did not, in this case, engage Article 8. The prosecutor had raised questions with the Home Office about the application of s 31, and could not, at the date of the initial decision to prosecute, be expected to have in mind all the consequences including extended detention before trial. The appellant might have been granted bail.

11.4.3 Those who assist or arrange entry

Section 25 Immigration Act 1971 was originally titled 'Assisting illegal entry and harbouring'. It consisted of knowingly 'making or carrying out arrangements for securing or facilitating the entry into the United Kingdom of anyone whom he knows or has reasonable cause for believing to be an illegal entrant' and of harbouring such a person, and carried a maximum sentence increased of seven years. The Nationality, Immigration and Asylum Act 2002 extended this offence and split it into three parts. The offence in s 25 now is to do an act 'which facilitates the commission of a breach of immigration law by an individual who is not a citizen of the European Union'. The definition of immigration law is wide, covering any provision which controls entitlement to enter or be in a Member State. The maximum sentence is increased to 14 years, and there are powers in ss 25C and D to seize vehicles owned by a person convicted. Section 25(5) provides for British nationals to be liable for the offence whether committed inside or outside the UK. Individuals are prosecuted under this section for assisting in immigration breaches (see chapter 6) and where people are smuggled or trafficked for illegal working (see chapter 9). The use of deception generally is covered in chapter 16. Here we focus on the application to seeking asylum.

The section was used to prosecute a married couple who facilitated the entry of the man's brother and his friend. The defendants were each sentenced to two years' imprisonment for that offence. The fact that the two entrants claimed asylum the day after their entry was irrelevant (*R v Javaherifard and Miller* [2005] EWCA Crim 3231).

Section 25A has the extraordinary heading of 'helping asylum seeker to enter UK'. Amended by the UK Borders Act 2007, the offence is 'knowingly and for gain' to facilitate the arrival or entry of someone the defendant knows or has reasonable cause to believe is an asylum seeker. There is a defence for someone acting on behalf of an organization which aims to help asylum seekers and does not charge for its services. Javaherifard and Miller could not be charged under this section because they did not act for gain.

Controlling those who profit from arranging illegal entry is a matter of some priority in the immigration law of the EU. Relevant European provisions are Directive 2002/90 (Defining the Facilitation of Unauthorised Entry, Transit and Residence) and Framework Decision 2002/946 (on strengthening the penal framework for unauthorized entry etc.), and the UK has opted in, but the offences under the expanded s 25 go beyond what is required by European measures. Notably, the s 25A offence of 'helping an asylum seeker to enter the UK' does not entail that the entry be illegal, simply that the entrant is an asylum seeker, whereas the Directive and Framework Decision requires criminal sanctions for the facilitation of entry or transit 'in breach of the laws of the state concerned', not penalties on the travel arrangements of asylum seekers per se. Directive 2002/90 Article 1.2 allows any Member State not to apply sanctions where the 'aim of the behaviour is to provide humanitarian assistance to the person concerned'. The British statutory defence is limited to organizations which do not charge for their services, although the Court in *Javaherifard and Miller* confirmed that facilitating the continued presence of refused asylum seekers by provision of services or accommodation in order to enable them to avoid destitution, is not an offence under s 25 (para 50).

In *Kapoor v R* [2012] EWCA Crim 435 the Court of Appeal held that the defence to a charge in s 25A, that no money was received, should not be circumvented by charging under s 25 simply because the evidence of profit was lacking. In this case, the appellants in India obtained visas to enter the UK via Bangkok. In Bangkok asylum seekers took their place on the second leg of the journey, using false passports in the appellants' names. On the plane the passports were retrieved by an escort. The travellers claimed asylum on arrival. The appellants were not charged under s 25A since there was insufficient evidence of gain. The asylum seekers were liable to prosecution under s 2 Asylum and Immigration Act 2004 because they could not show passports.

The appellants were initially convicted of conspiracy to commit the offence in s 25 Immigration Act 1971. The Court of Appeal held that section 25 entails a breach of immigration law, and that this is a law which determines whether a person is lawfully or unlawfully either entering, or in transit or in, the UK (s 25(2)). This does not include s 2 of the 2004 Act, which concerns the manner in which entry is exercised or determined, not the legality of the entry itself. The asylum seekers were not illegal entrants because they claimed asylum on arrival. Therefore, there was no breach of immigration law and thus no conspiracy to commit an offence under s 25. The convictions were overturned and replaced with conspiracy to commit an offence under s 2 Asylum and Immigration Act 2004. The sentences were radically reduced, since the offence in s 2 carries a maximum penalty of 2 years' imprisonment.

A distinction between *Javaherifard* and *Kapoor* is that in *Javaherifard* the travellers passed into the UK by train from Ireland, and their false documents were only inspected and identified after a sea crossing from Belfast to Birkenhead. They claimed asylum the following day, not on arrival.

11.5 Protection for victims of trafficking

Another group of people who risk being prosecuted and are in need of protection are those who have been trafficked. Trafficking is defined in the United Nations 2000 Protocol to Prevent, Suppress and Punish Trafficking in Persons, especially Women and Children (the Palermo Protocol) Article 3 as:

the recruitment, transportation, transfer, harbouring or receipt of persons, by means of the threat or use of force or other forms of coercion, of abduction, of fraud, of deception, of the abuse of power or of a position of vulnerability or of the giving or receiving of payments or benefits to achieve the consent of a person having control over another person, for the purpose of exploitation. Exploitation shall include, at a minimum, the exploitation of the prostitution of others or other forms of sexual exploitation, forced labour or services, slavery or practices similar to slavery, servitude or the removal of organs. This underpins the definition of offences in the Modern Slavery Act 2015. The Modern Slavery Act 2015 makes it a criminal offence to hold another person in slavery or servitude, or require them to perform forced or

Table 11.2 Smuggling and trafficking

Smuggling	Trafficking
The smuggled person in broad terms consents or agrees to what is done by the smuggler. They may have no control over specifics such as route or documentation, but they want to make the journey. Any deception is practised on third parties, such as an immigration officer	Trafficking is carried out by coercion or deception of the trafficked person
Relationship with smuggler ends when smuggled person reaches their destination	Trafficking entails subsequent exploitation of trafficked person
Smuggling entails movement across international borders	Trafficking can take place within and across national frontiers
Entry is illegal. If legal entry were possible, the smuggler would not be required	Trafficking may entail legal or illegal entry

compulsory labour (s.1). The offence of trafficking is committed where a person arranges for another to travel for the purposes of exploitation. Exploitation is slavery, servitude, forced labour, removal of organs, undue pressure to obtain services, or the person being involved in or a victim of a sexual offence (s.2).

It is important to distinguish between people smuggling and human trafficking. The Joint Parliamentary Committee on Human Rights (twenty-sixth report 2005–06) identifies some differences, which can be elaborated as shown in Table 11.2.

People smuggling involves infringement of immigration law. Trafficking entails human rights violations over and above the migration and criminal issues involved. The deaths of 23 Chinese cockle-pickers who drowned in Morecambe Bay in February 2004 focused public attention on labour exploitation by traffickers and gangmasters, and from this point government began to set up mechanisms to prevent labour exploitation and identify trafficking victims. After extensive discussion and lobbying, the UK opted into EU Directive 2011/36 on preventing and combating trafficking in human beings and protecting its victims, which requires the Member States to have criminal penalties for trafficking offences and powers to refrain from prosecuting victims of trafficking for offences committed 'as a direct consequence' of coercive acts of traffickers.

Similar provisions are contained in the Council of Europe's Convention against Human Trafficking, which took effect in the UK on 1 April 2009. In *LM, MB, DG, Talbot and Tijani v R* [2010] EWCA Crim 2327 the Court of Appeal held that the defence should have been available to women forced into prostitution who then controlled others.

The UK implemented the protective obligations of the Convention and Directive by setting up a National Referral Mechanism (NRM). The two Competent Authorities within the NRM are the UK Human Trafficking Centre and UK Visas and Immigration in the Home Office. UKVI is the Competent Authority when immigration issues are involved, and this includes where trafficking or modern slavery may be an issue as part of an asylum claim. Referrals to the Competent Authority can be made by First Responders. These include a number of NGOs as well as the police, UKVI and local authorities. The Competent Authority must decide whether there are reasonable grounds to believe that the person is a potential victim of trafficking (the 'reasonable grounds' decision). The low standard entailed at that stage is described in *R (on the application of Minh) v SSHD* [2015] EWHC (Admin) 1725.

If a 'positive' reasonable grounds decision is made, a person who has no other permission to be in the UK must be given 45 days' temporary admission as a reflection period. They will be maintained on asylum support in specialist supported accommodation. The Home Office has a discretion to extend this period, or curtail it if they consider it is no longer warranted. A reasonable grounds decision can be made whether the person has been trafficked into the UK, or has been trafficked abroad and escaped to the UK. An asylum application can proceed in parallel with an application to the NRM. Trafficking as a ground for protection is discussed in chapter 12.

The Court of Appeal held in *AS (Afghanistan) v SSHD* [2013] EWCA Civ 1469 that the fact that the Competent Authority has made a decision cannot prevent the First Tier Tribunal judge from considering the evidence, and if a perverse decision has been reached the judge may assess the facts differently for the purpose of an asylum appeal. The Tribunal cannot be used as an appeal mechanism against the Competent Authority's decision. However, a failure by the Secretary of State to apply her own policy is an error of law (following *Abdi* see chapter 7), and so 'where, as here, it is arguable that, on the facts found or accepted, the Competent Authority has reached a decision which was not open to it, that argument should be heard and taken into account' (para 18).

After information has been gathered, the Competent Authority must make a 'conclusive grounds' decision. This means that on the balance of probability the person is a victim of trafficking. The person cannot be removed from the UK until a conclusive grounds decision has been made. If conclusive grounds are found, the authority may grant discretionary leave up to 30 months depending on the circumstances, and 12 months + 1 day is standard where the applicant has agreed to help the police with inquiries. There is no appeal against a reasonable grounds or conclusive grounds decision. The only form of challenge is judicial review. See *R (on the application of AA (Iraq)) v SSHD* [2012] EWCA Civ 23 for a leading exposition of the application of the Trafficking Convention and judicial review of a decision that the applicant was not trafficked.

If there is also a successful asylum or human rights claim (see chapter 12), the trafficked person may be granted refugee status or humanitarian protection. The grant of 12 months + 1 day discretionary leave preserves an asylum seeker's appeal right against the refusal of refugee status (s 83(1)(b) 2002 Act).

Remedies for victims of trafficking not only relate to immigration status. Damages have been awarded in civil actions for false representations, false imprisonment, battery, assault, and harassment (*AT, NT, ML and AK v Dulghieru* [2009] EWHC 225 (QB)). The claimants' mental health was still suffering some years after these events, and for this they were awarded damages for pain, suffering, and loss of amenity: £125,000, £117,000, £82,000, and £97,000 to the claimants, respectively. The judge awarded further sums for injury to feelings, humiliation, loss of pride and dignity, and feelings of anger or resentment: £35,000 each to AT and ML and £30,000 each to NT and AK by way of aggravated damages.

The Modern Slavery Act 2015 includes a provision for a person who is convicted of an offence of trafficking or slavery to be ordered to pay compensation to their victim. This is a reparation order which can be made by the criminal court, and may avoid the need for the victim to take separate civil proceedings to get compensation.

Although the law has developed since ratification of the Council of Europe Treaty, practical difficulties remain in attaining protection for victims of trafficking. The Joint Committee on Human Rights reported that 'people who have been trafficked into the UK may not be asked appropriate questions by officials, and as a result will fail to be identified as victims' (para 145). Through mistrust of officials, not understanding what is happening to them, fear of reprisals, or of being returned to their home state, victims may also be unwilling to talk about being trafficked. The JCHR report cites instances of trauma to victims in giving evidence when their privacy was not respected. The Committee emphasizes the role to be played by support workers. Proper weight should be given to the evidence of professionals experienced in working with trafficking victims. In *AB v SSHD* [2015] EWHC 1490 (Admin) the trafficking decision was set aside in judicial review as the decision maker had not engaged with the opinions of psychiatrists, or Ashiana, an organization experienced in working with victims of trafficking. In *IO (Congo) v SSHD* [2006] EWCA Civ 796, social workers asserted that the appellant had probably been trafficked. All the circumstantial evidence pointed to this. The appellant herself denied it. The Court of Appeal held that there was 'real risk' that she had been trafficked, but that in order to treat this as established for the purposes of assessing her asylum claim it would have to be proved on the balance of probabilities as it was against her own assertions. In *LM, MB, DG, Talbot and Tijani*, mentioned earlier, it was clear that details of the women's experience of being trafficked only emerged slowly through the legal process. It demonstrates the need for caution in prosecuting women where there is a suspicion that they themselves may have been trafficked.

When the domestic system does not protect the victim, the ECtHR may step in, as it did in *LR v UK* (Application no. 49113/09), in which the ECtHR granted a Rule 39 (interim measures) order to LR, preventing her expulsion to Albania, where she was at risk of harm from her own family and from those who had trafficked her. LR had cooperated with the police but through no fault of hers, this did not lead to a conviction, leaving her vulnerable to retaliation from her traffickers. After the Rule 39 order, the applicant was granted refugee status.

11.6 After an asylum decision

11.6.1 Refugee status

In the cases where refugee status is granted (currently around 37 per cent of initial decisions and 35 per cent of appealed cases), five years' leave to remain in the UK is granted. At the end of that period an application can be made for indefinite leave to remain, which is likely to be granted if there has been no significant change in the refugee's country of origin or circumstances and if they do not have a criminal record.

The Refugee Convention and the Qualification Directive set out the legal consequences of recognition. Refugees have a right to the issue of a travel document, an important right bearing in mind that they may well not have a passport of their country of origin or be able to travel using it. Travel documents issued pursuant to the obligation in the Refugee Convention are recognized by signatory states, although visas are required for countries not implementing the Council of Europe Agreement on the Abolition of Visas for Refugees.

According to the Refugee Convention, refugees are entitled to social rights on favourable terms and the intention is that they should be integrated into the host society. In *ZN (Afghanistan) v ECO (Karachi)* [2010] UKSC 21 the Supreme Court ruled, interpreting the immigration rules, that a refugee who had obtained British citizenship did not need to fulfil the more onerous requirements for maintenance and accommodation in order for their family members to join them in the UK. They were still a person who had been granted refugee status, and as such should benefit from the more favourable rules applying to refugees. The government responded to this by changing the immigration rules, so as to reverse the effect of *ZN (Afghanistan) v SSHD*. The rules now say that refugee status automatically ceases upon acquisition of British citizenship (para 339BA), and that the more favourable family reunion rules only apply to those with current refugee status.

The rights listed in the Convention include civil and political rights and fundamental freedoms such as that of religion and religious education (Article 4). The Directive concentrates on social and economic rights: employment, education, accommodation, health care, and social welfare. Denial of fundamental rights would be unconstitutional in the EU, but social and economic rights have very limited protection. Some social rights in the Directive are granted on the same terms as to nationals—for example, education for children. Some are on the same terms as other third country nationals—for example, accommodation. For a really comprehensive account of Convention provisions, see Hathaway (2005).

A refugee is protected by the principle of *non-refoulement*, that is, that they may not be sent to a territory in which their life or freedom is threatened (Article 33 Refugee Convention). In addition, a recognized refugee 'lawfully in the territory' of the host state must not be expelled save on grounds of national security or public order. In *ST (Eritrea) v SSHD* [2012] UKSC 12 the Supreme Court held that the appellant, who had been found by the Tribunal to be a refugee in relation to her country of nationality, Eritrea, could nevertheless be removed to her country of former residence, Ethiopia, where it was found that she was not at risk. Although she had succeeded in the Tribunal, she had not yet been granted any form of leave to remain by the Secretary of State. Thus she was not yet 'lawfully in the territory' of the UK and so not protected by Article 32. The Supreme Court accepted that the Secretary of State was not obliged to grant her leave to remain in the UK if she could be safe in her country of former residence. ST had never lived in Eritrea.

11.6.2 Subsidiary protection

Arguments under the European Convention on Human Rights, as enacted in the Human Rights Act, run alongside an asylum appeal and must be put forward at the same time as the grounds of appeal against a refusal of asylum (often required by a 'one stop notice').

Many signatory states to the Refugee Convention make provision for a safety net status where a person is held not to qualify for asylum, but there are compelling reasons why they should not be returned to their home state. The Refugee Qualification Directive 2004/83 provides for 'subsidiary protection' (Article 18) where there are 'substantial grounds' for believing that the person concerned, if returned to their country of origin, would face a real risk of serious harm. Serious harm is defined in Article 15 as:

(a) death penalty or execution;

(b) torture or inhuman or degrading treatment or punishment;

(c) serious and individual threat to a civilian's life or person by reason of indiscriminate violence in situations of international or internal armed conflict.

One of the first decisions in the CJEU on the interpretation of the Qualification Directive concerned Article 15(c).

Key Case

C–465/07 *Elgafaji*

Mr and Mrs Elgafaji were nationals of Iraq. Mr Elgafaji, who was a Shiite Muslim, had worked for a British firm providing security for personnel transport between the airport and the 'Green Zone' in Baghdad. Mr Elgafaji's uncle, employed by the same firm, had been killed by militia, his death certificate stating that his death followed a terrorist act. A short time later, a letter threatening 'death to collaborators' was fixed to the door of the residence which Mr Elgafaji shared with his wife, a Sunni Muslim.

Mr and Mrs Elgafaji applied for temporary residence permits in the Netherlands but were refused. They challenged the refusal, arguing that Article 15(c) did not require the high degree of individualization of the threat required by Article 15(b). The Raad van State referred the question to the ECJ for a preliminary ruling.

The ECJ found that:

- the existence of a serious and individual threat to the life or person of an applicant for subsidiary protection did not require proof that the applicant was specifically targeted because of factors particular to them;
- the existence of such a threat could exceptionally be established where the degree of indiscriminate violence characterizing the armed conflict reached such a high level that there were substantial grounds for believing that a civilian would, solely on account of their presence, face a real risk of being subject to that threat.

This judgment was applied in the UK in *QD and AH (Iraq) v SSHD, UNHCR intervening* [2009] EWCA Civ 620. QD was a former Ba'ath Party member, and feared reprisals. AH's claim concerned the level of violence in his locality. The Court of Appeal held that the Directive must be given an autonomous meaning. Protection under Article 15(c), which was additional to that given by the Refugee Convention or ECHR, was derived not from international humanitarian law (as the Tribunal had found in an earlier case) but from the practice of states. The Court accepted UNHCR's submission that, for the purposes of Article 15(c), there was no requirement that the armed conflict itself must be exceptional. What was required was an intensity of indiscriminate violence great enough to meet the test spelt out by the ECJ. It followed that 'civilian' meant, not simply someone not in uniform—which might include terrorists—but only genuine non-combatants. Article 15(c) could be invoked whether the source of the violence was a single entity or two or more warring factions. The judgment of the CJEU in C-285/12 *Diakité* develops the law of Article 15 (c) consistently with the earlier cases. The CJEU held that an internal armed conflict exists, for the purposes of Article 15(c):

if a State's armed forces confront one or more armed groups or if two or more armed groups confront each other. It is not necessary for that conflict to be categorised as 'armed conflict not of an international character' under international humanitarian law; nor is it necessary to carry out, in addition to an appraisal of the level of violence present in the territory concerned, a separate assessment of the intensity of the armed confrontations, the level of organisation of the armed forces involved or the duration of the conflict. (para 35)

In country guidance cases on Afghanistan, the Upper Tribunal has determined that there is not such a high level of indiscriminate violence that a civilian would, solely by being present there, face a risk which entitled them to protection under Article 15(c)

(*AK (Article 15(c): indiscriminate violence) Afghanistan* CG [2012] UKUT 163 (IAC)). In re-lation to Iraq, the Tribunal's country guidance is that there is a state of internal armed conflict in the so-called 'contested areas' of Iraq such that 'there are substantial grounds for believing that any civilian returned there, solely on account of his or her presence there, faces a real risk of being subjected to indiscriminate violence amounting to seri-ous harm within the scope of Article 15(c) of the Qualification Directive' (*AA (Article 15(c)) Iraq* CG [2015] UKUT 544 (IAC)). They held that return to other parts of Iraq does not engage Article 15(c) as a general rule.

Subsidiary protection is called humanitarian protection in the UK, and is incorporated in the immigration rules at paras 339C–H. It may be granted when there is a finding of a risk of breach of Article 3 ECHR if the person is removed. The Directive requires that a year is the minimum leave given as humanitarian protection. In the immigration rules, five years is the norm, as for asylum. Like refugees, in the immigration rules, those with humanitarian protection are unrestricted in employment and have a right to a travel document (though not a Refugee Convention document).

Principles of internal flight and sufficiency of protection (see next chapter) are ap-plied in considering whether to grant humanitarian protection. Exclusions also apply, but are more severely drawn than for refugee status (see chapter 13). Persons excluded from humanitarian protection may be considered for a six-month period of discretion-ary leave.

Where a person fears breach of their human rights but does not qualify for asylum or humanitarian protection, it is still possible for the Secretary of State to grant leave outside the rules. From April 2003 to July 2012, leave granted because of family ties or private life in the UK was called discretionary leave, the conditions for which were set out in policy and guidance. Guidance on discretionary leave now emphasizes that its use is intended to be exceptional. The initial grant of discretionary leave has been re-duced from a norm of three years to 30 months. It does not lead to settlement until ten years have elapsed (API *Discretionary Leave* August 2015). Where children are involved their best interests must be taken into account as a primary, though not necessarily the only, consideration (s.55 Borders Citizenship and Immigration Act 2009, *ZH (Tanzania)* applied in the API para 1.4). Leave to remain on human rights grounds is discussed in chapter 5.

Where practical obstacles prevent a person from leaving the UK or being removed, for example, there are no flights to their home country, or travel documents cannot be obtained, this in itself will not entitle the person to be granted discretionary leave. A person in this situation is likely to remain on temporary admission. Discretionary leave does not give a right to be joined by family members.

11.6.3 Cessation

The Refugee Convention Article 1C makes provision for refugee status to end in certain circumstances. Most refer to the voluntary actions of the refugee. The exception is Article 1C(5), that 'because the circumstances in connection with which he has been recognized as a refugee have ceased to exist' he can no longer 'refuse to avail himself of the protection of the country of his nationality' or, if stateless, his former residence. The host state bears the burden of proving this, and refugees should not be subject to continual examination of their status as this undermines the very security the Conven-tion aims to give (see the *UNHCR Handbook* para 135). These conditions are reproduced in the Qualification Directive, and in the immigration rules implementing it. The rules include that there has been a 'significant and non-temporary change' in the conditions in the refugee's country of origin. The Directive and rules omit one provision of the Convention, which is that there are 'compelling reasons arising from previous persecution' for not returning to the country of origin. This means that the Directive and rules do not give the refugee the opportunity to argue against losing their refugee status because of the severity of their previous experience. However, in the first case exercising its new jurisdiction in refugee law, the CJEU set a high standard for domestic authorities who wish to assert that refugee status has ceased:

 **Key Case**

C–175/08 *Aydin Salahadin Abdulla*

The appellants in the main proceedings had been granted refugee status in Germany, as people subject to persecution from the former regime in Iraq. When the regime changed, their refugee status was revoked. The German courts referred the interpretation of the cessation clause to the CJEU, which ruled that:

- refugee status ceases to exist when, having regard to a change of circumstances of a significant and non-temporary nature in the home state, the circumstances which justified the person's fear of persecution no longer exist and that person has no other reason to fear being persecuted within the meaning of Article 2(c) of Directive 2004/83;

- for the purposes of assessing a change of circumstances, the competent authorities of the Member State must verify, having regard to the refugee's individual situation, that the actors of protection have taken reasonable steps to prevent the persecution, that they operate an effective legal system for the detection, prosecution, and punishment of acts constituting persecution, and that the national concerned will have access to such protection if he ceases to have refugee status.

11.7 Fresh claims

If new evidence comes to light after an appeal has been lost, or there is a change of circumstances for the asylum seeker or in their country of origin, a fresh claim for asylum or human rights protection may be made. This will only be considered when new submissions are significantly different from the material which has previously been considered, as prescribed in para 353 of the immigration rules:

The submissions will only be significantly different if the content:

1. has not already been considered;

2. is taken together with the previously considered material creates a realistic prospect of success, notwithstanding its rejection.

Given the length of time spent in the UK by many asylum seekers whose claim has failed, and the developments that can happen in that time, the opportunity to make a fresh claim is important. A fresh claim is made by taking further representations in person to a designated regional office of the Home Office. Since March 2015 this is Liverpool. There is no time limit for a decision to be made, though many refusals are issued quickly. Possible outcomes are: the claim is accepted and status granted, the claim is rejected, or the representations are accepted as constituting a fresh claim, but rejected on the merits. In the last-mentioned case there is a right of appeal to the Tribunal. There is no right of appeal against a decision not to recognize representations as constituting a fresh claim, and the only avenue to challenge this refusal is judicial review.

R (on the application of MN(Tanzania)) v SSHD [2011] EWCA Civ 193 confirmed that the proper approach for the courts when considering a challenge to a refusal to treat representations as a fresh claim is the usual judicial review standard (the *Wednesbury* standard) applied with 'anxious scrutiny'. This means in this context that the Court must ask itself whether the Secretary of State was entitled, on the evidence, to reach the conclusion that there was no realistic prospect of an immigration judge, applying the rule of anxious scrutiny, thinking that the appellant would be exposed to a real risk of persecution on return.

The House of Lords in *ZT (Kosovo)* held that the Secretary of State should have applied para 353 to further submissions made in a case where the earlier claim had been certified as clearly unfounded. The difference in practice between certifying a claim certified as clearly unfounded and using para 353 is that the former attracts an out of country right of appeal, whereas a refusal to treat further submissions as a fresh claim attracts no right of appeal. The majority thought that there was a difference between the question of whether there was no realistic prospect of success (para 353), and whether a claim was clearly unfounded (s 94). The Court of Appeal in *MN (Tanzania)* endorsed that difference.

In *ZA (Nigeria) v SSHD* [2010] EWCA Civ 926 the Court of Appeal confirmed that the refusal to treat further submissions as a fresh claim did not amount to an immigration decision attracting a right of appeal. Furthermore, the Court held that the existence of the power to certify clearly unfounded claims (s 94 of the 2002 Act) did not deprive para 353 of meaning, because s 94 referred to claims which had been decided on their merits, whereas para 353 gave a power not to consider submissions to be a claim at all. This decision followed on the Supreme Court judgment in *BA (Nigeria) and PE (Cameroon) v SSHD* [2009] UKSC 7 that where there had been an appealable decision (a refusal to revoke a deportation order) the Secretary of State could not deny the appellants a right of appeal by treating the appellants' representations as further submissions not amounting to a fresh claim.

In *R (on the application of ST) v SSHD* [2012] EWHC 988 (Admin) the Court reviewed and applied the authorities on the judicial review standard for challenging the refusal to treat representations as a fresh claim. The Court observed:

[A] claim may be significantly different if its factual or legal basis is significantly different from the first claim. It may also be significantly different if the decision-maker, exercising anxious scrutiny, considers that the new claim and anything else reasonably known to the decision-maker shows that there is a reasonable prospect of showing that significant adverse credibility findings made when the first claim was rejected were not justified or that there is uncertainty as to the reasonableness or fairness of those findings. (para 71(7))

Given the importance of credibility findings, this is a significant observation.

For a full account of the law relating to fresh claims, reference should be made to a practitioner work such as Macdonald.

11.8 Administration of asylum claims

The administration of the asylum system has suffered from massive problems. These were characterized by the Home Affairs Select Committee in 2013 as the length of time taken to receive a decision; the continuation of thousands of cases in a backlog, despite programmes to clear them; the 'culture of disbelief'; the quality of decision-making and lack of auditing; the inappropriateness or difficulty of procedures, for instance the requirement that all asylum seekers claim in Croydon; provision of interpreters with the wrong language or dialect; persistent inefficiency, such as people who reported regularly to the Home Office nevertheless being recorded as untraceable, and so on (House of Commons Home Affairs Committee, *Asylum,* Seventh Report of Session 2013–14 HC 71).

The issues about the quality of decision-making have been addressed earlier in this chapter. Applicants have also used the courts to challenge some of the persistent problems in the administration of the system, although the opportunities to do so seem to be narrowing.

11.8.1 Delays and mistakes

The administration of asylum claims has been subject to significant delays and mistakes. On the whole, the approach of the courts is that it is not their role to intervene in the asylum process to provide a remedy for maladministration. For instance, in *R (on the application of S, H & Q) v SSHD* [2009] EWCA Civ 14, S's Statement of Evidence (SEF) was not linked to his file. His claim was refused on the basis that he had not sent the SEF (a 'non-compliance' refusal) but he was not notified of that. In 2002, his solicitors were informed both that his claim had been refused because of a failure to return the SEF, and that the claim was being considered. In 2005, S applied for indefinite leave on the basis that he should have been granted exceptional leave based on a policy in existence at the time of the original non-compliance refusal, in which case he would now have qualified for ILR. The Court held that the Home Office's failure to implement its policies correctly did not mean that ILR should be granted.

S and the other applicants in that case were attempting to rely on the case of *Rashid*.

 **Key Case**

R (on the application of Rashid) v SSHD [2005] EWCA Civ 744

Mr Rashid was an Iraqi Kurd who sought asylum in the UK in December 2001. At that time there was a Home Office policy that people who had a well-founded fear in other parts of Iraq would not be forcibly returned on the basis they could find safety in the Kurdish Autonomous Zone (KAZ). The policy was based on the stance of the Kurdish authorities who, because of a lack of infrastructure and resources after the 1991 Gulf War, were not able to admit people who had been living in other parts of Iraq. The policy was not applied to Mr Rashid and his asylum claim was refused within a week on the basis he could relocate in the KAZ.

Six months later, in correspondence, the Home Office reiterated the refusal. A year later, on appeal to the adjudicator, relocation to the KAZ was fully argued by the Home Office Presenting Officer. The policy was still in force. The Home Office resisted an application for leave to appeal, then unsuccessfully opposed an application for permission for judicial review on the same point. Until late February 2003, the argument was maintained. There were two other applicants in a situation legally identical to Mr Rashid, M and A. By letter of 6 March 2003, A's legal representatives were told that the Secretary of State was not, 'as a matter of policy . . . relying on the availability of internal relocation' to the KAZ and that A would be granted refugee status. On 12 March 2003, Mr Rashid's solicitors wrote to the Treasury solicitors asking that he too be granted refugee status, as the Home Office had already accepted that his case was on the same point. On 21 March 2003, it was announced that, because of the military action in Iraq, decision-making on Iraqi nationals had been suspended. The suspension lasted until June 2003. The Home Office agreed in March to reconsider Mr Rashid's case, but did not do so until January 2004, by which time, they said, he could return, and he was refused refugee status.

The Court of Appeal found that Mr Rashid had a legitimate expectation that the KAZ policy would be applied to him, and that the repeated failure to do so, without explanation, was 'conspicuous unfairness amounting to an abuse of power'.

A number of attempts to follow *Rashid* have failed in cases where delay in making a decision has meant that a different policy has been applied to the applicant than would have been if the decision had been made more promptly. *Rashid* was followed successfully, if success is an appropriate word, where once again, three Iraqi Kurds had been refused asylum on the basis they could relocate in the KAZ, in ignorance of the same policy (*A, H and AH v SSHD* [2006] EWHC 526 (Admin)). As in *Rashid*, the Court held that only a finding of extreme unfairness could warrant going against the *Ravichandran* principle, which entails that asylum decisions are to be made on the basis of the situation as it stands at the time of the hearing. Application of that principle would mean that if it is safe at the time of the hearing the claimants would be expected to return.

In 2006, the Home Office issued a policy bulletin to provide guidance to decision-makers on the implications of the judgments in *Rashid* and *R (A) (H) and (AH)*. It said that:

we should not seek to enforce the removal of failed asylum seekers whose cases have the potential to fall within the scope of the *Rashid* judgment and/or the cases of *R (A): (H) and (AH)*, pending consideration of their cases.

An Annex to the Iraq policy bulletin set out factual requirements for inclusion within it, namely that the application was decided between April 1991 and 20 February 2003, that the applicant was accepted as being from government-controlled Iraq (GCI), that s/he was found to have no well-founded fear of persecution for a Convention reason, and had not been granted four years' ELR.

In subsequent case law the courts have generally declined to widen the application of the concept of 'conspicuous unfairness amounting to an abuse of power'. Most recently, in the context of a judgment on systemic failure to conduct family tracing the Supreme Court took the opportunity to say that the *Rashid* exception lacks a satisfactory principle and should no longer be followed. The Supreme Court reiterated that a grant of leave is not a remedy for administrative failures, and that a grant of asylum should be made based on the question of whether the individual is a risk of persecution, not as compensation for Home Office failures. The challenge in the Supreme Court came about as the culmination of challenges by young people from Afghanistan in particular after it came to light that from 2006 to 2010 the Home Office had systematically failed to comply with the duty to attempt to trace the family of unaccompanied asylum-seeking children. This duty is imposed by the Asylum Seeker Reception Conditions Regulations 2005, implementing the EC Reception Conditions Directive. It had been argued that the failure to attempt to trace family members undermined or jeopardized the position of the young people concerned, to the extent that the *Ravichandran* principle should be set aside, and leave granted to them. The Supreme Court held that the fact that the Secretary of State failed properly to discharge the obligation to trace family members did not affect the credibility of the asylum claim. The purpose of tracing a child's family was for the child's welfare in promoting reunification. In the same appeal the Supreme

Court also held that the appellants were not deprived of their right to appeal against asylum refusal by virtue of the fact that they were given a short period of UASC leave.

11.8.2 **The legacy programme**

Challenges relating to the so-called legacy programme were a special instance of delays and mistakes. In 2006 the Home Office identified that there was a backlog of some 450,000 unresolved asylum cases. A new unit, the Casework Resolution Directorate, was set up to resolve all these cases by July 2011. Resolution meant grant of leave or removal (ICIBI 2012b and *R (on the application of Prenga) v SSHD* [2013] EWHC 1891 (Admin)). Included within the programme were cases where the asylum claim had been refused, but where the applicant had not yet left the UK or where further representations had been made. Cases were also considered as concluded because of data errors, duplicate records, or because applicants could not be traced. To cut a long story short, not all cases were resolved by that date, and in April 2011 147,000 unresolved cases (this included both migration and asylum cases) were transferred to a new 'Case Assurance and Audit Unit', since renamed the 'Older Live Cases Unit'.

Legal challenges relating to the legacy programme centred on the following main issues:

- failure to prioritize a case according to the published criteria;
- from July 2011 a practice of granting three years' discretionary leave instead of indefinite leave to remain;
- failure to resolve a case before the July 2011 deadline.

Since the legacy programme promised to deal with a backlog, it was frustrating for those whose cases had been waiting many years, but who did not fit its published priorities. In *HG, AK, AM, MN, IR, HW v SSHD* [2008] EWHC 2685 (Admin), the Court held that the claimants, whose claims had been outstanding since 2000, and who had missed the benefit of a policy which would have been applied to them if they had had an earlier decision, could not claim priority in the legacy system to move their cases further up the queue. It was not a breach of public law principles for their cases to be dealt with in accordance with the priority accorded them by the legacy policy.

The question of what constituted a lawful conclusion of a case within the legacy programme was concluded in *SH (Iran) & Anor v SSHD* [2014] EWCA Civ 1469. The Court of Appeal said:

The position with regard to legacy cases on these particular points is now to be taken as laid to rest. There have been many decisions in the last two years on the salient points, all of which are in substantial accord. There is no separate legacy 'policy'. There is no basis for relying on delay as, in itself, a ground for obtaining leave to remain. There is in the ordinary case no relevant legitimate expectation, other than that the case will be considered on applicable law and policy at the time the decision is made. There is no basis for saying that there is a commitment on the part of the Secretary of State to 'conclude' a case either by effecting actual removal or by granting leave to remain. (para 65)

11.9 **Conclusion**

This chapter may illustrate that the procedural hurdles to be overcome are just as much of a challenge to establishing a refugee claim as satisfying the legal definition.

QUESTIONS

1 What would be your priorities for change in the asylum system?

2 Critically assess para 339L(iv) of the Immigration Rules.

 online resource centre For guidance on answering questions, visit the Online Resource Centre www.oxfordtextbooks.co.uk/orc/clayton7e/.

FURTHER READING

ADCS and Home Office (2015) *Age Assessment: Joint Working Guidance.*

Amnesty International (2004) *Get it Right: How Home Office Decision-making Fails Refugees,* Amnesty International UK.

Asylum Aid (1995) *No Reason at all.*

Asylum Aid (1999) *Still no Reason at all.*

Briddick, Catherine (2010) 'Trafficking and the National Referral Mechanism' *Women's Asylum News* (London: Asylum Aid), pp. 1–4.

Cohen, Juliet (2001) 'Questions of Credibility: Omissions, Discrepancies and Errors of Recall in the Testimony of Asylum Seekers' *International Journal of Refugee Law* vol. 13, no. 3, pp. 293–309.

Costello, Cathryn (2005) 'The Asylum Procedures Directive and the Proliferation of Safe Country Practices: Deterrence, Deflection and the Dismantling of International Protection?' *European Journal of Migration and Law* vol. 7, no. 1, March 2005, pp. 35–70 (36).

Den Heijer, Maarten (2010) 'Europe Beyond its Borders: Refugee and Human Rights Protection in Extraterritorial Immigration Control' *Extraterritorial Immigration Control: Legal Challenges* Ryan, Bernard and Shah, Prakash (eds) (Leiden: Martinus Nijhoff).

Detention Action (2011) *Fast Track to Despair; The unnecessary detention of asylum seekers* (London: Detention Action).

Ensor, Jonathan, Shah, Amanda and Grillo, Mirella (2006) 'Simple Myths and Complex Realities—Seeking Truth in the Face of Section 8' *Journal of Immigration, Asylum and Nationality Law* vol. 20, no. 2, pp. 95–111.

Errera, Roger (2011) 'The CJEU and subsidiary protection: reflections on *Elgafaji* and after' *International Journal of Refugee Law* vol. 23, no. 1, pp. 93–112.

Hathaway, James C. (2005) *The Right of Refugees under International Law* (Cambridge: Cambridge University Press).

Herlihy, Jane and Turner, Stuart W. (2009) 'The Psychology of Seeking Protection' *International Journal of Refugee Law* vol. 21, no. 2, pp. 171–92.

Home Affairs Committee: *Asylum,* Seventh Report of 2013–14, HC 71, 11 October 2013.

Independent Asylum Commission (2008) *Fit for Purpose Yet?*

Independent Asylum Commission (2008) *Saving Sanctuary.*

Independent Chief Inspector of Borders and Immigration (2012a) *Asylum: A Thematic Inspection of the Detained Fast Track,* ICIBI.

Independent Chief Inspector of Borders and Immigration (2012b) *UK Border Agency's Handling of Legacy Asylum and Migration Cases, March to July 2012,* ICIBI.

Millbank, Jenni (2009) '"The Ring of Truth": A Case Study of Credibility Assessment in Particular Social Group Refugee Determinations' *International Journal of Refugee Law* vol. 21, no. 1, March, pp. 1–33.

National Audit Office (2004) *Improving the Speed and Quality of Asylum Decisions,* report by the Comptroller and Auditor General HC 535 Session 2003–04, 23 June 2004.

Norman, Steve (2007), 'Assessing the Credibility of Refugee Applicants: A Judicial Perspective' *International Journal of Refugee Law* vol. 19, no. 2, pp. 273–92.

Ryan, Bernard and Mitsilegas, Valsamis (2010) *Extraterritorial Immigration Control: Legal Challenges* (Leiden: Martinus Nijhoff).

Shaw, Jan and Kaye, Mike (2013) *A Question of Credibility: Why so many initial asylum decisions are overturned on appeal in the UK* Amnesty International and Still Human Still Here.

Smith, Ellie (2004) *Right First Time* (London: Medical Foundation).

Sweeney, James (2009) 'Credibility, Proof and Refugee Law' *International Journal of Refugee Law* vol. 21, no. 4, pp. 700–26.

Thomas, Robert (2009) 'Consistency in Asylum Adjudication: Country guidance and the asylum process in the United Kingdom' *International Journal of Refugee Law* vol. 20, pp. 489–532.

Tsangarides, Natasha (2009) 'The Politics of Knowledge: An Examination of the Use of Country Information in the Asylum Determination Process' (2009) *Journal of Immigration, Asylum and Nationality Law* vol. 23, no. 3, pp. 252–63.

Tsangarides, Natasha (2010) *The Refugee Roulette: The Role of Country Information in Refugee Status Determination* (London: Immigration Advisory Service).

Trueman, Trevor (2009), 'Reasons for Refusal: An Audit of 200 Refusals of Ethiopian Asylum Seekers in England' *Journal of Immigration, Asylum and Nationality Law* vol. 23, no. 3, pp. 281–308.

UNCAT (2013) *Concluding observations on the fifth periodic report of the United Kingdom*, adopted by the Committee at its fiftieth session (6–31 May).

UNHCR (2013) *Beyond Proof: Credibility Assessment in EU Asylum Systems*.

UNHCR (2011) *Statistical Online Population Database, United Nations High Commissioner for Refugees* (UNHCR), data extracted: 12 October 2011.

Yeo, Colin (ed.) (2005) *Country Guideline Cases: Benign and Practical?* (London: IAS).

12

....

Claims for international protection

SUMMARY

This chapter examines what needs to be established in order to obtain the status of 'refugee', according to Article 1A of the UN Convention Relating to the Status of Refugees 1951 and the Refugee Qualification Directive (QD) EC 2004/83, referred to as the QD. It also considers applications for protection by victims of trafficking, who may go through a parallel process to the asylum system. The chapter begins with setting out the legal context of refugee claims in the UK, and the body of the chapter follows the structure of Article 1A of the Refugee Convention.

12.1 Refugees and asylum seekers

Millions of people face persecution worldwide. This is often on account of their political or religious beliefs, their race or nationality, or another fundamental quality such as their gender or sexuality. The purpose of refugee law is to protect people in this position. In the UK, whilst someone is applying for this protection, they are called an 'asylum seeker', although the term 'refugee' is also correct, as refugee status is declaratory, that is, a grant of refugee status is a recognition that someone is already (and probably has been since they left their home country) a refugee.

The main present-day causes of refugee movements are armed conflict, large-scale human rights abuses, and environmental degradation exacerbated by conflict and climate change. People leaving their homes for any of these reasons may or may not be in fear of persecution as defined within the 1951 UN Convention Relating to the Status of Refugees, known as the Refugee Convention.

The UN High Commission for Refugees, UNHCR, is the body given the task, worldwide, of protecting refugees and addressing the issues which give rise to refugee movements. By the middle of 2015, the total population of displaced people was the highest since 1992. This included 20.2 million refugees, 993,600 asylum seekers, and 34 million people forced to flee within the borders of their own countries. The figure for refugees includes people in 'refugee-like situations' and those who have been granted protective status under international provisions including the 1951 Refugee Convention. In 2014, forced displacement was at the highest levels on record. For over three decades Afghanistan was the country producing the highest number of refugees, but in 2014 it was overtaken by Syria. The country hosting the largest number of refugees is Turkey (UNHCR 2015).

12.1.1 Asylum and migration

The distinction between seeking asylum and other reasons for migration is a modern one, imposed in law, politics, and administration. In the experience of those who are moving, however, the distinction is not necessarily clear cut, and in earlier times, no such distinction was made even in law. Stevens (in Nicholson and Twomey 1998) says:

> There is evidence to suggest that England was acting as a country of refuge from as early as the 13th century. Until the late 18th century, however, the word 'refugee' had not become a generic term; rather, individuals fleeing from persecution or oppression were viewed, alongside other foreigners, as 'aliens' with nothing to distinguish the normal migrant from those with cause to escape their countries of origin.

In Shah's discussion of the consequences of the Africanization polices pursued by Kenya, Tanzania, and Uganda in the 1960s he makes the point that those Asian citizens of the UK and Colonies who were forced to leave East Africa were, in a practical sense, refugees (2000:77). The focus at the time was on Britain's obligations to its nationals, but flight from such discrimination is a search for asylum. As we have seen in chapters 1 and 3, the situation was dealt with by way of immigration restrictions. However, the Africanization policies which forced them out may be compared with the Serbianization policies which forced those of Albanian descent to leave Kosovo in search of asylum in the 1990s and who were treated as asylum seekers in the UK. The policies were characterized by favouring Africans (or Serbs) over Asians (or Albanians) in matters such as employment, business, and public office.

The House of Commons Home Affairs Committee noted:

> The difficulty of distinguishing between economic and non-economic causes of migration is compounded by the fact that the two categories may frequently overlap. Some refugees are undoubtedly motivated solely by the impossibility of continuing to live without persecution in their own countries. Some may be fleeing persecution in their homeland and be seeking a better job and income than is available there. Some may be primarily seeking to improve their economic position which is limited by the political or economic instability in their country of origin. Yet others will have identified the asylum system as a means of gaining access to the economic prosperity and welfare systems of Western Europe. (Session 2003–04 Second Report, *Asylum Applications*, HC 218 para 42)

However, the law draws a bright line, and whether a person gets refugee status is a matter of whether they are found to fit the legal definition in the Refugee Convention.

12.1.2 Political nature of asylum

The grant of asylum implies criticism of the state of origin, as recognized by the Court of Appeal in *Krotov v SSHD* [2004] EWCA Civ 69: 'it is in the very nature of adjudication upon asylum issues that the tribunals or courts concerned with them are, for the purposes of surrogate protection underlying the 1951 Convention, obliged to examine and adjudicate upon events internal to another state' (para 42). Accepting that someone has a well-founded fear of being persecuted in their country of origin is an acknowledgement that the host state is offering protection where the country of origin has failed to do so. This is a humanitarian act, and thus should not be construed as a hostile action. As Dummett and Nicol say, quoting Lauterpacht: 'An enemy of his government is not an enemy of mankind' (1990:144). Unfortunately, sometimes an asylum claim which fails is treated as a hostile act committed by the asylum seeker themselves. In such a case there is a risk that someone whose asylum claim has failed may face persecution on returning to their country of origin for having made a claim. The question then is whether the failed asylum claim itself can give rise to a claim for asylum (see e.g., *BK (DRC) v SSHD* [2008] EWCA Civ 1322 and *KB (Failed asylum seekers and forced returnees) Syria* CG [2012] UKUT 00426, at 12.4.4.1).

It follows from Lauterpacht's principle that, not only should a home state allow an asylum claim to be made without taking revenge, but also that governments should not band together against the asylum seeker. Lauterpacht also says that the international community is not one of mutual insurance for the maintenance of established governments and that treason is not an international crime. However, in today's political climate, countries increasingly work together in the interests of national security and the fight against terrorism. For instance, the definition of 'national security' used in the House of Lords judgment in *Rehman v SSHD* [2001] 3 WLR 877 asserts that a threat to the security of one nation is a threat to all. This theme is explored more in chapter 13 in the context of exclusion from asylum and membership of organizations proscribed as terrorist.

Despite the humanitarian principles, there is no doubt that the grant of asylum is intimately connected with politics. Macdonald makes no bones about this:

The recognition rate for refugees has less to do with merits than with politics. Thus between 1989 and 1998 Canada granted refugee status to over 80% of applicants from Sri Lanka, France to 74%, and the UK to 1%: Refugee Council response to the Home Secretary's Lisbon Proposals, January 2001. (2001:468 n 2)

More recently, the European Court of Human Rights observed that '[a]n asylum system with a rate of recognition not exceeding 1 percent is suspect per se in terms of the fairness of the procedure', contrasting Greece's 1 per cent recognition rate with that of 60 per cent in Malta (*MSS v Belgium and Greece* [2011] ECHR 108).

12.1.3 Refugees in the European Union

The asylum system of the European Union (EU) faced an overwhelming challenge in 2015 when an unprecedented one million people crossed the Mediterranean or land borders into the EU, fleeing 'persecution, conflict and poverty' (UNHCR 2015). The so-called 'refugee crisis' has brought a new challenge to the operation of the 'Dublin' system (see chapter 11), the capacity of asylum processing systems, the provision of reception facilities, the open borders within the Schengen group of countries and the common operation of a European Asylum System. European politicians have questioned whether the people arriving are indeed refugees or economic migrants. Commentators have pointed out that for instance in the case of Syria, those fleeing are generally in fear of being killed because of the religious or political agenda of the attacker. This would make them refugees. Refugee law, as well as well as the physical systems, is under pressure.

12.2 Legal basis of asylum

The legal concept of asylum is nowhere near as old as the practice of seeking it. Dummett and Nicol (1990:143) say that 'the granting of asylum to refugees is as old as the concept of sovereign states'. The legal idea was originally conceived as a matter between states, not, as we tend to see it now, as a matter of an individual's claim for protection from a particular country. The original idea still has importance.

A national has the right to expect protection from their government. One way of looking at refugee status is that it steps in when that relationship has broken down to the extent that the state is not giving protection. Traditionally, the right involved in asylum is the right of the state to grant asylum, not the right of the asylum seeker to receive it (see, for instance, Grahl-Madsen, *The Status of Refugees in International Law* (1972)). The state owes its nationals a duty of protection, and nationals owe a duty of allegiance, but the state cannot insist on its nationals being returned to its territory (except in legally controlled extradition proceedings); another state can assert the right to give them asylum. The Universal Declaration of Human Rights 1948 Article 14 recognizes the right to 'seek and enjoy' asylum, but this is not a right to *be granted* asylum. Indeed, Shah (2000:61) recounts how at the stage of negotiating the terms of the Declaration a British amendment removed the words 'to be granted', substituting 'enjoy'. This means to be able to benefit from the status once it is granted, but not to be granted it. Member States of the EU are bound by the Refugee QD Article 13, which says that Member States 'shall grant' asylum to those who qualify for it. Also, in the EU, Article 18 of the Charter of Fundamental Rights says that the right to asylum 'shall be guaranteed with due respect for the rules of the Refugee Convention'.

12.2.1 Refugee Convention

The 1951 Refugee Convention sets out an internationally agreed definition of who is a refugee and standards for treatment of refugees. The Convention was originally drafted to deal with the displacement of people as a result of the Second World War. It restricted the definition of refugees to those whose fear of persecution arose from events occurring in Europe before 1 January 1951. The Protocol of 1967 removed the time restriction and promoted a gradual removal of the geographical restriction but the refugee definition was not changed. The Convention was also drafted in the light of growing tension between East and West Europe, and was an instrument by which Western governments could prevent Communist ones from compelling the return of political dissidents.

The terms of the Refugee Convention do not lend themselves easily to some of the present-day situations which force people to leave their homes, and the majority of uprooted people in the world do not apply for legal status through the Refugee Convention. People who have fled intolerable conditions but not used the Convention are referred to as *de facto* refugees, a much larger group than Convention, called *de jure*, refugees.

According to UNHCR figures, around 1.7 million people submitted individual applications for asylum or refugee status in 2014 (the highest on record). Applications for individual status under the Refugee Convention in the UK, at around 25,000 per annum, are a tiny part of this global situation.

As the case law of the Refugee Convention is developed in signatory states rather than an international court, there are some differences in interpretation between states. Consistency, however, is considered desirable. As the House of Lords in *Adan v SSHD* [2001] 1 All ER 593 affirmed, the meaning of the Convention is an autonomous meaning, in accordance with its purposes to provide an effective system of refugee protection, and should not differ between states. In the EU, it is intended that there will be consistency of meaning to give effect to the Common European Asylum System (CEAS). The relationship between the Refugee Convention, EU, and domestic law is considered at 12.2.2. Case law of other jurisdictions, particularly New Zealand and Australia, is referred to in UK courts and tribunals as an aid to developing the law on new or contested points. The *UNHCR Handbook on Procedures and Criteria for Determining Refugee Status* is a recognized international aid to interpretation of the Refugee Convention.

12.2.1.1 Non-refoulement: Refugee Convention Article 33

The obligation which is central to the whole scheme of refugee protection is that of *non-refoulement*, imported into the QD by Article 21. Article 33 says:

No Contracting State shall expel or return (*refouler*) a refugee in any manner whatsoever to the frontiers of territories where his life or freedom would be threatened on account of his race, religion, nationality, membership of a particular social group or political opinion.

Refoulement can happen directly, by putting someone on a plane to their home country, or more controversially it is said that it may be done indirectly, by making their life so miserable and impossible that the better choice is to return and risk persecution. In this latter respect, some of the UK's legal provisions denying welfare support to asylum seekers have attracted adverse comment (see, for instance, Harvey in Twomey and Nicolson 1998). The obligation of *non-refoulement* applies to people seeking refugee status as well as those who are granted it, until their claim is determined (Goodwin-Gill 1996:141).

One of the most difficult issues in present refugee law and practice is the question of whether Article 33 is limited to those who have arrived in the territory of the contracting state. It is clear that the Refugee Convention does not apply to people who are still in their country of origin (*R v Immigration Officer at Prague Airport ex p European Roma Rights Centre* [2004] UKHL 55) and does apply once the asylum seeker reaches the territory of a destination state. However, the question of responsibility when asylum seekers are in transit is less clear. We have seen in chapters 6 and 11 how visa rules, airline liaison schemes, juxtaposed controls, and carrier sanctions can prevent asylum seekers from ever reaching the territory (see Blake in Twomey and Nicholson 1998). Australia has openly adopted policies of offshore processing (the 'Pacific solution'), beginning with its notorious refusal to land the Norwegian ship the *Tampa*, which had rescued hundreds of asylum seekers from drowning. Despite international criticism and partially successful constitutional challenges in the Australian courts, the Refugee Convention did not avail the travellers. 'Offshore processing' continues in Nauru and Papua New Guinea although it is controversial.

The US Supreme Court in *Sale, Acting Commissioner, INS v Haitian Centers Council* 113 S Ct 2549 (1993) ruled that the Convention did not apply outside US territorial waters, and so the US did not act unlawfully in intercepting refugees on board ships from Haiti and returning them to Haiti. This decision has been criticized but no binding alternative authority has been established, although an Advisory Opinion requested from UNHCR cogently argues that the prohibition of *refoulement* applies 'wherever a State exercises jurisdiction, including at the frontier, on the high seas or on the territory of another State' (UNHCR 2007:12). Den Heijer argues that the US Supreme Court placed too much importance on minority comments in the drafting history of the Convention, that it mistook the meaning of the word *refoulement*, and that the decision conflicts with the generally accepted notion that obligations in human rights treaties are not usually restricted to the territory of contracting states.

In an important judgment in 2012, the ECtHR held that it was a breach of the ECHR Protocol 4 prohibition against the collective expulsion of aliens when Italy intercepted refugees at sea and returned them to Libya (*Hirsi Jamaa v Italy* Application no. 27765/09). The events took place on board ships that were flying the Italian flag. The ECtHR noted that international law stipulates that a vessel sailing on the high seas is subject to the exclusive jurisdiction of the state whose flag it is flying. This meant that the actions of officials on board the ship were an exercise of Italy's jurisdiction. Thus those officials were bound to respond to the claims of the passengers for asylum and human rights protection, and not return them to the port they had left. The basis of the decision in the ECtHR is different from that of the Refugee Convention. The Refugee Convention contains no provision on the extent of jurisdiction, and the only guide to the limits of the state's responsibility is judicial interpretation of Article 33. The ECtHR contains a provision on jurisdiction which is accepted to be primarily territorial but with exceptions which *Hirsi Jamaa* developed.

Despite this ruling, responsibility for the safety of travellers by sea continues to be contentious and problematic. In August 2013 the Italian government ordered a Liberian commercial ship to take rescued passengers back to their port of departure in Libya. The vessel was on the high seas heading for Malta, but Malta was reported to have denied the vessel entry to its waters (Migrants at Sea August 2013). In October 2013 300 people died near the Italian coast when a boat carrying 500 travellers, mainly from Eritrea and Somalia, caught fire and sank. The people on board were burning a sheet to catch the attention of rescuers.

EU bodies including its border agency, Frontex, have not established a single clear mechanism for attempting to prevent these tragedies. This is partly because search and rescue continues to be outside the competence of the EU, and is the responsibility of coastal states. Italy instituted its Mare Nostrum programme which rescued migrants and arrested traffickers. After a year, in November 2014, Italy ended the programme, citing lack of international support. Frontex, the EU border agency, followed Mare Nostrum with a low level coastal patrol (Operation Triton). At the same time the UK, along with other EU governments, controversially withdrew its support for the Frontex mission. European governments were ambivalent about devoting resources to saving lives since they claimed that increasing the chance of a safe landing would act as a 'pull factor' to Europe. In 2015, over 3,700 people died at sea trying to reach Europe.

International law (e.g., the International Convention for the Safety of Life at Sea 1974) imposes obligations on the masters of ships which are alerted to those in danger at sea, and in the first half of 2015 merchant ships rescued more people in distress than did Frontex. The obligations on ships' masters are limited and are purely humanitarian. They apply regardless of the nationality of the person or the circumstances in which they are found. Current case law in the UK holds that the protection from *refoulement* does not prevent someone who would qualify for refugee status from being sent to another country which would accept them and where they are not at risk. This can arise in the case of dual nationality or where a refugee was habitually resident in a different country from that of which they are a national (*RR (refugee—safe third country) Syria* [2010] UKUT 422 (IAC) and *ST (Eritrea) v SSHD* [2012] UKSC 12).

12.2.2 Directly effective EU law

In the EU, the Refugee QDs govern the interpretation of the Convention in Member States. The first QD (2004/83) was implemented in the UK by the Refugee or Person in Need of International Protection (Qualification) Regulations 2006, SI 2006/2525 ('the 2006 regulations') and changes to the immigration rules. The effect is that asylum law has been placed on a legislative footing and the Home Office and courts must follow the regulations which implement the Directive. The UK has not opted into the recast QD 2011/95 EU. Additionally, with the Lisbon Treaty, the Court of Justice of the EU acquired jurisdiction in immigration and asylum matters. Accordingly, judgments of the CJEU are binding. See, for instance, *NS* at 11.3.3 and *Elgafaji* at 11.6.2 in chapter 11.

The immigration rules now set out in unprecedented detail the criteria for granting asylum or humanitarian protection in the UK. They state that asylum claims will be decided in accordance with the Refugee Convention (para 328) and that asylum will be granted if the claimant is found to be a refugee in accordance with the regulations (para 334).

Where there are gaps in the rules or regulations, the Directive is directly effective and can be drawn upon (e.g., in *AD* [2007] UKAIT 00065 the Directive's definition of 'family member' was relied upon as there was none in the immigration rules).

The QD gives an EU-wide interpretation of all aspects of the definition of a refugee. The relationship between the Refugee Convention and the QD is addressed in general terms in Joined Cases C-199/12 to C-201/12, *X, Y and Z v Minister voor Immigratie en Asiel* where the CJEU says:

39 It is apparent from recitals 3, 16 and 17 in the preamble to Directive 2004/83 that the Geneva Convention constitutes the cornerstone of the international legal regime for the protection of refugees . . .
40 The Directive must, for that reason, be interpreted in the light of its general scheme and purpose, and in a manner consistent with the Geneva Convention and the other relevant treaties referred to in Article 78(1) TFEU.

Where the Directive is more favourable to refugees than the Refugee Convention and its case law, it is binding (*SS (Libya) v SSHD* [2011] EWCA Civ 1547 para 25). The rights for refugees once status is awarded are, in the QD Article 20, made explicitly subject to any greater rights granted by the Convention. This includes, in Article 21, the right to *non-refoulement*.

The CJEU jurisdiction over immigration and asylum offers the first binding supranational source of refugee law. The Court's judgments have the potential to establish Europe-wide norms which integrate human rights protection into immigration and asylum law (see discussion of C-411/10 *NS v SSHD* at 12.3.3). In for example, Case C-364/11 *Abed El Karem El Kott and Others* [2012] ECR I-0000, the Court said:

As is apparent from recital 10 in the preamble thereto, the directive must also be interpreted in a manner consistent with the rights recognised by the Charter . . . (para 43)

Challenges to the UK's secondary legislation need not go as far as the EU. The Court of Appeal in *EN (Serbia) v SSHD* [2009] EWCA Civ 630 agreed with the Parliamentary Joint Committee on Human Rights that delegated legislation which conflicted with the Refugee Convention and was made under a statutory power that purported to give effect to the Convention was ultra vires (see chapter 13 re Specification of Particularly Serious Crimes Order 2004, SI 2004/1910).

The QD has affected the way in which asylum and human rights claims are structured. The applicant needs to argue:

- first, that the Appellant deserves refugee status under the Directive;
- second, that they merit subsidiary protection;
- third, other human rights issues which could prevent their removal from the UK albeit not falling with the Directive's confines (e.g., Article 8).

The substance of arguments for subsidiary or human rights protection is covered in chapter 5.

12.3 **Definition of 'refugee'**

Refugee status is determined by applying the definition found in Article 1A(2) of the Refugee Convention, as interpreted by the QD, implemented in the UK by the 2006 regulations. Article 1A(2) says that a 'refugee' is a person who:

owing to a well-founded fear of being persecuted for reasons of race, religion, nationality, membership of a particular social group, or political opinion, is outside his country of nationality and is unable or, owing to such fear, is unwilling to avail himself of the protection of that country; or who, not having a nationality and being outside the country of his former habitual residence . . . is unable or, owing to such fear, is unwilling to return to it.

The QD provides for refugee claims only from third-country (i.e., non-EEA) nationals and those who are stateless. The UK's implementing regulations apply to anyone who is not a British Citizen, but immigration rules effective from 19 November 2015 require a claim from an EU national to be declared inadmissible unless exceptional circumstances apply. The exceptions are defined in the rules (HC 395 para 326C–F). This does not make a significant practical difference, as before November 2015 very few asylum applications were made by EU nationals, and those that were made were routinely certified as clearly unfounded. The rest of this chapter consists of an exploration of the refugee definition as it has been interpreted by courts and tribunals.

12.4 **The fear**

The centrality of the requirement of fear places a greater emphasis on the experience and circumstances of the individual than the refugee protection measures which preceded the 1951 Convention. The fear has both a subjective and objective aspect.

12.4.1 **Subjective fear**

The subjective aspect is the refugee's own experience of fear. Paragraphs 40 and 41 of the *UNHCR Handbook* discuss the way in which the subjective element may be evaluated, and suggest that the requirement of subjective fear gives scope for taking account of the effect of circumstances on an individual. For instance, 'one person may have strong political or religious convictions, the disregard of which would make his life intolerable; another may have no such strong convictions' (para 40). Similar circumstances may bear differently on different people. The assessment of the subjective state of fear, according to para 40, involves engaging in 'an assessment of the personality of the applicant . . . since the psychological reactions of different individuals may not be the same in identical conditions'. However, tribunals tend to steer away from too intense a psychological scrutiny of the subjective fear. The proper and usual approach was expressed as follows by the Tribunal in *Asuming v SSHD (11530)*:

we understand 'fear' in an asylum claim to be nothing more nor less than a belief in that which the appellant states is likely to happen if he returns to his country of origin . . . one should not approach the issue on the basis of a need to assess whether a person is 'afraid' in the sense of being fearful rather than courageous.

In law and practice, subjective fear is secondary to objective fear. The objective aspect of the fear is the question of whether or not it is well-founded, that is, whether or not the events that the claimant fears are indeed likely to come about.

Hathaway says that 'the use of the term "fear" was intended to emphasize the forward-looking nature of the refugee claim, not to ground refugee status in an assessment of the claimant's state of mind' (1991:75). This approach supports the purpose of the Convention which is to protect people from actual persecution and was approved in the leading Tribunal case of *Gashi and Nikshiqi* [1997] INLR 96. The same standard of proof applies to the subjective and objective aspects of fear (*Asuming*). The third colloquium on challenges in international refugee law produced the Michigan Guidelines on Well-Founded Fear (adopted 28 March 2004). These took a further step in this same direction by suggesting that the different psychological effects of the same circumstances should be considered not in relation to establishing the 'fear' but only in relation to persecution. The Guidelines in effect develop *Gashi and Nikshiqi* and Hathaway's earlier work by saying, not only that there is no need to look for a state of trepidation, but that doing so is harmful, discriminatory, and wrong (see Hathaway and Hicks 2005). For a contrary view, see Tuitt (1996:96–7) who argues that the central importance accorded to the test of objectively well-founded fear may be seen as part of a legal trend which enables the state to make generalized statements about safety to defeat an asylum claim.

We can summarize by saying that the subjective aspect of the fear is an anticipation that persecution would result if the asylum seeker returned to their home country. In general, it will not come into question where there is evidence that the fear is well founded.

12.4.2 Objective fear

The applicant has the burden of proving that their fear is well founded, that is, that there are objective grounds for believing that the fear will materialize. In proving that they face a risk of persecution in their country of origin, the refugee faces substantial difficulties. Not only are they outside their country of origin, in an unfamiliar environment, without access to common reference points, witnesses, or documents, but also, communication with their country of origin may be difficult or impossible. The very nature of their claim means that governmental sources in their own country will not be willing to provide supporting evidence. The refugee is not likely to have substantial documentary evidence proving their claim; they may not even have documents proving their identity. On the other hand, the consequences of refusing a valid claim could be extremely serious. As the Tribunal said in *Asuming*, 'Asylum cases differ from most other cases in the seriousness of the consequences of an erroneous decision, in the focus of the decision on the future, and the inherent difficulties of obtaining objective evidence.' In such a situation, the question of what standard of proof must be reached by the asylum claimant is all-important.

12.4.2.1 Standard of proof

The House of Lords' judgment in *R v SSHD ex p Sivakumaran* [1988] AC 958 established that the asylum seeker should be required to establish a reasonable degree of likelihood that their fear will materialize, that is, that persecution will take place. The standard of proof to be applied was variously described in that case as 'a reasonable chance', 'substantial grounds for thinking', 'a serious possibility', and 'a one in ten chance'. In law the standard has remained the same since that time, but is now usually more simply expressed as a 'real risk' (see *PS (Sri Lanka) v SSHD* [2008] EWCA Civ 1213).

What has happened in the past is an important indicator of what may happen in the future. The QD says:

The fact that an applicant has already been subject to persecution or serious harm or to direct threats of such persecution or such harm, is a serious indication of the applicant's well-founded fear of persecution or real risk of suffering serious harm, unless there are good reasons to consider that such persecution or serious harm will not be repeated. (Article 4.4)

It must still be determined what *has* happened in the past, and in the case of *Kaja (11038)*, an experienced Tribunal convened for the purpose of resolving the question held that the *Sivakumaran* standard of proof should be applied to the question of whether past events had taken place as well as to whether persecution would take place in the future. So, if the applicant claimed that they had been beaten in custody and that this would recur, both matters need to be proved to be a reasonable likelihood. In fact, the Tribunal said, past events and future risks were all part of the same question. To divide past events from assessment of future risks is artificial as assessment of future risk will depend to a great extent on an evaluation of what has happened in the past. *Kaja* has been relied upon since as authority for the proposition simply as stated earlier, that the lower standard of proof should be applied to past events as well as the chance of future occurrences. Brooke LJ in *Karanakaran* [2000] Imm AR 271 suggested that this is an oversimplification of the Tribunal's judgment which amounts to misstating it, and that the decision should be applied using its full reasoning. This was that a decision-maker in an asylum claim will be faced with four kinds of evidence:

1. evidence whose validity they are certain about;
2. evidence they think is probably true;
3. evidence to which they are willing to attach some credence, but would not go so far as to say that it is probably true; and
4. evidence to which they are not willing to attach any credence at all.

The contentious area is the third category of evidence, as this falls below the standard of proof that would warrant reliance upon it in a civil claim. The Tribunal's view in *Kaja* was that the asylum decision-maker should not exclude such evidence from their mind.

Karanakaran steers decision-makers away from a mechanistic approach to the standard of proof. It is not that the asylum seeker must prove the matters alleged to the standard of reasonable likelihood. In itself, this can become a rather meaningless word game, as though the phrase had the precision of a percentage and as though events and risks could be proved to a quantifiable degree. A refugee claim is not like a civil claim in which there are two competing sets of evidence, one of which the judge must prefer. A refugee claim should not be an adversarial process at all (although see discussion of decision-making in chapter 11). Rather, although *Sivakumaran* and *Kaja* represent appropriate standards if standards are required, the inherent uncertainty of future possibilities and of the evaluation of evidence must be understood. Assessing an asylum claim is not a matter simply of fact-finding but, crucially, of evaluation. It must be approached as a whole, as a public law enquiry into the need for protection rather than as an exercise in proving facts to a standard. The risks of over-applying a formulation were identified by Sedley LJ in *Batayav v SSHD* [2003] EWCA Civ 1489: 'Great care needs to be taken with such epithets. They are intended to elucidate the jurisprudential concept of real risk, not to replace it' (para 38). He used the example of a faulty type of car. Even if only one car in ten actually crashes, most people would think there was a real risk of travelling in such a car. There do not have to be frequent or routine failures for this to be the case. In *PS (Sri Lanka)* the Court of Appeal said:

The single test of whether a fear of persecution or ill-treatment is well-founded is whether on the evidence there is a real risk of its occurrence or recurrence. This straightforward formula now replaces the sometimes confusing variants which have been used over the years.

The application of this approach is a question of assessing the evidence in every case. Evidence of likelihood or of risk involves evidence of context and surrounding factors which may suggest for instance trends of behaviour by police or security forces. Asylum cases therefore rely not only on evidence concerning the particular applicant, but also on evidence of what has happened to people who are in a comparable situation in the country concerned. As discussed in the previous chapter, these kinds of evidence are procured by using expert evidence and regularly produced reports on the overall situation in particular countries by organizations such as Human Rights Watch, Amnesty International, the US State Department, and the Home Office's Country of Origin Information Service.

In *Hariri v SSHD* [2003] EWCA Civ 807, the Court of Appeal said that the appellant's case depended entirely on whether he would suffer ill-treatment as a member of a class, either of draft evaders or of those who had left Syria without authority. Therefore, the question of whether there was generally a pattern of ill-treatment of such people was crucial to establishing whether there was a real risk to the appellant.

12.4.3 Timing of fear

The well-founded fear must, at the time of the claim, be an operative cause of the asylum seeker's being away from their country of origin. In the case of *Adan* [1998] Imm AR 338, the House of Lords considered whether historic fear, that is, fear in the past, would be sufficient to found refugee status, and concluded that it would not. Article 1(A)(2) says that it is 'owing to a well-founded fear' that the refugee 'is' outside their country of nationality. In Mr Adan's case, he could not, at the time of his claim, avail himself of the protection of his country (Somalia) as there was no effective government to offer that protection. However, the initial fear which had caused him to flee had subsided as President Barré had fallen and the risk to him of persecution was accordingly lessened. The House of Lords said that there were two parts to a refugee claim, the 'fear test' and the 'protection test', and held that Mr Adan could not obtain refugee status because the fear did not still exist, even though no governmental protection was available and there were risks to him consequent on the continuing civil war.

In *In re B; R v Special Adjudicator ex p Hoxha (UNHCR intervening)* [2005] UKHL 19, the House of Lords considered an argument centred on the cessation clause in Article 1C of the Refugee Convention. As discussed in the last chapter, this clause provides for the ending of refugee status when there has been such a radical change in the circumstances in the refugee's country of origin that they can no longer fail to avail themselves of their country's protection. There is an exception in Article 1C where a refugee is able to 'invoke compelling reasons arising out of past persecution'. The appellants in *Hoxha* had not obtained refugee status because of the changed circumstances in Kosovo. They argued that the persecution they had suffered in the past was nevertheless so severe that they should not be obliged to return. The House of Lords rejected this argument. An exception to the cessation clause could not be used to achieve refugee status for someone who had not achieved it on their asylum application. Their fear was not current, as was required in order to obtain protection.

12.4.4 **Refugee** *sur place*

The opposite situation also arises, where a refugee has left their country of origin without fear for some other purpose, for example, a holiday or study, but during their absence an event such as a change of government takes place which causes them to fear persecution should they return. In this case the fear is the operative cause of their remaining outside their country of nationality, even though it was not the cause of their leaving it. They are thus entitled to claim refugee status and are referred to, following the French, as a refugee *sur place*.

It follows that if events since the applicant's arrival in the UK may give rise to a well-founded fear, these events may take place not only in the applicant's home country but equally in the UK, in fact they may be the actions of the applicant themselves. This was established by the Court of Appeal in *Danian* [2000] Imm AR 96, in which it was confirmed that refugee status could be granted after the applicant was at risk of persecution in his country of nationality because of his activities in the UK.

This decision does not necessarily mean that a person may create their own refugee status cynically by undertaking political activities in the UK when they have no genuine political interest. The Court of Appeal in *Iftikhar Ahmed v SSHD* [2000] INLR 1 explained that *Danian* simply brings the decision back to the essential question, 'is there a serious risk that on return the applicant would be persecuted for a Convention reason?' In *Danian* itself, the Court endorsed the view of the UNHCR:

[I]t should be borne in mind that opportunistic post-flight activities will not necessarily create a real risk of persecution in the claimant's home country either because they will not come to the attention of the authorities of that country or because the opportunistic nature of such activities will be apparent to all including to those authorities.

The QD permits the decision-maker to take into account 'whether the applicant's activities since leaving the country of origin were engaged in for the sole or main purpose of creating the necessary conditions for applying for international protection,' but it does so 'so as to assess whether these activities will expose the applicant to persecution or serious harm if returned to that country' (Article 4.3(d)).

Mr Danian himself ultimately lost his appeal when the case came back to the Tribunal, after the Court of Appeal decision. The Tribunal considered that lack of good faith undermined the credibility of a well-founded fear of persecution. It took the view that if Mr Danian's motives were cynical, then he did not have a fear, and on the facts of his political involvement in the UK, the Nigerian authorities would not impute to him a political opinion. The *sur place* option is included in the QD, which says that a fear of being persecuted may be based on events which have taken place since the applicant left the country of origin and on activities undertaken since then by the applicant, in particular where these 'constitute the expression and continuation of convictions or orientations held in the country of origin' (Article 5.2). This leaves all aspects of *Danian* intact. In *YB (Eritrea)* [2008] EWCA Civ 360 Sedley LJ applied the QD, observing that even if the sole or main purpose of *sur place* activities was to create the conditions for international protection, the claim should succeed unless the authorities in the home state were likely to treat the activities as insincere and opportunistic.

Cases may turn on evidence of monitoring by the home country's government of nationals abroad. In *KS (Burma) v SSHD* [2013] EWCA Civ 67 the Court of Appeal held that the Upper Tribunal was wrong to find that the Burmese government would distinguish between genuine political activity in the UK and 'hangers-on'. The former ambassador to Burma had given evidence that the then Burmese government:

relied on random persecution of the civilian population who never knew whom they could trust because of the belief that the MI had thousands of informers. Any sign of dissent, even minor, was savagely punished. . . . There was no evidence that a distinction between minor and major actions would be made for those Burmese citizens returning home who had engaged in anti-government activity abroad . . . pro-democracy demonstrations outside the Burmese Embassy were anathema to the regime. (para 24)

The Upper Tribunal had accepted evidence of routine photography and video recording of demonstrations outside the Embassy and of efficient identification processes which result in the relaying of information to Burma, but doubted that the government would be concerned with someone of no political profile. The Court of Appeal held that their rejection of the former ambassador's evidence on this point was flawed, and that they were not justified to assume that the Burmese authorities in Rangoon operate 'a rational decision-making process which can reliably be trusted to distinguish between a genuine political opponent and a hanger-on' (para 31). The specific position concerning Burma (or, properly, Myanmar) was later the subject of country guidance in *TS (Political opponents—risk) Burma* CG [2013] UKUT 00281 (IAC).

Where a first claim for asylum has failed and the applicant submits a further application, the Directive permits Member States to introduce a presumption against the grant of refugee status on such a basis (Article 5.3). The UK government made it known that it would not instate such a presumption, and there is none in the implementing rules or regulations.

12.4.4.1 Rejected asylum claims

A related issue is the effect of a refused asylum claim itself on what treatment the individual might face on return. In the past the Home Office occasionally accepted as a matter of policy that returning people to particular countries was not possible because the fact of having made an asylum claim created a risk of reprisals from their home government. In the case of Libya, the Home Office previously adopted a policy of this kind in 2001 (see *Hassan* [2002] UKIAT 00062) and in relation to Zimbabwe. When the Home Office lifted the Zimbabwe moratorium in November 2004, Zimbabwean Information Minister, Jonathan Moyo, said that returnees should be treated with suspicion as they could be 'trained and bribed malcontents', sent to disrupt the election (newsvote.bbc.co.uk 17 December 2004). The resumption of returns caused not only a political and legal storm, but also scores of asylum seekers to go on hunger strike in detention. After seven Tribunal determinations and six Court of Appeal judgments, the legal situation at the time of writing is that failed asylum seekers per se are not held to be at risk on return to Zimbabwe.

It is now uncommon for the Home Office to adopt a policy of this kind. The risk to refused asylum seekers is sometimes dealt with by country guidance cases, however, refused asylum seekers from some countries in particular (e.g., Democratic Republic of Congo, Iraq, and Iran) have continued to argue that they face risks because of having made an asylum claim and the resources to bring country guidance cases are not readily available. Lobbying by NGOs (non-government organizations) has played a part, and sometimes the courts have intervened. Reports by the NGO Justice First found evidence of ill-treatment on return to DRC (*Unsafe Return* 2011 and Unsafe Return II 2013). Ultimately Justice First's reports have not prevailed, and the present country guidance on DRC is that returnees are not, per se, at risk (*BM and Others (returnees—criminal and non-criminal) DRC* CG [2015] UKUT 00293 (IAC)).

Flights returning refused asylum seekers to Iraq were stopped in June 2011 after evidence given in the High Court of ill-treatment of returnees at Baghdad airport. The suspension of flights ended after later country guidance.

The Home Office's Operational Guidance Notes for some countries include a section on the treatment of returning refused asylum seekers, and in the case of some countries (e.g., Syria) this is accepted as a risk factor.

NGOs lobby for monitoring of what happens to refused asylum seekers who are returned, but the government accepts no formal responsibility for monitoring, having not opted into the Returns Directive 2008/115/EC (*House of Commons* 2011 *Hansard Written Answers for 21 June 2011* Col. 208W Damien Green MP).

In addition to general country policies, it may be necessary to argue that the return of a particular refused asylum seeker is not safe. In *Degirmenci v SSHD* [2004] EWCA Civ 1553, the Court of Appeal held that there needed to be a full assessment of the evidence relating to the treatment on return to Turkey of a Kurdish failed asylum seeker such as the appellant. Where, for instance, as in *Yapici* (see 12.5.2.1) the appellant had left the country in breach of reporting conditions, this would increase the risk of their coming to the notice of the authorities. Risk may also be established where the asylum seeker left their country illegally (e.g., *MO (illegal exit—risk on return) Eritrea* CG [2011] UKUT 00190 (IAC)).

12.5 **Persecution**

The concept of persecution is central to the recognition of refugee status. It is not conclusively defined, and in fact the *UNHCR Handbook* expressly avoids attempting to lay down any such definition, saying that whether threats or actions will amount to persecution 'will depend on the circumstances of each case' (para 52) and 'it is not possible to lay down a general rule as to what cumulative reasons can give rise to a valid claim to refugee status' (para 53).

The QD however represents a development by identifying persecution in more detail. Article 9 says that to amount to persecution acts must be 'sufficiently serious by their nature or repetition' to constitute 'a severe violation of basic human rights' particularly those which are non-derogable under the ECHR, or must be an accumulation of measures, including violations of human rights, which is severe enough to affect an individual similarly to a severe violation of non-derogable rights. Paragraph 2 states:

2. Acts of persecution as qualified in paragraph 1, can, inter alia, take the form of:
   (a) acts of physical or mental violence, including acts of sexual violence;
   (b) legal, administrative, police, and/or judicial measures which are in themselves discriminatory or which are implemented in a discriminatory manner;
   (c) prosecution or punishment, which is disproportionate or discriminatory;
   (d) denial of judicial redress resulting in a disproportionate or discriminatory punishment;
   (e) prosecution or punishment for refusal to perform military service in a conflict, where performing military service would include crimes or acts falling under the exclusion clauses as set out in Article 12(2);
   (f) acts of a gender-specific or child-specific nature.

We shall return to this list as the matters arise.

One approach to identifying persecution, in a line of cases of which *Jonah* [1985] Imm AR 7 is the oft-quoted authority, has been reliance on the dictionary definition: 'to pursue with malignancy or injurious action'. However, this implies a focus on the motive and actions of the persecutor. It might be said that a person tortured once in a police station and then released has not been 'pursued' and that a person who would be prosecuted for any expression of their sexuality is not the target of malignancy but of government policy. Whereas the dictionary definition would work for some cases, it does not for others. This approach has been falling into disuse in favour of an emphasis on the acts or their effects rather than the motive. This approach is implicitly endorsed by the QD which does not attempt to define persecution as such, but acts of persecution.

The Tribunal in *Gashi* adopted the submission of the UNHCR that: 'for the Convention to be a living instrument of protection, the term "persecution" must be interpreted in a manner that best achieves its humanitarian object and purpose'. The Tribunal went on to say that 'it would be a mistake to attempt a definition of persecution which could in any way restrict its power to meet the changing circumstances in which the Convention has to operate'. A simple formulation is that persecution = serious harm + failure of state protection (set out in this way by the Refugee Women's Legal Group (*Women as Asylum Seekers* 1997:9)). This is a workable formulation which underscores the crucial aspect of state responsibility and has been used by the courts, for instance by Lord Hoffmann in *R v IAT & SSHD ex p Shah and Islam v IAT* [1999] 2 AC 629.

There must be an analysis of whether what is feared in a particular case is persecution. However, the decision-maker does not so much *define* persecution as *identify* it. The difference is that a definition is an attempt to provide in the abstract a statement that will apply in a wide range (preferably all) circumstances, whereas identification starts with a set of circumstances and asks whether these amount to persecution. The QD approach to acts of persecution is consistent with the commonly used starting point proffered by Hathaway:

The sustained or systemic violation of basic human rights demonstrative of a failure of state protection in relation to one of the core entitlements which has been recognized by the international community. The types of harm to be protected against include the breach of any rights within the first category, a discriminatory or non-emergency abnegation of a right within the second category or the failure to implement a right in the third category which is either discriminatory or not grounded in the absolute lack of resources. (1991:112)

The three categories to which he refers he sets out in the following way:

Category one:
Freedom from arbitrary deprivation of life, from torture, cruel, inhuman or, degrading treatment or punishment, from slavery, imprisonment for breach of a contractual obligation, retroactive criminal prosecution, freedom of thought, conscience and religion, and the right to be recognized as a person in law.

Category two:
Freedom from arbitrary arrest and detention, right to a fair trial, equal treatment including in access to public employment, freedom of expression, assembly and association, of movement inside a country, to leave and return to one's country of origin, to form and join trade unions, to take part in public affairs and vote, and protection for privacy and the family.

Category three:
The right to work, including just and favourable conditions of employment, to an adequate standard of living including food, clothing and housing, to the highest attainable standard of health, to education, and to engage in cultural, scientific, literary, and artistic expression.

This human rights approach to persecution was broadly adopted by the UNHCR and from them by the Tribunal in *Gashi and Nikshiqi*. It has been used and endorsed by the higher courts for instance the House of Lords in *Horvath v SSHD* [2000] 3 All ER 577 and *Sepet and Bulbul v SSHD* [2003] UKHL 15. It is an extremely useful framework though not final or definitive, and it has some limitations (see for instance Wilsher 2003).

Goodwin-Gill proposes a formulation of 'reasons, interests and measures': the reasons for persecution would be race, religion and so on; the interests affected would be fundamental ones such as life and liberty; and the measures are the infliction of harm, arbitrary arrest and so on (2007:132). This formulation steers away from focusing on persecution as a special kind of activity, but rather emphasizes the actual consequences and the denial of rights. See also summarized points on the relationship between the Refugee Convention and human rights in Ní Ghráinne 2015.

Whatever approach is taken to identifying persecution, it requires both 'serious harm' and a failure of state protection.

In the leading case of *Horvath*, Lord Hope said: 'The general purpose of the Convention is to enable the person who no longer has the benefit of state protection against persecution for a Convention reason in his own country to turn for protection to the international community'. This is known as the principle of surrogacy. The underlying idea is the breakdown in the relationship between citizen and state, so that the citizen can no longer rely on the state for the protection which is their due, and must look instead to the international community. This may entail that the state is actively the persecutor, as when the police torture people in their custody. Alternatively, it may entail that others perpetrate the serious harm, as when skinheads attack Roma people, but the state fails to protect them. Persecution by such non-state actors is discussed at 12.5.4.2.

Professor Hathaway's reference to the 'systemic violation' of rights suggests that the violation is part of the functioning of the state system, the state endorses the violations, implicitly by not providing redress or explicitly by for instance oppressive legislation, or covertly, by promoting brutal interrogation by security services.

This may be distinguished from, although it is connected to, the question of whether ill-treatment must be *systematic* to amount to persecution. This is sometimes used in the same way as 'systemic', but may also be used to mean 'repeated' or 'persistent', which will often be appropriate but not always. Where the violation feared is sufficiently serious, for example, killing or torture, there is no necessity for repetition in order for this to be persecution.

The QD follows the earlier EU Joint Position of 4 March 1996, in saying that acts feared will be persecution if sufficiently serious by reason of 'their nature *or* their repetition'. Either severity or repetition is required, but not both.

The authorities on a single instance of ill-treatment as persecution were comprehensively reviewed in the case of *Doymus* 00/TH/01748, expanding upon the Court of Appeal judgment in *Demirkaya* [1999] Imm AR 498, where Stuart-Smith LJ said:

At one end of the scale there may be arbitrary deprivation of life, torture and cruel, inhuman and degrading treatment or punishment. In such a case the conduct may be so extreme that one instance is sufficient, but less serious conduct may not amount to persecution unless it is persistent. (para 15)

That a single violation of a first category right would constitute persecution is so, not only in common sense (a single threat to life is enough) but also by reference to the human rights instruments from which these standards are derived. For instance, 'no one shall be subjected to torture or to cruel, inhuman or degrading treatment or punishment' (Article 9 ICCPR as well as Article 3 ECHR). This does not allow an exception if the torture happens only once, and case law under these Articles treats single acts of torture or cruel, inhuman or degrading treatment, or punishment as violations. The Tribunal in *Doymus* cited other academic writers, the UNHCR, and case law of other jurisdictions also as authorities that, while persistency is a usual characteristic of persecution, it is not an inevitable one.

There is no requirement to be 'singled out' for persecution (*R v SSHD ex p Jeyakumaran* [1994] Imm AR 45). If the persecutory treatment is for a reason included in the Convention (see 12.8), the fact that others who share the same characteristic are treated similarly may be evidence that supports the asylum claim but it does not detract from it. As Lord Lloyd said in *Adan* at 348: 'It is not necessary for a claimant to show that he is more at risk than anyone else in his group, if the group as a whole is subject to oppression.' Conversely, there is no need for all those sharing the characteristic to be persecuted (*Shah and Islam*). However, in situations of civil war, there will not be a refugee claim where *all* sections of society are similarly in fear (*SSHD v Adan* [1999] 1 AC 293). Where the refugee's country of origin has been in a state of armed conflict for many years, there are particular difficulties in assessing an asylum claim. The House of Lords in *Adan* required, for a successful claim, that where society had broken down into continual conflict 'the individual or group has to show a well-founded fear of persecution over and above the risk to life and liberty inherent in civil war' (para 349). However, as discussed in chapter 11, Article 15c of the QD contains a provision which has created a new possibility of protection in limited instances as a result of war.

12.5.1 Severe ill-treatment

As discussed in *Doymus* and *Demirkaya*, a single instance of sufficiently severe ill-treatment may amount to persecution. Loss of life and torture admit of no justification or derogation. This was made very clear by the House of Lords in *R v SSHD ex p Sivakumar* [2003] 1 WLR 840 where even the applicant's suspected involvement in terrorism could not justify the appalling torture he had experienced.

The UN Convention against Torture and Other Cruel Inhuman or Degrading Treatment Article 1(1) defines torture as:

An act by which pain or suffering, whether physical or mental, is intentionally inflicted on a person for such purposes as obtaining from him or a third person a confession, punishing him for an act which he or a third party has committed or is suspected of having committed, or intimidating him or a third person, or for any reason based on discrimination of any kind, when such pain or suffering is inflicted by or at the instigation of or with the consent of public officials or other person acting in an official capacity.

This Article has not been widely referred to in refugee cases, though it was used as guidance by the High Court in *R v SSHD ex p Javed and Ali* [2000] EWHC (Admin) 7. It suggests that not only the conduct but also who carried it out and the reason are significant in determining whether it amounts to torture. However, Goodwin-Gill and McAdam (2007:96) point out that there is no need for an asylum claimant to prove any particular intention on the part of their persecutor, nor that any particular person carries it out. Indeed, as *Sivakumar* makes plain, intention may be irrelevant, and the discussion which follows will show that who carries it out is less important than whether the state can provide protection.

In *Doymus*, the Tribunal recognized that it was not just the level of ill-treatment that was relevant but also the psychological effects. The applicant had described being stripped naked, sprayed with cold water from a hose, and beaten with a stick while his hands were tied behind his back. The Tribunal held that this was likely to 'give rise to feelings of fear, anguish, and inferiority capable of humiliating and debasing him and possibly breaking his physical and moral resistance'. This would be a breach of Article 3 ECHR or Article 9 ICCPR, it was degrading treatment, and it was unnecessary to determine whether it amounted to torture. The judgment in *Doymus* thus links an act of persecution explicitly to human rights norms. In *Demirkaya* the Court of Appeal expressly disapproved trying to categorize behaviour such that a particular level of ill-treatment would amount to persecution. The question should be looked at in the round. 'Is this person at risk of persecution for a Convention reason?' The Court said that this was a question of fact.

In a case such as *Doymus*, there is no examination of the motives of the police. It was an essential and undisputed element of Mr Doymus' claim that he was at risk because of his political affiliations, and the precise anticipated motives of the police on any particular occasion do not require inquiry. This is all the more so the case as torture cannot be justified and so even if their motive was to preserve law and order this would not prevent the feared action being persecution. If motive is unimportant, rape and other serious sexual assault receive anomalous treatment in refugee law.

12.5.1.1 Rape and other sexual violence

The QD and UK implementing regulations include, in their list of acts of persecution, 'acts of physical or mental violence, including acts of sexual violence'. In practice there has been a persistent failure at all stages of asylum decision-making to recognize rape and other sexual violence as forms of persecution (see Ceneda and Palmer 2006, Asylum Aid 2011 (Muggeridge and Maman), Dorling, Girma, and Walter 2012). Various organizations have produced guidelines on gender issues in asylum claims, including sexual violence, for example, the Refugee Women's Legal Group in 1998, the Immigration Appellate Authority in 2000, and UNHCR in 2002. UKVI developed their own guidance to decision-makers (API Gender issues in the asylum claim, revised 2010).

The guidelines produced by a small group of immigration judges for the Immigration Appellate Authority in 2000 addressed directly and with authority the use of sexual violence as a form of torture or cruel inhuman or degrading treatment or punishment, refuting 'the myth that rape is sexually motivated—it is usually intended to inflict violence and humiliation' (Assistant Commissioner Wyn Jones of the Metropolitan Police).

They cited the Statutes of the International Tribunals for Former Yugoslavia and Rwanda, which list rape as a crime against humanity, and the Article 3 ECHR case of *Aydin v Turkey* (1997) 25 EHRR 251 para 83 in which the Court said:

Rape of a detainee by an official of the State must be considered to be an especially grave and abhorrent form of ill-treatment given the ease with which the offender can exploit the vulnerability and weakened resistance of his victim.

The IAA gender guidelines however were quietly dropped. A Parliamentary Question (HL 1596) elicited the response on 5 February 2007 (WA93) that the gender guidelines were out of date, replaced by case law, and non-binding in any event. There is a Joint Presidential Guidance note (no. 2 of 2010) on the conduct of hearings involving child, vulnerable, or sensitive witnesses. This gives some guidance on the assessment of evidence from people who have been traumatized. The Home Office guidance, represented by the API also deals with sensitivity to trauma, in the context of the asylum interview. However, neither the guidelines for tribunals nor for Home Office caseworkers cover the same ground as the IAA guidelines in that they do not explain the political uses of sexual violence (Ceneda and Palmer 2006 and see Women's Asylum News no. 96).

In the absence of this understanding, research shows that the harm to the asylum seeker is often minimized (see Baillot, Cowan, and Munro). As in other contexts, accounts of sexual abuse including rape are often not believed (see for instance *R (on the application of AM) v SSHD* [2012] EWCA Civ 521). Also, there is much confused thinking about the motivation of the persecutor. This may be illustrated by the case of *R v Special*

Adjudicator ex p Okonkwo [1998] Imm AR 502, where Collins J supported the distinction made by the adjudicator between rape committed 'merely to seek sexual gratification' and rape committed for some other motive. If it was 'merely to seek sexual gratification', then it was a common crime on a par with assault, and would not amount to torture unless repeated. It was argued for the applicant that rape constituted torture in part because the psychological effects can be similar to those referred to in *Doymus*, namely of fear, anguish, humiliation, and inferiority, and also because of the severity of the physical ill-treatment. Of course, the necessary element of state involvement must exist, as a crime which is investigated and punished is not persecution. In *Okonkwo*, the assailant was an army officer who had previously threatened the applicant. She had suffered violence before from the authorities. She was not in detention at the time of the rape, but was attacked by the roadside and left there. The location and the lack of formal relationship between the assailant and applicant influenced Collins J in his agreement with the adjudicator. However, this leaves out of account the exercise of power by a member of the military forces and the lack of redress.

The reasoning in *Okonkwo* has been followed in later cases, and the case law in the UK has been slow to recognize the political nature of much sexual violence. Even systematic rape by armed forces has not necessarily been recognized as persecution, as in *R (N) v SSHD* [2002] EWCA Civ 1082, where the claimant had suffered double rape by armed forces who took away her son (and had probably killed him). *PS (Sri Lanka) v SSHD* [2008] EWCA Civ 1213 departed from this trend.

 Key Case

PS (Sri Lanka) v SSHD [2008] EWCA Civ 1213

The appellant was a Tamil living in the Jaffna Peninsula, where the insurgent LTTE was active. In 2006, she was raped in her home, which was also her father's grocery shop, by two Sri Lankan soldiers who used to make purchases there. Five days later, one of them returned with another soldier, and both of them raped her. A week or so later, the same two returned and again raped her, holding her father at gunpoint so that he would witness it. The appellant tried to kill herself. She failed, and her father took her to the home of her uncle with a view to her fleeing the country. Before she was able to do so, she found herself pregnant and then miscarried or aborted. In the interim, the soldiers had returned to her home, looking for her. In the UK, she was refused asylum and humanitarian protection.

The Tribunal on reconsideration upheld the Home Office's refusal, saying that the fact that she had been raped three times had no bearing on whether it would happen again; the rapes were the actions of rogue officers not sanctioned by the authorities, and if they did come back she could seek the protection of the authorities.

The Court of Appeal overturned that decision. Sedley LJ said that with perpetrators in the uniform of the state, there was no sensible possibility of state protection. The characterization of the soldiers' conduct as no different from that of civilian rapists was unsustainable. The whole point was that, unlike ordinary criminals, the soldiers were in a position to repeat their crime with no apparent prospect of detection or punishment.

This case is important in considering the issue of state protection, discussed at 12.5.4, and also demonstrates the issue under discussion. The UNHCR Global Consultations Summary Conclusions on gender-related persecution say that one of the main problems facing women asylum seekers is 'failure to recognize the political nature of seemingly private acts of harm to women' (para 4).

As appears from this, the recognition of sexual violence as persecution is bound up with the recognition of gender-based persecution, which is discussed further in relation to the Convention reason for persecution at 12.8.4.1. A more recent Sri Lankan case illustrates that the risk of repeated sexual violence may need to be understood in the context of a militarized situation and where women are systemically vulnerable, for example, as here where they are heads of households that is, there is no male protector in the family (*PP (Sri Lanka) v SSHD* [2014] EWCA Civ 1828).

A fundamental issue is that much violence perpetrated on the basis of gender is socially sanctioned either by law or by practice, whether or not it is violence committed by a sexual act. Recognition of an asylum claim on such a basis therefore involves a political judgment which may go against the tide of public thinking either in the country of origin or the host country or both. An example of increasing importance is the practice known variously as female genital cutting or mutilation, or female circumcision (FGM). Case law concerning this practice went in all directions until the Court of Appeal in *P and M v SSHD* [2004] EWCA Civ 1640 accepted that forcible subjection to female genital mutilation was severe ill-treatment which, combined with the absence of state intervention to prevent or punish it, amounted to persecution. This has been put beyond doubt in the House of Lords' judgment in *SSHD v Fornah* [2006] UKHL 46, in which Lord Bingham described FGM as 'an extreme and very cruel expression of male dominance'. This case is discussed further at 12.8.4.1.

The use and effects of sexual violence as a weapon of war are simply and eloquently described in an obiter passage of the judgment of Baroness Hale in *In re B & R v Special Adjudicator ex p Hoxha* [2005] UKHL 19. She explains that the effect may be compounded by a society which:

adds to the earlier suffering she has endured the pain, hardship and indignity of rejection and ostracism from her own people. There are many cultures in which a woman suffers almost as much from the attitudes of those around her to the degradation she has suffered as she did from the original assault. (para 32)

12.5.2 Second category rights

In relation to violations of rights in Hathaway's second category, for instance detention, ill-treatment in detention short of torture, or denial of a fair trial, international human rights' instruments give states some limited power to derogate or to justify infringements. For example, detention may be justified for one of a number of listed reasons in Article 5 ECHR. This is reflected in refugee law. The leading case which demonstrates this is *Sandralingham and Ravichandran* [1996] Imm AR 97, CA.

 **Key Case**

Sandralingham and Ravichandran **[1996] Imm AR 97, CA**

This case arose from periodic round-ups by the Sri Lankan police of young Tamil men and their detention for questioning, sometimes for periods of days. The appellants had been so detained, and had also been ill-treated in custody. They alleged that ill-treatment in custody and arbitrary arrest and detentions each separately constituted persecution. It was accepted that the situation had improved since the time when they were detained. There was therefore no reasonable likelihood of repetition of ill-treatment in detention and so this part of the claim fell out of the picture.

In considering detention as possible persecution, the Court of Appeal held following factors were relevant:

(i) the frequency of round-ups and the length of the detentions resulting;

(ii) the situation prevailing in Colombo at the material time and the Sri Lankan government's need to combat Tamil terrorism;

(iii) the true purpose of the round-ups and the efforts made to arrest and detain only those realistically suspected of involvement in the disturbances.

The Court of Appeal endorsed the respondent's argument that:

young male Tamils are not arrested and detained because they are Tamils but rather because they may have been involved in some outrage. The round-ups are not arbitrary. The very fact that the particular sub-groups identified by the Amnesty Report are especially vulnerable to arrest shows that the true objective of the round-ups is to combat terrorism rather than discriminate against Tamils as such. (at 108)

It accepted that the authorities' attempts to control disorder had affected Tamils the most because more of the disorder had occurred in areas where Tamils lived. Detention of excessive length could amount to persecution, repeated detention of the same person could amount to persecution if it was not justified by an appropriate level of suspicion of that individual's having committed a criminal offence, and ill-treatment in detention would normally amount to persecution. However, if innocent people were accidentally caught up in a legitimate policing exercise, this was not persecution even if they were likely to be of a particular minority. This last point shows that it is difficult to consider persecution separately from the reason for the persecution. For instance, a prison sentence imposed for a discriminatory reason amounts to persecution:

the term of imprisonment which accompanies a legislative provision which, like those at issue in the main proceedings, punishes homosexual acts is capable, in itself of constituting an act of persecution within the meaning of Article 9(1) of the Directive, provided that it is actually applied in the country of origin which adopted such legislation. (CJEU Joined Cases C-199/12 to C-201/12, *X, Y and Z*)

Where there is a prison sentence provided for in law, but prosecutions are rare, the existence of that offence does not amount to persecution (*OO (gay men—risk) Algeria* CG [2013] UKUT 63 (IAC)). The reason for persecution is discussed later under the heading of 'Convention reason'.

Although Hathaway places freedom of thought, conscience, and religion in his first category of rights, both the International Covenant on Civil and Political Rights (Article 18) and the ECHR (Article 9) allow some limitations by the state on *the practice of* that freedom where these are prescribed by law and 'necessary to protect public safety, order, health, or morals or the fundamental rights and freedoms of others' (ICCPR Article 18(3)). Whether restrictions on the right to express beliefs amount to persecution depends on the severity of sanctions, and 'the importance or centrality of the practice within the religion and/or to the individual concerned' (UNHCR Eligibility Guidelines for Assessing the International Protection Needs of Members of Religious Minorities from Pakistan dated 14 May 2012). The case law is discussed at 12.8.2. The QD list of acts of persecution includes 'legal, administrative, police, and/or judicial measures which are in themselves discriminatory or which are implemented in a discriminatory manner'.

12.5.2.1 Prosecution or persecution?

Continuing the consideration of second category rights, it is undeniable that the state has a right to prosecute its citizens, even a duty to do so in order to maintain law and order for the benefit of others. The *UNHCR Handbook* puts it in this way:

Persecution must be distinguished from punishment for a common law offence. Persons fleeing from prosecution or punishment for such an offence are not normally refugees. It should be recalled that a refugee is a victim—or potential victim—of injustice, not a fugitive from justice. (para 56)

However, prosecution may amount to persecution in certain circumstances. If a punishment is excessive, this may turn prosecution into persecution. For instance, it may be within lawful bounds of state action for there to be some penalty for adultery, but stoning to death goes beyond that (*Shah and Islam*).

The discriminatory application of the law may also turn prosecution into persecution, as suggested in the quotation from *Ravichandran*. If people had been detained *because* they were Tamils, then this could have amounted to persecution. The *Handbook* gives the example of prosecution for an offence of public order for the distribution of pamphlets, which could be 'a vehicle for the persecution of the individual on the grounds of the political content of the publication' (para 59). In *Sivakumar* in the Court of Appeal [2002] INLR 310, Dyson LJ used the following words which were quoted with approval by the House of Lords:

Where a person to whom a political opinion is imputed or who is a member of a race or social group is the subject of sanctions that do not apply generally in the state, then it is more likely than not that the application of the sanctions is discriminatory and persecutory for a Convention reason. (para 30)

The House of Lords added the caveat that this should not be used to suggest a rebuttable inference in the legal sense. There are many examples of cases in which the reason for prosecution is the political opinion imputed to the applicant, and this renders the prosecution persecutory for Convention purposes (e.g., *Asante* [1991] Imm AR 78).

The issue is less clear when an individual is not targeted for enforcement for a discriminatory reason, but enforcement of the law has a discriminatory impact. On the face of it, the claims of Turkish Kurds for refugee status on account of conscription into the military raise this issue as a significant proportion of the work of the military may be engaged in action against the minority to which they belong. However, these claims have on the whole not been successful. This is dealt with further at 12.8.5.1 in relation to the Convention reason for persecution and the implications of objection to military service.

Prosecution may also amount to persecution where there is a lack of due process or fairness in the criminal process. Hathaway says that where 'the decision to prosecute, the process under which the charge is heard, or the nature of the sentence imposed is politically manipulated' (1991:172) then the prosecution may found a refugee claim. The allegations were of this kind in *Khan v SSHD* [2003] EWCA Civ 530 where the appellant fled Bangladesh after a violent demonstration, as a result of which he had been charged and a warrant issued for his arrest. He believed that he would not be granted bail, would be detained in inhuman and degrading conditions for a long period of time, and would not receive a fair trial. The adjudicator had held that what he feared was prosecution rather than persecution, but the Court of Appeal agreed that the case must be reconsidered by the IAT when Mr Khan was able to prove that he had been sentenced to ten years' imprisonment in his absence. Where an individual is prosecuted for exercising fundamental human rights, then the prosecution may well be persecutory, but this will depend additionally on whether, in the circumstances, some curtailment of freedom is justified in the public interest, and if so, whether the curtailment imposed by the criminal law has exceeded what is justified. In Mr Khan's case, there may have been grounds for charging a public order offence, but this could not justify an unfair trial. The QD recognizes this form of persecution by listing 'prosecution or punishment which is disproportionate or discriminatory' including if through 'lack of judicial redress'.

A conviction in their absence will not always prevent an asylum seeker from being removed from the UK or create a new ground of asylum where a previous one has failed. In *QJ (Algeria) v SSHD* [2010] EWCA Civ 1478 the issue before the Court was the appellant's deportation following offences relating to terrorism in the UK. He had also been convicted in his absence in Algeria. There was no evidence that a second trial in Algeria would not comply with the standards required by Article 6 ECHR, and the Court held that double jeopardy, while normally prohibited in UK law, was not prohibited as such by Article 6.

As mentioned earlier in relation to refused asylum seekers, many cases have concerned the question of whether dissidents will attract the attention of the authorities on return and so be at risk. In *Yapici v SSHD* [2005] EWCA Civ 826, the Court of Appeal held that a proper decision must have regard to the effect of the appellant's leaving the country in breach of reporting conditions. Although the appellant was in breach of an administrative requirement, his reason for being in breach and the fact that it could bring him to the notice of the authorities were relevant to whether he would be at risk on return. As mentioned earlier, a fear of prosecution that may amount to persecution on return is punishment faced by a refused asylum seeker who left their country illegally, as for instance in *MO (illegal exit—risk on return) Eritrea CG* [2011] UKUT 00190 (IAC).

12.5.3 Discrimination as persecution

The violation and threatened violation of rights in Hathaway's third category gives rise to difficult questions in refugee claims. The Refugee Convention protects against persecution, but not against discrimination in delivery of social rights. In an age of bitter inter-ethnic wars and discrimination against minorities so fundamental that in some cases they have been obliterated from social and political life, when does one become the other? This is one of the challenges to the international framework of human rights and refugee protection which was probably not contemplated in this form when the Convention was first drafted.

Gashi and Nikshiqi [1997] INLR 96 demonstrated how pervasive discrimination could amount to persecution.

 **Key Case**

Gashi and Nikshiqi [1997] INLR 96

The appellants were ethnic Albanians from Kosovo. They had evaded military service, and their claim was based in part on the consequences for them of this evasion if they were to return and in part on the level of discrimination they would face as ethnic Albanians in Kosovo. There was an abundance of evidence before the Tribunal about the situation of ethnic Albanians in land, such as Kosovo, under Serb control. The government policy was referred to as 'Serbianization', implemented by, for instance (quoting from the Tribunal's summary of evidence):

the removal of senior Albanians in the courts and public sector generally and restrictions in even the most menial of employment, e.g. street vendors. 80% of Albanians lost their posts . . . There is no control or evidence of any intended control by the central authority of the police in Kosovo and the police are all Serbians. There is a systematic state policy which, it is said, permits this police misbehaviour. In day to day life Albanians are harassed, subjected to house searches, beating, torture at police stations, constant checks carried out at random without any recourse to courts with an effective system to provide adequate remedies and protection to ethnic Albanians.

As a consequence, the Tribunal found that Mr Gashi and Mr Nikshiqi, in addition to prosecution for draft evasion, faced physical abuse, inability to obtain employment, and constant and persistent harassment by police uncontrolled by government.

In considering whether this would amount to persecution, the Tribunal drew on the internationally accepted view of the Convention as a living instrument. It said: 'it would be a mistake to attempt a definition of "persecution" which could in any way restrict its growth to meet the changing circumstances in which the Convention has to operate'. The prospects faced by Mr Gashi and Mr Nikshiqi amounted to persecution.

Where discrimination in social rights is feared, the assessment of whether this amounts to persecution and whether the individual will be protected necessarily involves questions that are concerned with the normal functioning of a society. In the case of, for instance, torture, any nation would say that this was an out of the ordinary occurrence. In the case of, for instance, exclusion from mainstream schooling, an assessment of social policies and practices enters the frame. These decisions are potentially more intrusive on the values and government of the country of origin than cases based on non-derogable rights. For instance, a number of Roma people from Eastern European countries made asylum claims in the UK based on severe life-long discrimination. The British Home Office Minister, Mike O'Brien, appeared on television to say that the majority of these claims would not be entertained as it was the job of the asylum seekers' own governments to resolve issues of discrimination, and they would not interfere in the internal matters of another state.

Evidence of severe discrimination against Roma continued to appear in cases in the ECtHR. For instance, in *DH v Czech Republic* (Application no. 57325/00) Judgment 15 November 2007, the ECtHR found by 13 votes to four that there had been discrimination against Roma children in the provision of education by placing the majority of them in special schools for children with learning disabilities or particularly low intelligence. In *Kalanyos v Romania* (Application no. 57884/00) Judgment 26 July 2007, the houses of Roma people had been burned down after threats to do so and the prosecution of the attackers was closed down partly on the basis that the Roma were alleged to have brought it on themselves. The families affected lived in stables without heat or water as no alternative housing was provided. The case was settled because the Romanian government accepted that there had been violations of Articles 3, 6, 8, 13, and 14 of the ECHR.

The list of acts of persecution in the QD Article 9 is not exhaustive, so the fact that socio-economic rights are not on the list is indicative but not conclusive. There is scope for persecution to arise from 'an accumulation of various measures, including violation of human rights, which is sufficiently severe as to affect an individual in a similar manner to' severe violation of non-derogable human rights. The Directive may indicate a retreat at European level from countenancing claims with a socio-economic basis. The *UNHCR Handbook* suggests that discrimination may amount to persecution where:

measures of discrimination lead to consequences of a substantially prejudicial nature for the person concerned, e.g. serious restrictions on his right to earn a livelihood, his right to practise his religion, or his access to normally available educational facilities. (para 54)

Where this question has been considered in the Tribunal, it has been described as whether the denial of social rights, education, housing, and so forth, is such that it interferes 'with a basic human right to live a decent life' (*Gujda* (18231)). It must also be grounded in discrimination, not an absolute lack of resources in the state; citizens of countries where the majority live in extreme poverty cannot claim asylum on this basis. In *Harakal (also known as Harakel) v SSHD* [2001] EWCA Civ 884, the Court of Appeal found that a lifetime of serious discrimination should be taken into account in allowing the asylum claim of a Roma from the Czech Republic. The Court of Appeal described it as 'significant discrimination in all facets of his life throughout his life'. In *Chiver* (10758), the asylum application succeeded before the adjudicator where the claimant was a miner from Romania who had refused to take government orders to take part in breaking up anti-government demonstrations. He was dismissed from his job as a result, and refused a work card. Without this he was unable to obtain a job or any state benefits. He went on hunger strike, and was arrested and beaten by a policeman. His claim was based substantially on the denial of the right to a livelihood, and succeeded on this. It is noteworthy that although discrimination amounting to persecution is on the whole a more recent use of the Refugee Convention, a claim like this is a classic political refugee claim such as might have been envisaged by the drafters of the Convention.

As findings of discrimination require significant evidence of the law and practice in the refugee's country of origin, cases based on discrimination may become country guidance cases. For instance, in *SA (Divorced woman—illegitimate child) Bangladesh CG* [2011] UKUT 00254(IAC) the Tribunal was concerned with the question of what level of discrimination an unmarried mother might face in Bangladesh.

In more recent case law in which discrimination has played a part, a finding of risk of persecution tends to be based on risk of violence and/or denial of a fundamental right such as that of freedom of religion or expression of sexuality rather than an accumulation of socio-economic or political disadvantages. For instance, in *MS (Coptic Christians—Egypt) CG* [2013] UKUT 611 (IAC) the Tribunal found that there was not a general risk to Coptic Christians, but that there could be a risk to certain Coptic Christians in certain circumstances. The Home Office's Operational Guidance Note was quoted:

> 3.9.18: Christians in Egypt do face generalised societal discrimination and in recent years, levels of violence and ill-treatment have become increasingly severe and more overt. Christians may face intimidation and serious harassment which in many cases will amount to persecution. Case owners must carefully consider each case on its facts. The authorities frequently fail to provide effective protection to Christians, or to investigate and prosecute instances of serious harassment and ill-treatment. Where an individual is able to demonstrate that they are at serious risk of persecution on account of their particular individual circumstances and internal relocation is unavailable, a grant of asylum will be appropriate. (para 25)

In this kind of situation, the context of discrimination may affect the likelihood of persecutory acts, and the sufficiency of state protection. In *MN and others (Ahmadi—country conditions—risk—Pakistan) CG* [2012] UKUT 389, the Tribunal quoted the

UNHCR Eligibility Guidelines for Assessing the International Protection Needs of Members of Religious Minorities from Pakistan 14 May 2012. These guidelines cited discrimination against Ahmadis in public sector employment, denial of shelter and/or relief aid to forcibly displaced Ahmadis, and said: 'Areas where discrimination against the Ahmadi community is institutionalized reportedly include issuance of passports and national identity cards, voting, property rights, access to education and freedom of expression and press' (para 40). However, the country guidance which governs Ahmadi claims relates to the restrictions on religious practice, not on the ability to get a job or live the normal life of a citizen (see 12.8.2).

Although the possibility has not generally developed of attaining refugee status based on an accumulation of discrimination in socio-economic rights, an exception is the case of undocumented Kuwaiti Bidoons. Kuwaiti Bidoons who are denied documents are thereby prevented from participating in almost every aspect of Kuwaiti society (*NM documented or undocumented Bidoon: risk) Kuwait* CG [2013] UKUT 356 (IAC). The Tribunal quoted the Kuwait OGN:

they could not legally own property and their family relationships were effectively illegitimate. Those adults who did succeed in obtaining Kuwaiti ID cards reported that the renewal process was tantamount to interrogation, and the authorities made the process as difficult as possible . . . they had no right to work and were consequently disproportionately affected by poverty. They were not allowed to participate in the political process and, being disenfranchised, they were unable to improve their conditions through political pressure, except by public protest or demonstrations. Undocumented Bidoon were constantly at risk of arrest or detention on grounds of being stateless or illegal residents. (paras 50–1)

Proof that a person is an undocumented Bidoon (which of course is a difficult thing to establish) will normally result in a grant of refugee status.

12.5.4 **Effective state protection**

So far we have been considering the serious harm aspect of persecution. This is closely bound up with the second aspect, that of lack of state protection. Assessing state protection requires consideration of three questions:

1. Who will perpetrate the feared harm?
2. What kind of protection is available against that?
3. What kind of body is capable of delivering effective protection?

12.5.4.1 Perpetrators—agents of the state

The feared persecution may be carried out by those who are part of the state machinery. Examples are the police, the military, security services, or perhaps a combination of branches of government, such as when the judiciary implement discriminatory laws passed by the legislature. An agent of the state may remain an agent of the state for Convention purposes, even though their actions do not necessarily reflect official government policy. For instance, the Turkish police who tortured Mr Doymus were not implementing a policy which the Turkish government would acknowledge; in fact, rather the reverse, as Turkey is anxious to improve its human rights record. However, if such actions are not controlled and prevented, then they amount to persecution by the state. Where there is proper redress for such incidents then there would be no fear of repetition and thus no real risk of persecution in the future. The crucial question is whether the individual can obtain protection.

 **Key Case**

Svazas v SSHD [2002] 1 WLR 1891

Both appellants were Lithuanian communists who had been repeatedly detained. Ms B had been raped in custody by the police. Mr Svazas had been beaten and kicked. The evidence before the Tribunal 'depicted a police force which systematically or endemically abuses its power despite the law and the will of the government to stop it'.

Sedley LJ said:

Whether singling out Communist prisoners for assault . . . is systemic or endemic or sporadic, it necessarily represents an initial failure of protection on the part of the state. If so, the critical question . . . will be whether what the state does to stop it happening reaches a practical standard appropriate to the duty it owes all of its citizens . . . [this] does not require a guarantee against police misconduct, but it does . . . call for timely and effective rectification of the situation which is allowing the misconduct to happen.

Simon Brown LJ said:

The ultimate question in all cases is whether or not the asylum seeker can establish the need for surrogate protection by the international community for want of sufficient protection in his home state . . . [T]he more senior the officers of state concerned, and the more closely involved they are in the refugee's ill-treatment, the more necessary it will be to demonstrate clearly the home state's political will to stamp it out and the adequacy of their systems for doing so and for punishing those responsible, and the easier it will be for the asylum seeker to cast doubt upon their readiness, or at least their ability, to do so.

The legal questions are more complex where those from whom the refugee fears persecution are not agents of the state.

12.5.4.2 Perpetrators—non-state actors

Goodwin-Gill and McAdam point out that 'neither the 1951 Convention nor the *travaux préparatoires* say much about the source of the persecution feared by the refugee, and no necessary linkage between persecution and government authority is formally required' (2007:98). The *UNHCR Handbook* at para 65 says: 'where serious discriminatory or other offensive acts are committed by the local populace, they can be considered as persecution if they are knowingly tolerated by the authorities, or the authorities refuse, or prove unable, to offer effective protection'. Thus, in *R v SSHD ex p Jeyakumaran*, Tamils resident in Colombo were the victims of reprisals by local Sinhalese (majority ethnic) residents, and were not protected by the state. Although the victims were not 'singled out' for persecution by the government, the High Court held that they were nevertheless persecuted, as the state failed to protect them.

12.5.4.3 What protection is available?

The leading case on the question of persecution by non-state actors is the House of Lords case of *Horvath v SSHD* [2000] 3 All ER 577.

Key Case

Horvath v SSHD [2000] 3 All ER 577

The appellant was a Roma from the Slovak Republic who based his asylum claim on fear of violence by skinheads and on discrimination in employment, the right to marry, and education. The Tribunal concluded that any failure of these social rights in his case did not amount to persecution. The Court of Appeal agreed, and the appeal went to the House of Lords only on the question of the failure of state protection against the skinhead violence.

Three questions were considered by the House of Lords.

First: does the concept of 'persecution' refer simply to serious harm, or does it necessarily incorporate a failure of state protection?

Second: the refugee definition requires that a person is 'unwilling' to avail himself of state protection. Does this mean that they fear being persecuted precisely because they have gone to the police?

Third: if persecution implies a lack of state protection, what is the test for determining whether there is sufficient protection against a person's persecution in the country of origin? Is it sufficient that there is in that country a system of criminal law which makes violent attacks by the persecutors punishable and a reasonable willingness to enforce that law on the part of the law enforcement agencies? Or must the protection be such that it cannot be said that the applicant has a well-founded fear? The first alternative focuses on whether the state is doing its best, the second on whether risk is actually minimized or eliminated for the applicant.

Lord Hope said that the proper approach to this task was not 'to construe its language with the same precision as one would if it had been an Act of Parliament' but rather to give the words 'a broad meaning in the light of the purposes which the Convention was designed to serve'. He identified the key relevant Convention purpose as:

> to be found in the principle of surrogacy. The general purpose of the Convention is to enable the person who no longer has the benefit of protection against persecution for a Convention reason in his own country to turn for protection to the international community. (at 383)

This approach is known as the protection theory. It is to be contrasted with the attribution theory previously followed in, for instance, France and Germany, according to which persecution is not recognized as such unless it can be attributed to the state. This way of setting out the issue by Lord Hope seems to be a classic endorsement of the protection theory. However, there is a curious contradiction. The House of Lords found, in relation to the three questions, that:

1. persecution included by definition a failure of state protection,
2. the applicant needed to be unable or unwilling to avail themselves of the protection of the state because they feared persecution for doing so, and
3. a system with a reasonable willingness to enforce it was sufficient for protection.

The net result of this is much closer than Lord Hope's statement suggests to the attribution theory. The effect is not to focus on the failure of state protection for the asylum seeker, but rather on whether the state should be regarded as culpable.

The QD 2004/83 recognizes persecution by non-state actors where the state is unable or unwilling to protect (Article 6). Article 7 states that there will be protection when reasonable steps are taken to prevent the suffering or persecution by, *inter alia*, the operation of an effective legal system. In the UK this has been interpreted to mean the same as *Horvath*, but its effects and application have been mitigated and refined in later decisions. Schiemann LJ in *Noune v SSHD* [2000] EWCA Civ 306 made these points in relation to *Horvath:*

As a study of the many judgments and speeches in that case shows, the law in relation to persecution by non-state actors was unsettled and difficult to understand . . . [if it was interpreted to mean] . . . that where the law enforcement agencies are doing their best and are not being either generally inefficient and incompetent (as that word is generally understood implying a lack of skill rather than a lack of effectiveness) this was enough to disqualify a potential victim from being a refugee [this would be] an error of law. (para 28)

Schiemann LJ goes on to say that the crucial question is whether there was a reasonable likelihood of the appellant being persecuted for a Convention reason.

Horvath is generally quoted and applied in subsequent case law up to the present time as a 'practical standard which takes proper account of the duty which the state owes its nationals' relying also on the words of Lord Clyde:

the sufficiency of state protection is not measured by the existence of a real risk of an abuse of rights but by the availability of a system for the protection of a citizen and a reasonable willingness of the state to operate it.

The Court of Appeal in *Bagdanavicius v SSHD* [2003] EWCA Civ 1605 emphasized that punishment after the event was not sufficient protection. They said:

Sufficiency of state protection, whether from state agents or non-state actors, means a willingness *and* ability on the part of the receiving state to provide through its legal system a reasonable level of protection from ill-treatment of which the claimant for asylum has a well-founded fear.

The courts have elaborated the requirement for both willingness and effectiveness. The Federal Court of Canada in *Annan v Canada (Minister for Citizenship and Immigration)* IMM 215–95 said that 'pious statements of intent' about outlawing genital mutilation had not resulted in any action to do so and so not in protection for the asylum claimant. The Court of Appeal in *R (on the application of Atkinson) v SSHD* [2004] EWCA Civ 849 held that a lack of effectiveness would entail a systematic failure applying to individuals in the same group as the applicant, here, people who were or were seen to be informers for the People's National Party. It was not just a failure in relation to some individuals.

In *P and M v SSHD*, the IAT held that evidence that the police prosecuted due to public pressure after a woman had been killed by her husband and another had been seriously burned with acid suggested there was state protection against domestic violence. The Court of Appeal said this was to 'miss the point'. Where the police had to be compelled by such extreme circumstances to act (para 26), this did not amount to protection.

In *SA (political activist—internal relocation) Pakistan* [2011] UKUT 30 (IAC) the Tribunal said that judge must address not only whether there is a general sufficiency of protection in a country but also the question of whether the particular appellant would receive adequate protection. In this case there had already been highly dangerous incidents in which the appellant was targeted, and his brother had been killed; it could be inferred from this that the authorities were not able to protect him. The history also suggested a one-sided attitude by the police who therefore could also not be regarded as *willing* to protect him. See also *AW (sufficiency of protection) Pakistan* [2011] UKUT 31 (IAC), *Mishto v SSHD* [2003] EWCA Civ 1978, and *Hussein v SSHD* [2005 CSIH 45] for examples of how the particular circumstances must be investigated, in the light of the general situation in the country, in order to ascertain whether protection is sufficient.

In *DK v SSHD* [2006] EWCA Civ 682, the Court of Appeal held that evidence about the capacity of the KDP police to protect DK from being killed in a blood feud had not been properly considered. The question was not whether they had provided a sufficiency of protection within their capacity but whether the KDP police were actually capable of providing DK with adequate protection. Following *Noune*, it was not necessary to show that the state machinery had collapsed before being able to claim refugee status (para 27). See also *PS (Sri Lanka)* discussed at 12.5.1.1.

The full or partial collapse of state machinery, and the effect of ongoing conflict, are live issues in relation to many asylum claims now. Changing and unstable conditions are difficult for refugee decision-makers to assess. Substantial evidence is needed. The case of *AT and Others (Article 15c; risk categories) Libya* CG [2014] UKUT 318 (IAC) gives an example of what is needed to consider sufficiency of protection in the context of asylum claims and other claims to face a real risk of serious harm contrary to Article 15c QD.

 **Key Case**

AT and Others (Article 15c; risk categories) Libya CG [2014] UKUT 318 (IAC)

The Tribunal accepted evidence that the government in Libya was weak and relied on unaccountable militias to keep law and order. These militias were themselves a source of risk, and there was evidence of severe ill-treatment in detention. With regard to the courts there was:

> lack of enforcement capability, lack of competency of the courts, and confusion over the applicability of new and old laws . . . . The most significant human rights problems resulted from the absence of effective justice and security institutions . . . . The new government fell short of establishing a consistent rule of law.

> . . .

> Impunity was a serious problem. Although militias detained abusive Qadhafi-era officials, the scarcely functioning criminal courts struggled to try them, and when they did attempt to conduct trials, judges often faced threats of violence. In the same vein, with the judiciary not fully functioning, the government had not taken concrete steps by year's end to advance transitional justice. There were rarely investigations and still fewer prosecutions of those believed to have committed abuses.

The Tribunal accepted evidence that, although Libya had the legal facilities to carry out the prosecution of the Director of Intelligence of the former regime of Colonel Qadhafi, 'that could easily be interrupted if a sufficiently powerful local militia had cause to intervene'. There was 'no effective policing capability by uniformed officers under the authority of national or municipal institutions. Faced with the overwhelming firepower of militias and the widespread availability of weapons among the general population, the official police cannot guarantee protection for individuals, nor can they provide recourse for individuals who have encountered problems. To secure protection individuals can turn to militia leadership and declare their support for the militia.'
The Tribunal concluded that:

> The situation currently in Libya is that of a highly decentralised state in which the primary sources of protection are localised, through family and tribe. In these circumstances, and given the need to take a factual approach, we are satisfied that there is a general sufficiency of protection for the ordinary citizen. However, . . . the evidence establishes that an individual who succeeds in establishing a 'risk profile' will, in general, not be afforded a sufficiency of protection.

The spectrum of actors of persecution referred to in *Svazas* also potentially is a useful lens through which to consider protection. Where there is substantial corruption, or where the unofficial ideology of the state endorses the persecution, protection against non-state actors may not be available. The Tribunal in *AZ (Trafficked women) Thailand CG* [2010] UKUT 118 (IAC) held that trafficking is widespread and a serious problem all over Thailand and, applying *Horvath*, the problem is more than inefficiency or incompetence. Corruption was rife and the involvement of officials, whether at the border, at immigration counters at airports, or in other government departments, with traffickers and criminals had weakened the impact of the steps taken by the government to combat human trafficking. Shelters were run by men and were like detention centres.

12.5.4.4 Sources of protection

The final question here is whether protection must be offered by the state itself, or whether it may be offered by an entity which is capable of providing protection. *R (on the application of Vallaj) v Special Adjudicator and Canaj v Secretary of State for the Home Department* [2001] INLR 342 CA concerned the proposed return of the appellants, who were Kosovar Albanians, to Kosovo. The Court held that UNMIK (the United Nations Interim Administration Mission in Kosovo) supported by KFOR (the internal security force in Kosovo) had an international law obligation to protect Kosovans, which it was in fact discharging with the host country's consent, and this was enough to satisfy the Convention requirement for protection.

The QD, followed by the UK's implementing regulations, goes further than *Vallaj and Canaj*. The Directive allows that protection may be provided by 'parties or organisations, including international organisations, controlling the State or a substantial part of the territory of the State' (Article 7.1b). The European Council on Refugees and Exiles (ECRE) is concerned by this inclusion on the grounds that such authorities 'are not and cannot be parties to international human rights instruments and therefore cannot be held accountable for non-compliance with international refugee and human rights obligations' (ECRE information note October 2004). This argument was considered by the Tribunal in *DM (Majority Clan Entities can Protect) Somalia* [2005] UKAIT 00150, which concluded that all that was essential was effective protection. It could, in that case, be provided by a majority clan which had a militia. Somalia was a state in international law, and even if the function of government was fragmented, if a majority clan militia could provide protection, issues about the effectiveness of government would not need to be decided. *DM* predates the QD and later cases concerning Somalia have moved away from that conclusion (*AMM and others (conflict; humanitarian crisis; returnees; FGM) Somalia CG* [2011] UKUT 00445 (IAC)). In *AT and Others (Article 15c; risk categories) Libya CG* the Tribunal said that whether an individual could obtain protection from a militia would need to be decided on the evidence of an individual case.

12.6 Internal relocation

The concept of internal flight or internal relocation completes the consideration of persecution and state protection. Simply put, the internal flight or relocation doctrine, also called the internal protection alternative, is an assertion that, although they may risk persecution or breach of fundamental rights in their home area, the asylum seeker could find safety somewhere else in their own country. If established, then the asylum claim will be lost as there is no well-founded fear of persecution. The Michigan Guidelines on the Internal Protection Alternative (the product of an international consultation and colloquium in 1999) say that internal protection analysis must be 'directed to the identification of a present possibility of meaningful protection within the boundaries of the home state' (para 8).

The foundational case in relation to internal relocation is that of *Robinson* [1997] 3 WLR 1162.

Key Case

Robinson [1997] 3 WLR 1162

The appellant was a Tamil from northern Sri Lanka and had connections with the LTTE (Tamil Tigers). He claimed asylum in the UK following the assassination of the President of Sri Lanka by Tamil militants in May 1993, but his claim was refused. The Special Adjudicator held that, while he might risk persecution in an area controlled by the Tamil Tigers as he might be recruited against his will to support them, he could safely return to Colombo as it was controlled by the Sri Lankan authorities. He was in Colombo at the time of the President's assassination and had been briefly detained there. The Special Adjudicator did not expressly consider whether it was *reasonable* to expect the appellant to relocate in Colombo on the basis that this was an unreviewable matter of the Secretary of State's discretion.

The Court of Appeal decided that appellate authorities do have jurisdiction to consider the reasonableness of the internal flight alternative. As for the question of what is reasonable, that must be decided by looking at all the circumstances.

The Court of Appeal took guidance from the Australian case of *Randhawa* 124 ALR 265, suggesting that factors to be taken into account in determining whether it was reasonable to expect the appellant to relocate would include, for instance, the accessibility of the 'safe' part of the country, any danger or hardship of travelling there, the quality of internal protection in the country, that is, does it meet 'basic norms of civil, political and socio-economic human rights'?

The question to be answered was, it suggested, that posed in the Canadian case, *Thirunavukkarasu* (1993) 109 DLR (4th) 682, namely: 'would it be unduly harsh to expect this person, who is being persecuted in one part of his country, to move to another less hostile part of the country before seeking refugee status abroad?' The Canadian court had given the following examples:

While claimants should not be expected to cross battle lines or hide out in an isolated region of their country, like a cave in the mountains, a desert or a jungle, it will not be enough for them to say that they do not like the weather in a safe area, or that they have no friends or relatives there, or that they may not be able to find suitable work there.

These are extremes to illustrate the principle, which has been expanded upon in English case law. Nolan J in *R v IAT ex p Jonah* [1985] Imm AR 7 considered that it was unreasonable to expect a senior Ghanaian trade union official to go back to what was in effect a hideaway, a very remote village accessible only by a 15-mile walk through the jungle. On the other hand, in both *R v SSHD ex p Yurekli* [1991] Imm AR 153 (CA) and *R v SSHD ex p Gunes* [1991] Imm AR 278, the courts held that it was not unreasonable to expect Turkish Kurds to relocate in a part of Turkey away from the villages where they faced persecution. The size of the country is often treated as relevant. In *MM (Lebanon) v SSHD* [2009] EWCA Civ 382, the Court held that it was unrealistic to talk of the appellant being safe in an area of Lebanon not controlled by Hezbollah. It was a small country without restrictions on freedom of movement, every part of which was within 30 minutes' drive of a Hezbollah stronghold. The accessibility of the safe area includes being able to enter the country without a violation of rights. In *Degirmenci v SSHD* [2004] EWCA Civ 1553 the Court of Appeal accepted that if the appellant was at risk of being detained and interrogated on arrival in Turkey, then internal relocation was not relevant. This is not a 'technical obstacle to return', but a question of substantive rights. A 'technical obstacle' (such as difficulty obtaining travel documents) does not prevent reliance by the State on internal relocation, according to the 2004 QD Article 8.3. This leeway for states was removed in the 2011 QD, but the UK is bound only by the 2004 version.

Since *Robinson*, case law has not changed the basic question of whether it would be unduly harsh to expect the claimant to relocate, but the quality of life and of protection that the claimant should be expected to accept in the area of relocation has been hotly contested.

12.6.1 Replicating persecution in 'safe haven'

The internal protection alternative must not be used so as to require the refugee to live in a way that replicates the persecution they flee if they live normally, exercising basic human rights. The Court held in *Hysi v SSHD* [2005] EWCA Civ 711 that the Tribunal had given insufficient consideration as to whether it would be unduly harsh to expect a young man to return to Kosovo and hide his mixed ethnicity. The Court thought that the Australian case of *Appellant S 395 v Minister for Immigration and Multicultural Affairs* [2004] INLR 233 cited the correct principle:

It would undermine the object of the Convention if a signatory country required [refugees] to modify their beliefs or opinions or to hide their race, nationality or membership of particular social groups before those countries would give them protection.

In a similar vein, the Tribunal in *SA (political activist—internal relocation) Pakistan* [2011] UKUT 30 (IAC) held that:

[r]equiring a political activist to live away from his home area in order to avoid persecution at the hands of his political opponents has never been considered a proper application of the internal relocation principle: see e.g. Nolan J in *R v Immigration Appeal Tribunal, ex p. Jonah* [1985] Imm AR 7. And (since October 2006) such a requirement cannot be considered to be consistent with para 3390 of the Immigration Rules (Article 8 of the Qualification Directive). Indeed, the pitfalls of requiring a person to act contrary to his normal behaviour in order to avoid persecution have been further emphasised by the Supreme Court in *HJ (Iran)* [2010] UKSC 31.

In *HC v SSHD* [2005] EWCA Civ 893, the Court of Appeal held that the adjudicator, in considering that the appellant could return to a different part of Lebanon, had failed to take sufficient account of the cumulative effect of being homosexual and a Palestinian refugee. She had also not taken into account significant evidence of conditions in that country for homosexuals when holding that he would be safe in a place other than the refugee camp where he grew up.

In a similar vein, UNHCR Guidelines on Internal Protection 23 July 2003 say:

Where internal displacement is a result of 'ethnic cleansing' policies, denying refugee status on the basis of the internal flight or relocation concept could be interpreted as condoning the resulting situation on the ground, and therefore raises additional concerns.

12.6.2 **Past persecution by the state and non-state agents**

Is internal protection automatically debarred when past persecution was by the state? The Michigan Guidelines on the Internal Protection Alternative (para 16) say that there should be 'a strong presumption against finding an "internal protection alternative" where the agent or author of the original risk of persecution is, or is sponsored by, the national government'. UNHCR Guidelines 2003 take a similar position.

In *Januzi, Hamid, Gaafar and Mohammed v SSHD* [2006] UKHL 5, Lord Bingham said 'there is no absolute rule' or presumption of this kind (para 21). He referred to the spectrum of state responsibility we noted earlier in the case of *Svazas*, and said that the relationship between the state and the act(s) of persecution must be assessed: 'The more closely the persecution in question is linked to the state, and the greater the control of the state over those acting or purporting to act on its behalf, the more likely (other things being equal) that a victim of persecution in one place will be similarly vulnerable in another place within the state' (para 21). Lord Hope said that 'where the state is in full control of events and its agents of persecution are active everywhere' internal relocation is obviously not an option (para 48). The severity of past persecution has repeatedly been argued to have a bearing on internal relocation. Amnesty International evidence to the New Zealand Refugee Status Appeals Authority suggested it should (see Symes and Jorro p. 219). The reasons for this are indicated by Elias J, in *R v IAT ex p Sellasamy* CO/3238/99:

the fact that on his return he is protected by a state which has, albeit through a different agency and in a different area, inflicted great pain and humiliation on him, is potentially highly material to the question of whether it would be unduly harsh to expect him to return. (para 33)

Such a person might have developed a 'distrust of the country itself and a disinclination to be associated with it as its national' (Grahl-Madsen, quoted in *In re B & R v Special Adjudicator ex parte Hoxha* [2005] UKHL 19). In *FK (Kenya) v SSHD* [2008] EWCA Civ 119, Sedley LJ remarked, obiter, that there might be cases where, objectively, the appellant could be safe, but was so traumatized by past events that she remained in genuine terror of being returned there. This could be relevant to whether relocation was unduly harsh.

Where the persecution is feared from non-state actors, a careful evaluation of the evidence of their reach and influence is needed. In *PO (Nigeria)* [2011] EWCA Civ 132 the Court of Appeal considered that the Tribunal's failure to evaluate the evidence correctly infected their view that internal relocation was reasonable. The evidence included for instance that the man who arranged the appellant's trafficking was a 'professional violent criminal with a power base in Nigeria and probably in the UK'.

In some cases, particularly those concerning women, although the acts of persecution are by non-state actors, the underlying political or value system which perpetuates those actions may be so pervasive that the possibility or concept of a safe area is as inappropriate as it would be if a state agent were the direct persecutor. See *K and others (FGM) The Gambia* CG [2013] UKUT 00062 (IAC), in which the risk factors for FGM in Gambia are analysed in detail. In relation to internal relocation the Tribunal held that 'an individual at real risk of FGM in her home area is unlikely to be able to avail herself of internal relocation, although this is always a question of fact'. The power structures in the country of origin were also critical, and analysed in *AM and BM (Trafficked women) Albania* CG [2010] UKUT 80 (IAC), where the Tribunal said:

Much of Albanian society is governed by a strict code of honour which not only means that trafficked women would have very considerable difficulty in reintegrating into their home areas but also will affect their ability to relocate internally.

Another difficulty for women faced with a decision that they can internally relocate from a non-state persecutor is that the networks and means by which a private persecutor may trace the woman are not well evidenced or understood outside the country, but are nonetheless powerful (again see *K and others (FGM) The Gambia* CG [2013] UKUT 00062 (IAC)).

12.6.3 Risks in site of internal protection and basis of comparison

A case can be made that the Refugee Convention sets the standard of protection that is appropriate for a refugee. This standard should therefore be available in the site of alternative protection. The Michigan Guidelines support this view. However, in *E v SSHD* [2003] EWCA Civ 1032, the Court of Appeal held that what is required in the site of relocation is protection from persecution, not delivery of other human rights. The House of Lords in *Januzi, Hamid, Gaafar and Mohammed* agreed. It endorsed the UNHCR Guidelines in saying that relocation:

requires, from a practical perspective, an assessment of whether the rights that will not be respected or protected are fundamental to the individual, such that the deprivation of those rights would be sufficiently harmful to render the area an unreasonable alternative. (para 28, in [2006] UKHL 5 para 20)

The Refugee Convention requires delivery of political and socio-economic rights, and integration into the host state. However, in internal relocation, the question would be whether what is lacking is the 'the real possibility to survive economically'. The Refugee Convention was not intended to define rights in the claimant's home country.

In reaching its conclusion, the Court was supported by the QD which, it said, imposed a 'standard significantly lower' than the Michigan Guidelines and New Zealand cases would require (para 17). The QD permits internal relocation 'if in a part of the country of origin there is no well-founded fear of being persecuted . . . and the applicant can reasonably be expected to stay in that part of the country'. In order to determine this, the Member State must 'have regard to the general circumstances prevailing in that part of the country and to the personal circumstances of the applicant' (Article 8).

Januzi also held that the basis of comparison in assessing internal protection is between the proposed location and the refugee's home area, not with the country of asylum. The appeal of Mr Januzi was dismissed, but the appeals of Messrs Hamid, Gaafar, and Mohammed were sent back from the House of Lords to the Tribunal for decision. In the space of 18 months, the cases went back up the appeal chain and were heard again in the House of Lords. The cases concern the situation of people from Darfur. While, on the one hand, the situation in Darfur has caused alarm worldwide and has been characterized as one of the greatest human rights disasters of the present age, on the other hand the question of whether such a situation can or should be contained within Africa, what kind of material standards a rural Sudanese person can expect, and whether refugee camps are tolerable places, all raise issues that go to the heart of global inequities.

 **Key Case**

AH (Sudan), IG (Sudan), NM (Sudan) v SSHD [2007] UKHL 49

All three appellants were black Africans formerly living in Darfur in western Sudan. They had been victims of serious persecution by Arab bands known as the Janjaweed, persecution which the government of Sudan had connived in or at the very least not restrained. It was accepted that by reason of the well-known facts about the desperate situation of black Africans in Darfur, all of the appellants were *prima facie* entitled to international protection. The Secretary of

State's case was that they could safely return to Sudan, provided that they return not to Darfur but to Khartoum. The appellants' case was that they would still be in danger of persecution in any part of Sudan; alternatively, even if they were not in danger of persecution if returned to Khartoum, it would be unduly harsh to require them to return there. They were village people and subsistence farmers. If they returned to Khartoum they would be in a camp outside the city in conditions of urban or sub-urban poverty. In the judgment, one expert is quoted as follows:

In the Al-Fatah camp where the victims of forced relocation were living at the time of my visit, I was struck with their most desperate situation and appalling conditions of extreme poverty. They had scarcely been able to erect makeshift huts from plastic sheets and cardboard as they had been left without any building material. While there was a water bladder no food or other life-sustaining goods had been provided . . . The camp is situated some 50km outside of Khartoum in the desert, where without water agricultural activities are impossible. (para 43)

The Tribunal held that they would not be at risk of persecution anywhere in Sudan, and conditions in Khartoum would not be unduly harsh because they were no different from the conditions of rural poverty elsewhere in squatter camps and slums. The appeal continued to the Court of Appeal and House of Lords on the question of whether return to Khartoum was unduly harsh.

The Court of Appeal held it would be unduly harsh to expect them to relocate to Khartoum, including a principle that '[t]raumatic changes of life-style, for instance from a city to a desert, or into slum conditions, should not be forced on the asylum-seeker' (para 33).

The House of Lords allowed the Secretary of State's appeal. They said the proper approach remained that in *Januzi*:

The decision-maker, taking account of all relevant circumstances pertaining to the claimant and his country of origin, must decide whether it is reasonable to expect the claimant to relocate or whether it would be unduly harsh to expect him to do so. (para 21)

Lord Bingham agreed that 'enquiry must be directed to the situation of the particular applicant, whose age, gender, experience, health, skills and family ties may all be very relevant'. However, this did not mean that certain considerations should be mandated, prohibited or prioritized:

There is no warrant for excluding, or giving priority to, consideration of the applicant's way of life in the place of persecution. There is no warrant for excluding, or giving priority to, consideration of conditions generally prevailing in the home country. (*AH* para 5)

Internal relocation of non-Arab Darfuris to Sudan is now dealt with by a country guidance case: *AA (Non-Arab Darfuris—relocation) Sudan* CG [2009] UKAIT 00056, which says that all non-Arab Darfuris are at risk of persecution in Darfur and cannot reasonably be expected to relocate elsewhere in Sudan.

12.6.4 What is reasonable or not unduly harsh

The question of internal relocation nevertheless remains a two-part question:

1. Are there real risks of serious harm or persecution in the proposed site of relocation?
2. If not, is it reasonable (i.e., not unduly harsh) to expect this claimant to relocate there?

In *AZ (Thailand)* internal relocation was not reasonable. The shelters were run by men and were like detention centres. The appellant was also extremely fragile psychologically. There was a lack of facilities for psychological support for someone in her situation in Thailand.

Internal relocation presents many problems for women applicants (see *Relocation, Relocation* Asylum Aid). Guidance to Home Office caseworkers is that:

In certain countries, financial, logistical, social, cultural and other factors may mean that women face particular difficulties. This may be the case for divorced women, unmarried women, widows or single/lone parents, especially in countries where women are expected to have male protection. If women face discrimination in a possible place of relocation and are unable to work or obtain assistance from the authorities, relocation would be unreasonable. Where the fear is of members of her family, relocation is clearly not appropriate if the situation a woman would be placed in would be likely to leave her with no alternative but to seek her family's assistance and thus re-expose her to a well-founded fear of persecution or a real risk of serious harm. Caseworkers must consider whether the claimant, if unaccompanied, would be able to safely access the proposed relocation area. Gender specific risks include the risk of being subjected to sexual violence. (API *Assessing Credibility and Refugee Status*, January 2015, para 8.2).

The question of what standard is appropriate to judge conditions in the site of relocation remains contested (see Ní Ghráinne).

12.6.5 Safety of home area

Finally, if persecution has ceased in the home area, refugee status is not available, even if conditions remain risky elsewhere in the country (*Canaj and Vallaj v SSHD and Special Adjudicator* [2001] INLR 342). However, risks elsewhere in the country may make the home area inaccessible and thus invoke the doctrine of *non-refoulement*. The question of safe routes of return is often critical and is considered in more detail in chapter 16.

12.6.6 Summary and burden of proof in relation to internal flight

As the internal flight alternative is raised by the Secretary of State, it could seem appropriate that the Secretary of State would have the burden of proving that it would *not* be unduly harsh to return the claimant. This is strongly suggested by the Michigan Guidelines (para 14). Alternatively, if the Secretary of State raises the point, does the burden then shift to the claimant to show that it would be unduly harsh, and if so, to what standard of proof? The Court of Appeal in *Karanakaran v SSHD* [2003] 3 All ER 449 held that there was no standard of proof in the civil sense, as discussed earlier in relation to establishing a well-founded fear of persecution. The claimant did not have to prove to a certain standard that particular events were likely to occur, but the decision-maker should take into account all the evidence and decide whether it was unduly harsh for the claimant to return to a different area. This point was refined by Sedley LJ in *Salam Jasim v SSHD* [2006] EWCA Civ 342, where he said that:

Once the judge of fact is satisfied that the applicant has a justified fear of persecution or harm if returned to his home area, the claim will ordinarily be made out unless the judge is satisfied that he can nevertheless be safely returned to another part of his country of origin. Provided the second issue has been flagged up, there may be no formal burden of proof on the Home Secretary (see *GH* [2004] UKIAT 00248); but this does not mean that the judge of fact can reject an otherwise well-founded claim unless the evidence satisfies him that internal relocation is a safe and reasonable option. (para 16)

The risks of persecution in the claimant's home area must be considered first, because it is against these that the proposed location must provide protection. Symes and Jorro (p. 221) point out that this means a claim should not be certified as unfounded (see chapter 11) on the basis of internal protection.

Reading case law on internal flight can be confusing. Who is arguing what? It may be seen like this:

Step 1 : Asylum claim is assessed. Risk may or may not be found of persecution in home area.

Step 2 : Secretary of State asserts that the claimant would not face persecution or a real risk of serious harm in another area of their home country.

Step 3 : Secretary of State, looking at all relevant factors, determines that it would not be unduly harsh for the claimant to return to a different area.

Step 4 : Claimant on appeal may argue that there is a risk of persecution or serious harm elsewhere.

Step 5 : Whether or not there is a risk of persecution or serious harm elsewhere, the claimant may additionally argue that it would be unduly harsh and not reasonable for them to go to that area.

Step 6 : Undue harshness is assessed, bearing in mind whether the risks in the alternative site would amount to indirect *refoulement*, and the effect on the individual, as set out in *Januzi*.

Step 7 : The refugee claim may succeed if the claimant would face persecution in their home area *and* it would be unduly harsh to force them to live elsewhere.

Step 8 : A claim for humanitarian protection may succeed, even if the refugee claim has failed, if the claimant would face a real risk of serious harm in their home area *and* it would be unreasonable to return them elsewhere.

In practice, the Home Office often uses internal relocation as an alternative argument even when they have found there is no risk in the home area. Internal relocation often follows an adverse credibility finding as a kind of 'belt and braces' refusal (see Asylum Aid 2014).

12.7 **Causal link**

Returning to the Article 1A definition, we see that a refugee is one who is 'outside his country of nationality, and owing to a well-founded fear of being persecuted *for reasons of*', and then the list of Convention reasons appears. This apparently simple connecting phrase has significance in the case law of the Convention and in the determination of who is a refugee. The QD requires only a 'connection' between the Convention reason and the persecution. The UK's implementing regulations require that the act of persecution is committed 'for' Convention reasons. The Tribunal in *SB (Moldova) CG* [2008] UKAIT 00002 reviewed these formulations and that of Baroness Hale in *ex p Hoxha*, who said persecution must be 'for reasons which are related to one of the Convention grounds', and accepted that in that case it was sufficient that the persecution was related to the Convention reason.

As the *UNHCR Handbook* points out, 'Often the applicant himself may not be aware of the reasons for the persecution feared. It is not, however, his duty to analyze his case to such an extent as to identify the reasons in detail' (para 66). The reasons in detail in fact may not all be important as there is no requirement that the persecution is carried out solely for Convention reasons (see *SB (Moldova) CG* [2008] UKAIT 00002). Reasons may in reality be very mixed and the personal motivation of the persecutor is not the key (see Goodwin-Gill and McAdam 2007:101). For instance, in the case of *Sivakumar* referred to earlier, the House of Lords were aware that the persecutors might have the suppression of terrorism among their motives for torturing the appellant. However, the reason that he was tortured was a mixture of his ethnicity and supposed political stance. The personal motivations of the persecutor are an aspect of individual criminal-ity but are not connected with the failure of the state to protect. The relevant reason for the persecution is the structural reason in that society, not the personal reason of the persecutor. Again, we can see that the case of sexual attacks is treated quite differently as in *Okonkwo* and other cases discussed earlier, the supposed personal motive of the persecutor was regarded as overriding. Musalo (2003) proposes that some of this in-consistency in relation to gender-based claims would be resolved by a more widespread adoption of what she calls a 'bifurcated approach' to causation—namely, that there will be persecution for a Convention reason if either the ill-treatment or the failure of protection is for a Convention reason.

The question of the causal link, or *nexus*, was considered at length by the House of Lords in *Shah and Islam*. It considered the Canadian approach which is to use the 'but for' test, as in UK discrimination law. This is by asking the question: 'but for their gen-der, would these people be persecuted?' It is tempting to say that this is sufficient, and that in *Shah and Islam* (see 12.8.4) the two women would not have been persecuted but for their gender. However, this approach is not favoured as, following its use in tort law, it brings with it the question of how much of the cause the Convention reason needs to be, that is, 60 per cent, 40 per cent, and so on (see discussion in Hathaway and Foster 2003). This is a fruitless path which, it is generally accepted, is better not to tread.

Lord Hoffmann suggested that drawbacks in the 'but for' test were revealed by the example of women raped in a situation of general lawlessness. The women would not be raped but for gender but the reason for this treatment would also be the breakdown in law and order, and not their gender. This analysis is open to question in that men are subject to rape, but the power imbalance between men and women suggests that women are more likely to be raped, therefore one might argue that women would not be raped but for this imbalance which is left uncontrolled by the breakdown of law and order. They would not be raped but for their gender not because they are women but because they are women in a society where lawlessness exposes them to the underly-ing power imbalance. Nevertheless, one can disagree with the example and still see the point Lord Hoffmann is making, which is that causation should be sought at the structural level, in the lack of protection. He demonstrates this with the example of a Jew in Germany punished for failing to obey the racial laws, who is thereby perse-cuted for their race. The reason for this is that there is no state protection against such punishment and the state's lack of protection is also grounded in race. Whether the individual who initiates the prosecution hates Jews or not is irrelevant. Whether there are additional reasons, such as conducting a census, for identifying Jews is irrelevant. The reason in that society in which that person is suffering that treatment is that they are a Jew.

The effects of taking a subjective approach to causation are illustrated in the case of *Omoruyi v SSHD* [2001] Imm AR 175, in which the appellant sought asylum following death threats from the Ogboni cult as he refused to comply with their demands in relation to his father's burial. The Court of Appeal found against the appellant on the grounds that the Ogboni were not motivated by the appellant's religion (Christianity) to persecute him but by his non-compliance with their requirements. Anyone else who had similarly failed to comply would be treated in the same way. Simon Brown LJ said: 'The Nigerian State Authorities in the present case were not unable or unwilling to protect the appellant because of his being a Christian but rather because he was at risk for having crossed this particular cult.' Simon Brown LJ thus looked for motivation, first in the non-state persecutors, and, second, in the state, and finding none, concluded that there was no causal link to the appellant's religion. Hathaway and Foster (2003) provide a different analysis of this decision. The question, they suggest, should be 'why is the applicant in the predicament he is in?' rather than 'why does the persecutor wish to harm the applicant or the state refrain from protecting him?' The answer then would be 'because he was a Christian'. Hathaway and Foster contrast *Omoruyi* with the similar Australian case of *Okere v MIMA* 157 ALR 678 (Aust Fed C Sept 21 1998). In this case, the Court held that the causal nexus was satisfied. It noted that religious persecution often takes indirect forms, and if this form of causation were not accepted:

Persons who have a well-founded fear of persecution for reasons of their refusal to work on the Sabbath could be found not to have a well-founded fear of persecution for reasons of their religion; the persecution feared by them would be related to their refusal to work and not to their religion.

Lord Hoffmann in *Shah and Islam* also identified a fallacy in the judgment of the Court of Appeal, namely the idea that all members of a group have to be persecuted in order for the reason for persecution to be membership of that group. The reason these two women were persecuted was because they were women in a society that discriminates against women. Not all women in the society need to be discriminated against for this to be the case.

The question of causal nexus was briefly considered by the House of Lords in *Sepet and Bulbul*. The result is not entirely clear. Lord Bingham reiterated the generally accepted view that the motive of the perpetrator is not the reason. The question is, 'what is the real reason?' It is not clear how the real reason is ascertained, though the question may be approached consistently with *Okere*. In *Gaoua v SSHD* [2004] EWCA Civ 1528, the Court of Appeal held that the question of what was the real reason for the risk of detention and persecution upon return could be answered in the following way. If it was because he was perceived to hold radical opinions, this would found an asylum claim. If it was 'just' to obtain information about Algerian terrorists in the UK, then 'arguably' it would not. This case should be compared with *Sivakumar*.

Reference was made earlier to the particular difficulties of proving a refugee claim in the context of a war, and this was evident, for reasons related to causation, in *XZ (Russia) v SSHD* [2008] EWCA Civ 180. A Chechen mother and son were subjected to horrific atrocities, but the Tribunal did not consider it proved that they had been targeted because of their husband and father's political activities in the Chechen Parliament. The atrocities were carried out during the Chechen War. The perpetrators were believed to be Russian security forces. The Court of Appeal accepted there had been no error of law. If Hathaway and Foster's question had been asked—'why are the appellants in the position they are in?'—it is at least possible that the outcome might have been different.

The question of causal nexus may be simplified under the QD, but still overlaps with a key question in refugee law, identification of the Convention reason for the persecution.

12.8 **Convention reason**

Persecution only gives rise to refugee status if it is 'for reasons of race, religion, nationality, particular social group or political opinion'. The first three reasons can be briefly dealt with; the other two require closer examination.

12.8.1 **Race**

Convention law does not require a technical definition of race. The *Handbook* says that race 'is to be understood in its widest sense to include all kinds of ethnic groups that are referred to as "races" in common usage' (para 68). It is not impossible for there to be persecution of members of the same race for reasons of race. The Federal Court of Australia in the case of *Perampalam v Minister for Immigration and Multicultural Affairs* (1999) 55 ALD 431 notes that the LTTE (Tamil Tigers) would approach Tamils for financial support. The implication is that pressure could be brought to bear.

The *Handbook* also emphasizes the seriousness of racial discrimination, and that where such discrimination interferes with the exercise of fundamental rights, or has serious consequences, this is likely to amount to persecution. Goodwin-Gill comments that 'Persecution on account of race is all too frequently the background to refugee movements in all parts of the world' (2007:70). For instance, Buxton LJ identified the persecution in Darfur which has given rise to many asylum claims as 'one of the most serious and extensive examples of racial persecution to have occurred in recent years' in *AH (Sudan), IG (Sudan), NM (Sudan) v SSHD* [2007] EWCA Civ 297.

It may be recalled that the European Commission on Human Rights found the state's action in passing racially discriminatory legislation capable in itself of amounting to a violation of Article 3 ECHR (*East African Asians v UK* (1973) 3 EHRR 76). Claims of persecution of Roma have been accepted as being for reasons of race (e.g., *Horvath, Harakal*), although also commonly Roma cases have failed, and in the case reports the emphasis is rather on questioning or establishing the seriousness of the violations of other human rights (to physical security, housing, etc.). The racial dimension, rather than being seen as an aggravating factor, seems invisible.

Claims by Palestinians have also not succeeded on this basis. In *MM and FH (Stateless Palestinians—KK, IH, HE CG reaffirmed) Lebanon* [2008] UKAIT 00014, the Tribunal held that differential treatment of Palestinians in refugee camps in Lebanon did not arise from their race, but from their statelessness. It could be justified under international conventions and human rights norms.

A recurring issue faced by Palestinian refugees is the difficulty of actually obtaining re-entry to their homeland. In *MA (Palestinian Territories) v SSHD* [2008] EWCA Civ 304, the Court of Appeal held that it was not persecutory to turn a stateless person away at the borders of his country of former habitual residence. MA had lived all his life in the Palestinian Territories. According to the law of Israel, he had no nationality, and could not compel any state to grant him entry after the failure of his asylum claim. This in itself, the Court held, was not persecutory. The appellants in *MT (Palestinian Territories) v SSHD* [2008] EWCA Civ 1149 and *SH (Palestinian Territories) v SSHD* [2008] EWCA Civ 1150 argued that the Court in *MA* had not considered the refusal of entry in the light of its being for reasons of race (being a Palestinian Arab). The Court disagreed. They held that this must have been in the contemplation of the Court in *MA*.

12.8.2 **Religion**

Religion is widely defined in the QD, to include atheistic beliefs and both participation in and abstention from worship. The definition of religion has not been a major issue in asylum case law. More common issues have been what degree of self-restraint might be expected of the asylum seeker, what level of constraint is acceptable by a government, and therefore what kinds of religious activities should be absolutely free from state interference.

The ICCPR Article 18 provides: 'No one shall be subject to coercion which would impair his freedom to have or to adopt a religion or belief of his choice.' The freedom includes the freedom to change faith, or to hold a different faith from the official state religion. Another common issue in claims based on religion is the question of whether a person can be expected to only practise their faith in private so as to avoid persecution. This issue is now dealt with in *HJ (Iran) and HT (Cameroon)*, discussed at 12.8.4.3. This Supreme Court decision was applied in the country guidance case *MN and others (Ahmadis—country conditions—risk) Pakistan* CG [2012] UKUT 00389 (IAC) with the effect that a person of the Ahmadi faith cannot be required to practise in private so as to avoid persecution. Applying *HJ (Iran)*, it is necessary first to establish whether the person is a committed Ahmadi, and whether it is important to them to exercise the public aspects of their faith, but if it is, they cannot be required to desist. The relationship between state and non-state persecution is also described in the case, in which the Tribunal held that:

The legislation . . . prohibits preaching and other forms of proselytising . . . also in practice restricts . . . holding open discourse about religion with non-Ahmadis . . . openly referring to one's place of worship as a mosque and to one's religious leader as an Imam. In addition, Ahmadis are not permitted to refer to the call to prayer as azan nor to call themselves Muslims or refer to their faith as Islam. Sanctions include a fine and imprisonment and if blasphemy is found, there is a risk of the death penalty which to date has not been carried out although there is a risk of lengthy incarceration if the penalty is imposed. . . . this legislation is used by non-state actors to threaten and harass Ahmadis. This includes the filing of First Information Reports (FIRs) (the first step in any criminal proceedings) which can result in detentions whilst prosecutions are being pursued. Ahmadis are also subject to attacks . . .

If an Ahmadi is able to demonstrate that it is of particular importance to his religious identity to practise and manifest his faith openly in Pakistan in defiance of the restrictions in the Pakistan Penal Code (PPC) under sections 298B and 298C . . . he or she is likely to be in need of protection . . .

12.8.3 **Nationality**

This Convention reason is given a loose interpretation, not restricted to citizenship, as in the QD Article 10(1)(c) which includes 'cultural, linguistic or ethnic identity, common geographical or political origins or its relationship with the population of another State'. The *UNHCR Handbook* notes that in conflict within a state where there are 'two or more national (ethnic, linguistic) groups . . . It may not always be easy to distinguish between persecution for reasons of nationality and persecution for reasons of political opinion.'

Persecution on grounds of nationality can in theory include where citizenship is denied to a minority. Though Czech and Slovak Roma have been in this position (see O'Nions 1999), once again there was little evidence of this being used to their advantage in asylum claims.

12.8.4 **Particular social group**

This Convention reason is more open to interpretation than the preceding ones. It has the capacity to some extent to enable the Convention to meet needs not originally envisaged, but is not a cure-all or catch-all category. As the Tribunal said in *Montoya* [2002] INLR 399 para 24:

The convention is not intended to protect all suffering individuals, only those who can show that the risk of persecution in their case is for an enumerated Convention ground. If ignoring this principle the PSG grounds were read too widely, the enumeration of grounds would be superfluous; the definition of 'refugee' could have been limited to individuals who have a well-founded fear of persecution without more.

As a starting point for determining whether a claimant comes within a social group which could be protected by the Convention, it is useful though not essential to consider the principle of *ejusdem generis*. In other words, to construe 'particular social group' as being of the same kind as the other Convention reasons. This does not mean that social group repeats the other reasons, but that by having regard to the defining characteristics of the other reasons it may be possible to identify a social group for Convention purposes.

The key characteristics of the other Convention reasons were identified by the US Board of Immigration Appeals in the case of *Acosta* (1985) 19 I and N 211 as follows:

Each . . . describes persecution aimed at an immutable characteristic: a characteristic that either is beyond the power of the individual to change or is so fundamental to individual identity or conscience that it ought not to be required to be changed . . . The shared characteristic might be an innate one such as sex, colour, or kinship ties, or in some circumstances it might be a shared experience such as former military leadership or land ownership.

Very similar qualities were identified in *Attorney General for Canada v Ward* (1993) 2 SCR 689, an application by a member of the Irish National Liberation Army for asylum in Canada. The Supreme Court suggested the following 'working rules' for identifying a particular social group:

1. groups defined by an innate or unchangeable characteristic;
2. groups whose members voluntarily associate for reasons so fundamental to their human dignity that they should not be forced to forsake the association;
3. groups associated by a former voluntary status, unalterable due to historical permanence.

What we shall refer to as the *Ward* criteria have been extensively relied on by the courts.

The leading case in the UK on identifying particular social groups is *Shah and Islam v SSHD* [1999] 2 AC 629, to which reference has already been made in the context of causal nexus. The case resolved a number of disputed points.

 Key Case

Shah and Islam v SSHD **[1999] 2 AC 629**

Mrs Shah's husband was violent and turned her out of their home in Pakistan. She arrived in the UK and gave birth to a child shortly afterwards. She was afraid that her husband might accuse her of adultery and denounce her under Sharia law for the offence of sexual immorality. The Court accepted evidence from an Amnesty International report on the position of women in Pakistan that the legal system discriminated against women in particular in its rules of evidence, and for the most severe charges of sexual immorality the evidence of women would not be heard. Arrests on such a charge could be made without preliminary investigation and could result in prolonged detention. For those convicted 'there is the spectre of 100 lashes or stoning to death in public' (549e).

Mrs Islam also had a violent marriage, but she had remained in it for 20 years. She was a schoolteacher. One day, a fight broke out at the school between two young supporters of rival political factions. She intervened and one faction became hostile and accused her of infidelity. These accusations were repeated to her husband, who was a member of the same political faction. Mrs Islam's husband assaulted her and she was admitted to hospital twice. She left her husband and stayed briefly with her brother, but unknown men then threatened him and she could not stay.

The Court of Appeal held that they were not members of a particular social group. One reason for this was a view that the members of the group must associate with each other, there must be some cohesiveness, interdependence, or cooperation, this was what made them a *social* group. None of the possible ways of defining a group of which Mrs Shah and Mrs Islam were members produced groups with this characteristic. The House of Lords dealt with this unambiguously. Contact among group members was not required. The examples given in *Ward* of characteristics which might form a social group (e.g., language, sexuality) do not suggest such contact. The groups are social groups in the sense of being recognizable in the context of the society in which they arise (per Lords Hoffmann, Hope, and Millett at 571a and 569e).

The second reason that the Court of Appeal held that the women were not part of a social group was the difficulty of defining the group without reference to the persecution. It is settled law, for example, in *Savchenkov* [1996] Imm AR 28, that the group must exist independently of the persecution, and groups such as 'women subject to death by stoning for adultery' or 'women subject to domestic violence without redress' incorporate the persecution into the definition.

The problem was resolved by asking what the reason was for the persecution. It was because they were women, but not only this. They were women in a society that discriminates against women. This was not to use the persecution as a way of defining the group, but to use discrimination, and to acknowledge that women may be perceived as a group in a society which discriminates against them. Their Lordships explained by taking the example of left-handed people in a society that discriminates seriously against left-handedness. It may readily be seen that, in such a society, left-handed people would be regarded as a group in a way that they are not in a society that does not so discriminate.

To summarize, the group is a social group in the sense of being a group in the context of a society. The group may (but need not) be identified by discrimination against them in relation to a characteristic identified in the *Ward* criteria. There is no need for social cohesiveness in the group. The upshot in *Shah and Islam* was that the social group was found to be 'women in Pakistan', or 'women in a society that discriminates against women'.

12.8.4.1 Gender-based persecution

In the absence of gender as a listed reason in the Convention itself, case law has developed ways of including gender-specific persecution, and *Shah and Islam* was a significant step in this process. Women have faced enormous difficulty in establishing asylum claims. As discussed earlier, decision-makers at all levels have been very slow to recognize the political uses of rape and its place in the persecution of women. The nature of much gender-based persecution of women has not been recognized and neither have the forms of political activity in which women frequently engage. The Home Office's Guidance on Gender Issues in the Asylum Claim sets out some of the issues.

A woman may experience:

i) gender-specific persecution for reasons unrelated to gender (e.g. raped because of her activity in a political party)
ii) non-gender-specific persecution for reasons relating to her gender (e.g. flogged for refusing to wear a veil)
iii) gender-specific persecution because of her gender (e.g. female genital mutilation).

In connection with political opinion the API identifies that:

gender roles in many countries mean that women will more often be involved in low level political activities, for instance hiding people, passing messages or providing community services, food, clothing or medical care. Decision-makers should beware of equating so-called 'low-level' activity with low risk.

As discussed earlier in relation to sexual violence, although the guidance is limited, research also reveals a widespread failure to follow the guidance. Decisions still fail to recognize the political activities of women as political, or the possibility of applying *Shah and Islam* to identify a particular social group of women, persecuted for reasons connected to their gender (Ceneda and Palmer 2006, Ali et al 2012, Dorling et al 2012).

While *Shah and Islam* broke new ground, to succeed in a refugee claim a woman must still show that she is a member of a particular social group which can be defined without reference to the feared persecution. This requires evidence of the situation of women in a comparable situation to herself in the society she is in. Where extensive evidence is given of social conditions, cases concerning the risks facing women may become country guidance cases.

For instance, in Bangladesh, the Tribunal in 2011 found:

There is a high level of domestic violence in Bangladesh. Despite the efforts of the government to improve the situation, due to the disinclination of the police to act upon complaints, women subjected to domestic violence may not be able to obtain an effective measure of state protection by reason of the fact that they are women and may be able to show a risk of serious harm for a Refugee Convention reason. Each case, however, must be determined on its own facts. (*SA (Divorced woman –illegitimate child) Bangladesh CG* [2011] UKUT 00254 (IAC)

In *P and M v SSHD*, P had been subject to serious violence by her husband including death threats and received no state protection. Her husband was a police officer who had friendships with high-ranking police officers. The evidence was that violence against women was taken as normal in Kenya, and that death or life-threatening injuries would have to occur before police would take action. The particular social group was 'women, who are disadvantaged in Kenya because of their position in society' (para 21, quoting the adjudicator).

Claims based on FGM may succeed where societal discrimination and lack of protection is proved. In *P and M*, the Court defined the particular social group of which M was a part as women in Kenya, particularly Kikuyu women under 65 years of age. They had immutable characteristics of age and sex which existed independently of persecution and could be identified by reference to their being compelled to undergo FGM (para 41). The appellant's father had joined the Mungiki sect which enforces FGM. He and about 20 other members of the sect had performed a forced FGM on the appellant's mother, who died as a result. He then married another member of the sect who insisted that the appellant and her sister should be circumcised. Both refused. Five members of the sect were involved in raping M and violently assaulting her. Her sister was forcibly circumcised and M was told she would be next.

In the light of *P and M*, it was surprising that another FGM case went as far as the House of Lords (*Fornah v SSHD* [2006] UKHL 46).

 **Key Case**

Fornah v SSHD [2006] UKHL 46

In 1998, the appellant and her mother were living in her father's family village to escape the civil war, and she overheard discussions of her undergoing FGM as part of her initiation into womanhood. In order to avoid this, she ran away, but she was captured by rebels and repeatedly raped by a rebel leader, by whom she became pregnant. An uncle arranged her departure from Sierra Leone to the UK. She feared that if she was returned she would have nowhere to live except her father's village, where she feared she would be subjected to FGM. It was common ground that FGM constitutes persecution if the appellant was found to be a member of a particular social group. The Secretary of State argued that women in Sierra Leone could not be a social group because the cutting only happened once, and once it was done such women could no longer be in fear of persecution. But to hold that uninitiated women were the social group would be to define the group by the (fear of) persecution, therefore they could not be a social group for Convention purposes.

Baroness Hale pointed out the fallacy: 'It is the persecution, not the fear, which has to be "by reason of" membership of the group . . . [and] . . . It is well settled that not all members of the group need be at risk' (para 113). She defined the group as 'Sierra Leonean women belonging to those ethnic groups where FGM is practised' (para 114) although she added that 'it matters not whether the group is stated more widely, as all Sierra Leonean women, or more narrowly, as intact Sierra Leonean women from those ethnic groups. For all of them, the group has existence independent of the persecution' (para 114).

The House of Lords found that Ms Fornah was a member of a particular social group, though they defined it in a variety of ways. Lord Bingham's approach was interesting:

women in Sierra Leone are a group of persons sharing a common characteristic which, without a fundamental change in social mores is unchangeable, namely a position of social inferiority as compared with men. (para 31)

This is an interesting integration of the *Ward* criteria. Lord Bingham found the social group, on the basis of this reasoning, to be women in Sierra Leone. Most of their Lordships added some further qualifying characteristic such as not having undergone FGM (being 'intact' or 'uninitiated'). Since *Fornah* it is established that a risk of FGM is for a Convention reason. See *K and others (FGM) The Gambia*, mentioned in the context of internal relocation, in which the risk factors for FGM in Gambia are analysed in detail.

The discrimination in *Shah and Islam* was in part because of the law itself, which was discriminatory. In many cases, however, the question is not the law but the practice. In *P and M*, P could not obtain protection because of social attitudes and the power and practice of the police, not because violence was formally legal. In *RG (Ethiopia) v SSHD* [2006] EWCA Civ 339 the societal discrimination against women was combined with the non-enforcement of the law, and with a particular law which provided immunity from prosecution for rapists if their victims could be persuaded to marry them. The Court followed *P and M* in saying that societal discrimination and lack of police protection were crucial, and found that young women in Ethiopia were a particular social group.

In *NS (Afghanistan) CG* [2004] UKIAT 00328, the Tribunal found that lone women in Afghanistan were at risk of abuse, without adequate judicial redress and protection, and that the appellant could establish a fear of persecution as a member of the particular social group of women in Afghanistan (see *Women's Asylum News* issue no. 49 February 2005). In *HM (Somalia)* [2005] UKIAT 00040 the Tribunal held that '[w]omen in Somalia form a PSG not just because they are women, but because they are extensively discriminated against'. In *NM and Others (Lone women—Ashraf) Somalia CG* [2005] UKIAT 00076 the Tribunal found that a woman on her own and of a minority tribe would be at risk in Somalia. However, in *AI (Nigeria) v SSHD* [2007] EWCA Civ 707, the Court of Appeal rejected an argument on behalf of a young single woman with a child. She might face discrimination, but this did not amount to persecution. The generally stated evidence of Amnesty International that violence against women was widespread did not, the Court thought, give sufficient evidence that the appellant was at risk from 'harmful practices'.

12.8.4.2 Social perception

The UNHCR Guidelines identify two approaches to the recognition of a particular social group. One is the 'protected characteristics' approach, which we have used and referred to as the application of the *Ward* criteria. The other is based on social perception. They recommend the adoption of a single standard that incorporates both approaches (2002 para 10). Goodwin-Gill and McAdam suggest that there is a value in recognizing 'groups in society, in the ordinary everyday sense'. By way of example, they refer to 'the landlord class, the working class, the ruling class' (2007: 85). Even without the connection to fundamental characteristics required by the *Ward* criteria, the identity of the group might be well-known and acknowledged in society.

A requirement for recognition *by* the society in which the persecution arises would present serious pitfalls. For instance, it is unthinkable that Pakistani society, whether government or otherwise, should be required to identify women in that country as discriminated against and thus a social group. Opinion on the matter would obviously be divided. The particular social group is a legal construct in the hands of the decision-maker in the refugee claim, not a naturally arising phenomenon. Its identification is a matter for those decision-makers *in the context* of the society in which it is said to arise. The Australian case of *S v MIMA* [2004] HCA 25 sets out the difference between recognizing a group *in the context of* that society (here, young, able-bodied men in Afghanistan, who might as a consequence be subject to forcible recruitment by the Taleban), and their recognition as a group *by* that society. The latter was an unnecessary requirement, they thought, for a refugee claim.

Shah and Islam suggests that the group should be identifiable *within* that society, and this is demonstrated in the CJEU in Joined Cases C-199/12 to C-201/12 *X, Y and Z* where the Court said that the existence of a criminal penalty for homosexuality in Sierra Leone, Uganda, and Senegal was evidence that gay people were regarded as a social group in those societies (paras 48 and 49).

The QD seems to require the group to be recognized using both social perception and immutable characteristics. It says that a group shall be considered to form a particular social group where in particular the *Ward* criteria are met, *and* 'that group has a distinct identity in the relevant country, because it is perceived as being different by the surrounding society'. The UK implementing regulations repeat the two approaches, though say that groups will be recognized 'for example' where these are met, instead of 'in particular', which softens the requirement to apply both approaches. Lord Bingham in *Fornah* regarded an interpretation of the Directive which would require both the *Ward* criteria *and* the social perception approach as wrong, although these remarks were obiter (as the Tribunal noted in *SB (Moldova) CG* [2008] UKAIT 00002). In the House of Lords' judgment, the group is recognized in the context of the society, but the group that would be recognized *by* the society is uninitiated women, who were regarded as particularly inferior.

The Tribunal in *AZ (Trafficked women) Thailand* CG [2010] UKUT 118 (IAC) noted that the QD permits Member States to apply standards 'more favourable to the applicant than the minimum laid down'. Also, they noted that UNHCR advised that 'to avoid any protection gaps, member states should reconcile the two approaches to permit alternative rather than cumulative application of the two concepts'. The Tribunal declined to accept that they should do this; nevertheless, in reliance on the 'broad humanitarian purpose' of the Refugee Convention, as described by Sedley LJ in *Shah and Islam* and Lord Hope in *Hoxha*, they found that the appellant was a member of a particular social group of 'young women who have been victims of trafficking for sexual exploitation' (*AZ* para 140).

Having considered some of the follow-on from *Shah and Islam* and the construction of social group, we shall now consider some other particular social groups, and issues in defining social groups which arise in these contexts.

12.8.4.3 Sexuality

Shah and Islam laid the foundation for establishing inclusion within the Refugee Convention of asylum claims based on sexuality. Sexuality is clearly within the *Ward* criteria, either as an innate or unchangeable characteristic or else as something fundamental to human dignity which a person should not be required to forsake (see, for example, New Zealand Refugee Status Appeals Authority *Re GJ* [1998] (1995) INLR 387, 420).

This is confirmed by the QD, which says 'depending on the circumstances in the country of origin, a particular social group might include a group based on a common characteristic of sexual orientation' (Article 10(1)(d)). This does not include acts considered criminal in the national law of Member States. So, for instance, a common sexual orientation as a paedophile would not constitute a particular social group.

In *SSHD v Z, A v SSHD, M v SSHD* [2002] Imm AR 560, Schiemann LJ emphasized that such cases are very 'fact sensitive' and that general pronouncements about particular countries should be avoided. However, the advance of country guidance cases has made inroads upon this view. Indeed, social attitudes and governmental or legal penalties relating to sexuality are an obvious field for general evidence, with the risk to the individual being case-specific. For instance, in *SW (lesbians—HJ and HT applied) Jamaica CG* [2011] UKUT 00251(IAC) the Tribunal held that:

Jamaica is a deeply homophobic society. There is a high level of violence, and where a real risk of persecution or serious harm is established, the Jamaican state offers lesbians no sufficiency of protection. Lesbianism (actual or perceived) brings a risk of violence, up to and including 'corrective' rape and murder.

A recurring issue in claims based on sexuality has been the question of whether the claimant may be required to 'exercise discretion', that is, conceal their sexuality, on their return. The law on this point has now been settled by *HJ (Iran) and HT (Cameroon)* [2010] UKSC 31.

 **Key Case**

HJ (Iran) and HT (Cameroon) [2010] UKSC 31

The Court unanimously overturned the Court of Appeal's judgment, and set out the proper approach to an application for asylum on the ground of a well-founded fear of persecution for being gay:

- Is the decision-maker satisfied on the evidence that the applicant is gay, or would be treated as gay by potential persecutors in his country of nationality?
- If so, is the decision-maker satisfied on the evidence that gay people who live openly are liable to persecution in the applicant's country of nationality?
- If so, the decision-maker must consider what the applicant would do if he were returned to that country.
- If the applicant would in fact live openly and thereby be exposed to a real risk of persecution, then he has a well-founded fear of persecution—even if he could avoid the risk by living 'discreetly'.
- If, on the other hand, the applicant would in fact live discreetly and so avoid persecution, the decision-maker must ask *why* he would do so. If the applicant would choose to live discreetly simply because that was how he himself would wish to live, or because of social pressures, then his application should be rejected. If a material reason for the applicant living discreetly would be a fear of persecution which would follow if he were to live openly as a gay man, then such a person has a well-founded fear of persecution. To reject his application on the ground that he could avoid the persecution by living discreetly would be to defeat the very right which the Convention exists to protect—to live freely and openly as a gay man without fear of persecution. (para 82)

The Supreme Court judgment represents a new era in treatment of refugee claims on the grounds of sexuality. Other important statements in the judgment include:

- the use of the word 'discretion' is a euphemism and the more accurate description of what is being discussed is 'concealment'; (para 22)
- a straight person is not required to conceal their sexual identity—neither should a gay one be required to do so; (para 76)
- in any event, a decision-maker in the English legal system cannot lay down such a 'requirement'. There can be no such requirement; all that exists is a prediction of how the applicant will in fact behave, and what will be the consequences of that.

Their Lordships remarked that the Court of Appeal judgment would return Anne Frank to the attic, on the basis she could stay there and avoid persecution. This made the point clear that she was not afraid of being in an attic, but of persecution by the Nazis as a Jew. So with a gay man required to conceal his identity for fear of persecution.

The protection given by *HJ (Iran)* has now been endorsed fully by the CJEU in Joined Cases C–199/12 to C–201/12 *X, Y and Z*. The Court said:

an applicant for asylum cannot be expected to conceal his homosexuality in his country of origin in order to avoid persecution (para 71)

and so

must be granted refugee status, in accordance with Article 13 of the Directive, where it is established that on return to his country of origin his homosexuality would expose him to a genuine risk of persecution within the meaning of Article 9(1) thereof. The fact that he could avoid the risk by exercising greater restraint than a heterosexual in expressing his sexual orientation is not to be taken into account in that respect. (para 75)

12.8.4.4 Families

The identification of a family as a particular social group has slowly been established in the courts. Clearly, the first element in the *Ward* criteria is satisfied. There is an innate characteristic which is the blood tie, or there is a characteristic so fundamental that the person should not be required to change it in marriage or a comparable relationship. Lord Bingham in *K v SSHD* [2006] UKHL 46 (heard and decided with *Fornah*) said, 'the family is the quintessential social group' (para 3). The family has civil status in that its ties are recognized and even created by law. Article 23 International Covenant on Civil and Political Rights says: 'The family is the natural and fundamental group unit of society and is entitled to protection by society and the State.'

Prior to *K*, cases on family as a social group had often failed. One reason, now disposed of in the UK by *K*, was the argument that if Y is persecuted for being a family member of X, X must have been targeted for a Convention reason in order for Y to claim the family relationship as a Convention reason (*Quijano v SSHD* [1997] Imm AR 227, in which the first person in the family was targeted because he had refused to cooperate with a drugs cartel, which was not a Convention reason). The House of Lords in *K* preferred the earlier case of *R v IAT ex p De Melo* [1997] Imm AR 43, in which Laws J found two sisters to be members of a particular social group as the family members of a Brazilian farmer who had refused to grow drugs. K feared persecution because her husband had been detained and ill-treated, and after his detention the Revolutionary Guard had visited their home and raped her. She and her family were royalists associated with the late Shah of Iran. The adjudicator had not found evidence that the husband's persecution was for a Convention reason. The House of Lords held that this was an unnecessary requirement. Likewise, it was unnecessary that all members of the family should be at risk for the same Convention reason or that all members of the family should be at risk at all. The reason in K's case was that she was a family member of her husband. Lord Rodgers of Earlsferry said:

Even if Mr K was detained for completely valid reasons, singling out the members of his family for mistreatment simply because they are members of the family of a detainee would amount to persecution for the purposes of the Convention. (para 63)

One context in which family membership is the explicit reason for persecution is in a blood feud. Since *K* it can no longer be said, as it was in *Hurtado* [2002] UKIAT 03158, that it would be artificial to regard the family as a particular social group. Despite this, the Home Office argued in *EH (blood feuds) Albania* CG [2012] UKUT 00348 (IAC) that the family did not constitute a particular social group. The Tribunal regarded this as unarguable, and said that 'where there is an active feud affecting an individual and self-confinement is the only option, that person will normally qualify for Refugee status'. The difficult issue was not whether the family was a particular social group, but to establish whether the feud existed, and the Tribunal gave detailed guidance on that.

It is certainly a mistake to require that all members of the family be at risk in order to qualify as a particular social group. This was already the case following *Shah and Islam*, and *K* reinforces the point.

12.8.4.5 Other status

There is a wealth of case law relating to a wide range of possible social groups. Here, we seek to give an understanding of some further categories which demonstrate general principles.

The quotation given earlier from *Acosta* is a principle that those people protected from persecution are those who cannot, if they remain in their homeland, make a choice which would prevent the treatment they fear. This was addressed directly in *Ouanes v SSHD* [1998] Imm AR 76, a Court of Appeal case concerning an Algerian mid-wife who, as she was required to do, gave contraceptive advice as part of her practice. As a result, she received threats from religious fundamentalist groups opposed to this advice. The question was whether her employment was something so fundamental to her conscience that she should not be required to change it. The leading judgment was given by Pill LJ who said at 82:

A common employment does not ordinarily have that impact upon individual identities or conscience necessary to constitute employees a particular social group within the meaning of the Convention. I accept the possibility that fellow employees may constitute a particular social group if, by reason by the nature of their employment or the addition of other links to those of employment, the above principle applies. Employment as a member of a religious order could be an example.

Wealthy people have generally been held not to be a particular social group. Arguments were made by a Colombian landowner (*Montoya*), a wealthy educated Sierra Leonean mine owner (*Diallo* 00/TH/01231), a rich Lithuanian entrepreneur (*R v Special Adjudicator ex p Roznys* [2000] Imm AR 57). The words of Burton J in the last-named case probably sum up the courts' and tribunals' approach: 'I do not consider that it is arguable that possession of money puts you into a particular social group, namely a particular social group with money as opposed to those who do not have money.'

Other groups which have been recognized include women who have given birth in breach of China's family planning policy (*AX (family planning scheme) China* CG [2012] UKUT 00097 (IAC)) and victims of trafficking.

12.8.4.6 Victims of trafficking

The third limb of the *Ward* criteria, in the words of the QD, sharing 'a common background that cannot be changed', opened the way to identifying as a particular social group 'former victims of trafficking for sexual exploitation'. In the case of *SB (Moldova) CG* [2008] UKAIT 00002, the claimant was held to be a member of the particular social group of former victims of trafficking for sexual exploitation in Moldova. She had given evidence against her trafficker in his prosecution in the UK. After his prison sentence he was now free, and she feared reprisals from his network if she were to return to Moldova. The Tribunal confirmed that discrimination did not need to be an identifying characteristic of the group, providing it was formed according to the *Ward* criteria (here, common history) and (following the QD) the group was recognizable in that society.

The decision in *SB (Moldova)* paved the way for other decisions concerning former victims of trafficking, depending on the evidence concerning their treatment in the particular society. Baroness Hale of Richmond had said in *Hoxha* [2005] UKHL 19 that 'women who have been the victims of sexual violence in the past are linked by an immutable characteristic which is independent of and the cause of their current ill-treatment'. In *AM and BM (Trafficked women) Albania* CG [2010] UKUT 80 (IAC) the Tribunal relied on this and evidence about the situation in Albania to accept that former victims of trafficking were a particular social group there. This case gives detailed guidance on Albanian trafficking cases, and offers a model for issues that should be considered in assessing sufficiency of protection for trafficked women, and the viability of internal relocation. These issues were also considered in detail in *AZ (Trafficked women) Thailand* CG [2010] UKUT 118 (IAC) (see 12.5.4.3) where corruption and the involvement of officials with traffickers and criminals meant that it was not safe for former victims of trafficking.

As mentioned in chapter 11, in the context of special procedures for trafficking victims, human rights claims are also possible. The ECtHR in *Siliadin v France* [2005] ECHR 545 held that Article 4 entailed a positive obligation to penalize slavery and forced labour. In that case, a domestic worker had been held in conditions akin to slavery. The protective obligation was reinforced by a historic case in the ECtHR, the first on cross-border human trafficking in Europe.

 Key Case

Rantsev v Cyprus and Russia **Application 25965/04, [2010] ECHR 22**

The applicant was the father of a young Russian woman who had obtained an artiste's visa to work in Cyprus. After a short while, she announced to her flatmates that she was leaving her employment in a cabaret. Her employer found her and took her to the police, asking for her to be deported. They checked their list of those who were wanted, declared that her status was not illegal, but held her in detention until her employer came to collect her. He took her to his colleague's apartment. Just over an hour later, she was found dead on the pavement, having fallen from the balcony of the apartment.

The ECtHR found Cyprus to have violated Article 4. They accepted that trafficking was prohibited under Article 4. They noted that the police had failed to investigate whether she might have been trafficked, for instance by enquiring about her reasons for wanting to leave her employment. They had also failed to release her, even though they had concluded that they had no outstanding matter to pursue with her and therefore had no authority to detain her. They had, instead, insisted on delivering her back into the hands of the person who might have trafficked her.

The Court's judgment in *Rantsev* contains a careful consideration of the facts, and identifies a number of ways in which the authorities failed in their protective duties under Article 4. It is potentially ground-breaking in establishing a strong human rights standard as a benchmark for states' protection duties. (Compare discussion of the withdrawal of immigration rules concerning domestic workers in chapter 9.)

The High Court held in *OOO and others v The Commissioner of Police for the Metropolis* [2011] EWHC 1246 (QB) that *Rantsev* defined the duty of investigation for UK police to 'carry out an effective investigation of an allegation of a breach of Article 4 once a credible account of an alleged infringement had been brought to its attention. The trigger for the duty would not depend upon an actual complaint from a victim or near relative of a victim. The investigation, once triggered, would have to be undertaken promptly' (para 154).

In *C.N. v UK* 4239/08 [2012] ECHR 1911 the ECtHR found that the UK was in breach of Article 4 because of its failure to criminalize domestic forced labour. The applicant had been held in forced labour in the UK, but her asylum claim failed, and the case did not contain all the elements of the offence of trafficking. The investigating authorities had failed to pay attention to the applicant's conditions and thus failed to protect her. In *EK (Article 4 ECHR: Anti-Trafficking Convention) Tanzania* [2013] UKUT 00313 (IAC) the Tribunal confirmed that trafficking falls within the ambit of Article 4, and held that there is no distinction, for the purposes of Article 4, between a domestic worker who was trafficked by way of forced labour and one who arrived voluntarily and was then subjected to forced labour.

Humanitarian protection on the basis of a feared breach of Article 4 may be warranted where there is a real risk of being re-trafficked if the person is returned to their country of origin but former trafficking victims cannot be identified as a particular social group there.

12.8.5 Political opinion

A political dissident was a typical figure of a refugee who was the focus of the Refugee Convention when it was first drafted and political dissent continues to play a significant part in establishing refugee claims. Political opinion as a Convention reason however goes much wider than this.

Political expression is valued as an essential requirement of democracy as without debate and freedom of political speech, democracy cannot thrive. In the case law of the ECHR, political speech is protected more fully than other forms of expression as the Court allows a narrower margin of appreciation to states which seek to restrict it (see, e.g., *Lingens v Austria* (1986) 8 EHRR 407). In refugee claims, the question arises as to whether an opinion is political. Sometimes, this is obvious, such as support for a political party. Sometimes, it is less obvious, for instance a woman in Iran who refused to conform to a strict dress code and wore make-up was regarded by the Tribunal in *Fathi and Ahmady (14264)* as expressing a political opinion. Guidance was given in the Tribunal case of *Gomez* 00/TH/02257 on the characteristics of a political opinion: 'To qualify as political the opinion in question must relate to the major power transactions taking place in that particular society.' This makes it clear that not only party politics is intended, so, for instance, attending an anti-globalization protest would be an expression of political opinion. The University of Michigan, under the leadership of Professor James Hathaway, from time to time invites leading experts on refugee law to a colloquium at which, following debate, guidelines are drawn up on an issue of refugee law. These are not binding, but are respected. In 2015 they drew up guidelines on political opinion, and said:

A 'political' opinion is an opinion about the nature, policies, or practices of a state or of an entity that has the capacity, legitimately or otherwise, to exercise societal power or authority. A relevant non-state entity is one that is institutionalized, formalized, or informally systematized and which is shown by evidence of pattern or practice to exercise *de facto* societal power or authority. (*Michigan Guidelines on Risk for Reasons of Political Opinion*)

A political opinion may be expressed or it may be imputed by the persecutor. Hence, it is not the holding of the opinion which is important, but how the claimant is perceived by the persecutor. This is not to reverse all that was said earlier about the motivation of the persecutor. A detailed enquiry into their motives is not required. What is required is to ascertain what the reason is for the persecution.

A number of relevant principles are cited in the case of *Noune v SSHD* [2000] All ER (D) 2163.

 Key Case

Noune v SSHD [2000] All ER (D) 2163 CA

The appellant was an Algerian worker with a responsible position in the national Post Office. She was approached on numerous occasions by masked men asking her to send messages to Japan and the Soviet Union, offering her 'protection' in return. She was threatened with

> violence or other serious consequences if she did not comply and the suggestion made to her was that it was her duty to help. Those who approached her wore religious dress, whereas her appearance and demeanour were of a Westernized woman. There was plentiful evidence of killings by religious extremists in Algeria, and there was evidence of 'Westernized' women being targeted, but no evidence that she had been threatened for this reason, rather for her non-cooperation.

The Court of Appeal held inter alia that:

(i) The motives of the persecutor may be mixed, and they can include non-Convention reasons: it is not necessary to show that they are purely political.

(ii) Political opinion may be express or imputed.

(iii) It follows that in order to show persecution on account of political opinion it is not necessary to show political action or activity by the victim: in some circumstances mere inactivity and unwillingness to co-operate can be taken as an expression of political opinion. (*UNHCR Handbook* para 80)

(iv) If it is shown that there is a reasonable likelihood that the persecutor will attribute a political opinion to the victim and persecute him because of it, the fact, if it be a fact, that the persecutor would be in error in making that attribution does not disqualify the victim from refugee status. (para 8)

The Court of Appeal held that the facts were capable of giving rise to a claim on the basis of political opinion and remitted the case to a tribunal for decision.

As referred to previously, cases concerning witnesses of crimes and people refusing to cooperate with criminal activity have been argued under both social group and political opinion. For such claims to be seen as relating to the 'major power transactions in a society', the criminal activity in question must have a relationship to those power transactions. Like social group, political opinion must be construed in the context of the society in which it arises. Goodwin-Gill suggested a wider definition of political opinion as one 'on any matter in which the machinery of the state, government and policy may be engaged' (Goodwin-Gill and McAdam 2007:87). This definition has been approved by the courts. The QD definition is wider, as it includes holding an opinion, thought or belief on a matter related to the potential actors of persecution, which includes non-state actors (Article 10(1)(e)).

In *Acero-Garces* (21514), the appellant had witnessed the murder of a policeman and since then had been subject to serious threats and harassment. This had to be seen against the background in Colombia of the drugs cartels, in the words of the Tribunal 'a power unto themselves. The links between the narcotic industry, crime and the government is very thoroughly documented.' The Tribunal found that she risked persecution for reasons of political opinion, 'that the appellant is seen to be on the side of law, order and justice and against disorder, chaos and injustice; and it is these dark forces that control government'.

There was a different result in *Storozhenko v SSHD* [2002] Imm AR 329, CA. Here, the appellant had witnessed drunken police officers driving a speeding car which knocked down and injured a young girl. When he remonstrated with them, one of them hit him in the face with a baton, breaking his jaw. He made a formal complaint at the police station but there was no action taken, and after this he began to receive serious threats and was attacked. The Court of Appeal accepted that he was being persecuted for attempting to bring a police officer to justice, but said it was 'manifestly artificial to talk in terms of imputed political opinion' (para 44).

The case of *Gomez v SSHD* is a starred appeal which sets out a number of points intended to clarify issues in cases where some attitude may be imputed to the victim by a non-state perpetrator but it is arguable as to whether this is a political opinion. *Gomez* was heard before *Storozhenko* but would support the conclusion in that case.

The Tribunal confirmed established case law that the fundamental rights of the victim must be protected. So a person should not be in fear because they have exercised the rights to freedom of thought, conscience, opinion, expression, association, and assembly. As mentioned earlier, political opinions may be imputed to asylum seekers by their country of origin because they have made a failed asylum claim elsewhere. The risks of returning to Zimbabwe have been challenged on this basis, since previous country guidance indicated that a returnee would have to demonstrate loyalty to the government, and that inability to do so could generate a risk of persecution.

That requirement to demonstrate loyalty gave rise to a question as to whether the Supreme Court's decision in *HJ (Iran)* would apply to political opinion, and whether it would apply to someone who did not have political opinions. Will a returned asylum seeker from the UK lie about their political affiliation on return to Zimbabwe and should they be expected to?

 **Key Case**

RT (Zimbabwe) and others [2012] UKSC 38

In this case the appellants had been denied asylum because they were not politically active and did not hold strong political beliefs. The Supreme Court drew upon *HJ (Iran)* and held that 'the Convention affords no less protection to the right to express political opinion openly than it does to the right to live openly as a homosexual' (para 25). As regards a person without political opinions the Supreme Court held:

> the right to freedom of thought, opinion and expression protects non-believers as well as believers and extends to the freedom *not* to hold and *not* to have to express opinions. (para 32)
>
> This is as important as the freedom to hold and (within certain defined limits) to express such beliefs as they do hold. One of the hallmarks of totalitarian regimes is their insistence on controlling people's thoughts as well as their behaviour. (para 43)

12.8.5.1 Conscientious objection

Conscientious objection as a form of political opinion has generated a volume of case law from which certain principles may be distilled. Guidance is found in paras 167–74 of the *UNHCR Handbook*, though in places this is tentative.

Conscription and conscientious objection

There is a tension between the right of the state to demand military service from its citizens, and the right of the individual not to be forced to do something that goes against their conscience. All states have the right to demand military service from their nationals; some have a system of compulsory military service for all, some employ conscription only in times of war. In each case, it is usually a criminal offence either to refuse to join up or to desert the armed forces. An exemption from prosecution and an alternative to military service is given in an increasing number of countries to those who can establish a genuine conscientious objection to military action. In *Bayatyan v Armenia* [2011] ECHR 1095 the ECtHR noted that only two members of the Council of Europe did not have provisions for conscientious objection.

Prosecution for avoidance of normal military service for reasons other than conscience is not regarded as persecution unless the punishment is disproportionate or is inflicted or impacts in a discriminatory way. For instance, some countries, including the USA, still maintain the possibility of the death penalty for refusal to serve. In some countries, avoiding military service for whatever motive is seen as political dissent which warrants severe punishment. Country guidance cases on Eritrea hold that people who will be perceived as draft evaders are at risk on return to Eritrea, and that 'the issue of military service has become politicised and actual or perceived evasion of military service is regarded by the Eritrean authorities as an expression of political opinion' (*IN (Draft evaders—evidence of risk) Eritrea* CG [2005] UKIAT 00106).

 Key Case

Sepet and Bulbul [2003] UKHL 15

The two appellants were Turkish Kurds who objected to military service for the Turkish government. They did so because they opposed the Turkish government's policy towards the Kurds, and feared that they might be sent to a Kurdish area and required to commit atrocities against their own people. Turkey provided no alternative to military service. Draft evaders were liable to a prison sentence of between six months and three years, which was not thought disproportionate.

Their claim was framed as conscientious objection, but it was clear that they did not have a conscientious objection to military service as such, but only in the present circumstances. Nevertheless, their objection was evidently a political opinion and could not unreasonably be regarded as a reason of conscience. The Convention reason was therefore established, but the question was whether imprisonment because of this political opinion could amount to persecution, when imprisonment for refusal not based on such an opinion would not.

Their Lordships considered the submission for the appellants that there was a recognized human right of conscientious objection, for instance implied in the Universal Declaration of Human Rights Article 18. If there was such a right, then it could be argued that a discriminatory denial of the right could amount to persecution. They concluded that the weight of the evidence was that to date there is no such human right although there were developments in that direction.

The House of Lords made the distinction between 'absolute' and 'partial' conscientious objectors. Absolute objectors would object to all military action for reasons of conscience. This would include people who were pacifists without a religious belief, and people whose pacifism arose from a belief system which normally entailed it, such as Quakers or Buddhists. There was authority to suggest that in the case of absolute objectors at least that prosecution could amount to persecution (*Zaitz v SSHD* [2000] INLR 346). In the light of their finding that there was no human right of conscientious objection their Lordships considered that punishment for refusal of military service would *not* amount to persecution per se, reversing *Zaitz* to the extent that that case could be regarded as deciding otherwise.

Partial objection referred to people such as the appellants in these cases whose objection was a political one based on the practices and policy of the Turkish military, not on military action as such. In this case, the greater includes the less, because if there is no right of conscientious objection then even less will punishment of 'partial objectors' amount to persecution.

As the appellants Sepet and Bulbul were partial objectors, the case must be taken to decide that partial objection per se will not found a claim to refugee status. Comments that absolute objection does not give rise to a refugee claim must be regarded as obiter and would now be subject to review in the light of the ECtHR's Grand Chamber judgment in *Bayatyan v Armenia*.

 **Key Case**

Bayatyan v Armenia [2011] ECHR 1095

The applicant was a Jehovah's witness who objected to engaging in military action on the basis of his religious faith. He avoided conscription by leaving home, and was convicted for draft evasion. The Court held that 'opposition to military service, where it is motivated by a serious and insurmountable conflict between the obligation to serve in the army and a person's conscience or his deeply and genuinely held religious or other beliefs, constitutes a conviction or belief of sufficient cogency, seriousness, cohesion and importance to attract the guarantees of Article 9'.

The Court found that Article 9 had been violated.

In effect, in this judgment, the ECtHR, in harmony with the EU Charter of Fundamental Rights and Freedoms and the interpretation given by the UN Human Rights Commission to the ICCPR, found a human right to conscientious objection.

Action in breach of international norms

Refusal to undertake military action which is against international law can found refugee status. Lord Bingham in *Sepet and Bulbul* states established law in this way:

There is compelling support for the view that refugee status should be accorded to one who has refused to undertake compulsory military service on the grounds that such service would or might require him to commit atrocities or gross human rights abuses or participate in a conflict condemned by the international community, or where refusal to serve would earn grossly excessive or disproportionate punishment. (para 8)

This is partly endorsed in the QD, where the acts listed as persecution include prosecution or punishment for refusing to perform military service which would entail committing war crimes, crimes against peace, crimes against humanity or against the purposes and principles of the UN or serious non-political crimes. In such cases the political opinion of the refuser would readily be imputed if not expressed. Earlier drafts of the Directive allowed for broader grounds of conscience to found a refugee claim, but these were lost in the negotiation process. The cases of *Radivojevic and Lazarevic* [1997] 2 All ER 723 concerned objection to military service in the former Yugoslavia in an action that was internationally condemned. However, it was held in the Court of Appeal (and this point was not pursued to the House of Lords) that even in such a conflict, the individuals themselves must object to the condemned action on principle, not just be 'opportunistic draft evaders' in order to obtain asylum.

Paragraph 171 of the *UNHCR Handbook* suggests that where military action has drawn the condemnation of the international community, punishment for refusal may amount to persecution. In *Krotov v SSHD* [2004] EWCA Civ 69, the Court of Appeal considered a Russian soldier's refusal to participate in the Chechen War. The Secretary of State argued that the British asylum decision-making and appeal process could not be drawn into the kind of international judgments that would be required in order to grant refugee status on this basis. The Court of Appeal disagreed. They held that there were plenty of norms of international law to which reference could be made, and refugee status could be founded on objection to military service where that service would involve participation in acts which were contrary to basic rules of conduct as defined by international law. It was not necessary to wait for formal condemnation of the conflict by the international community. The claim could succeed if combatants could be punished for refusing to act in breach of basic rules of human conduct or if the genuine fear of such punishment was a reason for refusing to serve.

This was applied in *BE (Iran) v SSHD* [2008] EWCA Civ 540, where an Iranian soldier repeatedly refused orders to plant landmines in a populated area, despite three months' imprisonment, demotion, and death threats. There was no state of war or insurgency in Iranian Kurdistan at that time. The appellant did not want to cause civilian deaths. He deserted and fled to the UK.

His asylum claim reached the Court of Appeal, where he argued that the irreducible minimum of civilized conduct should not be lower in peace than in war, and his refusal to go below that minimum made him a refugee.

The Court said that the seeding of terrain with anti-personnel explosive devices was one of the most vicious tactics in modern warfare and also in state security. Sedley LJ reviewed research on the effect of landmines, and drew the conclusion that anyone who, and any state which, sowed unmarked anti-personnel mines in terrain from which civilians were not excluded was responsible for the deaths and injuries that would result.

The Home Secretary had defended the case mainly on the basis that there was no breach of 'hard law'. The Court held, however, that international agreements showed that by 1999, the almost universal condemnation of anti-personnel mines had placed their use in the category of gross atrocities or gross abuse of the human right to life and bodily integrity. In *Sepet and Bulbul*, Lord Bingham said:

There is compelling support for the view that refugee status should be accorded to one who has refused to undertake compulsory military service on the grounds that such service would or might require him to commit atrocities or gross human rights abuses, or participate in a conflict condemned by the international community, or where refusal to serve would earn grossly excessive or disproportionate punishment. (para 58)

This was BE's case, and he was entitled to asylum.

The case of *Aydogdu* [2002] UKIAT 06709 also succeeded because the appellant left Turkey at a time when the military action he would have been called upon to undertake would have been condemned by the international community. This was in 1997–98 when, in the Tribunal's words, 'The policy of the Turkish army, albeit against a determined and vicious enemy, did result in international condemnation as it involved a programme of compulsory village clearances and the large-scale displacement of the Kurdish civilian population' (para 18).

A number of American conscientious objectors to the war in Iraq sought refugee status in Canada but have been refused. Other soldiers who objected to the war but did not flee have been sentenced in the US to imprisonment or hard labour (Amnesty International press release 13 May 2005).

A soldier cannot claim refugee status on account of risks from terrorists (*Fadli v SSHD* [2001] Imm AR 392). Being a soldier entails taking the risk of losing one's life in the service of one's country, and this is no different if the enemy is an internal one (here, the GIA, a fundamentalist group in Algeria). However, conditions of military service may be such as to amount to persecution if they are inhuman (*Foughali 00/TH/01513* and now see *ZQ (serving soldier) Iraq* CG [2009] UKAIT 00048).

12.9 Conclusion

This chapter has given an introduction to refugee law in the UK, but no more. This field is now so vast, that a glance at some key issues and an examination of some of the key cases is all that is really possible in a small part of a larger book. The next chapter examines some of the legal restrictions upon refugee claims.

QUESTIONS

1 What are the benefits and the problems of operating with an international definition of who is a refugee?

2 Should gender be a Convention reason?

3 Is discrimination in relation to social rights a suitable basis for an asylum claim?

4 Would it be helpful to generalize about whether those fleeing the Middle East and Africa and coming to Europe in 2015 are refugees within the terms of the Refugee Convention?

 online resource centre For guidance on answering questions, visit the Online Resource Centre www.oxfordtextbooks.co.uk/orc/clayton7e/.

FURTHER READING

Ali, Hana Cheikh, Querton, Christel, and Soulard, Elodie, (2012) *Gender-related Asylum Claims in Europe: a comparative analysis of law policies and practice focusing on women in nine EU Member States* (Gensen Project).

Baillot, Helen, Cowan, Sharon, and Munro, Vanessa, (2014) 'Reason to (Dis)Believe? Evaluating the Rape Claims of Women Seeking Asylum in the UK' 10 (1) *International Journal of Law in Context* 104–37.

Bennett, Claire (2008) 'Relocation Relocation' (London: Asylum Aid).

Carrera,Sergio and den Hertog, Leonhard, (2015) 'Whose Mare? Rule of Law Challenges in the field of European Border Surveillance in the Mediterranean' *Liberty and Security*, no. 79 January 2015 (Centre for European Policy Studies, Brussels).

Ceneda, Sophia (2006) 'The Role of Gender Guidelines in the Determination of Asylum Claims' *Immigration Law Digest* vol. 12, no. 2, pp. 23–5.

Ceneda, Sophia and Palmer, Clare (2006) 'Lip Service or Implementation? The Home Office Gender Guidance and Women's Asylum Claims in the UK', *Refugee Women's Resource Project* (London: Asylum Aid).

Chaudhry, Mehvish (2007) 'Particular Social Group Post *Fornah*' *Journal of Immigration, Asylum and Nationality Law* vol. 21, no. 2, pp. 137–46.

Chandran, Parosha ed. (2011) *Human Trafficking Handbook—Recognising Trafficking and Modern-Day Slavery in the UK* (London: Lexis Nexis).

Clayton, Gina (2014) *'Even if . . . ' The use of the Internal Protection Alternative in asylum decisions in the UKC* (PL London:PN Asylum AidC).

Dorling, Kamena, Girma, Marchu, and Walter, Natasha, (2012) *Refused: the experiences of women denied asylum in the UK* (London: Women for Refugee Women).

Goodwin-Gill, Guy and McAdam, Jane (2007) *The Refugee in International Law*, 3rd edn (Oxford: Clarendon Press).

Hathaway, James (2002) 'The Causal Nexus in International Refugee Law' *Michigan Journal of International Law* Winter, vol. 23, pp. 207–21.

Hathaway, James and Foster, Michelle (2003) 'The Causal Connection (Nexus) to a Convention Ground' *International Journal of Refugee Law* vol. 15, no. 3, pp. 461–76.

Hathaway, James and Hicks, William S. (2005) 'Is there a Subjective Element in the Refugee Convention's Requirement of Well-founded Fear?' *Michigan Journal of International Law* Winter, vol. 26, pp. 505–25.

Hathaway, et al. 'Michigan Guidelines on Risk for Reasons of Political Opinion' *International Journal of Refugee Law*, 2015, Vol. 27, No. 3, 504–7.

Kelly, Brendan, 'What is a 'Particular Social Group'? A Review of the Development of the Refugee Convention in England' *Journal of Immigration, Asylum and Nationality Law* vol. 24, no. 1, pp. 11–25.

Krivenko, E. (2010) 'Muslim Women's Claims to Refugee Status within the Context of Child Custody upon Divorce under Islamic Law' *International Journal of Refugee Law* vol. 22, no.1, pp. 48–71.

Lambert, Helene (2001) 'The Conceptualisation of "Persecution" by the House of Lords: Horvath v SSHD' *International Journal of Refugee Law* vol. 13, no.1/2, pp. 16–31.

Migrants at Sea (2013) *Italy Conducted de facto push-back of migrants by ordering cargo ship to rescue and transport migrants to Libya* August 2013, accessed at: http://migrantsatsea. wordpress.com/2013/08/13/italy-conducted-de-facto-push-back-of-migrants-by-ordering-cargo-ship-to-rescue-and-transport-migrants-to-libya/.

Muggeridge, Helen and Maman, Chen (2011) *Unsustainable* (London: Asylum Aid).

Musalo, Karen (2003) 'Revisiting Social Group and Nexus in Gender Asylum Claims: A Unifying Rationale for Evolving Jurisprudence' *DePaul Law Review* vol. 52, Spring, pp. 777–808.

Ní Ghráinne, Bríd (2015) 'The Internal Protection Alternative Inquiry and Human Rights Considerations—Irrelevant or Indispensable?' *International Journal of Refugee Law* vol. 27, no. 1, pp. 29–51.

O'Nions, Helen (1999) 'Bona fide or Bogus? Roma Asylum Seekers from the Czech Republic' *Web Journal of Current Legal Issues* 3.

Pearce, Hannah (2002) 'An Examination of the International Understanding of Political Rape and the Significance of Labelling it Torture' *International Journal of Refugee Law* vol. 14, no. 4, pp. 534–60.

Schnöring, Katharina (2001) 'Deserters in the Federal Republic of Yugoslavia' *International Journal of Refugee Law* vol. 13, pp. 153–73.

Shah, Prakash (2000) *Refugees, Race and the Legal Concept of Asylum in Britain* (London: Cavendish).

Stevens, Dallal (2004) *UK Asylum Law and Policy* (London: Sweet & Maxwell), chapters 1 and P 2.

Storey, Hugo (2008) 'EU Refugee Qualification Directive: A Brave New World?' *International Journal of Refugee Law* vol. 20, no. 1, pp. 1–49.

UNHCR *Handbook on Procedures and Criteria for Determining Refugee Status* (UNHCR; re-edited, Geneva: UNHCR, 1992).

UNHCR (2002) 'UNHCR Guidelines on International Protection', 7 May 2002, Membership of Particular Social Group and Gender-related Persecution (UNHCR),C accessed at: www.unhcr.org/3d58ddef4.html.

UNHCR (2003) 'Guidelines on Internal Protection' (UNHCR), accessed at: www.unhcr. org/3f28d5cd4.html.

UNHCR (2011) *Safe at Last? Law and Practice in Selected EU Member States with Respect to Asylum Seekers Fleeing Indiscriminate Violence* (Brussels: UNHCR).

UNHCR (2015) *World at War: Global Trends: Forced Displacement in 2014*, accessed at: www. unhcr.org.

Wilsher, Dan (2003) 'Non-State Actors and the Definition of a Refugee in the UK: Protection, Accountability or Culpability?' *International Journal of Refugee Law* vol. 15, no. 1, pp. 68–112.

Yeo, Colin (2002) 'Agents of the State: When is an Official of the State an Agent of the State?' *International Journal of Refugee Law* vol. 14, no. 4, pp. 509–33.

Yeo, Colin (2006) 'Qualification Directive: A new Era?' *Immigration Law Digest* vol. 12 no. 3, pp. 26–7.

13

Exclusion from asylum

SUMMARY

This chapter is concerned with the provisions whereby an individual can be excluded from refugee status because of their conduct. It also deals with the situations in which refugees can be removed from the host country.

13.1 Exclusion from refugee status

The Refugee Convention provides both for the exclusion of individuals from initially obtaining refugee status (Art 1F), and the expulsion of recognized refugees and asylum seekers from the host state as a result of their actions there (Articles 32 and 33(2)). These provisions, with some additions, are found in the Qualification Directive (QD) Articles 12 (exclusion), 14 (revocation and refusal), and 21 (*refoulement*).

These powers were little used in the twentieth century, but now are used increasingly often in the context of the escalation in international action against terrorism. Their interpretation and application is also affected by domestic legislation, now in the UK the Nationality Immigration and Asylum Act 2002, the Immigration Asylum and Nationality Act 2006, and the Terrorism Acts of 2000 and 2006.

Exclusion from refugee protection is not only a question of refugee law. As advised by the Lisbon Expert Roundtable, held as part of the 2001 UNHCR Global Consultations on International Protection, interpretation and application of Art 1F also draws on 'developments in other areas of international law since 1951, in particular international criminal law and extradition law as well as international human rights law and international humanitarian law' (para 34). The provisions for expelling recognized refugees are considered later in this chapter. We begin with the examination of Article 1F Refugee Convention (Article 12 of the QD). Article 1F makes exclusion from refugee status mandatory for a person with respect to whom there are serious reasons for considering that s/he has committed:

(a) A crime against peace, a war crime, or crime against humanity as defined in international instruments . . .

(b) A serious non-political crime outside country of refuge prior to admission to that country as a refugee . . .

(c) Acts contrary to purpose and principles of UN. Article 12 QD adds 'as set out in the Preamble and articles 1 and 2 of the Charter of the UN'.

Some general principles have evolved in the application of Article 1F, and these continue to develop in the application of Article 12 QD.

13.1.1 **Restrictive interpretation**

The UNHCR says that the Article should be construed restrictively because it deprives a person of protection who would otherwise qualify for refugee status. This is set out both in *Guidelines on International Protection: Application of Exclusion Clauses: Article 1F of the 1951 Convention relating to the Status of Refugees*, 2003, and the *UNHCR Handbook* para 180.

This principle was endorsed by the Supreme Court both in *R (JS (Sri Lanka)) v SSHD* [2010] UKSC 15 and in *Al-Sirri and DD (Afghanistan) v SSHD* [2012] UKSC 54. In the context of a potential exclusion under Article 1F(c) the Court in *Al-Sirri* said:

The article should be interpreted restrictively and applied with caution. There should be a high threshold 'defined in terms of the gravity of the act in question, the manner in which the act is organised, its international impact and long-term objectives, and the implications for international peace and security'. And there should be serious reasons for considering that the person concerned bore individual responsibility for acts of that character. (para 16)

The impact of exclusion is expressed in a 2013 set of Michigan Guidelines on exclusion:

[D]ecisions on refugee exclusion are binary: an individual either is, or is not, excluded from refugee status. In contrast, the ramifications of a finding of guilt in the context of international criminal law can be tempered by the sentencing process –an option not available to the refugee decision maker. This contextual difference should be recognized and, to the greatest extent possible, accommodated in the assessment of criminal responsibility for purposes of exclusion from refugee status. (para 3)

The Immigration Asylum and Nationality Act 2006 s 54 requires an interpretation of Article 1F(c) which is wide rather than restrictive. The Court in turn has read down that requirement. This is discussed in relation to Article 1F(c) later.

13.1.2 **Inclusion before exclusion**

Another established principle formerly was that inclusion should be considered before exclusion. In other words, the question of eligibility for refugee status should be considered before the question of whether the person should be excluded from it. The Lisbon Expert Roundtable conclusions give a number of reasons for this:

- Exclusion before inclusion risks criminalizing refugees.
- Exclusion is exceptional and it is not appropriate to consider an exception first.
- If a person does not qualify for refugee status, it is not then necessary to address the question of exclusion, thereby avoiding having to deal with complex issues.
- Inclusion first enables consideration to be given to protection obligations to family members.
- Inclusion before exclusion allows proper distinctions to be drawn between prosecution and persecution.
- Textually, the 1951 Convention would appear to provide more clearly for inclusion before exclusion.
- Interviews which look at the whole refugee definition allow for information to be collected more broadly and accurately.

However, in the UK, the Immigration, Asylum and Nationality Act 2006 s 55 enables the Secretary of State to certify that an asylum claim is excluded under Article 1F or 33(2), and that the applicant is not entitled to the protection of Article 33(1) of the

Refugee Convention. The statute makes no concession to the principle of 'inclusion before exclusion' as once the Secretary of State has certified, the Tribunal must begin its deliberations by considering the statements in the Secretary of State's certificate. If the Tribunal agrees with those statements, it must dismiss the claim for asylum.

The application of this section was considered in *AS (s. 55 'exclusion' certificate— process) Sri Lanka* [2013] UKUT 571 (IAC). The Tribunal held that s 55 did not require a decision on exclusion to be made at the outset of a hearing. The evidence for exclusion was substantially the same evidence as that for the asylum claim, and it would be artificial to hear and decide the issues sequentially. They held that the effect of s 55 was to require exclusion to be considered first in the written determination, not in the hearing. The Tribunal thought this was 'common sense, regardless of whether there was a s. 55 certificate', as this would determine whether substantive consideration of the asylum claim was necessary. The Tribunal also held that, since the criteria in the immigration rules for exclusion from humanitarian protection are very similar to those in Article 1F, a Tribunal should also decide on exclusion from humanitarian protection before considering it substantively, although there is no statutory provision requiring this.

The Tribunal may of its own motion raise the issue of exclusion even where the Home Office has not. The Court of Appeal made this clear in *A (Iraq) v SSHD* [2005] EWCA Civ 1438, in which the appellant's asylum claim had been based on fear of reprisals because he had personally tortured many people under Saddam Hussain's regime in Iraq. The Court held that it was obvious that he was liable to be excluded under Article 1F and the adjudicator should have raised it. The Tribunal in *MT (Article 1F(a)—aiding and abetting) Zimbabwe* [2012] UKUT 15 (IAC) held (obiter) that this practice was subject to the requirements of procedural fairness (para 98). The Tribunal is not in a position to consider exclusion if the Secretary of State has not advanced any evidence as to the claimant's individual involvement in the alleged acts (see *DK v SSHD* [2015] UKAITUR AA084062014).

13.1.3 Standard of proof

The standard of proof of allegations which would lead to exclusion is a matter of importance, even more so following the application of s 55, which prevents an asylum decision from being made. The Article says that a person will be excluded if 'there are serious reasons for considering' that they have committed one of the acts discussed. The Lisbon Expert Roundtable said this should be interpreted as a minimum to mean 'clear evidence sufficient to indict'. The UNHCR in its statement for the CJEU references C-57/09 and C-101/09 suggests that the standard of proof is a high one:

Although the application of the exclusion clauses does not require a determination of guilt in the criminal justice sense, and therefore the standard of proof required would be less than 'proof of guilt beyond reasonable doubt', it must be sufficiently high to ensure that refugees are not erroneously excluded.

In *Al-Sirri and DD (Afghanistan) v SSHD* [2012] UKSC 54 the Supreme Court reviewed decisions in Canada, Germany, and New Zealand and held that:

(1) 'Serious reasons' is stronger than 'reasonable grounds'.
(2) The evidence from which those reasons are derived must be 'clear and credible' or 'strong'.
(3) 'Considering' is stronger than 'suspecting' [and] . . . 'believing'. It requires the considered judgment of the decision-maker.

(4) The decision-maker need not be satisfied beyond reasonable doubt or to the standard required in criminal law.

(5) It is unnecessary to import our domestic standards of proof . . . However, if the decision-maker is satisfied that it is more likely than not that the applicant has *not* committed the crimes in question or has *not* been guilty of acts contrary to the purposes and principles of the United Nations, it is difficult to see how there could be serious reasons for considering that he had done so. The reality is that there are unlikely to be sufficiently serious reasons for considering the applicant to be guilty unless the decision-maker can be satisfied on the balance of probabilities that he is. But the task of the decision-maker is to apply the words of the Convention (and the Directive) in the particular case. (para 75)

This approach was consistent with the UK Supreme Court's previous decision in *JS Sri Lanka* [2010] UKSC 15 and the New Zealand Supreme Court in *Tamil X* [2010] NZSC 107.

13.1.4 **Proportionality**

The question of whether proportionality has a role to play in exclusion decisions is partly settled in UK law by s 34 of the Anti-terrorism, Crime and Security Act 2001 (ATCSA). This section says that Article 1F 'shall not be taken to require consideration of events or fear by virtue of which Article 1A would or might apply to a person if Article 1F did not apply'. In other words, the asylum seeker cannot argue that they should not be excluded from refugee status because of the severity of the persecution they would face.

UNHCR, in Cases C-57/09 and C-101/09 *Bundesrepublik Deutschland v D and B*, argued that the degree and likelihood of persecution feared should be measured against the seriousness of the acts committed. They say that this balance is derived from 'the nature and rationale of the exclusion clauses and the overriding humanitarian object and purpose of the 1951 Convention'. However, the CJEU did not accept this view, and held that the question of exclusion was separate from the question of whether the person would be returned to their country of origin. The CJEU said:

Since the competent authority has already, in its assessment of the seriousness of the acts committed by the person concerned and of that person's individual responsibility, taken into account all the circumstances surrounding those acts and the situation of that person, it cannot . . . be required, if it reaches the conclusion that Article 12(2) applies, to undertake an assessment of proportionality, implying as that does a fresh assessment of the level of seriousness of the acts committed. (para 109)

The Court of Appeal in *AH (Algeria)* [2015] EWCA Civ 1003 relied on this in rejecting an argument that the appellant's behaviour since the conviction (including serving a prison sentence) could expiate the crime.

The Tribunal in *MT (Article 1F(a)—aiding and abetting) Zimbabwe v SSHD* [2012] UKUT 15 (IAC) held that proportionality was only relevant to the consideration of whether a crime was serious and non-political, an issue which is discussed at 13.2.2.

13.1.5 **Autonomous meaning**

It is generally accepted that the text of the Refugee Convention must be given an autonomous meaning, not dependent on equivalent terms in the domestic legal systems of signatory states. This was affirmed in the UK by the Supreme Court in *R (on the application of JS) (Sri Lanka) v SSHD* [2009] UKSC 15. In *AH (Algeria) v SSHD* [2012] EWCA Civ

395 the Court of Appeal applied this to the meaning of 'serious non-political crime' in Article 1F(b). The notion of a serious crime must be given an autonomous meaning. The appellant had received a two-year prison sentence for falsifying documents, in a context in which he was alleged to have terrorist connections. Rix LJ said 'I have been left uncertain as to the gravamen of the offence of which AH was convicted by the French court of appeal' (para 45). This was an issue which needed specific assessment by the Tribunal aside from the descriptors of domestic law, and in the context of the purpose of this Article and of the whole of the Refugee Convention. The sentence imposed by a domestic court could be relevant, but the treatment of the offence in a domestic system was not conclusive for the purposes of exclusion from the Refugee Convention.

Likewise, in *Al-Sirri*, discussed at 13.2.4, the Supreme Court stated that it was concerned with ascertaining the autonomous meaning of 'serious reasons for considering', as the standard of proof for exclusion clauses (para 75).

We will consider each of the Article 1F grounds in turn.

13.2 Grounds for exclusion

13.2.1 Article 1F(a): Crime against peace, war crime, crime against humanity

As Article 1F(a) suggests, the definition of these crimes is to be found in international instruments. The main contemporary source is the statutes of international tribunals. These incorporate key provisions of the UN Convention on the Protection and Punishment of Genocide (1948) and the four 1949 Geneva Conventions for the Protection of Victims of War. The Rome Statute of the International Criminal Court 1998 (ICC) contains extensive definitions of crimes against humanity and war crimes. The Statute of the International Criminal Tribunal for the former Yugoslavia (ICTY), (1993 but amended numerous times) has generated significant case law and is also an important source.

The statutes create jurisdiction to try the crimes of genocide, crimes against humanity, war crimes, and crimes of aggression. The Rome Statute's definition of war crimes includes, for instance, intentional attacks on undefended civilians, humanitarian bodies and buildings dedicated to religion, education, art or science, and killing prisoners of war. The ICTY established that war crimes may be committed during a civil war (see *Dusko Tadic* case no IT 94 I T). The ICC Article 7 enumerates crimes against humanity, including murder, extermination, enslavement, deportation, imprisonment, torture, rape, enforced disappearance of persons, the crime of apartheid, persecutions on political, racial, and religious grounds; and other inhumane acts committed knowingly against any civilian population.

Article 6 of the Charter of the International Military Tribunal includes in the definition of a crime against peace 'planning, preparation, initiating or waging a war of aggression, or a war in violation of international treaties, agreements or assurances'. In *JS Sri Lanka* [2010] UKSC 15, the Court of Appeal (affirmed in the Supreme Court) held that there could be no exclusion under Article 1F(a) without evidence of actual war crimes or crimes against humanity having been committed. In order to establish this, reference should be made to the ICC statute, and the crimes alleged should be identified. This is now the accepted approach, entailing findings in lower courts and tribunals about atrocities in other countries. Although these findings carry no legal weight outside the particular case, they demonstrate in a striking way the international context in which asylum law operates. For instance, in *AA (Art 1F(a)—complicity—Arts 7 and 25 ICC Statute) Iran* [2011] UKUT 00339 (IAC) the Upper Tribunal found that the First-tier Tribunal did not err in law in holding that the Bassij, whom they defined as a 'volunteer paramilitary force', committed crimes against humanity falling within Article 7 of the ICC Statute (para 51). The Court of Appeal confirmed the appellant's exclusion. In *B v Refugee Appeals Board & another* [2011] IEHC 198 the Irish High Court had no doubt that the Taliban committed crimes against humanity. In *SK (Zimbabwe) v SSHD* [2012] EWCA Civ 807 the Court of Appeal held that the appellant was rightly excluded under Article 1F(a). As a member of the Zanu-PF youth wing she had participated in:

severe beatings and joint enterprise responsibility in . . . two farm invasions as . . . described by the Upper Tribunal as brutal and terrifying, designed to force farmers and farm workers off the land on which they live by the use of violence and terror and the burning of their homes and the destruction of their livelihoods, and where this is done as part of a widespread and systematic attack on such farms for political and discriminatory aims such as can fairly be described as persecutory and as involving the forcible transfer of populations (whether or not amounting to those separate crimes).

These were held by the Tribunal and the Court of Appeal to be 'other inhumane acts of a similar character' to those listed, according to the Rome Statute Article 7(1)(k).

In *MT (Article 1F (a)—aiding and abetting) Zimbabwe* [2012] UKUT 00015(IAC) the Upper Tribunal held that the requirement in Article 7(1) of the ICC Statute that acts be 'committed as part of a widespread or systematic attack directed against any civilian population with knowledge of the attack' (the 'chapeau requirement') was an essential element in the definition of a crime against humanity. The appellant was a police officer in the Zimbabwe police force. Under pressure from her superiors she had participated in acts against political opponents of ZANU PF, including two incidents in which torture was used. Drawing on international criminal law jurisprudence, the Tribunal held that a crime against humanity could be committed as an aider and abettor. This encompassed any assistance, physical or psychological, that had a substantial effect on the commission of the crime. Individual acts of police brutality such as the ones she had been involved in would not amount to crimes against humanity if they were not committed in the context of a widespread or systematic attack against the civilian population (the chapeau requirement).

13.2.1.1 Complicity

Case law in the UK has turned to a great extent on the question of complicity. The authority is *JS (Sri Lanka) v SSHD* [2010] UKSC 15.

 **Key Case**

JS (Sri Lanka) v SSHD **[2010] UKSC 15**

The appellant had served as second-in-command of the LTTE Intelligence Division's combat unit. The main issue was what degree of responsibility JS could be said to have for any international crimes that had been committed or planned by the LTTE. There was no evidence that he had committed such crimes himself, so any responsibility had to turn on the question of his complicity in the acts of others. The Court held that this must be determined by reference to the detailed provisions on liability in the Rome Statute. These dealt with the whole range of involvement in a criminal act, for instance, acting as a principal or co-principal, soliciting or procuring the crime, engaging in a joint criminal enterprise (Article 25). All the authorities were agreed that mere membership of an organization some part or members of which had committed crimes against humanity did not make a person liable for those crimes. This was the case in refugee law as well as criminal law. Article 1F required 'serious reasons for considering' that the person had committed such a crime. The Court of Appeal concluded:

> The fact that he was a bodyguard of the head of the intelligence wing . . . shows that he was trusted to perform that role, but not that he made a significant contribution to the commission of international crimes or that he acted as that person's bodyguard with the intention of furthering the perpetration of international crimes. . . . there was no evidence of international crimes committed by the men under his command for which he might incur liability under article 28. His own engagement in non-criminal military activity was not of itself a reason for suspecting him of being guilty of international crimes.

The Supreme Court rejected the Secretary of State's appeal, but held that the Court of Appeal's approach to complicity was too restricted. Lord Brown said:

> I would hold an accused disqualified under Article 1F if there are serious reasons for considering him voluntarily to have contributed in a significant way to the organization's ability to pursue its purpose of committing war crimes, aware that his assistance will in fact further that purpose. (para 38)

These words of Lord Brown are now the test for establishing complicity.

In *MH (Syria) and DS (Afghanistan) v SSHD* [2009] EWCA Civ 226, the Secretary of State had held that DS was excluded from refugee status under Article 1F(a) on the basis of atrocities committed by the KhAD, the Afghani intelligence service. It was found on the basis of the evidence that the torture and brutality of the KhAD was directed towards insurgents, not towards civilians. Accordingly, the Court of Appeal found that these acts did not constitute crimes against humanity according to the international statutes. DS' refugee claim could not be excluded on this basis. In *AA (Iran) v SSHD* [2013] EWCA Civ 835, the Court of Appeal held that even though the appellant had not himself tortured or abused civilians, as a long-serving local commander of the Bassij, on his own evidence he had handed individuals over knowing that they would be seriously ill-treated and 'closed his eyes' to abuses by others. He had seen the injuries resulting from torture and beatings and had felt uneasy but had continued to hand people over. Applying the test laid down in *JS Sri Lanka*, the appellant was found to be complicit. He had 'contributed in a significant way to the organisation's ability to pursue its purpose of committing war crimes, aware that his assistance will in fact further that purpose' (*JS (Sri Lanka)* para 38). The situation was similar in *AN (Afghanistan) v SSHD* [2015] EWCA Civ 684 in which the appellant had been a commander in Hizb-e-Islami, with his main role being to ensure that security was maintained; he had not been deployed on the front line and had not been personally involved in committing war crimes. The judge found that he would have known about the atrocities committed elsewhere, and that, although he 'did not actively engage in the types of human rights atrocities detailed in the country information reports before me, such individuals were part of the organised machinery of [HI] which allowed the leadership to be in a position to deploy some individuals to maintain security in captured areas (which the appellant claimed was his role), whilst allowing others to carry out the kinds of violations and war crimes detailed in the country information reports.' (para 80, quoted in CA para 15)

In *Attorney General (Minister of Immigration) v Tamil X* [2010] NZSC 107 the New Zealand Supreme Court held that the respondent could not be regarded as complicit in crimes against humanity for having worked on board a ship which was transporting arms for the LTTE. Although acts committed by the LTTE in the past could be identified as crimes against humanity, it could not be shown that Tamil X's conduct had contributed to these acts, bearing in mind that the LTTE was engaged in armed struggle, and that his knowledge of the ship's cargo was not established prior to the last voyage.

The CJEU in *Bundesrepublik Deutschland v D and B* took a similar view to that in *JS* and *Tamil X*:

Any authority which finds . . . that the person concerned has—like D—occupied a prominent position within an organisation which uses terrorist methods is entitled to presume that that person has individual responsibility for acts committed by that organisation during the relevant period, but it nevertheless remains necessary to examine all the relevant circumstances before . . . excluding that person from refugee status . . . the finding . . . is conditional on an assessment on a case-by-case basis of the specific facts. (paras 98 and 99)

13.2.1.2 Superior orders or duress

The applicant may seek to avoid exclusion based on acts they have committed on the grounds that they were acting on superior orders. The appellant in *CM (Article 1F (a)—superior orders) Zimbabwe* [2012] UKUT 00236 (IAC) was excluded from the protection of the Refugee Convention under Article 1F(a). He was a sergeant in the Zimbabwe army who had been involved in beatings and he had given orders for other soldiers to participate in similar beatings. The Tribunal held that these acts were crimes against humanity within the Rome Statute. As such, he was debarred from relying on any defence of superior orders.

The defence of duress is available in international criminal law where, 'resulting from a threat of imminent death or of continuing or imminent serious bodily harm against that person or another person, . . . the person acts necessarily and reasonably to avoid this threat, provided that the person does not intend to cause a greater harm than the one sought to be avoided' (Article 31 ICC Statute). Given these restricted circumstances, the defence is rarely made out, and was not in *CM (Zimbabwe) or MT (Zimbabwe)*.

13.2.2 Article 1F(b): Serious non-political crimes

A serious non-political crime may be so either because it never had any political connection or motivation, or because the consequences of it are so severe that it can no longer be treated as political.

 **Key Case**

T v SSHD [1996] 2 All ER 865

T was a member of an organization in Algeria that intended to secure power, was prepared to use violence to achieve its ends, and had been declared illegal in 1992. The special adjudicator found that the appellant was involved in and had had prior knowledge of a bomb attack on the airport in Algiers in which ten civilians had been killed, although there was a dispute about the level of intended damage and of the appellant's knowledge of that. He had also been engaged in planning a raid on an army barracks to seize arms in which one person had died. The House of Lords endorsed the *UNHCR Handbook* paras 151–161 which suggests that a 'serious' crime in this context 'must be a capital crime or a very serious punishable act' (para 155). The common law character of the crime must be weighed against its political nature. The killing of ten civilians was too great a crime to warrant being called 'political'. Lord Lloyd suggested that for a crime to be political it must be committed for a political purpose, 'that is to say, with the object of overthrowing or subverting or changing the government of a state or inducing it to change its policy'. Second, there must be:

> sufficiently close and direct link between the crime and the alleged political purpose. In determining whether such a link exists, the court will bear in mind the means used to achieve the political end, and will have particular regard to whether the crime was aimed at a military or governmental target, on the one hand, or a civilian target on the other, and in either event whether it was likely to involve the indiscriminate killing or injuring of members of the public. (at 787)

T had not planted the bomb or carried out the raid, but he had planned the raid and was a political organizer for the group which planted the bomb. He had sufficient knowledge of the plan to exclude him from refugee status, even if it did not extend to details.

The QD adds that 'particularly cruel actions, even if committed with an allegedly political objective, may be classified as serious non-political crimes'.

The approach of the Tribunal to implementing these principles has not always been consistent. In *Hane* [2002] UKIAT 03945, the appellant was a Maoist Party member in Nepal who had been involved in an armed raid on a police station in which two policemen were injured. There was a high level of violence between Maoists and state authorities. For a period of time reported by Amnesty International, the official figures were 548 Maoists, three soldiers, and one policeman killed. The appellant was excluded from refugee protection by Article 1F, as the criminal nature of his act outweighed the political context in which it was committed. By comparison, in *Gnanasegaran* [2002] UKIAT 00583, the appellant was an active member of the LTTE (Tamil Tigers) in Sri Lanka. He and two other members were wanted for the murder of one or two policemen. The Tribunal concluded, following *T*, that this was a political crime. It concluded:

Disturbing though we find it in the circumstances of this case that 'the perpetrator of a repellent crime should insist on the hospitality and protection of any nation whose borders he can manage to penetrate' (from the judgment of Lord Mustill in *T* . . .) we consider that this appeal must be allowed.

The comparison of *Hane* and *Gnanasegaran* illustrates the old adage that 'one person's terrorist is another's freedom fighter'. This is now a key issue in the application and interpretation of Article 1F. The UK government, in common with other governments, since September 2001 in particular, has attempted to exclude from refugee status people who for a range of reasons might be given the label 'terrorist'.

 **Key Case**

Joined Cases C-57/09 and C-101/09, *Bundesrepublik Deutschland v D and B*

B had been a sympathizer of Dev Sol (now DHKP/C) when a schoolboy and had supported armed guerrilla warfare in the mountains. After being arrested he had been subjected to serious physical abuse and had been forced to give a statement under torture and sentenced to life imprisonment. In 2001, while he was in custody, B confessed to killing a fellow prisoner suspected of being an informant. D had been a guerrilla fighter for the PKK and one of its senior officials. Because of political differences with its leadership, D had left the PKK in May 2000 and since then had been under threat. He had been granted asylum in Germany, but after a change in the law this was revoked.

The German court sought a preliminary ruling which the CJEU answered as follows:

- the fact that a person has been a member of an organisation which, because of its involvement in terrorist acts, is on the [proscribed] list . . . and that that person has actively supported the armed struggle waged by that organisation does not automatically constitute a serious reason for considering that that person has committed 'a serious non-political crime' or 'acts contrary to the purposes and principles of the United Nations';
- the finding . . . that there are serious reasons for considering that a person has . . . been guilty of such acts is conditional on an assessment on a case-by-case basis of the specific facts, with a view to determining whether the acts committed by the organisation concerned meet the conditions laid down in those provisions and whether individual responsibility for carrying out those acts can be attributed to the person concerned, regard being had to the standard of proof required under Article 12(2) of the Directive.

The New Zealand Supreme Court in *Attorney General (Minister of Immigration) v Tamil X* [2010] NZSC 107 revived the recognition of serious *political* crimes. Tamil X had been recruited to work on board a ship, the *Yahata*. He claimed to be unaware that in addition to its legitimate commercial activities the ship transported arms for the LTTE. He was aware of this on what became its last voyage. When challenged by the Indian navy there was an exchange of fire, and those on board, including Tamil X, scuttled the ship, the *Yahata*. The Court held that this was a serious crime, involving risk to the life of the Indian navy, but its purpose was clearly political. It did not consist of indiscriminate violence to civilians such as in the case of *T*, and Tamil X should not be excluded from refugee status.

Paragraph (b), unlike the other two paragraphs, only applies to acts that were committed before entry to the country of refuge. This in part explains the recent increased resort to para (c) (discussed at 13.2.4). The QD extends Article 1F(b):

He or she has committed a serious non-political crime outside the country of refuge prior to his or her admission as a refugee; which means the time of issuing a residence permit based on the granting of refugee status . . . (Qualification Directive) Article 12.2(b)

This means that a crime committed while waiting for refugee status to be granted may give rise to liability for exclusion under Article 1F(b), although it must be committed outside the country of refuge.

In *AH (Algeria) v SSHD* [2012] EWCA Civ 395 the appellant had been excluded from refugee status under Article 1F(b) and (c) on the basis that 'he was knowingly part of a criminal conspiracy or grouping formed with a view to committing terrorist acts' (para 35 of the Tribunal's determination). The Court of Appeal held that there was an error of law in excluding the appellant on this basis. He had convictions in a French court for falsifying a passport and an identity card, and he had connections with people who were involved in terrorism, but the Tribunal had not examined the appellant's role in the 'criminal conspiracy or grouping'. The Tribunal had not, independently of the conviction in France, examined whether there were serious reasons for considering that he had been involved in a serious non-political crime.

As mentioned earlier, in *MT (Article 1F(a)—aiding and abetting) Zimbabwe* the Tribunal considered, obiter, the question of the appellant's exclusion under Article 1F(b). In this context the proportionality of the harm committed was relevant. As a police officer she had participated in acts of torture and ill-treatment. The Tribunal said:

Such acts are contrary to peremptory norms of international law and in our judgement they cannot for that reason be regarded as proportionate, non-political, enforcement of the law. (para 134)

The appellant had argued that the crimes were political, because they were committed as a state actor 'involved in a political struggle with other organised groups' (para 73). The Tribunal's reasoning, though brief, implies that a government agent cannot, any more than a freedom fighter, take advantage of a political purpose to justify gross acts.

13.2.2.1 Complicity

The question of complicity in the context of para (b) is not necessarily settled by reference to the international statutes as discussed earlier, as the matter under consideration is generally not covered by the international statutes. It is still a question of how implicated the claimant is in the wrongful acts. In the case of *T*, although the appellant had not planted the bomb or carried out the raid, he had taken part in the planning and preparation of the latter and as a political organizer had at minimum an incriminating level of knowledge of the former. The degree of complicity that will result in exclusion is related to the nature and seriousness of the offence. Knowledge in advance that a demonstration may well erupt into stone-throwing and damage to property is a very different matter from knowledge in advance that a bomb will be planted in a densely populated area. The CJEU's judgment in *D and B* made it clear that mere membership of a proscribed organization at the time of the commission of acts or crimes proscribed by Article 1F is not enough to mean that an appellant is excluded, but membership of certain organizations is an important factor. What then becomes critical is how such an organization is identified.

13.2.3 **Membership of proscribed organizations**

The list that was relevant in the judgment in *D and B* was an EU list, forming the Annex to Common Position 2001/931/CFSP on the application of specific measures to combat terrorism. The UK uses a national list of organizations which are proscribed. The UK's list is made under the Terrorism Act 2000. The grounds for proscription are that the organization is concerned in terrorism (s 3) and this is defined as committing, preparing for, participating in, promoting or encouraging, or otherwise engaging in terrorism. The Terrorism Act 2006 added that an organization promotes or encourages terrorism if it glorifies it. This means to praise or celebrate it in such a way as to give people to understand that such conduct should be emulated (see chapters 2 and 15). Sixty-seven organizations were proscribed by the end of 2015. These include Al-Qa'ida, the LTTE, the PKK, and ETA.

The Secretary of State has publicized the following as the criteria for proscription:

1. the nature and scale of the organization's activities;
2. the specific threat that it poses to the UK;
3. the specific threat that it poses to British nationals overseas;
4. the extent of the organization's presence in the UK; and
5. the need to support 'other members of the international community' in the fight against terrorism.

By Terrorism Act 2000 ss 11, 12, and 13 it is an offence to belong to a proscribed organization or to profess to do so, to invite support for a proscribed organization which is not restricted to money or other property, to arrange or support or address a meeting in order to support a proscribed organization, or to wear an item of clothing or display an article suggesting support for a proscribed organization. There is a defence under Terrorism Act 2000 s 11(2) that the organization was not proscribed when the person charged became a member and that the person has not taken part in the activities of the organization since it was proscribed. However, such defences can only be raised in the course of prosecution of an individual, and challenging proscription of an organization is a more difficult process. David Anderson QC, Independent Reviewer of Terrorism Legislation found that proscription was at best a blunt instrument, and that the expense and complexity of applications make it unduly difficult to challenge a designation which was politically advantageous to government but damaging for the organization. As an alternative he recommended that proscription be for a fixed period of five years, but the recommendation was not accepted, and currently proscription is indefinite.

The use of the word 'terrorist' as a description of an organization begs the questions that must be answered. The Supreme Court in *JS (Sri Lanka)* rejected an earlier idea that an organization could be placed in a continuum from violence to working for democratic change in order to determine whether it should be described as 'terrorist'. The Court of Appeal in *JS (Sri Lanka)* did not regard the continuum as helpful because, firstly, the Tribunal had 'rolled up a number of factors which might cause somebody wedded to the ideals of western liberal democracy to take a more or less hostile view of the organisation and to use an assessment of where the organisation stood in relation to those values in deciding whether its armed acts were "proportionate"'. This provided a subjective and unsatisfactory basis for determining whether as a matter of law an individual was guilty of an international crime. Secondly, some of the factors identified were not relevant to the question of guilt of an international crime, for example, whether the organization's long-term aims embraced a democratic mode of government. Thirdly, the continuum approach took the decision-maker's eye off the critical questions of whether the evidence provided serious reasons for considering the applicant to have committed the *actus reus* of an international crime with the requisite *mens rea* (Toulson LJ paras 112–114). In general, it is not so easy to identify 'an extremist terrorist group'. There is an all too obvious danger that a national list will include groups for political reasons. Without scope to recognize that 'one man's terrorist is another man's freedom fighter', the Refugee Convention would be undermined, as persecution for reasons of political opinion is an archetypal qualification for refugee status. It is easy to recognize the events of 11 September 2001 as an atrocity, but it is not easy to derive a generalizable principle from this.

The judgment of the CJEU in *D and B* makes it clear that membership of an organization deemed 'terrorist' is not enough in itself to warrant exclusion from refugee status. The application of this judgment is complicated by rules permitting closed evidence where national security is in issue. In *SS (Libya) v SSHD* [2011] EWCA Civ 1547, SS was excluded from refugee status. The only open allegation against him was that he was a member of the Libyan Islamic Fighting Group (LIFG). He denied this, but the remaining evidence was closed and so he did not have access to it (see SIAC procedures discussed in chapter 7). As mentioned, the LTTE and PKK are included in the UK's list, but the Supreme Court in *JS (Sri Lanka)* said that the LTTE was neither 'predominantly terrorist in character' nor an 'extremist terrorist group' (para 27). B was a PKK member and guerrilla fighter, initially awarded refugee status in Germany. In the UK membership of the PKK as a proscribed organization is a crime, but this in itself cannot be regarded as grounds for exclusion under Article 1F(b) as the crime is clearly political, and goes nowhere near the level of seriousness described by Lord Mustill in *T*.

13.2.4 **Article 1F(c): Acts contrary to purpose and principles of UN**

The purpose of this paragraph was summarized in the Canadian case of *Pushpanathan* [1998] 1 SCR by Bastarache J: 'The rationale is that those who are responsible for the persecution which creates refugees should not enjoy the benefits of a Convention designed to protect refugees' (para 63).

UNHCR and others had suggested that the drafters of the Convention had in mind 'those operating on a state level and perpetrating crimes of national or international significance' (Pretzell et al 2002:149 and UNHCR Guidelines 2003). However, it is now clear that the acts of individuals not operating at state level are included within Article 1F(c) (*Al-Sirri v SSHD* [2009] EWCA Civ 222, and the CJEU in *B and D*).

Nevertheless, the acts must have an international dimension. The Supreme Court in *Al-Sirri* adopted para 17 of the UNHCR Guidelines:

Article 1F(c) is only triggered in extreme circumstances by activity which attacks the very basis of the international community's coexistence. Such activity must have an international dimension. Crimes capable of affecting international peace, security and peaceful relations between states, as well as serious and sustained violations of human rights would fall under this category.

The source of the purpose and principles of the UN is made explicit by the Qualification Directive Article 12, extending the text of Article 1F(c) to say: 'Acts contrary to purpose and principles of UN *as set out in the Preamble and Articles 1 and 2 of the Charter of the United Nations*' (emphasis added).

It was earlier suggested that paragraph (c) was limited to actions committed before arrival in the country of refuge. If its purpose was to exclude state actors as stated earlier, this limitation would be too obvious to need stating. However, case law has established that no such limitation exists, and paragraph (c), which had been little used, began to be far more often invoked to deny or revoke refugee status where refugees are suspected of international terrorist activity in the country of refuge.

These developments began with *Singh and Singh v SSHD* (SIAC 31 July 2000), where the Special Immigration Appeals Commission held that Sikh activists who were supporting armed struggle in India from the UK could be excluded from refugee status under Article 1F(c). The fact that these actions were in pursuance of a fight for self-determination did not provide a defence against exclusion. They could not have been excluded under Article 1F(b) because these acts were committed after arrival in the country of refuge. The SIAC found that as there was no express limitation of Article 1F(c) to individuals carrying governmental authority, none should be implied. The crucial finding was that the UN unequivocally condemns terrorism. The actions of Singh and Singh could be brought within the definition of terrorism in the UK (Terrorism Act 2000 s 1). Therefore, terrorist acts such as these were contrary to the purpose and principles of the UN. Following this, in *KK (Article 1F(c)), Turkey* [2004] UKIAT 00101 the act that KK had committed came within the UK's controversial and wide definition of terrorism under Terrorism Act 2000 s 1. The UN condemned terrorism and so his action brought him within Article 1F(c). The approach was developed in *AA (Palestine)* [2005] UKIAT 00104, in which the appellant had been arrested while on a suicide-bombing mission. The Tribunal held that para (c) contains no requirement that the crime in question be non-political in order to attract exclusion, therefore if an act is accepted to come within this paragraph there does not need to be any enquiry into whether the common law criminal element outweighs any political motivation. Ironically, this now seems to result in a lesser crime giving rise to exclusion under Article 1F(c) than under 1F(b), even though the apparent intention is the other way round.

Para (c) became the exclusion clause of choice for government, keen to ensure that those who could attract the label 'terrorist' were not given refugee status. To create greater certainty, they introduced legislation, the Immigration, Asylum and Nationality Act 2006 s 54, which says:

In the construction and application of Article 1F(c) of the Refugee Convention the reference to acts contrary to the purposes and principles of the United Nations shall be taken as including, in particular –

(a) acts of committing, preparing or instigating terrorism (whether or not the acts amount to an actual or inchoate offence), and

(b) acts of encouraging or inducing others to commit, prepare or instigate terrorism (whether or not the acts amount to an actual or inchoate offence).

The interpretation and application of s 54 was dealt with by the Supreme Court in *Al-Sirri and DD (Afghanistan) v SSHD*.

 **Key Case**

Al-Sirri v SSHD [2012] UKSC 54

Mr Al-Sirri was an Egyptian national, who claimed asylum in the UK and was excluded by the application of Article 1F(c). He had written a foreword to a book by a member of an organization proscribed in the UK, EU, Canada, and US. He possessed an unpublished manuscript by the leader of another proscribed organization. He possessed books and videos relating to Osama bin Laden and Al-Qaeda, and he had transferred money to and from foreign countries, allegedly in sums greater than his known income could explain. He had been indicted for conspiracy to murder General Masoud, the Vice-President and Defence Minister of Afghanistan, two days before the attacks of September 11, 2001. However, the evidence against him was inconclusive, and the charge was dismissed.

The Tribunal upheld Mr Sirri's exclusion from refugee status.

The argument in the Supreme Court concerned whether the fact that his actions could be classified as contraventions of the UK terrorism legislation was sufficient to bring them within Article 1F(c). The Court held that 'acts contrary to the purpose and principles of the UN' must have an autonomous meaning for the purposes of the Refugee Convention. Sedley LJ had been correct to say in the Court of Appeal that 'the adoption by section 54(2) of the 2006 Act of the meaning of terrorism contained in the 2000 Act has where necessary to be read down in an article 1F(c) case so as to keep its meaning within the scope of article 12(2) (c) of the Directive' (para 36). There is no internationally agreed definition of terrorism. The purpose of the UN is an international purpose. In the light of all this, the Court adopted the UNHCR guideline.

Mr Al-Sirri had argued that any international element would not be satisfied just by doing an act in one state which jeopardized security in another. The Supreme Court held that it must depend on the circumstances:

the test is whether the resulting acts have the requisite serious effect upon international peace, security, and peaceful relations between states. (para 40)

DD Afghanistan was considered together with *Al-Sirri* by the Supreme Court since they raised similar issues about the interpretation of Article 1F(c).

 **Key Case**

DD (Afghanistan) v SSHD [2012] UKSC 54

The basis of DD's asylum claim was that he feared persecution because of his association with his brother AD, who was a well-known Jamiat-e-Islami commander in Afghanistan. Following US military intervention in Afghanistan, the appellant and his brother fled to Pakistan. In 2004, the appellant's brother was assassinated by his enemies who held positions in the Karzai government of Afghanistan. The appellant was also a target of the assassination attempt and sustained gunshot injuries. He returned to Afghanistan and sought protection by joining Hizb-e-Islami. He commanded 10–15 people and engaged in both offensive and defensive military operations against both the Afghan government and the forces of ISAF.

His argument against exclusion was that participation in an armed attack against forces operating under and carrying out a United Nations mandate does not without more engage Article 1F(c). ISAF was a NATO-led force, not a UN body. The Supreme Court held that ISAF

> was mandated by the United Nations for the express purpose of maintaining peace and security in Afghanistan, thereby assisting in the maintaining of international peace and security . . . . This is one of the most important purposes set out in article 1 of the United Nations Charter (para 63).

Accordingly, the Court concluded that 'an attack on ISAF is in principle capable of being an act contrary to the purposes and principles of the United Nations' (para 68).

The Supreme Court's judgment in Al-Sirri's case puts a brake on some of the expansion of the use of Article 1F(c). In DD's case at the Court of Appeal stage, the Court confirmed that 'participation in military actions against the government was not terrorism' (*SSHD v DD (Afghanistan)* [2010] EWCA Civ 1407 para 54). This had been doubted by SIAC in *SS* but the Court of Appeal may have stemmed the tide that was turning towards the erosion of even the concept of 'freedom fighter' by asserting 'it is difficult to hold that every act of violence in a civil war, the aim of which will usually be to overthrow a legitimate government, is an act of terrorism within the 2000 Act' (para 55). As they said, 'terrorism is indiscriminate'. DD was nevertheless excluded from refugee status under Article 1F(c), as described in the Supreme Court judgment earlier in this section because in Jamait-e-Islami, the Taliban, and Hizb-e-Islami he had fought also against the ISAF, the International Special Assistance Force. See Sivakumaran 2014 for commentary on the implications of this.

The Supreme Court's judgment in *Al-Sirri* did not address the effect of s 54 except to say that Sedley LJ was right to say that it must be read down where necessary 'to keep its meaning within the scope of article 12(2)(c) of the Directive'.

AH Algeria applied s 54, but predated *Al-Sirri*. In that case there was no evidence of instigation, encouragement, or inducement of acts of terrorism so as to bring the appellant within s 54(1).

13.3 **Article 33(2)**

The Michigan Guidelines quoted at the beginning of the previous section pithily say:

The fundamental object and purpose of Article 1(F)(a) is to exclude persons whose international criminal conduct means that their admission as a refugee threatens the integrity of the international refugee regime. This goal is to be distinguished from the advancement of host state safety and security, a matter addressed by Article 33(2) of the Convention.

Article 33(2) of the Refugee Convention provides an exception to the *non-refoulement* obligation. This is where there are 'reasonable grounds' for regarding the refugee as 'a danger to the security of the country in which he is' or in relation to a person 'who, having been convicted by a final judgment of a particularly serious crime constitutes a danger to that country'. The CJEU in *D and B* made the distinction plain between Article 1F and Article 33.2 by holding that exclusion from refugee status pursuant to Article 12(2)(b) or (c) of Directive 2004/83 (equivalent to Article 1F(b) and (c) of the Refugee Convention) was 'not conditional on the person concerned representing a present danger to the host Member State'.

Article 33.2 can be applied in case of serious common crime as well as threats to national security. For example, it was applied to the appellant in *A v SSHD* CA 16/2/2004, who had been convicted in the UK of a serious sexual assault on his daughter, and of the rape of a woman.

The emphasis is on danger to the country, that is, conviction of a particularly serious crime should not of itself warrant exclusion if the person would not constitute a danger to the country. Goodwin-Gill says:

an exception to *non-refoulement* ought necessarily to involve an assessment of all the circumstances, the nature of the offence, the background to its commission, the behaviour of the individual, and the actual terms of any sentence imposed. (2007:240)

The Qualification Directive Article 14 permits Member States to 'revoke, end or refuse to renew' refugee status on terms similar to Article 33.2, and Article 21 provides additionally for *refoulement* in the same circumstances as Article 33.2. The effect of Article 33.2 is to allow *refoulement*, rather than, as with Article 1F, exclusion from refugee status; because of the absolute nature of Article 3 ECHR, the distinction is rather theoretical. The presumption of Article 33 is that the offender is a person whose life or liberty is in danger if they are returned to their home state. If the risk of this is accepted at the time of a decision under Article 33.2, Article 3 will prevent their actual return. Of course, the need for protection from danger to the individual on return cannot be a licence for them to inflict serious harm on the host state. The creation of a 'special immigration status' by the 2008 Act, discussed at 13.4, is part of the UK's response to this tension.

13.3.1 **UK legislation related to Article 33.2**

UK statute contradicts the principles of proportionality and individual assessment. First, as in the case of exclusion, ATCSA s 34 provides that any threat to the person in the event of return need not be taken into account when the Secretary of State certifies that Article 33(2) applies. Section 34 is generally worded, and despite its inclusion in a statute rushed through Parliament as an emergency response to terrorism, it is not restricted to terrorist cases.

Second, Nationality, Immigration and Asylum Act 2002 s 72(2) resiles from the obligation to make the necessary judgment under Article 33(2) as to danger to the community. It says:

A person shall be *presumed* to have been convicted by a final judgment of a particularly serious crime and to constitute a danger to the community of the United Kingdom if he is –

(a) convicted in the United Kingdom of an offence, and
(b) sentenced to a period of imprisonment of at least two years. (emphasis added)

By s 72(11) this does not include a suspended sentence but does include a hospital order. The section also includes an offence committed abroad where the person is sentenced to a period of imprisonment of at least two years, and conviction for a similar offence in the UK would have carried a sentence of at least two years. The Tribunal in *HAA (s. 72: overseas conviction) Somalia* [2012] UKUT 00366 (IAC) held that this information on sentencing must be available for the presumption to be maintained. A general statement about a drugs offence was not sufficient.

Referring back to the earlier discussion of exclusion under Article 1F(b), it is worth noting that the offence of belonging to a proscribed organization under Terrorism Act 2000 s 11 carries a maximum sentence of 10 years. This risks making membership of the LTTE, PKK, and so on grounds for *refoulement* without the commission of any serious non-political crime. What saves it from this is that the presumption in s 72(2) is rebuttable (*IH (s 72 'Particularly Serious Crime') Eritrea* [2009] UKAIT 00012 confirmed in *EN (Serbia) v SSHD* [2009] EWCA Civ 630). Section 72(8) provides that the gravity of the fear or threat of persecution, as in s 34 ATCSA, is not to be taken into account in considering whether the presumption is rebutted.

In *AQ (Somalia)* [2011] EWCA Civ 695 the Court of Appeal held that the presumption in s 72 applies whether or not the Secretary of State issues a certificate. However, in order to apply and test the presumption, the issue must be raised one way or another before the Court or Tribunal. It was held to be an abuse of power to issue a s 72 certificate *after* judicial proceedings were concluded. (*TB v SSHD* [2008] EWCA Civ 977). Where for instance the danger of reoffending is low, the presumption can be rebutted (*Mugwagwa (s.72—applying statutory presumptions) Zimbabwe* [2011] UKUT 00338 (IAC)).

The Nationality, Immigration and Asylum Act 2002 (Specification of Particularly Serious Crimes) Order 2004, SI 2004/1910 was made under the power in s 72(4) to specify further crimes, having the same effect as a conviction under s 72(2). The order specified 183 offences, including not only rape, murder, and stockpiling biological weapons, but also theft, entering a building as a trespasser intending to steal, and aggravated taking of a vehicle. Section 72 is stated to be 'for the purpose and construction of article 33.2 of the Refugee Convention'. The Parliamentary Joint Committee on Human Rights advised the government that the Order was incompatible with Article 33(2) of the Refugee Convention 'because it includes within its scope a number of offences which do not amount to "particularly serious crimes" within the meaning of Article 33(2)' (Joint Committee on Human Rights Session 2003–04 Twenty-second Report). As the Human Rights Committee pointed out, legislation which is designed to give effect to international obligations must be interpreted compatibly with those obligations. If the order is incompatible with the Convention, then it follows that it is *ultra vires* the 2002 Act. This was held to be so in *EN (Serbia) v SSHD* [2009] EWCA Civ 630.

 **Key Case**

EN (Serbia) v SSHD [2009] EWCA Civ 630

EN was a national of Serbia who claimed asylum in the UK. After appeals, he was granted indefinite leave to remain. In 2002 and 2005, he was convicted of minor offences and in 2006 of burglary and possessing an offensive weapon. The longest of his prison sentences was 12 months. The Secretary of State decided to deport him. After he had given notice of appeal, the Secretary of State notified EN that it had been decided to issue a notice under s 72 of the 2002 Act against him and that he was not entitled to humanitarian protection.

The Court of Appeal confirmed that Article 33(2) imposed two requirements: conviction by a final judgment of a particularly serious crime *and* constituting a danger to the community. Both of these must be present in order for the person to be subject to *refoulement*. The Court held that a rebuttable presumption could in principle be compatible with Article 33.2 and Article 14 of the Directive. The Court said that the 2004 Order specified not only offences that could sensibly be regarded as particularly serious crimes, but also many that could not. Even on the basis that the presumption was rebuttable, the 2004 Order was objectionable. The power conferred by s 72(4)(a) was impliedly qualified by its context and purpose. The Order was ultra vires.

The 2004 Order was struck down by the Court of Appeal and there has been no new order under the section.

The Joint Committee on Human Rights had expressed doubts about the compatibility of s 72 itself with the Refugee Convention (their report predated the Qualification Directive) on the grounds that a presumption undermined the case by case basis of refugee determination, reversed the burden of proof as stated in Article 33.2, and precluded the application of a proper proportionality test to each case (paras 32–36). Goodwin-Gill and McAdam consider the section incompatible for these reasons (2007:183). The provisions also drew strong criticism from the UNHCR (see press release 7 November 2004). The Court of Appeal, however, as the case summary shows, did not go as far as saying that the presumption contained in the section conflicted with the Directive. They accepted the earlier decision of the Tribunal in *IH (s 72 'Particularly Serious Crime') Eritrea* [2009] UKAIT 00012, that the presumption in s 72 should be read as rebuttable, and this was enough to make it compatible with the Directive and the Convention.

In *EN (Serbia)* the appellant argued that the Qualification Directive Article 14.4 was incompatible with the Refugee Convention and thus with Article 63 of the EC Treaty. This was because it permitted revocation, ending, or refusal of refugee status, while Article 33.2 only allowed for *refoulement* where 'there are reasonable grounds for regarding him or her as a danger to the security of the Member State'. This would deprive the refugee of status while the issue was being considered. The Court did not have jurisdiction to decide this question. The UK's immigration rules para 334(iii) reflect Article 14.4(a).

13.4 Immigration status after s 72 and the Criminal Justice and Immigration Act 2008

Given the ineradicable obligation not to return a person to their own country to face treatment contrary to Article 3 ECHR (see in particular chapter 5), what is the practical impact of exclusion from refugee status or a decision under s 72, applying the exception to *refoulement*?

The immigration rules, in accordance with the Qualification Directive, provide that exclusion and Article 33.2 apply to humanitarian protection just as to refugee status. Humanitarian protection is the status which may be granted to a person whose return would breach Article 3, and, as mentioned in chapter 11, a person excluded from humanitarian protection by Article 1F may be granted a shorter period of discretionary (or 'restricted') leave. This is renewable, but short term and insecure, and may cause additional chaos and instability in the person's life if reviews and renewals do not take place.

A more draconian option is available, since ss 130–7 of the Criminal Justice and Immigration Act 2008 created a status of being a 'designated person'. Such a person has no leave to remain in the UK and is not on temporary admission (see chapter 14). They may be subject to conditions as to residence and work, reporting conditions, and electronic monitoring. They are not entitled to mainstream welfare benefits, but may be supported by way of vouchers. This 'special immigration status' (which is the heading to this Part of the 2008 Act) may only be imposed on someone who falls within the exclusion criteria of Article 1F of the Refugee Convention, or has been convicted of a crime to which s 72 of the 2002 Act applies. Falling within one of these groups makes the person a 'foreign criminal' according to the terminology of s 131. The other condition for designation is that the person is liable to deportation but cannot be removed from the UK because to do so would breach their human rights under the ECHR. These provisions are not yet in force.

13.5 Article 32

This Article, in contrast to Article 1F and 33(2), gives a refugee protection against expulsion and in that respect complements Article 33(1), but its terms are surprisingly weak. It applies to recognized refugees, lawfully present, and says that they shall not be expelled save on grounds of national security or public order. Proper legal process for appeal must be allowed. In effect, this makes a refugee in the UK liable to deportation, but with a higher threshold to be reached by the state to justify expulsion. Also, this is not a *refoulement* provision. The state must allow the refugee a reasonable period within which to seek admission to another country.

In *SSHD v ST (Eritrea)* [2012] UKSC 12 the Supreme Court held that a refugee was not entitled to the protection of Article 32 unless she had been granted 'lawful presence' in the state in question, in other words, leave to enter and remain. ST was an Eritrean national who had lived most of her life in Ethiopia. She was granted refugee status on the grounds of fear of persecution in Eritrea, but the Supreme Court agreed that she could still be removed to Ethiopia. The destination country must however be safe for the refugee, and a place from which they will not be *refouled* to the country from which they have been granted asylum (*RR (refugee—safe third country) Syria* [2010] UKUT 422 (IAC)).

13.6 Conclusion

The trend is towards a less secure status for refugees and a greater willingness to exclude by reason of the threat posed by individuals. The linkage made between asylum and terrorism has been demonstrated in this chapter to be not only a matter of politics but also a matter of law.

QUESTIONS

1 Why does the Refugee Convention exclude from protection those who have committed a serious non-political crime? Is there still a justification for limiting this exclusion to non-political crimes? What would be the effect of excluding people from protection for any serious crime?

2 Does the law now strike the right balance between denying a safe haven to those who perpetrate atrocities and giving refuge to those who are in danger of persecution?

**online
resource
centre**
For guidance on answering questions, visit the Online Resource Centre www.oxfordtextbooks.co.uk/orc/clayton7e/.

FURTHER READING

Anderson, David (2015) *The Terrorism Acts in 2014: Report of the Independent Reviewer on the Operation of the Terrorism Act 2000 and Part 1 of the Terrorism Act 2006,* September 2015.

Bowring, Bill and Korff, Douwe (2004) '*Terrorist Designation with Regard to European and International Law: The Case of the PMOI*' Paper for International Conference of Jurists, 10 November 2004.

Bruin, René and Wouters, Kees (2003) 'Terrorism and the Non-derogability of *Non-refoulement*' *International Journal of Refugee Law* vol. 15, no. 1, pp. 30–67.

Dungel, Joakim, (2009) 'Defining Victims of Crimes against Humanity: *Martic* and the International Criminal Court' *Leiden Journal of International Law* vol. 22, pp. 727–52.

Gilbert, Geoff, (2003) 'Protection after September 11th' *International Journal of Refugee Law* vol. 15, no. 1, pp. 1–4.

Hathaway, James (2013) 'The Michigan Guidelines on the Exclusion of International Criminals' *Michigan Journal of International Law* vol. 35, no. 1, pp. 3–13.

Sivakumaran, Sandesh (2014) 'Exclusion from Refugee Status: The Purposes and Principles of the United Nations and Article 1F(c) of the Refugee Convention' *International Journal of Refugee Law,* 2014, vol. 26, no. 3, 350–81.

Symonds, Steve, (2008) 'The Special Immigration Status' *Journal of Immigration Asylum and Nationality Law* vol. 22, no. 4, pp. 333–49.

UNHCR (2015) *Addressing Security Concerns without Undermining Refugee Protection* (UNHCR) accessed at: http://www.refworld.org/pdfid/5672aed34.pdf.

UNHCR (2003) 'Guidelines on International Protection: Application of Exclusion Clauses: Article 1F of the Convention Relating to the Status of Refugees' (UNHCR), accessed at: www.unhcr.org/3f7d48514.html.

SECTION 6

Enforcement

14

....

Detention

SUMMARY

The deprivation of liberty is one of the most serious infringements of fundamental human rights. In immigration law, individuals lose their liberty through the exercise of a statutory discretion by the Home Office or immigration officers. Guidelines and safeguards for the exercise of this discretion are crucial, but notably in UK law there is no fixed time limit on immigration detention. The statutory powers and executive guidelines are examined here, together with human rights and common law rules. The use of detention has been, until very recently, an increasingly frequent phenomenon in the asylum process, and the key role of temporary admission is examined. The former use of indefinite detention for foreign terrorist suspects is discussed at the end of the chapter.

14.1 Introduction

'In English law every imprisonment is *prima facie* unlawful, and . . . it is for a person directing imprisonment to justify his act.' These well-known words of Lord Atkin in the wartime internment case of *Liversidge v Anderson* [1942] AC 206 at 245 are still a proper statement of legal principle. Detention is not lawful unless authorized by law. This is the reverse of the usual rule in English law, whereby anything is lawful providing it is not specifically prohibited. Detention, however, interferes with one of the most basic human rights, that of physical liberty, and the advent of the Human Rights Act 1998 strengthens the common law by providing in Article 5 a statutory right which may only be infringed in prescribed circumstances. The deprivation of physical liberty is regarded as the most serious punishment available in the criminal justice system in the UK. Nevertheless, in the immigration and asylum system, detention may be imposed upon people who are not charged with any crime nor even suspected of committing one.

In this chapter, we shall consider, first, human rights law having a bearing on immigration detention; second, who is detained in the UK presently under immigration powers; and third, the parameters of the domestic law power to detain.

14.2 Human rights standards

International human rights instruments show unanimity on the issue of detention. United Nations Declaration of Human Rights Article 9: 'No-one shall be subjected to arbitrary arrest, detention and exile'; International Covenant on Civil and Political

Rights Article 9(1): 'Everyone has the right to liberty and security of person. No one shall be subjected to arbitrary arrest or detention'; European Convention on Human Rights Article 5: 'Everyone has the right to liberty and security of person. No one shall be deprived of his liberty save in the following cases and in accordance with a procedure prescribed by law'.

All these three international human rights documents prohibit detention which is arbitrary. The United Nations Human Rights Commission (UNHRC) Working Group on Arbitrary Detention said that detention is arbitrary when:

- there is no legal basis for the detention;
- detention is imposed as a state response to the exercise of a fundamental right; or
- the total or partial non-observance of the norms of a fair trial is of such gravity as to make the resulting detention arbitrary.

The UNHRC Working Group visits countries to investigate their detention practice. They visited the UK in 1998 to examine the situation of migrants and asylum seekers in detention, and identified a number of concerns relating to:

- reasons for detention;
- duration of detention;
- availability of independent review of detention; and
- limited consideration of other options before resorting to detention.

These concerns about the UK's detention practices have persisted.

The Human Rights Act principles, contained in Article 5 ECHR (European Convention on Human Rights), are concerned with similar issues:

- Detention must be for a reason specified in Article 5, and no other.
- Detention must only imposed through a procedure prescribed by law.
- That law should protect the individual from arbitrariness, both in content and process.
- The detained person has a right to reasons for their detention.
- They must be able to challenge their detention.

14.2.1 Article 5 ECHR

Article 5 ECHR begins with a presumption of liberty: 'Everyone has the right to liberty and security of person.' The principles upon which this liberty may be curtailed, as contained in Article 5, begin with the following:

- Article 5.1 'No-one shall be deprived of his liberty save in the following cases . . .'

In other words, detention must be for a reason specified in Article 5, and no other. Unlike the qualified rights in the Convention which may be interfered with in the interests of broad public policy objectives, the right to liberty may be interfered with for specified purposes only. Two of these relate to immigration: 'to prevent unauthorized entry' into the country, and 'detention of a person against whom action is being taken with a view to deportation or extradition' (Article 5(1)(f)). The meaning of 'to prevent unauthorized entry' was considered for the first time by the ECtHR in the Grand Chamber in the case of *Saadi v UK* [2008] ECHR 79.

Key Case

Saadi v UK [2008] ECHR 79

The appellants were Iraqi Kurds who claimed asylum on arrival. They were detained for seven days in Oakington Reception Centre. This was a new procedure initiated in the UK, whereby people whose claims were thought to be capable of being decided quickly were detained to enable that decision to be made. They challenged their detention on the basis that it was not 'to prevent unauthorized entry'. The European Court of Human Rights (ECtHR) found, with the Court of Appeal and House of Lords, that until a state has 'authorized' entry to the country, any entry is 'unauthorized'. So, detention of a person in order to enable that authorization to take place can be to 'prevent his effecting an unauthorized entry'.

The Court rejected the argument which had been accepted in the English High Court, that, having presented themselves to the immigration authorities, stated their need to claim asylum, and complied with requirements, the claimants were in fact doing everything they could to make an *authorized* entry. As the House of Lords had also held, the entry was unauthorized until it was authorized. In the case of 'detention of a person against whom action is being taken with a view to deportation or extradition', the ECtHR in *Chahal* had decided that there was 'no requirement that the detention be reasonably considered necessary, for example, to prevent the person concerned from committing an offence or fleeing' in order for it to be permitted by Article 5. In *Saadi*, the Court noted that, to avoid arbitrariness, detention for some other reasons permitted under Article 5.1—to secure compliance with a court order, of a minor for supervisory reasons, and those which concerned public health and safety—required an assessment of whether detention was necessary to achieve the stated aim. They held that this did not apply to detention for immigration reasons, and held that the first limb of Article 5.1(f) should be interpreted in the same way as the second, so that detention was not required to be necessary in order to be lawful. The second part concerned control of the residence of aliens, and the first part concerned their entry. The state had the right to control both equally, so it would be 'artificial' to impose a different standard on entry from that on deportation.

The Court held by 11 votes to six that there had been no violation of Article 5.1. Helen O'Nions comments that 'the interpretation of the majority . . . appears to be at odds with the international legal provisions and also with regional statements from the Council of Europe and the European Union'. *Saadi* has remained a controversial decision. Some of the case law applying and distinguishing it is discussed in relation to detention on arrival at 14.4.1

The national authority must make it plain under which limb of Article 5.1(f) the applicant is detained. In *Ahmade v Greece*, Application no. 50520/09, paras 142–144, 25 September 2012 the Court held that detention, which had been imposed by the authorities to effect removal, was not authorized under the second limb of the paragraph, since the asylum claim was not yet determined and deportation could not lawfully be carried out. In *Aden Ahmed v Malta* [2013] ECHR 720 14 months' detention of a Somali woman pending removal to Somalia was unlawful because no removals had ever been effected from Malta to Somalia, and the government offered no evidence of steps taken to remove her.

14.2.1.1 Arbitrariness

- Article 5(1) says that detention must be '. . . in accordance with a procedure prescribed by law . . .'

This means that the detention is in accordance with substantive and procedural rules of national law (*Conka v Belgium* (2002) 34 EHRR 54). If not, it will also breach Article 5 as being not in accordance with a procedure prescribed by law (e.g., *Abdi v UK* [2013] ECHR 299). It also means that the quality of that law is compatible with the rule of law and that the legal provision in question be accessible and precise (*Amuur v France* (1996) 22 EHRR 533 para 50).

These requirements are integral, in the case of Article 5, to the principle that detention should not be arbitrary. This principle goes wider than the requirement for the detention to be prescribed by law, and is fundamental to the protection given by Article 5. The ECtHR has said that detention 'should be in keeping with the purpose of Article 5, namely to protect the individual from arbitrariness' (*Chahal v UK, Amuur v France, Conka v Belgium*). The case law of the ECHR on the question of arbitrariness shares some of the principles identified by that of the UN Working Group on Arbitrary Detention: procedural fairness, limits on the duration of detention, the legitimacy of reasons for detention, and the availability of review. The Court in *Saadi* drew together authorities on the concept, saying that detention would be arbitrary where, 'despite complying with the letter of national law, there has been an element of bad faith or deception on the part of the authorities' and where the detention did not genuinely conform with the purpose permitted by the relevant sub-paragraph of Article 5(1). There must be some relationship between the ground of permitted deprivation of liberty relied on and the place and conditions of detention.

In *Conka v Belgium* the Court found a breach of Article 5.1 in that the reasons given for detention were misleading. Notices were sent to about 70 asylum seekers, requiring them to attend police stations to enable the files concerning their asylum applications to be completed. At the police station they were served with an order to leave Belgium, a decision for their removal to their country of origin, and notice of their detention for that purpose. They were detained and removed.

The ECtHR found that the wording of the notice which brought them to the police station was a deliberate ploy by the authorities to mislead the applicants in order to ensure the compliance of the largest possible number. The Court said that the action of the police in misleading asylum seekers about the purpose for which they were requested to attend the police station and thereby detaining them by deception could be found to contravene the principle against arbitrariness.

The mass nature of the deception practised by the police in this case attracted particular criticism by the Court. In addition to Article 5.1, the Court by a narrow majority found a violation of Protocol 4 Article 4, which prohibits collective expulsion of aliens.

These requirements for fairness and transparency have resonances in the UK's domestic case law, as appears later in this chapter.

14.2.1.2 Limit on duration of detention

In *Chahal*, the ECtHR held that where a person was detained with a view to deportation, the principle of lawfulness required that the deportation proceedings should be 'prosecuted with due diligence' (para 113). If they were not, the detention would cease to be lawful. Mr Chahal had been in detention for four years by the time of his application to the ECtHR. Two further years were spent waiting for his case to reach the Court, bringing his total detention to six years, though the Court could only consider the legality of the first four. The domestic proceedings were complex, involving deportation proceedings, two refusals of asylum, two applications for judicial review, the second of which was also refused on appeal by the Court of Appeal, and then refusals of leave to appeal to the House of Lords by both its Judicial Committee and the Court of Appeal. The ECtHR commented that the case involved 'considerations of an extremely serious and weighty nature'. It went on to say, 'It is neither in the interests of the individual applicant nor in the general public interest in the administration of justice that such decisions be taken hastily' (para 117). While a lack of due diligence could give rise to a breach of Article 5.1(f) as a violation of the principle of lawfulness, the Court here held that there had not been undue delay on the part of the government.

In *Amuur v France*, four asylum seekers were detained at an airport in the international zone. Their conditions were fairly comfortable, and they were free physically to board another flight out of France, although their safety in the event of this could not be assured. The government argued that this did not amount to detention. The Court said that such conditions were a restriction on liberty. This might be necessary to prevent unauthorized entry, but should not be unduly prolonged. In this case, they were restricted for 20 days. This length of time turned a restriction into a deprivation of liberty, which is detention.

Much of the case law in the UK on detention now concerns challenges to the length of time the person has been detained, and we revisit this subject later in the chapter.

14.2.1.3 Quality of legal reasons

Article 5.2 requires that everyone 'should be informed promptly' in a language that they understand, of the reasons for their detention. In *Saadi*, the ECtHR unanimously found a breach of Article 5.2 as a delay of 76 hours in giving reasons was held not to be prompt. The quality of legal reasons for detention also has a bearing on whether detention is arbitrary.

In *Dougoz v Greece* (2002) 34 EHRR 61, the ECtHR considered the quality of the domestic law which authorized Mr Dougoz's detention, in the light of the Court's principles on arbitrariness and the rule of law. Mr Dougoz had been released from detention after a criminal sentence on the explicit view of the indictments chamber that he was not a danger, would be unlikely to commit further offences, and need not be detained. This being the case, his detention was not actually authorized by domestic law, and so would have fallen at the first hurdle. However, there was a purported authorization in domestic law, in that the Deputy Public Prosecutor offered the opinion that an executive rule, which enabled detention of those who were subject to expulsion by administrative order, could be applied by analogy. The ECtHR did not consider that the opinion of a senior public prosecutor "constituted a 'law' of sufficient 'quality' within the meaning of the Court's case law" (para 57). This case has parallels in the UK, as we shall see in the discussion of detention after a prison sentence.

The quality of legal reasons may initially be accepted, but may become unlawful if the reasons cease to apply. In the case of *Chahal*, the alleged threat to national security posed by Mr Chahal was accepted by the Court to be a sufficient reason, but to avoid arbitrariness there needed to be a check on the continuing application of this reason. This check was provided by the former advisory panel (see chapter 7).

14.2.1.4 Review of detention

The availability of review is a separate heading of challenge under the ECHR, as Article 5.4 provides:

Everyone who is deprived of his liberty by arrest or detention shall be entitled to take proceedings by which the lawfulness of his detention shall be decided speedily by a court and his release ordered if the detention is not lawful.

In the case of *Chahal v UK*, the former advisory panel procedure (see chapter 7) was held to be a sufficient guarantee against arbitrary reasons, in that the panel could review the grounds for detention and check that it was still warranted in the interests of national security. There was therefore no breach of Article 5.1. However, it did not satisfy the requirements of Article 5.4 as the panel did not have the qualities of a 'court'. It lacked the normal qualities of judicial procedure, the right to representation, to notice of the case against the appellant, and so on. Even allowing for the need of the state for secrecy in national security matters, some fairer procedure could be devised. This decision led to the demise of the advisory panel and the creation of the Special Immigration Appeals Commission. Detention must be capable of being challenged speedily in order for the means of challenge to meet the requirements of Article 5.4. The ECtHR's requirements are strict. In *Aden Ahmed v Malta* [2013] ECHR 720 the Court affirmed its previous case law concerning Malta, in which it held that the constitutional review process was too cumbersome to provide a speedy remedy. In this case the appeal had lasted six months by which time the applicant had been released.

14.2.2 **Detention of asylum seekers**

Additional humanitarian considerations may apply in the case of asylum seekers, who may have been tortured or come from a war zone or have otherwise already suffered in detention. Additional human rights considerations also apply. Article 14 of the Universal Declaration of Human Rights provides that the 'right to seek and enjoy asylum' is a basic human right. Clearly, a person should not be detained *for* seeking asylum (see the UNHRC's criteria of arbitrariness, earlier). In the absence of lawful routes to enter and claim asylum, it is sometimes difficult in practice to see the difference between being detained as an illegal entrant and being detained as an asylum seeker, despite *Naillie* (see chapter 11). As UNHCR acknowledges, asylum seekers 'may not be in a position to comply with the legal formalities for entry' and may be 'forced to arrive at, or enter, a territory without prior authorisation' (*Guidelines on applicable Criteria and Standards Relating to the Detention of Asylum Seekers and Alternatives to Detention* 2012). Detention of asylum seekers as illegal entrants, though widely accepted in Europe, looks like a *prima facie* breach of Article 31 of the Refugee Convention (see chapter 11). Article 31(2) permits 'necessary' restrictions on refugees' freedom of movement but only until their status is 'regularised'. Hathaway (2005:4.2.4) suggests that this means that the asylum seeker has satisfied formalities needed for status verification, for instance, ascertaining their identity and whether they present a security risk. After that, an asylum seeker may not be detained except on the same grounds as are applied to aliens generally (Article 26 of the Refugee Convention). This seems consistent with the UNHCR Guidelines. Although in the UK the same legal regime applies to all immigration detainees, and in this sense refugees are not treated less favourably, in practice the lack of practical recognition that making an asylum claim is a lawful act makes it difficult to compare the detention of refugees with that of other foreign nationals.

The UNHCR Guidelines say that, in exceptional circumstances, asylum seekers may be detained, subject to strict compliance with principles of non-discrimination and against arbitrariness. The 2012 Guidelines describe the circumstances which UNHCR considers permissible, provided these are 'clearly prescribed in national law' and properly applied:

(a) where there are strong grounds for believing that the particular individual asylum-seeker is likely to abscond or otherwise to refuse to cooperate with the authorities;

(b) to verify identity or carry out security checks, but only as long as reasonable efforts are being made and within strict time limits established in law;

(c) in connection with accelerated procedures for manifestly unfounded or clearly abusive claims;

(d) to record in a preliminary interview the essential elements of the claim for international protection but only where that information could not be obtained in the absence of detention;

(e) to protect national security and public safety or public health.

Unaccompanied minors and pregnant and nursing mothers should not be detained, and alternatives to detention should be actively sought in the case of unaccompanied elderly people, those who have suffered torture or trauma, or who have a mental or physical disability. People in these groups should only be detained after medical advice that detention would not adversely affect their health or well-being. The safety of LGBTI asylum seekers must be assured if they are detained, and special attention paid to the needs of victims of trafficking.

The Guidelines advise that asylum seekers should not be detained in prisons, and that where this is unavoidable they should not be detained with those who are detained for criminal justice reasons, that is, convicted or remand prisoners. Basic hygiene, medical, exercise, and legal facilities should be provided, and access to UNHCR. There should be segregation of women and men and the opportunity for religious activity and contact with friends and relatives. While the Guidelines do not have any binding effect, Simon Brown LJ, in *R v Uxbridge Magistrates' Court ex p Adimi, R v Crown Prosecution Service ex p Sorani, R v SSHD ex p Kaziu* [2000] 3 WLR 434 at 444, said that they should be given 'considerable weight'.

UNHCR's submissions to the ECtHR in *Saadi v UK* argued that to assimilate the position of asylum seekers to ordinary immigrants and reject the application of a necessity test 'permitted States to detain asylum seekers on grounds of expediency in wide circumstances that were incompatible with general principles of international refugee and human rights law'. Article 12 of the ICCPR suggested that asylum seekers who were making a claim and complying with what was required of them were lawfully within the territory. This was also the effect of the EC Procedures Directive 2005/85/EC Article 7 and the House of Lords case of *Szoma v Secretary of State for the Department of Work and Pensions* [2005] UKHL 64. International law required that the detention of asylum seekers be necessary in order to be lawful. The Court's decision makes no distinction between asylum seekers and others, which was one of the points upon which the dissenting judges departed from the majority.

The reality is rather different. The Independent Asylum Commission criticized excessive use of detention as part of the asylum process (*Deserving Dignity* 2008). The impact of detention, with its lack of a fixed endpoint, yet the fear of removal, can be very severe for asylum seekers. In 1989, Kurdish refugees went on hunger strike in protest at their mass detention on arrival. One detainee, who was released and subsequently detained again after refusal of his asylum claim, was suffering from a profound depression at the prospect of return to Turkey and set fire to himself with fatal consequences (see Shah 2000:167). The pressure group No Deportations publicizes the numbers of deaths in immigration detention, and requests quarterly figures on self-harm in immigration detention. On 20 January 2014 they reported 19 deaths since 1989 in immigration detention, though in some cases the cause is unknown, as is whether the person was an asylum seeker. At least nine were accepted to be suicide. Instances of self-harm requiring medical attention have increased. There were 94 in the third quarter of 2013 and 624 individuals were recorded as being at risk during that quarter. Sometimes, deaths have sparked large-scale protests in removal centres. There have been other protests, too, about conditions in immigration detention, such as lack of legal advice and medical care, including hunger strikes at Yarl's Wood and Morton Hall. In 2013 it was found that there had been sexual abuse of women detainees in Yarl's Wood.

14.3 Who is detained in the UK?

While much of the policy described earlier focuses on the detention of asylum seekers, this is a more recent use of detention. In the first decade after the Immigration Act 1971 came into force, the power to detain, granted by that Act, was used mainly as a way of enforcing a refusal of leave to enter. For instance, a visitor or student who had been refused at the port might be detained overnight (see, e.g., Weber and Gelsthorp 2000). Lengthy detention beyond this was rare.

From the mid-1980s, the number of asylum applications began to rise, and the Home Office was not able to process asylum applications quickly enough to prevent a backlog arising. A survey by the Joint Council for the Welfare of Immigrants revealed an increasing resort to detention as a matter of course to manage asylum applications (Ashford 1993). From a few hours to resolve some outstanding point, or to effect removal, immigration detention quite commonly extended to weeks or months. From the early 2000s until 2008, Home Office figures showed that although asylum seekers numbered less than a quarter of the people removed from the UK each year, they constituted nearly three-quarters of the people in immigration detention. For the last full three years published (2010–12 inclusive) less than half of immigration detainees had sought asylum at some stage.

Other immigration detainees include those who have served a criminal sentence and are to be deported, and people arrested for removal after overstaying their leave or perhaps working in breach of a condition.

Most of the eleven immigration removal centres are for men only. Three include facilities for women and children, and a twelfth 'family-friendly' centre is discussed at 14.6. The Home Office published a research paper in 2005 which examined in detail a sample of 'the illegally resident population in detention'. Three-quarters of those interviewed had worked illegally in the UK. Around half were in detention as a result of a raid on their workplace, for most it was their first immigration detention and they were previously not in contact with the Home Office (Home Office online report 20/05). The researchers attempted to distinguish between those illegally resident and asylum seekers whose claim had failed, but this distinction was difficult to make.

Other information about who is detained using immigration powers emerges from the case law discussed in this chapter.

Until July 2015, the trend was towards the increasing use of detention. In the year to September 2015 32,741 people entered immigration detention and the number of detention places available increased to around 3,500, partly by the extension of Harmondsworth unfortunately in prison style. A second centre built near Gatwick, was to 'send a very clear message' to new arrivals (Immigration Minister 24 July 2007). There was fierce opposition in Parliament to this clear message when Nationality, Immigration and Asylum Act 2002 s 66 renamed detention centres as 'removal centres', but it was too late. It was revealed in the House of Lords that road and building signs had already been changed before the clause had even been debated in Parliament. However, even before the recent suspension of the detained fast track, there were some indications that the government is willing to consider moving away from the current wide use of detention (*A month on: assessing the political landscape post-election*, Detention Action, 3 June 2015; Lords Hansard text, 26 March 2015 (pt 0002)). The planned expansion of one detention centre has been cancelled and another has been closed and so it seems possible that when the government reviews its position following the judgment in *The Lord Chancellor v Detention Action* [2015] EWCA Civ 840 policy could finally be moving back towards reducing the use of detention, which has been shown to be both very expensive and notoriously inefficient in terms of removals.

14.4 Statutory basis of powers to detain

The power to detain for immigration purposes is found in Immigration Act 1971 Schedules 2 and 3 and in Nationality, Immigration and Asylum Act 2002 s 62. No distinction is made in the statutes between asylum seekers and others. Powers to detain are possessed both by immigration officers and by officials in the Home Office, though as a matter of policy, the immigration officer's power to detain is normally exercised by a Chief Immigration Officer. In broad terms, we can think of there being two stages at which detention may occur:

- before a decision is made to grant leave to enter; and
- in order to remove someone.

In terms of the legality of detention under domestic law, there are three main questions to consider:

- Does the power to detain exist in this situation? In other words, is the decision made 'pending examination' (before a decision to give leave is made), or pending removal or a decision to remove or deportation?
- Are there sufficient *reasons* to exercise the power?
- How long has this person been detained already?

Immigration officers have powers to detain, which follow from their border control functions. They may detain pending examination, pending a decision whether to remove, and pending removal (Sch 2 of the 1971 Act). An original division of powers in the 1971 Act that made the Secretary of State responsible for 'in-country' decisions and immigration officers responsible for decisions on entry has been largely eroded, and the Secretary of State now has similar powers (s 62(1) and (2)). These powers have been augmented in the UK Borders Act 2007 by a power for a designated immigration officer to detain someone for three hours at a port if they think that person may be arrestable under criminal law powers of arrest. This may have nothing to do with any immigration matter.

Until the 2002 Act, the Secretary of State only had power to detain pending deportation (Sch 3 to the 1971 Act) and this power remains.

14.4.1 Detention on arrival—pending examination

This power to detain 'pending examination and pending a decision to give or refuse leave to enter' (1971 Act Sch 2 para 16.1) may be exercised by immigration officers or

Table 14.1 Powers to detain on arrival

Person arriving	May be detained in these circumstances
Entry clearance holder	Only if leave is cancelled or suspended and reasons exist*
Non-visa national visitor, requiring leave on entry	If further investigations needed in order to decide whether to grant leave to enter, and if reasons exist*
Claims asylum on entry	In order to decide whether to grant leave to enter or reasons exist*
Clandestine entrant	Pending decision whether to remove, and reasons exist*
Arriving on false documents	Will depend on application made and nature of documents. May transfer into criminal remand if prosecution brought

* 'Reasons exist' refers to an assessed risk of absconding, the need to verify identity, etc.

the Secretary of State whenever the decision or examination takes place. In other words, a person may be detained on arrival, perhaps as a clandestine entrant at a port, but they may also be detained at any stage before leave to enter is given (see Table 14.1). An asylum seeker may wait many months or even years for a decision on their application for leave to enter. The power to detain continues throughout this time, although it is a discretion which must be exercised in accordance with proper criteria.

The power to detain pending examination is potentially mitigated by the relevant reason in Human Rights Act Article 5: 'to prevent his effecting an unauthorized entry'. As we have seen, this provision was widely construed by the ECtHR in *Saadi v UK*. In effect, the only constraint upheld by the Court upon the power to detain new arrivals in order to process an application was that implied by the principle against arbitrariness.

In domestic law detention on arrival must be for an authorized reason. In *AAM (a child) v SSHD* [2012] EWHC 2567 the Secretary of State accepted that detention was unlawful because local immigration officers applied a presumption that an asylum seeker who had arrived clandestinely by lorry should be detained. The detention was in breach of Article 5 also because it was not prescribed by domestic law.

In the UK, the *Saadi* case was an unsuccessful challenge to a significant plank of government policy, the precursor of the now suspended detained fast track. The regime at the Oakington Reception Centre was for newly arriving asylum seekers in the UK who did not come within the existing criteria for detention because there was no risk attached to their being at liberty. The regime at Oakington was described in the Home Office Operational Enforcement Manual as 'relaxed'. It was a kind of 'soft' detention. However, residence there was compulsory (by an amendment to Immigration Act 1971 Sch 2 para 21), and there could be no doubt that in terms of Article 5, it amounted to a deprivation of liberty. The new Oakington criterion, as announced in Parliament, was that 'it appears that their application can be decided quickly' (HC written answers 16 March 2000 col 263). It was apparent from guidance issued on applications at Oakington that the expectation of dealing with a claim quickly arose chiefly from judging it ill-founded.

The detention was lawful in domestic law under Immigration Act 1971 Schedule 2 para 16(1) 'pending examination'. Collins J in the High Court found it unlawful under Article 5, but the Court of Appeal and House of Lords disagreed (*R v SSHD ex p Saadi, Maged, Osman and Mohammed* [2002] 1 WLR 3131, HL).

The House of Lords resorted to the principle of sovereignty, which statute and human rights law are to a degree designed to mitigate, and quoted *Oppenheim's International Law*:

The reception of aliens is a matter of discretion, and every state is by reason of its territorial supremacy competent to exclude aliens from the whole, or any part, of its territory. (para 31)

On this basis, the House of Lords reasoned, similarly to the later decision of the ECtHR, that: every entry is unauthorized until it is authorized. The entry of the appellants was therefore, quite simply, unauthorized because it had not been authorized. The House of Lords was influenced in its decision by considerations of proportionality. Lord Slynn, giving the only reasoned judgment, said that the methods of selection of Oakington cases ('are they suitable for speedy decision?'), the objective of speedy decision-making, and 'the way in which people are held for a short period . . . and in reasonable conditions' were not arbitrary or disproportionate and therefore did not fall outside the Article 5 requirements of lawfulness (para 45). He accepted the 'need for highly structured and tightly managed arrangements' in the interests of speed (para 46). The ECtHR took a similar view. The 'proportionality' of this detention for administrative convenience persuaded both the House of Lords and the ECtHR that it was lawful.

Later decisions of the ECtHR have begun to address the lawfulness of detention of asylum seekers on arrival in situations where the detention is longer and the conditions harsher than in *Saadi*. In *Suso Musa v Malta* [2013] ECHR 721 a Chamber of the ECtHR held that whether an asylum seeker's entry had been authorized or not was largely dependent on national law, but regardless of this, six months in detention exceeded a period which could be regarded as reasonable for the purposes of deciding the asylum claim and thus granting any authorization required. This was particularly the case as the conditions of detention were poor (para 102).

Oakington closed in November 2010. However, it established that the government was entitled to have a fast-track policy, and was the forerunner of the fast-track procedures, discussed in chapter 11. In the fast-track system, unlike Oakington, detention is maintained throughout the decision-making process. At the time of writing, fast track detention of asylum seekers has been suspended. This follows the judgment of the Court of Appeal in the case of *The Lord Chancellor v Detention Action* [2015] EWCA Civ 840.

 **Key Case**

The Lord Chancellor v Detention Action [2015] EWCA Civ 840

The claimant challenged the legality of the Fast Track Rules 2014 that governed appeals to the First-tier Tribunal (Immigration and Asylum Chamber) against refusals by the Secretary of State for the Home Department of asylum applications. Essentially, the time scale of only seven days to prepare and present a full appeal as well as all the other tasks that must be completed was argued not to allow enough time in cases that can often be factually and legally complex.

In their judgment, the Court of Appeal agreed with a previous judgment of the High Court that the fast track rules are 'systematically unfair and unjust.' In the leading judgment, the Master of the Rolls stated that 'justice and fairness should not be sacrificed on the altar of speed and efficiency' and that the current rules do not strike the correct balance. The Home Office sought permission to appeal to the Supreme Court but was refused. The Government will now have to review its position but it already seems to be taking small steps to reduce its over-reliance on detention, which was severely criticized by a cross-party Parliamentary inquiry in March (*The APPG Inquiry into the Use of Immigration Detention in the United Kingdom* March 2015).

14.4.2 **Detention pending removal or deportation**

In the 1971 Act, as originally enacted, the power to detain pending removal was a power to detain someone 'in respect of whom directions may be given' (Sch 2 para 16(2)). In other words, someone who had already been deemed subject to removal, and before the Immigration and Asylum Act 1999 this meant someone upon whom notice had been served that they were deemed an illegal entrant. The 1999 Act, as well as widening the grounds for removal (see chapter 16), also amended para 16(2) to permit detention where there were 'reasonable grounds to suspect' that a person might be subject to removal. This means that, even where the removal decision has not been taken, for instance because the claim is not decided, or it is not clear to which country the claimant may be removed, they may still be detained. The discretion must still be exercised in accordance with the criteria discussed in 14.5.

One of the most pressing questions concerning the jurisdiction to detain pending removal is whether detention is lawful when there are obstacles in the way of removal. Schedule 2 para 16 of the 1971 Act permits detention when there are reasonable grounds for suspecting that a person may be removed. However, what if the person may be removable at some point, but at present is not?

It is a breach of the Refugee Convention (Article 33) to remove an asylum seeker from the UK until their claim has been determined. This is confirmed in Nationality, Immigration and Asylum Act 2002 s 77, which prevents removal while an asylum claim is pending. As we have seen in chapter 11, an exception is made when an asylum seeker can be returned to a third country which is deemed safe. Where an asylum seeker is detained before their claim is finally determined, it could be argued that, as the removal cannot be implemented, detention on this basis is unlawful. However, the 2002 Act makes it clear that it is only the removal itself which cannot happen while the claim is pending. Removal directions can be issued, and other preparatory steps taken (s 77). This means that statute permits a person to be detained for the entire duration of determination of the asylum claim, as was the case in the (now suspended) fast track, providing the common law and policy constraints are not breached, and providing either determination of the claim or removal is, in fact, pending.

In a Privy Council case, *Tan Te Lam and others v Superintendent of Tai A Chau Detention Centre and others* [1996] 4 All ER 256, the applicants were among those who fled from Vietnam to Hong Kong in the late 1970s, the 1980s, and early 1990s. They were of Chinese ethnic origin, and under the agreed repatriation arrangements it was the policy of the Vietnam government not to accept repatriation of non-Vietnam nationals. Therefore, although they were detained pending removal under the Immigration Ordinance of Hong Kong, as non-Vietnamese nationals they would not be removable. The Privy Council said there was no jurisdiction to detain 'pending removal' people whom there was no power to remove.

By way of illustration, in *R (on the application of Sino) v SSHD* [2011] EWHC 2249 (Admin) the Algerian claimant served a criminal sentence and then was detained under immigration powers in 2006. He had been in immigration detention for 4 years and 11 months by the time his case came before the High Court. His detention was found to be unlawful from the beginning by John Howell QC as there were applications by the Home Office for travel documents dating back to 2003 which had never been responded to by the Algerian authorities. When he was first detained under immigration powers there was no realistic prospect of deportation being achieved. Therefore, the statutory purpose was not being served even at the very beginning of his long immigration detention.

Now, where an automatic deportation order has been made under s 32(5) UK Borders Act there is a duty to detain pending removal unless the Secretary of State thinks it is inappropriate (s 36(2)).

The majority of challenges to detention in the UK are to the length of detention pending removal. The UK is one of the few Western democracies which do not place a statutory limit on the length of time that, at least, certain categories of people may be detained for immigration reasons. Case law on the length of detention is discussed in 14.7.

14.4.3 Detention after a criminal sentence has been served

Continued detention after a criminal sentence has been served is authorized either when the criminal court which passed the sentence of imprisonment itself recommended deportation (Immigration Act 1971 Sch 3 para 2.1), or when the Secretary of State has made and served a decision to deport, which might or might not follow a recommendation of the Court (para 2.2). And now there is a more far-reaching power to detain 'while the Secretary of State considers' whether the automatic deportation provisions apply (s 36 UK Borders Act 2007). The effect of para 2.1 and s 36 is that a person may remain in detention at the end of their criminal sentence, but before the Secretary of State has decided whether to deport them. Such a person is in a kind of limbo between criminal and immigration powers. In *R (on the application of Sedrati, Buitrago-Lopez and Anaghatu) v SSHD* [2001] EWHC Admin 418, Moses J granted a declaration to confirm an agreement reached between the parties that Schedule 3 para 2 did not create a presumption in favour of detention upon completion of a sentence of imprisonment. The effect of *Sedrati* was that the Secretary of State must actively decide in each case whether the prospective deportee should be detained, as demonstrated in *R (on the application of Vovk and Datta) v SSHD* [2006] EWHC 3386 (Admin). Mr Vovk was sentenced to 28 days in prison for using a false identity to gain employment. After his release date, he was detained for a further six weeks *before* being given notice of deportation which authorized his detention for that purpose. Mr Datta received an eight-month prison sentence for using a false passport. He was detained past his release date and later served with a notice authorizing his detention pending deportation. The High Court held that, until the decision had been made and notified to the two claimants, their detention was unlawful.

In *Vovk and Datta*, the Secretary of State argued that the claimants knew they were recommended for deportation, so it must have been obvious to them why they were not released (cf. *Dougoz*). There was jurisdiction, or power, to detain. However, the Secretary of State had acted unlawfully in his exercise of that power by not taking a decision and informing Vovk and Datta of it, and had breached Article 5 by not operating the presumption of liberty.

In s 36 of the UK Borders Act, the Secretary of State acquired the power that he seemed to aspire to in *Vovk and Datta*. Additionally, s 34 provides that a deportation order is made 'at a time chosen by the Secretary of State'. The statute makes no requirement for the decision to be made even within a reasonable period, let alone a specified one. However, the Court of Appeal in *R (on the application of Saleh (Sudan)) v SSHD* [2013] EWCA Civ 1378 approved the application of the *Hardial Singh* principles (see 14.7) to detention pending a decision as to whether to make an 'automatic' deportation. The Court made a number of observations about factors relevant to the reasonableness of the length of detention in the context of the s 36 power:

- the individual has no statutory right to challenge the Secretary of State's decision to proceed with deportation, until that decision has been made;

- determination by the Secretary of State of whether, despite the strong policy and statutory impetus favouring deportation, an individual should be given leave to remain is a serious and important matter requiring proper and careful evaluation which, of necessity, will occupy a period of time. Any evaluation of the reasonableness of that period of time must, therefore, reflect the gravity of the decision that is to be taken.

The first reported challenge to detention under s 36 was in *R (on the application of Hussein) v SSHD* [2009] EWHC 2492. The judge in the Administrative Court held that such detention did not breach Article 5. It was still detention with a view to deportation, even though the decision to deport had not yet been taken. The 2007 Act power is without regard to whether the criminal court has recommended deportation. It applies to *anyone* who has served a term of imprisonment (s 36(1)).

The Court of Appeal in *R (on the application of Nouazli) v SSHD* [2013] EWCA Civ 1608 held that the s 36(1) power to detain did not breach Article 27.1 of the Citizens Directive (see chapter 4). Article 27, the Court said, was cast in general terms and 'capable of applying to any measures restricting freedom of movement which can be justified by reference to the provisions of the Directive' (para 16). There was a safeguard in that deportation of the family members of an EEA national could only be carried out in accordance with EEA regulations which implemented and were consistent with the Directive (s 33(4)). The Court based this on the view that the detention power is 'exercised only for the purposes of implementing the provisions for automatic deportation contained in section 32(5)'. This was despite the fact that the power in s 36(1) (unlike s 36(2)) expressly allows detention 'while the Secretary of State considers *whether* s. 32(5) applies'.

Before the 2007 Act was passed, as mentioned in chapter 2, a large number of foreign national prisoners were detained, under a blanket policy which was a response to press agitation. The Supreme Court held that this was unlawful.

 **Key Case**

Mighty & Lumba v SSHD [2011] UKSC 12

Mr Mighty was at liberty when he was served with a decision to deport him and then detained. Mr Lumba was serving a custodial sentence when the Secretary of State gave him notice that he was to be deported. The day before he was due to be released at the end of his criminal sentence he was detained under Schedule 3 of the Immigration Act, pending deportation. In response to press criticism, the Home Office had in practice begun routinely detaining foreign national prisoners after the end of their sentence:

> Between April 2006 and 9 September 2008 the Secretary of State's published policy on detention of FNPs under her immigration powers was that there was a 'presumption' in favour of release . . . In fact, during this period the Secretary of State applied a quite different unpublished policy which was described as a 'near blanket ban' by the Secretary of State . . . to the Prime Minister. (para 5)

This was not disclosed as a policy until September 2008.

On the evidence of internal Home Office correspondence, the Supreme Court endorsed the conclusion of the Court of Appeal that this was a blanket policy admitting of almost no exceptions. This was in conflict with the basic rule of public law prohibiting rigid policies. The policy was also unlawful because it was secret, and in conflict with the published one. This breached the requirements of the rule of law for transparency.

Mr Lumba and Mr Mighty also challenged the policy on the basis that it entailed a presumption in favour of detention, contrary to common law principles and para 2 of Schedule 3 to the 1971 Act as interpreted in *Sedrati*. The Supreme Court held that a policy could entail that it was normal practice to detain, provided that each detention was justified with reasons that related closely to the statutory purpose of effecting deportation. The concept of a presumption was not applicable, as a presumption applies to a burden of proof in judicial proceedings, not an administrative decision.

Although the policy was unlawful, the minority in the Supreme Court held that the detentions were not unlawful because there was a statutory power to detain, and if it had been correctly exercised then, 'detention of the appellants would have been inevitable in the light of the risk of absconding and re-offending that they both posed' (para 60). The majority in the Supreme Court held that the detention was nevertheless unlawful. The tort of false imprisonment required only that there was a detention without lawful authority. As with any trespass, no damage need to be shown for the tort to be committed. The fact that they would have been detained if the discretion had been exercised lawfully led the majority to conclude that they should only receive nominal damages, though a minority thought that a small award between £500 and £1,000 would have been appropriate.

In *R (on application of Hindawi & Headley) v SSHD* [2006] UKHL 54, the House of Lords, overturning the Court of Appeal, unanimously found that the right of prisoners who were subject to a deportation order to have their case referred to the Parole Board came within the ambit of Article 5. Denying referral to the Parole Board on grounds of their nationality (as prisoners subject to deportation, which British national prisoners were not) was discrimination contrary to Article 14. It was objectively unjustifiable, as individual decisions about prisoner release were for the body experienced in this task, and were not (interestingly) 'political' decisions to be made by a government minister.

14.5 Exercise of the discretion

The BID Submission to the UN Working Group on Arbitrary Detention argued for statutory criteria for detention. These would be subject to parliamentary debate and thus democratic control, and would be more readily enforceable. However, the position remains that where the statutory power to detain exists, it is still a discretion, and the criteria for its exercise are contained mainly in policy and operational guidance. Additionally, the Detention Centre Rules govern a number of matters in the conduct of detention. The House of Lords' judgment in *Saadi* accepted that: 'the Home Office is entitled to adopt a policy in relation to procedures to be followed, a policy which may be changed from time to time as long as it does not conflict with relevant principles of law' ([2002] UKHL 41 para 11). Their Lordships did not elaborate on what these relevant principles are, but the principle against arbitrariness is undoubtedly one, and for the elaboration of this, reference should be made back to the human rights standards set out at 14.2. Helen O'Nions argues that 'what is required is not simply an assessment of legality but . . . should be defined as a broader test of substantive arbitrariness to include decisions which are unreasonable, unjust, delayed and unpredictable'. More recently the Bingham Centre for the Rule of Law has published an extensive report arguing for 25 safeguarding principles to be applied to immigration detention, including, of course, a maximum period (Fordham, Stefanelli, and Eser 2013). Many of these recommendations were echoed in the APPG Inquiry into the Use of Immigration Detention in 2015.

Guidance to immigration officers on detention decisions may be found in the Home Office's Enforcement Instructions and Guidance, chapter 55. Officers are advised:

[t]o be lawful, detention must not only be based on one of the statutory powers and accord with the limitations implied by domestic and Strasbourg case law but must also accord with stated policy.

The heart of the instructions is a list of factors to take into account in making a detention decision (55.3.1). Much depends on the immigration officer's perception of the width of their discretion. Weber and Gelsthorpe in 2000 found that 38 per cent of officers thought they did not have a wide discretion, whereas 28 per cent thought that they did. As the researchers comment, within an organization decision-making rapidly becomes routinized so that decision-makers easily lose sight of the amount of discretion they actually (or theoretically) hold. Local practices develop.

The policy and guidance found in the Enforcement Instructions do not represent the total policy in relation to detention. Where statements and usual practices are communicated to practitioners they are entitled to rely upon these (*Nadarajah & Amirthanathan v SSHD* [2003] EWCA Civ 1768).

14.5.1 Disclosure of guidance

The disclosure of guidance upon which a detention decision is based is required by the principle that a constraint on liberty must be prescribed by law according to Article 5 ECHR (see *Nadarajah and Amirthanathan* in which the operation of unpublished policy rendered the detentions in breach of Article 5). Following *Lumba and Mighty*, detention pursuant to an undisclosed policy which is inconsistent with a published policy is unlawful in domestic law too, because it contravenes basic principles of public law.

14.5.2 Content of guidance

The three main approved policy reasons for detention, as set out in the 1998 White Paper, *Fairer, Faster and Firmer—A Modern Approach to Immigration and Asylum* (Cm 4018), are still incorporated in current guidance as the policy foundation for detention decisions (EIG 55.1.1). These crystallize out as five approved reasons (EIG 55.6.3):

(a) the person is likely to abscond if given temporary admission or release;

(b) there is currently insufficient reliable information to decide on whether to grant temporary admission or release;

(c) removal from the United Kingdom is imminent;

(d) the person needs to be detained whilst alternative arrangements are made for their care;

(e) release is not considered conducive to the public good.

In order to be lawful, detention must not only be based on one of the statutory powers and accord with the limitations set by human rights law, but must also be for one of these reasons. The decision to detain must also be taken in accordance with the principles set out in EIG 55.3:

1. There is a presumption in favour of temporary admission or temporary release.

2. There must be strong grounds for believing that a person will not comply with conditions of temporary admission or temporary release for detention to be justified.

3. All reasonable alternatives to detention must be considered before detention is authorised.

4. Each case must be considered on its individual merits, including consideration of the duty to have regard to the need to safeguard and promote the welfare of any children involved.

These principles give priority to the presumption of liberty, but para 55.3A puts a gloss on this in criminal deportation cases where the presumption 'may well be outweighed by the risk to the public of harm from re-offending or the risk of absconding, evidenced by a past history of lack of respect for the law'. Particular factors that must be taken into account are also set out as follows:

- What is the likelihood of the person being removed and, if so, after what timescale?
- Is there any evidence of previous absconding from detention?
- Is there any evidence of previous failure to comply with conditions of temporary admission or bail?
- Has the subject taken part in a 'determined attempt' to breach the immigration laws (examples given here include attempted or actual clandestine entry)?
- Is there a history of complying with requirements of immigration control (e.g., by applying for a visa, further leave, etc.)?
- What are the person's ties with the UK? Are there close relatives (including dependants) here? Does anyone rely on the person for support? Does the person have a settled address or employment?
- What are the individual's expectations about the outcome of the case? Are there factors such as an outstanding appeal, an application for judicial review or representations which afford incentives to keep in touch?
- Is there a risk of offending or harm to the public (this requires consideration of the likelihood of harm *and* the seriousness of the harm if the person does offend)?

Ultimately, these enquiries must, if the person is to be detained, crystallize into one or more of the five listed reasons for detention which are ticked on a standard form (EIG 55.6.3). These reasons, and 14 listed factors that are used to determine whether the reason exists, were referred to in *Amirthanathan and Nadarajah* as 'an important part of the published policy' (para 55).

The policy also lists those who are unsuitable for immigration detention:

- the elderly, particularly where supervision is required;
- pregnant women, unless there is the clear prospect of early removal and medical advice suggests that there is no question of the baby arriving before this;
- unaccompanied children and young people under 18;
- persons identified by the Competent Authorities as victims of trafficking;
- where there is independent evidence that they have been tortured.

Other people who are considered not suitable for detention are people with serious disabilities or serious medical conditions or who are mentally ill. This policy was amended in 2010 to add that they should not be detained where their condition 'cannot be satisfactorily managed within detention' (55.10). This amendment should be read in the light of reports from NGOs (e.g., Medical Justice) and Independent Monitoring Boards about the severe limitations on the provision of and access to medical facilities in immigration detention.

Those with a violent or serious criminal background are among the very few immigration detainees who may or should be held in prison. Others include 'where there is specific (verified) information that a person is a member of a terrorist group or has been engaged in terrorist activities' (EIG 55.10.1). *Idira v Secretary of State for the Home Department* [2015] EWCA Civ 1187 raised important issues regarding the compatibility with Article 5(1)(f) ECHR of holding immigration detainees (specifically, post-sentence ex-offenders) in the prison estate. The Court of Appeal held that there was no principle that immigration detention in prison per se breaches Article 5 albeit 'detention in an IRC is generally more appropriate for immigrant detainees than detention in prison' and '[f]or some vulnerable detainees, detention in prison may be seriously inappropriate and on that account arbitrary'. Any claim on this basis would turn on its own facts, in particular 'the vulnerability of the detainee and the nature of the prison conditions'.

This case makes clear that the fact that listed factors and reasons exist does not mean that the detention decision can be reduced to a box-ticking exercise. The principles stated earlier are the basis of lawfulness, and without adherence to these principles oppressive practice may occur.

14.5.3 Detention in breach of guidance

Although policy guidance does not have statutory force, failure to have regard to it gives grounds for challenge in administrative law (*R v SSHD ex p Khan* [1985] 1 All ER 40). Non-compliance with the detention criteria or failure to have regard to a policy may render detention unlawful. Both substantive and procedural guidance is important to the legality of the detention decision. By way of example, to detain a person who has been tortured breaches the detention criteria and is unlawful unless there are exceptional circumstances. To fail to carry out regular reviews may also mean that there is no active decision as to whether the criteria for detention continue to be met, and may also be unlawful. Whether breaches of procedure or of the Detention Centre Rules render the detention unlawful depends largely on how closely connected the provision is with the power to detain.

Misuse of the power to detain was amply demonstrated in *Karas and Miladinovic v SSHD* [2006] EWHC 747 (Admin).

 **Key Case**

Karas and Miladinovic v SSHD [2006] EWHC 747 (Admin)

Mr Karas had lost his asylum claim, but made a request to have a fresh claim considered in 2001. Time passed. He married Ms Miladinovic. His solicitors wrote making representations about his family life and asking for her to be added to his asylum claim. There was no response. He continued to report weekly to the Croydon immigration office as he was required to do. Ms Miladinovic became pregnant. On 10 October 2004, he reported as usual. Unbeknown to him or them, on that day removal directions had been faxed to Heathrow for a flight at 7.40 a.m. on 12 October. At 8.30 p.m. on 11 October, the couple were detained by immigration officers at their home and told that they were to be removed the next morning. It turned out that Mr Karas' claim had been refused by fax sent to his solicitor shortly before the close of business on 11 October, four hours before the couple were detained.

Munby J. held that 'detention in the circumstances of this case was . . . oppressive, unreasonable and unnecessary' (para 65). It was done as it was in order to prevent the claimants from obtaining legal advice or being able to apply to a judge (para 81). The guiding principles of policy require detention to be used as a last resort. This detention was used in the opposite way—as a pre-emptive strike.

People who have been tortured are clearly among those who should not be detained. The issues are generally not whether that is a correct principle, but rather whether there is evidence which can be gathered within the time specified and what standard of proof is in practice employed. The current EIG says that where there is 'independent evidence' that a person has been tortured, they are 'normally considered suitable for detention in only very exceptional circumstances'. What was meant in this situation by independent evidence of torture was considered in *R (on the application of D and K) v SSHD* [2006] EWHC 980 (Admin).

 Key Case

R (on the application of D and K) v SSHD **[2006] EWHC 980 (Admin)**

D and K both sought asylum on arrival in the UK and were detained in Oakington. The Detention Centre Rules contained two provisions for medical examination on arrival. First, all detainees should be medically screened including an assessment for risks of self-harm within two hours of their arrival. Second, all detainees must have a physical and mental examination by a medical practitioner within 24 hours of arrival (rule 34). The Secretary of State initially argued that this did not constitute independent evidence of torture, but Davis J held that the emphasis placed upon the need for medical examination must mean that it was an essential part of the assessment as to whether a person was suitable to remain in fast-track detention. In that case, it must be capable of constituting independent evidence of torture.

This was an important outcome for detainees, who are not in a position to substantiate their claim of having been tortured in any other way at such an early stage after arrival, and it underscores the importance of the provision of medical services in detention centres.

In 2000, the evidence of Amnesty International and the Medical Foundation was that those who have suffered torture were still being detained (Dell and Salinsky 2000), and up to the present this is still the case. In *R (on the application of RT) v SSHD* [2011] EWHC 1792 (Admin) the Court held that there was a breach of rule 34 where the claimant had said that she had been tortured, but had not been offered a medical examination. Scars she bore were later found to be consistent with the torture she described. Kenneth Parker J held that her detention was unlawful following *Lumba and Mighty* and *Kambadzi* as the breach of the rules in not examining her meant that the authority to detain her was assumed improperly. As a victim of torture she should not have been detained.

Rule 35 of the Detention Centre Rules requires the medical practitioner at the detention centre to report to the centre manager any concern that a detainee may have suffered torture. The manager is required to report to the Secretary of State immediately and the person's detention must then be reviewed. The system was said to be failing; in 2012 983 rule 35 reports were made, but only 74 resulted in the detainee being released (House of Commons Hansard 24 Jan 2013: Col 431W).

Detainees supported by the charity Medical Justice challenged the failure of rule 35 to protect them. The High Court did not give permission for judicial review of an alleged systemic failure of rule 35, but in relation to the individual cases considered a number of issues about the operation of rule 35. In the case of EO, a doctor had reported scarring typical of and diagnostic of the ill-treatment which EO said had occurred. These are the highest standards of evidence in the Istanbul protocol relating to the assessment of scars. The Home Office rejected the rule 35 report on the basis that the ill-treatment he alleged was not torture because not inflicted by state actors and that the claimant's credibility was in doubt. The Court said that these factors were irrelevant for the purposes of a rule 35 report, and the detention was unlawful (*R (on the application of EO, RA, CE, OE and RAN) v SSHD* [2013] EWHC 1236 (Admin)).

Other groups also who should very rarely be detained are in fact detained in circumstances which are not justified as being exceptional. The interpretation of the guidelines has become more complex and open to judgment since they were amended to require that an illness or disability must be not capable of being satisfactorily managed in detention, and generates a higher risk of inappropriate detention of vulnerable people. Even under the previous form of the policy, the Court of Appeal rejected the contention that a diagnosed mental illness was sufficient to make the person *prima facie* unsuitable for detention (*R (on the application of LE (Jamaica)) v SSHD* [2012] EWCA Civ 597). The claimant in that case had a diagnosis of paranoid schizophrenia, but this was controlled by medication and the Court considered that it was not a breach of policy to detain him because his symptoms could be 'satisfactorily managed' in detention. The Court accepted the Home Office argument that the post-2010 formulation of the policy only made explicit what was intended before. In *R (on the application of Das) v SSHD* [2014] EWCA Civ 45 the Court of Appeal overturned a High Court decision which equated serious mental illness with one which required hospital admission, and agreed that in order for the condition to be satisfactorily managed, it must not be required that the detainee's state of mind was reduced to the point where they could not cope with ordinary life.

The continued practice of detaining people with mental illnesses has attracted a number of actions in damages, and findings of the High Court that the detention constituted a breach of Article 3. A recent example was in *R (on the application of S) v SSHD* [2014] EWHC (Admin) 50 where the claimant had florid symptoms of psychosis, which attracted the attention of the police and brought about his detention. He was taken from police custody into immigration detention and then placed in a fast-track process. Two independent psychiatric reports had been ignored until the hearing of his fast-track appeal (unrepresented) in Harmondsworth detention centre, where it was apparent to the judge 'from his appearance, behaviour, demeanour and from reading the two psychiatric reports that had been prepared for the hearing that he was unfit to participate in the hearing, was lacking in capacity and was incapable of representing himself' (para 4). His detention was unlawful throughout in domestic law and a breach of Articles 3 and 8. He was entitled to damages. In *R (on the application of Lamari) v SSHD* [2013] EWHC 3130 the claimant had been diagnosed with a mental illness and had made at least two serious suicide attempts. He was in immigration detention for 17 months and there was no significant progress in arranging his removal to Algeria. At a hearing at which the lawfulness of his detention was considered, the Secretary of State undertook to release him. After the hearing she changed that decision, in breach of the undertaking. The claimant was awarded exemplary damages as well as compensatory and aggravated damages.

Guidance says that the exceptions to the general rule that pregnant women should not be detained are:

where removal is imminent and medical advice does not suggest confinement before the due removal date (EIG para 55.9.1)

An audit by Medical Justice suggested that very few pregnant women were in fact removed, and their 2013 report makes the case for ending detention of pregnant women altogether. In research for a report by Women for Refugee Women (WRW), 46 women detainees were interviewed. Nineteen women, or 41 per cent, had been tortured, most by state officials. Thirty-three women, or 72 per cent, had been raped, 11 of them by soldiers, police, or prison guards. Forty women, over 80 per cent, had been either raped or tortured (WRW 2014). These figures are supported by damning reports from HM Inspector of Prisons on Yarl's Wood and The Verne in 2015 which revealed that 99 pregnant asylum seekers were detained in 2014 but 90 per cent of them were released back into the community. In October 2015, the Guardian carried a report that the Home Office had settled an unlawful detention claim by a pregnant asylum seeker detained at Yarl's Wood for an undisclosed sum and has said that it will review its policy. The litigation that led to this settlement noted that detention had a significant and detrimental effect on the woman's maternity care. Maternity records were not taken and GPs and midwives were not notified. The Royal College of Midwives and Medical Justice are now calling for consideration of a process similar to the new family returns process for pregnant women with proper safeguards in place (see 14.6).

Challenges to detention on the basis, for instance, that the person has been tortured or is pregnant are made on the basis that this person should not be detained at all. If someone is not given a medical examination promptly, or their detention is not reviewed when it should be according to the Detention Centre Rules, clearly it is possible that they will be detained or continue to be detained when they would otherwise have been released. Thus, a breach of Detention Centre Rules may affect the fact of detention as well as its conditions.

That a breach of the Detention Centre Rules which goes to the basis of the detention renders the detention unlawful is now established in *Kambadzi v SSHD* [2011] UKSC 23.

 Key Case

Kambadzi v SSHD [2011] UKSC 23.

The claimant's detention had not been reviewed at the intervals required by the Detention Centre Rules. By the date of the High Court hearing, the claimant's detention should have been subject to 22 monthly reviews but in fact had had only ten. Of these, four were not carried out by an officer of the right level of seniority, and two were vitiated by errors of fact. The Supreme Court held that the reviews required by the policy were the authority on which the continued legality of the detention rested. Policy could be departed from if good reason were shown, but there was no such reason in this case. Following *Lumba*, there was a public law duty to give effect to the policy on reviews, and when this duty was breached, the detention became unlawful. Unless the authority to detain was renewed, the detention became unlawful. The Court accepted that if the reviews had been properly conducted, continued detention would have been warranted. Thus, Mr Kambadzi was not entitled to significant damages.

14.6 **Detention of families**

Prior to 2001, established policy in relation to the detention of families was that it should generally be avoided, and should, if at all, take place 'only to be as close as possible to removal so as to ensure that it lasted no longer than a few days' (Cm 4018 para 12.5). In October 2001, the Home Office announced an increase in family detention provision, and the detention criteria for families were brought more closely into line with the criteria for detention of people without children, although the Home Office also stressed that this would only be where it was considered necessary, particularly in view of the possible breach of Article 8 (see Cole 2003). Family detention places in 2005 reached 456.

In December 2003, the government began to publish statistics on children in detention in the quarterly figures. The figures showed that, at any one time, there were scores of children in detention, and in 2009 over 1,000 children were detained. Inevitably, figures only show those children who are detained with their families, as those whose age was disputed would be shown as adults. Although the policy was that children should only be detained as a last resort, in a study done by BID and the Children's Society, 61 per cent of families were eventually released, their detention having served no purpose (Campbell et al 2011). Families were detained when there was little risk of their absconding. Families cited reasons to maintain contact with the Home Office: their children's welfare, access to health care, the need to avoid destitution, the desire to preserve their dignity, and pursuit of legal status. Often their removal was not imminent, and there were barriers to their removal—as with adults in fact. There was a significant adverse impact on the health of children, and the practice of detaining families was heavily criticized. In January 2010, the Home Office paid £100,000 in damages to a family that had been unlawfully detained for 42 days ('Family Wins £100,000 for Detention Ordeal' *The Guardian* 30 January 2010), and in January 2012 the Ay family settled out of court for a possibly higher figure.

The detention of children is now subject to the government's duty under s 55 Borders Citizenship and Immigration Act 2009, to make arrangements to ensure that in making any immigration decision affecting them the best interests of the child are taken into account. Guidance on implementing this section repeats that families must be encouraged to leave voluntarily and detention should be used only 'as a last resort and for the shortest possible time' ('Every Child Matters: Change for Children' November 2009).

The detention of children is clearly an interference with private and/or family life. The damage to children by being detained has been recognized in the UK courts (*S, C and D (by their litigation friend S) v SSHD* [2007] EWHC 1654 (Admin)), and is taken seriously by the ECtHR.

In *Mayeka and Mitunga v Belgium* (2008) 46 EHRR 23, the ECtHR found violations of Articles 3, 5.1, 5.4, and 8 in the detention of a five-year-old girl in adult detention facilities without the company of any adult known to her. Travelling with a relative she was due to join her mother who had been granted asylum in Canada. During the child's two months of detention, a legal tangle surrounding the child in Belgium even entailed her being deported, unaccompanied, back to the Democratic Republic of Congo before she was finally able to join her mother. The violations were of the mother's Articles 3 and 8 rights as well as the child's, since not knowing what was happening to her child and being unable to influence the course of events from Canada, despite daily telephone calls, was acutely distressing. In *Kanagaratnam v Belgium* (Application no. 15297/09) the Strasbourg Court held that the detention of a mother and her three children for four months during the determination of her asylum claim was a breach of Article 5. In relation to the children, it was also a breach of Article 3. They were detained in a centre that the Court had already held to be inappropriate for children. The Court said:

[B]y placing the children in a closed facility, the Belgian authorities subjected them to feelings of anxiety and inferiority and knowingly took the risk of compromising their development. (para 68)

In *Popov v France* (Application nos 39472/07 and 39474/07) detention of a family (parents with children) for 15 days was disproportionate and a breach of Article 8, unless there was a risk of absconding (see Weiss and Lieu 2012).

In May 2010, the Coalition government announced that the detention of children for immigration purposes would be ended. However, making this a reality took longer. Arguably, the case of *Suppiah v SSHD* [2011] EWHC 2 (Admin) brought the matter to a head. The two families were detained by immigration officers arriving unexpectedly at their home in the early hours of the morning. The families, including a two-year-old, were searched. The children quickly became sick in detention. They were detained on 10 February 2010 for removal on 13 February. The removals were cancelled, but the families were not released until 22 February. There was an enormous volume of evidence before the Court that 'detention is inherently and seriously harmful to the health and development of children' (para 106). The Court's judgment refers to the reports of the Children's Commissioner and the Chief Inspector of Prisons, both highly critical of the practice of detaining children, and to the report of the House of Commons Home Affairs Select Committee, which recommended a significant reduction in child detention. The Court quoted this passage from the HASC:

We do not understand why, if detention is the final step in the asylum process, and there is no evidence of families systematically 'disappearing or absconding', families are detained pending judicial reviews and other legal appeals. The detention of children for indeterminate periods of time (possibly for 6–8 weeks), pending legal appeals must be avoided.

The criticisms and recommendations of the Chief Inspector of the former UKBA were also quoted in full.

The judge concluded that the families were detained initially for the purpose of removal, but he was not satisfied that they had been given any meaningful option of voluntary return, or that there was any significant risk of their absconding. The Home Office had failed to have regard to their duty under s 55 of the Borders Citizenship and Immigration Act 2009, and this made the detention of the families unlawful.

In August 2011 the institution of a new process was completed with the opening of The Cedars, a 'last resort' detention facility for families. See chapter 16 for an outline of the family returns process.

Security at the Cedars is run by G4S, and there is a high perimeter fence, as well as 24-hour guards escorting detainees to and from the visitors' lounge. The Cedars is locked and detainees are searched on arrival. At the same time, The Cedars has play areas for small children, a library for different age groups, access to gardens, a pets' corner, and basketball court with equipment for ball games. HMIP confirms that it is still detention, but the conditions for children are significantly better than in previous facilities (*Report on an announced inspection of Cedars Pre-Departure Accommodation* 30 April–25 May 2012).

Numbers of children in detention have dropped since May 2010, but children are still detained. In 2014, 126 children were detained, most in either The Cedars or Tinsley House.

The UNHCR Guidelines say that 'in principle' children should not be detained at all, but if they are their education should continue and an

ethic of care—and not enforcement—needs to govern interactions with asylum-seeking children, including children in families, with the best interests of the child a primary consideration. (para 52)

The UN Working Group on Arbitrary Detention also states that children should not be detained. The UN Convention on the Rights of the Child Article 22 says:

States Parties shall take appropriate measures to ensure that a child who is seeking refugee status or who is considered a refugee in accordance with applicable international or domestic law procedures shall, whether unaccompanied or accompanied by his or her parents or by any other person, receive appropriate protection and humanitarian assistance in the enjoyment of applicable rights set forth in the present Convention and in other international human rights or humanitarian instrument to which the said States are Parties.

The UK has lifted its reservation to the Convention in relation to immigration and asylum matters, in tandem with introducing the duty under s 55 of the Borders Citizenship and Immigration Act 2009 to make arrangements to ensure that the best interests of the child are taken into account.

According to policy, an unaccompanied person under 18 is not generally detained. In *R (on the application of AA) v SSHD* [2013] UKSC 49 the Supreme Court held that the detention of AA while he was a minor was lawful and did not breach the duty to have regard to a child's welfare (s 55 Borders Citizenship and Immigration Act 2009) since the Secretary of State reasonably believed him to be an adult, even though that reasonable belief was wrong. The procedure for dealing with age disputes is discussed in chapter 11.

14.7 Length of detention

As mentioned at the start of this chapter, one of the chief concerns about immigration detention in the UK, voiced by many including the UN Working Group on Arbitrary Detention, is that there is no fixed statutory limit on the length of time a person can be detained. The Independent Chief Inspector of the former UKBA in a report of a thematic inspection of how the Home Office manages foreign national prisoners found that the average length of detention had increased from 143 days in February 2010 to 190 days in January 2011. Twenty-seven per cent of foreign national prisoners who were detained after their custodial sentence had been detained for longer than 12 months.

In earlier case law challenging the length of detention, it was considered that lengthy detention could undermine the jurisdiction to detain, so that if obstacles to removal persisted, the power to detain a person expired, and they must be released. However, in *R v SSHD ex p Khadir (Appellant)* [2005] UKHL 39, Lord Brown of Eaton-under-Heywood, giving the only reasoned judgment, found that the '*Hardial Singh* line of cases', which revolved around the length of detention, referred to the *exercise* of the power to detain and not to its *existence*. In other words, length of detention affects the exercise of the discretion to detain, which becomes unreasonable if it goes on too long. It does not affect the power to detain: '"pending" in paragraph 16 means no more than "until"' (para 32). The significance of this distinction will become apparent shortly. As noted in case law earlier in this chapter, if the purpose for which detention is authorized ceases to apply, then the detention is no longer authorized. There is an implied limitation of a reasonable time to achieve the purpose sought by the detention, as was held in *R v Governor of Durham Prison ex p Hardial Singh* [1983] Imm AR 198. This case remains the authority on this point, though Lord Dyson's judgment in *Lumba and Mighty* clarified a number of issues about how it is applied. In *Hardial Singh*, Woolf J said, 'if there is a situation where it is apparent to the Secretary of State that he is not going to be able to operate the machinery provided in the Act for removing persons who are intended to be deported within a reasonable period, it seems to me that it would be wrong for the Secretary of State to exercise his power of detention' (at 200). Woolf J directed the applicant's release, finding that 'the Home Office have not taken the action they should have taken and nor have they taken that action sufficiently promptly' (at 202). Mr Singh had been in detention for five months and had attempted to take his own life. The Court similarly intervened in the case of *Wafsi Suleman Mahmod* [1995] Imm AR 311, in which Laws J held that ten months was too long to try to persuade Germany to take back a man granted asylum in Germany who had been convicted of a criminal offence whilst on a visit to the UK. The Home Office activity during the ten months was described as 'nothing but fruitless negotiations'.

In *Tan Te Lam*, in which the applicants had been in detention for 44 months, Lord Browne-Wilkinson summarized the law as follows:

First, the power can only be exercised during the period necessary, in all the circumstances of the particular case, to effect removal. Secondly, if it becomes clear that removal is not going to be possible within a reasonable time, further detention is not authorised. Thirdly, the person seeking to exercise the power of detention must take all reasonable steps within his power to ensure the removal within a reasonable time.

The House of Lords regarded *Tan Te Lam* as an exception in which length of detention *did* remove the jurisdiction to detain, 'because there was simply no possibility of the Vietnamese government accepting the applicants' repatriation' (para 33).

The Court of Appeal applied these principles in *R (on the application of I) v SSHD* [2002] EWCA Civ 888, and added that the length of time a person has already been in detention was relevant to whether detention should be continued, taking into account whether there was a reasonable prospect that deportation would be achieved within a reasonable period. This has recently been confirmed in *ZA (Iraq)* [2015] EWCA Civ 168. Like the applicants in *Sedrati, Buitrago-Lopez, and Anaghatu*, Mr I was detained under 1971 Act Schedule 3 para 2 after the end of his criminal sentence and pending deportation. However, in his case, removal was not practically possible as there were no flights from the UK to his home country of Afghanistan. The Home Office was engaged in activity which might still have resulted in his removal in that they were engaged in negotiations with countries neighbouring Afghanistan for the return of Afghani asylum seekers whose claims had failed. The *Hardial Singh* point, the second in Lord Browne-Wilkinson's formulation in *Tan Te Lam*, was the crucial one for Simon Brown LJ in the Court of Appeal. He held that the Home Office's 'hope' that negotiations with neighbouring countries would bear fruit was not sufficient, given the time that Mr I had already spent in detention. By the time the case came before the Court of Appeal, he had been in administrative detention (i.e., after the end of his criminal sentence) for 16 months. Dyson LJ thought that the time already spent in detention was enough to justify release.

Appellant A v SSHD [2007] EWCA Civ 804 followed *Khadir* in the formulation that there must be 'some prospect' of A being removed within a reasonable period in order for the power to detain to exist. The level at which this prospect may be doubted was set extremely high. After two years of lawful detention, A was detained for a further 19 months during which he could not be removed because no airlines were willing to take enforced removals to Somalia, and he was not willing to go. The parties were agreed that this degree of practical obstruction and length of time did not affect the *existence* of the power to detain but only its exercise. There was still 'some prospect' of A being removed. *Appellant A* was distinguished from *I* in that the danger to the public posed by A was greater than that posed by I, and this was a factor which weighed in the exercise of discretion to continue to detain him.

In *Lumba and Mighty* Lord Dyson dealt with two further issues that commonly arise in cases based on *Hardial Singh*: detention during appeals pursued by the detainee, and the detainee's lack of cooperation. *R (on the application of Rostami) v SSHD* [2009] EWHC 2094 (QB) was a remarkable example of the latter. The claimant was detained in October 2006. He said that his father had been killed as a member of the Kurdish Democratic Party and his mother and sisters ill-treated by government agents. He had been unsuccessful in his asylum claims and had made suicide attempts in detention and refused to cooperate with steps to obtain travel documents to enable his return to Iran. He was convicted under s 35 of the Asylum and Immigration (Treatment of Claimants, etc.) Act 2004 (see chapter 11) of failing to cooperate with re-documenting procedures to effect his return. He was given a conditional discharge for 12 months.

He maintained his refusal to cooperate with re-documentation, and remained in detention, with no clarity as to whether he was on criminal remand or detained pending removal. He pleaded guilty to a further s 35 charge and breach of the conditional discharge, and received a prison sentence of four months. He refused again and was prosecuted again. He pleaded not guilty, and was sentenced to eight months in prison and recommended for deportation. Finally, in August 2009, the Administrative Court held that his detention had become unlawful. The Secretary of State had been unable to show that there was a reasonable prospect of removing Mr Rostami. He might abscond, but he was no danger to the public. His only breach of the law was his failure to cooperate with arrangements for his return to Iran.

Lord Dyson in *Lumba and Mighty* held that there was no exclusionary rule which prevented time spent in detention pending appeals from counting as part of the whole time spent in detention when this was considered for *Hardial Singh* purposes. The detainee's lack of cooperation was also just one relevant factor to take into account in deciding whether detention had gone on too long. It would be of limited weight and not conclusive, and would not be relevant if it was not in fact the reason for the extended detention. The ECtHR in *Abdi v UK* approved the remarks of Lord Dyson in *Lumba and Mighty* in the following way:

[R]efusal to return voluntarily was relevant to the assessment of the reasonableness of the period of detention because a risk of absconding could be inferred from the refusal . . . it [was] necessary to distinguish between cases where the return to the country of origin was possible and cases where it was not. Where return was not possible for reasons extraneous to the person detained, the fact that he was not willing to return voluntarily could not be held against him since his refusal had no causal effect. If return was possible, but the detained person was not willing to go, it would be necessary to consider whether or not he had issued proceedings challenging his deportation. If he had done so, it would be entirely reasonable that he should remain in the United Kingdom pending the determination of those proceedings, unless they were an abuse of process, and his refusal to return voluntarily would be irrelevant. If there were no outstanding legal challenges, the refusal to return voluntarily could not be seen as a trump card which enabled the Secretary of State to continue to detain until deportation could be effected, otherwise the refusal would justify as reasonable any period of detention, however long. (para 73)

Commonly, there are other complex obstacles to achieving deportation, including the lack of a safe route of return or the non-cooperation of home state embassies. Detention Action (then the London Detainee Support Group) carried out research on long-term detention and found that people who were in immigration detention for more than a year were unlikely to be removed. Latest statistics suggest this is still the case: in the third quarter of 2013, of the 48 people detained for 12 months or more, 17 (35 per cent) were removed, 13 (27 per cent) were granted temporary admission or release, and 17 (35 per cent) were bailed.

In *Saleh (Sudan)* the Court of Appeal held that although there was no obligation on the Secretary of State to start the removal process in a deportation case before the expiry of a criminal sentence, whether that had been done could be relevant to the overall assessment of the reasonableness of the length of detention. The Court said it is relevant that the individual has already served the sentence imposed by the criminal court. Their past criminal offending, of itself, is not a justification for implementing or extending time in immigration detention.

The use of assurances to enable a removal which would otherwise breach Article 3 is discussed in chapter 5. Another aspect of the use of assurances is the length of time that a person may spend in detention while they are negotiated. Reading the judgment in *Youssef v Home Office* gives a rare insight into such negotiations. The claimant was a leading member of Egyptian Islamic Jihad, which mounted high profile terrorist attacks. He claimed asylum and was excluded under Article 1F, but faced likely torture on return, in breach of Article 3. For comment on the political process see, for example, *The Guardian* 16 November 2004.

The Secretary of State sought to show that there was a realistic prospect of obtaining such assurances, so as to justify Mr Youssef's continuing detention until 9 July 1999, when negotiations were accepted to have failed and Mr Youssef was released. Detention remained lawful while it was reasonable for the UK to be negotiating with the Egyptian government, but ceased to be so, following *Hardial Singh*, when there was no realistic prospect of his being removed. If there is a period of inactivity, the Secretary of State must show reasons. The Court in *Saleh* said:

There is no requirement upon the Secretary of State to account for every single day or every single week . . . but, where, as here, a significant proportion of the total period of detention is marked by an apparent absence of any administrative activity, and no explanation for that state of affairs is proffered, then a court . . . is entitled to come to the view that a proportion of the total period of detention was unreasonable and therefore unlawful. (para 60)

In order for detention to be lawful pending removal, the proposed removal must not only be foreseeably feasible at some point, but also lawful. In *R (on the application of K v SSHD)* [2008] EWHC 1321 (Admin), the Court held that the detention of the claimant was unlawful as it was said to be for the purpose of removing him to Irbil. His asylum claim had been turned down on the basis of a possible internal relocation (see chapter 12). It had been accepted that he was at risk in Irbil, so detention for the purpose of removing him there was unlawful.

Detention can become arbitrary if it continues 'beyond the period for which the State can provide justification'. So said the UN Human Rights Committee in finding Australia to be in breach of Article 9.1 of the International Covenant on Civil and Political Rights (*A v Australia* (1997) 4 BHRC 210). The UK has not accepted the right of individual petition for breaches.

14.8 **Alternative to detention—temporary admission**

The practical meaning and importance of cases like *Khadir* cannot be understood without appreciating the important part played in present-day immigration control by the status of temporary admission.

Wherever there is a power to detain there is also power to grant temporary admission (Immigration Act 1971 Sch 2 para 21 and Nationality, Immigration and Asylum

Act 2002 s 62(3)). People are temporarily admitted when their applications for entry or asylum claims have not been determined. Once a claim is determined and refused, the person may remain on temporary admission. They were initially liable to detention pending examination. They are now liable to detention pending either a decision to remove or removal. The vast majority of asylum seekers are at liberty in the UK on temporary admission.

Temporary admission is granted for a fixed period which is normally renewed. The person admitted must report back to the Home Office or immigration service at the expiry of the period. Many people on temporary admission are required to report regularly, often weekly or monthly, to the Home Office. The day of reporting is an anxious time, as each time there is a risk of detention. There is no right of appeal against a refusal to extend temporary admission, because in itself it is not a status awarded, it is more like being on licence while being theoretically subject to a prison sentence.

Temporary admission may be subject to residence or employment restrictions and requirements to report to the police or an immigration officer (1971 Act Sch 2 para 21(2)). Residence restrictions may include the requirement to reside in accommodation provided under Immigration and Asylum Act 1999 s 4 or Nationality, Immigration and Asylum Act 2002 s 26. A prohibition on employment is routinely imposed. The restrictions may be varied, and the power to detain continues throughout the period of temporary admission. If a person is re-detained, although a breach of conditions is not specifically required by the schedule, the lack of such reasons would give rise to a finding of arbitrariness, unless, as is common, it is to carry out removal.

Temporary admission is a curious kind of limbo status, and this is where its importance lies. The person on temporary admission has no right to appeal against their limbo status, and only very minimal welfare rights. While people on temporary admission are 'lawfully present' (*Szoma v Secretary of State for the Department of Work and Pensions* [2005] UKHL 64) they are not 'lawfully resident'. This distinction excludes them from most rights to health and social assistance and will exclude them from legal aid if a residence test is imposed (see chapter 7). Any rights to health and welfare depend on separate statutory schemes creating exceptions to the general rule of non-entitlement, most notably the statutory scheme for the support of asylum seekers discussed in chapter 2.

The extended use of temporary admission creates a group of people without rights and security. Many people are destitute; typically, their asylum claim has failed, but for practical reasons they cannot be returned to their country of origin. Prior to 2002, many people in this position would have been granted exceptional leave to remain (ELR). This status could, after some years, allow reunion with family members, and eventually indefinite leave to remain. It allowed the person to work and claim benefits. Although by nature temporary and insecure, it could be extended and could eventually bring security. This is the background to the case of *Khadir*.

 **Key Case**

Khadir v SSHD *[2005] UKHL 39*

Mr Khadir's asylum application had been refused but he could not be returned to the Kurdish Autonomous Area of Iraq as there were no direct flights, and any travel via Baghdad would not be safe. The British government had been in negotiation with Turkey over the return of Iraqi Kurds, but they were not enthusiastic to permit travel of Kurdish people through their territory, and discussions had stalled. Usual practice at that time would have been to grant exceptional leave to remain, on the basis that return was not safe or possible. The Home Office's initial refusal to do so was quashed in the High Court. Mr Khadir was not in reality subject to removal and therefore it was not lawful to detain him. If there was no basis for detention, there was no basis for temporary admission. His status should change to ELR. This decision was overturned in the House of Lords.

When the High Court decision was given, the government was in the process of drafting the 2002 Bill and took the opportunity of inserting s 67(2) and (3). Section 67(2) provides that a reference to a person who is liable to detention shall be taken to include a person if the only reason why they cannot be removed is because of a 'legal impediment' concerning the UK's obligations under an international agreement, or practical difficulties in arranging the removal. This means that a person in Mr Khadir's situation may continue to be treated as liable to detention. In other words, they may remain on temporary admission despite the fact they cannot at present be removed. The subsection removed the obligation to grant ELR (now discretionary leave). Section 67(3) gave s 67(2) retrospective effect. The House of Lords held that the subsections were not even necessary. A person who could not for practical or legal reasons be removed was still liable to be removed and thus the power to detain existed.

The result dovetails with the Asylum Policy Instructions (see chapter 11): 'Discretionary leave is not to be granted on the basis that, for the time being, practical obstacles prevent a person from leaving the UK or being removed.'

Lord Brown raised a question, 'how the fact that someone has been temporarily admitted rather than detained can be said to lengthen the period properly to be regarded as "pending . . . his removal"' (para 31). Ironically, this is one effect of this judgment, as it is possible for people to be maintained for even longer periods in the limbo state of temporary admission, yet without the Home Office being required to concede that removal is unrealistic, and grant a more beneficial status. The periods spent on temporary admission can be far longer than any reasonable (and thus lawful) length of actual detention. On release from such excessive detention, however, removal would still be possible in law, and this appears to be Lord Brown's point. Length of time was not intended to displace the removal. Compatibility with Article 5 was not considered by the Court, as physical liberty was not in issue.

The importance of *Khadir* may now be appreciated. If their Lordships had accepted that length of detention affected the jurisdiction to detain, that would mean that temporary admission also could expire simply through length of time. There would come a point when a challenge in judicial review would accept that the jurisdiction to keep someone on temporary admission had expired because it had gone on too long. If length of time only affects the discretion to detain, as the House of Lords found, then there is always jurisdiction to detain while ever there is 'some prospect' of effecting a removal. Thus temporary admission, which subsists along with the jurisdiction to detain, may continue even while it would be a wrong use of discretion to actually detain the person.

In the context of European law, the ECJ was not prepared to regard someone on temporary admission as not having entered (C-357/98 *R v SSHD ex p Yiadom* [2003] ECR I-9265). She had been present in the UK for months and to regard her as not having entered was a legal fiction. Time spent on temporary admission in some circumstances counts towards a period of residence for obtaining British nationality (see chapter 3).

The current Immigration Bill 2015 seeks to give the Home Office new powers to manage those without leave (those whose claims have been refused or persons waiting, as in an asylum case, for an initial decision). It is intended that the concept of temporary admission will be repealed and replaced by a system whereby a person without leave who is waiting for a decision will be on immigration bail. This new scheme of immigration bail will be managed by the Home Office and not by the Tribunal (see further 14.9.3.2). Given that temporary admission is most commonly used for those seeking asylum, it is arguable that the proposal to repeal temporary admission and its replacement with a concept of bail is a further example of the government 'criminalizing' asylum seeking contrary to Article 31 of the Refugee Convention and creating a hostile environment for those who come to the UK to seek asylum.

14.9 Judicial supervision

The availability of judicial safeguards is central to the lawfulness of detention, and the major criticism by the UN Working Party and others is that although these exist in the UK, none is automatic.

14.9.1 Judicial review

As there is no statutory appeal against the decision to detain (it is not listed in s 82 Nationality Immigration and Asylum Act 2002), challenges to the length and the legality of detention are made by judicial review. Although judicial review is not an appeal on the merits, in the case of challenges to detention a more liberal approach to the Court's jurisdiction is applied. 'Where the liberty of the subject is concerned the court ought to be the primary decision-maker as to the reasonableness of the executive's actions, unless there are compelling reasons to the contrary' (*Youssef* [2004] EWHC 1884 QB). *Youssef* was a High Court case, and an action for false imprisonment, but its reasoning was adopted and approved by the Court of Appeal in *R (A (Somalia)) v SSHD* [2007] EWCA Civ 804, which is treated as 'binding authority that the court must assume the role of primary decision maker when considering the lawfulness of detention' (*Anam v SSHD* [2010] EWCA Civ 1140 and *R (AM) v SSHD* [2012] EWCA Civ 521). It has been suggested that review is limited to traditional public law grounds (*R (OM) v SSHD* [2011] EWCA Civ 999 and *R (on the application of LE (Jamaica)) v SSHD* [2012] EWCA Civ 597) but this does not seem to accord with the practice of the Supreme Court in leading cases.

14.9.2 Right to reasons for detention

Notice of reasons for detention may help the detainee to challenge the decision. The Human Rights Act gives a right in primary legislation to reasons for detention in Article 5.2: a detained person 'shall be informed promptly, in a language which he understands, of the reasons for his arrest'. There is an obligation in secondary legislation to give reasons on initial detention, and monthly thereafter (Detention Centre Rules 2001, SI 2001/238 r 9). As mentioned previously, the UNHCR Guidelines on Applicable Criteria and Standards relating to the Detention of Asylum Seekers carries similar advice. The Home Office produces a checklist of reasons—those detailed in the EIG (see

55.6.3). This is given by immigration officers to detainees on form IS91R, with boxes ticked to show which standard reasons for detention apply in their case.

These standard forms were first introduced during the period of the Cambridge research project in 2000, and were discussed with immigration officers during the research. They represented an attempt to ensure that only sanctioned reasons were actually used. Failure to use appropriate reasons may invalidate the detention if it can be shown that there were in fact no sustainable reasons for it. For instance, in *C, S and D*, standard reasons that they were likely to abscond was ticked, but this was contrary to all the available evidence.

14.9.3 **Bail**

A crucial safeguard for anyone in detention is the possibility of applying for bail. A bail application does not address the question of jurisdiction to detain. In a bail application, the argument is principally that the discretion to detain should not continue to be exercised in the particular case; the applicant should therefore be released, but a bail hearing does not consider the lawfulness of the detention. An effect of this in an ECtHR decision was that an application for bail did not engage Article 5.4 ECHR (*Ismail v UK* 48078/09 Admissibility Decision [2013] ECHR 1153) and thus the fact that it was not decided 'speedily' did not fall within the Court's jurisdiction.

Immigration and asylum detainees have a right to apply for bail, but unlike the position in criminal cases there is no automatic period of detention which triggers a bail hearing (Immigration Act 1971 Sch 2 paras 22 and 29 and Immigration and Asylum Act 1999 s 54). Those people detained pending examination under 16(1) do not have a right to apply for bail until they have been in the UK for seven days (para 22 (1B)). The Immigration and Asylum Act 1999 contained a scheme for a system of automatic bail hearings, but this was never implemented and was repealed by s 68(6) of the 2002 Act. There is no statutory presumption of a right to bail. In the Bail Guidance for Immigration Judges released by the President of the Tribunal in June 2012 the common law right to liberty appears as the first point, as a right enjoyed by all. However, in the specific Guidance this does not translate into a presumption in favour of liberty when making individual decisions. The Guidance says:

By contrast with criminal proceedings, there is no statutory presumption in favour of release in immigration detention cases. Nevertheless, bail should not be refused unless there is good reason to do so, and it is for the respondent to show what those reasons are. (para 27)

The Guidance characterizes a bail decision as a 'risk assessment'. The underpinning is the statutory power to detain, and whether it should continue to be exercised, not the liberty of the individual and whether this should continue to be restricted.

14.9.3.1 Power to grant bail

An immigration officer of ordinary rank does not have power to grant bail. Under paras 22, 29, and 34 bail may be granted by a chief immigration officer or an immigration judge. However, the Nationality, Immigration and Asylum Act 2002 s 68 gives the power to grant bail to anyone who has been detained for more than eight days to the Secretary of State. Immigration judges have the power to grant bail, however, there are difficulties in obtaining legal aid to be represented before them. The report of the Chief Inspector of Borders and Immigration noted that between February 2010 and January 2011 109 foreign prisoners were released from detention by executive decision, compared with 1,102 released by the Tribunal (2011:24). Section 7 of the Immigration

Act 2014 introduced some new restrictions on the availability of bail. Firstly, a detainee cannot be released on bail if their removal is scheduled to take place within the next 14 days, unless the Home Secretary consents. Secondly, the Tribunal must dismiss a bail application without a hearing if it is submitted within 28 days of a previous decision, unless there has been a material change in circumstances.

14.9.3.2 Conditions for the grant of bail

Bail may be granted on condition that the person bailed reports at a specified time and place, usually a police station or immigration office. Bail will be made subject to recognizances. These are pledges of money, which will be forfeited if the person does not report to bail. Further recognizances may be taken from people who are willing to stand as surety for a fixed sum proportionate to their means. The guidelines for immigration judges make it clear that sureties are not essential, and should not be routinely required. Immigration judges are reminded that 'people recently arrived in the country may have nobody whom they could expect to stand surety for them'. The guidelines advise that the purpose of requiring a surety is to increase confidence that the applicant will comply with all the conditions of bail. 'If there are no reasonable grounds for concluding that the applicant will abscond, a surety may well be unnecessary' (para 39). Research on the conduct of bail hearings together with the guidance notes for immigration judges make it clear that sureties can be excluded from the hearings, although some sureties are required to go to considerable lengths to demonstrate that they have the funds to pledge.

Conditions may be fixed such as that the bailee resides in a certain place, and other conditions may be imposed, but these should only be imposed if they are strictly necessary. The Secretary of State may pay for travelling expenses incurred in meeting reporting restrictions or bail conditions (2002 Act s 69). Under s 4 of the Immigration and Asylum Act 1999 the Secretary of State also has power to provide accommodation to a refused asylum seeker who has no address to enable them to get bail.

New provisions in the Immigration Bill 2015 seek to amend existing legislation in order to create a single simplified power to grant immigration bail, which would apply to all persons in detention at the time of commencement. The new scheme would consolidate and replace existing legislation surrounding the use of immigration bail, temporary admission, temporary release, and release on restrictions. The proposed scheme provides that that people who are being detained or who are liable to being detained under immigration powers may be given immigration bail by the Secretary of State or First-tier Tribunal and sets out a number of factors to be considered by the Home Secretary or Tribunal when deciding whether to grant bail. It is suggested that a grant of immigration bail would be subject to at least one of the named conditions. These include restrictions on work or study, residence, reporting, and electronic monitoring ('tagging'). The Home Secretary would also, controversially, be given some powers to substitute immigration bail conditions imposed by the First-tier Tribunal.

The Home Office factsheet on the Bill states that the Government intends to make use of these powers in order to ensure that foreign national ex-offenders who are released on immigration bail pending deportation from the UK are subject to an electronic monitoring condition. The Government anticipates that using GPS tagging technology will improve public protection and allow for a faster re-detention of foreign national ex-offenders when their deportation becomes imminent ('Immigration Bill 2015: Factsheet—Immigration Bail', Home Office, December 2015)

Under the Bill, s 4 of the Immigration and Asylum Act 1999 would be replaced by a more restrictive provision granting the Home Secretary power to provide accommodation facilities to a person on immigration bail, *in certain circumstances*. Facilities for the accommodation of the person at a specified address may be provided for, if the Home Secretary imposes a residence requirement as a condition of bail at an address that the person did not propose or cannot support themselves at (e.g., due to insufficient finances), and the Home Secretary considers that there are 'exceptional circumstances which justify the use of the power'. Similarly travelling expenses incurred by the person in order to comply with a bail condition may be paid for by the Home Secretary, where justified due to 'exceptional circumstances'. The implication of these changes is that all migrants applying for leave, including asylum seekers, will be considered in the same way as those convicted of a criminal offence. The transfer of power to impose conditions on leave from the tribunals to the Secretary of State is in danger of further removing judicial scrutiny from this area as without access to asylum support, (which will also be restricted if the Bill becomes law), many migrants in detention would be unable to apply for bail. Potentially, this could make an expensive challenge to detention in the High Court the only available option for many in order to seek release.

14.9.4 *Habeas corpus*

The lawfulness of detention may be challenged by the prerogative writ of *habeas corpus*. This is an ancient remedy which has been regarded as constitutionally important as it is a means whereby a court can inquire into the reasons for any detention and order immediate release. The basis of the jurisdiction is 'a detention or imprisonment which is incapable of legal justification' (*Halsbury's Laws* vol. 1(1), para 208). Although a foreign national has as much right as a subject to apply for *habeas corpus* (see *Khawaja v SSHD* [1984] AC 74 at 111: 'He who is subject to English law is entitled to its protection'), it is of little use in challenging immigration detention. The reason for this is there is nearly always a jurisdiction to detain, that is, the basic statutory precondition is in existence. The question is usually how that jurisdiction has been exercised. This is a matter for judicial review, not *habeas corpus*. The amendment brought in by Immigration and Asylum Act 1999 s 140(1), permitting detention where there is a reasonable suspicion that directions for removal may be given means that it is even more unlikely that jurisdiction can be questioned.

Where there is a question of the jurisdiction to detain, this can be argued in both judicial review and *habeas corpus* proceedings and where appropriate both sets of proceedings can be pursued simultaneously. The relationship between the two was considered by the Court of Appeal in *R v SSHD ex p Sheikh* [2001] Imm AR 219, who pointed out that *habeas corpus* proceedings may be brought at any time that an applicant is detained, and are not subject to the strict time limits applicable in judicial review. Furthermore, *habeas corpus* is a writ of right, whereas permission must be sought for judicial review. Where the challenge is really to the underlying immigration decision, for example, the refusal of leave to enter, then judicial review is the appropriate procedure, not habeas corpus (*R v SSHD ex p Muboyayi* [1991] 4 All ER 72). Finally, Macdonald's view on the 1999 Act amendment was that 'this change sounds the death-knell for habeas corpus in removal cases, save where there is no reasonable suspicion (i.e. *mala fides* is alleged) or where detention is excessively lengthy (the *Hardial Singh* situation)' (2001:762). This latter point would now be displaced by *Khadir* in relation to immigration detention, but not where individuals are moved across borders against their will (*Rahmatullah v Secretary of State for the Foreign and Commonwealth Affairs and the Ministry of Defence* [2011] EWCA Civ 1540).

14.9.5 **False imprisonment and breach of statutory duty**

At the time of *Youssef v Home Office* [2004] EWHC 1884 QB, an action in tort for immigration detention was relatively unusual. However, this is now an established cause of action, in particular following *Lumba and Mighty* and *Kambadzi* (see 14.4.3 and 14.5.3). In these cases, the Supreme Court accepted that errors of public law invalidated the detention such that it became unlawful. Without statutory authority, the tort of false imprisonment was committed. Following these two cases, where an error in the decision to detain or the procedure governing the detention is such as to remove the statutory basis of the detention, there may be remedies not only in public law but also in tort. In tort actions, damages can be claimed on a broader basis (although the claimants in the Supreme Court cases did not succeed in that respect) and there is greater scope for disclosure of evidence and cross-examination. Actions for unlawful detention were brought in a number of the cases discussed earlier, and this enables the claimant to sue for damages. The principles were also established in an earlier case of *ID and others v Home Office, BID & ILPA intervening* [2005] EWCA Civ 38.

Here the Court of Appeal reinstated particulars of claim that had been struck out in the lower court, allowing the appellants to proceed with an application for false imprisonment. A family on arrival in the UK had been detained in Oakington for a week. Following *Saadi*, they could not succeed in any action challenging that detention. Their asylum claim was then refused, and they were moved to Yarl's Wood detention centre. A major fire there started the night that they arrived. They lost their possessions, and were lucky to escape with their lives as they had been locked in and the guards forgot to let them out. In a state of shock, they were then transferred to Harmondsworth. The Court of Appeal held that their action in tort concerning the latter two periods of detention should be heard by the courts. The Home Office had argued that immigration officers were immune from suit in making decisions pursuant to statute. The Court of Appeal (Brooke LJ giving the only reasoned judgment) considered the limited immunities from suit still available in the case of decisions to detain, and concluded that there was no such immunity for immigration officers.

The Home Office relied also on an argument that 'the power of a state to control immigration . . . extends beyond the simple control of entry to encompass the treatment of aliens and the control of their activities while they are present or resident in the State' (para 71). This amounted to an attempt to argue that foreign nationals are not subject to the same law as nationals and do not have full redress in the courts. This argument was dealt with in *Khawaja* [1984] AC 74 and so the Court of Appeal held in *ID*. The Court also rejected an argument that the claim was an abuse of process: 'there is nothing in the slightest bit peculiar about an individual bringing a private law claim for damages against an executive official who has abused his private rights' (para 57).

14.10 **Detention centres as public authorities**

The management and running of detention centres, and of transport and escort services to effect removals, are contracted out to private bodies. An important question in terms of redress is whether these contractors act as public authorities for the purposes of the Human Rights Act 1998. In *R (on the application of D and K) v SSHD* [2006] EWHC (Admin) 980, GSL UK (formerly Group 4 Total Security), the contractors running Oakington, accepted that they were bound by the Detention Centre Rules and were a functional public authority for the purposes of the Human Rights Act. GSL contracted out the provision of medical services at Oakington to a company called Forensic Medical Services Ltd, a subsidiary of another company called PCFM. There was a failure to provide medical services according to the standard in the Detention Centre Rules, but this failure had been known to all parties for a long time. GSL said they were not funded to provide it. However, theirs was the obligation to ensure compliance with the contract, and so declarations were made against GSL and the Home Office, though not against PCFM.

Bacon (2005) examines the growth in involvement of private prison companies in running immigration detention centres. At that time, seven of the ten removal centres were run by private companies, but only 10 per cent of prisons. She cites the attractiveness of immigration detention to such enterprises, it being less regulated than prisons in the criminal justice system, and thus offering more opportunities for increasing the profit margin. No doubt the financial attractiveness of immigration detention is one reason why government policy to build more has been able to prosper.

On the other hand, there have also been some serious disturbances at detention centres, and in such a case, unsurprisingly, neither private contractors nor the government are eager to shoulder all responsibility for the cost of damage, for the causes of the problems or for human rights violations that may have occurred during disturbances. In February 2002, a riot occurred at Yarl's Wood Immigration Detention Centre. Group 4 and their insurers claimed to recover the cost of the damage from the Bedfordshire Police Authority under the provisions of the Riot (Damages) Act 1886. The claim had been quantified at some £32 million. The Police Authority resisted this on the basis that the Group 4 companies acted as public authorities in running the centre, and so were debarred from claiming against the police under the Act. As a preliminary issue, the Court of Appeal in *Yarl's Wood Immigration Limited; GSL UK Limited; Creechurch Dedicated Limited v Bedfordshire Police Authority* [2009] EWCA Civ 1110 held that such a claim was in principle allowable. If it were found that Group 4 were to any extent responsible for the riot or the damage, the Act itself made provision for exclusion or reduction of the police's liability.

Following disturbances at Harmondsworth Detention Centre, complaints were made by some uninvolved detainees, that they were:

kept in confinement while water from the sprinkler system entered their cells, then ordered out into the exercise yard in the cold while many of them were still wet, then readmitted and locked into cells. There AM and others were affected by smoke from a fire started by other inmates in an adjacent room; others were soaked by the sprinklers; there was reduced ventilation and, for many, a complete absence of toilet facilities. Some inmates spent well over 12 hours in these conditions without food or water. Two of the claimants, HM and LM, were assaulted by detention officers or rapid response personnel. The dispersal of detainees which followed was in many cases carried out callously; some were transported long distances without their belongings. (*R (on the application of AM) and others v SSHD and Kalyx, BID intervening*) [2009] EWCA Civ 219 para 7)

The three judges of the Court of Appeal each took different views of the responsibility of the Secretary of State and Kalyx Ltd, which managed the centre. Their majority conclusion was to make a declaration that the Secretary of State ought to have conducted an independent investigation when he was alerted to the possibility that the appellants may have been the subject of infringements of their Article 3 rights. The investigation that had been ordered was not independent and did not have a remit to investigate the impact on uninvolved detainees.

14.11 **Indefinite detention in the 'War on Terror'**

In a sense, the detention without trial of foreign nationals that took place from 2001 to 2005 does not belong in a textbook on immigration and asylum law. It has a place in this chapter because immigration powers were used to justify it, and the development has historical importance. When that foundation in immigration law was held by the House of Lords to be a misuse the provisions were declared unlawful. Nevertheless, these provisions in the Anti-terrorism, Crime and Security Act 2001 (ATCSA) were not an aberration. They were only the most extreme end of a number of measures we have noted already, the designated status in the Criminal Justice and Immigration Act, and UK Borders Act provisions for detention pending automatic deportation. All these lead towards a limbo without rights for foreign nationals whom the government wishes to deport but currently may not.

The Anti-terrorism, Crime and Security Act 2001 was the UK Parliament's legislative response to the attack on the World Trade Centre on 11 September of that year. The government claimed that intelligence information suggested that there were people operating within the UK who had international terrorist connections, but against whom there was insufficient evidence to bring a prosecution. Against British nationals operating in such a way there would be no sanction. Foreign nationals could be deported on the grounds that their deportation was conducive to the public good (see *Rehman v SSHD* [2001] 3 WLR 877) but not if they faced torture or inhuman or degrading treatment or punishment contrary to Article 3 EHCR (*Chahal v UK*) in the destination country. ATCSA s 23 gave a power to detain a foreign national who could not be deported if the Secretary of State reasonably believed their presence in the UK to be a risk to national security and reasonably suspected that person of international terrorist activities or connections.

The provision clearly had the potential to breach Article 5.1 as detention was not pending deportation or extradition or a criminal trial. Accordingly, the UK government derogated from Article 5 to the extent that it would be breached by this Act (Human Rights Act 1998 (Designated Derogation) Order 2001). This meant that Article 5 was suspended to the extent that it conflicted with 2001 Act provisions, both for the purposes of action in Strasbourg (Article 15 ECHR) and under the Human Rights Act (HRA s 1(2)). The validity of the derogation was challenged by the first twelve people to be detained under s 23. The challenge initially came before the Special Immigration Appeals Commission (SIAC) who granted a declaration under Human Rights Act 1998 s 4 that the detention power was incompatible with Article 14 ECHR.

The Court of Appeal overturned SIAC's declaration (*A, X, Y and others v SSHD* [2002] EWCA Civ 1502). Its approach follows in the footsteps of the House of Lords in the national security case of *Rehman*, considering that in measures concerning 'a public emergency threatening the life of the nation' it was appropriate to accord deference to the Home Secretary who is in a special position to be able to assess the evidence and take the decision. It was therefore prepared to accept the Home Secretary's assertion that only the detention of non-nationals was necessary.

The UK's continued detention of eleven men under these powers attracted criticism from the committee of Privy Counsellors (the Newton Committee) convened to review the legislation, the Parliamentary Joint Committee on Human Rights (in its Fifth, Sixth, and Eighth Reports of 2003–04), the UN Human Rights Committee, the European Commissioner on Human Rights (Opinion 1/2002, August 2002), and many NGOs and other commentators.

The House of Lords overturned the Court of Appeal's decision in a momentous judgment (*A v SSHD* [2004] UKHL 56). The nine judges who sat in the Lords reiterated the fundamental constitutional importance of the right to liberty, and that the law applies equally to all.

They noted that SIAC had found as fact that 'there are many British nationals already identified—mostly in detention abroad—who fall within the definition of suspected international terrorists, and . . . there are others at liberty in the UK who could similarly be defined' (para 32). Also, 'allowing a suspected international terrorist to leave our shores and depart to another country, perhaps a country as close as France, there to pursue his criminal designs, is hard to reconcile with a belief in his capacity to inflict serious injury to the people and interests of this country' (para 33). The lack of rational connection to the aim to be achieved made the measures both disproportionate and discriminatory.

The derogation was not, they thought, limited to what was strictly required by the exigencies of the situation. Lord Bingham of Cornhill referred to the very strict bail conditions upon which one detainee had been released. These were less draconian than detention, but presumably considered sufficient. As the derogation was discriminatory and so in breach of Article 14, it was also in breach of Article 26 ICCPR and thus not consistent with the UK's other international obligations, as required by Article 15.

Lord Hoffmann alone found that there was no threat to the life of the nation warranting derogation under Article 15. The life of the nation should not be equated with individual human lives, but rather with the values and practices that constitute the collective life. He said, most memorably: 'The real threat to the life of the nation, in the sense of a people living in accordance with its traditional laws and political values, comes not from terrorism but from laws such as these' (paras 96 and 97).

The majority found that s 23 was disproportionate and thus in breach of Article 15, and discriminatory and thus in breach of Article 14. They issued a quashing order in relation to the derogation order and a declaration of incompatibility in relation to s 23. Only Lord Walker of Gestingthorpe dissented.

This conclusion was endorsed by the ECtHR in *A v UK* (2009) 49 EHRR 29, who additionally found the provisions unlawful under Article 5.1 in relation to nine of the 11 applicants. The Court said that: 'one of the principal assumptions underlying the derogation notice, the 2001 Act and the decision to detain the applicants was that they could not be removed or deported "for the time being"'. Action 'with a view to deportation', as permitted by Article 5.1(f) could not therefore provide a reason for their detention (but see the contrary view of Finnis).

The Prevention of Terrorism Act 2005 was the government's response to the House of Lords' judgment, and this enabled the detainees' bail conditions to be swiftly transposed into control orders under that Act. A special provision exempted them from judicial oversight (PTA 2005 s 3(1)(c)). The most draconian were found to be in breach of Article 5. These entailed confinement, alone to a one-bedroomed flat in an unknown area for 18 hours a day, limited telephone, and no internet access, no visitors who had not been vetted by the Home Office, a limited radius of travel, a prohibition on attending any gatherings of people except once a week in an approved mosque, wearing an electronic tag at all times, and reporting to a monitoring centre on leaving and returning to the flat. The majority of the House of Lords thought that this amounted to a deprivation of liberty rather than merely a restriction on liberty (*SSHD v JJ* [2007] UKHL 45). It may be doubted whether such a draconian system would have come into being without the more severe detention regime first being imposed on foreign nationals. In 2012 control orders were in turn replaced by Terrorism Prevention and Investigation Measures (TPIMs), which expire after two years.

This section would not be complete without a reference to *R (on the application of Abbassi) v Secretary of State for Foreign and Commonwealth Affairs* [2003] UKHRR 76, a challenge to the Foreign Secretary's exercise of prerogative in interceding for the British prisoners held in the American military base in Guantanamo Bay, Cuba. In essence, the case concerns the impotence of the British government to intervene in the affairs of another nation and of the citizen to challenge that. However, it proceeded on the accepted basis that the detainees had access to no legal review of their detention, that detention was indefinite and that they had no access to legal advice or representation. Within the confines of the legal principles available to it, the Court of Appeal could only reiterate the primacy of liberty, and that every detention is a *prima facie* breach of law (para 60). They were powerless to intervene as the matter was political, not legal. As discussed in chapter 2, the impasse resulted in a break with constitutional convention when Lord Steyn spoke in a non-judicial setting to criticize the detentions (*The Independent* 26 November 2003). See also *R (on application of Al-Rawi) v FCO and SSHD* [2006] EWHC 972 (Admin), discussed in chapter 3.

14.12 Conclusion

We end this chapter as we began, *Liversidge v Anderson*, dealing with wartime internment, and *A v SSHD*, dealing with internment in a different kind of public emergency. In *Liversidge v Anderson*, although the House of Lords found for the executive, the case is remembered more for Lord Atkin's dissent than it is for its ratio. As *A v SSHD* takes its place in legal history, so far it is the majority judgment which has left a stronger print. The 8:1 decision that the detentions were unlawful has given the case a claim to be 'one of the most constitutionally significant ever decided by the House of Lords' (MLR Belmarsh special issue p. 654). Lord Bingham's leading judgment carefully marshals international law to reach the majority conclusion, and this is important, not only for the outcome, but also because it shows that the UK is subject to international restraints upon government. The judgment of the ECtHR in *A v UK* upheld the right to liberty for the same appellants in one of the most politically charged of cases. They did so partly on the basis that lesser constraints could and should have been considered. However, the contrary effect is achieved by the ECtHR decision in *Saadi v UK*. Here, international law restraint is more or less abandoned, and remarkably, lesser constraints than loss of liberty were not considered. The Court's failure to distinguish between asylum seekers and other entrants can be seen as negating the lawful status of seeking asylum. Ironically, it also means that the same principles are in human rights law applicable to other lawful applicants at ports of entry, such as visitors without entry clearance.

In the UK, *Khadir* entrenches the capacity of the government to maintain a limbo status for asylum seekers. Although *prima facie* unlawful, detention has been on the increase, and even statutorily enshrined human rights can be defeated by a judicial assertion of the state's power to control foreign nationals. The administrative power to detain pending determination of a claim has grown far beyond its original use for visitors overnight, and become the foundation for a whole new system of detention. Whilst the Court of Appeal appears to have sounded the death knell for the current system of fast track detention, it remains to be seen how the government will respond. The Supreme Court's judgments in *Mighty and Lumba* and in *Kambadzi* place a legal stop on the expansion of executive freedom, but the absence of any real sanction may limit the effect on detention practice.

QUESTIONS

1 Do the judgments in the case of *Saadi* recognize the right in Article 14 UDHR to claim asylum?

2 Is it appropriate that the decision to detain should be a discretionary one without statutory criteria to guide its exercise?

3 Should asylum seekers have automatic bail hearings as criminal suspects do?

 online resource centre For guidance on answering questions, visit the Online Resource Centre www.oxfordtextbooks.co.uk/orc/clayton7e/.

FURTHER READING

All Party Parliamentary Group on Refugees and Migration (2015) *The Report of the Inquiry into the Use of Immigration Detention in the United Kingdom*.

Bacon, Christine (2005) 'The Evolution of Immigration Detention in the UK: The Involvement of Private Prison Companies' *Refugee Studies Centre*, Working Paper no. 27.

Bail for Immigration Detainees (BID) (2002) *Immigration Detention in the United Kingdom, Submission to the United Nations Working Group on Arbitrary Detention* (London: BID).

Bail for Immigration Detainees (BID) (2005) *Fit to be Detained? Challenging the Detention of Asylum Seekers and Migrants with Health Needs* (London: BID).

Bail for Immigration Detainees (BID) (2012) *The Liberty Deficit: Long-Term Detention and Bail Decision-Making* (London: BID).

Black, Richard, Collyer, Michael, Skeldon, Ronald, and Waddington, Clare (2005) *A Survey of the Illegally Resident Population in Detention in the UK*, Home Office Research Paper 20/05.

Campbell, Sarah, Baqueriza Maria and Ingram James (2011) 'Last Resort or First Resort? Immigration Detention of Children in the UK' (BID and The Children's Society).

Fordham, Michael with Justine N. Stefanelli and Sophie Eser (2013) *Immigration Detention and the Rule of Law, National Report: United Kingdom*, (London: The British Institute of International and Comparative Law).

Independent Asylum Commission (2008) *Deserving Dignity* (London).

Independent Chief Inspector of UKBA (2011) *Thematic Inspection Report of How the Agency Manages Foreign National Prisoners February to May 2011* (London: Independent Chief Inspector of UKBA).

Johnston, Connor (2009) 'Indefinite Immigration Detention: Can it be Justified?' *Journal of Immigration and Nationality Asylum Law* vol. 23, no. 4, pp. 351–64.

London Detainee Support Group (2009) *Detained Lives* (London).

Modern Law Review (2005) 68(4) Cases Section: Special Issue on Belmarsh.

O'Nions, Helen (2008) 'No Right to Liberty: the Detention of Asylum Seekers for Administrative Convenience' *European Journal of Migration and Law* vol. 10, no. 2, pp. 149–85.

Phelps, Jerome (2015) 'End of the Line for the Detention of Asylum Seekers' *Huffington Post* 30 July 2015.

Poole, Tom (2005) 'Harnessing the Power of the Past? Lord Hoffmann and the *Belmarsh Detainees* Case' *Journal of Law and Society* vol. 32, no. 4, pp. 534–61.

Pourgourides, Christina K., Sashidharan, Sashi P., and Bracken, Pat J. (1996) *A Second Exile: The Mental Health Implications of Detention of Asylum Seekers in the United Kingdom* (Birmingham: Northern Birmingham Mental Health Trust).

Sawyer, Caroline (2007) 'Elephants in the Room, or: A Can of Worms: *Szoma v DWP*' *Journal of Social Security Law* vol. 86, pp. 86–104.

Sawyer, Caroline, and Turpin, Philip (2005) 'Neither Here nor There: Temporary Admission to the UK' *International Journal of Refugee Law* vol. 17, no. 4, December, pp. 688–728.

Shah, Prakash (2002) *Refugees, Race and the Concept of Asylum* (London: Cavendish), chapter 8.

Tsangarides, Natasha and Grant, Jane (2013) *Expecting Change: The Case for Ending the Detention of Pregnant Women* (Medical Justice).

UNHCR (2012) *Revised Guidelines on Applicable Criteria and Standards Relating to the Detention of Asylum Seekers* (Geneva: UNHCR).

Weber, Leane and Gelsthorpe, Loraine (2000) *Deciding to Detain: How Decisions to Detain Asylum Seekers are Made at Ports of Entry* (Cambridge: Cambridge Institute of Criminology).

Weiss, Adam and Lieu, Esther, (2012) 'Detention of Children' *Journal of Immigration Asylum and Nationality Law* vol. 26, no. 4, pp. 349–58.

Wilsher, Daniel (2012) *Immigration Detention: Law, History, Politics* (Cambridge: Cambridge University Press).

Women for Refugee Women (2014) *Detained: Women Asylum Seekers Locked up in the UK.*

15

....

Deportation

SUMMARY

This chapter gives a brief history of the power of deportation, then discusses in some detail the application of the ground that the deportation is conducive to the public good. This includes discussion of so-called automatic deportation under the UK Borders Act 2007, and of national security cases.

15.1 Introduction

Deportation has a long history. The word conjures up images of forced removals, divided families, and poor conditions on board crowded ships. Deportations had become uncommon, but underwent a revival as the government introduced a policy in 2006 to increase deportations after media revelations that not all those were considered for deportation who might be (see chapter 2). The Home Office's published statistics no longer distinguish between those removed administratively as an immigration enforcement (discussed in chapter 16) and those removed following a deportation order. The figures for deportation are now included in a group called 'foreign national offender'—a non-British national who has been convicted and received a prison sentence for any offence. In 2014, 5,022 people so described were forcibly removed. Deportation has traditionally offered more rights to the person removed than does the process of removal, though as this chapter will show, these have gradually been eroded almost to vanishing point.

Although the effects of deportation and removal have become similar, it is still important to understand them as distinct legal processes. Deportation may only take place where the grounds for it are either proved or deemed proved by statute. Removal by contrast, despite its devastating effect, is in essence an enforcement process. The 'grounds' for it are concerned with immigration control. Deportation is based on the personal conduct of the person concerned, even though in national security cases wrongdoing need not be proved (see 15.7.3). A person with any kind of immigration leave, including indefinite, may be deported. Although this means that a person subject to immigration control is subject to a sanction following a criminal offence which does not apply to a British citizen, the ECtHR does not treat this as an unlawful double jeopardy because expulsion is regarded not as a punishment but as an administrative sanction (*Maaouia v France*). This approach has been confirmed in the UK courts. In *AT (Pakistan) v SSHD* [2010] EWCA Civ 567 the Court of Appeal rejected an argument that deportation was a punishment. It was 'preventative rather than punitive' (para 25). Extradition sometimes interacts with asylum claims but is a means of enforcing non-immigration criminal processes, and will not be considered in this book. Voluntary departure is considered later in this chapter.

15.2 **What is deportation?**

Deportation is an enforced departure from the UK, pursuant to an order which also prevents the deportee from returning to the UK unless and until the order is revoked. Paragraph 362 of the immigration rules sets out the effects of a deportation order:

(i) it requires the person who is the subject of the order to leave the UK;

(ii) it authorizes that person's detention until they leave the UK (subject to a common law restraint on the length of detention, as discussed in the previous chapter);

(iii) it prohibits that person's re-entry for as long as the order is in force;

(iv) it invalidates any leave to enter or remain given to the person before the order was made or while it was in force.

The first formal step in the deportation process is the notice of decision to deport, which gives the reasons for the decision, the country to which it is proposed to deport the person, and notice of appeal rights. Appeal is against the notice of decision to deport. Once the deportation order is signed, it takes effect and there is no further appeal, though it may be possible to appeal a refusal to revoke the order (Nationality, Immigration and Asylum Act 2002 s 82(2)).

Entry while the deportation order is still in force makes that person an illegal entrant (Immigration Act 1971 s 33A).

15.3 **History and development of the power to deport**

As we have seen, in early times those regarded as enemies, such as Jews by Edward I or Irish by Elizabeth I, were expelled by royal decree. Deportation as a regulated process carried out by government officials was only instituted by the Aliens Act 1905. Under the statute, deportation could only take place after conviction of an imprisonable offence, or if a magistrates' court certified that the person had been sentenced elsewhere for an extradition offence, or had:

[b]een found in receipt of any such parochial relief as disqualifies a person for the parliamentary franchise, or found wandering without ostensible means of subsistence, or been living in insanitary conditions due to overcrowding.

Criminality, poverty, and the spread of disease have often been mixed in with immigration policy, as discussed in chapter 1. The operation of appeal boards was suspended in 1914, and although for a short time there was a review panel, its decisions were unpopular with the Home Office and it was abolished again. Effectively, from 1914 to 1969, people who were to be deported had no access to appeal or independent review.

We have seen that the Commonwealth Immigrants Act 1962 marked a historic shift in the relationship between the UK and its Commonwealth citizens. Not only did it provide the first powers to refuse them entry and impose conditions, it also provided the first powers to deport Commonwealth citizens, though originally only for criminal offences on the recommendation of a criminal court (s 6). The 1962 Act s 7 provided protection against deportation for anyone who could prove they had been ordinarily resident in the UK for five years prior to conviction. This exemption was preserved by the Immigration Act 1971 for existing residents, but otherwise abolished. The importance of long-term residence has remained a live issue in Europe, both in debates in the Council of Europe (see chapter 5) and in increased protection for long-term residents in EU law (see chapter 4). Such protection has diminished in the UK. Periods of residence accrued under some immigration rules may give settled status but give no protection against deportation.

The Immigration Appeals Act 1969 gave power to the Secretary of State to deport Commonwealth citizens who were in breach of their conditions of admission (s 16), again with an exemption for those who had been ordinarily resident for five years, and from 1969 until 1999 deportation could also be a means of enforcing immigration rules, not only a means of excluding people who were considered socially undesirable. The Immigration Act 1971 made the position of aliens and Commonwealth citizens broadly the same, in that deportation became possible for both groups for breach of condition or overstaying, when conducive to the public good and after recommendation by a criminal court (s 3). From that time onwards, apart from the exemptions, the distinction between Commonwealth citizens and aliens for deportation purposes has vanished. The main distinction now is between EU nationals and others.

The Immigration Act 1988 s 5 restricted the grounds for appeal against deportation so that people who had been in the UK less than seven years who were being deported for breach of condition or overstaying could not argue their case on the merits of whether they personally should be deported, but only on whether there was power in law to deport them. The Asylum and Immigration Act 1996 added a further ground for deportation—obtaining leave to remain by deception. Despite the widened grounds and the restricted appeal rights, a person who was to be deported still had a right to appeal from inside the UK which the person to be removed did not. The Immigration and Asylum Act 1999 translated most of the grounds for deportation into grounds for removal, thereby substantially eradicating the distinction between deportation and removal. The same Act introduced the human rights appeal against removal and deportation.

In summary, until the implementation of the 1999 Act, the scope of the power to deport increased, while the rights of people who were to be deported decreased. In the Nationality, Immigration and Asylum Act 2002 a new right of appeal was introduced against a decision to deport following the recommendation of a criminal court (s 82(2) (j)). Deportation powers were publicly linked to the national security agenda, though not for the first time, in 2005 in the Prime Minister's statement following the bombings in London that year. He proclaimed a 'list of unacceptable behaviours' and an intention to make these grounds for deportation and speed up the deportation process. The list includes writing, producing, publishing, or distributing material; public speaking including preaching; running a website; using a position of responsibility to express views which 'foment terrorism, justify or glorify terrorism, foster hatred which may lead to intra-community violence in the UK or other serious criminal activity, or seek to provoke others to serious criminal acts'. This list is not exhaustive. It is now part of a policy which can inform a decision to deport (IDI chapter 13). In May 2006, the press disclosed that, over a seven-year period, 1,000 foreign national prisoners had been released without being considered for deportation (see chapter 2 for discussion of the incident). This turned out to be due to failures of management, organization, and communication within what was then the Immigration and Nationality Directorate. It was not that it would necessarily have been appropriate to deport these prisoners, but rather that whether they should be deported had not been considered. Over 100 were the subject of a court recommendation. As a response, the government announced that there would be automatic deportation of serious offenders, a proposal which was supported by the House of Commons Home Affairs Committee (Fifth Report 2005–06).

The immediate result was a rule change in July 2006, HC 1337, abolishing consideration of the merits of the case in favour of a presumption that a deportation which the

Secretary of State considered to be conducive to the public good would be in the public interest. Most recently, UK Borders Act 2007 ss 32–39 created a statutory obligation to make a deportation order in many criminal cases, and deemed these to be conducive to the public good, as explained more fully in 15.7.1.

15.4 Rationale for deportation

The power to deport is most commonly used in relation to people who have been convicted of a criminal offence. The traditional and liberal view is that its use is not intended to be a further punishment for the criminal offence, but should only be considered when the person's continued presence in the country impinges on the life of the public in a way that is contrary to the public interest (Immigration Act 1971 s 3(5) (a) and *R v Nazari* [1980] 3 All ER 880). Every society contains a certain level of criminal activity and so crime in itself does not warrant deportation. The Court of Appeal in *Raghbir Singh* [1996] Imm AR 507 said that the Secretary of State should consider 'whether it is bad for the country for him to remain'. The rule change in 2006 and provision for automatic deportation in the UK Borders Act 2007 demonstrate a move towards a policy which in an extreme form would say that any non-British person who commits a criminal act should be removed. This is in the context of a growing government policy which creates categories of 'belongers' and 'non-belongers'. It is not really a penal policy as such, in that it regards criminality as secondary to nationality. It has echoes of the ATCSA experiment discussed in the last chapter, treating criminal matters as immigration matters wherever possible. Regarded as a penal policy, it could be summarized as 'out of sight, out of mind', rather like transportation of British subjects who had committed criminal offences to North America or Australia in the eighteenth century.

At the other end of the spectrum of opinion, it would be said that removing the criminal from society does not address the causes of crime and the wrongdoing of a non-citizen is no greater than the wrongdoing of a citizen. The possession of citizenship (and so exemption from deportation) is an irrelevant technicality given that one may apply for naturalization and so become a citizen after five years' residence in the UK, or on the other hand have lived here all one's life and still not have citizenship. Furthermore, nationality is now more easily removed (see chapter 3). The discrimination which results from the deportation of the non-citizen, combined with the harm to family and social networks, is a greater fracturing of the social fabric than the continued presence of someone who has committed a criminal offence. Punishment as meted out by the Court is already intended to deter others and prevent reoffending and if it fails to do so that is a matter for criminal policy, not immigration control.

Since deportation which interferes with Article 8 rights must be necessary in a democratic society (see chapter 5), these underlying concepts of society and criminality inevitably affect decision-making.

15.5 Exercise of the power to deport

Section 5(1) Immigration Act 1971 expresses the power to make a deportation order as a power of the Secretary of State. However, in accordance with the *Carltona* principle (*Carltona Ltd v Commissioner of Works* [1943] 2 All ER 560 CA), properly authorized officials may carry out the function of the Secretary of State and in doing so their actions count as the actions of the Secretary of State. In the context of deportation, the *Carltona* principle authorizes deportation action to be taken by officials of the Home Office. In 1988, the Secretary of State authorized certain nominated immigration officers of the rank of inspector also to make deportation decisions. This delegation was challenged in the case of *Oladehinde and Alexander v Secretary of State for the Home Department* [1991] 1 AC 254, but the House of Lords upheld the delegation. The Court's concern about procedures being properly applied was met by the practice of making written records of the decision-making process, ensuring that immigration officers who had been involved in the investigation process were not involved in the deportation decision, and referring to the Home Office any proposed deportation where the person had compassionate circumstances or had been in the UK for a long time.

Deportation orders will usually be signed by the 'Chief Executive or Deputy Chief Executive', presumably of the Immigration Enforcement Directorate, and 'certain' cases may be signed by a minister. Usual practice has been for the Home Secretary to sign deportation orders which are made on what we may loosely call national security grounds. These grounds are discussed at 15.7.3, and may only be challenged through the restricted appeal procedure before the Special Immigration Appeals Commission, discussed in chapter 7.

15.6 Who may be deported?

Section 3(5) Immigration Act 1971 says that 'a person who is not a British citizen' may be deported. Here, the term 'British citizen' has the meaning given to it by s 2 Immigration Act, as substituted by British Nationality Act 1981 s 39. It therefore includes, not only those who have British citizenship, but also Commonwealth citizens who retained right of abode when the British Nationality Act 1981 came into force, as discussed in chapter 3. However, s 2A Immigration Act 1971, inserted by the Immigration Asylum and Nationality Act 2006, provides for this right of abode to be removed from Commonwealth citizens if the Secretary of State thinks that their removal or exclusion from the UK would be conducive to the public good—the same grounds as deportation. Given the greater ease with which British citizenship is also now removed (see chapter 3), this too does not provide a complete protection from being considered for deportation except in the case of British citizens by birth or descent who have no other nationality (chapter 3).

There are other exemptions. By Immigration Act 1971 s 7, Commonwealth and Irish citizens are exempt if they were ordinarily resident in the UK on 1 January 1973 (the date that the 1971 Act came into force) and have been ordinarily resident for five years before the decision to deport was taken (s 7(1)(b) and (c)) (*Lawrence Kane v SSHD* [2000] Imm AR 250). Unusually in counting periods of residence, according to Immigration Act s 7(2), remaining 'in breach of immigration laws' counts towards this five-year period. Case law has established that this only applies to people who overstay their period of leave, and not to those who entered illegally in the first place. Time spent in prison however does not count (*Lawrence Kane*). Section 8(3) provides an exemption from deportation for diplomats and their families.

There used to be an exemption for Commonwealth wives of Commonwealth men settled in the UK before 1973, but this was abolished by s 1 Immigration Act 1988. The abolition of this security for Commonwealth women was in breach of a guarantee which had been given by s 1(5) of the Immigration Act 1971, that Commonwealth citizens would be no less free to come and go after the 1971 Act than they were before. The 1988 Act repealed that section and caused a furore by removing the rights of Commonwealth citizens. However, without constitutional protection, given the UK's doctrine of the legislative supremacy of Parliament, such promises cannot be relied upon. Even the Human Rights Act does not give a constitutional guarantee of the right to family life of Commonwealth citizens living in the UK (see generally chapter 8).

As discussed more fully in chapter 4, European Economic Area (EEA) nationals are only liable to be deported on the limited grounds allowed by Directive 2004/38. Developments in both EU and domestic law leave little room for doubt that EEA nationals have greater protection. Deportation of EEA nationals is an exception to the underlying right of freedom of movement and as such should be interpreted restrictively (Case 41/74 *Van Duyn v Home Office* [1974] ECR 1337). No such right can be claimed by non-EEA nationals. Leave to remain in the UK carries no protective power in itself comparable with European freedom of movement. Protection for an established life in the UK may only be argued through Article 8 European Convention of Human Rights (ECHR) or the very demanding immigration rules on private life (para 276ADE et seq). However, in *Omojudi v UK* [2009] ECHR 1942 the Court attached 'considerable weight to the fact that the Secretary of State for the Home Department, who was fully aware of his offending history, granted the applicant Indefinite Leave to Remain in the United Kingdom' (para 42).

15.7 Deportation 'conducive to the public good'

Since overstaying and breach of condition became grounds for removal instead of deportation, the remaining principal ground for deportation is that the Secretary of State deems the deportation to be conducive to the public good (s 3(5)(a)). In case law and literature prior to the 1999 Act, deportations under what is now s 3(5)(a) are referred to as 's 3(5)(b)' deportations.

It has been noted in the introduction to this chapter that deportation conducive to the public good has a long history. The power to deport on s 3(5)(a) grounds is a broad one, not confined to any one interpretation of the meaning of the public good. In practice, the commission of criminal offences is the most common basis, although as described earlier, the decision can be based on the Secretary of State's judgment that someone has engaged in the 'unacceptable behaviours' which might foster terrorism, without any criminal offence being charged (see *Mahajna v Home Secretary (deportation hate speech—unacceptable behaviour)* [2012] UKUT B1 (IAC)).

Case law on the question of whether deportation is conducive to the public good has included evaluation of matters such as the seriousness of the offence, the likelihood of reoffending, and any deterrent effect on others. The evaluation of these factors entered a new era with the case of *N (Kenya) v SSHD* [2004] EWCA Civ 1094, which, although only a majority decision, became a leading authority. *N (Kenya)* required that weight be given to the Secretary of State's policy on the deportation of serious criminals. As the one holding government responsibility for deportation policy, the Secretary of State could be assumed to have developed a policy which took proper account of the deterrent effect of deportation, and its function as an expression of public revulsion at the crime(s) in question. There is a tension in evaluating the public good argument in deportation appeals between the impact of the actual individual's continued presence in the UK, most often considered to be demonstrated by their likelihood of reoffending, and the wider social impact of the deportation. This latter factor is evaluated, not only by the deterrent effect on other would-be offenders (which is inherently difficult to prove), but also since *N (Kenya)*, by considering the deportation as a signal of society's revulsion at the crime(s). The ECtHR stresses taking all the circumstances into account, and would only weigh as one factor the use of deportation as a signal of revulsion at the crime. See *AA v UK* [2011] ECHR 1345:

where, as in the present case, the interference with the applicant's rights under Article 8 pursues the legitimate aim of 'prevention of disorder or crime', the above criteria ultimately are designed to help evaluate the extent to which the applicant can be expected to cause disorder or to engage in criminal activities. (para 58)

Deterrence of others and the signal to society have little to do with the individual deportee, except to the extent that their crime may be described as belonging to a category. It is in relation to categories (e.g., 'violent crime') that the Secretary of State develops policy. In the case of deportees with families, the public interest in maintaining family unity and avoiding the social cost of severed families is rarely weighed on this side of the balance. Disruption of the family is mainly considered as it impacts on the Article 8 rights of the individual family in question (see chapter 5).

In *N (Kenya)* itself, the adjudicator had given decisive weight to the low risk of reoffending. The Tribunal on reconsideration had held that this was the wrong approach, and that more weight should have been given to the Secretary of State's policy of deporting those who committed very serious offences (as N had). The majority of the Court of Appeal agreed with the Tribunal. This approach was reiterated and became established in *OH (Serbia) v SSHD* [2008] EWCA Civ 694, where the Court of Appeal held that the risk of reoffending was only one aspect of the public interest. Other matters included deterrence, and *as an independent factor*, the view of the Secretary of State of the public interest. Where the Tribunal had not given due weight to this, their decision was not lawful. The appellant was a 19-year-old Kosovan refugee who had been severely traumatized by the violence he had seen in Kosovo. He had seen one of his brothers blinded in one eye by picking up a hand grenade, and Serbian troops shoot his grandfather in the head, killing him. In the UK, he and a friend were accosted by two other youths and his friend was subjected to a brutal attack. When the assailants ran away, the appellant followed and, armed with a razor knife, which he had in his possession, he slashed the neck of one, narrowly missing the jugular vein. The evidence was that this response was induced by the effect of trauma. The Court of Appeal held that the low risk of reoffending should not outweigh what they considered to be a deterrent effect, nor the policy of the Secretary of State that those who committed serious offences should be deported.

Subsequent case law has relied on and applied *N (Kenya)* and *OH (Serbia)*, now referred to by the Court of Appeal in *PK (Congo) v SSHD* [2013] EWCA Civ 1500 as the 'threefold criteria of risk of re-offending, the need for deterrence and public revulsion in relation to serious criminal activity' (para 24). The cases may identify policy engaged by the particular facts, for example, in *AL (Jamaica) v SSHD* [2008] EWCA Civ 482 it was the Secretary of State's policy of deporting people who committed drugs offences which the Court held must be given independent weight. In *DS (India) v SSHD* [2009] EWCA Civ 544, in the case of a reformed gambler, the Court of Appeal upheld the Tribunal's decision that, even if he did not reoffend, the public interest extended to deterring serious crime generally, and to upholding public abhorrence of offences of dishonesty, and in particular the armed robbery he had committed to finance his gambling. In *SSHD v Omar* [2009] EWCA Civ 383, the Court of Appeal held that the Secretary of State's nine-month delay in filing notice of appeal did not indicate that she was serious in her assertion that the public good necessitated removing Mr Omar from the UK.

All of these deportation decisions except that in *DS (India)* were taken before July 2006, and thus were governed by what we may call the 'old' deportation rules. Paragraph 364 of these rules required that the public interest in deportation be balanced against a list of personal factors relating to the proposed deportee which concerned their life and connections in the UK and was arguably broader than Article 8. The weighting given by the Court of Appeal in *N (Kenya)* to the Secretary of State's policy was a parallel development to a rule change in 2006, which abolished that list and provided as follows:

- where a person is liable to deportation
- the presumption is that the public interest requires it
- SSHD will consider all relevant factors in each case BUT
- only in exceptional cases will public interest in deportation be outweighed
- EXCEPT where deportation is contrary to Human Rights or Refugee Convention.

This rule change was an interim step, and in 2007 the UK Borders Act continued the direction of travel by giving statutory approval to the Secretary of State's deportation decisions.

15.7.1 **UK Borders Act 2007 ss 32–39**

Section 32 provides that, where a person is sentenced to a period of imprisonment of at least 12 months, or is sentenced to a period of imprisonment of any length but has committed an offence specified under Nationality, Immigration and Asylum Act 2002 s 72(4) (none are presently specified), their deportation is automatically deemed to be conducive to the public good and the Secretary of State is obliged to make a deportation order (s 32(5)). The exceptions are where deportation would breach a person's ECHR or EC law rights, or breach the Refugee or Trafficking Convention, or they are subject to hospital orders or extradition proceedings, or the person was a minor at the date of conviction. The exceptions do not mean that no deportation order will be made (s 33), but rather that there is no duty to make the deportation order, and that there is a right of appeal on the grounds of the exceptions. There is no right of appeal against an 'automatic' deportation outside the exceptions, though the decision that s 32(5) applies is itself appealable (2002 Act s 82 (3A)).

Section 33(7) provides that in the case of exceptions based on EU law, ECHR rights, or the Refugee Convention, the presumption remains intact that the deportation is for the public good, even if the deportation is overturned by the Court on the basis of the exceptions. The effect of this was taken into account by the Court of Appeal in *SS (Nigeria) v SSHD* [2013] EWCA Civ 550 to make the point in the context of an Article 8 argument that:

[t]he pressing nature of the public interest here is vividly informed by the fact that by Parliament's express declaration the public interest is injured if the criminal's deportation is not effected. (para 54)

In *RS (immigration and family court proceedings) India* [2012] UKUT 00218(IAC) the Tribunal mentioned this presumption in the course of deciding that there was no bar to making a deportation decision pursuant to the UK Borders Act after a period of discretionary leave (para 41). The deportation remained for the public good. The effect of s 33(7) is perhaps most lucidly explained by Aikens LJ in *RU (Bangladesh) v SSHD* [2011] EWCA Civ 651, where he says that the presumption means that it is not open to the appellant to argue that their deportation is not conducive to the public good, and it is not necessary for the Secretary of State to argue that it is (para 34).

The more difficult issue is to determine the relationship between the statutory presumption and the weighing of public interest in Article 8 cases. After a number of Court of Appeal cases the matter was not entirely clear. In *RU (Bangladesh) v SSHD* [2011] EWCA Civ 651 the Court held that both the SSHD and any reviewing tribunal must take into account the public interest factors specified in *OH Serbia* when considering the proportionality of deportation under Article 8. See also *AP (Trinidad and Tobago) v SSHD* [2011] EWCA Civ 551 and *Gurung v SSHD* [2012] EWCA Civ 62. Chapter 5 discusses the Tribunal case of *Sanade*, which treated Article 8 as unaffected by the statutory presumption. Guidelines in *Masih (deportation—public interest—basic principles) Pakistan* [2012] UKUT 00046 (IAC) state the principles as:

(i)   In a case of automatic deportation, full account must be taken of the strong public interest in removing foreign citizens convicted of serious offences, which lies not only in the prevention of further offences on the part of the individual concerned, but in deterring others from committing them in the first place;

(ii) Deportation of foreign criminals expresses society's condemnation of serious criminal activity and promotes public confidence in the treatment of foreign citizens who have committed them;

(iii) The starting-point for assessing the facts of the offence of which an individual has been convicted, and their effect on others, and on the public as a whole, must be the view taken by the sentencing judge;

(iv) The appeal has to be dealt with on the basis of the situation at the date of the hearing;

(v)   Full account should also be taken of any developments since sentence was passed, for example the result of any disciplinary adjudications in prison or detention, or any OASys or licence report;

(vi) In considering the relevant facts on private and family life under article 8 of the European Convention on Human Rights, 'for a settled migrant who has lawfully spent all or the major part of his or her childhood and youth in [this] country, very serious reasons are required to justify expulsion';

(vii) Such serious reasons are needed 'all the more so where the person concerned committed the relevant offences as a juvenile' but 'very serious violent offences can justify expulsion even if they were committed by a minor' Other very serious offending may also have this consequence.

However, as discussed in chapter 5, new immigration rules were introduced in 2012 attempting to limit the scope of Article 8 in automatic deportation cases (para 398 to 399A IR). This was followed by an amendment to the Immigration Bill in January 2014 designed to remove all ECHR exceptions bar Articles 2 and 3 from the automatic deportation regime. This was hotly debated both in terms of the sovereignty of parliament and as to whether it would increase appeals to Strasbourg. In any event, the amendment was defeated but the political imperative to close down Article 8 appeals in foreign national prisoner cases remained a live issue and Part 5A of the Immigration Act 2014 returned to this issue.

Section 19 of the Immigration Act 2014, brought into force as from 14 July 2014, now adds to the Nationality, Immigration and Asylum Act 2002 a new Part 5A entitled 'Article 8 of the ECHR: public interest considerations' comprising four new sections, 117A, 117B, 117C, and 117D. Section 117A states that Part 5A applies where a court or tribunal has to determine whether a Home Office immigration decision breaches a person's right to respect for private and family life under Article 8 and as a result would be unlawful under s 6 of the Human Rights Act 1998. In such a case the court or tribunal must have regard to the 'public interest question', which means the question whether an interference with a person's right to respect for private and family life is justified under Article 8.2.

Section 117C sets out the additional matters that must be taken into account in considering the public interest question in relation to foreign criminals. 'Foreign criminal' for this purpose means a person who is not a British citizen, who has been convicted in the UK of an offence, and who has been sentenced to a period of imprisonment of at least 12 months or has been convicted of an offence that has caused serious harm or is a persistent offender.

Subsections (1) and (2) of s 117C state that the deportation of foreign criminals is in the public interest and the more serious the offence committed, the greater the public interest in deportation. Further factors to be taken into consideration are set out in the Criminality Guidance s 2.3 (*Immigration Directorate Instructions: Criminality Guidance in Article 8 ECHR cases, 28 July 2014*) and include:

- the more criminal convictions a foreign criminal has, the greater the public interest in deportation;
- it is in the public interest to deport a foreign criminal even where there is evidence of remorse or rehabilitation or that he presents a low risk of offending;
- the role of deportation as an expression of society's revulsion at serious crimes, and in building public confidence in the treatment of non-British nationals who have committed serious crimes is a very important facet of the public interest in deporting a foreign criminal.

Subsection (3) provides for the case of a foreign criminal who has not been sentenced to a period of imprisonment of four years or more. The public interest requires the deportation unless one of two specific exceptions applies. The first exception is the case where the individual has been resident in the UK for most of his/her life, is socially and culturally integrated, and would face significant obstacles to integration in the country to which it is proposed that s/he be deported. The second exception is where the foreign criminal has a genuine and subsisting relationship with a partner who is settled in the UK or with a qualifying child and the effect of that person's deportation on the partner or child as the case may be would be unduly harsh.

The meaning of 'unduly harsh' has been considered in the Upper Tribunal but with conflicting results. In *MAB (para 399; 'unduly harsh') USA* [2015] UKUT 435 (IAC) it was held that unduly harsh does not require any sort of balancing exercise between the public interest and the circumstances of the individual child or partner of the deportee. However, in the more recent case of *KMO (section 117—unduly harsh)* [2015] UKUT (IAC) it was held that these words do import a balancing exercise that requires consideration of the statutory presumptions. Arguably, the first decision should be preferred as it is unclear how an assessment of the effect on a child or partner could include consideration of an offence committed by a different person. Further, the rule is framed as an exception to deportation and so it is difficult to find a legal justification for carrying out a balancing exercise not required in the rule itself.

Controversially, the Act also grants a power to the Secretary of State to certify deportation appeals so that they can only be heard from abroad on the grounds that (in particular) the appellant would not, before the appeals process is exhausted, face a real risk of serious irreversible harm if removed to the country or territory to which s/he is proposed to be removed (s 94B NIAA 2002).

The guidance observes that the test of irreversible harm relates to the period between deportation and the conclusion of any appeal, after which the person will return to the UK if successful, and that the test requires that the harm be serious AND irreversible. It then goes on to suggest situations that in the opinion of the Home Office would not meet the test: (s 94B of the Nationality, Immigration and Asylum Act 2002, Version 5, 30 October 2015)

- a person will be separated from their child/partner for several months while the individual appeals against a human rights decision;
- a family court case is in progress;
- a child/partner is undergoing treatment for a temporary or chronic medical condition that is under control and can be satisfactorily managed through medication or other treatment and does not require the person liable to deportation to act as a full time carer;
- the FNO has a medical issue which does not lead to an Article 3 breach;
- a person has strong private life ties to a community that will be disrupted by deportation (e.g. they have a job, a mortgage, a prominent role in a community organization etc.) (para 3.17).

It might be thought that the family court case suggestion is clearly wrong. A person usually needs to be physically present in the UK in contested family court proceedings as various assessments are often needed that will be impossible if the person is not present in the UK.

The guidance also gives examples of situations that in the view of the Home Office would meet the test:

- the person has a genuine and subsisting parental relationship with a child who is seriously ill, requires full-time care, and there is no one else who can provide that care;
- the person has a genuine and subsisting long-term relationship with a partner who is seriously ill and requires full-time care because they are unable to care for themselves, and there is no one else who can provide that care (para 3.18).

The Court of Appeal has recently given guidance on the correct test to be applied when a claim is to be certified in *R (On the application of Kiarie) v Secretary of State for the Home Department* [2015] EWCA Civ 1020.

 Key Case

***R (On the application of Kiarie) v Secretary of State for the Home Department* [2015] EWCA Civ 1020.**

This was a test case on the meaning and effect of s 94 B of the Nationality, Immigration and Asylum Act 2002 as amended by the Immigration Act 2014. Lord Justice Richards giving the leading judgment noted that the correct test to be applied is that in subsection 2, namely the power to certify arises only 'if the Secretary of State considers that . . . removal of (the foreign national) ... would not be unlawful under s 6 of the Human Rights Act 1998'. Under subsection 3, a ground for certification is that the person would not, before the appeals process is exhausted, face a 'real risk of serious, irreversible harm' if removed but this does not displace the statutory condition in subsection 2. Effectively, the correct test is therefore whether removal for the duration of the appeal will breach the appellant's human rights, not whether it will cause serious irreversible harm.

Further, in relation to the public interest in removal pending an appeal, Richards LJ notes as Parliament has specifically legislated to remove foreign criminals pending their appeals, there is a strong public interest in such an outcome.

It was argued on behalf of Mr Kiarie not that out of country appeals would breach a person's human rights in all cases but that in this case, it would deprive the appellant of effective involvement in the appeals process and would result in unfairness because:

(a) Out of country appeals are generally less effective than in country appeals.
(b) Removal during the appeals process would create significant practical difficulties in obtaining, preparing and presenting evidence, particularly if no video link was available.
(c) It would impact on the overall fairness and appearance of fairness of the proceedings.
(d) It would diminish the appellant's chances of success and enhance the Secretary of State's prospects of successfully resisting the appeal.

These arguments were rejected by the court on the basis that, whilst one party would be at a disadvantage, Article 8 merely requires access to a procedure that meets the essential requirements of effectiveness and fairness. Out of country appeals have been in place in entry clearance cases for many years and are said to be favourable to appellants (although the success statistics were not disclosed in the judgment). It was held that 'The Secretary of State is entitled . . . to rely on the specialist immigration judges . . . to ensure that an appellant is given effective access to the decision making process and the process is fair to the appellant, irrespective of whether the appeal is brought in country or out of country.'

Lawyers acting for appellants have expressed concern at this judgment on a number of grounds. Firstly, some reports, such as an independent social worker's report on a parent's relationship and interaction with their children, would be impossible to obtain from abroad. Further, whilst Lord Justice Richards referred to the possibility of exceptional legal aid funding as considered in *R (Gudanaviciene) v Director of Legal Aid Casework* [2014] EWHC 1840 (Admin) if a case is particularly complex, the court did not consider how this funding could be obtained without considerable pro bono assistance from a lawyer in the UK. Finally, despite the fact that the Tribunal may be willing to hear evidence by video link (*Nare (evidence by electronic means) Zimbabwe* [2011] UKUT 443 (IAC)), it will be extremely difficult for litigants in person to make arrangements for and bear the cost of video link evidence from abroad.

Automatic deportation goes in exactly the opposite direction to the development of EC law, in which, as we have seen in chapter 4, deportation must be based on the personal conduct of the individual and the risk they present to society, and is a last resort for very serious reasons, in fact intended to be rare where the individual has lived in the host country for more than five years.

15.7.2 **Deportation outside the UK Borders Act**

In cases outside the UK Borders Act, the Secretary of State still has discretion to decide whether deportation is 'conducive to the public good'. These include minors, where the proposed deportee has not received a prison sentence of the kind covered by the section, or in cases not based on criminal convictions. An accumulation of shorter sentences can be relied on as grounds for a decision that deportation is in the public interest.

The Tribunal case of Bah *(EO (Turkey)—liability to deport)* [2012] UKUT 00196 (IAC) held that, in a non-Borders Act case, it was necessary to apply the approach set out in *EO (Turkey)*, the definitive case interpreting the pre-Borders Act (post-2006) immigration rules on deportation. This reasoning begins with the question of whether the person is liable to be deported. Where the facts are contested, as in the present case, this requires a variation on *EO (Turkey)*, and the Tribunal held that it means that the factual basis for the Secretary of State's allegations must be established, to a standard of balance of probabilities, flexibly applied. The Tribunal affirmed its power to consider any evidence before it, and, rather than to exclude evidence which was not sourced, to decide what weight to give to such evidence. It was for the Tribunal to make its own decision as to whether the discretion to deport had been correctly exercised, and whether the appellant was liable to deportation. The Tribunal was 'entitled to have regard to the precautionary and preventative principles rather than to wait until directly harmful activities have taken place' (para 61, quoting *Rehman*). The Tribunal approved the application of a standard of a reasonable degree of likelihood to this part of the decision. In so doing, the Tribunal approximated the approach in ordinary deportation appeals to that in national security deportations, treating the determination of what is conducive to the public good as a judgment based on future risk as much as past conduct. However, unlike cases in the Special Immigration Appeals Commission (SIAC), there is no power for the First-tier Tribunal to base a decision on evidence submitted by the Home Office and not disclosed to the appellant.

15.7.3 **Political reasons**

Interestingly, the deeming sections in the UK Borders Act do not necessarily apply to deportations under s 3(5)(a) where the ground of the decision is that deportation is conducive to the public good as being in the interests of national security or of the relations between the UK and any other country (Nationality, Immigration and Asylum Act 2002 s 97(2)). The reason for this is that proposed deportees do not necessarily have criminal convictions; the decision is based on the Secretary of State's assessment of the risk that the person poses to national security. However, an amendment in the Crime and Courts Act 2013, described below, has an even more draconian effect.

Before the 2002 Act the national security ground also included 'other reasons of a political nature'. Unlike other deportations under s 3(5)(a), national security appeals do not go through the ordinary appeal process, but only to the SIAC (see chapter 7). The Secretary of State also has power to take proceedings out of the ordinary appeal process and transfer them to the SIAC if s/he certifies that the decision was made wholly or partly in reliance on information that ought not to be disclosed for reasons of public interest or national security or relations with other states (s 97(3)). Where a deportation case is transferred to the SIAC, the Crime and Courts Act 2013 s 54 (amending the 2002 Act) permits the Secretary of State to certify that removal of the person would not breach the ECHR. The effect of such a certificate is that the appeal against deportation (on any grounds) may not be brought or continued while the person is in the UK. The grounds on which such a certificate may be issued include that:

(a) the person would not, before the appeals process is exhausted, face a real risk of serious irreversible harm if removed . . . ;

(b) the whole or part of any human rights claim made by the person is clearly unfounded. (2002 Act s. 97A (2C) as substituted)

As in other areas of law, where national security is in issue, the balance between the state and the individual shifts further towards the state, involving curtailment of the rights of the individual.

15.7.3.1 Basis of political deportation

Although so-called 'political' or 'national security' deportations are treated differently from others, the formal grounds for such a deportation are still that the deportation is conducive to the public good. National security and international relations may overlap. The Secretary of State is not obliged to settle the allegations in such a way that they fit into one or another category (*SSHD v Rehman* [2001] 3 WLR 877). The decision to deport may be described for instance as being 'in the interests of national security, namely the likelihood of your involvement in terrorist activity'. The specificity of allegations depends upon the view that the Secretary of State takes of any risks of disclosing sources. See discussion of evidence in the next section and chapter 7.

Before the case of *Chahal v UK* (1997) 23 EHRR 413 (see chapter 7), there was no right of appeal to a judicial body against a political or national security deportation. As described in chapter 7, the SIAC was the UK's response to the *Chahal* judgment, and the first case in the SIAC holds an important place in the development of the law on national security deportations.

15.7.3.2 Rehman's case—standard of proof and evidence in national security cases

 Key Case

SSHD v Rehman **[2001] 3 WLR 877**

Mr Rehman was a Muslim minister of religion who had limited leave to remain under the immigration rules in that capacity. He was married and had two children born in the UK. He was refused indefinite leave to remain on the grounds that the Secretary of State was satisfied that Mr Rehman was involved with a terrorist organization, and that in the light of that association his continued presence in the country represented a danger to national security.

The Secretary of State added that his deportation from the UK would be conducive to the public good in the interests of national security because of his association with Islamic terrorist groups. The organization was named, though the Secretary of State's view was formed on the basis of information received from confidential sources.

The SIAC found that the evidence did not establish the acts alleged, namely that Mr Rehman had recruited British Muslims to undergo militant training, or engaged in fundraising for Lashkar Tayyaba (LT), or knowingly sponsored individuals for militant training camps. It was accepted that he had provided sponsorship, information, and advice to people going to Pakistan for training. Such training he had regarded as purely religious and developmental. It had not been proved that he was aware of any militant content in such training.

In addition to the question of the jurisdiction of the Commission, two questions of law were appealed to the Court of Appeal and House of Lords. The first was the standard of proof to be applied. The SIAC took the view that these were serious allegations which had important repercussions for the individual involved and which impugned his good character. For these reasons, a standard of proof such as that laid down in *Khawaja* [1984] AC 74 should be applied, that is, a high civil standard of proof. Using this standard, they found that the matters alleged against Mr Rehman were not proved. The Court of Appeal and some members of the House of Lords approved the standard as applied to the appellant's actual involvement in alleged terrorist activities, but all found that the question of danger to national security required an all-round assessment of the situation, not just a finding of, as it were, guilt or innocence in relation to past events. The Court of Appeal said: 'it is necessary not only to look at the individual allegations and ask whether they have been proved. It is also necessary to examine the case as a whole against an individual and then ask whether on a global approach that individual is a danger to national security' ([2000] 3 All ER 778 at 791). The House of Lords approved this view and said that the Secretary of State was 'entitled to have regard to precautionary and preventative principles rather than to wait until directly harmful activities have taken place' (para 22). In fact, the idea of a standard of proof was, said Lords Steyn and Hoffmann, not really appropriate to a case where the central question was not, as in a civil or criminal trial, whether something had happened in the past, but rather whether something was likely to happen in the future. It was an evaluation of risk. The effect of this is that the Secretary of State is entitled to make a decision that an individual who cannot be proved to a criminal standard to have taken part in any unlawful activities should be deported because there is, in the words of Lord Slynn, a 'real possibility' that their presence may in the future constitute a danger.

The second issue in the appeals was the question of the definition of national security. First, there was the question of whether the SIAC had jurisdiction to engage in the question of defining national security. The House of Lords held that this could be within the jurisdiction of a judicial body; it was a question of construction and therefore a question of law. The area of contention between the parties was whether activities in the UK that furthered the cause of an organization abroad that could use violence which was not directed at the UK, could be said to endanger the security of the UK. The SIAC accepted the appellant's argument that for an activity to endanger the national security of the UK there must be some direct link between the activity and a danger to the UK. The House of Lords and Court of Appeal rejected this view. They adopted the approach of Auld LJ in *Raghbir Singh* [1996] Imm AR 507, who said at 511, 'all sorts of consequences may flow from the existence of terrorist conspiracies or organizations here, whether or not their outcome is intended to occur abroad. Who knows what equally violent response here this sort of conduct may provoke?' and of Lord Mustill in the asylum case of *T* [1996] Imm AR 443, that 'terror as a means of gaining what might loosely be described as political ends poses a danger not only to individual states but also to the community of nations'. Lord Slynn said:

It seems to me that, in contemporary world conditions, action against a foreign state may be capable indirectly of affecting the security of the United Kingdom. The means open to terrorists both in attacking another state and attacking international or global activity by the community of nationals, whatever the objectives of the terrorist, may well be capable of reflecting on the safety and well-being of the United Kingdom or its citizens . . . To require the matters in question to be capable of resulting 'directly' in a threat to national security limits too tightly the discretion of the executive in deciding how the interests of the state . . . need to be protected.

This approach is an international one, in which the fight against terrorism is seen as something in which nations have a common interest. National security is bound up with international security, and in the context of terrorism this enables the Secretary of State to justify a decision on national security by reference to damage to relations between countries.

The House of Lords made a distinction between deciding what national security is, which the courts could decide, and what is *in the interests of national security*, which they regarded as a matter for the Secretary of State to decide. In the words of Lord Hoffmann: 'the question of whether something is "in the interests" of national security is not a question of law. It is a matter of judgment and policy' (para 50). Such judgments should be made by someone who was democratically accountable, not by the courts.

Macdonald commented on this case at the Court of Appeal stage: 'Not since the majority decision *Liversidge and Anderson* has the executive been given such deference; one can hear the Secretary of State saying "I can make national security mean anything I want it to mean"' (2001:724).

Macdonald was commenting in May 2001, and his comparison with *Liversidge and Anderson* [1942] AC 206 was prophetic. That decision is often explained on the basis that it was taken during wartime, when the government needs to be given more scope to act as it sees fit, even in breach of people's ordinary civil liberties. The response of the UK and US to the attack on the World Trade Center, on 11 September 2001, was to legislate in a way that is reminiscent of wartime, in the extent of inroads made into civil liberties.

This approach to the standard of proof and assessment of national security risk is similar to that used in refugee claims to assess future risk should the asylum seeker return to their country of origin, and the authority on that point, *Karanakaran*, is used also in national security appeals. For instance, in *Y v SSHD* [2006] UKSIAC 36/2004, SIAC held that the proceedings were not civil proceedings, requiring acts to be proved on a balance of probabilities. 'They are public law proceedings the focus of which is risk, that is an evaluation of what harm may happen in the future' (para 128). This draws directly on *Karanakaran* and remains the approved approach in the SIAC for deportations based on national security considerations. Y was arrested on suspicion of being concerned in the instigation, preparation, or commission of acts of terrorism. He was tried as a defendant in the 'ricin' or 'poisons plot' trial but acquitted on all charges. Like other potential deportees on national security grounds, he did not hear all the evidence against him, as some was considered in 'closed' sessions of the SIAC. He was shown to be linked to militant organizations in Algeria, indeed facts related to this had formed the basis of his asylum claim which had succeeded on appeal some years earlier. Y could be shown to have connections and associations with people who were found culpable. For instance, he ran the bookshop at the mosque associated with extremist activity, and appeared to have photocopied the poison recipes. As the SIAC said, in isolation, each matter might be explicable as 'innocent'. Crucially, they decided that treating the matters as separate was not the right approach. They should be regarded cumulatively, and in that way they built a picture of someone the Secretary of State could legitimately regard as a risk. This approach was confirmed in *ZZ*, quoting from *Rehman*:

the whole concept of a standard of proof is not particularly helpful in a case such as the present . . . the question . . . is not whether a given event happened but the extent of future risk. This depends upon an evaluation of the evidence of the appellant's conduct against a broad range of facts with which they may interact. The question of whether the risk to national security is sufficient to justify the appellant's deportation cannot be answered by taking each allegation seriatim and deciding whether it has been established to some standard of proof. It is a question of evaluation and judgment, in which it is necessary to take into account not only the degree of probability of prejudice to national security but also the importance of the security interest at stake and the serious consequences of deportation for the deportee. (para 56)

In considering the correct standard of proof, the SIAC has cited its own expertise as a source of authority in matters of national security. For instance, in refusing an application to debar an ex-Director General of the security service from hearing a deportation appeal as a member of the SIAC, Mitting J said that the involvement of someone with experience of the use of high-level intelligence information was essential to the proper functioning of the SIAC. He pointed out that the SIAC was not a 'passive referee of evidence, material and arguments submitted to it by the parties' but an expert tribunal (*Zatuliveter v SSHD(Deportation—The hearing of an application by the appellant—Refused*) [2011] UKSIAC 103/2010. In the substantive appeal, the crucial issue was whether or not the appellant was a Russian intelligence agent. If she was, she was liable to be deported in the interests of national security. It was unusual for a SIAC deportation to be based solely on a finding of fact about events that had occurred, and SIAC observed that *Rehman* did not solve the question of the standard of proof to be applied. Continuing the theme of SIAC's expertise, Mitting J did not accept Lord Hoffmann's premise in *Rehman*

that the Secretary of State 'has the advantage of a wide range of advice from people with day to day involvement in security matters which the Commission, despite its specialist membership, cannot match'. For the reasons explained in paragraphs 3–11 of *Al-Jedda* SC/66/2008, 7th April 2009, we believe that we are able to, and do, give more careful and detailed scrutiny to the risk posed by an individual appellant to national security than the Secretary of State can reasonably be expected to do.

Mitting J said that the SIAC routinely made findings of fact on the balance of probabilities and would do so in that case.

Although the deportation of Abu Qatada (see chapter 5) was held lawful on grounds of national security by the SIAC and upheld along with others by the House of Lords (*RB (Algeria), U and OO (Jordan) v SSHD* [2009] UKHL 10), the questions of law in these appeals did not turn on the question of whether the deportation was conducive to the public good, but on the nature of SIAC proceedings and admissible evidence, discussed in chapter 7, and on the government's reliance on assurances of fair treatment in the country to which they were to be deported. The Court of Appeal in *W (Algeria)* held that despite this, the approach of their Lordships to the evidence required before the SIAC could be applied when the evidence required to justify a deportation on the grounds of national security was directly in issue (para 56).

Procedural rules are restrictive in national security cases. In some proceedings concerning national security, case law has established a right to disclosure of an 'irreducible minimum' of evidence (see chapter 7). The UK courts have held that this does not apply where deportation or exclusion are challenged, because Article 6 ECHR does not apply (see *Maaouia*, chapter 5), and civil rights in the ECHR sense are not at stake (*W and others (Algeria) v SSHD* [2010] EWCA Civ 898 and *IR (Sri Lanka)*). The appellants in *W (Algeria)* argued that the common law principles of a fair trial required the SIAC rules to be read down so as to enable disclosure of the gist of the case against them. The Court of Appeal held that they were not empowered to read down SIAC's explicit rules where the enabling statute clearly contemplated that priority could be given to the need to protect national security. Parliament had approved the rules by affirmative resolution (para 51). The only procedural right for the deportee or excluded person is to 'independent scrutiny of the claim' (*IR (Sri Lanka) and others v SSHD* [2011] EWCA Civ 704 (para 19)). This has now been mitigated in the case of EU nationals—see *ZZ v SSHD* Case C-300/11 in chapter 7.

The Immigration, Asylum and Nationality Act 2006 includes a provision that deportation orders may be made on the grounds of threat to national security while an appeal is pending or may be brought, in contrast with other deportations in which no order may be made until the appeal process is exhausted (s 7, excluding application of s 79 of the 2002 Act).

15.7.4 Family members

Apart from deportations conducive to the public good, the only other people who may be deported since the implementation of the 1999 Act are family members of people who are deported under s 3(5)(a). Note that these deportations now take place under s 3(5)(b) of the 1971 Act, whereas in case law prior to October 2000 they will be referred to as s 3(5)(c). 'Family members' are defined by the 1971 Act s 5(4), as amended by the 1996 Act, as the husband or wife and children of the person to be deported. 'Children' include adopted children. When parents are unmarried, children are regarded as children of only their mother. Although the entry of second or further wives is not permitted under the immigration rules, in the context of deportation polygamy is recognized, as 'wife' includes each of two or more wives.

Paragraphs 365–6 of the immigration rules give guidance on the deportation of family members, including civil partners, though these are not mentioned in the Act. According to these paragraphs, the Secretary of State will not normally decide to deport the partner of a deportee where they have qualified for settlement in their own right or have been living apart from the deportee. If a child is living apart from the deportee either with their other parent or because they have established themselves on an independent basis, the Secretary of State will not normally decide to deport the child. This is also the case where the child married before the deportation 'came into prospect'. Additional factors previously taken into account in the deportation of family members have been deleted from the immigration rules.

Following *Beoku-Betts* and s 55 Borders Citizenship and Immigration Act 2009, factors concerning the welfare of family members should have already been taken into account when finalizing the deportation, and considering an Article 8 defence to it.

According to s 5(3) of the 1971 Act, a deportation order may not be made against family members if more than eight weeks have elapsed since the principal deportee left the country. Again, this in practical terms only applies where the family member has a viable life in the UK aside from their deported relative. In the case of a child who attains the age of 18 during appeal proceedings, it would not be appropriate to continue a para 3(5)(b) deportation against them. This is apparent from the facts of *LH (Nigeria) v SSHD* [2013] EWCA Civ 26 though not at issue in that case, as the Secretary of State granted the appellant's son discretionary leave when he attained 18.

15.7.5 Criminal court's recommendation

Section 3(6) of the 1971 Act gives the power to the Secretary of State to deport following the recommendation of a criminal court. The power to make such a recommendation is a sentencing power which may be exercised by the courts in relation to a non-British citizen over the age of 17 who has been convicted of an offence that is punishable with imprisonment. Appeals against the recommendation itself are appeals against sentence and are made through the criminal appeals process.

The decision whether to follow the recommendation is a separate step, and this is the responsibility of the Secretary of State. Apart from exceptional cases, a sentence of the Court is the only circumstance in which an Irish national will be deported (EIG Service of Notice of Intention to Deport 15.9). The recommendation of the sentencing judge does not bind the Secretary of State. Case law held that s/he has a different constitutional role in the decision-making process and is better placed to take a wider policy-based view of whether deportation is the right course (*R v SSHD ex p Dinc* [1999] Imm AR 380 CA).

15.7.5.1 Criminal courts and deportation

The general powers of the criminal courts include sentencing for immigration offences. On the other hand, people who are liable to deportation for an offence which has nothing to do with immigration may not have a flawless immigration history. There is plenty of scope for confusion here. Macdonald used some choice words to describe an aspect of the problem:

Matters have not been assisted by the tendency of the courts to describe any non-citizen guilty of an offence under the Immigration Act as an 'illegal immigrant'. The phrase is meaningless and has pejorative connotations of status that may be misleading. A student who fails to get the Department of Employment's permission before getting a summer job, a husband who forgets to apply in time for permission to remain with a wife, an alien who fails to inform the police of a change of address, are doubtless all guilty of offences which may be described as regulatory, but it would be as inappropriate to describe them as 'illegal immigrants' as it would be to describe the company which fails to make expeditious VAT returns as an illegal business. (1995:489)

Deportation as a sentence for an immigration offence is not appropriate unless it would be warranted in accordance with the proper criteria for deportation.

15.7.5.2 Guidelines

Guidelines for the criminal courts in exercising their power to recommend deportation were set out initially in *R v Caird* (1970) 54 Cr App Rep 499, CA and developed in *R v Nazari* [1980] 3 All ER 880. These, of course, now apply only in cases where the sentence is of less than 12 months' imprisonment, and yet the Court considers that deportation may be appropriate. The Court of Appeal in *R v Kluxen* [2010] Crim CA 1081 noted that such cases will be rare. The Court held that the threshold for a recommendation of deportation in *Nazari* is a high one, corresponding to the test in the leading EU case of *Bouchereau* (see chapter 4).

The first guideline from *Nazari* is that criminal courts are concerned with the potential detriment to the UK of the person remaining in the country. This has been regarded as nothing to do with their immigration status as the detriment is through criminal activity. However, in *R v Benabbas* [2005] EWCA Crim 2113, the Court of Appeal held that where deportation was for using a forged passport, immigration status is 'not entirely irrelevant: it is part of the defendant's personal conduct . . . a matter of public interest' (para 40) and 'detriment is intimately bound up with the protection of public order afforded by confidence in a system of passports' (para 41). The risk of reoffending is a key matter to be assessed, and the Court will also have regard to the nature of the offence and the defendant's past record.

Second, the Court in *Nazari* thought that they should not be concerned with the political situation or regime or any political threat in the defendant's home country. The Home Office rather than the criminal court was the place to assess such matters.

The Court in *Kluxen* then sets out the matters that a court recommending deportation should not take into account. These are:

i) the rights of the offender under the ECHR. As explained by Stanley Burnton J. in *R. v. Carmona* [2006] 2 Cr. App. R. (S.) 662: the Secretary of State and, in the event of an appeal, the Asylum and Immigration Tribunal, are able and better placed than a sentencing court to consider the offender's Convention rights;

ii) the effect that a recommendation for deportation might have on innocent persons not before the Court, such as members of the family of the offender concerned (*Carmona* overturned *Nazari* in this regard);

iii) the political situation in the country to which the offender may be deported (following both *Nazari* and *Carmona*).

The Court in *Kluxen* rejected the view that a criminal court, if considering a deportation order against an EU national, should take into account the period of the offender's residence in the UK, and other personal circumstances listed in Article 28 of the Citizens Directive. Taking a similar approach to the Court in *Carmona*, the Court held that these were matters to be considered when a deportation order was made, not when the Court made a recommendation for deportation. The same consideration applied to factors under the 2006 EEA Regulations. In any event, it was highly unlikely that the Court would be considering such a recommendation, as the Secretary of State's policy was that no citizen of the European Economic Area would be removed unless the prison sentence imposed was two years or more (para 30).

15.8 **Revocation**

A deportation order does not expire after a period of time. It runs until it is revoked, unless the person who is the subject of the order becomes a British citizen (1971 Act s 5(2)). However, it may be revoked on application in accordance with paras 390–2 of the immigration rules. The factors which will be taken into account are:

(i) the grounds on which the order was made;

(ii) any representations made in support of revocation;

(iii) the interests of the community, including the maintenance of effective immigration control; and

(iv) the interests of the applicant, including any compassionate circumstances.

In the case of deportation based on criminal convictions, para 391 provides for a normal minimum period of time that should elapse after making the deportation order before revocation is considered. This is now ten years in the case of offences for which the person was sentenced to prison for less than four years. In the case of offences which attracted a longer sentence, deportation is indefinite, unless human rights or the Refugee Convention require otherwise. The limit of four years is the new maximum sentence which is capable of being spent under the Rehabilitation of Offenders Act 1974. The same statute which increased the maximum sentence also provided that immigration and nationality decisions are exempt from the Rehabilitation of Offenders Act 1974, so that even spent convictions must be declared for immigration applications, and may be taken into account in deportation decisions and revocation of deportation orders (Legal Aid Sentencing and Punishment of Offenders Act 2012 s 141 inserting s 56A into the UK Borders Act 2007).

The rule goes on to say 'in other cases' revocation will not normally be authorized, unless there is a change of circumstances or fresh information which might materially alter the situation. The passage of time in itself may amount to a change of circumstance (para 391A). 'Other cases' are those not based on criminal convictions. Clearly, there is some discretion in criminal cases, too, as the ten-year and indefinite provisions are the norm, not the rule, and even without such provision in the immigration rules, public law principles would require it (e.g., *British Oxygen v Minister of Technology* [1971] AC 610). Even before the 2008 rule change, the Home Office's internal guidance on deportation suggested that ten years should elapse before revoking deportation orders against people convicted of serious offences. These were defined as offences of violence, persistent, or large-scale burglary or theft, blackmail, forgery, drug offences, and public order offences including riot and affray. However, some of these offences could easily attract a sentence which would now place the individual at risk of indefinite deportation. Under s 82 of the 2002 Act, there may be a right of appeal against the refusal to revoke a deportation order, but under s 92 this right may only be exercised from outside the country unless it is based on asylum or human rights grounds that have not been certified as clearly unfounded (*BA Nigeria v SSHD* [2009] UKSC 7). According to para 391 of the rules, time is counted before which an application can be made to revoke from the date of making the order. Occasionally successful public campaigns are mounted to avoid deportation even at this late stage (see, for instance, 'Resistance from Below' in *No one is Illegal* (Cohen 2003)). An application to revoke a deportation order can be made on the basis of the impact that separation has had on family left in the UK (e.g., see *Lee v SSHD* [2011] EWCA Civ 348).

Revocation of a deportation order does not entitle the successful applicant to enter the UK. It only means that an application may be made for leave to enter under the immigration rules and this will be considered on its merits. However, note *R (on the application of) George v SSHD* [2012] EWCA Civ 1362 referred to in chapter 6. In that case Mr George had not left the UK when the deportation order was revoked.

15.9 Voluntary departures

Once a person is aware that they may be subject to deportation, if there are no strong grounds to challenge the deportation they may wish to leave the country as quickly as possible to avoid a deportation order being made. If they leave before the order is made, even without contact with the Home Office, any deportation order made after that date will be invalid.

If the person leaves after the deportation order was made, they are still regarded as deported, even if they were not aware of it, and the order will have the same validity as if the Home Office had enforced it. Alternatively, a person may sign a formal disclaimer of appeal rights and agree to leave, which gives rise to the possibility of the immigration service paying for their passage (Immigration Act 1971 s 5(6)). This is known as 'supervised departure'.

The International Organisation for Migration operates voluntary return programmes for 'irregular migrants' as well as people whose asylum claims have failed. These are now conspicuously advertised by the Home Office in the case of failed asylum claims, but have no application in the case of deportation.

Voluntary departures still have an impact on re-entry—see chapter 6 at 6.8.6.

15.10 Conclusion

The increased use of deportation in recent years reflects a government policy of something approaching zero tolerance towards foreign nationals who commit criminal offences. The interaction of the automatic deportation regime with criminal sanctions for use of false documents and working without permission generates a further route to removing those whose asylum claims have failed, and who may resort to illegal working when they have no other means of support. One interesting question though is how policy is being implemented. In October 2014, the National Audit Office published a damning report on the UK's deportation process. The numbers of foreign criminals deported had actually declined since 2008–9 despite a tenfold increase in the number of staff dealing with these cases at the Home Office, from below 100 in 2006 to over 900 in 2013–14. It was apparently only in 2012 that the Government started to take preventative measures to prevent foreign criminals entering the UK. Even today the UK remains outside critical European government intelligence networks.

The report follows a similar damning indictment in March 2014 of the management of detention and deportation at the Home Office by the Chief Inspector of Borders and Immigration, John Vine. In the experience of lawyers working in the field, months at a time go by before anyone at the Home Office takes any action on a case once a decision to deport has been made and immigration bail is eventually granted to foreign criminals who cannot lawfully be detained any longer.

The important changes brought about by the Immigration Act 2014 mean that many foreign criminals will be removed whilst waiting for their appeals to be heard and only re-admitted if they later win (which is inherently less likely as they will not be present to give evidence).

QUESTIONS

1 The European Court of Human Rights in the case of *Maaouia v France* said that deportation is not a criminal penalty imposed upon a foreign national. It is not a punishment for a crime for which they have already served a prison sentence, but is an administrative matter. Consider the arguments for and against that view.

2 Is it justifiable to treat European nationals more favourably in the context of deportation?

 online resource centre For guidance on answering questions, visit the Online Resource Centre www.oxfordtextbooks.co.uk/orc/clayton7e/.

FURTHER READING

Bevan, Vaughan (1986) *The Development of British Immigration Law* (London: Croom Helm), pp. 305–9.

Cohen, Steve (2003) 'Resistance from Below' in S. Cohen (ed.) *No-one is Illegal* (Stoke-on-Trent: Trentham Books).

Farbey, Judith (2007) 'Foreign National Prisoners: Current Law and Practice' *Journal of Immigration, Asylum and Nationality Law* vol. 21, no. 1 pp. 6–13.

Independent Chief Inspector of Immigration (2014) 'An Inspection of the Emergency Travel Document Process May-September 2013'.

National Audit Office (2014) 'Managing and Removing Foreign National Offenders' HC 441 Session 2014–15, 22 October.

Shah, Ramnik (2007) 'The FNP Saga' *Journal of Immigration, Asylum and Nationality Law* vol. 21, no. 1, pp. 27–31.

16

....

Removal

SUMMARY

This chapter describes the development of the grounds in law for exercising the power to remove a person from the UK. The chapter also examines the practical obstacles to removal, which are often as important to the individual as the legal ones.

16.1 Introduction

The power of removal is the fullest exercise of the Crown's power to control the movement of foreign nationals, though this does not mean that it is an untrammelled power. It is exercised within a statutory framework. Prior to 2014, the framework for removal could be found in the Immigration Act 1971, amended and supplemented by the Asylum and Immigration Act 1996, the Immigration and Asylum Act 1999, the Nationality, Immigration and Asylum Act 2002, the Asylum and Immigration (Treatment of Claimants etc.) Act 2004, and the Immigration Asylum and Nationality Act 2006. The Immigration Act 2014 s 1 abolishes the historic distinction between overstayers and illegal entrants and replaces a number of separate powers with a single power to remove a person who requires leave to enter or remain in the UK but does not have it. The power is tempered by human rights and asylum considerations; nevertheless, in 2014, 38,767 people were removed from the UK or departed voluntarily after the initiation of a removal decision (Migration Observatory Briefing on deportations, removals and voluntary departures from the UK, 2015).

Notice of removal may be given without, necessarily, any kind of judicial process. A person may be put onto an aeroplane or a ship and taken to another country without any opportunity to challenge this course of action. Because of the abrupt and potentially speedy nature of this process, and its lack of judicial oversight, it can be described as 'summary removal'. It is difficult to imagine a more dramatic exercise of power by the executive over the individual.

Where human rights or asylum claims are made, there may be an in-country right of appeal, but not if the claim is certified as clearly unfounded by the Secretary of State (Nationality, Immigration and Asylum Act 2002 Parts 4 and 5, see chapter 11). There are other limited appeal rights, but these may only be exercised after removal. As a consequence, judicial review is often the only recourse to suspend removal.

16.1.1 Terminology

There is scope for a great deal of confusion in the use of the term 'removal' and associated phrases. One use of the term 'administrative removal' is to refer to removal on the grounds which used to be grounds for deportation, discussed at 16.2.3. This distinguishes it from removal of illegal entrants and those who are refused entry. Another use of the term 'administrative removal' is to refer to all removals, using 'administrative' to distinguish it from deportation. Finally, all enforced departures including deportation end in removal, as this term is used to describe the actual embarkation on transport that takes the person away, and all such departures are preceded by either a notice of removal or removal directions. These are served on the captain of a ship or aircraft or on a train operator, and on the person themselves, telling them when and where to report in order for their removal to take place. The term 'removal' is used in this chapter to refer to all removals as distinct from deportations. The term 'administrative removal' is not used.

16.1.2 Growth of the power to remove

The current power of removal is found in s 10 of the 1999 Immigration Act as replaced by s 1 of the Immigration Act 2014. The previous power of removal had existed since 1 January 1973, when the Immigration Act 1971 came into force. The Act made Commonwealth citizens and aliens subject to the same legal regime, and this included the power to remove anyone who had entered in breach of immigration laws (Sch 2 and s 33). *Azam v SSHD* [1974] AC 18 confirmed that this statutory power applied even to Commonwealth citizens who had entered before the Act came into effect, and who would have been immune from removal or deportation under the previous law.

The power to remove was implemented straight away. Evans charts the growth in its use from 80 people in the first year of operation to a peak of 910 in 1980, dropping again to 640 in 1981. The starting figure of 80 was, he points out, a significant increase on the steady annual figure of around 60 people removed each year from 1968 to 1972. As we shall see, the increased number of removals reflected expansion of the law governing removal at that time. After the 1971 Act extended power to Commonwealth citizens, the courts took hold of the concept of 'illegal entrant' and extended it in a way not foreseen by Parliament. In 1983, the House of Lords put the brake on this expansion. However, as described at 16.2.3, with the 1999 Act many of those previously subject to deportation became subject to removal.

The number of people removed as illegal entrants doubled from 1987 to 1988, and the UK Immigration Advisory Service suggested that this increase was part of an attempt to curtail asylum appeals (Dummett and Nicol 1990:255). The number of removals combined with voluntary departures after enforcement proceedings reached a peak in 2008 at 67,980 (Control of Immigration Statistics 2008 Home Office August 2009). The Home Office explains that the drop since that peak:

can be mostly accounted for by the significantly lower number of non-asylum cases refused entry at port and subsequently removed and has also been affected by decreasing numbers of asylum cases (Immigration Statistics published August 2011).

Although the majority of people removed have never sought asylum, the desire to process asylum claims quickly and to remove unsuccessful applicants are significant policy drivers behind the law and practice on removal. It was considered in the Home Affairs Select Committee Report on Asylum Removals that the integrity of the asylum process relies on the capacity to effect the removal of those whose claim has failed (e.g., para 8). The Committee's report also describes the practical and legal complexities of effecting removals. In 2014, only 4,372 of the 12,627 people forcibly removed had sought asylum at some stage (Immigration Statistics October 2015). See also the discussion in chapter 2.

Although governments repeatedly promise to increase the number of refused asylum seekers removed each year, there continue to be important questions about whether removals to certain countries are safe and feasible. See 16.6 on Viability of Return. The manner in which removals are carried out is also an issue of public concern.

16.2 Grounds for removal

Previously, there were two sets of powers of removal. Immigration Act 1971 Schedule 2 gave power to immigration officers to remove people who had been refused leave to enter (para 8) and illegal entrants (para 9). Immigration and Asylum Act 1999 s 10 gave power to remove people who overstayed the limit of their leave, or breached conditions of leave or obtained leave to remain by deception, and the families of such people. Additionally, Immigration Asylum and Nationality Act 2006 s 47 gave power to make a removal decision while an immigration appeal was pending. The 2014 Immigration Act replaced these separate powers with a single power (in a new s 10 of the Immigration and Asylum Act 1999) to remove a person who requires leave to enter or remain in the UK but does not have it. This could be because they never had such leave (entered illegally) or they did have leave but stayed on after it expired or was revoked.

Whilst the new power completely abolishes the historic distinction between overstayers and illegal entrants, it is still valuable to consider how these grounds had developed under the previous framework, particularly as the relevant chapters of the Enforcement Instructions and Guidance still refer to these categories.

16.2.1 Illegal entrants

The definition of an illegal entrant is found in s 33, the definition section of the 1971 Act, and the power to remove an illegal entrant was found in Schedule 2. A power which forms a major plank of immigration control would have been more appropriately located in the body of the statute. However, the power to remove was envisaged as an administrative matter, an action which could be taken speedily by immigration officers without judicial involvement.

An 'illegal entrant' is defined in s 33(1) of the 1971 Act, as amended by the Asylum and Immigration Act 1996, as a person:

(i) unlawfully entering or seeking to enter in breach of a deportation order or of the immigration laws; or

(ii) entering or seeking to enter by means which include deception by another person,

and includes a person who has entered by these means.

A person may be termed an 'illegal entrant' without actually entering, as s 33 covers those who 'seek to enter' as well as those who actually do. A person may be apprehended, say, at a port, and may be subject to removal as an illegal entrant if they were seeking to enter in breach of immigration laws but had not yet done so. A clandestine entrant may come within this category.

Second, a person may be deemed an illegal entrant if they do actually enter illegally. We shall consider shortly what this means. Third, an illegal entrant is a person 'who has so entered'. The effect of this is that there is no cut-off date for designation as an illegal entrant. Under the Commonwealth Immigrants Act 1962, a person who remained un-detected for 24 hours could not be removed; the 1968 Act extended this to 28 days but there are no such periods of grace in present law. Now, a person may live for years in insecurity, not knowing whether they will be subject to enforcement action. While a long residence in this country may affect whether enforcement action is taken or is successful, the possibility of that action remains until their status is regularized. There are a number of ways in which a person may be considered to enter illegally, and thus a person seeking to do any of these may also be an illegal entrant.

16.2.1.1 Entering without leave

'Entering in breach of the immigration laws' was initially interpreted as meaning sim-ply 'entering without leave'. The immigration laws were primarily concerned with the regulation of entry, so someone who entered in breach of those laws entered without having gone through that regulatory process. Specifically, 1971 Act s 3(1)(a) states:

Except as otherwise provided by or under this Act, where a person is not a British Citizen (a) he shall not enter the UK unless given leave to do so in accordance with this Act.

Entry without leave by someone who needs leave is therefore a breach of immigration laws in that it is a breach of s 3 of the 1971 Act. Entry without leave does not require any particular state of mind or of knowledge in order to result in a person being an illegal entrant (*R v Governor of Ashford Remand Centre ex p Bouzagou* [1983] Imm AR 69). The breach of immigration laws does not need to be deliberate or even known to a person in order for them to have entered without leave and thus be deemed an illegal entrant.

This kind of illegal entry includes clandestine entrants who arrive in the back of lor-ries or land by night in a small boat on a secluded beach. It also includes people who mistakenly enter without leave, even if the mistake is that of the immigration officer. This surprising conclusion was reached in the case of *Rehal v Secretary of State for the Home Department* [1989] Imm AR 576 CA. Mr Rehal was a British overseas citizen. The immigration officer, glancing at his British passport, thought he was a British citizen and waved him through. Without a stamp in his passport, Mr Rehal had no leave to enter. The immigration officer's invitation for him to pass through was not a grant of leave but a (barely considered) decision that he did not need leave.

The same result comes about when the mistake, though still not the fault of the passport holder, is in the passport rather than the action of the immigration officer. This was apparent in the case of *Mokuolo and Ogunbiyi v SSHD* [1989] Imm AR 51 CA, in which the passports of two Nigerian sisters mistakenly stated that they were Brit-ish citizens. Accordingly, they were not granted leave to enter on the assumption that they did not need it. Although, like Mr Rehal, they were not guilty of any deception or wrongdoing, they, like him, were found to be illegal entrants.

The Court of Appeal's decision in *Rehal* turned on the meaning they gave to 1971 Act Schedule 2 para 6, the obligation to make a decision within 24 hours, failing which the entrant has six months' deemed leave. It applies where a person 'is to be given' limited leave. The Court of Appeal interpreted this to mean where the immigration officer intends to make a decision on the question of leave. This means that if the immigra-tion officer has not thought about it because, for instance, as in Mr Rehal's case, they did not realize it was necessary to do so, the deemed leave provision does not apply, so the person is considered an illegal entrant. Macdonald puts forward an alternative and surely preferable interpretation that the words 'is to be given' refer to someone who needs leave, that is, does not have right of abode (1995:70). This objective interpreta-tion would bring within para 6 those who are deemed illegal entrants through the immigration officer's mistake. The Enforcement Instructions and Guidance 2.3 says that the unwitting nature of any such illegal entry is a 'mitigating factor'. If a person enters using a British passport, the immigration officer has the burden of proving any suspicion that the person is not British.

Leave to enter is normally endorsed on a passport and will usually have been granted by entry clearance in advance except in the case of non-visa national visitors (Leave to Enter and Remain Order 2000, SI 2000/1161, see 6.4.1). Section 11(5) of the 1971 Act provides that an air or sea crew member who seeks to remain beyond the time allowed (s 8(1)) will be treated as seeking to enter the UK. If they do so in breach of immigration laws they will be regarded as an illegal entrant.

16.2.1.2 Entry in breach of a deportation order

The s 33 definition of an illegal entrant includes someone who enters in breach of a deportation order. This means that any person who is the subject of a deportation order is subject to removal as an illegal entrant if they enter the UK while the deportation order is still in force against them. The order is in force unless it has been revoked. A deportation order completely prohibits re-entry, whether or not the person would normally require leave to enter, for example, if they were a European Economic Area (EEA) national they would otherwise be able to enter without leave, but as a deportee they are an illegal entrant if they do so (*Shingara v SSHD* [1999] Imm AR 257 CA).

If the person who is the subject of the deportation order had leave when the deportation order was made, the leave, whether limited or indefinite, is invalidated by the deportation order. Any leave granted during the currency of the deportation order, whether to enter or remain, is also invalidated (1971 Act s 5). The result of this is that if someone enters while a deportation order is in force against them, they enter without leave. This is the case whether they enter clandestinely or whether, by mistake or deception, they manage to obtain an apparent leave, as any such leave will have no effect.

It might therefore be suggested that these words are redundant in the definition of an illegal entrant. A person subject to a deportation order is without leave anyway. This argument was advanced for the appellants in *Khawaja v SSHD* [1984] AC 74 (see next section) as evidence that 'in breach of the immigration laws' should be given a narrow interpretation, that is, restricted only to those who entered without leave. If it was open to a wider interpretation, there would be no need to specify 'in breach of a deportation order', as that would be included. However, the House of Lords rejected that argument, opening the way to a wider interpretation of who is an illegal entrant.

16.2.1.3 Entry by deception

As indicated earlier, the possibility of becoming an illegal entrant by deception was not in the contemplation of Parliament at the time of the passing of the Immigration Act 1971. Illegal entrants were those entering in breach of a deportation order or without leave (see, for instance, discussion in Grant and Martin, *Immigration Law and Practice* (1982) and Evans, *Immigration Law* (1983)). The courts, however, began to interpret 'in breach of the immigration laws' as including people who had passed through immigration control and had obtained leave to enter, but had done so by deception. In a series of cases, leave obtained by deception contrary to s 26(1)(c) was treated as invalid. Section 26(1)(c) sets out a criminal offence, committed where a person:

Makes or causes to be made . . . a return, statement or representation which he knows to be false or does not believe to be true.

The courts decided that leave obtained in this way was obtained 'in breach of the immigration laws' and therefore not leave which would entitle a person to enter.

This judicial invention was ratified by the House of Lords in July 1980 in *Zamir* [1980] 2 All ER 768. Their Lordships held that leave granted through the use of deception was not leave granted in accordance with the Immigration Act and could rightly found a removal as an illegal entrant. Disturbingly, they considered that the duty of a potential immigrant was a 'duty of candour', analogous to the duty of utmost good faith imposed upon parties in the law of contract. This meant that the applicant must disclose all potentially relevant information, and was under a duty to volunteer information, not just to answer questions. This put the applicant in the position of being responsible for deciding what was relevant, and risking being removed as an illegal entrant if they made a wrong judgment on that matter.

This decision 'provoked widespread academic criticism and a storm of protest from the ethnic communities and bodies concerned with improving race relations' (Evans 1983:314). It was reversed in important respects by the House of Lords in *Khawaja* [1984] AC 74, which held that there was no duty of utmost good faith. There must be actual or attempted deception before illegal entry could be established, not just a failure to interpret correctly the requirements of the immigration rules. This judgment put beyond doubt that entry obtained by deception could give rise to removal as an illegal entrant, while tempering the more extreme aspects of the *Zamir* judgment. The House of Lords found that the burden of proof that the person was an illegal entrant was upon the Secretary of State, and the standard was the civil standard, but this should be interpreted as being at the high end of the balance of probabilities, bearing in mind the serious consequences for the individual and the quasi-criminal nature of the allegations. Importantly, the House of Lords in *Khawaja* reversed the 'hands-off' approach which had characterized earlier judicial decisions concerning illegal entrants. The courts had tended not to investigate the facts, and in judicial review held that such investigation was outside the Court's scope of enquiry as the jurisdiction is one of review of the decision-making process, not an appeal on the merits. The House of Lords in *Khawaja* held that the fact that someone was an illegal entrant was a matter which determined whether or not there was jurisdiction to act. Such 'jurisdictional facts' *did*, they said, come within the scope of the Court's inquiry. The Court would therefore examine for itself the evidence as to whether the person was an illegal entrant.

Following *Khawaja*, the inclusion of a person who gained entry by deception in the definition of illegal entrant was here to stay. Obtaining entry by deception became explicitly part of the statutory definition with the Asylum and Immigration Act 1996. The offence was created of using deception to obtain or seek to obtain leave to enter or remain in the UK (now in 1971 Act s 24A). An offence under that section, like an offence under s 26(1)(c) is 'in breach of immigration laws' and so makes the perpetrator an illegal entrant as found in *Khawaja*.

However, this left open a number of issues surrounding deception. These included the effect of deception by a third party, the use of false documents, the relationship between any deception and the leave granted, and what conduct may give rise to a finding of deception, in the absence of a duty of utmost good faith.

Third-party deception and use of false documents
The Asylum and Immigration Act 1996 added to the definition of illegal entrant in s 33(1) para (b): 'entering or seeking to enter by means which include deception by another person'. This puts beyond doubt that deception by a third party will make the entry illegal and means that earlier case law on this point no longer has any effect.

Deception by a third party includes for instance preparing a false passport or a false offer of housing or employment.

The use of invalid documents is also covered by the statutory provisions introduced by the 1996 Act. If the entrant produces a false document knowing it to be false, this is deception contrary to s 24A(1). If they are not aware of its falsity but this is the result of the deliberate act of a third party, the deception is covered by s 33(1).

Relationship between deception and leave granted

The effect of the deception is a matter of some importance. At one extreme, some acts of deception might be about a peripheral fact, which had very little bearing on the decision to grant entry. It would be inappropriate then to regard entry as illegal. At the other extreme, misrepresentation about a central fact such as whether the sponsor and applicant did in fact intend to marry would render the entry illegal. The question to be addressed is whether, to make an entry illegal, the deception has to be the effective cause of leave being granted, or just a factor which contributed to the decision.

In *Khawaja* the Court held that the deception must be the effective means of obtaining leave in order for the entry to be regarded as illegal. It relied on the earlier case of *R v SSHD ex p Jayakody* [1982] 1 All ER 461, in which the Court of Appeal had held that in order to render the entry illegal the fraud should be the decisive factor in the application. In other words, if there had been no deception then the application would probably have been refused. In *Bugdaycay v SSHD* [1987] 1 AC 514, the House of Lords said that the question was, if the true facts were known, whether the decision-maker would have been 'bound to refuse' the application. Since then the courts have tended to treat deception as creating illegal entry if it is material rather than decisive. For instance, in *Durojaiye v Secretary of State for the Home Department* [1991] Imm AR 307, the Court of Appeal considered that giving false answers to questions about a student's attendance at college was 'material in the sense that it was likely to influence their decision'. This is not the same as saying that they were a matter without which a different decision would necessarily have been made.

At the time of *Khawaja*, a person was an illegal entrant by deception if they made representations which they knew to be false (1971 Act s 26(1)(c)). The causal relationship with the leave then granted was matter for the courts to consider. Since the 1996 Act, however, ss 24A and 33(1) both refer to entry obtained or sought 'by means which include' deception. It does not mean that, apart from the deception, the decision-maker would have been 'bound to refuse'. On the other hand, 'by means' implies that the deception is operative. The net result is that, in order for the deception to give rise to a finding of illegal entry, it must have played a part in the decision to grant entry, but need not necessarily have been the only factor.

In *Ofordu, Re Judicial Review* [2012] NICA 9 the Northern Ireland Court of Appeal pointed out that in order to be material the deception must have taken place at one of two points in time: applying for the visa or entering the UK.

Conduct—deception by silence

If the applicant says nothing about a relevant matter, it may be because they are deliberately concealing it or it may be because they are not aware that it is relevant and have not been asked about it. In the latter case, there is no deception. Which of these is the case is a matter of inference for the Tribunal from available evidence. To establish illegal entry from a failure to mention something, it needs to be established how much the applicant should have been expected to say. As there is not a duty of candour, what can the applicant be expected to know is relevant?

In *Cendiz Doldur v SSHD* [1998] Imm AR 352, the Court of Appeal held there was no duty on the applicant to disclose his marriage on arrival when he was not asked about it or about any change of circumstances. He was still dependent, in fact, on his father and could not be expected to know that this did not mean that he was still dependent in law after he had married. In *R v Secretary of State for the Home Department ex p Kuteesa* [1997] Imm AR 194, the applicant obtained leave to enter for two years as a student, subject to the condition that he was not to take employment. He decided not to enrol on the course for which he had been given leave, but enrolled on a later course and worked in the meantime. Shortly before he was due to start the new course his father died, and he went home to Uganda for the funeral. On his re-entry to the UK, he produced his passport and a letter from the college saying:

This student is going home as a result of a bereavement in the family and will be returning to college to continue his studies. I confirm that [there is] a place reserved for him.

The High Court held that by his silent presentation of his passport he had made a representation that he had previously fulfilled his conditions of entry. As this was false, contrary to s 26(1)(c), he was an illegal entrant. He argued that if he had revealed the true facts, he would still have been granted leave to enter as to refuse would have been unreasonable. However, Harrison J disagreed. He found that the immigration officer would have refused leave to enter if he had known the full history. This was at least in part because the applicant had had leave to enter as a student on a previous occasion and had worked in breach of conditions. This argument illustrates how engagement with the question outlawed by *Bugdaycay* (whether leave would have been granted had the true facts been known) merges into the question of materiality (what was relevant) and, in this case, what would have been a proper exercise of discretion.

Unlike Mr Doldur, Mr Kuteesa had done something (presented his passport) which was a positive action and could thus amount to a representation. However, the case turned more on what the entrant in each case could be expected to have known was relevant. This kind of reasoning survives the amendments made by the 1996 Act as the question of whether there has been deception must involve the question of the entrant's state of mind.

In *R (on the application of Efenure) v SSHD* [2013] EWHC 3072 (Admin) the decision that the applicant was an illegal entrant was irrational and was quashed. He was a student, but he had to extend his leave in order to complete and thus needed to extend his visa. He could not afford the application fee. He found on the internet that he could apply for discretionary leave without a fee, so enquired about this at the Home Office. He was advised that he could only obtain discretionary leave if he applied for asylum, so he did that. His asylum claim was certified as unfounded and he was immediately detained for removal as an illegal entrant. The High Court found that this decision was irrational. Mr Efenure had not used deception at any stage. He had been open about his reasons and circumstances. The suspicion that he intended to claim asylum when he first became a student had no foundation.

Standard of proof

The burden of proof that a person is an illegal entrant is on the Home Office. The standard of proof, first laid down in *Khawaja*, has been developed but not substantially altered by subsequent cases. It was said to be the civil standard, that is, on the balance of probabilities, but at the higher end of that scale in view of the gravity of the matters in question. If the person is found to be an illegal entrant they are liable to detention and removal from the country; as liberty is at stake the burden of proof should be strictly applied.

However, an inference against the applicant may be drawn from the evidence if it meets the standard. For instance, in *Kesse* TH/00419, the appellant had obtained entry on the basis of marriage to a person who was subsequently found to have never been married. The Tribunal upheld the finding of deception, using the standard of proof laid down in *Khawaja*, which they described as being 'a high degree of probability'.

In *R (on the Application of Ullah) v SSHD* [2003] EWCA Civ 1366 the case had proceeded without the benefit of a witness statement from the person who would have been the appellant's first wife had that marriage been valid. The Court of Appeal held that the Secretary of State could, in theory, proceed without such a statement, but in this case there was insufficient evidence to meet the high standard of proof that the appellant must have known of the invalidity of his marriage.

The majority of recent case law concerning obtaining entry by what might broadly be called deception is brought and decided under provisions relating to false representations as a ground for refusal or cancellation of leave, or in the context of prosecution for documents offences (see chapter 6). The law relating to illegal entrants is now relatively settled.

16.2.2 Refused leave to enter

The Immigration Act 1971 Schedule 2 para 8(1) says that where a person arriving in the UK is refused leave to enter, then they may be removed on the direction of an immigration officer. While some people have a right of appeal, it is also the case that those without that right may be refused entry and returned forthwith to the country from which they came. The UK Immigration Statistics show that 16,255 people were removed in this fashion from UK ports in the year ending March 2015. This includes those removed from juxtaposed controls (see chapter 6). The most common nationality of those refused at the port and departing was US (2,009), with Albania and Brazil second and third highest. Note that Albania is a visa national country whereas the US and Brazil are not.

This power refers to people arriving, and does not include people such as asylum seekers who may be given temporary admission on arrival, but are technically refused leave to enter much later, as a consequence of the refusal of their asylum claim. The power to remove someone refused leave to enter on arrival is subject to any in-country appeal right they may have, though as we have seen in chapter 7, this is restricted, broadly speaking, to people with a human rights claim, or who make an asylum claim on arrival, or EEA nationals. It is also subject to any in-country right of administrative review. See chapter 5.

16.2.3 Removal for overstaying, deception, and breach of conditions

From 1 January 1973 until 2 October 2000, those subject to removal were restricted to illegal entrants and people refused entry at the port. On 2 October 2000, Immigration and Asylum Act 1999 s 10 came into effect, and changed a number of grounds for deportation under Immigration Act 1971 s 3(5) into grounds for removal.

In the 1971 Act as originally passed, breach of condition and overstaying were grounds for deportation. Deportation carried a full right of appeal while summary removal attracted a right of appeal only from out of the UK, that is, after the event. There was a rationale for that distinction as the original target of the removal provisions was those who were refused entry at the port and people who had arrived clandestinely but were apprehended soon after arrival. People who had overstayed or breached their condition have had some period of residence, and some connection with the UK, perhaps brief, but maybe of many years. It would therefore be legitimate to treat them differently. However, in practice this rationale broke down because the courts developed the category of illegal entrant to include a person who had entered using deception. This could include a person whose original leave had been gained years earlier. This put a person deemed an illegal entrant and an overstayer in a similar position.

Parliament's response to this was to level down the rights of overstayers to those of illegal entrants. First, as discussed in chapter 15, by the Immigration Act 1988 s 5, then the Immigration and Asylum Act 1999. Section 10 made those who had overstayed, breached condition, or obtained leave by deception subject to removal and not deportation. The distinction between overstayers and illegal entrants has now been completely removed in the new s 10 Immigration and Asylum Act 2009 as amended by the Immigration Act 2014.

16.2.3.1 Obtaining leave to remain by deception

This was introduced into 1971 Act s 3 as a new ground of deportation by the 1996 Act but was changed into a ground for removal along with overstaying and breach of condition by 1999 Act s 10.

It refers to situations where, for instance, a person obtains indefinite leave to remain by misrepresenting that their marriage is still subsisting whereas in fact it has broken down, as for instance in *R v SSHD ex p Chaumun* CO/3143/95 (unreported).

16.2.3.2 Overstaying and breach of condition

As mentioned earlier, these two grounds, applicable only to limited leave, were formerly grounds for deportation and are now, under Immigration and Asylum Act 1999 s 10 grounds for removal.

Staying beyond the time allowed by a grant of limited leave is a factual matter. There may be issues of proof, for instance of the duration of the leave, but there is little scope for legal interpretation. When a person applies for a variation of their leave, the Immigration Act 1971 s 3C (as substituted by the 2002 Act s 118) continues the original leave until the end of the period set for appealing against a decision on the variation application. If an appeal is made, the same section continues the leave while the appeal is pending. It is only once these time limits are exhausted and the applicant has been unsuccessful that they may be treated as an overstayer. However, s 47 of the Immigration Asylum and Nationality Act 2006 allowed a decision to remove to be made during this period of extended leave, even though it could not be enforced until the appeal was withdrawn or lost. This amendment, in accordance with the policy of both the 2002 and the 2006 Act, aimed to speed up immigration processes. Section 47 has now been repealed by Schedule 9, para 5 of the Immigration Act 2014 as the new single power of removal has made it redundant.

Section 10 of the 1999 Act permits removal for breach of conditions imposed under 1971 Act s 3(1)(c). The conditions which may be imposed are: restricting employment or occupation, requiring the subject to maintain and accommodate himself and any dependants without recourse to public funds, registration with the police, reporting to an immigration officer or the Secretary of State, and a condition about residence. The Enforcement Instructions and Guidance (EIG) say that a breach of conditions relating to work must be of sufficient gravity to warrant removal and require 'firm and recent evidence' of such a breach (chapter 50, 3.1).

In *SSHD v R (on the application of Lim)* [2007] EWCA Civ 773, Sedley LJ described as a 'colossal overreaction' an arrest and decision to remove Mr Lim who was found working for the employer for whom he had permission to work, but present in a different restaurant in the same city. He said he had gone there to collect food for the Lucky Star, his specified work place, but was disbelieved. Mr Lim would have had an out-of-country right of appeal, but attempted unsuccessfully a challenge by judicial review proceedings to protect himself and his wife from having to leave the country (see chapter 7). The Court of Appeal pointed out that a modest change to his work permit was the most that was needed.

In *R (on the application of Thapa) v Secretary of State for the Home Department* [2014] EWHC 659 (Admin) Mr Thapa sought judicial review of the Secretary of State's decision to make directions for his administrative removal, in the exercise of her discretion under the Immigration and Asylum Act 1999, s 10(1)(a) (IAA 1999). Mr Thapa had worked in a restaurant while he had permission to work as a student. When his leave was varied to prohibit work, he says he stopped working. He was detained by immigration officers in the same restaurant—he said he was socializing with his friends, the immigration officer said he was working. He was detained and served with a decision summarily to remove him, as a person with limited leave in breach of his conditions, under IAA 1999, s 10(1)(a). Allowing the claim, the Administrative Court decided that there had been no evidence that the Secretary of State had appreciated that she had been exercising a discretion, rather than taking action which had followed automatically from her belief that there had been a breach of Mr Thapa's visa. The High Court stated clearly that Home Office officials should make decisions fairly, transparently and in line with published policy. However, it remains to be seen whether asserting these public law principles will in fact put any brake on the Home Office interest in removing people as quickly as possible.

16.2.3.3 Removal of families

The power to remove also applies to members of the family facing removal (s 10(2)). Family member is widely defined to include partner, parent, adult dependent relative or child living in the same household where the person facing removal has care of the child. The Immigration Act 2014 s 2 inserts a new section 78A in the 2002 Act to provide a 28-day grace period from exhaustion of appeal rights during which actual removal is forbidden for the child and the adult where 'if as a result, no relevant parent or carer would remain in the UK'.

A peculiar feature of UK law is that children of a person to be removed or deported from the UK may be British. This may occur when the partner of the person to be expelled is British, or when one or both parents have indefinite leave to remain at the time of the child's birth (see chapter 3). This situation was addressed by the Supreme Court in *ZH (Tanzania) v SSHD* [2011] UKSC 4. The case is discussed more fully in chapter 8. The particular point of importance for this chapter is the potential that the case has to make inroads into the practice of removing British children. ZH's children, aged 12 and 9, were born in the UK and had lived all their lives here. The Supreme Court held that their British nationality was 'of particular importance' in determining what were their best interests. The Court said that the intrinsic importance of citizenship should not be played down:

As citizens these children have rights which they will not be able to exercise if they move to another country. They will lose the advantages of growing up and being educated in their own country, their own culture and their own language. They will have lost all this when they come back as adults. (para 32)

Since *ZH (Tanzania)*, where British children are included in a removal decision, their British nationality is a factor of particular importance in determining whether the removal should go ahead.

In every family returns case and where the family is going to be detained, s 3 of the 2014 Act inserts a new s 54A into the Borders, Citizenship and Immigration Act 2009 and provides that the Independent Family Returns Panel must be consulted in relation to how best to safeguard and promote the welfare of the children in the family (see 16.7.1). There is no duty on the Secretary of State to follow any recommendations, only to consult, which means that recommendations or comments could be disregarded by the Secretary of State. However, this might call into question whether the Secretary of State was abiding by the duty under s 55 regarding the welfare of the child.

16.3 Effect of decision to remove

If a person is actually removed, this has an effect on future applications for entry to the UK. Mandatory grounds for refusal of entry clearance and leave to enter, discussed in chapter 6, include that the person has previously been removed for overstaying, breach of condition, obtaining or seeking to leave to remain by deception, or being an illegal entrant. This remains a mandatory ground for refusal for ten years from the actual removal (para 320 (7B)). The re-entry ban eliminates one of the distinctions between deportation and removal. There remains an important distinction that mandatory refusal of entry after removal does not apply where the new application is to join family in the UK (para A320), whereas an application for re-entry after deportation is not subject to that exception.

Section 48 of the Immigration Asylum and Nationality Act 2006 inserted a provision into the 1999 Act, that a decision to remove made under s 10 invalidated any leave that had been granted. The effect seemed to be that if a person, following receipt of the decision to remove them for breach of conditions, continued to work within what would have been their lawful limits, they were working illegally since they have no leave. Also, entitlement to any benefits stopped on service of the decision. In this way, the 2006 Act radically increased the impact of a decision to remove, as a person can rapidly be in a position where they have no means of support. This enacted the government's policy of being 'tougher' on infringements of immigration law. Section 48 has been repealed by the Immigration Act 2014 as the effect of the new single removal power has made it redundant. If the person does not have the resources to travel, but leaves at government expense, they will be subject to the maximum ten-year period of restriction on re-entry.

16.4 EEA nationals and removal

As EEA nationals may enter as of right on production of a passport or identity documents in order to exercise Treaty rights, it is rare that an EEA national may be deemed an illegal entrant. In C-215/03 *Oulane*, the ECJ held on a reference for a preliminary ruling that detention of a European national with a view to deportation was an unjustified restriction on free movement where his offence was principally lack of documentary proof of his status. So, while an EEA national may be deported on public policy grounds, removal is only likely to occur if the EEA national enters in breach of an exclusion or deportation order (*Shingara v SSHD* [1999] Imm AR 257 CA).

The Immigration (European Economic Area) Regulations 2006, SI 2006/1003 Regulations 19(3) and 24(2) provide that an EEA national or their family member who does not have or ceases to have a right to reside may be removed as if they fell within s 10 of the 1999 Act. This regulation is contentious. See chapter 4 at 4.3.1 for a discussion of the stringent new regulations from 1 January 2014, providing for a re-entry ban.

16.5 Removal power

Prior to the introduction of the new removal power, the person who was to be removed received a copy of removal directions. These were instructions by an immigration officer or the Secretary of State to the captain of a ship or aircraft to remove the person in question to a country or territory:

(i)   of which s/he is a national or citizen;

(ii) in which s/he has obtained a passport or identity document;

(iii) from which s/he embarked for the UK; or

(iv) to which there is reason to believe s/he will be admitted (Immigration Act 1971 Sch 2 para 8).

Removal directions had no duration or continuing legal effect beyond the moment when they were put into practice. They were enforceable in the very real sense that a person may be arrested and detained in order to give them effect. In law, they were themselves a form of enforcement (see, for instance, Burnton J in *SSHD v Kariharan* [2001] EWHC Admin 1004 likening them to a bailiff's warrant).

The Immigration Act 2014 section 1 removes the need for separate removal directions to enforce removal. The effect of the new removal power is that a person with no leave, who is required to have it, may simply be removed from the UK with no further notice or legal step being required. Essentially, the new power replaces the need for removal directions as it confers a general power to remove rather than one linked to a particular type of immigration decision. This means that, in many cases, no piece of paper needs to be served on the person to be removed in order to effect their removal. This is clear from Chapter 60 of the *Enforcement Instructions and Guidance*. A detained person removed under this power will usually be informed of their arrival time in their country of origin shortly before departure and as a matter of courtesy only.

On the face of the statute, there is no legal need for advance warning of removal under the new s 10 power. However, as Colin Yeo has argued, this would appear to go against the decision in the case of *R (on the application of Medical Justice) v SSHD* [2011] EWCA Civ 1710 in which the Court of Appeal upheld the High Court's decision that 'no notice' removals were unlawful. In practice, there is a new regime of forms to be served on people in relation to curtailing leave or notifying them that they have no leave (EIG, chapter 50, 1.3 Notice of liability for removal) and chapter 60 EIG s 2 sets out three forms of notice of removal. Chapters 50 and 60 therefore appear to create a policy of serving notice on the person to be removed, even though the statute requires no legal step to be taken.

There is no right of appeal under the new appeal provisions because there is no formal decision as such under the new s 10. However, an intimation that removal is going to take place under this power, whether through service of a notice or simply by detention, might be challenged by a person who does possess leave or who wishes to apply for it by judicial review seeking either a declaration that s/he does in fact possess leave or an injunction while making out some other basis for remaining in the UK, such as on human rights or international protection grounds.

16.6 Viability of return

Many of the more recent issues concerning removal have concerned the viability of return. As a thematic briefing for the Independent Asylum Commission relates, there may be practical and institutional barriers to removal. These include:

- lack of travel documents and identification;
- lack of institutional coordination;
- lack of an international airport, safe route, or carrier (ICAR 2007).

Not all of these issues are within the remit of courts or tribunals or come before them, but they are at least as important as legal issues in explaining why, although someone may be an illegal entrant or their asylum claim may have failed, they cannot necessarily be removed from the UK. The gap between the numbers of people who have no right in law to remain and the numbers removed is not just due to government inefficiency or non-compliance by those to be removed.

16.6.1 Risks *en route*

The Court of Appeal has considered the question of whether risks entailed in the actual route of return should form part of the human rights or asylum decision.

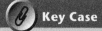 **Key Case**

HH, AM, J and MA (Somalia) v SSHD [2010] EWCA Civ 426

The appellants challenged their removal to Somalia on various grounds, including that for some of the appellants there was no safe route of return. The Court of Appeal accepted their argument that 'in any case in which it can be shown either directly or by implication what route and method of return is envisaged, the Tribunal is required by law to consider and determine any challenge to the safety of that route or method' (para 58). This 'must be considered as part of the decision on entitlement' to international protection (para 81). 'Postponement of such consideration until the Secretary of State is in a position to set safe removal directions would effectively be to postpone the decision until . . . cessation' (para 81). This, the Court held (obiter), was consistent with the Qualification Directive and the Procedures Directive. Only technical matters such as documentation and availability of flights could be deferred until the moment of issuing removal directions (para 84).

The only point of return to Somalia from the UK was Mogadishu. Accordingly, in order for someone to be safe on return it would need to be shown either that they were returning to Mogadishu itself, and would be safe there, or that they would have safe travel from Mogadishu to their home area. An Amnesty International report had described the road from Mogadishu to AM's home of Jowhar as 'one of the most dangerous', controlled by terrorist groups and freelance militias. This and other evidence must be considered by the Tribunal in determining whether he should be awarded a protective status.

The Court of Appeal said that its judgment in *HH and others* was consistent with that in *GH v SSHD* [2005] EWCA Civ 1182. Here, the Court held that, where removal directions are given as part of, or incidental to, an appealable decision, or where the Secretary of State adopts a routine procedure for removal or return so that the method or route is implicit in the decision to remove, the directions may also be considered as part of the appeal, though normal practice is to give the removal directions well after any appealable decision. *GH* concerned an Iraqi Kurd who, it was decided, could live safely in the area of northern Iraq from which he came, but who argued that he would face risks when travelling within Iraq from the point of arrival to his home area. As no removal directions had been set, the Court held that this question could not be considered on appeal.

Note that in cases of internal relocation, discussed in the context of asylum claims in chapter 12, risks in travelling to the new safe area may be taken into account to determine that the proposed relocation is 'unduly harsh'. In cases such as *GH*, we are considering a different situation, where the appellant is held *not* to be at risk in their home area. In this case, risks on travelling there will only engage the UK's legal system of protection if they amount to a risk of violation of Article 3 (e.g., torture on return at the airport) or if, once removal directions have been set, they are so unreasonable as to be challengeable by judicial review.

In *AK v SSHD* [2006] EWCA Civ 1117, in a similar vein the Court held that as there were no proven obstacles to the appellant's re-entering the Palestinian Territories via Jordan, even though he might encounter some difficulty, this was not a matter the Court could engage with. Inconvenience is not an objection to removal, unless it amounts to treatment in breach of Article 3. The Supreme Court in *MS (Palestinian Territories)* held that nothing in its judgment affected *HH (Somalia)*, AK or *GH (Iraq)*.

16.6.2 Obtaining travel documents

A further practical difficulty in the way of removal may be obstacles to obtaining travel documents. Asylum and Immigration (Treatment of Claimants, etc.) Act 2004 s 35 makes it a criminal offence for an asylum seeker to fail to comply, without reasonable excuse, with obtaining a travel document. Guidance to immigration officers suggests that reasonable excuse would be something like a need for emergency medical care or transport problems which prevented a person from getting to an interview. This does not include the claimant's fear of contact with authorities in their home country (*R v Tabnak* [2007] EWCA Crim 380). It must be something which made the asylum seeker unable to comply, not unwilling. The Court of Appeal in *Tabnak* pointed out that the criminal court was not able to assess risks in the country of return, which would have already been assessed by the immigration authorities. There is a caveat to this, which is that if the asylum seeker's claim has not been finally determined, they should not be exposed to questioning by the authorities of their home state. This practice has been challenged in particular in relation to the questioning of Sudanese asylum seekers by embassy officials (see *Waging Peace* 2007).

Obstacles to obtaining travel documents to effect a removal may result in extended detention while the authorities attempt to resolve the problems. Even where the asylum seeker contributes to the obstacles, they may nevertheless be insoluble. See the case of *Rostami* in chapter 14. Obstacles may equally come about because of the requirements of the proposed receiving state, which neither the individual nor the Home Office can fulfil, or repeated delays and other obstructions raised by the authorities of the receiving state. Even aside from the reluctance of the individual to go, it may be impossible to achieve a removal. Sedley LJ summarized the difficulties: 'Obstacles to return are commonly an amalgam of fact, governmental practice and policy, international law and local law, often in a form which is impossible to disentangle' (*R (MS, AR and FW) v SSHD* [2009] EWCA Civ 1310 at 26). As we have seen in chapter 14, people may remain in detention for extended periods because of these difficulties.

Longstanding problems in obtaining documents for Iranians and Eritreans in particular are discussed in chapter 2.

With the consent of the receiving government, alternative documentation can be used to effect a return. There are provisions for EU travel documents to be issued, or letters under the Chicago Convention, and the Home Office publishes details of the documentation requirements of receiving governments from time to time.

It is obvious that steps to obtain a travel document from the appellant's embassy should not be taken before an appeal has been concluded because of risk to the appellant. In *R (on the application of Sidibe) v SSHD* [2007] EWCA Civ 191, Home Office officials had taken the claimant to the Guinean Embassy to arrange travel documents, despite the fact that there were serious allegations of the risk he faced as a member of the military, an expert's report was pending on the risk to him, and his appeal had not yet been heard. Moses J made it clear that this was highly irregular and that it would be necessary to discover:

why it happened because if there was no good reason for it to be done that raises doubts as to the bona fides of those responsible for this applicant in the circumstances of his particular case, and may indeed add force to the contention that he was deliberately exposed to a risk by those responsible for his detention. (para 4)

16.6.3 **Other reasons**

The other obstacle referred to by ICAR, and discussed by Phuong (see chapter 2) is that the airlines may be unwilling to take enforced removals. This was so in *Appellant A v SSHD* [2007] EWCA Civ 804, in which after two years of lawful detention, A was detained for a further 19 months during which time he could not be removed because no airlines were willing to take enforced removals to Somalia, and he was not willing to go (now in *Abdi v UK* [2013] ECHR 299).

The case law on practical obstacles to return is the tip of an iceberg. Under the water are many other factors which do not readily enter the court room. In addition to all the human reasons that an asylum seeker whose claim has failed may have for not wanting to return to their home country, are the interests of the country of return. It is easy to lose sight when studying the UK's system that the return of an asylum seeker is an international action. The country of return may have social, economic, or political reasons for not wanting to accept the returnee. As the ICAR report says, 'in times of conflict they may be reluctant to re-admit supporters of resistance groups' or they may fear that returnees will not be absorbed economically, or may compromise fragile security situations.

The other major issue which follows is the status of an asylum seeker once the legal process has ended unsuccessfully, where the UK is unwilling to give any leave to remain, but return cannot be achieved. Issues about lack of status and resulting destitution underlie some of the cases dealing with the feasibility of return (and see chapter 2). In *HH (Somalia)* the Court of Appeal referred to an important implication of its judgment. If the safety of the route of return is considered by the Tribunal and a real risk is found of treatment that would violate human rights, this has the potential to change a refusal of asylum or humanitarian protection to a decision in the claimant's favour. This means that, although the individual may still be refused asylum, if there is currently no safe route of return the individual may be entitled to asylum support instead of being left entirely destitute. It also opens the possibility of some form of leave to remain, even if temporary.

Reference should also be made to discussion of temporary admission in chapter 14.

16.7 **The process of removal**

Practical and political aspects of this subject have already been discussed in chapter 2. Standard policy is to give 72 hours' notice of removal, including two working days. The last 24 hours before removal must include a working day unless the notice period already includes three working days. This policy is subject to exceptions, including shorter notice where the family removal process has reached its final stage, and where the person to be removed consents or removal is within seven days of refusal of entry at a port (EIG, chapter 60). Removal is only suspended if judicial review grounds are lodged in full (Policy notice, 2 March 2007), and in some cases only if the Court grants an injunction.

Medical Justice challenged former exceptions to the 72-hour notice period for those at risk of suicide and for young people, and these were held to be unlawful (*R (on the application of Medical Justice) v SSHD* [2010] EWHC 1925).

Even an injunction has on occasion not stopped a person being removed (see Thomas 2008), and in some cases the Home Office has been ordered to return to the UK a person unlawfully removed.

For concerns about excessive force used in removals, see 16.7.2.

16.7.1 **Family removals**

There is a special process for removing families, which was developed alongside a policy announcement in 2010 that the government aimed to end the immigration detention of children (see chapter 14). This includes an independent family returns panel, and the following stages:

- assisted return including family conferences to discuss welfare and medical concerns and the availability of tailored assisted voluntary return packages to help families resettle;
- required returns for families who fail to take up assistance packages, allowing them to remain in the community, but giving two weeks' notice to board their flight, allowing self check-in without enforcement action; and
- ensured return, as a last resort for families who refuse to depart. The family returns panel will advise the Home Office to ensure the welfare of the child is taken properly into account. Options include a limited notice removal, open accommodation, and as a last resort 'family friendly, pre-departure accommodation' (see chapter 14).

A review of the family returns process concluded that there was no statistically significant difference between the number of voluntary returns in the new and the old process, but children spent less time in detention and families had a better understanding of their options. Most families complied with the process (only 10 per cent absconded). The new process took longer, but there was a better impact on family welfare and the safety of children (Home Office Research Paper 78).

16.7.2 **Safety during removal**

Force used during removal was the main criticism of practice at The Cedars in an otherwise positive report from Her Majesty's Inspector of Prisons (2012). The inspectorate found that force had been used on six of the 39 families going through The Cedars. As regards the use of force on a pregnant woman they said 'There is no safe way to do this while protecting the unborn child and it is simply not acceptable to initiate force for such purposes.'

The use of force during removal has been a source of public concern since the death of Jimmy Mubenga who was being forcibly removed to Angola and died on the flight due to the use of inappropriate restraints. Monitoring and public scrutiny of the conduct of flights and achieving accountability has become more of a public concern. In *R (on the application of Salimi) v SSHD and IPCC* [2012] EWCA Civ 422 the appellant's asylum claim had failed, and he was removed from the UK on a charter flight to Baghdad. As is common practice, there were escorts on the flight. He asserted that, on arrival at Baghdad, three British escorts forced him face down onto the floor of the aircraft, and Iraqi police beat him on the head, shoulders, and back before forcibly removing him from the aircraft. The British Embassy in Iraq became concerned about his treatment and arranged to return him to the UK two weeks later. Mr Salimi wanted to complain to the Independent Police Complaints Commission about the conduct of the British escorts. The IPCC has jurisdiction to hear complaints about the exercise of powers under the Immigration Acts, but not those relating to enforcement (s 41(3) Police and Justice Act 2006). It was argued for Mr Salimi that once the aircraft had left British airspace, at latest, the escorts were no longer carrying out a removal—that is, immigration enforcement. From then the statutory responsibility passed to the carrier. The Court of Appeal did not accept this argument. They held that the escorts continued to exercise a statutory function until the removal was completed, and that Mr Salimi's proper recourse was to the prisons ombudsman.

The Joint Committee on Human Rights in 2007 heard evidence of violence, for instance people on the way to removal being beaten in the back of vans. The Committee recommended that people should be properly prepared for removal and that the removals should be carried out with dignity (HL 81 HC 60 para 337). Since then, the report *Outsourcing Abuse* in 2008 documented nearly 300 assaults against asylum detainees.

Although the UK has not opted into the EU Returns Directive which requires removal flights to be monitored, it has begun a non-statutory process of occasional monitoring of return flights by HMIP and by Independent Monitoring Boards attached to immigration removal centres. Each of these bodies monitored three return flights in 2013, consisting of five charter flights and one family removal. Inspectors voiced concerns about excessive restraints used on individuals who offered no resistance, and racist and offensive language used at what is a very distressing time for most people who are removed.

In October 2010, Jimmy Mubenga died in the course of restraint by G4S escorts while being placed on a plane for deportation to Angola. He is the second person to have died in the course of deportation from the UK. At a coroner's inquest the jury recorded a verdict of unlawful killing. Mr Mubenga's death prompted an inquiry by the HASC (HC 563). The Committee was not persuaded that a restraint position like the one that killed Jimmy Mubenga was not still used, despite being unauthorized. They said: 'The use by contractors of unauthorised restraint techniques, sanctioning their use, or failing to challenge their use, should be grounds for dismissal' (para 18). The guards who restrained Jimmy Mubenga were found to have very offensive racist jokes on their mobile phones, and these inspections and inquiries have exposed the danger of the situation if racist attitudes have free rein in a process such as removal where those being removed are exceptionally vulnerable.

16.8 **Conclusion**

Removal is a major plank of government immigration policy. There are 'targets' for removals, questions by Opposition MPs about the number of removals, and promises to do more. The law on removal is often tortuous and technical and its implementation may cause enormous human distress. Nevertheless, it has become a key measure of whether the government is able to maintain a firm immigration policy. There is no lack of legal powers to remove, and no increase in the law can answer questions such as 'Why are people willing to undergo significant hardship in the UK in order to avoid removal?' and 'Why is it that such a small percentage of people with irregular immigration status are in fact removed?'

QUESTIONS

1 Was it appropriate for the courts to develop the definition of 'illegal entrant' to include someone who entered by deception? What would have been the alternative?

2 What are the implications of the new removals policy? Should there be a right of appeal against removal and if so, on what grounds?

 online resource centre For guidance on answering questions, visit the Online Resource Centre www.oxfordtextbooks.co.uk/orc/clayton7e/.

FURTHER READING

Evans, John M. (1983) *Immigration Law*, 2nd edn (London: Sweet & Maxwell), chapter 6.

Granville-Chapman, Charlotte, Smith, Ellie, and Moloney, Neil (2005) *Harm on Removal: Excessive Force against Failed Asylum Seekers* (London: Medical Foundation).

Her Majesty's Inspector of Prisons (2012) *Expectations: Criteria for assessing the conditions for and treatment of immigration detainees. Section 6: overseas escorts,* accessible at: www.justice. gov.uk/downloads/about/hmipris/immigration-expectations.pdf.

Her Majesty's Chief Inspector of Prisons (2013) *Detainees under escort: Inspection of a family escort and removal to Ghana,* 23–4 March.

Independent Family Returns Panel (2013) *Annual Report 2011/12.*

Independent Family Returns Panel (2015) *Annual Report 2012–2014.*

Lane, Mike, Murray, Daniel, Smith, Terry *et al* (2013) *Evaluation of the New Family Returns Process* Home Office Research Report 78.

Thomas, Robert (2008) 'Judicial Review Challenges to Removal Decisions' *Immigration Law Digest* vol. 14, no. 1, Spring, pp. 2–6.

Waging Peace (2007) *'I felt like I had been brought into a lion's den.' How Darfuri asylum seekers are being illegally interviewed by Sudanese Embassy officials at Home Office facilities* (London: Waging Peace).

BIBLIOGRAPHY

Amnesty International (2007) *United Kingdom: Deportations to Algeria at all costs*, AI Index: EUR 45/001/2007.

Ashford, Mark (1993) *Detained Without Trial: A Survey of Immigration Act Detention* (London: JCWI).

Bevan, Vaughan (1986) *The Development of British Immigration Law* (Beckenham: Croom Helm).

Buck, Trevor G. (2006) 'Precedent in Tribunals and the Development of Principles' *Civil Justice Quarterly* vol. 25, no. 4, pp. 458–84.

Castles, Flynn, Lawson, Ryan et al (2007) *'Towards a Progressive Immigration Policy'* (Migrant Rights Network).

Clayton, Richard (2004) 'Judicial Deference and Democratic Dialogue: the Legitimacy of Judicial Intervention under the Human Rights Act' *Public Law* Spring, pp. 33–47.

Cornelisse, Galina (2004) 'Human Rights for Immigration Detainees in Strasbourg: Limited Sovereignty or a Limited Discourse?' *European Journal of Migration and Law* vol. 6, pp. 93–110.

Cutler, Sarah (2007) *Refusal Factory: Women's experiences of the detained fast track asylum process at Yarl's Wood Immigration Removal Centre* (Bail for Immigration Detainees).

Dummett, Ann and Nicol, Andrew (1990) *Subjects, Citizens, Aliens and Others* (London: Weidenfeld and Nicolson).

Goodwin-Gill, Guy and McAdam, Jane (2007) *The Refugee in International Law* 3rd edn (Oxford: Clarendon Press).

Gorlick, Brian (2002) *Common burdens and standards: legal elements in assessing claims to refugee status*, New Issues in Refugee Research, Working Paper no. 68 (Stockholm: UNHCR).

Hathaway, J. (1991) *The Law of Refugee Status* (Ontario: Butterworths Canada Ltd).

Her Majesty's Inspector of Prisons (HMIP) (2014) *Report on an unannounced inspection of Harmondsworth Immigration Removal Centre* 5–16 August.

Her Majesty's Inspector of Prisons (HMIP) (2010) *Report on an announced inspection of Harmondsworth Immigration Removal Centre* 11–15 August.

Human Rights Watch (2005) *Still at Risk: Diplomatic Assurances No Safeguard Against Torture.*

Hynes, Patricia (2011) *The Dispersal and Social Exclusion of Asylum Seekers* (Bristol: Policy Press).

Information Centre about Asylum and Refugees (ICAR) (2007) (London) Thematic Briefings: *Removals; Vulnerable groups in the asylum determination process; Asylum support and destitution.*

Joint Committee on Human Rights (2010) *Counter-Terrorism Policy and Human Rights (Seventeenth Report): Bringing Human Rights Back* in Sixteenth report of 2009–10 HL Paper 86 HC 111.

Juss, Satvinder (1993) *Immigration, Nationality and Citizenship* (London: Mansell).

Kostakopoulou, Dora and Thomas, Robert (2004) 'Unweaving the Threads: Territoriality, Asylum Policy and National Ownership of Land' *European Journal of Migration and Law* vol. 6, pp. 5–26.

Lester, Anthony and Bindman, Geoffrey (1972) *Race and Law* (London: Penguin).

London Detainee Support Group (2010) *No Return, No Release, No Reason* (London).

Macdonald, Ian and Blake, Nicholas (1995) *Macdonald's Immigration Law and Practice* 4th edn (London: Butterworths).

Macdonald, Ian and Webber, Frances (2001) *Macdonald's Immigration Law and Practice* 5th edn (London: Butterworths).

Macdonald, Ian and Webber, Frances (2005) *Macdonald's Immigration Law and Practice* 6th edn (Edinburgh: Lexis Nexis Butterworths).

Macdonald, Ian and Toal, Ronan (2008) *Macdonald's Immigration Law and Practice* 7th edn (London: Lexis Nexis).

Macdonald, Ian and Toal, Ronan (2010) *Macdonald's Immigration Law and Practice* 8th edn (London: Lexis Nexis, Butterworths).

Macdonald, Ian and Toal, Ronan (2014) *Macdonald's Immigration Law and Practice* 9th edn (London: Lexis Nexis, Butterworths).

Nandy, Lisa (2009) *An evaluative report on the Millbank Alternative to Detention Pilot* (London: BID and the Children's Society).

Nicholson, Frances and Twomey, Patrick (1998) *Current Issues of UK Asylum Law and Policy* (Ashgate: Dartmouth).

O'Nions, Helen (2014) *Asylum: A Right Denied* (Farnham: Ashgate)

Pretzell, Andreas, Krushner, Damian, and Hruschka, Constantin (2002) 'Terrorism and the 1951 Refugee Convention' *Journal of Immigration, Asylum & Nationality Law* vol. 16, no. 3, pp. 148–65.

Thomas, Robert (2011) *Administrative Justice and Asylum Appeals: A study of tribunal adjudication* (Oxford: Hart).

Wade, William and Forsyth, Christopher (2014) *Administrative Law* 11th edn (Oxford: OUP).

Webber, Frances (2012) *Borderline Justice* (London: Pluto).

INDEX